Oxford
Phrasal Verbs
Dictionary

for learners of English

OXFORD
UNIVERSITY PRESS

OXFORD
UNIVERSITY PRESS

Great Clarendon Street, Oxford OX2 6DP

Oxford University Press is a department of the University of Oxford.
It furthers the University's objective of excellence in research, scholarship,
and education by publishing worldwide in

Oxford New York

Athens Auckland Bangkok Bogotá Buenos Aires Cape Town
Chennai Dar es Salaam Delhi Florence Hong Kong Istanbul Karachi
Kolkata Kuala Lumpur Madrid Melbourne Mexico City Mumbai Nairobi
Paris São Paulo Shanghai Singapore Taipei Tokyo Toronto Warsaw
with associated companies in Berlin Ibadan

Oxford and Oxford English are registered trade marks of Oxford University Press
in the UK and in certain other countries

ISBN 0–19–431543–6
10 9 8 7 6 5 4 3 2 1

Acknowledgements

Advisory Board: Dr Keith Brown; Dr Alan Cruse; Ms Moira Runcie;
Prof. Gabriele Stein; Dr Norman Whitney; Prof. Henry Widdowson

Phonetics editor: Michael Ashby
Guide to the Particles: Graham Workman

A–Z pages designed by Peter Burgess
Non A–Z pages designed by Sarah Nicholson
Cover design by Richard Morris

Data capture and processing by Oxford University Press
Printed in Spain

CONTENTS

Short forms and symbols used in the dictionary   inside front cover

Labels used in the dictionary   iv

Key to the dictionary entries   v

Guide to using the dictionary   vi

Dictionary A–Z   **1–348**

STUDY PAGES   between pages 182–3

Tips on learning phrasal verbs   S2–4

Phrasal verb or single word?   S5

Are you a natural born student?   S 6–7

Sport   S 8–9

Computers   S10

Environmental problems   S11

Phrasal verbs in newspapers   S12

Phrasal verbs in business   S13

Phrasal verbs in informal language   S14–15

Using phrasal verbs in writing   S16–17

Using phrasal verbs in the passive   S18–19

New phrasal verbs   S20–21

The most common phrasal verbs   S22–25

Test yourself   S26

Guide to the particles   349–71

Key to the study pages   372–7

Pronunciation   inside back cover

Labels Used in the Dictionary

AmE describes verbs, expressions, spellings and pronunciations used in American English and not in British English, for example *beat on sb, blimp out/up, duke it out.*

approving verbs show that you feel approval or admiration.

BrE describes verbs, expressions, spellings and pronunciations that are mainly used in British English and not in American English, for example *beaver away (at sth), doss down, put (the clocks) back.*

disapproving verbs show that you feel disapproval or contempt, for example *dumb sth down, flash sth about.*

figurative a figurative example is one in which language is used in a non-literal or metaphorical way, as in *His anger blazed up* (= suddenly became very strong) *uncontrollably.*

formal verbs are usually only used in serious or official language and would not be appropriate in normal everyday conversation. Examples are *abide by sth, embark on/upon sth, vie for sth.*

humorous expressions are intended to be funny, for example *toddle off* and *We've rounded up some good speakers for the conference.*

informal verbs are used between friends or in a relaxed or unofficial situation. They are not appropriate for formal situations. Examples are *bang on about sth, kick back, tuck into sth.*

less formal synonyms are verbs that have a similar meaning to the main phrasal verb, but are used in less official situations or are more common in normal everyday conversation.

less frequent verbs or grammar patterns are not used as often as the main phrasal verb or the other grammar patterns given.

literary verbs are used mainly in literature and imaginative writing. Examples are *yearn for sb/sth, eke out sth.*

more formal verbs have a similar meaning to the main phrasal verb, but are usually used in more serious or official situations, or in a less casual way.

old-fashioned verbs are passing out of current use, for example, *buck up, gad about/around, run along.*

rare verbs or grammar patterns are not commonly used.

slang is very informal language, mainly used in speaking and sometimes restricted to a particular group of people, for example people of the same age or those who have similar interests or do the same job. Examples are *want in, want into sth, juice sth up.*

spoken verbs are used mainly in informal conversations, for example *Tea's up! chuck sth out.*

taboo verbs and expressions are likely to be thought by many people to be obscene or shocking and you should avoid using them.

written verbs are used mainly in written language, for example *abound in/with sth, spring from sth.*

Key to the Dictionary Entries

Information in the dictionary is given in **entries**, arranged in the alphabetical order of the key words and then in the alphabetical order of the particles.

Main parts of an entry

Key word with pronunciation and irregular forms.

Phrasal verb. The main forms of the verb + particle are given with the stress.

Definition. The meanings of the verb.

Examples (in *italic type*).

Grammar patterns to show how the verb is used.

blow /bləʊ; *AmE* bloʊ/ (**blew** /bluː/**blown** /bləʊn; *AmE* bloʊn/)

,blow a'way; ,blow sth a'way to be moved or carried away by the force of the wind or by sb's breath; to move in this way: *It was so windy the tent nearly blew away!* ◇ *A sudden breeze blew his newspaper away.* ◇ *She blew away the dust on the lid.*
◈ v + adv ◆ v + n/pron + adv ◆ v + adv + n

,blow sb a'way **1** (*informal*) to impress sb a lot; to surprise or please sb: *I saw this play last year and it just blew me away.* **2** (*AmE, informal, sport*) to defeat sb easily: *Mitchell blew away the other runners.*
◈ v + n/pron + adv ◆ v + adv + n

Further information in an entry

Special symbols show **synonyms** and **opposites**.

Information on prepositions frequently used with the verb.

Common phrase in **bold type**.

Idiom related to the verb.

Derivative adjective related to the verb.

Information on grammar and usage.

,stand 'out **1** (against/from sth) to be clearly visible: *His yellow jacket stood out clearly against the grey hillside.* ◇ *The church tower stands out against the sky.* ◇ *A small figure in red stood out from the rest of the group.* ⓢⓎⓃ **stick out 2** (as/from sb/sth) to be much better or more important than other people or things: *This building stands out from the rest because of its superior design.* ◇ *She's the sort of person who always stands out in a crowd.* **3** (against/for sb/sth) to oppose or refuse to accept sth that you believe is wrong: *Parents often stand out against troublesome behaviour for some time, then give in.* ⓢⓎⓃ **stick out for sth; hold out against/for sth**
◈ v + adv

ⒾⒹⓂ stand out like a sore thumb to be very noticeable in an unpleasant way: *Dressed like that, you'll stand out like a sore thumb.*

▶ **out'standing** *adj* **1** excellent: *an outstanding young actress* **2** [usually before noun] very obvious or important: *Lake Baykal is one of earth's outstanding features.* **3** (of payment, work, problems, etc.) not yet paid, done, solved, etc: *to repay outstanding debts* ◇ *I don't have any urgent work outstanding.*

▶ **out'standingly** *adv* **1** used to emphasize the good quality of sth: *outstandingly beautiful/successful* **2** extremely well: *Owen has played outstandingly this season.*

GUIDE to USING the DICTIONARY

Finding Verbs in the dictionary

1 What is in the dictionary?

In this dictionary we include several different types of verbs that are used with adverbs or prepositions, (often called 'particles').

a **Idiomatic verb + particle combinations**. Sometimes when you meet combinations of verb and particle, it is impossible to guess the meaning in the context from the meaning of the verb and the meaning of the particle. Examples of these are *fall through* (meaning '*not happen*') and *put up with somebody* (meaning '*accept somebody who is annoying without complaining*'). There is often a single-word verb with the same meaning. For example, instead of '*The meeting was **put off** until the next day*', we could say '*The meeting was postponed until the next day*'. Single-word verbs, however, may be more formal than the phrasal verb, or used in slightly different contexts.

b **Verbs which are always followed by a particular particle**. Examples of these are *rely on*, *crop up*, *abide by*. These cannot be used without the particle.

c **Verbs that are followed by a particle in a particular meaning**. These verbs can be used on their own without a particle, but have a different meaning when they are used with one. *Brush sth up* is an example of a verb like this. *Brush sth* can be used on its own meaning '*clean, polish or make sth smooth*'. *Brush sth up* means '*study or practise sth to get back the skill or knowledge that you had in the past*': *You should brush up your French before you go to France*. Other examples are *nod/nod off*, *grow/grow up*, *walk/walk out*.

Many very common verbs fall into this group. *Look*, for example, can be used with several different particles, and it has a special meaning with each one that is different from *look* on its own. *Look up the word in your dictionary.* ◇ *I'm really looking forward to the trip.* ◇ *Look out! There's a car coming.*

Some more formal verbs also fall into this group. For example you can '*furnish a room*', that is, put furniture in it, but if you '*furnish somebody with something*' you are giving them some useful information.

d **Verbs with a particle, where the particle adds to, but does not change, the basic meaning of the verb**. The particle often adds something to the meaning, such as completeness. For example, you can say '*I'll finish my work and then I'll go out*' or '*I'll finish off my work and then I'll go out.*' *Finish off* emphasizes that you are completing your work. Another example is *wake/wake up*. You can either say '*I woke at 6.30*' or '*I woke up at 6.30.*' *Woke up* is much more common than *woke*, which is used in more formal or written English. Other examples are *spread/spread out*, *fade/fade away*, *slave/slave away*. You will find more information about the meaning of the particles in the **Guide to the Particles** at the back of the dictionary.

e **Verbs plus particles where each has their normal meaning**. *Phone back* (meaning '*telephone sb again*') is an example of a verb like this. The meaning of *phone back* can be worked out from the meaning of *phone* and *back*. Verbs of this type have been included in the dictionary where the combination of verb and particle are very common, or where there is something unusual or interesting about the verb. For example, ***phone back*** can mean two slightly different things (*'telephone somebody who has called you'*, or *'telephone sb for a second time'*); ***pin sth up*** means *'fasten something to a wall with pins'*, but there is also a noun ***pin-up***, meaning *'a picture of an attractive person designed to be put up on a wall for people to look at'*, or *'the person who appears in a picture like that'*.

All these types of verbs can cause problems for learners, and so they have been included in this dictionary.

2 Particles

These are the particles used with phrasal verbs in this dictionary. The * shows you which are the most common. You will find more information about those particles in the **Guide to Particles** at the back of the dictionary.

aback	*about	above	across	after	against	ahead	ahead of
along	among	apart	*around	as	aside	*at	*away
*back	before	behind	between	by	*down	*for	forth
forward	from	*in	*into	*of	*off	*on	onto
*out	*out of	*over	past	*round	*through	*to	together
towards	under	*up	upon	*with	without		

3 Long verbs

Some verbs, such as ***come***, ***go***, ***put*** and ***take*** are used with many different particles. In these cases you will find literal meanings of the verb plus particle included for completeness. These meanings can also help you understand the idiomatic uses of the verb plus particle. For example, at ***run around***, you will find the literal meaning *'run in different directions'* (*It's a lovely park to run around in*) as well as the idiomatic meaning *'move very quickly from place to place, being very busy'* (*I've been running around all day trying to organize the meeting.*).

At the beginning of many of these verbs you will find a menu box with a list of all the particles that can be used with the verb, in the order they appear in the dictionary.

These verbs are:

break	bring	call	come	cut	do	fall	get	give
go	hang	hold	keep	kick	knock	lie	live	look
make	move	pass	play	pull	push	put	run	send
set	sit	stand	stay	stick	take	talk	throw	turn

It is also possible to add many different particles to verbs of movement to create 'multi-word' verbs with literal meanings. For example, we can use the verb ***walk*** in these sentences: *We **walked down** the road.* ◇ *He **walked up to** me and asked me for a light.* ◇ *We sang as we **walked along**.* ◇ ***Walk across** the road, don't run*. These are straightforward combinations of verb and particles.

4 Finding the verb you want

The phrasal verbs are arranged in the dictionary under their key verbs (for example, **give**, **move**, **sit**) and then in alphabetical order of the particles. Within each particle you will first find the verb + particle, with no object. Then there are meanings of the verb that can be used both without an object and with an object. After that, there are meanings of the verb used only with an object, first verbs with people as objects (sb), then verbs that can have people or things (sb/sth) and then verbs with only things as objects (sth). Verbs with itself, yourself, etc. come at the end of those, and verbs that are only used in passive forms will be last. For example:

give up; give sth up	break in	put sb out
give sb up	break sb/sth in	put sth out
give sth up	break sth in	put yourself out
give yourself up	break into sth	be put out

Using Phrasal Verbs

1 The phrasal verb

The arrangement of the verbs in the dictionary will tell you whether they can be used without an object, (INTRANSITIVE), with an object (TRANSITIVE) or both with and without an object.

Look at the beginning of the entry for **break down**:

> **break 'down 1** if a vehicle, etc. breaks down, it stops working because of a fault: *The washing machine has broken down again.* ◇ *We (= our car) broke down twice on the way home.* **2** if talks,

This shows you that in this meaning **break down** is an intransitive verb, used without an object: *My car broke down on the way to work this morning.*

There are two forms of the verb at **burn down**:

> **burn 'down**; **burn sth 'down** if a building burns down, or sb burns it down, it is destroyed by fire: *The palace burnt down in the nineteenth century.* ◇ *She threatened to burn the house down.*

This shows you that you can use **burn down** as a transitive and an intransitive verb in this meaning. The definition also shows you how to use it.

Look at the beginning of the entry for **wake up**.

> **wake 'up**; **wake sb 'up**; **wake yourself 'up 1** to stop sleeping; to make sb stop sleeping: *How many times does the baby wake up in the night?* ◇ *I usually wake up early in the summer.* ◇ *You look as if you've only just woken up!* ◇ *Can you wake me up at 8?* ◇ *He was woken up by the sound of*

This tells you that you can use it as an intransitive verb (*What time did you wake up this morning?*), and as a transitive verb with an object (*I'll wake you up at 6.30.*) or with **yourself** (*I must have shouted so loudly while I was dreaming that I woke myself up.*)

At **keep out**, you will see:

> **keep 'out**; **keep 'out of sth** to not enter a place; to remain outside: *There was a sign saying 'Keep out!'.* ◇ *Please keep out of the office while I'm working.*
> ⊕ v + adv ◆ v + adv + prep

This tells you that in this meaning you can use the verb on its own (*Danger! Keep out*) or as a transitive verb with the adverb + preposition **out of**, followed by a noun or pronoun (***Keep out of** my way*).

If the verb can also be used with an **-ing** form of a verb that follows it, this is given at the beginning:

> **,rush 'into sth**; **,rush 'into doing sth**; **,rush sb 'into doing sth** to do or decide sth quickly without thinking about it carefully; to make sb do this: *Don't go rushing into anything.* ◊ *You*

This tells you that all these sentences are possible: *Don't **rush into** anything.* ◊ *Don't **rush into leaving** your course.* ◊ *Don't **rush me into making** a decision.*

▶ More information about the grammar of phrasal verbs is given in the section on Grammar Patterns (page x)

2 Common subjects and objects

At the end of many of the verbs, or at the end of a numbered meaning, you will find some common subjects or objects. These show you the type of contexts that the verb is often used in, so that you can use it correctly yourself.
For example, at ***break out***, you will see:

> **,break 'out 1** if sth unpleasant such as a fire, a war, etc. breaks out, it starts suddenly: *They would have got married in 1939 if war had not broken out.* ◊ *A fire broke out on a ferry yesterday.*
> [SUBJ] **war, fire, fighting, row, violence   2** (*also*

Sentences such as ***Fighting** has broken out on the border*; ***Fire broke out** in a warehouse.* ◊ *A furious **row broke out** over the ownership of the painting* are therefore very common and acceptable in English.

You can use these subjects and objects to help you use the verbs in the right context.

3 Synonyms and opposites.

When there are helpful synonyms or opposites, these are given in alphabetical order, synonyms and opposites that are phrasal verbs first and then single-word verbs. These will help you understand the verb and add to your vocabulary. Information is also given about the formality of the

> **,pull 'in**; **,pull 'into sth 1** if a train or a bus pulls in, it arrives somewhere and stops: *The express pulled in on time.* ◊ *The coach pulled into bay 27.* **2** (*BrE*) if a vehicle or a driver pulls in, they move to the side of the road and stop: *Pull in in front of the bus.* ◊ *He pulled into the parking lot and turned off the engine.*
> [SYN] **draw in, draw into sth**
> [OPP] **pull out, pull out of sth**

synonym or opposite and whether it is British or American. As the contexts that the synonyms are used in may not always be exactly the same as the original phrasal verb, it is worth looking them up in this dictionary or another dictionary to be sure that you understand them and how they are used. For example, while ***knock down*** can be used instead of ***break down*** in the examples given there, ***break down*** cannot always be used instead of ***knock down***.

✓ *They had to get the police to **break/knock** the door **down**.* ✓ *If you don't open up, I'm going to **knock/break** the door **down**.* ✓ *These old houses are going to be **knocked down**.* ✗ *These old houses are going to be **broken down**.*

4 Notes

Notes are given in two places. Before a definition you will find information about the tenses or a particular use of a phrasal verb:

> **be'long to sb** (*not used in the progressive tenses*)
> **1** to be the property of sb; to be owned by sb: *The house belonged to my cousin.* ◇ *That land belongs*

Notes are also given after the examples where there is a particular point of grammar or use to draw your attention to. This is often something about the passive, or where the verb without the particle can also be used with a similar meaning.

> **,blaze a'way 1 (at sb/sth)** if guns or people blaze away, the guns fire continuously: *The guns kept blazing away at the enemy.* **2** if a fire blazes away, it burns brightly
> **NOTE** Blaze is used with the same meanings.
> **☯** v + adv

5 Grammar patterns of phrasal verbs

To help you use the verbs correctly, a simple system of grammar patterns is given after each one. These show you how the verb combines with an adverb, a preposition, a noun or a pronoun, an infinitive, etc. and the order in which these words can occur. The short forms used are these:

adv	= adverb		**n/pron**	= noun or pronoun
inf	= infinitive (without 'to' e.g. do)		**prep**	= preposition
-ing	= a verb form ending in -ing (e.g. doing)		**pron**	= pronoun
			to inf	= infinitive with 'to' (e.g. to do)
n	= noun		**v**	= verb

Frequent patterns

The following are the most common types of verb patterns used in the dictionary.

v + adv	Intransitive verbs, for example:	
	break down	*My car broke down this morning.*
	hang around	*There was a group of kids hanging around outside.*
	sit down	*Come in and sit down.*
v + prep	These are verbs followed by a preposition. For example:	
	rely on sb/sth	*You can rely on me.*
	call for sb	*I'll call for you at 8.*
	come across sth	*I came across an interesting book in the library.*
v + adv + prep	Some verbs are followed by an adverb and a preposition:	
	put up with sb/sth	*How do you put up with him?*
	settle down to sth	*Come on children, settle down to work now.*
	keep out of sth	*Keep out of the kitchen until I've finished cooking.*

These last two groups are sometimes called INSEPARABLE verbs as the object always follows the particle.

v + n/pron + adv   v + adv + n   v + pron + adv

These three patterns are all used with transitive verbs. In order to be able to use these verbs correctly, you need to know where to put the object. The patterns show you this. The most frequent patterns come first at each verb.

v + n/pron + adv   v + adv + n

Verbs that can be used with these patterns , where the object can go either between the verb and the particle or after the particle, are sometimes called SEPARABLE verbs. They are shown in the dictionary as, for example, **tear sth up**:

*She **tore** the letter **up**.   She **tore up** the letter.   She **tore** it **up**.*

When the object is a long phrase, it usually comes after the particle: *She **tore up** all the letters he had sent her*.

When the object is a pronoun, it **must** come between the verb and the particle.

v + adv + n   v + pron + adv

With some phrasal verbs the object can only come between the verb and the particle when it is a pronoun. A noun must follow the particle. They are given in the dictionary as, for example, **fight back sth**; **fight it/them back**

fight back sth   I tried to **fight back** my tears.

fight it/them back   I had an urge to scream but managed to **fight** it **back**.

v + n/pron + adv

There are a few phrasal verbs in which the two parts of the verb **must** be separated by the object. An example is **mess sb about/around**:

*They changed the flight time and **messed** all the passengers **around**.*

v + n/pron + prep

An example of a verb that is used in this pattern is **drill sth into sb**

drill sth into sb *The teacher **drilled** grammar **into** us right from the start.*

Passive

A few phrasal verbs are only used in the passive, for example: **be/get carried away**. The verb patterns will show you how to use these verbs. **be/get carried away** will have the pattern **be/get + v + adv**. **be/get stuck with sth** will have a pattern **be/get + verb + prep**.

Other phrasal verbs that are used with objects can also be used in the passive for example: *The deal **has been called off***. Where this is common you will find an example of the passive and a note. Verbs with the pattern **v + prep** are not usually used in the passive. If they are, you will find a note about this (see **rely on sb/sth**).

Other patterns

You can easily work out how to use verbs with different patterns. For example, if you look at **take sb up on sth**, you will see the pattern **v + n/pron + adv + prep**. This shows you that the verb is used in sentences like this:

*I'd like to   **take**   **you**   **up**   **on**   your offer of a bed for the night.*
      v + pron + adv + prep

At **set out**, you will see the pattern **v + adv + to inf**. This describes sentences such as: *He **set out to become** a millionaire by the time he was thirty*.

Boom out sth has two patterns:

v + adv + n   *She boomed out instructions.*
v + adv + speech   *A voice boomed out, 'Nobody move!'*

6 Building your vocabulary

Idioms

Many phrasal verbs have idioms related to them. You will find these immediately after the grammar patterns. The idioms in the dictionary are ones that are related in some way to the meaning of the phrasal verb where you find them. For example:

,bite sth 'off to cut sth off by biting it: *She bit off a piece of chocolate*. ◇ *His finger had been bitten off by a dog.*
⊕ v + adv + n ◆ v + n/pron + adv
IDM **bite/snap sb's 'head off** (*informal*) to shout at sb or speak to them angrily, often for no good reason: *I only asked him when the work would be finished and he almost bit my head off.* **bite off more than you can 'chew** (*informal*) to try to do too much or sth that is too difficult for you: *This time he's bitten off more than he can chew.*

Derivative nouns and adjectives.

Nouns and adjectives that are related in meaning to a particular phrasal verb are given after the grammar patterns or any idioms. Sometimes the derivative has more than one meaning, each one relating to different uses of the phrasal verb. You will find the meaning at the appropriate entry, with a link to show you where to find the same derivative with a different meaning.

For example, you will find one meaning of the adjective **mixed-up** at the verb it is related to, **mix sb up; be/get mixed up** and another meaning at **mix sth up (with sth)**, with a link from one to the other.

,mix sb 'up; be/get ,mixed 'up to make sb unable to think clearly or understand what is happening: *Now you've mixed me up completely! I'm really confused.* ◇ *He got mixed up and caught the wrong train.*
▶ ,mixed-'up *adj* (*informal*) confused because of social or emotional problems: *She's a very mixed-up kid.*
→ *see also* MIXED-UP *at* MIX STH UP (WITH STH)

Further Information and Practice

Study pages

There is a 25-page section of study pages in the middle of this dictionary. You can use these on your own or in class with a teacher. They will help you to learn phrasal verbs and give you practice in using them.

Guide to the particles

At the end of the dictionary is a guide to the most common particles used in the verbs in this dictionary and their main meanings. This will help you understand verbs better and be able to guess the meaning of new ones that you meet.

Aa

abide /əˈbaɪd/

a'bide by sth (*formal*) to accept rules, a law, an agreement, a decision, etc. and obey them/it: *Members must abide by the rules of the club.*
[OBJ] **rules, decision, the law**
⟩SYN⟨ **comply (with sth)**
◈ v + prep

abound /əˈbaʊnd/

a'bound in/with sth (*written*) to have a lot of sth; to contain a lot of sth: *The rivers there abound in/with fish.*
◈ v + prep

accede /əkˈsiːd/

ac'cede to sth (*formal*) to agree to or allow sth that sb has asked for, often after you have opposed it for a while: *The government acceded to public pressure to review the tax.*
[OBJ] **request, demands, pressure**
[NOTE] **Accede to sth** can be used in the passive: *Have all our requests been acceded to?*
◈ v + prep

account /əˈkaʊnt/

ac'count for sb/sth 1 to know where sb/sth is or what has happened to them, especially after an accident or a natural disaster: *All the people who were working in the building have now been accounted for.* ◊ *There are three files that I can't account for.* [NOTE] **Account for sb/sth** is often used in the passive in this meaning. 2 (*old-fashioned*) to destroy sth or kill sb: *Our guns accounted for five enemy planes.*
◈ v + prep

ac'count for sth 1 to explain how or why sth happened; to be the explanation for sth: *How do you account for the fact that the box has disappeared?* ◊ *Poor hygiene may have accounted for the increase in cases of the disease.* [OBJ] **the fact that… 2** to be a particular part of sth; to be a particular amount: *Car crime accounted for 28% of all reported offences.* ◊ *Wages account for less than half of the budget.* [OBJ] **a large amount, a (particular) proportion, (so many) per cent** ⟩SYN⟨ **make up sth; represent sth 3** to keep a record of how the money in your care will be spent or has been spent: *Every penny of the funds is accounted for.* **4** to consider particular facts or circumstances when you are making a decision about sth, especially when you are calculating the cost of sth: *The cost of the film and the processing were all accounted for in the calculation of the cost of the service.* ⟩SYN⟨ **take sth into account**

[NOTE] **Account for sth** can be used in the passive: *This increase is accounted for by rising taxes.*
◈ v + prep

[IDM] **there's no accounting for 'taste(s)** used to say that it is impossible to know why sb likes sb/sth that you do not like at all: (*humorous*) 'She seems to like you.' 'Well — there's no accounting for taste!'

accustom /əˈkʌstəm/

ac'custom sb/yourself to sth; ac'custom sb/yourself to doing sth (*formal*) to make sb/yourself familiar with sth; to become used to sth: *It shouldn't take long to accustom your students to working in groups.* ◊ *It took a while for her eyes to accustom themselves to the dark.*
◈ v + n/pron + prep

ache /eɪk/

'ache for sb/sth to have a strong desire for sb/sth or to do sth: *I was aching for home.*
⟩SYN⟨ **long for sb/sth**
◈ v + prep

acquaint /əˈkweɪnt/

ac'quaint sb/yourself with sth (*formal*) to make sb/yourself familiar with or aware of sth: *He decided to take his son along and acquaint him with the business.*
◈ v + n/pron + prep

act /ækt/

'act as sth to perform a particular role or function: *Will you act as interpreter for us?* ◊ *Large fines act as a deterrent to motorists.*
[OBJ] **agent, consultant, intermediary/go-between, deterrent** ⟩SYN⟨ **serve as sth**
◈ v + prep

'act for sb (*also* ˌact on be'half of sb, ˌact on sb's be'half) if sb acts for you or acts on behalf of you, they deal with your affairs for you, for example by representing you in a court of law, or by doing your duty when you are not able to: *Do you have a solicitor acting for you?* ◊ *The Prince was acting on behalf of the Queen.* ◊ *The Prince was acting on the Queen's behalf.*
[OBJ] **client**
◈ v + prep

'act on sth (*also* 'act upon sth *more formal*) 1 to do sth as a result of advice, information, instructions, etc. that you have received: *The police were acting on information from a member of the public.* ◊ *I was just acting on instructions.* ◊ *If my advice had been acted upon, this would never have happened.* [OBJ] **advice, information, instructions**

NOTE Act on/upon sth can be used in the passive in this meaning. **2** to have an effect on sth: *The drug acts on the central nervous system.* **NOTE** Act can be used on its own with this meaning: *The drug acts quickly.*
◈ v + prep

,act on be'half of sb; ,act on sb's be'half = ACT FOR SB

,act sth 'out 1 to perform a story or events that have happened or might happen, as if you are performing a play: *The teacher read a story and the children acted it out.* ◇ *She acted out her fantasies of pop stardom in front of her bedroom mirror.* ◇ (*figurative*) *The whole nation was following the drama being acted out on the football field.* **OBJ** story, fantasy **2** to act a part in real life: *I found myself acting out the role of good, brave patient.* **3** (*technical*) to express your thoughts and feelings in your behaviour, often without being aware of it
◈ v + adv + n ◆ v + n/pron + adv

,act 'up (*informal*) **1** to make sb annoyed by behaving badly, trying to get attention, etc: *The kids have been acting up all day.* **2** if a machine or part of the body **acts up**, it does not work properly: *The car's acting up again.* ◇ *My ankle is acting up* (= is painful and causing problems).
SYN play up
NOTE Act up is often used in the progressive tenses.
◈ v + adv

'act upon sth = ACT ON STH

add /æd/

,add sth 'in to include sth with sth else; to put sth into sth else or between two things: *Send me the new figures when the additional costs have been added in.* ◇ *I've added in two extra paragraphs.*
NOTE Add can also be used with this meaning: *I've added a couple of extra paragraphs.*
◈ v + adv + n ◆ v + n/pron + adv

,add 'on; ,add 'on to sth (*AmE*) to build an extra room or rooms on to a house or other building: *They decided to add on rather than move.*
◈ v + adv ◆ v + adv + prep

,add sth 'on; ,add sth 'on to sth to include sth or attach sth extra: *He added £2 on to the bill.*
NOTE Add (**to sth**) can also be used with this meaning: *He added £2 to the bill.*
◈ v + n/pron + adv ◆ v + adv + n ◆
  v + n/pron + adv + prep

▶ **'add-on** *n* a thing that is added to or included with sth else: *The catalogue advertised add-ons such as extra memory and software.* ◇ *add-on products/pockets/units*

'add to sth to increase the size, amount, number, etc. of sth: *Taking the children with us would only add to our problems.* ◇ *Music playing in the background added to the atmosphere.* ◇ (*BrE*) *The house has been added to over the years.* ◇ *The food at the hotel is of a very high standard.* **Add to this** the quality of the rooms and the service and it is clear why this is such a popular hotel.
OBJ problems, number, knowledge, enjoyment
NOTE Add to sth can be used in the passive.
◈ v + prep

,add to'gether; ,add sth to'gether to come together to produce sth; to join two or more things, numbers, etc. together to produce sth: *The games, the dancing and the good food all added together to make a memorable occasion.* ◇ *When all the different factors are added together, I can understand her decision.* ◇ *Add the two numbers together and divide by three.*
OBJ factors, numbers, costs
◈ v + adv ◆ v + adv + n ◆ v + n/pron + adv

,add 'up (*informal*) **1** to seem reasonable; to make sense; to have all the different parts agreeing with each other: *There are things in her story that just don't add up.* ◇ *Now that I know where she was last night, it's all beginning to add up.* **NOTE** Add up with this meaning is used especially in negative sentences. **2** to increase gradually to make a large number or amount: *Save a small amount each month; it'll soon add up.* **3** if two or more numbers **add up**, they come to the total that they should or that you would expect: *These figures just don't add up.*
◈ v + adv

,add 'up (*especially BrE*), **,add sth 'up** to calculate the total of two or more numbers or amounts: *I never could add up.* ◇ *She's very good at adding up in her head.* ◇ *She added the figures up in no time.* ◇ *I needed to use a calculator to add up the bill.*
OBJ numbers, figures, score, cost
◈ v + adv ◆ v + adv + n ◆ v + n/pron + adv

,add 'up to sth 1 if two or more numbers or figures **add up to** sth, they make a total of sth when they are added together: *Can you arrange the numbers in groups that add up to 10?* ◇ *The cost of all the equipment you need for a baby adds up to a considerable sum.* **2** (*informal*) to show sth; to have a particular meaning or result: *His evidence didn't really add up to very much* (= gave us very little information). ◇ *All in all, it adds up to a pretty desperate situation.*
SYN amount to sth
◈ v + adv + prep

address /ə'dres/

ad'dress yourself to sth (*formal*) to think about a problem or a situation and decide how you are going to deal with it: *We must address ourselves to the problem of traffic pollution.*
◈ v + pron + prep

adhere /əd'hɪə(r)/

ad'here to sth (*formal*) to act in the way that a particular law, rule or set of instructions says that you should; to follow or support a particular opinion or set of beliefs: *They have adhered strictly to the terms of the treaty.* ◇ *He found the diet very difficult to adhere to.* ◇ *How many people actually adhere to this view?*
[OBJ] **principles, rules, guidelines** [SYN] **keep to sth** (*less formal*)
[NOTE] **Adhere to sth** can be used in the passive: *All safety requirements must be adhered to.*
◈ v + prep

admit /əd'mɪt/ (-tt-)

ad'mit of sth (*formal*) to show that sth such as an explanation or an answer is possible; to allow sth to happen: *The situation admits of only one explanation.*
[OBJ] **explanation, answer** [SYN] **allow of sth**
◈ v + prep

agree /ə'gri:/

a'gree with sb to make you feel happy or healthy: *You look great! Marriage obviously agrees with you.* ◇ *Mushrooms don't agree with me* (= they make me feel ill/sick).
[NOTE] **Agree with sb** is often used in negative sentences.
◈ v + prep

a'gree with sth; **a'gree with doing sth** to approve of sth, especially a policy or a belief: *I don't agree with capital punishment.*
[OPP] **disagree with sth, disagree with doing sth**
◈ v + prep

aim /eɪm/

'aim at sth; **'aim at doing sth** to try to achieve sth; to have sth as your aim: *She's aiming at a sports scholarship.* ◇ *We need to aim at increasing exports.*
[NOTE] **Aim to do sth** is also used with the same meaning: *What do you aim to achieve?*
◈ v + prep

'aim sth at sb/sth if you **aim sth at** a particular person or group, you do or say sth that you intend to have an effect on them: *The advertising campaign is aimed primarily at young people.* ◇ *I was not aiming my remarks at you.*
[OBJ] **remarks, criticism, campaign**
[NOTE] **Aim sth at sb** is often used in the passive.
◈ v + n/pron + prep

be 'aimed at sth; **be 'aimed at doing sth** to have sth as an aim or purpose: *The new scheme is aimed at reducing unemployment.*
◈ be + v + prep

alight /ə'laɪt/

a'light on/upon sb/sth (*formal*) to notice sb/sth suddenly; to find or think of sth by chance: *My eye alighted on an old book.* ◇ *He finally alighted on a solution.*
[SYN] **light on/upon sb/sth**
◈ v + prep

align /ə'laɪn/

a'lign yourself with sb/sth to publicly support a person, a group of people or a set of opinions: *The senator aligned himself with the critics of the proposed reforms.*
◈ v + pron + prep

allow /ə'laʊ/

al'low for sth to include sth when you are calculating sth or planning sth: *Add an extra ten minutes to your journey time to allow for the traffic.* ◇ *I've bought a large size to allow for the fact that it may shrink in the wash.*
[OBJ] **the possibility, the fact that…, differences**
[NOTE] **Allow for sth** can be used in the passive: *This had not been allowed for in the budget.*
◈ v + prep

al'low of sth (*formal*) to show that sth such as an explanation or an answer is possible; to make sth possible: *The facts allow of only one explanation.*
[SYN] **admit of sth**
◈ v + prep

allude /ə'luːd/

al'lude to sb/sth (*formal*) to mention sb/sth indirectly or in a few words: *He hated his mother's way of alluding to Jean but never actually saying her name.*
[NOTE] **Allude to sb/sth** can be used in the passive: *Do you know the person who was alluded to in the report?*
◈ v + prep

amount /ə'maʊnt/

a'mount to sth (*not used in the progressive tenses*) **1** to add up to sth; to result in a final total of sth: *The cost of the trip amounted to well over £500.* ◇ *The money I pay in tax and insurance contributions amounts to about 40% of my salary.* [SYN] **come to sth 2** to be equal to or the same as sth: *What they did amounted to a breach of contract.* ◇ *It doesn't matter whether I pay or my husband pays — it amounts to the same thing in the end.* ◇ *It all amounts to a lot of hard work.* [SYN] **come to sth 3** if you say that sb/sth **doesn't amount to much**, you mean that he/she/it is not very important: *He'll never amount to anything.* ◇ *The information we have doesn't amount to much.*
[SYN] **add up to sth**
◈ v + prep

angle /'æŋgl/

'angle for sth (*often used in the progressive tenses*) to try to obtain sth without asking for it directly: *She's angling for an invitation to the party.*
⟩SYN⟨ **fish for sth**
◆ v + prep

answer /'ɑːnsə(r); AmE 'æn-/

,answer 'back to defend yourself against sth bad that sb has said about you: *It's not fair to criticize without giving her the chance to answer back.*
◆ v + adv

,answer 'back; ,answer sb 'back if a child **answers back** or **answers you back** when you are telling them to do sth, for example, they reply rudely: *Don't answer back! ◇ He's a rude little boy, always answering his mother back.*
◆ v + adv ◆ v + n/pron + adv

'answer for sb to speak on behalf of sb and say what they will do or what they think: *I can't answer for my colleagues, but I can manage a meeting next week.*
⟩SYN⟨ **speak for sb**
NOTE Answer for sb is usually used in negative sentences.
◆ v + prep

'answer for sth 1 to be responsible for sth bad; to accept the blame for sth: *She has a lot to answer for. ◇ He's old enough to answer for his own actions. ◇ When it comes to violence among young people, television has a great deal to answer for.* OBJ **the consequences, sb's actions 2** to say that you are certain that sb has a particular quality or can be trusted or relied on: *I can answer for her honesty.* ⟩SYN⟨ **vouch for sth**
◆ v + prep

'answer to sb (for sth) to have to explain your actions to sb or show that they are right or reasonable: *You will answer to me for any damage to the car. ◇ If anything happens to her, you'll have me to answer to.*
◆ v + prep

'answer to sth to be called sth; to recognize a name as your own: *I answer to either Susan or Sue. ◇ I'm afraid there's no one here answering to that name. ◇ They have a cat answering to the name of Bill.*
OBJ only **name**
◆ v + prep

appeal /ə'piːl/

ap'peal for sth/sb; ap'peal for sb to do sth to make a serious and urgent request for sth or for sth to be done: *The government has appealed for calm. ◇ The police appealed for witnesses to*
come forward. ◇ The victim's family has appealed for help in tracking down the killer.
OBJ **witnesses, help, information, calm, funds**
◆ v + prep ◆ v + prep + n/pron + to inf

ap'peal to sb if sth **appeals to** you, you like it or find it interesting and attractive: *The 'Harry Potter' books appeal to readers of all ages. ◇ The prospect of camping didn't appeal to me.*
◆ v + prep

ap'peal to sth to try to persuade sb to do sth by reminding them that it is a good, reasonable thing to do: *Maybe if you appeal to her better nature (= her kindness), you can get her to help.*
OBJ **sb's better nature, sb's sense of justice**
◆ v + prep

appertain /,æpə'tem; AmE -pər't-/

apper'tain to sth (*formal*) to belong to sth; to be connected with sth: *the duties appertaining to the post*
NOTE This verb is usually only used in written English.
◆ v + prep

apprise /ə'praɪz/

ap'prise sb of sth (*formal*) to tell or inform sb of sth: *We were fully apprised of the situation.*
◆ v + n/pron + prep

argue /'ɑːgjuː; AmE 'ɑːrg-/

,argue sb 'into sth; ,argue sb 'into doing sth to persuade sb to do sth by giving them a large number of reasons why they should do it: *I managed to argue him into going back home to talk to his parents.*
⟩OPP⟨ **argue sb out of sth, argue sb out of doing sth**
◆ v + n/pron + prep

,argue sth 'out to discuss all the details of an idea, a plan, etc., often in an excited or angry way, until you reach a decision: *I'm sure they'll manage to argue out any differences that arise. ◇ I'm too tired to argue it out with you now. ◇ The issues have all been argued out at great length.*
◆ v + adv + n ◆ v + n/pron + adv

,argue sb 'out of sth; ,argue sb 'out of doing sth to persuade sb not to do sth by giving them a large number of reasons why they should not do it: *I argued her out of her crazy idea.*
⟩OPP⟨ **argue sb into sth, argue sb into doing sth**
◆ v + n/pron + adv + prep

'argue with sth to disagree with what sb says; to say or show that sth is not right: *'It's cold today, isn't it?' 'I can't argue with you there! (= I agree with you).' ◇ It's a lovely jacket — and you couldn't argue with the price.*

NOTE **Argue with sth** is often used with *can't* or another negative.
◈ v + prep

arrive /əˈraɪv/

arˈrive at sth to agree on sth or to find sth after discussing and thinking about it: *They had both arrived at the same conclusion.* ◇ *It didn't take long to arrive at a decision.*
OBJ conclusion, decision, agreement
SYN reach sth
◈ v + prep

arse /ɑːs; AmE ɑːrs/

,arse aˈbout/aˈround (*BrE*, △, *slang*) to behave in a silly or annoying way and waste time instead of doing what you are supposed to be doing: *Stop arsing about and give me my bag back.*
NOTE **Mess around** and **play around** are more polite verbs to use to express this.
◈ v + adv

ascribe /əˈskraɪb/

aˈscribe sth to sb to consider, perhaps wrongly, that sth has been written, painted, spoken or created by a particular person: *This play is usually ascribed to Shakespeare.*
SYN attribute sth to sb
◈ v + n/pron + prep

aˈscribe sth to sb/sth (*formal*) **1** to consider that sth is caused by a particular person or thing: *He ascribed his exhaustion to the heat and an unfamiliar diet.* **2** to consider that a person or a thing has a particular quality: *I am reluctant to ascribe supernatural powers to a fortune teller.* ◇ *The government ascribe great importance to these policies.*
SYN attribute sth to sb/sth
◈ v + n/pron + prep

ask /ɑːsk; AmE æsk/

ˈask after sb to ask for news about sb and how they are, etc: *Did she ask after me in her letter?*
SYN enquire after sb (*formal*)
◈ v + prep

,ask sb aˈlong to ask sb if they would like to go with you to an event or activity: *Jane and Ed are going to a movie tonight, and they've asked me along.*
SYN invite sb along (*more formal*)
◈ v + n/pron + adv ♦ v + adv + n (*rare*)

,ask aˈround to ask a number of different people in order to find out sth: *I don't know if there's any work, but I'll ask around for you.*
◈ v + adv

,ask sb aˈround (*AmE*) = ASK SB OVER/ROUND

,ask sb ˈback (to sth) (*especially BrE*) to invite sb to come back to your house with you for a drink, etc. when you are both out together: *I asked him back for a coffee.*
SYN have sb back; invite sb back (to sth) (*more formal*)
◈ v + n/pron + adv

ˈask for sb to say that you want to see or speak to sb: *There's somebody at the door asking for Pete.*
◈ v + prep

ˈask for sth **1** to say that you want sb to give you sth: *Jodie asked for a guitar for her birthday.* ◇ *If you get into trouble, don't hesitate to ask for help.* ◇ *We couldn't have asked for better weather.* ◇ *A beautiful house, husband and children. What more could you ask for?* **SYN** request sth (*formal*) **2** (*informal*) if sb is **asking for trouble** or **asking for it**, they are behaving in a way that is likely to cause sth bad to happen to them: *You're asking for trouble walking home alone at night.* ◇ *'You asked for it!'* (= you deserve what I am going to do to you)' *she said, pouring a bucket of water over his head.* **OBJ** trouble, it **3** to say that you want to speak to sb or be directed to a place: *When you arrive, go to reception and ask for George.* ◇ *Ask for the station if you get lost.*
◈ v + prep

,ask sb ˈin/ˈup to invite sb to come into the room or building that you are in, especially your home: *Aren't you going to ask me in? It's cold out here.* ◇ *She asked me into her office for a chat.* ◇ *Once we get settled, we must ask the neighbours in for coffee.*
SYN invite sb in/up (*more formal*)
◈ v + n/pron + adv

,ask sb ˈout to invite sb to go out with you, especially when you would like a romantic relationship with them: *Has he asked you out yet?*
SYN invite sb out (*more formal*)
◈ v + n/pron + adv

,ask sb ˈover/ˈround (*BrE*) (*AmE* ,ask sb aˈround) to invite sb to come and visit you in your home: *She's asked me round for dinner.*
SYN invite sb over/round (*more formal*)
◈ v + n/pron + adv

,ask sb ˈup = ASK SB IN/UP

aspire /əˈspaɪə(r)/

aˈspire to sth to have a strong desire to gain or achieve sth: *He's never really aspired to great wealth.*
◈ v + prep

associate /əˈsəʊʃieɪt; AmE əˈsoʊ-/

asˈsociate with sb to be involved with or spend a lot of time with sb or with a group of people, especially people that sb else does not approve of: *I don't like the people you associate with.*
◈ v + prep

as'sociate yourself with sb/sth (*formal*) to say that you agree with sb or with their ideas: *It was unreasonable to expect the Democrats to associate themselves with spending cuts and tax increases.*
OPP **dissociate yourself from sb/sth**
✦ v + pron + prep

attend /ə'tend/

at'tend to sb/sth (*formal*) to deal with or take responsibility for sth; to give practical help and care to sb who needs it: *I have some urgent business to attend to.* ◇ (*BrE*) *Are you being attended to?*
OBJ **business, needs, customer**
SYN **look after sb; look after sth; see to sb/sth** (*less formal*)
✦ v + prep

attribute /ə'trɪbjuːt/

at'tribute sth to sb to consider, perhaps wrongly, that sth has been written, painted, spoken or created by a particular person: *This painting is usually attributed to Goya.*
SYN **ascribe sth to sb**
✦ v + n/pron + prep

at'tribute sth to sb/sth to consider that sth is caused by a particular person or thing: *His success can be largely attributed to hard work.* ◇ *She said she was not going to attribute blame or seek revenge for what had happened.*
SYN **ascribe sth to sb/sth; put sth down to sth** (*less formal*)
✦ v + n/pron + prep

auction /'ɔːkʃn, *BrE also* 'ɒk-/

auction sth 'off to sell sth at an auction, especially sth that sb no longer needs or wants: *The house and all its contents will be auctioned off next week.*
✦ v + adv + n ◆ v + n/pron + adv

avail /ə'veɪl/

a'vail yourself of sth (*formal*) to make use of sth; to take advantage of sth, usually to improve your situation: *Guests are encouraged to avail*

themselves of all the hotel's services. ◇ *I'd like to avail myself of this opportunity to thank you all.*
OBJ **facilities, opportunity**
✦ v + pron + prep

average /'ævərɪdʒ/

average 'out to result in a fair or equal amount over a period of time or after several occasions: *Sometimes I do the cooking and sometimes my flatmate does. It averages out over a month* (= results in us each doing the same amount of cooking).
✦ v + adv

average sth 'out (**at sth**) to calculate the average of sth: *If you average it out, there's one car stolen every three minutes.* ◇ *The tax authorities averaged out his profit at £10 000 a year over five years.*
✦ v + adv + n ◆ v + n/pron + adv

average 'out at sth to have a particular amount as the average over a period of time: *The time she spends practising the piano averages out at about an hour a day.*
✦ v + adv + prep

awake /ə'weɪk/ (**awoke** /ə'wəʊk/; *AmE* ə'woʊk/, **awoken** /ə'wəʊkən/; *AmE* ə'woʊkən/)

a'wake to sth (*formal*) to become aware of sth and its possible results; to realize or understand sth: *They finally awoke to the full extent of the problem.* ◇ *I suddenly awoke to the fact that I had the answer in front of me.*
→ *see also* AWAKEN TO STH, AWAKEN SB TO STH
✦ v + prep

awaken /ə'weɪkən/

a'waken to sth; a'waken sb to sth (*formal*) to become aware of sth, or to make sb become aware of sth, and its possible results: *People are gradually awakening to their rights.* ◇ *The public has been awakened to the full horror of the situation.*
→ *see also* AWAKE TO STH
✦ v + prep ◆ v + n/pron + prep

Bb

back /bæk/

,back a'way; **,back a'way from sb/sth** to move backwards away from sb/sth frightening or unpleasant: *He stepped forward and she backed away in alarm.* ◇ *The child backed away from the dog nervously.*

[SYN] **retreat (from sb/sth)** (*more formal*)

→ *see also* BACK OFF 2

⬥ v + adv ◆ v + adv + prep

,back a'way from sth; **,back a'way from doing sth** to avoid doing sth unpleasant or difficult; to show that you no longer support an action or an idea: *We will not back away from tough measures.* ◇ *The union has backed away from calling a strike.*

⬥ v + adv + prep

,back 'down (on/from sth) to take back a claim or a demand that you have made, or sth that you have said, usually because sb forces you to: *Neither of them will back down on this issue.* ◇ *His critics were forced to back down.*

[SYN] **climb down (over sth)**; **give in (to sb/sth)**

→ *see also* BACK OFF (FROM STH/FROM DOING STH), BACK OFF STH

⬥ v + adv

,back 'off 1 (*informal*) to stop threatening or annoying sb: *Back off and let me make my own decisions.* ◇ *The press have agreed to back off and leave the couple alone.* **2** to move away from sb/sth frightening or unpleasant: *As the head teacher approached the children backed off.* [SYN] **retreat (from sb/sth)** → *see also* BACK AWAY, BACK AWAY FROM SB/STH

⬥ v + adv

,back 'off (from sth/ from doing sth), **,back 'off sth** (*especially AmE*) to decide not to continue to do sth or support an idea, in order to avoid a difficult or unpleasant situation: *The government backed off in the face of strong opposition.* ◇ *He refused to back off from his earlier statement.* ◇ *The rebels backed off their demand for meeting with the President.*

→ *see also* BACK DOWN (ON/FROM STH)

⬥ v + adv ◆ v + prep

,back 'onto sth (*BrE*) if a building **backs onto** sth, it has sth behind it: *The hotel backs onto the golf course.*

⬥ v + prep

,back 'out; **,back 'out of sth**; **,back 'out of doing sth** to decide not to do sth that you had agreed or promised to do: *Everything's arranged. It's too late to back out now.* ◇ *There's still time to back out of selling the house.*

[SYN] **pull out, pull out of sth, pull out of doing sth; withdraw (from sth)** (*more formal*)

⬥ v + adv ◆ v + adv + prep

,back 'up; **,back sb/sth 'up** to move backwards a short distance, especially in a vehicle; to make sb/sth move backwards a short distance: *You can back up another two metres or so.* ◇ *Jeff backed the van up and drove off quickly.* ◇ (*figurative*) *The woman was backed up against the wall.*

[SYN] **reverse, reverse sth** (*more formal*)

⬥ v + adv ◆ v + n/pron + adv ◆ v + adv + n

,back 'up; **,back sth 'up** if traffic **backs up** or is **backed up**, it cannot move and forms a long line: *Two lanes were closed by the accident, causing cars to back up for miles.* ◇ *The traffic is backed up to the traffic lights.*

[NOTE] **Back sth up** is nearly always used in the passive.

⬥ v + adv ◆ v + n/pron + adv ◆ v + adv + n

,back sb/sth 'up 1 to say or show that what sb says is true: *If I tell my parents I was with you, will you back me up?* ◇ *His version of events is not backed up by the evidence.* [OBJ] **statement, claim 2** to support or help sb/sth: *Mel complained that her husband never backed her up in the control of the children.* ◇ *Backing her up* (= playing music to support her) *was the band 'Midnight Express'.*

[SYN] **support sb/sth**

⬥ v + n/pron + adv ◆ v + adv + n (*less frequent*)

▶ **'backup** *n* [C] [U] (*AmE, music*) (*usually used as an adjective*) music that supports the main singer or player in popular music or jazz: *a backup singer for Stevie Wonder* ◇ *She once sang backup for Madonna.*

→ *see also* BACK-UP at BACK STH UP

,back sth 'up 1 (*computing*) to make a copy of a file, a program, etc. that can be used if the original one is lost or damaged: *We back up all the files every night.* [OBJ] **file 2** to add sth extra to sth, especially as a support: *The lectures will be backed up by practical work.* ◇ *They backed up their demands with threats.*

⬥ v + n/pron + adv ◆ v + adv + n

▶ **'back-up** *n* **1** [U] support or help that you can use in order to do sth: *military back-up* ◇ *They have a huge back-up team.* **2** [C] a second piece of equipment, set of plans, person, etc. that can replace another if necessary: *He's our back-up if another player isn't available.* ◇ *the back-up plan* **3** [C] (*computing*) a copy of a file, program, etc. for use in case the original is lost or damaged: *Have you kept a back-up of this file?* ◇ *a back-up disk*

→ *see also* BACKUP at BACK SB/STH UP

bag /bæg/ (-gg-)

,bag sth 'up to put sth, usually large amounts of sth, into a bag or bags: *The vegetables are bagged up on the farm and then sent out to the shop.*
NOTE Bag sth can also be used with this meaning.
◈ v + adv + n ◆ v + n/pron + adv

bail /beɪl/

,bail 'out; ,bail 'out of sth 1 (*BrE also* ,bale 'out, ,bale 'out of sth) to jump out of a plane that is going to crash, using a parachute (= a large piece of cloth that opens out like an umbrella and makes people fall slowly and safely): *The crew just had time to bail out.* **2** (*AmE*) to stop doing sth or taking part in sth because it is difficult or unpleasant: *The actor who was supposed to be playing the part bailed out.* → *see also* BACK OUT, BACK OUT OF STH, BACK OUT OF DOING STH
◈ v + adv + prep

,bail 'out; ,bail sth 'out (*BrE also* ,bale 'out, ,bale sth 'out) to throw water out of a boat with a container or with your hands: *The boat will sink unless we bail out.* ◇ *They started bailing the boat out.*
OBJ boat, water
◈ v + adv ◆ v + n/pron + adv ◆ v + adv + n

,bail sb 'out (*law*) to pay sb's bail (= the money that sb accused of a crime has to pay if they do not appear at their trial) for them, so that they can be set free until their trial
◈ v + n/pron + adv ◆ v + adv + n

,bail sb/sth 'out; ,bail sb/sth 'out of sth (*BrE also* ,bale sb/sth 'out, ,bale sb/sth 'out of sth) (*informal*) to rescue sb/sth from difficulties, especially financial difficulties: *The government has refused to bail the company out again.*
◈ v + n/pron + adv ◆ v + adv + n ◆ v + n/pron + adv + prep
▶ **'bailout** *n* (*especially AmE, finance*) an act of giving financial help to a company, economy, etc. to save it from failing: *government/bank bailouts* ◇ *a bailout package*

balance /'bæləns/

'balance A against B to compare the value or importance of one plan, argument, etc. against another: *You must balance the high salary against the long working hours.*
SYN set sth against sth
◈ v + n/pron + prep

,balance 'out; ,balance sth 'out/'up if things that are very different or have opposite effects balance out or you balance them out, they become equal in amount or value: *If you eat a variety of food, protein and carbohydrate will balance out over a week.* ◇ *We need to invite three more girls to balance up the numbers* (= so that there are equal numbers of boys and girls).
◈ v + adv ◆ v + adv + n ◆ v + n/pron + adv

bale /beɪl/

,bale 'out; ,bale 'out of sth (*BrE*) = BAIL OUT, BAIL OUT OF STH 1

,bale 'out; ,bale sth 'out (*BrE*) = BAIL OUT, BAIL STH OUT

,bale sb/sth 'out; ,bale sb/sth 'out of sth (*BrE*) = BAIL SB/STH OUT, BAIL SB/STH OUT OF STH

balk /bɔːk/

'balk at sth; 'balk at doing sth (*especially AmE*) = BAULK AT STH, BAULK AT DOING STH

balls /bɔːlz/

,balls sth 'up (*BrE*, △) to spoil sth; to do sth very badly
NOTE A more polite, informal way of saying this is foul sth up or bungle sth.
◈ v + n/pron + adv ◆ v + adv + n
▶ **'balls-up** *n* (△, *slang, especially BrE*) something that has been done very badly: *I made a real balls-up of my exams.*
NOTE A more polite, informal way of saying this is foul-up.

band /bænd/

,band to'gether to form a group and act together in order to achieve sth, etc: *We need to band together to fight these reforms.*
◈ v + adv

bandage /'bændɪdʒ/

,bandage sb/sth 'up to wrap a bandage (= a long narrow strip of material) around a part of the body that is injured: *Joe bandaged me up until the doctor came.* ◇ *I didn't see the burns because her fingers were all bandaged up.*
OBJ wound, sb's leg/arm, etc.
NOTE Bandage sb/sth up is often used in the passive. ◆ Bandage sb/sth is also used with this meaning.
◈ v + n/pron + adv ◆ v + adv + n

bandy /'bændi/ (bandies, bandying, bandied, bandied)

,bandy sth a'bout (*also* ,bandy sth a'round *especially BrE*) if a word, a name, etc. is bandied about, it is mentioned or talked about by many people, often in a careless way: *The stories being bandied about are completely false.* ◇ *He's not paid anything like the £4 000 a week figure being bandied around.*
OBJ story, figures, word/term
NOTE Bandy sth about/around is usually used in the passive.
◈ v + adv + n ◆ v + n/pron + adv

bang /bæŋ/

bang a'round (*also* **bang a'bout** *especially BrE*) to move around noisily: *We could hear them banging about upstairs, moving things.*
◆ v + adv

bang a'way 1 (*informal*) to hit sth repeatedly with lots of force or energy: *She picked up the hammer and began banging away with enthusiasm.* **2** if sth such as your heart **bangs away**, it makes very loud regular sounds: *My heart was banging away unhealthily.*
◆ v + adv

bang a'way at sth (*AmE, informal*) to work very hard at sth: *She banged away all day at her assignment.*
SYN **bash away (at sth)** (*BrE*)
◆ v + adv + prep

bang sth 'down to put sth down quickly and with a lot of force so that it makes a loud noise: *He banged his fist down on the table.* ◇ *He banged the phone down* (= ended the telephone conversation) *before I could explain.*
◆ v + n/pron + adv ◆ v + adv + n

bang 'into sb/sth to crash into or hit sb/sth violently, usually by mistake: *He ran around the corner and banged into an old lady who was coming the other way.*
◆ v + prep

bang 'on about sb/sth (*BrE, informal*) to talk or write a lot or in a boring way about sth: *Pat is always banging on about politics.* ◇ *She keeps banging on about how wonderful her son is.*
SYN **go on (about sb/sth)**
◆ v + adv + prep

bang 'out sth; **bang it/them 'out** (*informal*) **1** to play music very loudly: *He banged out the tune on the piano.* **2** to write sth very quickly and without taking much care: *She was banging out four novels a year.* SYN **bash sth out** (*BrE*); **churn sth out**
NOTE A noun must always follow **out**, but a pronoun comes between the verb and **out**.
◆ v + adv + n ◆ v + pron + adv

bang sb/sth 'up (*AmE, informal*) to damage or injure sb/sth, especially by hitting sth else: *I banged up my knee when I fell off the bike.*
◆ v + adv + n ◆ v + n/pron + adv

be/get ,banged 'up (*BrE, informal*) to be locked up or put in prison: *He was banged up in a Singapore jail for six months.*
◆ be/get + v + adv

bank /bæŋk/

bank on sb/sth; **bank on doing sth**; **bank on sb/sth doing sth** to rely on sb/sth; to be confident that sth will happen: *I'm banking on your help.* ◇ *I'm banking on you to help me.* ◇ *I'd*

banked on getting a cup of coffee at the airport, but everything was closed. ◇ *He was banking on the train being on time.* ◇ *She might already have cleaned up but I wouldn't bank on it.*
SYN **count on sb/sth, count on doing sth, count on sb/sth doing sth; reckon on sb/sth, reckon on doing sth, reckon on sb/sth doing sth**
◆ v + prep ◆ v + prep + n/pron + to inf

bank 'up; **bank sth 'up** (*BrE*) to form into a large pile; to make sth form a large pile: *The snow had banked up on either side of the road.*
◆ v + adv ◆ v + n/pron + adv ◆ v + adv + n

bargain /'bɑːgən; AmE 'bɑːrgən/

bargain sth a'way (*rare*) to give away sth valuable or important in exchange for sth less valuable or important: *The leaders refused to bargain away the freedom of their people.*
◆ v + adv + n ◆ v + pron + adv ◆ v + n + adv (*less frequent*)

bargain for/on sth; **bargain for/on doing sth**; **bargain for/on sb/sth doing sth** to expect or be prepared to do sth; to expect sth to happen or sb to do sth: *We hadn't bargained for such bad weather.* ◇ *I hadn't bargained on taking the kids with us.* ◇ *I didn't bargain for Jake being at the party.* ◇ *When he tried to argue with Kate, he got more than he had bargained for.* ◇ *What I hadn't bargained for was that very few people would speak English.*
SYN **reckon on sb/sth, reckon on doing sth, reckon on sb/sth doing sth**
NOTE These phrasal verbs are usually used in negative sentences.
◆ v + prep

barge /bɑːdʒ; AmE bɑːrdʒ/

barge 'in (on sb/sth), **barge 'into sth** (*informal*) **1** to enter a place or join a group of people quickly and rudely, without being asked: *Sorry to barge in, but…* ◇ *She barged in on our meeting without knocking.* ◇ *He just barged (his way) into the room.* **2** to interrupt what sb is doing or saying, especially when you have not been invited to join in: *As soon as I paused for breath, Bart barged in.* ◇ *You can't just come barging into our conversation!*
◆ v + adv ◆ v + prep

bark /bɑːk; AmE bɑːrk/

bark sth 'out to shout sth loudly: *She barked out instructions to her secretary.*
OBJ **orders, instructions** SYN **rap sth out**
NOTE **Bark sth** can also be used with the same meaning: *He barked orders at Tim.*
◆ v + adv + n ◆ v + n/pron + adv ◆ v + adv + speech

barricade /ˌbærɪˈkeɪd/

barriˌcade yourself/sb 'in; barriˌcade yourself/sb 'in/'into/in'side sth to put up a line of objects at the entrance to a room or building, so that nobody can get in or out, usually to protect or defend yourself or sb else: *The police were called when he barricaded himself in.* ◇ *They barricaded themselves inside their house.* ◇ *Families had to be barricaded inside a restaurant while students protested outside.*
OBJ **room, house**
⊕ v + n/pron + adv ♦ v + n/pron + prep

base /beɪs/

'base sth on sth (*also* **'base sth upon sth** *more formal*) to use or have an idea, an experience, etc. as the point from which sth can be developed: *The novel is based on a true story.* ◇ *She is basing the prosecution case on the evidence of two witnesses.* ◇ *What's the design based on?* ◇ *The report has been based upon inaccurate information.* ◇ *Sue's knowledge of Japan was based only on what she had read in books.*
OBJ **decision, theory, design, opinion, etc.**
NOTE **Base sth on/upon sth** is often used in the passive.
⊕ v + n/pron + prep

bash /bæʃ/

bash sb/sth a'bout (*BrE, informal*) to hit or strike sb/sth and treat them/it in a rough way: *The mugger had bashed her about.*
⊕ v + n/pron + adv

bash a'way (at sth) (*BrE*) to work very hard at sth for a period of time: *I bashed away at the article without a break from 11 until 6.*
⊕ v + adv

bash sth 'down (*informal, especially BrE*) to destroy sth and make it fall by hitting it violently: *The firefighters had to bash the door down.*
OBJ **door** SYN **break sth down** (*more formal*), **knock sth down** (*more formal*)
⊕ v + n/pron + adv ♦ v + adv + n

bash sth 'in (*informal, especially BrE*) to break or destroy sth by hitting it violently: *The window had been bashed in.*
OBJ **window, head, skull, nose**
SYN **smash sth in**
NOTE **Bash sth in** is often used in the passive.
⊕ v + n/pron + adv ♦ v + adv + n
IDM **bash sb's 'head/'brains in** (*informal*) to hit sb very hard: *Shut up or I'll bash your brains in!*

bash 'on (with sth) (*BrE, informal*) to continue working hard at sth: *Let's bash on.* ◇ *I'd better bash on with my work.*
SYN **get on (with sth)** (*more formal*)
⊕ v + adv

bash sth 'out (*BrE, informal*) to write sth very quickly, without taking much care: *I don't do drafts of articles. I just bash them out.*
SYN **bang out sth**
⊕ v + adv + n ♦ v + n/pron + adv

bash sb 'up (*BrE, informal*) to attack sb violently
SYN **beat sb up** (*more formal*)
NOTE **Bash sb up** is used less often than the synonym **beat sb up**.
⊕ v + n/pron + adv ♦ v + adv + n

bat /bæt/ (**-tt-**)

bat sth a'round (*informal*) to talk about or discuss plans or ideas, etc. before you decide what to do: *We're just batting some ideas around.*
OBJ **ideas, figures**
⊕ v + n/pron + adv ♦ v + adv + n

batten /ˈbætn/

batten sth 'down to fasten sth firmly in order to prevent damage by storms or winds: *They managed to batten down the shutters and doors before the hurricane hit.*
⊕ v + adv + n ♦ v + n/pron + adv
IDM **batten down the 'hatches** to prepare for difficult times ahead: *Businesses are battening down the hatches and preparing for a difficult year.*

batter /ˈbætə(r)/

batter sth 'down to hit sth repeatedly until it breaks and falls down: *The only way to get in was to batter the door down.*
OBJ **door** SYN **break sth down; beat sth down**
⊕ v + n/pron + adv ♦ v + adv + n

baulk (*especially BrE*) (*AmE usually* **balk**) /bɔːk/

'baulk at sth; 'baulk at doing sth to be unwilling to do sth or to get involved in sth because it is difficult, dangerous, expensive, etc: *He baulked at the idea of telling his parents where he was going.*
OBJ **idea, expense**
⊕ v + prep

bawl /bɔːl/

bawl sb 'out (*informal*) to speak angrily to sb because they have done sth wrong: *My boss bawled me out for being late.*
SYN **tell sb off (for sth/for doing sth)**
⊕ v + n/pron + adv ♦ v + adv + n
▶ **bawling-'out** n [usually sing.] (*informal*) an act of speaking angrily to sb because they have done sth wrong

,bawl sth 'out (*informal, especially BrE*) to say or sing sth very loudly or in a harsh voice: *She doesn't give you an order. She bawls it out.* ◇ *The children bawled out the songs.*
  ✦ v + adv + n ♦ v + pron + adv ♦ v + n + adv (*rare*) ♦ v + adv + speech

be /bi; strong form biː/ (**is/are**, **being**, **was** /wəz, wɒz; *AmE* wɑːz, wʌz/, **were** /wə(r), wɜː(r)/, **been** /biːn, bɪn/)

~ after	~ on
~ at　　　　12	~ on about
~ away	~/go/keep on at
~ before	~ onto
~ behind	~ out
~ behind with	~ out for
~ down	~ out of
~ down on	~ over
~ down to	~ past
~/go down with	~ through
~ in	~ up
~ in for	~ up against
~/get in on	~ up before
~ (well) in with	~ up for
~ into	~ up to
~ off　　　　13	~ upon
~ off for	

be 'after sth to try to get or obtain sth: *Several people in the office are after the same job.* ◇ *She's being too nice. I wonder what she's after.*
  ✦ v + prep

be 'at sb (*informal, especially BrE*) = BE/GO/KEEP ON AT SB

be 'at sth to be busy doing sth: *He's been at his essay all night.* ◇ *I'll be at it all day tomorrow.*
  ✦ v + prep
  IDM **be 'at it** to behave badly; to argue or fight: *The kids are at it again.*

be a'way to not be at home, especially when you are on holiday/vacation or on a business trip: *We'll be away for the month of August.* ◇ *He's away on business at the moment.*
  ✦ v + adv

be before sb = BE UP BEFORE SB

be be'hind sb to give sb your support: *Don't forget that we're behind you all the way.*
  ✦ v + prep

be be'hind with sth to be late doing sth, such as paying a bill, your rent, etc: *We're behind with the mortgage repayments.* ◇ *I'm behind with my college assignments.*
  ✦ v + adv + prep

be 'down if a computer system **is down**, it is not working temporarily: *Surely your computer isn't down again?*
  ✦ v + adv

be 'down on sb to treat sb severely or unfairly: *He's been really down on me lately.*
  ✦ v + adv + prep

be 'down to sb to be the responsibility of sb; to be sb's fault: *It's down to you to help them now.*
  ✦ v + adv + prep

be 'down to sth to have only a little money left: *I'm down to my last dollar.*
  ✦ v + adv + prep

be/go 'down with sth to have or catch an illness: *Gill's down with flu.*
  ✦ v + adv + prep

be 'in 1 to be in fashion: *Miniskirts are in this season.* **2** to be elected to a political position: *The Democrats are in for another term.*
  ✦ v + adv

be 'in for sth (*informal*) to be going to experience sth soon, especially sth unpleasant: *She's in for a shock.* ◇ *It looks like we're in for a storm.*
  ✦ v + adv + prep

be/get 'in on sth (*informal*) to have a share in or knowledge of sth; to be or become involved in sth: *Are you in on the secret?* ◇ *I'd like to be in on the deal.*
  ✦ v + adv + prep

be (well) 'in with sb to be (very) friendly with sb and likely to get an advantage from the friendship
  ✦ v + adv + prep

be 'into sth to have a taste for or an interest in sth: *Are you into jazz music?* ◇ *He's been into trains since he was a small boy.*
  ✦ v + prep

be 'off 1 to leave; to go, especially in a hurry: *I must be off.* **2** to have gone bad and not be fit to eat or drink: *This milk is off.*
  ✦ v + adv

be 'off sth 1 to have no interest in sth; to have stopped liking sth: *She can't be well. She's been off her food all week.* ◇ *That's it. I'm off men for life.* **2** to have finished speaking on the telephone: *Isn't he off the phone yet?*
  ✦ v + prep

be ,off for 'sth (*informal*) to have a particular amount of sth: *How are we off for coffee* (= how much have we got)?
  ✦ v + adv + prep

be 'on 1 (of an event, a show, a performance, etc.) to be happening; to take place: *Is the party still on?* **2** (of a performer) to be on the stage; to perform: *Who's on next?* ◇ *We're on after the support band.* **3** (of food) to be cooking: *Are the potatoes on?*
  ✦ v + adv
  IDM **you're 'on** (*spoken, informal*) used when you are accepting a bet or a challenge

be 'on sb if sth such as drinks, food, tickets, etc. **are on** sb, they are paid for by that person: *The drinks are on me tonight.*
  ✦ v + prep

be 'on sth 1 to be taking medicine, a drug, etc: *She's been on the pill for ten years.* ◇ *I'm on strong painkillers.* **2** to be talking to sb on the telephone: *She's been on the phone for hours.* **3** to be eating or drinking sth: *I'm on my third coffee already this morning.*
◈ v + prep

IDM **what are you 'on?** (*spoken, informal*) used when you are very surprised at sb's behaviour and are suggesting that they are acting in a similar way to sb using drugs

be 'on about sth (*informal, especially BrE*) to talk about sth, often in a boring way; to mean sth: *He's always on about how much money he earns.* ◇ *What are you on about?* (= I don't really understand).
◈ v + adv + prep

be/go/keep 'on at sb (*also* **be 'at sb**) (*informal, especially BrE*) to try to persuade sb to do sth by talking about it very often and in an annoying way: *I've been on at my husband to go to the doctor, but he won't.*
SYN **nag sb**
◈ v + adv + prep ◆ v + prep

be 'onto sb (*informal*) **1** to become aware that sb has done sth wrong or illegal and be trying to catch them: *The police aren't onto us yet.* **2** to talk to sb about sth, especially to complain about sth or ask them to do sth: *I've been onto the council about the noise.*
◈ v + prep

be 'onto sth to find or discover sth that could have very good results for you or for sb else: *She could be onto something* (= she might have discovered sth that will prove important).
◈ v + prep

be 'out 1 to have stopped work as a protest and be on strike: *The postal workers are still out.* **2** to be no longer in prison: *I've heard Smith's out now.* **3** if a jury (= a group of people who decide the results of a competition or whether or not sb is guilty of a crime) **is out**, they are still trying to make a decision **4** to no longer be in fashion: *Black is out this year.* ◇ *Politeness seems to be out of fashion these days* (= no one is polite any more). **5** if an action, for example, **is out**, it is not possible or is not allowed: *Shall we get together one evening next week? Monday's out — I've got a French class.*
◈ v + adv

IDM **the jury is (still) 'out on sth** used when you are saying that sth is still not certain: *The jury is still out on whether wine can be good for you.*

be 'out for sth; **be 'out to do sth** to be trying very hard to do sth or to get sth: *He's out for revenge.* ◇ *Everyone's just out for what they can get these days* (= they are trying to get things for themselves). ◇ *The German team want to win this game, but Brazil are out to stop them.*
◈ v + adv + prep ◆ v + adv + to inf

be 'out of sth to have used up a supply of sth and have nothing left: *We're out of sugar.*
◈ v + adv + prep

be 'over sb to have returned to your usual state of happiness after the end of a relationship: *It was hard at first, but I'm over him now.*
◈ v + prep

be 'over sth to have returned to your normal state of health after an illness: *He's over the flu now.*
◈ v + prep

be 'past it (*informal*) used to show that you think sb is so old that they can no longer do anything useful or interesting: *The children laughed at him and said he was past it.*
◈ v + prep + it

be 'through (to sb) to be connected to sb on the telephone: *You're through now.* ◇ *You're through to the manager now.*
◈ v + adv

be 'through (with sb/sth) (*especially AmE*) to have finished using or doing sth; to have finished a relationship with sb: *Aren't you through yet? You've been ages!* ◇ *He promised he was through with drugs.* ◇ *Keith and I are through.*
◈ v + adv

be 'up 1 to be awake: *You're up early.* ◇ *I've been up all night.* **2** (of the wind, the sea, etc.) to increase in strength or become violent: *In the morning the wind was up and we got ready for a day's sailing.* **3** (*spoken, informal*) (of a drink, a meal, etc.) to be ready: *Tea's up! Come and get it.*
→ *see also* WHAT'S UP at BE UP TO STH
◈ v + adv

be 'up against sb/sth to be facing problems or difficulties: *We're up against tough competition.* ◇ *With three players injured, they were really up against it* (= in a difficult situation). ◇ *Do you realize what you're up against?*
◈ v + adv + prep

be 'up before sb (*also* **be be'fore sb**) to appear in court or before a judge: *He's up before the judge tomorrow.*
◈ v + adv + prep ◆ v + prep

be 'up for sth 1 to be considered for sth, especially as a candidate for a job, in an election, etc: *She's up for promotion.* ◇ (*informal*) *There are 50 tickets up for grabs* (= available for people who ask quickly). **2** to be for sb to buy: *I see your house is up for sale.* ◇ *A Picasso is up for auction.* **3** (*informal*) to be ready to take part in an activity: *The new job will be a challenge, but I'm up for it.*
◈ v + adv + prep

be 'up to sb 1 to be sb's responsibility or duty: *It's up to you to make sure the house is kept tidy.* **2** to be left to sb to decide: 'Shall we go out?' 'It's up to you.'
◈ v + adv + prep

be 'up to sth (*informal*) **1** to be busy doing sth, especially sth bad: *What have you been up to lately?* ◇ *The kids are quiet — I'm sure they're up to no good* (= they are doing sth bad). **2** to be as good as people expect: *Was your meal up to standard?*
◆ v + adv + prep

IDM what's up? (*spoken, informal*) **1** used to ask sb if there is something wrong: *You look terrible! What's up?* ◇ *I couldn't understand what was up with George.* **2** used as a greeting to mean 'how are you?', 'what have you been doing?', etc.

be u'pon sb (*formal*) to be going to happen very soon: *The election is almost upon us.*
◆ v + prep

bear /beə(r); *AmE* ber/ (**bore** /bɔː(r)/ **borne** /bɔːn; *AmE* bɔːrn/)

bear 'down on sb/sth (*also* **bear 'down upon sb/sth** *more formal*) **1** (*especially BrE*) to move towards sb/sth in a determined or threatening way: *A crowd of journalists bore down on the minister.* ◇ *A hurricane is bearing down on central America.* **2** (*especially AmE*) if a problem or a difficult situation **bears down on** you, it makes you feel very worried and has a severe effect on you: *The drought is bearing down very hard on farmers.* **3** (*especially AmE*) to press or push on sb/sth: (*figurative*) *The government has announced it will bear down on* (= deal strictly with) *inflation.*
◆ v + adv + prep

bear on/upon sb/sth (*formal*) to be connected with sb/sth; to have an effect on sb/sth: *This decision bears directly on our everyday lives.*
〉SYN **affect sb/sth**
NOTE This verb is mainly used in written English.
◆ v + prep

bear sb/sth 'out (*especially BrE*) to show that sth is true or that what sb says is true; to support sb/sth: *I always said she'd do well. John will bear me out on this.* ◇ *John will bear out what I say.* ◇ *This theory is not borne out by the facts.*
◆ v + n/pron + adv ◆ v + adv + n

bear 'up (**under sth**) to remain cheerful and in control in a difficult situation: *'How is your mother?' 'She's bearing up very well.'* ◇ *'How are you?' 'Oh, bearing up.'*
◆ v + adv

bear upon sb/sth = BEAR ON/UPON SB/STH

bear with sb to be patient with sb: *If you'll just bear with me for a moment, I'll try to find her.* ◇ *She's under a lot of strain. Just bear with her.*
NOTE **Bear with sb** is usually used in the present tense or to ask sb to be patient.
◆ v + prep

beat /biːt/ (**beat, beaten** /ˈbiːtn/)

beat sb 'back to make sb move backwards away from sth: *She was beaten back by the flames.* ◇ *They tried to beat the enemy forces back.*
NOTE **Beat sb back** is usually used in the passive.
◆ v + n/pron + adv ◆ v + adv + n

beat 'down (**on/upon sb/sth**) **1** if the sun **beats down**, it shines with great heat: *The sun beat down all afternoon from a clear sky.* **2** if rain **beats down**, it falls with great force: *The rain was beating down on them.*
◆ v + adv

beat sb/sth 'down to persuade sb to reduce the price of sth; to get sb to accept a lower price for sth: *Chris tried to beat them down to a lower price.*
〉SYN **knock sb/sth down**
◆ v + n/pron + adv ◆ v + adv + n (*less frequent*)

beat sth 'down 1 to hit sth hard, often many times, until it falls down: *The police had to beat the door down.* ◇ *People are hardly beating the door down to get her latest book* (= they are not rushing to buy it). **OBJ door** 〉SYN **break sth down; batter sth down 2** to make sth flatter or lower by hitting it hard, usually with sth flat: *I used a spade to beat down the mud until it was flat and hard.* ◇ *Two women tried to beat down the flames on his back.* **OBJ flames**
◆ v + n/pron + adv ◆ v + adv + n

beat sb/sth 'off 1 to drive sb/sth back or away by fighting: *They beat off an attack by the rebel army.* ◇ *He tried to beat the thugs off with a stick.* **OBJ attack, attacker 2** to defeat sb/sth in a competition: *The company has beaten off very strong competition from abroad.* **OBJ challenge, competition**
◆ v + adv + n ◆ v + n/pron + adv

beat on sb (*AmE, informal*) to hit or kick sb repeatedly
→ *see also* BEAT SB UP; BEAT UP ON SB
◆ v + prep

beat sth 'out 1 to produce a rhythm by hitting sth such as a drum repeatedly **OBJ rhythm 2** to put out a fire by hitting it with sth such as a blanket, a jacket, a brush, etc: *He used his jacket to beat out the flames.* **OBJ flames, fire 3** to make a piece of metal flat by hitting it with a hammer, etc: *Pure gold can be beaten out to form very thin sheets.* **OBJ gold/iron, dent**
◆ v + adv + n ◆ v + pron + adv ◆ v + n + adv (*less frequent*)

beat sb 'out (**for sth**) (*AmE*) to defeat sb in a competition: *They beat out nine other companies for the contract.*
◆ v + n/pron + adv ◆ v + adv + n

beat sb to sth; beat sb 'to it to achieve sth or reach a place before sb else: *Beckham beat everyone else to the ball.* ◇ *Book now before somebody else beats you to it!*
◆ v + n/pron + prep

,beat sb 'up to hit or kick sb repeatedly: *Her husband used to beat her up.* ◇ *The gang went round beating up old ladies.*
  $\overline{\text{SYN}}$ **bash sb up** (*informal, less frequent*)
  → *see also* BEAT UP ON SB
  ✦ v + n/pron + adv ✦ v + adv + n
▶ ,beat-'up (*especially AmE*) (*BrE usually* ,beaten-'up) *adj* [usually before noun] (*informal*) old or damaged: *He drives a beat-up old van.*

,beat yourself 'up (*informal*) to blame yourself for sth; to criticize yourself: *If we don't succeed the first time, we shouldn't beat ourselves up, but try again.*
  ✦ v + pron + adv

,beat 'up on sb (*AmE, informal*) to attack sb physically or with words: *Of course it's not OK to beat up on your wife.* ◇ *He was accused of beating up on the President in the press.*
  → *see also* BEAT ON SB
  ✦ v + adv + prep

beaver /'biːvə(r)/

,beaver a'way (at sth) (*BrE, informal*) to work very hard at sth: *She's been beavering away at her homework for hours.*
  ✦ v + adv

become /bɪ'kʌm/ (became /bɪ'keɪm/ become)

be'come of sb/sth (*formal*) to happen to sb/sth: *I wonder what became of the people who lived next door.* ◇ *What will become of us if I lose my job?*
  NOTE Become of sb/sth is always used in a question with *what*.
  ✦ v + prep

bed /bed/ (-dd-)

,bed 'down (*BrE*) **1** to lie down to go to sleep somewhere you do not normally sleep: *Young people bedded down in doorways.* $\overline{\text{SYN}}$ **doss down** (*BrE, less formal*) **2** (*also* ,bed 'in) if sth/sb new **beds down**, it/they become settled and start to work well: *It'll take a while for the new system to bed down.* ◇ *The new players have bedded down well in the team.*
  ✦ v + adv

beef /biːf/

,beef 'up sth; ,beef it/them 'up (*informal*) to make sth bigger, stronger, more interesting, etc: *Security has been beefed up.* ◇ *The company has been trying to beef up its image.*
  NOTE A noun must always follow **up**, but a pronoun comes between the verb and **up**.
  ✦ v + adv + n ✦ v + pron + adv
▶ 'beefed-up *adj* [only before noun] improved; made bigger, stronger, more interesting, etc: *beefed-up security*

beg /beg/ (-gg-)

,beg 'off; ,beg 'off sth; ,beg 'off doing sth to ask to be excused from sth; to say that you cannot do sth that you are expected or have promised to do: *She was asked to work the weekend shift but she tried to beg off.* ◇ *He begged off visiting his grandparents.*
  $\overline{\text{SYN}}$ **pull out, pull out of sth, pull out of doing sth**
  → *see also* CRY OFF, CRY OFF STH, CRY OFF DOING STH
  ✦ v + adv ✦ v + prep

believe /bɪ'liːv/

be'lieve in sb/sth **1** to feel sure that sb/sth exists: *Do you believe in ghosts?* ◇ *I believe in God.* ◇ *I don't believe in aliens.* → *see also* DISBELIEVE IN SB/STH **2** to have confidence in sb/sth, to feel sure that they/it will be successful or achieve sth: *My parents always believed in me.* ◇ *I have to believe in a product before I can sell it.*
  ✦ v + prep

be'lieve in sth; be'lieve in doing sth to feel that sth is right or valuable; to approve of sth: *Do you believe in capital punishment?* ◇ *She doesn't believe in running risks.* ◇ *I've always believed in giving people a second chance.*
  ✦ v + prep

be'lieve sth of sb to accept that sb is capable of a particular action, etc., especially a bad or immoral one: *Taking drugs! I can't believe that of Lucy!* ◇ *If I hadn't seen him doing it, I would never have believed it of him.* ◇ *She is determined to believe the worst of me* (= think I am capable of doing, and likely to do, sth very bad).
  ✦ v + n/pron + prep

belong /bɪ'lɒŋ; *AmE* -'lɔːŋ/

be'long to sb (*not used in the progressive tenses*) **1** to be the property of sb; to be owned by sb: *The house belonged to my cousin.* ◇ *That land belongs to the golf club.* ◇ *Who does the van belong to?* **2** if a time or an event **belongs to** a team, a group of people, etc. they are the most successful, popular or important: *Britain did well in the athletics competition, but the day belonged to Norway.* ◇ *The second half of the twentieth century belonged to the young.* **3** if a job, a duty, etc. **belongs to** you, it is your responsibility: *The job of disciplining a child belongs to the parents.* ◇ *The credit for our success belongs to the staff* (= they made us successful, for example by working hard).
  ✦ v + prep

be'long to sth **1** to be a member of sth, for example, a club, an organization or a family: *I don't belong to any political party.* ◇ *Portugal already belongs to the European Union.* OBJ (trade) union, club, (political) party **2** to be part of a particular group or system: *Rattlesnakes belong to the viper family.* ◇ *These three turtles all*

belong to one species. OBJ **species, class, group, category 3** to be part of sth or connected with a particular time or place: *These things belong to the past.* ◇ *Writers like him belong to a different generation.* OBJ **the past, generation**
> ✦ v + prep

belt /belt/

,**belt sth 'down** (*AmE, informal*) to drink sth quickly: *He belted down his beer.*
> ⟩SYN⟨ **knock sth back**
> ✦ v + adv + n ◆ v + n/pron + adv

,**belt 'out sth**; ,**belt it/them 'out** (*informal*) if you **belt out** a song or a piece of music, you sing or play it very loudly: *Nobody can belt out a tune like she can.* ◇ *A radio belted out pop music.*
> NOTE A noun must always follow **out**, but a pronoun comes between the verb and **out**.
> ✦ v + adv + n ◆ v + pron + adv

,**belt 'up** (*BrE, informal*) **1** (*spoken*) used to tell sb not very politely to be quiet: *Belt up, will you?* ⟩SYN⟨ **shut up** (*informal*) **2** to fasten the belt that you wear in a car to keep you in your seat if there is an accident (a **seat belt**) ⟩SYN⟨ **buckle up**
> ✦ v + adv

bend /bend/ (**bent, bent** /bent/)

,**bend 'down** to lean down: *He bent down and kissed her on the cheek.*
> ✦ v + adv

,**bend 'over**; ,**bend 'over sth** to lean over; to bend from the waist: *Bend over and touch your toes.* ◇ *He was bending over his desk, writing.*
> ✦ v + adv ◆ v + prep
> IDM **bend over 'backwards** (**to do sth**) to do everything you can or make a great effort to do sth, especially to help sb: *We bend over backwards to be fair to all the children.*

bet /bet/ (**betting, bet, bet** or *less frequent* **betting, betted, betted**)

'**bet on sth**; '**bet on sb doing sth** to rely on sth or on sb doing sth and expect it to happen: *'Do you think she'll come?' 'I wouldn't bet on it* (= I don't think it is very likely).*' ◇ *Don't bet on me still being here when you get back!*
> ⟩SYN⟨ **count on sb/sth, count on doing sth, count on sb/sth doing sth**
> ✦ v + prep

bill /bɪl/

'**bill sb/sth as sth** to describe sb/sth in a particular way; to advertise sb/sth as sth: *Some patients are receiving what has been billed as a revolutionary treatment.* ◇ *The concert was billed as 'A Night of Magic'.*
> ✦ v + n/pron + prep

bind /baɪnd/ (**bound, bound** /baʊnd/)

,**bind sb 'over** (*law*) to warn sb that they will have to appear in court if they break the law again: *He was bound over to keep the peace.*
> NOTE **Bind sb over** is usually used in the passive.
> ✦ v + n/pron + adv ◆ v + adv + n

'**bind sb to sth** (*formal*) to force sb to do sth by making them promise to do it or making it part of a legal document: *The company directors are **bound to secrecy*** (= they have promised not to say anything) *about the future of the company.* ◇ *The band found they were bound to the contract.*
> NOTE **Bind sb to sth** is usually used in the passive.
> ✦ v + n/pron + prep

,**bind sth 'up** (**with sth**) to tie a long thin piece of fabric around sth to protect it: *She bound up his wounds with bandages.*
> ✦ v + adv + n ◆ v + n/pron + adv
> IDM **be bound 'up in sth** to be very busy with sth; to be very interested or involved in sth: *He's too bound up in his work to have much time for his children.* **bound 'up with sth** closely connected with sth: *The history of the mill is closely bound up with the history of the Wilkins family.*

bite /baɪt/ (**bit** /bɪt/, **bitten** /'bɪtn/)

'**bite at sth** to try to bite sth: *The dog bit at the boy's hand.*
> ✦ v + prep

,**bite 'back** (**at sb/sth**) to react when sb has harmed you and try to harm or criticize them: *If you criticize him, he'll bite back.*
> ⟩SYN⟨ **hit back** (**at sb/sth**)
> ✦ v + adv

,**bite sth 'back** to stop yourself from saying sth or from showing how you feel: *She struggled to bite back the tears of disappointment.* ◇ *Mike bit back his anger.* ◇ *The word 'idiot' came into her head, but she bit it back.*
> OBJ **words, anger, retort** ⟩SYN⟨ **suppress sth**
> NOTE **Bite sth back** is not used in the passive.
> ✦ v + adv + n ◆ v + pron + adv ◆ v + n + adv (*rare*)

,**bite 'into sth 1** to cut or press into the surface of sth: *The collar bit into his neck.* ⟩SYN⟨ **cut into sth 2** to have an unpleasant effect on sth, especially by making it smaller: *The recession is biting into our profits.*
> ✦ v + prep

,**bite sth 'off** to cut sth off by biting it: *She bit off a piece of chocolate.* ◇ *His finger had been bitten off by a dog.*
> ✦ v + adv + n ◆ v + n/pron + adv
> IDM **bite/snap sb's 'head off** (*informal*) to shout at sb or speak to them angrily, often for no good reason: *I only asked him when the work would be finished and he almost bit my head off.* **bite off more than you can 'chew** (*informal*) to try to do

too much or sth that is too difficult for you: *This time he's bitten off more than he can chew.* **I, etc. could have bitten my/his/her 'tongue off/out** used to say that you wish you hadn't said sth that you have just said: *Sam looked hurt and Maria could have bitten her tongue off.*

black /blæk/

black 'out to lose consciousness or lose your memory for a short time: *The pain hit him and he blacked out.*
◆ v + adv
▶ **'blackout** *n* a temporary loss of consciousness or of memory: *When did you start having these blackouts?*
→ *see also* BLACKOUT at BLACK STH OUT

black sth 'out to turn out lights completely or cover windows, etc. so that light cannot be seen from outside: *blacked out windows/houses* ◇ *The city was often blacked out* (= there were no lights because there was no electricity) *by power cuts.*
[OBJ] **window, city**
[NOTE] Black sth out is often used in the passive.
◆ v + adv + n ◆ v + pron + adv ◆ v + n + adv (*rare*)
▶ **'blackout 1** (*especially BrE*) (in the past) a period of time during a war when the streets and buildings were kept as dark as possible so that the enemy could not see what to bomb **2** [usually pl.] (*BrE*) a covering for windows that stops light from outside coming in, or that stops bright light being seen from outside: *blackout material* **3** (*also* **'outage** *AmE*) a period of time when the electricity supply to a place stops completely [NOTE] This is now the most common meaning of blackout. **4** a situation when the government or the police prevent a radio or television programme from being broadcast, or do not allow some news or information to be given to the public: *The government have been accused of maintaining a news blackout over election fraud.*
→ *see also* BLACKOUT at BLACK OUT

blank /blæŋk/

blank 'out (*AmE, informal*) if you or your mind **blanks out**, you can't remember anything or you become confused: *I hope I don't blank out in the exam.*
[NOTE] Blank has the same meaning.
◆ v + adv

blank sth 'out 1 to deliberately forget sth unpleasant: *Your childhood may have been difficult but you can't just blank it out.* **2** to cover sth written or printed, for example, with black ink so that it cannot be read: *All the names in the report had been blanked out.*
◆ v + adv + n ◆ v + pron + adv ◆ v + n + adv (*rare*)

blare /bleə(r); AmE bler/

blare 'out; blare sth 'out if music **blares out**, or a radio, etc. **blares out** music, it is produced or played very loudly: *Music was blaring out from somewhere.* ◇ *The radio was blaring out rock music.*
[SYN] **blast out, blast sth out** (*less frequent*)
◆ v + adv ◆ v + adv + n ◆ v + n/pron + adv

blast /blɑːst; AmE blæst/

blast a'way (at sb/sth) if a gun or sb using a gun **blasts away**, the gun fires loudly and continuously: *The machine guns blasted away all night.*
◆ v + adv

blast sb/sth a'way (*less frequent*) to kill sb or remove sth or break it apart violently, for example with a gun, explosives, etc: *They have blasted away the side of this beautiful valley to make a road.* ◇ (*figurative*) *This theory has been blasted away by the new evidence.*
[SYN] **blow sb/sth away**
◆ v + adv + n ◆ v + n/pron + adv (*rare*)

blast 'off when a spacecraft **blasts off**, it leaves the ground and goes up into space: *The rocket blasted off at 7.28 p.m.*
[SYN] **lift off**
◆ v + adv
▶ **'blast-off** *n* [U] the moment when a spacecraft leaves the ground: *Blast-off will be in 30 seconds.*

blast 'out; blast sth 'out if music **blasts out**, or a radio, etc. **blasts out** music, it is produced or played very loudly: *A Beatles song was blasting out at full volume.* ◇ *The radio was blasting out heavy rock music.*
[SYN] **blare out, blare sth out**
◆ v + adv ◆ v + adv + n ◆ v + n/pron + adv

blaze /bleɪz/

blaze a'way 1 (at sb/sth) if guns or people **blaze away**, the guns fire continuously: *The guns kept blazing away at the enemy.* **2** if a fire **blazes away**, it burns brightly
[NOTE] Blaze is used with the same meanings.
◆ v + adv

blaze 'up if a fire **blazes up**, it suddenly starts burning more strongly: (*figurative*) *His anger blazed up uncontrollably.*
◆ v + adv

blend /blend/

blend 'in (with sth) if something **blends in** with sth else or with its surroundings, it looks similar to it/them or matches well: *The curtains blend in perfectly with the carpet.* ◇ *The new office block doesn't blend in well with its traditional surroundings.* **2** (with sb) if sb **blends in** with other people, they become similar to the people around them: *He should try to blend in with the locals a bit more.*

→ *see also* BLEND INTO STH; MERGE IN (WITH STH), MERGE INTO STH

◈ v + adv

blend sth 'in 1 (in cooking) to add another substance to sth and mix them together: *Heat the butter gently and then blend in a little flour.* ⟨SYN⟩ **mix sth in 2** to make a substance mix with another so that you cannot see where one ends and the other starts: *Blend the eyeshadow in with your fingers.* ◇ *He blended in the charcoal lines to make the picture look softer.*

◈ v + adv + n ◆ v + pron + adv ◆ v + n + adv (*less frequent*)

blend 'into sth to look or sound so similar to sth that it is difficult for anyone to see or hear it separately: *The animals can become almost invisible by blending into the long grass.* ◇ *The new development should blend into its surroundings.*

⟨OBJ⟩ **background, surroundings**

→ *see also* BLEND IN; MERGE IN (WITH STH), MERGE INTO STH

◈ v + prep

blimp /blɪmp/

blimp 'out/'up (*AmE, informal*) to become fat; to gain weight

◈ v + adv

blink /blɪŋk/

blink sth a'way to clear sth from the eyes by blinking (= closing and opening your eyes quickly): *He blinked away a tear.*

⟨OBJ⟩ **tears**

◈ v + adv + n ◆ v + n/pron + adv

blink sth 'back to try to control your tears: *I found myself blinking back tears during his speech.*

⟨OBJ⟩ only **tear(s)**

◈ v + adv + n ◆ v + n/pron + adv

block /blɒk; *AmE* blɑːk/

block sb/sth 'in to stop a vehicle from being driven away by parking too close to it: *You're blocking that Mini in.* ◇ *Somebody had parked in front of me, blocking me in.* ◇ *I was blocked in by two lorries so I had to leave the car and walk.*

◈ v + n/pron + adv ◆ v + adv + n (*less frequent*)

block sth 'off 1 to close a road or another place by placing a barrier across it to stop sb/sth going in or coming out: *The police blocked the street off.* ◇ *The pipe had been blocked off to prevent further leaks.* ⟨OBJ⟩ **street, road, area, entrance** ⟨SYN⟩ **close sth off (to sth/sb) 2** (*especially AmE*) to reserve a period of time for a particular activity: *Thursday afternoons are blocked off for sports.*

◈ v + n/pron + adv ◆ v + adv + n

block sth 'out to stop light or noise from coming in; to cover or hide sth: *The trees blocked out much of the sunlight.* ◇ (*figurative*) *I'm so used to the traffic noise now I just block it out* (= I don't hear it).

⟨OBJ⟩ **light, sun, sound**

◈ v + adv + n ◆ v + pron + adv ◆ v + n + adv (*less frequent*)

block sb/sth 'out; block sb/sth 'out of sth to avoid remembering sb/sth or thinking about sb/sth, especially sth unpleasant: *He tried to block the incident out of his mind.*

⟨SYN⟩ **blot sb/sth out, blot sb/sth out of sth; shut sth out, shut sth out of sth; suppress sth**

◈ v + n/pron + adv ◆ v + adv + n ◆ v + n/pron + adv + prep

block sth 'up to fill sth such as a hole completely so that nothing can get through it: *All the windows had been blocked up.*

⟨OBJ⟩ **window, door, hole, fireplace**

◈ v + n/pron + adv ◆ v + adv + n

▶ **blocked 'up** *adj* completely full; not clear: *I've got a blocked-up nose.*

blot /blɒt; *AmE* blɑːt/ (**-tt-**)

blot sb/sth 'out; blot sb/sth 'out of sth to avoid remembering sb/sth or thinking about sb/sth, especially sth unpleasant: *He wanted to blot out the memory.*

⟨OBJ⟩ **memories, thoughts** ⟨SYN⟩ **block sb/sth out, block sb/sth out of sth; shut sth out, shut sth out of sth**

◈ v + n/pron + adv ◆ v + adv + n ◆ v + n/pron + adv + prep

blot sth 'out to stop light or noise coming in; to cover or hide sth: *Dark clouds were blotting out the sun.*

⟨OBJ⟩ **light, sun, stars, sound** ⟨SYN⟩ **block sth out**

◈ v + adv + n ◆ v + n/pron + adv

blow /bləʊ; *AmE* bloʊ/ (**blew** /bluː/ **blown** /bləʊn; *AmE* bloʊn/)

18	~ away	~ out
	~ down	~ over
	~ in, into	~ up
	~ off	

blow a'way; blow sth a'way to be moved or carried away by the force of the wind or by sb's breath; to move in this way: *It was so windy the tent nearly blew away!* ◇ *A sudden breeze blew his newspaper away.* ◇ *She blew away the dust on the lid.*

◈ v + adv ◆ v + n/pron + adv ◆ v + adv + n

blow sb a'way 1 (*informal*) to impress sb a lot; to surprise or please sb: *I saw her performance on Broadway last year and it just blew me away.*

2 (*AmE, informal, sport*) to defeat sb easily: *Mitchell blew away the other runners.*
◆ v + n/pron + adv ◆ v + adv + n

,**blow sb/sth a'way** to kill sb or remove or destroy sth with explosives or with a gun: *He threatened to blow us away.* ◇ *They blew his kneecaps away* (= by shooting them).
〉SYN〈 **blast sb/sth away**
◆ v + n/pron + adv ◆ v + adv + n

,**blow 'down**; ,**blow sth 'down** if sth **blows down**, or the wind **blows it down**, it falls to the ground because of the force of the wind: *An old oak tree had blown down in the storm.* ◇ *Hundreds of trees have been blown down this winter.*
◆ v + adv ◆ v + n/pron + adv ◆ v + adv + n

,**blow 'in**; ,**blow 'into sth** (*informal*) to arrive somewhere where you are not expected: *Look who's just blown in!* ◇ *Have you heard who's just blown into town?*
◆ v + adv ◆ v + prep

,**blow 'off**; ,**blow sth 'off**; ,**blow sth 'off sth 1** if sth **blows off**, or the wind **blows it off**, it is removed by the force of the wind: *My hat blew off.* ◇ *A gust of wind blew her cap off.* ◇ *The roof was blown off the Greens' house.* **2** if sth **blows off** in an explosion, or an explosion **blows sth off** it is violently removed: *The door blew off in the explosion.* ◇ *The explosion blew the roof off* (*the house*).
◆ v + adv ◆ v + n/pron + adv ◆ v + adv + n ◆ v + n/pron + prep
〉IDM〈 **blow/knock sb's 'socks off** to impress or surprise sb very much: *When I first heard the song, it blew my socks off.*

,**blow 'off sth**; ,**blow it 'off** (*AmE, informal*) to decide not to do sth you should do or were planning to do: *Jessica blew off her classes on Friday afternoon to go shopping.*
〉NOTE〈 A noun must follow **off**, but a pronoun comes between the verb and **off**.
◆ v + adv + n ◆ v + pron + adv

,**blow sb 'off** (*AmE, informal*) to disappoint sb by not meeting them as arranged; to end a relationship with sb: *We were supposed to go out yesterday, but he blew me off.*
〉SYN〈 **stand sb up**
◆ v + n/pron + adv ◆ v + adv + n

,**blow 'out 1** if a tyre **blows out**, it bursts suddenly: *One of the front tyres blew out.* 〉SYN〈 **burst 2** if an oil or gas well **blows out**, it suddenly sends out gas with great force
◆ v + adv
▶ '**blowout** *n* **1** an occasion when a tyre bursts on a vehicle while it is being driven **2** an occasion when oil or gas suddenly escapes from an oil well **3** (*BrE, informal*) a large meal at which people eat too much **4** (*AmE, informal*) a large party or social occasion
→ *see also* BLOWOUT at BLOW SB OUT

,**blow 'out**; ,**blow sth 'out 1** if a flame **blows out** or sb/sth **blows it out**, it is put out by the wind or some air: *There was a sudden gust of wind and the candle blew out.* ◇ *She took a deep breath and blew out all the candles.* **2** if a window **blows out**, or an explosion, etc. **blows it out**, the force makes it fall out: *All the windows blew out in the blast.* ◇ *The explosion blew out the windows in the building.*
◆ v + adv ◆ v + adv + n ◆ v + n/pron + adv

,**blow sb 'out** (*AmE, informal, sport*) to defeat sb easily: *The home team blew out the Suns by 30 points.*
◆ v + n/pron + adv ◆ v + adv + n
▶ '**blowout** *n* (*AmE, informal, sport*) an easy victory
→ *see also* BLOWOUT at BLOW OUT

,**blow sth 'out 1** to breathe sth out from your mouth: *She inhaled and then blew the smoke out.* 〉SYN〈 **exhale sth 2** to fill sth, especially your cheeks, with air: *She blew out her cheeks in exasperation.* 〉OBJ〈 **cheeks**
◆ v + n/pron + adv ◆ v + adv + n
〉IDM〈 **blow your/sb's 'brains out** (*informal*) to kill yourself/sb by shooting yourself/them in the head

,**blow itself 'out** if a storm **blows itself out**, it loses its force and stops: *By morning the storm had blown itself out.*
◆ v + pron + adv

,**blow 'over 1** if a storm **blows over**, it becomes less strong and stops: *We sheltered in a barn until the storm blew over.* 〉SYN〈 **die down**; **subside 2** if sth such as an argument **blows over**, it becomes less important and is forgotten: *Don't come back to work until the argument has blown over.* 〉SYN〈 **subside**
◆ v + adv

,**blow 'over**; ,**blow sb/sth 'over** if sb/sth **blows over** or the wind **blows sb/sth over**, they fall to the ground because of the force of the wind: *One of the trees had blown over in the storm.* ◇ *The fence had been blown over in a storm.*
〉NOTE〈 **Blow sb/sth over** is often used in the passive: *Pedestrians were blown over in gale force winds today.*
◆ v + adv ◆ v + n/pron + adv

,**blow 'up 1** to explode; to be destroyed by an explosion: *The bomb blew up as experts tried to defuse it.* ◇ *The car blew up when it hit the wall.* 〉SYN〈 **explode** (*more formal*) **2** to start suddenly and with force: *A storm blew up just after the ship left port.* ◇ *A row has blown up over the leaking of information to the press.* 〉OPP〈 **die down 3** (*at sb*) (*informal*) to become very angry: *My mum blew up at my dad for keeping me up so late.* ◇ *His attitude annoyed me and I blew up.*
◆ v + adv

IDM blow up in sb's 'face if a plan, a deal or a situation blows up in your face, it goes very badly wrong and causes you harm or embarrassment

▶ 'blow-up *n* **1** (*especially AmE*) an explosion **2** (*AmE*) an occasion when sb becomes very angry; an argument: *The tensions between them ended in a big blow-up.*

→ *see also* BLOW-UP *at* BLOW STH UP

,blow sb/sth 'up to kill sb or destroy sth with a bomb or an explosion: *The hijackers threatened to blow the plane up.* ◇ *A judge in Italy was blown up by a car bomb last week.*

NOTE Blow sb/sth up is often used in the passive.

◈ v + n/pron + adv ◆ v + adv + n

,blow sth 'up **1** to fill sth with air or gas: *You need to blow up the tyres on your bike.* **OBJ** balloon, tyre **⟨SYN⟩** inflate sth (*more formal*) **⟨OPP⟩** let sth down **2** to make sth larger: *What a lovely photo! Why don't you have it blown up?* **OBJ** photo **⟨SYN⟩** enlarge sth (*more formal*) **3** to make sth seem more important, better or worse than it really is: *The whole affair has been **blown up out of all proportion**.* **⟨SYN⟩** exaggerate sth (*more formal*)

◈ v + n/pron + adv ◆ v + adv + n

▶ 'blow-up *n* a larger picture made from a photo or picture: *The blow-up showed a scar on the attacker's cheek.*

→ *see also* BLOW-UP *at* BLOW UP

▶ 'blow-up *adj* [only before noun] that you can fill with air or gas

→ *see also* BLOW-UP *at* BLOW UP

bluff /blʌf/

,bluff sb 'out (*old-fashioned, informal, especially AmE*) to lie and pretend in order to deceive sb

◈ v + n/pron + adv ◆ v + adv + n

,bluff it 'out (*especially BrE*) to lie and deceive sb in order to get out of a difficult situation, especially when they suspect you are not being honest: *If he asks any difficult questions, you'll have to bluff it out.* ◇ *I know everything so there's no point trying to bluff it out.*

◈ v + it + adv

,bluff sb 'out of sth (*old-fashioned, AmE*) to deceive sb in order to get sth from them

⟨SYN⟩ cheat sb of sth, cheat sb out of sth

◈ v + n/pron + adv + prep

blunder /'blʌndə(r)/

,blunder a'round; ,blunder a'round sth (*also* ,blunder a'bout/'round, ,blunder a'bout/'round sth especially BrE*) to move about a place in an awkward or uncertain way, knocking into things: *He blundered about in the dark, feeling for the light switch.* ◇ *I blundered around the flat, trying to be quiet.*

◈ v + adv ◆ v + prep

,blunder 'into sth **1** to walk into sb/sth because you are awkward or unable to see: *She blundered into a tree.* **2** to accidentally find yourself in a difficult or dangerous place or situation: *She blundered into a dangerous area of the city after losing her way.* ◇ *He had innocently blundered into a private dispute.*

◈ v + prep

blurt /blɜːt; *AmE* blɜːrt/

,blurt sth 'out to say sth suddenly and without thinking carefully: *'There's been an accident,' she blurted out.* ◇ *He found himself blurting out the whole story to her.*

◈ v + adv + speech ◆ v + adv + n ◆ v + n/pron + adv

board /bɔːd; *AmE* bɔːrd/

,board sth 'up to cover a window or a door with boards: *All the windows had been boarded up.*

OBJ window, house, shop

NOTE Board sth up is often used in the passive.

◈ v + n/pron + adv ◆ v + adv + n

bob /bɒb; *AmE* bɑːb/ (-bb-)

,bob 'up **1** to come to the surface quickly: *She dived in and bobbed up a few seconds later in the middle of the pool.* **2** to appear suddenly: *She bobbed up from behind the fence.* **⟨SYN⟩** pop up

◈ v + adv

bog /bɒg; *AmE* bɔːg/ (-gg-)

,bog 'down (*AmE*) to be unable to make progress: *The bill bogged down after being passed by Congress.*

◈ v + adv

be/get ,bogged 'down (in sth) **1** to be/get stuck in mud or wet ground; to become stuck in sth and unable to make progress: *The car got bogged down in the mud.* **2** to be unable to make progress in an activity: *Don't get bogged down in details.* ◇ *I'm rather bogged down (with work) at the moment.*

◈ be/get + v + adv

,bog 'off (*BrE, slang*) used to tell sb rudely to go away: *Bog off, I'm trying to sleep!*

⟨SYN⟩ clear off (*informal*)

◈ v + adv

boil /bɔɪl/

,boil a'way if a liquid boils away, it boils until there is nothing left: *The water in the saucepan had all boiled away.*

⟨SYN⟩ evaporate (*more formal*)

◈ v + adv

,boil sth 'down **1** to make a liquid less in quantity by boiling it **⟨SYN⟩** reduce sth (*more formal*)

2 (to sth) to make sth smaller by removing unimportant parts and leaving only the essential things: *Boil the report down to the key points.*
[SYN] **condense sth** (*more formal*)
◆ v + n/pron + adv ◆ v + adv + n

boil 'down to sth (*not used in the progressive tenses*) if a situation, an issue, etc. **boils down to sth**, it has that as its main part: *It all boils down to money in the end.*
◆ v + adv + prep

boil 'over 1 if a liquid in a pan, etc. **boils over**, it boils and flows over the side of the pan: *Don't let the milk boil over.* **2 (into sth)** (*informal*) if anger, an argument, etc. **boils over**, it changes and becomes very violent and difficult to control: *The unrest could boil over into civil war.* ◇ *She interrupted swiftly before his temper could boil over again.* [SYN] **explode**
◆ v + adv

boil 'up if anger, an argument, etc. **boils up**, it starts to become stronger or more violent
◆ v + adv

boil sth 'up (*BrE*) to heat a liquid or some food until it boils: *I'll boil the kettle up again and we'll have a cup of tea.*
[NOTE] **Boil sth** can be used with the same meaning.
◆ v + n/pron + adv ◆ v + adv + n

bollix /'bɒlɪks; *AmE* 'bɑːl-/

bollix sth 'up (*AmE, slang*) to confuse or change sth; to spoil sth
[SYN] **mess sth up** (*informal*), **screw sth up** (*slang*)
◆ v + n/pron + adv ◆ v + adv + n

bolster /'bəʊlstə(r); *AmE* 'boʊl-/

bolster sb/sth 'up to support or encourage sb; to make sth better or stronger: *He tried to bolster up their morale.* ◇ *The high interest rates helped to bolster up the economy.*
[OBJ] **confidence, morale**
[NOTE] **Bolster sb/sth** is more frequent.
◆ v + n/pron + adv ◆ v + adv + n

bolt /bəʊlt; *AmE* boʊlt/

bolt sth 'down (*informal*) to eat sth very quickly: *I had to bolt down my breakfast.*
[OBJ] **food**
[NOTE] **Bolt sth** is also used with this meaning.
◆ v + n/pron + adv ◆ v + adv + n

bomb /bɒm; *AmE* bɑːm/

bomb a'long (*informal, especially BrE*) to move very fast, usually in a vehicle
◆ v + adv

bomb 'out (*informal, especially AmE*) to fail very badly: *The movie bombed out at the box office.*
[NOTE] **Bomb** is also used with the same meaning.
◆ v + adv

be/get ,bombed 'out; be/get ,bombed 'out of sth if a person is **bombed out**, their home is destroyed by bombs; if a building is **bombed out**, it is destroyed by bombs: *They got bombed out.*
◆ be/get + v + adv ◆ be/get + v + adv + prep

bone /bəʊn; *AmE* boʊn/

bone 'up on sth (*informal*) to study sth; to look again at sth you already know: *I must bone up on my French before we go to Paris.*
◆ v + adv + prep

book /bʊk/

book 'in (at sth), ,book 'into sth (*BrE*) to arrive at a hotel and arrange to have a room: *They booked in (at the St Francis Hotel) using a false name.* ◇ *She booked into a hotel in the centre of Boston.*
[SYN] **check in (at sth); check into sth**
[OPP] **check out, check out of sth**
◆ v + adv ◆ v + adv + prep

book sb/yourself 'in (at sth), ,book sb/yourself 'into sth (*BrE*) to reserve a room at a hotel, etc. for sb: *I've booked us in at the Plaza.* ◇ *The hotel I was booked into was awful.* ◇ *He's booked himself into a rehabilitation clinic.*
[OBJ] **hotel**
◆ v + n/pron + adv ◆ v + n/pron + prep

book 'up (for sth) (*especially BrE*) to reserve a place, for example on a trip or a course: *I booked up for the course months in advance.*
[NOTE] **Book (for sth)** can be used with the same meaning.
◆ v + adv

be ,booked 'up 1 if a plane, restaurant, theatre, etc. **is booked up**, there are no seats, tables, etc. available: *All the flights are booked up.* [NOTE] **Be fully booked** is often used with the same meaning. **2** (*informal*) if a person **is booked up**, they have no time available: *He can't see you tomorrow, he's booked up.*
◆ be + v + adv

boom /buːm/

boom 'out if a sound or sb's voice **booms out**, it makes a loud, deep noise: *His voice boomed out, announcing the winners.*
◆ v + adv

boom 'out sth to say sth in a loud deep voice: *She boomed out instructions through a loud hailer.* ◇ *A voice boomed out: 'Nobody move!'*
◆ v + adv + n ◆ v + adv + speech

boot /buːt/

‚boot sb 'out; ‚boot sb 'out of sth (*informal, especially BrE*) to force sb to leave a place, job, school, club, etc: *I'll have to boot you out soon — I want to lock up.* ◇ *The manager booted him out of the team.* ◇ *He was booted out of the house by his father.*
⟨SYN⟩ **kick sb out, kick sb out of sth** (*informal*), **throw sb out, throw sb out of sth**
⟦NOTE⟧ Boot sb out, boot sb out of sth are often used in the passive.
✦ v + n/pron + adv ♦ v + adv + n ♦ v + n/pron + adv + prep

‚boot 'up; ‚boot sth 'up (*computing*) if a computer **boots up**, or sb **boots it up**, it is turned on and becomes ready to use: *My machine isn't booting up properly.* ◇ *When you boot up, a menu will appear on the screen.* ◇ *Boot the computer up and enter your password.*
⟦OBJ⟧ **computer**
✦ v + adv ♦ v + n/pron + adv ♦ v + adv + n

border /'bɔːdə(r); AmE 'bɔːrd-/

'border on sth (*also* **'border upon sth** *more formal*) **1** to share a border with another country or region; to be next to a place: *Many states bordering on the EU are eager to join.* ◇ *Their garden borders on the River Severn.* **2** to come close to being sth: *Her self-confidence borders on arrogance.* ◇ *Our task borders on the impossible.* ⟨SYN⟩ **verge on sth**
✦ v + prep

bore /bɔː(r)/

‚bore 'into sb/sth (*literary*) if somebody's eyes **bore into** sb/sth, they stare in a way that makes sb feel uncomfortable: *His blue eyes seemed to bore into her.*
✦ v + prep

boss /bɒs; AmE bɔːs/

‚boss sb a'round (*also* ‚**boss sb a'bout** *especially BrE*) (*informal*) to tell sb what to do in a forceful or unpleasant way: *He's always bossing his wife around.*
✦ v + n/pron + adv

botch /bɒtʃ; AmE bɑːtʃ/

‚botch sth 'up (*informal*) to spoil sth by doing it badly; to do sth badly: *Instead of fixing my computer, he's botched it up completely.*
⟨SYN⟩ **mess sth up**
⟦NOTE⟧ Botch sth is used more frequently with the same meaning: *botched attempts at DIY*
✦ v + n/pron + adv ♦ v + adv + n
▸ **'botch-up** (*also* **botch**) *n* (*informal, especially BrE*) a piece of work that is badly done

bottle /'bɒtl; AmE 'bɑːtl/

‚bottle 'out; ‚bottle 'out of sth; ‚bottle 'out of doing sth (*BrE, informal*) to suddenly decide not to do sth because you are too frightened: *I bottled out of phoning him at the last minute.*
⟨SYN⟩ **chicken out, chicken out of sth, chicken out of doing sth**
✦ v + adv ♦ v + adv + prep

‚bottle sth 'up to keep your feelings, especially sadness or anger, hidden and not tell other people how you are feeling: *Tell someone how you're feeling, instead of bottling it all up.*
⟦OBJ⟧ **emotions, feelings**
✦ v + n/pron + adv ♦ v + adv + n

bottom /'bɒtəm; AmE 'bɑːtəm/

‚bottom 'out if markets, prices or bad situations **bottom out**, they reach their lowest point and then stop getting worse: *The recession has finally bottomed out.*
✦ v + adv

bounce /baʊns/

‚bounce sth a'round (*informal, especially AmE*) to discuss sth with other people: *We're bouncing some new ideas around.*
⟦OBJ⟧ **ideas**
✦ v + n/pron + adv ♦ v + adv + n

‚bounce 'back (from sth) (*AmE also* ‚**snap 'back (into sth)**) (*informal*) to recover well after you have been ill/sick or had a difficult time: *No matter what happens, she always bounces back very quickly.*
⟨SYN⟩ **recover (from sth)** (*more formal*)
✦ v + adv

‚bounce 'back; ‚bounce sth 'back if an e-mail **bounces back**, or the system **bounces it back**, it returns to the person who sent it because the system cannot deliver it
✦ v + adv ♦ v + adv + n ♦ v + n/pron + adv

‚bounce sb 'into sth; ‚bounce sb 'into doing sth (*especially BrE*) to make or force sb to do sth quickly without giving them time to think about it: *I felt I'd been bounced into supporting a proposal I didn't really agree with.*
⟦NOTE⟧ This phrasal verb is often used in the passive.
✦ v + n/pron + prep

‚bounce sth 'off sb (*informal*) to tell sb else your ideas to find out what they think about them: *We were able to share problems and bounce ideas off each other.*
⟦OBJ⟧ **ideas**
✦ v + n/pron + prep

bow /baʊ/

,bow 'down 1 (to/before sb/sth) to move your head or the top part of your body forwards or downwards as a sign of respect: *He refused to bow down before the king.* **2** (to sb/sth) to do what sb tells you to do without trying to resist: *We refuse to just bow down and let the government do whatever it wants.*
⊕ v + adv

,bow 'out; **,bow 'out of sth** to stop doing an activity or a job that you have been doing successfully, often for a long time: *After thirty years in politics, he feels it is time to bow out.* ◇ *Smith will bow out of professional football at the end of the season.*
⊕ v + adv ♦ v + adv + prep

'bow to sth to agree unwillingly to do sth or to accept sth that sb else wants you to: *The government eventually bowed to public pressure.*
OBJ **pressure, the inevitable**
SYN **give in (to sb/sth)**
⊕ v + prep

bowl /bəʊl; *AmE* boʊl/

,bowl sb 'out (in cricket) to make the person who is hitting the ball (the **batsman**) have to leave the field by throwing a ball that they cannot hit and that hits the wicket (= the three sticks behind the batsman); to dismiss a whole team in this way
⊕ v + n/pron + adv ♦ v + adv + n

,bowl sb 'over to surprise or impress sb a lot; to affect sb deeply: *We were bowled over by the news.* ◇ *Philip bowled us all over by deciding to go into advertising.*
NOTE **Bowl sb over** is often used in the passive.
⊕ v + n/pron + adv ♦ v + adv + n

box /bɒks; *AmE* bɑːks/

,box sb 'in to prevent sb from doing what they want, especially by creating rules or other difficulties: *The President was unable to act because the Democrats were boxing him in.* ◇ *She was boxed in by rules and regulations.*
NOTE **Box sb in** is often used in the passive.
⊕ v + n/pron + adv

,box sb/sth 'in to prevent a person or a vehicle from moving by surrounding them/it with other people or vehicles: *You can't park here — you're boxing that car in!* ◇ *He couldn't overtake the leader because he was boxed in by the other runners.*
NOTE **Box sb/sth in** is often used in the passive.
⊕ v + n/pron + adv ♦ v + adv + n

,box sth 'up to put sth in a box or boxes: *She boxed up all the old baby clothes to send to her niece.*
⊕ v + n/pron + adv ♦ v + adv + n

branch /brɑːntʃ; *AmE* bræntʃ/

,branch 'off 1 if a road or path **branches off**, it leaves a larger one and goes in a different direction: *She followed the path until it branched off.* ◇ *Over the bridge a road branches off to the right.* **2** if a person **branches off**, they leave a road or path and travel in a different direction: *Go past the farm and branch off towards the trees.*
⊕ v + adv

,branch 'out (into sth) to begin to do a new job or an activity that you do not usually do: *The company is branching out into Europe.* ◇ *She's leaving the company to branch out on her own.*
⊕ v + adv

brazen /'breɪzn/

,brazen 'out sth; **,brazen it 'out** to behave in a confident way as if you are not ashamed or embarrassed about sth you have done, even though you should be: *The senator brazened it out as the list of scandals grew.*
NOTE A noun must always follow **out**, but **it** comes between the verb and **out**.
⊕ v + it + adv ♦ v + adv + n

break /breɪk/ (**broke** /brəʊk; *AmE* broʊk/ **broken** /'brəʊkən; *AmE* 'broʊkən/)

	~ away	24	~ out
23	~ down		~ out in/into
	~ in		~ through
	~ into		~ up
	~ off	25	~ with

,break a'way 1 (from sth) if an object **breaks away** from sth that is holding it in place, it becomes separated from it: *The boat had broken away from its moorings.* **2** (from sb) to escape suddenly from sb who is holding you or keeping you prisoner: *The prisoner broke away from the guards.* **3** (from sb/sth) to leave a group or an organization, such as a political party or a state, because of a disagreement, usually in order to form a new one: *Several MPs broke away to form a new party.* ◇ *Two states broke away from the federation.* **4** (from sb/sth) to move away from a group of people or a crowd: *She managed to break away from the pack* (= in a race) *and establish a lead.* ◇ *He broke away from the group and came over to talk to us.* **5** (from sb/sth) to reject a tradition or the usual way of doing things and do sth new and different: *The company is trying to break away from its traditional image.*
⊕ v + adv

▸ **'breakaway** *adj* [only before noun] a **breakaway** group, political party or part of a country is one that leaves a larger group: *a breakaway faction/movement/republic*

▸ **'breakaway** *n* [sing.] an act of separating from a larger group/state, etc.

,break 'down 1 if a vehicle, etc. **breaks down**, it stops working because of a fault: *The washing machine has broken down again.* ◇ *We* (= our car) *broke down twice on the way home.* **2** if talks, a marriage, etc. **break down**, they fail: *Negotiations between the two sides have broken down.* ◇ *Their marriage broke down after three years.* **3** to lose control of your feelings and start crying: *As she drove away, I just broke down and wept.* **4** if your health **breaks down**, it becomes very bad: *Her health broke down as a result of the strain.* **5** **(into sth)** to be divided into parts so that it is easier to discuss, to analyse or to deal with: *My weekly budget breaks down as follows: 50% for rent, 20% for food, 10% for travel, and 20% for everything else.* ◇ *The job breaks down into seven parts.* → *see also* BREAK STH DOWN 3 **6 (into sth)** if a substance **breaks down**, it separates into different parts or changes into sth else in a chemical process: *Some pesticides break down safely in water.* → *see also* BREAK STH DOWN 4
◈ v + adv

▶ **'breakdown** *n* **1** [C] an occasion when a vehicle or a machine stops working: *We had a breakdown on the way home.* ◇ *a breakdown truck* **2** [C] [U] a failure of talks, a marriage, law and order, etc: *a breakdown in communication* ◇ *They were both responsible for the breakdown of their marriage.* **3** [C] a period of mental illness when sb becomes tired, depressed and unable to lead a normal life: *He had a **nervous breakdown** last year.* **4** [C, usually sing.] detailed information or figures that are the results of dividing sth into its parts to explain it more clearly: *Get me a breakdown of how the money was spent.* **5** [U] the act of dividing a substance into its parts in a chemical process

▶ **,broken-'down** *adj* [usually before noun] **1** (of a vehicle or a machine) not working: *a broken-down car* **2** in a poor condition: *a broken-down wall*

,break sth 'down 1 to make sth fall down or open by hitting it hard: *They had to get the police to break the door down.* OBJ **door** SYN **knock sth down 2** to destroy or remove sth, especially a problem or an attitude or opinion that sb has: *Our aim is to **break down barriers** that exist between teachers and parents.* OBJ **barriers 3** **(into sth)** to separate sth into smaller parts in order to analyse it or deal with it more easily: *I've broken down the costs by country.* ◇ *The company was broken down into smaller units.* ◇ *The question can be broken down into two parts.* → *see also* BREAK DOWN 5 **4 (into sth)** to make a substance separate into its parts or change in a chemical process: *Enzymes in the mouth and stomach break the food down.* → *see also* BREAK DOWN 6
◈ v + n/pron + adv ◆ v + adv + n

▶ **'breakdown** *n* = BREAKDOWN at BREAK DOWN
▶ **,broken-'down** *adj* = BROKEN-DOWN at BREAK DOWN

,break 'in 1 to enter a building illegally or by force: *Somebody broke in last night and stole the PC and video.* ◇ *The firefighters had to break in to rescue them.* → *see also* BREAK INTO STH 1 **2 (on sth)** to interrupt sb when they are speaking or doing sth: *He apologized for breaking in on their conversation.* ◇ *Mary broke in: 'It's not her fault!'*
◈ **1** v + adv
   2 v + adv ◆ v + adv + speech

▶ **'break-in** *n* an entry into a building using force, usually illegally: *There has been a series of break-ins in the area.*

,break sb/sth 'in to train a person so that they get used to a new job or situation; to train a horse so that you can ride it: *We try to break newcomers in gently.* ◇ *The horses hadn't been broken in.*
◈ v + n/pron + adv ◆ v + adv + n

,break sth 'in 1 if you **break in** new shoes or boots, you wear them until they become comfortable: *It took me weeks to break in these new boots.* OBJ **boots, shoes** SYN **wear sth in 2** (*AmE*) (in the past) to prepare the engine of a new car for normal use by driving it slowly and carefully OBJ **car** SYN **run sth in** (*BrE*)
◈ v + adv + n ◆ v + n/pron + adv

,break 'into sth 1 to enter a building, open a car, etc. illegally and by force: *A thief can break into a car in under ten seconds.* ◇ *Three houses in our street have been broken into this week.* OBJ **house, car** NOTE Break into sth can be used in the passive in this meaning. → *see also* BREAK IN 1 **2** to suddenly begin to do sth such as laugh, cheer, run, etc: *He broke into a run when he saw the police.* ◇ *Her face broke into a huge smile.* ◇ *The audience broke into applause.* OBJ **smile/grin, run/trot, song, laughter 3** (*BrE*) to use a banknote (= a piece of paper money) of high value to buy sth costing less: *I didn't want to break into a twenty-pound note.* **4** to interrupt sb's thoughts: *Her mother's voice broke into her thoughts.* OBJ **thoughts** SYN **disturb sth 5** to start to get involved in an activity that it is difficult to become involved in and to be successful at it: *The company is having difficulty breaking into new markets.* ◇ *She is trying to break into journalism.* OBJ **market 6** to open and use sth that you have been saving for an emergency or a special occasion: *I had to break into my savings to pay for the trip.*
◈ v + prep

,break 'off; ,break sth 'off 1 (*also* ,break sth 'off sth) to separate sth from sth else, using force; to become separated from sth in this way: *The leg of the table just broke off.* ◇ *A corner of*

her tooth had broken off. ◇ *He broke off a piece of chocolate and gave it to me.* **2** to stop speaking or stop doing sth suddenly before you have finished: *He broke off abruptly in the middle of a sentence.* ◇ *We had to break off our holiday and return home immediately.* ◇ *They broke off their conversation as I approached.*

◈ **1** v + adv ♦ v + adv + n ♦ v + n/pron + adv ♦ v + n/pron + prep
2 v + adv ♦ v + adv + n ♦ v + pron + adv ♦ v + n + adv (*rare*)

,**break sth 'off** to end sth such as a relationship: *They've broken off their engagement.* ◇ *Britain threatened to break off diplomatic relations.* ◇ *They were having an affair but she broke it off.*
[OBJ] **diplomatic relations, engagement, talks/ negotiations** [SYN] **terminate** (*formal*)

◈ v + adv + n ♦ v + pron + adv ♦ v + n + adv (*rare*)

,**break 'out 1** if sth unpleasant such as a fire, a war, etc. **breaks out**, it starts suddenly: *They would have got married in 1939 if war had not broken out.* ◇ *A fire broke out on a ferry yesterday.*
[SUBJ] **war, fire, fighting, row, violence 2** (*also* ,**break 'out of sth**) to escape from a place or from a situation: *Two terrorists have broken out of Blackwall Prison.* ◇ *She longed to break out of the daily routine.* **3** if sth **breaks out** on your skin, your skin becomes covered in sth: (*AmE*) *I keep breaking out* (= I keep getting lots of spots). ◇ *Sweat broke out all over his body.*

◈ v + adv **2** also v + adv + prep
▶ '**breakout** n an escape from prison
▶ '**outbreak** n the start of sth or the sudden appearance of sth unpleasant or violent: *the outbreak of war* ◇ *an outbreak of food poisoning* ◇ *outbreaks of rain*

,**break sth 'out** to get sth ready to be used, eaten, drunk, etc: *That's wonderful news! Let's break out the champagne!*
[OBJ] **champagne**

◈ v + adv + n ♦ v + pron + adv ♦ v + n + adv (*rare*)

,**break 'out in/into sth** to suddenly become covered in sth such as sweat: *He broke out in a cold sweat at the thought of the trial.* ◇ *My skin has broken out in an itchy rash.*
[OBJ] **sweat, rash**

◈ v + adv + prep

,**break 'through** (*especially AmE*) to achieve your first important success in sth; to make an important or new discovery: *Glenn Close broke through as a star with 'Fatal Attraction'.* ◇ *Scientists believe they have broken through in their fight against the disease.*
[NOTE] The phrase **to make a breakthrough** is used more often than **to break through**: *Scientists have made a major breakthrough in their fight against AIDS.*

◈ v + adv
▶ '**breakthrough** n an important discovery or development; sb's first important success in sth:

an important breakthrough in the negotiations ◇ *Jo was only 19 when he got his breakthrough as a DJ.*

,**break 'through**; ,**break 'through sth 1** to make a way through a barrier using force: *He ran towards the barrier in an attempt to break through.* ◇ *Demonstrators tried to break through the police cordon.* [OBJ] **barrier 2** (of the sun or moon) to appear from behind sth: *The sun finally broke through in the afternoon.* ◇ *It stopped raining and the sun broke through the clouds.*
→ *see also* BREAK THROUGH STH

◈ v + adv ♦ v + prep

,**break 'through sth 1** to become greater in size or quantity than a particular level: *Unemployment figures have broken through the three million barrier.* **2** to succeed in dealing with a problem such as an attitude that sb has and the difficulties that it makes: *I tried hard to break through his silent mood.* ◇ *Women are starting to break through the barriers that keep them out of top management.* [SYN] **overcome sth** (*more formal*)
→ *see also* BREAK THROUGH, BREAK THROUGH STH

◈ v + prep

,**break 'up 1** (*especially BrE*) if a school or the children in it **break up**, school closes for the holidays at the end of a period of the school year (a **term**): *We break up for Christmas next week.* ◇ *Have the schools broken up yet?* **2** (of a relationship, a band, etc.) to come to an end; to stop working together: *Their marriage broke up after ten years.* ◇ *There are rumours that the band are breaking up.* [SUBJ] **marriage 3** (*usually used in the progressive tenses*) if the connection between two telephones, or two radios that are used for sending and receiving messages, is **breaking up**, the people speaking can no longer hear each other clearly: *The signal was breaking up.* ◇ *I'm sorry — what did you say? You're breaking up.*

◈ v + adv

,**break 'up (with sb)**, ,**break sb 'up** to end a relationship with sb: *Rob and I broke up last week.* ◇ *She's just broken up with her boyfriend.* ◇ *I can't believe my best friend is really trying to break us up!*
[SYN] **split up (with/from sb), split sb up**

◈ v + adv ♦ v + n/pron + adv ♦ v + adv + n
▶ '**break-up** n [C] [U] the ending of a marriage or a relationship: *He moved away after the break-up of his marriage.* ◇ *marriage break-up*
→ *see also* BREAK-UP at BREAK UP, BREAK SB/STH UP

,**break 'up**; ,**break sb/sth 'up 1** (into sth) if a group of people or a family **breaks up**, or sb **breaks it up**, the members separate and do not stay together: *The conference broke up into discussion groups.* ◇ *She had never intended to break up his family.* ◇ *The Soviet Union began to break up in 1991.* [SYN] **split up (into sth), split**

sb/sth up (into sth) **2** if a group of people meeting **break up**, or sb **breaks them up**, they go away in different directions: *The meeting broke up after two hours.* ◇ *Police broke up the demonstration.* ◇ *I don't want to break up the party* (= I don't want to make everyone else leave)*, but I have to go.*
◆ v + adv ◆ v + pron + adv ◆ v + n + adv (*less frequent*)
▶ **'break-up** n [C] [U] the division of a company, a country, an organization or a group of people into smaller parts: *the break-up of the Commonwealth* ◇ *family break-up*
→ *see also* BREAK-UP at BREAK UP (WITH SB), BREAK SB UP

break 'up (into sth), **break sth 'up** (into sth) if sth **breaks up**, or sb/sth **breaks it up**, it becomes separated into smaller pieces: *The ship broke up on the rocks.* ◇ *Break the chocolate up into small pieces.* ◇ *Sentences can be broken up into clauses.*
◆ v + adv ◆ v + n/pron + adv ◆ v + adv + n

break sth 'up to make sth that is rather boring, such as a period of time or a pattern, more interesting by adding sth different to it: *I break up my day by going for a walk in the afternoon.* ◇ *Drawings were used to break up the page.*
[OBJ] **day, monotony**
◆ v + adv + n ◆ v + pron + adv ◆ v + n + adv (*less frequent*)

break with sb/sth (*formal*) to end your connection or relationship with sb/sth because you no longer agree with them: *Nick broke with his father to set up his own firm.*
◆ v + prep

break with sth (*formal*) to reject sth such as a tradition or the past and decide to do sth different: *The prince broke with tradition by going to study abroad.* ◇ *The new directors are eager to break with the past.*
[OBJ] **tradition, the past**
◆ v + prep

breathe /briːð/

breathe 'in to take air into your lungs through your nose or mouth: *Breathe in through your nose as you stretch up.* ◇ *He breathed in deeply and then spoke.*
[SYN] **inhale** (*more formal*) [OPP] **breathe out**
◆ v + adv

breathe sth 'in to take air, smoke, a smell, etc. in through your nose or mouth: *We walked along the beach, breathing in the sea air.*
[OBJ] **air, smoke** [SYN] **inhale sth** (*more formal*)
[OPP] **breathe sth out**
◆ v + adv + n ◆ v + n/pron + adv

breathe sth 'into sth to fill sth with life, energy or enthusiasm: *She has breathed fresh life into the movie industry.*
[OBJ] **life**
◆ v + n/pron + prep

breathe 'out to send air out of your lungs through your nose or mouth: *Breathe out slowly through your mouth as you stand up.*
[SYN] **exhale** (*more formal*) [OPP] **breathe in**
◆ v + adv

breathe sth 'out to send air, smoke, etc. out through your nose or mouth: *Breathe the air out slowly and steadily.*
[OBJ] **air, smoke** [SYN] **exhale sth** (*more formal*)
[OPP] **breathe sth in**
◆ v + adv + n ◆ v + n/pron + adv

breeze /briːz/

breeze 'in; breeze 'into sth (*informal*) to arrive somewhere or enter a place in a casual, cheerful and confident way: *She breezed in at eleven and greeted everyone with a smile.* ◇ *He breezed into the office and announced he was leaving.*
◆ v + adv ◆ v + prep

breeze 'through sth (*informal*) to succeed in doing sth very easily: *She breezed through the first exam.*
◆ v + prep

brew /bruː/

brew 'up; brew sth 'up (*BrE, informal*) to prepare a hot drink of tea or coffee: *Come into the kitchen while I brew up.* ◇ *I'll brew up a fresh pot of tea when they arrive.*
[OBJ] **tea**
◆ v + adv ◆ v + adv + n ◆ v + pron + adv ◆ v + n + adv (*rare*)
▶ **'brew-up** n (*BrE, informal*) an act of making a drink of tea; the drink that you make

brick /brɪk/

brick sth 'in/'up to fill in or block an opening with bricks: *The fireplace had been bricked in some years before.* ◇ *Somebody had bricked up all the doors and windows.*
[OBJ] **window, fireplace, door**
[NOTE] Brick sth in/up is often used in the passive.
◆ v + adv + n ◆ v + n/pron + adv

brighten /'braɪtn/

brighten 'up 1 if the weather **brightens up**, it becomes clearer and brighter: *After a dull start, it should brighten up later.* [SYN] **clear up 2** if a

person **brightens up**, they become happier and more cheerful: *He brightened up when they said he could go with them.* ⟩SYN⟨ **cheer up**
◈ v + adv

,**brighten sth 'up** to make sth more interesting, exciting or attractive: *I've brought some flowers to brighten the place up a bit.* ◇ *Brighten up your bedroom with a few posters.*
▢OBJ▢ **place, room** ⟩SYN⟨ **cheer sth up**
◈ v + n/pron + adv ♦ v + adv + n

brim /brɪm/ (-mm-)

,**brim 'over** (with sth) (*usually used in the progressive tenses*) if a cup or a container **brims over** with a liquid, it is so full that the liquid flows over the edge: *He filled my glass so full it was brimming over!* ◇ *Her eyes were brimming over with tears.*
⟩SYN⟨ **overflow** (with sth) (*more formal*)
◈ v + adv

,**brim 'over with sth** (*not used in the progressive tenses*) if sb **brims over with** sth, they show a lot of a particular quality: *She's brimming over with confidence and enthusiasm.*
▢OBJ▢ **confidence, excitement**
◈ v + adv + prep

bring /brɪŋ/ (brought, brought /brɔːt/)

26	~ about		~ on
	~ along	28	~ out
	~ around		~ out in
	~ around to		~ over
	~ back		~ round
	~ before		~ round to
	~ down		~ to
27	~ down on/upon		~ together
	~ forth		~ up
	~ forward		~ up against
	~ in	29	~ up to
	~ into		~ upon
	~ off		

,**bring sth a'bout** to make sth happen: *What has brought about this change?* ◇ *His nervous breakdown was brought about by stress.*
▢OBJ▢ **change, the end/collapse of sth** ⟩SYN⟨ **cause sth**
◈ v + adv + n ♦ v + n/pron + adv

,**bring sb a'long** (*AmE*) = BRING SB ON

,**bring sb/sth a'long** to bring sb/sth somewhere with you: *Can I bring my sister along to the party?* ◇ *She brought some CDs along.*
◈ v + n/pron + adv ♦ v + adv + n

,**bring sb a'round** (*AmE*) = BRING SB ROUND

,**bring sb/sth a'round** (*especially AmE*) = BRING SB/STH ROUND

,**bring sth a'round to sth** (*especially AmE*) = BRING STH ROUND TO STH

,**bring sb 'back** (to sth) **1** to return sb to a place; to take sb home: *I'll bring you back again after the party.* ◇ *She tried to bring him back* (= to make him return) *to the matter in hand.* ◇ *Putting the driver of the car in prison won't bring my sister back* (= return her to life after she has been killed). **2** to put sb back in their old job or position: *United have brought back their old manager.*
◈ v + n/pron + adv ♦ v + adv + n

,**bring sth 'back 1** (to sth) to return sth to the place it came from: *If the dress doesn't fit, bring it back to the shop and we'll change it for you.* **2** to make you remember sth or think about it again: *Talking about his death brought it all back to me.* ◇ *The photos brought back happy memories.*
▢OBJ▢ **memories 3** to make sth that existed or was done before be used or done again: *Are you in favour of bringing back the death penalty?* ⟩SYN⟨ **restore sth; reintroduce sth** (*both more formal*) **4** (for sb) to return with sth for sb: *What shall I bring back for the children from Paris?* ▢NOTE▢ In informal language **bring sb back sth** and, less often, **bring sb sth back** are also used in this meaning: *I brought the kids back some books.* ◇ *Can you bring me something back?*
◈ v + adv + n ♦ v + n/pron + adv

'**bring sb/sth before sb/sth** (*law*) to present sb for judgement; to present sth to sb/sth for discussion or a decision: *Children should not be brought before a court.* ◇ *The case was brought before the judge.*
▢OBJ▢ **case** ⟩SYN⟨ **haul sb before sb/sth, haul sb up before sb/sth** (*informal*)
▢NOTE▢ Bring sb/sth before sb/sth is usually used in the passive.
◈ v + n/pron + prep

,**bring sb 'down** (*informal*) to depress sb; to make sb unhappy: *Spending New Year alone brought me right down.*
⟩SYN⟨ **get sb down; depress sb** (*more formal*)
◈ v + n/pron + adv

,**bring sb/sth 'down 1** to take sb/sth from a higher to a lower level: *They brought all the boxes down from the attic.* **2** to make sb/sth fall to the ground: *He was brought down in the penalty area.* ◇ *Their plane was brought down by a violent storm.* ◇ *When she fell, she brought him down with her.* ◇ *He brought down the bird with a single shot.* **3** to make a government, a leader, etc. lose power or be defeated: *The scandal brought the government down.* ▢OBJ▢ **government**
◈ v + n/pron + adv ♦ v + adv + n

,**bring sth 'down 1** to make sth smaller in size or amount: *We are determined to bring down inflation.* ◇ *The price war is bringing the cost of flights down.* ▢OBJ▢ **inflation, prices** ⟩SYN⟨ **lower sth** (*more formal*) **2** to make an aircraft come

down to the ground (**land**): *The pilot brought the plane down safely.* OBJ **plane** SYN **land sth**
◈ v + n/pron + adv ♦ v + adv + n
IDM **bring the 'house down** to make an audience laugh or clap in an enthusiastic way: *Her performance brought the house down.*

,**bring sth 'down on/upon sb** (*formal*) to make sth unpleasant happen to sb as a result of your actions: *He had brought nothing but trouble down on the family.*
◈ v + n/pron + adv + prep ♦ v + adv + n + prep
IDM **bring down the 'curtain on sth**; **bring the 'curtain down on sth** to finish or mark the end of sth: *Her decision to retire brought down the curtain on a glittering 30-year career.*

,**bring sb 'forth** (*old-fashioned, formal, rare*) to give birth to sb: *She brought forth a son.*
OBJ **child**
◈ v + adv + n ♦ v + pron + adv ♦ v + n + adv (*less frequent*)

,**bring sth 'forth** (*formal*) **1** to produce sth; to make sth happen: *Her remarks brought forth a harsh response.* **2** (*old-fashioned*) to take sth out of a container
◈ v + adv + n ♦ v + pron + adv ♦ v + n + adv (*less frequent*)

,**bring sth 'forward 1** to move sth to an earlier date or time: *We'll have to bring the date of the final game forward.* OBJ **meeting, date** SYN **put sth forward** OPP **put sth back 2** to suggest a subject, an idea, etc. for discussion: *She brought forward proposals for a new school building.* OBJ **proposal** SYN **put sth forward 3** (*finance*) to move a total from the bottom of one page or column of numbers to the top of the next page OBJ **balance** SYN **carry sth forward** NOTE Bring sth forward is often used in the passive in this meaning. **4** (*technical*) to put a document in a file until the particular date when you need to deal with it: *a bring forward file* (= one that contains documents for a particular date) ◊ *With this software, the system will remind you when the bring forward date arrives.* NOTE Bring sth forward is only used in an office context with this meaning, and is usually used in front of a noun, as if it is an adjective.
◈ v + n/pron + adv ♦ v + adv + n

,**bring 'in sth**; ,**bring sb 'in sth** to make or earn money for sb: *How much is she bringing in every month?* ◊ *His job only brought him in a small income.*
◈ v + adv + n ♦ v + n/pron + adv + n

,**bring sb 'in 1** (**on sth**) to get sb involved in sth, especially to advise or help, etc: *Can we deal with this without bringing the police in?* ◊ *I'd like to bring Inspector Lacey in on this investigation.* ◊ *Experts were brought in to advise the government.*

OBJ **experts, police, troops 2** if the police **bring sb in** they take them to a police station to question them or arrest them: *Two men have been brought in for questioning.* OBJ **suspect**
◈ v + adv + n ♦ v + n/pron + adv

,**bring sb/sth 'in 1** to take sb/sth into a room, a house, an office, etc: *Could you bring in another chair?* ◊ *Bring him in!* NOTE In informal language **bring sb in sth** and, less often, **bring sb sth in** are also used: *Could you bring me in another chair?* ◊ *Could you bring us some tea in?* **2** to attract sb/sth to a place or a business: *The visitor centre is bringing in more and more people.*
OBJ **business, customers, tourism**
→ *see also* BRING SB/STH INTO STH
◈ v + adv + n ♦ v + n/pron + adv

,**bring sth 'in 1** to introduce a new law: *A new law was brought in to improve road safety.* ◊ *New controls were brought in to limit spending and borrowing.* OBJ **legislation, law** SYN **introduce sth** (*more formal*) NOTE Bring sth in is often used in the passive in this meaning. **2** (*law*) to give a decision in a court of law: *The jury brought in a verdict of guilty.* OBJ only **verdict, decision 3** to mention or include sth: *She brought in other evidence to support her argument.*
◈ v + adv + n ♦ v + n/pron + adv

,**bring sb/sth 'into sth 1** to take sb/sth into a place: *Bring that chair into the dining room.* **2** to include or mention sb/sth in a discussion, conversation, etc: *Why do you always have to bring Pete into it* (= mention Pete when we are discussing sth)? ◊ *I knew you'd manage to bring football into the conversation!* **3** to attract sb/sth to a place or business: *The advertising campaign should bring more people into the bookshops.*
→ *see also* BRING SB/STH IN
◈ v + n/pron + prep

,**bring sth 'off** (*informal*) to manage to do sth difficult successfully: *England were close to victory, but they couldn't quite bring it off.* ◊ *Thompson, the new goalkeeper, brought off a superb save.*
SYN **pull sth off**
◈ v + pron + adv ♦ v + adv + n ♦ v + n + adv

,**bring sb 'on** (*BrE*) (*AmE* ,**bring sb a'long**) to help sb to develop or improve when they are learning to do sth: *We need to bring on the young players quickly.* ◊ *There's no time to bring employees along gradually.*
◈ v + adv + n ♦ v + n/pron + adv

,**bring sth 'on** to make sth unpleasant happen: *The heart attack was brought on by stress.* ◊ *It's not like you to get so upset. What's brought this on* (= has made you so upset)?
OBJ **heart attack, depression** SYN **cause sth** (*more formal*)
◈ v + n/pron + adv ♦ v + adv + n

'bring sth on sb/yourself (*also* **bring sth upon sb/yourself** *more formal*) to be responsible for sth unpleasant that happens to sb/yourself: *You've brought shame on the whole family!* ◇ *Don't blame me! You've brought this on yourself.*
- **OBJ** **shame, disgrace**
- ◈ v + n/pron + prep

'bring sb 'out to help sb to be more confident and less shy: *He's good at bringing out nervous interviewees.* ◇ *A year at college has really brought her out of herself.*
- ◈ v + adv + n ◆ v + n/pron + adv

'bring sth 'out 1 (*also* **'bring sth 'out of sth**) to take sth out of sth; to remove sth from sth: *He brought a card out of his wallet and gave it to her.* **SYN** **take sth out, take sth out of sth 2** to produce or publish sth: *They're bringing out a new sports car this year.* ◇ *How many albums have the band brought out?* ◇ *The publishers are bringing out a new edition of the dictionary next spring.* **3** to make a particular quality easier to see, taste, or notice: *That dress brings out the colour of your eyes.* **OBJ** **colour, flavour** **SYN** **emphasize sth** (*more formal*) **4** to make sth appear that is usually hidden: *She always brings out the meanest in me!* ◇ *The situation brought out the viciousness in him.* **OBJ** **the best, the worst**
- ◈ v + n/pron + adv ◆ v + adv + n
- **1** also v + n/pron + adv + prep

'bring sb 'out in sth (*BrE*) to make sb's skin be covered in sth such as sweat or spots: *Tomatoes bring me out in a rash.*
- ◈ v + n/pron + adv + prep

'bring sb/sth 'over to take or bring sb/sth to a particular place, especially sb's home: *When your sister gets back from New York, bring her over to see us.* ◇ *Bring your chair over and sit with us!*
- ◈ v + n/pron + adv ◆ v + adv + n

'bring sb 'round (*BrE*) (*AmE* **'bring sb a'round**) **1** (*also* **'bring sb 'to**) to make sb conscious again: *She gently slapped his face to bring him round.* **2** (to sth) to persuade sb to agree with you, or to do what you want: *I brought him round to my way of thinking in the end.* **SYN** **win sb over (to sth)**
- ◈ v + n/pron + adv

'bring sb/sth 'round (*especially BrE*) (*AmE usually* **'bring sb/sth a'round**) to bring sb/sth to sb's home: *I'll bring the papers round to your house this evening.*
- ◈ v + n/pron + adv ◆ v + adv + n

'bring sth 'round to sth (*BrE*) (*also* **'bring sth a'round to sth** *AmE, BrE*) to direct a conversation, a discussion, etc. so that you are talking about the subject you want to talk about: *He always brings the conversation round to football.*
- **OBJ** **conversation, discussion**
- ◈ v + n/pron + adv + prep

'bring sb 'to = BRING SB ROUND 1

'bring A and B to'gether 1 to help two people or groups to end a quarrel; to unite two people or groups: *The crisis brought the family closer together.* **2** to introduce two people who have never met; to help two people come together socially: *It was me who brought them together.*
- **SYN** **get A and B together**
- ◈ v + n/pron + adv ◆ v + adv + n

'bring sb/sth to'gether to collect a group of people or objects together in one place: *This exhibition brings together many artists' work.*
- ◈ v + n/pron + adv ◆ v + adv + n

'bring sb 'up 1 to care for a child until he or she is grown up: *She was brought up by her aunt.* ◇ *I was brought up* (= I grew up) *on a farm.* **OBJ** **children, family, daughter, son** **SYN** **raise sb** (*AmE*) **NOTE** Bring up a child does not mean the same as look after a child. **2** to teach your child a particular way to behave, etc: *They brought their children up very strictly.* ◇ *We were brought up to be polite and do what we were told.* ◇ *a well brought up child* **OBJ** **children, family, daughter, son** **SYN** **raise sb** (*AmE*) **3** (*law*) to make sb appear for trial in a court of law
- **NOTE** Bring sb up is often used in the passive.
- ◈ v + n/pron + adv ◆ v + adv + n
- ▶ **'upbringing** *n* [sing.] [U] the way in which a child is cared for and taught, especially by parents, while he or she is growing up

'bring sb/sth 'up (to sth) to move sb/sth to a higher place, especially up the stairs: *Breakfast was brought up to our room.* ◇ *Callum is downstairs. Shall I bring him up?* ◇ *She brought her hand up and slapped him.* ◇ *I brought the cup up to my lips and took a sip of coffee.*
- ◈ v + n/pron + adv ◆ v + adv + n

'bring sth 'up 1 to move sth from a lower to a higher position: *She brought up her hand to protect her face.* **2** to mention a subject and start to talk about it: *Every time I bring the matter up, he changes the subject.* **OBJ** **subject, matter** **SYN** **raise sth** (*more formal*) **3** (to sth) to increase a total, a price, a number, etc. to a higher level or amount: *This donation brings the total up to $6 000.* ◇ *Owen got another goal, bringing the score up to 4-0.* **OBJ** **total** **SYN** **raise sth** (*more formal*) **4** to bring food from the stomach back out through the mouth: *The baby's just brought up her breakfast.* **SYN** **throw sth up** (*informal*), **vomit sth** (*more formal*) **5** to make sth appear on a computer screen: *Can you bring that file up on screen?*
- ◈ v + n/pron + adv ◆ v + adv + n

'bring sb 'up against sth to make sb realize sth or face sth and deal with it: *This case brings us up against the problem of punishment in schools.*
- ◈ v + n/pron + adv + prep

,bring sb/sth 'up to sth to help sb/sth to reach an acceptable level or standard: *They have now brought the football ground up to the required safety standards.*
⊕ v + n/pron + adv + prep

,bring sth u'pon sb/yourself = BRING STH ON SB/YOURSELF

bristle /'brɪsl/

'bristle with sth to be covered in sth; to have or contain a large number or amount of sth: *a roof bristling with TV aerials* ◊ *The staff bristle with efficiency.*
NOTE Bristle with sth is mainly used in writing.
⊕ v + prep

broaden /'brɔːdn/

,broaden 'out if a river, a road, etc. broadens out, it becomes wider
NOTE Broaden is also used with the same meaning, but less often.
⊕ v + adv

,broaden 'out; ,broaden sth 'out (*especially BrE*) if sth broadens out, or you broaden it out, it becomes more general or includes a larger number of people or things: *Let's broaden out the discussion to talk about education as a whole.*
NOTE Broaden is used more frequently with the same meaning.
⊕ v + adv ♦ v + adv + n ♦ v + n/pron + adv

browse /braʊz/

,browse 'through sth to look through a book, a magazine, etc. in a casual way, without reading everything: *She browsed through the newspaper while she waited.*
OBJ book, newspaper
⊕ v + prep

brush /brʌʃ/

,brush a'gainst/'by/'past sb/sth to touch sb/sth lightly when you move close to them/it: *A cat brushed against his leg.* ◊ *He brushed by/past me and ran out.*
⊕ v + prep

,brush sb/sth a'side 1 to push sb/sth to one side: *She brushed a strand of hair aside.* 2 to refuse to listen to sb/sth or treat them/it as important: *He brushed my protests aside and paid the bill.* ◊ *Every time I try to explain, you brush me aside.* ⎣SYN⎤ wave sth aside/away; dismiss sb/sth
→ *see also* BRUSH SB OFF 1; BRUSH STH OFF 2
⊕ v + n/pron + adv ♦ v + adv + n

,brush sth a'way (from sth) 1 to remove sth from a surface with a brush, your hand, etc: *She brushed a stray hair away from her face.* **OBJ** tears, hair, dust 2 to ignore an idea, a thought,

etc. because you do not want to think about it or you think it is not important: *She quickly brushed the idea away.* ⎣SYN⎤ dismiss sth
⊕ v + n/pron + adv ♦ v + adv + n

,brush 'by sb/sth = BRUSH AGAINST/BY/PAST SB/STH

,brush sb/yourself 'down (*especially BrE*) to clean sb/yourself by brushing their/your clothes with your hand, especially after they/you have fallen: *She stood up and brushed herself down.*
→ *see also* BRUSH SB/YOURSELF OFF
⊕ v + n/pron + adv

,brush sth 'down (*especially BrE*) to clean sth by brushing it thoroughly: *Brush your coat down to get the mud off.* ◊ *The children were taught how to brush down their ponies.*
OBJ coat, skirt, etc.
→ *see also* BRUSH STH OFF 1
⊕ v + n/pron + adv ♦ v + adv + n

,brush 'off; ,brush sth 'off if mud, dust etc. brushes off, or you brush it off, it is removed by brushing: *Don't worry about the mud — it'll brush off easily when it's dry.* ◊ *We were able to brush the dirt off quite easily.*
⊕ v + adv ♦ v + n/pron + adv ♦ v + adv + n

,brush sb 'off (*informal*) 1 to refuse to listen to sb; to ignore sb in a rude or unkind way: *He tried to explain to her, but she brushed him off impatiently.* ⎣SYN⎤ rebuff sb (*formal*) → *see also* BRUSH SB/STH ASIDE 2 2 to get rid of sb: *She couldn't brush Roger off after the party.*
⊕ v + n/pron + adv ♦ v + adv + n
▶ 'brush-off n (*informal*) rude or unkind behaviour that shows you do not want to be friendly: *to give sb the brush-off*

,brush sb/yourself 'off to clean sb/yourself by brushing their/your clothes quickly with your hand
→ *see also* BRUSH SB/YOURSELF DOWN
⊕ v + n/pron + adv ♦ v + adv + n

,brush sth 'off 1 to clean sth quickly by brushing it: *He picked up his hat and brushed it off quickly.*
→ *see also* BRUSH STH DOWN 2 to refuse to listen to, discuss or accept sth: *Roberts brushed off allegations of corruption.* ◊ *She brushed off offers of help from her friends.* → *see also* BRUSH SB/STH ASIDE 2
⊕ v + n/pron + adv ♦ v + adv + n

,brush sth 'out 1 to brush sth, especially hair, thoroughly to remove knots or to make it straighter: *She brushed out her hair, washed her face and got into bed.* **OBJ** hair 2 (*also* ,brush sth 'out of sth) to remove knots, etc. from your hair by brushing: *It took half an hour to brush out all the tangles in his hair.* **OBJ** tangles, knots
⊕ v + adv + n ♦ v + n/pron + adv
2 also v + n/pron + adv + prep

,brush 'past sb/sth = BRUSH AGAINST/BY/PAST SB/STH

,brush sth 'up; ,brush 'up on sth (*especially BrE*) to study or practise sth in order to get back the skill or knowledge that you had in the past but have not used for some time: *I need to brush up my computer skills.* ◇ *You should brush up on your French before you go to France.*

OBJ skills, French/English, etc. **SYN** polish sth up; review sth (*especially AmE*), revise sth (*BrE*)

NOTE Brush sth up cannot be used in the passive.

◈ v + adv + n ♦ v + pron + adv ♦ v + n + adv (*less frequent*) ♦ v + adv + prep

bubble /'bʌbl/

,bubble 'over (with sth) to be full of excitement, enthusiasm, ideas, etc: *They were bubbling over with excitement.*

◈ v + adv

,bubble 'under; ,bubble 'under sth if sth is bubbling under, it is already fairly successful but is not yet as successful as other things of the same kind, although it is likely to be so soon: *This is our list of tracks bubbling under — songs that may soon be in the Top 20.*

◈ v + adv ♦ v + prep

,bubble 'up 1 if a liquid bubbles up from the ground, etc. it rises up in the form of bubbles or making the sound of bubbles: *Water bubbled up from the pool.* ◇ (*figurative*) *Clouds will bubble up* (= start to form) *later this afternoon.* **2** if laughter or an emotion bubbles up, it becomes stronger and starts to be heard or seen: *I could feel the anger bubbling up inside me.* ◇ *Laughter came bubbling up.*

◈ v + adv

buck /bʌk/

,buck 'up (*old-fashioned*, *BrE*, *informal*) used to tell sb to hurry up: *Buck up! We'll be late.*

SYN hurry up

◈ v + adv

,buck 'up; ,buck sb 'up (*old-fashioned*, *BrE*, *informal*) to become, or to make sb, more cheerful: *Buck up! There's no school tomorrow!* ◇ *He bucked up when I said he could go.* ◇ *A day out will buck you up.*

SYN cheer up, cheer sb/yourself up

◈ v + adv ♦ v + n/pron + adv

IDM buck your i'deas up (*BrE*, *informal*) to start behaving in a more acceptable way, so that work gets done better, etc.

bucket /'bʌkɪt/

'bucket down (*BrE*, *informal*) to rain heavily: *It bucketed down all day.*

◈ v + adv

buckle /'bʌkl/

,buckle 'down (to sth) (*informal*) to start working or doing sth in a serious or determined way: *He tried to buckle down to some work/study.*

SYN knuckle down (to sth)

◈ v + adv

,buckle 'up (*especially AmE*) to fasten the belt that you wear in a car, etc. to keep you in your seat if there is an accident (a **seat belt**): *Buckle up, kids.*

SYN belt up (*BrE*)

◈ v + adv

buddy /'bʌdi/ (buddies, buddying, buddied, buddied)

,buddy 'up to/with sb/sth; be/get ,buddied 'up to/with sb/sth (*AmE*, *informal*) to become friendly with sb or work closely with another person: *She buddied up to Julie, hoping to get to know her brother.* ◇ *I asked to get buddied up with an experienced diver.*

◈ v + adv + prep ♦ be/get + v + adv + prep

budge /bʌdʒ/

,budge 'up (*BrE*, *informal*) to move up; to make more room for sb else: *Budge up a bit! I'd like to sit down too.*

SYN move up

◈ v + adv

budget /'bʌdʒɪt/

'budget for sth to plan to save or provide an amount of money for a particular purpose: *Don't forget to budget for the cost of textbooks.*

NOTE Budget for sth can be used in the passive: *These extra costs have not been budgeted for.*

◈ v + prep

bug /bʌg/ (-gg-)

,bug 'out (*AmE*, *informal*) to leave in a hurry: *I picked up my pay and then bugged out.*

◈ v + adv

bugger /'bʌgə(r)/

,bugger a'bout/a'round (with sth) (*BrE*, △, *slang*) to waste time doing stupid or unimportant things; to behave in a silly way: *Stop buggering about and let's get on with it.*

NOTE Mess around or, in British English, mess about is a more polite informal way to say this.

◈ v + adv

,bugger sb a'bout/a'round (*BrE*, △, *slang*) to treat sb badly or in a way that wastes their time: *I'm sick of being buggered about by my boss.*

NOTE Mess sb around or, in British English, mess sb about is a more polite informal way to say this.

◈ v + n/pron + adv

,**bugger 'off** (*BrE*, △, *slang*) to go away: *Bugger off and leave me alone.* ◇ *Clive's buggered off to the pub with Julie.*
NOTE Clear off is a more polite informal way to say this.
◈ v + adv

,**bugger sth 'up** (*BrE*, △, *slang*) to spoil sth; to do sth badly: *I'm not going to let her bugger things up for me.*
NOTE Mess sth up is a more polite informal way to say this.
◈ v + n/pron + adv ◆ v + adv + n

build /bɪld/ (**built, built** /bɪlt/)

,**build sth a'round sth** (*BrE also* ,**build sth 'round sth**) to create sth, basing it on a particular thing, person, idea, etc: *The story is built around the adventures of 12 knights.*
NOTE Build sth around/round sth is often used in the passive.
◈ v + n/pron + prep

,**build sth 'in**; ,**build sth 'into sth 1** to make sth a fixed and permanent part of a system, a plan, etc: *Safeguards against fraud are built into the system.* **2** to make sth a fixed and permanent part of sth larger: *The flash is built into the camera.* ◇ *This dishwasher can be built in.*
NOTE Build sth in and **build sth into sth** are often used in the passive.
◈ v + n/pron + adv ◆ v + adv + n ◆ v + n/pron + prep
▶ ,**built-'in** (*also* ,**in-'built** *less frequent*) *adj* [only before noun] forming a fixed part of a larger structure: *a built-in cupboard* ◇ *The camera has a built-in flash.*
▶ '**inbuilt** *adj* [only before noun] existing as an essential part of sth/sb: *the inbuilt survival instinct of animals*

'**build on sth** (*also* '**build upon sth** *more formal*) to develop further from sth that you have already achieved: *We need to build on last year's success.* ◇ *This course builds on existing skills.*
OBJ success, skills, strengths, achievements
NOTE Build on/upon sth can be used in the passive: *This success should be built on, not ignored.*
◈ v + prep

,**build sth 'on**; ,**build sth 'onto sth** to add sth such as an extra room to an existing building: *They had built on a large extension at the back of the house.*
OBJ extension
◈ v + adv + n ◆ v + n/pron + adv ◆ v + n/pron + prep

'**build sth on sth** (*also* '**build sth upon sth** *more formal*) to base sth on sth; to use sth as the basis or foundation for sth: *Our company has built its reputation on the quality of its products.*
◈ v + n/pron + prep

,**build sth 'round sth** (*BrE*) = BUILD STH AROUND STH

,**build 'up** to become greater, stronger or larger in number: *Queues of traffic are building up after the accident.* ◇ *I could feel the anger building up inside me.*
SYN accumulate (*more formal*)
◈ v + adv
▶ '**build-up** *n* [sing.] [U] an increase in the amount, strength or number of sth: *a build-up of carbon dioxide in the atmosphere*
→ *see also* BUILD-UP at BUILD UP (TO STH), BUILD YOURSELF UP (TO STH); BUILD-UP at BUILD SB/STH UP

,**build 'up** (to sth), ,**build yourself 'up** (to sth) to gradually prepare yourself for sth such as a race or competition: *Start gently and build up to the more strenuous exercises.* ◇ *Build up slowly until you can jog for 30 minutes.* ◇ *Build yourself up to the day of the performance.*
◈ v + adv ◆ v + pron + adv
▶ ,**build-'up** (to sth) *n* [C, usually sing.] the time before an important event, when people are gradually preparing for it: *the build-up to the Olympics*
→ *see also* BUILD-UP at BUILD UP; BUILD-UP at BUILD SB/STH UP

,**build sb/yourself 'up** to make sb healthier or stronger: *She gave me lots of vitamins and minerals to build me up.*
NOTE Build sb up cannot be used in the passive.
◈ v + n/pron + adv

,**build sb/sth 'up** to speak about sb/sth with great enthusiasm, often praising them more than they deserve: *He has been built up to be the answer to the nation's problems.*
NOTE Build sb/sth up is often used in the passive.
◈ v + n/pron + adv ◆ v + adv + n
▶ '**build-up** *n* [C, usually sing.] a very enthusiastic description, especially of a performance, that is intended to make people excited about it and want to see it: *The reviewers gave the play a big build-up.*
→ *see also* BUILD-UP at BUILD UP; BUILD-UP at BUILD UP (TO STH), BUILD YOURSELF UP (TO STH)

,**build sth 'up 1** to collect or create sth, often gradually over a period of time: *She has built up an impressive collection of paintings.* **OBJ collection, library 2** to develop sth: *The manager had built up a good relationship with his staff.* ◇ *My father built the business up from scratch.* ◇ *Harriet has built up quite a reputation for herself as a reporter.* ◇ *We are gradually building up a picture of what happened.* **OBJ business, reputation, picture 3** to increase sth or make sth stronger: *After an accident, most drivers need to build up their confidence again.* **OBJ confidence, trust, strength 4** to cover sth so that it is higher or stronger than before
◈ v + adv + n ◆ v + n/pron + adv

▶ **,built-'up** *adj* [usually before noun] **1** covered with many houses or buildings: *The speed limit is lower in built-up areas.* **2 built-up** shoes, boots, or heels have extra height added

,build yourself 'up 1 = BUILD UP (TO STH), BUILD YOURSELF UP (TO STH) **2** = BUILD SB/YOURSELF UP

'build upon sth = BUILD ON STH

'build sth upon sth = BUILD STH ON STH

bulk /bʌlk/

,bulk 'out/'up; **,bulk sb/sth 'out/'up** (*especially AmE*) to increase in size or weight; to make sb/sth increase in size or weight: *Griswold had bulked up for this match and won easily.* ◇ *Local businesses are helping to bulk up school computer labs* (= provide more computers).
◈ v + adv ◆ v + adv + n ◆ v + pron + adv ◆ v + n + adv (*rare*)

bully /'bʊli/ (bullies, bullying, bullied, bullied)

,bully sb 'into sth; **,bully sb 'into doing sth** to force sb to do sth by frightening them or threatening them: *You can't bully me into saying anything!*
◈ v + n/pron + prep

bum /bʌm/ (-mm-)

,bum a'round (*BrE also* **,bum 'round**) (*informal*) to travel around or to spend your time doing nothing in particular
◈ v + adv

,bum a'round/'round sth (*informal, especially BrE*) to travel somewhere with no particular plans: *After I left school, I bummed around the world for a year.*
[OBJ] the world, Europe, etc.
◈ v + prep

,bum sb 'out (*AmE, informal*) to annoy sb: *I was really bummed out that there were no tickets left.*
◈ v + n/pron + adv

,bum 'round (*BrE*) = BUM AROUND

,bum 'round sth (*especially BrE*) = BUM AROUND/ROUND STH

bumble /'bʌmbl/

,bumble a'round; **,bumble a'round sth** (*BrE also* **,bumble a'bout**, **,bumble a'bout sth**) to move around in an awkward and noisy way: *I could hear my father bumbling about downstairs.* ◇ *a film of two sisters bumbling around their home, making tea*
◈ v + adv ◆ v + prep

bump /bʌmp/

,bump 'into sb (*informal*) to meet sb by chance: *I bumped into an old friend in town today.*
SYN **run into sb**
◈ v + prep

,bump sb 'off (*informal*) to murder sb: *He admitted bumping off Baines.*
◈ v + n/pron + adv ◆ v + adv + n

,bump sb 'off; **,bump sb 'off sth 1** to not allow sb to have the seat on a plane that they have booked, because seats have been sold to more people than the plane will carry: *With more people flying these days, there is a greater chance of getting bumped off your flight.* ◇ *bumped off travellers* NOTE **Bump sb** can also be used with this meaning: *We were late arriving at the airport and the airline bumped us.* **2** (*especially AmE, computing*) to break the connection between sb's computer and the Internet, so that they can no longer use the Internet: *Some users couldn't log in, others kept getting bumped off.* ◇ *to be bumped off the Internet* [OBJ] the Internet, server, website SYN **kick sb off, kick sb off sth; disconnect sb (from sth)** (*more formal*)
NOTE These phrasal verbs are usually used in the passive: *I was worried about being bumped off the flight.*
◈ v + n/pron + adv ◆ v + n/pron + prep

,bump sb 'up (to sth) (*informal*) to move sb to a more expensive seat in a plane without charging them extra, because there are not enough seats at the price they have paid: *I got bumped up to business class.*
NOTE **Bump sb up** is often used in the passive.
◈ v + n/pron + adv

,bump sth 'up (*informal*) to increase or raise sth: *The company bumped their prices up by 10%.*
[OBJ] prices
◈ v + n/pron + adv ◆ v + adv + n

bunch /bʌntʃ/

,bunch 'up; **,bunch sth 'up** if material bunches up, or you bunch it up, it forms tight folds: *The sheets bunched up under him every time he moved.* ◇ *She bunched her skirt up and jumped.*
NOTE **Bunch sth up** is often used in the passive.
◈ v + adv ◆ v + n/pron + adv ◆ v + adv + n

,bunch 'up/to'gether; **,bunch sb/sth 'up/to'gether** to move closer together to make a tight group; to make sb/sth do this: *The children bunched together in little groups in the playground.* ◇ *All the runners were bunched up behind the leader.*
NOTE **Bunch sb/sth up/together** is often used in the passive.
◈ v + adv ◆ v + n/pron + adv ◆ v + adv + n

bundle /'bʌndl/

,bundle sb 'off (**to sth…**) to send sb somewhere in a hurry or when they do not want to go: *She bundled her son off to school.*
⟨SYN⟩ pack sb off (to…)
◆ v + n/pron + adv ◆ v + adv + n

,bundle 'up; **,bundle sb 'up** (**in sth**) to dress in warm clothes; to put warm clothes on sb: *Bundle up! It's freezing outside!* ◇ *I bundled Lucy up in a blanket and made her a cup of tea.*
⟨SYN⟩ wrap up (in sth), wrap sb up (in sth), wrap yourself up (in sth)
NOTE Bundle sb up is often used in the passive.
◆ v + adv ◆ v + n/pron + adv

,bundle sth 'up/to'gether to put or tie things together into a bundle: *She bundled up her clothes and pushed them into a cupboard.* ◇ *The papers were all bundled together, ready to be thrown away.*
◆ v + n/pron + adv ◆ v + adv + n

bung /bʌŋ/

,bung sth 'up (**with sth**) (*BrE, informal*) to stop sth from moving or flowing through sth by putting sth in or across it: *She's bunged the sink up with tea leaves.*
⟨SYN⟩ block sth up (*more formal*)
◆ v + n/pron + adv ◆ v + adv + n
▶ **,bunged 'up** *adj* blocked; not clear: *My nose is all bunged up this morning.*

bunk /bʌŋk/

,bunk 'down (*especially AmE*) to lie down to sleep somewhere, especially somewhere uncomfortable or for only one night: *We bunked down in an old barn for the night.*
⟨SYN⟩ doss down (*BrE, informal*)
◆ v + adv

,bunk 'off; **,bunk 'off sth** (*BrE, informal*) to stay away from school or work when you ought to be there; to leave school or work early, especially without permission: *Let's bunk off this afternoon and go shopping.*
OBJ school, work ⟨SYN⟩ skive off, skive off sth (*BrE*)
◆ v + adv ◆ v + prep

buoy /bɔɪ; *AmE also* 'buːi/

,buoy sb/sth 'up 1 to make or keep sb cheerful and confident: *Winning the match buoyed the team up.* ◇ *The party did little to buoy up her spirits.* ◇ *She was buoyed up by her father's praise.* **2** to keep sb/sth floating; to stop sb/sth from sinking: *I relaxed, letting the salt water buoy me up.*

NOTE Buoy sb/sth up is often used in the passive. **Buoy sb/sth** can also be used: *Buoyed by their recent victory, the team are convinced they can win the final.*
◆ v + n/pron + adv ◆ v + adv + n

,buoy sth 'up (*finance*) to make or keep prices at a high or satisfactory level: *Share prices were buoyed up by the news.* ◇ *to buoy up the economy*
OBJ prices
NOTE Buoy sth up is often used in the passive. ◆ **Buoy sth** is also used with this meaning.
◆ v + n/pron + adv ◆ v + adv + n

burn /bɜːn; *AmE* bɜːrn/ (**burnt, burnt** /bɜːnt; *AmE* bɜːrnt/ or **burned, burned** /bɜːnd; *AmE* bɜːrnd/)

,burn a'way; **,burn sth a'way** to disappear as a result of burning; to make sth do this: *Half the candle had burnt away.* ◇ *The fire had burned away part of the roof.*
◆ v + adv ◆ v + adv + n ◆ v + pron + adv ◆ v + n + adv (*less frequent*)

,burn 'down if a fire **burns down**, it becomes less strong and burns with smaller flames: *They sat by the fire, watching it slowly burn down.*
⟨OPP⟩ burn up
◆ v + adv

,burn 'down; **,burn sth 'down** if a building **burns down**, or sb **burns it down**, it is destroyed by fire: *The palace burnt down in the 19th century.* ◇ *She threatened to burn the house down.*
NOTE Burn sth down is often used in the passive.
◆ v + adv ◆ v + n/pron + adv ◆ v + adv + n

,burn sth 'off 1 to remove sth by burning: *Burn the old paint off before repainting the door.* **2** (*also* **,burn sth 'up**) to use energy by exercising: *Walking briskly can burn off a lot of calories.* **OBJ calories, fat**
◆ v + adv + n ◆ v + n/pron + adv

,burn 'out; **,burn sth 'out** if a machine or part of a machine **burns out** or sb **burns it out**, it stops working because it has been used too much or has got too hot: *The clutch has burnt out.* ◇ *I burnt out the motor in the first car I had.*
◆ v + adv ◆ v + n/pron + adv ◆ v + adv + n

,burn 'out; **,burn itself 'out** to stop burning because there is no more fuel: *Blow out the candles before they burn out.* ◇ *By the time the fire brigade arrived the fire had burnt (itself) out.*
→ *see also* BURN STH OUT
◆ v + adv ◆ v + pron + adv

,burn 'out; **,burn yourself 'out** to become very tired or sick and unable to continue your work by working too hard over a period of time: *It's a high pressure job and many people burn out at a young age.* ◇ *If he carries on working so hard, he'll burn himself out.*

→ *see also* BURN SB OUT, BURN SB OUT OF STH
✧ v + adv ◆ v + pron + adv

▶ '**burnout** *n* [C] [U] the state of being very tired or sick because you have worked too hard: *Burnout is common among teachers.*

▶ ,**burnt-'out** (*especially BrE*) (*AmE usually* ,**burned-'out**) very tired or sick because you have worked too hard: *burnt-out rock singers*
→ *see also* BURNT-OUT at BURN STH OUT

,**burn sb 'out**; ,**burn sb 'out of sth** to force sb to leave a building by setting fire to it: *A gang has tried to burn a woman out of her home.*
→ *see also* BURN OUT, BURN YOURSELF OUT
✧ v + n/pron + adv ◆ v + adv + n ◆ v + n/pron + adv + prep

,**burn sth 'out** to destroy sth completely by fire, so that only the outside or the frame is left: *Two cars were burnt out in the crash.*
NOTE Burn sth out is usually used in the passive.
→ *see also* BURN OUT, BURN ITSELF OUT
✧ v + n/pron + adv ◆ v + adv + n

▶ '**burnt-out** (*especially BrE*) (*AmE usually* '**burned-out**) *adj* [only before noun] completely destroyed or badly damaged by fire: *burnt-out buses* ◇ *burned-out houses*
→ *see also* BURNT-OUT at BURN OUT, BURN YOURSELF OUT

,**burn 'up 1** to be destroyed by heat: *The spacecraft burned up as it entered the earth's atmosphere.* **2** (*usually used in the progressive tenses*) to have a fever or a high temperature: *She is burning up — she needs a doctor.* **3** if a fire **burns up**, it gets stronger and has larger flames ᴼᴾᴾ **burn down**
✧ v + adv

,**burn sb 'up** (*AmE, informal*) to make sb very angry: *The way he treats me really burns me up.*
✧ v + n/pron + adv

,**burn sth 'up 1** to get rid of sth completely by burning: *I'm going to burn up all the rubbish/trash.* **2** = BURN STH OFF 2
✧ v + adv + n ◆ v + n/pron + adv

burrow /'bʌrəʊ; *AmE* 'bɜːroʊ/

'**burrow in sth** to search for sth among things in a container: *She burrowed in her pocket and eventually found a few coins.*
✧ v + prep

burst /bɜːst; *AmE* bɜːrst/ (**burst**, **burst**)

,**burst 'in** (on sb/sth), ,**burst 'into sth** to enter a room, a building, etc. suddenly and noisily, interrupting the people who are in it: *He apologized for bursting in on our meeting.* ◇ *The door suddenly flew open and Mia burst in.* ◇ *She ran down the stairs and burst into the kitchen.*
→ *see also* BURST INTO STH
✧ v + adv ◆ v + prep

'**burst into sth** to start producing or doing sth suddenly and with great force: *The aircraft burst into flames* (= suddenly started to burn). ◇ *I was so relieved I burst into tears* (= suddenly started to cry). ◇ *The cab's engine burst into life* (= suddenly started to work). ◇ *As the curtain fell, the audience burst into applause* (= suddenly started to clap).
OBJ tears, flames, laughter, life
→ *see also* BURST IN (ON SB/STH), BURST INTO STH
✧ v + prep

'**burst on/onto sth** (*also* '**burst upon sth** *more formal*) to appear somewhere suddenly in a dramatic or unusual way: *A major new talent has burst on/onto the tennis scene.*
OBJ scene
✧ v + prep

,**burst 'out** to say sth suddenly, loudly and with strong feeling: *'I hate you!' she burst out.*
ˢʸᴺ **exclaim** (*formal*)
→ *see also* BURST OUT DOING STH
✧ v + adv + speech

▶ '**outburst** *n* a sudden strong expression of an emotion; a sudden increase in an attitude or an activity: *an outburst of anger/laughter* ◇ *sporadic outbursts of violence* ◇ *She apologized for her outburst.*

,**burst 'out**; ,**burst 'out of sth** to leave a room, a building, etc. suddenly and noisily: *The door opened suddenly and a man burst out of the house.*
✧ v + adv ◆ v + adv + prep

,**burst 'out doing sth** to begin doing sth suddenly: *We looked at one another and burst out laughing.*
OBJ laughing, crying
→ *see also* BURST OUT; OUTBURST at BURST OUT
✧ v + adv + -ing

,**burst 'through**; ,**burst 'through sth** to move suddenly through a door, a barrier, etc. with great force: *The car drove fast up to the road block and burst through.* ◇ *She burst through the door pursued by two men.* ◇ *The sun burst through the clouds.*
✧ v + adv ◆ v + prep

'**burst upon sth** = BURST ON/ONTO STH

bury /'beri/ (**buries**, **burying**, **buried**, **buried**)

'**bury yourself in sth 1** to go to or be in a place where you will not meet many people: *He buried himself in the country to write a book.* **2** to involve yourself in sth completely; to spend all your time thinking about or doing sth and ignore everything else: *She buried herself in her work in an attempt to forget.* **OBJ** work, book
✧ v + pron + prep

bust /bʌst/ (bust, bust or busted, busted)

,bust 'out; ,bust 'out of sth; ,bust sb 'out; ,bust sb 'out of sth (*informal*) to escape from somewhere, usually prison; to help sb to do this: *His last movie was about a guy busting out of Alcatraz.* ◇ *His friends busted him out of jail.*
〈SYN〉 **break out, break out of sth** (*more formal*)
◈ v + adv ◆ v + adv + prep ◆ v + n/pron + adv ◆ v + n/pron + adv + prep

,bust 'up (with sb) (*BrE, informal*) if a couple or two friends **bust up**, they have a quarrel and separate: *They bust up after five years together.* ◇ *I bust up with Tim a while ago.*
〈SYN〉 **break up (with sb); split up (with/from sb)**
◈ v + adv
▸ **'bust-up** *n* (*BrE, informal*) **1** (with sb) an argument or a quarrel: *We had a huge bust-up and now we're not talking.* **2** the end of a relationship

,bust sth 'up (*informal*) **1** to end sth such as a meeting or a relationship by disturbing or ruining it: *The police busted up the meeting.* 〈SYN〉 **break sth up** (*more formal*) **2** (*AmE*) to injure, damage or break sth: *He busted up his knee in the accident.* **3** (*AmE*) to break a company or a larger organization into smaller parts 〈OBJ〉 **company** 〈SYN〉 **break sth up** (*more formal*)
◈ v + adv + n ◆ v + n/pron + adv

bustle /'bʌsl/

,bustle a'bout/a'round; ,bustle a'bout/ a'round sth (*especially BrE*) to move about somewhere in a busy or hurried way: *She was already bustling about, getting dinner ready.*
◈ v + adv ◆ v + prep

butt /bʌt/

,butt 'in (*informal*) **1** (on sb/sth) to rudely interrupt sb when they are speaking: *He apologized for butting in on our conversation.* ◇ *'His name's Terry, actually,' she butted in.* 〈SYN〉 **interrupt (sb/sth)** (*more formal*) **2** to interfere in a situation that does not concern you: *Stop butting in. It's nothing to do with you.* 〈SYN〉 **interfere (with sth)** (*more formal*)
◈ v + adv **1** also v + adv + speech

,butt 'out (*spoken, informal, especially AmE*) used to tell sb rudely not to interfere in sth or to go away: *Butt out! It's none of your business.*
◈ v + adv

butter /'bʌtə(r)/

,butter sb 'up (*informal*) to say nice things about sb because you want them to do sth for you or give you sth: *We'd better butter him up a bit before we ask for his help.*
〈SYN〉 **soften sb up**
◈ v + n/pron + adv ◆ v + adv + n

button /'bʌtn/

,button 'up; ,button sth 'up to be fastened with buttons; to fasten sth with buttons: *He buttoned up his coat.*
〈OBJ〉 **coat, jacket, etc.** 〈SYN〉 **do up, do sth up**
〈OPP〉 **unbutton, unbutton sth**
〈NOTE〉 **Button** and **button sth** are also used with this meaning.
◈ v + n/pron + adv ◆ v + adv + n
▸ **,buttoned-'up** *adj* **1** [usually before noun] not showing or expressing your feelings openly; not very friendly: *his buttoned-up calmness* **2** (*AmE*) very formal in appearance; traditional rather than new or exciting

buy /baɪ/ (bought, bought /bɔːt/)

,buy sth 'back if somebody **buys sth back**, they buy again sth that they have sold earlier to sb else: *The bank will supply and buy back foreign currency.* ◇ *He sold the car in 1949 for £400. To buy it back last year cost £31 000.*
◈ v + adv + n ◆ v + n/pron + adv
▸ **'buy-back** *n* **1** the action of buying again sth that you have sold earlier: *a book/equipment buy-back* (= when a shop/store or company buys back sth you have finished using) **2** (*business*) a form of borrowing money in which a company sells its shares with an agreement that it will buy them again at a later date: *a share buy-back* ◇ *a share buy-back programme*

,buy sth 'in (*BrE*) to buy sth or a large amount of sth for a special occasion or in order to have a supply for the future: *I'll have to buy in extra food if they're coming to stay for a while.*
〈OBJ〉 **food**
◈ v + adv + n ◆ v + n/pron + adv

,buy 'into sth 1 to buy shares in a company, for example to gain control over it: *They are looking to buy into another insurance company.* 〈OBJ〉 **company, business 2** (*informal*) to accept sth that many other people believe: *We don't buy into the myth that money is the answer to everything.*
◈ v + prep

,buy sb 'off to pay sb to stop them acting against you, causing trouble for you, etc: *They had to buy Brennan off to stop him from talking.*
◈ v + n/pron + adv ◆ v + adv + n

,buy sb/yourself 'out; ,buy sb/yourself 'out of sth (*BrE*) to pay money so that sb/you can leave an organization, especially the armed forces, before the time agreed: *After four years in the navy I bought myself out.*
◈ v + n/pron + adv ◆ v + n/pron + adv + prep

,buy sb/sth 'out to buy part of a company, business, etc. from sb else so that you own all of it and control it: *I want to buy her out and have the*

buzz

36

house to myself. ◇ *The company was bought out by two German businessmen.*
OBJ **partner, company**
◆ v + n/pron + adv ◆ v + adv + n
▶ **'buyout** *n* (*finance*) a situation when sb buys enough shares in a company to gain control of it

,buy sth 'up to buy quickly all of sth or as much as you can: *They've bought up all the land in the area.*
OBJ **company, land, property**
◆ v + adv + n ◆ v + pron + adv ◆ v + n + adv (*rare*)

buzz /bʌz/

,buzz a'round; ,buzz a'round sth (*also* ,buzz a'bout/'round, ,buzz a'bout/'round sth *especially BrE*) to move around quickly and busily: *She buzzed round (the kitchen).* ◇ *The photographer buzzed around, checking the light.* ◇ *Questions buzzed round inside my head.*
◆ v + adv ◆ v + prep

,buzz 'off (*informal*) used to tell sb, not very politely, to go away: *Buzz off, I'm trying to work!* ◇ *I wish he'd buzz off!*
SYN **clear off; go away** (*more formal*)
◆ v + adv

,buzz 'round; ,buzz 'round sth (*especially BrE*)
= BUZZ AROUND, BUZZ AROUND STH

Cc

call /kɔːl/

~ around		~ on
~ away		~ on/upon
~ back		~ out
~ by		~ out for
~ down		~ over
~ for		~ round
~ forth		~ up
~ in	39	~ upon
38 ~ off		

NOTE To call is the most common way to say 'to telephone' in American English. It is also used in British English, but **to phone** and **to ring** are more common.

,call a'round; **,call a'round sb/sth** (*AmE*) to telephone a number of different people, usually to try to get information: *He's been calling around trying to get the best price on a computer.* ◇ *I called around the neighbourhood to get support for my campaign.*
⊕ v + adv ◆ v + prep

,call sb a'way to ask sb to stop doing what they are doing and go somewhere else to deal with sth: *He was called away to the phone.* ◇ *She was called away from the meeting to deal with an emergency.*
NOTE Call sb away is almost always used in the passive.
⊕ v + n/pron + adv

,call 'back (*BrE*) to visit sb again: *I'll call back later when your wife's at home.*
⊕ v + adv

,call 'back; **,call sb 'back** to telephone sb again or to telephone sb who telephoned you earlier: *Call back in an hour — he'll be here then.* ◇ *Kate phoned. Can you call her back?* ◇ *I'll call you back with the details later.*
⊕ v + adv ◆ v + n/pron + adv
▸ **'callback** *n* **1** a device in a telephone that automatically calls again a number that was busy when you first called it: *a callback facility* **2** a telephone call that you make to sb who has called you earlier

,call sb 'back 1 to shout to sb to turn around and come back to a place they have just left: *I ran off, but he called me back.* ◇ *We started to walk off but were called back by the police officer.* **2** to ask sb who is applying for a job, etc. to return so that you can talk to them again: *Three people were called back for a second interview.*
⊕ v + n/pron + adv

,call 'by (*informal, especially BrE*) to visit a place or a person for a short time, usually when you are going somewhere else: *Could you call by on your way home?* ◇ *Jan called by to bring your gift.*
SYN **drop by**
⊕ v + adv

,call sb 'down to shout to sb to ask them to come down from a place which is higher than you: *I've called him down* (= to come downstairs) *to breakfast already.*
⊕ v + n/pron + adv

,call sth 'down (on/upon sb) (*literary*) to pray that sth unpleasant will happen to sb because of sth bad they have done to you; to make sth bad happen to sb: *He called down curses on them.*
OBJ **curses, wrath**
⊕ v + adv + n ◆ v + n/pron + adv

'call for sb (*BrE*) to go to sb's home, for example, and take them or go with them somewhere: *Shall I call for you at eight?*
⊕ v + prep

'call for sth if a situation **calls for** a particular action or quality, it needs or requires it: *This calls for a celebration!* ◇ *What she's doing calls for great skill and courage.*
NOTE Call for sth can be used in the passive: *Tougher action by the government is called for.*
⊕ v + prep
▸ **un'called for** *adj* (of remarks or behaviour) not fair or necessary in the circumstances: *I shall ignore that uncalled-for remark.*

'call for sth; **'call for sb/sth to do sth** to demand publicly that sth should be done: *The group has called for a boycott of the elections.* ◇ *The other directors have called for him to resign.*
NOTE Call for sth can be used in the passive: *A total ban on nuclear weapons has been called for.*
⊕ v + prep ◆ v + prep + n/pron + to inf

,call sth 'forth (*formal*) to produce a particular reaction: *Her remarks have called forth harsh criticism in the media.*
⊕ v + adv + n ◆ v + pron + adv ◆ v + n + adv (*rare*)

,call 'in 1 [+ adv/prep] (*especially BrE*) to visit a place or a person for a short time, usually when you are going somewhere else: *He called in at the office before he left for London.* ◇ *She often calls in for a chat.* **SYN** **drop in (on sb/at…)** (*informal*) **2** to telephone the place where you work: *She called in sick this morning* (= telephoned to say that she was ill/sick and would not be coming to work). **3** to make a telephone call to a radio or television programme: *Many listeners called in to complain.*
⊕ v + adv

► **'call-in** *n* (*AmE*) a television or radio show in which people can phone to talk to people on the show, ask questions, give their opinions, etc: *a call-in show*

,call sb 'in to ask sb to come and help, give advice, repair sth, etc: *He's threatened to call in the police.* ◇ *You'll have to call a plumber in to look at this.* ◇ *Bomb disposal experts were called in to get rid of the device.*
[OBJ] **police, expert** [SYN] **send for sb**
◈ v + adv + n ♦ v + n/pron + adv

,call sth 'in (*BrE*) to order or request the return of sth, especially a product that has a fault: *The manufacturers have called in the faulty goods.* ◇ *The bank have called in the loan* (= asked for the money to be paid back) *immediately.*
[SYN] **recall sth** (*more formal*)
◈ v + adv + n ♦ v + n/pron + adv

,call sb/sth 'off to order soldiers, dogs, etc. to stop attacking sb, searching for sb/sth, etc: *Please call your dog off.*
[OBJ] **dog**
◈ v + n/pron + adv ♦ v + adv + n

,call sth 'off to cancel or abandon sth that has been planned or that has already started: *The meeting was called off at the last minute.* ◇ *They've called off their engagement* (= they have decided not to get married). ◇ *Police called off the search for the climbers at dusk.*
[OBJ] **match/game, engagement/wedding, deal, search, strike**
◈ v + adv + n ♦ v + n/pron + adv

'call on sb 1 (*especially BrE*) to visit sb for a short time: *On our way back, we called on grandma.* [SYN] **drop in** (**on sb/at …**) **2** (*AmE*) to ask sb in a class, etc. to answer a question or give their opinion: *The math teacher always calls on the boys.*
◈ v + prep

'call on/upon sth (*formal*) to use your strength, courage, etc. in order to achieve sth or deal with a problem: *She had to call on all her reserves of courage to face the ordeal.*
[OBJ] **strength, courage**
◈ v + prep

'call on/upon sb to do sth (*formal*) **1** to make a serious or urgent request to sb to do sth: *I'm available in case I'm called on to help.* ◇ *We call upon all parties to respect the results of the election.* **2** to formally invite or request sb to speak, etc: *I now call upon Mr. Spring to give the vote of thanks.*
[NOTE] **Call on/upon sb to do sth** can be used in the passive: *I was called on to make a speech.*
◈ v + prep + n/pron + to inf

,call 'out (**to sb**), **,call sth 'out** (**to sb**) to shout or say sth loudly in order to get sb's attention or help: *He called out to her, but she carried on walk-ing.* ◇ *He woke in the night, calling out her name.* ◇ *They called out the numbers of the winning tickets.*
[OBJ] **name** [SYN] **shout out** (**to sb**), **shout sth out** (**to sb**)
[NOTE] **Call/call sth** can be used with a similar meaning, but **call out/call sth out** suggests sth louder or more urgent.
◈ v + adv ♦ v + adv + n/pron + adv ♦ v + adv + n ♦ v + adv + speech

,call sb 'out 1 to ask sb to come to help you, when there is an emergency: *I've never had to call the doctor out at night before.* ◇ *We had to call out an electrician.* ◇ *Troops were called out to deal with the riot.* [OBJ] **doctor, fire brigade, electrician 2** to order or ask workers to stop work as a protest: *Miners were called out on strike by union leaders.*
◈ v + n/pron + adv ♦ v + adv + n

► **'call-out** *n* (*BrE*) an occasion when you ask sb to come to help you in an emergency: *ambulance call-outs* ◇ *How much is the plumber's call-out charge?*
[NOTE] The noun **call** is also used.

,call 'out for sth (*AmE*) to telephone a shop, store, restaurant, etc. to ask them to deliver food to you at home or at work: *Let's call out for pizza.*
[SYN] **send out for sth**
◈ v + adv + prep

,call sb 'over to call sb to come over to where you are, because you want to speak to them, give or show them sth, etc: *Call the waiter over.*
◈ v + n/pron + adv ♦ v + adv + n (*rare*)

,call 'round (*BrE*) to visit sb at their home for a short time: *I just called round to say hello.*
[SYN] **drop round**
◈ v + adv

,call 'up; ,call sb/sth 'up (*especially AmE*) to make a phone call to a person or a place: *Call up and make a reservation for 8 o'clock.* ◇ *She called him up from the bus station.* ◇ *Call up the office and ask for Mr. Morgan.*
[NOTE] **Call** and **call sb** are also frequently used with this meaning. **Call up** and **call sb up** are very common in spoken English.
◈ v + adv ♦ v + n/pron + adv ♦ v + adv + n

,call sb 'up 1 to officially ask sb to go to do training in the army, navy or air force or to fight in a war: *When the war began, he was too old to be called up.* [SYN] **conscript sb** (*especially BrE*), **draft sb** (*AmE*) **2** (*especially BrE*) to ask sb to join sth or take part in sth; to choose sb to play in a team: *He's been called up for next week's match.*
[NOTE] **Call sb up** is often used in the passive.
◈ v + n/pron + adv ♦ v + adv + n

► **'call-up** *n* **1** an official order to join the army, navy or air force: *call-up papers/camps* **2** (*especially BrE, sport*) an official invitation to play in a team or in a particular game

,call sth 'up 1 (*computing*) to obtain information that is stored on a computer: *She called up all the files he had worked on.* OBJ **file, information 2** to bring sth back to your mind; to make you remember and think about sth: *The sound of their laughter called up memories of his own childhood.* OBJ **memory** SYN **recall sth** (*formal*) **3** to use a quality that you have: *He called up all his reserves of courage.* OBJ **reserves**
⬥ v + adv + n ♦ v + n/pron + adv

'call upon sth = CALL ON/UPON STH
'call upon sb to do sth = CALL ON/UPON SB TO DO STH

calm /kɑːm/

,calm 'down; ,calm sb/yourself 'down if sb **calms down**, or you **calm them down**, they stop being angry or excited and become calm: *Calm down! I've said I'm sorry.* ◊ *There was nothing we could do to calm her down.* ◊ *He went for a walk to calm himself down.* ◊ *Jack was so shocked that he had to be calmed down by his wife and son.*
⬥ v + adv ♦ v + n/pron + adv ♦ v + adv + n

,calm 'down; ,calm sth 'down to become calmer; to make a situation calmer: *The whole fuss will have calmed down by tomorrow.* ◊ *I've spoken to them to try to calm things down a bit.* NOTE **Calm sth down** cannot be used in the passive.
⬥ v + adv ♦ v + n/pron + adv ♦ v + adv + n

camp /kæmp/

,camp 'out (*informal*) to sleep outside, usually in a tent; to sleep on the floor somewhere for a short time: *If there is nowhere to stay, we'll have to camp out.* ◊ *People camped out in the school hall to escape the flood water.*
⬥ v + adv
▶ **'campout** *n* (*AmE*) a time when people sleep outside in a tent

,camp it 'up (*BrE, informal*) **1** (of a man) to move or behave deliberately in a way that people think is typical of a man who is sexually attracted to other men (a **homosexual**): *He enjoys camping it up.* **2** to exaggerate your behaviour or a performance to make people laugh: *I really camped it up in the final scene.*
⬥ v + it + adv

cancel /'kænsl/ (-ll-, *AmE* -l-)

,cancel 'out; ,cancel sth 'out if two or more things **cancel out** or one **cancels out** the other, they are equally important, but have an opposite effect on a situation so that the situation does not change: *The gains and losses are expected to cancel out.* ◊ *Our expenditure and profits cancel each other out.* ◊ *The job is hard work, but this is cancelled out by the fact that the people are so nice.*
⬥ v + adv ♦ v + n/pron + adv ♦ v + adv + n

cannon /'kænən/

,cannon 'into sb/sth (of a moving person, vehicle, etc.) to hit sb/sth by accident and with great force: *She stopped suddenly and I almost cannoned into her.*
⬥ v + prep

,cannon 'off sb/sth if sth moving **cannons off** sb/sth, it hits them/it by accident and with great force and then goes off in a different direction: *The ball cannoned off his leg into the goal.*
⬥ v + prep

capitalize (*also* capitalise) /'kæpɪtəlaɪz/

'capitalize on sth (*also* **'capitalize upon sth** *less frequent, more formal*) to use sth to gain further advantage for yourself: *They capitalized on their success by raising prices.* ◊ *The opposition tried to capitalize on popular discontent over the new law.* OBJ **success, opportunity, potential** SYN **take advantage of sth**
⬥ v + prep

care /keə(r); *AmE* ker/

'care for sb to like or love sb: *I care deeply for you.* NOTE **Care for sb** can be used in the passive: *I just want to be loved and cared for by somebody.*
⬥ v + prep

'care for sb/sth 1 to take care of and be responsible for sb who is very young, old or sick, etc. or for sth that is in danger or could be damaged: *The nurses give advice to the patients and those who care for them.* ◊ *She cares for several children with special needs.* ◊ *The company is committed to caring for the environment.* OBJ **children, the sick, the elderly** NOTE In this meaning **care for sb/sth** can be used in the passive: *The children were all clean and well cared for.* → *see also* LOOK AFTER SB/STH/YOURSELF; LOOK AFTER STH **2 not care for sb/sth** (*formal*) to not like sb/sth very much: *I don't care for opera.*
⬥ v + prep
IDM **would you care for ...** (*formal*) used to ask sb if they would like sth to eat or drink: *Would you care for a cup of tea?*
▶ **un'cared for** *adj* not looked after; neglected: *The children looked dirty and uncared for.* ◊ *uncared-for gardens*

carry /'kæri/ (carries, carrying, carried, carried)

,carry sth a'round (*also* **,carry sth a'bout/ 'round** *especially BrE*) (**with you**) to take sth from one place to another; to take sth everywhere with you: *I don't want to carry this bag about with me all day.* ◊ *The CD player is light enough to carry around in your pocket.*
⬥ v + n/pron + adv ♦ v + adv + n

,**carry sb/sth a'long** to take or move sb/sth forward: *His body had been carried along by the river.* ◇ *The crowd was so thick that she was carried along with it.* ◇ *(figurative) His immense enthusiasm carried us all along.*
◈ v + n/pron + adv

,**carry sb/sth a'way/'off** to support the weight of sb/sth and take them/it away: *A strong current carried the dinghy away.*
◈ v + n/pron + adv ◆ v + adv + n

be/get ,carried a'way to be so excited and enthusiastic about sth that you lose control of your feelings and may behave in a silly or thoughtless way: *I got so carried away with shopping that I completely forgot the time.* ◇ *Don't get carried away — it's not that exciting.*
◈ be/get + v + adv

,**carry sb 'back (to sth)** to remind sb of sth that happened in the past: *The song carried her back to her childhood.*
⟨SYN⟩ **take sb back (to sth)**
◈ v + n/pron + adv

,**carry sth 'forward 1** (*also* ,**carry sth 'over**) (*finance*) to move a total sum of money, or a total amount, from one page or column to the next, or from one week or year to the next: *The figures were carried forward from the previous page.* ⟨SYN⟩ **bring sth forward** NOTE In this meaning **carry sth forward** is often used in the passive. **2** to help sth to make progress or succeed: *She will carry the project forward after I leave.*
◈ v + n/pron + adv ◆ v + adv + n

,**carry sb 'off 1** if a disease **carries sb off**, they die as a result of it: *She was carried off by the epidemic.* **2** to capture sb: *The enemy carried off many prisoners.*
◈ v + n/pron + adv ◆ v + adv + n

,**carry sb/sth 'off** = CARRY SB/STH AWAY/OFF

,**carry sth 'off 1** to win sth: *She carried off most of the prizes.* **2** to succeed in doing sth difficult; to deal with a difficult situation successfully: *She's the only person I know who can wear a dress like that and carry it off!*
◈ **1** v + adv + n ◆ v + pron + adv ◆ v + n + adv (*less frequent*)
2 v + n/pron + adv ◆ v + adv + n

,**carry 'on 1 (with sth)** (*also* ,**carry 'on doing sth**) (*especially BrE*) to continue doing sth or moving in a particular direction, without stopping: *Carry on working/with your work while I'm away.* ◇ *If she carries on shoplifting, she'll end up in jail.* ◇ *She ignored me and carried on writing.* ◇ *I called out to him, but he carried on down the road.* ⟨SYN⟩ **go on, go on doing sth** → *see also* CARRY STH ON 1 2 to manage to continue living or working in your usual way in spite of difficult or unpleasant circumstances: *Life carried on as usual after the fire.* ◇ *We're all going to carry on*

as if nothing has happened. ⟨SYN⟩ **go on**; **continue 3 (with sth)** to continue speaking or doing sth after a short pause: *'Well', she carried on, 'then I realized where I'd met him before!'* ◇ *Ted looked up briefly, then carried on with what he was doing.* ⟨SYN⟩ **go on (with sth) 4** to last for a particular time: *How long can this situation carry on?* ⟨SYN⟩ **go on; last 5 (at sb) (about sth)** (*informal*) to argue, quarrel or complain noisily; to make a fuss: *Stop carrying on about how hard your life is.* ◇ *How long are they going to be shouting and carrying on like that?* ⟨SYN⟩ **go on (at sb) (about sth) 6 (with sb)** (*old-fashioned, informal*) to have a sexual relationship with sb: *She's carrying on with her boss.*
◈ v + adv
1 also v + adv + -ing
3 also v + adv + speech

▸ '**carry-on** n **1** [usually sing.] (*BrE, informal*) excited or noisy behaviour over sth that is not important; a fuss **2** (*AmE*) a small bag or case that you carry onto a plane with you: *I'm travelling light — I just have a carry-on.* ◇ *Do you have any carry-on luggage?*

,**carry sth 'on 1** to continue sth, especially sth that sb else has begun: *Our children will carry this tradition on after us.* → *see also* CARRY ON 1 2 ,**carry 'on sth,** ,**carry it/them 'on** to do the activity mentioned: *We're trying to carry on a very important conversation!* ◇ *They carried on a correspondence for over forty years.* ◇ *to carry on a business/trade* OBJ **conversation, correspondence, business** ⟨SYN⟩ **conduct sth** NOTE A noun must always follow **on**, but a pronoun comes between the verb and **on**.
◈ **1** v + adv + n ◆ v + n/pron + adv
2 v + adv + n ◆ v + pron + adv

,**carry sth 'out 1** to do sth that you said you would do or that you have been asked to do: *to carry out a plan/a promise/an order* ◇ *He had no intention of carrying out his threats.* ◇ *She had carried out all his instructions.* OBJ **threat, promise, order 2** to do and complete a task: *to carry out a survey/an investigation* ◇ *to carry out repairs/checks/tests* ◇ *to carry out research* ◇ *It is not yet clear who carried out the attack.*
◈ v + adv + n ◆ v + pron + adv ◆ v + n + adv (*less frequent*)

▸ '**carry-out** n (*AmE, ScotE*) a meal that you buy cooked from a restaurant and take away to eat somewhere else: *Let's get a carry-out.*

,**carry sth 'over 1** to delay sth until a later time: *The game had to be carried over until Wednesday.* ◇ *You can carry over 4 days' leave to next year.* ⟨SYN⟩ **postpone sth 2** to keep sth from one situation and use or deal with it in a new situation: *You should carry over what you learn in school into your everyday life.* **3** = CARRY STH FORWARD 1
◈ v + adv + n ◆ v + n/pron + adv

▶ **'carry-over** *n* **1** (*finance*) a total sum of money or an amount that is moved to the next column/page/year, etc. **2** something that is kept from one situation or time and used in another

,carry sth 'round (**with you**) (*especially BrE*) = CARRY STH AROUND (WITH YOU)

,carry 'through (**on/with sth**) (*AmE*) to do and finish what you have promised, agreed or arranged to do: *He convinced us that he would carry through with/on his promise.*
◈ v + adv

,carry sb 'through; **,carry sb 'through sth** to help sb to deal with a difficult period: *Her determination carried her through.* ◇ *His courage helped to carry them through the difficult times.*
◈ v + n/pron + adv ◆ v + n/pron + prep

,carry sth 'through to finish a task, a plan, etc. successfully: *She was determined to carry through her plans.* ◇ *Once Helen has started a task, she'll carry it through to the end.*
◻ **plan, proposal, decision, reforms**
◈ v + adv + n ◆ v + n/pron + adv

cart /kɑːt; *AmE* kɑːrt/

,cart sth a'round (*also* **,cart sth a'bout/'round** *especially BrE*) (**with you**) (*informal*) used to talk about carrying sth large, awkward or unimportant from one place to another or everywhere you go: *I had to cart my shopping around with me all day.* ◇ *He carts all sorts of useless stuff about.*
◻ **carry sth around** (**with you**) (*more formal*), **lug sth around** (**with you**)
◈ v + n/pron + adv ◆ v + adv + n

,cart sb/sth a'way/'off (*informal*) to take sb/sth away with some difficulty: *Two players were carted off to hospital.* ◇ *The police arrived and carted 40 rioters off to jail.*
◻ **take sb/sth away** (*more formal*)
◻ Cart sb/sth away/off is often used in the passive: *He was carted away by two policemen.*
◈ v + adv + n ◆ v + n/pron + adv

carve /kɑːv; *AmE* kɑːrv/

,carve sth 'out 1 (*also* **,carve sth 'out of sth**) (*geology*) to make a physical feature in the earth's surface over a long period of time through the action of water, ice, weather, etc: *The valley was carved out by glaciers.* ◻ In this meaning **carve sth out** is often used in the passive. **2** (**for yourself**) to build a successful career, a good reputation, etc., often with difficulty or hard work: *She carved out a unique niche for herself in the music business.* ◇ *He's carved out a successful career in the building industry.* ◻ **career, name, niche**
◈ v + adv + n ◆ v + n/pron + adv
   1 also v + n/pron + adv + prep

,carve sb/sth 'up (*BrE, informal*) **1** to wound sb or their face badly with a knife: *He got carved up outside the pub last night.* **2** to go past a moving vehicle ahead of you and then suddenly move in front of it in a dangerous way: *I was carved up by a lunatic in a Porsche.* ◇ *We saw the van carve up several cars, before turning left.* ◻ **person, car**
◻ **cut sb/sth up** (*BrE*)
◈ v + n/pron + adv ◆ v + adv + n

,carve sth 'up to divide a company, an area of land, etc. into parts and share them out: *They carved the territory up into three provinces.* ◇ *The thieves hurriedly carved up the loot.*
◈ v + adv + n ◆ v + n/pron + adv

▶ **'carve-up** *n* [sing.] (*BrE, informal*) the act of dividing sth up into parts and sharing them out

cash /kæʃ/

,cash 'in (**on sth**) (*informal*) to gain an advantage from a situation in a way that people think is wrong or dishonest: *Many businesses cashed in on the massive public interest in her death.* ◇ *The new law means video pirates can no longer cash in by selling illegal copies.*
◈ v + adv

,cash sth 'in to exchange sth for money: *Cash in any remaining travellers' cheques when you return.* ◇ *You will lose money if you cash your policy in early.*
◻ **shares, policy**
◈ v + adv + n ◆ v + n/pron + adv

,cash 'up (*BrE*) (*AmE* **,cash 'out**) to count the money that has been taken in a shop/store, restaurant, etc. at the end of the day: *We cash up at five o'clock.*
◈ v + adv

cast /kɑːst; *AmE* kæst/ (**cast, cast**)

,cast a'round (*BrE also* **,cast a'bout**) (**for sth**) (*formal*) to look around you to try to find sth; to try very hard to think of sth: *He cast about for an escape route.* ◇ *He was desperately casting around for an excuse.* ◇ *The company is having to cast around feverishly for ways to cut its costs.* ◻ This phrasal verb is usually used in written English.
◈ v + adv

,cast sb/sth a'side (*formal*) to get rid of, or give no attention to, sb/sth that you no longer want or need: *She just cast him aside when she got bored.* ◇ *She has been able to cast aside* (= stop using) *her wheelchair.*
◻ **discard sb/sth**
◈ v + adv + n ◆ v + n/pron + adv

,cast sth a'side (*formal*) **1** to throw sth to one side: *He cast aside the newspaper impatiently.* **2** to get rid of feelings, attitudes, etc. that are bad or

negative, or that stop you achieving sth: *He cast
aside all his inhibitions.* ◇ *The speakers cast mod-
esty aside and talked about their success.*
SYN **throw sth aside; toss sth aside** (*less
formal*)
◆ v + adv + n ◆ v + n/pron + adv

be ,cast a'way (on sth) to be left somewhere
after your ship has been destroyed at sea: *What
would you do if you were cast away on a desert
island?*
◆ be + v + adv
▶ **'castaway** *n* a person whose ship has been destroyed and who has managed to swim to an
island, etc.

,cast sth 'back (to sb/sth) to make yourself
think about a particular time, a situation in the
past, etc: *I cast my mind back to our first meeting all those years ago.*
OBJ only **your mind**
◆ v + n + adv

,cast sth 'down (*literary*) if you **cast** your eyes
down, you look down: *She cast her eyes down
modestly while Jack was talking about her.*
OBJ only **eyes** SYN **lower sth** (*less formal*)
◆ v + n/pron + adv ◆ v + adv + n
▶ **'downcast** (*also* ,cast **'down** *less frequent*) *adj*
(*literary*) downcast eyes are looking down
→ *see also* DOWNCAST at BE CAST DOWN

be ,cast 'down (by sth) (*formal*) to be sad or
unhappy about sth: *He is not easily cast down.*
◆ be + v + adv
▶ **'downcast** (*also* ,cast **'down** *less frequent*) *adj*
(*literary*) sad or unhappy: *a downcast expression*
◇ *He looked so downcast I took pity on him.*
→ *see also* DOWNCAST at CAST STH DOWN

,cast 'off; ,cast sth 'off 1 to undo the ropes that
are holding a boat in position so that it can start
to move **2** (in knitting) to remove a row of
stitches from the needle in a way that will make a
finished edge: *When the scarf is the right length,
cast off.* OBJ **stitches** OPP **cast on, cast sth on**
◆ v + adv ◆ v + adv + n ◆ v + pron + adv ◆
v + n + adv (*rare*)

,cast sth 'off (*formal*) **1** to take off a piece of
clothing and throw it to one side: *They cast off
their clothes and jumped in the pool.* OBJ **jacket,
shoes, clothes** SYN **take sth off** (*less formal*) **2**
to get rid of sth bad or sth that you do not like:
She tried to cast off her upbringing. ◇ *It's time to
cast off those winter blues and burst into spring!*
◆ v + adv + n ◆ v + pron + adv ◆ v + n + adv (*rare*)
▶ **'cast-off** (*especially BrE*) (*AmE usually* **'hand-
me-down**) *n* [usually pl.] a piece of clothing that
the original owner no longer wants to wear:
She's fed up with wearing her sister's cast-offs.
▶ **'cast-off** *adj* [only before noun] that the original owner no longer wants to wear or use: *cast-
off clothing* ◇ *cast-off plastic bags*

,cast 'on; ,cast sth 'on (in knitting) to make the
first row of stitches on a needle, or add new
stitches: *Cast on and knit 10 rows.*
OBJ **stitches** OPP **cast off, cast sth off**
◆ v + adv ◆ v + adv + n ◆ v + pron + adv ◆
v + n + adv (*rare*)

,cast sb/sth 'out; ,cast sb/sth 'out of sth
(*formal*) to drive sb away; to get rid of sb/sth,
especially by using force: *She was cast out by
society.* ◇ *He claimed to be able to cast out demons.*
◇ *The villagers had been cast out of their homes.*
NOTE **Cast sb out** is often used in the passive.
◆ v + adv + n ◆ v + n/pron + adv ◆
v + n/pron + adv + prep
▶ **'outcast** *n* someone who is rejected and
ignored by other people and often has to leave
their home and friends: *She felt like a social outcast.* ◇ *He was treated like an outcast by the other
children.*
▶ **'outcast** *adj* [only before noun] ignored or not
accepted by other people: *outcast members of
society*

,cast sb/sth 'up (on sth) (*literary*) **1** if the sea
casts sb/sth up on the land, it carries them/it in
and leaves them/it there: *A whale bone was cast
up on the beach.* SYN **wash up, wash sth up** (*less
formal*) NOTE **Cast sb/sth up** is often used in the
passive in this meaning. **2** if you **cast** your eyes
up, you look up: *She cast her eyes up to the ceiling
and sighed.* OBJ only **eyes**
◆ v + n/pron + adv ◆ v + adv + n

catch /kætʃ/ (caught, caught /kɔːt/)

'catch at sth/sb to try to get hold of sth quickly:
She tried to catch at a branch but couldn't reach.
OBJ **sb's hand/arm/sleeve** SYN **clutch at sb/sth;
grasp at sth/sb**
◆ v + prep

catch 'on (*informal*) **1 (to sth)** to understand sth;
to realize the truth of sth: *He's very quick to catch
on.* ◇ *The students soon caught on to the idea that
phrasal verbs are not really difficult.* ◇ *People are
catching on to the fact that he's a fraud.* SYN **cotton on (to sth) 2 (with sb)** to become popular or
fashionable: *It's a good idea, but it'll never catch
on.* ◇ *Paying by credit card has only caught on
recently here.* ◇ *3-D films never caught on with a
mass audience.*
◆ v + adv

catch sb 'out 1 to trick sb into making a mistake or doing sth wrong; to discover that sb does
not know much or is doing sth wrong: *The test
isn't designed to catch you out. It's to see how
much you've learnt.* ◇ *The interviewer may try to
catch you out with trick questions.* ◇ *She reacted
like a child caught out in a lie.* **2** (*especially BrE*) if
a situation, bad weather etc. **catches sb out**, it
surprises them and puts them into a difficult

situation: *The snow catches us out every year* (= we are not prepared for it). ◊ *Many investors were caught out by the collapse of the company.*

NOTE **Catch sb out** is often used in the passive.

◆ v + n/pron + adv ◆ v + adv + n (*less frequent*)

ˌcatch ˈup (with sb/sth) (*BrE also* ˌcatch sb/sth ˈup) **1** to reach sb/sth ahead of you by going faster than them/it: *She was walking so fast I had to run to catch up (with her).* ◊ *The police car finally caught up with the van at the junction.* **2** to reach the same level or standard as sb/sth else that was better or more advanced: *We need to catch up with our competitors in Europe.* ◊ *You'll have to work hard to catch up with the rest of the class.* ◊ *When I went back to school I found I had a lot of catching up to do.*

◆ v + adv ◆ v + n/pron + adv ◆ v + adv + n (*rare*)

ˌcatch ˈup (with sth) 1 to spend extra time doing all the work, tasks, etc. that you should have done earlier: *I'm so behind with my paperwork, it's going to take me a week to catch up.* **2** to find out about things that have happened: *Come and stay for a few days, so that we have a chance to catch up.* ◊ *I want to catch up with all your news.* ◊ *We've got a lot of catching up to do after all this time.* → *see also* CATCH UP ON STH

◆ v + adv

ˌcatch sb ˈup (on sth) (*AmE*) to tell sb about things that have happened: *You can catch me up on the news later.*

◆ v + n/pron + adv

ˌcatch sb/sth ˈup (*BrE*) **1** = CATCH UP (WITH SB/STH) 1 *You go ahead. I'll catch you up.* ◊ *She caught the leader up and then overtook her.* **2** = CATCH UP (WITH STH) 2 *This company is the most likely to catch up the market leader.* ◊ *She's training hard to catch her sister up.*

be/get ˌcaught ˈup in sth 1 to become involved in an unpleasant event or situation that you cannot escape from: *A number of tourists got caught up in the riots.* ◊ *children caught up in crime* ◊ *Sorry I'm late — I got caught up in a traffic jam.* OBJ **violence, war, events, traffic 2** to be completely absorbed in an activity, your own feelings, etc: *She got caught up in the excitement and drama of the auction.* ◊ *I didn't hear you come in; I was so caught up in this book.* OBJ **excitement, book**

◆ be/get + v + adv + prep

ˌcatch ˈup on sb = CATCH UP WITH SB 2 *Old age is catching up on me.*

ˌcatch ˈup on sth 1 to spend extra time doing all the work, tasks, etc. that you should have done earlier: *I've got a lot of work to catch up on.* ◊ *I spent the weekend catching up on lost sleep.* OBJ

work, sleep 2 to find out about things that have happened: *It was good to see Patsy and catch up on all the gossip.*

→ *see also* CATCH UP (WITH STH)

◆ v + adv + prep

ˌcatch ˈup with sb 1 if the police or people in authority **catch up with** sb, they finally find out that they have done sth wrong and punish them: *They were involved in burglary for years before the police caught up with them.* **2** (*also* **catch up on sb** *less frequent*) if sth you have done or sth that has been happening to you **catches up with** you, it starts to cause you problems that you have so far managed to avoid: *His past is finally catching up with him.* ◊ *The late nights were beginning to catch up with her.* **3** (*informal*) to meet sb you have not seen for a while and hear their news: *He just wants to rest and catch up with old friends.* ◊ *Catch up with you later!* ◊ *We've got a lot of catching up to do after all this time!* OBJ **friends**

◆ v + adv + prep

cater /ˈkeɪtə(r)/

ˈcater for sb/sth to provide everything that sb, a group of people or a situation needs or wants: *The careers service caters for the needs of young people and adults.* ◊ *The resort also caters for winter sports.*

OBJ **needs, children, interests**

NOTE **Cater for sb/sth** can be used in the passive: *All age groups are well catered for.*

◆ v + prep

ˈcater to sb/sth (*disapproving*) to provide sth that satisfies what a particular type of person wants: *Endless media coverage catered to the public's interest in the scandal.*

NOTE **Cater to sb/sth** can be used in the passive: *Their every need was catered to.*

◆ v + prep

cave /keɪv/

ˌcave ˈin 1 (on sb/sth) if a roof, wall, etc. **caves in**, it falls down and inwards: *The roof of the tunnel caved in on the workmen.* SUBJ **roof, wall 2 (to sth)** to finally do what sb wants you to do after you have resisted for a long time: *The management refused to cave in to their demands.* ◊ *Under his fierce questioning she caved in and told him the truth.* OBJ **demands, pressure**

◆ v + adv

▶ **ˈcave-in** *n* **1** the fact of a roof, wall, etc. falling down and inwards: *For the people inside the tunnel there was a serious risk of flooding or a cave-in.* **2** an instance of agreeing under pressure to do sth you do not want to do

centre (BrE) (AmE center) /'sentə(r)/

'centre around sb/sth; 'centre sth around sb/sth (BrE also **'centre round sb/sth, 'centre sth round sb/sth**) to be, or make sb/sth, the most important person or thing around which most activity takes place: *The debate centres around the question of power.* ◇ *The case centred around the couple's adopted children.* ◇ *Her life was centred entirely around her family.* ◇ *The night-life of the town is largely centred around the hotels.*
NOTE **Centre sth around/round sb/sth** is often used in the passive.
◈ v + prep ◆ v + n/pron + prep

'centre on sb/sth; 'centre sth on sb/sth (also **'centre upon sb/sth, 'centre sth upon sb/sth** more formal) to give a lot of attention or thought to one particular activity, idea or person, etc: *The discussions centred on the hostage issue.* ◇ *Public interest centred largely on the team's stars.* ◇ *The group has centred its attention on the need for reform.* ◇ *His research is centred on the effects of unemployment.*
NOTE **Centre sth on/upon sb/sth** is often used in the passive.
◈ v + prep ◆ v + n/pron + prep

chain /tʃeɪn/

,chain sb/sth 'up (to sth) to fasten sb/sth to sth else with chains to stop them escaping or being stolen: *I'd chain your bike up (to the fence) just in case.* ◇ *The prisoners were chained up in a dark cell.*
NOTE **Chain sb/sth (to sth)** can also be used with this meaning.
◈ v + n/pron + adv ◆ v + adv + n

chalk /tʃɔːk/

,chalk 'up sth; ,chalk it/them 'up (informal) to achieve a success, a victory, a score in a game, etc: *The team has chalked up its fifth win in a row.* ◇ *This week Dee Brothers chalked up 100 years of business in this town.*
OBJ **success, victory, win**
NOTE A noun must always follow **up**, but a pronoun comes between the verb and **up**.
◈ v + adv + n ◆ v + pron + adv

,chalk sth 'up to sth (informal) to think that sth happens as a result of sth else: *We can chalk our recent victories up to a lot of luck.* ◇ *When the goal was disallowed they chalked it up to a bad referee decision.*
SYN **attribute sth to sth** (formal), **put sth down to sth**
◈ v + n/pron + adv + prep
IDM **chalk it up to ex'perience** (spoken, especially AmE) used to say that you can learn from sth bad that has happened to you

chance /tʃɑːns; AmE tʃæns/

'chance on/upon sb/sth (formal) to meet sb or find sth when you do not expect to: *I chanced on an old school friend in town.* ◇ *He chanced upon a volume of Japanese poetry in a bookshop.*
◈ v + prep

change /tʃeɪndʒ/

,change sb/sth a'round (especially AmE) = CHANGE SB/STH ROUND

,change 'back 1 (into sth) to take off your clothes and put on what you were wearing earlier: *I'll just change back into my tracksuit.* **2 (into/to sth)** to return to an earlier state or form: *When you double click on SELECT, the screen changes back to the main design screen.* ◇ *Slowly the angry animal changed back into its normal calm self.*
◈ v + adv

,change sth 'back (into/to sth) to exchange an amount of money into the system of money (**currency**) that it was in before: *Can I change these dollars back into sterling?*
◈ v + n/pron + adv ◆ v + adv + n (less frequent)

,change 'down (into/to sth) (BrE) to move the stick that controls the speed in a vehicle into a position suitable for slower speeds (a **lower gear**): *Change down into second as you approach the corner.*
OPP **change up (into/to sth)**
◈ v + adv

,change 'into sth to put on different clothes: *We quickly changed into our swimsuits.* ◇ *I didn't bring anything to change into.*
◈ v + prep

,change 'into sth; ,change sb/sth 'into sth to change, or to make sb/sth change, into sth different: *The castle has changed into a hotel.* ◇ *The handsome prince was changed into a frog.*
SYN **turn into sth, turn sb/sth into sth**
◈ v + prep ◆ v + n/pron + prep

,change 'out of sth to take off the clothes you are wearing and put on different ones: *I must change out of these wet clothes before I get a chill.* ◇ *She changed out of her suit as soon as she came home.*
◈ v + adv + prep

,change 'over 1 (from sth) (to sth) to stop using one system or thing and start using another: *The magazine changed over from pink paper to white in 1917.* ◇ *We're changing over to a new computer system.* SYN **switch over (from sth) (to sth) 2 (to sth)** (BrE) to change from watching one television channel to watching another: *I changed over to BBC1 to see the football.* ◇ *Can we change over?* SYN **switch over (from sth) (to sth); turn over (to sth)**
◈ v + adv

▶ **'changeover** *n* a change from one system or thing to another: *The changeover to the new system will take place gradually.* ◇ *a changeover period*

,change 'over/'round (*BrE*) if two people **change over/round**, they move to where the other person was before or do what the other person was doing: *Can you and Phil change round? You're too tall to stand in the front row.* ◇ *When you get tired of driving we can change over.*
〉SYN〈 **swap around/over/round** (*informal, especially BrE*)
◈ v + adv

,change sb/sth 'round (*especially BrE*) (*AmE usually* **,change sb/sth a'round**) to move objects, such as furniture, or people into different positions: *Who's changed the desks around?* ◇ *You're always changing this room round!* (= making it look different by moving the furniture, etc.) ◇ *The Yankees keep changing their players around.*
OBJ **room, furniture** 〉SYN〈 **swap sb/sth around/over/round** (*especially BrE*)
◈ v + n/pron + adv ♦ v + adv + n (*less frequent*)

,change 'up (into/to sth) (*BrE*) to move the stick that controls the speed in a vehicle into a position suitable for faster speeds (a **higher gear**): *Change up into fourth gear now.*
〉OPP〈 **change down (into/to sth)**
◈ v + adv

charge /tʃɑːdʒ; *AmE* tʃɑːrdʒ/

'charge sb with sth; 'charge sb with doing sth (*formal*) to give sb a duty, responsibility or task: *A solicitor was charged with administering the estate.*
NOTE These phrasal verbs are often used in the passive.
◈ v + n/pron + prep

charm /tʃɑːm; *AmE* tʃɑːrm/

,charm sth 'out of sb if you **charm** money or information **out of** sb, you obtain it by using your power to please or attract people: *She managed to charm £20 out of him.*
◈ v + n/pron + adv + prep

chase /tʃeɪs/

,chase a'round (*BrE also* **,chase a'bout/'round**) to be very busy, rushing from one place to another: *I've been chasing around all morning trying to find a gift for my sister.*
◈ v + adv

,chase sb/sth a'way/'off/'out to force sb/sth to run away by running after them or threatening them: *He chased the attackers away by firing shots into the air.*
◈ v + n/pron + adv ♦ v + adv + n

,chase sb/sth 'down (*AmE, informal*) to try hard to get sth or find sb/sth that you need or want: *I've been trying to chase Sam down all day!*
〉SYN〈 **seek sb/sth out** (*more formal*), **track sb/sth down**
◈ v + n/pron + adv ♦ v + adv + n

,chase sb/sth 'off = CHASE SB/STH AWAY/OFF/OUT, ETC.

,chase sb/sth 'out = CHASE SB/STH AWAY/OFF/OUT, ETC.

,chase 'round (*BrE*) = CHASE AROUND

,chase sb/sth 'up (*informal*) **1** to contact sb and remind them to do sth they have said they would do or that they ought to do: *I'll chase him up and find out what's going on.* ◇ *It is his job to chase up clients with outstanding debts.* ◇ *Could you chase up those late replies* (= remind people to reply). **2** to try to find sth/sth that you need; to try to get more information about sb/sth: *We're chasing up two other people who were at the party.* ◇ *I'll chase up references to the battle in the library.*
◈ v + n/pron + adv ♦ v + adv + n

chat /tʃæt/ (**-tt-**)

,chat sb 'up (*informal*) **1** (*BrE*) to talk in a friendly way to sb because you are sexually attracted to them: *Who was that girl you were chatting up last night?* **2** (*especially AmE*) to talk to sb in a friendly way because you want them to do sth for you or to give you sth: *You'll have to chat the boss up if you want some days off.*
◈ v + n/pron + adv ♦ v + adv + n
▶ **'chat-up** *n* (*BrE, informal*) an attempt to talk in a friendly way to sb you are sexually attracted to: *He was trying some old chat-up lines.*

cheat /tʃiːt/

'cheat sb of sth (*also* **,cheat sb 'out of sth**) to prevent sb from having sth, especially in an unfair or dishonest way: *He had cheated the taxman of £60 000.* ◇ *He was cheated out of his rightful inheritance.*
◈ v + n/pron + prep ♦ v + n/pron + adv + prep

'cheat on sb to be unfaithful to your husband, wife or partner by secretly having sex with sb else: *He was the last to know that she had been cheating on him.*
OBJ **wife, partner, etc.**
◈ v + prep

'cheat on sth to fail to do sth you have agreed or promised to do: *The government have cheated on their commitment not to raise taxes.*
OBJ **agreement, commitment**
◈ v + prep

,cheat sb 'out of sth = CHEAT SB OF STH

check /tʃek/

ˌcheck ˈin 1 (at sth) to go to an official desk at a hotel, an airport, etc. and tell sb that you have arrived: *After checking in, we went out for a meal.* ◇ *You must check in at desk 25 an hour before take-off.* → *see also* CHECK INTO STH 1 **2** (with sb) (*especially AmE*) to contact sb to let them know where you are or what you are doing: *I have to check in with my boss every three hours.* ⓢⓎⓝ **report in (to sb/sth)**
⊕ v + adv

▶ **ˈcheck-in** *n* **1** [U] the act of telling an official at an airport that you have arrived, showing them your ticket, etc: *the check-in desk* **2** [C] [U] the place at an airport where you go to say you have arrived, show your ticket, etc: *There were long queues at the check-in.*

ˌcheck sb ˈin to take sb's name when they arrive at a hotel or an airport, look at their ticket, etc: *Write all the names of the guests in this book as they are checked in.* ◇ *All the passengers have been checked in.*
ⓞⒷⒿ **guests, passengers**
⊕ v + n/pron + adv ◆ v + adv + n

ˌcheck sth ˈin to leave or accept bags, cases, etc. to be put on a plane or a train: *When we arrived at the airport we checked our bags in straight away.*
ⓞⒷⒿ **luggage, bags**
⊕ v + n/pron + adv ◆ v + adv + n

ˌcheck ˈinto sth 1 to arrive at a hotel, private hospital, etc. to begin your stay there: *I arrived in Boston and checked into my hotel.* ◇ *She's checked into a private clinic for drug rehabilitation.* ⓞⒷⒿ **hotel, motel, clinic** ⓢⓎⓝ **book into sth** ⓄⓅⓅ **check out of sth** → *see also* CHECK IN 1 **2** to try to find out more about sth or discover the true facts about sth: *The police are checking into the cause of the crash.* ⓢⓎⓝ **look into sth**
⊕ v + prep

ˌcheck sth ˈoff 1 to put a mark beside items on a list to show that they are correct, present or have been dealt with: *I've checked off all the furniture on the list.* ◇ *He checked everyone's name off as they arrived.* ⓢⓎⓝ **tick sth off 2** (*especially AmE*) to put a mark in a box on a document to give an answer to a question, choose sb/sth, etc: *Some voters wrote in names instead of checking off the candidates listed.* ⓝⓄⓣⒺ Check sth is usually used with this meaning.
⊕ v + adv + n ◆ v + n/pron + adv

ˈcheck on sb/sth 1 to make sure that sb is safe, happy, etc. or that sth is progressing as it should be: *I'll just check on dinner.* ◇ *The doctor visited every day to check on my progress.* ⓞⒷⒿ **progress, children, patient 2** to find out if sth is true or correct, especially sth that sb has said about themselves: *Do you always check on future employees?* ◇ *Will you check on his address?* → *see also* CHECK UP

ⓝⓄⓣⒺ **Check on sb/sth** can be used in the passive: *The children were put to bed and then not checked on again.* ◆ **Check sth** can also be used with these meanings.
⊕ v + prep

ˌcheck ˈout (*especially AmE*) if facts, etc. **check out**, they can be shown to be correct or true: *His story doesn't check out.* ⓢⓤⒷⒿ **story, reference**
⊕ v + adv

ˌcheck ˈout; ˌcheck ˈout of sth 1 (*AmE, informal, becoming old-fashioned*) to leave a place or finish an activity: *The climb was too difficult so I checked out early.* ◇ *He can't just check out on us like that!* ◇ *Let's check out of here.* **2** to leave a hotel, a hospital, etc. where you have been staying: *She checked out this morning.* ◇ *He decided to check out of the hospital and go home.* ⓞⒷⒿ **hotel, motel, hospital** ⓄⓅⓅ **check in; check into sth**
⊕ v + adv ◆ v + adv + prep

▶ **ˈcheckout** *n* (*AmE*) [U] the act or time of leaving a hotel at the end of your stay: *Checkout is 10 a.m.* ◇ *checkout time*
→ *see also* CHECKOUT at CHECK OUT, CHECK SB OUT

ˌcheck ˈout; ˌcheck sb ˈout (*AmE*) if you **check out** in a shop/store, or sb **checks you out**, you find out how much you have to pay and give sb the money: *You can check out at aisle eight.* ◇ *The girl who checked me out looked at me strangely.*
⊕ v + adv ◆ v + n/pron + adv

▶ **ˈcheckout** *n* the place where you pay for the goods you are buying in a supermarket: *There were huge queues at the checkout.* ◇ *a supermarket checkout*
→ *see also* CHECKOUT at CHECK OUT, CHECK OUT OF STH

ˌcheck sb/sth ˈout 1 (*especially AmE*) to find out if sth is true or correct or if sb is honest, truthful, reliable, etc: *Check him out before you give him the job.* ◇ *Police have checked out his story.* ◇ *We need to check out whether the company is reliable.* ⓞⒷⒿ **story, claim, company 2** (*informal, especially AmE*) to look at sb/sth because they/it seem interesting or attractive: *Check out our new fashion range!* ◇ *It's worth checking out that new restaurant.* ◇ *Check out that gorgeous guy over there!*
⊕ v + adv + n ◆ v + n/pron + adv

ˌcheck sth ˈout (*AmE*) to borrow sth such as a book or a video from a library: *I checked out three books from the library.*
ⓞⒷⒿ **book, video**
⊕ v + n/pron + adv ◆ v + adv + n

ˌcheck sb/sth ˈover to examine a person or an animal to make sure that they are healthy; to examine a machine, etc. to make sure it is working correctly: *The doctor would like to check you over.* ◇ *I got the car checked over before the trip.* ⓢⓎⓝ **look sb/sth over; examine sb/sth** (*more formal*)
⊕ v + n/pron + adv ◆ v + adv + n

,check sth 'over (*also* ,check 'through sth) to examine sth written or printed carefully to make sure that it is correct: *I've got to check over my work for spelling before I hand it in.* ◇ *You should get someone to check the letter over for you.*
◈ v + adv + n ♦ v + pron + adv ♦ v + n + adv (*less frequent*) ♦ v + prep

,check 'through sth (*also* ,check it, them, etc. 'through *less frequent*) = CHECK STH OVER *Check through your notes carefully.* ◇ *There were 23 files to look at, and Tim spent half his day checking through them all.*
NOTE A noun must always follow **through**. A pronoun can come between the verb and **through** or after **through**.
◈ v + prep ♦ v + pron + adv (*less frequent*)

,check 'up (*especially BrE*) **1** (on sb) to make sure that sb is doing what they should be doing, or that what they have said about themselves is true: *They always check up on prospective employees.* ◇ *I won't have you checking up on me like that!* ◇ *I'd better check up to see the kids are OK.* **2** (on sth) to find out if sth is true or correct; to find out what is happening: *I think the train's at ten o'clock, but I'll phone the station to check up.* ◇ *I went to the library to check up on a few things.*
NOTE Check and check sth can also be used with these meanings.
→ *see also* CHECK ON SB/STH
◈ v + adv
▶ '**check-up** *n* an examination by your doctor to see how healthy you are: *to go for a check-up* ◇ *a routine check-up*

cheer /tʃɪə(r); *AmE* tʃɪr/

,cheer sb 'on to encourage sb, especially sb in a race or competition, by shouting: *The crowd cheered the runners on.*
◈ v + n/pron + adv ♦ v + adv + n

,cheer 'up; ,cheer sb/yourself 'up to become, or to make sb/yourself, happier or more cheerful: *She seems to have cheered up since Saturday.* ◇ *Cheer up!* ◇ *Nothing could cheer him up.* ◇ *She bought some chocolates to cheer herself up.*
SYN brighten up; liven up, liven sb/sth up
◈ v + adv ♦ v + n/pron + adv ♦ v + adv + n

,cheer sth 'up to make a room, etc. brighter and more cheerful: *Flowers always cheer up a room.*
OBJ room **SYN** brighten sth up; liven sth up
◈ v + adv + n ♦ v + n/pron + adv

chew /tʃuː/

'**chew on sth 1** (*also* 'chew at sth) to bite sth continuously, especially because you are nervous or to test your teeth: *He chewed on his bottom lip as he considered the question.* **2** (*informal*) = CHEW STH OVER *Why don't we chew on it for a while?*
◈ v + prep

,chew sb 'out (*AmE, informal*) to tell sb angrily that they have done sth wrong: *He got chewed out by his teacher for being late.*
SYN tell sb off (for sth/for doing sth); reprimand sb (*formal*)
◈ v + n/pron + adv ♦ v + adv + n

,chew sth 'over (*also* 'chew on sth) (*both informal*) to think about or discuss sth carefully and in detail: *He spent the weekend chewing over the problem.*
OBJ problem, idea
◈ v + adv + n ♦ v + n/pron + adv

,chew sth 'up 1 to bite sth until it is completely soft or destroyed: *The baby chewed the cookie up and swallowed it.* **2** (*informal*) if a machine **chews sth up**, it damages or destroys it: *The cassette player's chewed the tape up again.*
◈ v + n/pron + adv ♦ v + adv + n

chicken /'tʃɪkɪn/

,chicken 'out; ,chicken 'out of sth; ,chicken 'out of doing sth (*informal*) to decide not to do sth because you are afraid: *If I don't fight him, everyone will say that I chickened out.* ◇ *She chickened out of telling him the truth.*
SYN bottle out, bottle out of sth, bottle out of doing sth
◈ v + adv ♦ v + adv + prep

chill /tʃɪl/

,chill 'out (*informal*) to relax completely and not get upset or excited about anything: *Chill out! We'll get there on time!*
◈ v + adv
▶ '**chill-out** *adj* [only before noun] that helps you to relax or makes you feel relaxed: *chill-out music* ◇ *a chill-out room* (= a place at a club, etc. where you can relax when you do not want to dance)

chime /tʃaɪm/

,chime 'in (with sth) (*informal*) to join in a conversation suddenly or interrupt sb: *'Absolutely!' she chimed in eagerly.* ◇ *He kept chiming in with his own opinions.*
◈ v + adv ♦ v + adv + speech

,chime 'in with sth; 'chime with sth (*formal*) to agree with sth; to be similar to sth: *His policies chimed in with the national mood at the time.*
SYN fit in with sth
NOTE These phrasal verbs are usually used in written English.
◈ v + adv + prep ♦ v + prep

chip /tʃɪp/ (-pp-)

,chip a'way at sth (*used especially in the progressive tenses*) to make sth smaller or weaker by continuously breaking small pieces off it: *He* *was chipping away at the rocks, looking for fossils.* ◇ *(figurative) The government seems to be chipping away at people's rights.*

⊕ v + adv + prep

,**chip sth a'way/'off**; ,**chip sth 'off sth** to remove sth by continuously breaking off small pieces: *She used a hammer to chip away the stone.* ◇ *I chipped the rust off the box with a knife.*

⊕ v + adv + n ♦ v + n/pron + adv ♦ v + n/pron + prep

,**chip 'in (with sth)** *(informal)* **1** to join in or interrupt a conversation; to add sth to a conversation: *Feel free to chip in if I've forgotten to mention anything.* ◇ *She chipped in with some interesting remarks.* **2** *(also* ,**chip 'in sth)** to give some money so that a group of people can buy sth together: *Has everyone chipped in for the present?* ◇ *The company has chipped in with a $200 donation.* ◇ *Let's all chip in five dollars.* ⟩SYN⟨ **club together (to do sth)**

⊕ v + adv **2** also v + adv + n

,**chip sth 'off**; ,**chip sth 'off sth** = CHIP STH AWAY/OFF, CHIP STH OFF STH

,**chip 'off**; ,**chip 'off sth** if paint or a surface **chips off**, it comes off in small pieces: *The varnish is chipping off.* ◇ *Most of the paint had chipped off the gate.*

⊕ v + adv ♦ v + prep

chivvy /'tʃɪvi/ (**chivvies, chivvying, chivvied, chivvied**)

,**chivvy sb a'long** *(BrE, informal)* to try to make sb move faster or do sth more quickly: *The teacher chivvied the children along.* ⟩SYN⟨ **hurry sb/sth along**

⊕ v + n/pron + adv ♦ v + adv + n

choke /tʃəʊk; *AmE* tʃoʊk/

,**choke sth 'back** to try to stop yourself from showing a strong emotion, or saying sth that might upset sb: *He choked back his tears.* ◇ *A protest rose to her lips, but she choked it back.* ⟨OBJ⟩ **tears, sob(s)** ⟨NOTE⟩ **Choke sth back** is not used in the passive.

⊕ v + adv + n ♦ v + n/pron + adv

,**choke sth 'off 1** to prevent or stop sth: *High interest rates have choked off investment.* ⟨OBJ⟩ **demand, investment 2** to stop or interrupt sth: *His words were choked off by the sudden screams.*

⊕ v + adv + n ♦ v + n/pron + adv

,**choke 'up**; ,**choke sb 'up** to become, or to make sb, so upset that you/they are unable to speak: *That song really chokes me up.* ◇ *He gets choked up just remembering the day she left.* ⟨NOTE⟩ **Choke sb up** is usually used in the passive with *be* or *get*.

⊕ v + adv ♦ v + n/pron + adv

chop /tʃɒp; *AmE* tʃɑːp/ (-**pp**-)

'**chop at sth**; ,**chop a'way at sth** to aim blows at sth with a sharp heavy tool: *They chopped at the undergrowth with their machetes.*

⊕ v + prep ♦ v + adv + prep

,**chop sth 'down** to make sth such as a tree fall down by cutting it at the base with a sharp tool: *They're chopping down thousands of trees every year.* ⟨OBJ⟩ **tree** ⟩SYN⟨ **cut sth down**

⊕ v + adv + n ♦ v + n/pron + adv

,**chop sth 'off**; ,**chop sth 'off sth** to remove sth by cutting it with a sharp heavy tool: *The king had his head chopped off.* ◇ *She chopped a branch off the tree.* ⟩SYN⟨ **cut sth off, cut sth off sth**

⊕ v + n/pron + adv ♦ v + adv + n ♦ v + n/pron + prep

,**chop sth 'up** to cut sth into small pieces with a knife or a sharp tool: *Shall we chop these logs up for firewood?* ◇ *I shall have to chop her food up very small for her.* ◇ *Chop up the onion into small pieces.* ⟩SYN⟨ **cut sth up**

→ *see also* HACK STH UP

⊕ v + n/pron + adv ♦ v + adv + n

chow /tʃaʊ/

,**chow 'down (on sth)** *(AmE, informal)* to eat a lot of food: *We chowed down on fried chicken and salad.*

⊕ v + adv

chuck /tʃʌk/

⟨NOTE⟩ **Chuck** is an informal way of saying **throw.**

,**chuck sth a'way** *(BrE, informal)* **1** to not make good use of sth; to waste sth: *She's chucking all her money away on presents for him.* ◇ *It's too good an opportunity to chuck away.* **2** *(also* ,**chuck sth 'out)** to throw sth away because you no longer want or need it: *We chucked the old sofa away.* ◇ *Don't chuck yesterday's paper out. I still haven't done the crossword.* ⟩SYN⟨ **throw sth away**

⊕ v + n/pron + adv ♦ v + adv + n

'**chuck it down** *(also* '**chuck down,** '**chuck down sth** *less frequent) (BrE, informal)* to rain very heavily: *It was chucking it down outside.* ⟩SYN⟨ **pour down** *(BrE)*

⟨NOTE⟩ **Chuck it down** and **chuck down** are always used with the subject *it.*

⊕ v + it + adv ♦ v + adv ♦ v + adv + n

,**chuck sth 'in** *(BrE, informal)* to include sth extra with what you are selling or offering without increasing the price: *If you buy the freezer and the fridge we'll chuck in a toaster.* ⟩SYN⟨ **throw sth in**

⊕ v + adv + n ♦ v + n/pron + adv

‚chuck sth 'in/'up (*BrE*, *informal*) to decide to stop doing sth such as a job or a course of study: *What made you decide to chuck in your course?* ◇ *I feel like **chucking it all in** and going back to Africa.*
[OBJ] **job, course** [SYN] **jack sth in** (*BrE*), **pack sth in** (*BrE*), **give sth up**
[NOTE] **Chuck sth in/up** cannot be used in the passive.
◆ v + adv + n ♦ v + n/pron + adv

‚chuck sb 'out; ‚chuck sb 'out of sth (*informal*) to force sb to leave a place, a job, etc: *Her parents chucked her out when she got pregnant.*
[SYN] **throw sb out, throw sb out of sth; turn sb out (from sth), turn sb out of sth**
◆ v + n/pron + adv ♦ v + adv + n ♦
   v + n/pron + adv + prep

‚chuck sth 'out (*spoken*, *informal*) **1** to reject a plan, a proposal, etc: *The committee chucked my proposal out.* **2** = CHUCK STH AWAY 2
[SYN] **throw sth out**
◆ v + n/pron + adv ♦ v + adv + n

‚chuck sth 'up (*BrE*) = CHUCK STH IN/UP

chug /tʃʌg/ (**-gg-**)

‚chug a'long (*informal*) to make steady but slow progress: *'Hi! How are things?' 'Oh, fine, just chugging along.'*
◆ v + adv

churn /tʃɜːn; *AmE* tʃɜːrn/

‚churn sth 'out (*informal*) to produce sth quickly in large amounts: *She churns out trashy romantic novels.* ◇ *They churn out 3 000 identical toy trains every day.*
◆ v + adv + n ♦ v + n/pron + adv

‚churn sb 'up (*informal*) to make sb feel very upset, worried, frightened or angry: *When I drove away from the house for the last time, I was churned up inside.*
◆ v + n/pron + adv ♦ v + adv + n

‚churn sth 'up to move sth such as mud or water around and damage or disturb the surface: *Cars and motorbikes had churned up the field.* ◇ *seas churned up by the storm* ◇ (*figurative*) *His visit churned up bitter memories.*
[OBJ] **earth/ground, mud, water**
◆ v + adv + n ♦ v + n/pron + adv

claim /kleɪm/

‚claim sth 'back to ask for sth to be returned to you: *Claim your expenses back from the company.*
[OBJ] **tax, money**
◆ v + n/pron + adv ♦ v + adv + n

clam /klæm/ (**-mm-**)

‚clam 'up (on sb) (*informal*) to refuse to speak about sth because you are afraid, or want to keep it secret: *He always clams up when we ask about his family.*
◆ v + adv

clamp /klæmp/

‚clamp 'down; ‚clamp 'down on sb/sth (*informal*) to become strict about sth in order to prevent sth happening, especially a crime, a protest, etc: *The government intends to clamp down on drug smuggling.*
[SYN] **crack down, crack down on sb/sth**
◆ v + adv ♦ v + adv + prep
▸ **'clampdown (on sb/sth)** *n* sudden action that is taken by a government or other authority to stop a crime, a protest, etc.

'‚clamp 'on sth; ‚clamp sth 'on sb/sth (*especially AmE*) to force sb to accept sth unpleasant: *The army clamped on a curfew after the riots.* ◇ *The army clamped a curfew on the refugee camps.*
◆ v + adv + n ♦ v + pron + adv (*rare*) ♦
   v + n/pron + prep

claw /klɔː/

'claw at sb/sth to try to catch sb/sth or scratch or tear sb/sth with sharp, curved nails (**claws**) or with your fingernails: *The cat was clawing at the door.* ◇ *She tried to claw at his face.*
◆ v + prep

‚claw sth 'back (*especially BrE*) **1** to work hard to get sth back that you have lost: *They're trying to claw back their share of the market.* **2** if a government **claws back** money it has paid to people, it gets it back, usually by taxing them: *The government are clawing back age allowances in tax.*
◆ v + adv + n ♦ v + n/pron + adv
▸ **'clawback** *n* (*BrE*, *business*) the act of a government getting back in tax the money it has paid to people; the money that is paid back

clean /kliːn/

‚clean sth 'down (*BrE*) to clean sth thoroughly by wiping or brushing it: *Clean down all the walls before repainting them.*
◆ v + adv + n ♦ v + n/pron + adv

‚clean sth 'off; ‚clean sth 'off sth to remove sth from the surface of sth by brushing, wiping, etc: *She couldn't be bothered to clean her make-up off.* ◇ *How can I clean red wine off the carpet?*
◆ v + n/pron + adv ♦ v + adv + n ♦ v + n/pron + prep

‚clean sb/sth 'out; ‚clean sb/sth 'out of sth (*informal*) to use up or take all sb's money; to take or buy the whole supply of sth that sb has: *Buying drinks for everyone cleaned me out.* ◇ *It's been a great year for sales. We're completely* *cleaned out* (= we've sold all our supply). ◇ *The stall was cleaned out of newspapers by 8.00 a.m.* ◇ *Burglars had cleaned the place out* (= had stolen everything).

◈ v + n/pron + adv ◆ v + n/pron + adv + prep

,clean sth 'out to clean the inside of sth thoroughly: *We clean the stables out every day.*

◈ v + n/pron + adv ◆ v + adv + n

▶ **'clean-out** *n* [usually sing.] (*especially BrE*) an occasion when you clean a room, house, cupboard, etc. thoroughly; the activity of cleaning a room, house, cupboard, etc. thoroughly

,clean 'up (*informal*) to be very successful; to win a lot of money or prizes: *The movie cleaned up at the awards ceremony.*

◈ v + adv

,clean 'up; **,clean yourself 'up** to wash yourself or make yourself clean: *I'll just clean up before dinner.* ◇ *They cleaned themselves up and put on their best clothes.* ◇ *It's time you got cleaned up and ready for the evening.*

◈ v + adv ◆ v + pron + adv

,clean 'up; **,clean sth 'up** to remove dirt, etc. from a place and make it clean: *I've got to clean up before my parents get home.* ◇ *Who's going to clean the place up after you?* ◇ *How often is the trash and litter cleaned up?*

[OBJ] **mess, house, environment**

◈ v + adv ◆ v + adv + n ◆ v + n/pron + adv

▶ **'clean-up** *n* [usually sing.] the act of removing dirt, etc. from a place to clean it

→ *see also* CLEAN-UP at CLEAN STH UP

,clean sb 'up to clean sb thoroughly: *Dad cleaned me up after I fell over in the mud.*

◈ v + n/pron + adv ◆ v + adv + n

,clean sth up to remove criminals, crime or immoral behaviour from a place or an organization: *The mayor is determined to clean up the city and make it a safer place to live.* ◇ *The company is trying to clean up its image.*

[OBJ] **city, image**

◈ v + adv + n ◆ v + n/pron + adv

[IDM] **clean up your 'act** to start behaving in a responsible way

▶ **'clean-up** *n* [usually sing.] the act of removing crime or immoral behaviour from a place or an organization

→ *see also* CLEAN-UP at CLEAN UP, CLEAN STH UP

clear /klɪə(r); *AmE* klɪr/

,clear a'way; **,clear sth a'way** (*especially BrE*) to remove things that you have been using and no longer need in order to leave a clear space: *I'll help you to clear away after tea.* ◇ *to clear away the dishes* ◇ *Can you clear your books away?*

◈ v + adv ◆ v + n/pron + adv ◆ v + adv + n

,clear sb a'way (*AmE*) to make sb leave a place: *The police cleared the demonstrators away.*

◈ v + n/pron + adv ◆ v + adv + n

,clear 'off (*informal, especially BrE*) to go or run away: *You've no right to be here. Clear off!* ◇ *He cleared off as soon as he heard the police car.* ◇ *I asked if I could play with them, but they told me to clear off home.*

◈ v + adv

,clear 'out; **,clear 'out of sth** (*informal*) to leave a place quickly: *Would it be better for you if I just cleared out and went back to London?* ◇ *I told him to clear out of the house by Monday.*

[SYN] **get out, get out of sth**

◈ v + adv ◆ v + adv + prep

,clear sth 'out to make sth empty and clean by removing what you do not want: *I cleared out all the cupboards.*

[SYN] **tidy sth out** (*BrE*)

◈ v + adv + n ◆ v + n/pron + adv

▶ **'clear-out** *n* [usually sing.] (*informal, especially BrE*) the act of throwing away all the things you no longer want or need or of getting rid of people you no longer want: *a clear-out of staff to reduce the wages bill*

,clear 'up if the weather **clears up**, it becomes brighter and rain, etc. moves away: *For a week, it rained all day and cleared up in the evening.*

[SYN] **brighten up**

◈ v + adv

,clear 'up; **,clear sth 'up 1** to make sth clean and neat: *I'll help you clear up.* ◇ *Clear up the mess in here before you go.* [OBJ] **mess** [SYN] **tidy up, tidy sth up** (*especially BrE*) **2** if an illness, infection, etc. **clears up** or sth **clears it up**, it disappears: *The rash cleared up very quickly.* ◇ *The antibiotics should clear up the infection.* [OBJ] **rash, infection**

◈ v + adv ◆ v + n/pron + adv ◆ v + adv + n

,clear sth 'up to solve a problem; to find an explanation for sth: *to clear up a mystery* ◇ *I'm glad we've cleared that misunderstanding up.*

[OBJ] **confusion, matter, problem, mystery**

◈ v + adv + n ◆ v + n/pron + adv

climb /klaɪm/

,climb 'down (**over sth**) (*informal*) to admit that you are wrong or have made a mistake; to change your position in an argument: *The president was forced to climb down and issue an apology.*

[SYN] **back down (on/from sth); give in (to sb/sth)**

◈ v + adv

▶ **'climbdown** (**over sth**) *n* an act of admitting that you are wrong or have made a mistake; an act of changing your position in an argument

cling /klɪŋ/ (**clung, clung** /klʌŋ/)

'cling to sth; **cling 'on to sth** to be unwilling to stop doing, believing or thinking about sth; to be unwilling to get rid of sth: *I still cling to the hope that he's alive.* ◇ *She's clinging on to the past.*

OBJ **past, power, tradition**

◈ v + prep ◆ v + adv + prep

clock /klɒk; *AmE* klɑːk/

clock 'in/'on; **clock sb 'in/'on** (*BrE*) to record the time that you arrive at work, especially by putting a card into a machine; to do this for sb or check the time they arrive at work: *We arrived and clocked on for the night shift.*

SYN **punch in, punch sb in** (*AmE*)

OPP **clock off/out**

◈ v + adv ◆ v + n/pron + adv

clock 'in at sth to last or take a particular amount of time; to cost a particular amount of money: *The fastest runner clocked in at 3 minutes 40 seconds.*

◈ v + adv + prep

clock 'off/'out; **clock sb 'off/'out** (*BrE*) to record the time that you leave work, especially by putting a card into a machine; to do this for sb: *Don't forget to clock off when you leave.*

SYN **punch out, punch sb out** (*AmE*)

OPP **clock in/on, clock sb in/on**

◈ v + adv ◆ v + n/pron + adv

clock 'on; **clock sb 'on** (*BrE*) = CLOCK IN/ON, CLOCK SB IN/ON

clock 'out; **clock sb 'out** (*BrE*) = CLOCK OFF/ OUT, CLOCK SB OFF/OUT

clock sth 'up (*informal*) to win or achieve a particular number or amount: *We've clocked up 500 miles* (= we've travelled 500 miles) *today.* ◇ *The company has clocked up record exports this year.*

OBJ **miles, years** SYN **notch sth up**

◈ v + adv + n ◆ v + n/pron + adv (*rare*)

clog /klɒg; *AmE* klɑːg/ (**-gg-**)

clog 'up (**with sth**), **clog sth 'up** (**with sth**) to become, or to make sth, blocked so that nothing can move: *The pipe had clogged up (with mud).* ◇ *The roads were clogged up with traffic.*

OBJ **roads, pipes** SYN **block up, block sth up**

NOTE Clog and clog sth are used with a similar meaning.

◈ v + adv ◆ v + adv + n ◆ v + n/pron + adv

close /kləʊz; *AmE* kloʊz/

close a'round sb/sth (*BrE also* **close a'bout/'round sb/sth**) to surround sb/sth, holding them/it tightly: *His fingers closed around her wrist.* ◇ (*figurative*) *The darkness of the night was closing about him.*

◈ v + prep

close 'down (*BrE*) if a radio or television station **closes down**, it stops broadcasting programmes at the end of the day

◈ v + adv

▶ **'close-down** *n* [sing.] the end of broadcasting on television and radio until the next day

→ *see also* CLOSE-DOWN at CLOSE DOWN, CLOSE STH DOWN

close 'down; **close sth 'down** if a shop/ store, business, etc. **closes down**, or sb **closes it down**, it stops operating as a business, usually permanently: *Many businesses have closed down because of the recession.* ◇ *The government has closed down most of the mines.* ◇ *The hospital closed down last year.*

SYN **shut down, shut sth down**

OPP **open up, open sth up**

NOTE Close and close sth are also used with this meaning: *The factory was closed last year.*

◈ v + adv ◆ v + adv + n ◆ v + n/pron + adv

▶ **'close-down** *n* [U] [sing.] the stopping of work, especially permanently, in an office, factory, etc.

→ *see also* CLOSE-DOWN at CLOSE DOWN

close 'in 1 (**on sb/sth**) to come nearer to and surround sb/sth in a frightening way or in order to attack them: *The enemy is closing in.* ◇ *The fog was closing in on us.* **2** (*especially BrE*) when the days **close in**, they gradually become shorter: *The days/nights are closing in now that autumn/fall is here.* ◇ *The evenings are closing in fast.* SYN **draw in** (*BrE*)

◈ v + adv

close sth 'off (**to sb/sth**) to put sth across the entrance to a road, a room, etc. so that people cannot go in: *Police have closed the area off to traffic.* ◇ (*figurative*) *We don't want to close off any options.*

◈ v + n/pron + adv ◆ v + adv + n

close on sb/sth (*BrE*) to make the distance between you and sb/sth else smaller, for example in a race: *I was slowly closing on the runner ahead of me.*

◈ v + prep

close on/over sth to surround sth, covering it or holding it tightly: *His fingers closed over the money.*

◈ v + prep

close 'out (*AmE*) if a shop/store **closes out** it sells everything very cheaply before it stops operating as a business: *The store is closing out on Monday with discounts of up to 75%.*

◈ v + adv

▶ **'closeout** *n* (*AmE*) an occasion when a shop/store sells all remaining goods very cheaply before it stops operating: *a closeout sale*

NOTE In British English, this is called a **closing-down sale**.

,**close sth 'out 1** to prevent light, sound, etc. from entering a place: *We need a curtain up there to close out the light.* ⟨OBJ⟩ **light, noise** ⟨SYN⟩ **shut sb/sth out 2** (*AmE, informal*) to bring sth to an end: *The vote closed out the three-day debate.* **3** (*AmE*) if you **close out** a bank account, you stop keeping money in it: *I'd like to close out my savings account.* ⟨OBJ⟩ only **account** ⟨NOTE⟩ **Close sth** is also used with this meaning.
◆ v + adv + n ◆ v + n/pron + adv

,**close 'over sth** = CLOSE ON/OVER STH

,**close 'round sb/sth** (*BrE*) = CLOSE AROUND SB/STH

,**close 'up 1** to close completely: *His eye had swollen and closed up.* ◇ *The cut took a long time to close up* (= to heal). ⟨OPP⟩ **open up 2** to hide your thoughts and feelings: *She closed up when I mentioned her father.* ⟨OPP⟩ **open up 3** if people or vehicles **close up**, they move nearer to each other: *Traffic was heavy and cars were closing up behind each other.*
◆ v + adv

,**close 'up**; ,**close sth ,up** to shut and lock a building completely for a period of time: *You go on home. I'll close up* (= shut the shop/store). ◇ *He closes the shop up at 5.30.* ◇ *They closed the house up and rented an apartment in the city.*
⟨OPP⟩ **open up, open sth up**
◆ v + adv ◆ v + n/pron + adv ◆ v + adv + n

cloud /klaʊd/

,**cloud 'over 1** if the sky or the weather **clouds over**, clouds cover the sky and the sun disappears: *It's starting to cloud over.* ⟨SUBJ⟩ **it, the sky 2** if your face, expression, etc. **clouds over**, you start to look sad, worried or angry: *His face clouded over when she walked into the room.* ⟨SUBJ⟩ **face, expression, eyes**
◆ v + adv

clown /klaʊn/

,**clown a'round** (*BrE also* ,**clown a'bout**) to behave in a silly way to make other people laugh
⟨SYN⟩ **mess around** (*informal*)
◆ v + adv

club /klʌb/ (-bb-)

,**club to'gether** (**to do sth**) if people **club together**, they each give an amount of money so that the total can be used for a particular purpose: *They clubbed together to buy their teacher a present.*
⟨SYN⟩ **chip in** (**with sth**)
◆ v + adv

clue /kluː/

,**clue sb 'in** (**on/about sth**) (*AmE, informal*) to give sb reliable information about sth: *Can you clue me in on the facts of the case?*
◆ v + n/pron + adv
▶ ,**clued-'in** (**on/about sth**) *adj* having a lot of information about sth
⟨NOTE⟩ **Clued-up** is used in British English with this meaning.

cluster /'klʌstə(r)/

,**cluster a'round sb/sth** (*BrE also* ,**cluster a'bout/'round sb/sth**) to form a group around sb/sth: *People clustered around the market stalls.*
◆ v + prep

,**cluster to'gether** to come together in a small group: *The children clustered together in a corner of the room.*
◆ v + adv

clutch /klʌtʃ/

'**clutch at sth/sb** to try to get hold of sb/sth suddenly: *She clutched at her stomach, obviously in pain.*
⟨SYN⟩ **catch at sth/sb; grasp at sth**
◆ v + prep
⟨IDM⟩ **clutch at 'straws** to try every possible way to escape from a difficult situation even though there seems to be little hope of doing so

clutter /'klʌtə(r)/

,**clutter sth 'up** (**with sth**) to fill or cover sth with lots of things so that it looks very untidy: *I'm sick of all these books cluttering up my office.*
⟨NOTE⟩ **Clutter sth** is used with a similar meaning.
◆ v + adv + n ◆ v + n/pron + adv

coax /kəʊks; *AmE* koʊks/

,**coax sb 'into sth**; ,**coax sb 'into doing sth** to persuade sb to do sth by talking to them gently: *Can we coax you into singing for us?*
◆ v + n/pron + prep

,**coax sb 'out of sth**; ,**coax sb 'out of doing sth** to persuade sb not to do sth by talking to them gently: *Try to coax him out of resigning.*
◆ v + n/pron + adv + prep

,**coax sth 'out of sb**; ,**coax sth 'from sb** to persuade sb to do sth or to give you sth by talking gently: *She coaxed a smile from the baby.*
◆ v + n/pron + adv + prep ◆ v + n/pron + prep

cobble /'kɒbl; *AmE* 'kɑːbl/

,**cobble sth to'gether** (*informal*) to put sth together or to make sth quickly or carelessly, with whatever time and materials you have available: (*figurative*) *The government seems to have cobbled together these proposals.*

◈ v + adv + n ◆ v + n/pron + adv

cock /kɒk; *AmE* kɑːk/

,cock 'up; ,cock sth 'up (*slang, especially BrE*) to spoil or ruin sth by doing it badly or by making a mistake: *You've really cocked up this time.* ◇ *The travel agency completely cocked up the arrangements.* ◇ *Trust him to cock things up again!*

SYN **mess up, mess sth up; bungle sth** (*informal*)

◈ v + adv ◆ v + n/pron + adv

▶ 'cock-up *n* (*slang, especially BrE*) a mistake that spoils or ruins plans or arrangements; sth that has been spoilt because it has been badly done: *She's made a complete cock-up of the arrangements.*

coil /kɔɪl/

,coil 'up; ,coil sth 'up to wind into a series of circles; to make sth do this: *The snake coiled up in the sunshine.* ◇ *He coiled the rope up neatly.*

OBJ **rope, string**

◈ v + adv ◆ v + n/pron + adv ◆ v + adv + n

colour (*BrE*) (*AmE* **color**) /ˈkʌlə(r)/

,colour sth 'in to fill a shape, an area, etc. with colour, using pencils or pens: *Why don't you colour the pictures in?*

OBJ **picture, drawing**

◈ v + n/pron + adv ◆ v + adv + n

comb /kəʊm; *AmE* koʊm/

,comb sth 'out 1 to use a comb to remove knots from your hair or to make it neat: *My hair's so long that it takes me ages to comb it out.* OBJ **hair** 2 (*also* ,comb sth 'out of sth) to remove dirt, knots, etc. from hair or fur with a comb: *She brushed her hair and then combed out the tangles.*

OBJ **knots, tangles**

◈ v + n/pron + adv ◆ v + adv + n 2 also v + n/pron + adv + prep

come /kʌm/ (**came** /keɪm/ **come**)

,come a'bout to happen: *It's hard to understand how the accident came about.* ◇ *Can you tell us how it came about that you decided to strike?*

SYN **happen**

◈ v + adv

,come a'cross (*also* ,come 'over) 1 (*also* ,come 'through') [+adv/prep] (of an idea, an opinion or a feeling) to be expressed clearly and understood easily: *Do you think the film's message comes*

~ about	57	~ into
~ across		~ of
~ after		~ off
~ along	54	~ on
~ apart		~ on/upon
~ around	58	~ on to
~ at		~ out, out of
~ away		~ out at
~ away from		~ out in
~ away with		~ out with
~ back		~ over
~ back to		~ over to
~ before	59	~ past
~ between		~ round
~ by	55	~ through
~ down		~ to
~ down on		~ together
~ down to		~ under
~ down with	60	~ up
~ for		~ up against
~ forth	56	~ up for
~ forward		~ up on
~ from		~ up to
~ in		~ up with
~ in for		~ upon
~ in with	61	~ with

across clearly? ◇ *These themes come across very strongly in the novel.* ◇ *I could tell she was frightened. It came over in her voice.* ◇ *The feeling of solidarity among the people really came through.* **2** (*AmE also* ,come 'off *informal*) [+ adv/prep] (as sth) to make a particular impression on people: *She comes across well in interviews.* ◇ *At the press conference, he came over as cool and confident.*

◈ v + adv

,come a'cross (with sth) (*informal*) to provide or supply sth that sb asks for, especially money: *They eventually came across with another $250000.* ◇ *We still hope the company will come across for us.*

◈ v + adv

,come a'cross; ',come a'cross sth to cross a room, a road, a river, etc. towards the place where the speaker is: *When you've done your homework, come across to my house and we'll listen to some music.* ◇ *She waved and came across the room to talk to me.*

◈ v + adv ◆ v + prep

',come a'cross sb/sth to meet or find sb/sth by chance, without having planned or thought about it: *He's the most unpleasant man I've ever come across.* ◇ *She came across a pile of old photographs while she was clearing the attic.*

SYN **encounter sb/sth** (*formal*)

◈ v + prep

,come 'after sb/sth to chase or follow a person or an animal to try to catch them: *The farmer came after them, threatening to call the police.*

◈ v + prep

,**come a'long 1** to arrive or appear somewhere; to start to exist, happen or be available: *It's lucky you came along when you did or I'd have been stranded at the bus stop for an hour!* ◇ *When the right opportunity comes along, he'll take it.* ◇ *There are new designs coming along.* ⟨SYN⟩ **turn up 2** to go somewhere with sb: *We're going to the pub. Do you want to come along?* ◇ *You'd better come along with me to the police station.* **3** = COME ON 4 **4 come along!** (*especially BrE*) = COME ON 1
◈ v + adv

,**come a'long**; ,**come a'long sth** to move forward or from one end of sth to the other, towards the speaker: *I waited for ages for a bus, then three came along together!* ◇ *The lorry was coming along the road at great speed.*
⟨OBJ⟩ **road**
◈ v + adv ◆ v + prep

,**come a'part** to break or fall into pieces: *The teapot just came apart in my hands.* ◇ (*figurative*) *After the first act, the play begins to come apart at the seams* (= have a lot of problems).
⟨SYN⟩ **fall apart**
◈ v + adv

,**come a'round** (*especially AmE*) = COME ROUND

,**come a'round**; ,**come a'round sth** (*especially AmE*) = COME ROUND, COME ROUND STH

,**come a'round sth** (*BrE also* ,**come 'round sth**) to move or travel around a corner: *The bus came round the bend too fast.*
⟨OBJ⟩ only **corner, bend**
◈ v + prep

'**come at sb** to move towards sb as if you are going to attack them: *She came at me with a knife.* ◇ (*figurative*) *The questions came at me so fast that I didn't have time to think about them.*
◈ v + prep

'**come at sth** to approach, think about or try to deal with a question, problem, etc. in a particular way: *We're getting nowhere. Let's try coming at the problem from a different angle.*
⟨OBJ⟩ **problem**
◈ v + prep

,**come a'way**; ,**come a'way from sth 1** to leave a place or a person: *Come away, now. There's nothing to see.* ◇ *Jane came away from the meeting feeling angry and upset.* **2** to become separated from sth: *He pulled at the door handle until it came away in his hands.* ◇ *The plaster had started to come away from the wall.*
◈ v + adv ◆ v + adv + prep

,**come a'way with sth** to leave a place with a particular feeling, impression or result: *She came away from the championship with three medals.* ◇ *We came away with the impression that something was wrong.*
◈ v + adv + prep

come 'back 1 to return to the place where the speaker is: *Come back here at once!* ◇ *Did she say when she was coming back?* ◇ *Why don't you come back to my place for a coffee?* ◇ *They came back from the trip relaxed and happy.* ◇ *She went into the kitchen and came back with two glasses of milk.* ◇ *We'll come back for the car tomorrow.* ◇ (*figurative*) *Liverpool came back from being 2-0 down to win the game.* ⟨SYN⟩ **return** (*more formal*) **2** to begin to exist or happen again: *My headache has come back again.* ◇ *Her confidence is starting to come back slowly.* ⟨SYN⟩ **return** ⟨OPP⟩ **go away 3** to return to school or work after a break: *Do you know when Bill is coming back to work?* **4** to become popular, successful or fashionable again: *Punk hairstyles are coming back into fashion.* ◇ *Punk hairstyles are coming back in.* ◇ *Do you think trams will come back?* **5** (of a message or a reply) to be given in answer to a message, letter, etc. that you have sent or a question that you have asked: *I sent her an email and a message came back that she was away.* **6 (to sb)** to return to your memory, often suddenly: *It's all coming back to me now.* **7 (at sb) (with sth)** to reply to sb quickly, strongly or angrily: *She came back at the speaker with some questions.* ◇ *He came back straightaway, telling me what he thought of me.*
◈ v + adv

▶ '**comeback** *n* **1** [usually sing.] if a person makes a comeback they return to performing or to public life after a long time, or they become popular again: *The band's trying to make/stage a comeback.* **2** if something **makes a comeback** it becomes popular or fashionable again: *Cartoons seem to be making a comeback.* **3** a way of getting payment or a reward for sth unfair or wrong that has been done to you: *Will I have no comeback if the contract falls through?* **4** a quick reply that is often angry, insulting, clever or humorous: *For once in her life, she had no sharp comeback.*

,**come 'back to sth** to return to a particular subject, an idea, etc. and start to talk about it or think about it: *I'll come back to that point in a moment.* ◇ *It always seems to come back to the question of money.*
⟨SYN⟩ **return to sth** (*more formal*)
◈ v + adv + prep

,**come be'fore sb/sth** (*formal*) (of a legal case, a proposal or an issue) to be presented to sb/sth so that they can discuss it or make a decision or a judgement about it: *The case comes before the court next week.* ◇ *The bill came before parliament last month.*
⟨OBJ⟩ **the court(s), committee, judge, parliament**
◈ v + prep

,**come be'tween sb and sb**; ,**come be'tween sb and sth** to harm or disturb a relationship between two people; to prevent sb from doing, enjoying or having sth: *Nobody will ever come between them.* ◇ *I don't want to come between her and her work.*

◈ v + prep

,come 'by; ,come 'by sth 1 to pass sb/sth without stopping: *Some kids on bikes came by, but they didn't notice me.* **2** (*especially AmE*) to come to visit sb for a short time in a casual or informal way: *Thanks for coming by yesterday.* ◇ *Come by on your way home from work.* ◇ *If you come by the office tomorrow, I'll have it ready for you.* ⟨SYN⟩ **drop by; stop by, stop by sth**

◈ v + adv ♦ v + prep

'come by sth to manage to get sth; to receive sth by chance: *Jobs are hard to come by these days.* ◇ *Information about the company was not easy to come by.* ◇ *How did you come by that cut on your hand?*

⟨SYN⟩ **get sth; obtain sth** (*more formal*)

⟨NOTE⟩ **Come by sth** can be used in the passive, but this is not common: *Old postcards are fairly easily come by.*

◈ v + prep

,come 'down 1 (from…) (to…) to travel from one place to another, especially from the north of a country to the south: *When are you going to come down and see us?* **2** if a price, a level or an amount **comes down**, it becomes lower or less than before: *Oil is coming down in price.* ◇ *Inflation has come down twice in the last month.* ⟨SYN⟩ **decrease** (*more formal*), **drop; fall** ⟨OPP⟩ **go up** ⟨NOTE⟩ You can also use **come back up** with the opposite meaning if a price, etc. is increasing towards what it had been before: *Oil prices are coming back up* (= they have been high in the past, then they fell, but now they are rising again). **3** to break and fall to the ground: *Part of the ceiling had come down.* ⟨SYN⟩ **collapse 4** (of a plane, etc.) to fall from the sky; to be brought down to the ground: *The pilot was forced to come down in a field.* **5** (of rain, snow, etc.) to fall: *The rain was coming down harder now.* ⟨SUBJ⟩ only the **rain, the snow** ⟨SYN⟩ **fall 6** [+ adv/prep] to decide that you support or oppose sb/sth and say so publicly: *I knew my parents would come down on my sister's side.* ◇ *The committee came down against the proposal.* ◇ *Voters came down firmly in favour of reform.* **7** when the curtain in a theatre **comes down**, it is the end of the performance: *When the curtain came down, we all rushed for the exits.* ⟨OPP⟩ **go up 8** [+adv/prep] to reach down to a particular point: *My mother's hair comes down to her waist.* **9** (*informal*) to stop having the pleasant feelings and excitement that sth such as an enjoyable experience or a drug produces: *The party was so good I haven't really come down yet.* **10** (from sth) (to sth) (of a person selling sth) to suggest or agree to a lower price: *I wasn't prepared to pay £1500, but they eventually came down to £1350.* ◇ *Can you come down another $30?*

11 (from sth) (*BrE, formal*) to leave a university (especially Oxford or Cambridge) after finishing your studies: *When did you come down (from Oxford)?* ⟨OPP⟩ **come up (to sth)**

◈ v + adv **10** also v + adv + n

⟨IDM⟩ **come (back) down to 'earth (with a 'bang/'bump)** to return to the reality of everyday life after a period of great excitement or a time when you have been living in a way that is not very practical: *He came (back) down to earth with a bang when he discovered that all his money had run out.*

▶ **'comedown** n [usually sing.] (*informal*) a situation which is not as good, important or interesting as one that you have experienced previously: *It's a bit of a comedown after her previous job.*

,come 'down; ,come 'down sth to move from a higher place or position to a lower one, or from a distant place towards the speaker: *Come down from that tree!* ◇ *The car was coming down the road towards us.* ◇ *Jack came down the stairs two at a time.*

⟨OPP⟩ **come up, come up sth**

◈ v + adv ♦ v + prep

,come 'down on sb (*informal*) to punish sb or criticize sb severely: *The courts are coming down heavily on drug dealers.* ◇ *Don't come down too hard on him — he's young.*

⟨NOTE⟩ **Come down on sb** is always used with an adverb such as *hard* and/or a phrase with a similar meaning: *If it happens again, we'll come down on you so hard that you'll wish you'd never been born.* ◇ *He came down on me like a ton of bricks.*

◈ v + adv + prep

,come 'down to sb (from sb/sth) to be passed to sb from sb who lived in the past: *The estate came down to her from her grandfather.*

⟨SUBJ⟩ **story, name, tradition**

◈ v + adv + prep

,come 'down to sth to be able to be explained as one simple, important question or point: *It all comes down to a matter of priorities in the end.* ◇ *When it comes down to it* (= the most important fact is), *we can't afford to go.* ◇ *What it comes down to is a choice between money or happiness.*

◈ v + adv + prep

,come 'down with sth to get an illness, often not a very serious one: *I came down with a bad cold.* ◇ *I think I'm coming down with something.*

⟨OBJ⟩ **flu, a cold** ⟨SYN⟩ **go down with sth; catch sth; get sth**

◈ v + adv + prep

'come for sb/sth 1 to come to sb's home, or to the place where sb/sth is in order to take them/it somewhere: *The police came for him this morning.* ◇ *Have you come for the parcel?* **2** to attack sb/sth: *Sam came for me with his fists.*

◈ v + prep

,come 'forth (*literary*) to appear or be produced: *He struck the rock and water came forth.*
✥ v + adv

▶ **,forth'coming** *adj* **1** [only before noun] about to happen or appear very soon: *Who is in charge of promoting the band's forthcoming album?* **2** [not before noun] ready or made available when you need it: *Unfortunately money for the project has not been very forthcoming.* **3** [not before noun] (of a person) ready to give information when they are asked: *He's not very forthcoming about his love life.*

,come 'forward (with sth) to offer to give help, information, etc: *Police have asked witnesses to come forward.* ◇ *We're hoping that a sponsor will come forward with the extra money.* ◇ *No one came forward to claim the reward.*
✥ v + adv

'come from ... (*not used in the progressive tenses*) to be born in or live in a particular place: *Where do you come from?* ◇ *She comes from London.*
✥ v + prep

'come from sth to start in a particular place or be made from a particular thing: *Most of the wines that we sell come from France.* ◇ *Does your information come from a reliable source?* ◇ *I'm lazy? That's rich, coming from you!* (= you are lazy too) ◇ *He comes from a wealthy family.* ◇ *Where's that terrible noise coming from?* ◇ *93% of our energy comes from fossil fuels.*
✥ v + prep

IDM **where sb is 'coming from** (*spoken, informal*) a person's situation, attitude, ideas, etc. that make them say what they have said: *I know exactly where you're coming from.*

'come from sth; 'come from doing sth = COME OF STH, COME OF DOING STH

,come 'in 1 when the sea comes in it moves towards the land: *The tide was coming in fast.* **OPP** **go out 2** to finish a race in a particular position: *Which horse came in first?* **3** to arrive; to be received: *News is coming in of a train crash in Scotland.* ◇ *We've got more work coming in than we can handle.* ◇ *I met all the trains that came in from London.* ◇ *We've got just enough money coming in each month to pay the bills.* **4** to become available: *English strawberries usually come in in June.* ◇ *New jobs are coming in all the time.* **5** if a law or a rule **comes in**, it is introduced and begins to take effect: *New legislation coming in next month will tackle low pay.* **6** to take part in a discussion, sometimes by interrupting sb: *I'd like to come in here.* ◇ *I wish he wouldn't keep coming in with his stupid suggestions.* **7** to come to your home, office, etc. in order to repair sth, or do some work: *A plumber's coming in to look at*

the boiler. → *see also* COME IN, COME IN STH, COME INTO STH; COME IN, COME INTO STH; COME INTO STH
✥ v + adv

IDM **,come in 'handy/'useful** to be useful: *These boxes will come in handy when we move house.*

▶ **'income** *n* money that you receive regularly, especially as payment for work

▶ **'incoming** *adj* [only before noun] **1** travelling towards a place and arriving there: *incoming flights/passengers* **2** (of the sea) coming towards the land **3** (of a phone call, letter or message) that has been sent to you or received by you: *This phone only takes incoming calls.* **4** recently appointed or elected: *the incoming Socialist government*

,come 'in; ,come 'in sth; ,come 'into sth to enter a room or a building; to pass through sth such as a hole, a window, etc: *I knocked and heard her say 'Come in'.* ◇ *The rain's coming in through that hole.* ◇ *I'll ask him to call you as soon as he comes in* (= arrives home or at work). ◇ *The sun was coming in at the windows.* ◇ *When you come in the door, you'll find Reception on your left.* ◇ *She came into the room crying.*
→ *see also* COME IN; COME IN STH, COME INTO STH; COME INTO STH
✥ v + adv ✦ v + prep

,come 'in; ,come 'into sth 1 to go to an office or the place where you work, in order to do some work: *Are you coming into the office tomorrow?* **OBJ** **the office, work 2** to have a part to play in sth; to play a useful role: *I like the plan, but where do I come in* (= what is my role)? **3** to become fashionable; to start to be worn or used: *When did platform heels come in?* ◇ *Trolleybuses first came in in 1923.* ◇ *Punk clothes seem to be coming into fashion again.* **OPP** **go out 4** to go to a hospital to receive treatment, tests, etc: *Can you come in for the X-rays on Friday?*
→ *see also* COME IN; COME IN, COME IN STH, COME INTO STH; COME INTO STH
✥ v + adv ✦ v + prep

,come 'in for sth to receive sth, especially sth unpleasant: *The government has come in for severe criticism from all sides.* ◇ *The company came in for a lot of stick* (= a lot of criticism) *with their advertising campaign.*
OBJ **(severe) criticism**
✥ v + adv + prep

,come 'in with sb (on sth), **,come 'in** (with sb) **on sth** if somebody **comes in with** you, they join you in a particular project, activity, business, etc: *Do you want to come in with me on Joe's present?* ◇ *My brother hoped I would come in with him when he started his own business.* ◇ *Do you want to come in on the deal?*
✥ v + adv + prep

,**come 'into sth 1** to begin to exist, happen, etc: *The cherry trees are **coming into** blossom.* ◊ *The band only **came into being** in 1995.* ◊ *When do the new regulations **come into force/effect**?* ◊ *When did the Labour party **come into office**?* ◊ *A variety of factors **come into play** when choosing an employee.* **2** to receive a large sum of money when sb dies: *She unexpectedly **came into** a fortune when her cousin died.* OBJ **a fortune, money 3** to be important in a particular situation: *I got the job because I was the best. My looks didn't **come into it**.* ◊ *He took the job because he liked the work. Money didn't **come into** the equation.* OBJ **it, the equation**

→ *see also* COME IN; COME IN, COME IN STH, COME INTO STH; COME IN, COME INTO STH

✦ v + prep

IDM **come into 'line (with sb/sth)** to behave in the way other people behave, or in the way you should behave **come into your/its 'own** to have the opportunity to show your/its qualities or abilities: *After two rather poor games, he finally came into his own in the game against Germany.* ◊ *This bike really comes into its own on rough ground.*

'**come of sth**; '**come of doing sth** (*also* '**come from sth,** '**come from doing sth**) to happen as a result of sth: *He promised to help, but I don't think anything will **come of it**.* ◊ *That's what comes of not listening to my advice!* ◊ *I had the feeling of satisfaction that comes from doing a difficult job well.*

NOTE **Come of sth** is often used with a negative: *I told him no good would come of it.*

✦ v + prep

,**come 'off 1** to be able to be removed: *Does this knob come off?* **2** (*informal*) to take place; to happen: *Did your trip to New York ever come off?* **3** (*informal*) if a plan, etc. **comes off**, it is successful or it has the result that you intend: *Her attempt to break the world record nearly came off.* **4** [+ adv] (*informal*) if somebody **comes off** well or badly in a fight, a contest, etc. they finish the fight in a good or a bad condition: *He always comes off worst in fights.* **5** (*AmE, informal*) = COME ACROSS 2

✦ v + adv

,**come 'off**; ,**come 'off sth 1** to become detached or separated from sth: *The handle came off in my hand.* ◊ *A button has come off my coat.* **2** to fall from sth: *My glasses came off when I tripped.* ◊ *She braked sharply and came off her bike.* OBJ **bicycle, horse 3** to move away from sth large or important and go in a different direction: *A narrow road comes off on the left.* **4** to leave the stage, the sports field, etc. during a play or a game: *Two players came off just before half time.* **5** to leave sth such as a vehicle or a road: *She looked tired as she came off the plane.* ◊ *Come off (the motorway) at junction five.* **6** if an

amount of money **comes off** a price, the price becomes lower by that amount: *Two pence a litre is coming off the price of petrol/gasoline.*

✦ v + adv ◆ v + prep

,**come 'off sth 1** to stop using sth; to stop taking a drug, medicine, alcohol, etc: *It's time she tried to come off sleeping pills.* **2** (of heat, a smell, the wind, etc.) to start from a particular place or thing: *There was a mist coming off the sea.*

✦ v + prep

IDM ,**come 'off it!** used to tell sb that you think or know that what they have said is untrue or that you disagree with it: *Come off it! England will never win!*

,**come 'on 1** (*also* ,**come a'long** *especially BrE, less frequent*) used to encourage sb to do sth, for example, to hurry: *Come on, we'll be late.* ◊ *Come on, things can't be that bad!* **2** used to show that you do not believe what sb has said or that you disagree with them: *Come on! You don't really expect me to believe that do you?* **3** (of a light, the electricity, etc.) to begin working; to be switched on: *Does the heating come on automatically?* ◊ *I've set the oven to come on at five.* SUBJ **lights** OPP **go off 4** (*also* ,**come a'long**) to make progress; to improve or develop in the way that you want: *Your French is really coming on.* ◊ *Tim's come on well with the guitar.* ◊ *How's dinner coming along?* **5** (of an actor or a performer) to walk onto the stage and start to perform: *When are Westlife coming on?* **6** (in sport) (of a player) to join a team instead of another player during a game: *Robson came on in place of Wilkins.* **7** (of a television programme, etc.) to start to be shown: *What time does the news come on?* **8** (*especially BrE*) (of a season, a period of time, an illness, etc.) to begin: *It's getting colder. Winter's coming on.* ◊ *I think I've got a cold coming on.* ◊ *It came on to rain.* NOTE In this meaning, **come on** is usually used in the progressive tenses. **9** [+ adv] to go to a place: *Come on in and make yourself at home.* ◊ *My wife's coming on later.*

✦ v + adv

IDM ,**come on 'strong** to speak or behave in a very forceful way, especially in a way that shows sb you want to have a sexual relationship with them

▶ '**oncoming** *adj* [only before noun] advancing towards you; approaching you

,**come 'on**; ,**come 'on sth** to begin speaking to sb on the telephone: *I had a long talk with my mother, then my dad came on.* ◊ *Sue came on the line for a chat.*

✦ v + adv ◆ v + prep

'**come on/upon sb/sth** (*formal*) to meet or find sb/sth by chance: *I came upon this beautiful vase in the attic.*

✦ v + prep

,**come 'on to sb** (*informal*) to behave in a way that clearly shows sb that you want to have a sexual relationship with them

@ v + adv + prep

▶ **'come-on** *n* [usually sing.] (*informal*) a remark or an action that is intended to attract sb

,**come 'on to sth** to start talking about or discussing a topic: *I'll come on to the subject of exams in a minute.*

OBJ **question, topic, subject**

@ v + adv + prep

,**come 'out 1** when the sun, moon or stars **come out**, they appear in the sky: *The sun came out in the afternoon.* SYN **appear 2** when flowers **come out**, they open: *The daffodils came out late this year.* **3** to be published or produced: *Her new novel's just come out.* ◇ *When do the exam results come out?* SYN **appear 4** (of news, the truth, etc.) to become known after a time when it has been secret: *The truth finally came out.* ◇ *It came out that she'd made the whole thing up.* **5** to be shown clearly: *His arrogance comes out in every speech he makes.* **6** (**with sb**) to go somewhere with sb for a social event: *Will you come out to dinner with me tonight?* **7** if a photograph **comes out**, the picture can be seen clearly: *My photos didn't come out very well because there wasn't enough light.* **8** when words **come out** they are spoken: *I opened my mouth to apologize, but the words wouldn't come out.* ◇ *He tried to pay her a compliment but it came out all wrong.* **9** [+ prep] to state publicly that you do or do not support sth: *Members of the committee have come out in opposition to the proposal.* **10 come out and do sth** to be brave enough to say or do sth that other people might find it hard to say or do: *Has she actually come out and admitted it yet?* ◇ *Only one member of staff came out and said that the working conditions were unsatisfactory.* **11** (*BrE*) to stop work and go on strike: *The miners have come out on strike.* **12** to say openly that you are a homosexual (= a person who is sexually attracted to people of the same sex) **13** when a young girl **came out** in the past, she was formally introduced into society

@ v + adv

,**come 'out**; ,**come 'out of sth 1** to leave a place or appear from inside a place: *Come out! I know you're in there!* ◇ *I'll speak to her as soon as she comes out of the meeting.* **2** if an object **comes out** of sth, it is removed from the place where it is fixed or becomes separated from sth: *Her tooth came out when she bit into the apple.* ◇ *All the pages have come out of this book.* ◇ *This screw won't come out of the wall.* **3** if a mark or dirt **comes out**, it is removed from sth by washing or cleaning: *The bloodstains won't come out of my shirt.* ◇ *It was a very expensive skirt, but most of the colour came out when I washed it.*

4 [+ adv/prep/adj] to finish sth in a particular state; to have a particular result: *She came out on top in the exams.* ◇ *His reputation came out undamaged.* ◇ *The family didn't come out of the affair very well.* NOTE In this meaning, **come out** and **come out of sth** are always used either with an adverb, an adjective or a phrase beginning with a preposition.

@ v + adv ◆ v + adv + prep

IDM ,**come 'out of yourself** to relax and become more confident and friendly with other people

,**come 'out at sth** to add up to a particular cost or sum: *The total bill comes out at over a thousand pounds.*

@ v + adv + prep

,**come 'out in sth** if a person **comes out in** sth such as spots, their skin becomes covered in them: *The cream made her face come out in a rash.*

OBJ **spots, rash, lumps** SYN **break out in sth**

@ v + adv + prep

,**come 'out of sth 1** to return to normal after a difficult time: *The country is slowly coming out of recession.* **2** to result or develop from a process or an event: *At least some good came out of all our hard work.* ◇ *The book came out of her travels in Japan.* **3** to be taken away from a total amount: *The money will have to come out of your wages.*

@ v + adv + prep

,**come 'out with sth** (*informal*) to say sth, especially sth surprising or not polite: *I can't believe the things he comes out with!* ◇ *When I asked her why she was late, she just came out with a load of nonsense.*

@ v + adv + prep

,**come 'over 1** (**to sb/sth**) to move across a room, a road, an ocean, etc. towards where the speaker is: *Come over and meet my husband.* ◇ *When are you coming over to England again?* ◇ *Lots of people are coming over from America for the wedding.* **2** (**to sth**) to visit sb for a short time, usually at their home: *Her son only comes over to see her occasionally.* ◇ *Our new neighbours came over to our house last night.* **3** [+ adj] (*BrE, informal*) to suddenly start feeling sth: *to come over funny/dizzy/faint* ◇ *I come over all shy whenever I see her.* **4** = COME ACROSS 1 **5** = COME ACROSS 2

@ v + adv

,**come 'over sb/sth** (of a feeling, a mood, etc.) to affect sb/sth: *I'm sorry — I don't know what came over me* (= I don't know what made me behave in that way). ◇ *A remarkable change has come over the group since he left.*

@ v + prep

,**come 'over to sb/sth** to leave one group of people in order to join a competing group; to change from one opinion to another: *Some of their members have come over to our side.*

@ v + adv + prep

,come 'past; ,come 'past sb/sth to pass in front of the speaker or the place where the speaker is: *As I walked down the road, Charlie came past on his bike.* ◇ *I'll bring the book round this evening on my way to night school — I've got to come past your house.*
⊕ v + adv ◆ v + prep

,come 'round (*BrE*) (*also* ,come a'round *AmE, BrE*) **1** (to sth) to visit sb or a place; to come to sb's home to see them for a short time: *Come round and see us sometime.* ◇ *Do you want to come round for lunch?* → *see also* COME OVER 2 **2** (of a regular event) to arrive; to happen at the usual time: *I can't believe Christmas has come round again!* **3** to move among a group of people in order to give them sth: *The waiters came round with drinks.* **4** (to sth) (*informal*) to agree to sth that you were against before; to change your opinion about sth: *She'll never come round to our way of thinking.* ◇ *Don't push him; he'll come round in time.*
⊕ v + adv

,come 'round (*BrE*) (*AmE* ,come a'round) (*also* ,come 'to *BrE, AmE*) to become conscious again: *When she came round, her sister was sitting beside her bed.* ◇ *He hasn't yet come round after the anaesthetic.*
→ *see also* PASS OUT
⊕ v + adv

,come 'round; ,come 'round sth (*BrE*) (*also* ,come a'round, ,come a'round sth *AmE, BrE*) **1** (of a letter or a document) to be passed from one person to another: *The card came round for everyone to sign.* **2** to travel to where the speaker is by a longer route than usual, especially around the outside of sth: *The road was blocked so we had to come round by the fields.*
⊕ v + adv ◆ v + prep

,come 'round sth (*BrE*) = COME AROUND STH

,come 'through **1** (to sth) (*informal*) used especially to ask sb to enter a room or a building, or move from one room to another: *Come through to my office.* ◇ *Mr. Dole can see you now. Will you come through?* **2** (of news, a message, a document, etc.) to be received by telephone, radio, etc. or in an official way: *I've got an international call coming through for you.* ◇ *We're going to buy a new car when the insurance money comes through.* ◇ *He's still waiting for his divorce to come through.* **3** (with sth) to provide or do sth that people expect or that you have promised: *The insurance company has finally come through with the money.* **4** = COME ACROSS 1
⊕ v + adv

,come 'through; ,come 'through sth **1** to enter and cross a room, an area of land, a town, a country, etc.; to pass through sth: ◇ *Put sth over the hole to stop the rain coming through.* **2** to get better after a serious illness; to avoid serious injury or damage: *He's very ill but his doctors*

expect him to come through the operation. **3** to start to appear from under or behind sth: *The baby's front teeth are coming through.* ◇ *The sun's coming through the clouds at last.* ⟨SYN⟩ **emerge** (*more formal*) **4** to pass from one stage of a competition to the next; to be successful in a test or an exam: *Chris did well to come through the qualifying rounds of the tournament* (= for example in tennis). ◇ *Most of the students came through* (*the exam*) *with flying colours* (= were very successful).
⊕ v + adv ◆ v + prep + pron

,come 'to = COME ROUND

'come to sb **1** if an idea comes to you, it suddenly enters your mind: *The idea came to me in the middle of the night.* ◇ *It suddenly came to her that she had been wrong.* **2** (*especially BrE*) (of money, property, etc.) to pass to sb else when sb dies: *All my money will come to you when I die.*
⊕ v + prep

,come to your'self (*old-fashioned*) to return to your normal state: *It took her a while to come to herself again.*
⊕ v + prep + pron

'come to sth **1** to add up to sth; to be equal to sth: *The bill came to $50.* **2** to reach a particular state or condition; to arrive at sth: *We both came to the same conclusion.* ◇ *I don't know what the world's coming to* (= I think things are getting very bad and unpleasant). ◇ *All her dreams had come to nothing.* ⟨OBJ⟩ **this, that, nothing** ⟨NOTE⟩ In this meaning **come to sth** is often used with *this* or *that*: *The doctors will operate if necessary, but it may not come to that.*
⊕ v + prep

⟨IDM⟩ **when it comes to sth/to doing sth** when it is a case, matter or question of sth/of doing sth: *When it comes to cooking, he's much better than I am!*

,come to'gether if two or more people or things **come together**, they form one group or one piece: *Several local groups came together to fight the proposed housing development.* ◇ *During the last three days of rehearsals, everything came together.*
⊕ v + adv

,come 'under sth **1** be included within a particular group or collection of things: *Several different types of schools come under the heading of 'private schools'.* ⟨OBJ⟩ **heading, banner, category 2** to be managed, controlled or owned by a particular group or organization: *The prisons now come under central government control.* ⟨OBJ⟩ **control, authority, wing 3** if you **come under** attack, criticism, etc. sb attacks, criticizes, etc. you: *The government has come under attack over the new bill.* ◇ *She's come under intense pressure to change her mind.* ⟨OBJ⟩ **attack, pressure, fire, scrutiny, criticism**
⊕ v + prep

,**come 'up 1** (to …) (from …) to travel from one place to another, usually from a smaller place to a larger one, or from the south of a country to the north: *They've come up from Texas.* ◇ *We thought we'd go up to London for a weekend in the big city.* **2** (**to sb/sth**) to go towards a person in order to talk to them: *An old guy came up to me in the street and asked me for money.* ◇ *The group leader came up to the reception desk looking anxious.* **3** (of plants) to appear above the ground: *The first snowdrops are just coming up.* ⟨SYN⟩ **appear 4** when the sun or moon **comes up**, it rises in the sky: *We sat and watched the sun coming up behind the hills.* ⟨SUBJ⟩ only **the sun, the moon** ⟨SYN⟩ **rise** ⟨OPP⟩ **go down 5** to rise to the surface of water or another liquid: *I came up gasping for air.* ◇ *Bubbles were coming up to the surface.* **6** to happen, especially when you do not expect it: *Something urgent has come up; I have to go.* ◇ *Opportunities like this don't come up every day.* ⟨SYN⟩ **crop up 7** (*always used in the progressive tenses*) (of an event or a time) to be going to happen very soon: *Our exams are coming up soon.* ◇ *Coming up next is the news.* **8** to be talked about or discussed: *The subject didn't come up in conversation last night.* ◇ *Mary's name keeps coming up.* ⟨SUBJ⟩ **name, question, subject 9** to be dealt with by a court of law: *Her case comes up next month.* **10** if your name, number or ticket **comes up** in a betting game, it is chosen and you are one of the winners: *My numbers came up and I won a million pounds!* **11** (*spoken, informal*) (*usually used in the progressive tenses*) to be ready soon; to be coming soon: 'A cup of tea please.' 'Coming up!' **12** (of information) to appear on a computer screen or a board, for example in an airport: *Her flight has just come up on the arrivals board.* **13** [+ adj/adv] (*BrE*) (of an object or a substance) to appear in a particular way at the end of a period of time or when sth has been done to it: *When the wool is washed, it comes up beautifully soft and fluffy.* ◇ *I've given it a good clean and it's come up like new.* **14** (of lights in a cinema, a theatre, etc.) to become brighter after the film/movie, play, etc. has finished: *The lights came up to loud applause.* **15** (**to sth**) (*BrE, formal*) to begin your studies at a university (especially Oxford or Cambridge): *She came up (to Oxford) in 1982.* ⟨OPP⟩ **come down (from sth) 16** (**to sth**) to reach as far as a particular point or level: *The water came up to my chin.* ◇ *My sister hardly comes up to my shoulder.* ◇ *His scarf came up over his eyes.* ⟨SYN⟩ **reach sth**
⊕ v + adv

⟨IDM⟩ **be coming up 'roses** (*informal*) (of a situation) to be developing in a successful way: *Everything's coming up roses!* **come 'up in the world** to become more important in society or more successful in your career: *She's really come up in the world since she left school.* **come up/turn up 'trumps** to do more than people expect and so make a situation very successful: *The team's new player came up trumps and scored three goals.* ◇ *That was a wonderful meal! You've come up trumps again.*

▶ ,**up-and-'coming** *adj* [only before noun] (*informal*) making good progress and likely to be successful in the future: *an up-and-coming young actor*

▶ '**upcoming** *adj* [only before noun] (*especially AmE*) about to happen soon: *the upcoming presidential election*

,**come 'up;** ,**come 'up sth** to move from a lower place or position to a higher one, or upstairs in a building, especially with the speaker or towards the place where the speaker is: *Who wants to come up to the top of the hill with me?* ◇ *My apartment is on the third floor. Are you coming up?* ◇ *I can hear somebody coming up the stairs.*
⟨OBJ⟩ **road, stairs** ⟨OPP⟩ **come down, come down sth**
⊕ v + adv ♦ v + prep

,**come 'up against sb/sth** if you **come up against sb/sth**, you have to face sb/sth difficult: *We expect to come up against a lot of opposition to the scheme.* ◇ *You'll come up against the reigning champion in the next round.*
⊕ v + adv + prep

,**come 'up for sth 1** to come to the time when sth must be done: *He's coming up for retirement soon.* ◇ *She comes up for re-election next year.* ◇ *When does your contract come up for renewal?* ⟨OBJ⟩ **renewal 2** to become available for a particular purpose: *That house you like has come up for sale.*
⟨OBJ⟩ **sale, auction**
⊕ v + adv + prep

,**come 'up on sth** (*AmE*) to be almost a particular time or age: *It's coming up on your bedtime.*
⊕ v + adv + prep

,**come 'up to sth 1** to approach a particular place, an age or a period of time: *You're coming up to a busy road now.* ◇ *It's just coming up to half past twelve.* **2** to reach an acceptable level or standard: *The performance didn't come up to our expectations.* ◇ *You may lose your job if you don't come up to scratch.* ⟨OBJ⟩ **standard, expectations** ⟨NOTE⟩ In this meaning **come up to sth** is usually used in the negative.
⊕ v + adv + prep

,**come 'up with sth 1** to think of an idea, an answer to a question or a solution to a problem: *She came up with a great idea for increasing sales.* ⟨OBJ⟩ **idea, answer, suggestion, explanation 2** to find or produce sth that sb needs: *If you want to buy my car, you must come up with the money.* ◇ *He always comes up with the goods* (= does what he is expected to do) *on the day.*
⊕ v + adv + prep

'**come upon sb/sth** = COME ON/UPON SB/STH

'come with sth to be included with or as part of sth: *A new car comes with the job.*
◈ v + prep

commune /kə'mjuːn; *AmE* 'kɑːm-/

com'mune with sth (*formal*) if you **commune with** sth such as nature, you spend time thinking deeply about it and so feel close to it
[OBJ] **nature**
◈ v + prep

complain /kəm'pleɪn/

com'plain of sth to say that you feel ill or are suffering from a pain: *Several children complained of severe stomach pains.*
[OBJ] **pain, headache, symptoms**
◈ v + prep

condemn /kən'dem/

con'demn sb to sth 1 to say what sb's punishment will be: *to be condemned to death/hard labour* **2** to force sb to accept a difficult or unpleasant situation: *They were condemned to a life of hardship.* [SYN] **doom sb (to sth)**
[NOTE] **Condemn sb to sth** is usually used in the passive.
◈ v + n/pron + prep

cone /kəʊn; *AmE* koʊn/

,cone sth 'off to close a road or part of a road with special coloured plastic objects that have a round base and a point at the top (**traffic cones**): *Part of the road was coned off while repairs were done.*
[NOTE] **Cone sth off** is usually used in the passive.
◈ v + adv + n ◆ v + n/pron + adv

confide /kən'faɪd/

con'fide in sb to tell sb a secret or a piece of information that you wouldn't tell other people: *Can I confide in you?* ◊ *Do you have a friend that you can confide in?*
[OBJ] **mother, friend**
◈ v + prep

confine /kən'faɪn/

con'fine sb/sth to sth; con'fine yourself to sth to keep sb/sth/yourself inside the limits of a particular activity, subject, area, etc: *The work will not be confined to the Glasgow area.* ◊ *I will confine myself to looking at the period from 1900 to 1916.*
[SYN] **limit sth to sb/sth; restrict sb/sth/yourself (to sth)**
[NOTE] **Confine sb/sth/yourself to sth** is often used in the passive.
◈ v + n/pron + prep

be con'fined to sth 1 if a person or an animal **is confined to** a place, they are kept in a small or closed space and not allowed to go out: *The children were confined to their rooms for the evening.* ◊ *The soldiers concerned were confined to barracks* (= had to stay in the barracks, as a punishment). **2** if a person **is confined to** bed, etc., they have to stay in bed, etc. because they are ill/sick or injured: *She was confined to bed with the flu.* ◊ *He was confined to a wheelchair after the car accident.*
◈ be + v + prep

confront /kən'frʌnt/

con'front sb with sth to make sb face or deal with an unpleasant or difficult person or situation: *He confronted her with a choice between her career or their relationship.*
◈ v + n/pron + prep

be con'fronted with sth to have sth in front of you that you have to deal with or react to: *Most people when confronted with a horse will pat it.*
◈ be + v + prep

conjure /'kʌndʒə(r)/

,conjure sb/sth 'up to make sb/sth appear suddenly or unexpectedly, as if by magic: *She conjured up a three-course meal in half an hour!*
◈ v + adv + n ◆ v + pron + adv ◆ v + n + adv (*less frequent*)

,conjure sth 'up 1 to make a picture, a memory, etc. appear in your mind: *The word 'birthday' conjures up images of presents and parties.* ◊ *The song conjured up memories of warm summer evenings.* [OBJ] **image, picture, visions, memories** [SYN] **evoke sth** (*more formal*) **2** to ask a spirit of a dead person to appear, by using a magic ceremony
◈ v + adv + n ◆ v + pron + adv ◆ v + n + adv (*less frequent*)

conk /kɒŋk; *AmE* kɑːŋk, kɔːŋk/

,conk 'out (*informal or humorous*) **1** if a vehicle or a machine **conks out**, it stops working: *Our car conked out 5 miles from home.* **2** if a person **conks out**, they fall asleep because they are very tired: *She was so tired she came home and conked out at eight o'clock.* **3** (*old-fashioned, BrE*) (of a person) to collapse or become unconscious **4** (*AmE*) to die: *The old guy looks as if he's going to conk out any minute.*
◈ v + adv

connect /kə'nekt/

con,nect sth 'up (to sth); con,nect 'up (to sth) to join sth to a supply of electricity, gas, water, etc. or to another piece of equipment; to be joined to sth in this way: *Connect the computer up* (*to the power supply*). ◇ *Many canals connected up to major ports.*

OPP **disconnect sth (from sth)**; **disconnect (from sth)**

NOTE **Connect sth** and **connect** are often used with the same meaning.

✦ v + n/pron + adv ♦ v + adv + n ♦ v + adv

connive /kəˈnaɪv/

conˈnive at/in sth (*formal*) to ignore or seem to allow sth that you know is wrong: *The general is accused of conniving in a plot to topple the government.* ◇ *Her brother is believed to have connived at her murder.*

✦ v + prep

consign /kənˈsaɪn/

conˈsign sb/sth to sth (*formal*) **1** to get rid of or put somewhere sb/sth that you do not want: *She consigned his letter to the waste basket.* ◇ (*figurative*) *They can't just consign me to the scrap heap because I'm over fifty!* **2** to put sb/sth in an unpleasant situation: *Orphaned children were consigned to institutions.*

NOTE **Consign sb/sth to sth** is often used in the passive: *The report was consigned to the dustbin.*

✦ v + n/pron + prep

consist /kənˈsɪst/

conˈsist in sth; **conˈsist in doing sth** (*formal*) (*not used in the progressive tenses*) to have sth as the main or only feature: *A home does not consist in the quality of its architecture and decoration.*

✦ v + prep

conˈsist of sth/sb; **conˈsist of doing sth** (*not used in the progressive tenses*) to be formed from the things or people mentioned: *The exam consists of two parts: a written test and an oral.* ◇ *The group consists of senior people from education and business.* ◇ *His job consists of answering the phone and making coffee.*

SYN **be made up of sth**; **comprise sth** (*formal*)

✦ v + prep

consort /kənˈsɔːt; AmE kɑːnˈsɔːrt/

conˈsort with sb (*formal or humorous*) to spend time with sb, especially sb that other people do not approve of: *The nurses are instructed not to consort with their patients.*

✦ v + prep

contend /kənˈtend/

conˈtend with sb/sth to have to deal with a difficult person or situation: *If we leave at 8, we'll have to contend with the rush-hour traffic.* ◇ *Any-*

one who criticizes her will have me to contend with! ◇ *He's had a lot of serious problems to contend with.*

OBJ **problems**

NOTE **Contend with sb/sth** can be used in the passive.

✦ v + prep

content /kənˈtent/

conˈtent yourself with sth to accept and be satisfied with sth and not try to have or do sth better: *Martina contented herself with a single glass of wine.* ◇ *The crowd contented themselves with shouting insults.*

SYN **make do with sth**

✦ v + pron + prep

contract /kənˈtrækt/

conˌtract ˈin; **conˌtract ˈinto sth** (*BrE*) to choose to become involved in and formally agree to a system, plan, etc: *Employees can contract into the company pension scheme.*

OBJ (**pension**) **scheme** **OPP** **contract out**, **contract out of sth**

✦ v + adv ♦ v + prep

conˌtract ˈout; **conˌtract ˈout of sth** (*BrE*) to choose and formally state that you do not want to be involved in a system, plan, etc: *Only a few employees have contracted out (of the pension scheme) so far.*

OBJ (**pension**) **scheme** **OPP** **contract in**, **contract into sth**

✦ v + adv ♦ v + adv + prep

conˌtract sth ˈout (**to sb**) to arrange for work to be done by another company rather than your own: *The company contracts the printing out to an outside firm.*

OBJ **work**

✦ v + n/pron + adv ♦ v + adv + n

contribute /kənˈtrɪbjuːt; BrE also ˈkɒntrɪbjuːt/

conˈtribute to sth to help to cause sth: *The stress of losing his job contributed to his death.* ◇ *The Prime Minister contributed to his own downfall by failing to control his government.*

OBJ **death, decline, downfall**

✦ v + prep

convert /kənˈvɜːt; AmE ˈvɜːrt/

conˈvert into/to sth; **conˈvert sth into/to sth** to be able to be changed from one form, purpose, or system to another; to make sth do this: *a sofa that converts into a bed*

SYN **turn into sth, turn sb/sth into sth**

✦ v + prep ♦ v + n/pron + prep

cook /kʊk/

ˌcook sth 'up 1 to cook sth, especially very quickly: *In half an hour she had managed to cook up some delicious chilli.* OBJ **meal 2** (*informal*) to invent a story, an excuse or a plan, especially a very clever or dishonest one: *She cooked the plan up while he was away.* ◇ *They cooked up the story between the two of them.* OBJ **plan**, **story**, **scheme** SYN **concoct sth** (*more formal*)
◈ v + adv + n ◆ v + n/pron + adv

cool /kuːl/

ˌcool 'down; **ˌcool sb 'down 1** (*also* ˌcool 'off, ˌcool sb 'off) to become, or to make sb become, cool or cooler: *I'm going for a swim to cool down.* ◇ *A shower will cool you down.* **2** to become, or to make sb become, less angry or excited: *She's very angry. Give her some time to cool down.* ◇ *He tried to cool her down but she carried on shouting.*
◈ v + adv ◆ v + n/pron + adv

ˌcool 'down; **ˌcool sth 'down** to become, or to make sth become, cooler: *He waited for the soup to cool down a bit.* ◇ *Once it had cooled down outside, we went for a walk.* ◇ *Cool the soup down by stirring it.* ◇ *The rain had cooled everything down.*
NOTE **Cool** and **cool sth** are also used with this meaning, but less often.
◈ v + adv ◆ v + n/pron + adv ◆ v + adv + n (*rare*)

ˌcool 'off 1 to become less interested or enthusiastic: *Our relationship was going well, but then Laura seemed to cool off.* **2** to become less angry or excited: *When I'm angry, I go for a walk to cool off.* **3** if sth hot **cools off**, it becomes cooler: *Leave the engine to cool off before you touch it.*
◈ v + adv
▸ ˌcooling-'off period *n* **1** a period of time in which two sides in a dispute try to come to an agreement before taking any further action: *There is to be a six month cooling-off period before divorce proceedings begin.* ◇ *The union and the employers failed to reach an agreement within the cooling-off period.* **2** a period of time when you can change your mind about buying sth, such as an insurance plan, that you have agreed to buy: *Customers have a 14-day cooling-off period in which to cancel the agreement.*

ˌcool 'off; **ˌcool sb 'off** = COOL DOWN, COOL SB DOWN 1

coop /kuːp/

be ˌcooped 'up (in sth) if a person or an animal **is cooped up**, they/it are kept in a small place or inside a building: *We've been cooped up (indoors) for hours because of the rain.*
◈ be + v + adv

cop /kɒp; AmE kɑːp/ (-pp-)

ˌcop 'off (with sb) (*BrE, slang*) to meet sb and start a sexual relationship with them
◈ v + adv

ˌcop 'out; **ˌcop 'out of sth** (*informal*) to avoid or not do sth that you should be doing, because you are afraid, shy, lazy, etc: *Lots of people said they'd help but they've all copped out.* ◇ *You can't just cop out of difficult decisions.*
◈ v + adv ◆ v + adv + prep
▸ **'cop-out** *n* (*informal, disapproving*) a way of, or an excuse for, avoiding sth you should be doing: *You're not too busy to come! That's just a cop-out.*

copy /'kɒpi; AmE 'kɑːpi/ (copies, copying, copied, copied)

ˌcopy sth 'down to write sth exactly as it is written somewhere else: *If I don't copy the phone number down, I'll forget it!* ◇ *We copied down what the teacher had written on the blackboard.*
SYN **write sth down**
◈ v + n/pron + adv ◆ v + adv + n

ˌcopy sb 'in (on sth) to make sure that sb receives a copy of a letter, an electronic message, etc. that you are sending to sb else: *Please copy me in on all correspondence.*
◈ v + n/pron + adv ◆ v + adv + n (*rare*)

ˌcopy sth 'out to write sth out again; to make a copy of sth that is already written or printed: *She copied out a recipe she found in a library book.*
SYN **write sth out**
◈ v + adv + n ◆ v + n/pron + adv

cordon /'kɔːdn; AmE 'kɔːrdn/

ˌcordon sth 'off to stop people going into an area by forming a line or ring around it with police, soldiers, objects, etc: *Police cordoned off the area until the bomb was defused.*
OBJ **area**, **street** SYN **close sth off (to sb/sth)**
NOTE **Cordon sth off** is often used in the passive: *The roads were cordoned off.*
◈ v + adv + n ◆ v + n/pron + adv

cost /kɒst; AmE kɔːst/

ˌcost sth 'out to estimate how much money will be needed for sth: *We'll have to cost the work out before we make a decision.* ◇ *Have you costed out how much it will be to hire another member of staff?*
NOTE **Cost sth** is usually used with this meaning.
◈ v + n/pron + adv ◆ v + adv + n

cosy (*BrE*) (*AmE* **cozy**) /'kəʊzi; *AmE* 'koʊzi/ (**cosies, cosying, cosied, cosied**)

,**cosy 'up to sb** (*informal, especially AmE*) to try to become friendly with sb, especially in order to gain an advantage for yourself: *She's only cosying up to him because she needs his help.*
ⓢⓨⓝ **cuddle up to sb** (*BrE, less frequent*)
✦ v + adv + prep

cotton /'kɒtn; *AmE* 'kɑːtn/

,**cotton 'on (to sth)** (*informal*) to come to understand or realize sth without being told directly: *She cottons on very quickly.* ◇ *It took him a while to cotton on to what I was trying to say.*
ⓢⓨⓝ **catch on (to sth)**
✦ v + adv

'**cotton to sb/sth** (*old-fashioned, AmE, informal*) to begin to like or approve of sb/sth: *I didn't much cotton to the idea at first.*
ⓝⓞⓣⓔ Cotton to sb is often used in negative sentences.
✦ v + prep

cough /kɒf; *AmE* kɔːf/

,**cough 'up**; ,**cough sth 'up** (*informal*) **1** (*especially BrE*) to pay for sth or give sb money unwillingly: *You owe me £20. Come on, cough up!* ◇ *Don't cough up the money until the job's finished.*
ⓢⓨⓝ **pay up 2** (*BrE*) to admit sth or give sb information unwillingly: *Come on, cough up: where've you been?* ⓢⓨⓝ **own up (to sth/to doing sth)**; **confess (to sth/to doing sth)** (*more formal*)
✦ v + adv ◆ v + adv + n ◆ v + n/pron + adv

,**cough sth 'up** to force sth out of the throat or lungs by coughing: *He's been coughing up blood.*
ⓞⓑⓙ **blood**
✦ v + adv + n ◆ v + n/pron + adv

count /kaʊnt/

,**count a'gainst sb** to be a disadvantage to sb: *I'm sure that being late for the interview counted against me.*
ⓢⓨⓝ **weigh against sb** (*formal*)
✦ v + prep

,**count a'mong sb/sth**; ,**count sb/sth a'mong sth** to be considered, or to consider sb/sth, to be part of the group mentioned: *She counts among the top ten marathon runners in the country.* ◇ *The band count John Lennon among their influences.* ◇ *I no longer counted myself among his friends.*
ⓝⓞⓣⓔ Count sb/sth among sb/sth is more frequent than count among sb/sth: *Egypt was counted among the most powerful countries in the world.*
✦ v + prep ◆ v + n/pron + prep

,**count 'down (to sth)**, ,**count sth 'down** to be waiting for an important or exciting day, event, etc. and be counting the number of days, minutes, etc. there are before it: *The whole world was counting down to the new millennium.* ◇ *I'm counting down the days until my trip.*
✦ v + adv ◆ v + adv + n ◆ v + n/pron + adv (*rare*)
▸ '**countdown (to sth)** *n* **1** the act of counting backwards to zero, for example before a spacecraft is sent into space **2** the period immediately before sth important happens

,**count sb 'in** to include sb in a group or an activity: *If you're going to the theatre, you can count me in.*
ⓢⓨⓝ **deal sb in** (*less formal*) ⓞⓟⓟ **count sb out**
✦ v + n/pron + adv

,**count 'off** (*AmE*) if people **count off**, they say loudly in order the numbers they have been given: *He made everyone count off.*
✦ v + adv

'**count on sb/sth**; '**count on doing sth**; '**count on sb/sth doing sth** (*also* '**count upon sb/sth**, '**count upon doing sth**, '**count upon sb/sth doing sth** *more formal*) to rely on sb to do sth; to expect sth to happen and make plans in an appropriate way: *You can count on me!* ◇ *'I'm sure he'll help us.' 'Don't count on it.'* ◇ *She hadn't counted on going swimming when she packed.* ◇ *I'm counting on your support.* ◇ *I'm counting on you to support me.*
ⓢⓨⓝ **bank on sb/sth, bank on doing sth, bank on sb/sth doing sth; reckon on sb/sth, reckon on doing sth, reckon on sb/sth doing sth**
ⓝⓞⓣⓔ These phrasal verbs can be used in the passive: *She can be counted upon to contribute good ideas.*
✦ v + prep ◆ v + prep + n/pron + to inf

,**count sb 'out**; ,**count sb 'out of sth** (*informal*) to not include sb in a group or an activity: *You may enjoy those games, but you can count me out.*
ⓢⓨⓝ **deal sb out, deal sb out of sth**
ⓞⓟⓟ **count sb in**
✦ v + n/pron + adv ◆ v + n/pron + adv + prep

,**count sth 'out** to count coins, etc. one by one and put them somewhere: *He counted out the exact money (on the counter).*
ⓞⓑⓙ **money, change, notes/coins**
✦ v + adv + n ◆ v + n/pron + adv

,**count to'wards sth** (*also* ,**count to'ward sth** *especially AmE*) to be included as part of sth you hope to obtain or achieve: *Marks from this test count towards your final grade.* ◇ *These sales will not count toward meeting the target.*
ⓝⓞⓣⓔ Count towards/toward sth can be used in the passive: *These payments may be counted towards your pension.*
✦ v + prep

,count sb/sth 'up to add together the number of things or people in a group: *Count up the number of times you've been abroad.*
[OBJ] **number**
[NOTE] **Count sb/sth** is used with the same meaning.
◆ v + adv + n ◆ v + n/pron + adv

'count upon sb/sth; 'count upon doing sth; 'count on sb/sth doing sth = COUNT ON SB/STH, COUNT ON DOING STH, COUNT ON SB/STH DOING STH

couple /'kʌpl/

'couple sb/sth with sb/sth to link one person, thing or situation with another: *The large number of new graduates, coupled with high unemployment, means that there is fierce competition for jobs.*
[NOTE] **Couple sb/sth with sb/sth** is usually used in the passive.
◆ v + n/pron + prep

cover /'kʌvə(r)/

,cover sth 'over (with sth) to cover sth completely, especially to hide or protect it: *Put the bulbs in a bowl and cover them over with soil.* ◇ *The shopping mall is covered over with an enormous glass roof.*
[NOTE] **Cover sth (with sth)** is used more often with this meaning.
◆ v + n/pron + adv ◆ v + adv + n

,cover 'up; ,cover yourself 'up (with sth) to put on more clothes: *Make sure you cover up before going out in the sun.* ◇ *Cover yourself up. It's cold.*
◆ v + adv ◆ v + pron + adv

,cover 'up (for sb/sth), ,cover sth 'up to try hard to stop people finding out about a mistake, a crime, etc.; to hide the truth about sth: *He's always covering up for her.* ◇ *The government's attempts to cover up the scandal failed.*
[OBJ] **scandal, mistake, truth** [SYN] **conceal sth** (*more formal*), **hide sth**
◆ v + adv ◆ v + adv + n ◆ v + pron + adv ◆ v + n + adv (*less frequent*)
▶ **'cover-up** *n* [usually sing.] an act of hiding a mistake, a crime, etc: *The opposition accused the government of a cover-up.*

,cover sb/sth 'up to put sth over sb/sth in order to hide or protect them/it: *You can cover up ugly pipes with wooden boxes.* ◇ *There was something on the table covered up with a cloth.*
◆ v + adv + n ◆ v + n/pron + adv

cozy /'kəʊzi; AmE 'koʊzi/ (cozies, cozying, cozied, cozied)

,cozy 'up to sb (*AmE*) = COSY UP TO SB

crack /kræk/

,crack 'down; ,crack 'down on sb/sth to try harder to prevent people breaking a rule, using sth harmful, committing a crime, etc. and deal severely with those who do: *Police are cracking down hard on drug dealers.* ◇ *The government is cracking down on misleading food labelling.*
[SYN] **clamp down, clamp down on sb/sth**
◆ v + adv ◆ v + adv + prep
▶ **'crackdown (on sb/sth)** *n* severe action that is taken to prevent people committing a crime, opposing the government, etc: *a police crackdown on car crime*

,crack 'on (with sth) (*BrE, informal*) to work hard and do sth quickly: *We'd better crack on with the painting before it gets dark.*
[SYN] **get on (with sth)**
◆ v + adv

,crack 'up (*informal*) to become physically or mentally ill because you are under pressure: *She's cracking up under the strain.*
◆ v + adv
▶ **'crack-up** *n* (*informal, especially AmE*) a period of mental illness caused by pressure

,crack 'up; ,crack sb 'up (*informal*) to start laughing a lot; to make sb laugh a lot: *Everybody cracked up when he fell over.* ◇ *She's so funny — she cracks me up!*
[SYN] **crease up, crease sb up** (*BrE*)
[NOTE] **Crack sb up** is not used in the passive.
◆ v + adv ◆ v + n/pron + adv
[IDM] **be ,cracked 'up to be sth** (*informal*) to be as good, clever, exciting, etc. as people think or say sb/sth is: *Stardom is not all it's cracked up to be.* ◇ *She's not as good as she's cracked up to be.*

cram /kræm/ (-mm-)

,cram 'into sth; ,cram sb/sth 'in; ,cram sb/sth 'in/'into sth to go into a place or space that is too small for everyone/everything; to push or force sb/sth into a place or space that is too small: *Six of us crammed into Rob's Mini.* ◇ *I only had three days in New York, but I crammed in as much sightseeing as I could.* ◇ *He crammed all the sweets into his mouth.* ◇ *You can't cram eight children into the car!*
◆ v + prep ◆ v + n/pron + adv ◆ v + adv + n ◆ v + n/pron + prep

crank /kræŋk/

,crank sth 'out (*informal, especially AmE*) to produce sth quickly and in large amounts: *The plant can crank out about 63 cars an hour.*
[SYN] **churn sth out; turn sth out**
◆ v + adv + n ◆ v + n/pron + adv

,crank sth 'up (*informal*) **1** to make a machine start working or work better: *It's time to crank up the air conditioning.* **2** to make music, etc. louder:

They cranked the music up when the party started. **OBJ music, volume** **SYN** **turn sth up** (*more formal*)
◈ v + n/pron + adv ♦ v + adv + n

crash /kræʃ/

,**crash a'round** (*also* ,**crash a'bout/'round** *especially BrE*) (*informal*) to move around making a lot of noise: *I heard her crashing about in the bathroom.*
◈ v + adv

,**crash 'down** to fall with a very loud noise: *Passengers had a lucky escape when a huge tree crashed down onto a bus.* ◇ *John's hand came crashing down on the table* (= he hit the table hard with his hand). ◇ (*figurative*) *All my dreams came crashing down around me* (= I completely failed in what I wanted to do).
NOTE Crash down is usually followed by a phrase beginning with a preposition.
◈ v + adv

,**crash 'out** (*informal, especially BrE*) to go to sleep because you are very tired: *I was so tired I crashed out in an armchair.*
SYN **flake out** (*BrE*)
◈ v + adv

,**crash 'out of sth** (in sport) to lose a game very badly and so not be able to continue to take part in a competition: *England crashed out of the World Cup.*
NOTE This phrasal verb is used especially in newspapers.
◈ v + adv + prep

,**crash 'round** (*especially BrE*) = CRASH AROUND

crawl /krɔːl/

'**crawl with sb/sth** (*usually used in the progressive tenses*) to be full of moving people, animals, insects, etc. in an unpleasant way: *The place is crawling with cops!*
OBJ police, insects
◈ v + prep

cream /kriːm/

,**cream sb/sth 'off** to take away the best people or things in a group or an amount of money, usually for your own advantage: *The best pupils are creamed off into special classes.* ◇ *The company's directors are creaming off the profits.*
◈ v + adv + n ♦ v + n/pron + adv

crease /kriːs/

,**crease 'up**; ,**crease sb 'up** (*BrE, informal*) to start laughing; to make sb start laughing: *We all creased up when we saw her hat!* ◇ *His programme always creases me up.*
SYN **crack up, crack sb up**
◈ v + adv ♦ v + n/pron + adv

credit /'kredɪt/

'**credit A with B**; '**credit B to A 1** to believe that sb/sth is responsible for sth or for doing sth, especially sth good: *Bach is credited with performing the first solo on a piano.* ◇ *She credits her good looks and intelligence to her father's side of the family.* **2** to consider that sb/sth has a particular good quality or characteristic: *I had credited him with more sense.* ◇ *Numerous health benefits are credited to this natural oil.*
NOTE Credit A with B is often used in the passive. ♦ You can also use the pattern **credit sb/sth as sth**, especially in the passive: *The cheetah is generally credited as the world's fastest animal.*
◈ v + n/pron + prep

creep /kriːp/ (**crept, crept** /krept/)

,**creep 'in**; ,**creep 'into sth** to start happening or affecting sb/sth gradually: *I thought I'd decided, but then doubts started to creep in.* ◇ *A hint of sarcasm crept into his voice.* ◇ *More and more foreign words are creeping into the language.*
◈ v + adv ♦ v + prep

,**creep 'over sb/sth** if a feeling **creeps over** you, or an expression **creeps over** your face, it gradually affects you: *A feeling of tiredness began to creep over her.* ◇ *A sly smile crept over her lips.*
SYN **steal over sb/sth**
◈ v + prep

,**creep 'up 1** if a price, an amount, etc. **creeps up**, it rises very gradually: *House prices are starting to creep up.* **2** (**on sb**) to move nearer to sb/sth slowly and quietly without being seen or heard: *Don't creep up on me like that!* ◇ *Jack crept up behind me.* **SYN** **steal up (on sb)**
◈ v + adv

,**creep 'up on sb 1** if an event, a date, etc. **creeps up on** you, it arrives before you are really ready for it: *The exams just seemed to creep up on me.* **2** if a feeling, etc. **creeps up on** you, it starts to affect you before you realize it: *Anorexia can creep up on young girls when they least expect it.*
◈ v + adv + prep

crop /krɒp; AmE krɑːp/ (-pp-)

,**crop 'up** (*informal*) to appear, happen, etc. when it is not expected: *I can't make it tonight — something's cropped up.* ◇ *Her name keeps cropping up everywhere.*
SYN **come up**
◈ v + adv

cross /krɒs; AmE krɔːs/

,**cross sb/sth 'off**; ,**cross sb/sth 'off sth** to remove sb's name or an item from a list by drawing a line through it because you have dealt with them/it or they/it are no longer involved: *Cross off any items we've already got. ◇ Jane won't be coming, so we can cross her off the list.*

$\overline{\text{SYN}}$ **delete sth** (*more formal*)

◈ v + n/pron + adv ◆ v + adv + n ◆ v + n/pron + prep

,**cross sth 'out/'through** to remove words from a text by drawing a line through them, usually because they are wrong: *I crossed his name out and wrote mine instead. ◇ You've spelt it wrong. Cross it out and try again.*

$\overline{\text{OBJ}}$ **word, name** $\overline{\text{SYN}}$ **delete sth** (*more formal*)

◈ v + n/pron + adv ◆ v + adv + n

,**cross 'over 1** (*also* ,**cross 'over sth**) (*especially BrE*) to go from one side of sth, for example a road/street, a room, etc. to the other: *Let's cross over to the other side. ◇ She crossed over the road.*

$\overline{\text{OBJ}}$ **road, bridge 2** (**into/to sth**) to move from one style or type of music, culture, politics, etc. to another; to combine parts of different styles or types: *They're a blues band who have succeeded in crossing over to jazz.*

◈ **1** v + adv ◆ v + prep
   2 v + adv

▶ '**crossover** *n* a successful combination of different styles or types of music or culture; a successful change from one style or type to another: *a fresh and exciting rock-dance crossover ◇ a crossover artist*

,**cross sth 'through** = CROSS STH OUT/THROUGH

crouch /kraʊtʃ/

'**crouch over sb/sth** to bend over sb/sth so you are near them/it: *She crouched over the injured man, checking his wounds.*

◈ v + prep

crowd /kraʊd/

,**crowd a'round**; ,**crowd a'round sb/sth** (*especially AmE*) = CROWD ROUND, CROWD ROUND SB/STH

,**crowd 'in**; ,**crowd 'into sth** to move in large numbers into a small place: *As soon as the doors opened people began to crowd in. ◇ We all crowded into the lift. ◇ (figurative) Memories she would rather forget came crowding in. ◇ (figurative) Doubts crowded into my mind.*

$\overline{\text{SYN}}$ **pile in, pile into sth**

◈ v + adv ◆ v + prep

,**crowd sb/sth 'in**; ,**crowd sb/sth 'into/'onto sth** to put a large number of people or things into a small space: *I doubt if we can crowd any more people in — the place is packed already. ◇ We were all crowded into a small area behind the goal.*

$\overline{\text{SYN}}$ **cram sb/sth in, cram sb/sth in/into sth; pack sb/sth in, pack sb/sth into sth**

◈ v + n/pron + adv ◆ v + adv + n ◆ v + n/pron + prep

,**crowd 'in** (**on sb**) if high buildings, mountains, etc. **crowd in**, they seem to surround you and threaten you or have a strong effect on you: *The high walls seemed to crowd in (on her). ◇ (figurative) He tried to resist the fears that were crowding in on him.*

◈ v + adv + prep

,**crowd sb/sth 'onto sth** = CROWD SB/STH IN, CROWD SB/STH INTO/ONTO STH

,**crowd sb/sth 'out**; ,**crowd sb/sth 'out of sth** if a number of people or things **crowd out** other people or things, they are present in such large numbers that there is no room for anyone or anything else: *Tourists are crowding the regular customers out of the bar. ◇ (figurative) Small shops are increasingly being crowded out by the big supermarkets.*

$\overline{\text{SYN}}$ **squeeze sb/sth out, squeeze sb/sth out of sth**

◈ v + n/pron + adv ◆ v + adv + n ◆
   v + n/pron + adv + prep

,**crowd 'round**; ,**crowd 'round sb/sth** (*especially BrE*) (*AmE usually* ,**crowd a'round**, ,**crowd a'round sb/sth**) to gather in large numbers around sb/sth: *People were crowding around to see what was going on. ◇ Fans crowded round him to ask for his autograph.*

◈ v + adv ◆ v + prep

crumple /'krʌmpl/

,**crumple sth 'up** to crush sth, especially a piece of paper, into a ball: *She crumpled his letter up without even looking at it.*

$\overline{\text{OBJ}}$ **paper**

◈ v + n/pron + adv ◆ v + adv + n

cry /kraɪ/ (**cries, crying, cried, cried**)

'**cry for sth** to ask for or demand sth in a forceful or urgent way: *The families of the victims are crying for justice. ◇ Listen! That sounds like somebody crying* (= calling) *for help.*

$\overline{\text{OBJ}}$ **help, mercy**

◈ v + prep

,**cry 'off**; ,**cry 'off sth**; ,**cry 'off doing sth** (*BrE*) to decide not to do sth you have promised or agreed to do: *We'd arranged to go together but Luis cried off at the last moment. ◇ Why did you cry off training last night?*

$\overline{\text{SYN}}$ **pull out, pull out of sth, pull out of doing sth**

→ *see also* BEG OFF, BEG OFF STH, BEG OFF DOING STH

◈ v + adv ◆ v + prep

,**cry 'out** to make a loud sound without words because you are hurt, afraid, surprised, etc: *She cried out in/with pain.*

◈ v + adv

,cry 'out sth to shout sth loudly: *He suddenly cried out, 'Stop at once!'* ◇ *She could hear a voice crying out her name.*
  ⊕ v + adv + speech ♦ v + adv + n
IDM for ,crying out 'loud! (*spoken, informal*) used to show that you are surprised or angry about sth: *For crying out loud! What did you do that for?*

,cry 'out against sth to protest strongly about sth: *People have been crying out against this abuse for years.*
  ⊕ v + adv + prep
▶ 'outcry (against/at/over sth) *n* [C] [U] a public reaction of strong protest against sth: *There is sure to be a massive outcry against the proposals.*

,cry 'out for sth (*usually used in the progressive tenses*) to clearly need sth very quickly: *The group is crying out for new members.* ◇ *The whole system was crying out for a radical review.*
  ⊕ v + adv + prep

cuddle /'kʌdl/

,cuddle 'up (to/against sb), ,cuddle 'up together if children, pets, etc. cuddle up, they sit or lie close to each other or sb else, because they need warmth or comfort, or want to show affection: *Jack cuddled up to his mother.* ◇ *The cubs cuddle up together for warmth.*
  SYN snuggle up (to/against sb/sth)
  ⊕ v + adv ♦ v + adv + adv

,cuddle 'up to sb/sth (*BrE, informal, rare*) to try to be friendly to sb in order to gain an advantage for yourself: *Just before the election they started cuddling up to the government.*
  SYN cosy up to sb
  ⊕ v + adv + prep

culminate /'kʌlmɪneɪt/

'culminate in sth (*also* 'culminate with sth *less frequent*) (*formal*) to end with a particular result or conclusion, or at a particular point: *The negotiations culminated in an agreement acceptable to all sides.*
  ⊕ v + prep

curl /kɜːl; *AmE* kɜːrl/

,curl 'up; be ,curled 'up 1 to lie down or sit down with your back curved and your knees and arms close to your body: *I love curling up in an armchair with a good book.* ◇ *The cat was curled up asleep under the bush.* 2 if the edges of pages, leaves, etc. curl up they bend towards the middle: *The pages had all curled up at the corners.*
  ⊕ v + adv ♦ be + v + adv

,curl sth 'up; ,curl yourself 'up to bend sth/yourself into a tight curved shape: *She curled her legs up under her on the sofa.* ◇ *He curled himself up under the covers and went to sleep.*
  ⊕ v + n/pron + adv

curse /kɜːs; *AmE* kɜːrs/

be 'cursed with sth to have or suffer from sth bad: *He was cursed with poor health from childhood.* ◇ *I've always been cursed with bad luck.*
  ⊕ be + v + prep

curtain /'kɜːtn; *AmE* 'kɜːrtn/

,curtain sth off (from sth) to separate part of a room with a curtain or curtains: *A corner of the room was curtained off.*
  ⊕ v + n/pron + adv ♦ v + adv + n

cut /kʌt/ (cutting, cut, cut)

	~ across		~ off
	~ away	70	~ out, out of
	~ back		~ out for
69	~ down		~ through
	~ in		~ up
	~ into		

,cut a'cross sth 1 (*also* ,cut 'through sth) to take a short route (a short cut) across a place instead of going around it: *We'll get there quicker if we cut across the fields.* 2 to affect or be true for people in different groups that usually remain separate: *Opposition to the proposal cuts across party boundaries.* **OBJ** boundary, division 3 to interrupt and stop sth: *The sound of the fire alarm cut across his attempt to explain.*
  ⊕ v + prep

,cut sth a'way (from sth) to remove sth by cutting with a knife or a sharp tool: *Cut away any dead branches.*
  ⊕ v + adv + n ♦ v + n/pron + adv

,cut 'back (on sth) 1 to reduce sth such as the amount sb spends or produces: *The recession means that everyone is cutting back.* ◇ *We've had to cut back on staff to save money.* 2 (*especially AmE*) to eat, drink or use less of a particular thing, usually for your health: *I smoke too much. I must cut back.* ◇ *The doctor's told me to cut back on red meat.*
  → *see also* CUT STH BACK 1; CUT DOWN
  ⊕ v + adv
▶ 'cutback (in sth) *n* [usually pl.] a reduction in sth: *cutbacks in public spending*

,cut sth 'back 1 to reduce sth a lot, especially to save money or improve the environment or your health: *Government funding is being cut back.* ◇ *We have agreed to cut back CFC emissions by the end of the century.* **OBJ** production, spending, pollution **SYN** pare sth down (to sth), pare sth back (to sth) **NOTE** Cut sth back is often used in the passive in this meaning. 2 to reduce the size of a plant, a bush, etc. by cutting parts off: *That rose bush needs cutting back a lot.* **OBJ** bush, tree **SYN** prune sth
  ⊕ v + adv + n ♦ v + pron + adv ♦ v + n + adv (*less frequent*)

,cut 'down (on sth) **1** to reduce the amount or quantity of sth: *Recycling cuts down on waste.* ◇ *I've spent too much already this month — I'll have to cut down a bit* (= spend less money). **2** to consume, use or buy less of sth: *The doctor's told me to cut down on fatty foods.* ◇ *I haven't stopped smoking, but I've cut down to five a day.*
→ *see also* CUT STH DOWN 1; CUT BACK
⊕ v + adv

,cut sb 'down (*formal, BrE*) to kill sb: *He was cut down by pneumonia at an early age.*
NOTE Cut sb down is often used in the passive in this meaning.
⊕ v + n/pron + adv ♦ v + adv + n

,cut sb/sth 'down (*AmE, informal*) to make sb feel or look stupid, especially in front of other people: *He always cuts her down in front of his friends.* ◇ *She's always cutting down my lifestyle.*
SYN put sb down
⊕ v + n/pron + adv ♦ v + adv + n
IDM cut sb down to 'size to show sb that they are not as important as they think they are
▶ 'cutdown (*AmE*) (*BrE* 'put-down) *n* (*informal*) a remark or criticism that is intended to make sb feel or look stupid

,cut sth 'down **1** to reduce the amount or quantity of sth: *Measures were introduced to cut down the number of road accidents involving children.* ◇ *The policy aims at cutting down exhaust emissions.* **OBJ** number, costs, amount **SYN** reduce sth (*more formal*) **NOTE** Cut sth can also be used with this meaning. Cut sth, not cut sth down is used for reducing the cost or the price of sth: *Petrol/gas prices have been cut.* → *see also* CUT DOWN; CUT STH BACK 1 **2** to make a tree, etc. fall down by cutting it at the base: *Every time we cut a tree down, we plant a new one.* **OBJ** tree **SYN** chop sth down; fell sth (*more formal*) **3** to reduce the length of sth: *Please cut your article down to 1 000 words.* **SYN** shorten sth (*more formal*) **NOTE** Cut sth can also be used with this meaning.
⊕ v + adv + n ♦ v + n/pron + adv

,cut 'in (on sb/sth) to interrupt sb/sth: *'Listen to me!' she cut in impatiently.* **SYN** interrupt (sb/sth) → *see also* CUT INTO STH 2 **2** (on sb/sth) (of a vehicle or a driver) to move suddenly in front of another vehicle in a dangerous way, leaving little space between the two vehicles: *The lorry cut in (on me) suddenly and I had to brake sharply.* **3** (of an engine, a motor or a piece of equipment) to start working automatically, especially after another source of power has failed: *If the power fails, the generator will cut in.* **SYN** kick in **4** (*AmE, informal*) to push in front of people who have been waiting in a line: *Someone tried to cut in in front of us.* ◇ *She saw some friends in line and cut in with them.* **SYN** push in (*BrE*)
⊕ v + adv **1** also v + adv + speech

,cut sb 'in (on sth) (*informal*) to include sb in a deal and give them a share of the profits: *Do you think we can cut Harris in on the deal?*
⊕ v + n/pron + adv

,cut 'into sth **1** to make a mark, an opening or a wound in sth with a knife or a sharp object: *Make some pencil guidelines before you cut into the wood.* ◇ *The rope was cutting into her wrists* (= because it was very tight). **OBJ** cake, meat, etc. **2** to interrupt sth: *His voice cut into her thoughts.* **OBJ** thoughts **3** to begin to use part or too much of sb's time, sth that belongs to sb else, etc: *My work's cutting into my free time at the moment.* ◇ *The independent stations are cutting into our audience.* **OBJ** time **SYN** encroach on/upon sth (*more formal*)
⊕ v + prep

,cut sb 'off **1** to refuse to let sb have any of your money or property after you die: *He cut his son off without a penny.* **OBJ** son, daughter **SYN** disinherit sb (*more formal*) → *see also* CUT SB OUT, CUT SB OUT OF STH **2** to end a relationship with sb because you do not want to see or talk to them any more: *His family have cut him off since he told them what he'd done.* **3** to interrupt a telephone conversation by breaking the connection: *Operator, I've just been cut off.* **NOTE** Cut sb off is usually used in the passive in this meaning.
⊕ **1,2** v + n/pron + adv ♦ v + adv + n (*less frequent*) **3** v + n/pron + adv
IDM be cut off in your 'prime to die suddenly when you are still young, strong and successful

,cut sb/sth 'off **1** (*also* ,cut yourself 'off) (from sb/sth) to separate sb/sth/yourself physically or socially from other people or things: *His deafness cut him off from his family and friends.* ◇ *She cut herself off from music after her marriage.* ◇ *Why has he cut off all contact with his family?* ◇ *The farm gets completely cut off in the winter.* ◇ (*figurative*) *Politicians are cut off from the reality of poverty.* **SYN** isolate sb/sth/yourself (from sb/sth) **NOTE** Cut sb/sth/yourself off is often used in the passive in this meaning: *The children were cut off by the tide.* **2** to interrupt sb when they are speaking: *He cut me off in mid-sentence.* ◇ *My explanation was abruptly cut off.* **3** to stop the supply of gas, water or electricity to sb's home: *The gas company threatened to cut them off if they didn't pay the bill.* ◇ *The water supply had been cut off.* **4** (*AmE*) = CUT SB/STH UP *A sports car cut me off as I turned into the road.* **5** to prevent sb from reaching or leaving a place; to stop sb: *Try to cut him off at the traffic lights.*
⊕ v + n/pron + adv ♦ v + adv + n
▶ 'cut-off *n* an act of stopping sth
→ *see also* CUT-OFF at CUT STH OFF; CUT-OFF at CUT STH OFF, CUT STH OFF STH

,**cut sth 'off** to block or get in the way of sth, etc: *The police cut off all their escape routes.* ◇ *The new hotel cuts off our view of the sea.*

OBJ **route, aid, supplies**

◆ v + adv + n ◆ v + n/pron + adv

▶ **'cut-off** *n* a point or a limit when you stop sth: *a cut-off in aid* ◇ *What is the cut-off date for registration?*

→ *see also* CUT-OFF at CUT SB/STH OFF; CUT-OFF at CUT STH OFF, CUT STH OFF STH

,**cut sth 'off**; ,**cut sth 'off sth** to remove sth by cutting it with a knife or a sharp tool: *He cut off a metre of cloth from the roll.* ◇ *Mind you don't cut your fingers off!* ◇ *She's **had** all her hair cut off.* ◇ *If the photo is too large for the frame, cut a bit off the top.* ◇ *(figurative) Five seconds has been cut off the world record.*

SYN **chop sth off, chop sth off sth**

◆ v + n/pron + adv ◆ v + adv + n ◆ v + n/pron + prep

▶ **'cut-offs** *n* [pl.] trousers/pants that have been made shorter by cutting off part of the legs

▶ **'cut-off** *adj* [only before noun] **cut-off** trousers/pants have been made shorter by cutting off part of the legs

→ *see also* CUT-OFF at CUT SB/STH OFF; CUT-OFF at CUT STH OFF

▶ **'offcut** *n* (*especially BrE*) a piece of wood, paper, etc. that remains after the main piece has been cut

,**cut yourself 'off** (from sb/sth) = CUT SB OFF 1

,**cut 'out** if an engine or a motor **cuts out**, it suddenly stops working: *One of the aircraft's engines cut out.*

◆ v + adv

▶ **'cut-out** *n* (*especially BrE*) a safety device that stops an electric current from flowing through sth: *A cut-out stops the kettle boiling dry.*

→ *see also* CUT-OUT at CUT STH OUT, CUT STH OUT OF STH

,**cut 'out**; ,**cut 'out of sth** (*AmE*) **1** (of a vehicle or a driver) to move suddenly sideways out of a line of traffic: *Did you see the way the car in front cut out?* **2** (*old-fashioned, slang*) to leave: *I'm cutting out* (*of here*). *See you later.*

◆ v + adv ◆ v + adv + prep

,**cut sb 'out**; ,**cut sb 'out of sth** to not allow sb to be involved in sth: *If we deliver the goods ourselves, we can cut out the middleman.* ◇ *Don't cut your parents out of your lives!* ◇ *She cut me out of her will* (= refused to let me have any of her money or property after she died).

→ *see also* CUT SB OFF 1

◆ v + adv + n ◆ v + n/pron + adv ◆ v + n/pron + adv + prep

,**cut sth 'out 1** to make sth unnecessary: *Cut out some of the administration by computerizing your records.* ◇ *The new fast train service cuts out the need for a long bus journey.* **OBJ** **need 2** (*informal*) to stop doing, using or eating sth: *I've cut out sweets to try to lose weight.* **OBJ** **smoking,**

drink, sweets 3 (*informal*) to block light or sound: *That tree in front of the window cuts out the light.* **OBJ** **light, noise** **SYN** **block sth out 4** (*informal*) used to tell sb to stop doing or saying sth that is annoying you: *I'm sick of you two arguing — just cut it out!* ◇ *Now cut out the jokes and pay attention!* **OBJ** **it, that 5** to make sth by cutting: *They managed to cut out a path through the jungle.*

◆ v + n/pron + adv ◆ v + adv + n

,**cut sth 'out**; ,**cut sth 'out of sth 1** to remove sth you want from sth larger by cutting; to cut the shape of sth from a piece of fabric, paper, etc: *Simply cut out and return the coupon.* ◇ *She cut the article out of the newspaper.* ◇ *The children enjoy cutting shapes out of coloured paper.* **OBJ** **article, picture 2** to remove sth bad from sth by cutting: *I cut out the bad parts of the apple.* **3** (*informal*) to leave sth out of a piece of writing, etc: *You can cut out the unimportant details.* **SYN** **omit sth**

◆ v + n/pron + adv ◆ v + adv + n ◆ v + n/pron + adv + prep

IDM **have your 'work cut out (for you)** (*formal*) to face a difficult task or situation: *You'll have your work cut out to beat him.*

▶ **'cut-out** *n* a shape cut out of paper, wood, etc: *a cardboard cut-out*

→ *see also* CUT-OUT at CUT OUT

be ,**cut 'out for sth**; be ,**cut 'out to do/be sth** (*informal*) to have the qualities and abilities needed for sth: *I don't think I'm cut out for country life.* ◇ *He's not cut out to be a politician.*

NOTE This phrasal verb is usually used in negative sentences.

◆ be + v + adv + prep ◆ be + v + adv + to inf

,**cut 'through sth 1** = CUT ACROSS STH 1 *The path cuts through the wood.* ◇ *It should be quicker if we cut through town.* **2** to pass through sth by cutting: *Will this saw cut through metal?* ◇ *(figurative) The sharp wind cut through his shirt.* ◇ *(figurative) The pain cut through him like a knife.* **3** to overcome a difficulty that is preventing you from making progress: *Once you cut through the technical language the report is easy to understand.* ◇ *The yacht cut smoothly through the waves.* **4** to interrupt sth: *His voice cut through her thoughts.*

→ *see also* CUT STH THROUGH STH

◆ v + prep

,**cut 'through sth** to make a path or passage through sth by cutting: *They had to use their knives to cut a path through the undergrowth.*

OBJ **path**

→ *see also* CUT THROUGH STH

◆ v + n/pron + prep

,**cut sb 'up** (*informal*) **1** to injure sb by cutting them with a knife, a piece of glass, etc: *He was very badly cut up in the fight.* **2** to make sb very emotionally upset: *She's still very cut up about the divorce.* NOTE **Cut sb up** is usually used in the passive in this meaning.

◆ **1** v + n/pron + adv ◆ v + adv + n
  2 v + n/pron + adv

,cut **sb/sth 'up** (*BrE*) (*AmE* ,cut **sb/sth 'off**) (of a vehicle or a driver) to suddenly drive in front of another vehicle in a dangerous way: *Did you see how he cut me up?*

SYN **carve sb/sth up** (*BrE*)

◆ v + n/pron + adv ◆ v + adv + n

,cut **sth 'up** to divide sth into small pieces with a knife or a sharp tool: *Who's going to cut up the vegetables?*

SYN **chop sth up**

◆ v + n/pron + adv ◆ v + adv + n

Dd

dab /dæb/ (-bb-)

'dab at sth (with sth) to touch sth, especially your face, several times, quickly and lightly: *She was crying and dabbing at her eyes with a handkerchief.* ◇ *He gently dabbed at his cuts with a piece of cotton wool.*

OBJ **my, your, etc. eyes**
NOTE **Dab sth** can be used with the same meaning: *She dabbed her eyes with a handkerchief.*
⊕ v + prep

dab sth 'off to remove sth such as a stain, sth you have spilled on sth, etc. with quick, light movements: *Dab the coffee off with your handkerchief.*
⊕ v + n/pron + adv ♦ v + adv + n

dab sth 'on (with sth) to put sth on a surface with quick, light movements: *Dab the paint on with a sponge.* ◇ *She dabbed on a little perfume.*
⊕ v + n/pron + adv ♦ v + adv + n

dabble /'dæbl/

'dabble in sth to take part in an activity or a sport, but not very seriously: *She swims twice a week and has been dabbling in weight training.*
⊕ v + prep

dally /'dæli/ (dallies, dallying, dallied, dallied)

'dally with sth/sb (old-fashioned) to think about sth, do sth or treat sb in a way that is not serious enough: *They've been dallying with the idea for years.*
OBJ **idea, thought** SYN **toy with sth**
⊕ v + prep

dam /dæm/

dam sth 'up to stop the water flowing in a river by building sth across it (a **dam**): *The stream was dammed up to form ornamental lakes.* ◇ *(figurative) I tried to dam up my tears.*
⊕ v + adv + n ♦ v + n/pron + adv

damp /dæmp/ (*also* **dampen** /'dæmpən/)

damp sth 'down 1 to make a fire burn more slowly or stop burning: *Firefighters were damping down the embers hours later.* ◇ *He put sand on the fire to try to damp it down.* ◇ *The fire had been damped down but not extinguished.* OBJ **fire 2** if somebody or something **damps down** an emotion or a feeling, it becomes less strong: *She tried to damp down her feelings of despair.* OBJ **emotions 3** if somebody or something **damps down** a situation or an activity, it becomes slower or weaker: *The latest increase in interest rates has* damped down activity in the housing market. **4** (*rare*) to make a surface slightly wet by spraying a small amount of water over it
⊕ v + adv + n ♦ v + pron + adv ♦ v + n + adv (*rare*)

dangle /'dæŋgl/

dangle sth be'fore sb/sth to offer sb sth very attractive to try to persuade them to do sth: *It's the biggest financial incentive ever dangled before British footballers.*
NOTE **In front of** can be used instead of **before**.
⊕ v + n/pron + prep

dash /dæʃ/

dash a'bout (*especially BrE*) = DASH AROUND

dash a'gainst sth (of rain, waves, the sea, etc.) to beat violently against a surface
⊕ v + prep

dash a'round (*also* **dash a'bout/'round** *especially BrE*) to move very quickly from place to place, being very busy: *I've been dashing around all day!* ◇ *At the scene of the accident, people were dashing about all over the place.*
SYN **rush around**
⊕ v + adv

dash a'way/'off to go away from a place in a hurry: *He dashes off every day at 4 o'clock.*
⊕ v + adv

dash sth a'way if you **dash** tears **away**, you remove them quickly from your face: *He dashed away the tears welling up in his eyes with an impatient hand.*
⊕ v + n/pron + adv ♦ v + adv + n

dash 'off = DASH AWAY/OFF

dash sth 'off to write or draw sth very quickly: *I dashed off a quick letter to my brother.*
SYN **scribble sth**
⊕ v + adv + n ♦ v + pron + adv ♦ v + n + adv (*rare*)

dash 'round (*especially BrE*) = DASH AROUND

date /deɪt/

date 'back ... (*also* **date 'back to sth**) to have existed since a particular time in the past or for the length of time mentioned: *It's a tradition that dates back at least a thousand years.* ◇ *Her problems date back to her childhood.* ◇ *The town dates back to Roman times.*
⊕ v + adv ♦ v + adv + prep

'date from sth to have existed since a particular time in the past: *It is a beautiful vase dating from about 1715.* ◇ *The strike was the latest stage in a dispute which dated from 1990.*
⊕ v + prep

dawn /dɔ:n/

'dawn on sb (*also* **'dawn upon sb** *more formal*) if an idea, the truth or a fact **dawns on** you, you realize it for the first time: *It suddenly dawned on us that we were lost.* ◇ *The answer finally dawned on me.*
SYN **strike sb**
◈ v + prep

deal /di:l/ (**dealt**, **dealt** /delt/)

'deal in sth 1 to do business; to make money by buying and selling a particular product or kind of goods: *He made a fortune dealing in stocks and shares.* ◇ *They deal exclusively in Chinese art.* ◇ *The company deals in computer software.* OBJ **shares**, **art 2** to make money by buying and selling goods illegally, especially drugs: *They're rumoured to be dealing in stolen goods.* OBJ **drugs**, **arms 3** to be concerned with or involved in sth: *This newspaper doesn't deal in gossip, only in facts.* ◇ *She's not the type to deal in rumours.*
◈ v + prep

,deal sb 'in (*informal, especially AmE*) to include sb in an activity: *It sounds like a great plan! Deal me in!*
SYN **count sb in**
OPP **deal sb out**, **deal sb out of sth**
◈ v + n/pron + adv

,deal sb 'out; **,deal sb 'out of sth** (*AmE, informal*) to not include sb in an activity: *You can deal me out of this. I don't want to get involved in anything illegal.*
SYN **count sb out**, **count sb out of sth**
OPP **deal sb in**
◈ v + n/pron + adv ♦ v + n/pron + adv + prep

,deal sth 'out (**to sb**) **1** to share sth among a number of people, groups of people or organizations: *We'll deal out the proceeds to several charities.* ◇ *The profits were dealt out among the investors.* SYN **distribute sth** (*more formal*) **2** (in a game of cards) to give cards to each player: *She dealt out seven cards to each player.* NOTE **Deal sth** can also be used with this meaning. **3** to give sb a particular punishment; to say what punishment sb should have: *She dealt out the same punishment to all the children.* ◇ *Severe penalties are dealt out to persistent offenders.* OBJ **punishment** SYN **administer sth** (*formal*)
◈ **1,2** v + adv + n ♦ v + n/pron + adv
   3 v + adv + n ♦ v + n/pron + adv

'deal with sb 1 to look after, talk to or control people in an appropriate way, especially as part of your job: *Her job involves dealing with young offenders.* ◇ *They're very difficult people to deal with.* SYN **handle sb 2** to take appropriate action in a particular situation or according to who you are talking to, etc: *Can you deal with this*

customer? ◇ *We have to deal with students and handle a load of paperwork as well.* ◇ *Most patients are dealt with within four weeks.* **3** to take appropriate action to punish sb who has done sth wrong: *Your father will deal with you when he gets home.* ◇ *Athletes found guilty of taking drugs were swiftly dealt with.* SYN **sort sb out**
◈ v + prep

'deal with sb/sth 1 to do business regularly with a person, an organization, a government, etc: *We prefer to deal only with reputable companies.* ◇ *It is best to deal directly with foreign suppliers.* OBJ **business**, **company 2** to talk to sb, an organization, a government, etc. in order to reach an agreement or settle a dispute: *I prefer to deal with somebody in authority.* ◇ *It would help if I knew exactly who I'm dealing with.*
◈ v + prep

'deal with sth 1 to solve a problem, carry out a task, etc: *to deal with enquiries/issues/complaints* ◇ *The police dealt with the incident very efficiently.* ◇ *There's some urgent correspondence here that hasn't been dealt with.* OBJ **problems**, **matter**, **situation**, **crisis 2** (of a book, poem, article, etc.) to be about sth: *The next programme deals with the subject of divorce.* OBJ **subject**, **question**, **issue** SYN **cover sth 3** if you **deal with** an emotion such as anger or sadness, you learn to control it or become less affected by it: *He is beginning to deal with his anger in a constructive way.* ◇ *'You've got to try and forget her and get on with your life.' 'I'm dealing with it!'* ◇ *She's good at dealing with pressure.*
OBJ **anger**, **grief**, **loss** SYN **cope** (**with sth**)
NOTE **Deal with sth** can be used in the passive.
◈ v + prep

debar /dɪˈbɑː(r)/ (**-rr-**)

deˈbar sb from sth; **deˈbar sb from doing sth** (*formal*) to prevent sb from doing sth, joining an organization, going somewhere, etc: *Students who have not paid their fees will be debarred from taking examinations.* ◇ *He was debarred from holding public office.*
◈ v + n/pron + prep

decide /dɪˈsaɪd/

deˈcide on sb/sth (*also* **deˈcide upon sb/sth** *more formal*) to choose sb/sth after careful thought: *We haven't decided on a date for the wedding yet.* ◇ *Have you decided on whether to take the job or not?*
SYN **settle on/upon sth**
NOTE **Decide on/upon sb/sth** can be used in the passive: *Nothing has yet been decided on.*
◈ v + prep

deck /dek/

,deck sb 'out; **,deck yourself 'out (in/as/like sth)** to put on interesting and colourful clothes or jewellery, usually for a special occasion: *He decked himself out in his best suit.* ◇ *A lot of supporters were decked out in the team's colours.*
〔SYN〕 **dress up (as sth)**, **dress sb/yourself up (as sb/sth)**
〔NOTE〕 Deck sb out is usually used in the passive.
◆ Deck sb/yourself (in/with sth) is also used with this meaning.
◈ v + adv + n ◆ v + n/pron + adv

,deck sth 'out (with/in/like sth) to decorate sth, especially a room or a building, for a special occasion: *The canteen was decked out with Christmas decorations.* ◇ *The room was decked out to look like the inside of a spaceship.*
〔OBJ〕 **room**
〔NOTE〕 Deck sth out is usually used in the passive.
◆ Deck sth can also be used with this meaning.
◈ v + adv + n ◆ v + n/pron + adv

dedicate /'dedɪkeɪt/

'dedicate sth to sb to say at the beginning of a book, a piece of music or a performance that you are doing it for sb, as a way of thanking them or showing respect: *This book is dedicated to my parents.*
〔OBJ〕 **book, work, song**
◈ v + n/pron + prep

'dedicate yourself/sth to sth; **'dedicate yourself/sth to doing sth** to give a lot of your time and effort to a particular activity or purpose because you think it is important: *She dedicates herself to her work.* ◇ *He dedicated his life to helping the poor.*
◈ v + n/pron + prep

defer /dɪ'fɜː(r)/ (-rr-)

de'fer to sb/sth (rather formal) to accept sb's opinion or do what they suggest because you respect them: *I defer to your judgement in these matters.* ◇ *We are happy to defer to the committee's wishes.*
〔OBJ〕 **judgement, wishes**
〔NOTE〕 Defer to sb/sth can be used in the passive: *They were deferred to just because they were men.*
◈ v + prep

delight /dɪ'laɪt/

de'light in sth; **de'light in doing sth** to get a lot of pleasure from sth or from doing sth, especially sth that annoys or upsets other people: *She seemed to delight in making her parents angry.* ◇ *(rather formal) From childhood, she delighted in reading.*
◈ v + prep

deliver /dɪ'lɪvə(r)/

de'liver on sth if you deliver on a promise, a threat or an agreement, you do what you have said you would do, or what you are expected to do: *Can he be trusted to deliver on his promises?* ◇ *They failed to deliver on the agreement.*
〔OBJ〕 **promise, agreement**
◈ v + prep

de,liver sb/sth 'over/'up (to sb); **de,liver yourself 'over/'up (to sb) (formal)** to give sb/sth/yourself to sb in authority, often because you have been ordered to do so: *The defendant has been ordered to deliver up the goods.* ◇ *She delivered the baby over to the care of her sister.* ◇ *He delivered himself up to the authorities.*
〔SYN〕 **hand sb/sth over (to sb)**, **hand yourself over (to sb) (less formal)**
◈ v + adv + n ◆ v + n/pron + adv

delve /delv/

,delve 'into sth to try hard to find out more information about sth: *We should not delve too deeply into this painful matter.*
〔OBJ〕 **subject, reasons** 〔SYN〕 **probe (sth/into sth)**
◈ v + prep

depart /dɪ'pɑːt; AmE dɪ'pɑːrt/

de'part from sth to behave in a way that is different from what is usual or expected: *The teachers are not encouraged to depart from the syllabus.* ◇ *They departed from tradition and got married in a hotel.*
〔OBJ〕 **principles, rules, tradition, decision**
〔NOTE〕 Depart from sth can be used in the passive: *This rule should only be departed from in exceptional circumstances.*
◈ v + prep

depend /dɪ'pend/

de'pend on sb/sth (also de'pend upon sb/sth more formal) 1 (for sth) (not usually used in the progressive tenses) to need help or support from sb/sth in order to live or to manage in a particular situation: *The organization depended heavily on voluntary help.* ◇ *She came to depend on her daughter for support.* ◇ *He depends on medication to stay alive.* 〔SYN〕 **rely on/upon sb/sth (for sth) 2 (not used in the progressive tenses)** to be affected by or decided by sb/sth: *I don't know if I'll come or not. It all depends on how tired I feel this evening.* ◇ *This may be a welcome change or not, depending on your point of view.* 〔NOTE〕 In informal English it is quite common to say **depend** rather than **depend on** before words like *what*, *how*, or *whether*: *It depends how tired I feel.* ◇ *It all depends what happens.* **3** to rely on sb/sth; to be able to trust sb: *I hope you'll be able to come — I'm depending on you to help me.* ◇ *We*

need someone who can be depended on. SYN
count on/upon sb/sth; rely on/upon sb/sth NOTE
In this meaning **depend on/upon sb/sth** can be
used in the passive. **4** (*not used in the progressive
tenses*) to be sure that sth will happen: *You can
depend on my sister to spoil things* (= she always
does). SYN **count on/upon sb/sth; rely on/upon
sb/sth** NOTE In this meaning **depend on/upon
sb/sth** can be used in the passive.
◆ v + prep ◆ v + prep + n/pron + to inf

deprive /dɪˈpraɪv/

deˈprive sb/sth/yourself of sth to prevent
sb/sth from having sth important; to take sth
away from sb: *In prison they were starved and
deprived of sleep.* ◇ *The baby's brain had been
deprived of oxygen during the birth.* ◇ *There is no
need to deprive yourself of food on this diet.* ◇
(*humorous*) *I couldn't deprive you of* (= take away
from you) *your last few pence.*
◆ v + n/pron + prep

derive /dɪˈraɪv/

deˈrive from sth to come or develop from sth:
*The word history derives from the Latin word
'historia' meaning story.* ◇ *The criticism derives
from a misunderstanding of our aims.*
◆ v + prep

deˈrive sth from sth 1 (*formal*) to get or obtain
sth from sth: *She derived a great deal of satisfaction from this achievement.* OBJ **pleasure, satisfaction, information, benefits 2** to obtain a
substance from sth: *These remedies are derived
mainly from the natural world.* **3** to come or
develop from sth: *The Rubik cube derives its
name from its inventor.* ◇ *The name of the mountain appears to be derived from an old Norse
word.* OBJ **name, word**
NOTE In meanings 2 and 3, **derive sth from sth** is
frequently used in the passive.
◆ v + n/pron + prep

descend /dɪˈsend/

be desˈcended from sb/sth to be related to sb
who lived a long time ago: *He claimed he was descended from the Vikings.*
OBJ **ancestors, line, family**
◆ be + v + prep

desˈcend into sth to get into a very bad condition or state: *The situation has descended into
total chaos.* ◇ *There were fears that the country
was descending into turmoil or even civil war.*
◆ v + prep

desˈcend on sb/sth (*also* **desˈcend upon
sb/sth** *more formal*) **1** to arrive somewhere, especially suddenly and unexpectedly and in large
numbers: *Dozens of police descended on the
building.* ◇ (*humorous*) *My sister and her family
are descending on us this weekend.* **2** to go

towards sb/sth as if you are going to attack
them/it: *The mosquitoes descended on us as soon
as night fell.* ◇ (*humorous*) *A large woman in a
hat was descending on them.*
◆ v + prep

desˈcend to sth to do or say sth that makes
people lose their respect for you: *If you insult
him back, you descend to his level.*
SYN **stoop to sth, stoop to doing sth**
◆ v + prep

despair /dɪˈspeə(r); AmE dɪˈsper/

deˈspair of sb/sth; deˈspair of doing sth
(*formal or humorous*) to feel that there is no hope
that sb/sth will improve, get better, etc. or that
sth will happen: *I despair of you, Ian — act your
age!* ◇ *I'd begun to despair of ever seeing him
again.*
◆ v + prep

detract /dɪˈtrækt/

deˈtract from sth (*not usually used in the progressive tenses*) to make sth seem less good than it
really is: *These revelations should not detract
from his achievements.* ◇ *Her tattered clothes in
no way detracted from her beauty.*
SYN **diminish sth**
◆ v + prep

devolve /dɪˈvɒlv; AmE -ˈvɑːlv/

deˈvolve on/to/upon sb/sth (*formal*) (of work,
duties, power or responsibility) to be given to a
person or an organization by sb at a higher level
of authority: *All the responsibility has devolved
upon him.* ◇ *Additional powers will devolve to the
regional governments.*
◆ v + prep

deˈvolve sth to sb/sth to give work, duties,
power or responsibility to sb with less authority
than you: *More powers are gradually being
devolved to the regions.*
◆ v + n/pron + prep

devote /dɪˈvəʊt; AmE dɪˈvoʊt/

**deˈvote sth to sb/sth; deˈvote sth to doing
sth** to give an amount of time, energy or attention to sb/sth: *He devoted his life to the struggle for
justice.* ◇ *She gave up work to devote more time to
her children.* ◇ *The museum is hosting an exhibition devoted to her work.* ◇ *Several courses are
devoted to improving customer care.*
OBJ **time, attention, energy, life, chapter**
◆ v + n/pron + prep

**deˈvote yourself to sb/sth; deˈvote your-
self to doing sth** to spend a large part of your
time, energy and attention on a particular activity, especially sth good: *After her marriage, she*

couldn't devote herself totally to her music. ◇
*They had devoted themselves entirely to building
up their business.*

  ✦ v + pron + prep

dial /'daɪəl/ (-ll-, *AmE* -l-)

,dial 'in; ,dial 'into sth (*also* ,dial 'up sth) (*computing*) to make a connection between one computer and another using a telephone line: *I dial
in from my PC at home to get the files I need.* ◇
*Every time I try to dial into the Internet I can't get
a connection.*

  ✦ v + adv ✦ v + prep

,dial 'out to make a call to sb outside the building
you are in: *You can't dial out from that phone —
it's for internal calls only.*

  ✦ v + adv

,dial 'up sth; ,dial it/them 'up 1 (*AmE*) to call
sb/sth on the telephone: *Would you dial up the
doctor's office for me?* ⟨SYN⟩ **call sb/sth up; call
sb/sth** (*AmE*) **2** = DIAL INTO STH *Customers can
dial up the central computer from home and
access the database.*

  NOTE A noun must always follow **up**, but a pronoun comes between the verb and **up**.

  ✦ v + adv + n ✦ v + pron + adv

dictate /dɪk'teɪt; *AmE* 'dɪkteɪt/

dic'tate to sb to give orders to sb, especially in a
rude or aggressive way: *You can't dictate to
people how they should live.* ◇ *I'm not going to be
dictated to by my little brother!*

  NOTE Dictate to sb can be used in the passive.

  ✦ v + prep

diddle /'dɪdl/

,diddle a'round (*AmE, informal*) to spend your
time doing things that are not important: *Stop
diddling around and do some work!*

  ⟨SYN⟩ **fiddle about/around** (*BrE*), **mess around**

  ✦ v + adv

die /daɪ/ (dies, dying, died, died)

,die a'way 1 (of a sound) to become so faint or
weak that you can no longer hear it: *The sound of
the car engine died away.* ◇ *Her laughter died
away when she saw how angry he was.* ⟨SYN⟩ **fade
away 2** (*also* ,die 'out) (of rain, wind or a storm)
to gradually become weaker and stop: *The rain
will largely die away overnight.* **3** (of a feeling or
an emotion) to gradually become weaker and
disappear: *The excitement over their affair soon
died away.* ⟨SYN⟩ **fade away**

  ✦ v + adv

,die 'back (*also* ,die 'down) if a plant **dies back**,
its leaves die, although the roots are still alive:
The leaves die back in winter.

  ✦ v + adv

,die 'down 1 (of a sound or flames) to gradually
become less loud or strong: *He waited for the
applause to die down.* ◇ *The fire had died down by
the morning.* **2** (of wind, rain or a storm) to gradually become less strong or violent: *As it got
dark, the wind died down.* ⟨SYN⟩ **subside 3** if
something such as excitement or confusion **dies
down**, it gradually becomes less: *When all the
fuss had died down, he just quietly went back
home.* ⟨SYN⟩ **subside 4** = DIE BACK

  ✦ v + adv

,die 'off if a group of people or animals **die off**,
they die one by one over a short period of time
until there are none left: *The survivors are dying
off daily.*

  ✦ v + adv

,die 'out 1 if a family, race or species **dies out**,
there are no longer any members left alive: *There
are several theories about why dinosaurs died out
so suddenly.* ◇ *Many plants and animals are in
danger of dying out.* ⟨SYN⟩ **become extinct 2** (of
a custom, tradition or skill) to no longer be used
or practised: *Many New Year and May Day ceremonies have virtually died out now.* **3** = DIE AWAY
2 *The outbreaks of rain will die out later in the
day.*

  ✦ v + adv

dig /dɪg/ (digging, dug, dug /dʌg/)

,dig 'in 1 (*informal*) to begin to eat: *Dig in while it's
hot!* ◇ *As soon as the food arrived he dug in hungrily.* ⟨SYN⟩ **tuck in** (*especially BrE*) NOTE Dig in
is used especially to tell sb to start eating. **2** if
soldiers **dig in**, they make a safe place in the
ground and prepare for the enemy to attack: *The
troops dug in and organized their defences.* **3** to
wait for or deal with a difficult situation with
great patience: *Hospital workers dug in, prepared
for a long battle with management over pay
increases.*

  ✦ v + adv

,dig 'in; ,dig 'into sth (*AmE, informal*) to begin
to do sth in a way that shows that you are determined to continue or finish it, even if it is difficult: *He looked at the stack of work and dug in
straight away.* ◇ *She dug into the reports and finished them before the meeting.*

  ✦ v + adv ✦ v + prep

,dig sth 'in; ,dig sth 'into sth 1 to push sth into
sth: *The bird dug its claws in and held onto its
prey.* ◇ *She dug her nails into my arm.* **2** to mix a
substance into soil by digging: *I've dug the
fertilizer into the soil.*

  ✦ v + n/pron + adv ✦ v + adv + n ✦ v + n/pron + prep

  IDM dig your 'heels/'toes in to refuse to do sth or
to change your ideas or plans: *He dug his heels in
and insisted she went with him.*

,**dig yourself 'in** to make a safe place for yourself in the ground and prepare for the enemy to attack: *The marines were dug in on the front line.* **NOTE** **Dig yourself in** is used especially in the passive.
◈ v + pron + adv

,**dig 'into sth 1** (*informal*) to begin to eat in an enthusiastic way: *They dug into the pizza hungrily.* **SYN** **tuck into sth** (*especially BrE*) **2** to examine sth carefully to find out information: *It isn't a good idea to dig too deep into his past.* **3** (*AmE, informal*) = DIG IN, DIG INTO STH
◈ v + prep

IDM ,**dig (deep) into your 'pocket(s), 'savings, etc.** to spend some of the money you have or have been saving: *I'll have to dig into my savings to buy a new car.* '**dig your 'hands into your 'pockets** to put your hands deep inside your pockets

,**dig sb/sth 'out**; ,**dig sb/sth 'out of sth** to get sb/sth out of a place by digging the ground around them/it: *It took them three hours to dig him out of the rubble.* ◊ *The car was buried in snow and had to be dug out.*
◈ v + n/pron + adv ♦ v + n/pron + adv + n ♦
v + n/pron + adv + prep

,**dig sth 'out 1** (*informal*) to find sth that has been hidden or not used for a long time: *He dug out the shoes he'd bought 20 years before.* **SYN** **unearth sth** (*more formal*) **2** (*informal*) to find out facts or information by searching or asking questions: *I took the opportunity to dig out some interesting facts and figures about the island.* **SYN** **hunt sth down/out**; **root sb/sth out**
◈ v + adv + n ♦ v + n/pron + adv

,**dig sth 'over** to prepare the ground thoroughly for plants by digging the soil: *The flower beds should be dug over in the spring.* **OBJ** **ground, garden**
◈ v + n/pron + adv ♦ v + adv + n

,**dig sth 'up 1** to break the ground into small pieces, especially before building sth, taking sth from underneath it, etc: *Some Roman remains were found under a car park which was being dug up.* **OBJ** **road, garden 2** to remove sth from the ground by digging: *Archaeologists have dug up some human remains.* **OBJ** **weeds, roots** **SYN** **unearth sth** (*more formal*) **3** (*informal*) to discover information about sb/sth by searching or asking questions: *See what you can dig up on this man's past.* **SYN** **unearth sth** (*more formal*)
◈ v + n/pron + adv ♦ v + adv + n

dine /daɪn/

'**dine on sth** to eat a particular type of food: *We dined on freshly-caught fish in a floating restaurant.* ◊ *They dined on a bland diet of soup and bread.*
◈ v + prep

,**dine 'out** (*formal*) to have dinner away from your home, for example at a restaurant or in sb else's home: *We dined out every night when we stayed in Paris.*
SYN **eat out** (*less formal*)
◈ v + adv

,**dine 'out on sth** (*BrE, humorous*) to tell people of something that has happened to you in order to impress them: *She only actually said one sentence to Brad Pitt but she dined out on it for years.*
◈ v + adv + prep

dip /dɪp/ (**-pp-**)

,**dip sth 'in/'into sth**; ,**dip sth 'in** to put sth very quickly into a liquid and take it out again: *She dipped her toes cautiously into the sea.* ◊ *She took off her shoes and cautiously dipped a toe in.* ◊ *The fruit had been dipped in chocolate.*
◈ v + n/pron + prep ♦ v + n/pron + adv ♦ v + adv + n

,**dip 'into sth 1** to read or watch only small parts of a book, magazine, programme, etc: *I've only had time to dip into the report.* ◊ *The continuous news services are intended for people to dip into.* **OBJ** **book, report 2** to put your hand into a container to take sth out of it: *She dipped into her purse and took out a coin.*
◈ v + prep

IDM **dip into your 'pocket, 'savings, etc.** to take an amount from money that you have been keeping or saving: *They have dipped into their savings to pay for the shares.*

disagree /ˌdɪsəˈgriː/

,**disa'gree with sb** (*not used in the progressive tenses*) if something such as food or the weather disagrees with you, it has a bad effect on you or makes you feel ill: *I feel terrible — something I ate must have disagreed with me.*
SYN **upset sb**
NOTE **Not agree with sb** is used more often: *Mushrooms don't agree with me.*
→ *see also* AGREE WITH SB
◈ v + prep

,**disa'gree with sth**; **disa'gree with doing sth** to disapprove of sth and think it is bad or wrong: *We totally disagree with the ban on fox hunting.* ◊ *She disagrees with keeping animals locked up in cages.*
OBJ **decision, statement, principle** **OPP** **agree with sth, agree with doing sth**
◈ v + prep

disassociate /ˌdɪsəˈsəʊʃieɪt, -ˈsəʊs-; *AmE* -ˈsoʊ-/

,**disas'sociate yourself from sb/sth** (*formal*) = DISSOCIATE YOURSELF FROM SB/STH

disbelieve /ˌdɪsbrˈliːv/

disbelieve in sb/sth to not believe that sb/sth exists: *to disbelieve in God/devils*
NOTE Not believe in sb/sth is used more frequently.
→ *see also* BELIEVE IN SB/STH
◆ v + prep

discourse /dɪsˈkɔːs; AmE -ˈkɔːrs/

discourse (with sb) on sth (*formal*) to talk for a long time on a subject; to make a long speech about sth: *He was able to discourse at great length on the problems of education.*
◆ v + prep

dish /dɪʃ/

dish sth 'out (to sb) 1 (*informal*) to give sth out to large numbers of people or in large amounts: *He's always dishing out advice to people.* **SYN** hand sth out (to sb) (*more formal*) **NOTE** In informal spoken language **dish sb out sth** is also used: *He dished me out a few vitamin pills.* **2** to serve food to sb by putting it on plates: *He's busy dishing out the dinner.* **SYN serve sth (to sb)** (*more formal*)
◆ v + adv + n ◆ v + pron + adv ◆ v + n + adv (*rare*)
IDM dish it 'out (*disapproving*) to criticize sb or attack them: *He was good at dishing it out. It was time he learned what it felt like.*
dish 'up; dish sth 'up (*BrE, informal*) to serve food by putting it on plates: *You pour the wine while I dish up.* ◇ *Come and wash your hands — I'm just going to dish up the dinner.* **SYN serve sth out; serve, serve sth** (*more formal*)
◆ v + adv ◆ v + adv + n ◆ v + pron + adv ◆ v + n + adv (*less frequent*)
dish 'up sth; dish it/them 'up (*informal*) to present or offer sth to sb, usually sth not very good: *She keeps on dishing up the same old jokes in her shows.* **SYN serve sth up**
NOTE A noun must always follow up, but a pronoun comes between the verb and up.
◆ v + adv + n ◆ v + pron + adv

dispense /dɪsˈpens/

dispense with sb/sth (*formal*) to get rid of sth; to stop using sb/sth because they/it are no longer necessary: *The programme dispensed with its most popular presenter.* ◇ *The spread of PCs has dispensed with the need for typists.*
OBJ services, need, requirement
NOTE Dispense with sb/sth can be used in the passive: *His services can now be dispensed with.*
◆ v + prep

dispose /dɪˈspəʊz; AmE dɪˈspoʊz/

dispose of sb to defeat or kill sb: *The league champions quickly disposed of the opposition.*
◆ v + prep
dispose of sb/sth (*formal*) to get rid of sb/sth that you do not want: *She tried to dispose of the evidence.* ◇ *They decided to dispose of much of their property.*
OBJ waste, property, assets
NOTE Dispose of sb/sth can be used in the passive: *Ensure that all the waste is properly and safely disposed of.*
◆ v + prep
dispose of sth (*formal*) to successfully deal with or finish with a problem, etc: *There just remains the matter of funding to dispose of.*
OBJ problem, matter, argument SYN deal with sth (*less formal*)
NOTE Dispose of sth can be used in the passive.
◆ v + prep

dissociate /dɪˈsəʊʃieɪt, -ˈsəʊs-; AmE -ˈsoʊ-/ (*also* disassociate /ˌdɪsəˈsəʊʃieɪt, -ˈsəʊs-; AmE -ˈsoʊ-/)

dissociate yourself from sb/sth (*formal*) to say or do sth to show that you have no connection with sb/sth and do not support or agree with them/it: *The President dissociated himself from the report.*
OPP associate yourself with sb/sth
◆ v + pron + prep

dissolve /dɪˈzɒlv; AmE -ˈzɑːlv/

dissolve into sth 1 to suddenly start to laugh or cry: *They dissolved into fits of laughter.* ◇ *I dissolved into giggles.* ◇ *When I mentioned his name, she dissolved into tears.* **OBJ laughter, giggles, tears 2** to change gradually into a very bad state: *His surprise slowly dissolved into fury.*
◆ v + prep

dive /daɪv/ (dived, dived, AmE also dove /dəʊv; AmE doʊv/dived)

dive 'in; dive 'into sth 1 (*informal*) to start doing sth with enthusiasm and without stopping to think: *She dived in with a question before I had finished speaking.* ◇ *They had dived into the new business without thinking it through.* **2** (*informal*) to start eating with enthusiasm: *As soon as the food was served, she dived in.* **OBJ food, dinner SYN dig in; dig into sth**
◆ v + adv ◆ v + prep
'dive into sth to move your hand quickly into sth such as a pocket or bag to try to find sth: *She dived into her handbag for the keys.*
OBJ bag, pocket
◆ v + prep

divest /daɪˈvest/

di'vest sb/yourself of sth (*formal*) to take clothes off sb/yourself: *He swiftly divested himself of his clothes.*
⬥ v + n/pron + prep

di'vest sb/sth of sth (*formal*) to take sth away from sb/sth: *The court order divests the company of all its assets.*
⟨SYN⟩ **strip sb/sth of sth** (*less formal*)
⬥ v + n/pron + prep

di'vest yourself of sth (*formal*) to get rid of sth you no longer want or that is no longer useful: *She managed to divest herself of the unwanted property.*
→ *see also* DIVEST SB/YOURSELF OF STH
⬥ v + pron + prep

divide /dɪˈvaɪd/

di'vide by sth if a number **divides by** another number, the second number is contained in the first an exact number of times: *Does 612 divide by 13?* ◇ *148 doesn't divide by 12.*
⬥ v + prep

di'vide sth by sth if you **divide** a number **by** another number, you find out how many times the second number is contained in the first: *What's 48 divided by 3?* ◇ *48 ÷ 3 = 16.*
⬥ v + n/pron + prep

di'vide into sth if a number **divides into** another number, it is contained in the second number a particular number of times: *Does 300 divide into 1270?*
⬥ v + prep

di'vide sth into sth if you **divide** a number **into** another number, you find out how many times the first number is contained in the second: *Can you divide 300 into 1270?*
⬥ v + n/pron + prep

di,vide sth/sb 'off (**from sth/sb**) to separate two things or two people with a barrier such as a wall or fence; to form a barrier between two things or people: *A fence divided off one side of the garden.* ◇ *They put up a barrier to divide the women's section off from the men's.*
⬥ v + adv + n ◆ v + n/pron + adv

di,vide 'up; di,vide sb/sth 'up (**into sth**) to separate, or to make sb/sth separate, into groups or parts: *Divide up into two teams.* ◇ *They divided the children up into groups.* ◇ *Divide up your time so that you don't spend too long on any of the questions.*
⬥ v + adv ◆ v + n/pron + adv

di,vide sth 'up (**among/between sb**) to separate sth into parts and give one part to each of a number of people: *We divided the work up between us.* ◇ *The money was divided up among all three winners.*
⟨OBJ⟩ **work, money, land**
⬥ v + n/pron + adv ◆ v + adv + n

divorce /dɪˈvɔːs; *AmE* dɪˈvɔːrs/

di'vorce sb/sth from sth to separate a person, an idea, a subject, etc. from sth; to keep two things separate: *They believed that art should be divorced from politics.* ◇ *When he was depressed, he felt utterly divorced from reality.*
⟨SYN⟩ **separate sb/sth (from/and sth)**
⬥ v + n/pron + prep

divvy /ˈdɪvi/ (**divvies, divvying, divvied, divvied**)

,divvy sth 'up (*informal, especially AmE*) to divide or share sth, especially money, between a number of people: *They divvied up the bill.*
⟨OBJ⟩ **money** ⟨SYN⟩ **share sth out (among/between sb)** (*more formal*)
⬥ v + adv + n ◆ v + pron + adv ◆ v + n + adv (*rare*)

do /du; strong form duː/ (**does** /dʌz/ **did** /dɪd/ **done** /dʌn/)

,do a'way with sb/yourself (*informal*) to kill sb/yourself: *She tried to do away with herself.*
⬥ v + adv + prep

,do a'way with sth (*informal*) **1** to get rid of sth; to stop doing or having sth: *They've done away with the uniform at our school.* ⟨SYN⟩ **abolish sth** (*more formal*) **2** to make sth no longer necessary: *Computers have done away with a lot of the repetitive work.* ⟨SYN⟩ **eliminate sth; end sth** (*both more formal*)
⟨NOTE⟩ **Do away with sth** can be used in the passive: *A lot of the paperwork could easily be done away with.*
⬥ v + adv + prep

,do sb 'down; ,do yourself 'down (*BrE, informal*) to criticize sb or yourself in a way that makes them/you appear more stupid or less able than they/you really are: *Don't do him down, he's a good worker.* ◇ *She's always doing herself down.*
⟨SYN⟩ **put sb down, put yourself down** (*more formal*)
⬥ v + n/pron + adv ◆ v + adv + n (*less frequent*)

'do for sb/sth (*BrE, informal*) to damage or destroy sth; to injure or kill sb; to put sb/sth in a situation so bad that they/it have no chance of returning to normal: *The last bout of pneumonia nearly did for her.*
⬥ v + prep

▶ **'done for** *adj* (*informal*) in serious trouble or danger; having no chance of succeeding at sth: *If anyone recognizes us, we're done for!* (= we will not be able to escape and will be in trouble) ◇ *After three days trapped in the cave they thought they were done for* (= they thought they would die).

,do sb 'in (*informal*) **1** if sth **does you in**, it makes you feel extremely tired: *That's done me in, lifting all those boxes.* **2** (*also* **,do yourself 'in**)

(*informal, especially BrE*) to kill sb/yourself: *When we split up I felt like doing myself in.* ◊ *Does he get done in at the end of the film?*
◆ v + n/pron + adv ♦ v + adv + n (*rare*)
  2 also v + pron + adv
▶ **done 'in** *adj* (*informal*) very tired: *I felt absolutely done in by the end of the day!* ◊ *Come and sit down — you look done in.*

do sth 'in (*BrE, informal*) to injure a part of your body: *He did his back in playing tennis.*
◆ v + n/pron + adv ♦ v + adv + n (*less frequent*)
IDM **do sb's 'head in** (*BrE, informal*) to make you feel confused, upset and/or annoyed: *Shut up! You're doing my head in.*

do yourself 'in = DO SB IN 2

do sth 'out (*BrE, informal*) to clean or paint and decorate a room, a house, etc: *He's done the whole house out in yellows and greens.* ◊ *They had the hall done out in striped wallpaper.*
◆ v + n/pron + adv ♦ v + adv + n

do sb 'out of sth (*informal*) to prevent sb from getting or keeping sth they ought to have, in an unfair or dishonest way: *She tried to do me out of my inheritance.* ◊ *The residents of the home have been done out of a lot of money.*
◆ v + n/pron + adv + prep

do sb 'over (*BrE, informal*) to attack sb and beat them severely: *They threatened to do her over if she didn't pay.*
◆ v + n/pron + adv ♦ v + adv + n

do sth 'over 1 (*BrE, informal*) to enter a house, flat/apartment, etc. by force and steal things from it: *I got back to find the house had been done over.* **NOTE** In this meaning **do sth over** is frequently used in the passive. **2** (*AmE*) to do sth again: *Your handwriting is too messy — you'd better do it over* (= write it out again). ◊ *I'm glad the campaign was successful, but I wouldn't want to do it over.* **SYN** **do sth again**; **redo sth** (*more formal*) **3** (*AmE*) to clean or paint and decorate a room, house, etc: *They've done over the whole store.*
◆ **1,3** v + n/pron + adv ♦ v + adv + n
  2 v + n/pron + adv

do 'up; **do sth 'up** (*especially BrE*) to be fastened with buttons, straps, etc.; to fasten or close sth in this way: *This skirt does up at the back.* ◊ *Could you do up my dress?* ◊ *I can't do the zip up.*
OBJ **jacket, buttons, zip** **SYN** **fasten up, fasten sth up** (*BrE*); **fasten, fasten sth** **OPP** **undo, undo sth**
◆ v + adv ♦ v + adv + n ♦ v + n/pron + adv

do sth 'up 1 (**in sth**) to make sth into a parcel or package: *She was carrying some books done up in brown paper.* **SYN** **wrap sth up** (**in sth**) **2** (*especially BrE*) to repair or decorate a room, a house,

etc. to make it look better and more modern: *They're looking for an old house so that they can do it up.* ◊ *We're having the kitchen done up.* **OBJ** **house** **SYN** **fix sth up** (*especially AmE*), **decorate sth**; **renovate sth**
◆ v + n/pron + adv ♦ v + adv + n

do yourself 'up (*informal*) to make yourself more attractive by putting on make-up, attractive clothes, etc: *She spent hours doing herself up for their first date.*
◆ v + pron + adv

do with sb/sth
◆ v + prep
IDM **be/have 'done with it** to finish dealing with sth unpleasant, especially as quickly as possible: *Just tear up the contract and be done with it.* **I, you, etc. can't/couldn't be 'doing with sb/sth** (*BrE, informal*) used to say that you do not like sb/sth and find them/it very annoying: *I can't be doing with people like that.* ◊ *He couldn't be doing with her untidiness.* **I, you, etc. could 'do with sth/sb** used to say that you need or would like sth/sb: *I could do with a drink!*

do sth with sth used with negatives and in questions to talk about where sb has put sth: *What have you done with my shoes?* ◊ *I haven't done anything with your keys* (= I haven't moved them).
◆ v + pron + prep

do sth with yourself used in questions to talk about how sb spends their time: *She doesn't know what to do with herself while they're at school.*
◆ v + pron + prep + pron

do with'out; **do with'out sb/sth** to manage without sb/sth: *If you can't afford a car, you'll just have to do without.* ◊ *I could do without* (= I wish I didn't have) *all this hassle.*
SYN **go without, go without sth**
◆ v + adv ♦ v + prep

dob /dɒb; *AmE* dɑːb/ (**-bb-**)

dob sb 'in (**to sb**) (*informal*) to tell sb about sth bad that another person has done: *Kay wasn't sure who had dobbed her in to the teachers.*
◆ v + n/pron + adv

dole /dəʊl; *AmE* doʊl/

dole sth 'out (**to sb**) (*informal*) to give money, food, etc. to a group of people: *She quickly doled out the food.* ◊ *The money was doled out to them on a weekly basis.*
OBJ **money, bread, etc.**
◆ v + adv + n ♦ v + pron + adv ♦ v + n + adv (*less frequent*)

doll /dɒl; AmE dɑːl/

doll yourself 'up (in sth) (*informal*) to make yourself look attractive by putting on fashionable clothes, doing your hair, etc: *Every Friday she dolls herself up and goes out to a nightclub.*
◈ v + pron + adv

be/get ,dolled 'up (in sth) (*informal*) to be/get ready for a special occasion by putting on fashionable clothes, doing your hair, etc: *She was all dolled up in a black dress and pearls.* ◇ *I got dolled up for the party.*
◈ be/get + v + adv

dope /dəʊp; AmE doʊp/

be/get ,doped 'up (*informal, especially AmE*) to be in a state where you cannot think clearly or act normally because you are under the influence of drugs: *Some of the patients were kept doped up most of the time.*
◈ be/get + v + adv

dose /dəʊs; AmE doʊs/

,dose sb/yourself 'up (with sth) to give sb/yourself a large amount of a medicine: *She dosed him up with aspirin and sent him to bed.*
NOTE Dose sb/yourself is used more often with the same meaning.
◈ v + n/pron + adv

doss /dɒs; AmE dɑːs/

,doss a'bout/a'round (*BrE, informal*) to spend your time doing nothing or very little: *Everyone dosses about in geography classes.* ◇ *He just dossed around for a year before he got a job.*
◈ v + adv

,doss 'down (*BrE, informal*) to sleep on the floor or somewhere uncomfortable because you have nowhere else to sleep: *We dossed down on Tony's floor after the party.*
SYN bed down (*BrE, more formal*)
NOTE Doss is sometimes used with the same meaning.
◈ v + adv

dot /dɒt; AmE dɑːt/ (-tt-)

be ,dotted a'bout/a'round; be ,dotted a'bout/a'round sth (*especially BrE*) if things or people are dotted about/around, they are in several different places over an area: *A few farms were dotted about in the valley.*
◈ be + v + adv ♦ be + v + prep

'dot A on/over B; 'dot B with A to spread very small amounts of sth in different places on a surface: *Dot the suncream on your face in tiny quantities and rub it in well.* ◇ *Dot the top of the cake with small sweets.*
◈ v + n/pron + prep

be 'dotted with sth if an area is dotted with things or people, they are spread around in several places: *The hillside was dotted with houses.*
◈ be + v + prep

dote /dəʊt; AmE doʊt/

'dote on sb (*also* **'dote upon sb** *more formal*) to feel or show very great love for sb and ignore their faults: *They dote on their daughter.*
OBJ daughter/child/mother, etc.
NOTE Dote on/upon sb can be used in the passive: *He was doted on (by his sisters).*
◈ v + prep

double /'dʌbl/

'double as sth; ,double 'up as sth to have a second function in addition to the main use: *The garage doubles as his workshop.* ◇ *The school secretary doubled up as the nurse.*
◈ v + prep ♦ v + adv + prep

,double 'back (on yourself, itself, etc.) to turn around and go back in the direction you have come from: *The road ahead was flooded so we had to double back to find another way around.* ◇ *The line of trees doubles back on itself at a bend in the river.*
◈ v + adv

,double 'over; ,double sb 'over = DOUBLE UP/OVER, DOUBLE SB UP/OVER (IN/WITH STH)

,double sth 'over to bend or fold sth in the middle: *Use an A4 sheet doubled over.*
◈ v + n/pron + adv ♦ v + adv + n

,double 'up 1 (with sb/on sth) to form pairs in order to share sth: *We've only got one room left; you'll have to double up with Peter.* ◇ *There were enough guitarists to double up on parts* (= two played each part). **2** (on sth) (*rare*) to do sth in addition to your main role: *The band are looking for a singer who can double up on guitar* (= who can also play the guitar).
◈ v + adv

,double 'up as sth = DOUBLE AS STH, DOUBLE UP AS STH

,double 'up/'over (in/with sth); **,double sb 'up/'over** (in/with sth) to bend your body suddenly or quickly because you are in pain, for example; to make sb bend their body in this way: *He doubled up in/with pain.* ◇ *She doubled up with laughter.* ◇ *The punch hit him in the stomach, doubling him over.*
◈ v + adv ♦ v + n/pron + adv ♦ v + adv + n (*rare*)

doze /dəʊz; AmE doʊz/

,doze 'off to go to sleep, especially during the day: *He dozed off during the film.* ◇ *I must have dozed off for a few minutes because I didn't hear her come in.*
SYN nod off (*informal*)
◈ v + adv

draft (*also* **draught** *especially BrE*) /drɑːft; *AmE* dræft/

,**draft sb 'in**; ,**draft sb 'into sth** to choose people and send them somewhere for a special task: *Extra police are being drafted in to control the crowds.* ◇ *Williams was drafted into the team to play France.*
◈ v + adv + n ♦ v + pron + adv ♦ v + n + adv (*less frequent*) ♦ v + n/pron + prep

drag /dræg/ (**-gg-**)

,**drag sb/sth/yourself a'way** (**from sb/sth**) to make sb or yourself stop doing sth when they/you do not really want to: *She was enjoying herself at the party so much, I couldn't drag her away.* ◇ *I find it difficult to drag myself away from my computer.* ◇ *He couldn't **drag his eyes away** from her face.*
[SYN] **tear sb/sth/yourself away** (**from sb/sth**)
◈ v + n/pron + adv

,**drag sb/sth 'down 1** (**to sth**) to bring sb down to a lower standard of behaviour, or a lower social or economic level: *I'm worried the other children will be dragged down to his level* (= because his behaviour is so bad). **2** to make sb feel depressed or weak: *Her parents' constant criticism began to drag her down.*
◈ v + n/pron + adv ♦ v + adv + n (*less frequent*)

,**drag sb/sth 'in**; ,**drag sb/sth 'into sth 1** to make sb or sth become involved in a difficult or unpleasant situation when they do not want to be involved: *When violence breaks out in the streets, innocent people are always dragged in.* ◇ *Don't drag me into your argument!* [SYN] **involve sb** (**in sth**) (*more formal*) **2** to start talking about a person or a subject that has nothing to do with what is being talked about: *Do you have to drag politics into every conversation?*
◈ v + n/pron + adv ♦ v + adv + n ♦ v + n/pron + prep

,**drag sb 'off** (**to sth/…**) to take sb somewhere by force: *I was dragged off to the head teacher's office.*
◈ v + n/pron + adv

,**drag 'on** (*disapproving*) to progress very slowly and take too long: *The day dragged on interminably.* ◇ *Negotiations between the two sides dragged on through the summer.*
[SUBJ] **months, time, meeting, negotiations**
◈ v + adv

,**drag sth 'out** to make sth last longer than it should: *She dragged the meeting out for as long as possible.*
[SYN] **prolong sth** (*more formal*)
◈ v + n/pron + adv ♦ v + adv + n

,**drag sth 'out of sb** to make sb give you information they do not want to give you: *They eventually dragged a confession out of her.*
[OBJ] **confession, truth**
◈ v + n/pron + adv + prep

,**drag sth 'up** to mention in a conversation an unpleasant fact from the past that sb would prefer to forget: *It all happened years ago. There's no point dragging it up now.* ◇ *She's dragged up that story just to embarrass me.*
[SYN] **bring sth up**
◈ v + n/pron + adv ♦ v + adv + n

dragoon /drəˈguːn/

dra'goon sb into sth; **dra'goon sb into doing sth** (*written* or *humorous*) to force sb to do sth that they do not want to do: *We were dragooned into the football team.*
[NOTE] **Dragoon sb into sth/into doing sth** is usually used in the passive.
◈ v + n/pron + prep

drain /dreɪn/

,**drain a'way** (of feelings or colours) to disappear gradually: *As she lay in the warm bath all the tension drained away.* ◇ *The colour had drained away from her face.*
[SUBJ] **anger** [SYN] **fade**
◈ v + adv

,**drain a'way/'off**; ,**drain sth a'way/'off** (**from sth**) if a liquid **drains away/off**, or sb **drains it away/off**, it flows away: *The water drained away down the plughole.* ◇ *I drained the water away and hung up the blouse to dry.* ◇ (*figurative*) *Paying for private education for the children was draining away their resources.*
◈ v + adv ♦ v + adv + n ♦ v + n/pron + adv

draw /drɔː/ (**drew** /druː/ **drawn** /drɔːn/)

,**draw 'back 1** to move away from sb/sth, especially sb/sth that makes you feel frightened: *She drew back from the window in case anyone saw her.* **2** (**from sth/from doing sth**) to decide not to do sth, because you are afraid of what might happen: *The government has drawn back from making a commitment to reform the voting system.*
◈ v + adv

,**draw sth 'down** (*AmE, business*) to reduce the amount of sth, especially money, by using it and spending it: *Higher production costs will draw down cash gains from rising farm prices.*
[OBJ] **funds**
◈ v + adv + n ♦ v + n/pron + adv

'**draw sth from sth** to get sth from a particular source: *Many artists and poets have drawn their inspiration from the landscape.* ◇ *At times of crisis, we drew strength from each other.*
[OBJ] **inspiration, comfort, support**
◈ v + n/pron + prep

,**draw 'in** (*BrE*) (*usually used in the progressive tenses*) when evenings or nights are **drawing in**, it is gradually becoming darker earlier in the evening because winter is coming: *The nights*

are drawing in fast now. ◇ *Evening was already drawing in.* ◇ *It was the end of September and the days had begun to draw in.*
SYN **close in** OPP **draw out** (*BrE*)
◈ v + adv

draw 'in; **draw 'into sth** (*especially BrE*) if a train **draws in**, or **draws into** a station, it slowly enters a station and stops at the platform: *The London train drew in late.* ◇ *I got to the platform just as the train was drawing into the station.*
SYN **pull in, pull into sth**
OPP **draw out, draw out of sth**
◈ v + adv ◆ v + prep

draw sb 'in; **draw sb 'into sth**; **draw sb 'into doing sth** to make sb become involved or take part in sth, although they do not want to: *I didn't like the book when I started it, but the strange story soon drew me in.* ◇ *I refuse to be drawn into this argument.*
OBJ **conversation, discussion, argument, situation** SYN **involve sb (in sth)**
NOTE This phrasal verb is often used in the passive.
◈ v + n/pron + adv ◆ v + adv + n ◆ v + n/pron + prep

draw sth 'in if you **draw in** a breath, you breathe deeply or quickly: *She drew in a deep breath at the magical sight of the city below.* ◇ *He drew in his breath sharply.*
OBJ only **a/your, etc. breath**
◈ v + adv + n ◆ v + n/pron + adv

draw sth 'off to remove some liquid from a larger amount: *He drew off a glass of beer.*
◈ v + n/pron + adv ◆ v + adv + n

draw 'on (of a time or a season) to slowly pass: *As night drew on, it became clear he wasn't coming.*
◈ v + adv

'**draw on sth 1** (*also* '**draw upon sth** *more formal*) to use sth that you have or that is available to help you do sth: *The assignment asked us to draw on our experiences while we were in England.* ◇ *I'll have to draw on my savings to pay for the car.* OBJ **experience, work, resources, savings, tradition** NOTE Draw on/upon sth can be used in the passive in this meaning: *Sections of the book should be drawn on as required.* **2** if you **draw on** a cigarette or a pipe, etc. you breathe smoke into your mouth from it: *He drew on his cigar.* OBJ **cigar, cigarette, pipe**
◈ v + prep

draw 'out (*BrE*) (*usually used in the progressive tenses*) when evenings or nights are **drawing out**, it is gradually becoming lighter for longer in the evening because spring is coming: *After March the evenings started drawing out.*
OPP **draw in** (*BrE*)
◈ v + adv

draw 'out; **draw 'out of sth** (*especially BrE*) if a train **draws out** or **draws out of** a station, it begins to move and slowly leaves the station: *I arrived in time to see the train drawing out.* ◇ *The train drew slowly out of the station.*
SYN **pull out, pull out of sth**
OPP **draw in, draw into sth**
◈ v + adv ◆ v + adv + prep

draw sb 'out to encourage sb who is shy to talk freely: *I tried to draw him out on the subject of his life in Africa.*
◈ v + n/pron + adv

draw sth 'out to make sth such as a meeting or an event last longer than usual or longer than it should: *They drew the interview out to over an hour.* ◇ *The process is likely to be drawn out over several months.*
▶ **drawn-'out** (*also* **long-drawn-'out**, '**long-drawn** *less frequent*) *adj* lasting longer than you expect or too long: *The negotiations were difficult and drawn-out.* ◇ *It was another long-drawn-out meeting.*
◈ v + n/pron + adv ◆ v + adv + n

draw sth 'out; **draw sth 'out of sth** to take money out of a bank account: *How much money did you draw out?* ◇ *Several thousand pounds had been drawn out of the account.*
SYN **take sth out, take sth out of sth; withdraw sth (from sth)** (*more formal*)
◈ v + n/pron + adv ◆ v + adv + n ◆ v + n/pron + adv + prep

draw 'up; **draw sth/sb/yourself 'up** to come to a stop; to make sth/sb/yourself stop: *A taxi drew up outside.* ◇ *He drew the car up at the front door.* ◇ *He was walking towards the door when a loud knock drew him up sharply.*
SYN **pull up; pull sb up; pull yourself up**
→ *see also* DRAW YOURSELF UP
◈ v + adv ◆ v + n/pron + adv

draw sth 'up 1 to make or write sth that needs careful planning: *My solicitor is drawing up the contract.* ◇ *Clear guidelines need to be drawn up.* ◇ *We've drawn up a plan of action.* OBJ **contract, agreement, plan** SYN **formulate sth** (*more formal*) **2** to bring sth nearer to sb/sth: *She drew up another chair and sat with them.* ◇ *He drew his knees up to his chest.* OBJ **chair, knees** SYN **pull sth up**
◈ v + adv + n ◆ v + n/pron + adv

draw yourself 'up to stand up very straight so that you are as tall as possible: *She drew herself up to her full height, hands on hips, and glared at me.*
SYN **pull yourself up**
→ *see also* DRAW UP, DRAW SB/STH/YOURSELF UP
◈ v + pron + adv

'**draw upon sth** = DRAW ON STH 1

dream /dri:m/ (**dreamt, dreamt** /dremt/ or **dreamed, dreamed**)

,dream sth a'way to spend time in a lazy way thinking about things you would like to do but not actually doing anything: *She dreamt her life away, never really achieving anything.*
⬛ᴼᴮᴶ **life**
✦ v + n/pron + adv ◆ v + adv + n

'dream of sth
✦ v + prep
⬛ᴵᴰᴹ **wouldn't 'dream of sth/of doing sth** used to emphasize the fact that you would not even think about doing sth: *'Don't go without me, will you?' 'I wouldn't dream of it!'*
▶ **un'dreamed of** *adj* much more or much better than you thought was possible: *undreamed-of happiness*

,dream 'on (*spoken, informal*) used to tell sb that you are certain that what they have just said will not happen: *You want a pay rise? Dream on!*
✦ v + adv

,dream sth 'up (*informal*) to have an idea or think of a plan, especially one that is not very practical: *The scheme was dreamed up by a local businessman.* ◇ *Trust you to dream up a crazy idea like this!*
⬛ᴼᴮᴶ **idea, scheme**
✦ v + adv + n ◆ v + pron + adv ◆ v + n + adv (*rare*)

dredge /dredʒ/

,dredge sth 'up (*usually disapproving*) **1** to mention sth that sb has forgotten or wants to forget because it is unpleasant or embarrassing: *She always dredges up that embarrassing story.* ⬛ᴼᴮᴶ **the past 2** to remember sth or to do sth with difficulty: *She was dredging up the little she knew about babies.* ◇ *He managed to dredge up a smile.*
✦ v + adv + n ◆ v + pron + adv ◆ v + n + adv (*less frequent*)

dress /dres/

,dress 'down (in sth) to wear clothes that are less formal than those you usually wear or those that are usually worn in a particular situation: *He deliberately dressed down for the party.* ◇ *More and more people are dressing down for the office these days.*
⬛ᴼᴾᴾ **dress up** (in sth)
✦ v + adv

,dress sb 'down to criticize sb angrily for sth wrong that they have done: *The sergeant dressed down the new recruits.*
✦ v + adv + n ◆ v + n/pron + adv
▶ **,dressing-'down** n [sing.] (*old-fashioned, informal*) an occasion when sb speaks angrily to a person because they have done sth wrong

,dress 'up (as sb/sth), **,dress sb/yourself 'up** (as sb/sth) to put on special clothes in order to pretend to be sb else: *The kids love dressing up.* ◇ *They dressed themselves up as cartoon characters.* ◇ (*BrE*) *dressing-up clothes* ◇ (*AmE*) *dress-up clothes*
✦ v + adv ◆ v + n/pron + adv ◆ v + adv + n (*less frequent*)

,dress 'up (in sth), **,dress yourself 'up** (in sth) to wear special or more formal clothes than you usually do or than those usually worn in a particular situation: *Don't bother to dress up — come as you are.* ◇ *She dressed herself up in a grey suit for the court appearance.*
⬛ᴼᴾᴾ **dress down** (in sth)
⬛ᴺᴼᵀᴱ Do not confuse this phrasal verb with **get dressed** or **dress, dress sb/yourself**, which just mean 'to put on clothes': *I jumped out of bed and got dressed quickly.*
✦ v + adv ◆ v + pron + adv

,dress sth 'up (as sth) to make sth seem different or better than it really is by the way that you present it: *You're sacking me. Don't try to dress it up as a career move.*
✦ v + n/pron + adv ◆ v + adv + n

drift /drɪft/

,drift a'part to become less close or less friendly with sb: *Over the years we just drifted apart.*
✦ v + adv

,drift 'off to fall asleep: *She soon drifted off.* ◇ *I drifted off to sleep on the sofa while I was watching the football.*
⬛ˢʸᴺ **doze off**
✦ v + adv

drill /drɪl/

,drill sth 'into sb to make sb learn or understand sth by repeating it frequently: *We had multiplication tables drilled into us at school.* ◇ *There's no need to drill things into them — they'll learn as they go along.*
⬛ˢʸᴺ **drum sth into sb**
⬛ᴺᴼᵀᴱ **Drill sth into sb** is often used in the passive.
✦ v + n/pron + prep

drink /drɪŋk/ (**drank** /dræŋk/, **drunk** /drʌŋk/)

,drink sth 'down to drink all of sth quickly: *He filled a cup with cold water and drank it down in one gulp.*
✦ v + n/pron + adv ◆ v + adv + n

,drink 'in sth; ,drink it/them 'in to look at, listen to or experience sth with great pleasure and interest: *She wandered the streets, drinking in the atmosphere.* ◇ *We sat gazing at the view, drinking it all in.*
⬛ᴼᴮᴶ **sight, view, atmosphere, beauty**

NOTE A noun must always follow **in**, but a pronoun comes between the verb and **in**. ◆ **Drink in sth** can not be used in the passive.
◆ v + adv + n ◆ v + pron + adv

'drink to sb/sth to wish sb/sth good luck, success or happiness, by raising your glass and then drinking: *They all drank to the couple's health.* ◇ *'Things can only get better.' 'I'll drink to that!'*
SYN toast sb/sth
◆ v + prep

drink 'up; **drink sth 'up** to finish all of a drink: *Drink up. It's time to go.* ◇ *Drink your milk up — it's good for you.*
NOTE Drink sth up is not used in the passive.
◆ v + adv ◆ v + n/pron + adv ◆ v + adv + n

drive /draɪv/ (**drove** /drəʊv; *AmE* droʊv/, **driven** /'drɪvn/)

'drive at sth to try to express or say sth: *I'm not sure I understand what you're driving at.* ◇ *What's he driving at?*
SYN get at sth
NOTE Drive at sth is only used in the progressive tenses and in direct or indirect questions with 'what'.
◆ v + prep

drive a'way/'off; **drive sb/sth a'way/'off** (of a car or a driver) to go away in a vehicle; to take sb away in a vehicle: *The cab drove slowly away.* ◇ *There's someone to drive your car away and park it.* ◇ *They were driven away in a police van.*
◆ v + adv ◆ v + n/pron + adv

drive sb/sth a'way (from sth) to make sb not want to go to a particular place or be with a particular person; to make sb/sth leave a place: *Rising prices are driving our customers away.* ◇ *His temper and his violent behaviour have driven all his family away.*
OBJ business, customers
◆ v + n/pron + adv ◆ v + adv + n

drive 'off (in golf) to hit the ball to begin a game
◆ v + adv

drive 'off; **drive sb/sth 'off** = DRIVE AWAY/OFF, DRIVE SB/STH AWAY/OFF *The van drove off at high speed.* ◇ *The car was driven off at speed.* ◇ *Then he drove her off to the airport.*

drive sb/sth 'off; **drive sb/sth 'off sth** to force sb/sth to move away from a particular place: *The army was driven off by the fierce attacks of the rebels.* ◇ *We were driven off the island by the new owner.*
◆ v + n/pron + adv ◆ v + adv + n ◆ v + n/pron + prep

drive 'on to continue driving either without stopping or after stopping for a short time: *We drove on until we came to an open square full of cafés.* ◇ *Paula stopped to let Philip out of the car before driving on.*
◆ v + adv

drive sb/sth 'out; **drive sb/sth 'out of sth** to make sb/sth leave or disappear: *They're hoping that their competitive prices will drive out the rival company.* ◇ *They tried to drive her out of the village.*
◆ v + n/pron + adv ◆ v + adv + n ◆ v + n/pron + adv + prep

drone /drəʊn; *AmE* droʊn/

drone 'on (about sth) to talk about sth for a long time in a boring way: *I nearly fell asleep while he was droning on!* ◇ *She droned on for hours about the uses of the present tense.*
◆ v + adv

drool /druːl/

'drool over sb/sth to look at sb/sth in a way that shows you like and admire or want them/it, often in a silly or exaggerated way: *He was drooling all over you at the party!* ◇ *The boys drooled over the sports cars in the showroom.*
◆ v + prep

drop /drɒp; *AmE* drɑːp/ (**-pp-**)

drop a'round (*AmE*) = DROP BY
drop sth a'round (*AmE*) = DROP STH ROUND
drop a'way (*especially BrE*) **1** if the ground drops away, it slopes down steeply away from where you are: *The seabed suddenly dropped away and I was waist deep in the water.* **2** to become less strong or disappear: *He felt his dark mood dropping away.*
◆ v + adv

drop 'back if a person in a group drops back, they move to a position further back behind other people, often because they are not able to stay at the front: *The original leader in the race has now dropped back to third place.*
SYN fall back
◆ v + adv

drop be'hind; **drop be'hind sb/sth** if sb drops behind or drops behind sb/sth, they move to a position behind other people: *He dropped behind to walk with Sam.* ◇ *We cannot afford to drop behind our competitors.*
SYN fall behind, fall behind sb/sth
◆ v + adv ◆ v + prep

drop 'by (*also* **drop 'round** *BrE*, **drop a'round** *AmE*) (*informal*) to pay a short, informal visit to sb, often without arranging this in advance: *I just dropped by to check you were OK.* ◇ *I'm dropping round to Kate's later.*
SYN call by (*especially BrE*), stop by
→ *see also* DROP IN (ON SB/AT…), DROP INTO STH; DROP OVER
◆ v + adv

drop sth 'by (*AmE*) = DROP STH IN (TO SB/STH), DROP STH INTO STH

,**drop 'in** (on sb/at…), ,**drop 'into sth** (*informal*)
to pay a short, informal visit to sb, often without
arranging this in advance: *Drop in any time
you're passing.* ◊ *She drops in on her parents at
least once a week.* ◊ *I dropped into the coffee shop
for a quick drink on my way home.*
>SYN< **call in**
→ *see also* DROP BY
◈ v + adv ◆ v + prep
▶ '**drop-in** *adj* [only before noun] used to describe
a place where you can go without making an
appointment: *a drop-in centre/surgery/clinic*

,**drop sb/yourself 'in it** (*BrE, informal*) to put sb
in a difficult or embarrassing situation: *She got
herself out of trouble by dropping Laura in it.*
◈ v + n/pron + prep + it

,**drop sth 'in** (to sb/sth), ,**drop sth 'into sth**
(*especially BrE*) (*AmE usually* ,**drop sth 'by**)
(*informal*) to deliver sth, especially when you are
on the way to somewhere else: *She dropped the
report in on her way out.* ◊ *I'll drop a note in to
you when I know the arrangements.* ◊ *Could you
drop my coat into the cleaner's on your way to
work?* ◊ *I'll drop the brochures by later.*
◈ v + n/pron + adv ◆ v + adv + n ◆ v + n/pron + prep

,**drop 'into sth** = DROP IN (ON SB/AT…), DROP INTO
STH

,**drop sth 'into sth** = DROP STH IN (TO SB/STH),
DROP STH INTO STH

,**drop 'off** (*informal, especially BrE*) to fall into a
light sleep: *He's always dropping off in front of
the TV.* >SYN< **doze off**; **nod off** (*informal*) **2** if a
number, an amount or a quality **drops off**, it
decreases: *The numbers applying for membership have dropped off sharply.* >SYN< **fall off**
◈ v + adv
▶ '**drop-off** (in sth) *n* a decrease: *Managers are
concerned by a recent drop-off in sales.*
→ *see also* DROP-OFF at DROP OFF

,**drop sb/sth 'off** to stop and let sb get out of a car,
etc.; to deliver sth to a place, often when you are
on the way to somewhere else: *Could you drop me
off at the station?* ◊ *I'm going past Jan's house —
I could drop the cake off.* ◊ *She dropped off some
clothes at the dry-cleaner's.*
◈ v + n/pron + adv ◆ v + adv + n
▶ '**drop-off** *n* a place where vehicles can stop for
people to get out, or where sth can be left; the
action of doing this: *It is easier to get a taxi at passenger drop-off points than at flight arrival
stands.*
→ *see also* DROP-OFF at DROP OFF

,**drop 'out**; ,**drop 'out of sth 1** to stop taking
part in an activity, being a member of a group,
etc: *Several members of the team had to drop out
at the last minute.* ◊ *She had to drop out of the
race half way through.* ◊ *The company had to
drop out of the deal due to rising costs.* >SYN< **pull**

out, **pull out of sth**; **withdraw** (from sth) (*more
formal*) **2** to leave school, college, university, etc.
without finishing your studies: *She dropped out
of college after only a few weeks.* ◊ *Many students
drop out or fail because they're not enjoying the
course.* **3** to reject the accepted ideas, morals and
values of society: *There's a danger that when
people lose their jobs they drop out (of society)
altogether.*
◈ v + adv ◆ v + adv + prep
▶ '**dropout** *n* **1** a person who leaves school, college or university before they have finished their
studies: *He might be a college dropout but he's
made a fortune in business.* ◊ *There is a high
dropout rate from some college courses.* **2**
(*usually disapproving, especially BrE*) a person
who rejects the accepted ideas, morals and values of society: *Many of the town's dropouts hang
around the square.*

,**drop 'over** (*especially AmE*) to visit sb for a short
time at their home, without arranging a time in
advance: *I think I'll just drop over to Jim's for a
while.* ◊ *Why don't you drop over this evening?*
>SYN< **pop over/round**
→ *see also* DROP BY
◈ v + adv

,**drop 'round** (*BrE*) = DROP BY

,**drop sth 'round** (*BrE*) (*AmE* ,**drop sth a'round**)
(*informal*) to deliver sth to sb's home, etc: *I'll
drop those papers round later.*
→ *see also* DROP STH IN (TO SB/STH), DROP STH
INTO STH
◈ v + n/pron + adv

drown /draʊn/

,**drown sb/sth 'out** if a sound **drowns out**
sb/sth, it is so loud that they/it cannot be heard:
*The music was playing at full volume, drowning
out conversation.* ◊ *Her reply was drowned out by
a passing motorbike.*
|SUBJ| **noise**, **sound**, **roar**, **music**
|NOTE| **Drown sb/sth** can also be used with the
same meaning. *Her voice was drowned by the
crashing waves.*
◈ v + adv + n ◆ v + pron + adv ◆ v + n + adv (*less
frequent*)

drum /drʌm/ (**-mm-**)

,**drum sth 'into sb** to make sb remember sth by
repeating it often: *He drummed road safety into
them before letting them out on their bicycles.* ◊
*Traditional values were drummed into him from
an early age.* ◊ *I had it drummed into me that I
shouldn't talk to strangers.*
>SYN< **drill sth into sb**
◈ v + n/pron + prep

,**drum sb 'out**; ,**drum sb 'out of sth** to force sb
to leave a group or an organization, usually

because they have done sth wrong: *He was drummed out of the club.*

SYN **throw sb out, throw sb out of sth**

◆ v + n/pron + adv ◆ v + n/pron + adv + prep

,drum sth 'up to work hard to get sth: *We're launching a campaign to drum up more business.* ◇ *We couldn't drum up enough cash to keep the club going.*

OBJ **business, support, customers**

◆ v + adv + n ◆ v + pron + adv ◆ v + n + adv (*rare*)

dry /draɪ/ (**dries, drying, dried, dried**)

,dry 'off; ,dry sb/sth 'off; ,dry yourself 'off to become dry; to make sb/sth/yourself dry: *We lay beside the pool to dry off in the sun.* ◇ *You can use this towel to dry yourself off.* ◇ *I dried the car off with a soft cloth.*

◆ v + adv ◆ v + n/pron + adv ◆ v + adv + n

,dry 'out; ,dry sb 'out (*informal*) to receive treatment to help you stop drinking alcohol or taking drugs; to cure sb of drinking too much alcohol or of taking drugs: *She went into a clinic to dry out.*

◆ v + adv ◆ v + n/pron + adv

,dry 'out; ,dry sth 'out to become very or too dry; to make sth become very or too dry: *Water the plant regularly and don't let the soil dry out.* ◇ *The wind and the sun had dried out my skin.*

◆ v + adv ◆ v + n/pron + adv ◆ v + adv + n

,dry 'up 1 if a supply of sth **dries up**, it is no longer available: *The plan was abandoned when the money dried up.* **SUBJ** **investment, supply, funds** **SYN** **run out 2** (*informal*) to stop talking suddenly because you cannot remember what to say next or are very nervous: *She dried up during the second act.* ◇ *I just dried up halfway through the interview.* **3** (*informal*) used to tell sb rudely to be quiet or stop talking

◆ v + adv

,dry 'up; ,dry sth 'up 1 if a river or a lake, etc. **dries up**, or sth **dries it up**, it becomes completely dry: *The well dried up for the first time in a century.* ◇ *The sun dried up all the puddles.* **2** (*BrE, informal*) to dry dishes after they have been washed: *I'll dry up if you wash the dishes.* ◇ *He dried all the dishes up and put them away.* **NOTE** **Dry** and **dry sth** are also used with this meaning.

◆ v + adv ◆ v + adv + n ◆ v + pron + adv ◆ v + n + adv (*rare*)

▸ **,dried 'up** *adj* **1** completely dry: *They camped in a dried-up river bed.* **2** [only before noun] (*disapproving*) (of a person) old, with many folds and lines on the skin, small and usually bitter or bad-tempered: *The librarian was a dried-up, bitter old man.*

▸ **,drying 'up** *n* [U] (*BrE, informal*) the act of drying dishes after they have been washed: *to do the drying up*

duck /dʌk/

,duck 'out; ,duck 'out of sth; ,duck 'out of doing sth (*informal*) to avoid a responsibility or duty, especially an unpleasant one: *She ducked out of visiting him in hospital.* ◇ *You have to go, so don't try ducking out.*

NOTE **Duck** can be used with an object with the same meaning: *Don't try to duck the issue.*

◆ v + adv ◆ v + adv + prep

dude /duːd/

,dude yourself 'up (*AmE, slang*) to make yourself more attractive and try to impress people by wearing expensive or special clothes: *He really duded himself up for the party.*

◆ v + pron + adv

duff /dʌf/

,duff sb 'up (*BrE, informal*) to hit or kick sb severely: *A couple of guys duffed him up.*

SYN **beat sb up**

◆ v + n/pron + adv

duke /djuːk; *AmE* duːk/

,duke it 'out (**with sb**) (*AmE, slang*) to fight with sb using your hands tightly closed: *You can't settle every argument by duking it out.* ◇ (*figurative*) *You'll have to duke it out over the last cookie.*

◆ v + it + adv

dumb /dʌm/

,dumb 'down; ,dumb sth 'down (*disapproving*) to make sth too simple and therefore less accurate and of poorer quality, by trying to make it easier for people to understand: *The programme producers claimed they had to dumb down.* ◇ *The new producer has really dumbed the show down.*

◆ v + adv ◆ v + n/pron + adv ◆ v + adv + n

▸ **,dumbing 'down** *n* [U] the act or policy of making sth too simple and therefore less accurate and of poorer quality

dummy /'dʌmi/ (**dummies, dummying, dummied, dummied**)

,dummy 'up (*AmE*) to say nothing: *If he dummies up, just try a little persuasion.*

SYN **clam up**

◆ v + adv

dump /dʌmp/

'dump on sb (*slang*) **1** to treat sb unfairly, especially by giving them too much to do or unpleasant tasks: *The boss dumps on Jane and she dumps on the junior staff.* **2** (*AmE*) to criticize sb and

make them feel unimportant or stupid: *Quit dumping on me, I'm trying my best.*
NOTE **Dump on sb** can be used in the passive: *Why do I always get dumped on?*
◆ v + prep

'dump on sb; **'dump sth on sb** (*slang, especially AmE*) to tell sb all your problems: *He dumps on me every time she throws him out.* ◇ *She keeps phoning me and dumping all her problems on me.*
◆ v + prep ◆ v + n/pron + prep

dust /dʌst/

,dust sb/sth 'down (*BrE*) = DUST SB/STH OFF, DUST YOURSELF OFF

,dust sth 'down (*BrE*) = DUST STH OFF

,dust yourself 'down (*BrE*) **1** = DUST SB/STH OFF, DUST YOURSELF OFF **2** = DUST YOURSELF OFF

,dust sb/sth 'off; **,dust yourself 'off** (*BrE also* **,dust sb/sth 'down**, **,dust yourself 'down**) to remove the dust or dirt from sb/sth/yourself, for example with your hand or a brush: *She stood up and dusted herself down.*
→ *see also* DUST YOURSELF OFF
◆ v + n/pron + adv ◆ v + adv + n

,dust sth 'off (*BrE also* **,dust sth 'down**) to bring sth out after it has not been used for a long time and start to use it again: *The government is dusting off its plans for offshore gas and oil exploration.* ◇ *Some of their early songs have been brought out and dusted down for re-release.*
◆ v + adv + n ◆ v + pron + adv ◆ v + n + adv (*less frequent*)

,dust yourself 'off (*BrE also* **,dust yourself 'down**) to recover after a difficult or unpleasant experience and begin again: *After every disappointment I just dust myself down and start again.*
→ *see also* DUST SB/STH OFF, DUST YOURSELF OFF
◆ v + pron + adv

dwell /dwel/ (**dwelt, dwelt** or **dwelled, dwelled**)

'dwell on sth (*also* **'dwell upon sth** *more formal*) **1** to think or talk about sth for too long, especially sth unpleasant: *It's time you stopped dwelling on the past.* **OBJ** **the past, problems 2** (*literary*) to look at sth for a long time: *He smiled, his eyes dwelling on her face.*
◆ v + prep

Ee

ease /i:z/

,ease 'back 1 (*business*) if profits, prices, etc. **ease back**, they become a little lower, especially after they have been high: *The company's profits eased back from £15.1 million to £14.7 million.* **2** (**on sth**) if somebody **eases back**, they go a little slower, do sth with a little less energy, are less strict, etc. than before: *The team played aggressively in the first half of the game, but were able to ease back in the second.* ◇ *The government should ease back on farming restrictions.*
  ✦ v + adv

,ease 'back into sth; **,ease sb/yourself 'back into sth** to gradually become familiar again with sth you have not done for some time; to help sb become familiar again with sth they used to do: *Smith is gradually easing back into running after his injury.* ◇ *It's time to ease the kids back into the school routine.* ◇ *The **ease back process** is designed to reduce the chance of re-injury.*
  → *see also* EASE INTO STH, EASE SB/YOURSELF INTO STH
  ✦ v + adv + prep ✦ v + n/pron + adv + prep

,ease 'into sth; **,ease sb/yourself 'into sth** to gradually become, or help sb become, familiar with sth new, especially a new job: *to ease into retirement* ◇ *a course for easing people into the world of computing*
  → *see also* EASE BACK INTO STH, EASE SB/YOURSELF BACK INTO STH
  ✦ v + prep ✦ v + n/pron + prep

,ease 'off 1 to gradually become less strong or unpleasant: *Eventually the rain started to ease off.* ◇ *The pain eased off after a few hours.* **2** to go slower or make less effort: *He eased off in the last lap and still won.* ⟩SYN⟨ **slack off**
  ✦ v + adv

,ease sb 'out; **,ease sb 'out of sth** to make sb leave their job or position, especially by making it difficult or unpleasant for them over a period of time: *He was eased out of his job as presidential adviser.*
  NOTE **Ease sb out** is often used in the passive.
  ✦ v + n/pron + adv ✦ v + adv + n ✦ v + n/pron + adv + prep

,ease 'up 1 (**on sth**) to go slower or make less effort; to do sth less: *The doctor told me to ease up.* ◇ *I'd ease up on the training a bit if I were you.* **2** (**on sb**) to start being less severe with sb: *I think you should ease up on the kids a bit.*
  ✦ v + adv

eat /i:t/ (**ate** /et, eɪt (*especially AmE*)/, **eaten** /'i:tn/)

,eat sth a'way to gradually damage or destroy sth over a period of time: *Something was eating away the foliage.* ◇ *Some of the stone had been eaten away by pollution.* ◇ *The sea is eating away the coastline.*
  → *see also* EAT AWAY AT STH
  ✦ v + adv + n ✦ v + n/pron + adv

,eat a'way at sb to worry sb over a long period of time: *Jealousy is eating away at him.*
  ✦ v + adv + prep

,eat a'way at sth to gradually damage or destroy sth over a period of time: *Pollution is eating away at the stone.* ◇ *Resentment ate away at their relationship.*
  → *see also* EAT STH AWAY
  ✦ v + adv + prep

,eat 'in 1 to have a meal at home rather than at a restaurant: *Are you eating in tonight?* ⟩OPP⟨ **eat out 2** (*also* **,eat sth 'in**) (*especially BrE*) to buy and eat food at a restaurant, rather than taking it away to eat: *Is this food to eat in or take away?* ⟩OPP⟨ **take sth away** (*especially BrE*)
  ✦ v + adv **2** also v + n/pron + adv

'eat into sth 1 to gradually damage or destroy sth: *Woodworm had eaten into most of the furniture.* **2** to use or take away a large part of sth valuable, especially money or time: *My work began to eat into the weekends.* ⟨OBJ⟩ **profits, time**
  ✦ v + prep

,eat 'out to have a meal in a restaurant, etc. rather than at home: *We ate out almost every night.*
  ⟩SYN⟨ **dine out** (*formal*) ⟩OPP⟨ **eat in**
  ✦ v + adv

,eat 'up used to tell sb to eat quickly or to eat everything they have been given: *Eat up! You'll be late for school.*
  → *see also* EAT STH UP 1
  ✦ v + adv

,eat sb 'up if an emotion such as anger, guilt, etc. **eats sb up**, it worries them all the time and they cannot think of anything else: *The anger was eating her up inside.*
  ⟩SYN⟨ **consume sb** (*formal*)
  NOTE **Eat sb up** is often used in the passive: *He's eaten up by jealousy.*
  ✦ v + n/pron + adv ✦ v + adv + n

,eat sth 'up 1 to eat all the food you have been given: *Eat up your broccoli. It's good for you.* → *see also* EAT UP **2** (*informal, especially BrE*) to use large quantities of sth, for example fuel or electricity: *His extravagance is eating up our profits.* ◇ *The van really eats up petrol/gas.*

◈ v + adv + n ◆ v + pron + adv ◆ v + n + adv (*rare*)

ebb /eb/

,ebb a'way to gradually become weaker and begin to disappear: *His confidence ebbed away.*
[SUBJ] **strength, enthusiasm, anger**
◈ v + adv

edge /edʒ/

,edge sb/sth 'out; ,edge sb/sth 'out of sth to gradually move sb out of their job or position, especially by taking their place yourself; to gradually defeat sb: *Be careful he doesn't edge you out of your job altogether.* ◇ *She was edged out of the semi-final by her younger rival.*
◈ v + n/pron + adv ◆ v + adv + n ◆
v + n/pron + adv + prep

,edge 'up if prices, etc. **edge up**, they gradually increase: *Inflation is edging up.*
◈ v + adv

edit /'edɪt/

,edit sth 'out; ,edit sth 'out of sth to remove words or phrases from a book, programme, etc. before it is published or shown: *The swear words were edited out (of the song).* ◇ *He must have edited a lot of the interview out.* ◇ *Read through your work and edit out anything repetitive or irrelevant.*
◈ v + n/pron + adv ◆ v + adv + n ◆
v + n/pron + adv + prep

eff /ef/

,eff 'off (*BrE*, △) a rude way of telling sb to go away, used instead of *fuck off*
◈ v + adv

egg /eg/

,egg sb 'on (to do sth) to encourage sb to do sth, especially sth foolish or wrong: *Egged on by his classmates, he climbed a bit higher.* ◇ *The other lads were egging them on to fight.*
[SYN] **urge sb/sth on (to sth/to do sth)**
◈ v + n/pron + adv ◆ v + adv + n

eke /i:k/

,eke sth 'out 1 to make a small supply of sth last longer by using only a little at a time or by adding sth else to it: *She eked out the stew to make another meal.* [OBJ] **income, supplies 2** ,eke 'out sth, ,eke it/them 'out (*literary*) to manage to live with very little money: *She eked out a living by selling what she could grow.* [OBJ] **living, exist-**

ence [NOTE] A noun must always follow **out**, but a pronoun comes between the verb and **out**.
◈ **1** v + adv + n ◆ v + pron + adv ◆ v + n + adv (*less frequent*)
2 v + adv + n ◆ v + pron + adv

elaborate /ɪ'læbəreɪt/

e'laborate on/upon sth to explain or describe sth in a more detailed way: *He said he was resigning but did not elaborate on his reasons.*
[SYN] **enlarge on/upon sth**
◈ v + prep

elbow /'elbəʊ; *AmE* -boʊ/

,elbow sb/sth a'side/'out; ,elbow sb/sth 'out of sth to force sb or sth out of a position or job: *The story was on the front page, elbowing aside the peace talks.* ◇ *Wrestling elbowed judo out of the 1994 Games.* ◇ *He was elbowed out of power.*
◈ v + adv + n ◆ v + n/pron + adv ◆
v + n/pron + adv + prep

embark /ɪm'bɑːk; *AmE* ɪm'bɑːrk/

em'bark on/upon sth (*formal*) to start to do sth new, important or difficult: *The government has embarked upon a programme of reforms.* ◇ *He travelled for a year, before embarking on graduate studies.*
[OBJ] **programme, career, course, journey**
◈ v + prep

empty /'empti/ (**empties, emptying, emptied, emptied**)

,empty 'out; ,empty 'out of sth if a place **empties out**, or people **empty out of** a place, it becomes empty of people: *At 11.30 the restaurant emptied out (= people left it).* ◇ *People were emptying out of bars and clubs.*
[NOTE] **Empty** and **empty sth** are also used with this meaning.
◈ v + adv ◆ v + adv + prep

,empty sth 'out; ,empty sth 'out of sth to remove all the things from inside a container: *He emptied the bag out onto the table.* ◇ *Don't empty the bath water out!* ◇ *I was asked to empty everything out of my pockets.*
[NOTE] **Empty sth** is used more frequently with this meaning than **empty sth out**.
◈ v + n/pron + adv ◆ v + adv + n ◆
v + n/pron + adv + prep

encroach /ɪn'krəʊtʃ; *AmE* ɪn'kroʊtʃ/

en'croach on sth (*also* en'croach upon sth *more formal*) **1** to use up too much of sb's time, personal life, etc.; to begin to affect sb: *She tried to prevent her work from encroaching too far on her private life.* [SYN] **cut into sth** (*less formal*)

2 to gradually spread over more and more of an area: *New housing is starting to encroach upon the surrounding fields.* [OBJ] **territory**, **land**
◆ v + prep

end /end/

'end in sth to have sth as an ending or as a result: *Many adverbs in English end in -ly.* ◇ *His first attempt to run a marathon ended in disaster.* ◇ *The partnership between the two companies could all end in tears* (= have an unhappy or unpleasant result).
[OBJ] **failure**, **disaster**, **divorce**, **a draw**
◆ v + prep

,end 'up; **,end 'up doing sth** to reach or come to a particular place or situation that you did not expect or intend to be in: *He ended up in prison.* ◇ *I don't want to end up worse off than when I started.* ◇ *I expect I'll end up paying, as usual.* ◇ *If you drive like that, you could **end up dead**!*
[SYN] **finish up**, **finish up doing sth**; **wind up**, **wind up doing sth** (*informal*)
[NOTE] In this meaning, **end up** is nearly always used with either an adjective, a phrase beginning with a preposition, or *doing sth.* ◆ Note that this phrasal verb does not mean the same as **end**: *Classes end at 4 p.m.*
◆ v + adv ◆ v + adv + -ing

endear /ɪnˈdɪə(r); AmE -ˈdɪr/

en'dear sb/yourself to sb (*formal*) to make sb/yourself loved or liked by sb: *He managed to endear himself to my entire family.* ◇ *The government's record on employment did not endear them to the voters.*
◆ v + n/pron + prep

endow /ɪnˈdaʊ/

en'dow sb/sth with sth (*formal*) **1** to give sb sth, such as a particular quality, responsibility, etc: *They endowed their children with remarkable names.* ◇ *The job endows its holder with great prestige.* **2** to imagine or believe that sb/sth has a particular quality: *They endowed certain plants with almost magical healing qualities.*
◆ v + n/pron + prep

be en'dowed with sth to naturally have a particular skill, quality, feature, etc: *He is endowed with both intelligence and good looks.* ◇ *machines endowed with amazing powers* ◇ *The islands are well endowed with ponds, lakes and streams.*
◆ be + v + prep

engage /ɪnˈɡeɪdʒ/

en'gage in sth; **en'gage in doing sth**; **en'gage sb in sth**; **en'gage sb in doing sth** (*formal*) to take part in sth; to make sb take part in sth; to be busy doing sth: *Lecturers engage in teaching and research.* ◇ *She tried to engage him in conversation.* ◇ *He was engaged in running a small business.*
[OBJ] **activities**, **research**, **business**, **discussion**
◆ v + prep ◆ v + n/pron + prep

be en'gaged on/upon sth (*formal*) to do sth; to be involved in doing sth: *He is engaged on a biography of his father.*
◆ be + v + prep

enlarge /ɪnˈlɑːdʒ; AmE -ˈlɑːrdʒ/

en'large on/upon sth (*formal*) to say or write more about sth you have mentioned: *I'll enlarge on this point later.*
[SYN] **elaborate on/upon sth**
◆ v + prep

enquire (*also* inquire *especially AmE*) /ɪnˈkwaɪə(r)/

en'quire after sb (*formal*) to ask about sb's health or about what they are doing: *My mother enquired after you and the baby.*
[SYN] **ask after sb** (*less formal*)
◆ v + prep

en'quire into sth (*formal, especially BrE*) to try to find out the facts about sth: *The committee are enquiring into the employment of children.*
[SYN] **investigate sth**
[NOTE] **Enquire into sth** can be used in the passive.
◆ v + prep

en'quire sth of sb (*formal*) to ask sb sth: *'Are you able to come with us?' she enquired of Will.*
◆ v + speech + prep

enter /ˈentə(r)/

'enter into sth (*formal*) **1** (with sb) to begin to discuss or deal with sth: *The government agreed to enter into negotiations.* ◇ *The examiners cannot enter into any correspondence over the results.*
[OBJ] **negotiations**, **correspondence**, **contract**
[NOTE] **Enter into sth** can be used in the passive in this meaning. **2** (with sb) to begin or become involved in a formal agreement: *The government has entered into an agreement with the World Bank.* ◇ *It is vital that the contract be freely entered into.* [OBJ] **agreement** [NOTE] **Enter into sth** can be used in the passive in this meaning. **3** to affect a situation or be an important part of it: *Luck didn't enter into it; I won because of my skill.* [OBJ] **it**
◆ v + prep

'enter on/upon sth (*formal*) to make a start on sth; to begin sth: *The economy entered on a period of sustained growth.* ◇ *In 1991, he entered upon a turbulent political career.*
[NOTE] **Enter on/upon sth** can be used in the passive.
◆ v + prep

entitle /ɪnˈtaɪtl/

enˈtitle sb to sth to give sb a right to have or do sth: *This ticket entitles you to a free meal.* ◇ *All children are entitled to education.* ◇ *I think I'm entitled to an explanation.*
> **NOTE** Entitle sb to sth is often used in the passive.
> ◈ v + n/pron + prep

entrust /ɪnˈtrʌst/

enˈtrust A to B; **enˈtrust B with A** to make sb responsible for doing sth or for taking care of sb: *I couldn't entrust my children to strangers.* ◇ *Can you entrust an assistant with the task?*
> ◈ v + n/pron + prep

equate /iˈkweɪt/

eˈquate to sth to be equal to sth: *Do my qualifications equate to any in your country?* ◇ *Production costs for the movie equated to around 30% of income.*
> ◈ v + prep

eˈquate sth with sth to consider that sth is the same as sth else, or equal in value or importance: *He equates success with material wealth.*
> ◈ v + n/pron + prep

etch /etʃ/

be ˈetched into/on sth; **be ˈetched with sth** if a feeling is etched into/on sb's face or sb's face is etched with a particular feeling, that feeling can be seen very clearly: *Tiredness and despair were etched into his face.* ◇ *Anthea's face was etched with horror.*
> ◈ be + v + prep
> **IDM** **be etched on your ˈheart/ˈmemory/ˈmind** if sth is etched on your memory, you remember it because it has made a very strong impression on you

even /ˈiːvn/

even ˈout if sth evens out, it becomes level or steady after a period when it has gone up and down or changed a lot: *The path evens out further on.* ◇ *House prices will eventually even out.*
> ◈ v + adv

even sth ˈout to spread sth equally over a number of people or a period of time: *She tried to even out the work among the staff.*
> ◈ v + adv + n ♦ v + n/pron + adv

even sth ˈup to make a situation, a competition, etc. more equal: *If I give you another £5, that will even things up a bit.*
> ◈ v + n/pron + adv ♦ v + adv + n

expand /ɪkˈspænd/

exˈpand on sth (*also* **exˈpand upon sth** *more formal*) to give more information or details about sth you have said or written: *Could you expand on your earlier statement?*
> **OBJ** point, statement
> **NOTE** Expand on/upon sth can be used in the passive.
> ◈ v + prep

explain /ɪkˈspleɪn/

exˌplain sth aˈway to give reasons why you should not be blamed for sth or why sth is not as important or as bad as people think: *How will you explain away the loss of two cars?*
> ◈ v + adv + n ♦ v + n/pron + adv

eye /aɪ/ (eyeing *or* eying, eyed, eyed)

ˌeye sb ˈup (*informal, especially BrE*) to look at sb in a way that shows that you are interested in them, especially in a sexual way: *She's eyeing me up as a potential customer.* ◇ *He was eyeing up all the women at the party.*
> ◈ v + n/pron + adv ♦ v + adv + n

ˌeye sth ˈup (*informal, especially BrE*) to look closely at sth, because you want it or are interested in it: *Are you eyeing up that strawberry tart?*
> **NOTE** **Have your eye on sth** has a similar meaning.
> ◈ v + adv + n ♦ v + n/pron + adv

Ff

face /feɪs/

,face sb 'down (*especially AmE*) to oppose or defeat sb by dealing with them directly and confidently: *The President is determined to face down his critics.*

◈ v + adv + n ◆ v + n/pron + adv

,face 'off (*AmE*) **1** (*sport*) to start a game such as ice hockey: *The teams face off at 2.30.* **2** to get ready to argue, fight or compete with sb: *The candidates face off in a Democratic primary today.*

◈ v + adv

▸ **'face-off** *n* (*AmE*) **1** a method of beginning a game such as ice hockey **2** an argument or a fight

,face 'onto sth if a room or a building **faces onto** sth, the windows look in that direction: *The front bedroom faces onto a main road.*

◈ v + prep

,face 'up to sth to accept and deal with a difficult or unpleasant situation: *When is she going to face up to her responsibilities?* ◇ *He must face up to the fact that he is no longer young.*

OBJ fact, reality, problem, responsibilities
SYN square up (to sb/sth)
NOTE Face up to sth can be used in the passive: *This problem has got to be faced up to.*

◈ v + adv + prep

factor /'fæktə(r)/

,factor sth 'in; ,factor sth 'into sth (*especially AmE*) to include a particular fact or situation when you are calculating sth, or thinking about or planning sth: *When you estimated the cost of the repairs, you forgot to factor in the labour.* ◇
OPP factor sth out, factor sth out of sth

◈ v + adv + n ◆ v + n/pron + adv ◆ v + n/pron + prep

,factor sth 'out; ,factor sth 'out of sth (*especially AmE*) to not include a particular fact or situation when you are calculating sth, or thinking about or planning sth: *When inflation is factored out, the trade deficit fell 12.8%.*

OPP factor sth in, factor sth into sth

◈ v + n/pron + adv ◆ v + adv + n ◆
v + n/pron + adv + prep

fade /feɪd/

,fade a'way 1 to gradually become less strong, clear or frequent and disappear: *His footsteps gradually faded away.* ◇ *Her enthusiasm will soon fade away.* **SYN** die away **NOTE** Fade can also be used with this meaning, especially in more formal English. **2** (of a person) to become weaker and die: *She's fading away rapidly.*

◈ v + adv

,fade 'in; ,fade sth 'in if a sound or a picture in a film/movie, etc. **fades in**, or sb **fades it in**, it gradually becomes louder or clearer

OPP fade out, fade sth out

◈ v + adv ◆ v + n/pron + adv ◆ v + adv + n

▸ **'fade-in** *n* [U] [C] an act of gradually making a picture appear at the beginning of a scene in a film/movie

,fade 'out; ,fade 'out of sth to become quieter, weaker, etc. and gradually disappear: *The protest eventually faded out.* ◇ *She looked a strong candidate, but then faded out of the picture.*

◈ v + adv ◆ v + adv + prep

,fade 'out; ,fade sth 'out if a sound or a picture in a film/movie, etc. **fades out** or sb **fades it out**, it gradually becomes quieter or less clear: *Near the end of the song he faded out the music.*

OPP fade in, fade sth in

◈ v + adv ◆ v + n/pron + adv ◆ v + adv + n

▸ **'fade-out** *n* [U] [C] an act of gradually making a picture disappear at the end of a scene in a film/movie

faff /fæf/

,faff a'bout/a'round (*BrE, spoken, informal*) to waste time doing unimportant things and not get very much done: *Stop faffing about.*

◈ v + adv

fake /feɪk/

,fake sb 'out (*AmE, informal*) to deceive or trick sb; to make sb think you are going to do one thing and then do another: *He thought I was going to turn left, but I faked him out.*

◈ v + n/pron + adv ◆ v + adv + n

fall /fɔːl/ (fell /fel/ fallen /'fɔːlən/)

94	~ about		~ in with
	~ apart		~ into
	~ away	95	~ off
	~ back		~ on
	~ back on		~ out
	~ behind		~ over
	~ behind with/in		~ through
	~ down		~ to
	~ down on		~ under
	~ for		~ upon
	~ in		

,fall a'bout (*BrE, informal*) to laugh a lot: *We all fell about at her idea.* ◇ *He's rude to the audience and yet they fall about laughing.*

◈ v + adv

,**fall a'part 1** to be old or in bad condition and break or break into pieces: *If you buy cheap shoes, they'll fall apart after a few months.* ◇ *My dictionary is falling apart now, I've used it so much.* ⟨SYN⟩ **come apart 2** to have so many problems that it is no longer possible to exist or operate: *The whole country's falling apart.* ◇ *After my marriage fell apart I moved away.* **3** (*informal*) to have so many problems or worries that you can no longer think or behave normally: *I fell apart when she left.*
✦ v + adv

▣ **be falling apart at the 'seams** to have a lot of problems and is starting to fail

,**fall a'way 1** (**from sth**) to break off or separate from a surface: *The plaster was falling away in big chunks.* **2** (of land, a road, etc.) to slope down: *The ground falls away abruptly to the right.* **3** to gradually disappear: *Gradually, all his cares and worries fell away.* ◇ *When things got difficult, his supporters all fell away.* **4** (*especially BrE*) to get less or smaller: *The number of applicants has fallen away sharply.* → *see also* FALL OFF
✦ v + adv

,**fall 'back 1** to fail to stay with people at the front in a race: *Betts had been leading, but fell back with 10 laps to go.* ⟨SYN⟩ **drop back** → *see also* FALL BEHIND, FALL BEHIND SB/STH **2** to move or turn back away from sth or sb: *When the troops moved forward, the crowd fell back.* ⟨SYN⟩ **retreat** (*more formal*) **3** (*BrE, finance*) to decrease in value or amount: *Prices rose by more than 10% before falling back slightly.*
✦ v + adv

,**fall 'back on sb/sth** (*also* ,**fall 'back upon sb/sth** *more formal*) to use sb/sth when the situation is difficult or other people/things have failed: *It's very hard if you have no family to fall back on.* ◇ *He could always fall back on his old jokes.*
✦ v + adv + prep

▸ **'fallback** *n* a plan or course of action that you can use if sth else fails: *a fallback position*

,**fall be'hind** ; ,**fall be'hind sb/sth** to fail to stay with other people or things, especially in a race or competition: *I fell further and further behind.* ◇ *The industry is falling behind the rest of Europe.* ◇ *He fell behind the rest of the class.*
⟨SYN⟩ **drop behind, drop behind sb/sth**
→ *see also* FALL BACK 1
✦ v + adv ◆ v + adv + prep

,**fall be'hind with/in sth** to not do sth or pay sth at the right time: *She fell behind with the rent.* ◇ *He began falling behind in his schoolwork.*
▣ **payments, school work**
✦ v + adv + prep

,**fall 'down 1** to suddenly stop standing: *I thought the whole house was falling down.* ◇ *Her legs were so weak that she fell down on her knees.* **2** to drop to the ground: *His trousers were falling down.* ◇ *A lump of the ceiling fell down.* **3** (*only used in the progressive tenses*) (of a building) to be in extremely bad condition: *It's a beautiful house but it's falling down.* **4** (of an idea, an argument, a method, etc.) to be shown to be not true or not good enough: *That's where the theory falls down.*
✦ v + adv

▸ **'downfall** *n* the loss of sb's power, position, money, etc.; the thing that causes this

,**fall 'down on sth** (*BrE, informal*) to fail to do sth correctly or successfully: *The suggestion was that he was falling down on the job.*
▣ **job**
✦ v + adv + prep

'**fall for sb/sth** (*informal*) to be attracted to sb/sth; to fall in love with sb/sth: *He fell for a young student.* ◇ *We fell for the farmhouse as soon as we saw it.*
✦ v + prep

'**fall for sth** (*informal*) to be tricked into believing sth is true when it is not: *You didn't fall for that old trick, did you?*
✦ v + prep

,**fall 'in 1** if a roof or a ceiling **falls in**, it drops to the ground: *The roof of the cave fell in.* **2** (of soldiers) to move into a line ⟨OPP⟩ **fall out**
✦ v + adv

,**fall 'in with sb** (*informal*) to join sb; to become involved with sb: *She fell in with a bad crowd.*
✦ v + adv + prep

,**fall 'in with sth** (*BrE*) to agree to or support a plan or an idea, especially when you do not really want to: *He always expects me to fall in with his plans.*
▣ **plans** ⟨SYN⟩ **go along with sb/sth**
✦ v + adv + prep

,**fall 'into sth 1** to begin to be in a particular state: *He fell into a deep sleep.* ◇ *The tramway fell into disuse in the 1920s.* ◇ *We mustn't fall into this error* (= make this mistake). ◇ *He's fallen into arrears with the rent* (= he is late in paying it). ▣ **disuse, disrepair 2** to begin to do sth or become involved in sth: *I fell into the habit of having a nap after dinner.* ◇ *She fell into conversation with her neighbour.* ▣ **the habit of...**, **conversation 3** to be able to be divided into sth: *Computer viruses fall into three broad categories.* ▣ **two groups, three categories, etc. 4** to belong to a particular group or class: *Only 25% of people fall into this group.* ▣ **category, group, class, etc.**
✦ v + prep

,**fall 'off** to decrease in quantity or quality: *Attendance has fallen off recently.* ◇ *The standard of cooking fell off when the old chef left.*

SYN **drop off**

→ *see also* FALL AWAY 4

◈ v + adv

▶ **'fall-off** (*BrE also* **'falling-off** *less frequent*) (**in/of** sth) *n* [sing.] a decrease in the quality of sth: *a fall-off in attendance/interest/sales*

,**fall 'off**; ,**fall 'off sth** if something **falls off** or **falls off** sth, it becomes separated from the thing it is joined to: *The door handle has fallen off.* ◇ *Put the picture up properly — we don't want it to fall off the wall.*

◈ v + adv ◆ v + prep

'**fall on sb/sth** (*also* '**fall upon sb/sth** *more formal*) (*especially BrE*) **1** to be the responsibility or duty of a particular person or organization: *Most of the cost fell on us.* ◇ *When he died, the responsibility of the business fell on his son.* **2** if your eyes **fall on** sb/sth, you suddenly see or notice them/it: *My eye fell on a letter she had left on the table.* **3** to attack sb/sth with energy or enthusiasm: *The children fell on the food with cries of delight.* ◇ (*figurative*) *He fell on the drawings and examined them closely.* OBJ **food**

◈ v + prep

,**fall 'out 1** (of hair, teeth etc.) to become loose and drop out: *The chemotherapy made her hair fall out.* **2** (**with sb**) (**over/about** sth) (*especially BrE*) to have an argument with sb and stop being friendly with them: *It's not worth falling out about this.* ◇ *Why have you fallen out with him?* ◇ *They fell out over their father's will.* **3** (of soldiers) to move out of lines OPP **fall in**

◈ v + adv

▶ ,**falling-'out** *n* [sing.] (*especially BrE*) a quarrel: *We've had a bit of a falling-out.*

▶ '**fallout** *n* [U] **1** dangerous (**radioactive**) dust that is in the air after a nuclear explosion or accident **2** the bad results of a situation: *the current crisis and its political fallout*

,**fall 'over** to be unable to stay standing and fall to the ground: (*especially BrE*) *He lost his balance and fell over.* ◇ *His bike fell over.*

◈ v + adv

,**fall 'over sb/sth** to hit sb/sth with your foot when you are walking or running and fall or almost fall: *Mind you don't fall over the boxes.*

SYN **trip over sb/sth**

◈ v + prep

IDM ,**fall 'over yourself to do sth** (*informal*) to be very eager to do sth: *Recording companies were falling over themselves to sign the band.*

,**fall 'through** to fail to be completed; to not happen: *Our travel plans have fallen through.* ◇ *The deal fell through.*

SUBJ **deal**

◈ v + adv

'**fall to sb** (**to do sth**) to become the duty or responsibility of a particular person: *The task of telling them the news fell to me.* ◇ *It falls to the police to ensure that demonstrations are well organized.*

◈ v + prep

'**fall to sth**; '**fall to doing sth** (*literary*) to start doing sth: *Little Red Riding Hood and the wolf fell to talking.* ◇ *They fell to it with gusto.*

◈ v + prep

'**fall under sth 1** to belong to or be included in a particular group of things: *What heading do these items fall under?* OBJ **heading 2** to begin to be controlled or influenced by sb/sth: *I realized I was falling under her spell.* ◇ *The education system fell under the control of the church.* OBJ **spell**

◈ v + prep

'**fall upon sb/sth** = FALL ON SB/STH

familiarize (*also* **familiarise**) /fəˈmɪliəraɪz/

fa**'miliarize sb/yourself with sth** to teach sb about sth or to learn about sth until you know it well: *I familiarized myself with everyone's name before the meeting.*

◈ v + n/pron + prep

fan /fæn/ (**-nn-**)

,**fan 'out** to spread out over an area from a central point: *Searchers fanned out over the area where the missing child was last seen.* ◇ *Five main roads fan out from the village.*

◈ v + adv

,**fan sth 'out** if a bird **fans out** its feathers, it spreads them out: *The peacock fanned out its tail.*

◈ v + adv + n ◆ v + n/pron + adv

fancy /ˈfænsi/ (**fancies, fancying, fancied, fancied**)

,**fancy sth 'up** (*AmE, informal*) to make sth look more attractive by adding decoration to it: *I fancied up the dress with some pearls.* ◇ *You don't need to fancy up your web pages.*

◈ v + adv + n ◆ v + n/pron + adv

farm /fɑːm; *AmE* fɑːrm/

,**farm sb 'out** (**to sb**) (*informal, disapproving*) to arrange for sb you are responsible for, especially a child, to be cared for by other people: *When he was little, he was often farmed out to family friends.*

◈ v + n/pron + adv ◆ v + adv + n

,**farm sth 'out** (**to sb**) (*informal*) to send or give work to other people to do: *We farm a lot of the work out to other companies.*

◈ v + n/pron + adv ◆ v + adv + n

fart /fɑːt; AmE fɑːrt/

‚fart a'round (*BrE also* ‚**fart a'bout**) (△, *slang*) to waste time, especially by behaving in a silly way: *Stop farting around and behave yourself!*

NOTE A more polite, informal way to express this is **mess around** or, in British English, **mess about**.

◆ v + adv

fasten /'fɑːsn; AmE 'fæsn/

'fasten on sb/sth; 'fasten sth on sb/sth if your eyes **fasten on** sb/sth, or you **fasten** your eyes **on** sb/sth, you look at them for a long time: *All eyes in the room fastened on me.* ◇ *She fastened her gaze on him.*

◆ v + prep ◆ v + n/pron + prep

'fasten on sth (*also* '**fasten upon sth** *more formal*) **1** to hold sth firmly: *The cheetah's jaw fastened on the gazelle's throat.* **2** to choose sth and give it all your attention or interest: *When she fastens on an idea, there's no stopping her.* **OBJ** **idea, word, fact**

◆ v + prep

'fasten sth on/onto sb/sth to direct feelings such as blame, hope, etc. towards sb: *The blame hasn't been fastened on anybody yet.* **OBJ** **blame, hopes**

◆ v + n/pron + prep

‚fasten 'up; ‚fasten sth 'up (*BrE*) to close, or to make sth close, with buttons, straps, etc: *The dress fastens up at the front.* ◇ *Fasten your jacket up — it's getting cold.* **OBJ** **jacket, coat** **SYN do up, do sth up** (*especially BrE*)

NOTE **Fasten** and **fasten sth** can also be used with the same meaning.

◆ v + adv ◆ v + n/pron + adv ◆ v + adv + n

'fasten upon sth = FASTEN ON/ONTO STH

fathom /'fæðəm/

‚fathom sb/sth 'out (*BrE*) to understand how sb thinks and acts; to find an explanation for sth: *I can't fathom her out — she says one thing then does another.* ◇ *Have you fathomed out how to work the video yet?*

SYN work sb out; work sth out

NOTE **Fathom sb/sth out** is not used in the passive.

◆ v + n/pron + adv

fatten /'fætn/

‚fatten 'up; ‚fatten sb/sth 'up to become fatter; to give an animal or a person a lot of food so that they become fatter: *The sheep fattened up quickly.* ◇ *We're fattening the livestock up for slaughter.*

◆ v + adv ◆ v + n/pron + adv ◆ v + adv + n

fax /fæks/

‚fax 'in; ‚fax sth 'in to send a fax (= a message sent using a machine that sends and receives messages or documents along telephone wires and then prints them) to an organization, a company, a television or radio programme, etc: *Viewers are invited to fax in with their comments.* ◇ *Orders can be either phoned or faxed in to us.*

◆ v + adv ◆ v + n/pron + adv ◆ v + adv + n

‚fax sth 'on (**to sb/sth**) to send a fax (= a message sent using a machine that sends and receives messages or documents along telephone wires and then prints them) that you have received to sb else for them to see or deal with: *Please email or fax this on to a friend.*

◆ v + n/pron + adv ◆ v + adv + n

‚fax sth 'out to send a fax (= a message sent using a machine that sends and receives messages or documents along telephone wires and then prints them) to a large number of people at the same time: *Draft proposals will be faxed out for comment at the end of May.*

◆ v + n/pron + adv ◆ v + adv + n

‚fax sth 'through to send sb a fax (= a message sent using a machine that sends and receives messages or documents along telephone wires and then prints them) with details of or information about sth

◆ v + n/pron + adv ◆ v + adv + n

fear /fɪə(r); AmE fɪr/

'fear for sb/sth (*literary*) to be anxious or worried about sb/sth: *I fear for her safety.* ◇ *When he's away at sea, I really fear for him.* **OBJ** **life, safety, future**

◆ v + prep

feed /fiːd/ (**fed, fed** /fed/)

‚feed 'back (**into/to sth**) if sth **feeds back** to/into sth, it returns to the place, situation, idea, etc. that it started from and has an effect, usually a good one, on its development: *Rising import prices tend to feed back into domestic prices.* ◇ *What the audience says feeds back into the development of the programme.*

◆ v + adv

‚feed sth 'back (**to sb**) to give information, advice or opinions about a product, sb's work, etc., especially so that it can be improved: *We will feed this information back to the company.* ◇ *The results of the tests will be fed back to the schools.* **OBJ** **information**

◆ v + n/pron + adv ◆ v + adv + n

▶ **'feedback** *n* [U] **1** information, advice or opinions about how good a product, sb's work, etc. is: *We got a lot of positive feedback about the programme.* **2** an unpleasant noise produced by some electrical equipment when some of the power returns to the system

,**feed sth 'in**; ,**feed A 'into B**; '**feed B with A**
to put sth into a machine: *You'll need to feed the
paper in by hand.* ◊ *to feed information into a
computer* ◊ *He fed coins into the meter.* ◊ *He fed
the meter with coins.*
◈ v + n/pron + adv ◆ v + adv + n ◆ v + n/pron + prep

'**feed on/off sth 1** (of an animal, etc.) to use sth
as food; to eat sth; to be nourished or strength-
ened by sth: *This bat feeds on fruit.* **2** (*often disapproving*) to become stronger because of sth else:
The media feed off each other's stories.
◈ v + prep

,**feed 'through** (**to sb/sth/into sth**) to reach sb/sth
after going through a process or a system: *Rises
in prices feed through to higher wage claims.* ◊ *It
will take time for the higher rates to feed through
to invesetors.*
◈ v + adv

,**feed sb/sth 'up** (*BrE*) to give extra food to a person or an animal to make them stronger and
more healthy: *You look as if you need feeding up a
bit.*
◈ v + n/pron + adv ◆ v + adv + n

'**feed B with A** = FEED STH IN, FEED A INTO B,
FEED B WITH A

feel /fiːl/ (**felt, felt** /felt/)

'**feel for sb** to have sympathy for sb: *I really felt
for her, bringing up her children alone.* ◊ *I do feel
for you, honestly.*
◈ v + prep

,**feel sb 'up** (*informal*) to touch sb in a sexual way
when they do not want you to
◈ v + n/pron + adv

,**feel 'up to sth**; ,**feel 'up to doing sth** to feel
capable of doing sth, physically or mentally: *If
you feel up to it, we could walk into town.* ◊ *I
don't really feel up to seeing anyone.*
◈ v + adv + prep

fence /fens/

,**fence sb 'in** to restrict sb's freedom: *We've been
fenced in by rules and regulations for too long.*
〉SYN〉 **hem sb/sth in**
NOTE **Fence sb in** is often used in the passive.
◈ v + n/pron + adv ◆ v + adv + n

,**fence sth 'in** to surround sth with a fence: *The
grounds are fenced in by barbed wire.*
NOTE **Fence sth in** is often used in the passive.
◈ v + n/pron + adv ◆ v + adv + n

,**fence sth 'off** to separate one area from another
with a fence, often to stop people or animals from
entering: *We've fenced off the vegetable patch to
stop the rabbits from getting in.*
◈ v + adv + n ◆ v + n/pron + adv

fend /fend/

,**fend for your'self** to take care of yourself without needing any help from other people: *We were
brought up to fend for ourselves when we were still
quite young.*
◈ v + prep + pron

,**fend sb/sth 'off** to defend or protect yourself
from sb/sth: *The minister had to fend off some
awkward questions.* ◊ *She managed to fend her
attackers off for some time.* ◊ *She held up her arm
to fend him off.*
OBJ **attack, question, criticism**
◈ v + adv + n ◆ v + pron + adv ◆ v + n + adv (*less
frequent*)

ferret /'ferɪt/

,**ferret 'out sth**; ,**ferret it/them 'out** (*informal*)
to discover sth by searching thoroughly or asking a lot of questions: *She's determined to ferret
out the truth.*
OBJ **information, the truth**
NOTE A noun must always follow **out**, but a pronoun comes between the verb and **out**.
◈ v + adv + n ◆ v + pron + adv

fess /fes/

,**fess 'up** (**to sth**)/(**to sb**) (**about sth**) (*informal,
especially AmE*) to admit that you have done sth
wrong: *Come on, fess up. I know there's something
you're not telling me.* ◊ *How many stolen cars did
they fess up to?*
〉SYN〉 **own up** (**to sth/to doing sth**); **confess** (**to
sth/to doing sth**) (*more formal*)
◈ v + adv

fetch /fetʃ/

,**fetch 'up** (*informal, especially BrE*) to arrive
somewhere by chance: *The boat finally fetched up
on a sandy beach.* ◊ *He travelled around Europe
for a while and finally fetched up in Naples.*
〉SYN〉 **end up**
◈ v + adv

fiddle /'fɪdl/

,**fiddle a'bout/a'round** (*BrE, informal*) to spend
your time doing nothing or doing sth that is not
important: *He's fiddling around in the garage.*
〉SYN〉 **mess around**
◈ v + adv

fight /faɪt/ (**fought, fought** /fɔːt/)

,**fight 'back** (**against sb/sth**) to defend yourself
with actions or words when sb attacks you or
causes you problems: *The team fought back to
win the game.* ◊ *Don't let them bully you. Fight
back!*
◈ v + adv

,**fight 'back sth**; ,**fight it/them 'back** to try hard not to show your feelings or not to do sth: *She tried to fight back the tears.*
OBJ tears, urge
NOTE A noun must always follow **back**, but a pronoun comes between the verb and **back**.
◆ v + adv + n ◆ v + pron + adv

,**fight 'down sth**; ,**fight it/them 'down** to try hard not to show an emotion that you are starting to feel: *He fought down a rush of panic.* ◇ *She fought down the anger that was rising in her.*
OBJ desire, impulse, panic
NOTE A noun must always follow **down**, but a pronoun comes between the verb and **down**.
◆ v + adv + n ◆ v + pron + adv

,**fight sb/sth 'off** to resist sb/sth or make them/it go away, by fighting against them/it: *She managed to fight her attackers off.* ◇ *The company fought off tough competition.*
OBJ attack, illness
◆ v + n/pron + adv ◆ v + adv + n

,**fight 'out sth**; ,**fight it 'out** to fight or argue about sth until it is settled: *We mustn't interfere. Let them fight it out between themselves.* ◇ *The teams fought out a 0-0 draw.*
OBJ battle, struggle, draw
NOTE A noun must always follow **out**, but a pronoun comes between the verb and **out**.
◆ v + adv + n ◆ v + pron + adv

figure /'fɪgə(r); AmE 'fɪgjər/

'**figure on sth**; '**figure on sb/sth doing sth** (*informal, especially AmE*) to include sth in your plans; to plan sth: *We hadn't figured on a long delay at the airport.* ◇ *I figure on being in New York in January.*
◆ v + prep

,**figure sb/sth 'out** to come to understand sb/sth by thinking carefully: *I never could figure him out.* ◇ *Can you figure out what's going on?*
SYN work sb out; work sth out
NOTE Figure sb/sth out is often followed by a question word such as *how, what, why,* etc: *I can't figure out why he quit his job.*
◆ v + n/pron + adv ◆ v + adv + n

,**figure sth 'out** to calculate the total amount of sth: *Have you figured out how much it will cost?*
SYN work sth out
NOTE Figure sth out is often followed by a question word such as *what, how much,* etc.
◆ v + adv + n ◆ v + n/pron + adv

file /faɪl/

,**file sth a'way** to put papers, documents, etc. away in a place where you can find them easily: *Everything is filed away in drawers.*
◆ v + n/pron + adv ◆ v + adv + n

fill /fɪl/

,**fill 'in (for sb)** to take sb's place for a short time and do the work they normally do: *Who's filling in for you while you're away?*
◆ v + adv

,**fill sb 'in (on sth)** to give sb all the details about sth that has happened: *Can you fill me in on what's been happening while I was away?*
◆ v + n/pron + adv ◆ v + adv + n

,**fill sth 'in 1** (*also* ,**fill sth 'out** *especially AmE*) to complete a form, etc. by writing information on it: *You could fill in an application form now.* ◇ *Fill in the blank spaces with one of these words.* ◇ *I've left gaps on the sheet for you to fill in the details.* **OBJ** form, details **2** to fill sth, such as a hole, a crack, etc. completely with a substance: *We'll have to fill the holes in with cement.* **OBJ** hole, crack **3** (*especially BrE*) to spend time while you are waiting for sb/sth: *How shall we fill in the time until he arrives?*
◆ v + adv + n ◆ v + n/pron + adv (*less frequent*)

,**fill 'out** to become larger, rounder or fatter: *The baby's filled out a lot recently.*
◆ v + adv

,**fill sth 'out 1** to make sth larger or more complete: *We'll need to fill the story out to make a full page article.* **2** (*especially AmE*) = FILL STH IN 1
◆ v + n/pron + adv ◆ v + adv + n

,**fill 'up**; ,**fill sth 'up 1 (with sb/sth)** if a container or a place **fills up** or sb **fills it up**, it becomes completely full: *The restaurant was beginning to fill up.* ◇ *She filled her glass up again.* ◇ *People began filling up the empty seats.* **2 (with sth)** to fill your vehicle with petrol/gas, etc: *I need to fill up with petrol before we go.* ◇ *Fill the tank up with diesel.*
◆ v + adv ◆ v + n/pron + adv ◆ v + adv + n
▶ '**fill-up** *n* (*AmE*) the action of filling sth, particularly of filling a car with petrol/gas

,**fill sb/yourself 'up** to give sb a lot of food so that they feel full; to eat as much as you can: *The meals at school never fill me up.* ◇ *Eat lots of pasta to fill yourself up.*
◆ v + n/pron + adv

filter /'fɪltə(r)/

,**filter sth 'out** to remove sth from a substance by passing it through a special substance or device: *Use a sun cream to filter out ultraviolet rays.*
◆ v + adv + n ◆ v + n/pron + adv

find /faɪnd/ (found, found /faʊnd/)

'**find against sb** (*law*) to decide in a court of law that sb is guilty: *The court found against the defendant.*
◆ v + prep

'find for sb (*law*) to decide in a court of law that sb is innocent: *The jury found for the defendant.*
◆ v + prep

find 'out (about sth/sb, that..., how..., etc.), **find sth 'out** (about sth/sb) to learn a fact, a piece of information, or the truth about sth/sb: *She won't be happy when she finds out about this.* ◊ *'What did she say?' 'You'll find out soon enough.'* ◊ *When did you find out (that) she was ill?* ◊ *I never found out exactly what happened.* ◊ *How did you find that out?*
NOTE Find out is often used with question words such as *how, what, when,* etc: *It took me a while to find out what he was really like.* ◊ *Did you ever find out who did it?* ◆ If you **find sth out**, you do so either by chance or by asking or studying. You can **discover** a piece of information that other people know but you didn't. You can also **discover sth** before anyone else does.
◆ v + adv ◆ v + adv + n ◆ v + pron + adv ◆ v + n + adv (*rare*)

find sb 'out (*informal*) to discover that sb has been dishonest or has done sth wrong: *If you're ever found out, you'll go to prison.*
NOTE Find sb out is often used in the passive.
◆ v + n/pron + adv

finish /'fɪnɪʃ/

finish 'off (with sth), **finish sth 'off** (with sth) (*informal*) to have sth as the last part of sth; to make sth end by doing one last thing: *After a delicious meal we finished off with coffee and mints.* ◊ *The concert finished off with the band's latest hit.* ◊ *The band finished off the show with their latest hit.* ◊ *I have to go now, can I leave you to finish off?* ◊ *Her outfit was finished off with navy shoes.*
NOTE Finish and finish sth are also used with almost the same meaning.
◆ v + adv ◆ v + n/pron + adv ◆ v + adv + n

finish sb 'off (*informal*) to make sb so unhappy, tired, etc. that they cannot continue what they are doing: *Running in that heat nearly finished him off.*
NOTE Finish sb can also be used with almost the same meaning.
◆ v + n/pron + adv ◆ v + adv + n (*rare*)

finish sb/sth 'off (*informal*) **1** to destroy or kill sb/sth, especially sb/sth that is already injured: *He thought the soldiers would come back and finish him off.* ◊ *We ought to finish the poor animal off.* ◊ (*figurative*) *The business had been finished off by financial difficulties.* **2** (in sport) to defeat a person or team that you are competing against: *Agassi finished him off in three sets.*
◆ v + n/pron + adv ◆ v + adv + n

finish sth 'off 1 to complete sth: *I'm going to try and finish off my work tonight.* **2** to use the last part of sth, especially food or drink: *He's finished off all the ice cream!*

NOTE Finish sth is used with almost the same meaning.
◆ v + n/pron + adv ◆ v + adv + n

finish 'up 1 [+ adj/prep] (*also* **finish 'up doing sth**) (*especially BrE*) to reach or come to a particular place, state or situation after a long series of events, often without planning it: *He lost control of the car and finished up in the river.* ◊ *She started out washing dishes and finished up as a chef.* ◊ *They all went home and I finished up doing most of the clearing up.* **SYN** **end up, end up doing sth; wind up, wind up doing sth** (*informal*) **NOTE** In this meaning, **finish up** is always used with either an adjective, a phrase beginning with a preposition, or *doing sth*. Note that **finish up** does not mean the same as **finish**: *Classes finish at 4 p.m.* **2** (*AmE*) to complete what you are doing; to do the last part of sth: *I'll finish up here and join you later.*
◆ **1** v + adv ◆ v + adv + -ing
◆ **2** v + adv

finish sth 'up (*especially AmE*) to do the last part of sth; to use what is left of sth: *He stayed home to finish up his assignment.*
NOTE Finish sth up is not used in the passive.
◆ v + adv + n ◆ v + pron + adv ◆ v + n + adv (*less frequent*)

finish with sb (*informal*) **1** (*BrE*) to end a relationship with sb: *I've finished with Antonia.* **SYN** **break up** (with sb) **2** to stop punishing sb: *He'll never do that again once I've finished with him!*
◆ v + prep

finish with sth 1 to no longer need to use sth: *Can you wash your cup when you've finished with it?* ◊ *Can I keep the book a little longer? I haven't finished with it yet.* **NOTE** Finish with sth is usually used in the perfect tenses in this meaning. **2** (*BrE, informal*) to stop doing sth because you no longer want to do it or enjoy it: *He said he was finished with football.* **NOTE** Finish with sth is usually used in the perfect tenses or in the form **be finished with sth** in this meaning.
◆ v + prep

fire /'faɪə(r)/

fire a'way (*spoken, informal*) used to tell sb to begin asking questions or to begin to speak: *'Can I ask you some questions?' 'Fire away!'*
◆ v + adv

fire sth 'off 1 to shoot a bullet from a gun: *He fired off a volley of shots.* **OBJ** **gun, shot 2** to ask a lot of questions, etc. quickly, one after the other: *He fired off a series of questions.* **OBJ** **questions 3** to write a letter, report, etc. quickly, often because you are angry: *She would fire off a letter of protest in the morning.* **OBJ** **letter 4** if you **fire off** an email, you send it: *I'm going to fire off an email to a newsgroup.* **OBJ** **email**
◆ v + adv + n ◆ v + pron + adv ◆ v + n + adv (*rare*)

,**fire sb/sth 'up** to make sb/sth become excited or enthusiastic about sth: *The manager fired the team up at half-time.*
◆ v + n/pron + adv ◆ v + adv + n

,**fire sth 'up 1** (*AmE*) to light a fire; to make sth hot: *I'll get the burgers — you fire up the grill.* **2** (*especially AmE*) to make an engine start operating: *She fired up the engine.* OBJ **engine**
◆ v + adv + n ◆ v + n/pron + adv

firm /fɜːm; *AmE* fɜːrm/

,**firm sth 'up** (*also* ,**firm 'up** *less frequent*) **1** if sb **firms up** an arrangement, an agreement, etc. it becomes more definite or less likely to change: *I'll phone on the 25th to firm up the details of the meeting.* ◇ *Prices will firm up later this year.* OBJ **plans**, **agreement 2** to make sth, especially part of the body, harder or more solid: *These exercises will firm up those difficult areas of your body.*
◆ v + adv + n ◆ v + pron + adv ◆ v + n + adv (*rare*) ◆ v + adv

fish /fɪʃ/

'**fish for sth** (*often used in the progressive tenses*) to try to make sb tell you sth, say sth nice to you, etc. by asking them a question: *Are you fishing for compliments?*
OBJ **information**, **compliment** SYN **angle for sth**
◆ v + prep

,**fish sb/sth 'out**; ,**fish sb/sth 'out of sth** to take or pull sb/sth out of somewhere: *He fished some change out of his pocket.* ◇ *Several days later his car was fished out of the river.*
◆ v + n/pron + adv ◆ v + adv + n ◆ v + n/pron + adv + prep

fit /fɪt/ (**fitting**, **fitted**, **fitted**, *AmE usually* **fitting**, **fit**, **fit** except in the passive)

,**fit 'in** (**with sth**) if sth **fits in**, it looks pleasant or suitable with other things or in a particular place: *The building doesn't fit in with the surrounding area.* ◇ *It's an old house, but our furniture fits in well.*
◆ v + adv

,**fit 'in**; ,**fit 'into sth 1** to be the right size or shape to go in a particular place: *Will all your furniture fit in?* ◇ *The piano wouldn't fit into the room.* **2** to live or work easily and naturally with a group of people: *Tim never fitted in at college.* ◇ *Jane fitted in well with the rest of the staff.* ◇ *She's fitted into the team well.* **3** to have a particular role or part in a plan, a situation, etc: *Where does he fit in?* ◇ *I like to know where I fit in and what I have to do.* ◇ *Where do I fit into all this?*
◆ v + adv ◆ v + prep

,**fit sb/sth 'in**; ,**fit sb/sth 'into sth 1** to find a place for sb/sth, especially when there is not much space: *We can't fit a sofa in here.* ◇ *We will try to fit you in somewhere in the organization.* SYN **get sb in**, **get sb into sth**; **get sth in**, **get sth into sth 2** to manage to find time to see sb or to do sth: *The nurse will fit you in between other appointments.* ◇ *How do you manage to fit so much into your day?*
◆ v + n/pron + adv ◆ v + adv + n ◆ v + n/pron + prep

,**fit 'in with sth 1** if an activity or event **fits in with** sth else, they exist or happen together in an easy or convenient way: *My job fits in with looking after my family.* **2** to adapt to what sb else is planning or to sb else's way of doing things: *They've got to learn to fit in with our methods.* ◇ *I'll fit in with what you want to do.* **3** to agree with ideas or information that you already have about sb/sth: *That fits in with everything I've heard about her.*
◆ v + adv + prep

,**fit sb/sth 'out** (*also* ,**fit sb/sth 'up**) (**with sth**) to supply sb/sth with the clothes, food, equipment, etc. they need: *The ship had to be fitted out before the voyage.* ◇ *the high cost of fitting out offices* ◇ *We fitted him out with a set of dry clothes.*
NOTE **Fit sb/sth out** is often used in the passive.
◆ v + adv + n ◆ v + n/pron + adv

,**fit sb 'up** (**for sth**) (*BrE*, *informal*) to make sb appear to be guilty of a crime that they have not committed: *They're trying to fit me up for the theft.*
SYN **frame sb** (*more formal*)
◆ v + n/pron + adv ◆ v + adv + n

,**fit sb/sth 'up** (**with sth**) = FIT SB/STH OUT (WITH STH)

fix /fɪks/

'**fix on sth** to decide to choose sth: *We haven't fixed on a date for the meeting yet.*
SYN **decide on/upon sth**; **settle on/upon sth**
◆ v + prep

'**fix sth on sb/sth** if you **fix** your eyes or your mind **on** sb/sth, you look at or think about them/it with great attention: *She fixed her eyes on his face.* ◇ *His attention was fixed on a large dark car.*
OBJ **eyes**, **gaze**, **attention**
NOTE **Fix sth on sb/sth** is often used in the passive.
◆ v + n/pron + prep

,**fix sb 'up**; ,**fix yourself 'up** (*informal*) **1** (**with sth**) to arrange for sb to have sth; to provide sb with sth: *I can fix you up with somewhere to stay.* ◇ *I hope she soon gets herself fixed up with a job.*
NOTE In informal spoken language **fix sb up sth** is also used: *Can you fix me up an appointment for tomorrow?* **2** (**with sb**) to arrange for sb to meet sb who might become a boyfriend or girlfriend: *My brother says he wants me to fix him up with one of my friends.*

→ *see also* FIX YOURSELF UP; FIX STH UP 1; FIX UP
TO DO STH, FIX UP FOR SB TO DO STH

✥ v + n/pron + adv ◆ v + adv + n (*less frequent*)

ˌfix sth ˈup 1 to arrange or organize sth; to
arrange for sb to have sth: *Have you fixed your
holiday up yet?* ◇ *Shall we fix up a meeting for
next week?* OBJ **meeting** SYN **arrange sth** → *see
also* FIX UP TO DO STH, FIX UP FOR SB TO DO STH 2
(*especially AmE*) to repair, decorate, etc. a room of
a house: *They spent £30 000 fixing up their house.* ◇
We fixed up the attic as a study. OBJ **house, room**
SYN **do sth up** (*BrE*) 3 (*especially BrE*) to build
or make something quickly; to make sth ready:
We fixed up a shelter for the night.

✥ v + adv + n ◆ v + pron + adv ◆ v + n + adv (*less
frequent*)

ˌfix yourself ˈup (*AmE, informal*) to make yourself neat and attractive: *Can you wait? I'll just go
and fix myself up.*

→ *see also* FIX SB UP, FIX YOURSELF UP

✥ v + pron + adv

ˌfix ˈup to do sth; ˌfix ˈup for sb to do sth
(*BrE, informal*) to make arrangements to do sth
or for sb to do sth: *He's fixed up for her to see the
doctor on Thursday.* ◇ *I've fixed up with the
school to start in September.*

SYN **arrange to do sth; arrange for sb to do
sth**

→ *see also* FIX STH UP 1; FIX SB UP, FIX YOURSELF
UP

✥ v + adv + to inf ◆ v + adv + prep + n/pron + to inf

ˌfix sb with sth (*formal*) if you **fix sb with** a
look, etc., you look at them directly for a long
time: *She fixed him with a cold stare.*

✥ v + n/pron + prep

fizzle /ˈfɪzl/

ˌfizzle ˈout (*formal*) to fail or to end in a weak or
disappointing way, often after having started
strongly: *The romance fizzled out after a month.*
◇ *The coup attempt soon fizzled out.*

✥ v + adv

flag /flæɡ/ (-gg-)

ˌflag sb/sth ˈdown to signal to the driver of a
moving vehicle to stop, usually by waving your
arm: *He managed to flag down a passing motorist.* ◇ *The police were flagging down all heavy
goods vehicles.*

OBJ **taxi/cab, motorist** SYN **wave sb/sth down**

✥ v + adv + n ◆ v + n/pron + adv

flake /fleɪk/

ˌflake ˈout (*informal*) 1 to collapse or fall asleep
because you are very tired: *I was so exhausted
that I flaked out on the sofa.* 2 (*AmE*) to begin to
behave in a strange way

✥ v + adv

flare /fleə(r); *AmE* fler/

ˌflare ˈup 1 (of flames, a fire, etc.) to suddenly
burn more strongly: *The fire flared up as I added
more wood.* 2 if fighting, tension, anger, etc.
flares up, it starts very suddenly and violently:
Violence flared up in several cities. ◇ *The dispute
could flare up into a major crisis.* 3 if a person
flares up, they show sudden anger towards sb:
He flared up in a fury and shouted at her. 4 if an
illness or injury **flares up**, it suddenly starts
again or becomes worse: *Her asthma has flared
up again.*

✥ v + adv

▶ ˈflare-up *n* [usually sing.] 1 a sudden expression of anger, violent feeling, etc: *the latest flare-
up between the two countries* 2 an occasion when
an illness or injury starts again or quickly
becomes worse

flash /flæʃ/

ˌflash sth aˈround (*also* ˌflash sth aˈbout *especially BrE*) (*disapproving*) to show sth valuable,
especially money or jewellery to people, or let
them see it, to impress them: *Stop flashing your
money around.*

✥ v + n/pron + adv

ˌflash ˈback (to sth) if your mind or your
thoughts **flash back** to sth that happened in the
past, you suddenly remember it: *My mind
flashed back to my first day at college.*

✥ v + adv

▶ ˈflashback *n* 1 [C] [U] a scene in a film/movie,
book, etc. which shows sth that happened earlier
2 a sudden, very clear, strong memory of sth that
happened to you in the past that is so real you feel
that you are living through the experience
again: *She still has nightmares and vivid flash-
backs of the accident.*

ˌflash ˈby/ˈpast; ˌflash ˈby/ˈpast sb/sth to go
or pass very quickly; to go very quickly past
sb/sth: *The days just flashed by.* ◇ *She watched
the scenery flash past the train window.*

✥ v + adv ◆ v + prep

flatten /ˈflætn/

ˌflatten sth/yourself aˈgainst/ˈon sb/sth to
press your body or part of your body on or
against sb/sth: *She flattened her nose and lips
against the window.* ◇ *I flattened myself against
the wall to let them pass.*

✥ v + n/pron + prep

ˌflatten ˈout 1 if a road, an area of land, etc. **flattens out**, it gradually becomes flat: *After Oxford the
countryside flattens out.* 2 to stop growing or going
up: *Sales have flattened out in the last few years.*

ˌflatten sth ˈout to make sth completely flat: *She
flattened out the crumpled letter on the desk.*

✥ v + adv + n ◆ v + n/pron + adv

flesh /fleʃ/

flesh sth 'out (with sth) to add more details or
information to an argument, an idea, a drawing,
etc: *You need to flesh out the bones of your idea a
bit more.* ◇ *They must be prepared to flesh out
their strategy with some details.*
  ◈ v + adv + n ♦ v + n/pron + adv

flick /flɪk/

flick sth 'off to switch sth off quickly: *He flicked
the light off.*
  [OBJ] **light** [SYN] **switch sth off** [OPP] **flick sth on**
  ◈ v + n/pron + adv ♦ v + adv + n

flick sth 'on to switch sth on quickly: *He flicked
on the air-conditioning.*
  [OBJ] **light** [SYN] **switch sth on** [OPP] **flick sth off**
  ◈ v + n/pron + adv ♦ v + adv + n

flick 'through sth to turn the pages of a book,
etc. quickly, or look through a pile of papers, etc.
without reading everything: *He flicked through a
magazine while he waited.*
  [OBJ] **pages, book, papers** [SYN] **flip through sth**;
  leaf through sth; thumb through sth
  ◈ v + prep

fling /flɪŋ/ (flung /flʌŋ/, flung)

'fling yourself at sb (*informal, disapproving*) to
try too hard to show sb that you are interested in
them in a sexual way and make them interested
in you
  [SYN] **throw yourself at sb**
  ◈ v + pron + prep

'fling yourself into sth to start to do sth with a
lot of energy, enthusiasm and effort: *When they
split up she flung herself into her work to try to
forget him.*
  [SYN] **throw yourself into sth**
  ◈ v + pron + prep

fling sth 'off (*informal*) to take clothes off
quickly and carelessly: *Flinging off her coat, she
sank into an armchair.*
  [SYN] **throw sth off** [OPP] **fling sth on**
  ◈ v + n/pron + adv ♦ v + adv + n

fling sth 'on (*informal*) to put clothes on quickly
and carelessly: *Just fling a coat on over your
pyjamas.*
  [SYN] **throw sth on** [OPP] **fling sth off**
  ◈ v + n/pron + adv ♦ v + adv + n

flip /flɪp/ (-pp-)

'flip for sb/sth (*AmE, slang*) to begin to like sb
very much; to suddenly become very excited
about sth attractive, pleasant, etc: *She flipped for
his red hair and freckles.*
  ◈ v + prep

'flip for sth; 'flip sb for sth (*AmE*) = TOSS FOR
STH, TOSS SB FOR STH

flip sb 'off (*AmE, slang*) to raise your middle finger to sb in a very rude gesture
  ◈ v + n/pron + adv ♦ v + adv + n

flip 'out (*informal, especially AmE*) to become
very angry or excited, or lose control
  [NOTE] **Flip** is often used with this meaning, especially in British English.
  ◈ v + adv

flip 'over; flip sth 'over to turn over, or to turn
sth over, onto the other side or upside down: *The
dolphin flipped over onto its back.* ◇ *A huge wave
flipped the dinghy over.*
  ◈ v + adv ♦ v + n/pron + adv ♦ v + adv + n

'flip through sth to turn over the pages of a
book, etc. quickly, or look through a pile of
papers, etc. without reading everything: *He
flipped through the photos quickly.*
  [OBJ] **pages, magazines** [SYN] **flick through sth**;
  leaf through sth
  ◈ v + prep

flirt /flɜːt; AmE flɜːrt/

'flirt with sth (*written*) **1** to think about or be
interested in sth for a short time, but not very
seriously: *I flirted briefly with the idea of emigrating.* [OBJ] **idea, thought** [SYN] **toy with sth 2**
to take risks or not worry about a dangerous
situation: *to flirt with danger/death/disaster* [OBJ]
danger, disaster
  ◈ v + prep

float /fləʊt; AmE floʊt/

float a'round; float a'round sth (*BrE also
float a'bout/'round, float a'bout/'round sth*) **1**
(*usually used in the progressive tenses*) if an idea
or a piece of news is **floating around/about**, it
is being talked about by a lot of people: *There's a
rumour floating about* (*the office*) *that she's leaving.* [SUBJ] **rumour, idea** [SYN] **go around, go
around sth 2** if you say that an object is **floating
around/about** you mean that you have seen it
somewhere but do not know exactly where it is:
Is there a pen floating about here somewhere?
  ◈ v + adv ♦ v + prep

flood /flʌd/

flood 'back if a thought or a memory **floods
back**, you remember sth suddenly and it affects
you strongly: *Suddenly all my fears came flooding back.*
  [NOTE] **Flood back** is often used with the verb
  come: *His words came flooding back to me.*
  ◈ v + adv

flood 'in; flood 'into sth 1 if water, etc. **floods
in** or **floods into** a place, it moves to fill or cover
it: *He opened the door and water came flooding in.*
◇ *Sunshine flooded into the room.* **2** to come to or

arrive at a place in large numbers or great quantities: *Letters of support have been flooding in from all over the country.*
>SYN> **pour in, pour into sth**
✛ v + adv ◆ v + prep

,**flood sb 'out** to force sb to leave their home because of a flood: *We were flooded out by a burst water main.*
NOTE **Flood sb out** is often used in the passive.
✛ v + n/pron + adv ◆ v + adv + n

,**flood 'over/'through sb** if a feeling **floods over/through** you, it affects you very strongly: *A great sense of relief flooded through her.*
SUBJ **relief**
✛ v + prep

'**flood sth with sth** to send sth somewhere in large numbers or amounts, sometimes more than is necessary: *The switchboard was flooded with calls after the programme.* ◇ *(figurative) The room was flooded with evening light.*
NOTE **Flood sb/sth with sth** is often used in the passive: *The office was flooded with complaints.*
✛ v + n/pron + prep

flounder /'flaʊndə(r)/

,**flounder a'round** (*BrE also* ,**flounder a'bout**) to struggle to move or get somewhere because it is difficult, or because you do not know where you are going: *People were floundering about in the water, shouting and screaming.* ◇ *(figurative) I floundered around trying to decide what I ought to do next.*
✛ v + adv

flow /fləʊ; *AmE* floʊ/

'**flow from sth** (*formal*) to come or result from sth: *What benefits might flow from having a single European currency?*
SUBJ **benefits/advantages, consequences**
✛ v + prep

fluff /flʌf/

,**fluff sth 'out/'up** to shake or brush feathers, fur, hair, etc. so that they look bigger or softer: *The bird fluffed out its feathers.* ◇ *Let me fluff up your pillows for you.*
OBJ **feathers**
✛ v + adv + n ◆ v + n/pron + adv

flunk /flʌŋk/

,**flunk 'out;** ,**flunk 'out of sth** (*AmE, informal*) to have to leave school or college because your marks/grades are not good enough: *He flunked out (of college) last year.*
✛ v + adv ◆ v + adv + prep

flush /flʌʃ/

,**flush sth a'way** to get rid of sth with a sudden quick flow of water: *She flushed the unused tablets away.*
✛ v + n/pron + adv ◆ v + adv + n

,**flush sb/sth 'out;** ,**flush sb/sth 'out of sth** to force a person or an animal to leave the place where they are hiding: *The dogs flushed out the deer that were left in the wood.* ◇ *The police flushed the gunmen out of the building.*
✛ v + adv + n ◆ v + n/pron + adv ◆ v + n/pron + adv + prep

,**flush sth 'out;** ,**flush sth 'out of sth** to wash sth out; to get rid of sth with a rush of water: *Drink lots of water to flush the poisons out of your body.*
✛ v + n/pron + adv ◆ v + adv + n ◆ v + n/pron + adv + prep

flutter /'flʌtə(r)/

,**flutter a'round;** ,**flutter a'round sth** (*also* ,**flutter a'bout,** ,**flutter a'bout sth** *especially BrE*) **1** if a bird or an insect **flutters around**, it flies somewhere moving its wings very quickly: *Butterflies fluttered around (the garden).* **2** if a person **flutters around**, they move quickly in a nervous or excited way: *My mother fluttered about picking things up and putting things away.*
✛ v + adv ◆ v + prep

,**flutter 'down** to move gently through the air to the ground: *Wind shook the branches and several leaves fluttered down.*
✛ v + adv

fly /flaɪ/ (**flies, flying, flew** /fluː/ **flown** /fləʊn; *AmE* floʊn/)

,**fly a'round;** ,**fly a'round sth** (*also* ,**fly a'bout,** ,**fly a'bout sth** *especially BrE*) (*usually used in the progressive tenses*) if a story or a piece of news is **flying around**, it is being talked about by a lot of people and passed from one person to another: *Stories about his past are flying around among the students.* ◇ *Rumours have been flying around the office.*
✛ v + adv ◆ v + prep

'**fly at sb** (of a person or an animal) to attack sb suddenly and violently: *She flew at him, hitting and kicking.*
✛ v + prep

,**fly 'by/'past 1** when time **flies by/past**, it seems to pass very quickly: *My three years at college flew by.* ◇ *When you have lots of things to do, time just flies past.* SUBJ **time, days, hours, etc.** NOTE **Fly** can also be used with this meaning, especially with the subject *time*: *There was so much to do the time just flew.* **2** when miles, etc. **fly by/past**, a journey by car, bus, train or bicycle

seems to pass very quickly: *As the miles flew past and we got closer and closer to the sea, the kids got more and more excited.* ⟨SUBJ⟩ **miles, countryside**
◆ v + adv

,fly 'in/out; ,fly 'into sth; ,fly 'out of sth to arrive/leave a place by plane: *She's flying out to join him in Nairobi next week.* ◇ *Several heads of state flew into London last night for talks with the Prime Minister.*
→ *see also* FLY SB/STH IN/OUT, FLY SB/STH INTO/OUT OF STH
◆ v + adv ◆ v + prep ◆ v + adv + prep

,fly sb/sth 'in/'out; ,fly sb/sth 'into sth; ,fly sb/sth 'out of sth to bring sb/sth by plane to a place or take them away: *They flew us in by helicopter.* ◇ *Food supplies are being flown out immediately.* ◇ *The travel company is flying 200 people out of the area tomorrow.*
→ *see also* FLY IN/OUT, FLY INTO STH, FLY OUT OF STH
◆ v + n/pron + adv ◆ v + adv + n ◆ v + n/pron + prep ◆ v + n/pron + adv + prep

,fly 'into sth if sb **flies into** a temper, etc., they suddenly become extremely angry: *He flies into a rage when you mention her.*
⟨OBJ⟩ **rage, temper, panic**
◆ v + prep

,fly 'off; ,fly 'off sth to come off sth suddenly and with force: *The jolt caused her glasses to fly off.*
◆ v + adv ◆ v + prep
⟨IDM⟩ **fly off the 'handle** (*informal*) to become suddenly very angry

,fly 'out; ,fly 'out of sth = FLY IN/OUT, FLY INTO STH, FLY OUT OF STH

,fly sb/sth 'out; ,fly sb/sth 'out of sth = FLY SB/STH IN/OUT, FLY SB/STH INTO STH, FLY SB/STH OUT OF STH

,fly 'past = FLY BY/PAST

fob /fɒb; *AmE* fɑːb/ (**-bb-**)

,fob sb 'off (with sth) (*BrE*) **1** to try to make sb stop asking questions or complaining by giving them answers or excuses that are not true: *Don't try to fob me off with excuses.* **2** to give sb sth that is different from or not as good as what they want: *We thought we'd been fobbed off with inferior goods.*
⟨SYN⟩ **palm sb off (with sth)**
◆ v + n/pron + adv ◆ v + adv + n

,fob sth 'off on/onto sb (*BrE, informal*) to trick sb into accepting sth that you do not want or sth that is not genuine: *She tried to fob all her junk off onto me.*
◆ v + n/pron + adv + prep

focus /ˈfəʊkəs; *AmE* ˈfoʊ-/ (**-s-** or **-ss-**)

'focus on sb/sth; 'focus sth on sb/sth (*also* **'focus upon sb/sth, 'focus sth upon sb/sth** *more formal*) **1** to give all your attention, effort, etc. to a particular problem, subject or person: *Suspicion focused on her husband.* ◇ *The programme was intended to focus attention on global warming.* **2** (of eyes, a camera, etc.) to be adjusted so that things can be seen clearly; to adjust sth so that you can see things clearly: *Rest your eyes by letting them focus on distant objects.* ◇ *The camera was focused on an old woman.*
◆ v + prep ◆ v + n/pron + prep

fog /fɒg; *AmE* fɔːg, fɑːg/ (**-gg-**)

,fog 'up if a glass surface **fogs up** it becomes covered with steam or drops of water so that it is difficult to see in or through it: *The windscreen started to fog up.*
⟨SYN⟩ **mist up, mist sth up; steam up, steam sth up**
◆ v + adv

foist /fɔɪst/

'foist sth/sb/yourself on sb (*also* **'foist sth/sb/yourself upon sb** *more formal*) to force sb to accept sth that they do not want, or take care of sb that they do not want to: *He doesn't try to foist his beliefs on everyone.* ◇ *She resented having the child foisted on her while the parents went travelling abroad.*
⟨NOTE⟩ **Foist sth on sb** is often used in the passive.
◆ v + n/pron + prep

fold /fəʊld; *AmE* foʊld/

,fold a'way/'down; ,fold sth a'way/'down to be able to be bent or arranged into a smaller or flatter shape that you can store or carry more easily; to bend or arrange sth in this way: *The bed can fold away.* ◇ *You can fold the table away to make more room.*
⟨NOTE⟩ If you want to talk about a newspaper, a piece of paper, etc. use **fold up**.
◆ v + adv ◆ v + n/pron + adv ◆ v + adv + n
▶ **'foldaway** (*also* **'fold-down, 'fold-up**) *adj* [only before noun] that can be folded so that you can carry it or store it more easily

,fold sth a'way to fold sth and put it away: *She folded the newspaper away.*
◆ v + n/pron + adv ◆ v + adv + n

,fold sth 'back, 'over, 'down, etc. to bend sth back, over, down, etc. so that one part of it lies flat on another: *He folded the corner of the page over to mark his place.*
◆ v + n/pron + adv ◆ v + adv + n

,fold 'down; ,fold sth 'down = FOLD AWAY/DOWN, FOLD STH AWAY/DOWN

,fold sth 'into sth; ,fold sth 'in (in cooking) to mix one substance gently with another, usually with a spoon: *Gently fold the flour into the mixture.* ◇ *Fold in two egg whites.*
◆ v + n/pron + prep ◆ v + adv + n ◆ v + n/pron + adv

'fold A in B; **'fold B round/over A** to wrap
sb/sth in sth: *She gently folded the baby in a blanket.* ◊ *She folded a blanket round the baby.* ◊ *He
folded her in his arms* (= he put his arms
around her).
 ◈ v + n/pron + prep

,fold 'up; **,fold sth 'up** to bend sth or fold it so
that it is smaller: *The map folds up quite small.* ◊
She folded the letter up and put it in her pocket.
 ̄OPP ̄ unfold, unfold sth
 ◈ v + adv ♦ v + adv + n ♦ v + n/pron + adv
 ▶ **'fold-up** *adj* = FOLDAWAY at FOLD AWAY/DOWN,
FOLD STH AWAY/DOWN

follow /'fɒləʊ; *AmE* 'fɑːloʊ/

,follow 'on 1 (**from sth**) to continue or result from
sth in a natural or logical way: *Listen carefully to
the answer and make sure that your next question
follows on.* ◊ *Following on from what Jill has
said, I'd like to talk about the future of the company.* **2** to leave a place after sb else and meet
them later: *You go now. I'll follow on later.*
 ◈ v + adv
 ▶ **'follow-on** *n* (*especially BrE*) something that
continues or results from sth; the action of following on from sth: *The movie 'Arthur 2' was a
successful follow-on to 'Arthur'.* ◊ *follow-on treat-
ment/talks* ◊ *a follow-on call*

,follow 'through (*sport*) to complete a stroke in
tennis, golf, etc. by continuing to move the club,
etc. after you have hit the ball
 ◈ v + adv
 ▶ **,follow-'through** (*also* **'follow-through** *especially AmE*) *n* (*sport*) (in tennis, golf, etc.) the
final part of a stroke after the ball has been hit
 → *see also* FOLLOW-THROUGH at FOLLOW THROUGH
 (WITH STH), FOLLOW STH THROUGH

,follow 'through, **,follow sth 'through** to
complete sth you have begun or already done:
*The store did not follow through with the prosecu-
tion.* ◊ *He never follows things through.*
 ◈ v + adv ♦ v + adv + n ♦ v + n/pron + adv
 ▶ **,follow-'through** *n* the actions that sb takes to
complete or continue sth: *Your follow-through on
the project was not very satisfactory.*
 → *see also* FOLLOW-THROUGH at FOLLOW THROUGH

,follow 'up; **,follow sth 'up 1** (**with sth**) to take
further action about sth: *You should follow your
letter up with a phone call* (= you should write
first and then telephone). **2** to find out more
about sth sb has told you or suggested to you: *The
police are following up all the leads.* ◊ *It's worth
following up his idea.* ̄OBJ ̄ **lead, idea, complaint,
matter** ̄SYN ̄ **investigate sth** (*more formal*)
 ◈ v + adv ♦ v + n/pron + adv ♦ v + adv + n
 ▶ **'follow-up** (**to sth**) *n* [usually sing.] something
that continues sth: *The survey is a follow-up to
the questionnaire.* ◊ *follow-up treatment/studies*

fool /fuːl/

,fool a'round 1 (*BrE also* **,fool a'bout**) (**with sth**)
to waste time or behave in a silly way: *Stop fooling about with that knife!* **2** (**with sb**) (*especially
AmE*) to have a casual sexual relationship with
another person's partner or with sb who is not
your partner: *He's been fooling around with other
women.* **3** (*AmE*) if two people **fool around**, they
kiss and touch each other in a sexual way: *We
were fooling around on the couch when my dad
walked in.*
 ◈ v + adv

force /fɔːs; *AmE* fɔːrs/

,force 'back sth; **,force it/them 'back** to try
very hard not to show an emotion: *Forcing back
the tears, she nodded and smiled.*
 ̄OBJ ̄ **tears**
 ̄NOTE ̄ A noun must always follow **back**, but a pronoun comes between the verb and **back**. ♦ **Force
back sth** is not used in the passive.
 ◈ v + adv + n ♦ v + pron + adv

,force sth 'down to make yourself eat or drink
sth when you do not want to: *She forced down her
breakfast.*
 ◈ v + adv + n ♦ v + n/pron + adv

'force sth on sb (*also* **'force sth upon sb** *more
formal*) to make sb accept sth they do not want to:
*I didn't want to take the money, but she forced it on
me.* ◊ *Teachers feel that changes are being forced
on them.*
 ̄OBJ ̄ **change, cuts, decision**
 ◈ v + n/pron + prep

'force itself/themselves on sb (*also* **'force
itself/themselves upon sb** *more formal*) if sth
forces itself on you, you cannot avoid becoming
aware of it: *When he read the letter, the truth
forced itself on him.*
 ◈ v + pron + prep

'force yourself on sb (*also* **'force yourself
upon sb** *more formal*) to force sb to have sex with
you when they do not want to, by using violence
or by threatening them
 ̄SYN ̄ **rape sb**
 ◈ v + pron + prep

'force sth upon sb = FORCE STH ON SB

'force itself/themselves upon sb = FORCE
ITSELF/THEMSELVES ON SB

'force yourself upon sb = FORCE YOURSELF ON SB

forge /fɔːdʒ; *AmE* fɔːrdʒ/

,forge a'head 1 to move forward quickly: *He
forged ahead, panting and breathless.* **2** (**with sth**)
to make progress quickly: *The company is forg-
ing ahead with its plans.* ◊ *Jane's language skills
enabled her to forge ahead on the career ladder.*
 ̄SYN ̄ **press ahead/on** (**with sth**)
 ◈ v + adv

fork /fɔːk; AmE fɔːrk/

,fork 'out (for sth), ,fork sth 'out (for/on sth) (informal) to pay a lot of money for sth, especially when you do not want to: *I had to fork out for a cab home.* ◇ *I had to fork out $30 for a cab home.*

〉SYN〈 **shell out (for sth), shell sth out (for sth)**

⊕ v + adv ♦ v + adv + n ♦ v + pron + adv ♦
v + n + adv (*rare*)

,fork sth 'over (AmE, informal) to pay for sth, especially when you do not want to: *I had to fork over the $10 I owed her.*

⊕ v + adv + n ♦ v + pron + adv ♦ v + n + adv (*less frequent*)

form /fɔːm; AmE fɔːrm/

,form 'up; ,form sb 'up if soldiers **form up**, or sb **forms them up**, they get into position in lines: *The general formed up his troops.* ◇ *The teams formed up into lines.*

⊕ v + adv ♦ v + adv + n ♦ v + pron + adv ♦
v + n + adv (*rare*)

foul /faʊl/

,foul 'up; ,foul sth 'up (informal) to do sth badly; to spoil sth, especially by making mistakes: *The team can't afford to foul up in this game.* ◇ *He admitted he'd completely **fouled things up**.*

〉SYN〈 **mess up, mess sth up**

⊕ v + adv ♦ v + adv + n ♦ v + n/pron + adv

▶ '**foul-up** n (informal) a problem caused by bad organization or a stupid mistake: *an administrative foul-up* ◇ *There was a computer foul-up at the bank and customers were sent the wrong statements.*

found /faʊnd/

'found sth on sth (also 'found sth upon sth more formal) to base sth on sth: *Their conclusions were largely founded on guesswork.*

〉SYN〈 **base sth on/upon sth**

NOTE Found sth on/upon sth is usually used in the passive.

⊕ v + n/pron + prep

freak /friːk/

,freak 'out; ,freak sb 'out (informal) if sb **freaks out** or if sth **freaks them out**, they react very strongly to sth that shocks, angers, excites or frightens them: *I don't know what happened in the exams. I just freaked out.* ◇ *I thought I'd seen a ghost — it really freaked me out.*

NOTE Freak and freak sb are used less often with the same meaning.

⊕ v + adv ♦ v + n/pron + adv ♦ v + adv + n (*less frequent*)

free /friː/

,free sb/sth 'up to do sth so that sb is able to do sth else; to make money, time, etc. available for a particular purpose: *Having a secretary frees me up to work on other things.* ◇ *I need to free up more disk space.*

NOTE Free sb/sth is also used with the same meaning.

⊕ v + adv + n ♦ v + pron + adv ♦ v + n + adv (*less frequent*)

freeze /friːz/ (froze /frəʊz; AmE froʊz/ frozen /ˈfrəʊzn; AmE ˈfroʊzn/)

,freeze sb/sth 'out; ,freeze sb/sth 'out of sth (informal) to prevent sb from being part of a group or taking part in an activity, business, etc. by being very unfriendly or making things very difficult for them: *My colleagues were freezing me out.* ◇ *American rice farmers complained that their crops were being frozen out of the market.*

NOTE This phrasal verb is often used in the passive.

⊕ v + n/pron + adv ♦ v + adv + n ♦
v + n/pron + adv + prep

▶ '**freeze-out** n (informal, especially AmE) an act of preventing sb from being part of a group or from taking part in an activity, a business, etc.

,freeze 'over to become covered by ice: *The river sometimes freezes over.*

〉SYN〈 **ice over/up**

⊕ v + adv

,freeze 'up 1 if sth **freezes up**, it becomes blocked with frozen liquid so that it cannot be used: *The pipes had frozen up.* 2 if sb **freezes up**, they are so nervous, frightened or excited that they are unable to move: *I was so nervous I froze up.*

⊕ v + adv

freshen /ˈfreʃn/

,freshen 'up; ,freshen yourself 'up to wash and make yourself look clean and tidy after a journey, before a meeting, etc: *I'll just freshen (myself) up before dinner.*

⊕ v + adv ♦ v + pron + adv

,freshen sth 'up to make sth look cleaner and more attractive: *A coat of paint will freshen this room up.*

⊕ v + n/pron + adv ♦ v + adv + n

frighten /ˈfraɪtn/

,frighten sb/sth a'way/'off; ,frighten sb/sth a'way from sth 1 to make a person or an animal go away by making them feel afraid: *The noise frightened the birds away.* ◇ *I sometimes use a gun to frighten dogs away from the hens.* 2 to make a person or an organization so nervous

that they are no longer interested in sth or no longer want to do sth: *Investment companies have been frightened off by fear of losing money.*
>SYN< **scare sb/sth away/off**
⬥ v + n/pron + adv ◆ v + adv + n ◆ v + n/pron + prep

fritter /'frɪtə(r)/

fritter sth a'way (on sth) to waste time or money on things that are not useful or important: *He's frittered away the money his father left him.*
[OBJ] **money, time**
⬥ v + adv + n ◆ v + n/pron + adv

front /frʌnt/

'front for sb/sth to represent a group or an organization in order to hide a secret or an illegal activity or protect the person who is controlling it: *The police could not discover who he was fronting for.*
⬥ v + prep

front 'onto sth if a building **fronts onto** sth, it faces it: *The apartment fronts onto the beach.*
⬥ v + prep

frost /frɒst; *AmE* frɔːst/

frost 'over/'up to become covered with frost: *All the windows frosted up overnight.*
⬥ v + adv

frown /fraʊn/

'frown on sb/sth (*also* **'frown upon sb/sth** *more formal*) to disapprove of sb/sth: *Some restaurants frown on men not wearing jackets.*
[NOTE] **Frown on/upon sth** is often used in the passive: *Such behaviour is frowned upon.*
→ *see also* SMILE ON/UPON SB/STH
⬥ v + prep

fry /fraɪ/ (fries, frying, fried, fried)

fry sth 'up to cook food in oil especially in order to make a meal quickly: *He fried up some eggs and potatoes.*
⬥ v + adv + n ◆ v + n/pron + adv
▶ **'fry-up** *n* (*BrE*, *informal*) a meal of fried food, especially bacon, eggs, etc.

fuck /fʌk/

fuck a'bout (with sth) (*BrE*) = FUCK AROUND (WITH STH)

fuck sb a'bout (*BrE*) = FUCK SB AROUND

fuck a'round (*BrE also* **fuck a'bout**) **(with sth)** (△, *slang*) to waste time by behaving in a silly way: *Stop fucking around and give me a hand.*
[NOTE] A more polite informal way of saying this is **mess around** or, in British English, **mess about**.
⬥ v + adv

fuck sb a'round (*BrE also* **fuck sb a'bout**) (△, *slang*) to treat sb badly or in an unhelpful way, causing them a delay: *Don't fuck me around.*
[NOTE] A more polite informal way of saying this is **mess sb around** or, in British English, **mess sb about**.
⬥ v + n/pron + adv

fuck 'off (△, *slang*) used to tell sb very rudely to go away: *Fuck off and leave me alone!*
⬥ v + adv

fuck sb 'over (*AmE*, △, *slang*) to treat sb very badly or unfairly: *The company promised me a big pay-off but they really fucked me over.*
[NOTE] A more polite informal way to say this is **mess sb around**.
⬥ v + n/pron + adv ◆ v + adv + n (*less frequent*)

fuck 'up; fuck sth 'up (△, *slang*) to spoil sth or do sth badly; to make a stupid mistake: *It was my fault — I fucked up.* ◇ *He's fucked everything up.*
[NOTE] A more polite informal way to say this is **mess (sth) up** or **foul (sth) up**.
⬥ v + adv ◆ v + n/pron + adv ◆ v + adv + n
▶ **'fuck-up** *n* (△, *slang*) **1** a problem caused by bad organization or a stupid mistake [NOTE] A more polite informal way to say this is **foul-up**. **2** (*AmE*) a person who does sth badly or makes stupid mistakes

fuck sb 'up (△, *slang*) **1** to upset or confuse sb so much that they are not able to deal with problems in their life [NOTE] A more polite informal way to say this is **mess sb up**. **2** (*AmE*) to hit or kick sb hard many times [NOTE] A more polite informal way to say this is **beat sb up**.
⬥ v + n/pron + adv ◆ v + adv + n
▶ **fucked 'up** *adj* (△, *slang*) thoroughly confused or disturbed
[NOTE] A more polite informal way to say this is **messed up**.

'fuck with sb to treat sb badly in a way that makes them annoyed
[NOTE] A more polite way to express this is **mess with sb**.
⬥ v + prep

fuel /'fjuːəl/ (-ll-, *AmE* -l-)

fuel 'up; fuel sth 'up to put fuel into a vehicle: *I need to fuel up before I begin the trip.* ◇ (*figurative*) *On a cold morning I like to fuel up with a hot breakfast.* ◇ *People in a hurry can fuel up their cars and themselves in one stop.*
⬥ v + adv ◆ v + n/pron + adv ◆ v + adv + n

fumble /'fʌmbl/

fumble a'round (*also* **fumble a'bout** *especially BrE*) to move awkwardly, especially using your hands to do sth or to find sth: *He fumbled around in the dark trying to find the lamp.*
⬥ v + adv

furnish /ˈfɜːnɪʃ; *AmE* ˈfɜːrnɪʃ/

'furnish sb/sth with sth (*formal*) to supply or
provide sb/sth with sth: *She furnished him with
the facts surrounding the case.*
SYN supply sb/sth (with sth)
✣ v + n/pron + prep

fuss /fʌs/

'fuss at sb (*AmE*) to complain to sb about sb/sth
very often in an annoying way: *She's always fuss-
ing at me about my smoking.*
✣ v + prep

'fuss over sb/sth to pay a lot of attention, or too
much attention, to sb/sth: *She likes to have someone to fuss over.* ◇ *When she gets nervous she
fusses over unimportant details.*
NOTE Fuss over sb can be used in the passive: *I
hate being fussed over.*
✣ v + prep

futz /fʌts/

,futz a'round (*AmE, spoken, slang*) to spend time
doing unimportant things: *I just futzed around
all morning and got nothing done.*
SYN mess around (*BrE*)
✣ v + adv

Gg

gabble /'gæbl/

,gabble a'way/'on (about sth) to talk quickly and for a long time about sth so that people find it difficult to understand you or become bored: *Someone on the radio was gabbling away in a foreign language.* ◇ *Nicola gabbled on about her boyfriend for hours.*
⬥ v + adv

gad /gæd/ (-dd-)

,gad a'bout/a'round (*old-fashioned, informal, humorous, especially BrE*) to go to different places looking for fun and excitement, especially when you should be doing sth else: *It's about time he stopped gadding about and settled down.*
⬥ v + adv

gag /gæg/ (-gg-)

be 'gagging for sth (*BrE, slang*) (*only used in the progressive tenses*) if somebody is **gagging** for sth, they want it very much: *We were all gagging for a burger.* ◇ *Not all rock stars are gagging for it* (= wanting to have sex with sb).
NOTE You can also use **be gagging to do sth**: *footballers gagging to play for their country*
⬥ v + prep

gain /geɪn/

'gain in sth to get more of a particular quality: *The students are slowly gaining in confidence.*
OBJ popularity, confidence, strength
⬥ v + prep

'gain on sb/sth (*often used in the progressive tenses*) to come closer to sb/sth, especially sb/sth that you are chasing: *We were gaining on the car in front.*
⬥ v + prep

gallop /'gæləp/

,gallop 'through sth to do or say sth very quickly: *Don't gallop through your speech as if you can't wait to finish.*
⬥ v + prep

gamble /'gæmbl/

,gamble sth a'way to lose sth such as money, your possessions, etc. by risking it/them on a card game, horse race, etc: *She gambled away all our money.*
OBJ money
⬥ v + adv + n ◆ v + n/pron + adv

'gamble on sth; 'gamble on doing sth; 'gamble on sb/sth doing sth to take a risk with sth, hoping that you or it will be successful: *She's had two kidney transplants and now her family are gambling on one last operation.* ◇ *We're gambling on the weather being fine on Saturday.*
⬥ v + prep

gang /gæŋ/

,gang 'up (against/on sb) (*informal*) to join together, especially to oppose, threaten, hurt or frighten sb: *My brothers are always ganging up on me.*
⬥ v + adv

gas /gæs/ (-ss-)

,gas 'up; ,gas sth 'up (*AmE, informal*) to put fuel in a vehicle: *I'll have to gas up before we leave.* ◇ *Have you gassed up the car?*
SYN fuel up, fuel sth up
⬥ v + adv ◆ v + adv + n ◆ v + n/pron + adv

gather /'gæðə(r)/

,gather a'round; ,gather a'round sb/sth (*BrE also* ,gather 'round, ,gather 'round sb/sth) to come together in one place, forming a group around sb/sth: *Everyone gathered around to hear the song.* ◇ *They all gathered round the table.*
⬥ v + adv ◆ v + prep

,gather sth 'in to collect a quantity of things, especially crops, and put them all together in one place
OBJ harvest, crop
⬥ v + n/pron + adv ◆ v + adv + n

,gather 'round; ,gather 'round sb/sth (*BrE*) = GATHER AROUND, GATHER AROUND SB/STH

,gather sth to'gether/'up to bring together objects that have been spread around: *She gathered together her belongings and left.*
OBJ papers, belongings, things
NOTE Gather sth is used less often with the same meaning.
⬥ v + adv + n ◆ v + n/pron + adv

gear /gɪə(r); AmE gɪr/

'gear sth to/towards sb/sth; 'gear sth to/towards doing sth to make or change sth so that it is suitable for a particular need or an appropriate level or standard: *The programme is clearly geared to a teenage audience.* ◇ *We try to gear our services to customers' requirements.* ◇ *The policy is geared towards attracting nurses back to work.*
NOTE This phrasal verb is usually used in the passive.
⬥ v + n/pron + prep

,**gear 'up** (for sth/to do sth), ,**gear sb/sth/yourself 'up** (for sth/to do sth) to be prepared, ready and able to do sth; to become or make sb/sth/yourself ready, prepared or able to do sth: *The players are gearing up for the big game.* ◊ *The hospital is gearing itself up to deal with new patients.*
NOTE Gear sb/sth up is usually used in the passive.
◆ v + adv ◆ v + n/pron + adv ◆ v + adv + n

gee /dʒiː/

,**gee 'up** (*BrE*) used to tell a horse to start moving or to go faster
◆ v + adv

,**gee sb 'up** (*BrE*) to encourage sb to work harder or faster or to perform better: *Their success last week will gee the team up.*
◆ v + n/pron + adv ◆ v + adv + n

gen /dʒen/ (-nn-)

,**gen 'up**; ,**gen sb/yourself 'up** (on sth) (*old-fashioned, BrE, informal*) to find out about sth; to get or give sb information on sth: *I must gen myself up for the interview.*
◆ v + adv ◆ v + n/pron + adv

get /get/ (getting, got, got /gɒt/; *AmE* gɑːt/)

NOTE In spoken American English, the past participle **gotten** is almost always used.

	~ about		~ in
	~ above	114	~ in on
	~ across		~ in with
	~ after		~ into
	~ ahead, ahead of	115	~ off
111	~ along		~ off on
	~ around		~ off together
	~ around to		~ off on doing
	~ at		~ off with
	~ away	116	~ on
	~ away from		~ on at
	~ away with		~ onto, on to
	~ back	117	~ out, out of
112	~ back at		~ out of
	~ back into	118	~ over
	~ back to		~ past
	~ back together		~ round
	~ back with		~ round to
	~ behind		~ through
	~ beyond	119	~ to
	~ by		~ together
113	~ down	120	~ up
	~ down on		~ up as/in
	~ down to		~ up to

,**get a'bout 1** (*BrE also* ,**get a'round**) if sb who is old or ill **gets about**, they are able to move from place to place without difficulty: *She gets about with the help of a stick.* **2** (*BrE*) = GET AROUND
◆ v + adv

,**get a'bout sth** (*BrE*) = GET AROUND STH

,**get a'bove yourself** (*especially BrE*) (*often used in the progressive tenses*) to have too high an opinion of yourself; to behave as if you are better than other people: *She's been getting a bit above herself since winning that award.*
◆ v + prep + pron

,**get a'cross** (to sb) to be communicated to sb or understood by sb: *The message is finally getting across to the public.*
◆ v + adv

,**get a'cross**; ,**get a'cross sth** to move from one side of a river, a bridge, a street, etc. to the other: *How can we get across to the island?* ◊ *The only way to get across the lake is by boat.* ◊ *Can we get across the city without having to use the subway?*
◆ v + adv ◆ v + prep

,**get sth a'cross** (*also* ,**get sth 'over** *less frequent*) (to sb) to communicate sth to sb; to make sth clear to sb: *He's not very good at getting his ideas across to the class.* ◊ *You'll have to think of new ways of getting your message across effectively.*
OBJ message, point, idea **SYN** put sth across
NOTE Get sth across is not used in the passive.
◆ v + n/pron + adv ◆ v + adv + prep

,**get sb/sth a'cross sth** (*also* ,**get sb/sth 'over sth**) to move sb/sth, or to help sb/sth move, from one side of sth such as a road, river, bridge, wall, etc. to the other: *We've got to get supplies across the border somehow.* ◊ *We got all the injured soldiers across the river.* ◊ *Billy got the pony over the jumps with difficulty.*
NOTE Get sb/sth across sth is not used in the passive.
◆ v + n/pron + prep

,**get 'after sb** (*informal, especially AmE*) **1** to keep asking or telling sb to do sth, often in an annoying way: *She's been getting after me to take a vacation.* ◊ *I had to get after Jack to clean his room.* **2** to try to catch sb, especially after they have committed a crime: *We need to be tougher on those who commit crime and get after drug users more.*
◆ v + prep

,**get a'head**; ,**get a'head of sb** to make more progress than other people, companies, etc.; to become successful in your life or your career: *It isn't easy to get ahead in the movie business.* ◊ *By doing extra homework, he soon got ahead of his classmates.*
◆ v + adv ◆ v + adv + prep

IDM **get a'head of yourself** to tell sb sth before you have fully explained the background or the details that they need to know first

,get a'long (*informal*) **1** (*often used in the progressive tenses*) to leave a place: *It's late. We'd better be getting along.* ◇ *One more coffee and then I must get along.* → *see also* GET ON 5 **2** (**with sb/together**) = GET ON 1 **3** (**with sth**) = GET ON 4
◆ v + adv

,get a'round (*BrE also* **,get a'bout**) **1** (*informal*) to move from place to place; to go to lots of different places: *You certainly get around! Paris one minute, Bonn the next.* ◇ *She can use my car to get around while she's here.* **2** (of news, a piece of information, etc.) to become known by a lot of people: *The news of her resignation soon got around.* ◇ *Word soon got around that they were having an affair.* **3** to have an active social life and be aware of what is happening: *It's time you got around more.* → *see also* GET OUT 2 **4** (*informal, disapproving*) to have sexual relationships with lots of different people **5** = GET ABOUT 1
◆ v + adv

,get a'round; **,get a'round sth** = GET ROUND, GET ROUND STH

,get a'round sb (*especially AmE*) = GET ROUND SB

,get a'round sth (*BrE also* **,get a'bout sth**, **,get 'round sth**) **1** to move around a city, a country, etc: *It's easy to get around Amsterdam on a bicycle.* **2** (of news, a piece of information, etc.) to become known by a lot of people: *News soon gets round the office.* ◇ *It didn't take long for the rumour to get all around town.* **3** (*especially AmE*) = GET ROUND STH 3
◆ v + prep

,get a'round to sth; **,get a'round to doing sth** = GET ROUND/AROUND TO STH, GET ROUND/AROUND TO DOING STH

'get at sb (*informal*) **1** (*usually used in the progressive tenses*) to keep criticizing sb: *Sam's parents are always getting at him.* ◇ *She feels she's being got at.* **2** to influence sb, especially illegally, for example by threatening them or offering money, in order to persuade them to say sth untrue or act in an unfair way: *One of the witnesses had been got at.* ◇ *They even tried getting at the judge.*
NOTE Get at sb can be used in the passive.
◆ v + prep

'get at sb/sth to reach or obtain sb/sth; to find a way of entering a place, talking to sb, looking at sth, etc: *The files are locked up and I can't get at them.* ◇ *I can't get at my inheritance until I'm 21.*
NOTE Get at sb/sth can be used in the passive: *Put it in a place where it can be got at easily.*
◆ v + prep

'get at sth to learn, discover or find out sth: *We've got to get at the truth.*
OBJ truth **SYN** find sth out
◆ v + prep

IDM what are you, was he, etc. 'getting at? (*spoken*) used to ask, often in an angry way, what sb is/was suggesting: *What exactly are you getting at?* ◇ *I see what you're getting at, but I'm afraid I can't help you with that.*

,get a'way 1 to have a holiday/vacation: *We're hoping to get away for a few days at Easter.* ◇ *Will you manage to get away this year?* **2** (**from sth/…**) to succeed in leaving a place: *It was midday before we finally managed to get away.* ◇ *I won't be able to get away from the office before 7.* **3** (**from sb/sth/…**) to escape from sb or a place: *The thieves got away in a blue van.* ◇ *You're not getting away from me so easily!* **4** **,get 'away** (**with you!**) (*BrE, spoken, becoming old-fashioned*) used to show that you find it difficult to believe what sb has just said: *Get away! You could never run that far!* ◇ *'I'm going to live in China.' 'Get away with you!'* **SYN** go on
◆ v + adv

▶ **'getaway** n [usually sing.] **1** the act of leaving a place in a hurry, especially after committing a crime: *They made a quick getaway.* **2** a short holiday/vacation; a place for this: *the popular island getaway of Penang*

,get a'way from sth; **,get a'way from doing sth** to start doing sth in a different way or talking about a different subject: *The club should get away from its old-fashioned image and try to attract younger people.* ◇ *I tried to get away from the subject of babies.*
◆ v + adv + prep

IDM get a'way from it all (*informal*) to have a short holiday/vacation in a quiet place where you can relax **there's no getting a'way from sth**; **you can't get a'way from sth** you have to admit that sth unpleasant is true: *There's no getting away from the fact that his mistake lost the game for his team.*

,get sb/sth a'way from sth to remove sb/sth from somewhere. *Get that dog away from me!* ◇ *Someone was trying to get Angela away from the window.*
NOTE Get sb/sth away from sth is not used in the passive.
◆ v + n/pron + adv + prep

,get a'way with sth 1 to steal sth and escape with it: *Thieves raided the bank and got away with £50000.* **2** (*also* **,get a'way with doing sth**) (*informal*) to do sth wrong and not be punished or criticized for it: *I can't believe you cheated in the exam and got away with it!* ◇ *Nobody gets away with insulting me like that.* **3** to receive a relatively light punishment: *For such a serious offence he was lucky to get away with a fine.* **OBJ** fine, warning
◆ v + adv + prep

,get 'back 1 (**from/to sth/…**) to return, especially to your home: *What time did you get back last night?* ◇ *We only got back from our trip yesterday.*

◇ *It'll take us ten minutes to get there and five minutes to get back.* **2 (from sb/sth)** *(used especially to give orders)* to move away from a place, a person or sth that is happening: *Get back or I'll shoot!*
)SYN(**stand back; back off**
✪ v + adv

,**get sb 'back 1** to persuade sb to begin a romantic relationship with you again, after you have been apart for some time: *I've done everything I can to get her back.* **2 (for sth/for doing sth)** *(informal)* = GET BACK AT SB
NOTE **Get sb back** is not used in the passive.
✪ v + n/pron + adv

,**get sb/sth 'back (to sth/…)** to take sb/sth back to a place after they have been away from it: *We'll get her back home before midnight.*
NOTE **Get sb/sth back** is not used in the passive.
✪ v + n/pron + adv

,**get sth 'back** to obtain sth again after you have lost it, spent it, lent it to sb, etc: *She's got her old job back.* ◇ *I never lend people books; you never get them back.* ◇ *If I don't like the dress, can I get my money back?* ◇ *There isn't much of a chance of getting the wallet back (= it has been stolen).*
NOTE **Get sth back** cannot be used in the passive.
✪ v + n/pron + adv ◆ v + adv + n *(rare)*
IDM **get your 'breath back** *(BrE)* to start breathing normally again after physical exercise: *It took me a while to get my breath back after running for the bus.* ◇ *(figurative)* *I haven't had a moment to get my breath back (= I've been very busy) since we came back from Prague.*

,**get 'back at sb** *(also* ,**get sb 'back) (for sth/for doing sth)** *(informal)* to punish or hurt sb because they have done sth unpleasant to you: *This is his way of getting back at me for arguing with him.* ◇ *I'll get her back for what she's done.*
)SYN(**pay sb back (for sth/for doing sth)**
✪ v + adv + prep ◆ v + n/pron + adv

,**get back 'into sth** to start being interested or involved in a particular activity again: *She'll try to get back into journalism when the kids start school* ◇ *How soon should I get back into serious training?*
✪ v + adv + prep

,**get 'back to sb** to reply to sb or contact them again by letter or by telephone: *Leave a message and I'll get back to you as soon as I can.* ◇ *They never got back to me about my order.*
✪ v + adv + prep

,**get 'back to sth** to start doing or talking about sth again; to return to sth: *To get back to what I was saying earlier…* ◇ *Once I was awake I couldn't get back to sleep.* ◇ *Let's get back to the point.*
✪ v + adv + prep

,**get 'back with sb**; ,**get back to'gether** to begin a romantic relationship with sb again, after you have been apart for some time: *Jack's getting back with his ex-girlfriend.* ◇ *Jack and his girlfriend are getting back together.*
→ *see also* GET TOGETHER 2
✪ v + adv + prep ◆ v + adv + adv

,**get be'hind (with sth)** to not go as fast as is necessary or as other people; to not produce sth at the right time: *Once I get behind (with my work) it's very hard to catch up.* ◇ *We're getting behind with the rent.*
)SYN(**drop behind, drop behind sb/sth; fall behind, fall behind sb/sth**)OPP(**get ahead**
✪ v + adv

,**get be'hind sb/sth 1** to move into a position behind sb/sth: *If you get behind the tree, she won't see you.* ◇ *He seems to go mad when he gets behind the wheel of a car.* **2** to reveal the person or thing responsible for starting or developing sth: *This is a programme that really gets behind the world of pop music.* **3** *(especially AmE)* to support sb/sth and help them to succeed: *The whole town got behind him/the campaign.*
✪ v + prep

,**get be'yond sth 1** *(also* ,**get 'past sth)** to move or advance further than a particular place: *I haven't been able to get beyond chapter one.* ◇ *When we got beyond York, it started to snow.* **2** *(also* ,**get 'past sth)** to make progress so that you no longer do or are interested in a particular thing: *Hasn't she got beyond/past the stage of sucking her thumb yet?* **3** to become more than sth: *What if our losses get beyond 10%?*
✪ v + prep
IDM **get beyond a 'joke** to become annoying and no longer acceptable: *This rain is getting beyond a joke. Let's go inside.*

,**get 'by** to manage to live or do a particular thing using the money, knowledge, equipment, etc. that you have: *How does she get by on such a small salary?* ◇ *'Are you earning more money now?' 'I get by.'* ◇ *She's got a deadline to meet, so she's getting by on virtually no sleep.* ◇ *I don't know a lot of Italian, but I can get by.* ◇ *To begin with, you can get by with a few simple tools.* ◇ *Getting by isn't good enough for me. I want to be successful.*
✪ v + adv

,**get 'by**; ,**get 'by sb/sth** = GET PAST, GET PAST SB/STH

,**get 'down 1 (from sth)** to move from a higher position to a lower one: *The driver got down from his truck to help me.*)OPP(**get up 2** to bend downwards from a standing position and sit, kneel or lie on the ground: *The children got down on their hands and knees and pretended to be lions.* ◇ *He's going to shoot! Get down!*)OPP(**get up 3 (to sth/…)** to visit or arrive at a place further south

in the country than the place where you live: *How long did it take you to get down here?* ⟨OPP⟩ **get up 4 (from sth)** (*BrE*) (of children) to leave the table after a meal: *Please may I get down (from the table)?* **5 (to sth)** (*spoken, informal*) to go to a place: *I'll get down there straight away.* ◇ *I've got five minutes to get down to the store.* **6** (*AmE, informal*) to relax and enjoy yourself, especially in a very lively way: *Let's get down and party!*
⊕ v + adv

‚get 'down; **‚get 'down sth** to move from a higher place to a lower one, for example using stairs, a rope, a ladder, etc: *What are you doing on the table? Get down now!* ◇ *Did you get down the hill without any difficulty?* ◇ *How does water get down the back of the sink?*
⟨OPP⟩ **get up, get up sth**
⊕ v + adv ◆ v + prep

‚get sb 'down (*informal*) to make sb feel sad or depressed: *This weather is really getting me down.* ◇ *Don't let it get you down too much.*
⟨SYN⟩ **depress sb**
NOTE Get sb down is not used in the passive.
⊕ v + n/pron + adv

‚get sb/sth 'down 1 (to sth/…) to send or move sb/sth to a place, often a place further south in a country: *Get somebody down here straight away.* ◇ *We'll need to get the boat down to the south coast.* ⟨OPP⟩ **get sb/sth up 2 (from sth)** to move sb/sth from a higher position to a lower one: *Can you get a jar down from the shelf for me?* ◇ *He got the baby down from the high chair and put her on the floor.* ◇ *Get your head down!* (= bend so that your head is low) *He's going to shoot!* NOTE In informal spoken language **get sb down sth** and, less often, **get sb sth down**, are also used: *Can you get me down that book?* ◇ *Can you get me that book down?*
NOTE Get sb/sth down is not used in the passive.
⊕ v + n/pron + adv

‚get sth 'down 1 (*also* **‚get sth 'down sb/you** *informal*) to swallow sth, usually with difficulty: *The medicine was so horrible I could hardly get it down.* ◇ *Get this tea down you, then you'll feel better.* ⟨SYN⟩ **swallow sth 2** to make a note of or record sth: *Get it down in writing.* ◇ *I just managed to get down the car's registration number.* ◇ *Did you get his name and telephone number down?* ⟨SYN⟩ **note sth down; take sth down; write sth down 3** to reduce sth, especially the cost or price of sth: *If we bargain, we may be able to get the price down.* ◇ *How can I get my blood pressure down?* ⟨SYN⟩ **bring sth down; lower sth** NOTE Get sth down cannot be used in the passive.
⊕ v + n/pron + adv ◆ v + adv + n (*less frequent*)
1 also v + n/pron + prep

‚get sb/sth 'down sth to manage to move sb/sth from a higher place to a lower one, for example using stairs, a rope, a ladder, etc: *I can't get the bookcase down the stairs on my own.*
NOTE Get sb/sth down sth cannot be used in the passive.
⊕ v + n/pron + prep

‚get sth 'down sb/you (*informal*) = GET STH DOWN 1

‚get 'down on sb/sth (for sth) (*AmE, slang*) to think that sb/sth is wrong and to criticize them: *She's always getting down on me for coming in late.* ◇ *It's easy to get down on kids from day to day and forget their good points.*
⊕ v + adv + prep

‚get 'down to sth; **‚get 'down to doing sth** to begin to do sth; to give serious attention to sth: *Let's get down to business straight away.* ◇ *Isn't it about time you got down to work?* ◇ *Read the text all the way through before you get down to translating it.*
OBJ **business, work**
⊕ v + adv + prep

‚get 'in; **‚get 'into sth 1** to arrive at a place: *When do you normally get in* (= arrive home) *from work?* ◇ *What time do you get into work in the morning?* ◇ *The train got in late.* ◇ *What time does your flight get into Heathrow?* **2** (*also* **‚get 'in sth** *informal*) to succeed in entering a place, especially a building: *How did the burglars get in?* ◇ *They broke a window to get into the house.* ◇ *You can't get in* (= to a concert, party, etc.) *without a ticket.* ◇ *Maybe we can get in the window?* ⟨OPP⟩ **get out, get out of sth 3** (*also* **‚get 'in sth**) to enter or go inside sth: *He ran to the car, got in and drove off.* ◇ *I saw Jan getting into a cab.* ◇ *Hurry up and get into bed.* ◇ *Get in the car!* ◇ *He needs help getting in the bath.* ◇ *Luckily the poison hasn't got into her bloodstream.* ◇ *The smell of smoke got into all my clothes.* ⟨OPP⟩ **get out, get out of sth 4** to be elected to a political position: *They need 326 seats to get in.* ◇ *The Republican candidate got in with a small majority.* ◇ *When did she first get into Parliament?* **5** to gain a place at a school, college, university, etc: *She's applied for Cambridge, but doesn't know if she'll get in.* ◇ *I tried to get into Harvard, but I wasn't accepted.* **6** (*also* **‚get 'in sth** *informal*) (*BrE, sport*) to be chosen as a member of a sports team: *He played well at the trials for the football team and got in.* ◇ *I'll never get into the senior side.* ◇ *Did you get in the team?*
→ *see also* GET INTO STH; GET INTO STH, GET SB/YOURSELF INTO STH
⊕ v + adv ◆ v + prep

‚get 'in sth = GET IN, GET INTO STH 2,3,6

‚get sb 'in 1 to call sb to your home, etc. to do a job for you: *We'll have to get a plumber in to mend the pipe.* **2** to attract a large audience: *A pantomime*

usually gets the crowds in. ⟨SYN⟩ **pull sb in 3** (*also* **get sb 'into sth**) to fit sb in a small place: *Can you get another person in* (= in a car, for example)? ⟨SYN⟩ **fit sb/sth in, fit sb/sth into sth 4** (*also* **get sb 'into sth**) to make it possible for sb to get into a place, attend an event, etc: *If I come to the stage door, can you get me in?*
NOTE Get sb in cannot be used in the passive.
◈ v + n/pron + adv ♦ v + adv + n (*rare*)

get sth 'in 1 to collect or gather sth and bring it inside a place: *Did you get in the washing when it started raining?* ◇ *Can you get the bags in from the car?* ◇ *We worked hard all week to get the corn in.* ⟨SYN⟩ **bring sth in 2** to buy a supply of sth: *Have you got your coal in for the winter yet?* ◇ *Will you be getting any more of these dresses in?* ◇ (*informal*) *Who's going to get the beers in* (= buy beer for everybody)? **3** to manage to do, have, etc. sth, although there is not much time: *I can only get in an hour's piano practice a day.* ◇ *We ought to get in another meeting before the end of the month.* ⟨SYN⟩ **fit sth in 4** to manage to say sth, usually when there are lots of people talking: *She talks so much that it's impossible to **get a word in**.* ◇ *'Excuse me', I eventually got in, 'I think I can help you.'* **OBJ** **word 5** to manage to finish a piece of work and give it to sb in authority, for example your teacher: *Did you manage to get your project in on time?* **6** (*also* **get sth 'into sth**) to fit sth in a small place: *How are we going to get everything in?* ⟨SYN⟩ **fit sth in, fit sth into sth**
NOTE Get sth in cannot be used in the passive.
◈ v + n/pron + adv ♦ v + adv + n
    3 v + adv + n ♦ v + n/pron + adv (*less frequent*)
    4 also v + adv + speech

IDM **(not) get a word in 'edgeways** (*BrE*) (*AmE* **(not) get a word in 'edgewise**) to (not) be able to say anything because sb else is talking too much: *When those two get together, you can't get a word in edgeways.*

get 'in on sth (*informal*) to become involved or take part in an activity: *How did she manage to get in on the deal?* ◇ *He's hoping to get in on any discussions about the new project.*
→ *see also* BE IN ON STH
◈ v + adv + prep
IDM **get in on the 'act** (*informal*) to become involved in an activity that sb else has started, especially to get sth for yourself: *Since the success of the first four-wheel drives, other companies are getting in on the act too.*

get 'in with sb (*informal*) to try to become friendly with sb, especially in order to gain an advantage for yourself: *Have you noticed how he's trying to get in with the boss?* ◇ *She got in with a bad crowd at school.*
◈ v + adv + prep

get 'into sb
◈ v + prep

IDM **what has got into sb?** (*spoken*) used to say that sb has started to behave in a strange or different way: *What's got into you?* ◇ *I don't know what's got into Georgia recently — she's so bad-tempered.*

get 'into sth 1 to put on a piece of clothing, especially with difficulty: *I can't get into these shoes; they're too small.* ◇ *She wants to get into a size 40.* ◇ *Go upstairs and get into your pyjamas.* **2** to start a career in a particular profession: *Can you give me any advice on getting into advertising?* **3** (*also* **get into doing sth**) to become involved in an activity; to start sth: *We got into a conversation about pollution.* ◇ *He got into taking drugs at school.* ◇ *Sam's always getting into fights.* ◇ *Are you sure you know what you're getting into?* **OBJ** **conversation, fight, argument 4** to develop a habit, a routine, etc: *I don't want to get into bad habits.* ◇ *We've got into a good routine with the baby now.* ◇ *Get into the habit of checking your work carefully.* **OBJ** **habit, routine** ⟨OPP⟩ **get out of sth 5** (*informal*) to develop a taste for or an interest in sth: *I'm really getting into jazz these days.* **6** to become familiar with sth; to learn sth: *I haven't really got into my new job yet.* **7** to be found and used in a particular way or by particular people: *I hope the story doesn't get into the papers.* ◇ *I don't want this file **getting into the wrong hands** (= getting to people who should not see it).*
→ *see also* GET IN, GET INTO STH; GET INTO STH, GET SB/YOURSELF INTO STH
◈ v + prep

get 'into sth; get sb/yourself 'into sth to reach a particular state or condition, especially a bad or unpleasant one; to make sb do this: *Jerry was always getting into trouble as a boy.* ◇ *Her little brother was always getting her into trouble.* ◇ *My sense of humour often gets me into trouble!* ◇ *The company has got into difficulties* (= financial problems). ◇ *His passion for sailing has got him into debt.* ◇ *That's another fine mess I've got myself into!* ◇ *Do you realize what you're getting (yourself) into?'*
⟨OPP⟩ **get out of sth; get sb/yourself out of sth**
NOTE Get sb into sth cannot be used in the passive.
→ *see also* GET IN, GET INTO STH; GET INTO STH
◈ v + prep ♦ v + n/pron + prep
IDM **get sb into 'bed** to persuade sb to have a sexual relationship with you

get sb 'into sth = GET SB IN 3,4

get sth 'into sth = GET STH IN 7

get 'off 1 to leave a place or start a journey: *We ought to get off straight after breakfast.* ◇ *to get off to bed/work* **2** (**with sth**) to escape or nearly escape punishment: *He got off with a small fine.* ◇ *Companies who pollute the environment have been **getting off lightly**.* **3** (**with sth**) to escape or nearly escape injury in an accident: *She was* *lucky to get off with just a few bruises.* **4** (*BrE, informal*) to go to sleep: *I couldn't get off to sleep last night.* **5** (*AmE, informal,* usually *disapproving*) to be bold enough to say or do sth: *I don't know where you get off saying that musicians don't make much money.* **6** (*AmE,* △) to have an orgasm (= strong feelings of sexual pleasure)

◆ v + adv

IDM **get off to a flying 'start; get off to a 'flyer** to make a very good start: *The team have got off to a flying start this season.* **get off on the right/wrong 'foot** (*informal*) to start a relationship well/badly: *Mark and I managed to get off on the wrong foot.*

,**get 'off; ,get 'off sb** (*informal*) used to tell sb to stop touching sb: *Get off (me)! You're hurting my arm!*

◆ v + adv ♦ v + prep

,**get 'off; ,get 'off sth 1** to leave a bus, train, plane, etc. that you are travelling in: *Ask the driver where to get off.* ◇ *Let's get off the bus and walk the rest of the way.* ⟨OPP⟩ **get on, get on sth** → *see also* GET OUT, GET OUT OF STH 2 **2** to move your body from sth you are sitting, standing, lying, etc. on, down to the ground: *Get off the table at once!* ◇ *Your bike's got a flat tyre. You'd better get off and walk.* **3** to leave work with permission: *I normally get off at 5.30, but I'll try to get off earlier.* ◇ *What time do you get off work tomorrow?* **4** to stop touching sth: *Get off those cakes! They're for your grandparents.*

◆ v + adv ♦ v + prep

,**get 'off sth 1** to leave a place where you shouldn't really be: *Get off my land!* ⟨OBJ⟩ **land, property 2** to stop discussing a particular subject: *Doesn't she ever get off the subject of money?* ⟨OBJ⟩ **subject 3** to stop using the telephone: *Can you tell me when you get off the phone?* ◇ *Get off that phone! I'm waiting for a call.* ⟨OBJ⟩ **phone, line** ⟨OPP⟩ **get on sth 4** to stop using or doing sth that you have been using or doing as a habit: *I'm determined to get off the drugs.* ⟨OBJ⟩ **drugs, drink** → *see also* GET SB OFF STH 1 **5** (*AmE*) to say or write sth amusing

◆ v + prep

IDM **get off my 'back/'case** (*spoken, informal*) used to ask sb to stop annoying you by criticizing you or telling you to do things **get (sth) off the 'ground** to start happening successfully; to make sth do this: *The project was slow to get off the ground.* ◇ *to get a new company off the ground*

,**get sb 'off 1** (to ...) to make or help sb leave a place or start a journey: *I'll come after I've got the children off to school.* **2** to make a baby, a child, etc. fall asleep: *She got the baby off to sleep by rocking her.* ◇ *When did you eventually get him off?* ⟨OBJ⟩ **baby 3** (*also* ,**get sb 'off sth**) to help sb

to escape punishment: *She's relying on clever lawyers to get her off.* ◇ *They managed to get him off the charge.*

NOTE **Get sb off** is not used in the passive.

◆ v + n/pron + adv **3** also v + n/pron + prep

,**get sth 'off 1** to send sth by post/mail: *I must get these letters off tonight.* ⟨SYN⟩ **send sth off (to sb) 2** to remove sth from sth; to manage to remove sth from sth: *Get your coat off and come and sit down.* ◇ *Her finger was so swollen that she couldn't get her ring off.* ⟨OBJ⟩ **clothes, coat** ⟨SYN⟩ **take sth off 3** to have permission from your employer not to go to work for a particular period of time: *Can you get some time off next week?* ◇ *I'll see if I can get the day off.* ⟨OBJ⟩ **time, day, week** ⟨SYN⟩ **take sth off** → *see also* GET STH OFF STH 2

NOTE **Get sth off** is not used in the passive.

◆ v + n/pron + adv

IDM **get it 'off (with sb)** (*AmE,* △, *slang*) to have sexual relations with sb; to have strong feelings of sexual pleasure

,**get sb 'off sth 1** to help sb to stop using or doing sth that they are in the habit of using or doing: *I need professional help to get me off the alcohol.* → *see also* GET OFF STH 4 **2** to stop sb from discussing a particular subject: *I couldn't get him off politics once he'd started* **3** = GET SB OFF STH 3

⟨OPP⟩ **get sb onto sth**

NOTE **Get sb off sth** cannot be used in the passive.

◆ v + n/pron + prep

,**get sth 'off sb** (*informal*) to succeed in getting sb to give you sth: *Did you get that money off him?* ◇ *Our team couldn't get the ball off them.*

NOTE **Get sb off sth** cannot be used in the passive.

◆ v + n/pron + prep

,**get sth 'off sth 1** to manage to remove sth from sth; to remove sth from somewhere: *Can you get the top off this bottle?* ◇ *She got a jar of coffee off the shelf.* ◇ *Get your feet off the chair!* **2** to get permission from your employer not to go to work during a particular period of time: *Do you think you can get the week off work?* ⟨OBJ⟩ **time, day, week** → *see also* GET STH OFF STH 3

⟨SYN⟩ **take sth off sth**

NOTE **Get sth off sth** cannot be used in the passive.

◆ **1** v + n/pron + prep
2 v + n/pron + prep + n

,**get 'off on sth; ,get 'off on doing sth** (*informal*) to become very excited by sth, often in a sexual way or because of drugs: *She seems to get off on shouting at people.*

◆ v + adv + prep

,**get 'off with sb; ,get 'off together** (*informal, especially BrE*) to start a sexual or romantic rela-

tionship with sb: *Sam got off with Kate at the party.* ◇ *Sam and Kate got off together at the party.* ◇ *He was trying to get off with her.*
⊕ v + adv + prep ◆ v + adv + adv

,get 'on 1 (*also* **,get a'long**) (**with sb/together**) to have a friendly relationship with sb: *My mum and I never really got on (together).* ◇ *Do you get along all right with your boss?* ◇ *Do you and your boss get along all right?* ◇ *I'm glad you get on so well with her.* **2** (**with sth**) to start an activity or continue doing sth, especially after an interruption: *Be quiet and get on with your dinner!* ◇ *Let's get on with the meeting.* ◇ *She got on with the job quietly.* ◇ *If you're going to tell us, just get on with it!* ◇ *I'd love to talk but I must get on.* ◇ *All I want is to get on with my life.* **3** (**in sth**) to be successful in your career: *She's keen to get on in her career.* ◇ *Having contacts is the only way to get on in the art world.* **4** (*also* **,get a'long**) (**with sth**) used to talk about how well sb is doing a task, managing a situation, etc: *How's Jan getting on at college?* ◇ *Are you getting on alright with your project?* ◇ *I can get along without him easily.* ◇ *I'm not getting on very fast with this job.* ◇ *How did you get on in your exams?* **5** (*often used in the progressive tenses*) to leave a place, because you have lots to do: *It's time we were getting on.* → *see also* GET ALONG 1
⊕ v + adv

IDM **be getting 'on 1** (of a person) to be becoming old **2** (of time) to be becoming late: *The time's getting on — we ought to be going.* **be, getting 'on for…** to be near a particular time, age or number: *It must be getting on for midnight.* ◇ *I think he's getting on for 40.* **be, getting 'on towards/ toward…** (*especially AmE*) to be near a particular time, especially a time that is late: *It must be getting on toward midnight by now.*

,get 'on; ,get 'on sth 1 (*also* **,get 'onto sth**) to get into a bus, plane, train, etc: *How did he manage to get on the wrong plane?* ◇ *Did Jack manage to get on?* ◇ *Did anyone see Sue getting onto the bus?* **OBJ** **plane, bus, train** **SYN** **board, board sth** (*more formal*) **OPP** **get off, get off sth** **NOTE** Enter sth cannot be used with this meaning. **2** (*also* **,get 'onto sth**) to move your body so that you are standing, sitting or lying on sth: *He got on his bike and rode off.* ◇ *How did the rabbit get onto the table?* **OPP** **get off, get off sth 3** to leave one road and join another: *You'll need to get on the motorway at Birmingham.*
⊕ v + adv ◆ v + prep

,get 'on sth 1 (**to sb**) to pick up the telephone and try to call sb: *Get on the phone (to them) and tell them you can't come.* **OBJ** **phone, telephone, line** **OPP** **get off sth 2** (*also* **,get 'onto sth**) to be successful in being chosen to do sth such as be on a radio or television programme, etc: *She'd do anything to get on the telly.* **3** (*also* **,get 'onto sth**) to gain a place on a course, a committee, etc: *I*

was very lucky to get onto the course. **4** (*also* **,get 'onto sth**) to be dropped, rubbed, etc. on sth; to fall on sth: *How did that mud get on the carpet?* ◇ *Be careful that the oil doesn't get onto your clothes.*
⊕ v + prep

,get on sth; ,get sb on sth used especially in offices to mean to make telephone calls, or to contact sb by phone: *I'll get on the phone and find out exactly what he wants.* ◇ *I couldn't get him on the phone all day.* ◇ *Shall I get her on the line?*
NOTE Get sb on sth is not used in the passive.
⊕ v + prep ◆ v + n/pron + prep

,get sth 'on 1 to put on, or to manage to put on, an item of clothing, jewellery, etc: *Get your coat on and we'll go for a walk.* ◇ *My finger's swollen and I can't get my ring on.* **OBJ** **coat, shoes** **OPP** **get sth off 2** to start preparing or cooking a meal, a drink, etc: *It's nearly 6 o'clock. I must get the dinner on.* ◇ *Get the kettle on and make us a nice cup of tea.* **OBJ** **dinner, kettle**
SYN **put sth on**
NOTE Get sth on is not used in the passive.
⊕ **1** v + n/pron + adv ◆ v + adv + n (*less frequent*)
2 v + n/pron + adv
IDM **,get it 'on (with sb)** (*slang, especially AmE*) to have sex with sb

,get sb/sth 'on sth (*also* **,get sb/sth 'onto sth** *less frequent*) **1** to manage to put sb/sth onto a place: *It took four people to get the piano on the stage.* ◇ *Get him onto a chair and call an ambulance.* **2** to make sth reach a particular state or condition: *How did you get mud on your coat?*
NOTE Get sb/sth on sth is not used in the passive.
⊕ v + n/pron + prep
IDM **get your 'hands on sb/sth** to find, obtain or catch sb/sth: *I'll need anything I can get my hands on.* ◇ *Just wait until I get my hands on him!*

,get 'on at sb to criticize sb a lot: *She's always getting on at me.*
⊕ v + adv + prep

,get 'on to = GET ONTO

,get 'onto sb; ,get 'on to sb 1 (*informal*) to contact sb, especially by telephone or letter: *If you've got a complaint you'd better get onto the manager.* **2** to become aware of sb's activities, especially ones they want to keep secret: *I don't want the police getting onto me.* → *see also* BE ONTO SB
⊕ v + prep ◆ v + adv + prep

,get 'onto sth 1 = GET ON STH 2,3,4 **2** (*also* **,get 'on to sth**) to begin to discuss a new subject: *We somehow got onto the subject of exams.* ◇ *It's time we got onto the question of cost.* **OBJ** **subject, question 3** (*also* **,get 'on to sth**) (*spoken, informal*) to start working on or thinking about sth: *I'll get onto it right away.* → *see also* BE ONTO STH **4** = GET ON, GET ON STH 1,2
⊕ v + prep

,get sb 'onto sth; **,get sb 'on to sth 1** to introduce sb to sth, especially sth harmful: *Who got her onto drugs in the first place?* **2** to make sb start discussing a particular subject: *Don't get Ken onto politics or we'll be here all night!*
OPP get sb off sth
NOTE Get sb onto sth cannot be used in the passive.
✦ v + n/pron + prep ✦ v + n/pron + adv + prep

,get sb/sth 'onto sth = GET SB/STH ON STH

,get 'out 1 if news, etc. **gets out**, it becomes known, even though people are trying to keep it a secret: *If word gets out there'll be trouble.* ◊ *When it got out that we'd won the lottery, we couldn't escape press photographers.* **SYN leak out 2** to have a social life outside your home: *You need to get out more.* **SYN go out** → *see also* GET AROUND 3 **3 Get out!** (*AmE, informal*) used to show that you do not believe sth: *Get out! Ed actually said that?*
✦ v + adv

,get 'out; **,get 'out of sth 1** to leave or go out of a place such as a car, a lift, a room or a house: *The car door opened and a tall man got out.* ◊ *I have a lot of trouble getting out of bed in the mornings.* ◊ *Close the door to stop the heat getting out.* ◊ *Get out and don't come back!* ◊ *Do you need help getting out of the bath?* **OPP get in, get into sth 2** to leave a bus, train, plane, etc. that you are travelling in: *The bus driver will tell you where to get out.* **OPP get on, get on sth** → *see also* GET OFF, GET OFF STH 1 **3** to manage to find a way out of a place: *It's very difficult getting out of the city in the rush hour.* ◊ *The thieves must have got out through the window.* **4** to leave a place, an organization, etc. in order to avoid difficulty or danger: *They were able to get out of the country before the war started.* ◊ *The company's in trouble — you should get out while you can.*
✦ v + adv ✦ v + adv + prep

get sb 'out (in cricket) to end the time when sb is hitting the ball, for example by forcing them to make a mistake: *If England can get Richards out, they might win the match.*
✦ v + n/pron + adv ✦ v + adv + n (*less frequent*)

get sb 'out; **,get sb 'out of sth** to help or make sb leave a place: *Get everyone out* (= out of a building) *quickly!* ◊ *I couldn't get the kids out of bed this morning.* ◊ (*figurative*) *I can't get her out of my mind.*
✦ v + n/pron + adv ✦ v + n/pron + adv + prep

get sth 'out 1 to say sth with difficulty: *She was laughing so much she could hardly get the words out.* ◊ *I wanted to tell him how I felt, but I couldn't get it out.* **OBJ words 2** to produce or publish sth: *Will we get the book out by the end of the year?*
NOTE Get sth out is not used in the passive.
✦ v + n/pron + adv ✦ v + adv + n (*less frequent*)

,get sth 'out; **,get sth 'out of sth 1** to remove or take sth out of a place, a container, etc: *Get your violin out and we'll start the lesson.* ◊ *He started to get his wallet out* (*of his pocket*) (= to pay) *but I insisted on paying.* ◊ *I'll need to get some money out* (= out of the bank). ◊ *She got out her cigarettes and offered me one.* ◊ *I'll try and get that book out of the library.* ◊ (*figurative*) *I can't get the argument out of my mind.* **SYN take sth out, take sth out of sth 2** to remove a stain, etc. from sth: *Did you manage to get out that oil stain?* ◊ *I can't get the red wine out of the carpet.* **OBJ stain**
✦ v + n/pron + adv ✦ v + adv + n (*less frequent*) ✦ v + n/pron + adv + prep
IDM get sth out of your 'system (*informal*) to do or say sth so that you no longer feel a very strong emotion or have a very strong desire: *I need to get the anger out of my system.* ◊ *You'll feel better once you've got it all out of your system.*

,get 'out of sth 1 (*also* ,get 'out of doing sth) to avoid a responsibility or duty; to not do sth that you ought to do: *We promised we'd go — we can't get out of it now.* ◊ *I'll see if I can get out of going to the meeting.* **2** to stop having a particular habit: *I can't get out of the habit of waking up early.* ◊ *I don't want the children to get out of their routine.* ◊ *Try to get out of the habit of eating between meals.* **OBJ habit, routine OPP get into sth 3** to escape from a difficult situation: *Sometimes I feel I'll never get out of debt.* ◊ *How are we going to get out of this mess?* **OBJ debt, mess, trouble OPP get into sth 4** to remove an item of clothing: *Come in and get out of those wet clothes.* **OPP get into sth**
✦ v + adv + prep
▶ **'get-out** n [usually sing.] a way of avoiding sth; an excuse: *They're looking for a good get-out.* ◊ *The agreement contains a number of **get-out** clauses.*

,get 'out of sth; **,get sb/yourself 'out of sth** to escape from a particular state or condition, especially a bad or unpleasant one; to make or help sb do this: *Jack always uses his wits to get out of trouble.* ◊ *The situation is getting out of control.* ◊ *Who can get us out of this mess?* ◊ *This new job should help me get out of debt.*
OPP get into sth; **get sb/yourself into sth**
NOTE Get sb out of sth cannot be used in the passive.
✦ v + adv + prep ✦ v + n/pron + adv + prep

,get sth 'out of sb to obtain sth from sb, usually by persuading or threatening them: *The police have got a confession out of her.* ◊ *It's not worth trying to get money out of him!* ◊ *I couldn't get a word out of her.*
OBJ word, money, the best
✦ v + n/pron + adv + prep

,**get sth 'out of sth**; ,**get sth 'out of doing sth** to gain, obtain or achieve sth from a particular occasion, situation or activity: *She seems to get a lot out of life.* ◇ *He gets a lot of pleasure out of buying presents for the children.* ◇ *I didn't get much out of the conference.* ◇ *I don't feel she's getting the most out of her studies.* ◇ *John **gets a kick out of** (= gets a lot of pleasure and excitement from) driving fast cars.*

[OBJ] **pleasure, enjoyment**

◈ v + n/pron + adv + prep

,**get 'over** (*also* ,**get yourself 'over** *informal*) [+adv/prep] to go to a place or to arrive somewhere: *How much will it cost you to get over to Ireland?* ◇ *I'd better get over there right now to see her.* ◇ *Get yourself over there now and tell him how you feel.*

◈ v + adv ◆ v + pron + adv

,**get 'over sb/sth** to return to your usual state of health, happiness, etc. after the end of a relationship with sb, an illness, a shock, etc: *He never really got·over Jennifer* (= when their relationship finished). ◇ *I'm still getting over my cold.* ◇ *My pride was hurt, but I'll get over it.*

◈ v + prep

,**get 'over sth 1** to deal with or gain control of sth: *Eddy's got to learn to get over his shyness.* [OBJ] **shyness, problem** [SYN] **overcome sth** [NOTE] Get over sth can be used in the passive in this meaning: *I think the problem can be got over without too much difficulty.* **2** (*informal*) (*usually used in a negative sentence with can't or couldn't*) to believe that sth surprising or unexpected really did happen or is true: *I can't get over* (= I'm very surprised or shocked by) *how much she's changed!* [SYN] **believe sth 3** to climb or cross sth high: *Can you get over the wall on your own?*

◈ v + prep

,**get sb 'over** [+adv/prep] to arrange for sb to go or come to a place: *Get a reporter over here straight away!* ◇ *Shall we get my parents over for dinner tonight?* [NOTE] Get sb over is not used in the passive

◈ v + n/pron + adv

,**get sth 'over 1 (to sb)** = GET STH ACROSS (TO SB) **2** (*informal*) to complete sth necessary and usually unpleasant: *Can we just get this test over?* ◇ *Let's tell her the news now and get it over with.* ◇ *I'll be glad to get the exam over and done with.* [NOTE] Get sth over is not used in the passive.

◈ **1** v + n/pron + adv ◆ v + adv + n
　2 v + n/pron + adv

,**get yourself 'over** [+adv/prep] = GET OVER

,**get sb/sth 'over sth** = GET SB/STH ACROSS STH

,**get sth 'over sth** to make sth reach a particular state or condition: *How did you manage to get chocolate all over your clean T-shirt?* [NOTE] Get sth over sth is not used in the passive.

◈ v + n/pron + prep

,**get 'past**; ,**get 'past sb/sth** (*also* ,**get 'by**, ,**get 'by sth** *less frequent*) **1** to manage to move past sb/sth: *He tried to get past them and run for the door.* ◇ *Once we get past this truck I can speed up.* **2** to pass sb/sth without being noticed, caught or stopped: *It'll be difficult to get past the ticket collector without paying.* ◇ *The movie will never get past the censors.* ◇ *Very few goals get past the goalkeeper.*

◈ v + adv ◆ v + prep

,**get 'past sth** = GET BEYOND STH 1, 2

,**get sb/sth 'past sb/sth 1** to manage to move sb/sth past sb/sth: *I couldn't get the baby's buggy past the car parked on the pavement.* **2** to make sb/sth go past sb/sth without being noticed, stopped or caught: *You won't get any goals past him!* ◇ *How did you get your article past the editor?*

[NOTE] Get sth past sb/sth is not used in the passive.

◈ v + n/pron + prep

,**get 'round**; ,**get 'round sth** (*BrE*) (*also* ,**get a'round**, ,**get a'round sth** *AmE, BrE*) **1** (in sport, a race, etc.) to complete a course and return to the beginning: *How long did it take you to get round (the course)?* **2** to fit in a circle around a table, etc: *Can we all get round (the table)?*

◈ v + adv ◆ v + prep

,**get 'round sb** (*also* ,**get a'round sb** *especially AmE*) to persuade sb to let you do or have sth, or to do what you want, often by being nice to them *I'll try and get round my dad tonight and persuade him to give us a lift.*

[NOTE] Get round/around sb can be used in the passive, but this is not common: *Do you think your brother can be got around?*

◈ v + prep

,**get 'round sth** (*BrE*) **1** = GET AROUND STH 1 **2** = GET AROUND STH 2 **3** (*also* ,**get a'round sth** *especially AmE*) to deal with a problem successfully to avoid sth: *There's no getting round it. We're just going to have to pay.* ◇ *A clever lawyer might be able to get round that clause.* [NOTE] In this meaning, get round can be used in the passive: *There must be a way these rules can be got round.*

◈ v + prep

,**get ,round/a'round to sth**; ,**get 'round a'round to doing sth** to find the time to do sth: *I haven't got round to asking him yet.* ◇ *One of these days I'll get around to buying a new car.* ◇ *I'm going to write to Uncle Joe, but I haven't got around to it yet.*

◈ v + adv + prep

,**get 'through 1 (to sb)** to make contact with sb by telephone: *I tried ringing you but I couldn't get through.* ◇ *We had great trouble getting through to the right person on the phone.* **2 (to sb)** to make sb understand or accept what you say to them especially when you are trying to help them:

don't feel I'm getting through (to her). ◇ *Do you think the message is getting through?* ◇ *How can I* **get it through to** *him that he's wasting his life in that job?* **3** (**to sb/sth**) to succeed in reaching a place or a person: *Thousands of refugees will die if these supplies don't get through (to them).* **4** (**to sth**) to reach the next stage of a competition: *Henman got through to the final.* ◇ *I really wasn't expecting to get through!*

◆ v + adv

get 'through; **get 'through sth 1** to survive a difficult or unpleasant experience or period in your life: *He wouldn't have got through (it) without her.* ◇ *I don't know how I got through the day.* OBJ **day** ⟩SYN⟩ **survive**, **survive sth** NOTE **Get through sth** can be used in the passive in this meaning: *These difficult times just have to be got through.* → *see also* GET SB THROUGH, GET SB THROUGH STH 1 **2** to be successful in an examination, a test, etc: *Tom failed but his sister got through.* ◇ *The whole class got through the exam.* OBJ **exam** ⟩SYN⟩ **pass**, **pass sth 3** to manage to pass through a hole, gap, etc. to reach the other side: *The gap's not very wide. Do you think you can get through?* ◇ *Sophie's probably small enough to get through the window.* ◇ *The sun was still trying to get through (the clouds).* OBJ **window** → *see also* GET STH THROUGH, GET STH THROUGH STH 2 **4** to be officially approved or accepted: *Do you think the bill will get through (Congress)?* OBJ **Parliament**, **Congress** → *see also* GET STH THROUGH, GET STH THROUGH STH 1

◆ v + adv ◆ v + prep

get 'through sth 1 (*especially BrE*) to use up the amount or quantity of sth mentioned: *She gets through forty cigarettes a day.* ◇ *Have we got through all that milk already?* **2** to manage to do or complete sth: *I've got a lot of work to get through today.* ◇ *We must get through the syllabus before the end of the year.* OBJ **work**

NOTE **Get through sth** can be used in the passive: *There are a lot of jobs to be got through.*

◆ v + prep

get sb 'through; **get sb 'through sth 1** to help sb survive a difficult or unpleasant experience or period in their life: *I'm depending on luck to get me through.* ◇ *A good breakfast will help you get through the morning.* → *see also* GET THROUGH, GET THROUGH STH 1 **2** to help sb to be successful in an examination, a test, etc: *My mum got me through my driving test.* ◇ *These grades should just get me through.* → *see also* GET THROUGH, GET THROUGH STH 2 **3** (**to sth**) to help a player or team to reach the next stage of a competition: *He was responsible for getting them through that round.* ◇ *A stroke of luck may get us through to the final.*

NOTE **Get sb through** and **get sb through sth** are not used in the passive.

◆ v + n/pron + adv ◆ v + n/pron + prep

get sth 'through (**to sb/sth**) to manage to send sth to a person or place: *I really need to get a message through to them.* ◇ *We must get food through to Ethiopia.*

NOTE **Get sth through** is not used in the passive.

◆ v + n/pron + adv

get sth 'through; **get sth 'through sth 1** to make sth be officially approved or accepted: *I'm still trying to get the proposal through.* ◇ *Will he manage to get the bill through parliament?* OBJ **bill 2** to cause sth to pass through sth: *Can you get your car through the gate?* ◇ *My hair was so tangled that I couldn't get a comb through it.*

NOTE **Get sth through** and **get sth through sth** are not used in the passive.

→ *see also* GET THROUGH, GET THROUGH STH 3

◆ v + n/pron + adv ◆ v + n/pron + prep

'get to sb (*informal*) to begin to annoy, anger, upset or affect sb, even though they try not to let it: *His constant nagging is beginning to get to her.* ◇ *Don't let her get to you.* ◇ *Seeing him so sad really got to me.*

◆ v + prep

'get to sth to arrive at a place or reach a particular situation, age, time, etc: *The train gets to London at 6 o'clock.* ◇ *I didn't get to bed until after midnight last night.* ◇ *It's got to the stage/point where I don't want to go home.* ◇ *When you get to my age you're a bit more relaxed about things.* ◇ *It got to 4 o'clock and she still hadn't arrived.* ◇ *I wonder where Anthony's got to* (= where he is/what he is doing)?

OBJ **bed**, **stage**, **point**

◆ v + prep

'get to doing sth to reach the point where you do sth; to begin to do sth: *He got to thinking that perhaps she wouldn't come after all.*

◆ v + prep

get to'gether (**with sb**) **1** to meet with sb for social purposes or to discuss or organize sth: *We must get together for a drink some time.* ◇ *The management should get together with the union to discuss their differences.* ◇ *Local residents have got together and started a petition.* **2** to begin a relationship with sb: *Did you two get together (with each other) at university?* → *see also* GET BACK WITH SB, GET BACK TOGETHER

◆ v + adv

▶ **'get-together** *n* (*informal*) an informal social meeting; a small party: *a family get-together* ◇ *We're having a little get-together to celebrate Jane's exam results.*

get A and B to'gether to help two people begin a romantic relationship with each other: *I was the one who got them together.*

⟩SYN⟩ **bring A and B together**

NOTE **Get sb together** is not used in the passive.

◆ v + n/pron + adv

,get sb/sth to'gether to bring people or things together in one place: *She's getting her things together ready to leave.* ◇ *Do you think you could get together a team for Saturday's match?* ◇ *We're getting a band together.* ◇ *(figurative) We'll need some time to get our ideas together and come up with a plan.* ◇ *Can you get the money together by Friday?* ◇ *Do you think you can get together a proposal by next week?* ◇ *I haven't got anything together for the trip.*
◈ v + n/pron + adv ♦ v + adv + n

IDM **get your 'act together** (*informal*) to become properly organized in order to be able to deal with or achieve sth: *If he gets his act together he could be very successful.* ◇ *The government needs to get its act together on unemployment.* **get it to'gether (with sb)** (*informal*) **1** to start a romantic or sexual relationship with sb: *I didn't know Bill and Gina had got it together!* **2** to become properly organized in order to be able to deal with or achieve sth: *The team needs to get it together if they want to win the match.*

,get yourself to'gether to manage to control your feelings in a difficult situation: *She paused outside the door to get herself together.*
SYN **pull yourself together**
◈ v + pron + adv

,get 'up 1 to stand after sitting, kneeling, etc: *Everyone got up when the President came in.* ◇ *He got up slowly from his chair.* ◇ *Get up off the floor!* **2** [+ adv/prep] to visit or travel to a place (usually somewhere further north in the country): *When are you going to get up to Glasgow for a visit?* ◇ *He doesn't get up to see me very often.* ◇ *I won't be able to get up there until Wednesday.* **OPP** **get down 3** if the sea or the wind **gets up**, it increases in strength and becomes violent: *As the sun went down, a breeze got up.*
◈ v + adv
▶ **,get-up-and-'go** *n* [U] (*informal*) the quality of being energetic and determined: *She's got lots of get-up-and-go.*

,get 'up; ,get sb 'up to get out of bed; to make sb get out of bed: *What time do you usually get up?* ◇ *Could you get me up early tomorrow?* ◇ *Get up, you lazy thing!*
◈ v + adv ♦ v + n/pron + adv

,get 'up; ,get 'up sth to climb to the top of sth such as a hill, steps, etc: *How did the cat get up there?* ◇ *He can't really get up the stairs on his own.* ◇ *We used ropes to get up the mountain.* ◇ *I had to get up on the desk and shout to get somebody's attention.*
OBJ **mountain, hill, stairs, steps** **OPP** **get down, get down sth**
◈ v + adv ♦ v + prep

,get 'up sth 1 to make yourself feel excited, full of energy, etc: *I'm trying to get up the enthusiasm to do some Christmas shopping.* **OBJ** **enthusiasm,**

energy 2 to organize sth such as a public event or action: *Parents are getting up a petition against the closure of the local school.* ◇ *We're getting up a party for her birthday.*
◈ **1** v + adv + n
2 v + adv + n ♦ v + n/pron + adv ♦ v + n + adv (*rare*)
IDM **get up 'speed** to start to go faster: *We'll be able to get up speed once we get onto the motorway.*

,get sb/sth 'up 1 (to sth) to send or move sb/sth to another place, often a place further north in the country: *We need to get somebody up there straight away.* ◇ *How can we get all our equipment up to Leeds?* **OPP** **get sb/sth down 2** (*also* **,get sb/sth 'up sth**) to move sb/sth from a lower position to a higher one: *Can you get me up onto the chair?* ◇ *How did you get the bed up the stairs?* **OPP** **get sb/sth down; get sb/sth down sth**
NOTE Get sb/sth up is not used in the passive.
◈ v + n/pron + adv **2** also v + n/pron + prep

,get sth 'up 1 to build sth; to put sth into an upright position: *They got the building up in just a few months.* ◇ *Can you get the tent up while I go and find water?* **2** if sb **gets** their hopes **up**, they start to hope and believe that sth they want will happen: *I don't want to get your hopes up, but there will probably be a place on the course for you.* **OBJ** only **hopes**
NOTE Get sth up is not used in the passive.
◈ v + n/pron + adv

IDM **get sb's 'back up** (*informal*) to annoy sb: *He really gets my back up when he behaves like that!* **get it 'up** (*slang*) (of a man) to become sexually excited so that the penis is hard and upright

,get sb/yourself 'up as/in sth to dress sb/yourself in unusual or strange clothes: *She was got up as an Indian princess.*
◈ v + n/pron + adv + prep
▶ **'get-up** *n* (*old-fashioned, informal*) a set of clothes, usually an unusual or strange one: *He looked ridiculous in that get-up!*

,get 'up to sth 1 to reach a particular point: *We got up to page 72 last lesson.* ◇ *I've got to get up to intermediate level in French in a year.* **2** (*informal*) to be doing or be involved in sth, especially sth that is surprising or unpleasant: *What on earth will he get up to next?* ◇ *What have you kids been getting up to?* ◇ *The boys are lively and get up to mischief all day.* ◇ *She's been getting up to her old tricks again!*
◈ v + adv + prep

ginger /'dʒɪndʒə(r)/

,ginger sb/sth 'up (*BrE*) to make sb/sth more active, interesting or exciting: *Some dancing would ginger up the party.* ◇ *They need some excitement to ginger them up a bit.*
◈ v + adv + n ♦ v + n/pron + adv

give /gɪv/ (**gave** /geɪv/ **given** /'gɪvn/)

~ away		~ out
~ back	122	~ over
~ for		~ over to
~ in		~ up
~ of		~ up on
~ off		~ up to
~ onto		

,**give sb a'way 1** (in a marriage ceremony) to lead the woman who is getting married to the man she is going to marry and formally allow her to marry him: *Her father gave her away.* **2** (*BrE*) to give a baby or a child to another person to take care of as their own child: *She had never understood why her mother had given her away.*
→ *see also* GIVE SB UP 2
✦ v + n/pron + adv ◆ v + adv + n

,**give sb/sth/yourself a'way** to do or say sth that shows sth about sb/sth/yourself that was a secret: *It was her eyes that gave her away* (= showed how she really felt). ◇ *He never gives very much away about himself.* ◇ *She had given away state secrets to the enemy.* ◇ *I found I could tell lies confidently without giving myself away.*
[OBJ] **nothing, anything, little** [SYN] **betray sb/sth/ yourself** (*more formal*)
✦ v + adv + n ◆ v + n/pron + adv

[IDM] **give the 'game away** to tell a secret, especially by accident; to show sth that has been hidden: *I don't want to give the game away by telling you how the movie ends.*
▶ '**giveaway** *n* (*informal*) something that makes you guess the real truth about sth: *He said he was French, but his accent was a dead giveaway!* (= showed clearly that he was not French)
→ *see also* GIVEAWAY at GIVE STH AWAY

,**give sth a'way** to give sth to sb as a gift: *He decided to give most of his money away.* ◇ *We have 200 tickets to give away free to our viewers.*
✦ v + n/pron + adv ◆ v + adv + n
▶ '**giveaway** *n* (*informal*) something that a company gives free, usually with a product for sale, to persuade people to buy it
→ *see also* GIVEAWAY at GIVE SB/STH/YOURSELF AWAY
▶ '**give-away** *adj* [only before noun] (*informal*) (of prices) very low

,**give sb 'back** (**to sb**) to return a child to its parents: *We love our grandchildren dearly, but we are happy to give them back at the end of the day!*
✦ v + n/pron + adv ◆ v + adv + n

,**give sth 'back** (**to sb**) to return sth to its owner: *You can't have it. Give it back!* ◇ *Have you given back the money you borrowed from your father?* ◇ *Can you lend me $20? I'll give it back to you later.* ◇ *The new law gives some power back to the people.* ◇ (*figurative*) *The operation gave him back the use of his legs.*

[SYN] **hand sth back** (**to sb**); **return sth** (**to sb**) (*more formal*)
[NOTE] In informal language **give sb back sth** and, less often, **give sb sth back** are also used: *Could you give me back my pen?* ◇ *Could you give me my pen back?* In very informal spoken English, you can also say: *I'll give you it back tomorrow* or *I'll give it you back tomorrow.*
✦ v + n/pron + adv ◆ v + adv + n

'**give sth for sth** to pay or give a particular amount to have or do sth: *How much did you give for the car?* ◇ *I'd give anything for a cold beer.*
[NOTE] **Give sth for sth** is not used in the passive.
✦ v + n/pron + prep

,**give 'in** (**to sb/sth**) **1** to accept that you have been defeated or persuaded by sb: *I give in — you'll have to tell me the answer.* ◇ *Eventually I gave in to temptation and had an ice cream.* **2** to finally agree to do sth that you do not want to do: *We mustn't give in to terrorist demands.* ◇ *She gives in to the children all the time to avoid arguments.*
[OPP] **hold out** (**against sb/sth**)
✦ v + adv

,**give sth 'in** (**to sb**) to hand sth to sb in authority, for example a teacher: *Please give your test in* (*to the teacher*) *when you've finished.*
[SYN] **hand sth in** (**to sb**)
✦ v + n/pron + adv ◆ v + adv + n

'**give of sth**; '**give of yourself** (*formal*) to give your time or money willingly to help other people without expecting them to do anything for you: *She's always willing to give of her time to help the homeless.* ◇ *The teacher encourages all the children to give of their best.*
[OBJ] **time, best**
✦ v + prep ◆ v + prep + pron

,**give 'off sth**; ,**give it/them 'off 1** to produce sth such as heat, light, smoke, etc: *Burning apple wood gives off a pleasing smell.* [OBJ] **smell, aroma, light, gas** → *see also* GIVE STH OUT 2 **2** to give a particular impression by the way you look or behave: *She gave off an air of confidence.*
[NOTE] A noun must always follow **off**, but a pronoun comes between the verb and **off**.
✦ v + adv + n ◆ v + pron + adv (*less frequent*)

'**give onto sth** (*BrE*) if a door, a window, etc. **gives onto** sth, it has a view of it or leads directly to it: *French windows give onto a balcony.*
✦ v + prep

,**give 'out 1** to come to an end; to be used up: *My patience finally gave out.* ◇ *We were fine until the batteries in the torch gave out.* [SYN] **run out 2** if an engine, a machine, etc. **gives out**, it stops working, especially if it is old or damaged: *One of the plane's engines gave out.* ◇ (*figurative*) *His heart gave out just before his eightieth birthday.* [SYN] **break down**
✦ v + adv

,give sth 'out 1 to hand sth to a lot of people: *The teacher gave out the exam papers.* ◇ *I'll write up the report and give it out to the whole department.* **OBJ cards, leaflets** ⟨SYN⟩ **hand sth out** (to sb) **NOTE** In informal spoken language **give sb out** sth is also used: *I'll give you out the cards later.* **2** to produce sth, such as light or heat: *That lamp doesn't give out a lot of light.* **OBJ light, heat, noise** → *see also* GIVE OFF STH, GIVE IT/THEM OFF 1 **3** (*BrE*) to tell people sth or broadcast sth: *No details of the accident have been given out yet.* ◇ *The leader of the opposition has given out that she is resigning.* **OBJ information NOTE** Give sth out is often used in the passive in this meaning.
◆ v + adv + n ♦ v + n/pron + adv

,give 'over (*BrE, spoken, informal*) used to tell sb to stop doing sth: *Give over! I can't work with you shouting like that.*
◆ v + adv

,give sb/sth 'over to sb to let sb have sb/sth so that they can look after or have responsibility for them/it: *We gave the house over to my uncle when we went to live abroad.*
◆ v + n/pron + adv + prep ♦ v + adv + n + prep

,give sth 'over to sth to use sth only for a particular activity or purpose: *The newspapers gave six pages over to the tragedy.* ◇ *Much of the countryside is given over to agriculture.*
NOTE Give sth over to sth is often used in the passive.
◆ v + n/pron + adv + prep ♦ v + adv + n + prep

,give yourself 'over/up to sth; **,give yourself 'over/up to doing sth** to spend all your time and energy on sth; to allow sth to completely control your life: *After his wife's death, he seemed to give himself over to despair.* ◇ *I want to give myself over to writing full-time.*
◆ v + pron + adv + prep

,give 'up; **,give sth 'up**; **,give 'up doing sth 1** to stop trying to do sth, usually because it is too difficult: *She doesn't give up easily — she keeps on trying.* ◇ *I tried to fix the car myself, but gave up the attempt after a couple of hours.* ◇ *I've given up trying to understand her.* → *see also* GIVE IN (TO SB/STH) **2** to stop doing or having sth that you consider unhealthy: *It's about time you gave up smoking.*
◆ v + adv ♦ v + adv + n ♦ v + pron + adv ♦ v + n + adv (*less frequent*) ♦ v + adv + -ing

,give sb 'up 1 to stop having a friendship or a relationship with sb: *I'm not going to give up all my friends just because I'm getting married.* ◇ *He gave her up for a younger woman.* **2** to give a baby to sb else to bring up: *She gave the baby up for adoption.* → *see also* GIVE SB AWAY 2 **3** (*also* ,give 'up on sb *especially AmE*) to stop hoping that sb will arrive or is still alive: *Where have you been? We'd given you up!*
◆ v + n/pron + adv ♦ v + adv + n **2** also v + adv + prep

IDM give sb up for 'lost/'dead (*formal*) to no longer hope or expect that sb will arrive or is still alive

,give sth 'up 1 to stop doing or having sth: *He's given up the idea of becoming a model.* ◇ *She'd given up all hope of seeing him again.* **2** (to sb) to let sb else have sth, sometimes because they need it more than you: *Children rarely give up their seats to older people on buses now* (= stand up so that they can sit down). **3** (to sb) to hand sth over to sb else: *Do I have to give up my old passport when I apply for a new one?* **4** to spend time doing sth when you would normally be doing sth else: *Thanks for giving up your time to come and help us.* **OBJ time, the morning, etc. 5** (for sb/to do sth) to stop doing or having sth that you enjoy so that you can do or achieve sth that you consider more important: *I gave up everything for my family.* ◇ *She gave it all up to be with him.*
NOTE Give sth up is not often used in the passive.
◆ v + adv + n ♦ v + pron + adv ♦ v + n + adv (*less frequent*) **3** v + n/pron + adv ♦ v + adv + n

IDM let's give it up for sb (*spoken, informal, especially AmE*) used to ask people to hit their hands together several times (to **clap**) to show they approve of sb or have enjoyed sth

,give yourself 'up (to sb/sth) to allow yourself to be arrested or captured: *After a week on the run he gave himself up to the police.*
⟨SYN⟩ **surrender** (to sb/sth)
◆ v + pron + adv

,give 'up on sb (*informal*) **1** to lose hope that sb will get better, change, etc: *I've given up on her. She never replies to my letters.* ◇ *His teachers seem to have given up on him.* **2** (*especially AmE*) = GIVE SB UP 3
◆ v + adv + prep

,give 'up on sth (*informal*) to stop hoping that sth will be successful or will happen: *I haven't given up on my marriage yet* (= I think we can save it). ◇ *Have you given up on the idea of emigrating?*
◆ v + adv + prep

,give yourself 'up to sth; **,give yourself 'up to doing sth** = GIVE YOURSELF OVER/UP TO STH, GIVE YOURSELF OVER/UP TO DOING STH

glance /glɑːns; *AmE* glæns/

,glance 'off sth if a ball, etc. glances off sth, it touches it lightly and moves away from it in a different direction: *The ball glanced off the goal post into the net.*
◆ v + prep

,glance 'off/'on sth if light glances off/on sth, it flashes on a surface or is reflected from it: *the sun glancing on water*
◆ v + prep

'glance 'over/'through sth to look at or read sth very quickly and not very thoroughly: *Could you glance over this document for me?* ◇ *I glanced through a magazine while I waited.*
[OBJ] **book, list**
◈ v + prep

glaze /gleɪz/

,glaze 'over if a person's eyes **glaze over**, the person begins to look very bored or tired: *Her eyes glazed over when they started talking about football.* ◇ *I started to glaze over at that point.*
[NOTE] Glaze can also be used with the same meaning: *Her eyes glazed with tears.*
◈ v + adv

glom /glɒm; AmE glɑːm/ (-mm-)

,glom 'onto sth (*AmE, slang*) to become very interested in sth such as a new fashion or an idea: *The whole nation glommed onto the scandal.*
◈ v + prep

glory /'glɔːri/ (glories, glorying, gloried, gloried)

'glory in sth (*literary*) **1** to get great pleasure or enjoyment from sth: *He gloried in his son's success.* ◇ *I gloried in the beauty of the scenery.* **2** to take pleasure in sth: *She seemed to glory in his failure.*
◈ v + prep

gloss /glɒs; AmE glɔːs, glɑːs/

,gloss 'over sth to treat sth such as a problem, mistake, etc. as if it was not important and avoid discussing it in detail: *The manager glossed over the team's recent defeat.* ◇ *The movie glosses over the real issues of the war.*
[NOTE] Gloss over sth can be used in the passive: *This question has been glossed over by politicians.*
◈ v + prep

gnaw /nɔː/

'gnaw at sb to make sb feel gradually more anxious or annoyed over a long period of time: *These doubts had been gnawing at him for some time.*
◈ v + prep

,gnaw a'way at sth to gradually have a harmful effect on sth over a long period of time: *His attitude towards her gnawed away at her confidence.*
◈ v + adv + prep

go /gəʊ; AmE goʊ/ (goes /gəʊz; AmE goʊz/ went /went/ gone /gɒn; AmE gɔːn, gɑːn/)

[NOTE] Been is used as the past participle of go when sb has gone somewhere and come back.

,go a'bout; ,go a'bout sth (*BrE*) = GO AROUND, GO AROUND STH 3

	~ about	128	~ in for
	~ about together		~ in with
	~ about with		~ into
	~ across		~ off
	~ after	129	~ off with
124	~ against		~ on
	~ ahead	130	~ out, out of
	~ along		~ out for
	~ along with		~ out of
	~ around		~ over
	~ around together	131	~ over to
	~ around with		~ past
125	~ at		~ round
	~ away		~ round together
	~ away with		~ round with
	~ back		~ through
	~ back on	132	~ through with
	~ back over		~ to
	~ back to		~ together
126	~ before		~ towards
	~ beyond		~ under
	~ by		~ up
	~ down		~ up against
127	~ down on		~ up to
	~ down to		~ with
	~ down with		~ without
	~ for	133	~ up against
	~ forth		~ up to
	~ forward		~ with
	~ in		~ without

,go a'bout; ,go a'bout sth; ,go a'bout doing sth (*BrE*) = GO AROUND, GO AROUND STH, GO AROUND DOING STH

'go about sth to continue to do sth in your usual way, especially after sth unusual has happened; to keep busy with sth: *Everybody was going about their business as usual.*
[OBJ] **your business, the business of..., work, task**
◈ v + prep

,go a'bout sth; ,go a'bout doing sth to start to work at sth; to approach or deal with sth: *I want to help, but I don't know how to go about it.* ◇ *How should I go about finding a job?* ◇ *You're not going about it the right way.* ◇ *It seems a strange way of going about things.*
[OBJ] **things** [SYN] **set about sth, set about doing sth; tackle sth**
◈ v + prep

,go a'bout with sb; ,go a'bout together (*BrE*) = GO AROUND WITH SB, GO AROUND TOGETHER

,go a'cross; ,go a'cross sth to cross a room, a road, a river, etc. in order to get to the other side: *We borrowed a boat and went across to the island.* ◇ *Can you go across the road to the store for me?*
◈ v + adv ◆ v + prep

,go 'after sb/sth 1 to chase or follow a person or an animal to try to catch them: *He went after the burglars.* ◇ *Aren't you going to go after her to see if she's all right?* **2** to try to get or obtain sb/sth: *We're both going after the same job.*
◈ v + prep

,**go a'gainst sb** if a result, a judgement, etc. **goes against** sb, it is not in their favour or to their advantage: *The jury's verdict went against him.* ◇ *The war is going against us.*
◈ v + prep

,**go a'gainst sb/sth** to resist or oppose sb/sth; to act in a different way from what sb tells you or advises you to do: *Anyone who goes against me will be punished.* ◇ *He was going against his doctor's advice by continuing to work.* ◇ *Don't go against your parents' wishes.*
◈ v + prep

,**go a'gainst sth** to be opposed or contrary to sth; to not fit or agree with sth: *This goes against everything I believe in.* ◇ *Paying for my children's education goes against my principles.*
OBJ **principles, beliefs**
◈ v + prep
IDM **go against the 'grain** to be sth different from what is normal or natural for you and so sth you do not like doing: *It went against the grain to have to agree with my brother.*

,**go a'head 1** (*also* ,**go a'head of sb**) to go in front of other people who are going in the same direction as you and arrive before them: *She went ahead of him into the house.* **2** (of a plan, a project, a deal, etc.) to be carried out or happen: *The building of the new bridge will go ahead as planned.* ◇ *Filming went ahead in spite of the bad weather.* **SYN** **proceed** (*formal*) **3** (**with sth**) if sb **goes ahead** with sth, they do it, although there may be a problem, or sb may have objected or expressed doubts: *In spite of her illness, Anna decided to go ahead with the wedding.* ◇ *'May I start now?' 'Yes, go ahead* (= I give you permission).*' **SYN** **proceed** (**with sth**)
◈ v + adv **1** also v + adv + prep
▶ the '**go-ahead** n [sing.] permission or approval for sth to start: *Has the boss given you the go-ahead for the project?*
▶ '**go-ahead** adj [usually before noun] (*BrE*) very ambitious; trying hard to succeed, often by using new methods and ideas: *a go-ahead young designer*

,**go a'long 1** to progress; to develop or improve: *Things are going along nicely.* **2** (**to sth**) (**with sb**) to go somewhere or to an event with sb: *I went along to the club a couple of times.* ◇ *Sam said he'd go along to the party with us.* **3** (*especially AmE*) to do what sb else suggests or does: *Whatever Ed said, Max went right along.*
◈ v + adv
IDM **as you go a'long** while you are doing sth: *He made the story up as he went along.* ◇ *I was never taught how to use a computer. I just picked it up as I went along.*

,**go a'long**; ,**go a'long sth** to move forward or from one end of sth towards the other: *The bus rattled as it went along.* ◇ *I went along a dark narrow passage, past several doors.*
◈ v + adv ◆ v + prep

,**go a'long with sb/sth 1** (*especially BrE*) to agree with sb/sth: *I can't go along with you on that point.* **2** to accept sth or do sth, especially when you do not really want to: *They didn't like the idea, but they went along with it.* ◇ *I didn't want to make him angry, so I just went along with him* (= I didn't argue with him). **SYN** **fall in with sth** (*BrE*)
◈ v + adv + prep

,**go a'round** (*AmE*) = GO ROUND

,**go a'round**; ,**go a'round sth** (*BrE also* ,**go 'round**, ,**go 'round sth**) **1** to visit a group of people or places, one by one: *I'll go around and check all the doors are locked.* ◇ *We spent all afternoon going round the shops.* ◇ *She went round the table and said goodbye to everyone.* **2** (of a note, etc.) to be sent round a group of people so that everyone can read it: *A card's going around for people to sign.* ◇ *A memo went around the department.* **3** (*BrE also* ,**go a'bout**, ,**go a'bout sth**) if a piece of news, an illness, etc. **goes around**, it spreads from one person to another: *There's a rumour going around that Sam and Kate are having an affair.* ◇ *There's a nasty virus going round the school.* **SYN** **float around, float around sth 4** to move or be placed in a circle: *The cyclist was going round the roundabout the wrong way.* ◇ *The earth goes round the sun.* ◇ (*figurative*) *We're going round in circles in this argument.* **5** to be enough for everyone to have a share: *There aren't enough chairs to go round.* ◇ *Is there enough food to go around all the guests?* **6** to move around the outside of sth in order to get past sth or get to the other side: *We didn't go into the city. We went around it.* ◇ *Because of the flood, we had to go round by the minor roads to get to school.* **7** to travel in a country or place and visit lots of different things: *We travel around by bus.* ◇ *They're saving up to go around the world.* ◇ *We're planning to go round visiting all the temples.* **8** to visit every part of a room or building: *How long does it take to go around the museum?* ◇ *A guide will go round with you.*
◈ v + adv ◆ v + prep
IDM **what ,goes around 'comes around** whatever happens now will have an effect in the future

,**go a'round** [+ adv/prep], ,**go a'round sth** [+ adv/prep], ,**go a'round doing sth** (*BrE also* ,**go 'round/about** [+ adv/prep] ,**go 'round/about sth** [+ adv/prep] ,**go 'round/a'bout doing sth**) to dress or behave in a particular way; to do sth regularly: *She goes around barefoot most of the time.* ◇ *It's not safe to go about the streets alone.* ◇

You can't go round spreading rumours like that. ◇ *The kids went around in gangs, dressed completely in black.*

NOTE Go around/round/about and go around/round/about sth are used with an adverb or a phrase beginning with a preposition.

◈ v + adv ◆ v + prep

,go a'round sb/sth (*BrE also* ,go 'round sb/sth) to surround or go in a circle around sb/sth: *I felt his arm going around my shoulder.* ◇ *The belt won't go round my waist!*

◈ v + prep

,go a'round sth (*BrE also* ,go 'round sth) to move or travel around a corner: *The car's tyres screeched as it went round the bend.* ◇ *Maggie watched until Jess had gone around the corner and was out of sight.*

OBJ only **corner, bend**

◈ v + prep

IDM **go round the 'bend/'twist** (*informal, especially BrE*) to go crazy: *If I have to stay in this place another day, I'll go round the bend!*

,go a'round with sb; ,go a'round together (*BrE also* ,go a'bout/'round with sb, ,go a'bout/ 'round together) (*becoming old-fashioned*) to spend a lot of time with sb or with a group of people: *Ann goes around with Sue.* ◇ *Ann and Sue go around together.* ◇ *These are the people I used to go around with.*

SYN **hang around with sb, hang around together**

◈ v + adv + prep ◆ v + adv + adv

'go at sb to attack sb: *He went at me like a wild animal.*

◈ v + prep

'go at sth to make great efforts to do sth; to work hard and with enthusiasm at sth: *They went at the job as if their lives depended on it.* ◇ *He was going at the food as though he hadn't eaten for days.*

◈ v + prep

IDM **go at it ,hammer and 'tongs** if two people **go at it hammer and tongs**, they argue or fight with a lot of energy and noise

,go a'way 1 to leave a place or a person: *Go away! You're annoying me!* ◇ *Go away and think about it a bit.* **2** to leave home for a period of time, especially for a holiday/vacation: *They went away for the weekend.* ◇ *Are you going away on holiday this year?* ◇ *She goes away on business a lot.* **3** to disappear gradually: *The smell still hasn't gone away.* ◇ *Has your headache gone away?* ◇ *The longing never went away.*

OPP **come back**

◈ v + adv

,go a'way with sth to leave a place with a particular feeling or impression: *I don't want people to go away with the wrong idea.*

◈ v + adv + prep

,go 'back 1 (to sth/...) to return to a place where you were before: *Can we go back inside?* ◇ *I made a cup of tea and went back to bed.* ◇ *When are you going back to Australia?* **2** (to sth) to return to school or work after a break: *The children have to go back to school next week.* **3** (to sth/sth) to be in a situation that you were in before: *We can never go back to how things were before* (= in a relationship, for example). ◇ *Once you have taken this decision, there's no going back.* ◇ *I don't think Emily will go back to her husband* (= live with him again). **4** (to sth) to return to work after being on strike: *The strikers won't go back* (to work) *until they get a pay rise.* **5** (to sth) (*informal*) (of sth that you have bought or borrowed) to be returned to the place where you got it: *This toaster will have to go back to the shop — it doesn't work properly.* ◇ *When does this video have to go back?* **6** (of clocks and watches) to be set to an earlier time when the time changes at the end of summer: *The clocks go back tonight. We get an extra hour in bed.* **OPP** **go forward**

◈ v + adv

,go 'back... 1 if two people **go back** a period of time, they have known each other and have been friends for that time: *Adam and I go back a long way.* **2** (*also* ,go 'back to sth) to have existed since a particular time in the past: *Our friendship goes back fifteen years.* ◇ *This tradition goes back to medieval times.* **SYN** **date back..., date back to sth 3** (*also* ,go 'back to sth) to consider sth that happened in the past: *To trace the origins of the problem, we have to go back to the 18th century.* ◇ *I'm going back a few years now...* (= I'm talking about sth that happened some years ago)

◈ v + adv **2,3** also v + adv + prep

,go 'back on sth to fail to keep a promise; to change your mind about sth: *She never goes back on her word* (= fails to do what she has said she will do). ◇ *He went back on his promise.* ◇ *I don't like to go back on what I said.*

OBJ **your promise, your word**

◈ v + adv + prep

go 'back over sth to think about sth again or often: *I went back over the day's events in my mind.*

◈ v + adv + prep

,go 'back to sth 1 to start talking about sth again: *To go back to what you were saying before...* **SYN** **return to sth 2** = GO BACK... 2 **3** = GO BACK... 3

◈ v + adv + prep

,go 'back to sth; ,go 'back to doing sth 1 to start doing sth again that you had stopped doing: *Tom turned over and went back to sleep.* ◇ *I wouldn't go back to living in the city.* ◇ *She's decided to go back to teaching.* ◇ *John's going back to college to get some more qualifications.*

2 (of a situation) to return to what it was before sth else happened: *Things haven't gone back to normal yet.*

⟨SYN⟩ **return to sth**

◈ v + adv + prep

,go be'fore (*literary*) (*not used in the progressive tenses*) to exist or happen in an earlier time: *The present crisis is worse than any that have gone before.*

〖NOTE〗 Go before is usually used in the past or perfect tenses.

◈ v + adv

'go before sb/sth (of a legal case, a proposal or an issue) to be presented to sb/sth so that they can discuss it or make a decision or a judgement about it: *When does his case go before the judge?*

◈ v + prep

,go be'yond sth to be greater, better, etc. than sth: *The price we got for the painting went beyond all our expectations* (= was much better than we had expected). ◇ *The matter has gone beyond a joke* (= has become very serious and is no longer amusing).

⟨SYN⟩ **exceed sth** (*formal*)

◈ v + prep

,go 'by (of time) to pass: *As time goes by, my memory seems to get worse.* ◇ *The weeks went slowly by.* ◇ *Hardly a day went by without Anthony's name being mentioned.*

◈ v + adv

'go by; **'go by sb/sth 1** to pass sb/sth without stopping: *Did you see a boy go by on a bicycle?* ◇ *We sat and watched the world go by* (= watched people passing). ◇ *They waved to us as we went by the window.* ⟨SYN⟩ **pass by, pass by sb/sth 2** (*AmE*) to stop somewhere or visit sb for a short time, often on your way to somewhere else: *I'll go by and see him on my way home.* ◇ *Would you go by the grocery store for me?* ⟨SYN⟩ **drop by; stop by**

◈ v + adv ◆ v + prep

'go by sth 1 to be guided or directed by sth; to form an opinion or a judgement from sth: *That's a good rule to go by.* ◇ *If past experience is anything to go by, Tom will be late!* ◇ *I shall go entirely by what my solicitor says.* **2** to call yourself a particular name, which may not be your real name: *For her crime novels, she goes by the name of Monica Simon.* 〖OBJ〗 only **the name of**…

◈ v + prep

,go 'down 1 (**to**…/**sth**) (**from**…/**sth**) to travel from one place to another, especially from the north of a country to the south: *We're going down to London next week.* ⟨OPP⟩ **go up 2** to fall to the ground: *She tripped and went down with a bump.* **3** to become lower or smaller; to fall: *The price of petrol is going down/Petrol is going down* (in price). ◇ *The temperature went down by 10 degrees overnight.* ◇ *Rental costs have gone down* (£50) *since last year.* ◇ *The flood waters are going down.* ◇

Membership numbers have gone down recently. ◇ *The swelling has gone down a little.* ⟨SYN⟩ **drop**; **fall** ⟨OPP⟩ **go up 4** [+ adv] if a remark, a performance, an action, etc. **goes down** well or badly, etc. it gets a good or bad reaction from people: *Did your performance go down all right* (= did people like it)? ◇ *The movie went down well in America.* ◇ *Jokes don't go down too well with my mother* (= she does not like them). ◇ *The band went down a storm* (= people liked them very much). **5** (of the sun and moon) to disappear below the point where the sky seems to meet the land or the sea (the **horizon**): *We watched the sun go down.* ⟨SYN⟩ **set** ⟨OPP⟩ **come up**; **rise 6** to get worse: *The quality of the product has gone down since the company was sold.* ◇ *He's certainly gone down in my estimation* (= I don't have the good opinion of him that I used to). ◇ *The food's gone down since the restaurant changed hands.* ⟨SYN⟩ **deteriorate** (*more formal*) ⟨OPP⟩ **go up 7** (*computing*) if a computer system **goes down**, it stops working temporarily: *I lost all my work when the computer went down.* **8** (of food, a meal, etc.) to be digested or partly digested: *Let your food go down before you go swimming.* **9** [+ adv] if food or drink will/will not **go down**, it is easy/difficult to swallow, or you enjoy it/do not enjoy it: *My drink went down the wrong way and I started coughing.* ◇ *A cup of tea would go down nicely* (= I would like one). **10** when the curtain in a theatre **goes down**, it is the end of the performance: *The audience were cheering as the curtain went down.* ◇ (*figurative*) *After 25 years, the curtain has finally gone down on his sparkling career.* ⟨OPP⟩ **go up 11** when lights **go down** in a theatre, the performance is about to start: *She quickly found a seat before the lights went down.* ⟨OPP⟩ **go up 12** [+ adv/prep] to reach down to a particular point: *Pepita's coat is so big it goes right down to her ankles.* **13** (of a tyre) to lose air: *My tyre's gone down again.* **14** (*BrE*, *informal*) to be sent to prison: *He's gone down for twenty years.* **15** (of a carpet) to be put on the floor: *It'll feel a lot warmer when the carpet goes down.* **16** (of a plane) to fall from the sky; to be brought to the ground: *'The plane's going down!' he cried.* **17** (of a ship) to sink: *Hundreds died when the ferry went down.* **18** to fail; to behave badly and lose people's respect: *If the business goes down, we go down with it.* **19** to be defeated by sb, especially in a sports game or competition: *Liverpool went down 2-0 to Everton.* **20** (**to sth**) (*especially BrE*) to be made to move to a lower position, rank, class, status, etc: *We need to win the next two games to avoid going down.* ⟨OPP⟩ **go up 21** (**in sth**) (**as sth**) to be written down; to be recorded or remembered in a particular way: *Everything I said went down in his little book.* ◇ *1998 will go down as the company's best year.* ◇ *He will go down in history as a great statesman.* **22** (*slang, especially AmE*) to be happening: *She always*

knows what's going down. ◇ *What's going down?*
23 (from…) (*BrE, formal*) to leave a university
(especially Oxford or Cambridge) at the end of a
term or after finishing your studies: *She went
down (from Cambridge) in 1984.* OPP **go up**
◈ v + adv

,**go 'down**; ,**go 'down sth** to move from a higher
position to a lower one; to go along sth from one
end towards the other: *One end of the see-saw
goes up while the other end goes down.* ◇ *The pain
goes down my arm.* ◇ *I've just got to go down to
Jim's office with these papers.* ◇ *Will we go down
any steep hills?* ◇ *You'll see the museum if you go
down the road a bit.* ◇ *It was hard enough to get
up here* (= a mountain, for example), *and now
we've got to go down!* ◇ *Their company has
decided to go **down the same path*** (= do the same
things) *as ours.*
OBJ **road, stairs, hill** OPP **go up, go up sth**
◈ v + adv ◆ v + prep
IDM **go down the 'drain** (*BrE also* **go down the
'plughole**) to be wasted; to get much worse **go
down 'that road** to follow a particular course of
action, especially a difficult or harmful one: *He
said he'd never used drugs because he'd seen too
many talented kids go down that road.*

,**go 'down on sth** to lower your body towards the
ground, especially so that you are kneeling: *I
went down on my hands and knees to look for
the pen.* ◇ *I'm not going to go down on my knees
and beg him to forgive me.*
OBJ **hands and knees, knees, one knee, all
fours**
◈ v + adv + prep

,**go 'down to …/sth** to go to a place near where
you are, or a place you often go to: *Shall we go
down to the beach for a swim?* ◇ *I'm going down to
the corner shop for some milk.*
◈ v + adv + prep

,**go 'down with sth** (*especially BrE*) to become ill
with sth: *I think I'm going down with a cold.*
SYN **come down with sth; sicken for sth;
catch sth; get sth**
◈ v + adv + prep

'**go for sb/sth 1** to attack sb/sth: *She went for him
with a knife.* ◇ (*figurative*) *The newspapers really
went for him over his defence of terrorism.* **2** to
apply to sb/sth; to be true of sb/sth: *What I said
about Tim helping goes for you too, Alex.* ◇ *We
may have high unemployment, but the same goes
for many other countries.* ◇ *Terry needs to relax
more, and the same goes for you.* **3** to go to get
sb/sth: *Shall I go for a doctor?* ◇ *She's gone for
some milk.* **4** to be attracted by sb/sth; to like or
prefer sb/sth: *He's not the type I usually go for.* ◇
Children usually go for colourful packaging.
◈ v + prep

IDM (have) **a lot, nothing, etc. 'going for it/you**
(to have) many/not many advantages: *She has a
good job, she's attractive and intelligent — she
has a lot going for her.* ◇ *The town doesn't really
have much going for it.*

'**go for sth 1** to choose sth: *I think I'll go for the
steak.* ◇ *Which computer system are they going
for?* **2** to try to get or achieve sth: *Did you go for
that job?* ◇ *He's going for the world record.* ◇ **Go
for it!** *You've got nothing to lose.* ◇ *That's a great
idea! Go for it!* **3** to be sold for the price mentioned: *These computers usually go for under
£1 000.*
◈ v + prep

,**go 'forth** (*literary*) to leave a place and go somewhere, especially in order to do sth good or brave
◈ v + adv

,**go 'forward 1** to make progress; to begin to happen or be successful: *The project is going forward
nicely.* ◇ *Now that we have his agreement, the deal
can go forward.* **2** (of clocks and watches) to be
set one hour ahead at the beginning of summer:
*The clocks go forward tonight. We have an hour
less in bed.* OPP **go back 3** to be suggested as a
candidate for a job or an elected position, etc: *Her
name has gone forward for the job.* **4 (to sth)** to
win one stage of a competition, etc. and be able
to take part in the next stage: *Which teams will go
forward to the second round?*
◈ v + adv

,**go 'in 1** (of the sun or moon) to disappear behind a
cloud: *The sun went in and it grew colder.* OPP
come out 2 (*informal*) (of facts, information,
etc.) to be absorbed, understood and remembered: *I keep studying, but these dates just won't
go in.* SYN **sink in 3** (of a piece of equipment,
furniture, etc.) to be built or fitted in a place: *The
kitchen will be finished once the fridge has gone in.*
→ *see also* GO IN, GO IN STH, GO INTO STH; GO IN,
GO INTO STH; GO INTO STH
◈ v + adv

,**go 'in**; ,**go 'in sth**; ,**go 'into sth 1** to enter a
room, a house, etc: *It's getting cold; let's go in.* ◇
Let's go in the kitchen — it's warmer. ◇ *Why did
you go into my office?* ◇ *Are you going into town
today?* **2** to fit into a container, etc: *The suitcase is
full already — those shoes definitely won't go in.* ◇
I'm amazed that all the luggage went in the car. ◇
All the photos will go into this box. **3** (*informal*) to
join an organization, especially one of the armed
forces or the police: *He was 17 when he went in the
army.* ◇ *Ed wants to go into the Marines.* **4** (of the
ball in sports played with a ball, etc.) to enter the
goal, net, hole, etc. and score points: *Did you see if
the ball went in?* ◇ *He kicked the ball hard enough
to go into the back of the goal.*
→ *see also* GO IN; GO IN, GO INTO STH; GO INTO STH
◈ v + adv ◆ v + prep

,go 'in; **,go 'into sth 1** to go to an office or another place of work in order to work, do a particular task, have some work done for you, etc: *I've got to work tomorrow, but I can always go in late.* ◇ *The car needs to go in* (= into the garage) *for a service.* ◇ *Are you going into work tomorrow?* **2** to go to a hospital to receive treatment, tests, etc: *I'm going in on Friday for an X-ray.* ◇ *When is Cara going into hospital?* **3** (of soldiers, an army, etc.) to go to a place where there is fighting or a war and become involved in it: *Troops are going in tonight.*

→ *see also* GO IN; GO IN, GO IN STH, GO INTO STH; GO INTO STH

◆ v + adv ◆ v + prep

,go 'in for sth (*especially BrE*) **1** to take part in a competition; to take an exam: *She goes in for all the competitions in the magazines and never wins anything.* ◇ *Which events are you going in for at the school sports?* ◇ *She's going in for the Cambridge First Certificate.* **2** = GO INTO STH 3 *He decided to go in for politics.*

[SYN] **enter sth**

◆ v + adv + prep

,go 'in for sth; **,go 'in for doing sth** to like sth and regularly use it, do it, etc.; to have sth as an interest or a hobby: *She goes in for very bright colours.* ◇ *He doesn't really go in for making long speeches.* ◇ *My family don't go in for that sort of thing.* ◇ *She never went in for dancing.*

◆ v + adv + prep

,go 'in with sb (**on sth**) to join sb in a particular project, activity, business, etc: *Jack went in with some friends to start a car hire business.* ◇ *I'll go in with you on* (= I'll give you some money for) *Mary's present.* ◇ *My brothers are opening a garage and they want me to go in with them.*

◆ v + adv + prep

,go 'into sth 1 (of a vehicle) to hit sth violently; to crash into sth: *The car skidded and went into a tree.* **2** (of a vehicle or driver) to start a particular movement: *The truck went into a spin on a patch of ice.* ◇ *The plane went into a nosedive.* **3** (*also* **,go 'in for sth**) to decide to do a particular kind of work as your job or career: *When did you decide to go into politics?* ◇ *She's going into publishing.* ◇ *Sanjay's gone into business with his father.* [OBJ] **politics** [SYN] **take sth up 4** to begin to be in a particular state or situation: *She went into a coma after the accident.* ◇ *The country is going into a decline.* ◇ *The company has gone into liquidation.* ◇ *The family has gone into hiding.* [OBJ] **liquidation, production, decline, hiding, exile, a coma 5** to begin to act or behave in a particular way: *He went into a long explanation of the affair.* ◇ *Divers were there, ready to go into action if the stunt went wrong.* **6** to examine or discuss sth carefully: *I won't go into details now.* ◇ *We need to go into the question of costs.* ◇ *She's not coming, for reasons which I won't go into*

now. **7** (*also* **,go 'into doing sth**) (of money, time, effort, etc.) to be spent on sth; to be used to do sth: *More money needs to go into rebuilding the inner cities.* ◇ *I can see that a lot of time and effort has gone into your project.* ◇ *A huge amount of work went into making the occasion a success.* ◇ *A lot of skill, love and work had gone into the garden.* **8** to start taking part in an exam, a competition, an election, etc: *I can't go into the exam unprepared.* **9** if one number **goes into** a larger number, it is contained in that number the number of times mentioned: *5 goes into 25 five times.* ◇ *Does 13 go into 39?* [NOTE] Notice also the example: *5 into 24 won't go.*

→ *see also* GO IN; GO IN, GO IN STH, GO INTO STH; GO IN, GO INTO STH

◆ v + prep

,go 'off 1 (**to sth**) to leave a place, especially in order to do sth: *You go off and have fun.* ◇ *When are you going off on your trip?* ◇ *Have the children gone off to school yet?* ◇ *Everyone went off happy.* ◇ *I can't believe Ed went off without saying goodbye!* ◇ *My parents have just gone off to bed.* **2** (of a weapon, etc.) to be fired; to explode: *The gun went off by accident.* ◇ *The bomb went off in a crowded street.* [SUBJ] **gun, bomb 3** (of an alarm) to make a sudden loud noise or flash: *She got up as soon as the alarm clock went off.* ◇ *The thieves ran away when the burglar alarm went off.* [SUBJ] **alarm, alarm clock, fire alarm 4** if a light, the electricity, etc. **goes off**, it stops working: *Suddenly all the lights went off.* ◇ *The heating comes on at 6 and goes off at 9.* [SUBJ] **lights** [OPP] **come on**; **go on 5** [+ adv] if a performance, etc. **goes off** well/badly, it is successful/not successful: *The show went off very well.* ◇ *How did the concert go off?* ◇ *The performance went off without a hitch* (= without any problems at all). **6** (*BrE*) if food or drink **goes off**, it becomes bad and not fit to eat or drink: *This milk has gone off.* [SUBJ] **milk, meat 7** (*especially BrE*) to become worse in quality: *Her books have gone off in recent years.* **8** (*informal, especially BrE*) to fall asleep: *Hasn't the baby gone off (to sleep) yet?* [SYN] **drop off**

◆ v + adv

,go 'off; **,go 'off sth 1** to move away from sth large or important and go in a different direction: *The road you want goes off on the right.* ◇ (*figurative*) *She's always going off the point* (= not talking about the main topic). **2** to leave the stage, the sports field, etc. during a play or a game: *Hamlet goes off in the middle of the scene.* ◇ *Johnson went off at half-time.*

◆ v + adv ◆ v + prep

,go 'off sb/sth (*informal, especially BrE*) to lose interest in sb/sth; to stop liking sb/sth: *I think she's going off me.* ◇ *He's gone off his food.* ◇ *I've gone off the idea of a holiday in Scotland.*

◆ v + prep

,go 'off with sb to leave your husband, wife, partner, etc. in order to have a relationship with sb else: *Eddie's gone off with his wife's best friend.*
[SYN] **run away/off with sb**
♦ v + adv + prep

,go 'off with sth to leave a place with sth that does not belong to you: *Who's gone off with my new pen?*
[SYN] **make off (with sth)**
♦ v + adv + prep

,go 'on 1 (of a situation or a state of affairs) to continue to happen or exist without changing: *We can't let this dispute go on.* ◇ *Things can't go on as they are.* ◇ *In spite of everything, life must go on.* ◇ *We can't go on like this!* [SYN] **carry on**; **continue 2** to last for a particular time: *The meeting went on for hours.* ◇ *How much longer will this hot weather go on (for)?* [SYN] **carry on**; **last 3** (with sth) to continue an activity, especially after a pause or a break: *I'm sorry I interrupted. Go on with your story.* ◇ *The children quietly went on with their work.* ◇ *Let's take a break. We'll go on when you're ready.* [SYN] **carry on (with sth) 4** (with sth) (also ,go 'on doing sth) to continue an activity without stopping: *When I came into the room, the boss just went on with what she was doing and didn't look up.* ◇ *I could have gone on listening to Ted's stories all night.* ◇ *I'd prefer to go on doing things my own way.* [SYN] **carry on (with sth), carry on doing sth 5** to continue speaking after a short pause: *'You know', he went on, 'I never liked her.'* ◇ *Go on then! Tell me what happened.* ◇ *She hesitated for a moment, and then went on.* [SYN] **carry on 6** (of a light, the electricity, etc.) to start to work; to be switched on: *Suddenly all the lights went on.* [OPP] **go off 7** (of time) to pass: *Things will improve as time goes on.* ◇ *She became more miserable as the evening went on.* [SYN] **go by 8** (usually used in the progressive tenses) to take place; to happen: *What's going on here?* ◇ *Who knows what goes on when I'm away.* ◇ *There must be a party going on next door.* ◇ *She ignores a lot of what goes on.* **9** (to sth/to do sth) to do sth after you have finished sth else: *Do all the students go on to work in catering?* ◇ *Let's go on to the next item on the agenda.* ◇ *The boys went on to a club, but I decided to go home.* **10** ,go 'on! (informal) used to encourage or dare sb to do sth: *Go on! Have another cake.* ◇ *Go on! Try it!* ◇ *Go on! Ask her out! I dare you!* **11** (about sb/sth) to continue talking to sb for a long time about the same person or thing, usually in an annoying way: *They keep going on about their trip.* ◇ *What is she going on about?* ◇ *My parents went on and on about how successful my sister is.* [SYN] **bang on about sb/sth** (BrE, informal) **12** (at sb) (about sth) (especially BrE) to complain to sb about their behaviour, work, etc: *My dad went on at me about not having a job.* ◇ *Stop going on at me!* ◇ *She keeps going on at me to dress better.* [SYN] **carry on (at sb) (about sth); criticize sb 13** to continue to travel in the direction you are going: *I'm too tired to go on.* ◇ *They had an accident and couldn't go on.* [SYN] **carry on 14** (ahead/to sth) to travel in front of sb else: *Jack's going on ahead to get the house ready.* ◇ *Shall we wait for Ray or shall we go on into town without him?* **15** (of a road, a piece of land, etc.) to cover a particular distance in a particular direction: *The desert seemed to go on forever.* **16** (of an actor or a performer) to walk onto the stage to begin their performance: *She doesn't go on till Act 2.* **17** (in sport) (of a player) to join a team instead of another player during a game: *Allen went on (in place of Brown) just before half-time.* **18 go on** (spoken, informal, especially BrE) used to agree to do or allow sth that you do not really want to do or allow, after sb has persuaded you: *'Are you sure you won't come?' 'Oh go on then, but I won't be able to stay long.'* **19 go on!** (old-fashioned, BrE, spoken, informal) used to show that you do not believe what sb is saying: *Go on! You didn't eat it all yourself!* [SYN] **get away (with you)**
♦ v + adv
4 also v + adv + -ing
5 also v + adv + speech
[IDM] **be ,going 'on (for) sth** (BrE) to be nearly a particular age, time or number: *It was going on (for) midnight.* ◇ *She's 15, going on 21!* (= she acts as if she's 21) **enough, plenty, etc. to be going 'on with** enough, plenty, etc. for our present needs: *That should be enough food to be going on with.*
▶ **,goings-'on** n [pl.] (informal) activities or events that are strange or amusing: *There have been some strange goings-on at their house.*
▶ **'ongoing** adj [usually before noun] continuing to exist or develop: *an ongoing process* ◇ *the ongoing debate* ◇ *an ongoing situation* ◇ *The problem is ongoing.*

,go 'on; ,go 'on sth to fit or be put on top of another object: *The lid won't go on.* ◇ *This shoe won't go on my foot at all.*
♦ v + adv ♦ v + prep

'go on sth 1 (used in negative sentences and questions) to base an opinion or a judgement on sth: *The police don't have much evidence to go on.* ◇ *I'm only going on what she told me.* **2** to begin doing, following, enjoying or using sth: *to go on a course/trip* ◇ *I'm going on a diet on Monday.* ◇ *When are you going on holiday?* ◇ *to go on the dole* (= to start to receive government unemployment benefit) ◇ *When do the band go on tour?*
♦ v + prep

'go on sth; 'go on doing sth (of money, time, energy, etc.) to be spent or used for sth: *All his money goes on drink.* ◇ *Most of the electricity we use goes on running the computers.*
→ see also GO ON 4
♦ v + prep

go out

,go 'out 1 (for/to sth) to leave your house to go to social events, etc: *Shall we go out for a meal tonight?* ◇ *Ellie goes out a lot.* ◇ *She goes out dancing most weekends.* ◇ *Jenny usually goes out with her friends on Friday evenings.* OPP **stay in 2** (with **sb/together**) (*informal*) (especially of young people) to spend time with sb and have a romantic or sexual relationship with them: *Sam has been going out with Kate for six months.* ◇ *How long have Sam and Kate been going out together?* ◇ *When did they start going out?* SYN **date, date sb 3** (of a letter, a message, etc.) to be sent, announced, etc: *Have the invitations gone out yet?* ◇ *A memo went out about the director's resignation.* **4** (of news, information, etc.) to be made public; to be published: *Word went out that the Prime Minister had resigned.* ◇ *The magazine goes out six times a year.* **5** (*especially BrE*) (of a radio or television programme) to be broadcast: *The first episode goes out next Friday at 8.00 pm.* ◇ *The show will go out live from the studio.* **6** (of a fire or a light) to stop burning or shining: *The fire has gone out.* ◇ *There was a power cut and all the lights went out.* SUBJ **lights, fire** SYN **be extinguished** (*formal*) **7** if money **goes out**, it is spent on bills and expenses: *We need to have more money coming in than going out.* OPP **come in 8** (**to …**) to leave your country and travel to another one, especially one far away: *We went out to see him when he was living in Australia.* ◇ *Have you been out to India recently?* **9** if the tide or the sea **goes out**, it moves away from the land: *When does the tide go out?* SUBJ only **the tide** SYN **ebb** (*more formal*) OPP **come in 10** to fail in a competition, contest, etc: *She went out in the first round of the tournament.*
⊕ v + adv

IDM **go out like a 'light** to fall asleep very quickly: *I went out like a light as soon as my head hit the pillow.* **your heart goes 'out to sb** used to say that you feel a lot of sympathy for sb: *Our hearts go out to the families of the victims.*

▶ '**outgoing** *adj* **1** out'going very friendly and liking to meet and talk to other people: *Annie's sister is much more outgoing than she is.* **2** [only before noun] about to leave a position of responsibility: *the outgoing government* **3** [only before noun] going away from a particular place rather than coming in to it: *outgoing calls/flights/passengers* ◇ *the outgoing tide*

▶ '**outgoings** *n* [pl.] (*BrE*) the money which a person or a company spends regularly on bills and other necessary expenses: *They haven't got enough money to cover their outgoings.*

,go 'out; ,go 'out of sth 1 to leave a room, building, etc: *It's too cold to go out.* ◇ *The talking started as soon as the teacher went out of the room.* ◇ *It isn't a good idea to go out alone at night.* ◇ *I'm going out for a walk.* ◇ *He's just gone out to get a newspaper.* ◇ *My grandmother never went out to work* (= away from the home). ◇ *She*

went straight out and spent £200 on a new coat. OPP **go in, go in sth, go into sth 2** to become no longer fashionable or used: *That hairstyle went out of fashion years ago.* ◇ *Styles like that have completely gone out now.* ◇ *The word 'leathern' has gone out of use in modern English.* OPP **come in, come in sth, come into sth**
⊕ v + adv ♦ v + adv + prep

,go 'out for sth (*AmE*) to try to gain a place in a sports team, a band or a group that does some other activity: *I had to talk Greg into going out for the basketball team.* ◇ *'Did she make the band?' 'She didn't go out for it.'*
SYN **try for sth** (*especially BrE*), **try out (for sth)** (*especially AmE*)
⊕ v + adv + prep

,go 'out of sb/sth (of a quality or feeling) to no longer be present in sb/sth; to disappear from sb/sth: *He relaxed and the tension went out of him.* ◇ *The heat had gone out of the day.*
⊕ v + adv + prep

,go 'over 1 (to sb/sth) to move towards sb/sth, especially crossing a room, etc: *He went over to the window for a closer look at the parade.* ◇ *I went over and sat beside Jane.* **2** (to sth) to visit sb for a short time, usually at their house: *I'm going over to my daughter's for lunch.* → *see also* GO ROUND 1 **3** (to …) to travel to a place overseas: *My family live in Belgium and I'm going over to see them next week.*
⊕ v + adv

,go 'over; ,go 'over sth to pass above or over the top of sb/sth: *Planes were going over all night.* ◇ *We were shaken as the car went over the bumps in the road.*
⊕ v + adv ♦ v + adv + prep

,go 'over sth 1 to do more, spend more, etc. than a particular amount or than you are allowed to do: *Don't go over the speed limit.* ◇ *Did you go over budget on your project?* SYN **exceed sth** (*more formal*) **2** to examine the details of sth; to check sth: *I'll go over the figures again to make sure they're right.* ◇ *Go over your work carefully before you hand it in.* **3** to study sth carefully; to repeat sth: *I've gone over and over what happened in my mind.* ◇ *She went over her lines* (= in a play) *until she knew them perfectly.* **4** to look at or inspect sth carefully: *Police went (back) over all the evidence again.* ◇ *My dad went over the car thoroughly and advised us not to buy it.* **5** to draw, paint, etc. over the top of sth that has already been drawn or painted: *I've gone over the original drawing in pen.* **6** to clean sth by passing sth across the surface: *He went over the surfaces with a duster.*
NOTE **Go over sth** can be used in the passive in meanings 2, 4, 5 and 6: *These details have been gone over already.*
⊕ v + prep

▶ ,going-'over *n* [sing.] (*informal*) **1** an act of examining, cleaning or repairing sth thoroughly: *I've given the flat a good going-over* (= a thorough clean). ◊ *The garage gave the car a thorough going-over* (= a careful inspection). **2** a serious physical or verbal attack on sb: *The gang gave him a real going-over.*

,go 'over to sb/sth **1** to leave a group of people in order to join a competing group; to change from one side, opinion, habit, system, etc. to another; to start using sth different: *Two Conservative MPs went over to the opposition.* ◊ *We've recently gone over to* (= we've started using) *semi-skimmed milk.* **2** (in broadcasting) to transfer to a different person, place, etc. for the next part of a programme: *Let's go over to the news desk for an important announcement.*
◆ v + adv + prep

,go 'past (of time) to pass: *Half an hour went past while we were sitting there.*
◆ v + adv

,go 'past; ,go 'past sb/sth to pass in front of sb/sth: *I stood back to let Jack go past.* ◊ *The shop is empty whenever I go past it.*
◆ v + adv ♦ v + prep

,go 'round (*BrE*) (*AmE* ,go a'round) **1** (to sth) to visit sb for a short time, usually at their house: *Why don't you go round and see Annie?* ◊ *I've got to go around to my sister's* (= to her house) *in the morning.* → *see also* GO OVER 2 **2** to spin or turn: *When I found the bicycle, the wheels were still going round.* ◊ (*figurative*) *I've got so many ideas going around in my head at the moment.*
◆ v + adv

,go 'round; ,go 'round sth (*BrE*) = GO AROUND, GO AROUND STH

,go 'round; ,go 'round sth; ,go 'round doing sth (*BrE*) = GO AROUND, GO AROUND STH, GO AROUND DOING STH

,go 'round sb/sth (*BrE*) = GO AROUND SB/STH

,go 'round sth (*BrE*) = GO AROUND STH

,go 'round with sb; ,go 'round together (*BrE*) = GO AROUND WITH SB, GO AROUND TOGETHER

,go 'through **1** (to sth) (*informal*) used especially to ask sb to enter a room, etc: *Shall we go through to my office?* ◊ *Go through and make yourself comfortable.* **2** if a law, a contract, etc. **goes through**, it is officially approved, accepted or completed: *The bill went through without any objections.* ◊ *The adoption* (= of a child) *has finally gone through.* **3** if a business deal, etc. **goes through**, it is completed successfully: *We are almost certain the deal will go through.* ◊ *If the merger goes through, we may lose our jobs.* **4** (to sth) to pass to the next stage of a competition, etc., having won the first part(s): *Four teams will go through to the semi-final.*
◆ v + adv

,go 'through; ,go 'through sth to enter and cross a room, an area of land, a town, a country, etc.; to pass through sth: *The gates opened and we went through.* ◊ *Lots of huge trucks go through the town.* ◊ *You have to go through the lounge to reach the kitchen.* ◊ *The defence was weak, and the ball went through into the goal.* ◊ *The bullet went straight through the window.* ◊ *This is the hole where the bullet went through.*
◆ v + adv ♦ v + prep

,go 'through sb **1** if a feeling **goes through** you, it passes through your body: *A shudder went through her.* **2** if a particular type of food **goes through** you, you find it difficult to digest and it is emptied from your bowels quickly or in liquid form: *I can't eat sushi — it goes right through me.*
◆ v + prep

'go through sb/sth to ask a person or an organization to deal with sth for you or give you permission to do sth: *If you want to book the cruise, you'll have to go through a travel agent.*
◆ v + prep

,go 'through sth **1** to pass through sth from one end to the other: *We went through the woods to get to the lake.* ◊ (*figurative*) *What went through your mind when you saw John standing there after all this time?* **2** if you **go through** an event, a period of time, etc., you pass through it from the beginning to the end: *He went through the day in a state of shock.* ◊ *She can't go through life always depending on her parents.* **3** to experience or suffer sth: *You don't realize what I've been going through.* ◊ *She's been through a bad patch recently.* ◊ *We've been through a lot together.* ◊ *It's a phase/stage all teenagers go through.* ᴼᴮᴶ **phase, experience, a bad, difficult, etc. patch** ⓈⓎⓃ **undergo sth** (*more formal*) **4** to look at, check or examine sth closely and carefully, especially in order to find sth: *I've gone through all my pockets but I can't find my keys.* ◊ *After his death, his daughter had to go through his papers.* ᴼᴮᴶ **pockets, papers 5** to discuss or study sth in detail, especially repeating it: *Let's go through the arguments again.* ◊ *Could we go through Act 2 once more?* ⓈⓎⓃ **run through sth 6** to perform a series of actions; to follow a method: *This is the process you have to go through to become a club member.* ◊ *I made a mistake when I was logging out and had to go through the whole process again.* ◊ *Have you seen him go through his exercise routine in the mornings?* ᴼᴮᴶ **process, routine, procedure 7** to use up sth: *I seem to be going through a lot of money at the moment.* ◊ *Have we gone through all that milk already?* ⓈⓎⓃ **get through sth 8** to wear or make a hole in sth: *I've gone through the elbows of my jumper.*

ᴺᴼᵀᴱ Go through sth can be used in the passive in meanings 4, 5 and 6: *The formalities have to be gone through.*
◆ v + prep

IDM **go through the 'motions (of sth/of doing sth) 1** to pretend to do sth: *He just went through the motions of being a poet.* **2** to do or say sth without being serious or sincere about it: *Her heart wasn't in the game — she was just going through the motions.* **go through the 'roof 1** (of prices, etc.) to rise very quickly: *House prices have gone through the roof.* **2** to become very angry: *My mum will go through the roof if she finds out!*

,go 'through with sth to do what is necessary to complete sth or achieve sth, even though it may be difficult or unpleasant: *She decided not to go through with the operation* (= she decided not to have it). ◇ *He says he'll take us to court, but he'll never go through with it.*
  ◆ v + adv + prep

,go 'to it (*AmE, spoken, informal*) used to tell sb to start doing sth: *You need to get it finished by 6. Go to it!* ◇ *We better go to it before it gets dark.*
  ◆ v + prep + it

'go to sb/sth to be given to sb/sth; to pass to sb else when sb dies: *Proceeds from the concert will go to charity.* ◇ *Some of the credit for the book should go to the illustrator.* ◇ *The first prize went to Peter.* ◇ *The contract has gone to a private firm.* ◇ *The property went to his eldest daughter* (= when he died).
  ◆ v + prep

'go to sth 1 to start to do sth; to begin to be in a particular state or condition: *The two countries are set to go to war over the dispute.* ◇ *I hate to see food going to waste.* ◇ *My brain went to work on* (= started to think about) *what I should do next.* **OBJ** only **war, waste, work 2** to make a lot of effort, spend a lot of money, etc. in order to do or achieve sth: *Don't go to any trouble on my behalf.* ◇ *Why go to the expense of buying a car?* ◇ *He went to great pains to persuade us.* ◇ *It's amazing the lengths people will go to to get a job.* **OBJ** only **trouble, expense, pains, lengths**
  ◆ v + prep + n

IDM **go to the 'dogs** (*informal*) to get into a very bad state: *Some people think this country is going to the dogs.* **go to your 'head 1** (of alcohol) to make you feel drunk **2** (of success, praise, etc.) to make you feel very proud of yourself, especially in a way that other people find annoying **go to 'pieces** (*informal*) if somebody goes to pieces, they become so upset or frightened that they cannot live or work normally: *It seems he goes to pieces in a crisis.* **go to 'pot** (*informal*) to be spoiled because people are not working hard or taking care of things: *His plan to make money had gone to pot.* **go to 'sleep 1** to fall asleep **2** if part of your body goes to sleep, you lose the sense of feeling in it **go to 'town (on sth)** to do sth with a lot of energy and enthusiasm, especially spending a lot of money: *They hadn't got a garden, so they really went to town on indoor*

plants. **go to the 'wall** if a company or a business goes to the wall, it fails because of a lack of money

,go to'gether 1 (of two or more things) to exist at the same time; to be often found together: *Money and happiness don't always go together.* → *see also* GO WITH STH 2 **2** to look, taste, sound, etc. good together; to combine well with sth: *These colours go together well.* ◇ *Curry and pasta don't really go together.* **NOTE** **Go** is also used with this meaning: *Curry and pasta don't really go.* ◇ *These colours don't really go.* → *see also* GO WITH STH 1 **3** (*old-fashioned, especially AmE*) (*usually used in the progressive tenses*) (of two people) to spend time with each other and have a romantic or sexual relationship: *They haven't been going together long.* → *see also* GO OUT 2
  ◆ v + adv

'go towards sth; 'go towards doing sth to be used as part of the payment for sth; to be used as part of sth: *The money will go towards buying a computer.* ◇ *All these marks go towards my final diploma.*
  ◆ v + prep

,go 'under 1 to sink below the surface of the water: *They had to swim to shore when the boat went under.* ◇ *Someone rushed to help him when he went under.* **2** (*informal*) to fail, lose power, etc.; to be unable to pay what you owe: *A large number of small companies have gone under.*
  ◆ v + adv

'go under sth to be known by a particular name or title: *Does he go under any other names?*
  OBJ **the name of…, a different, etc. name, the title of…**
  → *see also* GO BY STH 2
  ◆ v + prep

,go 'up 1 to become higher in price, level, etc.; to rise: *The price of cigarettes is going up.* ◇ *Cigarettes are going up (in price).* ◇ *My pension has gone up (by) £5 a week.* **SUBJ** **price, temperature** **SYN** **rise** **OPP** **come down**; **go down 2** (**to sb/sth**) to go towards sb/sth: *He went up to the house and knocked on the door.* **3** (**to…**) to travel from one place to another, especially from the south of a country to the north: *She's gone up to Scotland to see her son.* ◇ *Are you going up to London tomorrow?* **4** to be built; to be put up: *New office blocks are going up everywhere.* **5** to be destroyed by fire or an explosion: *If one of the gas tanks goes up, there will be massive damage.* ◇ *The whole building went up in flames.* **6** to be fixed in a public place: *Notices have gone up all over the university.* **7** if the curtain across the stage in a theatre **goes up**, it is raised or opened: *The stage was empty when the curtain went up.* **SUBJ** **curtain** **OPP** **come down 8** if a loud sound such as a shout or a cheer **goes up**, it is made by lots of people: *A huge cheer went up from the crowd.* **SUBJ** **cheer, cry 9 (to/into sth)** (of a sports

team or a student) to move to a higher rank, position or class: *Liverpool have gone up into the second division.* ◇ *Is she going up into the sixth form this year?* ⟨OPP⟩ **go down 10 (to…)** (*BrE*) to begin your studies at a university, especially Oxford or Cambridge; to begin a term at university: *She went up (to Oxford) in 1976.* ⟨OPP⟩ **go down**
◈ v + adv

,go 'up; **,go 'up sth** to move from a lower position to a higher one or upstairs in a building: *The lift goes up and down all day.* ◇ *Go up the ladder.* ◇ *She went up the stairs very slowly.* ◇ *Julie's gone up to her room to change.*
⟨OBJ⟩ **stairs**, **hill**, **road** ⟨SYN⟩ **ascend, ascend sth** (*formal*)
⟨OPP⟩ **go down, go down sth; descend, descend sth** (*formal*)
◈ v + adv ◆ v + prep

,go 'up against sb/sth (*AmE, informal*) to face sb/sth difficult, for example in a competition: *He went up against the champion in the second round.* ◇ *In a consumer taste test, Coke went up against Pepsi.*
◈ v + adv + prep

,go 'up to sth to come close to a particular point or time, or go in a particular direction: *This diary only goes up to November.* ◇ *The road goes up to the school.*
◈ v + adv + prep

'go with sb (*old-fashioned, informal*) to have a sexual or romantic relationship with sb; to have sex with sb: *She's been going with him for quite a while.*
→ *see also* GO OUT 2
◈ v + prep

'go with sb/sth (*informal, especially AmE*) to support a plan, an idea, etc. or the person suggesting it: *I'm prepared to go with her decision.* ◇ *I like Ted's idea. Let's go with it.* ◇ *Which candidate shall we go with?*
◈ v + prep

'go with sth 1 to look, taste, sound, etc. good with sth; to combine well with sth: *This sauce goes well with lamb.* ◇ *Does this skirt go with my jumper?* → *see also* GO TOGETHER 2 **2** (of two or more things) to exist at the same time or in the same place as sth; to be often found together: *Disease often goes with poverty.* ◇ *She loves all the attention that goes with being famous.* → *see also* GO TOGETHER 1 **3** to be included with or as a part of sth: *A new car goes with the job.*
◈ v + prep

,go with'out; **,go with'out sth**; **,go with'out doing sth** to manage without sth which you usually have: *I never want the children to have to go without.* ◇ *She went without sleep for three days.*
⟨SYN⟩ **do without, do without sth**
◈ v + adv ◆ v + prep

goad /ɡəʊd; *AmE* ɡoʊd/
,goad sb 'on to drive and encourage sb to do sth: *They goaded him on to break the window.* ◇ *The boxers were goaded on by the shrieking crowd.*
◈ v + n/pron + adv

gobble /'ɡɒbl; *AmE* 'ɡɑːbl/
,gobble sth 'down/'up (*informal*) to eat food very quickly: *I gobbled down my breakfast and ran out of the house.*
⟨SYN⟩ **wolf sth down**
◈ v + adv + n ◆ v + n/pron + adv

,gobble sth 'up (*informal*) **1** to use all of sth, especially money, very quickly: *The rent gobbles up half his earnings.* **2** if a business, company, etc. **gobbles up** a smaller one, it takes control of it: *Small family businesses are being gobbled up by larger firms.*
⟨SYN⟩ **swallow sth up**
◈ v + adv + n ◆ v + n/pron + adv

goof /ɡuːf/
,goof a'round (*informal, especially AmE*) to waste your time doing silly or stupid things: *Come on, quit goofing around — this is serious.*
⟨SYN⟩ **mess around**
◈ v + adv

,goof 'off (*AmE, informal*) to waste time when you are supposed to be working
◈ v + adv
▶ **'goof-off** n (*AmE, informal, disapproving*) a lazy person who does not work hard

,goof 'up (on sth), **,goof sth 'up** (*AmE, informal*) to make a mistake; to spoil sth by making a mistake or doing it badly: *He always goofs up (on exams).* ◇ *He really goofed up his exam.*
⟨SYN⟩ **mess up, mess sth up**
◈ v + adv ◆ v + n/pron + adv ◆ v + adv + n

gouge /ɡaʊdʒ/
,gouge sth 'out; **,gouge sth 'out of sth** to remove sth, or form sth, by digging into a surface with a sharp tool, your fingers, etc: *I wanted to gouge her eyes out.* ◇ *Glaciers gouged out valleys from the hills.*
⟨OBJ⟩ **eyes**
◈ v + adv + n ◆ v + n/pron + adv ◆
v + n/pron + adv + prep

grab /ɡræb/
'grab at sb/sth to try to take hold of sb/sth: *She grabbed at the branch, missed and fell.*
⟨SYN⟩ **clutch at sb/sth**
◈ v + prep

'grab at sth to take advantage of an opportunity to do or have sth: *He'll grab at any excuse to avoid doing the dishes.*
[OBJ] **chance, opportunity, excuse** [SYN] **seize on sth**
◆ v + prep

grapple /'græpl/

'grapple with sth to try to deal with a difficult situation or solve a difficult problem: *I've spent all afternoon grappling with these accounts.*
[OBJ] **problem, issue** [SYN] **wrestle with sth**
[NOTE] **Grapple with sth** can be used in the passive: *This is an issue that is being grappled with by the council.*
◆ v + prep

grasp /grɑːsp; *AmE* græsp/

'grasp at sth/sb to try to take hold of sth/sb in your hands: *She grasped at his coat.*
[SYN] **catch at sth/sb; clutch at sth/sb**
◆ v + prep

'grasp at sth to try to take advantage of an opportunity, especially because you are unhappy with the present situation: *He grasped at any hope of escape.*
[SYN] **clutch at sth**
◆ v + prep
[IDM] **grasp at 'straws** to try very hard to find a solution to a problem or some hope in a difficult or unpleasant situation, even though this seems very unlikely

grass /grɑːs; *AmE* græs/

,grass sth 'over to cover an area of ground with grass: *The garden had been grassed over.*
[NOTE] **Grass sth over** is often used in the passive.
◆ v + adv + n ♦ v + n/pron + adv

,grass sb 'up (*BrE, informal*) to inform the police or sb in authority about a crime or sth bad that sb has done: *My girlfriend grassed me up.*
[NOTE] It is also possible to say: *My girlfriend grassed (on me).*
◆ v + n/pron + adv ♦ v + adv + n

gravitate /'grævɪteɪt/

'gravitate to/toward(s) sb/sth to move towards sb/sth that you are attracted to: *Most visitors to New York gravitate to Times Square.*
◆ v + prep

grind /graɪnd/ (**ground, ground** /graʊnd/)

,grind sb 'down to treat sb in a harsh way or annoy them for a long time until they can no longer defend themselves or fight back: *Don't let*

your colleagues grind you down! ◇ *The villagers had been ground down by years of poverty.*
[SYN] **wear sb down**
◆ v + n/pron + adv ♦ v + adv + n

,grind sth 'down to rub sth against a hard surface in order to make it smooth and shiny
[SYN] **wear sth down**
◆ v + n/pron + adv ♦ v + adv + n

,grind 'on to continue for a long time in a boring or unpleasant way: *The negotiations ground on for months.*
◆ v + adv

,grind sth 'out 1 to produce sth in large quantities over a long period of time, especially sth that is not interesting or of good quality: *He grinds out a novel a month.* [SYN] **churn sth out 2** to press a burning cigarette down firmly with your hand or your foot in order to stop it burning: *He ground out the cigarette with his heel.*
[SYN] **stub sth out**
◆ v + adv + n ♦ v + n/pron + adv

grope /grəʊp; *AmE* groʊp/

'grope for sth to try hard to find sth: *I stepped in the door and groped for the light switch.* ◇ (*figurative*) '*Yes, but....*' *He was groping for words.*
[OBJ] **light, word, answer**
◆ v + prep

'grope towards sth (*rare*) to try to find an agreement, an answer to a problem, etc: *The two parties are groping towards a compromise.*
◆ v + prep

gross /grəʊs; *AmE* groʊs/

,gross sb 'out (*AmE, informal*) to make sb feel disgusted: *His greasy hair really grosses me out!*
◆ v + n/pron + adv ♦ v + adv + n (*less frequent*)

ground /graʊnd/

be 'grounded in/on sth to be based on sth: *Is the story grounded in fact?*
◆ be + v + prep

grow /grəʊ; *AmE* groʊ/ (**grew** /gruː/**grown** /grəʊn; *AmE* groʊn/)

,grow a'part to become less close to sb in a relationship: *We used to be good friends, but we've grown apart.*
◆ v + adv

,grow a'way from sb to come to have a less close relationship with sb; to depend on sb less: *She has grown away from her parents.*
◆ v + adv + prep

,grow 'back if hair, fur, etc. **grows back**, it starts to grow again after it has been cut or damaged: *His hair grew back thicker after he shaved his head.*
SUBJ **hair**
✦ v + adv

,grow 'into sth 1 to gradually become sth over a period of time: *She had grown into a beautiful young woman.* **2** if a child **grows into** clothes, he/she becomes big enough to fit into them: *This coat's too big for him now, but he'll grow into it.* OBJ **coat, trousers, etc.** OPP **grow out of sth 3** to become familiar with and confident in a new job, activity, etc: *He needs time to grow into the job.* OBJ **job, role**
✦ v + prep

'grow on sb if sb/sth **grows on** you, you gradually like them/it more and more: *That painting's really grown on me.*
✦ v + prep

,grow 'out if the colour or style of your hair **grows out**, it disappears as your hair grows: *I had my hair coloured six weeks ago, but it's growing out now.*
✦ v + adv

,grow sth 'out to let your hair grow so that the colour or style changes or disappears: *I've decide to grow the layers out.*
✦ v + n/pron + adv ◆ v + adv + n

,grow 'out of sth 1 if a child **grows out of** clothes, he/she becomes too big to wear them: *She grows out of her clothes so fast!* OBJ **coat, trousers, etc.** SYN **outgrow sth** OPP **grow into sth 2** to stop doing something or suffering from sth as you become older: *He grew out of his eczema as he got older.* ◇ *He was a very rebellious teenager, but he grew out of it.* SYN **outgrow sth 3** to develop from sth: *These laws grew out of a need to protect children.*
✦ v + adv + prep

,grow 'up 1 when a person **grows up**, they become an adult: *Kate's growing up fast.* ◇ *Oh, grow up* (= behave in a more sensible way) *and stop making such a fuss!* ◇ *He was a difficult teenager, but grew up to be a responsible adult.* **2** [+adv/prep] to spend the time you are a child in a particular place or in a particular way: *He grew up in Portugal.* ◇ *Mel and I grew up together.* ◇ *This generation has grown up on MTV.* **3** to develop gradually: *The town had grown up around the abbey.* ◇ *A cult had grown up around him.* SYN **develop**
NOTE Do not confuse this phrasal verb with **grow**. **Grow** can be used without an object to mean 'increase in size, number, cost, etc.' **Grow**, but not **grow up**, can be used with an object: *to grow vegetables.* Use **bring sb up** to refer to parents caring for their children until they are grown up and teaching them how to behave, etc.
✦ v + adv

▶ **,grown-'up** *adj* (*informal*) **1** mentally and physically an adult: *He has two grown-up children.* **2** adult, mature: *Susie is very grown-up for her age.*
▶ **'grown-up** *n* (*informal*) (*used especially by adults when talking to children, or by children*) an adult person: *The grown-ups will sit at one table and the children at another.*

grub /grʌb/ (-bb-)

,grub sth 'out/'up (*rare*) to dig sth out of the ground: *Thousands of miles of hedgerows have been grubbed up.*
SYN **dig sth out; dig sth up**
✦ v + adv + n ◆ v + n/pron + adv

guard /gɑːd; *AmE* gɑːrd/

'guard against sth; 'guard against doing sth to do sth to prevent sth happening or to protect yourself from sth: *Clean the wound to guard against the danger of infection.* ◇ *We should guard against the possibility of this happening again.* ◇ *Regular exercise can help to guard against heart disease.*
OBJ **danger, risks, possibility**
NOTE **Guard against sth/against doing sth** can be used in the passive: *This danger must be guarded against.*
✦ v + prep

guess /ges/

'guess at sth to try to imagine sth or make a judgement without knowing all the facts: *We can only guess at the reason for his actions.*
NOTE **Guess at sth** can be used in the passive: *Her feelings can only be guessed at.*
✦ v + prep

gulp /gʌlp/

,gulp sth 'back (*rare*) to stop yourself showing that you are upset by swallowing hard: *She gulped back her tears.*
OBJ **tears**
✦ v + adv + n ◆ v + n/pron + adv

,gulp sth 'down to swallow sth quickly and noisily: *He gulped down a glass of water.*
OBJ **water, coffee, etc.**
NOTE **Gulp sth** can also be used with a similar meaning.
✦ v + adv + n ◆ v + n/pron + adv

gum /gʌm/ (-mm-)

,gum sth 'up (*BrE, informal, rare*) to fill sth with a sticky substance so that it cannot move or work: *My eyes were all gummed up.* ◇ *The substance gummed the machine up.*
NOTE **Gum sth up** is often used in the passive.
✦ v + n/pron + adv ◆ v + adv + n

gun /gʌn/ (**-nn-**)

,**gun sb 'down** (*informal*) to shoot sb, especially so as to kill or seriously injure them: *He was gunned down outside his home.* ◇ *Terrorists gunned down six people in the town last month.*
〉SYN〈 **shoot sb**
NOTE **Gun sb down** is often used in the passive.
◆ v + adv + n ◆ v + pron + adv ◆ v + n + adv (*rare*)

'**gun for sb** (*informal*) (*only used in the progressive tenses*) to try to blame sb or cause trouble for them: *She's been gunning for me since I came to work here.*
◆ v + prep

'**gun for sth** (*informal*) (*only used in the progressive tenses*) to try hard to get sth; to aim for sth: *They are both gunning for places in the championship.*
◆ v + prep

gussy /'gʌsi/ (**gussies, gussying, gussied, gussied**)

,**gussy sb/sth 'up**; ,**gussy yourself 'up** (*AmE, informal*) to dress sb/yourself in special, attractive clothes; to decorate sth to make it look attractive: *She gussied herself up for the big party.* ◇ *Jim's got all gussied up!* ◇ *My dress was plain, but I gussied it up with some jewellery.* ◇ *The city was gussied up for the President's visit.*
〉SYN〈 **doll yourself up** (**in sth**); **be/get dolled up** (**in sth**)
NOTE **Gussy sb/sth up** is usually used in the passive with *be* or *get*.
◆ v + adv + n ◆ v + pron + adv

H h

hack /hæk/

,hack sth a'bout (*BrE, informal, disapproving*) to cut or change sth in a rough and careless way: *The hairdressers have hacked her hair about a bit.* ◊ *(figurative) The script was hacked about by several people before the movie was finished.*
⊕ v + n/pron + adv

'hack at sth; **,hack a'way (at sth)** to try to cut sth using strong rough blows with an axe, a knife, scissors, etc: *She's really hacked at my hair. It's a complete mess.* ◊ *He was hacking away at the trees with an axe.* ◊ *Don't hack at it! Cut it carefully!*
⊕ v + prep ♦ v + adv

,hack sth 'down to cut a tree, etc. roughly so that it falls to the ground: *They are hacking down the forests to sell the timber.*
OBJ tree **SYN** chop sth down
⊕ v + n/pron + adv ♦ v + adv + n

,hack 'into sth (*computing*) to find a way of looking at or changing the information on sb else's computer without their knowledge or permission: *A teenage girl managed to hack into the bank's computer.*
⊕ v + prep

,hack sb 'off (*BrE, informal*) to make sb feel extremely annoyed or irritated: *He was hacked off with the whole situation.* ◊ *She always wants her jobs done in the next 10 minutes. That really hacks me off.*
NOTE Hack sb off is usually used in the passive or as an adjective.
⊕ v + n/pron + adv ♦ v + adv + n

,hack sth 'off; **,hack 'off sth** to cut sth off sth with rough heavy blows: *They hacked off the dead branches.* ◊ *He hacked the padlock off the door.* ◊ *She was always threatening to hack her lovely long hair off with the kitchen scissors.*
SYN chop sth off, chop sth off sth
⊕ v + adv + n ♦ v + n/pron + adv ♦ v + n/pron + prep

,hack sth 'up to cut sth very roughly into large pieces: *He hacked up the meat with a large knife.*
SYN chop sth up
⊕ v + adv + n ♦ v + n/pron + adv

hail /heɪl/

'hail from … (*formal*) (*not used in the progressive tenses*) to come from or to live in a particular place: *Which part of Ireland does he hail from?*
⊕ v + prep

ham /hæm/ (-mm-)

,ham it 'up (*informal*) to act in a deliberately artificial or exaggerated way: *The actors were really hamming it up.*
⊕ v + it + adv

hammer /'hæmə(r)/

,hammer a'way at sth to work hard in order to finish or achieve sth; to repeat sth again and again: *He kept hammering away at the same point all through the meeting.*
⊕ v + adv + prep

,hammer sth 'in; **,hammer sth 'into sb** to force sb to learn sth by repeating it many times: *I'll manage to hammer the point in somehow.* ◊ *They have had English grammar hammered into them.*
⊕ v + n/pron + adv ♦ v + adv + n ♦ v + n/pron + prep

,hammer sth 'out 1 to discuss a plan, a deal, etc. for a long time and with great effort, until sth is decided or agreed on: *It took weeks to hammer out an agreement.* **OBJ** deal, agreement, policy **2** to produce a sound, play a tune, etc. especially on a piano, loudly and not very well: *She hammered out 'Happy Birthday' on the piano.*
⊕ v + adv + n ♦ v + n/pron + adv

hand /hænd/

,hand sth a'round (*especially AmE*) = HAND STH ROUND

,hand sb 'back to sb/sth used by a television or radio reporter at the end of a report from a particular place to show that the main presenter will continue: *Now I'll hand you back to Trevor in the studio.*
⊕ v + n/pron + adv + prep

,hand sth 'back (to sb) 1 to give sth back to the person, country, etc. who used to have it or who owns it legally: *The territory was handed back to Egypt.* ◊ *We will not press charges if the stolen money is handed back.* **OBJ** money, control **2** to give sth back to the person who gave it to you: *She looked quickly at my passport and then handed it back.* **OBJ** passport, letter, glass **NOTE** In informal spoken language hand sb back sth and, less often, hand sb sth back are also used: *I handed her back her pen.* ◊ *I handed her her pen back.*
SYN give sth back (to sb); return sth (to sb)
⊕ v + n/pron + adv ♦ v + adv + n

,hand sth 'down 1 (*also* ,hand sth 'on) (to sb) to give or leave sth to a younger person: *All my clothes were handed down to me by my brother.* ◊ *These skills have been handed down from*

generation to generation. ◇ *He's got no one to hand the family house on to.* OBJ **tradition, custom, skills** SYN **pass sth down (to sb)** NOTE In this meaning **hand sth down** is usually used in the passive. **2** (*especially AmE*) (of a court of law or other official body) to announce an official decision: *The judge handed down a sentence of six years.* OBJ **decision, sentence, verdict**
◆ v + n/pron + adv ◆ v + adv + n

▶ '**hand-me-down** *n* [usually pl.] (*especially AmE*) clothing that is no longer wanted and is given to sb else, especially a younger brother or sister: *I used to hate wearing my brother's hand-me-downs.*

,**hand sth 'in (to sb) 1** to give a piece of work to sb, such as a teacher, so that they can correct, read or deal with it; to give sth to sb in authority because it belongs to them or is lost: *Make sure you hand in your homework on time.* ◇ *Hand your room keys in by 10 a.m* OBJ **essay, homework** SYN **give sth in (to sb) 2** to tell sb officially that you intend to leave your job: *I've just handed in my notice.* OBJ only **your notice, your resignation** SYN **give sth in (to sb); resign**
◆ v + adv + n ◆ v + n/pron + adv

,**hand sth 'on (to sb) 1** to send or give sth to another person after you have finished with it: *Hand on the magazine to your friends.* ◇ *The task has been handed on to me.* **2** = HAND STH DOWN 1 SYN **pass sth on (to sb)**
◆ v + adv + n ◆ v + n/pron + adv

,**hand sth 'out (to sb) 1** to give sth to each person in a group: *She handed textbooks out to the new students.* OBJ **leaflets, money** SYN **give sth out; pass sth out (to sb) 2** to give advice, criticism, a punishment, etc. to sb: *The courts are handing out tough sentences to frequent offenders.* OBJ **information, punishment, sentence** SYN **dish sth out (to sb)** (*informal*)
◆ v + n/pron + adv ◆ v + adv + n

▶ '**handout** *n* **1** something that is given free to people, especially food, money or clothes **2** a document giving information about sth, especially one that is given to a group or a class by a teacher, speaker, etc.

,**hand 'over to sb**; ,**hand sb 'over to sb** (*especially BrE*) to give sb else a turn to speak when you have finished talking: *I'd like to hand over now to our guest speaker.* ◇ *I'll hand you over to dad for a chat.*
◆ v + adv + prep ◆ v + n/pron + adv + prep

,**hand 'over to sb**; ,**hand sth 'over to sb** to give sb else your position of power or authority; to give sb else the responsibility for dealing with a particular situation: *I am resigning and handing over to my deputy.* ◇ *My father has handed over the business to me.*
◆ v + adv + prep ◆ v + adv + n + prep ◆
v + n/pron + adv + prep

▶ '**handover** *n* [C] [U] the act of moving power or responsibility from one person or group to another; the period during which this happens
→ *see also* HANDOVER at HAND SB/STH OVER (TO SB), HAND YOURSELF OVER (TO SB)

,**hand sb/sth 'over (to sb)**, ,**hand yourself 'over (to sb)** to give sb/sth officially to sb else, especially sb in authority: *They handed him over to the police.* ◇ *He forced me to hand over the keys to the safe.*
SYN **deliver sb/sth over/up (to sb), deliver yourself over/up (to sb)** (*more formal*)
◆ v + n/pron + adv ◆ v + adv + n

▶ '**handover** *n* [C] [U] the act of giving a person or a thing to sb in authority
→ *see also* HANDOVER at HAND OVER TO SB, HAND STH OVER TO SB

,**hand sth 'round** (*especially BrE*) (*AmE usually* ,**hand sth a'round**) to offer or pass sth (especially food and drink) to each person in a group of people or in a room: *Could you hand sth round the sandwiches, please?*
◆ v + adv + n ◆ v + n/pron + adv

hang /hæŋ/ (**hung, hung** /hʌŋ/)

~ about	~ out
~ about together	~ over
~ about with	~ round
~ around	~ round together
~ around together	~ round with
~ around with	~ together
139 ~ back	~ up
~ on	140 ~ with
~ onto, on to	

,**hang a'bout** (*BrE*) **1** (*informal*) = HANG ON 3 **2** = HANG AROUND

,**hang a'bout**; ,**hang a'bout sth** (*BrE*) = HANG AROUND, HANG AROUND STH

,**hang a'bout with sb**; ,**hang a'bout together** (*BrE*) = HANG AROUND WITH SB, HANG AROUND TOGETHER

,**hang a'round** (*BrE also* ,**hang a'bout/'round**) (*informal*) **1** to wait: *Sorry to keep you hanging around for so long.* ◇ *I won't hang about for you if you're late.* SYN **wait around (for sb/sth) 2** to delay doing sth; to be slow to do sth: *Have you finished already? You don't hang about do you?*
◆ v + adv

,**hang a'round**; ,**hang a'round sth** (*BrE also* ,**hang a'bout/'round**, ,**hang a'bout/'round sth**) (*informal*) to spend time somewhere, without doing very much: *We spent most of the day hanging about doing nothing.* ◇ *Children hang around the streets because there's nowhere for them to play.* ◇ *Why are they always hanging round our house?*
◆ v + adv ◆ v + prep

,hang a'round with sb; ,hang a'round together (BrE also ,hang a'bout/'round with sb, ,hang a'bout/'round together) (informal) to spend a lot of time with sb or with a group of people: Bob hangs around with Tim. ◇ Bob and Tim hang around together. ◇ I don't like the kind of people she hangs about with.
SYN go around with sb, go around together
♦ v + adv + prep ♦ v + adv + adv

,hang 'back 1 to not move forwards because you are nervous or afraid: She hung back, afraid to go near the dog. 2 to stay behind in a place such as a school or an office after most of the other people have left: My friends rushed out, but I hung back to talk to the teacher. 3 to be unwilling to do sth; to hesitate: This is a great opportunity. We can't afford to hang back.
♦ v + adv

,hang 'on 1 to hold sb/sth firmly: Hang on tight and you won't fall off. ◇ The horse suddenly galloped off and I tried to hang on as best as I could.
→ see also HANG ONTO STH/SB, HANG ON TO STH/SB 2 (BrE, spoken, informal) used to ask sb to wait for a short time: Hang on a minute — I'm nearly ready. ◇ The line's engaged. Would you like to hang on? 3 (BrE also ,hang a'bout) (spoken, informal) used to tell sb to stop what they are doing or saying, because you have just realized sth, or because you do not understand sth: Hang on! I've had an idea. ◇ Hang on! How much did you say it was? ◇ Hang on! That's not what I said! 4 to continue doing sth even when the situation is difficult: How much longer can their troops hang on in that position? 5 to wait for sth to happen: I need an answer soon — don't keep me hanging on.
SYN hold on
♦ v + adv

IDM hang (on) 'in there (informal) to continue trying to do sth, even though it is very difficult: Hang in there! The exams will soon be over.

'hang on sth to depend on sth: My whole future hung on his decision.
OBJ decision SYN depend on sth
♦ v + prep

'hang sth on sb (informal, especially AmE) to blame sb for sth, often unfairly: You can't hang the damage to your computer on me — I wasn't even there!
♦ v + n/pron + prep

,hang 'onto sth/sb; ,hang 'on to sth/sb to hold sth/sb tightly: Hang onto my hand while we cross the road.
SYN hold on, hold onto sth/sb, hold on to sth/sb
→ see also HANG ON
♦ v + adv ♦ v + prep ♦ v + adv + prep

,hang 'onto sb/sth; ,hang 'on to sb/sth (informal) to keep sth/sb; to not sell, give away or lose sth: Hang on to the receipt in case you want to change the dress. ◇ You can hang on to the book

for a bit longer if you want. ◇ I hope she manages to hang on to her job. ◇ The company seems to be incapable of hanging on to its staff. ◇ He's a great guy — you should hang on to him!
SYN hold onto sb/sth, hold on to sb/sth
♦ v + prep ♦ v + adv + prep

,hang 'out (informal) 1 [+adv/prep] to spend a lot of time in a place or with a person or a group of people: Where does he hang out these days? ◇ She used to hang out with the Beatles in the sixties. 2 to spend time relaxing, doing very little: We've just been hanging out and listening to music.
♦ v + adv
▶ 'hang-out n (informal) a place where you live or enjoy spending time with friends: a popular hang-out for teenagers

,hang sth 'out to attach things that you have washed to a piece of string or rope outside so that they can dry; to put sth such as a flag, etc. out of a window or in a street by attaching it to a piece of string or rope: Have you hung the washing out? ◇ Many houses hung out a banner supporting the march.
OBJ washing, clothes, flags, banner
→ see also HANG UP, HANG STH UP 1
♦ v + n/pron + adv ♦ v + adv + n

,hang 'over sb/sth if a problem, a threat or sth sad hangs over you, you think about it or worry about it a lot: A question mark hangs over the future of the club (= no one knows what is going to happen). ◇ The threat of dismissal hung over our heads.
SUBJ question mark, threat OBJ head, future
♦ v + prep

,hang 'round (BrE, informal) = HANG AROUND

,hang 'round; ,hang 'round sth (BrE, informal) = HANG AROUND, HANG AROUND STH

,hang 'round with sb; ,hang 'round together (BrE, informal) = HANG AROUND WITH SB, HANG AROUND TOGETHER

,hang to'gether to be well organized and fit together well; to have parts that all agree with each other: The book doesn't really hang together. ◇ This account of what happened doesn't hang together.
♦ v + adv

,hang 'up; ,hang sth 'up 1 to attach sth from the top to a hook, a piece of string, etc. so that the lower part is free or loose; to be attached in this way: My dress is hanging up in the wardrobe. ◇ Shall I hang your coat up? ◇ He took off his suit and hung it up carefully. OBJ coat, clothes → see also HANG STH OUT 2 (on sb) to end a telephone conversation, often very suddenly, by putting down the part of the telephone that you speak into (the receiver) or switching the telephone off: She hung up on me. ◇ Don't hang up. I'd like to talk to Dad too. ◇ I was so upset I hung up the phone. OBJ phone, receiver 3 to finish using sth

for the last time; to give up a particular activity, profession, etc: *After twenty years playing football, he's finally hanging up his boots.* OBJ **boots**
◈ v + adv ◆ v + adv + n ◆ v + n/pron + adv

get ,hung 'up (*AmE*) to be delayed: *I got hung up in traffic.* ◇ *Sorry I'm late — I got hung up at the office.*
◈ get + v + adv

'hang with sb (*AmE, slang*) to spend a lot of time with sb: *Are you still hanging with those guys?*
◈ v + prep

hanker /'hæŋkə(r)/

'hanker after/for sth to want sth very much: *He hankered after big city life.*
SYN **long for sth**
◈ v + prep

happen /'hæpən/

,happen a'long/'by (*informal*) to arrive or appear unexpectedly: *A police car happened along just at that moment.*
◈ v + adv

'happen on/upon sb/sth (*old-fashioned*) to find or meet sb/sth by chance: *I happened upon the book I wanted in a second-hand bookshop.*
SYN **come across sb/sth**
◈ v + prep

hark /hɑːk; AmE hɑːrk/

'hark at sb (*spoken, humorous*) used only in the form **hark at** sb, to show that you think what sb has just said is stupid, or shows too much pride: *'I need to lose some weight.' 'Hark at her! She's so thin I can hardly see her!'*
◈ v + prep

,hark 'back to sth 1 to talk about or remember sth that happened in the past or was mentioned before: *You can't keep harking back to the past.* OBJ **the past, youth** NOTE In this meaning **hark back to sth** is often used in the progressive tenses. **2** (*BrE*) to remind you of or to be like sth in the past: *The melody harks back to one of his earlier symphonies.* NOTE In this meaning **hark back to sth** is not used in the progressive tenses.
◈ v + adv + prep

harp /hɑːp; AmE hɑːrp/

,harp 'on (about sth), **'harp on sth** (*informal*) to keep talking about sth in a way that other people find annoying: *He's still harping on about having his bike stolen.* ◇ *He's always harping on the same theme.*
SYN **go on (about sth)**
◈ v + adv ◆ v + prep

hash /hæʃ/

,hash sth 'out (*AmE, informal*) to discuss sth in detail for a long time in order to reach an agreement: *They are still hashing out the details of the contract.*
SYN **thrash sth out**
◈ v + adv + n ◆ v + n/pron + adv

hatch /hætʃ/

,hatch 'out (*BrE*) when a bird, an insect, etc. **hatches out**, it comes out of the egg; when an egg **hatches out**, it breaks open and a bird, an insect, etc. comes out: *The chicks hatch out after fifteen days.* ◇ *Have the eggs hatched out yet?* ◇ *When will the caterpillars hatch out?*
NOTE **Hatch** is used instead of **hatch out** in American English. It can also be used in British English.
◈ v + adv

haul /hɔːl/

,haul sb be'fore sb/sth (*also* **,haul sb 'up before sb/sth**) (*informal*) to make sb appear in a court of law in order to be judged: *They were hauled before the courts.* ◇ *They hauled her up in front of senior officers.*
SYN **bring sb before sb/sth** (*more formal*)
NOTE **In front of** can be used instead of **before**: *They hauled her up in front of senior officers.* ◆ **Haul sb (up) before/in front of sb/sth** is often used in the passive.
→ *see also* HAUL SB UP
◈ v + n/pron + prep

,haul sb 'off (to sth/...) (*informal*) to take sb somewhere by force: *They hauled him off to jail.*
SYN **drag sb off (to sth/...)**
◈ v + n/pron + adv ◆ v + adv + n (*rare*)

,haul sb 'up (*informal*) to make sb appear in a court of law in order to be judged: *He was hauled up on a charge of dangerous driving.*
NOTE **Haul sb up** is often used in the passive.
→ *see also* HAUL SB BEFORE SB/STH
◈ v + n/pron + adv ◆ v + adv + n (*rare*)

have /həv, əv, hæv/ (has, having, had, had)

,have sth a'gainst sb/sth (*also* **have ,got sth a'gainst sb/sth**) (*not used in the progressive tenses*) to dislike sb/sth for a particular reason: *I've got nothing against her family personally — it's just that there are so many of them!* ◇ *I don't know what she had against me.*
OBJ **nothing, anything, something**
NOTE **Have sth against sb/sth** is not used in the passive.
◈ v + pron + prep

,**have sb a'round** (*especially AmE*) = HAVE SB OVER

,**have it a'way** (**with sb**) (*BrE*, *slang*) = HAVE IT OFF (WITH SB)

,**have sb 'back** (*especially BrE*) **1** to allow a husband, wife or partner that you are separated from to return: *He had his wife back time and time again.* $\overline{\text{SYN}}$ **take sb back 2** to invite sb to your house after you have been somewhere with them: *After the cinema we had everybody back for coffee.* $\overline{\text{SYN}}$ **ask sb back**; **invite sb back** (*more formal*)
 NOTE Have sb back is not used in the passive.
 ✦ v + n/pron + adv

,**have sth 'back** to receive sth that has been borrowed or taken from you: *Can I have the book back by Thursday?*
 NOTE Have sth back is not used in the passive.
 ✦ v + n/pron + adv ◆ v + adv + n (*rare*)

,**have sb 'down as sth** (*especially BrE*) to think that sb is a particular type of person, especially when in fact they are not: *I didn't have you down as the jealous type.*
 NOTE Have sb down as sth is not used in the passive.
 ✦ v + n/pron + adv + prep

,**have sb 'in** (*also* **have ,got sb 'in**) to have sb doing some work in your home or office: *They've got the builders in all week.* ◊ *We had the inspectors in on Tuesday.*
 NOTE Have sb in is not used in the passive.
 ✦ v + n/pron + adv

,**have sth 'in** (*also* **have ,got sth 'in**) (*not used in the progressive tenses*) to have a supply of sth in your home, etc: *Do we have enough food in for the holiday?* ◊ *I wanted to get a new swimsuit, but the store didn't have any in yet.*
 NOTE Have sth in is not used in the passive.
 ✦ v + n/pron + adv

have it 'off (*also* ,**have it a'way** (**with sb**)) (*BrE*, *slang*) to have sex with sb
 ✦ v + it + adv

,**have sb 'on** (*informal*) (*usually used in the progressive tenses*) to joke with sb by pretending sth is true when it is not: *'We've won a new car!' 'You're having me on!'*
 ✦ v + n/pron + adv

,**have sth 'on** (*also* **have ,got sth 'on**) **1** (*not used in the progressive tenses*) to be wearing sth: *She's got her best dress on.* ◊ *He had nothing* (= no clothes) *on!* ◊ *He had on a blue and white checked shirt and jeans.* $\overline{\text{OBJ}}$ **clothes, coat, hat, etc.** $\overline{\text{SYN}}$ **be wearing sth 2** to have a piece of electrical equipment switched on: *I didn't hear you come in because I had the radio on.* $\overline{\text{OBJ}}$ **television, radio 3** to have something planned or arranged: *I've had a lot on recently.* ◊ *What do you have on* (*for*)

tomorrow? $\overline{\text{OBJ}}$ **nothing, something, a lot**
 ✦ **Have sth on** is not used in the passive.
 ✦ v + n/pron + adv
 1 also v + adv + n (*less frequent*)

,**have sth 'on sb/sth** (*also* **have ,got sth 'on sb/sth**) (*informal*) (*not used in the progressive tenses*) to know sth bad about someone that can be used against them: *The police had nothing on him* (= no evidence that he had committed a crime).
 $\overline{\text{OBJ}}$ **something, nothing**
 NOTE Have sth on sb/sth is not used in the passive.
 ✦ v + n/pron + prep

,**have sth 'out 1** to have a tooth or an organ of your body removed: *I had to have a tooth out.* $\overline{\text{OBJ}}$ **tooth, appendix, tonsils 2** (**with sb**) to talk to sb openly to try to settle a dispute or disagreement: *She finally decided to have it out with him.* $\overline{\text{OBJ}}$ **it**
 NOTE Have sth out is not used in the passive.
 ✦ v + n/pron + adv

,**have sb 'over** (*also* ,**have sb a'round** *especially AmE*) (*BrE also* ,**have sb 'round**) to invite sb to come to your house: *They had some friends over last night.* ◊ *We're having people round for dinner tonight.*
 NOTE Have sb over/around/round is not used in the passive.
 ✦ v + n/pron + adv

,**have sb 'up** (**for sth**) (*BrE*, *informal*) to accuse sb of sth and bring them to a court of law to be examined by a judge: *He was had up for dangerous driving.*
 NOTE Have sb up is usually used in the passive.
 ✦ v + n/pron + adv

hawk /hɔːk/

,**hawk sth a'bout/a'round/'round**; ,**hawk sth a'bout/a'round/'round sth** (*BrE*) to try to sell things by going from place to place asking people to buy them: *Pirate copies of their CD were being hawked around.* ◊ *They hawked their newsletter around student bars.*
 ✦ v + n/pron + adv ◆ v + adv + n (*less frequent*) ◆ v + n/pron + prep

head /hed/

'**head for/towards sth** (*also* **be 'headed for/towards sth** *especially AmE*) (*often used in the progressive tenses*) **1** to be going in a particular direction or to a particular place: *It's time I was heading for home.* ◊ *Jane headed for the door.* $\overline{\text{SYN}}$ **make for sb/sth 2** to be likely to experience sth, especially sth bad: *They're heading for trouble.* ◊ *The country is headed for an economic disaster.* $\overline{\text{OBJ}}$ **trouble, defeat, disaster, victory, a fall**
 ✦ v + prep ◆ be + v + prep

head 'off to leave a place to go somewhere else or do sth else: *It's time we headed off to get the train.*
◈ v + adv

head sb 'off to get in front of sb in order to make them turn back or go in a different direction: *Police tried to head off the demonstrators before they got to the city hall.*
⟩SYN⟨ **intercept sb** (*more formal*)
◈ v + adv + n ◆ v + n/pron + adv

head sb/sth 'off to prevent sth; to stop sb from doing sth: *Their attempts to head off criticism have failed.*
◈ v + adv + n ◆ v + n/pron + adv

head towards sth (*also* **be 'headed towards sth** *especially AmE*) = HEAD FOR/TOWARDS STH, BE HEADED FOR/TOWARDS STH

head 'up sth; **head it/them 'up** to be in charge of sth such as a department, a company, an organization, etc: *She heads up our finance division.*
OBJ **operation, company**
NOTE A noun must always follow **up**, but a pronoun comes between the verb and **up**. ◆ This phrasal verb is also used in the passive: *The new company will be headed up by Graham Hart.*
NOTE **Head sth** is also used with the same meaning: *She heads our finance division.*
◈ v + adv + n ◆ v + pron + adv

heal /hi:l/

heal 'up/'over if a cut, a wound, etc. **heals up/over**, it closes and becomes healthy again: *Her leg took a long time to heal up.* ◇ *The cut has healed over now.*
NOTE **Heal** is often used with the same meaning.
◈ v + adv

heap /hi:p/

heap A on B; **heap B with A** (*also* **heap A upon B** *more formal*) **1** to put a lot of sth in a pile on sth: *She heaped food on my plate.* ◇ *The food was heaped on the plate.* ◇ *The chairs were heaped with cushions.* **2** to offer or give sb a lot of sth, especially praise or criticism: *They heaped scorn upon his proposal.* ◇ *Praise was heaped on the police for their handling of the case.* **OBJ** **praise, scorn**
NOTE These phrasal verbs are often used in the passive.
◈ v + n/pron + prep

heap sth 'up to put sth into a pile: *A huge pile of washing was heaped up in a corner.*
⟩SYN⟨ **pile sth up**
◈ v + n/pron + adv ◆ v + adv + n

hear /hɪə(r); *AmE* hɪr/ (**heard, heard** /hɜːd; *AmE* hɜːrd/)

'hear about sb/sth to be told news or information about sb/sth: *I'm so sorry to hear about your mother* (= for example, that she is ill). ◇ *Have you heard about your job yet* (= if you have got it or not)*?*
◈ v + prep

'hear from sb; **'hear sth from sb 1** to receive news or information from sb, usually by letter or telephone: *Do you ever hear from any of your school friends?* ◇ (*written*) *I look forward to hearing from you.* ◇ *I haven't heard anything from Kate for ages.* **2** to formally get sb's opinion about sth or their description of sth that has happened, such as an accident, etc: *Can we hear from some of the women in the audience?* ◇ *The police would like to hear from anyone who witnessed the accident.* ◇ *I'd like to hear something from somebody who's had experience of studying abroad.*
◈ v + prep ◆ v + n/pron + prep

'hear of sb/sth to know about sb/sth because you have been told about them/it: *I've heard of the Alexander technique, but I don't know anything about it.* ◇ *I've never heard of him.*
NOTE **Hear of sb** is often used in the present perfect tense with *have*.
→ *see also* UNHEARD-OF at HEAR OF SB/STH, HEAR STH OF SB/STH
◈ v + prep

'hear of sb/sth; **'hear sth of sb/sth** to have news of sb/sth: *I was sorry to hear of your accident.* ◇ *He was last heard of in Liverpool.* ◇ *You're going abroad? This is the first I've heard of it!* ◇ *From what I've heard of Andy, he's become very successful.* ◇ *I expect we'll hear more of this band in the future.*
NOTE **Hear of sb** is often used in the passive.
→ *see also* NOT HEAR OF STH, NOT HEAR OF SB DOING STH
◈ v + prep ◆ v + n/pron + prep

▶ **un'heard-of** *adj* that has never been known or done; surprising: *It's almost unheard-of for it to rain there in July.*

not 'hear of sth; **not 'hear of sb doing sth** to not allow something or not allow sb to do sth: *I offered to go but she wouldn't hear of it.* ◇ *They wouldn't hear of us postponing the trip.*
→ *see also* UNHEARD-OF at HEAR OF SB/STH, HEAR STH OF SB/STH
◈ v + prep

hear sb 'out to listen until sb has finished saying what they want to say: *I know you don't believe me, but please hear me out!*
◈ v + n/pron + adv

heat /hiːt/

,heat 'up (*AmE*) = HOT UP

,heat 'up; ,heat sth 'up to become warm or hot; to make sth warm or hot: *The pipes will expand as they heat up.* ◇ *We can heat up the soup in the microwave.*

> SYN **warm up, warm sth up**

⊕ v + adv ◆ v + adv + n ◆ v + n/pron + adv

hedge /hedʒ/

,hedge sth a'bout/a'round/'round with sth (*BrE, formal*) to surround and limit sth with conditions or restrictions: *Employment is hedged around with legislation nowadays.*

> NOTE **Hedge sth about/around/round with sth** is usually used in the passive.

⊕ v + n/pron + adv + prep

,hedge sb/sth 'in to surround sb/sth with sth; to restrict the freedom of sb to do sth: *The cathedral is hedged in by other buildings.* ◇ *He felt hedged in by all the rules and regulations.*

> SYN **fence sb in; hem sb/sth in**

> NOTE **Hedge sb/sth in** is often used in the passive.

⊕ v + n/pron + adv ◆ v + adv + n

help /help/

,help sth a'long to try to make sth happen more quickly or easily: *My mother always says that a cup of tea **helps things along**.* ◇ *His father's name helped along his career in the early days.*

⊕ v + n/pron + adv ◆ v + adv + n (*less frequent*)

,help sb 'off/'on with sth to help sb to take off or put on a piece of clothing, such as a coat: *Can I help you off with your coat?* ◇ *She helped him on with his dressing gown.*

⊕ v + n/pron + adv + prep

,help 'out (with sth), **,help sb 'out** (with sth) to help sb in order to make things easier for them, for example by doing some of their work or by giving them money: *Thank you for helping out.* ◇ *My dad said he'd help me out with money.*

> NOTE **Help** (with sth) and **help sb** (with sth) can be used with the same meaning.

⊕ v + adv ◆ v + n/pron + adv ◆ v + adv + n (*rare*)

'help sb to sth; 'help yourself to sth to give sb/yourself some food or drink: *Can I help anyone to more chicken?* ◇ *Please help yourselves to salad.*

⊕ v + n/pron + prep

hem /hem/ (-mm-)

,hem sb/sth 'in to surround sb/sth with sth so that they cannot move freely: *The thick trees hemmed them in on all sides.* ◇ *The ship was hemmed in by the ice.* ◇ (*figurative*) *We felt*

hemmed in by restrictions.

> SYN **fence sb in**

> NOTE **Hem sb/sth in** is often used in the passive.

⊕ v + n/pron + adv ◆ v + adv + n

herd /hɜːd; AmE hɜːrd/

,herd to'gether; ,herd sb/sth to'gether to move or make sb/sth move in a particular direction: *They were herded together into trucks and driven away.*

> NOTE **Herd sb/sth together** is often used in the passive.

⊕ v + adv ◆ v + n/pron + adv ◆ v + adv + n

hide /haɪd/ (hid /hɪd/ hidden /'hɪdn/)

,hide a'way; ,hide yourself a'way to go to a place secretly because you do not want anyone to find you: *She used to hide away in her room when she got depressed.* ◇ *She hid herself away until she felt better.*

⊕ v + adv ◆ v + pron + adv

▶ **'hideaway** *n* a place where sb goes to be alone

,hide sb/sth a'way to put sb/sth in a secret place so that no one else can find them/it: *You won't find your present — I've hidden it away!*

⊕ v + n/pron + adv ◆ v + adv + n (*less frequent*)

,hide 'out to go to a secret place to escape from sb who is trying to find you: *He hid out in the woods.*

⊕ v + adv

▶ **'hideout** *n* a place where sb goes when they do not want to be found

hike /haɪk/

,hike sth 'up 1 (*informal*) to lift or pull up a piece of clothing that you are wearing: *He hiked up his trousers and waded into the water.* > SYN **hitch sth up 2** to increase a price or rate suddenly and by a large amount: *They hiked up the price by 40%.* > SYN **jack sth up** (*informal*), **put sth up** > NOTE **Hike sth** is used less often with this meaning.

⊕ v + adv + n ◆ v + pron + adv ◆ v + n + adv (*rare*)

hinge /hɪndʒ/

'hinge on sth (*also* **'hinge upon sth** *more formal*) if an action, a result, etc. **hinges on/upon** sth, it depends on it completely or is strongly influenced by it: *My whole career could hinge on the results of these exams.* ◇ *The success of the project hinges on how well everyone works together.*

⊕ v + prep

hint /hɪnt/

'hint at sth to suggest in an indirect way that sth is true or likely: *In his speech the Prime Minister hinted at an early election.*

> NOTE **Hint at sth** can be used in the passive: *The problem was only hinted at.*

⊕ v + prep

hire /'haɪə(r)/

ˌhire sb 'out; **ˌhire yourself 'out** (to sb) (as sth) to arrange for sb to work for sb else; to arrange to work for sb: *The agency hires out cleaning staff.* ◇ *He hires himself out to farmers at harvest time.* ◇ *He had been hired out to them as an expert.*
◈ v + adv + n ♦ v + n/pron + adv

ˌhire sth 'out to allow sb to use sth for a short period of time in return for payment: *The club will hire out tennis rackets to guests.*
[OBJ] **equipment, boat** [SYN] **let sth out (to sb)**; **rent sth out (to sb)**
◈ v + adv + n ♦ v + n/pron + adv

hit /hɪt/ (hitting, hit, hit)

ˌhit 'back (at sb/sth) to criticize or attack sb who has criticized or attacked you: *In an interview she hit back at her critics.*
[SYN] **bite back (at sb/sth)**; **strike back (at/against sb/sth)**
◈ v + adv

'hit sb for sth (also **ˌhit sb 'up for sth**) (slang, especially AmE) to ask sb for sth, especially money: *They hit us for a commission as well.* ◇ *She's always hitting me up for the cab fare home.* ◇ *Does he always hit you for cash when he wants new clothes?*
◈ v + n/pron + prep ♦ v + n/pron + adv + prep

ˌhit it 'off (with sb) (informal) if two people **hit it off** with each other, they like each other and become friendly immediately: *We hit it off from the start.* ◇ *She didn't really hit it off with the office manager.*
◈ v + it + adv

'hit on sb (AmE, slang) to talk to sb in a way that shows you are sexually attracted to them: *He was hitting on my girlfriend!*
◈ v + prep

'hit on sth (also **'hit upon sth** more formal) (not used in the progressive tenses) to think of a plan, a solution, etc. suddenly or by chance: *She hit on an idea for raising money.* ◇ *I realized I'd hit upon a solution to one of our main problems.*
[OBJ] **idea, method, formula, solution** [SYN] **light on/upon sb/sth**
◈ v + prep

ˌhit 'out (at sb/sth) **1** to attack sb violently, especially sb who is trying to hit or capture you: *She hit out at the policeman as he tried to arrest her.* ◇ *I just hit out blindly in all directions.* [SYN] **strike out (at sb/sth) 2** to criticize sb or sth strongly: *He hit out at the government's decision.*
[SYN] **lash out (at sb/sth)**
◈ v + adv

ˌhit sb 'up for sth (especially AmE) = HIT SB FOR STH

'hit upon sth = HIT ON STH

hitch /hɪtʃ/

ˌhitch sth 'up to pull up a piece of your clothing: *We hitched up our skirts and climbed over the wall.*
[SYN] **hike sth up** (informal)
◈ v + adv + n ♦ v + n/pron + adv

hive /haɪv/

ˌhive sth 'off (into/to sth) (business) to separate sth from a larger group; to sell part of a company: *Some of the firm's operations have been hived off into a separate company.*
[NOTE] **Hive sth off** is often used in the passive.
◈ v + adv + n ♦ v + pron + adv ♦ v + n + adv (rare)

hold /həʊld; AmE hoʊld/ (held, held /held/)

	~ against		~ out
	~ back	146	~ out for
145	~ back on		~ out on
	~ down		~ over
	~ forth		~ to
	~ in		~ together
	~ off		~ up
	~ on		~ up as
	~ onto, on to		~ with

ˌhold sth a'gainst sb to allow sth bad that sb has done to make you like or respect them less: *I know I was stupid — I hope you won't **hold it against** me.* ◇ *Do you hold any grudges against him?* ◇ *I don't **hold it against** him that he lied to me twice.*
[OBJ] **it, grudge**
[NOTE] **Hold sth against sb** is often used with a negative such as *don't* or *won't*.
◈ v + n/pron + prep

ˌhold 'back (from doing sth); **ˌhold sb 'back** (from doing sth) to hesitate, or to make sb hesitate, to act or speak: *Don't hold back! This opportunity is too good to miss!* ◇ *Phil walked forward confidently but something held Ben back.* ◇ *I nearly told him what I thought of him, but I held back.*
◈ v + adv ♦ v + n/pron + adv

ˌhold sb/sth 'back 1 to prevent sb/sth from moving forward or from entering or leaving a place: *The police were unable to hold back the fans.* **2** to prevent the progress or development of sb/sth: *Now that he's got this job, there'll be **no holding him back**.* ◇ *Teaching all the children together can hold the brighter children back.* ◇ *Low rates of investment will hold back technical progress.* ◇ *Parents claim the tests are being used to hold children back* (= not let them progress to the next class).
◈ v + n/pron + adv ♦ v + adv + n

ˌhold sth 'back 1 to stop yourself from expressing or showing how you feel: *They couldn't hold back their laughter.* ◇ *He struggled to hold*

back his tears. OBJ **your tears, your laughter** SYN **keep sth back; contain sth** (*more formal*) **2** to not tell sb sth that you wish to keep secret: *I think he's holding something back; he knows more than he's admitting.* OBJ **something, anything, information** SYN **withhold sth** (*more formal*) **3** to keep sth such as money to use later: *£1 000 of the grant will be held back until the project is completed.* NOTE **Hold sth back** is often used in the passive in this meaning.
◆ v + adv + n ◆ v + n/pron + adv

,hold 'back on sth to try to spend only a little time, money, etc. on sth; to show control in what you do: *My grandmother never held back on the tea and cakes when we visited.* ◇ *She held back on her questioning* (= she did not ask too many questions).
◆ v + adv + prep

,hold sb 'down to prevent sb from having their freedom or rights
◆ v + adv + n ◆ v + n/pron + adv

,hold sb/sth 'down to use force to hold sb/sth in a particular position and stop them/it from moving: *He was held down and kicked by the two men.* ◇ *Hold the mouse button down as you move the cursor.*
◆ v + n/pron + adv ◆ v + adv + n

,hold sth 'down 1 to manage to keep a job, position, etc. even though it may be difficult for you to do so: *He doesn't seem able to hold down a full-time job.* OBJ **a job 2** (*especially BrE*) to keep sth at a low level: *The company is trying to hold down costs.* ◇ *The rate of inflation must be held down.* OBJ **prices, wages, inflation, costs** SYN **keep sth down 3** (*AmE, informal*) to limit sth, especially a noise: *Hold it down, will you? I'm trying to sleep!* **4** (*usually used in negative sentences*) to be able to eat food without bringing it back out of your mouth: *She hasn't been able to hold any food down since the operation.* OBJ **food** SYN **keep sth down 5** to not allow yourself to show or express a strong emotion: *I had to hold down the urge to hit him.*
◆ v + adv + n ◆ v + n/pron + adv

,hold 'forth (on/about sth) (*formal* or *humorous*) to speak for a long time and often in a boring or annoying way: *He was holding forth about how successful his business is.*
◆ v + adv

,hold sth 'in 1 to keep sth inside a place so that it cannot fall out or escape: *The straps hold the baby in securely.* ◇ *I had to hold my stomach in* (= pull the muscles flat) *to zip up my jeans.* OBJ **your stomach, your tummy 2** to not show or express how you feel: *I couldn't hold in my anger any longer.* OPP **let sth out**
◆ v + n/pron + adv ◆ v + adv + n

,hold 'off 1 if rain or a storm, etc. **holds off**, it does not start: *I hope the rain holds off for the wedding.* SYN **keep off 2** (*also* ,hold 'off sth, ,hold 'off (from) doing sth) to delay doing sth: *I need to make a decision soon, but I'll hold off until next week.* ◇ *The committee will hold off their decision until they receive the report.* ◇ *I'm holding off buying a dress until the sales start.* NOTE **Hold off sth** is not used with a pronoun.
◆ **1** v + adv
  2 v + adv ◆ v + adv + n ◆ v + adv + -ing

,hold sb/sth 'off to resist an attack by an enemy or an opponent: *How long do you think you can hold off the attack?* ◇ *He held off a late challenge from Davies to win the race.*
◆ v + n/pron + adv ◆ v + adv + n

,hold 'on 1 (*spoken, informal*) used to ask sb to wait or stop for a short time: *Hold on a minute — I'm not quite ready.* ◇ *Hold on! That doesn't sound right.* **2** to survive in a difficult or dangerous situation; to continue doing sth although it is difficult: *They managed to hold on until help arrived.*
SYN **hang on**
◆ v + adv

,hold 'on; ,hold 'onto sth/sb; ,hold 'on to sth/sb to hold sth/sb tightly; to not let go of sth/sb: *Hold on tight — I'm going to speed up!* ◇ *Hold onto your hat or it'll blow away.* ◇ *I had to hold onto the chair for support.*
SYN **hang on, hang onto sth/sb, hang on to sth/sb**
◆ v + adv ◆ v + prep ◆ v + adv + prep

,hold sth 'on to keep sth in position so that it cannot fall off: *It is these nuts and bolts that hold the wheels on.*
◆ v + n/pron + adv ◆ v + adv + n

,hold 'onto sb/sth; ,hold 'on to sb/sth to keep sth/sb; to not lose sth/sb: *Hold on to the magazines for as long as you like.* ◇ *The party will hold on to its majority at the next election.* ◇ *She's a good worker. You should hold on to her.* ◇ *You must pass the ball else and not hold onto it.*
SYN **hang onto sb/sth, hang on to sb/sth** (*informal*)
◆ v + prep ◆ v + adv + prep

,hold 'out 1 if money or supplies, etc. **hold out**, they last or remain: *I'm staying here for as long as my money holds out.* ◇ *Do you think the fine weather will hold out?* SYN **last out 2** (**against sb/sth**) to resist an attack: *The town continues to hold out against enemy bombing.* **3** (**against sth**) to refuse to accept sth that you not agree with: *We can't hold out against industrialization any longer.* OPP **give in (to sb/sth)**
◆ v + adv

▶ 'holdout n (*AmE*) someone who resists an attack, an enemy or an opponent, or who refuses to accept sth

,**hold 'out sth** to offer a chance, hope or possibility of sth: *He may come, but I don't **hold out** much hope.* ◇ *This method seems to hold out the greatest promise of success.*
OBJ **the promise/prospect/possibility of..., hope**
NOTE **Hold out sth** is never used with a pronoun.
◈ v + adv + n

,**hold sth 'out** to hold sth such as your hand or sth in your hand, in front of you towards sb else: *She held her cup out for more coffee.* ◇ *'You must be Kate,' he said, holding out his hand.*
OBJ **hand**
◈ v + n/pron + adv ◆ v + adv + n

,**hold 'out for sth** to deliberately delay reaching an agreement in the hope that you will gain sth; to refuse to accept anything less than what you are asking for: *Union leaders are holding out for a better deal.*
◈ v + adv + prep

,**hold 'out on sb** (*informal*) to refuse to tell or give sb sth: *You promised to give me the money. Stop holding out on me.*
◈ v + adv + prep

,**hold sth 'over 1** to leave sth to be dealt with later: *We decided to hold the matter over until the next meeting.* SYN **postpone sth 2** (*AmE*) to show a film/movie or play for longer than planned because it is so successful: *The show is being held over for another month.*
NOTE **Hold sth over** is often used in the passive.
◈ v + n/pron + adv ◆ v + adv + n
▶ '**holdover** *n* (*AmE*) a person who keeps a position of power, for example sb who had a particular position in one government and who still has it in the next

,**hold sth 'over sb** to use sth that you know about sb in order to threaten them and to make them do what you want: *I don't want to give him anything to hold over me.*
◈ v + n/pron + prep

'**hold to sth** if you **hold to** an opinion, a belief, etc., you do not change it: *She always holds to her principles.*
SYN **keep to sth; stick to sth**
◈ v + prep

'**hold sb to sth 1** to make sb keep a promise: *'I promise I'll take you out to dinner if we win.' 'I'll hold you to that!'* **2** (*sport*) to stop your opponent in a sports competition winning more points than you: *Spain held France to a 1-1 draw.*
◈ v + n/pron + prep

'**hold sth to sth** to place sth close to sth else: *He held a knife to her throat.*
◈ v + n/pron + prep

,**hold to'gether**; ,**hold sth to'gether 1** to remain, or to keep sb/sth, united: *The coalition has held together for longer than expected.* ◇ *Strong bonds of loyalty hold the family together.* **2** if ideas, arguments, etc. **hold together**, or

sth **holds them together**, they are logical and the parts agree with each other: *His ideas don't really hold together.* ◇ *Words like 'however', 'therefore', 'although', etc. can hold your text together.* **3** to remain in one piece; to stay in good condition: *It's a miracle that his car is still holding together.* ◇ *His trousers were held together by safety pins.*
◈ v + adv ◆ v + n/pron + adv ◆ v + adv + n

,**hold 'up 1** to remain healthy, in good condition or working effectively, especially when there are difficulties: *Sales have held up well, in spite of economic difficulties.* ◇ *How did your tent hold up in the storm?* **2** if an idea, an argument, etc. **holds up**, it remains strong when you analyse it carefully: *I don't think his argument really holds up.* SYN **stand up**
◈ v + adv

,**hold sb/sth 'up 1** to raise sb/sth in the air: *She held up her hand to stop him.* ◇ *He held up his trophy as the crowd applauded.* **2** to support sb/sth and prevent it/them from falling: *Her trousers were held up with string.* ◇ *The two pillars were holding the ceiling up.* SYN **keep sth up 3** to block or delay the progress of sb/sth: *Roadworks on the motorway are holding up traffic.* ◇ *She phoned to say she'd been held up at the office.* ◇ *I don't want to hold you up.* **4** to rob a person, a bank, a shop/store, etc. using a gun: *Have they caught the people who held up the bank?*
NOTE **Hold sb/sth up** is often used in the passive.
◈ v + adv + n ◆ v + n/pron + adv
   4 v + adv + n ◆ v + pron + adv ◆ v + n + adv (*rare*)
▶ '**hold-up** *n* **1** a delay or sth which causes a delay: *What's the hold-up?* **2** an act of robbing a person, a bank, a shop/store, etc. using a gun

,**hold sb/sth 'up as sth** to present sb/sth as an example of sth: *My mother held up my cousin as an example of a good student.*
◈ v + n/pron + adv + prep ◆ v + adv + n + prep

'**hold with sth** to agree with or approve of sth: *I don't hold with these new theories on education.*
NOTE **Hold with sth** is only used in negative sentences and questions.
◈ v + prep

hole /həʊl; *AmE* hoʊl/

,**hole 'up; be ,holed 'up** (*informal*) to hide somewhere: *The thieves holed up in an empty warehouse.* ◇ *The police couldn't find out where the gang were holed up.*
◈ v + adv ◆ be + v + adv

hollow /'hɒləʊ; *AmE* 'hɑ:loʊ/

,**hollow sth 'out 1** to make a space inside sth by removing part of it: *We hollowed out the pumpkin and put a candle in it.* ◇ *a hollowed-out tree*

trunk **2** to form sth by making a hole in something else: *The waves have hollowed out caves along the cliff.*
◆ v + adv + n ◆ v + pron + adv ◆ v + n + adv (*rare*)

home /həʊm; *AmE* hoʊm/

home 'in on sb/sth 1 to move or be aimed straight towards sb/sth: *She homed in on me as soon as she saw me.* **2** to turn all your attention to sth: *The lawyer homed in on the inconsistencies in her story.*
◆ v + adv + prep

hook /hʊk/

hook sb 'into sth; **hook sb 'into doing sth** (*AmE, informal*) to persuade sb to do sth when they do not want to: *I didn't want to be involved but I got hooked into helping.* ◊ *He tried to hook me into going with them.*
NOTE Hook sb into sth/into doing sth is nearly always used in the passive.
◆ v + n/pron + prep

hook 'up (with sb) 1 (*informal*) to agree to work with sb: *We've hooked up with a firm in Ireland.* **2** (*informal, especially AmE*) to meet sb and spend time with them: *On vacation we hooked up with some Texans.* ◊ *Let's hook up when you get back from your trip.* **3** (*AmE, informal*) to start a relationship with sb: *They hooked up at Kyle's party.*
◆ v + adv

hook 'up; **hook sb/sth 'up (to sth)** to connect sb/sth to a piece of electronic equipment or to a power supply: *All the speakers hook up to a single amplifier.* ◊ *The boat was hooked up to the shore power supply.* ◊ *They've hooked him up to a life-support machine.*
◆ v + adv ◆ v + adv + n ◆ v + n/pron + adv
▶ **'hook-up** *n* a connection between two or more pieces of equipment: *an international phone hook-up*

hoover /'huːvə(r)/

hoover sth 'up (*BrE*) to remove dust, dirt, etc. from a carpet or floor with a vacuum cleaner (= an electrical machine that cleans floors and carpets by sucking up dust and dirt): (*figurative*) *The US and Canada usually hoover up all the gold and silver medals at the Olympic Games.*
◆ v + adv + n ◆ v + n/pron + adv

horse /hɔːs; *AmE* hɔːrs/

horse a'round (*BrE also* **horse a'bout**) (*informal*) to play in a noisy and careless way that is likely to damage sth or hurt sb: *If you two don't stop horsing around you'll hurt yourselves.*
SYN **mess around** (*BrE*)
◆ v + adv

hose /həʊz; *AmE* hoʊz/

hose sth 'down to wash or clean sth using water from a long rubber or plastic tube (a **hose**): *I hosed the car down to get rid of the mud.*
◆ v + n/pron + adv ◆ v + adv + n

hot /hɒt; *AmE* hɑːt/ (**-tt-**)

hot 'up (*BrE*) (*AmE* **heat 'up** *informal*) to become more lively or exciting: *Things are hotting up as the election approaches.* ◊ *As the pace hotted up, he dropped back into third place.*
◆ v + adv

hound /haʊnd/

hound sb 'out; **hound sb 'out of sth**; **'hound sb from sth** to force sb to leave a place or their job: *They were hounded out of the town.* ◊ *She was hounded from politics by her rivals.*
NOTE Hound sb out is usually used in the passive.
◆ v + n/pron + adv ◆ v + adv + n (*rare*) ◆ v + n/pron + adv + prep ◆ v + n/pron + prep

huddle /'hʌdl/

huddle to'gether to move, stand or sit close to one another for warmth or protection: *We huddled together for warmth.*
◆ v + adv

huddle 'up (against/to sb/sth) to press yourself into a small space for warmth or protection: *She huddled up against him to keep warm.*
◆ v + adv

hunger /'hʌŋgə(r)/

'hunger after/for sth (*literary*) to have a strong desire for sth and try to get it: *She hungers after wealth and prestige.*
◆ v + prep

hunker /'hʌŋkə(r)/

hunker 'down (*especially AmE*) **1** to sit on your heels with your knees bent up in front of you: *We hunkered down around the fire.* **SYN** **squat 2** to refuse to change an opinion, a way of behaving, etc: *The Democrats have hunkered down and won't be moved.* **3** to start to work at sth or study very hard: *It's time you hunkered down and started studying.*
◆ v + adv

hunt /hʌnt/

hunt sb 'down to search for sb until you find or catch them: *He vowed to hunt down the killer.*
◆ v + adv + n ◆ v + n/pron + adv

,**hunt sth 'down/'out** to find sth after a long and difficult search: *I managed to hunt out those files you wanted.* ◇ *Can you hunt down his phone number for me?*

▷**SYN** **dig sth out; root sb/sth out**

◆ v + adv + n ◆ v + pron + adv ◆ v + n + adv (*rare*)

,**hunt sb/sth 'up** to search for sb/sth, especially sb/sth that is hidden or difficult to find: *We hunted up anyone who might have known him.*

◆ v + adv + n ◆ v + pron + adv ◆ v + n + adv (*rare*)

hurry /'hʌri; *AmE* 'hɜːri/ (**hurries, hurrying, hurried, hurried**)

,**hurry sb/sth a'long** to do or say sth to make sb move or work faster; to do sth to make sth happen faster: *Hurry the kids along or we'll miss the train.* ◇ *We should try to* **hurry things along** *a bit.*

◆ v + n/pron + adv

,**hurry 'on (to sth)** to continue speaking, without allowing anyone to interrupt or speak: *She hurried on to the next topic before I could object.* ◇ *'Just leave that to me,' she hurried on.*

◆ v + adv ◆ v + adv + speech

,**hurry 'up** (*spoken*) used to tell sb to move or do sth more quickly: *Hurry up, we have to leave in five minutes!* ◇ *I wish the bus would hurry up and come.* ◇ *I wish the waiter would hurry up with our soup.*

◆ v + adv

,**hurry sb/sth 'up** to encourage sb to move or work faster; to do sth to make sth happen faster: *Hurry your brother up or we'll be late.* ◇ **Hurry it up** — *we haven't got all day!* ◇ *Is there a way of* **hurrying things up**?

◆ v + n/pron + adv ◆ v + adv + n (*rare*)

hush /hʌʃ/

,**hush sth 'up** to hide information about a situation, especially sth bad or shocking, because you do not want people to know about it: *The government tried to hush the affair up.*

NOTE Hush sth up is often used in the passive: *The scandal was hushed up.*

◆ v + n/pron + adv ◆ v + adv + n

hype /haɪp/

,**hype sb/sth 'up** (*informal*) to advertise or talk about sb/sth in an exaggerated way in order to get a lot of public attention for it: *His latest movie is being hyped up by the media.*

NOTE Hype sb/sth up is often used in the passive. ◆ **Hype sb/sth** is also used with the same meaning.

◆ v + n/pron + adv ◆ v + adv + n

▶ ,**hyped 'up** *adj* (*informal*) **1** (of a person) very excited or worried about sth: *She gets very hyped up before a race.* **2** (of a film/movie, a book, an event, etc.) advertised or talked about in an exaggerated way to get public attention: *a hyped-up movie*

I i

ice /aɪs/

,ice 'over/'up; be ,iced 'over/'up to become
covered by a layer of ice: *The road had iced over
during the night.* ◇ *The windscreen had iced up.* ◇
The lake was iced up.
[SYN] **freeze over, freeze up**
◈ v + adv ◆ be + v + adv

identify /aɪ'dentɪfaɪ/ (**identifies, identifying,
identified, identified**)

i'dentify with sb/sth to feel that you can understand and share the feelings of sb else: *He's a
character that readers feel they can identify with.*
◈ v + prep

i'dentify sb with sb/sth to consider sb to be sth
or to be closely connected with sb/sth: *The last
thing she wanted was to be identified with her parents.* ◇ *Many of these artists were closely identified with Cubist painting.*
[NOTE] **Identify sb with sb/sth** is often used in the
passive.
◈ v + n/pron + prep

i'dentify sth with sth to consider sth to be the
same as sth else: *Beauty is often identified with
youth.*
◈ v + n/pron + prep

**i'dentify yourself with sb/sth; be
i'dentified with sb/sth** to support sb/sth; to
be closely connected with sb/sth: *He refused to
identify himself with the new political party.*
→ *see also* IDENTIFY SB WITH SB/STH

idle /'aɪdl/

idle sth a'way to spend time doing nothing very
important: *They idled away their time watching
television.*
[OBJ] **day, time**
◈ v + adv + n ◆ v + n/pron + adv

imbue /ɪm'bjuː/

im'bue sb/sth with sth to fill sb/sth with a
strong feeling, quality, etc: *He managed to imbue
his employees with team spirit.* ◇ *The painting is
imbued with energy and life.*
[SYN] **infuse B with A**
[NOTE] **Imbue sb/sth with sth** is often used in the
passive.
◈ v + n/pron + prep

immerse /ɪ'mɜːs; *AmE* ɪ'mɜːrs/

im'merse sb/yourself in sth to become, or to
make sb become, completely involved in sth: *He
immersed himself in his studies.* ◇ *I was completely immersed in the story.*

[NOTE] **Immerse sb in sth** is often used in the
passive.
◈ v + n/pron + prep

impact /ɪm'pækt/

im'pact on sb/sth (*also* **im'pact upon sb/sth**
more formal) to have an effect on sb/sth: *Government cuts will impact directly on education.* ◇
This decision may impact on the unemployed.
[SYN] **affect sb/sth**
◈ v + prep

impinge /ɪm'pɪndʒ/

im'pinge on sb/sth (*also* **im'pinge upon sb/sth**
more formal) to have a strong effect on sb/sth,
especially a bad one: *She didn't allow her personal problems to impinge on her work.*
[SYN] **affect sb/sth**
◈ v + prep

impose /ɪm'pəʊz; *AmE* ɪm'poʊz/

im'pose on sb to expect sb to do sth for you or
spend time with you when they do not have much
time, or when it may not be convenient for them:
*Tim never says 'No', so people are always impos-
ing on him.*
◈ v + prep

impress /ɪm'pres/

im'press sth on sb (*also* **im'press sth upon sb**
more formal) to emphasize to sb how important
or serious sth is: *I wanted to impress on him that
it was a very serious offence.* ◇ *She impressed on
her staff the importance of keeping accurate
records.*
[NOTE] The object of **impress** usually comes after
on sb.
◈ v + n/pron + prep

im'press sth/itself on sth (*also* **im'press
sth/itself upon sth** *more formal*) if sb **impresses
sth on** or sth **impresses itself on** your mind,
memory, etc. it has a great effect on you so that
you do not forget it: *Her beauty impressed itself
on everyone who met her.* ◇ *His words impressed
themselves on my memory.*
◈ v + n/pron + prep

imprint /ɪm'prɪnt/

im'print A in/on B; im'print B with A 1 to
have a great effect on sth so that it cannot be forgotten, changed, etc: *The scene was imprinted on
my mind.* ◇ *The picture is imprinted with his own
style.* **2** to print or press a mark or design on sth:
T-shirts imprinted with the logos of sports teams

NOTE Imprint sth in/on/with sth is often used in the passive.
◆ v + n/pron + prep

improve /ɪmˈpruːv/

im'prove on sth (*also* im'prove upon sth *more formal*) to achieve or produce sth of a better standard or quality than sth else: *There are a few points in your work that you could improve on.* ◇ *The Kenyan girl improved on her previous best performance* (= in a race).
NOTE Improve on/upon sth can be used in the passive: *These results must be improved upon.*
◆ v + prep

impute /ɪmˈpjuːt/

im'pute sth to sb/sth (*formal*) to say, often unfairly, that sb/sth is responsible for sth, or has a particular quality: *Why do you impute selfish motives to her?*
◆ v + n/pron + prep

incline /ɪnˈklaɪn/

in'cline to/towards sth; in'cline sb to/towards sth (*formal*) to tend to think or behave in a particular way; to make sb do this: *I incline to the view that we should take no action.* ◇ *Her love of languages inclined her towards a career as a translator.*
◆ v + prep ◆ v + n/pron + prep

indulge /ɪnˈdʌldʒ/

in'dulge in sth **1** to allow yourself to have or do sth that you like, often sth that is bad for you: *She indulged in the luxury of a long bath.* ◇ *He now has time to indulge in his favourite hobby: photography.* ◇ *I'm going to indulge in a chocolate cake!* **2** to take part in an activity, especially sth bad or illegal: *We shouldn't indulge in speculation as to what really happened.*
NOTE Indulge in sth can be used in the passive: *It's a luxury that can only be indulged in from time to time.*
◆ v + prep

inform /ɪnˈfɔːm; AmE ɪnˈfɔːrm/

in'form on sb to give evidence about sb or make an accusation against sb, to the police or sb in authority: *One of the gang informed on the rest.*
◆ v + prep

infringe /ɪnˈfrɪndʒ/

in'fringe on sth (*also* in'fringe upon sth *more formal*) to limit sb's freedom, rights, etc: *The media is accused of infringing on people's privacy.*
OBJ liberty, rights

NOTE Infringe on/upon sth can be used in the passive.
◆ v + prep

infuse /ɪnˈfjuːz/

in'fuse A into B; in'fuse B with A (*formal*) to fill sb/sth with a particular quality: *His arrival infused new life and energy into the team.* ◇ *Her work is infused with anger.*
SYN imbue sth with sth
◆ v + n/pron + prep

ink /ɪŋk/

,ink sth 'in (*BrE*) to write or draw in ink over sth that has been written or drawn in pencil: *I did the answers in pencil first and then inked them in.* ◇ (*figurative*) *The company has inked in June 1st* (= made it definite) *for the launch.*
◆ v + n/pron + adv ◆ v + adv + n

inquire /ɪnˈkwaɪə(r)/

in'quire after sb/sth (*especially AmE*) = ENQUIRE AFTER SB/STH
in'quire into sth (*especially AmE*) = ENQUIRE INTO STH
in'quire sth of sb (*especially AmE*) = ENQUIRE STH OF SB

insinuate /ɪnˈsɪnjueɪt/

in,sinuate yourself 'into sth (*formal, disapproving*) to get yourself into a position of advantage, especially by clever talk or by gaining the favour or respect of sb important: *She cleverly insinuated herself into his family.*
◆ v + pron + prep

insist /ɪnˈsɪst/

in'sist on sth; in'sist on doing sth (*also* in'sist upon sth, in'sist upon doing sth *more formal*) to demand sth and refuse to be persuaded to accept anything else: *They are insisting on a meeting tomorrow.* ◇ *I always insist on skimmed milk.* ◇ *He insisted on walking home with her.*
NOTE Insist on/upon sth can be used in the passive: *This format must be insisted on.*
◆ v + prep
in'sist on doing sth (*also* in'sist upon doing sth *more formal*) to continue doing sth even though other people find it annoying: *She will insist on shouting at the top of her voice.*
◆ v + prep

insure /ɪnˈʃʊə(r), -ˈʃɔː(r); AmE -ˈʃʊr/

in'sure against sth **1** to buy an insurance policy which will pay you money if the event mentioned happens: *Everyone needs to insure agains*

fire. **2** to take action to prevent sth unpleasant happening: *This is to insure against a repetition of previous disasters.*
◈ v + prep

interest /'ɪntrəst, -trest/

'**interest sb in sth** to persuade sb to buy, do or eat sth: *Could I interest you in this model* (= of car)*, Sir?*
◈ v + n/pron + prep

interfere /ˌɪntəˈfɪə(r); AmE ˌɪntərˈfɪr/

inter'**fere with sb** (*BrE*) to touch a child in a sexual way
NOTE Interfere with sb can be used in the passive.
◈ v + prep

inter'**fere with sth 1** to get in the way of sth; to prevent sth from being done or making progress: *Don't let anything interfere with your training.* ◇ *We don't want to interfere with your plans.* **2** to touch, adjust or change sth without permission, and damage it: *Who's been interfering with the clock?* **SYN** **tamper with sth 3** if sth **interferes with** radio or sound waves, etc., it stops them being heard easily or clearly: *The computer is interfering with the radio.*
NOTE Interfere with sth can be used in the passive: *The evidence has been interfered with.*
◈ v + prep

inure /ɪˈnjʊə(r); AmE ɪˈnjʊr/

i'**nure sb/yourself to sth** to make sb/sth get used to sth unpleasant so that they are no longer strongly affected by it: *The prisoners quickly became inured to the harsh conditions.*
◈ v + n/pron + prep

invalid /'ɪnvəlɪd, 'ɪnvəli:d/

invalid sb 'out; **invalid sb 'out of sth** (*BrE*) to make sb leave a job, especially in the armed forces, because they are ill/sick or injured: *He was invalided out of the army because of his injuries.*
NOTE Invalid sb out is usually used in the passive.
◈ v + n/pron + adv ♦ v + adv + n ♦ v + n/pron + adv + prep

invest /ɪnˈvest/

in'**vest in sth** (*informal, often humorous*) to buy sth or spend money on sth useful, especially sth expensive: *It's time we invested in a new sofa — this one is falling to bits.*
◈ v + prep

in'**vest sb/sth with sth** (*formal*) to make sb/sth seem to have a particular quality: *Being the boss invests her with a certain glamour.*

NOTE Invest sb/sth with sth is often used in the passive.
◈ v + n/pron + prep

invite /ɪnˈvaɪt/

in,**vite sb a'long** to ask sb if they would like to go with you to an event or activity: *Shall I invite Dave along (to the concert)?*
SYN ask sb along (*less formal*)
◈ v + n/pron + adv ♦ v + adv + n (*rare*)

in,**vite sb a'round** (*AmE*) = INVITE SB OVER/ROUND

in,**vite sb 'back (to sth)** (*especially BrE*) to ask sb to go back to your home after you have been out somewhere together: *She invited me back to her flat for coffee after the movie.*
SYN ask sb back (to sth); have sb back (*both less formal*)
◈ v + n/pron + adv ♦ v + adv + n (*less frequent*)

in,**vite sb 'in/'up** to politely ask sb to enter a room, your house, etc: *Aren't you going to invite me in for a coffee?*
SYN ask sb in/up (*less formal*)
◈ v + n/pron + adv ♦ v + adv + n (*less frequent*)

in,**vite sb 'out** to ask sb to go out with you, especially as a way of beginning a romantic relationship: *We've been invited out for dinner this evening.* ◇ *He eventually found the courage to invite Julia out.*
SYN ask sb out (*less formal*)
◈ v + n/pron + adv ♦ v + adv + n (*less frequent*)

in,**vite sb 'over/'round** (*BrE*) (*AmE* ,invite sb a'round) to ask sb to come and visit you in your home: *I've invited a few friends round to watch the game with us on TV.* ◇ *We ought to invite the new neighbours over for coffee.*
SYN ask sb over/round (*less formal*)
◈ v + n/pron + adv

in,**vite sb 'up** = INVITE SB IN/UP

involve /ɪnˈvɒlv; AmE ɪnˈvɑːlv/

in'**volve sb in sth** to make sb experience or do sth, especially sth unpleasant: *The new exams have involved teachers in a lot of extra paperwork.*
◈ v + n/pron + prep

iron /'aɪən; AmE 'aɪərn/

,**iron sth 'out 1** to remove the folds that you do not want from clothes, etc. by using a tool with a flat metal base that can be heated (an **iron**): *Iron out all the creases.* **OBJ** creases **2** to get rid of any problems or difficulties that are affecting sth: *We must iron out the problems before next week.* **OBJ** difficulties, problems **SYN** resolve sth (*more formal*)
◈ v + adv + n ♦ v + pron + adv ♦ v + n + adv (*rare*)

issue /ˈɪʃuː (*BrE also*)ˈɪsjuː/

'issue from sth (*formal*) to come, go or flow out of sth or somewhere: *I could see smoke issuing from the window.*
◈ v + prep

itch /ɪtʃ/

'itch for sth (*usually used in the progressive tenses*) to want sth very much: *They were just itching for a fight.*
OBJ **a fight**, **a chance**
NOTE **Itch to do sth** can also be used with the same meaning: *He was itching to find out more.*
◈ v + prep

Jj

jab /dʒæb/ (-bb-)

'jab at sb/sth (with sth) to push a sharp or pointed object quickly or roughly into sb/sth or in the direction of sb/sth: *He kept jabbing at the paper cup with his pencil.* ◇ *She jabbed at the papers with her finger.*
◈ v + prep

jabber /'dʒæbə(r)/

jabber a'way (*informal*) to speak or talk quickly in an excited way: *She jabbered away, trying to distract his attention.* ◇ *He was jabbering away in Russian.*
◈ v + adv

jack /dʒæk/

jack sth 'in (*BrE, informal*) to stop doing sth, especially your job: *She decided to jack in her job.* ◇ *After such a bad day I feel like jacking it all in.*
OBJ **job** SYN **chuck sth in/up; pack sth in**
NOTE **Jack sth in** can not be used in the passive.
◈ v + adv + n ◆ v + n/pron + adv

jack 'off (*AmE, △, slang*) if a man **jacks off** he gives himself sexual pleasure by rubbing his sexual organs
◈ v + adv

jack 'up (*slang*) to take an illegal drug by putting it into your body using a plastic or glass tube with a long hollow needle (a **syringe**)
◈ v + adv

jack sth 'up 1 to lift sth such as a vehicle off the ground using a special device (a **jack**) OBJ **car 2** (*informal*) to increase the cost or the price of sth: *The wholesalers have jacked up their prices.* OBJ **cost, price** SYN **put sth up; increase sth** (*more formal*)
◈ v + adv + n ◆ v + n/pron + adv

jam /dʒæm/ (-mm-)

jam sth 'on if you **jam on** the brakes on a vehicle you operate them suddenly and with force: *A child ran into the road and I jammed on the brakes.*
OBJ only **the brakes, the handbrake** SYN **slam sth on**
◈ v + adv + n ◆ v + n/pron + adv

jam 'up; jam sth 'up (with sth) (*especially BrE*) if a machine, a road, etc. **jams up**, or sth **jams it up**, it becomes blocked, stops working, etc: *Let's get moving before the traffic jams up.* ◇ *People were jamming up the aisles in their rush to get out of the theatre.* ◇ *That photocopier is always getting jammed up.*
◈ v + adv ◆ v + adv + n ◆ v + pron + adv ◆ v + n + adv (*less frequent*)

jazz /dʒæz/

jazz sth 'up (with sth) (*informal*) **1** to make sth more lively or interesting: *Jazz up that plain dress with some jewellery.* SYN **liven sth up; spice sth up** (*more formal*) **2** to make a piece of music sound more modern, or more like jazz or popular music: *jazzed up Bach*
◈ v + adv + n ◆ v + n/pron + adv

jerk /dʒɜːk; AmE dʒɜːrk/

jerk sb a'round (*informal, especially AmE*) to treat sb badly and cause them problems, especially by deceiving them: *He won't give us an answer — he keeps jerking us around.*
SYN **mess sb about/around** (*BrE*)
◈ v + n/pron + adv ◆ v + adv + n

jerk 'off (*BrE, △, slang*) if a man **jerks off**, he gives himself sexual pleasure by rubbing his sexual organs
◈ v + adv

jet /dʒet/ (-tt-)

jet 'off (to …) to fly somewhere, especially somewhere far away: *They're jetting off to Florida tomorrow.*
◈ v + adv

jibe /dʒaɪb/

'jibe with sth (*AmE*) to agree with sth; to be the same as sth or match sth: *Her story didn't jibe with the witnesses' account.*
◈ v + prep

jockey /'dʒɒki; AmE 'dʒɑːki/

'jockey for sth to try very hard to gain an advantage, a favour, etc. for yourself and stop other people getting it: *Several employees are jockeying for the manager's position.*
OBJ **position, power**
◈ v + prep

jog /dʒɒg; AmE dʒɑːɡ/ (-gg-)

jog a'long (*BrE, informal*) to continue in a steady way, with little or no excitement or progress: *For years the business just kept jogging along.*
◈ v + adv

join /dʒɔɪn/

join 'in (with sb/sth), **join 'in sth** to become involved in sth; to take part in an activity with other people: *Can I join in (the game)?* ◇ *We all joined in with the singing.*
SYN **participate** (in sth) (*more formal*)
◈ v + adv ◆ v + prep

join 'up 1 (with sb/sth) to meet or combine with sb/sth to do sth together: *They joined up with the rest of the party later.* **2** to become a member of the armed forces: *We both joined up in 1939.* ⟨SYN⟩ **enlist** (*more formal*)
◆ v + adv

join 'up; join sth 'up (*especially BrE*) to be connected to sth; to connect sth to sth: *The dots join up to form a solid line.* ◇ *Join up the dots to see the picture.*
⟨SYN⟩ **connect** (sth) (*more formal*)
◆ v + adv ◆ v + adv + n ◆ v + n/pron + adv
▶ **joined 'up** *adj* [usually before noun] (*especially BrE*) things that are **joined up** are connected or linked together: *joined-up writing* ◇ (*figurative*) *joined-up thinking* ◇ (*figurative*) *the government's joined-up policy on health care*

'join with sb (in sth/in doing sth) (*formal*) to do or say sth with sb else or with a group of people: *I'm sure you'll join with me in congratulating Isla and Jake.* ◇ *Parents joined with teachers to protest against the closure of the school.*
◆ v + prep

jolly /'dʒɒli; *AmE* 'dʒɑːli/ (**jollies, jollying, jollied**)

jolly sb a'long (*BrE, informal*) to keep encouraging sb in a friendly way: *She tried to jolly him along but he couldn't forget his problems.*
◆ v + n/pron + adv

jolly sb/sth 'up (*BrE*) to make sb/sth brighter or more cheerful: *Do you think you can jolly Anthony up a bit?*
⟨SYN⟩ **cheer sb/sth up; liven sb/sth up**
◆ v + n/pron + adv ◆ v + adv + n

jostle /'dʒɒsl; *AmE* 'dʒɑːsl/

'jostle for sth to compete strongly and forcefully with other people for sth: *People in the crowd were jostling for the best positions.*
◆ v + prep

jot /dʒɒt; *AmE* dʒɑːt/ (**-tt-**)

jot sth 'down to write sth down quickly: *I'll jot down their address before I forget it.*
⟨SYN⟩ **note sth down**
◆ v + adv + n ◆ v + n/pron + adv

juice /dʒuːs/

juice sth 'up (*AmE, slang*) **1** to make sth more lively, exciting or interesting: *Juice up your presentations with colourful graphics.* ⟨SYN⟩ **jazz sth up** (*informal*) **2** to make sth more powerful: *I could juice up the engine for you.* ⟨SYN⟩ **soup sth up 3** to put petrol in a vehicle: *We need to juice up the car before we leave.* ⟨OBJ⟩ **car** ⟨SYN⟩ **fill sth up**
◆ v + adv + n ◆ v + n/pron + adv

jumble /'dʒʌmbl/

jumble sth 'up/to'gether to mix things up in a confused way: *Make sure you don't jumble everything up.* ◇ *The details of the accident were all jumbled together in his mind.*
⟨SYN⟩ **mix sth up**
⟨NOTE⟩ **Jumble sth up/together** is often used in the passive: *All her papers had been jumbled up.*
◆ v + n/pron + adv ◆ v + adv + n

jump /dʒʌmp/

'jump at sb (*AmE*) = JUMP ON SB

'jump at sth to accept an opportunity, a chance, etc. with enthusiasm: *I jumped at the chance of a trip to Italy.*
⟨OBJ⟩ **chance, idea** ⟨SYN⟩ **leap at sth**
◆ v + prep

jump 'in 1 (with sth) to interrupt a conversation: *I jumped in while there was a brief pause in the conversation.* **2** to become involved in a situation suddenly or quickly: *She had jumped in to help while he was ill.*
◆ v + adv

'jump on sb (*AmE also* **'jump at sb**) (*informal*) to criticize sb sharply: *She jumped on me before I had a chance to explain.*
◆ v + prep

jump 'out at sb to be very easy to see; to be noticeable: *The headline jumped out at me.* ◇ *The mistakes are so obvious they jump out at you.*
⟨SYN⟩ **leap out at sb**
◆ v + adv + prep

jump 'up to stand quickly and suddenly when you have been sitting: *He jumped up off the floor.*
⟨SYN⟩ **leap up**
◆ v + adv
▶ **'jumped-up** *adj* [only before noun] (*BrE, informal, disapproving*) thinking that you are more important than you really are, particularly when you have risen in social status but do not deserve to: *I won't take orders from a jumped-up office girl!*

jut /dʒʌt/ (**-tt-**)

jut 'out (from sth), **jut 'out of sth** to stand out from sth; to stick out further than the surrounding surface: *The tops of the flooded houses jutted out of the water.*
⟨SYN⟩ **stick out, stick out of sth**
◆ v + adv ◆ v + adv + prep

Kk

keel /kiːl/

keel 'over 1 (*informal*) to fall over: *I'm so tired, all I want to do is keel over and sleep for a week.* ⟨SYN⟩ **collapse 2** (of a boat) to turn on its side: *The boat keeled over in the strong winds.* ⟨SYN⟩ **capsize**
◆ v + adv

keep /kiːp/ (**kept, kept** /kept/)

~ after		~ in with
~ ahead, ahead of		~ off
~ at		~ on
~ away	157	~ out, out of
~ back		~ to
~ behind		~ together
~ down		~ under
156 ~ from		~ up
~ in		158 ~ up with

keep 'after sb (about sth/to do sth) (*AmE*) to ask or tell sb repeatedly to do sth: *She keeps after me to fix the TV.*
→ *see also* KEEP ON 2
◆ v + prep

keep a'head; keep a'head of sb/sth to continue to be more advanced or successful than other people, groups, etc: *We need to keep ahead of our competitors.* ◇ *If you want to keep ahead in this industry, you have to be ruthless.*
⟨SYN⟩ **stay ahead, stay ahead of sb/sth**
◆ v + adv ◆ v + adv + prep

keep 'at sth; keep sb 'at sth to continue to work hard at sth, or to make sb work hard at sth, particularly sth which is difficult or takes a long time: *Keep at it, you've nearly finished!* ◇ *He kept them at the job until it was finished.*
◆ v + prep ◆ v + n/pron + prep

keep a'way (from sb/sth) to not go near sb/sth: *Keep away from me!* ◇ *The police told us to keep well away from the area.*
⟨SYN⟩ **stay away (from sb/sth)**
◆ v + adv

keep sb/sth a'way (from sb/sth) to prevent sb/sth from going near sb/sth: *Keep him away from the kitchen while we make his birthday cake.* ◇ *We turned off the lights to keep the mosquitoes away.* ◇ *Her parents are keeping her away from school for a few days.* ◇ (*figurative*) *A healthy diet can help to keep colds and flu away.*
◆ v + n/pron + adv ◆ v + adv + n (*less frequent*)

keep 'back (from sb/sth) to remain at a distance from sb/sth: *Keep back or I'll shoot!* ◇ *I kept well back from the road.*
⟨SYN⟩ **stay back**
◆ v + adv

keep sb 'back 1 (*BrE*) = KEEP SB IN 1 *I was kept back after school for being cheeky.* **2** (*AmE*) = KEEP SB DOWN 1

keep sb/sth 'back (from sb/sth) to make sb/sth remain at a distance from sb/sth; to prevent sb from moving forwards: *Keep the children back from the fire.* ◇ *The police were trying to keep back the crowds.*
◆ v + n/pron + adv ◆ v + adv + n

keep sth 'back 1 (*especially BrE*) to keep a part of sth to use later: *Have you kept some money back to pay the bills?* ◇ *Keep a piece of cake back for Alex.* **2** (from sb/sth) to refuse to tell sb sth; to hold sth back: *I'm sure she's keeping something back (from us).* ⟨OBJ⟩ **something, anything, nothing** ⟨SYN⟩ **withold sth** (*more formal*) **3** to try not to let other people see or know how you feel: *He could hardly keep back the tears.* ⟨OBJ⟩ **tears** ⟨SYN⟩ **hold sth back**
◆ **1,2** v + n/pron + adv ◆ v + adv + n
◆ **3** v + adv + n ◆ v + n/pron + adv

keep sb be'hind (*AmE*) **1** = KEEP SB IN 1

keep 'down to hide yourself by not standing up straight: *Keep down! Don't let anybody see you.*
⟨SYN⟩ **stay down**
◆ v + adv

keep sb 'down 1 (*BrE*) (*AmE* **keep sb 'back**) to make a student repeat a year at school, college, etc. because of poor marks/grades: *I was kept down because I failed the exam.* **2** to control a people, a nation, etc. so that they have no power or freedom: *The people have been kept down for years by a brutal regime.* ⟨SYN⟩ **repress sb**
◆ **1** v + n/pron + adv
◆ **2** v + n/pron + adv ◆ v + adv + n

keep sth 'down 1 to make sth remain at a low level; to avoid increasing sth: *We're trying to keep costs down.* ◇ *He exercises a lot to keep his weight down.* ◇ *Keep your voice down!* ◇ *Keep it down* (= the noise)! *I'm trying to concentrate.* ⟨OBJ⟩ **costs, prices, voice, noise** ⟨SYN⟩ **hold sth down 2** to manage to keep food or drink in your stomach and avoid bringing it back through the mouth: *He can't keep anything down.* ⟨OBJ⟩ **food** ⟨SYN⟩ **hold sth down 3** to not raise a part of your body: *Keep your head down!* ◇ *She kept her eyes down while he was talking.* ⟨OBJ⟩ **eyes, head, face** ⟨NOTE⟩ In meanings 2 and 3, **keep sth down** can not be used in the passive.
◆ **1,2** v + n/pron + adv ◆ v + adv + n
◆ **3** v + n/pron + adv

⟨IDM⟩ **keep/get your 'head down** to avoid attracting attention

'keep from doing sth; **'keep yourself from doing sth** to prevent yourself from doing sth: *She bit her lip to keep from laughing.*
   ❖ v + prep ♦ v + pron + prep

'keep sb from sth; **'keep sb from doing sth** to prevent sb from doing sth: *Don't let me keep you from your work.* ◊ *I've been trying to keep him from finding out the truth.* ◊ *Her pride kept her from crying in front of them.*
   ❖ v + n/pron + prep

'keep sth from sb to avoid telling sb sth: *I think he's keeping secrets from me.* ◊ *Are you keeping something from us?*
   ⊙BJ **secrets, something**
   ❖ v + n/pron + prep

‚keep 'in (*BrE*) to stay near the edge of the road or path while you are driving, walking, etc: *If you keep in, the van can overtake.*
   ❖ v + adv

‚keep sb 'in (*especially BrE*) **1** (*BrE also* ‚keep sb 'back) (*AmE also* ‚keep sb be'hind) to make a child stay after normal school hours as a punishment: *The teacher kept them all in after school.* **2** to not allow a child to go outdoors: *I'm keeping the children in because it's raining outside.* **3** to keep sb in hospital: *She's much better, but they're keeping her in overnight.*
   ❖ v + n/pron + adv

‚keep sth 'in 1 to stop yourself expressing an emotion: *He could hardly keep in his anger.* SYN **restrain sth 2** to not allow sth to escape, be lost or taken out: *Close the door to keep in the warmth.* ◊ *She wanted to cut the sex scene* (= in a play or film/movie), *but we kept it in.* ⊙BJ **warmth, heat 3** to not allow an animal to go outdoors
   ❖ v + n/pron + adv ♦ v + adv + n
   IDM **keep your 'hand in** to do an activity occasionally so that you do not lose your skill at it: *I play squash from time to time, just to keep my hand in.*

'keep sb/yourself in sth (*informal*) to give or allow sb/yourself a regular supply of sth: *This part-time job keeps me in cigarettes.*
   ❖ v + n/pron + prep

‚keep 'in with sb (*BrE*) to continue to be friendly with sb, especially in order to gain some advantage for yourself: *He keeps in with anyone who might be useful to him.*
   ❖ v + adv + prep

‚keep 'off (*especially BrE*) if rain, snow, etc. **keeps off**, it does not fall, even though it looks as if it might: *The party will go ahead provided the rain keeps off.*
   SYN **hold off**
   ❖ v + adv

‚keep 'off; **‚keep 'off sth** to not go onto a particular area: *Keep off* (*the grass*)! ◊ *We kept off the main roads to avoid the traffic.*
   ⊙BJ **grass**
   ❖ v + adv ♦ v + prep

‚keep 'off sth; **‚keep sb 'off sth 1** to not eat, drink or smoke sth; to not let sb eat, drink or smoke sth: *The doctor's told me to keep off red meat.* **2** to not mention a particular topic; to stop sb talking about a particular topic: *It's best to keep off the subject of politics with my father.* ◊ *Keep her off the subject of teenage girls!* ⊙BJ **subject, topic**
   SYN **stay off sth**
   ❖ v + prep ♦ v + n/pron + prep

‚keep sb/sth 'off; **‚keep sb/sth 'off sb/sth** to stop sb/sth from coming near or going into (a place); to stop sb/sth from touching or harming sb/sth: *He covered the sandwiches to keep the flies off.* ◊ *Keep your animals off my land!* ◊ *Working helps keep my mind off my problems.* ◊ *I kept the children off* (*school*) *until they felt better.*
   ⊙BJ **flies, hands, mind, eyes**
   ❖ v + n/pron + adv ♦ v + n/pron + prep

‚keep 'on 1 (*also* ‚keep 'on doing sth) to continue doing what you were doing, behaving in a certain way, etc., without stopping: *He'll get into trouble if he keeps on like this!* ◊ *Keep on trying — don't give up!* ◊ *The rain kept on* (= continued to fall) *all night.* SYN **carry on** (**with sth**), **carry on doing sth 2** (at sb) (about sb/sth) (*BrE*) to continue to talk about sb/sth in a boring or annoying way: *Don't keep on* (*about it*)*!* ◊ *My mum keeps on at me to cut my hair.* SYN **go on** (**about sb/sth**) → *see also* KEEP AFTER SB (ABOUT STH/TO DO STH)
   ❖ v + adv **1** also v + adv + -ing

‚keep 'on; **‚keep 'on sth** to continue to follow a particular route: *Keep on until you come to the road.* ◊ *Keep on the path until you see a gate.*
   ❖ v + adv ♦ v + prep

‚keep sb 'on to continue to employ sb, even though circumstances have changed: *We can only afford to keep a few workers on.*
   ❖ v + n/pron + adv ♦ v + adv + n (*less frequent*)

‚keep sth 'on 1 to continue to wear sth; to not take sth off: *It was so cold that we kept our socks on in bed.* ◊ *Keep the lid on while the tea is brewing.* OPP **take sth off 2** to not switch sth off: *Do you keep the heating on all day?* SYN **leave sth on** OPP **switch sth off 3** to stop sth coming or falling off: *How do you keep that bandage on?* **4** to continue to rent or be the owner of a house, flat/apartment, etc: *Can you afford to keep this place on while you're abroad?*
   ❖ v + n/pron + adv ♦ v + adv + n (*less frequent*)
   IDM **keep your 'hair on** (*BrE, spoken, informal*) used to tell sb not to become angry

'keep sth on sb/sth if you **keep** your mind, eyes, etc. **on** sb/sth, you fix your attention on them/it: *I can't keep my mind on my work.* ◇ *She kept one eye on the traffic and the other on the map.* ⟨OBJ⟩ **mind, attention, eye**

✦ v + n/pron + prep

⟨IDM⟩ **keep an eye on sb/sth** (*informal*) to watch or check sb/sth to make sure that they are safe, etc.; to look after sb/sth: *Will you keep an eye on the baby for five minutes?*

keep 'out; **keep 'out of sth** to not enter a place; to remain outside: *There was a sign saying 'Keep out!'.* ◇ *Please keep out of the office while I'm working.*

✦ v + adv ◆ v + adv + prep

keep 'out of sth; **keep sb 'out of sth 1** to avoid sth; to prevent sb/yourself from being affected by sth: *The doctor has advised me to keep out of the sun.* ◇ *They always kept their daughter out of the spotlight* (= away from the public). ◇ *I try to keep out of his way.* ⟨OBJ⟩ **the sun, sight, sb's/the way 2** to avoid becoming involved in sth; to stop sb from becoming involved in sth: *Keep out of this! It's got nothing to do with you!* ◇ *Try to keep the kids out of mischief while I'm out.*

✦ v + adv + prep ◆ v + n/pron + adv + prep

keep sth 'out to not put sth away that you have taken out of a cupboard, etc.; to keep sth ready to use: *Keep the butter out for your dad's breakfast.*

⟨OPP⟩ **put sth away**

✦ v + n/pron + adv ◆ v + adv + n (*less frequent*)

keep sb/sth 'out; **keep sb/sth 'out of sth** to prevent sb/sth from entering a place: *We hung a curtain at the door to keep out the cold.* ◇ (*figurative*) *She tried to keep the anger out of her voice.*

✦ v + n/pron + adv ◆ v + adv + n ◆
   v + n/pron + adv + prep

'keep to sth 1 to not leave a path, a road, etc: *Keep to the footpath.* ◇ *Keep to the left* (= on a road, etc.). ⟨OBJ⟩ **path 2** to talk or write only about a particular subject: *Keep to the point!* ◇ *Will you please keep to the subject under discussion?* ⟨OBJ⟩ **subject, point 3** to follow a plan, an agreement, a rule, etc. exactly as you are expected to do, or as you have promised to do: *She hasn't kept to the agreement, so neither will I.* ◇ *We must keep to the schedule.* ◇ *He never keeps to the speed limit.* ⟨OBJ⟩ **rules, agreement, schedule** ⟨SYN⟩ **adhere to sth** (*formal*)

⟨SYN⟩ **stick to sth**

⟨NOTE⟩ **Keep to sth** can be used in the passive: *Was the agenda kept to at the meeting?*

✦ v + prep

keep to your'self; **keep your'self to your'self** to avoid meeting people socially or becoming involved in other people's affairs: *He keeps* (*himself*) *to himself and nobody knows very much about him.*

✦ v + prep + pron ◆ v + pron + prep + pron

'keep to sth; **'keep sth to sth** to use only one thing or a limited number or amount of sth; to make sure that the number or amount of sth doesn't become any bigger than a particular size: *We've decided to keep to pale colours for the bedroom.* ◇ *I'm trying to keep the number of guests to a minimum.*

✦ v + prep ◆ v + n/pron + prep

keep sth to your'self to not tell anyone about sth or what you think about sth: *I know who's won, but I'm keeping it to myself.* ◇ *Keep your opinions to yourself in future!* ◇ (*figurative*) *Keep your hands to yourself!* (= do not touch me)

⟨OBJ⟩ **opinions**

✦ v + n/pron + prep + pron

keep to'gether; **keep sb/sth to'gether** to remain together in a group; to make sb/sth do this: *Keep together, kids, when we cross the road.* ◇ *Use a paper clip to keep your papers together.*

✦ v + adv ◆ v + n/pron + adv ◆ v + adv + n (*less frequent*)

keep sb 'under (*BrE*) to control sb: *The local people are kept under by the army.*

⟨SYN⟩ **oppress sb** (*more formal*)

✦ v + n/pron + adv

keep 'up 1 if rain, snow, etc. **keeps up**, it continues without stopping: *The rain kept up all afternoon.* **2** (with sb/sth) to move at the same rate or speed as sb/sth: *I had to run to keep up with him.* ⟨OPP⟩ **fall behind, fall behind sb/sth 3** to work at the necessary speed so that you progress at the same speed as other people: *She's having trouble keeping up with the rest of the class.* ◇ *Do keep up! I can't keep repeating everything.* **4** (with sth) to rise at the same rate as sth else: *Salaries are not keeping up with inflation.* **5** (with sth) to do all the work necessary in order to finish on time or deal successfully with a situation that changes rapidly: *We're finding it hard to keep up with demand.* ◇ *Things were happening too fast to keep up with.*

✦ v + adv

keep sb 'up to prevent sb from going to bed or from sleeping: *I hope we're not keeping you up.* ◇ *The baby kept us up half the night.*

✦ v + n/pron + adv

keep sth 'up 1 to continue sth at the same, usually high, level; to continue to practise or observe sth: *Keep up the good work!* ◇ *You're doing a great job! Keep it up!* ◇ *We kept up a fast pace all the way.* ◇ *We're having difficulty keeping up our mortgage payments.* ◇ *The press is keeping up the pressure on the government.* ◇ *Do you still keep up your Portuguese?* ⟨OBJ⟩ **it, pace, pressure, tradition 2** to prevent sth from falling down: *You'll have to wear a belt to keep your trousers up.* ⟨OBJ⟩ **trousers/pants** ⟨SYN⟩ **hold sth up**

3 to make sth stay at a high level: *High transport costs are keeping food prices up.* ◇ *They sang songs to keep their spirits up.* OBJ **price, spirits, strength, morale 4** to keep a house, garden/yard, etc. in good condition by spending money on it or working hard on it: *The house is becoming too expensive for them to keep up.* SYN **maintain sth**

⊕ v + n/pron + adv ◆ v + adv + n

IDM **keep up ap'pearances** to hide the true situation and pretend that things are better than they are: *There's no point keeping up appearances when everyone knows we've lost all our money.* **keep your 'chin up!** (*spoken, informal*) used to tell sb to remain cheerful in difficult circumstances

▶ **'upkeep** *n* [U] **1** the cost or process of keeping a building, piece of land, etc. in good condition: *Who is responsible for the day-to-day upkeep of the house?* **2** the cost or process of giving a child or an animal the things that they need

keep 'up with sb to continue to be in contact with sb by writing, phoning or seeing them regularly: *How many of your old school friends do you manage to keepup with?*

⊕ v + adv + prep

keep 'up with sth 1 to learn about the news, events, etc. that are happening: *I try to keep up with current affairs.* ◇ *Susie lies to keep up with the latest fashions.* **2** to continue to pay or do sth regularly: *He couldn't keep up with the repayments on the loan.* ◇ *Are you keeping up with your homework?*

⊕ v + adv + prep

key /kiː/

key sth 'in; **key sth 'into sth** to put information into a computer, using a keyboard: *Key in your personal number.* ◇ *All the information has been keyed into the computer.*

OBJ **data, information** SYN **enter sth** (into sth)
⊕ v + adv + n ◆ v + n/pron + adv ◆ v + n/pron + prep

key 'into sth 1 to use a computer or information stored on a computer: *A hacker keyed into a vital database at the newspaper's office.* SYN **access sth** (*more formal*) **2** if sth **keys into** sth else, it goes well with it and agrees with it, producing a good result: *remedies that key into the body's basic metabolism*

⊕ v + prep

'key sth to sth/sb to make sth suitable for sth/sb; to make sth consistent with sth else or to link sth with sth else: *The farm was keyed to the needs of the local people.* ◇ *The timing of the concerts was keyed to the World Cup soccer games.*

NOTE **Key sth to sth/sb** is usually used in the passive.

⊕ v + n/pron + prep

kick /kɪk/

kick a'bout; **kick a'bout sth** (*BrE*) = KICK AROUND, KICK AROUND STH

kick sb a'bout (*BrE*) = KICK SB AROUND

kick sth a'bout (*BrE*) = KICK STH AROUND

kick a'round; **kick a'round sth** (*BrE also* **kick a'bout, kick a'bout sth**) (*informal*) **1** (*usually used in the progressive tenses*) to be present or lying somewhere not being used: *His letter is kicking about somewhere.* ◇ *The idea has been kicking around for years.* **2** (of a person) to be somewhere, or to go from one place to another, with no particular purpose: *I decided to kick around the States for a couple of months.*

SYN **knock around, knock around sth**
⊕ v + adv ◆ v + prep

kick sb a'round (*BrE also* **kick sb a'bout**) (*informal*) to treat sb in a harsh or unfair way: *Don't let the boss kick you around.*

⊕ v + n/pron + adv

kick sth a'round (*BrE also* **kick sth a'bout**) **1** to play with a ball by kicking it with your foot: *They were kicking a ball around in the street.* OBJ **ball 2** (*informal*) to discuss plans, ideas, etc. in an informal way: *They're kicking around the idea of a merger.* OBJ **idea** SYN **discuss sth** (*more formal*)

SYN **knock sth around**
⊕ v + n/pron + adv ◆ v + adv + n

'kick against sth to protest about sth or resist sth: *It's no use kicking against the system.*

⊕ v + prep

kick 'back (*AmE, informal*) to relax: *I spent the evening kicking back in the hotel's piano bar.*

⊕ v + adv

kick sth 'back (**to sb**) (*AmE, informal*) to pay money illegally in order to get some advantage for yourself: *Contractors winning construction jobs had to kick back 2 per cent of the contract price to the mafia.* ◇

⊕ v + adv + n ◆ v + n/pron + adv

▶ **'kickback** *n* (*AmE, informal*) money that is paid to sb in order to get an advantage for yourself

kick sth 'down to break sth and make it fall inwards by kicking it: *If you don't open up, we'll kick the door down.*

OBJ **door**
⊕ v + n/pron + adv ◆ v + adv + n

kick 'in (*informal*) to start to work or have an effect: *After a couple of minutes the emergency electricity supply kicked in.* ◇ *You'll feel better when the antibiotics kick in.*

⊕ v + adv

kick sth 'in to break sth and make it fall inwards by kicking it: *They had kicked the front door in.*

OBJ **door**
⊕ v + n/pron + adv ◆ v + adv + n (*less frequent*)

IDM ˌkick sb's 'head/'teeth in (*informal*) to kick sb very violently

ˌkick 'off 1 when a football game or team **kicks off**, the game starts: *The game kicks off at 7.30.* 2 (with sth) (*informal*) to start: *The tour kicks off with a concert in Nottingham.*

◆ v + adv

▶ 'kick-off *n* [C] [U] the start of a football game: *It's an afternoon kick-off.*

ˌkick sb 'off; ˌkick sb 'off sth (*computing*) to break the connection between sb's computer and the Internet, so that they can no longer use the Internet: *I keep getting kicked off the Internet for no reason.*

OBJ the Internet, server, website **SYN** disconnect sb (from sth)

NOTE These phrasal verbs are usually used in the passive.

◆ v + n/pron + adv ◆ v + n/pron + prep

ˌkick sth 'off 1 to remove sth by kicking: *She kicked off her shoes and lay down on the bed.* 2 (with sth) to begin a meeting, an event, etc: *Who's going to kick off the discussion?*

◆ v + adv + n ◆ v + pron + adv ◆ v + n + adv (*rare*)

ˌkick 'out (at sb/sth) 1 to kick your foot into the air to try to hit sb, especially because you are angry or upset: *She kicked out wildly at him as he tried to grab her.* 2 to react violently to sb/sth that makes you angry or upset: *She kicked out against traditional ideas about painting portraits.*

◆ v + adv

ˌkick sb 'out; ˌkick sb 'out of sth (*informal*) to make sb leave; to send sb away by force: *His parents kicked him out* (= made him leave home) *when he was seventeen.* ◇ *They were kicked out of the nightclub for fighting.*

SYN boot sb out, boot sb out of sth (*informal*), throw sb out, throw sb out of sth

NOTE Kick sb out is often used in the passive.

◆ v + n/pron + adv ◆ v + adv + n ◆
  v + n/pron + adv + prep

ˌkick sth 'over to make sth fall on its side by kicking it: *She almost kicked the bucket over.*

SYN knock sth over

◆ v + n/pron + adv ◆ v + adv + n

ˌkick 'up if a wind, a storm, etc. **kicks up**, it becomes stronger

SUBJ only wind, storm

◆ v + adv

ˌkick sth 'up to make dust, sand, etc. rise into the air: *The horse kicked up a cloud of dust.*

OBJ dirt, dust

◆ v + adv + n ◆ v + pron + adv ◆ v + n + adv (*rare*)

IDM ˌkick up a 'fuss/'stink etc. (about sth) to complain loudly about sth

kid /kɪd/ (-dd-)

ˌkid a'round (*informal, especially AmE*) to behave in a silly way; to joke: *A lot of what I said was just kidding around, but people took me seriously.*

SYN mess around

◆ v + adv

kill /kɪl/

ˌkill sb/sth 'off 1 to make a lot of plants, animals, etc. die: *Antibiotics should kill off the bacteria.* ◇ *The plant life was killed off by air pollution.* 2 to get rid of sb/sth; to stop sth: *The hero is killed off in the last chapter.* ◇ *It is difficult to kill off old traditions or myths.* **NOTE** Kill sb/sth off is often used in the passive.

◆ v + adv + n ◆ v + pron + adv ◆ v + n + adv (*rare*)

kip /kɪp/ (-pp-)

ˌkip 'down (*BrE, informal*) to sleep in a place that is not your own bed: *Is there anywhere to kip down for the night?*

◆ v + adv

kiss /kɪs/

ˌkiss sth a'way to stop sb feeling sad or angry by kissing them: *Let mummy kiss away your tears.*

OBJ tears, worries

◆ v + adv + n ◆ v + pron + adv ◆ v + n + adv (*rare*)

ˌkiss 'up to sb (*AmE, informal*) if you **kiss up to** sb in authority, you try to please them in order to gain an advantage for yourself

SYN suck up to sb

◆ v + adv + prep

kit /kɪt/ (-tt-)

ˌkit sb/sth 'out (*also* ˌkit sb/sth 'up *less frequent*) (in/with sth) (*BrE*) to supply sb/sth with the clothes or equipment that they need for a particular purpose: *The kids are all kitted out for the new school year.* ◇ *The studio is kitted out with modern sound equipment.*

NOTE Kit sb/sth out is usually used in the passive.

◆ v + n/pron + adv ◆ v + adv + n

kneel /niːl/ (knelt, knelt /nelt/, *AmE also* kneeled, kneeled)

ˌkneel 'down to get into a position where one or both knees are resting on the ground: *He knelt down beside the chair.* ◇ *She was kneeling down, looking for something on the floor.*

◆ v + adv

knit /nɪt/ (-tt-)

,knit to'gether (*Knit is usually used for the past tense and past participle*) when broken bones **knit together**, they grow together again: *The ribs are broken, but they'll knit together.*
NOTE **Knit** is also used with the same meaning.
◈ v + adv

knock /nɒk; *AmE* nɑːk/

~ about	161	~ in	
~ about together		~ in/into	
~ about with		~ off	
~ around		~ out, out of	
~ around together	162	~ over	
~ around with		~ together	
~ back		~ up	
~ down			

,knock a'bout; ,knock a'bout sth (*BrE*) = KNOCK AROUND, KNOCK AROUND STH

,knock sb a'bout (*BrE*) = KNOCK SB AROUND

,knock sth a'bout (*BrE*) = KNOCK STH AROUND

,knock a'bout with sb; ,knock a'bout together = KNOCK AROUND/ABOUT WITH SB, KNOCK AROUND/ABOUT TOGETHER

,knock a'round; ,knock a'round sth (*BrE also* ,knock a'bout, ,knock a'bout sth) (*informal*) **1** (*especially BrE*) (*often used in the progressive tenses*) used to say that sb/sth is in a particular place, but is not doing anything or being used: *These chocolates have been knocking around since New Year.* ◇ *His book was knocking around the lounge for ages.* ◇ *There were a few kids knocking about in the street outside.* **2** to travel and live in various places: *He spent a few years knocking about Europe.* ◇ *Jeff will know what to do — he's knocked about a bit* (= has travelled and had a lot of experience of different situations).
SYN **kick around, kick around sth**
◈ v + adv ◆ v + prep

,knock sb a'round (*BrE also* ,knock sb a'bout) (*informal*) to hit sb again and again: *Her husband knocks her about.*
◈ v + n/pron + adv

,knock sth a'round (*BrE also* ,knock sth a'bout) **1** to treat sth roughly; to hammer or hit sth: *The builders have started knocking our kitchen about.* **2** (*BrE*) to kick sth around: *We spent a few hours knocking a ball about.* OBJ **a ball** SYN **kick sth around 3** (*informal*) to discuss an idea or a suggestion with several people: *We knocked a few ideas about at the meeting.* OBJ **idea** SYN **kick sth around**
◈ v + n/pron + adv ◆ v + adv + n
▶ 'knockabout *n* (*BrE*) a period of time spent kicking a ball around with other people: *We had a knockabout in the park.*

▶ 'knockabout *adj* [usually before noun] (*BrE*) knockabout entertainment involves people acting in a deliberately silly way, for example falling over or hitting other people, in order to make the audience laugh

,knock a'round/a'bout with sb; ,knock a'round/a'bout together (*BrE, informal*) to spend a lot of time with sb: *She knocks around with Sahan.* ◇ *She and Sahan knock around together.* ◇ *He knocks about with some strange people!*
SYN **hang around with sb, hang around together**
◈ v + adv + prep ◆ v + adv + adv

,knock sb 'back 1 to prevent sb from achieving sth or making progress, especially by rejecting them or sth that they suggest or ask: *He had been knocked back twice by the selection committee.* **2** to surprise or shock sb: *The news really knocked me back.*
◈ v + n/pron + adv ◆ v + adv + n (*rare*)
▶ 'knock-back *n* (*BrE*) an occasion when sb rejects you or sth that you suggest or ask; a refusal: *I don't think I could stand another knock-back.*

,knock sb 'back sth (*BrE, informal*) to cost sb a particular amount of money: *Those books knocked me back £50.* ◇ *That car must have knocked you back a bit!*
SYN **set sb back sth**
NOTE **Knock sb back sth** cannot be used in the passive.
◈ v + n/pron + adv + n

,knock sth 'back (*informal*) to drink sth quickly: *He knocked back two pints of beer.*
OBJ **beer, coffee, etc.** SYN **swig sth**
◈ v + adv + n ◆ v + n/pron + adv

,knock sb 'down 1 if a car or another vehicle **knocks sb down**, it hits them, often killing or injuring them: *She was knocked down by a bus.*
SYN **run sb over** NOTE **Knock sb down** is often used in the passive in this meaning. **2** to hit or push sb so that they fall to the ground or the floor: *The wind was strong enough to knock you down.* ◇ *He knocked down his opponent in the first round* (= in boxing).
→ *see also* KNOCK SB OVER
◈ v + n/pron + adv ◆ v + adv + n
IDM **you could have knocked me down with a 'feather** used to express great surprise
▶ 'knock-down *n* an occasion in boxing when one competitor hits the other so hard that they fall to the ground
→ *see also* KNOCK-DOWN PRICE at KNOCK STH DOWN

,knock sb/sth 'down to persuade sb to accept a lower price for sth; to make the price of sth lower: *He knocked Simon down to £5.* ◇ *We knocked the price down to £10.* ◇ *How did you manage to knock them down from £5 000 to £4 000?* ◇ *He managed to knock the price down from £350 to £320.*

SYN **beat sb/sth down**

NOTE **Knock sb down sth** and **knock sth down sth** can also be used: *We should be able to knock them down a few pounds.* ◇ *He knocked the price down five dollars.*

✥ v + n/pron + adv ♦ v + adv + n (*less frequent*)

knock sth 'down 1 to destroy sth and make it fall down: *If you don't open up, I'm going to knock the door down.* ◇ *These old houses are going to be knocked down.* OBJ **house, door** SYN **demolish sth** (*more formal*) **2** (**to sb**) to sell sth to the person who offers most money at a public sale (an **auction**): *The painting was knocked down to me for £5 000.* **3** (*AmE*) to take sth apart, especially furniture, so that it can be sent or carried somewhere more easily

✥ v + n/pron + adv ♦ v + adv + n

▸ **'knock-down price** *n* a much lower price than usual: *I got these books at a knock-down price.*

→ *see also* KNOCK-DOWN *at* KNOCK SB DOWN

knock sth 'in; knock sth 'in/'into sth 1 to make sth enter sth by hitting it, for example with a hammer: *She knocked some nails into the wall.* **2** to make sth go into sth by hitting or kicking it: *Barnes knocked in two goals.* ◇ *She knocked the ball into the net.* OBJ **goal, ball**

✥ v + n/pron + adv ♦ v + adv + n ♦ v + n/pron + prep

knock sth 'in sth to make sth such as a hole in sth by hitting: *They knocked a hole in the wall for the window.* OBJ **hole**

✥ v + n/pron + prep

knock 'off; knock 'off sth (*informal*) to stop doing sth, especially work: *What time do you knock off* (*work*) *today?* OBJ **work**

✥ v + adv ♦ v + prep

knock it 'off (*spoken, informal*) used to tell sb to stop doing sth annoying: *Knock it off! I'm trying to concentrate!*

✥ v + it + adv

knock sb 'off (*slang*) **1** to murder sb: *He was knocked off by another gang.* SYN **bump sb off** (*informal*) **2** (*BrE, △, slang*) to have sex with sb

✥ v + n/pron + adv ♦ v + adv + n

knock sb 'off; knock sb 'off sth to make sb fall off sth by hitting them: *I was knocked off my bike this morning* (= by a car).

✥ v + n/pron + adv ♦ v + n/pron + prep

knock sth 'off 1 (*also* **knock sth 'out**) (*informal*) to complete sth quickly and without much effort: *They expect me to knock off* (= write) *a thousand words a day.* SYN **churn sth out 2** (*BrE, slang*) to steal sth: *He's knocking off TVs and video recorders.* ◇ *These bikes have been*

knocked off. **3** (*AmE, slang*) to make a copy of a popular product to sell at a cheaper price, often illegally

✥ v + adv + n ♦ v + n/pron + adv

▸ **'knock-off** *n* (*AmE, informal*) a copy, often illegal, of a popular product sold at a cheaper price

knock sth 'off; knock sth 'off sth 1 to reduce the price, value, etc. of sth: *We've knocked £20 off the price.* ◇ *The short cut knocks about half an hour off the journey.* ◇ *That hairstyle knocks years off your age.* SYN **lop sth off, lop sth off sth 2** to remove sth, and usually make it fall to the ground, by hitting it: *Who knocked that glass off the table?* ◇ *She knocked my glasses off.*

✥ v + n/pron + adv ♦ v + adv + n ♦ v + n/pron + prep

IDM **I'll knock your 'block/'head off** (*BrE, spoken, informal*) used to show that you are very angry with sb, by threatening to hit them **knock/ blow sb's 'socks off** to impress or surprise sb very much

knock sb 'out 1 (*also* **knock yourself 'out**) to make sb fall asleep or become unconscious: *The bump on the head knocked me out cold.* ◇ *He was knocked out in the seventh round.* ◇ *He ran straight into a lamp post, knocking himself out.* **2** (in boxing) to hit an opponent so hard that they fall to the ground and cannot get up within a limited time, so losing the fight **3** (*also* **knock yourself 'out**) to make sb very tired, ill, etc: *The course completely knocked me out.* ◇ *She's knocking herself out with all that work.* **4** (*informal*) to surprise sb very much; to have a strong emotional effect on sb: *The movie was fantastic. It knocked me out.*

✥ **1,2,3** v + n/pron + adv ♦ v + adv + n (*less frequent*)
   4 v + n/pron + adv

▸ **'knockout** (*also* **'knock-out**) *n* **1** a person, a piece of clothing, a performance, etc. that is extremely attractive or impressive: *Her daughter's an absolute knockout.* **2** (in boxing) a blow that is so hard that your opponent falls to the ground and cannot get up within a limited time, so losing the fight

→ *see also* KNOCKOUT *at* KNOCK SB/STH OUT

▸ **'knockout drops** *n* [pl.] (*humorous*) medicine in liquid form that makes you sleep or feel sleepy

knock sb/sth 'out; knock sb/sth 'out of sth (*sport*) to defeat a person or a team so that they cannot continue in the competition: *France knocked Belgium out of the European Cup.*

✥ v + n/pron + adv ♦ v + adv + n ♦
   v + n/pron + adv + prep

▸ **'knockout** (*also* **'knock-out**) *n* (*especially BrE, sport*) a competition in which the winning player or team at each stage goes on to the next stage, but the losing one no longer takes part in the competition: *the European cup knockout* ◇ *a knockout competition*

→ *see also* KNOCKOUT *at* KNOCK SB OUT

,knock sth 'out 1 = KNOCK STH OFF 1 (*informal*) *Can you knock out a quick report for me?* **2** to remove sth with a hard blow: *She knocked out her front teeth in the fall.* [OBJ] **teeth**
⊕ v + adv + n ◆ v + n/pron + adv

,knock yourself 'out 1 = KNOCK SB OUT 1 **2** = KNOCK SB OUT 3 **3** (*informal, humorous, especially AmE*) used to encourage sb to do sth they have said they would like to do, even though you do not understand why they want to do it: *You want to help? Great, knock yourself out!* ◇ *Sure you can take over the cooking — knock yourself out!*
⊕ v + pron + adv

,knock sth 'out of sb to make sb lose their breath, because of a fall, a blow, etc: *The force of the impact knocked the breath out of her.* [OBJ] **breath, wind**
⊕ v + n/pron + adv + prep
[IDM] knock the 'stuffing out of sb (*informal*) to make sb lose their energy, enthusiasm or confidence

,knock sb 'over if a car or another vehicle **knocks sb over**, it hits them and often kills or injures them: *He got knocked over by a bus.*
[SYN] **run sb/sth over**
[NOTE] Knock sb over is often used in the passive. It is not used as often as **knock sb down** or **run sb over**.
→ *see also* KNOCK SB DOWN
⊕ v + n/pron + adv ◆ v + adv + n

,knock sth 'over to push or hit sth, making it fall or turn on its side: *You've knocked my drink over!* ◇ *I'll put the candle here so that it doesn't get knocked over.*
⊕ v + n/pron + adv ◆ v + adv + n

,knock to'gether (*especially BrE*) if two things **knock together**, they touch each other with some force and make a sound: (*figurative*) *His knees were knocking together with fright.*
⊕ v + adv

,knock sth to'gether 1 (*also* ,knock sth 'up) to make or complete sth quickly and often not very well: *I'll quickly knock some lunch together.* **2** (*BrE*) to join two or more rooms or houses to make a single one: *They've knocked the two rooms together to make one big living room.*
⊕ v + n/pron + adv ◆ v + adv + n

,knock 'up (*BrE, sport*) (in tennis, etc.) to practise for a short time before the beginning of a game: *We knocked up for a few minutes before the match.*
⊕ v + adv
▶ 'knock-up n (*BrE*) (in tennis, etc.) a short practice before a game

,knock sb 'up (*informal*) **1** (*BrE*) to wake sb by knocking on their door: *Would you like me to knock you up in the morning?* **2** (*especially AmE*) to make a woman pregnant
⊕ **1** v + n/pron + adv
2 v + n/pron + adv ◆ v + adv + n

,knock sth 'up = KNOCK STH TOGETHER 1

know /nəʊ; AmE noʊ/ (knew /njuː; AmE nuː/known /nəʊn; AmE noʊn/)

'know sb/sth as sth to call sb/sth by a particular name; to think that sb/sth has a particular characteristic or is a particular type of person or thing: *She is known to her friends as Beth.* ◇ *It became known as the worst local company to work for.*
[NOTE] Know sb/sth as sth is usually used in the passive.
⊕ v + n/pron + prep

be 'known for sth to be well known because of a particular characteristic, achievement or feature: *The town is best known for its ancient university.* ◇ *He is not known for his tact!* (= he is often rude)
⊕ be + v + prep

'know A from B to be able to recognize the difference between two things: *She doesn't know a Rolls Royce from a Renault.*
[NOTE] Know sth from sth cannot be used in the passive.
⊕ v + n/pron + prep
[IDM] not know your ,arse from your 'elbow (*BrE*, △, *slang*) used to say that you think sb is very stupid or completely lacking in skill

'know of sb/sth to have heard of sb/sth, but not have very much information about or experience of them/it: *'Has he ever been in trouble with the police?' 'Not that I know of.'* ◇ *I know of one student who failed the exam twice.* ◇ *I know of her, but we've never actually met.*
⊕ v + prep

knuckle /'nʌkl/

,knuckle 'down (to sth) (*informal*) to begin to work seriously at sth, usually after a period when you have not worked hard: *It's time to knuckle down (to some hard work).*
[SYN] **buckle down (to sth)**
⊕ v + adv

,knuckle 'under (to sb/sth) (*informal*) to accept or admit defeat and do what you are told or what you have to do: *Those who refused to knuckle under were imprisoned.*
⊕ v + adv

kowtow /,kaʊ'taʊ/

kow'tow to sb/sth (*informal*) to show sb/sth too much respect and be too willing to obey them: *I refuse to kowtow to anyone.*
⊕ v + prep

LI

labour (*BrE*) (*AmE* **labor**) /ˈleɪbə(r)/

'labour under sth (*BrE*) (*formal*) **1** (*often used in the progressive tenses*) to believe sth that is not true: *to be labouring under a delusion* ◇ *She was labouring under the impression that he loved her.* [OBJ] **misapprehension, delusion 2** to find a situation very difficult because of sth: *The new government is labouring under a huge debt.*
⬦ v + prep

lace /leɪs/

,lace 'up; **,lace sth 'up** to tie the strings that go through the holes on a shoe to fasten it (**shoe-laces** or **laces**): *She laced her shoes up.*
[OBJ] **shoes, boots** [SYN] **do up, do sth up**
[NOTE] **Lace sth** is also used with this meaning.
⬦ v + n/pron + adv ◆ v + adv + n
▶ **'lace-up** *n* [usually pl.] (*BrE*) shoes fastened with strings: *As a child, she always wore lace-ups.* ◇ *lace-up shoes*

'lace sth with sth 1 to put a small amount of sth, such as alcohol, a drug, poison, etc. into a drink: *Someone had laced the cat's milk with alcohol.* **2** (*especially BrE*) to put a lot of a particular quality into sth such as a speech, a piece of writing, etc: *The show is laced with black humour.* ◇ *She laces her stories with irony.* [NOTE] **Lace sth with sth** is usually used in the passive in this meaning.
⬦ v + n/pron + prep

ladle /ˈleɪdl/

,ladle sth 'out 1 to serve food with a large spoon or in large quantities: *He ladled out the soup.* **2** (*sometimes disapproving*) to give sb a lot of sth, especially money or advice
⬦ v + adv + n ◆ v + n/pron + adv

lag /læg/ (-gg-)

,lag be'hind; **,lag be'hind sb/sth 1** to be behind sb/sth because you are walking more slowly: *Everyone ran down to the beach, but Amy lagged behind.* ◇ *Susie lagged behind the other children.* **2** (**in sth/in doing sth**) to progress or develop more slowly than others: *We are lagging far behind our European competitors in using new technology.*
⬦ v + adv ◆ v + prep

land /lænd/

'land in sth; **'land sb/yourself in sth** (*informal*) to get sb/yourself into trouble or a difficult situation: *She landed in court for stealing a car.* ◇

Being too outspoken landed her in trouble. ◇ *How did I land myself in such a mess?* ◇ *He really landed us in it!* (= got us into trouble).
⬦ v + prep ◆ v + n/pron + prep

,land 'up (*BrE, informal*) **1** [+adv/prep] to reach a final position or situation: *She landed up in hospital with a broken leg.* ◇ *The train was diverted and we landed up in York.* ◇ *The dish slipped out of my hands and landed up on the floor.* ◇ *I landed up with more work than I could manage.* **2** **land up doing sth** to end by doing sth or having to do sth that you had not planned to do: *They landed up paying for the damage.* ◇ *We landed up spending the night at the airport.*
[SYN] **end up; finish up**
⬦ **1** v + adv
2 v + adv + -ing

'land sb/yourself with sb/sth; **'land sb/yourself with doing sth** (*informal, especially BrE*) to give sb/yourself an unpleasant or difficult task to deal with: *We've landed ourselves with the most boring job of the lot.* ◇ *I got landed with clearing up the mess.* ◇ *They landed the organization with a huge bill.*
[SYN] **saddle sb/yourself with sb/sth, saddle sb/yourself with doing sth**
[NOTE] **Land sb with sb/sth** and **land sb with doing sth** are often used in the passive, usually with **get**: *Guess who got landed with washing the dishes?*
⬦ v + n/pron + prep

lap /læp/ (-pp-)

,lap sth 'up 1 to receive sth such as praise or a kind remark with pleasure without thinking about whether it is true or not: *The baby was lapping up the attention he was getting.* ◇ *She lapped up his flattery.* **2** to drink all of sth with great enjoyment: *The cat lapped up the cream.*
⬦ v + adv + n ◆ v + pron + adv ◆ v + n + adv (*less frequent*)

lapse /læps/

'lapse into sth 1 to pass gradually into a worse or less active state or condition: *They lapsed into silence.* ◇ *The country lapsed into chaos.* ◇ *to lapse into unconsciousness/a coma* [OBJ] **silence, unconsciousness 2** to start speaking or behaving in a different way, often one that is less acceptable: *She lapses into French when she can't think of a word in English.*
⬦ v + prep

lard /lɑːd; AmE lɑːrd/

'lard sth with sth (*often disapproving*) to include a lot of a particular kind of words or expressions in a speech or in a piece of writing: *His conversation was larded with Russian proverbs.*
NOTE **Lard sth with sth** is nearly always used in the passive.
◆ v + n/pron + prep

lark /lɑːk; AmE lɑːrk/

,lark a'bout/a'round (*old-fashioned, BrE, informal*) to enjoy yourself by behaving in a silly way: *Some kids were larking about in the shopping centre.*
SYN **mess around**
◆ v + adv

lash /læʃ/

,lash 'down if rain **lashes down**, it falls heavily: *The rain lashed down.*
◆ v + adv

,lash 'out (at sb/sth) 1 to make a sudden violent attack on sb: *He lashed out at us.* ◇ *Jim lashed out with both fists.* **2** to criticize sb/sth in an angry way: *She lashed out at the company for treating her so badly.* SYN **hit out (at sb/sth)**
◆ v + adv

last /lɑːst; AmE læst/

,last 'out; ,last sth 'out 1 to survive for a period of time: *How long can we last out without water?* ◇ *The doctors thought he might not last out the night.* **2** to continue in the same situation or manage to do sth for a particular length of time: *He made it to the summit, but at one point I thought he wasn't going to last out.* ◇ *She lasted out for a week without smoking.* ◇ *Can you last out the day without using your phone?* **3** to be enough for a particular length of time: *Our supplies should last out until the end of the month.* ◇ *Will the food last out the week?* SYN **hold out**
NOTE **Last sth out** cannot be used in the passive.
♦ **Last** and **last sth** are used frequently with the same meanings.
◆ v + adv ♦ v + adv + n ♦ v + pron + adv ♦ v + n + adv (*less frequent*)

,last sb 'out (*often humorous*) to live or continue longer than sb else: *My grandmother is so fit and healthy she'll probably last us all out!*
◆ v + n/pron + adv

latch /lætʃ/

,latch 'on; ,latch 'onto sb (*also* ,latch 'on to sb) (*informal*) to follow sb around, often when they do not want you to be with them: *He latched onto us and we couldn't get rid of him.*
◆ v + adv ♦ v + prep ♦ v + adv + prep

,latch 'on; ,latch 'onto sth (*also* ,latch 'on to sth*) 1** to become attached to sth: *The virus latches onto the red blood cells.* **2** to be interested in an idea, a fashion, etc. and use it for your own purposes: *The government have latched onto environmental issues to win votes.* ◇ *They have a reputation for latching onto all the latest crazes.* ◇ *Young children latch onto phrases and repeat them over and over.* **3** (*BrE, informal*) to understand an idea, what sb is saying, etc: *It took him a while to latch onto their style of humour.* ◇ *She soon latched onto the idea.* ◇ *It was a difficult concept to grasp, but Sam latched on very quickly.*
◆ v + adv ♦ v + prep ♦ v + adv + prep

laugh /lɑːf; AmE læf/

'laugh at sb/yourself to make sb/yourself seem stupid by making jokes about them/yourself; to not be too serious about sb/yourself: *They were laughing at him behind his back.* ◇ *We all laughed at Jane when she said she believed in ghosts.* ◇ *I laughed at myself for believing such an unlikely story.*
NOTE **Laugh at sb** can be used in the passive: *Nobody likes to be laughed at.*
◆ v + prep

'laugh at sth 1 to show that you find sth funny or amusing: *You never laugh at my jokes.* ◇ *The whole class was laughing at him clowning around.* **2** to make sth seem stupid by making jokes about it: *He was laughing at my accent.* SYN **ridicule sth** (*more formal*)
NOTE **Laugh at sth** can be used in the passive: *He doesn't like his ideas being laughed at.*
◆ v + prep

,laugh sth 'off (*informal*) to try to make people think that you do not care about sth, or that it is not serious or important, by making a joke about it: *He laughed off suggestions that he had been approached to be manager of the England team.* ◇ *It was an embarrassing situation, but she managed to laugh it off.*
◆ v + adv + n ♦ v + pron + adv ♦ v + n + adv (*less frequent*)

launch /lɔːntʃ/

'launch into sth; 'launch yourself into sth to start doing sth in a very enthusiastic way; to start to attack sb physically or with words: *She launched into an explanation of how the machine worked.* ◇ *We don't want to launch ourselves into the wrong enterprise.* ◇ *The band launched into one of their best known songs.*
OBJ **speech, explanation, challenge**
◆ v + prep ♦ v + pron + prep

,launch 'out (into sth) to begin to do sth new or different in a confident way: *She's decided she has enough experience to launch out on her own.*
◆ v + adv

lavish /ˈlævɪʃ/

ˈlavish sth on sb/sth (*also* **ˈlavish sth upon sb/sth** *more formal*) to give a lot of sth, often too much, to sb/sth: *They lavished such care on that house!* ◇ *He was jealous of the attention lavished on his sister.* ◇ *Millions of pounds were lavished on restoring the building.*
> **OBJ** **attention**, **praise**, **care**
> **NOTE** **Lavish sth on/upon sb/sth** is often used in the passive.
> ✧ v + n/pron + prep

lay /leɪ/ (**laid**, **laid** /leɪd/)

ˌlay aˈbout sb (**with sth**) (*especially BrE*) to attack sb violently physically or sometimes with words: *He started to lay about me with his walking stick.*
> ✧ v + prep

ˌlay sth aˈside (*formal*) **1** to put sth to one side and not use it or think about it: *I laid my book aside and picked up the letter.* ◇ (*figurative*) *They laid aside their differences until the crisis was over.* **2** (*also* **ˌlay sth ˈby** *less frequent*) to keep sth to use in the future; to save sth: *Have you laid anything aside for your old age?*
> **SYN** **put sth aside; set sth aside**
> ✧ v + n/pron + adv ◆ v + n/pron + adv + n

ˌlay sth beˈfore sb/sth to present a proposal, some information, etc. to sb for them to think about and decide on: *The bill was laid before Parliament.*
> ✧ v + n/pron + prep

ˌlay sth ˈby = LAY STH ASIDE

ˌlay sth ˈdown 1 to put sth down or stop using it: *He stopped writing and laid down his pen.* ◇ *They refused to lay down their arms.* **SYN** **put sb/sth down 2** if you **lay down** a rule, or a principle, you state officially that people must obey it or use it: *The government has laid down procedures for negotiating teachers' pay.* ◇ *Clear guidelines have been laid down for religious teaching in schools.* **OBJ** **guidelines**, **rules**, **conditions 3** to establish sth that will develop or be useful in the future: *Good eating habits can be laid down in childhood.* **4** to produce sth that is stored and gradually increases: *If you eat too much, the surplus is laid down as fat.* **OBJ** **fat NOTE Lay sth down** is usually used in the passive in this meaning. **5** (*BrE*) to store sth, especially wine, to use in the future: *She has laid down hundreds of bottles of port.* **OBJ** **bottles**, **wine**
> ✧ **1,4** v + adv + n ◆ v + n/pron + adv
> **2,3,5** v + adv + n ◆ v + pron + adv ◆
> v + n + adv (*rare*)

> **IDM** **lay down the ˈlaw** to tell sb firmly what they can or cannot do **lay down your ˈlife** (**for sb/sth**) to die willingly in order to save sb or because of sth that you believe in

ˌlay sth ˈin (*formal*) to get a supply of sth and store it to use in the future: *I've laid in enough logs for the winter.*
> **SYN** **get sth in**
> ✧ v + adv + n ◆ v + n/pron + adv

ˌlay ˈinto sb/sth (**with sth**) (**for sth/for doing sth**) (*informal*) to attack sb/sth violently, with words or blows: *She laid into him with her fists.* ◇ *He laid into the government for spending millions of pounds on buildings nobody wanted.*
> **SYN** **rip into sb/sth** (**with sth**) (**for sth/for doing sth**)
> ✧ v + prep

ˌlay ˈoff; ˌlay ˈoff sb/sth; ˌlay ˈoff doing sth (*informal*) used to tell sb to stop doing sth that irritates or annoys you: *Lay off! You're messing up my homework!* ◇ *Lay off him, he's still learning.* ◇ *Lay off bullying your brother!*
> ✧ v + adv ◆ v + prep

ˌlay ˈoff sth; ˌlay ˈoff doing sth (*informal*) to stop doing or using sth harmful: *You should lay off alcohol/drinking for a while.*
> ✧ v + prep

ˌlay sb ˈoff to dismiss workers, usually for a short time, because there is not enough work: *We've had to lay off hundreds of workers.*
> ✧ v + n/pron + adv ◆ v + adv + n
> ▶ **ˈlay-off** *n* **1** [C] an act of dismissing workers because there is not enough work: *The crisis has caused thousands of lay-offs.* **2** [usually sing.] a period of time when sb is not able to take part in an activity or a sport that they usually do

ˌlay sth ˈon (*BrE, informal*) to provide or arrange sth for sb, for example food, transport or entertainment: *Extra buses were laid on during the train strike.* ◇ *She had laid on tea for the players.*
> ✧ v + adv + n ◆ v + n/pron + adv

> **IDM** **lay it/sth on with a ˈtrowel; lay it on ˈthick** (*informal*) to talk about sb/sth in a way that makes them seem much better or worse than they really are; to exaggerate sth: *He was laying on the flattery with a trowel.* ◇ *Calling him a genius is laying it on a bit thick!*

ˌlay sth ˈon sb (*informal*) **1** to force sb to deal with sth unpleasant or difficult: *I'm sorry to lay all this work on you.* **2** (*AmE*) to break bad or surprising news to sb: *Sorry to lay this on you, but he's never coming back.*
> ✧ v + n/pron + prep

ˌlay sb ˈout 1 (*informal*) to knock sb unconscious: *He laid his opponent out with a single blow.* **2** to prepare a dead body to be buried
> ✧ v + n/pron + adv ◆ v + adv + n

ˌlay sth ˈout 1 to spread sth out ready to use or so that it can be seen easily: *Lay out all the clothes you want to take.* ◇ *Lay all the cards out on the table.* **2** to plan how sth should look and arrange it in this way: *They laid the streets out on a grid pattern.* ◇ *a well laid out CV/resumé* **3** to present or explain sth clearly and carefully: *At the meet-ing, he laid out his plans for the company.* **4 (on sth)** (*informal*) to spend money: *He laid out thou-sands renovating the house.*

◆ v + n/pron + adv ♦ v + adv + n

▶ **'layout** *n* [usually sing.] the way in which sth is arranged: *He still recalled the layout of the house perfectly.* ◇ *The magazine has a very attractive layout.*

▶ **'outlay** *n* [C] [U] the money that you spend on sth, especially when you start a new project: *an outlay of $400 000* ◇ *What was your initial outlay on equipment?*

lay 'up to hide somewhere or do nothing for a while: *They lay up in a cave until it got dark.*

◆ v + adv

lay sb 'up (*informal*) if sb is **laid up** they are unable to work or take part in an activity because they are ill/sick or injured: *I was laid up for a month with a broken leg.* ◇ *He has been laid up with flu for a week.*

NOTE **Lay sb up** is nearly always used in the passive.

◆ v + n/pron + adv ♦ v + adv + n

lay sth 'up 1 (for yourself) (*BrE*) if you **lay up** trouble or problems for yourself, you do sth that will result in difficulties later: *You're laying up problems for yourself by not tackling this now.* **2** to stop using a vehicle, ship, etc. because you do not need it, or it has to be repaired: *Our boat is laid up during the winter months.* NOTE **Lay sth up** is often used in the passive in this meaning.

◆ v + adv + n ♦ v + n/pron + adv

laze /leɪz/

laze a'round; laze a'round sth (*BrE also* **laze a'bout, laze a'bout sth**) to spend your time relaxing and doing very little: *He lazed about all day.* ◇ *They lazed around the pool in the after-noon.*

SYN **lie around, lie around sth; lounge about/around, lounge about/around sth**

◆ v + adv ♦ v + prep

laze sth a'way to spend a period of time relax-ing and doing very little: *We lazed away the sum-mer on the beach.*

◆ v + n/pron + adv ♦ v + adv + n

lead /liːd/ (led, led /led/)

lead 'into sth 1 if a subject or a discussion **leads into** sth, it moves naturally into a second subject or discussion: *This led into a discussion on gender differences.* ◇ *Pair and group work often leads into a whole class discussion.* **2** if a

room, a door, a street, etc. **leads into** a place, it opens into it or connects with it: *The door led into a tiny kitchen.* SUBJ **door, room, road**

◆ v + prep

▶ **'lead-in (to sth)** *n* an introduction to a subject, a story, etc: *We want a striking lead-in to the new programme.*

lead 'off (with sth) (*especially AmE*) to start a dis-cussion, meeting, etc: *Everyone will have a chance to speak. Would you like to lead off?*

◆ v + adv

lead 'off sth; lead 'off from sth 1 if a street **leads off** (from) a place, it starts there and goes away from it: *He pointed to a street leading off (from) the corner of the square.* **2** if a room, a door, etc. **leads off** (from) a place, it connects dir-ectly with it: *All the rooms lead off the main hall.*

◆ v + prep ♦ v + adv + prep

lead sb 'on (*informal*) to deceive sb and make them believe sth that is not true, especially that you love them or find them attractive: *You shouldn't have led him on like that.*

◆ v + n/pron + adv ♦ v + adv + n (*less frequent*)

'lead to sth; 'lead sb to sth (*also* **lead 'on to sth, lead sb 'on to sth**) to result in a particular action or event; to force or persuade sb to take a particular action: *Living in damp conditions can lead to serious health problems.* ◇ *What led you to this conclusion?* ◇ *The increase in the number of motor vehicles has led to an increase in auto-crimes.* ◇ *The police have offered a reward for information leading to the conviction of the child's killers.* ◇ *She described how her early life had led her to her profession as an artist.* ◇ *One thing led to another and before long Sue and I were engaged.*

NOTE **Lead sb to do sth** can also be used with this meaning: *She described how her early life led her to become an artist.*

◆ v + prep ♦ v + n/pron + prep ♦ v + adv + prep ♦ v + n/pron + adv + prep

lead 'up to sth 1 to be the introduction to or the cause of sth: *The book describes the period lead-ing up to the start of the war.* ◇ *Police are investi-gating the chain of events that led up to her death.* **2** to prepare to talk about sth or ask a difficult question by gradually introducing the subject you want to talk about: *What exactly are you lead-ing up to?* ◇ *He seemed to be leading up to asking a difficult question.*

◆ v + adv + prep

▶ **lead-'up (to sth)** *n* [sing.] (*BrE*) a period of time or an event or series of events before another event or activity: *in the lead-up to the election*

leaf /liːf/

leaf 'through sth to turn over the pages of a book, a magazine etc. quickly without reading them carefully or in detail: *She picked up a brochure and leafed through it.*
OBJ **pages** SYN **flick through sth**
◈ v + prep

leak /liːk/

leak 'out if secret information **leaks out**, it becomes known to the public when it should remain secret: *He was worried about what might happen if the news leaked out.*
SYN **get out**
◈ v + adv

lean /liːn/ (**leaned, leaned,** *BrE also* **leant, leant** /lent/)

lean against/on sth/sb; lean 'up against sth to rest against or on sth/sb for support: *Laura leaned weakly against the door.* ◇ *We left our bikes leaning up against the wall.* ◇ *You can lean on my arm.*
→ *see also* LEAN ON SB/STH
◈ v + prep ◆ v + adv + prep

lean sth against/on sth; lean sth 'up against sth to make sth rest against or on sth in a sloping position: *He leaned his head on his hand and closed his eyes.* ◇ *Maggie leant the broom up against the wall.*
◈ v + n/pron + prep ◆ v + n/pron + adv + prep

lean on sb (*informal*) to try to make sb do sth by threatening them: *They are leaning on him to make him withdraw his complaints.*
NOTE **Lean on sb** can be used in the passive: *I was being leaned on.*
◈ v + prep

lean on sb/sth (*also* **lean upon sb/sth** *more formal*) to depend on sb/sth: *It's good to have someone to lean on.* ◇ *She was unsure of herself and leaned heavily on her friends for support.*
→ *see also* LEAN AGAINST/ON SB/STH
◈ v + prep

lean to'wards sth (*also* **lean to'ward sth**) to support or tend to prefer a particular idea or political party: *I'm not sure how I'm going to vote but I'm leaning towards the Democrats.*
◈ v + prep

lean up a'gainst sth
→ *see also* LEAN AGAINST/ON STH/SB

lean sth up a'gainst sth
→ *see also* LEAN STH AGAINST/ON STH

lean upon sb/sth = LEAN ON SB/STH

leap /liːp/ (**leapt, leapt** /lept/ or **leaped, leaped**)

leap at sth to accept sth eagerly, without hesitating: *She leapt at the chance of working in Paris.*
OBJ **chance, opportunity** SYN **jump at sth**
◈ v + prep

leap on sth (*also* **leap upon sth** *more formal*) (*especially BrE*) to suddenly become very interested in an idea or a suggestion, especially because you think it will give you an advantage: *The press leapt on the story.*
◈ v + prep

leap 'out at sb if sth, especially sth written, **leaps out at** you, you see it immediately: *His name leapt out at me from the page.*
SYN **jump out at sb**
◈ v + adv + prep

leap 'up to stand quickly and suddenly when you have been sitting: *He leapt up and ran to answer the door.*
SYN **jump up**
◈ v + adv

leap upon sth (*especially BrE*) = LEAP ON STH

leave /liːv/ (**left, left** /left/)

leave sth a'side to not discuss or consider a particular idea or issue: *Leaving aside car parking space, the housing development is well planned.* ◇ *Let us leave aside the question of costs for the moment.* ◇ *Leaving that aside…*
OBJ **question, that/this problem**
◈ v + adv + n ◆ v + pron + adv ◆ v + n + adv (*less frequent*)

leave sb/sth be'hind to make progress much faster than sb else: *The new car is going to leave the competition far behind.*
◈ v + n/pron + adv

leave sb/sth be'hind; leave sb/sth be'hind sb 1 to go away from a place without taking sb/sth because you have forgotten them/it: *Somebody has left their umbrella behind.* ◇ *Wait — don't leave me behind!* **2** to go away from a place while the result of sth you have done stays there: *They wore gloves so as not to leave any fingerprints behind* (*them*). **3** to leave a person or place permanently, especially in order to begin a new life: *He was anxious to leave the past behind* (*him*). ◇ *She disappeared a year ago leaving behind a boyfriend and a small baby.* **4** to have sb/sth remaining after your death: *He died at the age of 33, leaving behind a wife and three young children.*
NOTE **Leave sb/sth** is also often used with all these meanings: *They wore gloves so as not to leave any fingerprints.*
◈ v + n/pron + adv ◆ v + adv + n ◆ v + n/pron + prep

,**leave sth 'in** to not remove sth for example from a book, a piece of writing, etc: *Make sure you leave that paragraph in.*
OPP **leave sth out**
⊕ v + n/pron + adv ◆ v + adv + n

,**leave 'off**; ,**leave 'off sth**; ,**leave 'off doing sth** (*BrE*, *informal*) to stop doing sth: *Lee shouted at him, but he wouldn't leave off.* ◇ *Would you leave off what you are doing for a moment?* ◇ *We're going to try and begin where they left off.* ◇ *'Will you leave off nagging?' he shouted.*
⊕ v + adv ◆ v + adv + n ◆ v + adv +-ing

,**leave sb/sth 'off**; ,**leave sb/sth 'off sth** to not include or mention sb/sth, especially on a list: *Have I left anyone off the list?*
⊕ v + n/pron + adv ◆ v + adv + n/pron + prep

,**leave sth 'on 1** if you **leave** clothes **on**, you continue wearing them: *Leave your shoes on.* **2** to not switch sth off: *I found the television had been left on all night.*
SYN **keep sth on** **OPP** **leave sth off**; **switch sth off**
⊕ v + n/pron + adv ◆ v + adv + n

,**leave it 'out** (*BrE*, *informal*) **1** used to tell sb to stop doing sth silly or annoying **2** used to tell sb that you think what they have said is stupid, or that you do not believe it: *Two million dollars? Leave it out!*
⊕ v + it + adv

,**leave sb 'out**; ,**leave sb 'out of sth** to not include sb deliberately: *It seemed unkind to leave Daisy out, so we invited her too.* ◇ *There was an outcry when he was left out of the team.*
SYN **exclude sb** (*more formal*)
⊕ v + n/pron + adv ◆ v + adv + n ◆
v + n/pron + adv + prep
▶ **left 'out** *adj* unhappy because you have not been included in sth: *I felt a bit left out.*

,**leave sb/sth 'out**; ,**leave sb/sth 'out of sth 1** to not involve sb/sth in sth: *Leave my brother out of this — he had nothing to do with it.* **2** to not include sb/sth either accidentally or on purpose: *Have I left anyone out?* ◇ *You can leave out the gory details.* ◇ *This is spelt wrongly. You've left out the 'e'.* ◇ *You've left the second 'm' out of 'committee'.* ◇ *You've left out an 'm' in 'committee'.* **SYN** **omit sth** (*more formal*)
⊕ **1** v + n/pron + adv ◆ v + n/pron + adv + prep
2 v + adv + n ◆ v + n/pron + adv ◆
v + n/pron + adv + prep

be ,left 'over (from sth) (of food or money) if food, money, etc. is **left over**, it remains when the rest has been eaten or used up: *After I've paid my rent and bought food there isn't much left over to spend on books.* ◇ *There was plenty of food left over after the party.* ◇ *There's some rice left over from lunch.*
⊕ be + v + adv

▶ **'leftover** *n* (*BrE*) **1** [usually pl.] food that has not been eaten and remains after a meal **2** a custom, tradition, etc. that belongs to an earlier time but still exists: *These narrow roads are a leftover from the days of horse-drawn carriages.*
▶ **'leftover** *adj* [only before noun] remaining because it has not been eaten or used: *leftover vegetables/fabric*

'**leave sb to sth** to go away from sb so that they can continue what they were doing before you came, or do sth without your help: (*informal*) *If you don't need me any more, I'll leave you to it.* ◇ *I'll leave you to your lunch.*
⊕ v + n/pron + prep
IDM **leave sb to their own de'vices** to leave sb alone to do as they wish: *Once I've explained things to him I tend to leave him to his own devices.*

lend /lend/ (**lent, lent** /lent/)

,**lend sth 'out (to sb)** to allow sb to borrow sth for a period of time: *The reference books cannot be lent out.*
⊕ v + n/pron + adv ◆ v + adv + n

'**lend itself/themselves to sth** (*formal*) to be suitable for sth: *Science in elementary schools lends itself well to learning through play.* ◇ *Not all materials lend themselves to scientific dating.*

let /let/ (**letting, let, let**)

~ down	~ on
169 ~ in, into	~ out
~ in for	170 ~ past
~ in on	~ through
~ into	~ up
~ off	

,**let sb ' down 1** to fail to help or support sb in the way that they hoped or expected: *She said she would help, but let them down at the last minute.* ◇ *It's important our decision doesn't let down our customers.* ◇ *The car has never let me down.* ◇ *I felt I'd been badly let down by the company.* **2** to tell sb some bad news in a kind way so that they will not be too disappointed or upset: *The kids will be really upset the trip's been cancelled — try to let them down gently.*
⊕ v + n/pron + adv **1** also v + adv + n
IDM **let the 'side down** (*BrE*) to disappoint your family, friends, team, etc. by not being as successful as they expect, or not helping or supporting them: *John would never let the side down.* ◇ *I knew I was letting the side down* (= disappointing my family, etc.) *by not going to college.*
▶ '**let-down** *n* [C, usually sing.] [U] something that is not as good as you thought or hoped it would be: *The movie was great but the ending was a bit of a let-down.*

,let sb/sth 'down; **,let yourself 'down** to make sb/sth/yourself less successful or impressive than they/it/you should be: *Her knowledge of Italian is excellent, but her pronunciation lets her down.* ◊ *His clothes let him down.* ◊ *If you don't work hard for these exams, you'll come to be letting yourself down.*
◆ v + n/pron + adv ♦ v + adv + n

,let sth 'down 1 to make sth go lower: *We let the bucket down on a rope.* ⟨SYN⟩ **lower sth** (*more formal*) **2** to make sth longer, especially an item of clothing such as a skirt or a dress: *I'm going to let the hem down a couple of centimetres.* ⟨OPP⟩ **take sth up 3** (*BrE*) to allow the air to come out of sth, such as a tyre: *The tyres on his car had been let down during the night.* ⟨OBJ⟩ **tyre** ⟨SYN⟩ **deflate sth** (*formal*)
◆ v + n/pron + adv ♦ v + adv + n

⟨IDM⟩ **let your 'hair down** (*informal*) to relax and enjoy yourself, often in a wild or lively way: *I saw my parents letting their hair down on the dance floor.*

,let sb/sth 'in; **,let yourself 'in**; **,let sb/sth/ yourself 'into sth** to allow sb/sth/yourself to enter a room or a building: *Let me in! It's cold out here.* ◊ *The guard refuses to let anyone in without a security pass.* ◊ *She let herself into the flat.*
◆ v + n/pron + adv ♦ v + adv + n ♦ v + n/pron + prep

,let sth 'in to allow sth such as water or light to enter a place through a hole: *There was a hole in the roof that let the rain in.* ◊ *I drew the curtains back to let in some light.*
⟨OBJ⟩ **light, rain**
⟨NOTE⟩ **Let sth in** cannot be used in the passive.
◆ v + n/pron + adv ♦ v + adv + n
▶ **'inlet** *n* **1** a narrow strip of water which goes from the sea or a lake into the land: *a narrow/sheltered inlet* **2** the part of a machine through which air, gas or fuel enters: *a fuel/power inlet*

,let sb/yourself 'in for sth (*informal*) to allow yourself to become involved in sth difficult or unpleasant: *If I'd known what I was letting myself in for, I'd never have agreed to help.* ◊ *What have you let me in for?*
⟨NOTE⟩ **Let sb/yourself in for sth** cannot be used in the passive. It is often used in questions with *what*.
◆ v + n/pron + adv + prep

,let sb 'in on sth (*BrE also* **,let sb 'into sth**) (*informal*) to allow sb to share a secret: *Are you going to let them in on your plans?* ◊ *I wanted to let Chris in on the secret.* ◊ *I'll let you into a little secret.*
⟨OBJ⟩ **secret**
◆ v + n/pron + adv + prep ♦ v + n/pron + prep

be ,let 'into sth (*BrE*) to be put into the surface of sth: *A large window was let into the wall.*
◆ be + v + prep

,let 'off (*BrE, slang*) to let air from the bowels come out through your bottom
◆ v + adv

,let sb 'off (**with sth**) to punish sb lightly for sth wrong they have done; to not punish sb at all: *She was let off with a fine.* ◊ *I'll let you off this time, but don't do it again.*
◆ v + n/pron + adv

,let sb 'off; **,let sb 'off sth 1** to allow sb not to do sth or not to go somewhere: *You really ought to help with the shopping, but I suppose I could let you off.* ◊ *Mum let me off the household chores during exams.* **2** to allow sb to get out of a vehicle, especially a bus: *Can you let me off here?*
◆ v + n/pron + adv ♦ v + n/pron + prep

⟨IDM⟩ **let sb off the 'hook** to free sb from a difficult or unpleasant task or situation: *He wasn't going to let the senator off the hook easily; he kept asking difficult questions.*

,let sth 'off to fire a gun; to make a bomb explode: *The boys were letting off fireworks.* ◊ *He let off a warning shot.*
⟨OBJ⟩ **firework, shot**
◆ v + adv + n ♦ v + n/pron + adv
⟨IDM⟩ **,let off 'steam** to get rid of your energy, emotions, etc. by shouting or doing sth active: *He let off steam by hitting a pillow.*

,let 'on (**to sb**) (*informal*) to tell sb sth that is supposed to be a secret: *She doesn't know I've bought her a watch, so don't let on, will you?* ◊ *The children knew he was coming, but they didn't let on to anyone.* ◊ *There were holes in Jack's shoes, but Kate didn't let on (that) she'd noticed.*
◆ v + adv

,let 'out (*AmE*) when schools, classes, offices, etc. **let out**, they come to an end and students, workers, etc. go home at the end of a day or a term: *Classes let out in June.* ◊ *More than 30 000 people are expected in the square after work lets out.*
◆ v + adv

,let sb 'out; **,let sb 'out of sth 1** to allow sb not to do sth they have promised or are expected to do; to free sb from a difficult situation: *I've got school tomorrow, so that lets me out (of helping).* **2** to allow sb to leave a hospital, prison, etc., especially early or for a short time: *The doctors might let me out tomorrow.*
◆ v + n/pron + adv ♦ v + adv + n ♦
    v + n/pron + adv + prep
▶ **'let-out** *n* [sing.] (*especially BrE*) something that allows you to avoid an unpleasant or difficult situation: *a let-out clause* (= in a contract) ◊ *'I think it's too hot to go jogging today,' I said, looking for a let-out.*

,let sb/sth 'out; ,let sb/sth 'out of sth; ,let yourself 'out; ,let yourself 'out of sth to allow sb/sth/yourself to go out of a room or a building: *Can you let yourself out?* ◇ *I was amazed they let her out of hospital so soon.*
◆ v + n/pron + adv ◆ v + adv + n ◆
   v + n/pron + adv + prep

IDM **let the 'cat out of the bag** to tell a secret carelessly or by mistake: *I was trying to keep my promotion quiet, but Steve went and let the cat out of the bag.*

,let sth 'out 1 to give a cry; to make a sound: *She let out a scream of terror.* ◇ *He let out a sigh of relief.* **OBJ** **cry, sigh** **OPP** **hold sth in 2** to allow secret information to become known: *He's the only person who could have let the secret out.* ◇ *The company let out that they were putting in a bid for KFC.* **OBJ** **secret** **SYN** **reveal sth** (*more formal*) **3** (*to sb*) (*BrE*) to make a house, flat, apartment, etc. available for rent: *The apartment's been let out to a German couple.* **OBJ** **flat/apartment, house** **SYN** **hire sth out (to sb); rent sth out (to sb) 4** to make an item of clothing looser or larger: *I've eaten so much I'll have to let my belt out!* **OBJ** **skirt, trousers** **OPP** **take sth in 5** (*also* ,let sth 'out of sth) to allow air, liquid, etc. to escape or flow out of somewhere: *We need to let the air out of the radiator.*
◆ v + adv + n ◆ v + n/pron + adv
   5 also v + n/pron + adv + prep
▸ 'outlet *n* **1** (*for sth*) a way of expressing or using energy, strong feelings, ideas, etc: *Children need an outlet for all their energy.* **2** a shop/store or an organization that sells goods made by a particular company or of a particular type: *a retail/fast food outlet* **3** (*especially AmE*) a shop/store that sells goods of a particular make/makes at reduced prices: *designer outlets* **4** a pipe or hole through which water, steam, etc. can flow out **5** (*AmE*) a device in a wall that you use to connect a piece of electrical equipment to a power supply: *an electrical outlet* **6** the end of a river where it flows into a lake or the sea

,let sb/sth 'past to allow sb/sth to go past you: *Can you let me past, please?*
◆ v + n/pron + adv

,let sb/sth 'through 1 to allow sb/sth to pass or go through sth that is blocking the way: *The crowd moved aside to let the ambulance through.* ◇ *Let me through — I'm a doctor.* ◇ *These blinds don't let much light through.* **2** (*especially BrE*) to say that sb/sth is good enough for sth or is correct: *We were worried the council wouldn't let the plans for the new building through.*
◆ v + n/pron + adv ◆ v + adv + n (*rare*)

,let 'up (*informal*) **1** to become less strong: *The rain showed no sign of letting up.* **2** to do sth with less effort or energy than before, or stop doing it:

We mustn't let up, even though we're winning. ◇ *Doesn't she ever let up? She's been complaining all day.*
◆ v + adv
▸ 'let-up (in sth) *n* [U] [sing.] a reduction in the strength of something; a period of time when sth unpleasant stops: *There can be no let-up in the war against drugs.* ◇ *The rain continued all afternoon with no let-up.*

level /'levl/ (-ll-, *AmE* -l-)

'level sth at sb/sth 1 (*also* ,level sth a'gainst sb/sth) to say publicly that sb is to blame for sth, especially a mistake or a crime: *The charges levelled against him are unjust.* ◇ *Environmental groups have levelled a number of criticisms at the proposal.* **OBJ** **criticism, accusation, charge** **NOTE** **Level sth against/at sb/sth** is usually used in the passive in this meaning: *Accusations of incompetence have been levelled at the principal.* **2** to point sth, especially a gun, at sb: *She levelled the pistol at his head.*
◆ v + n/pron + prep

,level sth 'down/'up to make standards, amounts, etc. be the same low/high or lower/higher level: *The government is accused of levelling down standards in schools rather than levelling them up.*
◆ v + adv + n ◆ v + n/pron + adv

,level 'off/'out 1 to become level or steady after a period of sharp rises and falls: *House prices showed no sign of levelling off.* **2** to become level or horizontal after rising or falling: *The road began to level off as we approached the coast.* ◇ *The plane levelled off at 20 000 feet.*
◆ v + adv

,level sth 'off/'out to make something smooth or flat: *Level the ground out before sowing the seed.*
◆ v + n/pron + adv ◆ v + adv + n

,level sth 'up = LEVEL STH DOWN/UP

'level with sb (*informal*) to speak or deal with sb in an honest and direct way: *I'm going to level with you now — your work hasn't been up to standard for some time.* ◇ *I've got the feeling that he's not levelling with me.*
◆ v + prep

lick /lɪk/

,lick sth 'off/'up; ,lick sth 'off sth to eat or drink sth by moving your tongue over the surface of it: *She licked the jam off (the spoon).* ◇ *The cat licked up the milk from the dish.*
◆ v + n/pron + adv ◆ v + adv + n ◆ v + n/pron + prep

lie /laɪ/ (lies, lying, lay /leɪ/lain /leɪn/)

,lie a'bout; ,lie a'bout sth (*BrE*) = LIE AROUND, LIE AROUND STH

,lie a'head; ,lie a'head of sb to be in the future; to be in front of you: *Great opportunities lie ahead.* ◇ *Who knows what problems might lie ahead of us?*
◆ v + adv ♦ v + adv + prep

,lie a'round; ,lie a'round sth (*BrE also* ,lie a'bout, ,lie a'bout sth) 1 (of a person) to spend time being lazy and not doing anything in particular: *She's been lying around the house all day doing nothing.* ⟨SYN⟩ **laze around, laze around sth; lounge about/around, lounge about/around sth 2** (of a number of things) to be left somewhere in a careless or untidy way: *His clothes lay around all over the floor.* ◇ *'Have you seen my purse?' 'It was lying about in the kitchen when I last saw it.'* ◇ *You shouldn't leave valuables lying around the changing rooms.*
◆ v + adv ♦ v + prep
▶ 'layabout *n* (*old-fashioned, BrE, informal*) a lazy person who does very little work

,lie 'back (in/on sth) to rest, relax and do very little: *Just lie back and enjoy the peace and quiet.* ◇ *She lay back on the pillows and closed her eyes.*
◆ v + adv

,lie be'fore sb (*literary*) 1 to be in front of sb: *A terrible sight lay before them.* 2 to be in the future: *Your whole life lies before you.*
◆ v + prep

,lie be'hind sth to be the real explanation or reason for sth: *She understood the feelings that lay behind his angry words.* ◇ *We will probably never know what lay behind his decision to resign.*
◆ v + prep

,lie 'down to be or move into a horizontal position on a bed, etc. in order to sleep or rest: *Go and lie down for a while.* ◇ *He lay down on the sofa and went to sleep.* ◇ *The coughing is worse when he's lying down.* ◇ *She was lying down on the bed.*
NOTE Do not confuse this sense of **lie down** with **lay sth down**, which must always have an object: *Jack lay down on the sofa.* ◇ *Jack laid the pen down on the table.* ◇ *Jack was lying down on the sofa,* (*not* Jack was laying down on the sofa).
◆ v + adv
IDM take sth lying 'down to accept an insult, a criticism, a violent attack, etc. without protesting or reacting to it: *He has been accused of bribery, but he won't take this lying down.*
▶ ,lie-'down *n* [sing.] (*BrE, informal*) a short rest, especially in bed: *to have a lie-down*

lie 'in (*BrE, informal*) to stay in bed after the time you usually get up: *It's Saturday tomorrow, so you can lie in.*
⟨SYN⟩ **sleep in**
◆ v + adv
▶ ,lie-'in *n* [sing.] (*BrE, informal*) an act of staying in bed longer than usual in the morning: *to have a lie-in*

,lie 'up (*BrE*) to hide somewhere: *The fugitives lay up in the caves until it got dark.*
◆ v + adv

'lie with sb/sth (to do sth) (*formal*) to be the duty or responsibility of sb/sth: *It lies with you to accept or reject the proposal.* ◇ *The decision on whether to proceed lies with the minister.*
⟨SYN⟩ **rest with sb**
◆ v + prep

lift /lɪft/

,lift 'off when a rocket, etc. **lifts off** it rises from the ground into the air: *The rocket lifts off next Monday.*
◆ v + adv
▶ 'lift-off *n* [C] [U] the moment when a rocket or spacecraft leaves the ground and rises into the air: *We have lift-off!*

,lift sb/sth 'up; ,lift yourself 'up to raise sb/sth/yourself to a higher position or level: *I can't lift you up — you're too heavy!* ◇ *She lifted herself up on one elbow.* ◇ *She lifted up the box and put it on the table.*
NOTE Lift sb/sth/yourself can also be used with this meaning.
◆ v + n/pron + adv ♦ v + adv + n

light /laɪt/ (lit, lit /lɪt/)

'light on/upon sb/sth (*literary*) 1 to suddenly see sb/sth: *Her gaze lighted on her daughter.* 2 to suddenly find sb/sth or think of sb/sth: *The research team has lit upon important new material.* ⟨SYN⟩ **hit on sth**
NOTE Lighted is also used for the past tense and past participle.
⟨SYN⟩ **alight on/upon sb/sth**
◆ v + prep

,light 'up; ,light sth 'up 1 to become or to make sth bright with light or colour: *She switched the monitor on and the screen lit up.* ◇ *Flashes of lightning lit up the sky.* ◇ *The waterfall was lit up at night with pink and green floodlights.* 2 if a person's eyes or face **light up**, or sth **lights them up**, they become bright with excitement or happiness: *Her eyes lit up when she saw them.* ◇ *A smile of delight lit up his face.* ◇ *His face lit up with pleasure.* 3 (*informal*) to begin to smoke a cigarette, etc: *She took out a cigarette and lit up.* ◇ *He lit up one cigarette after another.*
◆ v + adv ♦ v + adv + n ♦ v + pron + adv ♦ v + n + adv (*less frequent*)

'light upon sb/sth = LIGHT ON/UPON SB/STH

lighten /'laɪtn/

,lighten 'up (*spoken*) used to tell sb to be less serious or to complain or worry less about sth: *Come on, lighten up! It was only a joke.*
◆ v + adv

,**lighten sth 'up** (*informal*) to make sth more cheerful and less serious or depressing: *He did his best to **lighten things up**.* ◇ *She tried to lighten up her speech with a few jokes.*
⬥ v + n/pron + adv ♦ v + adv + n

liken /'laɪkən/

'**liken sb/sth to sb/sth** (*formal*) to compare sb/sth to someone or something else and say that they are similar: *He has been likened to a young George Best.* ◇ *She likened the building to a ship.*
NOTE Liken sb/sth to sb/sth is often used in the passive.
⬥ v + n/pron + prep

limber /'lɪmbə(r)/

,**limber 'up** (**for sth**) to do exercise to prepare to take part in a sport, a race, etc.; to warm up: *The players were limbering up for the game.* ◇ (*figurative*) *The candidates are already limbering up for the election campaign.*
SYN warm up
⬥ v + adv

limit /'lɪmɪt/

'**limit sth to sb/sth** to make sth exist or happen only in a particular place or within a particular group: *Violent crime is not limited to big cities.* ◇ *The teaching of history should not be limited to dates and figures.*
SYN confine sth to sb/sth
NOTE Limit sth to sb/sth is usually used in the passive.
⬥ v + n/pron + prep

line /lam/

,**line 'up 1** (**for sth/to do sth**) if people **line up**, they form a line, standing one behind the other or beside each other: *A group of people were lining up for tickets.* ◇ *They lined up to shake the President's hand.* ◇ *The runners lined up at the starting line.* → *see also* QUEUE UP (FOR STH/TO DO STH) **2** to join with sb in order to do sth: *Local groups are lining up against the new development.* ◇ *Several newspapers lined up to demand his resignation.*
⬥ v + adv
▶ '**line-up** *n* [usually sing.] a row of people that is formed so that sb who saw a crime can try to recognize the person who did it: *She picked him out of a line-up* (= she recognized him as the person who committed the crime).
→ *see also* LINE-UP at LINE SB/STH UP

,**line 'up**; ,**line sth 'up** to be, or to put sth, in the correct position in relation to sth else: *The three holes should all line up* (*with each other*).
⬥ v + adv ♦ v + n/pron + adv ♦ v + adv + n

,**line sb/sth 'up 1** to arrange people or things in a line or a row: *She lined the children up for the photograph.* ◇ *His CDs were lined up on the shelf.* **2** (**for sb/sth**) to organize an event or an activity; to arrange for sb to do something at an event, a competition, etc: *He's lined up a band for the party.* ◇ *We've lined up a few things for the weekend.* ◇ *They already had a buyer for their car lined up.*
⬥ v + adv + n ♦ v + pron + adv ♦ v + n + adv (*less frequent*)
▶ '**line-up** *n* [usually sing.] **1** a group of people who have been chosen or invited to take part in an event: *an impressive line-up of performers* ◇ *The line-up for tonight's game is still not known.* **2** a set of events, people or things: *Several new dramas are included in the line-up of programmes for next year.*
→ *see also* LINE-UP at LINE UP

linger /'lɪŋɡə(r)/

,**linger 'on 1** to remain for a long time: *The memory of that day lingers on in the minds of local people.* ◇ *The smell lingered on for days after.* **2** to remain alive, but becoming gradually weaker: *We should be thankful that she didn't linger on.*
NOTE Linger is used more frequently with the same meanings.
⬥ v + adv

link /lɪŋk/

,**link 'up 1** (**with sb**) to join with sb in order to do sth together: *We are trying to link up with other charities working in the area.* **2** (**with sth**) to make a connection with sth: *The two spacecraft will link up in orbit.*
⬥ v + adv

,**link sb/sth 'up** (**to sth**) to connect sb/sth with someone or something else: *The alarm is linked up to the police station.* ◇ *The new network can link us up to similar organizations around the country.*
⬥ v + n/pron + adv ♦ v + adv + n
▶ '**link-up** *n* a connection between two systems or machines: *They did a live satellite link-up with the show.*

liquor /'lɪkə(r)/

be/get ,liquored 'up (*AmE, informal*) to be/get drunk: *We got liquored up on Saturday night.*
⬥ be/get + v + adv

listen /'lɪsn/

'**listen for sb/sth**; ,**listen 'out for sb/sth** to listen carefully to see if you can hear sb/sth: *She lay awake, listening out for the sound of the key in*

the lock. ◇ *Will you listen out for the phone while I'm in the bath?* ◇ *The children were asked to listen out for a word beginning with 'sh'.*
OBJ **sound, door**
⬥ v + prep ♦ v + adv + prep

,**listen 'in 1 (on/to sth)** to listen to sth or sb secretly: *Have you been listening in on my phone calls?* ◇ *They were sure that the police were listening in to their conversations.* **2 (to sth)** to listen to a radio programme, etc: *Listen in on Friday for our interview with George Michael.*
⬥ v + adv

,**listen 'out for sb/sth** = LISTEN FOR SB/STH, LISTEN OUT FOR SB/STH

,**listen 'up** (*spoken, especially AmE*) used to tell sb to pay attention to what you are going to say: *Listen up, everyone — this is important!*
⬥ v + adv

live /lɪv/

'**live by sth** to follow a particular belief or set of principles: *Some people live by the rule 'anything for the sake of peace'.* ◇ *Women working in a man's world have to live by men's rules.*
OBJ **principles, standards**
⬥ v + prep
IDM **live by your 'wits** to earn money or survive by clever and sometimes dishonest means: *He had no money and was living by his wits and by selling a few paintings.*

'**live by sth**; '**live by doing sth** to earn the money that you need by using or doing a particular thing: *people who live by the land* (= for example, farmers) ◇ *She lived by giving private lessons.*
⬥ v + prep

,**live sth 'down** to make people forget sth very embarrassing or bad that you have done in the past: *I can't believe I fell in the river — I'll never be able to live it down.*
NOTE Live sth down is not used in the passive.
⬥ v + n/pron + adv ♦ v + adv + n

'**live for sb/sth** to consider sb/sth as the main purpose of or the most important person or thing in your life: *She lives for her work.* ◇ *What have I got to live for now?*
⬥ v + prep

,**live 'in** to live at the place where you work or study: *They have a nanny living in.* ◇ (*BrE*) *Most students live in during their first year.*
OPP **live out**
⬥ v + adv
▶ '**live-in** *adj* [only before noun] **1** (of an employee) living in the house where they work: *a live-in housekeeper/position* **2** (of a boyfriend, girlfriend, etc.) living in the same house as their sexual partner: *a live-in lover/boyfriend*

'**live off sb/sth** (*disapproving*) to get the money or the things you need from sb/sth: *You can't live off your parents forever!* ◇ *He had to live off his savings.*
⬥ v + prep

'**live off sth** to eat one type of food very frequently or all the time: *When I was a student I lived off bread and cheese.*
→ *see also* LIVE ON STH 2
⬥ v + prep
IDM **live off the 'land** to eat food that you can grow, kill or find yourself: *The army was forced to live off the land.* ◇ *It's a farming area and most of the people still live off the land.* **live off the fat of the 'land** (*disapproving*) to have enough money to be able to buy expensive food, drink, clothes, etc: *It was a time when landlords and merchants lived off the fat of the land.*

,**live 'on** to continue to live or exist: *He may be dead but his music lives on.*
⬥ v + adv

'**live on sth 1** to have a particular amount of money with which to buy everything you need: *How did you manage to live on a student grant?* ◇ *They don't earn enough to live on.* **2** to eat a particular type of food very frequently or all the time: *She was living on fruit and raw vegetables.* ◇ *birds that live on insects* → *see also* LIVE OFF STH
⬥ v + prep

,**live 'out** (*BrE*) to live away from the place where you work or study: *I lived out during my final year at college.*
OPP **live in**
⬥ v + adv

,**live 'out sth**; ,**live it/them 'out 1** to do in reality sth that you think about, believe in, dream of, etc: *On holiday in Texas I lived out my childhood fantasy of being a cowboy.* **OBJ** **fantasy, dream 2** to spend your life or the rest of your life in a particular way: *She lived out the rest of her life in poverty.* ◇ *Maybe I'll live out my days in the peace of the mountains.* **OBJ** **life, days**
NOTE A noun must always follow out, but a pronoun comes between the verb and out.
⬥ v + adv + n ♦ v + pron + adv

,**live 'through sth** to experience sth difficult or unpleasant and survive: *He lived through both world wars.* ◇ *It's something I never want to live through again.*
⬥ v + prep

'**live together** (*also* '**live with sb**) **1** to live in the same house, flat/apartment, etc: *There are six students living together in the house.* ◇ *I'm living in a flat with Meg.* **2** to share a home and have a sexual relationship, but without being married
⬥ v + adv ♦ v + prep

,live it 'up (*informal*) to have a very exciting and enjoyable time, usually spending a lot of money: *I've heard that Tom's living it up in L.A.*
◈ v + it + adv

,live 'up to sth to behave as well as or be as good or successful as people expect: *The hotel failed to live up to expectations.* ◊ *Mr. Mean lived up to his name and died a millionaire.* ◊ *I've got a lot to live up to.*
[OBJ] **expectations, name, reputation**
◈ v + adv + prep

'live with sb = LIVE TOGETHER

'live with sth; 'live with yourself to accept an unpleasant situation and continue with your life and work: *You might not like the situation, but you'll have to learn to live with it.* ◊ *She wouldn't be able to live with herself if she hurt him.*
◈ v + prep

liven /'laɪvn/

,liven 'up; ,liven sb/sth 'up to become or to make sb/sth more lively, interesting or exciting: *She livened up when Alan asked her to dance.* ◊ *Put some music on to liven things up.* ◊ *A few pictures would liven up the room.*
[SYN] **brighten up; brighten sth up**
◈ v + adv ◆ v + n/pron + adv ◆ v + adv + n

load /ləʊd; AmE loʊd/

,load sb/sth 'down (with sth) **1** to give sb/sth too many things to carry: *She was loaded down with books.* **2** to give sb/sth too much work or too many responsibilities: *We've been loaded down with work recently.*
[NOTE] **Load sb/sth down** is usually used in the passive.
◈ v + n/pron + adv ◆ v + adv + n

,load 'up (with sth), **,load sth 'up** (with sth) to put a lot of things in/on sth, especially a vehicle: *Bring the car to the door and we'll help you load up.* ◊ *I loaded up the van with all my possessions.* ◊ *We've loaded up all the furniture and are just about ready to go.*
[NOTE] **Load** and **load sth** are used more frequently with this meaning.
◈ v + adv ◆ v + adv + n ◆ v + n/pron + adv

loaf /ləʊf; AmE loʊf/

,loaf a'round; ,loaf a'round sth (*BrE also ,loaf a'bout, ,loaf a'bout sth*) (*informal*) to spend your time in a lazy way, doing very little: *kids loafing about with nothing to do* ◊ *She just loafs around the streets all day.*
◈ v + adv ◆ v + prep

loan /ləʊn; AmE loʊn/

,loan sth/sb 'out (to sb) to lend sth/sb to sb, sometimes in return for money: *Several players have been loaned out to other teams.* ◊ *Sometimes we loan out these buses.*
◈ v + adv + n ◆ v + n/pron + adv

lock /lɒk; AmE lɑːk/

,lock sb a'way 1 = LOCK STH UP 1 **2** = LOCK SB UP/AWAY *He was locked away for the rest of his life.*

,lock sth a'way = LOCK STH UP *She locked the money away in a cupboard.*

,lock yourself a'way = LOCK STH UP 1 to shut yourself in a place away from other people so that you are not disturbed: *He locked himself away (in his room) until he'd finished his work.*
[SYN] **shut yourself away (from sb/sth)**
→ *see also* LOCK SB UP/AWAY
◈ v + pron + adv

,lock sb/sth 'in; ,lock yourself 'in to put sb/sth/yourself in a room or building and lock the door: *The prisoners are locked in every night.* ◊ *He rushed to his bedroom and locked himself in.*
◈ v + n/pron + adv ◆ v + adv + n
▶ **'lock-in** n (*BrE*) an occasion when customers are locked into a bar or pub after it has closed so that they can continue drinking privately

be 'locked in sth to be involved in a difficult or unpleasant situation, especially an argument or a legal dispute, that seems unlikely to end soon: *The parents are locked in a bitter legal battle over the future of the twins.*
◈ be + v + prep

,lock 'in on sth = LOCK ONTO STH

be ,locked 'into sth (*also* become/get ,locked 'into sth*) to be in a particular situation, or behave in a particular way, that you cannot change: *The government is locked into a policy of reducing taxes.* ◊ *Older horses can get locked into bad habits.*
◈ be + v + prep

,lock 'onto sth (*also ,lock 'in on sth*) if a weapon that is sent through the air **locks onto** sth that it is aimed at, it finds it and follows it: *The missile can lock onto a target from a kilometre away.*
[OBJ] **target**
[NOTE] **Lock onto sth** can be used in the passive: *The missile was locked onto the target.*
◈ v + prep ◆ v + adv + prep

,lock sb/sth 'out 1 (*also ,lock sb/sth 'out of sth*) to prevent sb/sth from entering a place by locking a door: *I arrived home to find the landlady had locked me out.* **2** to prevent workers from entering their place of work until they agree to the conditions given by the employer: *The management will lock out anyone who refuses to sign the new contract.*

⊕ v + n/pron + adv ◆ v + adv + n

   1 also v + n/pron + adv + prep

▶ **'lockout** *n* a situation when an employer refuses to let workers enter their place of work until they agree to particular conditions: *The strikers faced a lockout.*

,lock yourself 'out; ,lock yourself 'out of sth to accidentally leave your keys inside a car, building, etc. when you go out, so that you are unable to get inside again: *I've managed to lock myself out of my room three times!*

⊕ v + pron + adv ◆ v + pron + adv + prep

,lock 'up; ,lock sth 'up to make a building safe by locking the doors and windows: *Make sure you lock up before you leave.* ◇ *She locked the shop up and went home.*

⊕ v + adv ◆ v + n/pron + adv ◆ v + adv + n

▶ **'lock-up** *n* a small shop that the owner does not live in; a place that the owner does not need and rents to sb else, for example to keep a car in: *a lock-up garage/shop*

→ *see also* LOCK-UP at LOCK SB UP/AWAY

,lock sb 'up/a'way (*informal*) to put sb in prison or in a guarded hospital: *People like that should be locked up!* ◇ *They should lock her up and throw away the key.*

⊕ v + n/pron + adv ◆ v + adv + n

▶ **'lock-up** *n* a small prison where prisoners are kept for a short time

→ *see also* LOCK-UP at LOCK UP, LOCK STH UP

,lock sth 'up 1 (*also* **,lock sth a'way**) to put sth valuable in a safe place and lock it: *Lock your valuables up in the safe.* **2** (*in sth*) to invest money in sth and not be able to turn it into cash to spend: *Huge sums of money are locked up in pension funds.* OBJ **capital, money** SYN **tie sth up** NOTE In this meaning **lock sth up** is nearly always used in the passive.

⊕ v + n/pron + adv ◆ v + adv + n

log /lɒg; *AmE* lɔ:g, lɑ:g/ (-gg-)

log 'in/'on; ,log 'into/'onto sth (*computing*) to perform the actions that allow you to begin using a computer system: *I got an error message when I tried to log in/on.* ◇ *The password allows the user to log into the system.*

OBJ **system, network, computer** OPP **log off/out; log off/out of sth** NOTE Log into/onto sth can be used in the pattern: *I was logged onto the Internet.*

⊕ v + adv ◆ v + prep

log 'off/'out; ,log 'off/'out of sth (*computing*) to perform the actions that allow you to finish using a computer system: *Try logging off and logging on again.*

OBJ **system, computer** OPP **log in/on; log into/onto sth** NOTE Log off/out of sth can be used in the pattern: *Wait until all the users are logged off.*

⊕ v + adv ◆ v + prep

loll /lɒl/

,loll a'round; ,loll a'round sth (*BrE also* **,loll a'bout, ,loll a'bout sth**) to sit, lie or stand in a relaxed way, doing very little: *There were several kids lolling around outside the club.* ◇ *Jim should get a job instead of lolling around the house all day.*

⊕ v + adv ◆ v + prep

long /lɒŋ; *AmE* lɔ:ŋ/

'long for sb/sth; 'long for sb to do sth to want sb/sth very much: *to long for a baby* ◇ *I was longing for a chat and a good laugh.* ◇ *She found herself longing for her visitors to leave.*

⊕ v + prep ◆ v + prep + n/pron + to inf

▶ **'longed-for** *adj* [only before noun] that sb has been wanting or hoping for very much: *a longed-for child*

look /lʊk/

~ about	~ into
~ across	~ on
~ after	~ out
176 ~ ahead	~ out for
~ around	~ out on/over
~ at	~ over
~ away	~ round
~ back	178 ~ through
~ down	~ to
~ down on	~ up
~ for	~ up to
177 ~ forward to	~ upon
~ in	

,look a'bout; ,look a'bout sth; ,look a'bout you (*BrE*) = LOOK AROUND, LOOK AROUND STH, LOOK AROUND YOU

,look a'cross/'over (*at/to sb/sth*) to look quickly across a room: *I looked across to where they were sitting.* ◇ *She knew I was there, but she didn't look over at me.*

⊕ v + adv

,look 'after sb/sth/yourself (*especially BrE*) **1** to make sure that sb/sth is safe; take care of sb/sth: *His parents are looking after the children for the weekend.* ◇ *She doesn't look after her clothes.* ◇ *Sophie will look after the visitors.* ◇ *They're old enough to look after themselves now* (= they don't need any help). ◇ *Would you mind looking after my bag for a minute?* ◇ *See you soon — look after yourself* (= when saying goodbye to sb). NOTE Take care of sb is used in American and British English with the same meaning: *My mother is going to look after/take care of the kids*

while we're away. In more formal language you can also use **care for sb**: *His job involves caring for the elderly.* → *see also* BRING SB UP 1 **2** to make sure that things happen to sb's advantage: *He's good at looking after his own interests.*
NOTE Look after sb/sth can be used in the passive: *He needs to be properly looked after.*
✧ v + adv

,look 'after sth (*BrE*) to deal with sth; to be responsible for sth: *Their accountant looks after the financial side of things.*
SYN **attend to sth** (*more formal*)
NOTE Look after sth can be used in the passive: *Everything's being looked after.* ◆ **Take care of sth** is used in American and British English with the same meaning.
✧ v + prep

,look a'head (to sth) to think about what is going to happen in the future: *The team is looking ahead to next season.* ◊ *Looking ahead to the weekend, the weather will stay fine.*
✧ v + adv

,look a'round (*BrE also* ,look 'round) **1** (at sb/sth) to turn your head in order to see sb/sth behind you: *The people in front kept looking round at us.* ◊ *He looked round to see if I was still there.* **2** (for sb/sth) to examine various choices or possibilities: *We're looking around for a new car.*
✧ v + adv

,look a'round; ,look a'round sth (*BrE also* ,look 'round, ,look 'round sth) to visit a place or a building as a tourist: *Take your time looking around.* ◊ *They've gone to look round the cathedral.* ◊ *I spent the day looking around the town.*
✧ v + adv ◆ v + prep

,look a'round; ,look a'round sth; ,look a'round you (*BrE also* ,look a'bout/'round, ,look a'bout/'round sth, ,look a'bout/'round you) to turn your head in different directions so that you can see sth or see what is there: *She came into the room, looked around, then went out.* ◊ *He looked round the classroom angrily.* ◊ *I looked about me at the other passengers.*
✧ v + adv ◆ v + prep

'look at sb/sth **1** to turn your eyes towards sb/sth so that you can see them/it: *Don't look at me like that!* ◊ *What are you looking at?* **2** to examine sth/sb closely: *I'd like the doctor to look at him.* ◊ *Can you look at this watch for me? I think it might be broken.* **NOTE** In this meaning, **look at sb/sth** can be used in the passive: *I took the car to the garage to get it looked at.* **3** (*usually used in negative sentences or questions*) to consider or be prepared to accept sb/sth: *They wouldn't even look at someone wanting part-time work.* **4** used to draw sb's attention to sb/sth, often as an example that you want them to follow or not follow: *I wouldn't take advice from her — just look at the mess she's made of her own life!* ◊

He left school without any qualifications, but look at him now! (= he is very successful now) ◊ *Money doesn't always bring happiness — just look at Ian* (= he is rich but not happy).
✧ v + prep

'look at sth **1** to read sth, usually quickly, without reading all the details: *She sat in the waiting room, looking at a magazine.* **NOTE** In this meaning **look at sth** can be used in the passive: *Don't hand the form in until it's been looked at by a teacher.* **2** to think about or study sth: *Have you looked at the possibility of adopting a child?* ◊ *The film looks at the events leading up to the war.* **NOTE** In this meaning, **look at sth** can be used in the passive: *Four possible routes were looked at for the new road.* **3** to consider sth in a particular way: *If you look at it like that, it's a good thing we didn't go.* **4** (*informal*) (*always used in the progressive tenses*) to have to consider or deal with sth; to be faced with sth: *You're looking at £600 to get the car fixed.* ◊ *If he's found guilty he's looking at a six-year prison sentence.*
✧ v + prep

,look a'way (from sb/sth) to look in the opposite direction; to turn your eyes away from sb/sth: *She looked at him then looked away.* ◊ *He mumbled a reply and looked away from me.*
✧ v + adv

,look 'back (at/on/to sth) to think about sth that has happened in your past: *Looking back, I'm not surprised she left.* ◊ *He looked back on his time in England with a sense of nostalgia.*
✧ v + adv

IDM never/not look 'back (*informal*) to become more and more successful: *He started work on a market stall in 1970 and he's never looked back.*

,look 'down to turn your eyes downwards to the floor, especially because you are embarrassed, shy, etc: *The little boy blushed and looked down.* ◊ *She looked down at her hands.*
✧ v + adv

,look 'down on sb/sth to consider sb/sth as less good or important than yourself: *She tends to look down on people who haven't been to college.* ◊ *They looked down on our little house.*
NOTE Look down on sb/sth can be used in the passive: *He was looked down on at school.*
✧ v + adv + prep

'look for sb/sth to search for sb/sth, either because you have lost them/it, or because you need them/it: *Sue's been looking for you.* ◊ *'Can I help you?' 'Yes, I'm looking for this shirt in blue.'* (= in a shop/store)
NOTE Seek sb/sth is only used with this meaning in very formal language or in newspapers.
✧ v + prep

'look for sth **1** to hope for sth or expect sth: *The examiners will be looking for good grammar and spelling.* ◊ *This could be just the opportunity he* *been looking for.* **2** to search for sth; to try to find sth: *They were looking for an easy solution to the problem.* **NOTE** **Seek sth** is only used with this meaning in very formal language, or in newspapers.

✦ v + prep

IDM **look for 'trouble** to behave in a way that is likely to cause an argument, a fight, etc: *Are you looking for trouble?*

▸ **un'looked-for** *adj* (*formal*) not expected: *unlooked-for success*

,**look 'forward to sth**; ,**look 'forward to doing sth** to feel excited about sth that is going to happen because you expect to enjoy it: *Are you looking forward to your trip?* ◇ *I'm not looking forward to going to the dentist.* ◇ *We're looking forward to the concert!* ◇ *I look forward to hearing from you* (= at the end of a letter).

NOTE **Look forward to sth** can be used in the passive: *The President's visit is eagerly looked forward to.* ♦ Remember that **to** is a preposition in this phrasal verb and must be followed by a noun or the *-ing* form of a verb.

✦ v + adv + prep

,**look 'in** (**on sb**) to make a short visit to a place: *I asked Sarah to look in on her grandmother on her way home.* ◇ *The doctor will look in again this evening.*

✦ v + adv

,**look 'into sth** to examine sth or consider it carefully: *The committee is looking into the matter.* ◇ *The manager is looking into your complaint.* ◇ *We're looking into the possibility of moving to France.*

NOTE **Look into sth** can be used in the passive: *This situation should be looked into.*

✦ v + prep

,**look 'on 1** to watch an event or an incident without taking part in it yourself: *People looked on in alarm as the car began to roll down the hill.* ◇ *Passers-by just looked on as he was attacked.* **2** (**with sb**) (*AmE*) to share a book, etc. with another person in a group: *There aren't enough books so you'll have to look on with your neighbor.*

✦ v + adv

▸ **'onlooker** *n* a person who watches sth without becoming involved in it: *A crowd of onlookers formed around the fight.*

'**look on sb/sth** (*also* '**look upon sb/sth** *more formal*) [+ adv/prep] to consider sb/sth in a particular way: *I look on you as my friend.* ◇ *She looked upon the assignment as a challenge.* ◇ *I looked on life in a different way after that.* ◇ *She was always looked on with distrust.*

NOTE **Look on/upon sb/sth** can be used in the passive: *The job was looked upon as glamorous.*

✦ v + prep

,**look 'out** used to tell sb to be careful, especially when there is some danger: *Look out! There's a car coming.* ◇ *You're going to burn that food if you don't look out.*

SYN **watch out**

✦ v + adv

,**look sth 'out** (**for sb/sth**) (*BrE*) to search for something from among your possessions: *I'll look out that book for you.*

NOTE **Look sth out** cannot be used in the passive.

✦ v + adv + n ♦ v + n/pron + adv

,**look 'out for sb/yourself** to take care of sb/yourself and think about their/your own interests: *Once he was in London he had to look out for himself.* ◇ *Emily's brothers always looked out for her.*

✦ v + adv + prep

,**look 'out for sb/sth 1** to try to find sb/sth or meet sb: *I was looking out for Pete but I didn't see him.* ◇ *Look out for this film at your local cinema.* **2** to try to avoid sth bad happening or doing sth bad: *Look out for pickpockets.*

SYN **watch out for sb/sth**

✦ v + adv + prep

▸ **'lookout** *n* **1** a place where sb watches from to see if there is any danger: *a lookout post/tower* **2** a person who watches for danger: *The burglars posted a lookout outside the house.*

,**look 'out on/over sth** (of a room, etc.) to have a view of sth: *Our room looked out over the square.*

✦ v + adv + prep

,**look 'over** (**at/to sb/sth**) = LOOK ACROSS/OVER (AT/TO SB/STH)

,**look 'over sth 1** to make a tour of a place: *We were invited to look over the new classrooms.* **2** to read sth quickly: *I need to look over my notes before the test.* ◇ *Your tutor will look over your work with you.*

✦ v + prep

,**look sb/sth 'over** to inspect or examine sb/sth to see how good, big, etc. it is: *He looked the painting over carefully.* ◇ *I'd like the doctor to look him over.* ◇ *We'll get a mechanic to look the car over before we buy it.*

SYN **check sb/sth over; examine sb/sth**

NOTE When **look sb/sth over** is used with the pronouns *it* and *them* referring to things, these pronouns can also come after **over**: *We'd like a mechanic to look over it for us.*

✦ v + n/pron + adv ♦ v + adv + n

,**look 'round** (*BrE*) = LOOK AROUND

,**look 'round**; ,**look 'round sth** (*BrE*) = LOOK AROUND, LOOK AROUND STH

,**look 'round**; ,**look 'round sth**; ,**look 'round you** (*BrE*) = LOOK AROUND, LOOK AROUND STH, LOOK AROUND YOU

look 'through sb to look at sb and not show that you have seen or recognized them: *I smiled at him, but he just looked straight through me.*
◈ v + prep

look 'through sth 1 to read sth quickly: *She looked through her notes before the exam.* **2** to read sth quickly: *I looked through the paper while I was waiting.* **3** to examine a collection of things or what is inside sth: *What are you doing looking through my bag?*
◈ v + prep

look to sb/sth (for sth/to do sth) to rely on sb/sth or expect sb to provide sth or do sth: *They looked to us for help.* ◇ *We must look to other means to generate the funds we need.* ◇ *Many students can't look to their parents for financial support.*
SYN **turn to sb**
◈ v + prep

look to sth (*especially BrE*) **1** to think about something that will happen in the future: *We are looking to the future with confidence.* OBJ **the future 2** (*formal*) to make sure that sth is safe or in good condition; to think about how to improve sth: *You should look to your own behaviour before criticizing others.*
◈ v + prep

look 'up 1 (from sth) to raise your eyes: *She looked up from her book and smiled.* **2** (*informal*) (*usually used in the progressive tenses*) (of a business, a situation etc.) to become better; to improve: *Things started to look up for me after I got a job.* ◇ *Business is looking up at last.*
◈ v + adv

look sb 'up (*informal*) to visit or contact sb when you are in the place where they live, especially when you have not seen them for a long time: *Look me up next time you're in London.*
NOTE **Look sb up** cannot be used in the passive.
◈ v + n/pron + adv ◆ v + adv + n (*less frequent*)
IDM **look sb 'up and 'down** to look at sb suspiciously or in a careful or critical way

look sth 'up to search for a word or some information in a dictionary or another book: *I looked the word up in the dictionary.* ◇ *Hang on, I'll just look up her telephone number.*
◈ v + n/pron + adv ◆ v + adv + n

look 'up to sb to admire or respect sb: *She always looked up to her older sister.*
NOTE **Look up to sb** can be used in the passive: *She was looked up to by the rest of her family.*
◈ v + adv + prep

look upon sb/sth = LOOK ON SB/STH

loom /luːm/

loom a'head if sth dangerous, difficult or unpleasant **looms ahead**, it is likely to happen soon: *Further problems are looming ahead.*
◈ v + adv

loom 'up to appear as a large shape that is not clear, often in a way that seems frightening or threatening: *A dark shape loomed up out of the fog.*
NOTE **Loom up** is usually followed by an adverb or a phrase beginning with a preposition: *A man loomed up out of the darkness.* ◆ **Loom** is also used with this meaning.
◈ v + adv

loosen /ˈluːsn/

loosen 'up (*informal*) to become more relaxed and comfortable: *He began to loosen up and enjoy the evening.*
◈ v + adv

loosen 'up; **loosen sb/sth 'up** to relax your muscles or parts of the body, or make them relax, before taking exercise, etc: *I swam a short distance to loosen up.* ◇ *A massage will help loosen you up.* ◇ *These exercises will loosen up your shoulders.*
◈ v + adv ◆ v + n/pron + adv ◆ v + adv + n

lop /lɒp; *AmE* lɑːp/ **(-pp-)**

lop sth 'off; **lop sth 'off sth 1** to remove sth from sth, especially branches from a tree, by cutting it: *Several branches had been lopped off (the tree).* ◇ *They lopped 20p off the price of each unit.*
SYN **chop sth off, chop sth off sth**; **cut sth off, cut sth off sth 2** to make sth smaller or less: *The new rail link has lopped an hour off the journey.*
SYN **knock sth off, knock sth off sth**
◈ v + n/pron + adv ◆ v + adv + n ◆ v + n/pron + prep

lord /lɔːd; *AmE* lɔːrd/

lord it over sb to behave in a superior way to sb: *She likes to lord it over the junior staff.*
◈ v + it + prep

lose /luːz/ **(lost, lost** /lɒst; *AmE* lɔːst/**)**

lose yourself in sth to become so interested in sth that you are not aware of anything else: *I soon lost myself in the excitement of the play.*
◈ v + pron + prep

lose 'out (on sth) (*informal*) to be unsuccessful in getting sth that you want or think you should have: *Some youngsters are taking day jobs and losing out on schooling.* ◇ *If things go wrong, I'm the one who'll lose out.* ◇ *While the stores make big profits, it's the customers who lose out.*
◈ v + adv

lose 'out to sb/sth (*informal*) to not get the business you expected or hoped to get, because sb else has got it: *Small stores are losing out to the big supermarkets.*
◈ v + adv + prep

lounge /laʊndʒ/

ˌlounge aˈbout/aˈround; ˌlounge aˈbout/ aˈround sth to spend your time in a relaxed way doing very little: *She was always lounging about while the rest of us were working!* ◊ *They were lounging around the hotel pool.*
> **SYN** **laze around, laze around sth; lie about/ around, lie about/around sth**
> ✪ v + adv ✦ v + prep

louse /laʊs/

ˌlouse sth ˈup (*slang*) to spoil or ruin sth: *He loused up my promotion chances.*
> **SYN** **mess sth up** (*BrE*)
> ✪ v + adv + n ✦ v + n/pron + adv

luck /lʌk/

ˌluck ˈinto sth (*AmE, informal*) to get sth you want by chance: *I lucked into some free tickets.*
> ✪ v + prep

ˌluck ˈout (*AmE, informal*) to be very lucky: *We lucked out in a big way.* ◊ *We really lucked out with the weather.*
> ✪ v + adv

lug /lʌg/ (-gg-)

ˌlug sth aˈround (*BrE also* ˌlug sth aˈbout, ˌlug sth ˈround) (with you) (*informal*) to carry or pull sth large, awkward or heavy from one place to another, or everywhere you go: *Can I leave my bag somewhere? It's very heavy to lug around.*
> **SYN** **carry sth around** (with you) (*more formal*), **cart sth around** (with you)
> ✪ v + n/pron + adv ✦ v + adv + n

lull /lʌl/

ˌlull sb ˈinto sth; ˌlull sb ˈinto doing sth to make sb feel confident and relaxed, especially so that they do not expect it when sth bad happens: *Don't let success in the test lull you into thinking you do not need to work hard.* ◊ *His calm manner lulled me into a false sense of security* (= made me feel safe with him when I was not).
> ✪ v + n/pron + prep

lumber /ˈlʌmbə(r)/

be/get ˈlumbered with sb/sth (*BrE, informal*) to give sb a responsibility or a problem that they do not want and cannot get rid of: *I'm sorry you've been lumbered with driving me home.* ◊ *The movie was about sb who sees a murder and then gets lumbered with the dead man's child.*
> ✪ be/get + v + prep

lump /lʌmp/

ˌlump A and B toˈgether; ˈlump A with B; ˈlump A in with B (*informal*) to put or consider two or more people or things together in the same group: *A large number of plants are lumped together under the name of 'herbs'.* ◊ *You can't lump the elderly and the disabled together.* ◊ *You can't lump the elderly with the disabled.*
> **NOTE** **Lump sb/sth together** is often used in the passive.
> ✪ v + n/pron + adv ✦ v + adv + n ✦
>   v + n/pron + prep ✦ v + n/pron + adv + prep

lust /lʌst/

ˈlust after sb (*often disapproving*) to feel a strong sexual desire for sb
> **NOTE** **Lust after sb** can be used in the passive.
> ✪ v + prep

ˈlust after/for sth to have a strong desire to possess or have sth: *She was lusting after/for revenge.*
> **NOTE** **Lust after/for sth** can be used in the passive.
> ✪ v + prep

luxuriate /lʌgˈʒʊərieɪt; AmE -ˈʒʊr-/

luˈxuriate in sth (*formal*) to take great pleasure in sth that is very pleasant and relaxing: *I luxuriated in a long, hot bath.*
> ✪ v + prep

M m

magic /'mædʒɪk/ (**-ck-**)

magic sb/sth a'way/'up (*BrE*) to use magic to make sb/sth disappear or appear; to make sb/sth disappear or appear so quickly or suddenly that it seems as if you have used magic: *I wish my problems could be just magicked away.* ◇ *Sarah magicked up a wonderful meal in a very short time.*
⊕ v + adv + n ♦ v + n/pron + adv

mail /meɪl/

mail sth 'off (**to sb**) to send sth to sb by post/mail: *I mailed off an application the next day.*
OBJ **letter, package** **SYN** **post sth off** (*BrE*), **send sth off** (**to sb**)
NOTE You can also use **mail a letter**, etc., but this often refers to the action of putting the letter in the mailbox: *How much does it cost to mail a letter in Italy?*
⊕ v + n/pron + adv ♦ v + adv + n

mail sth 'out to send sth to a lot of different people or places at the same time: *Catalogues will be mailed out next week.*
SYN **send sth out**
NOTE Mail sth can also be used with this meaning.
⊕ v + n/pron + adv ♦ v + adv + n

major /'meɪdʒə(r)/

'major in sth (*AmE*) to study sth as your main subject at a university or college; to get a degree in that subject: *He majored in chemistry.*
⊕ v + prep

make /meɪk/ (**made, made** /meɪd/)

~ away with		181	~ over
~ for			~ over to
~ into			~ towards
~ of			~ up
~ off			~ up for
~ out		182	~ up to

make a'way with sth (*informal*) to steal sth and take it away with you: *Thieves made away with a computer and two televisions.*
→ *see also* MAKE OFF (WITH STH)
⊕ v + adv + prep

'make for sb/sth to move in the direction of sb/sth: *He jumped up and made for the door.* ◇ *She made straight for me.*
SYN **head for/towards sth**
⊕ v + prep

'make for sth (*not used in the progressive tenses*) to help to make sth possible; to produce a particular result: *The two-hour journey to work makes for a long day.* ◇ *The large print makes for easier reading.*
⊕ v + prep

'make sb/sth into sth to change sb/sth into sth: *They made the extra bedroom into a bathroom.* ◇ *You're trying to make her into something she isn't.* ◇ *Their story is being made into a movie.*
SYN **turn sb/sth into sth**
♦ v + n/pron + prep

'make sth of sb/sth to have an impression or an understanding of sb/sth: *What did you make of the play?* ◇ *I never knew quite what to make of Nick.* ◇ *The information we have is so confused, it's hard to make anything of it.*
⊕ v + n/pron + prep

make 'off (**with sth**) (*informal*) to hurry or rush away, especially when sb is trying to escape or has stolen sth: *The youths made off in a stolen car.* ◇ *Two boys made off with our bags.*
→ *see also* MAKE AWAY WITH STH
⊕ v + adv

make 'out (*informal*) **1** used to ask sb how they have managed or survived in a particular situation: *How are you making out in your new home?* ◇ *'Did you make out all right in the interview?' 'Yes, fine.'* **2** (**with sb**) (*AmE*) to kiss sb: *I saw her making out with Billy.*
⊕ v + adv

make 'out (**that ...**), **make sb/sth/yourself 'out to be ...** to claim that sth is true that may not be; to try to make people believe sth: *She made out (that) she was earning a fortune.* ◇ *Things aren't as bad as he makes out.* ◇ *The brochure made the place out to be a quiet resort.* ◇ *He makes himself out to be a big shot in the city.* ◇ *The hotel wasn't quite what it was made out to be* (= it was not as good as the brochure said it was).
⊕ v + adv ♦ v + n/pron + adv + to inf

make sb/sth 'out 1 to manage to see sb/sth or read sth: *I could just make out the shape of a house in the darkness.* ◇ *Can you make out his handwriting?* ◇ *She could just make out the sound of distant voices.* ◇ *I couldn't make out what he was saying.* **2** (*used in negative sentences and questions*) to understand sb/sth; to see the reasons why sth happens or why sb behaves in the way that they do: *She couldn't make out the expression on his face as he spoke.* ◇ *I can't make her out at all.* ◇ *He couldn't make out what was going on.* ◇ *You need to apply for a permit, as far as I can make out.* ◇ *How do you make that out*

(= how did you reach that conclusion)? NOTE
Make sb/sth out cannot be used in the passive
in this meaning.

✦ **1** v + adv + n ◆ v + pron + adv ◆ v + n + adv (*less frequent*)

2 v + adv + n ◆ v + n/pron + adv

,make sth 'out to write out or complete a form or
document: *He made out a cheque for £100.* ◇ *Who
shall I make the cheque out to* (= whose name
shall I write on it)? ◇ *Shall I make the invoice out
to the company?* ◇ *Would you make out a list for
me of everyone who's coming?*

OBJ **cheque, list**

NOTE In informal spoken language **make sb out
sth** can also be used: *I'll make you out a list.*

✦ v + adv + n ◆ v + n/pron + adv

,make sb/sth 'over (*informal, especially AmE*)
to change sb/sth to give them/it a new
appearance; to change sth to give it a new use:
*They decided to make over the whole house when
they moved in.*

✦ v + adv + n ◆ v + n/pron + adv

▶ **'makeover** *n* the process of improving the
appearance of a person or a place: *She won a complete makeover* (= new clothes, hairstyle, etc.) *in a
competition.*

,make sth 'over to sb to legally give sth you
own to sb else: *He made his estate over to his eldest
son.* ◇ *The government has made a lot of its
power over to the regions.* ◇ *The house was made
over to the charity three years ago.*

OBJ **estate, money**

✦ v + n/pron + adv + prep ◆ v + adv + n + prep

'make towards sb/sth to go in the direction of
sb/sth: *I saw them making towards the exit.*

✦ v + prep

**,make 'up; ,make sb/sth 'up; ,make your-
self 'up** (*BrE*) to put substances on your/sb's
eyes, lips and face to make them or yourself
attractive or to prepare for an appearance in the
theatre, on television, etc: *It takes her an hour to
make up before going on stage.* ◇ *She spends ages
making herself up.* ◇ *The children had been made
up to look like clowns.*

✦ v + adv ◆ v + n/pron + adv ◆ v + adv + n

▶ **,made-'up** *adj* wearing coloured substances on
the face: *a heavily made-up face* ◇ *She's always
carefully made-up.*

→ *see also* MADE-UP at MAKE STH UP

▶ **'make-up** *n* [U] substances that people put on
their eyes, lips and face to make themselves
more attractive, or that actors, etc. use: *to put on
your make-up* ◇ *a make-up bag*

→ *see also* MAKE-UP at MAKE STH UP

,make 'up; ,make it 'up (with sb) (*BrE*) to end a
quarrel or a dispute with sb: *Let's kiss and make
up.* ◇ *He's made it up with his parents.*

✦ v + adv ◆ v + it + adv

,make sth 'up 1 to invent sth, often in order to
deceive sb: *He was making up stories for the children.* ◇ *She made up an excuse for being late.* ◇
Did you think I was making it all up? OBJ **story,
excuse** NOTE It is much more common to say
make up a story than **invent** a story. **2** ,**make 'up
sth** to form a particular part of sth: *Rice makes
up a large part of their diet.* ◇ *Women make up
55% of the student population.* SYN **account for
sth; constitute sth** (*formal*) **3** ,**make 'up sth,
,make it/them 'up** to put sth together from several different things: *the cultures and races that
make up the nation* ◇ *The course is made up of
five modules.* SYN **constitute sth; be com-
posed of sth** (*formal*) NOTE A noun must always
follow **up**, but a pronoun comes between the verb
and **up**. → *see also* CONSIST OF STH/SB, CONSIST OF
DOING STH **4** to complete sth, especially a number or an amount: *We need one more player to
make up a team.* **5** to replace sth that has been
lost: *We need to make up lost time.* ◇ *He was late
for work but he made the time up the following
day.* **6** to prepare sth; to make sth ready to use:
The pharmacist made up the prescription (= the
medicine). ◇ *She made up a basket of food for the
picnic.* ◇ *The bed's already made up.* NOTE In
informal spoken language **make sb up sth** is
also used: *Can you make us up a packed lunch?*

✦ v + adv + n ◆ v + n/pron + adv

2 v + adv + n

3 v + adv + n ◆ v + pron + adv

IDM **make up your 'mind** to decide sth: *I like both
dresses — I can't make up my mind.* ◇ *Have you
made up your minds where to go for your honeymoon?* ◇ *You'll never persuade him to stay — his
mind's made up* (= he has definitely decided to
go). ◇ *Come on — it's make your mind up time!*

▶ **made-'up** *adj* invented; not true or real: *It was
a true story, not a made-up one.*

→ *see also* MADE-UP at MAKE UP, MAKE SB/STH UP,
MAKE YOURSELF UP

▶ **'make-up** *n* **1** the different things, people, qualities, etc. that combine to form something:
Aggression is part of our genetic make-up. ◇ *The
country has a complicated ethnic make-up.* **2**
(*AmE*) a school test that you were not present for
and that you take later: *The make-up will be on
Friday.* ◇ *a make-up test*

→ *see also* MAKE-UP at MAKE UP, MAKE SB/STH UP,
MAKE YOURSELF UP

,make 'up for sth; ,make 'up for doing sth
to do or provide sth good to balance or reduce the
effects of sth bad: *I bought myself a new dress to
make up for not getting the job.* ◇ *After two years
in prison he's now making up for lost time* (=
doing the things he was not able to do while he
was in prison).

SYN **compensate (for sth)** (*more formal*)

✦ v + adv + prep

make 'up for sth; **make it 'up to sb** (*informal*) to do sth good for sb because you have treated them badly or because they have done sth good for you: *An apology won't make up for the way you've behaved.* ◊ *He said he was sorry and promised to make it up to her.* ◊ *You've done me a real favour — I don't know how to make it up to you.*
⊕ v + adv + prep ♦ v + it + adv + prep

make 'up to sb (*BrE, informal, disapproving*) to be pleasant to sb in order to get an advantage for yourself: *He's always making up to the boss.*
[SYN] **kiss up to sb** (*AmE*), **suck up to sb**
⊕ v + adv + prep

map /mæp/ (-pp-)

map sth 'out to plan or arrange sth in detail: *I've mapped out a route for you.* ◊ *She felt as though her future had been mapped out for her.*
[OBJ] **future, route, strategy, plan**
⊕ v + adv + n ♦ v + pron + adv ♦ v + n + adv (*rare*)

march /mɑːtʃ; *AmE* mɑːrtʃ/

march 'on 1 to continue marching; to continue walking quickly: *I tried to speak to her but she just marched on.* **2** to move on or pass quickly: *Time marched on and we still hadn't finished.*
[SUBJ] **time**
⊕ v + adv

'march on sth to march to a place in order to attack it or make a protest: *Demonstrators marched on the American embassy.*
⊕ v + prep

march 'past; **march 'past sb/sth** (of soldiers) to march past an important person or building: *At 11 o'clock the army began to march past.*
⊕ v + adv ♦ v + prep
▶ **'march past** *n* a ceremony in which soldiers formally march past an important person, etc.

mark /mɑːk; *AmE* mɑːrk/

mark sb/sth 'down to reduce the marks given to sb in an examination, etc: *She was marked down for poor spelling.*
⊕ v + n/pron + adv ♦ v + adv + n

mark sth 'down 1 to reduce the price of sth: *All goods have been marked down by 15%.* [SYN] **reduce sth 2** to write something down; to make a note of something for future action: *The teacher had marked me down as absent.* ◊ *The council had the old square marked down for new development.*
⊕ v + n/pron + adv ♦ v + adv + n
▶ **'markdown** *n* a reduction in price: *a markdown of 12%*

mark sb 'down as sth (*BrE*) to consider sb a particular type of person: *I had him marked down as a promising player from the start.*
⊕ v + n/pron + adv + prep

mark sb/sth 'off (*BrE*) = MARK SB/STH OUT

mark sth 'off 1 to separate sth by marking a line between it and sth else: *We've marked the playing area off with a white line.* **2** to write or draw a mark beside a name or an item on a list, for example, for a particular reason: *The students I want to see are marked off on the list.*
⊕ v + n/pron + adv ♦ v + adv + n

mark sb/sth 'out (*BrE also* **mark sb/sth 'off** *less frequent*) to make sb or sth different from other people or things: *There was something about her which marked her out from the other students.*
⊕ v + n/pron + adv ♦ v + adv + n

mark sth 'out to draw lines to show the edges of sth: *She marked out a circle on the ground.*
⊕ v + adv + n ♦ v + n/pron + adv

mark sth 'up 1 to increase the price of sth: *Shares were marked up by 8%.* **2** to mark or correct a text: *The text had already been marked up with corrections* (= for printing).
[NOTE] **Mark sth up** is often used in the passive.
⊕ v + n/pron + adv ♦ v + adv + n
▶ **'mark-up** *n* [usually sing.] the difference between the cost of producing sth and the price it is sold at

marry /'mæri/ (**marries, marrying, married, married**)

marry be'neath you/yourself to marry sb who belongs to a lower social class than your own: *She thought her son was marrying beneath him.*
⊕ v + prep + pron

marry 'into sth to become a part of a family or a group because you have married sb who belongs to it: *She married into a wealthy family.*
[OBJ] **family, aristocracy**
⊕ v + prep

marry sb 'off (to sb) (*disapproving*) to get rid of a daughter or a son by finding a husband or wife for them: *He had married his daughter off to a man twice her age.*
⊕ v + n/pron + adv ♦ v + adv + n

marry 'up; **marry sth 'up (with sth)** (*BrE*) **1** to join up or connect successfully; to make two things or two parts do this: *The two halves of the structure didn't marry up.* ◊ *He couldn't marry up the two parts of the lock.* **2** to match; to make two things match: *The two versions of the story don't quite marry up.* ◊ *The lawyers couldn't marry up her story with the facts.*
⊕ v + adv ♦ v + adv + n ♦ v + n/pron + adv

STUDY PAGES

Tips on learning phrasal verbs   S2–4

Phrasal verb or single word?   S5

Are you a natural born student?   S6–7

Sport   S8–9

Computers   S10

Environmental problems   S11

Phrasal verbs in newspapers   S12

Phrasal verbs in business   S13

Phrasal verbs in informal language   S14–15

Using phrasal verbs in writing   S16–17

Using phrasal verbs in the passive   S18–19

New phrasal verbs   S20–21

The most common phrasal verbs   S22–25

Test yourself   S26

Phrasal verbs

Sometimes when you meet a multi-word verb, you can understand the meaning if you understand the verb and particle individually. For example, one meaning of **put down** is to place something somewhere: *Jack put the books down on the table.* But what does it mean in the following sentence? *She's always putting people down.* It does not mean that she places people somewhere, but that she is always criticizing them. When you see a verb followed by a particle but you cannot understand the meaning in the context from the meaning of the verb and the particle, you have found an idiomatic phrasal verb.

If you find other combinations of verbs and particles which seem to have a different meaning from the verb used on its own, this is likely to be a type of phrasal verb too. Verbs which are always followed by the same particle are another type. (For more information on the types of phrasal verbs found in this dictionary, look at page vi).

It is useful to learn these combinations of verbs and particles as a chunk of language. It is also essential to learn the context the verb usually appears in. For example, **put down** in the sense of *criticize* is used with a person or people as the object.

Recording Phrasal Verbs

The first thing you need to do is to find ways of recording the phrasal verbs you meet. It is a good idea to have a separate section for them in your vocabulary book. You should record the verb, its meaning and an example sentence to help you remember the context. Look at the example in the box.

You could also record a translation in your own language but you must make sure the context is the same.

verb	meaning
drop off	to fall asleep, often when you don't intend to
example:	He usually drops off in front of the television.
mess around	to do unimportant things rather than e.g. your work
example:	He failed his exams because he was messing around instead of studying.

The position of objects

If the verb has an object, it is useful to record the possible positions of the object. In this dictionary you will find this information about each verb after the definitions and examples. You can record the information as it is given in the dictionary, or by putting examples in your notebook.

try out	to test something
	v+n/pron+adv, v+adv+n
examples:	She tried out the new recipe on her children.
	She tried the new recipe out on her children.

Or you could record the verb as: **try sth out, try out sth** Remember that when the object is a pronoun, it must come between the verb and the particle: *She tried it out on the children.*

Collocations

Many phrasal verbs are typically used with particular nouns. It is a good idea to record these. This will help you with context and accuracy, e.g.

to find out <u>information</u>
to work out <u>a solution</u>
to phase in <u>changes</u>
to make up <u>a story</u>

to play down <u>a problem or the dangers of something</u>
to fill in <u>a document or form</u>
to break off <u>negotiations or formal talks</u>
to butt in on <u>a conversation</u>

You can use the common subjects or objects given in the dictionary to help you do this.

Organizing Phrasal Verbs

When you record the verbs there are ways of organizing them that may make them easier to remember.

a Organizing by particles

The particles which appear with phrasal verbs often have a general meaning of their own, which can help you to understand the meaning of the whole verb. For example, one

into	
entering:	break into, get into, check into, crowd into
changing:	grow into, turn into, make into
persuading:	talk into, pull into, draw into

meaning of the particle *over* is 'considering, thinking about or examining' and this can help you to understand verbs like *look over*, *talk over*, *go over*, *think over*, *read over*. The particle *up* is the most common particle with phrasal verbs but it has several meanings e.g. 'increasing', 'improving', 'preparing', 'completing and finishing'. Therefore, you should try and record verbs under all these separate meanings. Look at the examples for the particle *into* above:

b Organizing by meaning groups

Sometimes it can help you to remember verbs if you record them in meaning (or semantic) groups. This is because these verbs often appear together in the same context, for example 'feelings', 'travel', 'crime'. This means that when you need to talk or write about a particular situation you will have all the verbs you may need together. For example:

Feelings:	to get carried away; to open up; to fall out; to fall for; to get on with
Travel:	to take off; to set off; to check in; to touch down; to stop over
Crime:	to get away with; to break into; to take in; to track down

c Organizing by opposites

turn up/turn down
break up/get together

switch on/switch off
go away/come back

pass out/come round
bring forward/put back

d Organizing by different meanings and patterns for the same verb

For example: make up

to make up	– to put on make-up (lipstick, eye-shadow, etc)
to make something up	– to invent a story
to make up with somebody	– to become friends again after an argument
to make up something	– to form or compose a thing
to make up your mind	– to decide from a number of possibilities

e Organizing three-word verbs

You may want to record together the verbs that are followed by an adverb and a preposition. For example:

to cut back on	to catch up on	to go along with	to stand in for
to feel up to	to come in for	to get round to	to look back on
to run out of	to get on with	to look forward to	to take over from

NB However you organize your verbs, it is essential that you record them in the same way, that is with their meaning and context.

Learning Phrasal Verbs

These are some ideas for self-study that may help you to learn and remember phrasal verbs.

i	Try to read in English, especially informal writing such as tabloid newspapers and novels, and underline all the phrasal verbs you find. Check their meaning in your dictionary and make a note in your vocabulary book as suggested above.
ii	Learn the verbs in organized groups (as suggested on p S22–25) rather than randomly. Constantly look back through your vocabulary book — familiarity and repetition help you to learn more effectively.
iii	Think of a particle and then try and list the different 'meanings' that the particle has. When you have done this, see how many verbs you can list under each meaning. You can also do this exercise with a friend. If you can learn the meanings of the particles, it will help you to understand new verbs you come across. The Guide to Particles at the back of the dictionary will help you with this.
iv	Look at the verbs you have recorded in meaning groups. Try to learn all the verbs, then in your head or in writing, make up a story using as many of the verbs as possible. These 'stories' will help you to remember the context for the verbs. Try this with a friend. Tell each other stories and correct each other if necessary.
v	Write down ten example sentences of phrasal verbs that you want to learn. Then on another piece of paper write down a translation in your own language. Underline the verb in your language. One week later, take out your translated sentences. Look at the underlined verb and try to remember what the phrasal verb equivalent is in English. This will help you to 'think' in phrasal verbs, rather than using a more formal translation from your language.

S5 Phrasal Verb or Single Word?

Phrasal verbs are often the usual way of expressing something in everyday language. A single word which means the same is often more formal. Look at this description of an excursion from a printed brochure:

Day 4 Temple Tour The coach will <u>depart</u> at 09.00. Leaving the city, it will <u>ascend</u> the mountain passes to <u>reach</u> the temple at 10.30. A local guide will conduct the tour and will answer any questions that <u>arise</u>. Visitors will not be <u>admitted</u> unless they are wearing suitable clothing, and will be expected to <u>remove</u> their shoes before <u>entering</u> the temple. The group will return via the 'Lost Valley', where lunch will be <u>provided</u> for those who have <u>requested</u> it.

Now look at this letter, which Penny wrote to her friend when she got back from her holiday. In this letter the words that are underlined in the brochure text would be too formal. Use a form of one of each of the phrasal verbs in the box to fill the gaps in her letter:

ask for   come back
come up   get to
go in   go up   lay on
let in   set off
show round   take off

For me, the highlight of the whole holiday was the trip to the temple. We _____ at nine in the morning and were soon _____ some hair-raisingly steep roads. We _____ the temple about half ten. We had to wear long-sleeved tops and long trousers or they wouldn't have _____ us _____. Of course, we had to _____ our shoes _____ before we _____ the temple, too. A local guide _____ us _____, which was good, because lots of questions _____ about how we were supposed to behave, and about the history of the place. The temple itself was absolutely breathtaking, but that wasn't the best thing because we _____ through what they call the 'Lost Valley'. Lunch was _____ for the people who'd _____ it, but we'd taken a packed lunch with us and we agreed that it was the most spectacular picnic spot we'd ever seen!

Recording phrasal verbs

Here are some suggestions for your own vocabulary records.

Verb	position of pronoun/object	meaning	synonym/ translation	related noun
set off		start on a journey	depart (fml) (partire)	departure
go up	go up **sth**	climb	ascend (fml) (scendere)	ascent
take off	take **sth** off take off **sth**	when you are too hot you ~ your jumper	remove (fml) (togliere)	removal

S6-7 Are You a Natural Born Student?

Some people are born to study, others just think it's a bore. Here's a quiz for you to try to find which category you are in. First you'll need to complete the questions by choosing a verb from the box on the left to make a phrasal verb (you may need to change the form of the verb). The first one has been done for you. Then try the quiz. For each question tick the letter that best applies to you. The questions are written to someone who has finished school, so if you are still at school you will need to imagine the questions are in the present tense. You can check the completed questions on page 372 before you start the quiz.

mess pick keep tell	**1**	At school
		A did teachers always _pick_ on you and _____ you off for no reason? ___
		B did kids who _____ around in class annoy you? ___
		C did you ever get _____ back for extra study? ___
put get put	**2**	When you are given an essay to do, do you
		A _____ on with it straight away and finish it early? ___
		B _____ off starting it until the last possible moment? ___
		C do some work on it immediately then _____ it aside for a while? ___
hand jot plan type write	**3**	How do you go about writing the essay? Do you
		A _____ down some notes then write it and _____ it in? ___
		B do it in rough first, and then _____ it out neatly or _____ it up? ___
		C _____ it out carefully then write and edit it? ___
beaver get sail scrape	**4**	Do you
		A work steadily and _____ through your exams? ___
		B _____ through your exams despite _____ away all year? ___
		C just do enough to _____ by? ___
rattle go check hand move	**5**	When you do an exam, do you
		A _____ through it and _____ it in early? ___
		B _____ over each question carefully before _____ on to the next one? ___
		C answer all the questions then _____ through your answers? ___
read come look	**6**	If you're reading a newspaper article in English, do you reach for your English dictionary
		A as soon as you _____ across a word you don't know? ___
		B only to _____ up a word whose meaning you can't guess? ___
		C only after you've _____ through the article once without a dictionary? ___

throw sign swot	**7** Which of these methods is the best if you want to speak good English? **A** _____ up for evening classes? ____ **B** _____ away your books and find someone to talk with in English? ____ **C** _____ up on vocabulary every night? ____
fall get write	**8** When you had to stay off school when you were younger, **A** did you study while you were sick in order not to _____ behind? ____ **B** were you just happy to have _____ out of lessons? ____ **C** did you borrow a friend's notes and _____ them up? ____
scribble talk	**9** When you had homework did you **A** do it as well as you could? ____ **B** _____ it down as quickly as possible? ____ **C** _____ a friend into letting you copy theirs at the last minute? ____
read come work	**10** When you had a week of exams coming up did you **A** _____ out a revision timetable in plenty of time? ____ **B** _____ up the subject the night before each exam? ____ **C** just take it easy and hope easy questions _____ up? ____
switch shout come	**11** If there's a quiz on TV do you **A** _____ over to something more interesting? ____ **B** _____ out an answer quickly, even if you're not sure? ____ **C** get annoyed if the answer doesn't _____ to you quickly? ____
settle chill catch	**12** What do you like to do on a long train journey? **A** _____ out and gaze out of the window? ____ **B** buy a paper and _____ up on the news? ____ **C** _____ down with a good book? ____

Now check your score on page 372.

20–24 points:	You were born to study. You are the type of student teachers love. Remember to relax sometimes!
14–19 points:	You don't mind studying and you aren't frightened of exams, but sometimes you need a little push in the right direction.
9–13 points:	You can force yourself to study if you absolutely have to, but there are other things that you'd much rather be doing.
0–8 points:	Lazy bones! Studying is as natural to you as breathing air is to a fish!

If you are working in class, discuss your answers to the quiz with other students and give each other advice about how to improve your study methods. For example: 'You should **look up** words you don't know in the dictionary.' 'You shouldn't have **messed around** in class'.

If you enjoy sport, you will meet many of the phrasal verbs that are used to describe different sports.

Here are three extracts from a sports bulletin. Complete the extracts with phrasal verbs, using either a verb from the box on the left or a particle from the box on the right in each gap. You will need to change the form of the verb in some cases. Use your dictionary to help you if you need to. The first one has been done for you.

bring end play rule send	**F**ootball, and tonight's match in the European Cup ended in controversy after Italy *came* __back__ from 2–0 down to beat Spain. At 2–2, the Italian goalkeeper Alberti appeared to _____ *down* Rojas, the Spanish centre forward. As the Spanish players *appealed* _____ a penalty, the Italians _____ on and *broke* _____ to score. The Spanish captain Martín was then _____ _____ for arguing with the referee. Italy _____ *up* fortunate winners, but their goalkeeper Pollo *picked* _____ a hand injury and has been _____ *out* of the next two games.	away back for off up
catch drop hold urge	**T**he Tokyo marathon has been won by Takeshi Saito of Japan. _____ on by the home crowd, Saito *forged* _____ after just 5 kilometres and built up a 2-minute lead. The chasing runners did not *give* _____, and gradually reduced the lead. The hot weather and the fast pace caused several leading athletes to _____ out. Saito's recent training in the Sahara desert *paid* _____ as he _____ off the strong challenge of the Kenyan Daniel Nyanga, who _____ up with 5 kilometres to go, then *fell* _____ in the final kilometre.	ahead back off up
go hold knock pick settle take come	**T**ennis, and the unseeded Sofia Adamou of Greece has beaten Russia's Irena Markova in three sets to _____ _____ to the final of the French Open. Adamou said afterwards, "I've never _____ up _____ such a tough opponent. Before I came here I thought I'd get _____ out in the first round, but now I've got a chance of winning." Adamou, who only _____ _____ the sport four years ago, will _____ *up* a cheque for \$100,000. The loser will have to _____ *for* just \$50,000 !	against through up

Further practice

Now cover the left-hand page and match the definitions on the left with the phrasal verbs from the extracts on the right. One has been done for you as an example.

Extract 1	
1 *to reach a situation that you did not expect to be in*	**a** come back
2 to continue to play	**b** bring sb down
3 to return or recover	**c** end up
4 to make it impossible for somebody to do something	**d** play on
5 to escape from somebody who is keeping you somewhere	**e** break away
6 to get sth	**f** send sb off
7 to make somebody leave the field because they have broken the rules	**g** appeal for sth
8 to make somebody fall to the ground	**h** pick sth up
9 to make an urgent request for sth	**i** rule sb out of sth

Extracts 2 and 3	
1 to make progress quickly	**a** urge sb on
2 to stop taking part in an activity	**b** forge ahead
3 to defeat a person or a team so that they cannot continue in the competition	**c** give up
4 to encourage somebody	**d** drop out
5 to fail to stay with people at the front in a race	**e** pay off
6 to start to do a new activity	**f** hold sth off
7 to accept something that is not quite what you wanted	**g** catch up
8 to reach somebody ahead of you by going faster than them	**h** fall back
9 to stop trying to do something	**i** go through
10 to face somebody or something difficult	**j** come up against sb/sth
11 to resist an attack by an opponent	**k** knock sb out
12 to be successful and bring the results that you want	**l** take sth up
13 to pass to the next stage of a competition	**m** pick sth up
14 to obtain or win sth	**n** settle for sth

Have you noticed how many phrasal verbs are used in computing? Try this crossword to see how many you know. Use the dictionary to help you if you need to.

Use a verb from the top box and a particle from the lower box to complete each sentence. The missing word(s) can be a verb, an adjective or a noun. The solid lines in the crossword show the divisions between words.

switch hack type back scan boot shut
print pull pop go log scroll add click

down out on
up in in down
on down on into
up down up in

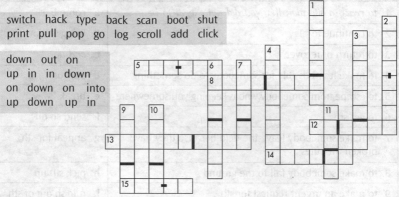

Down

1 _____ the link below to visit our web site.
2 Select 'options' from the _____ menu.
3 The printer didn't work because I'd forgotten to _____ it ___!
4 I stuck a _____ of the email on the wall.
6 Close all programs before you _____ your computer.
7 You can _____ your photos and email them to friends.
9 _____ vital documents on floppy disk to avoid losing them if your system crashes.
10 The computer sometimes takes ages to _____ when I turn it on.
11 You'll need a password to _____

Across

5 You can download various _____s that allow your existing software to do even more things.
8 A teenager managed to _____ the bank's main database.
12 I hope the computer doesn't _____ again or I'll never finish this work.
13 _____ the page until you find the item you want.
14 _____ your password and press 'enter'.
15 If you click on the right mouse button a _____ menu will appear.

The language used to talk about computers is often quite informal. Look out for phrasal verbs used in a figurative or creative way, such as 'crank up' a search engine' (= start it working) or 'wander around the web'; and keep an eye out for invented combinations, such as 'browsing off' (= starting to browse).

S11 Environmental Problems

Phrasal verbs are not necessarily informal. The ones on this page, for example, could appear in a text book or a magazine article on the environment.

Use your environmental knowledge and your phrasal verb dictionary to help you complete this exercise. Match the heads and tails of the sentences, then write the completed sentences in a logical order under the appropriate heading. The first one has been done for you.

The algae *uses*	_up_	.
Temperatures on earth *go*	_through_	the soil and end up in rivers and lakes.
Algae *feeds*	_off_	when fossil fuels are burned.
Carbon dioxide and other greenhouse gases are *given*	_up_	the oxygen in the water, and fish die.
Nitrates from fertilizers *soak*	_up_	heat that should escape into space.
Greenhouse gases *soak*	_on_	the nitrates and multiplies uncontrollably.

The Greenhouse Effect

1 Carbon dioxide and other greenhouse gases are given off when fossil fuels are burned.

2 _____

3 _____

Algae

1 _____

2 _____

3 _____

Some species of animals and plants lose their habitat and *die*	_down_	.
Less carbon dioxide is *soaked*	_into_	desert.
Some areas *turn*	_up_	by trees, which adds to global warming.
Too many trees are burnt or *cut*	_out_	.

Deforestation

1 _____

2 _____

3 _____

4 _____

If you are studying for an exam and the environment is a topic you need to know, you may find it useful to record these phrasal verbs together in your vocabulary notebook. Add a definition and an example. Use the dictionary to help you record some information about the grammar of the verbs.

© Oxford University Press photocopiable

S12 Phrasal Verbs in Newspapers

Some phrasal verbs are used more commonly in newspapers, etc. than in other kinds of writing. Look at these headlines and make sure that you understand the phrasal verbs in them.

a
Manager steps down after cup disaster

b
UNIONS TAKE ON MANAGEMENT OVER NEW SHIFTS

c
President aims to win back voters

d
PRESIDENT FLIES IN FOR TALKS

e
HOSTILITIES BREAK OUT IN DISPUTED TERRITORIES

f
DEMOCRATS CALL FOR TOUGHER SENTENCING

g
ROBBINS BOWS OUT AFTER 10 YEARS ON COUNCIL

h
GOVERNMENT CLIMBS DOWN OVER NEW ROAD

i
WAR OF NERVES PLAYED OUT ON HOSTAGE PLANE

k
Stars whisked away to honeymoon hideaway

l
United Romp Ahead

j
INFLATION SHOOTS UP

Try to guess what the stories might be about. If you are working in class, discuss your ideas with a partner. Then answer the questions below to match the headlines with the subject of the article that they go with.

1   Which headline goes with an article about somebody travelling to an important meeting?
2   Which reports that somebody was taken to a secret destination?
3   Which two headlines talk about somebody resigning?
4   Which headline refers to reports about the start of fighting?
5   Which article is about somebody trying to win an election?
6   Which is a report on rising prices?
7   Which comes from a sports report about a team winning a game easily?
8   Which headline is about people wanting new punishments?
9   Which article reports that somebody has changed their mind about something?
10 Which report is about events that are happening in a tense situation?

Further practice

On your own

When you see English newspapers, look for phrasal verbs in the headlines. In your vocabulary notebook, keep a record of any you find.

Class activity

Look through some English newspapers and find headlines containing phrasal verbs. Cut out the headlines with the articles. In groups, cut the headlines from your articles and mix them all up. Put the headlines and the articles in an envelope. Pass your envelope to another group. Their task is to try to match the headlines with the articles. Do the same for the headlines and articles in the envelope you receive.

The story of a company

Here is the outline history of Hall Motors. Fill in the missing particles and follow the rise and fall of this (fictional!) company. Use the phrasal verbs dictionary to help you.

1888 Frank Hall designs and builds the 'Hall safety cycle' in his back yard. The design really *catches* _____ and Hall soon has to *take* _____ five workers to help him produce bicycles.

1902 Hall, who now has a workforce of 50, *teams* _____ with his cousin Jack, a motor mechanic, and they build their first car. They set _____ 'Hall Motors' and *sell* _____ the bicycle side of the business.

1906 Hall Motors is the country's second biggest car manufacturer, *turning* _____ 20 cars a week.

1945 Frank Hall dies and his son Bill *takes* _____ the company.

1954 The company sees a market for a light 4-wheel drive vehicle, and *comes* _____ _____ the extremely successful 'Trail Ranger'.

1963 Hall Motors revolutionizes the design of the small car with the 'Townie'. Sales *take* _____ immediately, *bringing* _____ record profits.

1969 The company *buys* _____ its main rivals, Wallace Cars and Ryder-Pratt.

1974 Workers at the Leeds plant *walk* _____ in protest at the latest pay offer, *sparking* _____ several years of management-union unrest.

1987 The company just manages to avoid being *swallowed* _____ by American Motors, and announces healthy profits for the first time in many years. Thing seem to have *turned* _____ .

1992 Hall Motors' market share has been gradually *worn* _____ by cheaper foreign imports. With sales *falling* _____ as quickly as debts *mount* _____ , the company seems set to go _____ , but is *bailed* _____ by a last-minute government loan.

1999 As sales continue to decline, Europe Motors *takes* _____ the company, announcing that its aim is to break even within two years. After investing heavily in new models, Europe Motors is *caught* _____ as the value of the pound *shoots* _____ , causing exports to plunge. The decision is taken to *wind* _____ Hall Motors.

2000 6000 workers are *laid* _____ as the last remaining Hall Motors plant *closes* _____ .

Further practice

1 Sort the phrasal verbs above into three groups according to whether you feel their meaning is positive, negative or neutral.

+	–	+/–
catch on	close down	team up

2 Research and write 10 important dates in the history of a famous real company, using these and/or other phrasal verbs.

Using this Dictionary

Phrasal verbs are especially common in informal language, but it is important to know whether a phrasal verb is informal or not to help you use it more appropriately.

- Look at the dictionary entry below and notice how information on the formality of the phrasal verb is given:

> ,chuck sth a'way (*BrE, informal*) **1** to not make good use of sth; to waste sth: *She's chucking all her money away on presents for him.* ◊ *It's too good an opportunity to chuck away.* **2** (*also* ,chuck sth 'out) to throw sth away because you no longer want or need it: *We chucked the old sofa away.* ◊ *Don't chuck yesterday's paper out. I still haven't done the crossword.*
> ⟨SYN⟩ **throw sth away**
> ⊕ v + n/pron + adv ♦ v + adv + n

- Look up the following phrasal verbs in your dictionary and complete the table on the right.

a boot sb out
b provide for sth
c turn up
d barge into sb
e throw sth aside

f put sb down
g tune out
h attend to sb/sth

Formal	Informal	Neutral

Practice

- Read the following email from Helen to her friend Katy. Underline all the phrasal verbs that you can find. One has been done for you, there are 10 others:

From:	Helen	To:	Katy
Subject:			

Message: Hi Katy
I haven't heard from you for a while so I thought I'd take a break from work and write. I'm desperately trying to <u>swot up</u> for my exams at the moment – you know I had to retake them, after messing up so badly in June. So I spend my days beavering away at my desk, and my evenings vegging out in front of the television. Very unhealthy and very boring!

Anyway, how are you? How is the course going? Are they making you work hard? I'm sure you'll breeze through it!

Simon came to see me the other day. He seemed very well – he was jabbering away about his job for ages and telling me how wonderful it is.

Funny – I'm sure last time I spoke to him he was going to jack it all in and see the world! My Nick's doing pretty well too – he's swanning around having business lunches every other day while I'm stuck here. It's not fair! Still I suppose it's my own fault for mucking around last year when I should have been studying.

Are you coming to Brighton soon? Don't forget to look me up if you are. You could come and stay for a couple of days after my exams. It will be good to catch up with you after so long. What do you think? Phone or email me, OK?

Love Helen xx

- Now write one of the phrasal verbs from the email next to the definitions below according to its meaning. One has been done for you.

a work very hard (at sth)   _____
b study very hard, especially when you are preparing for an exam   _swot up_
c go from one place to another feeling pleased with yourself   _____
d speak or talk quickly in an excited way   _____
e visit or contact sb when you are in the place where they live   _____
f find out about things that have happened to somebody   _____
g stop doing sth, especially your job   _____
h succeed in sth very easily   _____
i relax in a lazy way and do very little   _____
j do sth very badly   _____
k behave in a silly way, especially when you should be working or   _____
   doing sth else

- Replace all the <u>unnecessary</u> information (in italics) with one phrasal verb from the box, remembering to change the verb into the correct form. The first one has been done for you.

                        level with you
a OK, ~~I'll tell you the situation in an honest way~~. I'm afraid we're not able to accept your proposals at this time.
b Greg was all ready to do the bungee-jump, but at the last moment he *decided not to do it because he was afraid*.
c We're going to *visit* the new bar in town *to see if it's any good*. Would you like to come?
d Dinner? I haven't had time to go the shops, but I guess I'll be able to *provide* something *quickly and without planning*.
e Our class was really behind the others, so we *did* the last three chapters *very quickly*.
f I don't like watching horror movies – they *make* me *feel* really *shocked and scared*.
g He's usually pretty quick, but it took him ages to *understand what I meant without being told directly*.
h As soon as I asked her about her family, she just *refused to speak because she didn't want to talk about it*.

freak out   cotton on   chicken out   ~~level with~~   check out   rustle up
whip through   clam up

S16–17 Using Phrasal Verbs in Writing

The following verbs are often used in essays and reports and are slightly more 'formal' than the majority of phrasal verbs. The verbs are listed below together with the context in which they typically appear in a piece of writing.

1	*refer to*	a particular subject	9	*write down*	the information
2	*report back*	to a person or committee about something	10	*file away*	the documents
			11	*go through*	a list or plan
3	*enlarge upon*	a problem	12	*set out*	the reasons why something should be done
4	*put forward*	a suggestion			
5	*draw up*	a plan or proposal	13	*edit out*	any unnecessary information
6	*consist of*	several sections			
7	*point out*	an important piece of information	14	*deal with*	a topic or idea
			15	*account for*	why something happened
8	*sum up*	the main points discussed			

Exercise 1

Read the following extract from a report and replace the underlined words with the phrasal verbs listed below.

This report [1]concerns the delivery services we wish to expand for our clients. Our market research company has already [2]given the information to the marketing department on their recent research. The main points of this information will be [3]given in a series of short reports for the committee to examine in their own time.

The marketing department has now [4]made a plan of action for increasing our delivery service. The Managing Director has [5]looked at this carefully and given it his approval. Essentially it [6]presents three suggestions for discussion and [7]explains the reasons why we should consider a slow rather than a rapid expansion.

This report summarises those reasons and [8]is in three parts: *(a)* it [9]gives more details about the difficulties we have had with recruiting staff, *(b)* it [10]explains why our delivery service had problems last month, *(c)* it [11]briefly discusses the problems caused by rising inflation. ....

consists of	gone through	summed up	deals with
puts forward	drawn up	refers to	sets out
enlarges upon	reported back	accounts for	

Exercise 2

Now write your own report using as many of the phrasal verbs above as possible. Imagine you have been studying English at a college in Britain and the Principal has asked you to write a short report explaining what you enjoyed about the course, discussing any problems you had and suggesting some improvements for next year.

Below is a short list of what you may have liked and another list of some problems. Remember to explain in the introduction what your report is about and to finish with your suggestions. There is a sample answer in the key (at the back of the dictionary).

Good points	Problems
■ enjoyed lessons	■ expensive cafeteria
■ helpful teachers	■ not enough books in library
■ meeting other students	■ boring trips and visits

Exercise 3

In the sentences below, choose the best verb to fill the gap.

1 This document _____ the brochures you were sent earlier this week.
  a consists of   b refers to   c accounts for

2 It is important to _____ that our prices have been reduced.
  a set out   b sum up   c point out

3 The director would like you to _____ the list carefully and check the figures.
  a go through   b draw up   c deal with

4 The secretary reported that the papers had been _____ in the wrong order.
  a filed away   b accounted for   c put forward

5 It is useful to _____ all the important points in a presentation.
  a draw up   b write down   c edit out

6 It is essential to _____ the main points discussed in your report.
  a put forward   b file away   c sum up

7 This afternoon the MD will _____ on our success in the new markets.
  a sum up   b write down   c report back

8 The presentation will _____ the issue of customer complaints.
  a deal with   b account for   c point out

Formal verbs

You will find many other verbs marked formal in this dictionary. Many of them have the pattern **v + n/pron + prep** and are often used in the passive. *To ascribe sth to sb, to preface sth by/with sth, to refer sb/sth to sb/sth* are examples of these. Other formal verbs are reflexive and have the pattern **v + pron + prep**. Examples are *to address yourself to sth, to avail yourself of sth* and *to dissociate yourself from sth*.

You may not always recognize them as 'phrasal verbs', but they must always be used in these patterns. They are often used in business or in spoken or written news reports. If you are studying at university or college, you may meet them in academic textbooks or journals. If you meet verbs like this, keep a note of them, with their patterns and an example, in your vocabulary book.

S18–19 Using Phrasal Verbs in the Passive

Forming the passive

Notice the word order of the passive phrasal verbs:

Active	You'll need to write down the details.	= **Verb + particle + Object**
	or Did you write the details down?	= **Verb + Object + Particle**
Passive	The details will need to be written down.	**Auxiliary verb 'to be' +**
	The details weren't written down correctly. =	**Verb (Past Participle) +**
	Have they been written down?	**Particle.**

Transitive and intransitive verbs

Verbs can be used either without an object, (**intransitive**), for example *sleep*:
I slept ~~the night~~. *I slept for 8 hours.*
or with an object, (**transitive**), for example *read* in the sentence:
She's reading the newspaper.

Combinations of verbs and particles can be used in the same way:
sit down (intransitive): *I sat down.*
put sth on (transitive): *I put on my coat. I put my coat on.*
rely on sb/sth (transitive): *You can rely on me.*

Exercise 1

Which of the following verbs + particles have an object and which do not?

1 He likes to stand out in the crowd.
2 I'm looking for a new job.
3 Turn off the TV if you don't want to watch it.
4 Our holiday plans fell through at the last minute.
5 I didn't get the job – they turned down my application.
6 Do you think the sun will come out this afternoon?

We can divide the **transitive** verbs + particles into two further groups:

■ those where the verb can be separated from its particle (**separable**)
■ those where the verb and particle must occur next to each other (**inseparable**)

In this dictionary, this information is shown in the grammar patterns following the verbs.
Sort sth out is separable:

| ✓ I'll **sort out** the accommodation. v+adv+n | ✓ I'll **sort** the accommodation **out**. v+n/pron+adv |

But *jump at sth* is inseparable:

| ✓ I'd **jump at** the chance to study abroad. v+prep | ✗ I'd **jump** the chance **at** to study abroad. |

Exercise 2

Now divide the verbs that have objects in the sentences above according to their grammar. Refer to the dictionary entries if you need help.

Separable	Inseparable

Exercise 3

The following sentences contain the same verbs, this time in the passive. Look at the table and then answer the question below.

✓ Passive possible	✗ Passive not possible
The television must **be turned off after** use. My application**'s been turned down**.	Jobs have **to be looked for** very carefully.

Which type of verbs can generally be used in the passive?
Complete this general 'rule' using the words '*separable*' or '*inseparable*':

_____ phrasal verbs can generally be used in the passive, whereas _____ phrasal verbs cannot.

However, there are many exceptions!
The verbs in the following sentences are all **separable**.

✓ Passive possible	✗ Passive not possible
Can the whole chapter **be left out**? The top floor **is being made into** a separate flat.	My meaning just can't **be got across** no matter how I try. We **were sat down** by the manager in his office.

Notes in the dictionary tell you when you **cannot** use the passive with this type of verb.
The following sentences all contain **inseparable** verbs.

✓ Passive possible	✗ Passive not possible
That remark **wasn't called for**! He hates **being fussed over**. Can this section **be improved on**?	The noise will just have to **be put up with**, I'm afraid.

Notes in the dictionary tell you when you **can** use a passive with verbs of this type.

Exericse 4

Some phrasal verbs are often used in the passive.
(Again, notes in the dictionary give you this information.) Choose one verb from the box and put it into the correct form to complete each sentence:

charge sb with	hear of sb
rip sb off	mix sb up
kick sb out	burn sth down

1 She's been _____ shoplifting.
2 If you carry on like this you'll be _____ of college.
3 The building was _____ in the riots.
4 No one knows where Jerry is. He hasn't been _____ since the summer.
5 The twins look so alike that they are often _____.
6 £10 for this? You've been _____!

When you look up a verb in the dictionary, look to see if there is a note about the passive.

Where do new phrasal verbs come from?

New phrasal verbs turn up in the language all the time, but where do they come from? One answer is of course that new inventions and activities appear and new names and verbs are invented to describe them. But in fact, they are not usually completely new verbs, but either new combinations of existing verbs and particles, or old phrases which have found new uses.

1 From literal meaning to figurative meaning.

Plough back originally meant to return a crop that you have grown to the soil. This was done to produce more. It is easy to see how this can change to being used about reinvesting profits in a business. Sometimes the connection is less obvious. An American student may **blow off** his or her classes (that is, not go to them) – perhaps because they seem as unimportant as a fly that you would blow off your face.

2 New opposites.

In the past we tended to **dress up** more for formal occasions, putting on special clothes and perhaps jewellery. Today, modern companies often try to foster a more creative and relaxed atmosphere by allowing staff to **dress down** once a week, that is, to wear more casual clothes.

3 New verbs from nouns or adjectives.

There are enormous possibilities for creating phrasal verbs because they don't have to be made from existing verbs. Nouns, too, can turn into verbs and be used with particles to make new phrasal verbs. These often come into the language first through American English where there seems to be more freedom for words to change grammatical class, or through informal spoken language. So from the noun **luck**, instead of 'getting lucky', we can **luck out** and cowards ('wimps', people who have no courage or 'bottle') might **wimp out** or **bottle out**.

4 Adding particles for emphasis.

Sometimes a simple verb can turn into a phrasal verb without any real change of meaning. We now often hear something like '*Professor Jones will head up an international team.*' where before we would have said that he will head the team, and it is difficult to see any reason for this change, except that the particle 'up' seems to strengthen the meaning of the verb.

Task A
Find phrasal verbs with **free**, **hype**, **tense**, **test** and **drown** that are similar to this.

New phrasal verbs in modern life.

Business and communication	Personal life	
fax out a document	work out in the gym	veg out with a pizza
fire off an email	chill out and watch TV	and a video
bump sb off the Internet	lighten up	pig out on junk food

You will find other new verbs on other study pages.

Being creative

In addition to forming new verbs in the ways we have looked at, it is also possible to form many other combinations of verbs and particles. Think, for example, of all the ways that movement can be described. Almost any verb of motion can team up with almost any particle. Because we can **go back** or **come back**, we can also **hurry back**, **amble back** or **tear back**. We can say '**I walked around** the town', so it's also possible to say '**I sauntered around**', or **wandered around**, or **strolled around**. If you are having a lazy day, perhaps you **sit around** at home. You might also **lie around** or **lounge around**. If we want to describe how somebody **came in**, did they **sneak in**, **burst in**, **creep in** or **storm in**? You can see how using combinations of verbs and particles in this way can make your speech and writing more interesting.

Task B

Combine a verb from the box on the left with a particle from a box on the right and make a verb that might describe one of these things that you might see when you are out. If you are working in class, see if your partner can guess which person or thing your verb is describing. Then write a sentence for each one.

a sports car	*a butterfly*
a boy with his leg in plaster	*a bee*
a train	*tourists visiting a palace*
a small child in a park	*a group of boys going to school*
a teacher going home at the end of a long day	

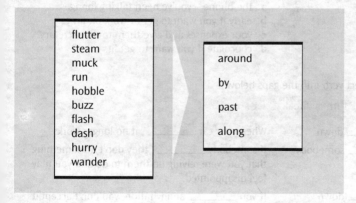

flutter
steam
muck
run
hobble
buzz
flash
dash
hurry
wander

around

by

past

along

Conclusion

We live in a fast-changing world and new expressions to describe it can be coined faster even than dictionaries can record them! However, we don't need to **freak out** when we meet a new phrasal verb, because we are usually already familiar with one or both of the parts when we hear a new addition to English. (The Guide to the Particles at the back of the dictionary will give you more information on the way particles are used.) No need, then, to panic – just **lighten up** and **chill out**!

Combinations of verbs and particles are extremely common in English, especially in the spoken language. Many of these verbs appear to have a single-word equivalent (a synonym). However, often the single-word equivalent is not used in the same context or has a slightly different meaning. For example, it is often said that *find out* means the same as *discover*, but in fact *find out* is generally used for facts and information, whereas *discover* can be used for something you are the first person to learn about, such as a place or scientific technique. It is therefore essential to learn the most frequently used phrasal verbs if you want to understand and speak English well. Here are some exercises to help you understand and learn the most common.

Particles

The following verbs are organized by their particle. You will find more about the meanings of the particles in the *Guide to the Particles* at the back of the dictionary.

Group A

Up

Match the item on the left with the item on the right.

(i) *increasing or improving:*

1	Many people	a	grow up so fast and soon leave home.
2	Students	b	bring up their children to be well-mannered.
3	Peter,	c	cheer up when their university exams are over.
4	Children	d	hurry up or we will miss the train.

(ii) *completing or finishing:*

1	Add up	a	the phone – you've been talking for ages.
2	Hang up	b	early if you want to get to work on time.
3	Give up	c	your expenses and give them to my secretary.
4	Wake up	d	chocolate if you want to get fit.

Down

Put the correct verb into the gaps below.

(i) *failing:*   turn   break   let

1	_____ down	When your car _____ , it no longer works.
2	_____ somebody down	If somebody _____ , they don't do something that you were relying on them to do and you may feel disappointed.
3	_____ down	If you _____ an invitation, you don't accept it.

(ii) *movement :*   bend   keep   lie   put   sit

1 Every day, at 8pm, we all _____ down to have dinner together.
2 If you don't want him to see you, you'd better _____ your head down.
3 That bag looks heavy! You can _____ it down over there.
4 The coach made us _____ down and touch our toes. It was quite difficult.
5 I'm so tired – I'm going to _____ down on the bed. Wake me up if I fall asleep.

Group B

Match the item on the left with the item on the right.

On
Continuing:

1 The professor   a went on for months until we resolved it.
2 The customer   b keeps on talking to me and interrupting my work.
3 My boss   c carried on talking even though the seminar had finished.
4 The problem   d held on for several minutes then put the phone down.

Off
Departing:

1 Get off   a early so you miss the traffic on the motorway.
2 Go off   b the bus at the next stop if you want the city centre.
3 Run off   c on holiday by yourself if you really want to relax.
4 Set off   d and play in the garden – you need some fresh air.

Group C

Put the correct verb into the gaps below.

In
Entering or arriving:

break in   check in   come in   let in

1 _____ in   When you _____ somewhere you enter a place, often somewhere familiar such as your home or when a friend invites you to their house.

2 _____ in   When you _____, you register at a hotel or an airport desk.

3 _____ somebody in   When you _____ you open the door and allow them to come in.

4 _____ in   If someone _____, they enter a building illegally.

NB *Break into* and *check into* mean the same as *break in* and *check in* but they must be followed by an object.

Out
Leaving:

break   come   fall   get

1 Some medical treatments can make your hair _____ out.
2 As I was _____ out of the car, I fell over.
3 Several prisoners have _____ out of jail.
4 As we _____ out of the hotel we saw the beach right in front of us.

Group D – verbs with an adverb and a preposition

Use the verbs to fill the gaps in the sentences below.

look forward to   get on with   hang on to   run out of   put up with

1 You should _____ your baggage at the airport in case it gets stolen.
2 I've been really _____ meeting your family.
3 Oh no, we've _____ milk again – will you go to the shop and get some?
4 I don't know how you _____ his temper – you must be very patient.
5 I _____ my father very well – we always have a laugh together.

Meaning Groups

The following verbs are organized into meaning groups because certain verbs are typically used in particular situations.

Group 1
Daily Routine

Put the following phrasal verbs in the gaps in the text below. Remember to use the right tense.

wake up	get off	look after	phone up	set off	have sth on
catch up	get to	come from	meet up	get back	

I ᵃ_____ a small town outside London and when I was younger, most days I ᵇ_____ at about 7am, showered and had breakfast. Then, when I ᶜ_____ my coat _____ I used to ᵈ_____ for school. I got the bus and I would ᵉ_____ at the stop just before the school. I usually ᶠ_____ with my friends but often I was late so I would have to run to ᵍ_____ with them. We ʰ_____ school before 9am. After a long day in school I used to ⁱ_____ home at about 4, and if my mother was at work I had to ʲ_____ my little sister. Most evenings I would ᵏ_____ my best friend and we would chat for ages. I was very happy then.

Group 2
Business

The following is a speech by a Marketing Director to some managers.
Put the sentences from the speech into the correct order.

> Good morning.
> **a** Then, when our Finance Director did the figures, he decided that it added up to too great an investment for us at this stage.
> **b** We were hoping that our meeting would lead to a partnership so that we too had access to these markets.
> **c** First of all, I'm sorry this meeting had to be put off until today but I was away in Germany last week.
> **d** I began my visit discussing this and dealing with the negotiations for a possible contract.
> **e** However, my visit was not a success – two important meetings were called off so I had no opportunity to speak to the Chief Executive.
> **f** I also gave out some leaflets to senior managers, which described our products.
> **g** I would, however, like to point out to you all that we will be visiting other companies in Europe next year and hope this will be more successful.
> **h** Now, as you know, the company I visited deals in stationery supplies and sells their products all over Europe.
> Thank you.

Opposites

The following verbs are organized into pairs with their opposites. Match the phrase on the right with the phrase on the left.

1 If we set off early
2 You must stand up when the teacher arrives
3 Put the box down in the corner
4 You've been lying down all day
5 I decided to carry on with tennis
6 If you're too hot, take your jumper off

a and put a T-shirt on.
b – get up and do something.
c we'll get back before dark.
d – I'll get someone to pick it up and move it later.
e – you can sit down when she has said hello.
f and give up volleyball. It was too much to do both.

Multi-Meaning Verbs

The following verbs have more than one meaning. Complete the pairs of sentences with one of the verbs listed below.

| catch up | give up | meet up | pick up | take off | come out | fall out |

1 If you want to _____ you will have to run.
  You will have to work hard to _____ with the other students.

2 That shampoo made my hair _____ in handfuls.
  I hate to have arguments and _____ with my friends.

3 My little daughter always _____ her clothes by herself.
  When the plane _____ we will be able to see the fields below.

4 I'm going to _____ smoking in the New Year.
  I don't think the rebels will _____ their fight easily.

5 If she waits by the station, I'll _____ (her) in my car.
  The cat was so light , I could _____ (it) with one hand.

6 The mark on my skirt wouldn't _____ even when I washed it.
  We know that the stars _____ at night but we can't always see them.

7 Do you want to _____ for dinner after work?
  I'm so surprised to _____ with you here – I haven't seen you for ages.

Further practice

You will find more meaning groups on the Are you a Natural Born Student, Sport, Computers, Environmental Problems, Phrasal Verbs in Newspapers, and Phrasal Verbs in Business study pages.

Exercise 1

These are all verbs that you have studied in the last four pages. Choose the best phrasal verb to fill the gaps in the sentences below.

1 I would love to be able to _____ my children in the country.
   a grow up b bring up c get up d wake up

2 I warned them to _____ , otherwise they would hit their heads.
   a put down b let down c bend down d lie down

3 The two boys _____ to the building easily because there was no security.
   a came in b broke in c put in d checked in

4 She was relieved to _____ of the party – it was so hot in there.
   a run out b come out c get out d break out

5 He will _____ leaving the door open – it drives me mad!
   a hold on b go on c keep on d carry on

6 We were so late, the plane nearly _____ without us!
   a went off b set off c took off d got off

7 He _____ her difficult behaviour even though it made him angry.
   a got on with b put up with c looked forward to d hung on to

8 I'm going to ask you to _____ the problem because you know the background to it.
   a deal with b point out c deal in d lead to

9 Give me your blouse and I'll see if the stain will _____ .
   a fall out b come out c get out d go out

Which meaning?

Exercise 2

List the following verbs under the meaning of their particle.

(i) grow up add up hang up bring up give up cheer up shut up wake up hurry up

   increasing or improving   **completing or finishing**
   ....
   ....

(ii) sit down let down lie down put down turn down keep down break down bend down

   failing   **movement**
   ....
   ....

marvel /'mɑːvl; *AmE* 'mɑːrvl/ (**-ll-**, *AmE* **-l-**)

'marvel at sth to be very surprised or impressed by sb/sth: *Everyone marvelled at his courage.* ◇ *Massimo marvelled at how quickly he had got used to life in Britain.*
  ⟨SYN⟩ **wonder at sth**
  ◈ v + prep

masquerade /ˌmæskə'reɪd; *BrE also* ˌmɑːsk-/

masque'rade as sb/sth to pretend to be sth that you are not: *commercial advertisers masquerading as private individuals* ◇ *The local paper is full of gossip masquerading as news.*
  ◈ v + prep

match /mætʃ/

'match sb/sth against/with sb/sth to make sb/sth compete with another person or thing: *Jobson will be matched against a far more experienced player.* ◇ *Match your skill against the experts in our weekly quiz.*
  ⟨NOTE⟩ **Match sb/sth against sb/sth** is often used in the passive.
  ◈ v + n/pron + prep

match sth against sth to compare sth to sth else to see how the two things are similar or different: *We are able to match the details he gave us against the information held on the computer.*
  ◈ v + n/pron + prep

match 'up 1 (**with sth**) to be the same or similar: *Do their names match up with any in our database?* ◇ *The two statements don't match up.* ⟨SYN⟩ **tally** (**with sth**) **2** (**to sb/sth**) (*especially BrE*) (*usually used in negative sentences*) to be as good as or equal to sb/sth: *The movie didn't match up to my expectations.* ◇ *He knows what he wants and I just don't match up.* ⟨SYN⟩ **measure up (to sb/sth)**
  ◈ v + adv

match sb/sth 'up (**with sb/sth**) to find things or people that are suitable for each other or fit well with each other: *The agency matched me up with a suitable job.* ◇ *They were unable to match up his tissue type with any of the possible donors.*
  ⟨NOTE⟩ **Match sb/sth** (**with sb/sth**) can be used with the same meaning.
  ◈ v + n/pron + adv ◆ v + adv + n

match sb/sth with sb/sth = MATCH SB/STH AGAINST/WITH SB/STH

max /mæks/

max 'out; max sth 'out (*AmE, slang*) to reach the limit at which nothing more is possible: *The car maxed out at 180 mph.* ◇ *I just maxed out my credit card.*
  ◈ v + adv ◆ v + adv + n ◆ v + n/pron + adv

measure /'meʒə(r)/

'measure sb/sth/yourself against sb/sth to compare sb/sth/yourself with somebody or something else: *The quality of the water is measured against EU standards.* ◇ *We have nothing to measure our performance against.* ◇ *She always measured herself against her sisters.* ◇ *I had no one to measure myself against.*
  ◈ v + n/pron + prep

measure sth 'off to mark out a particular length on sth such as a piece of cloth: *She measured off two metres of cloth.*
  ◈ v + adv + n ◆ v + pron + adv ◆ v + n + adv (*less frequent*)

measure sth 'out to measure the quantity of sth that you need from a larger amount: *He measured out the ingredients for the cake.*
  ◈ v + adv + n ◆ v + pron + adv ◆ v + n + adv (*less frequent*)

measure 'up (**to sb/sth**) (*informal*) to be of a good enough standard: *The new assistant didn't measure up* (= he was not good enough to do the job), *so we had to replace him.* ◇ *The procedures don't measure up to today's standards.*
  ⟨SYN⟩ **match up (to sb/sth)**
  ⟨NOTE⟩ **Measure up** is often used in negative sentences and questions.
  ◈ v + adv

measure 'up (**for sth**), **measure sb/sth 'up** (**for sth**) (*especially BrE*) to find the exact size of sth or of sth that you need by measuring: *We need to measure up and decide where the furniture can go.* ◇ *They've come to measure up* (*the room*) *for the new carpet.* ◇ *He was being measured up for a suit.*
  ◈ v + adv ◆ v + n/pron + adv ◆ v + adv + n

meet /miːt/ (**met, met** /met/)

meet 'up 1 (**with sb**) to meet sb by arrangement: *We're meeting up with Gary after work, if you want to come.* ◇ *Where shall we meet up?* **2** (**with sb**) to meet sb by chance: *It was lucky we met up with them.* ◇ *I expect we'll meet up again some time.* **3** (**with sth**) (of two or more roads, rivers, etc.) to join up: *The two paths meet up just below the summit.* ◇ *This road eventually meets up with the A40.* ⟨SYN⟩ **join up**
  ◈ v + adv

'meet with sb to have a meeting with sb: *The Prime Minister met with other European leaders this morning.*
  ◈ v + prep

'meet with sth (*formal*) **1** to experience sth unpleasant: *The chief witness met with an accident on his way to the court.* ◇ *Our attempts to save her met with failure.* ⟨OBJ⟩ **an accident, fate 2** to be received or treated by sb in a particular

way: *The proposal met with considerable opposition.* ◇ *My explanation met with a blank stare.*
OBJ **opposition**, **approval**, **hostility**, **resistance**
NOTE Meet **with sth** is mainly used in written English.
◆ v + prep

'meet sth with sth to react to sth in a particular way, especially a bad or negative way: *The proposal was met with anger and dismay.*
NOTE Meet **sth with sth** is usually used in the passive.
◆ v + n/pron + prep

mellow /'meləʊ; AmE -loʊ/

,mellow 'out (*informal, especially AmE*) to relax and do very little: *We could just put on some music and mellow out.*
SYN chill out
◆ v + adv

,mellow sb 'out (*informal, especially AmE*) to make sb more relaxed: *A week on the beach should mellow him out.*
◆ v + n/pron + adv ◆ v + adv + n

melt /melt/

,melt a'way; **,melt sth a'way** to disappear gradually; to make sth disappear gradually: *His anger melted away.* ◇ *The crowd dispersed, melting away into the side streets.* ◇ *His smile melted away all the tension.*
◆ v + adv ◆ v + adv + n ◆ v + n/pron + adv

,melt sth 'down to heat sth until it is in a liquid state, usually so that it can be made into sth else: *Aluminium cans can be melted down and recycled.*
OBJ gold, silver, etc.
◆ v + n/pron + adv ◆ v + adv + n
▸ **'meltdown** *n* [U] [C] a serious accident in which the central part of a structure that produces nuclear energy melts, causing harmful rays to escape: *A meltdown at the reactor had only just been avoided.* ◇ (*figurative*) *The meltdown on Wall Street caused chaos in markets worldwide.*

'melt into sth to gradually become part of sth and difficult to see: *I tried hard to melt into the background.*
◆ v + prep

merge /mɜːdʒ; AmE mɜːrdʒ/

,merge 'in (with sth), **,merge 'into sth** if something merges in (with sth) or merges into sth, it is so similar to the second thing that you cannot really see the differences between them or where one ends and the other begins: *The new college building does not merge in with the old buildings around it.* ◇ *Autumn is merging into winter.* ◇ *Saturday and Sunday seemed to merge into each other.*

→ *see also* BLEND IN; BLEND INTO STH
◆ v + adv ◆ v + prep
IDM merge into the 'background (of a person) to behave quietly when you are with a group of people so that they do not notice you

mess /mes/

,mess a'bout (*BrE*) = MESS AROUND
,mess a'bout with sb (*BrE*) = MESS AROUND WITH SB
,mess a'bout with sth (*BrE*) = MESS AROUND WITH STH
,mess sb a'bout/a'round (*BrE, informal*) to treat sb badly, making them waste time, changing your mind a lot, etc: *They messed us around so much, I wrote to complain.* ◇ *I don't like being messed about.*
SYN muck sb about/around (*BrE*)
◆ v + n/pron + adv

,mess a'round (*BrE also* ,mess a'bout) (*informal*) **1** (with sb/sth) to spend time and enjoy yourself doing sth with no particular purpose: *We just messed around at home all day.* ◇ *Children love to mess about in water.* **2** (with sb/sth) to behave in a silly way, especially when you should be working or doing sth else: *He got told off for messing around in class.* ◇ *She messed about all year and failed her exams.* ◇ *Stop messing around with Jo and get on with the work.* ◇ *'They fixed that quickly!' 'Yeah, they don't mess around.'* (= they do things quickly) **3** to joke, to say silly things: *I'm not messing about, it's true!* **SYN** kid around (*informal*)
SYN muck about/around (*BrE*)
→ *see also* MESS AROUND WITH STH
◆ v + adv

,mess sb a'round (*BrE*) = MESS SB ABOUT/AROUND
,mess a'round with sb (*BrE also* ,mess about with sb*) (*informal*) to have a sexual relationship with sb
◆ v + adv + prep

,mess a'round with sth (*BrE also* ,mess about with sth*) (*informal*) **1** to keep touching or moving sth in an annoying way: *Stop messing around with the video!* ◇ *Don't mess around with your food like that!* **2** to get involved in sth that you do not know much about or understand: *Who knows what might happen if we mess around with nature?* **3** to get involved with sth dangerous: *He started messing around with drugs when he was just a kid.*
SYN muck about/around with sth (*BrE*)
NOTE Mess about/around with sth can be used in the passive in meanings 1 and 2: *This package has been messed around with.*
→ *see also* MESS AROUND
◆ v + adv + prep

,mess 'up; **,mess sth 'up** (*informal*) to spoil sth; to do sth very badly: *I was so nervous I totally messed up at the interview.* ◇ *She messed up all our arrangements by arriving late.* ◇ *You've really messed things up for me.*
SYN) foul up, foul sth up; **screw up, screw sth up**
⬦ v + adv ♦ v + adv + n ♦ v + n/pron + adv

,mess sb 'up (*informal*) **1** to spoil sb's life; to make sb suffer emotionally or mentally: *His parents really messed him up.* ◇ *He came back into her life and messed her up again.* **2** (*AmE, spoken*) to physically hurt sb, especially by hitting them
SYN) screw sb up
⬦ v + n/pron + adv ♦ v + adv + n

▶ **,messed 'up** *adj* (*informal*) confused and upset, especially because of sth bad that has happened to you in the past: *He's just a messed-up kid.*

,mess sth 'up to make sth untidy or dirty: *She comes in, messes the place up and then goes out again.* ◇ *The wind is going to mess up my hair.*
SYN) muck sth up (*informal*)
⬦ v + n/pron + adv ♦ v + adv + n

'mess with sb (*informal*) (*usually used in negative sentences*) **1** to do or say sth that might annoy a particular person, as they may react in a violent or dangerous way: *I wouldn't mess with Frank if I were you.* **2** to have or try to have a sexual relationship with sb
→ *see also* MESS AROUND WITH SB
⬦ v + prep

'mess with sth (*informal, especially AmE*) **1** to use or treat sth carelessly, causing damage: *Who's been messing with the answering machine?* ◇ *Read the label carefully before you start messing with dangerous products.* **2** to get involved with sth dangerous: *How long has he been messing with drugs?* **OBJ) drugs**
→ *see also* MESS AROUND WITH STH
⬦ v + prep

mete /miːt/

mete sth 'out (to sb) (*formal*) to give sb a punishment, etc: *Schools should not mete out physical punishment to children.* ◇ *Severe penalties were meted out to the offenders.*
OBJ) punishment, treatment, justice
NOTE) Mete sth out is usually used in the passive.
⬦ v + adv + n ♦ v + pron + adv ♦ v + n + adv (*rare*)

militate /'mɪlɪteɪt/

militate a'gainst sth (*formal*) to prevent sth; to make it difficult for sth to happen: *Lack of funds militated against the success of the campaign.*
⬦ v + prep

mill /mɪl/

,mill a'round; **,mill a'round sb/sth** (*BrE also* **,mill a'bout**, **,mill a'bout sb/sth**) if a large group of people **mill around**, or **mill around** a place, they move around without going anywhere in particular, often while waiting for sth to happen: *Photographers milled around outside the hotel, waiting for the prince to appear.* ◇ *People milled about the room, shaking hands and chatting.*
⬦ v + adv ♦ v + prep

mind /maɪnd/

,mind 'out (*BrE*) **1** used to warn sb to be careful: *Mind out! You nearly knocked me off my bike!* ◇ *I've got you fish and chips. Mind out for the bones!*
SYN) watch out 2 (*informal*) used to tell sb to move so that you or sb else can pass: *Mind out Joe — you're in the way!*
⬦ v + adv

minister /'mɪnɪstə(r)/

'minister to sb/sth (*old-fashioned, formal*) to care for sb; to make sure that sb/sth has everything necessary: *She felt it was her vocation to minister to the sick.* ◇ *Servants ministered to his needs.*
OBJ) needs, the sick
NOTE) Minister to sb/sth can be used in the passive: *He would not be ministered to by strangers.*
⬦ v + prep

minor /'maɪnə(r)/

'minor in sth (*AmE*) to study another subject as well as your main subject at a university or college: *He minored in Art History.*
⬦ v + prep

miss /mɪs/

,miss 'out (on sth) to lose an opportunity to benefit from sth or enjoy yourself, by not doing sth or taking part in an activity: *I felt I missed out because I didn't go to college.* ◇ *She missed out on the school trip.* ◇ *He just missed out on a gold medal in the last Olympics* (= he was just beaten). ◇ *There are lots of things happening during Carnival, so don't miss out on the fun!*
⬦ v + adv

,miss sb/sth 'out (*BrE*) to not include sb/sth either deliberately or by accident: *Have I missed anybody out?* ◇ *You've missed out the most important piece of information!* (= you haven't mentioned it) ◇ *She missed out a few chapters in the middle.*
⬦ v + n/pron + adv ♦ v + adv + n

mist /mɪst/

,mist 'over 1 if glass **mists over**, it becomes covered with very small drops of water so that you cannot see through it: *As soon as I stepped inside, my glasses misted over.* **2** if your eyes **mist over**, they fill with tears: *His eyes misted over.*
NOTE Mist is often used with these meanings.
◆ v + adv

,mist 'up; **,mist sth 'up** to cover sth such as glass with small drops of water so that you cannot see through it: *The inside of the car was beginning to mist up.* ◇ *The windows were misted up.*
SYN fog up; steam up, steam sth up
NOTE Mist and mist sth are also used with this meaning.
◆ v + adv ◆ v + n/pron + adv ◆ v + adv + n

mistake /mɪ'steɪk/ (mistook /mɪ'stʊk/ mistaken /mɪ'steɪkən/)

mi'stake sb/sth for sb/sth to think wrongly that sb/sth is sb/sth else: *I mistook him for his brother.* ◇ *The toy could easily be mistaken for a real gun.*
◆ v + n/pron + prep

mix /mɪks/

,mix sth 'in (with sth**)**, **,mix sth 'into sth** to combine one substance with others, especially in cooking: *Mix the eggs in slowly.* ◇ *Mix a little cream into the sauce.*
SYN blend sth in; stir sth in, stir sth into sth
◆ v + n/pron + adv ◆ v + adv + n ◆ v + n/pron + prep

,mix sb 'up; be/get ,mixed 'up to make sb unable to think clearly or understand what is happening: *Now you've mixed me up completely! I'm really confused.* ◇ *He got mixed up and caught the wrong train.*
SYN muddle sb up (*informal, especially BrE*), confuse sb (*more formal*)
NOTE Mix sb up is often used in the passive with be or get: *I think you're getting mixed up.*
◆ v + n/pron + adv ◆ v + adv + n ◆ be/get + v + adv
▶ **,mixed-'up** *adj* (*informal*) confused because of social or emotional problems: *She's a very mixed-up kid.*
→ *see also* MIXED-UP at MIX STH UP (WITH STH)

,mix sb/sth 'up (with sb/sth**)** to think wrongly that sb/sth is sb/sth else; to be unable to distinguish between two or more people or things: *You're mixing me up with my brother.* ◇ *The hospital was accused of mixing up the babies' name tags.*
SYN muddle sb/sth up (with sb/sth) (*especially BrE*)
◆ v + n/pron + adv ◆ v + adv + n
IDM get A and B mixed up; get A mixed up with B to think wrongly that sb/sth is sb/sth else; to be unable to distinguish between two or more

people or things: *My bag got mixed up with somebody else's at the airport.* ◇ *People who are colour-blind usually get red and green mixed up.*

,mix sth 'up (with sth**)** to change the order or arrangement of things in a confused or untidy way: *I'd sorted those papers out and now you've mixed them all up again.* ◇ *My letters have all been mixed up with yours.*
SYN muddle sth up (with sth) (*especially BrE*)
NOTE Mix sth up is often used in the passive with be or get: *The clean clothes got all mixed up with the dirty ones.*
◆ v + n/pron + adv ◆ v + adv + n
▶ **'mix-up** *n* a mistake that causes confusion; a situation that is full of confusion: *There was a mix-up over the tickets.*
▶ **,mixed-'up** *adj* untidy; in a state of confusion: *She presented me with a mixed-up stack of files and asked me to put them in order.* ◇ *My papers were all mixed-up.*
→ *see also* MIXED-UP at MIX SB UP, BE/GET MIXED UP

be/get ,mixed 'up in sth to be/become involved in sth dangerous or illegal: *He would never have got mixed up in anything criminal.* ◇ *How did you get mixed up in all this?*
◆ be/get + v + adv + prep

be/get ,mixed 'up with sb to be/become friendly with or involved with sb dangerous or dishonest: *I'll never understand how she got mixed up with Phil.* ◇ *He was mixed up with the wrong crowd for a while.*
◆ be/get + v + adv + prep

'mix it with sb (*BrE, informal*) **1** to compete with sb; to argue or fight with sb: *He'll be mixing it with the world's best players.* ◇ *He can mix it with the best of them.* **2** to meet and spend time with people in a friendly way: *She loves mixing it with the rich and famous.*
◆ v + it + prep

mock /mɒk/

,mock sth 'up to produce a copy of sth that is going to be made, so that it can be tested or people can see what it will be like: *We mocked up the front page to see how it would look.*
◆ v + adv + n ◆ v + n/pron + adv
▶ **'mock-up** *n* a copy of sth that is produced to show people what it will be like, or to test it: *mock-up of the next day's front page*

model /'mɒdl; *AmE* 'mɑːdl/ (-ll-, *AmE* -l-)

'model sb/sth/yourself on sb/sth (*also* **'model sb/sth/yourself upon sb/sth** *more formal*) (*AmE also* **'model sb/sth after sb/sth**) to make or create sth that looks or behaves like sth else; to take sb, especially sb you like, as an example and copy them: *The house was modelled*

on a French chateau. ◊ He modelled the main
character on his friend. ◊ He still models himself
on Elvis.
NOTE Model sb/sth on/after sb/sth is often used
in the passive: *The ship was modelled after a
Greek pirate ship.*
◆ v + n/pron + prep

monkey /'mʌŋki/

monkey a'bout/a'round (with sth) (*BrE, informal*) to behave in a silly way; to touch or change
sth in a careless way: *They were monkeying
around in class.* ◊ *He's monkeyed about with the
original words of the song.*
SYN **mess around; mess around with sth**
◆ v + adv

mooch /muːtʃ/

mooch a'bout/a'round; **mooch a'bout/
a'round sth** (*informal, especially BrE*) to spend
time doing nothing in particular: *We went into
town and mooched about for a while.* ◊ *They
spent an hour mooching around the shops.*
◆ v + adv ◆ v + prep

moon /muːn/

moon a'bout/a'round; **moon a'bout/a'round
sth** (*BrE, informal*) to spend time doing nothing
in particular, often because you are feeling
unhappy: *He mooned around the streets, hoping to
see Anna.*
◆ v + adv ◆ v + prep

'moon over sb (*informal*) to spend your time
dreamily thinking about sb that you love: *He
spends most of his time mooning over Helen.*
◆ v + prep

mop /mɒp; AmE maːp/ (-pp-)

mop 'up; **mop sth 'up 1** to clean up liquid or
remove liquid from somewhere, using sth that
absorbs it: *I always have to mop up after he's had
a shower.* ◊ *Can you mop up the water on the bathroom floor?* ◊ *She mopped up the sauce with a
piece of bread.* ◊ *Mopping-up operations have
begun after the floods.* **2** to use up all of sth: *The
new factory should mop up the pool of surplus
labour.* **3** to take control of sth: *The company
started mopping up smaller firms.*
◆ v + adv ◆ v + adv + n ◆ v + pron + adv ◆ v + n + adv
(*less frequent*)

mop sb/sth 'up to get rid of the last few people
who continue to oppose you; to finish tasks that
remain: *The army mopped up some isolated
pockets of resistance.* ◊ *There are a few things to
mop up before we go.*
◆ v + adv + n ◆ v + pron + adv ◆ v + n + adv (*less
frequent*)

mope /məʊp; AmE moʊp/

mope a'round; **mope a'round sth** (*BrE also
mope a'bout, mope a'bout sth*) to walk about a
place in an unhappy way, with no particular purpose: *He's been moping about all day.* ◊ *You spend
too much time moping around the house.*
◆ v + adv ◆ v + prep

mount /maʊnt/

mount 'up (to sth) to increase gradually in size
or quantity: *The paperwork soon mounts up if
you don't deal with it immediately.* ◊ *My debts
have mounted up to over a thousand dollars.*
◆ v + adv

mouth /maʊð/

mouth 'off (at/about sb/sth) (*informal*) (*often
used in the progressive tenses*) to give your opinion about sb/sth loudly; to complain loudly about
sb/sth: *I could hear him mouthing off about how
they should have won.* ◊ *She was mouthing off at
all the other drivers on the road.*
◆ v + adv

move /muːv/

~ about	189	~ in
~ across		~ in together
~ ahead		~ in with
~ ahead of		~ into
188 ~ along		~ off
~ apart		~ on
~ around		~ out
~ aside		~ out of
~ away		~ over
~ away from	190	~ past
~ back		~ round
~ down		~ towards
~ forward	191	~ up

move a'bout; **move a'bout sth** (*especially
BrE*) = MOVE AROUND, MOVE AROUND STH

move sb/sth a'bout (*especially BrE*) = MOVE
SB/STH AROUND

move a'cross; **move a'cross sth** to move
from one side of sth to the other: *He moved across
to the window and looked out.*
OBJ **room**
◆ v + adv ◆ v + prep

move a'head to advance or develop, often after
there has been a delay: *The project is moving
ahead again now.*
SYN **proceed** (*more formal*)
◆ v + adv

move a'head of sb/sth to move faster than
sb/sth; to develop more quickly than sb/sth else:
'Speed up!' he said, moving ahead of her. ◊ *Our
foreign competitors are moving ahead of us.*
SYN **overtake sb/sth**
◆ v + adv + prep

,move a'long; **,move a'long sth** to go forward: *The convoy of cars was moving slowly along the road.*
[OBJ] **road**
◆ v + adv ◆ v + prep

,move a'long/'on; **,move sb a'long/'on** to leave a particular place or go to a new position; to make sb do this: *Move along now. You're blocking the entrance.* ◇ *The police arrived to move the demonstrators along.*
◆ v + adv ◆ v + n/pron + adv

,move a'long; **,move sth a'long** if a project, etc. **moves along**, or if sb **moves it along**, it continues to make good progress: *Can you move the story along a bit faster? What happened in the end?*
◆ v + adv ◆ v + n/pron + adv

,move a'part if two or more things or people **move apart**, they become separated by a distance: *They quickly moved apart when I walked in.* ◇ *(figurative) The two sides in the dispute are moving further and further apart.*
◆ v + adv

,move a'round; **,move a'round sth** (also **,move a'bout/'round**, **,move a'bout/'round sth** especially BrE) to keep moving from one place to another: *Use the mouse to move around the screen.* ◇ *I have to move around a lot with my job.* ◇ *She sang as she moved about the room.*
◆ v + adv ◆ v + prep

,move sb/sth a'round (also **,move sb/sth a'bout/round** especially BrE) to move sb/sth from one place to another: *It's not fair to keep moving the children around from school to school.* ◇ *The chair is light and easy to move about.*
◆ v + n/pron + adv

,move a'round sth (also **,move 'round sth** especially BrE) to move in a circle around sth that is blocking your path: *She moved round the table to open the window.*
[SYN] **go around sb/sth**
◆ v + prep

,move a'side to move to one side, usually to allow sb or sth to pass: *I moved aside to let her go past.*
◆ v + adv

,move sb/sth a'side to put sb/sth to one side away from the centre of a place, usually to make room for sb/sth else: *We moved the tables aside so that we could dance.*
◆ v + n/pron + adv

,move a'way to leave the place where you live to go and live in another place: *All her friends have moved away from the area.*
◆ v + adv

,move a'way (from sb/sth), **,move sth a'way (from sb/sth)** to leave the place or position you are in and go to another; to take sth from one place or position and put it in another: *Move away from the window in case anyone sees you.* ◇ *Can you move the scissors away from the baby?*
◆ v + adv ◆ v + n/pron + adv ◆ v + adv + n

,move a'way from sth to stop doing, following or believing sth: *The party seems to be moving away from its original aims.*
◆ v + adv + prep

,move 'back; **,move sth 'back 1** to go, or to move sth, to a new position at a distance away from the front or behind sb/sth: *He moved back a few steps.* ◇ *She moved her chair back from the fire.* [OPP] **move forward, move sth forward 2** to go, or to move sth, to the place or position it was in before: *His eyes moved back to her face.* ◇ *It took a long time to move the furniture back after the party.* [SYN] **return (sth) (to sth) 3** if an event **moves back**, or sb **moves it back**, it takes place at a later date or time than was first planned: *They've moved back the date of the wedding.*
→ see also PUT STH BACK
◆ v + adv ◆ v + n/pron + adv ◆ v + adv + n (less frequent)

,move 'down (of a level or an amount) to decrease: *Prices move up and down according to demand.*
[SYN] **go down** [OPP] **move up**
◆ v + adv

,move 'down; **,move 'down sth 1** to move from a higher position to a lower one: *I watched her move nervously down the slope.* [OBJ] **hill, ladder** [OPP] **go up, go up sth 2** to move to a new position to make more space for sb else: *Can you move down (the bus) so more people can get on?*
[OPP] **move up, move up sth**
◆ v + adv ◆ v + prep

,move 'down; **,move sb 'down** (at school) to move, or to move sb, to a lower class, grade or level: *I was worried that if I failed the test I would have to move down.* ◇ *If you don't work harder, you'll be moved down (to the class below).*
[OPP] **move up, move sb up**
◆ v + adv ◆ v + n/pron + adv

,move sb/sth 'down; **,move sb/sth 'down sth** to move sb/sth from a higher position to a lower one: *Move the boxes down from the top of the wardrobe.*
◆ v + n/pron + adv ◆ v + n/pron + prep

,move 'forward; **,move sth 'forward 1** to go, or to make sth go, to a place or position that is in front: *The car began to move forward slowly.* [OPP] **move back, move sth back 2** to develop, or to make sth develop, towards a good result: *It's time to move this project forward.* **3** to move, or to make sth move, towards the future: *The company must keep moving forward.* ◇ *The story then moves forward to 1999.* **4** if an event **moves forward**, or sb **moves it forward**, it takes place at

an earlier date or time than was planned: *My operation has been moved forward two weeks.*
OPP **move back, move sth back**
⊕ v + adv ◆ v + n/pron + adv

,move 'in 1 (on sb/sth) to move towards sb/sth, especially in a threatening way, or to make a dangerous situation calm: *I moved in close and stuck the gun in his back.* ◇ *The police moved in to control the crowd.* **SYN** **close in (on sb/sth) 2** to arrive and begin work, especially when people don't really want you there: *The developers moved in and built a housing estate in the grounds of the old house.* **3 (on sth)** to begin to try to have control of or responsibility for a company, a project, etc: *They are moving in on another drugs company.*
⊕ v + adv

,move 'in; **,move 'into sth** to go to a new house and begin to live there: *How soon can you move in?* ◇ *When are you moving into your new flat?*
OPP **move out, move out of sth**
⊕ v + adv ◆ v + prep

,move 'in together; **,move 'in with sb** to start living with sb, especially a partner: *They've decided to move in together.*
⊕ v + adv + adv ◆ v + adv + prep

,move 'into sth 1 = MOVE IN, MOVE INTO STH **2** to start to be involved in a new area of activity or business: *The company is looking to move into new markets.* ◇ *After teaching for ten years he moved into publishing.* **3** to develop or advance into a new position, stage, etc: *The project is now moving into its second year.* ◇ *The team has moved into fourth place after their victory.*
⊕ v + prep

,move sb/sth 'into sth to take sb/sth and put them/it in a new place: *We've moved the phone into the hall.* ◇ *The doctors at the hospital have moved my father into a room on his own.* ◇ *I've moved my savings into a different bank account.*
⊕ v + n/pron + prep

,move 'off (*especially BrE*) (especially of a vehicle) to start a journey; to begin to move: *Check in your mirrors before you move off.*
⊕ v + adv

,move 'off sth; **,move sb/sth 'off sth** to leave the place where you are; to remove sb/sth from a particular place: *Farmers are rapidly moving off the land.* ◇ *Can you move your car off the pavement please?*
⊕ v + prep ◆ v + n/pron + prep

,move 'on 1 to continue your journey after stopping for a short while; to leave the place where you are and go to a new place: *After a few minutes, the bus moved on again.* ◇ *The police told them to move on and go home!* ◇ *When I looked round, I realized everyone else had moved on.* **2** if ideas, beliefs, etc. **move on**, they change and develop: *Things have moved on a lot since my par-*

ents were young. ◇ *The debate does not seem to have moved on much.* ◇ *Fashions are moving on all the time.* **3 (to sth)** to start doing or discussing sth new: *I want to move on to my next point now.* ◇ *When her contract here runs out in April, Tessa will move on.* ◇ *She moved on to become senior editor of a magazine.* **SYN** **pass on (to sth)**
⊕ v + adv

,move 'on; **,move sb 'on** = MOVE ALONG/ON, MOVE SB ALONG/ON *Every time they stopped they got moved on by the police.*

,move 'out; **,move 'out of sth** to leave your home and go to live somewhere else: *The lodger moved out yesterday.* ◇ *He wants to move out of London.* ◇ *They've recently moved out of the city and gone to live in the country.*
OPP **move in, move into sth**
⊕ v + adv ◆ v + adv + prep

,move sb 'out; **,move sb 'out of sth 1** to make sb leave a place, especially their home: *The landlord is moving the tenants out.* ◇ *The emergency services are moving people out of their homes.* **2** to remove sb from a place: *Many countries are moving their troops out of the area.* **SYN** **withdraw sb (from sth)**
⊕ v + n/pron + adv ◆ v + adv + n (*less frequent*) ◆ v + n/pron + adv + prep

,move sth 'out; **,move sth 'out of sth** to remove sth from a place, especially in order to make more space: *We'll need to move some chairs out before the party to make more room.* ◇ *When can you move your belongings out of my apartment?* ◇ *That table will have to be moved out of the way.*
⊕ v + n/pron + adv ◆ v + adv + n (*less frequent*) ◆ v + n/pron + adv + prep

,move 'out of sth 1 to leave a particular place, area or situation: *We watched the boat moving out of the harbour.* ◇ *The country is moving out of recession.* **2** to stop being involved in a particular activity or area of business: *Many people have been forced to move out of farming.*
⊕ v + adv + prep

,move 'over 1 (to sb/sth) to go towards sb/sth: *He moved over to her.* **2 (to sth)** (*especially BrE*) to begin to do sth in a different way or with different people; to change the system you are using: *I'm an interpreter, but I'd like to move over to translation work.* ◇ *We've just moved over to a new computing system.* **3** to move to one side, usually to make room for sb/sth else: *I wish the car in front would move over and let me overtake.* ◇ *Move over! I want to sit down too.* ◇ (*figurative*) *Older managers should move over to make room for younger people.* → *see also* MOVE UP 2
⊕ v + adv

,move 'over sth; **,move sb/sth 'over sth 1** to go forward slowly across a surface; to make sth do this: *The tank adapts to the ground it is mov-*

ing over. ◇ *Just move the brush lightly over the paper.* **2** if somebody's hands, eyes, etc. **move over** sth, or sb **moves them over** sth, they slowly cross sth: *His eyes moved over her face.* ◇ *She moved her hands gently over his injured ankle.*

◈ v + prep ♦ v + n/pron + prep

,**move 'past sb/sth** to pass in front of sb/sth: *He moved past her into the lounge.*

〉SYN〉 **go past sb/sth**

◈ v + prep

,**move 'round**; ,**move 'round sth** (*especially BrE*) = MOVE AROUND, MOVE AROUND STH

,**move sb/sth' round** (*especially BrE*) = MOVE SB/STH AROUND

,**move 'round sth** (*especially BrE*) = MOVE AROUND STH

,**move to'wards sb/sth** to approach sb/sth: *She began to run as the car moved towards her.*

◈ v + prep

,**move to'wards sth**; ,**move to'wards doing sth** (*especially BrE*) (*AmE usually* ,**move to'ward sth**, ,**move to'ward doing sth**) (*often used in the progressive tenses*) to prepare to do or achieve sth; to approach or move nearer to sth: *We are moving towards a better understanding of the situation.* ◇ *Is the group moving towards finding a solution?*

〔OBJ〕 **understanding, settlement**

◈ v + prep

,**move 'up 1** (of a rate, a level or an amount) to increase: *What will we do if interest rates move up?* 〉SYN〉 **go up** 〈OPP〉 **go down 2** to change your position to make room for sb else: *Come on, move up a bit and let your mother sit down!* → *see also* MOVE DOWN, MOVE DOWN STH 2; MOVE OVER 3

,**move 'up**; ,**move sb 'up** to move, or to make sb move, to a higher level, grade or class: *She's been moved up into the Advanced class.* ◇ *I see Tim has moved up in the world* (= has got a better job, more money, a higher social position, etc.)

〈OPP〉 **move down, move sb down**

◈ v + adv ♦ v + n/pron + adv

,**move 'up**; ,**move 'up sth**; ,**move sb/sth 'up**; ,**move sb/sth 'up sth** to move from a lower to a higher position; to make sb/sth do this: *Hold the ladder tightly and move up a rung at a time.* ◇ *We watched the group moving up the hill.* ◇ (*figurative*) *This is your chance to move up the career ladder and get a better job.* ◇ *Move your hand up and down.* ◇ *We had to move the piano up three flights of stairs.*

〉SYN〉 **go up, go up sth** 〈OPP〉 **move down, move down sth**

◈ v + adv ♦ v + prep ♦ v + n/pron + adv ♦ v + n/pron + prep

mow /məʊ; *AmE* moʊ/ (**mowed**, **mown** /məʊn; *AmE* moʊn/ or **mowed**)

,**mow sb 'down 1** to kill sb, often large numbers of people, with a gun: *The demonstrators were mown down by the soldiers.* **2** (of a vehicle or a driver) to kill/hit sb, often because the driver has been driving carelessly or dangerously: *A mother and her two children were mown down by joyriders.* 〉SYN〉 **run sb down**

〔NOTE〕 **Mow sb down** is often used in the passive.

◈ v + adv + n ♦ v + n/pron + adv

muck /mʌk/

,**muck a'bout/a'round** (*BrE, informal*) **1** (with sb/sth) to spend time and enjoy yourself doing sth with no particular purpose: *They were mucking about outside, kicking a ball around.* **2** (with sb/sth) to behave in a silly way, especially when you should be working or doing sth else: *Stop mucking around and go to bed.* ◇ *She mucked around all year and failed her exams.* **3** to joke; to say silly things: *I thought he was mucking about until I saw it was real blood on his face.*

〉SYN〉 **mess around**

→ *see also* MUCK ABOUT/AROUND WITH STH

◈ v + adv

,**muck sb a'bout/a'round** (*BrE, informal*) to treat sb badly, making them waste time, changing your mind a lot, etc: *I'm sick of being mucked about by employers.*

〉SYN〉 **mess sb about/around**

◈ v + n/pron + adv

,**muck a'bout/a'round with sth** (*BrE, informal*) to keep touching, moving or changing sth in an annoying way: *Who's been mucking about with my computer?* ◇ *Don't muck around with the words of the song — I think they're fine.*

〉SYN〉 **mess around with sth, mess about with sth**

→ *see also* MUCK ABOUT/AROUND

◈ v + adv + prep

,**muck a'round** (*BrE*) = MUCK ABOUT/AROUND

,**muck sb a'round** (*BrE*) = MUCK SB ABOUT/AROUND

,**muck a'round with sth** (*BrE*) = MUCK ABOUT/AROUND WITH STH

,**muck 'in** (*BrE, informal*) **1** to join in with other people in order to complete a task: *If we all muck in, we'll soon get the job finished.* **2** to share food, accommodation, costs, etc. with other people: *Money was short, but we all mucked in together.*

◈ v + adv

,**muck 'out**; ,**muck sth 'out** to clean the place where an animal lives, especially a horse: *It's your turn to muck out today.*

◈ v + adv ♦ v + adv + n ♦ v + n/pron + adv

,muck sth 'up (*informal, especially BrE*) **1** to do sth very badly; to spoil sth: *This is your last chance, so don't muck it up.* ◇ *Her surprise visit totally mucked up my plans.* **2** to make sth dirty: *Take your shoes off! You're mucking up my floor!* **3** to make sth untidy: *Stop that, you're mucking up my hair.*

⟨SYN⟩ **mess sth up**

◈ v + adv + n ◆ v + n/pron + adv

muddle /'mʌdl/

,muddle a'long (*also* ,muddle 'on *less frequent*) (*especially BrE*) to continue living or doing sth with no clear purpose or plan: *We muddle along from day to day.*

◈ v + adv

,muddle 'through to achieve your aims although you are not efficient, do not know what you are doing, do not have the right equipment, etc: *I'll muddle through somehow.*

◈ v + adv

,muddle sb 'up (*especially BrE*) to make sb confused: *I won't explain how this works now — it might muddle you up.* ◇ *You're muddling me up!* ◇ *I got muddled up and took the wrong turning.*

⟨SYN⟩ **mix sb up**; **confuse sb** (*more formal*)

NOTE **Muddle sb up** is often used in the passive with the verb *get*. ◆ **Muddle sb** is used more frequently with the same meaning.

◈ v + n/pron + adv ◆ v + adv + n (*less frequent*)

,muddle sb/sth 'up (with sb/sth), ,muddle A 'up with B (*especially BrE*) to confuse one person or thing with another; to think that sb/sth is sb/sth else: *He muddled up our passports and gave me back the wrong one.* ◇ *I keep muddling her up with her sister.*

⟨SYN⟩ **mix sb/sth up** (with sb/sth)

NOTE **Muddle sb/sth** is also used with the same meaning.

◈ v + n/pron + adv ◆ v + adv + n

IDM **get A and B muddled 'up**; **get A muddled 'up with B** to confuse one person or thing with another: *I always get the twins muddled up.*

,muddle sth 'up (with sth) (*especially BrE*) to carelessly put things in the wrong order; to mix things together in an untidy way: *The money was muddled up with everything else in his pocket.* ◇ *The kids have muddled up all the photos.*

⟨SYN⟩ **mix sth up** (with sth)

NOTE **Muddle sth** is also used with the same meaning.

◈ v + adv + n ◆ v + n/pron + adv

IDM **get sth muddled 'up** (with sth) to put things in the wrong order; to mix things together in an untidy way: *The words seemed to have got muddled up.*

mug /mʌg/ (-gg-)

,mug 'up (on sth), ,mug sth 'up (*BrE, informal*) to quickly learn sth, especially sth that you should already know, before an exam, etc: *He spent the whole night mugging up for the exam.* ◇ *I'd better mug up on the subject before I meet her.* ◇ *I'm going to mug up as much as I can about Delhi before I go there.*

⟨SYN⟩ **swot up** (on sth) (*BrE*), **review sth** (*especially AmE*), **revise sth** (*BrE*)

◈ v + adv ◆ v + adv + n ◆ v + n/pron + adv

mull /mʌl/

,mull sth 'over to think about or consider sth for a long time before you decide to do sth: *I've been mulling over what you said last night.*

◈ v + n/pron + adv ◆ v + adv + n

muscle /'mʌsl/

,muscle 'in (on sb/sth) (*informal*) to get involved in a situation that you have no right to be involved in, especially sth that will give you an advantage or a profit: *I don't want Matt muscling in on our deal.*

◈ v + adv

muss /mʌs/

,muss sth 'up (*AmE*) to make sth look untidy: *My skirt got mussed up when I sat down.*

⟨SYN⟩ **mess sth up**

NOTE **Muss sth up** is often used in the passive. ◆ **Muss sth** is often used.

◈ v + n/pron + adv ◆ v + adv + n

muster /'mʌstə(r)/

,muster sth 'up to find the courage, strength, etc. that you need in order to do sth difficult or unpleasant: *She could barely muster up the strength to get out of bed.*

OBJ **strength, energy** ⟨SYN⟩ **summon sth up**

NOTE **Muster sth** is often used with the same meaning.

◈ v + adv + n ◆ v + n/pron + adv

Nn

naff /næf/

,naff 'off (becoming old-fashioned, BrE, slang)
used by some people to tell sb rudely to go away
and stop annoying them: Just naff off and leave
me alone!
⟩SYN⟨ clear off (especially BrE)
◈ v + adv

nag /næg/ (-gg-)

'nag at sb 1 to keep complaining to sb about their
behaviour; to keep asking sb to do sth: He keeps
nagging at me to get more exercise. 2 to worry or
irritate you continuously: The suspicion that she
was lying continued to nag at me.
◈ v + prep

nail /neɪl/

,nail sb 'down (to sth) to force sb to state exactly
what they think, what they intend to do, etc: He
says he'll come, but I can't nail him down to a
date.
⟩SYN⟨ pin sb down (to sth)
◈ v + n/pron + adv ◆ v + adv + n

,nail sth 'down 1 to fasten sth down with nails:
She got him to nail the loose floorboard down. 2 to
know or understand exactly what sth is: Something seems strange here, but I can't nail it down.
3 to reach an agreement or a decision, usually
after a lot of discussion: They managed to nail
down an agreement with the management. OBJ
agreement
◈ 1 v + n/pron + adv 2 v + adv + n ◆ v + n/pron + adv
3 v + adv + n ◆ v + n/pron + adv

,nail sth 'up 1 to attach sth to a wall, a post, etc.
with nails: I nailed up a notice saying: Keep out! 2
to fasten a door, a window, etc. with nails so that
it cannot easily be opened: He nailed up the door
to keep intruders out.
◈ v + adv + n ◆ v + n/pron + adv

name /neɪm/

'name sb/sth 'after sb/sth (AmE also 'name
sb/sth 'for sb/sth) to give sb/sth the name of
sb/sth else that you like or admire, for example a
family member or a famous person or place: We
named her after her grandmother. ◇ The Miller
fire was named for the canyon in which it began.
◈ v + n/pron + prep

narrow /'nærəʊ; AmE -roʊ/

,narrow sth 'down (to sth) to gradually reduce
the number of possibilities: I've narrowed the
list of candidates down to three.
◈ v + n/pron + adv ◆ v + adv + n

nestle /'nesl/

,nestle 'up (to sb/sth) to make yourself warm and
comfortable by moving close to sb: Jamie nestled
up to his mother on the sofa.
◈ v + adv

nibble /'nɪbl/

'nibble at sth 1 to eat sth by taking very small
bites: The mouse nibbled at the peanuts. ◇ You've
only nibbled at your lunch. 2 to show a slight
interest in sth: Several companies have nibbled at
our offer.
◈ v + prep

,nibble a'way at sth (especially BrE) to gradually reduce or use up the total amount of sth:
Inflation began to nibble away at their savings.
◈ v + adv + prep

nip /nɪp/ (-pp-)

,nip sth 'off to remove a part of sth by squeezing
it with your fingers, cutting it quickly with scissors, etc: She nipped off the dead leaves.
⟩SYN⟨ cut sth off
◈ v + adv + n ◆ v + n/pron + adv

nod /nɒd; AmE nɑːd/ (-dd-)

,nod 'off (informal) to fall asleep: She nodded off
in front of the television.
⟩SYN⟨ doze off (more formal)
◈ v + adv

nose /nəʊz; AmE noʊz/

,nose a'round (BrE also ,nose a'bout) (for sth)
(informal) to go around trying to find out sth
about sb/sth, particularly when you should not
do this: I'm just nosing about for clues.
◈ v + adv

,nose sb 'out (informal) to defeat sb by a small
amount, for example in a race or an election: She
was nosed out of first place by her old rival.
◈ v + n/pron + adv ◆ v + adv + n

,nose sth 'out (informal) to discover some information by searching for it: That man can nose a
news story out anywhere.
⟩SYN⟨ sniff sth out
◈ v + n/pron + adv ◆ v + adv + n

notch /nɒtʃ; AmE nɑːtʃ/

,notch sth 'up (informal) to achieve a win or a
high score: He notched up ten points in the first
five minutes of the game.
OBJ victory, points ⟩SYN⟨ clock sth up
◈ v + adv + n ◆ v + n/pron + adv

note /nəʊt; *AmE* noʊt/

,note sth 'down to write sth down so that you
will remember it: *The class noted down every
word she said.*
  ⟨SYN⟩ **take sth down; write sth down**
  ◈ v + adv + n ♦ v + n/pron + adv

number /'nʌmbə(r)/

'number sb/sth among sth (*formal*) to include
sb/sth in a particular group: *I number her among
my closest friends.* ◇ *He is numbered among the
world's top experts.*
  ⟨SYN⟩ **count sb/sth among sth**
  ◈ v + n/pron + prep

nuzzle /'nʌzl/

,nuzzle 'up against/to sb/sth to press your
head, face, etc. against sb/sth to show affection or
keep warm, etc: *He nuzzled up to his mother with
a happy sigh.*
  ◈ v + adv + prep

O o

object /əbˈdʒekt/

ob'ject to sb/sth; ob'ject to doing sth; ob'ject to sb doing sth to say that you disagree with, disapprove of or oppose sth: *Many local people object to the building of the new airport.* ◊ *I really object to being charged for parking at the hospital.*
◈ v + prep

occur /əˈkɜː(r)/

oc'cur to sb if an idea or a thought **occurs to** you it suddenly comes into your mind: *Hasn't it ever occurred to you that he might be lying to you?* ◊ *A strange thought suddenly occurred to me.*
[SUBJ] **thought, possibility**
◈ v + prep

offend /əˈfend/

of'fend against sth (*formal*) to go against what people believe is morally right: *The film offends against good taste.*
◈ v + prep

offer /ˈɒfə(r); AmE ˈɔːf-, ˈɑːf-/

,offer sth 'up (for sth) to give sth to God: *She offered up a prayer for her husband's safe return.*
[OBJ] **prayer, sacrifice**
◈ v + adv + n ◆ v + n/pron + adv (*less frequent*)

ooze /uːz/

,ooze 'out; ,ooze 'out of/'from/'through sth if a thick liquid **oozes out** or **oozes from**, etc. somewhere, it flows out slowly: *Cream was oozing out of the cake.* ◊ *cakes with cream oozing out at the sides* ◊ *Blood was oozing from the cut on her arm.*
◈ v + adv ◆ v + adv + prep ◆ v + prep

open /ˈəʊpən; AmE ˈoʊ-/

,open 'into/'onto sth if a door or a room **opens into/onto** sth, it leads directly to it: *The door opened onto a small yard.* ◊ *The kitchen opens into a large sitting room.*
◈ v + prep

,open 'off sth if a door or a room **opens off** sth, it connects directly with it: *Several doors opened off the hall.* ◊ *The offices opened off the reception area.*
◈ v + prep

,open 'out 1 (into/onto sth) to become wider or bigger; to become more open and not enclosed by anything: *The valley opened out in front of us.* ◊ *The narrow lane opened out into a field.* **2 (to sb)** (*BrE*) = OPEN UP 1 *He only opened out to her very*

slowly. **3** to spread out; to become open and larger or flatter: *The table opens out so that more people can sit at it.* ◊ *The buds on the trees have all opened out.*
◈ v + adv

,open sth 'out to spread sth out; to make sth open and flat: *He opened the map out.*
◈ v + n/pron + adv ◆ v + adv + n

,open 'up 1 (*BrE also* ,**open 'out**) **(to sb)** (*informal*) to talk freely and openly about what you feel or think: *Will you open up to me and tell me what's worrying you?* **2** to start firing: *The anti-aircraft guns opened up.* **3** (often used in orders etc.) to open a door: *Open up or we'll break the door down!*
◈ v + adv

,open sb 'up to cut sb open in order to do a medical operation: *They opened her up but didn't find anything wrong.*
◈ v + n/pron + adv ◆ v + adv + n

,open 'up; ,open sth 'up 1 to become or to make sth possible, available or able to be reached: *If you have good qualifications, a whole range of possibilities open up for you.* ◊ *The whole region has been opened up for trade by the new rail link.* ◊ *They opened up the sports hall to house the flood victims.* ◊ *Writing to penfriends can open up a whole new world.* **2** to start a new business: *The company are opening up a new factory in Wales.* [OPP] **close down, close sth down 3** to begin business for the day: *If you're feeling tired this morning, I'll open up (the store).* [OPP] **close up, close sth up 4** (usually in sport) to develop or start to happen; to produce sth or make sth start to happen: *An increasing gap is opening up between the achievements of girls and boys in exams.* ◊ *United have opened up a three-point lead after five games.* **5** to become wider; to make sth wider, especially sth that has been closed: *Coughing might open up your wound.* ◊ *She wished the floor would open up and swallow her* (= for example, because she felt very embarrassed about sth). ◊ *Cutting down the trees opened up the view from the house.*
◈ v + adv ◆ v + n/pron + adv ◆ v + adv + n

,open sth 'up to make sth that is shut, locked, etc. open: *Can you open up that box of books for me?*
◈ v + n/pron + adv ◆ v + adv + n

opt /ɒpt; AmE ɑːpt/

'opt for sth to choose sth; to make a decision about sth: *More students are now opting for computer science courses.* ◊ *You can stay in the main hotel or opt for one of the bungalows near the beach.*
◈ v + prep

,**opt 'in**; ,**opt 'into sth** to choose to take part in
sth: *We offer a pension plan, and all staff have the*
chance to opt. in. ◇ *The government decided to opt*
into the new European treaty.
 〉OPP〉 **opt out, opt out of sth**
 ✦ v + adv ◆ v + prep

,**opt 'out**; ,**opt 'out of sth 1** to choose not to take
part in sth: *You can opt out of the company's pen-*
sion plan. **2** (of a school or a hospital in Britain)
to choose not to be under the control of the local
authority: *A majority of parents were in favour of*
opting out.
 〉OPP〉 **opt in, opt into sth**
 ✦ v + adv ◆ v + adv + prep
 ▶ **'opt-out** n (*often used as an adjective*) **1** the act
 of choosing not to take part in sth **2** (in Britain)
 the action of a school or a hospital that decides to
 manage its own money and is therefore no
 longer controlled by a local authority: *Nurses*
 and health workers voted against the opt-out.
 ▶ ,**opted-'out** adj [only before noun] (in Britain)
 an **opted-out** school or hospital is one that has
 decided not to be under the control of the local
 authority

order /'ɔ:də(r); AmE 'ɔ:rd-/

,**order sb a'round** (BrE also ,**order sb a'bout**) to
keep on telling sb to do things in an unpleasant
way: *Stop ordering me around!* ◇ *Even as a child*
he ordered his friends about.
 ✦ v + n/pron + adv

,**order 'in**; ,**order 'in sth** (AmE) to telephone and
buy a meal from a restaurant that cooks the food
and brings it to your home: *I'm too tired to cook —*
let's order in. ◇ *Let's order in Chinese tonight.*
 ✦ v + adv ◆ v + adv + n

,**order sb 'off**; ,**order sb 'off sth 1** to tell sb to
leave sth such as a bus, a train, etc: *The driver*
ordered the boys off for messing around on the
bus. **2** (for sth) (*especially BrE*) (in a sports game)
to make sb leave the field because they have
broken the rules of the game: *He was ordered off*
for arguing with the referee. OBJ **player** 〉SYN〉
send sb off (for sth) (BrE) NOTE **Order sb off** is
often used in the passive in this meaning.
 ✦ v + n/pron + adv ◆ v + adv + n ◆ v + n/pron + prep

,**order 'out (for sth)** (AmE) to telephone and buy a
meal from a restaurant that cooks the food and
brings it to you: *We could order out for a Chinese.*
 ✦ v + adv

own /əʊn; AmE oʊn/

own 'up (to sth/to doing sth) to admit that you are
the person responsible for sth that has happened: *Nobody owned up to breaking the window.*
 〉SYN〉 **confess (to sth/to doing sth)** (*more formal*)
 ✦ v + adv

P p

pace /peɪs/

‚pace 'out sth; **‚pace it/them 'out** (*also* ‚pace 'off sth, ‚pace it/them 'off *less frequent*) to measure sth by taking regular steps across it: *She paced out the length of the room.*

NOTE A noun must always follow **out**, but a pronoun comes between the verb and **out**.

⚙ v + adv + n ♦ v + pron + adv

pack /pæk/

‚pack a'way if sth **packs away**, it can be folded up small when you are no longer using it: *The jacket packs away neatly into its own pocket.*

⚙ v + adv

‚pack sth a'way 1 to put sth into a box, cupboard, etc. when you are no longer using it: *We packed away the picnic things and put them in the car.* **2** (*informal*) to eat a lot of sth: *She can certainly pack it away!*

SYN put sth away

⚙ v + n/pron + adv ♦ v + adv + n

‚pack sb 'in to attract large numbers of people to a show, a play, etc: *The film is still packing in the crowds.*

OBJ the crowds

NOTE Pack sb in is not used in the passive.

⚙ v + adv + n ♦ v + pron + adv ♦ v + n + adv (*rare*)

‚pack sb/sth 'in; **‚pack sth/sb 'in/'into sth 1** to do a lot of things, see a lot of people, etc. in a limited period of time: *She managed to pack a lot of sightseeing into three days.* ◇ *We packed in a lot yesterday afternoon.* **2** to put a lot of things or people into a limited space: *Somehow we managed to pack everyone in.*

SYN cram sb/sth in, cram sb/sth in/into sth

⚙ v + n/pron + adv ♦ v + adv + n ♦ v + n/pron + prep

‚pack sth 'in (*BrE, informal*) **1** to give sth up, especially a job: *She's packed in her job as a teacher.* ◇ *Smoking's bad for you. You ought to pack it in.* ◇ *I was so depressed I felt like packing it all in.* **OBJ** job **SYN** chuck sth in/up (*BrE*), jack sth in (*BrE*), give sth up → *see also* PACK UP, PACK STH UP 2 **2** ‚pack it 'in used to tell sb to stop behaving badly or doing sth that is annoying you: *Just pack it in, will you?*

⚙ **1** v + adv + n ♦ v + n/pron + adv

   2 v + it + adv

‚pack 'into sth if people **pack into** a place, they go there in large numbers and fill it completely: *All six of us packed into the tiny car.* ◇ *More than 70 000 people packed into Trafalgar Square on New Year's Eve.*

SYN cram into sth

⚙ v + prep

‚pack sb/sth 'into sth = PACK SB/STH IN, PACK SB/STH IN/INTO STH

‚pack sb 'off (**to …**) (*informal*) to send sb away, especially because you do not want them with you: *She was packed off to boarding school at the age of eight.* ◇ *He packed the children off to bed.*

NOTE Pack sb off is often used in the passive.

⚙ v + n/pron + adv ♦ v + adv + n

‚pack sth 'out (*BrE*) if a show, a performer, etc. **packs out** a place, they attract large numbers of people to see it/them: *The band packs out venues all over the country.* ◇ *The movie has been packing out cinemas for weeks.*

⚙ v + adv + n ♦ v + n/pron + adv

▶ **‚packed 'out** *adj* (*BrE*) very full: *The town is packed out with tourists in the summer.* ◇ *a packed-out stadium*

‚pack 'up (*BrE, informal*) if a machine, an engine, etc. **packs up**, it stops working: *My car's packed up again.*

SYN break down; give out

⚙ v + adv

‚pack 'up; **‚pack sth 'up 1** to put your possessions, equipment, etc. into bags or boxes before you leave a place: *It's time to pack up and go home now.* ◇ *All our things were packed up waiting to be moved.* **OBJ** things, belongings **2** (*BrE, informal*) to stop doing sth, especially a job: *He used to smoke but he packed up last year.* ◇ *You'd feel better if you packed up smoking.* ◇ *When did you pack up your job at the bookshop?* **OBJ** smoking, work, job **SYN** give sth up → *see also* PACK STH IN 1

⚙ v + adv ♦ v + adv + n ♦ v + pron + adv ♦ v + n + adv (*rare*)

package /'pækɪdʒ/

‚package sth 'up (*especially AmE*) to wrap sth and make it into a parcel so that you can send it somewhere: *She packaged up his books and mailed them to him.*

SYN parcel sth up (*BrE*)

⚙ v + adv + n ♦ v + n/pron + adv

pad /pæd/ (**-dd-**)

‚pad sth 'out (**with sth**) **1** to put soft material into a piece of clothing in order to change its shape: *She padded the costume out with foam.* **2** to make sth, such as a book, an article, a speech, etc., longer by adding unnecessary material: *I padded out the article with lots of quotations.*

⚙ v + adv + n ♦ v + pron + adv ♦ v + n + adv

page /peɪdʒ/

page 'through sth (*AmE*) to turn the pages of a book, a magazine, etc. and look at them without reading them in detail: *She paged through the report looking for her name.*
~~SYN~~ **leaf through sth**
◈ v + prep

paint /peɪnt/

paint sth 'out (*especially BrE*) to cover sth, such as a mark, part of a picture, etc. by putting paint on top of it so that no one can see it: *The markings on the plane had been hurriedly painted out.*
◈ v + adv + n ◆ v + pron + adv ◆ v + n + adv (*rare*)

paint 'over sth to cover sth with a layer of paint: *We'll have to paint over the dirty marks on the wall.* ◇ *I don't like the way the painting has turned out so I'll just paint over it.*
~~NOTE~~ Paint over sth can be used in the passive: *The name had been painted over.*
◈ v + prep

paint sth 'up to paint sth, decorating it in a bright, attractive way: *Their house had been painted up in amazing colours.* ◇ *The bus was painted up with advertisements.*
◈ v + n/pron + adv ◆ v + adv + n

pair /peə(r); *AmE* per/

pair 'off; **pair sb 'off** (with sb) to form a pair or pairs, especially in order to have a romantic relationship; to bring two people together in this way: *By the end of the course, everyone had paired off.* ◇ (*especially BrE*) *They tried to pair their daughter off with the neighbour's son.*
◈ v + adv ◆ v + n/pron + adv ◆ v + adv + n

pair 'up; **pair sb 'up** (with sb/sth) to form a pair or pairs (with sb/sth) in order to work, play a game, etc. together; to bring two people together for this purpose: *The job is a lot easier if you pair up with someone else.* ◇ *Writers have been paired up with artists to write articles on paintings.*
◈ v + adv ◆ v + n/pron + adv ◆ v + adv + n

pal /pæl/ (-ll-)

pal a'round (with sb) (*AmE*) to become friends with sb and spend time with them: *I used to pal around with Brad.*
◈ v + adv

pal 'up (with sb) (*BrE*) to become friends with sb: *They palled up at college.*
◈ v + adv

palm /pɑːm/

palm sb 'off (with sth) (*informal*) **1** to persuade sb to believe an explanation for sth that is not true, in order to stop them asking questions or complaining: *Don't let him palm you off with an excuse.* **2** to persuade sb to accept sth that has little value or is not what they really want: *Make sure he doesn't palm you off with faulty goods.*
~~SYN~~ **fob sb off** (with sth)
◈ v + n/pron + adv ◆ v + adv + n

palm sth 'off as sth (*informal*) to persuade sb that sth is better than it really is, or is sth different, especially in order to sell it: *She was trying to palm copies off as original paintings.*
◈ v + n/pron + adv + prep

palm sb/sth 'off on/onto sb (*informal*) to get rid of sb/sth that you do not want by persuading sb else to accept them/it: *He tried to palm his uncle off on me for the whole afternoon.* ◇ *I think she palmed off the stolen necklace on some unsuspecting old lady.*
◈ v + n/pron + adv + prep ◆ v + adv + n + prep

pan /pæn/ (-nn-)

pan 'out (*informal*) (of events or a situation) to develop in a particular way: *I don't know why things panned out the way they did.* ◇ *How do you see your career panning out?*
~~SYN~~ **turn out**
◈ v + adv

pander /'pændə(r)/

'pander to sb/sth (*disapproving*) to try to please sb by doing or providing what they want although you know it is probably wrong to do so: *He panders to her every whim.* ◇ *His films never pandered to public taste.*
~~NOTE~~ Pander to sb/sth can be used in the passive: *I don't think children should be pandered to.*
◈ v + prep

panic /'pænɪk/ (-ck-)

'panic sb into sth; **'panic sb into doing sth** to make sb do sth too quickly because they are afraid: *Don't let them panic you into a decision.*
~~NOTE~~ Panic sb into sth/into doing sth is often used in the passive: *She refused to be panicked into making rash promises.*
◈ v + n/pron + prep

paper /'peɪpə(r)/

paper 'over sth 1 to cover sth such as a wall with thick paper in order to hide sth: *We papered over the stains on the wall.* **2** to hide sth such as a problem, a disagreement, etc., especially quickly or not very well: *The divisions in the party had been papered over during the election campaign.*
~~NOTE~~ Paper over sth can be used in the passive.
◈ v + prep
~~IDM~~ **paper over the 'cracks** (in sth) to try to hide a problem or fault, especially in a way that is unlikely to be successful

parcel /ˈpɑːsl; *AmE* ˈpɑːrsl/ (**-ll-**, *AmE* **-l-**)

,**parcel sth 'out** to divide sth into parts or portions: *They parcelled out the land into small plots.* ◊ *The work was parcelled out among the staff.*
◆ v + adv + n ♦ v + pron + adv ♦ v + n + adv (*rare*)

,**parcel sth 'up** (*BrE*) to wrap sth and make it into a parcel: *She parcelled up the books ready to send.*
[SYN] **package sth up** (*especially AmE*), **wrap sth up**
[NOTE] **Parcel sth** is used less often with the same meaning.
◆ v + adv + n ♦ v + n/pron + adv

pare /peə(r); *AmE* per/

,**pare sth a'way/'off** to remove the thin outer layer from sth in thin strips: *Pare off the rind from the orange using a sharp knife.* ◊ (*figurative*) *Their rights had been pared away under the last three kings.*
[NOTE] **Pare sth** can also be used with this meaning: *Pare the rind from the lemons.* ◊ *thinly pared rind*
◆ v + adv + n ♦ v + n/pron + adv

,**pare sth 'down** (*also* ,**pare sth 'back** *less frequent*) (**to sth**) to gradually reduce sth considerably in size or amount: *We've pared our expenses down to a minimum.*
[SYN] **cut sth back; cut sth down (to sth)**
[NOTE] **Pare sth** can also be used with this meaning: *We pared costs by doing much of the work ourselves.*
◆ v + n/pron + adv ♦ v + adv + n

parlay /ˈpɑːleɪ; *AmE* ˈpɑːrleɪ/

,**parlay sth 'into sth** (*AmE, informal*) to use an advantage that you have, such as money or a skill, in order to get sth or make it worth more: *He parlayed his relationship with his boss into an important job.*
◆ v + n/pron + prep

part /pɑːt; *AmE* pɑːrt/

'**part with sth** to give sth away that you would prefer to keep: *It was my grandmother's necklace and I'll never part with it.* ◊ (*humorous*) *We won't be sorry to part with that old sofa.* ◊ *He hates parting with* (= spending) *his money.*
[OBJ] **money**
◆ v + prep

partake /pɑːˈteɪk; *AmE* pɑːrˈt-/ (**partook** /-ˈtʊk/ **partaken** /-ˈteɪkən/)

par'take of sth (*old-fashioned* or *humorous*) to eat or drink sth: *Would you care to partake of some refreshment?*
◆ v + prep

partition /pɑːˈtɪʃn; *AmE* pɑːrˈt-/

par,tition sth 'off to separate one area, one part of a room, etc. from another with a wall or screen: *The dining area is partitioned off with screens.*
[NOTE] **Partition sth off** is often used in the passive.
◆ v + adv + n ♦ v + n/pron + adv

pass /pɑːs; *AmE* pæs/

	~ around		~ off as
	~ as		~ on
	~ away		~ on to
	~ between		~ out
	~ by		~ over
199	~ down	200	~ round
	~ for		~ through
	~ into		~ to
	~ off		~ up

,**pass sth a'round**; ,**pass sth a'round sth** (*BrE also* ,**pass sth 'round**, ,**pass sth 'round sth**) to offer sth to each person in a group: *Would you mind passing the sandwiches round?* ◊ *A picture was passed around the class.*
[SYN] **hand sth round, hand sth around**
◆ v + n/pron + adv ♦ v + adv + n ♦ v + n/pron + prep

'**pass as sb**
→ *see also* PASS FOR/AS SB

,**pass a'way 1** (*also* ,**pass 'on**) people say **pass away** to avoid saying 'die': *She passed away peacefully in her sleep.* **2** to disappear: *Many of these customs have passed away.*
◆ v + adv

,**pass be'tween sb** if sth such as a look, a word, etc. **passes between** two people, they look quickly at each other, speak to each other, etc: *A look of understanding passed between Ann and Carla.* ◊ *I never knew what passed between them* (= what they said to each other) *on that day.*
◆ v + prep

,**pass 'by** if time **passes by**, it goes past: *The weeks passed by and she didn't call.*
[SYN] **go by**
[NOTE] **Pass** is used more frequently with this meaning: *The weeks passed.*
◆ v + adv

,**pass 'by**; ,**pass 'by sb/sth** to go past sb/sth without stopping: *He saw the procession pass by.* ◊ *The boat passed close by the island.*
[SYN] **go by, go by sb/sth**
[NOTE] **Pass** and **pass sb/sth** are also used with this meaning: *We watched the procession pass.*
◆ v + adv ♦ v + prep

▶ '**bypass** *n* **1** a road that goes around a town, etc. and which is intended to keep traffic out of the town centre **2** a medical operation on the heart in which blood is directed along a different route so that it does not flow through a part that is damaged or blocked; the new route that the blood takes: *a bypass operation*

▶ ˌpasser-'by *n* a person who is walking past sb/sth, especially when sth unexpected happens: *Several passers-by stopped to help.*

ˌpass sb/sth 'by to happen without affecting sb/sth: *She feels that life is passing her by* (= that she is not enjoying the opportunities and pleasures of life). ◇ *The whole business passed him by* (= he was hardly aware that it was happening).
🔷 v + n/pron + adv

ˌpass sth 'down (to sb) to give sth or teach sth to your children or people who are younger than you, who will then give or teach it to their children, etc: *These stories were passed down from one generation to the next.* ◇ *Some of the furniture has been passed down through the family.*
ˢʸⁿ **hand sth down (to sb)**
ⁿᵒᵗᵉ Pass sth down is often used in the passive.
🔷 v + n/pron + adv ◆ v + adv + n

'pass for sth (*disapproving*) used to say that although sth is said to be a particular thing, you do not think it is good enough to be called that: *I got used to drinking what passes for tea in that part of the world.*
🔷 v + prep

'pass for/as sb to be so much like another person, or another type of person, that people could easily think you were that person or type: *He speaks French well enough to pass for a Frenchman.* ◇ *She's in her forties but she could pass for ten years younger.* ◇ *They could pass as twins.*
🔷 v + prep

'pass into sth to become a part of sth: *Many foreign words have passed into English.*
🔷 v + prep

ˌpass 'off (*BrE*) **1** [+ adv/prep] if an event **passes off** in a particular way, it takes place and is finished in the way mentioned: *The election has passed off without incident.* ◇ *The celebrations passed off peacefully.* **2** if pain, the effects of a drug, etc. **pass off**, they gradually disappear: *The symptoms should pass off within 24 hours.*
🔷 v + adv

ˌpass sth 'off to act as if a difficult or awkward remark or situation is less important than you really think it is: *He had really upset her, but she smiled and tried to pass it off.* ◇ *He managed to pass the question off lightly.*
🔷 v + n/pron + adv ◆ v + adv + n

ˌpass sb/sth 'off as sb/sth; ˌpass yourself 'off as sb/sth to pretend that sb or sth is something that they are not: *She tried to pass the picture off as an original.* ◇ *He succeeded in passing himself off as a doctor.*
🔷 v + n/pron + adv + prep ◆ v + adv + n + prep (*less frequent*)

ˌpass 'on 1 (to sth) (*BrE*) to begin a new activity, discussion, etc: *Let's pass on to the next item on the agenda.* ◇ *If you can't answer one question, pass on to the next.* ˢʸⁿ **move on (to sth) 2** = PASS AWAY 1
🔷 v + adv

ˌpass sth 'on (to sb) **1** to give sth to sb else, especially after receiving or using it yourself: *I'll pass this book on to you when I've finished with it.* ◇ *I'll pass on your news to the rest of the family.*
ˢʸⁿ **hand sth on (to sb) 2** to give sth that you have, such as a disease, a quality, etc. to sb else: *HIV can be passed on from parent to child.* ◇ *Parents pass these attitudes on to their children.* **3** if a company, a shop/store, etc. **passes on** higher or lower costs to its customers, it makes them pay more or less for sth: *The supermarket did not pass on its profit to customers by cutting prices.*
🔷 v + n/pron + adv ◆ v + adv + n

ˌpass sb 'on to sb to arrange for sb else to help or deal with a particular person: *I'm afraid I can't answer your question, but I'll pass you on to my colleague.*
🔷 v + n/pron + adv + prep

ˌpass 'out 1 to lose consciousness: *He almost passed out with the pain.* ˢʸⁿ **black out; faint** → see also COME ROUND/COME TO **2** (*also* ˌpass 'out of sth) (*BrE*) to leave a military college after completing a course of training
🔷 v + adv **2** also v + adv + prep

ˌpass sth 'out (to sb) to give something to each person in a group: *The teacher asked me to pass the books out.*
ˢʸⁿ **give sth out; hand sth out (to sb)**
🔷 v + n/pron + adv ◆ v + adv + n

ˌpass 'over sb (for sth), ˌpass him, them, etc. 'over (for sth) to not consider sb for a better job, especially when they deserve it or think they deserve it: *I was passed over for promotion again.* ◇ *He was passed over in favour of a younger man.*
ⁿᵒᵗᵉ A noun must always follow **over**, but a pronoun comes between the verb and **over**. ◆ This phrasal verb is often used in the passive.
🔷 v + adv + n ◆ v + pron + adv

ˌpass 'over sb/sth **1** to move over the top of sb/sth: *The planes pass directly over the hospital.* ◇ *The eye of the storm was passing over us.* **2** to ignore or avoid sth: *They chose to pass over her rude remarks.* ◇ *For years this painting was passed over by experts.* ˢʸⁿ **ignore sb/sth** ⁿᵒᵗᵉ Pass over sb/sth can be used in the passive in this meaning.
🔷 v + prep

▶ 'overpass *n* (*especially AmE*) a bridge that carries one road or railway above another; a bridge over a road for people who want to cross: *Don't try to cross the highway — use the overpass.*

,**pass sb/sth 'over** (to sb) **1** to give sth to sb, especially when they ask for it or you do not want it any more; to give sb, or the responsibility for sb, to sb else: *Jeff passed the phone over so that I could speak to Clare.* ◇ *The doctor passed the baby over to the nurse.* ◇ *Control of the budgets has been passed over to individual schools.* ⓢⓨⓝ **hand sb/sth over** (to sb) **2** to let sb listen or speak to sb else when you have finished talking: *If there are no more questions, I'll pass you over to Ted.* ⓢⓨⓝ **hand over to sb, hand sb over to sb**
  ✦ v + n/pron + adv ◆ v + adv + n

,**pass sth 'round**; ,**pass sth 'round sth** (*BrE*)
= PASS STH AROUND, PASS STH AROUND STH

,**pass 'through**; ,**pass 'through sth** to go or travel through a place, only stopping for a short time: *We're not staying here, we're just passing through.* ◇ *We passed through Pompeii on our way to Naples.*
  ✦ v + adv ◆ v + prep

,**pass 'through sth** (*especially BrE*) to experience a particular kind of situation or period of time, especially a difficult or unpleasant one, and develop during it: *She passed through a difficult period after her divorce.* ◇ *The industry is passing through a period of change.*
  ⓞⒷⒿ **period, stage** ⓢⓨⓝ **go through sth**
  ✦ v + prep

'**pass to sb/sth** to begin to be owned by sb new: *When she died, the house passed to her niece.*
  ✦ v + prep

,**pass sth 'up** (*informal*) to decide not to take advantage of an opportunity, an offer, etc: *She passed up the chance of a trip to Rome.* ◇ *Imagine passing up an offer like that!*
  ⓞⒷⒿ **opportunity, chance, offer**
  ✦ v + adv + n ◆ v + pron + adv ◆ v + n + adv (*less frequent*)

patch /pætʃ/

,**patch sb/sth 'through** to connect telephone or electronic equipment temporarily: *The radio was patched through to army headquarters*
  ✦ v + n/pron + adv

,**patch sth to'gether** to arrange sth quickly, especially by putting several different parts together, without taking any care over it: *An interim government was quickly patched together.*
  ✦ v + adv + n ◆ v + n/pron + adv

,**patch sb/sth 'up** to give quick or temporary medical treatment to someone who is injured: *They patched him up and sent him back onto the field* (= for example in a game of football). ◇ *The doctor did the best he could to patch up their wounds.*
  ✦ v + n/pron + adv ◆ v + adv + n

,**patch sth 'up 1** to repair sth, especially quickly or temporarily: *The car was patched up and resold.* ◇ *We patched up the hole in the roof and got it repaired the next day.* **2** to end a quarrel or dispute with sb and be friends again: *They patched up their differences.* ◇ *Can't you two try to* **patch things up?** ⓞⒷⒿ **differences, quarrel, things 3** to agree on sth, especially after long discussions and even though the agreement is not completely satisfactory: *They managed to patch up a peace.*
  ✦ **1** v + n/pron + adv ◆ v + adv + n
     2,3 v + adv + n ◆ v + n/pron + adv

paw /pɔː/

'**paw at sb/sth** (*informal*) if an animal **paws at** sb/sth, it touches sb/sth repeatedly with its foot: *a horse pawing at the ground* ◇ (*figurative*) *One of the children was pawing at my sleeve.*
  ✦ v + prep

pay /peɪ/ (**paid, paid** /peɪd/)

,**pay sb 'back** (for sth/for doing sth) to punish sb because they have made you or sb else suffer: *I'll pay him back for getting me into trouble!*
  ⓢⓨⓝ **get back at sb** (for sth/for doing sth)
  ✦ v + n/pron + adv ◆ v + adv + n (*less frequent*)
  ▶ '**payback** *n* [C] [U] a reward or a punishment that sb receives for sth they have done
  → *see also* PAYBACK at PAY SB BACK, PAY STH BACK (TO STH)

,**pay sb 'back**; ,**pay sth 'back** (to sb) to return money that you have borrowed from sb: *I'll pay you back next week.* ◇ *She's trying to pay the loan back over 5 years.* ◇ *He'll never be able to pay back the money.*
  ⓢⓨⓝ **repay sb** (sth), **repay sth** (to sb) (*more formal*)
  ⓝⓞⓣⓔ In informal language **pay sb back sth** and, less often, **pay sb sth back** are also used: *When are you going to pay me back that $100 you owe me?* ◇ *Can you pay me that money back soon?*
  ✦ v + n/pron + adv ◆ v + adv + n
  ▶ '**payback** *n* [C] [U] the money that you receive back on money that you have invested; the time that it takes to get your money back: *I'm waiting to get the maximum payback on my investment.* ◇ *a ten-year payback*
  → *see also* PAYBACK at PAY SB BACK (FOR STH/FOR DOING STH)

'**pay for sth** to suffer or be punished for sth wrong that you have done or said, or for sth you believe: *Someone's going to pay for this!* ◇ *They are **paying dearly for** their mistake.*
  ⓞⒷⒿ **mistake, crime**
  ✦ v + prep

,pay sth 'in; **,pay sth 'into sth** to put money into a bank account: *I had to go to the bank to pay a cheque in.* ◇ *Her wages are paid directly into her account.*

[OBJ] **cheque, money** [SYN] **deposit sth (in sth)** *(more formal)*

◆ v + n/pron + adv ◆ v + adv + n ◆ v + n/pron + prep

,pay 'off if sth that involves risk **pays off**, it is successful and brings the results that you want: *The gamble paid off.* ◇ *Their hard work is beginning to pay off.* ◇ *All the training you've been doing seems to have paid off handsomely* (= has had very good results).

◆ v + adv

▶ **'pay-off** *n* (*informal*) a reward or a benefit that you receive as a result of sth you do: *What are the pay-offs of working at home?*

→ *see also* PAY-OFF *at* PAY SB OFF

,pay sb 'off 1 to give sb money to persuade them not to do sth or not to tell sb about sth illegal or dishonest you have done: *She refused to be paid off.* [SYN] **buy sb off 2** to pay sb the money they have earned and dismiss them from their job: *The store has paid off many of the full-time staff and offered them part-time work.*

◆ v + n/pron + adv ◆ v + adv + n

▶ **'pay-off** *n* (*informal*) **1** a payment you make to sb to persuade them not to do sth or not to tell sb about sth illegal or dishonest you have done: *Police have been accused of receiving pay-offs from local gangs.* **2** a payment made to sb to persuade them to leave their job: *She has received a £10 000 pay-off.*

→ *see also* PAY-OFF *at* PAY OFF

,pay sth/sb 'off 1 to finish paying money that you owe for sth: *I used the money to pay off my overdraft.* ◇ *They're still paying off their mortgage.* ◇ *to pay off creditors/a bank manager* [OBJ] **mortgage, loan, debts** [SYN] **repay sth/sb** (*more formal*) **2** (*especially BrE*) to pay the fare for a taxi journey: *She paid the taxi off and walked the rest of the way.* [OBJ] **taxi/cab**

◆ **1** v + adv + n ◆ v + pron + adv ◆ v + n + adv (*less frequent*)
2 v + n/pron + adv ◆ v + adv + n

,pay 'out; **,pay sth 'out (for sth)** (*especially BrE*) to pay a large amount for sth: *The insurance company refused to pay out.* ◇ *The government pays out millions of pounds in benefits.* ◇ *I can't afford to pay out for private treatment.*

◆ v + adv ◆ v + adv + n ◆ v + pron + adv ◆ v + n + adv (*rare*)

▶ **'payout** *n* a large amount of money that is given to sb: *People injured in the crash won record payouts from the rail company.*

,pay sth 'out (*BrE*) to release or pass a length or rope, etc. through your hands: *He started paying out the rope.*

◆ v + adv + n ◆ v + pron + adv ◆ v + n + adv (*rare*)

,pay 'up (*informal*) to give somebody the money that you owe them, especially if you do not want to: *In the end we threatened to take them to court and they paid up.*

[SYN] **cough up** (*especially BrE*)

◆ v + adv

▶ **'paid-up** *adj* [only before noun] **1** having paid all the money necessary to be a member of a club or an organization **2** (*informal*) strongly supporting sth: *a fully paid-up football fan*

peck /pek/

'peck at sth to eat only very small amounts of sth, because you are not hungry: *He was so nervous he only pecked at his lunch.*

◆ v + prep

peel /piːl/

,peel a'way/'back (from sth), **,peel a'way/'back (from sth)** to come off the surface of sth; to remove a thin layer from the surface of sth: *The wallpaper had started to peel away.* ◇ *The paint was peeling away from the wood.* ◇ *She peeled back the blankets and jumped into bed.* ◇ *He peeled away the plastic wrapping.*

→ *see also* PEEL STH OFF, PEEL STH OFF STH

◆ v + adv ◆ v + n/pron + adv ◆ v + adv + n

,peel 'off 1 to come away from the surface of sth: *The wallpaper was peeling off.* [SUBJ] **paper, skin, paint 2** (of cars, aircraft, etc.) to leave a group and turn to one side: *The planes peeled off, one by one.*

◆ v + adv

,peel sth 'off 1 to remove some or all of your clothing, especially sth that fits tightly: *He peeled off his wet clothes.* [OBJ] **clothes, gloves, T-shirt, etc. 2** to remove some notes from a thick pile of folded or rolled paper money: *He peeled off two hundred dollars and handed them to her.*

◆ v + adv + n ◆ v + pron + adv ◆ v + n + adv (*rare*)

,peel sth 'off; **,peel sth 'off sth** to remove a thin layer from the surface of something: *He peeled off the sweet wrapper.* ◇ *She peeled all the wallpaper off the bathroom ceiling.*

[OBJ] **wallpaper, paint, wrapper**

◆ v + n/pron + adv ◆ v + adv + n ◆ v + n/pron + prep

peg /peg/ (**-gg-**)

,peg a'way (at sth) (*informal*) to continue to work hard at or try to achieve sth difficult: *He keeps pegging away at his novel.*

◆ v + adv

,peg sb/sth 'back (especially in sport) to stop sb/sth from winning or from increasing the amount by which they are ahead: *Italy were winning 2-0, but were pegged back to a draw by Spain's late goal.*

[NOTE] **Peg sb/sth back** is often used in the passive. ◆ It is common in newspapers.

◆ v + n/pron + adv ◆ v + adv + n (*less frequent*)

,peg 'out (*BrE, informal*) to die: *I thought she was going to peg out right in front of me!*
⊕ v + adv

,peg sth 'out (*BrE*) to fasten washing to a line with a wooden or plastic device (a **peg**): *He was outside, pegging the washing out.*
[OBJ] **washing, clothes** [SYN] **hang sth out**
⊕ v + n/pron + adv ♦ v + adv + n

pelt /pelt/

'pelt down (*informal*) to rain very heavily: *It's pelting down (with rain) outside.*
[SYN] **pour down**
⊕ v + adv

pen /pen/ (-nn-)

,pen sb/sth 'in; **,pen sb/sth 'in sth** to shut sb/sth in a small space with walls or fences, etc. all around: *We penned the sheep in the yard.* ◇ *The troublemakers were penned in by the police.* ◇ (*figurative*) *She felt penned in living in the heart of the city.*
[NOTE] This phrasal verb is often used in the passive.
⊕ v + n/pron + adv ♦ v + adv + n ♦ v + n/pron + prep

,pen sb/sth 'up (*especially BrE*) to shut sb/sth in a place with walls, fences, etc. all around, and not let them leave: *It was good to go outside after being penned up in the house all day.* ◇ *They penned us up in a little room and wouldn't let anyone leave.*
[NOTE] **Pen sb/sth up** is usually used in the passive.
⊕ v + n/pron + adv ♦ v + adv + n

pencil /'pensl/ (-ll-, AmE -l-)

,pencil sb/sth 'in (for sth) to write down sb's name for an appointment, or the details of an arrangement, although you know that this might have to be changed later: *Let's pencil in the third of May for the meeting.*
⊕ v + n/pron + adv ♦ v + adv + n

pension /'penʃn/

,pension sb 'off to allow or force sb to leave their job and stop regular work (to **retire**), especially because they are old or ill, and pay them a regular sum of money (a **pension**): *She was pensioned off at the age of 56.* ◇ (*figurative*) *We've pensioned our old TV off and bought a new one.*
[NOTE] **Pension sb off** is usually used in the passive.
⊕ v + n/pron + adv ♦ v + adv + n

pep /pep/ (-pp-)

,pep sb/sth 'up (*informal*) to make sb/sth more interesting; to make sb feel more lively or full of energy: *The company needs to pep up its image.*
⊕ v + adv + n ♦ v + n/pron + adv

pepper /'pepə(r)/

'pepper sb/sth with sth to hit sb/sth with lots of small things such as bullets: *They said they were peppered with shotgun pellets as they walked in the forest.* ◇ (*figurative*) *The interviewer peppered her with questions.*
[NOTE] **Pepper sb/sth with sth** is usually used in the passive.
⊕ v + n/pron + prep

'pepper sth with sth to include a large number of sth in sth: *She peppers her conversation with references to famous people.* ◇ *Her hair is peppered with grey.*
[NOTE] **Pepper sth with sth** is usually used in the passive.
⊕ v + n/pron + prep

perk /pɜːk; AmE pɜːrk/

,perk 'up; **,perk sb 'up** (*informal*) to become, or make sb, more lively or more cheerful, especially after they have been ill/sick: *You've perked up since this morning.* ◇ *A shower would soon perk you up.*
[SYN] **liven up, liven sb up**
⊕ v + adv ♦ v + n/pron + adv ♦ v + adv + n

,perk 'up; **,perk sth 'up** (*informal*) to improve or increase in value, to make sth increase in value, etc: *The weather seems to be perking up.* ◇ *The recent demand for houses has perked up the prices.* ◇ *House prices are expected to perk up.*
[SYN] **improve, improve sth**
⊕ v + adv ♦ v + n/pron + adv ♦ v + adv + n

,perk sth 'up (*informal*) to make sth more interesting or more attractive: *Perk up a dark kitchen with a coat of paint.* ◇ *A vegetable stew can be perked up with a dash of chilli sauce.* ◇ *ideas for perking up bland food*
[SYN] **liven sth up**
⊕ v + adv + n ♦ v + pron + adv ♦ v + n + adv (*less frequent*)

permit /pə'mɪt; AmE pər'm-/ (-tt-)

per'mit of sth (*formal*) to make sth possible; to allow sth to happen: *The situation does not permit of any delay.*
[NOTE] **Permit of sth** is usually used in negative sentences, and in written English.
⊕ v + prep

pertain /pə'teɪn; AmE pər't-/

per'tain to sth (*formal*) to be connected with a particular subject, person, event or situation: *The committee was reviewing all the laws pertaining to adoption.*
⊕ v + prep

peter /ˈpiːtə(r)/

ˌpeter 'out (into sth) to decrease or fade gradually before coming to an end: *The road petered out into a dirt track.* ◇ *By midday their enthusiasm had petered out.* ◇ *The conversation gradually petered out.*
◆ v + adv

phase /feɪz/

ˌphase sth 'in to introduce sth gradually or in stages: *The government will phase in the new tax.*
ᴼᴾᴾ **phase sth out**
ɴᴏᴛᴇ **Phase sth in** is often used in the passive: *The scheme will be phased in over 15 years.*
◆ v + adv + n ◆ v + n/pron + adv

ˌphase sth 'out to stop using sth gradually or in stages: *They agreed to phase out chemical weapons.*
ᴼᴾᴾ **phase sth in**
ɴᴏᴛᴇ **Phase sth out** is often used in the passive: *The old system is being phased out.*
◆ v + adv + n ◆ v + n/pron + adv

phone /fəʊn; *AmE* foʊn/
ɴᴏᴛᴇ **To phone** is the most common way to say 'to telephone' in British English. **To ring** and **to call** are also used. The most common verb in American English for this is **to call**.

ˌphone a'round/'round; ˌphone a'round/ 'round sb/sth (*especially BrE*) to make phone calls to several different people or places, usually to try to find out some information: *I spent the morning phoning round hotels, trying to book a room.* ◇ *He phoned around to tell everyone about the meeting.*
◆ v + adv ◆ v + prep

ˌphone 'back; ˌphone sb 'back (*especially BrE*) to telephone sb again or to telephone sb who telephoned you earlier: *I left a message but they never phoned back.* ◇ *Tom called while you were out. He asked if you could phone him back.* ◇ *The travel agent phoned back to confirm your booking.* ◇ *It's engaged — I'll phone back later.*
◆ v + adv ◆ v + n/pron + adv ◆ v + adv + n (*rare*)

phone 'in (*especially BrE*) **1** to telephone your place of work: *I'll phone in to say I won't be in until lunchtime.* ◇ *He **phoned in sick** (= to say he was ill/sick and could not go to work) this morning.* **2** to phone a television or radio programme: *Hundreds of listeners phoned in to complain.*
◆ v + adv

▶ 'phone-in n (*especially BrE*) a radio or TV programme in which people can phone and ask questions, give their opinions, etc. as the programme is being broadcast: *He hosts a radio phone-in.* ◇ *a phone-in programme*

ˌphone sth 'in (*especially BrE*) to make a telephone call to the place where you work in order to give sb some information: *Our reporter phoned the story in this afternoon.*
ᴼˢʸᴺ **ring sth in** (*BrE*)
◆ v + n/pron + adv ◆ v + adv + n

ˌphone 'round; ˌphone 'round sb/sth (*especially BrE*) = PHONE AROUND/ROUND, PHONE AROUND/ROUND SB/STH

ˌphone sth 'through (*especially BrE*) to phone sb with details of or information about sth: *Phone your order through to the store.*
◆ v + n/pron + adv ◆ v + adv + n

ˌphone 'up; ˌphone sb/sth 'up (*especially BrE*) to make a telephone call to sb/sth: *I'll phone up and cancel my appointment.* ◇ *Phone Mike up and ask him if he wants to come.* ◇ *I phoned up the bank this morning.*
ɴᴏᴛᴇ **Phone** and **phone sb** are also frequently used with this meaning. **Phone up** and **phone sb up** are very common in spoken English.
◆ v + adv ◆ v + n/pron + adv ◆ v + adv + n

pick /pɪk/

~ at	~ over
~ off	~ up
~ on	205 ~ up on
204 ~ out	

'pick at sth **1** to eat very small amounts of food because you are not hungry: *She picked at her food for a while, then left the table.* ᴼᴮᴶ **food, meal 2** to pull sth with your fingers several times: *She picked nervously at her skirt until she made a hole.*
◆ v + prep

ˌpick sb/sth 'off **1** to shoot a person, an animal, a bird, an aircraft, etc. especially one of a group, after aiming carefully: *One of our men was picked off by a sniper.* **2** to choose the best people or things for your own use: *The company continues to pick off the brightest young graduates.*
◆ v + adv + n ◆ v + n/pron + adv

ˌpick sth 'off; ˌpick sth 'off sth to remove sth from sth with your fingernails or a tool: *She watered the plants and picked off the dead leaves.*
◆ v + n/pron + adv ◆ v + adv + n ◆ v + n/pron + prep

'pick on sb **1** to treat sb badly or unfairly, especially repeatedly: *You're always picking on me!* ◇ *The manager was accused of picking on a member of the department.* ◇ *It's difficult being the younger sister — you always get picked on.* **2** (*especially BrE*) to choose sb for a task, especially an unpleasant one: *The teacher always picked on Tom to answer the difficult questions.*
ɴᴏᴛᴇ **Pick on sb** can be used in the passive: *She was picked on by the other children at school.*
◆ v + prep

,pick sb/sth 'out 1 to choose sb/sth from a number of people or things: *He picks out people from the audience to come up on stage.* ◇ *The brightest students were picked out for special training.* ◇ *He picked out the most expensive suit in the shop.* SYN **select sb/sth** (*more formal*) **2** to recognize sb/sth from among people or things: *Can you pick me out in this old school photo?* ◇ *The suspect was picked out at an identity parade.* **3** to manage to see sb/sth: *We could just pick out a car in the distance.* SYN **make sb/sth out** (*more formal*) **4** if a light, etc. **picks sb/sth out** it shines on sb/sth so that they/it are easier to see: *The car's headlights picked out a road sign.*
◆ v + adv + n ◆ v + n/pron + adv

,pick sth 'out 1 to discover or recognize sth after careful study: *It was difficult to pick out the important points from the mass of facts.* ◇ *They were asked to pick out exactly what it was that made his style so distinctive.* **2** if you **pick out** a tune on a musical instrument, you play a tune that you have heard or made up slowly, note by note, without using written music: *Buddie was picking out a simple tune on his guitar.* OBJ **melody, tune 3** usually be **,picked 'out** (*BrE*) to paint, draw or write sth in such a way that it is very easy to see, especially by using a colour that is different from the background: *The details of the flowers were picked out in blue and gold.*
◆ v + adv + n ◆ v + n/pron + adv

,pick sth 'over 1 (*also* **,pick 'through sth** *less frequent*) to look carefully at a group of things, choosing what you want and rejecting anything you do not want: *He picked over the apples, checking for bad ones.* ◇ *Bargain hunters picked over a pile of sale items.* **2** (*especially BrE*) to examine or analyse sth carefully: *We spent the meeting picking over last month's results.*
◆ v + adv + n ◆ v + pron + adv

,pick 'up 1 to become better; to improve: *The market always picks up in the spring.* ◇ *The game started very slowly but picked up in the second half.* ◇ *We're waiting until the weather picks up a bit.* **2** if the wind **picks up**, it starts to blow more strongly: *The wind seems to be picking up.* **3** to start again; to continue: *The new series picks up where the old one left off.* → *see also* PICK STH UP 10 **4** if your speed **picks up**, you start to go faster: *After the first mile* (= in a race) *I started to feel stronger and my speed picked up.* → *see also* PICK UP SPEED/MOMENTUM at PICK STH UP **5** if a bus, etc. **picks up** somewhere, it stops there to allow passengers to get on: *The bus picks up outside the Post Office* → *see also* PICK SB UP 3 **6** (*informal, especially AmE*) to collect things that have been dropped or left on the ground and put them away: *I shouldn't have to pick up after you!* → *see also* PICK STH UP 12
◆ v + adv

▶ **'pickup** *n* **1** an improvement: *There are no signs of a pickup in consumer spending.* **2** (*AmE*) the ability of a vehicle to increase its speed
→ *see also* PICKUP at PICK SB UP; PICKUP at PICK STH UP

,pick sb 'up 1 to take hold of and lift sb: *I always pick the baby up when she cries.* → *see also* PICK STH UP 1 **2** to go to sb's home or a place you have arranged and take them somewhere in your car: *I'll pick you up at seven o'clock.* ◇ *He picked up a hitch-hiker.* ◇ *I went to pick her up from the airport.* NOTE **Pick sb up** is used much more often than **collect sb** in spoken English. **3** ,**pick 'up sb,** ,**pick him, her, them, etc. 'up** if a bus, etc. **picks up** sb, it stops and allows them to get on: *The bus stopped to pick up some passengers.* NOTE A noun must always follow **up**, but a pronoun comes between the verb and **up**. → *see also* PICK UP 5 **4** to rescue sb, for example from the sea: *Lifeboats picked up all the survivors.* **5** to arrest sb; to take sb somewhere in order to question them: *She was picked up by the police as she was leaving her hotel.* **6** (*informal*) to start talking to sb you do not know, because you want to have a sexual relationship with them: *He picked her up at a club.* **7** if sth **picks you up**, it makes you feel better: *A cup of tea will soon pick you up.*
→ *see also* PICK YOURSELF UP
◆ v + n/pron + adv ◆ v + adv + n
   3 v + adv + n ◆ v + pron + adv

▶ **'pick-me-up** *n* (*informal*) something that makes you feel better or happier, etc: *The country air was the perfect pick-me-up.*

▶ **'pickup** *n* **1** an occasion when sb gets in a car, on a bus, etc. to be taken to another place: *The coach driver made several pickups before heading for the airport.* ◇ *a pickup point* **2** (*informal*) a situation in which sb is trying to start a sexual relationship with a person they do not know; the person they are trying to start a sexual relationship with: *Nothing ever came of his pickups.*
→ *see also* PICKUP at PICK UP; PICKUP at PICK STH UP

,pick sth 'up 1 to take hold of and lift sth: *I picked up your bag by mistake.* ◇ *Pick your coat up off the floor!* ◇ *Pick up* (= answer the phone) *if you're there, Tom!* → *see also* PICK SB UP 1 **2** to obtain or collect sth: *We can pick up the tickets an hour before the show starts.* **3** to learn a language a skill, etc., or to get information, without making an effort: *She picks up languages really easily* ◇ *I showed her how to use the software and she picked it up quickly.* ◇ *I picked up lots of tips or home entertainment from the magazine.* ◇ *She picked up the idea for the novel from a news story* OBJ **languages, French, tips, etc. 4** to get or obtain sth: *He picked up a virus at school.* ◇ *The children have picked up the local accent.* OBJ **cold, habits 5** to identify or recognize sth: *The early signs of the disease were not picked up.* OBJ signs SYN) **detect sth 6** if a machine **picks sth up**, it receives a sound, a signal or a picture: *The microphone picks up every sound.* ◇ *Signals from the satellite are picked up at ground stations.* ◇ *We were able to pick up the BBC World Service.* **7** to buy sth, especially cheaply or by good luck: *He picked up some amazing bargains in the sales.* ◇ *You can pick up a second-hand bike for about £60.* OBJ **bargain 8** to win a prize or an award: *The movie picked up several Oscars.* OBJ **award, cheque 9** to find and follow a route, etc: *A police dog picked up his scent.* ◇ *The French police picked up the trail and traced her to Lisle.* OBJ **trail, scent 10** to discuss something further; to return to a topic or theme and continue it: *Can I pick up the point you made earlier?* ◇ *We pick the story up again in London, five years later.* OBJ **point, story** → *see also* PICK UP 3 **11** to manage to see or hear sth that is not very clear: *I just picked up the sound of a car in the distance.* **12** (*especially AmE*) to collect things that have been dropped or left on the ground and put them away: *Will you pick up your toys now?* → *see also* PICK UP 6 **13** (*AmE*) to tidy a room, etc. and put things away: *Pick up your room before you go out.* OBJ **room** SYN) **tidy sth up** (*BrE*), **tidy sth** (*BrE*) **14** (*informal*) if you **pick up** a bill for sth you pay it for sb else: *We ended up picking up the bill.* OBJ **bill, tab**

⊕ v + adv + n ♦ v + adv + n/pron + adv **14** v + adv + n ♦ v + pron + adv ♦ v + n + adv (*rare*)

IDM **pick up the 'pieces** to return, or to help sb return, to a normal situation, particularly after a shock or a disaster: *He walked out on his family, leaving his wife to pick up the pieces.* **pick up 'speed/mo'mentum** to go faster: *The bus picked up speed as it went down the hill.*

▸ **'pickup 1** (*also* **'pickup truck**) a light motor vehicle with low sides and no roof at the back, used for example, by farmers **2** the part of a record player or musical instrument that changes electrical signals into sound, or sound into electrical signals

→ *see also* PICKUP at PICK UP; PICKUP at PICK SB UP

,**pick yourself 'up** to get to your feet, especially after a fall: *She picked herself up and stumbled on.* ◇ (*figurative*) *We have to pick ourselves up after yesterday's defeat and start again.*

→ *see also* PICK SB UP

⊕ v + pron + adv

,**pick 'up on sth 1** to notice sth: *He picked up on her feelings of unease.* ◇ *Children soon pick up on tensions between their parents.* **2** to return to a point in order to talk about it in more detail: *I'd like to pick up on Mr Finlay's point.* OBJ **point**

⊕ v + adv + prep

,**pick sb 'up on sth** (*BrE*) to correct sth that sb has said or done: *If you make a mistake, he always picks you up on it.*

⊕ v + n/pron + adv + prep

piece /piːs/

,**piece sth to'gether 1** to discover a story, etc. by putting together separate facts or pieces of evidence: *Detectives are piecing together the events of the last hours of his life.* ◇ *Investigators are still trying to piece together the evidence to find out what caused the crash.* OBJ **evidence, story, events 2** to make sth by putting a lot of separate parts together: *Archaeologists have worked for years to piece together the huge mosaic.*

⊕ v + adv + n ♦ v + pron + adv ♦ v + n + adv (*less frequent*)

pig /pɪɡ/ (-gg-)

,**pig 'out** (**on sth**) (*informal*) to eat too much or a lot of food: *We pigged out at lunch for four bucks each.* ◇ *It isn't a good idea to pig out on sugar.*

⊕ v + adv

▸ **'pig-out** *n* an occasion on which you eat too much or a lot of food: *We had a real pig-out last night.* ◇ *a pig-out party*

pile /paɪl/

,**pile 'in/out**; ,**pile 'into/'out of sth** to go in or out of somewhere without order or control: *The taxi arrived and we all piled in.* ◇ *Crowds of children piled out of the building.*

OBJ **car, taxi, room**

⊕ v + adv ♦ v + prep

,**pile 'into sb/sth** to crash into sb/sth: *She stopped dead in the middle of the pavement and we all piled into her.* ◇ *As many as 30 cars and trucks piled into each other in the fog this morning.*

→ *see also* PILE UP, PILE STH UP

⊕ v + prep

,**pile 'on** if sb's weight **piles on**, it increases rapidly: *The pounds have just piled on since I got married!*

⊕ v + adv

,**pile sth 'on 1** to express a feeling in a much stronger way than is necessary: *I admit I'm piling on the drama a bit, but I'm trying to make a serious point.* **2** to give sb a lot or too much of sth: *United piled on the pressure in the second half* (= of the football game). OBJ **pressure, guilt 3** to make sth increase rapidly: *As soon as she stops dieting she piles on the pounds.* ◇ *The team were piling on the points.* OBJ **pounds, weight**

⊕ v + adv + n ♦ v + n/pron + adv

IDM **pile on the 'agony/'gloom** (*informal, especially BrE*) to make an unpleasant situation worse

,**pile 'out**; ,**pile 'out of sth**

→ *see also* PILE IN/OUT, PILE INTO/OUT OF STH

,**pile 'up**; ,**pile sth 'up 1** to form a pile; to make a lot of things into a pile: *Snow was piling up against the windows.* ◇ *They piled the stones up in a corner of the yard.* **2** to increase or to make sth increase in quantity or amount: *Rubbish was piling up in the streets.* ◇ *The bills were piling up and we had no money to pay them.* ◇ *Liverpool should have gone on to pile up a big score* (= in a game of football).

◆ v + adv ◆ v + n/pron + adv ◆ v + adv + n

2 v + adv ◆ v + adv + n ◆ v + pron + adv ◆ v + n + adv *(rare)*

▶ **'pile-up** *n* a road accident in which several vehicles crash into each other: *Eleven cars were involved in a pile-up on the motorway.* ◇ *Three people were killed in a multiple pile-up.*

pin /pɪn/ (-nn-)

,pin sb 'down 1 to make sb unable to move, especially by holding them firmly: *The older boy had pinned Jimmy down on the floor.* ◇ *The rebels were pinned down* (= they could not move from their position) *just south of the border.* **2 (to sth/to doing sth)** to make sb say clearly exactly what they are going to do: *You'll find it difficult to pin him down to a price.* ◇ *They pinned the builders down to finishing by June.* ⓈⓎⓃ **nail sb down (to sth) 3** to find sb and make them answer a question or tell you what you need to know: *She tried to pin him down for an interview, but he was always busy.*

◆ v + n/pron + adv ◆ v + adv + n

,pin sth 'down to identify or understand sth exactly: *There's something wrong with this photograph but I can't quite pin it down.* ◇ *Doctors have been unable to pin down the cause of her symptoms.*

◆ v + n/pron + adv ◆ v + adv + n

'pin sth on sb to make sb seem responsible or take the blame for sth they have not done: *They tried to pin the blame on me!*

ⓄⒷⒿ **blame**

◆ v + n/pron + prep

ⒾⒹⓂ **,pin (all) your 'hopes on sb/sth; ,pin your 'faith on sb/sth** to rely on sb/sth completely for success or help: *Police are pinning their hopes on finding the murder weapon.*

,pin sth 'up 1 to fasten sth to a wall, etc. with pins: *He pinned up a notice on the board.* ◇ *Can I pin this poster up?* **2** to fix your hair in place with pins: *She was pinning her hair up in front of the mirror.* ⓄⒷⒿ **hair**

◆ v + n/pron + adv ◆ v + adv + n

▶ **'pin-up** *n* **1** a picture of an attractive person, designed to be put up on the wall for people to look at: *The walls of his room were covered in pin-ups.* ◇ *He was football's first pin-up boy.* **2** a person who appears in a pin-up

pine /paɪn/

,pine a'way to become very sad, and sometimes ill or weak because sb has died or gone away: *After his wife died, he just pined away.* ◇ *He seemed to be pining away from love.*

◆ v + adv

'pine for sb/sth to want or miss sb/sth very much: *She wasn't really pining for Brazil at all.* ◇ *a dog pining for its master*

◆ v + prep

pipe /paɪp/

,pipe 'down *(informal)* used to tell sb to be less noisy or to stop talking: *OK, everybody pipe down!*

◆ v + adv

,pipe 'up (with sth) *(informal)* to begin to speak: *Debbie suddenly piped up with 'I've seen this film before!'*

◆ v + adv ◆ v + adv + speech

piss /pɪs/

,piss a'bout/a'round *(BrE, △, slang)* to act in a silly or unhelpful way and waste time: *We haven't got time to piss about.*

ⓃⓄⓉⒺ A more polite, informal way of saying this is **mess around** or, in British English, **mess about**.

◆ v + adv

,piss sb a'bout/a'round *(BrE, △, slang)* to treat sb in an unhelpful way that wastes their time: *Don't piss me about, just tell me the truth!*

ⓃⓄⓉⒺ A more polite, informal way of saying this is **mess sb around** or, in British English, **mess sb about**.

◆ v + n/pron + adv

'piss down; 'piss it down *(BrE, △, slang)* to rain very heavily: *It's still pissing (it) down out there.*

ⓈⓊⒷⒿ only **it** ⓈⓎⓃ **pour down** *(BrE, more formal)*

ⓃⓄⓉⒺ **Piss (it) down** is always used with the subject **it**. ◆ A more polite, informal way of saying this is **chuck it down**: *It's still chucking it down outside.*

◆ v + adv ◆ v + it + adv

,piss 'off *(△, slang, especially BrE)* used to tell sb rudely to go away: *I told him to piss off.* ◇ *Piss off and leave me alone!*

◆ v + adv

,piss sb 'off *(△, slang)* to make sb annoyed or bored: *Everybody's pissed off with what's going on.* ◇ *It really pisses me off when I see people behaving like that.*

ⓃⓄⓉⒺ **Pissed off** *(BrE)* and **pissed** *(AmE)* are often used as adjectives: *I was really pissed off with him.* A more polite way of saying **piss sb off** is **get on sb's nerves**: *It really gets on my nerves when I see people behaving like that.*

◆ v + n/pron + adv ◆ v + adv + n *(rare)*

pit /pɪt/ (-tt-)

,pit sb/sth/yourself a'gainst sb/sth to test sb/sth/yourself in a struggle or competition with sb/sth: *It's a chance to pit yourself against the champion.* ◇ *I'd like to pit my wits against the*

best minds in the country (= to test my intelligence). ◇ I like sailing as I enjoy **pitting my strength** against the wind and the waves.
◆ v + n/pron + prep

pitch /pɪtʃ/

pitch 'in (with sb/sth) (informal) to join in willingly with sb to help with an activity: We all pitched in and soon finished the job. ◇ Lots of people pitched in with advice. ◇ Ruth pitches in with the adult workers at the stables before she goes off to school.
◆ v + adv

pitch 'into sb (informal, especially BrE) to attack or criticize sb: They really pitched into me when I refused to cooperate.
◆ v + prep

pitch 'into sth (informal, especially BrE) to start doing sth with energy and enthusiasm: I rolled up my sleeves and pitched into the cleaning. ◇ All of them pitched into the fight.
SYN launch into sth
◆ v + prep

pivot /'pɪvət/

'pivot on/around sth to depend on a central point; to develop from a central idea or point: The success of the project pivots on investment from abroad. ◇ The novel pivots around a long conversation between two characters.
SYN hinge on sth
◆ v + prep

plan /plæn/ (-nn-)

plan a'head (for sth) to make arrangements in advance: It's impossible to plan ahead when things keep changing! ◇ We need to plan ahead for our retirement.
◆ v + adv

'plan on sth; 'plan on doing sth; 'plan on sb doing sth 1 to intend to do sth: We'd planned on having a quiet evening at home tonight. ◇ I'm not planning on going to bed yet. **2** (often used in negative sentences) to expect sth to happen: We hadn't planned on a storm! ◇ They hadn't planned on so many people visiting the exhibition.
◆ v + prep

plan sth 'out to plan carefully and in detail sth that you are going to do in the future: to plan out your time/route ◇ I knew exactly where I was going — I'd got it all planned out.
◆ v + adv + n ◆ v + n/pron + adv

plant /plɑːnt; AmE plænt/

plant sth 'out to put plants in the ground so that they have enough room to grow
◆ v + adv + n ◆ v + n/pron + adv ◆ v + n + adv (less frequent)

plaster /'plɑːstə(r); AmE 'plæs-/

plaster 'over sth to cover sth such as a crack or a wall with a substance that is put on wet and dries to form a hard, smooth surface (**plaster**): The old brick had been plastered over.
NOTE Plaster over sth is often used in the passive.
◆ v + prep

play /pleɪ/

~ about	~ off
~ about with	~ off against
~ along	~ on
~ around	~ out
~ around with	~ up
~ at	~ up to
208 ~ back	~ upon
~ down	~ with

play a'bout (BrE) = PLAY AROUND

play a'bout with sth (BrE) = PLAY AROUND WITH STH

play a'long (with sb/sth) to pretend to agree with sb/sth, to believe sb/sth, etc., to gain an advantage for yourself, amuse yourself, avoid trouble, etc: He realized they'd mistaken him for the gardener, but decided to play along. ◇ I knew he was lying, but I decided to play along with him for a while.
◆ v + adv

play a'round (BrE also **play a'bout**) **1** (with sb/sth) to behave in a careless way, without thinking about the results: Stop playing about and get on with your work! ◇ Don't play around with matches! **SYN** mess around (with sb/sth); mess around with sth → see also PLAY AROUND WITH STH **2** (with sb) (informal) to have a sexual relationship with sb who is not your usual partner
◆ v + adv

play a'round with sth (BrE also **play a'bout with sth**) to test or try new ideas, methods, etc. to see how good or effective they are before you make a final decision: Play around with the spreadsheet until you find the best way to display the data. ◇ We're still playing around with ideas for a new programme.
◆ v + adv + prep

'play at doing sth (especially BrE) to do sth without any effort or real interest: He's just playing at being in love.
◆ v + prep

IDM **two can play at 'that game** used to tell sb who has played a trick on you that you can do the same to them **what is sb playing at?** (informal) used to ask in an angry way about what sb is doing: What do you think you're playing at?

,play sth 'back (to sb) to play music, sound, film, etc. that has been recorded on a tape or video: *Can you play back what we've just recorded?*
[OBJ] tape
 v + n/pron + adv ◆ v + adv + n
▶ 'playback n [U] [C] the act of playing music, showing a film/movie or listening to a telephone message that has been recorded before; a recording that you listen to or watch again: *A TV playback showed exactly what had happened.*

,play sth 'down to try to make sth appear less important than it is: *The government is trying to play down its involvement in the affair.*
[OPP] play up sth, play it/them up
[NOTE] Downplay sth is also used with the same meaning: *The report downplayed the effects of large class sizes in schools.*
 v + adv + n ◆ v + pron + adv ◆ v + n + adv *(rare)*

,play 'off *(especially BrE)* if two teams, players, etc. that have the same number of points in a competition play off, they play a final game to decide who has won: *The two Germans played off for a place in the final.*
 v + adv
▶ 'play-off n a game or games between two players or teams with equal points in a competition to decide who the winner is: *We're unlikely to reach the play-offs.* ◇ *The title was decided by a sudden-death play-off.* ◇ *a play-off final*

,play A 'off against B *(BrE)* *(AmE* 'play A off B) to make two people or groups oppose each other, especially in order to gain an advantage for yourself: *(BrE) He tries to play one parent off against the other.* ◇ *(AmE) The children played their parents off each other.* ◇ *She played her two rivals off against each other and got the job herself.*
 v + n/pron + adv + prep ◆ v + n/pron + prep

,play 'on 1 *(sport)* to continue to play; to start playing again: *They claimed a penalty but the referee told them to play on.* 2 to continue to play music: *Despite the uproar, the musicians played on.*
 v + adv

'play on sth *(also* 'play upon sth *more formal)* to deliberately use sb's fears, etc. for your own advantage: *He played on my feelings of guilt to make me stay.* ◇ *The government played on people's fears of rising crime to get support for their policies.*
[OBJ] fears [SYN] exploit sth *(formal)*
 v + prep

,play 'out *(informal)* if a band, etc. plays out, it performs in front of an audience: *Serious bands should be playing out regularly.* ◇ *Playing out is the best way for a DJ to build a following.*
 v + adv

,play 'out; ,play itself/themselves 'out *(formal)* to develop and come to an end or be no longer useful or important: *The crisis has yet to play out.* ◇ *The revolution soon played itself out.*

[NOTE] This phrasal verb is usually used in written English.
 v + adv ◆ v + pron + adv
▶ ,played 'out *adj* completely finished; too tired or weak to continue: *She was played out — too exhausted even to cry.*

,play sth 'out 1 when an event is played out, or sb plays it out, it happens: *The negotiations are being played out behind closed doors.* ◇ *She continued to play out her role of dutiful daughter.*
[NOTE] Play sth out is often used in the passive. 2 *(especially AmE)* to continue to play sth until it finishes: *We'll play out this game and then go to bed.* 3 to let a length of rope pass through your hands bit by bit
 v + adv + n ◆ v + n/pron + adv

,play 'up; ,play sb 'up *(informal, especially BrE)* 1 if a part of your body, a machine, etc. plays up or plays you up, it causes you problems: *My leg's playing up again* (= it is painful). ◇ *My back plays me up from time to time.* ◇ *The car started playing up* (= not working in a reliable way) *about six months ago.* ◇ *The computer's been playing me up recently.* 2 if children play up or play sb up, they behave very badly: *The kids have been playing up all day.* ◇ *All kids play new teachers up.*
[NOTE] Play up, play sb up are often used in the progressive tenses.
 v + n/pron + adv ◆ v + adv + n

,play 'up sth; ,play it/them 'up to try to make sth appear more important than it really is: *She played up her achievements in an attempt to impress us.*
[OPP] play sth down
[NOTE] A noun must always follow up, but a pronoun comes between the verb and up.
 v + adv + n ◆ v + n/pron + adv

,play 'up to sb *(BrE)* to behave towards sb in a way that you think they will like and will bring you an advantage: *She always played up to her father.*
 v + adv + prep

,play 'up to sth *(especially BrE)* to behave in the way that people expect you to: *She doesn't look 12. People think she's only 8 or 9, and she plays up to this all the time.*
 v + adv + prep

'play upon sth = PLAY ON STH

'play with sb/sth *(disapproving)* to behave towards sb in a way that is not serious, especially by pretending to feel sth you do not feel: *She was just playing with my emotions.*
 v + prep

'play with sth *(usually used in the progressive tenses)* if you play with an idea, you think about it, but do not really intend to do anything about it: *She's playing with the idea of starting her own business.*
[OBJ] idea [SYN] toy with sth
 v + prep

'**play with yourself** (*informal*) to touch your sexual organs in order to give yourself pleasure
✥ v + prep

plod /plɒd; *AmE* plɑːd/ (-dd-)

,**plod a'long/'on** to continue doing sth, especially difficult or boring work, at a very slow rate: *Keep plodding on — you'll soon be finished!* ◇ *They're still plodding along with their investigation.*
✥ v + adv

,**plod a'way** (**at sth**) to work steadily but slowly at a difficult or boring task: *He plodded away all night at his project to get it finished.*
✥ v + adv

plonk (*especially BrE*) /plɒŋk; *AmE* plɑːŋk, plɔːŋk/ (*AmE usually* plunk)

,**plonk 'down**; ,**plonk yourself 'down** (*informal*) to sit down heavily and quickly: *She plonked herself down in front of the telly.*
⟫SYN⟫ plump down, plump yourself down
✥ v + adv ◆ v + pron + adv

,**plonk sb/sth 'down** (*informal*) to drop sth or put sth down heavily without taking great care: *She plonked the food down in front of them.* ◇ *Don't just plonk the baby down on the floor.*
✥ v + n/pron + adv ◆ v + adv + n (*less frequent*)

plough (*BrE*) (*AmE* plow) /plaʊ/

,**plough sth 'back** (**into sth**), ,**plough sth back 'in** to put profits back into the business that produced them: *All the profits are ploughed back into the company.* ◇ *The director confirmed that every penny had been ploughed back in.*
OBJ profits, money
NOTE Plough sth back is usually used in the passive.
✥ v + n/pron + adv ◆ v + adv + n

,**plough 'into sb/sth** (of a vehicle or a driver) to crash violently into sb/sth: *The car hit a lamppost before ploughing into a wall.*
✥ v + prep

,**plough sth 'into sth**; ,**plough sth 'into doing sth** to invest a large amount of money on a project, a business etc: *$50 million will be ploughed into the area over the next five years.*
⟫SYN⟫ sink sth into sth
✥ v + n/pron + prep

,**plough 'on** (**with sth**) to continue to say or do sth even though it becomes difficult: *No one was listening to him but he **ploughed on regardless**.* ◇ *The path was steep, but we ploughed on until we got to the top.*
✥ v + adv

,**plough 'through sth**; ,**plough your way 'through sth 1** to force a way through sth: *The car ploughed its way through the snow and ice.* ◇ *The journey involved ploughing through 50 miles*

of swamp land. **2** (of a vehicle or an aircraft) to crash violently through sth: *The car ploughed through the hedge.* **3** to slowly do, read or eat all of sth even though it is difficult or boring: *It took me hours to plough through all the mail.* ◇ *I had to plough my way through a mountain of pasta because I didn't want to appear rude.*
✥ v + prep ◆ v + n + prep

,**plough sth 'up 1** to break the surface of an area of land that has not been used for growing crops before, and turn it over using a special piece of farming equipment (a **plough**): *He ploughed up the field ready for sowing.* ◇ *action to prevent farmers ploughing up footpaths* **2** to break up the surface of the ground by walking or driving across it again and again: *He got so angry he ploughed up his neighbour's lawn with his motorbike.*
✥ v + adv + n ◆ v + n/pron + adv

plow (*AmE*) /plaʊ/

,**plow sth 'back** (**into sth**), ,**plow sth back 'in** (*AmE*) = PLOUGH STH BACK (INTO STH), PLOUGH STH BACK IN

,**plow 'into sb/sth** (*AmE*) = PLOUGH INTO SB/STH

,**plow 'into sth**; ,**plow sth 'into doing sth** (*AmE*) = PLOUGH STH INTO STH, PLOUGH STH INTO DOING STH

,**plow 'on** (**with sth**) (*AmE*) = PLOUGH ON (WITH STH)

,**plow 'through sth**; ,**plow your way 'through sth** (*AmE*) = PLOUGH THROUGH STH, PLOUGH YOUR WAY THROUGH STH

,**plow sth 'up** (*AmE*) = PLOUGH STH UP

pluck /plʌk/

'**pluck at sth** to take hold of sth with your fingers and pull it towards you in a quick, sharp movement: *He plucked at my sleeve. 'Come and sit down.'*
✥ v + prep

plug /plʌg/ (-gg-)

,**plug a'way** (**at sth**) (*informal*) to work hard and steadily at sth for a long time, especially sth difficult or boring: *Scientists have been plugging away at the problem for years.*
✥ v + adv

,**plug 'in**; ,**plug 'into sth 1** to be able to be connected to a source of electricity or another piece of electrical equipment: *Where does the TV plug in?* ◇ *The guitar plugs into this amplifier.* **2** to become involved with a particular activity or group of people: *The company hopes to plug into new markets in Asia.*
✥ v + adv ◆ v + prep

,plug sth 'in; ,plug sth 'into sth to connect a piece of electrical equipment to the electricity supply or to another piece of electrical equipment: *Don't forget to plug the printer in.* ◊ *Where can I plug in my hairdryer?*

〉OPP〈 **unplug sth (from sth)**

⊕ v + n/pron + adv ♦ v + adv + n ♦ v + n/pron + prep

▶ '**plug-in** *adj* [only before noun] that can be connected to an electricity supply with a plug (= a small plastic object with two or three metal pins): *a plug-in kettle*

▶ '**plug-in** *n* (*computing*) a piece of software (= programs used to operate a computer) that can be added to a computer system to give extra features: *plug-ins for a palmtop computer* ◊ *a plug-in graphics card*

,plug sth 'into sth 1 = PLUG STH IN, PLUG STH INTO STH 2 to connect a computer to a computer system → *see also* PLUG-IN at PLUG STH IN, PLUG STH INTO STH

⊕ v + n/pron + prep

,plug sth 'up to fill or block a hole with a substance or a piece of material that fits tightly into it: *We plugged up all the holes around the window to stop the wind coming in.*

OBJ **hole** 〉SYN〈 **block sth up**

NOTE Plug sth is often used with the same meaning.

⊕ v + adv + n ♦ v + n/pron + adv

plumb /plʌm/

,plumb sth' in (*BrE*) to connect a washing-machine, a bath, etc. to a water system: *He's plumbed in the new washing machine for me.*

⊕ v + adv + n ♦ v + n/pron + adv

plump /plʌmp/

,plump 'down; ,plump yourself 'down (*informal*) to sit down quickly and heavily: *She plumped herself down in the armchair.*

〉SYN〈 **plonk down, plonk yourself down**

⊕ v + adv ♦ v + pron + adv

,plump sth 'down (*informal*) to put sth down suddenly and carelessly: *He plumped his books down on the table.*

⊕ v + n/pron + adv ♦ v + adv + n

'plump for sb/sth (*BrE, informal*) to choose or vote for sb/sth after thinking about it carefully: *I think I'll plump for the steak.*

⊕ v + prep

,plump 'up to become rounder or fatter: *Soak the raisins until they plump up.*

⊕ v + adv

,plump sth 'up to make sth such as a cushion rounder and softer by shaking it: *Let me plump up your pillows for you.*

OBJ **cushion, pillow**

⊕ v + adv + n ♦ v + n/pron + adv

plunge /plʌndʒ/

,plunge 'in; ,plunge 'into sth 1 to jump or fall in to sth, usually with some force: *He plunged into the pool.* ◊ *The car plunged into a gorge.* ◊ *We ran down to the sea and plunged in.* 2 to begin doing sth or talking about sth without preparing for it or thinking carefully: *He plunged into the task of clearing the office.* ◊ *I plunged in and started telling them all about it.*

⊕ v + adv ♦ v + prep

,plunge sth 'in; ,plunge sth 'in/'into sth to put sth quickly and with force into sth else: *She plunged the knife into his leg.* ◊ *He opened the sack and plunged his arm in.*

OBJ **knife, hand**

⊕ v + n/pron + adv ♦ v + adv + n ♦ v + n/pron + prep

,plunge 'into sth = PLUNGE IN, PLUNGE INTO STH

,plunge 'into sth; ,plunge sb/sth 'into sth to be or to make sb/sth suddenly be in a bad situation or state: *The country plunged into recession.* ◊ *The city was plunged into chaos as a result of the strike.* ◊ *The room was suddenly plunged into darkness.*

OBJ **recession, despair**

NOTE Plunge sb/sth into sth is often used in the passive.

⊕ v + prep ♦ v + n/pron + prep

,plunge sth 'into sth = PLUNGE STH IN, PLUNGE STH IN/INTO STH

plunk /plʌŋk/

,plunk 'down; ,plunk yourself 'down (*AmE, informal*) = PLONK DOWN, PLONK YOURSELF DOWN

⊕ v + adv

,plunk sb/sth 'down (*AmE, informal*) = PLONK SB/STH DOWN (*figurative*) *Movie goers* **plunked** *down $1.7 billion for tickets* (= spent that amount on tickets) *this summer.*

⊕ v + n/pron + adv ♦ v + adv + n

ply /plaɪ/ (plies, plying, plied, plied)

'ply sb with sth 1 to keep giving sb large amounts of sth, especially food and drink: *They plied us with tea and cakes.* 2 to keep asking sb questions: *They plied me with questions about my visit to England.*

⊕ v + n/pron + prep

point /pɔɪnt/

,point sb/sth 'out (to sb) to show sb which person or thing you are referring to, for example by moving your head, by describing them/it, etc: *Will you point his wife out to me if you see her?* ◊ *He drove them around Beverley Hills pointing out where the stars lived.* ◊ *The guide pointed out various historic monuments.*

⊕ v + n/pron + adv ♦ v + adv + n

,point sth 'out (to sb) to mention sth in order to give sb information about it or make them notice it: *He thanked me for pointing out the mistakes in his report.* ◇ *I must point out that my part in the rescue was very small.* ◆ *It must be pointed out that this new drug is not a miracle cure.* ◇ *He doesn't like having his faults pointed out to him.* ◇ *'He's not my father, he's my stepfather,' he pointed out angrily.*

NOTE Point sth out is often used in the pattern **point out that...**

◈ v + adv + n ◆ v + n/pron + adv ◆ v + adv + speech

'point to sth 1 to mention sth that you think is important and/or the reason why a particular situation exists: *She pointed to unemployment as a reason for rising crime.* **2** if a fact, event or situation **points to** sth, it suggests that this is true or likely to happen: *All the signs pointed to a successful year ahead.* ◇ *The facts seem to point to him having been murdered.* ◇ *She had symptoms which pointed to a diagnosis of kidney failure.*

◈ v + prep

,point 'up sth; ,point it/'them up (*BrE, formal*) to give special emphasis to one particular aspect of a problem, fact or opinion; to show sth very clearly: *This incident points up the hostility between the two sides.*

NOTE A noun must always follow **up**, but a pronoun comes between the verb and **up**.

◈ v + adv + n ◆ v + pron + adv

poke /pəʊk; *AmE* poʊk/

poke a'bout/a'round; ,poke a'bout/a'round sth (*informal*) **1** (*also* ,poke 'through sth especially AmE*) to look for sth, especially sth that is hidden among other things that you have to move: *They were poking around in the bushes, looking for their ball.* ◇ *What were you doing poking about in my room?* ◇ *He spent his weekends poking around dusty old bookshops.* ◇ *Customs officials poked through the containers looking for weapons.* **2** to try to find out information, especially secret or hidden information; to get involved in sth that does not concern you: *A reporter had been poking around, trying to discover something in my past.*

◈ v + adv ◆ v + prep

poke a'round; ,poke a'round sth (*AmE, informal*) to move or do things slowly, without hurrying: *I was just poking around in town all morning.*

◈ v + adv ◆ v + prep

poke at sth to push your finger, a stick, etc. into sth, often several times: *She poked at her salad with her fork.*

SYN prod at sth

◈ v + prep

,poke 'out; ,poke 'out of sth (*also* ,poke 'through, ,poke 'through sth**) if sth **pokes out** or **pokes out of** sth, you can see it because a small part is coming through a hole or is no longer covered: *His toes were poking through the holes in his socks.* ◇ *Two feet poked out from under the bed.* ◇ *There were flowers poking out of holes in the wall.*

SYN stick out, stick out of sth; stick through, stick through sth

◈ v + adv ◆ v + adv + prep ◆ v + prep

,poke sth 'out; ,poke sth 'out of sth to move sth suddenly forwards or out of sth: *The door opened and Max poked his head out.* ◇ *The pony poked its nose out of the door as I went past.*

OBJ head, tongue **SYN** stick sth out, stick sth out of sth

◈ v + n/pron + adv ◆ v + adv + n (*less frequent*) ◆ v + n/pron + adv + prep

,poke 'through; ,poke 'through sth = POKE OUT, POKE OUT OF STH

,poke 'through sth (*especially AmE*) = POKE ABOUT/AROUND, POKE ABOUT/AROUND STH 1

,poke 'up to become visible because a small part is coming through a hole, etc: *The grass had begun to poke up through the snow.*

SYN stick up

◈ v + adv

polish /'pɒlɪʃ; *AmE* 'pɑːl-/

,polish sb 'off (*informal, especially AmE*) to kill someone: *She hired an assassin to polish him off.*

◈ v + n/pron + adv ◆ v + adv + n

,polish sth 'off (*informal*) to finish sth quickly, especially food or drink: *They polished off the pudding in no time.* ◇ *I'll polish off this last bit of work, then we can go out.*

◈ v + adv + n ◆ v + n/pron + adv

,polish sth 'up 1 to make changes to sth in order to improve it: *The college needs to polish up its image.* **OBJ** act, image **2** to improve your skills in sth that you have learned but have not used for a long time: *She went on a course to polish up her German.* **OBJ** French, Italian, etc. **SYN** brush sth up

◈ v + adv + n ◆ v + pron + adv ◆ v + n + adv (*rare*)

ponce /pɒns; *AmE* pɑːns/

,ponce a'bout/a'round (*BrE, informal*) to do silly things in a way that looks ridiculous, especially to attract attention; to waste time: *He ponces around on the show, interviewing members of the audience.* ◇ *I could have finished that job while you've been poncing around!*

◈ v + adv

poop /puːp/

,poop 'out (*AmE, slang*) **1** (on sth) (*also* ,poop 'out of sth) to fail to do something that you have arranged to do; to stop doing sth because you are very tired or afraid: *I was supposed to go out last night but I pooped out.* **2** if a machine **poops out**, it stops working
◆ v + adv **1** *also* v + adv + prep

,poop sb 'out (*AmE, informal*) to make sb very tired: *A long day at the office poops me out.*
◆ v + n/pron + adv
▶ ,pooped 'out *adj* [not before noun] (*informal, especially AmE*) very tired: *I was pooped out after a long day at the office.*

pop /pɒp/; *AmE* pɑːp/ (-pp-)

,pop 'in (*informal, especially BrE*) to visit sb/sth for a short time: *She often pops in for coffee.* ◇ *I'll pop in to see you at the weekend.*
[SYN] drop in (on sb/at …)
◆ v + adv

,pop sth 'in/'round (*BrE*) to deliver sth to sb on your way to another place: *I'll pop the library books in on my way home.* ◇ *Could you pop those photos round later?*
[SYN] drop sth by; drop sth in (to sb/sth); drop sth off
◆ v + n/pron + adv

,pop 'off (*informal, especially BrE*) **1** to go or leave somewhere, especially for a short time: *I'm going to pop off early tonight* (= leave work early), *if it's all right with you.* ◇ *They just pop off to France whenever they feel like it.* **2** (*old-fashioned*) to die: *When I pop off, all my money goes to you.*
◆ v + adv

,pop sth 'on (*BrE, informal*) **1** to put on a piece of clothing quickly: *He popped on his jacket and went out.* **2** to turn on a piece of electrical equipment: *I'll pop the kettle on and we'll have some tea.*
◆ v + n/pron + adv ◆ v + adv + n

,pop 'out **1** (*also* ,pop 'out of sth) to come out from a place suddenly: *He just popped out from behind a tree.* ◇ (*figurative*) *I didn't mean to tell them — it just popped out* (= I spoke) *before I realized.* ◇ (*figurative*) *His eyes nearly popped out of his head* (= he was very surprised) *when he saw what she was wearing.* **2** (*especially BrE*) to leave somewhere for a very short time: *John's just popped out to get a newspaper.*
◆ v + adv **1** *also* v + adv + prep

,pop 'over/'round (*BrE*) to visit sb's home for a short time: *Pop over if you feel lonely.*
[SYN] drop by; drop over (*especially AmE*)
◆ v + adv

,pop 'up (*informal*) to appear or happen when you do not expect it: *He seems to pop up in the most unlikely places.* ◇ *When you click with the mouse, a menu pops up.*
◆ v + adv
▶ 'pop-up *adj* [only before noun] **1** (of a book, etc.) having pictures that stand up when you open the pages: *a pop-up book* **2** (*computing*) a pop-up function is one that appears quickly on the screen when you choose it while you are working on another document: *a pop-up menu/window*

pore /pɔː(r)/

'pore over sth to study sth by looking at it or thinking about it very carefully: *She was poring over an old map.*
◆ v + prep

post /pəʊst/; *AmE* poʊst/

,post sth 'off (to sb) (*BrE*) to send sth to sb by post/mail: *I posted a letter off to you this morning.*
[OBJ] letter, parcel [SYN] mail sth off; send sth off (to sb)
[NOTE] You can also use post a letter, etc., but this often refers to the action of putting the letter in the mailbox: *Did you remember to post my letter when you went out?*
◆ v + n/pron + adv ◆ v + adv + n

,post sth 'up to put a notice, etc. up on a wall so that people can see it: *The exam results will be posted up in the hall.*
◆ v + n/pron + adv ◆ v + adv + n

potter (*BrE*) /'pɒtə(r); *AmE* 'pɑːt-/ (*AmE* putter)

,potter a'bout/a'round; ,potter a'bout/ a'round sth to do things or move without hurrying, especially when you are doing sth that you enjoy and that is not important: *They spent the day pottering about by the river.* ◇ *She was happy just pottering around the house.*
[OBJ] the house, the garden
◆ v + adv ◆ v + prep

pounce /paʊns/

'pounce on sb/sth (*also* 'pounce upon sb/sth more formal*) to quickly notice sth that sb has said or done, and criticize it or use it for your own advantage: *As soon as I opened my mouth the teacher pounced on me.* ◇ *He said something silly and the other boys pounced on it at once.*
[SYN] seize on sth (*more formal*)
[NOTE] Pounce on/upon sb/sth can be used in the passive: *His mistake was pounced on by the press.*
◆ v + prep

'pounce on sth (*also* **'pounce upon sth** *more formal*) to accept an opportunity, etc. with enthusiasm: *She pounced on the opportunity to work with them.*
〉SYN〈 **seize sth** (*more formal*)
◈ v + prep

pound /paʊnd/

,pound sth 'out to play a tune on a musical instrument very loudly: *Cole was pounding out a tune on the piano.* ◇ (*figurative*) *She pounded out her poems on an old typewriter.*
◈ v + adv + n ♦ v + pron + adv ♦ v + n + adv (*less frequent*)

pour /pɔː(r)/

,pour sth a'way to get rid of a liquid by emptying it out of its container: *He poured the water away after he finished washing the car.*
◈ v + n/pron + adv ♦ v + adv + n

'pour down to rain heavily: *It's pouring down.* ◇ *The rain poured down all weekend.*
〉SYN〈 **pelt down**
NOTE **Pour** is also used with this meaning, but only with the subject *it*: *It's pouring (with rain).*
◈ v + adv
▶ **'downpour** *n* a heavy shower of rain

,pour 'forth; ,pour 'forth sth (*formal*) to appear or to produce sth from somewhere in large numbers or amounts: *The doors opened and a crowd of people poured forth.* ◇ *He poured forth a stream of bitter accusations.*
◈ v + adv ♦ v + adv + n

,pour 'in; ,pour 'into sth to arrive in large numbers or amounts: *Complaints poured in after last night's programme.* ◇ *Sunlight poured in through the windows.* ◇ *Fans were still pouring into the stadium.*
〉SYN〈 **flood in, flood into sth**
◈ v + adv ♦ v + prep

,pour sth 'into sth to provide a large amount of money for sth: *The council has been pouring money into the area.*
◈ v + n/pron + prep

pour sth 'off to remove some of the liquid from a container, cooking pot, etc. by pouring: *When the fish is cooked, pour off the water.*
◈ v + adv + n ♦ v + n/pron + adv

pour 'out; ,pour sth 'out 1 (*also* ,**pour 'out of sth**, ,**pour sth 'out of sth**) to come out or to produce sth from somewhere in large amounts or numbers: *Black smoke poured out of the engine.* ◇ *People poured out through the gates.* ◇ *Factory chimneys poured out smoke.* **2** when feelings or words **pour out**, or sb **pours them out**, they are expressed, usually after they have been kept hidden for some time: *All her feelings of resentment*

just came pouring out. ◇ *The whole story then poured out.* ◇ *He poured out his troubles to me.*
◈ v + adv ♦ v + adv + n ♦ v + pron + adv ♦ v + n + adv (*less frequent*)
  1 also v + adv + prep ♦ v + n/pron + adv + prep
▶ **'outpouring** *n* **1** [usually pl.] a strong and sudden expression of feeling: *She hated having to listen to his passionate outpourings.* **2** a large amount of sth produced in a short time: *a remarkable outpouring of scholarship*

power /'paʊə(r)/

,power 'up; ,power sth 'up if a machine **powers up**, or sb/sth **powers it up**, it is switched on and becomes ready to use: *Switch on the computer then wait for it to power up.* ◇ *This switch will power up the monitor.*
◈ v + adv ♦ v + adv + n ♦ v + n/pron + adv

precede /prɪ'siːd/

'precede sth with sth (*formal*) to do or say sth before the main thing that you want to do or say: *They often precede their performances with a short talk or display.*
◈ v + n/pron + prep

predispose /ˌpriːdɪ'spəʊz; *AmE* -'spoʊz/

predi'spose sb to sth (*also* **predi'spose sb towards sth** *less frequent*) (*formal*) to make sb more likely to do something or to suffer from a particular illness: *Cigarette advertising predisposes children to smoking.* ◇ *His lifestyle predisposed him to high blood pressure.* ◇ *Certain people may be predisposed to mental illness.*
NOTE **Predispose sb to/towards sth** is often used in the passive: *He believes that some people are predisposed to criminal behaviour.*
◈ v + n/pron + prep

preface /'prefəs/

'preface sth by/with sth; 'preface sth by doing sth (*formal*) to say sth before you start making a speech, answering a question, etc: *It is helpful if an interviewer prefaces each group of questions with a brief explanation.*
◈ v + n/pron + prep

prefix /'priːfɪks/

'prefix A to B; 'prefix A with B to add letters, numbers or words to the beginning of a number or word: *Prefix 020 to the number you want to call.* ◇ *Prefix the number you want to call with 020.*
◈ v + n/pron + prep

preside /prɪ'zaɪd/

pre'side over sth (*formal*) to lead or be in charge of a meeting, ceremony, etc: *She presided over the meeting.* ◇ *The court is presided over by a*

single judge. ◊ *(figurative) His government pre-sided over* (= were responsible for) *a massive increase in unemployment.*
NOTE **Preside over sth** can be used in the passive in its basic meaning.
🔁 v + prep

press /pres/

press a'head/'on (*also* **press 'forward** *less fre-quent*) **(with sth)** to continue moving forward quickly; to continue to do a task in a determined way: *He pressed on, even though it was now dark.* ◊ *They decided to press ahead with their plans.*
SYN **forge ahead (with sth)**
🔁 v + adv

'press for sth; **'press sb for sth** to make repeated and urgent requests for sth: *The unions are pressing for a pay rise.* ◊ *I must press you for a reply.*
SYN **push for sth, push sb for sth**
🔁 v + prep

press 'forward = PRESS AHEAD/ON

press 'in (on/upon sb) to move nearer to sb in a way that seems likely to cause harm: *He felt as if the walls were pressing in on him.*
SYN **close in (on sb/sth)**
🔁 v + adv

press 'on = PRESS AHEAD/ON

'press sth on sb to try to make sb accept sth, even though they may not want it: *She pressed cake and tea on us.*
🔁 v + n/pron + prep

presume /prɪˈzjuːm; AmE -ˈzuːm/

pre'sume on/upon sth (*formal*) to use sb's friendship or kindness for your own advantage in an unfair way: *I felt it would be presuming on our friendship to keep asking her for help.*
OBJ **friendship, hospitality**
NOTE **Presume on/upon sth** can be used in the passive.
🔁 v + prep

pretend /prɪˈtend/

pre'tend to sth (*formal*) (*usually used in nega-tive sentences and questions*) to claim to be or have sth, especially when it is not true: *I don't pretend to any great knowledge of the situation.*
🔁 v + prep

prevail /prɪˈveɪl/

pre'vail on/upon sb (to do sth) (*formal*) to per-suade sb to do sth: *Can I prevail on you to play the piano for us?*
NOTE **Prevail on/upon sb** can be used in the pas-sive: *She was prevailed upon to give one final per-formance.*
🔁 v + prep

prey /preɪ/

'prey on sb (*also* **'prey upon sb** *more formal*) to treat sb who is weaker than you in an unfair or dishonest way in order to get sth or gain an advantage for yourself: *The thieves have been preying on elderly people living alone.*
SYN **exploit sb**
NOTE **Prey on/upon sb** can be used in the passive
🔁 v + prep
IDM **prey on sb's 'mind** if a problem or a thought **preys on your mind**, you think and worry about it all the time

'prey on sth (*also* **'prey upon sth** *more formal*) if a bird or an animal **preys on/upon** another bird or animal, it hunts and kills it for food: *They prey on small mammals.*
NOTE **Prey on/upon sth** can be used in the pas-sive: *These small fish are preyed upon by sharks and other fish.*
🔁 v + prep

pride /praɪd/

'pride yourself on sth; **'pride yourself on doing sth** to be proud of sth such as a personal quality or a skill: *She had always prided herself on her appearance.*
🔁 v + pron + prep

print /prɪnt/

print sth 'off/'out to produce a document or information from a computer in printed form: *I'll print off enough copies for everyone to have one.* ◊ *I'm waiting for the results to be printed out.*
OBJ **copy**
🔁 v + adv + n ♦ v + n/pron + adv
▶ **'printout** *n* a printed copy of information in a computer file: *She asked for a printout of the pre-vious year's accounts.*

prise (*BrE*) (*AmE* **prize**) /praɪz/ (*also* **pry** /praɪ/ *especially AmE*)

prise sth 'out of sb; **'prise sth from sb** to obtain some information, etc. from sb with great difficulty: *I finally managed to prise his new address out of her.* ◊ *She had a way of prising secrets from people.* ◊ *You'll be lucky to prise any money out of him!*
🔁 v + n/pron + adv + prep ♦ v + n/pron + prep

prize (*AmE*) /praɪz/

prize sth 'out of sb; **'prize sth from sb** = PRISE STH OUT OF SB, PRISE STH FROM SB

proceed /prəˈsiːd; AmE proʊ-/

pro'ceed against sb (*formal, law*) to start a court case against sb: *I shall instruct my solicitor to proceed against you for trespass.*

NOTE Proceed **against sb** can be used in the passive.

♦ v + prep

pro'ceed from sth (*formal*) to be caused by or be the result of sth: *The dispute proceeded from a wrong interpretation of the law.*

♦ v + prep

prod /prɒd; *AmE* prɑːd/ (**-dd-**)

prod at sth to press sth with your finger or with a pointed object, especially to see what it is, or what it is made of, etc: *He prodded at the plate of fish with his fork.*

SYN poke at sth

♦ v + prep

pronounce /prə'naʊns/

pro'nounce for/against sb/sth to give a judgement in a court of law for or against sb/sth

♦ v + prep

pro'nounce on/upon sth (*formal*) to express an opinion or give a judgement on sth: *The minister will pronounce on the situation today.*

♦ v + prep

prop /prɒp; *AmE* prɑːp/ (**-pp-**)

prop sb 'up; **prop yourself 'up** to support a person by putting sth under or behind them: *We propped her up with a pillow.* ◊ *He tried to prop himself up on his elbow.*

♦ v + n/pron + adv ♦ v + adv + n

prop sth 'up 1 to keep sth upright or stop sth from falling by putting sth under or behind it: *A family photo was propped up against some books on her desk.* ◊ *The tree had to be propped up with thick posts.* **2** to support sth that is having financial, political, etc. difficulties: *The regime is being propped up by foreign aid.* ◊ *The government will no longer prop up inefficient industries.*

♦ v + n/pron + adv ♦ v + adv + n

provide /prə'vaɪd/

pro'vide against sth (*formal*) to make plans in order to deal with or prevent a bad or unpleasant situation: *Does your insurance provide against loss of income?*

NOTE Provide **against sth** can be used in the passive.

♦ v + prep

pro'vide for sb to give sb the things that they need to live, such as food, money and clothing: *How will she provide for six children?* ◊ *My family will be well provided for if I die.*

OBJ children, family

NOTE Provide **for sb** can be used in the passive.

♦ v + prep

pro'vide for sth (*formal*) **1** to make plans or arrangements to deal with sth that may happen in the future: *The budget provides for rising inflation.* **SYN** allow for sth **2** (of a law, etc.) to make it possible for sth to be done: *European legislation provides for expansion of the EU.*

NOTE Provide **for sth** can be used in the passive.

♦ v + prep

prowl /praʊl/

prowl a'round; **prowl a'round sth** (*also* **prowl a'bout/'round**, **prowl a'bout/'round sth** *especially BrE*) **1** to move quietly and carefully around an area, often with the intention of committing a crime: *There was someone prowling around outside.* ◊ *Why were you prowling about the building so late?* **2** to walk around a room, a building, etc., because you are worried, bored or unable to relax: *Her husband prowled about restlessly.* ◊ *She got up and prowled around the room.*

♦ v + adv ♦ v + prep

pry (*AmE*) /praɪ/ (**pries, prying, pried, pried**)

pry sth 'out of sb; **'pry sth from sb** = PRISE STH OUT OF SB, PRISE STH FROM SB

psych /saɪk/

psych sb 'out (*informal*) to make an opponent feel less confident by saying or doing things that make you seem better, stronger, etc. than them: *The other team tried to psych us out before the game started.*

♦ v + n/pron + adv ♦ v + adv + n

psych sb 'up; **psych yourself 'up (for sth)** (*informal*) to prepare sb/yourself mentally for sth difficult or unpleasant, such as a game, an exam, an interview, etc: *Boxers need to psych themselves up for the fight.* ◊ *I'd got psyched up for the interview but then it was cancelled at the very last minute!*

♦ v + n/pron + adv ♦ v + adv + n

puff /pʌf/

puff a'way (at/on sth) (*informal*) (*usually used in the progressive tenses*) to smoke a pipe, cigarette, etc., often when you are thinking deeply: *He stood looking out of the window, puffing away at his pipe.*

♦ v + adv

puff sth 'out to make sth larger and rounder by filling it with air: *She puffed out her cheeks in anger.* ◊ *Her hair was puffed out round her face.*

OBJ cheeks, chest

♦ v + n/pron + adv ♦ v + adv + n

‚puff 'up; **‚puff sth 'up** to swell or to make sth
swell and increase in size: *He could feel his face
puffing up where Mark had hit him.* ◇ *He puffed
up his chest like an exotic bird.* ◇ *The medicine
makes my ankles puff up.*
◆ v + adv ♦ v + adv + n ♦ v + n/pron + adv
**IDM be puffed up with 'pride, self-im'portance,
etc.** to be too full of pride, self-importance, etc:
*She was so puffed up with conceit she didn't notice
people were avoiding her.*

pull /pʊl/

~ ahead, ahead of	~ off
~ apart	~ on
~ aside	~ out, out of
~ at	~ over
~ away	~ through
~ back 218	~ to
~ down	~ together
~ for	~ under
217 ~ in	~ up
~ into	

‚pull a'head; **‚pull a'head of sb/sth** to move in
front of sb/sth, especially suddenly or unexpectedly: *I pulled ahead of the other runners on the
last straight.*
◆ v + adv ♦ v + adv + prep

‚pull sb/sth a'part 1 to separate sb/sth, often
people or animals that are fighting: *It took several of us to pull them apart.* SYN **separate
sb/sth** (*more formal*) **2** to severely criticize
sb/sth: *She pulled my work apart and made me do
it again.*
◆ v + n/pron + adv ♦ v + adv + n (*less frequent*)

‚pull sth a'part to destroy sth or separate sth
into pieces by pulling parts of it in different directions: *I pulled the machine apart, but couldn't
find what was wrong with it.* ◇ *The fox was pulled
apart by the dogs.*
◆ v + n/pron + adv ♦ v + adv + n (*less frequent*)

‚pull sb a'side to take sb to a quiet corner or
place to talk to them privately: *I pulled him aside
to warn him not to say anything.*
SYN **take sb a'side**
◆ v + n/pron + adv

‚pull sth a'side to move sth such as a curtain so
that you can see sth: *She pulled the curtain aside
to reveal a small door.*
OBJ **curtain**
◆ v + n/pron + adv ♦ v + adv + n

'pull at sth 1 to pull sth lightly several times
especially to gain attention: *The little boy pulled
anxiously at her sleeve.* **2** = PULL ON/AT STH
SYN **tug at sth**
◆ v + prep

‚pull a'way (from sth) 1 when a vehicle **pulls
away**, it begins to move: *The train was pulling
away as we reached the station.* ◇ *I started the
engine and pulled away from the kerb.* **2** to grad-

ually move further in front of sb/sth; to start to
win a game or competition by getting more
points than your opponent: *The British boat
began to pull away from the Italians* (= in a race).
◇ *The German pair pulled away to finish three
games ahead* (= in tennis). **3 (from sb/sth)** to
move quickly away from sb/sth: *She pulled away
from him in horror.*
◆ v + adv

‚pull sb/sth a'way (from sb/sth) to make sb/sth
move away from sb/sth: *I pulled her away from
the edge.*
◆ v + n/pron + adv ♦ v + adv + n

‚pull 'back 1 (from sb/sth) to move backwards
away from sb/sth: *He pulled back and stared at
her in disbelief.* ◇ *The camera then pulled back to
a wider view.* **2** to decide not to do sth you were
intending to do, usually because of possible
problems: *Their sponsors pulled back from finan-
cing the movie.* SYN **withdraw**
◆ v + adv

‚pull 'back; **‚pull sb/sth 'back 1** to move back
from a place; to make an army move back from a
place **2** (*BrE, sport*) to improve a team's position
in a game: *Rangers pulled back to 4–3.* ◇ *The
pulled back a goal in the last few minutes of the
game.*
◆ v + adv ♦ v + adv + n ♦ v + n/pron + adv

‚pull sb/sth 'back to hold sb/sth and move
them/it backwards, sideways or away from sth:
pulled the child back from the edge. ◇ *He pulle
back the curtain.* ◇ *She pulled the sheet back
show us the wound.*
◆ v + n/pron + adv ♦ v + adv + n

‚pull sb 'down (*informal, especially AmE*) to hav
a bad effect on sb's health or happiness: *Th
strain is really pulling me down.*
SYN **get sb down**
◆ v + n/pron + adv ♦ v + adv + n

‚pull sth 'down 1 to move sth from a higher to
lower position: *She pulled down the blinds an
locked the door.* ◇ *He dried his hands and pulle
down his sleeves.* OBJ **blinds, trousers, arm**
(*especially BrE*) to destroy a building complete
My old school has been pulled down. OBJ **hous
building** SYN **demolish sth** (*more formal*)
(*computing*) to make a list of possible choic
appear on a computer screen by pressing one
the buttons on the mouse **4** (*slang*) = PULL STH
◆ v + n/pron + adv ♦ v + adv + n
▶ **'pull-down** *adj* [only before noun] used
describe a list of possible choices that appea
on a computer screen below a title: *a pull-dor
menu*

'pull for sb/sth (*AmE*) to support and encoura
sb/sth and hope they will be successful: *Hang
there, we're all pulling for you to win!*
SYN **root for sb/sth**
◆ v + prep

,**pull 'in**; ,**pull 'into sth 1** if a train or a bus **pulls in**, it arrives somewhere and stops: *The express pulled in on time.* ◇ *The coach pulled into bay 27.* **2** (*BrE*) if a vehicle or a driver **pulls in**, they move to the side of the road and stop: *Pull in in front of the bus.* ◇ *He pulled into the parking lot and turned off the engine.*
> SYN draw in, draw into sth
> OPP pull out, pull out of sth
⊕ v + adv ◆ v + prep
▶ **'pull-in** *n* (*old-fashioned*, *BrE*) an area at the side of a road where drivers can stop; a restaurant for drivers at the side of a road

,**pull sb 'in 1** (*informal*) to bring sb to a police station in order to ask them questions: *The police have pulled him in for questioning.* SYN **bring sb in 2** if an event or a show **pulls** people **in**, it attracts people in large numbers: *The show is still pulling in the crowds.* OBJ **crowds, customers** SYN **get sb in**
⊕ **1** v + n/pron + adv ◆ v + adv + n
2 v + adv + n ◆ v + n/pron + adv

pull sth 'in (*also* ,**pull sth 'down** *slang*) (*informal*) to earn a particular amount of money: *He must be pulling in a hundred thousand.*
⊕ v + adv + n ◆ v + n/pron + adv (*rare*)

pull 'off; ,**pull 'off sth** (of a vehicle or its driver) to leave the road in order to stop for a short time: *He pulled off onto the verge.* ◇ *I pulled off the main road and stopped.*
⊕ v + adv ◆ v + prep + n

pull sb/sth 'off; ,**pull sb/sth 'off sb/sth** to forcefully pull away sb/sth attacking sb/sth else: *They tried to pull off the dogs with their hands.* ◇ *He had to be pulled off the older man by two policemen.*
⊕ v + adv + n ◆ v + n/pron + adv ◆ v + n/pron + prep

pull sth 'off 1 to remove an item of clothing quickly or with difficulty: *She pulled off her hat and gloves.* SYN **take sth off** OPP **pull sth on 2** (*informal*) to succeed in doing or achieving sth difficult: *The goalie pulled off a terrific save.* ◇ *If anyone can pull it off, I'm sure you can.* SYN **bring sth off**
⊕ **1** v + n/pron + adv ◆ v + adv + n
2 v + adv + n ◆ v + pron + adv ◆ v + n + adv (*rare*)

pull sth 'on to put an item of clothing on quickly or with difficulty: *I pulled my shorts on and ran outside.*
SYN **put sth on** OPP **pull sth off**
⊕ v + n/pron + adv ◆ v + adv + n

pull on/at sth to take long deep breaths from a cigarette, etc: *She pulled on her cigar.*
OBJ **cigarette, cigar**
⊕ v + prep

pull 'out 1 (*also* ,**pull 'out of sth**) if a train or bus **pulls out**, it leaves a place: *The train pulled out (of the station) on time.* SYN **draw out, draw out of sth** OPP **pull in, pull into sth 2** [+ adv/prep] (of a vehicle or its driver) to move away from the side of a road, from behind sth, etc: *I pulled out onto the main road.* ◇ *A white van suddenly pulled out in front of me.*
⊕ v + adv **1** also v + adv + prep

,**pull 'out**; ,**pull 'out of sth**; ,**pull sb/sth 'out**; ,**pull sb/sth 'out of sth 1** to move or to make sb/sth move away from sth or stop being involved in it: *They are pulling their troops out of the war zone.* **2** (*also* ,**pull 'out of doing sth**, ,**pull sb/sth 'out of doing sth**) to stop being involved in sth or decide not to do sth you had promised to do; to make sb do this: *The other firm wanted to pull out of the deal.* ◇ *The manager has pulled the team out of the competition.* ◇ *The company is pulling out of sponsoring the team.*
SYN **back out, back out of sth, back out of doing sth; withdraw (from sth), withdraw sb/sth (from sth)** (*more formal*)
⊕ v + adv ◆ v + prep ◆ v + n/pron + adv ◆ v + adv + n ◆ v + n/pron + adv + prep
▶ **'pull-out** *n* an act of taking an army away from an area; an act of taking an organization out of a system, a deal, etc: *their unexpected pull-out from the competition*
→ *see also* PULL-OUT at PULL STH OUT, PULL STH OUT OF STH

,**pull sth 'out**; ,**pull sth 'out of sth 1** to take sth out of somewhere by pulling: *He pulled an envelope out of his pocket.* ◇ *The woman suddenly pulled out a knife.* **2** to remove sth from sth else; to separate sth from sth else: *I pulled out the middle page of the magazine to show him.*
⊕ v + n/pron + adv ◆ v + n/pron + adv + prep
▶ **'pull-out** *n* a part of a magazine, newspaper, etc. that can be taken out easily and kept separately: *an eight-page pull-out* ◇ *a pull-out guide to health*
→ *see also* PULL-OUT at PULL OUT, PULL OUT OF STH, PULL SB/STH OUT, PULL SB/STH OUT OF STH

,**pull 'over**; ,**pull sb/sth 'over** to move or to make sb/sth move, to the side of the road and stop: *He pulled over and jumped out of the car.* ◇ *I pulled over to let the ambulance pass.* ◇ *A police car pulled me over.*
⊕ v + adv ◆ v + n/pron + adv ◆ v + adv + n

,**pull 'through**; ,**pull 'through sth**; ,**pull sb 'through**; ,**pull sb 'through sth 1** to get better after an illness; to help sb get better after an illness: *Few people expected him to pull through after the accident.* ◇ *She has pulled through the operation remarkably well.* ◇ *He suffered terrible injuries, but his courage pulled him through.* **2** to succeed in doing sth very difficult or in dealing with difficult problems; to help sb do this: *He's got his problems at school, but with help he'll pull through.* ◇ *It's going to be tough but we'll pull through it together.* ◇ *She relied on her business experience to pull her through.*
⊕ v + adv ◆ v + prep ◆ v + n/pron + adv ◆ v + n/pron + prep

,**pull sth 'to** if you **pull** a door or a window **to**, you close it or almost close it by pulling it towards you: *Pull the door to on your way out.*
OBJ **door, window**
SYN **shut sth** OPP **push sth to**
✦ v + n/pron + adv

,**pull to'gether** if a group of people **pull together**, they act or work together in order to achieve sth: *If we all pull together, we'll finish by Friday.*
✦ v + adv

,**pull sth to'gether 1** to make all the different parts of an organization, an activity, etc. work together in a successful way: *His inspired leadership pulled the party together.* **2** to organize a variety of ideas, etc. in a logical and careful way: *This lecture pulls together several recent theories.*
✦ v + n/pron + adv ✦ v + adv + n

,**pull yourself to'gether** to gain control of your feelings and start to act in a calm and sensible way: *She made a great effort to pull herself together.* ◇ *Stop crying and pull yourself together!*
✦ v + pron + adv

,**pull sb/sth 'under** to make sb/sth become completely covered in water: *He felt the waves pulling him under.*
✦ v + n/pron + adv

,**pull 'up** (of a vehicle, or its driver) to stop, especially for a short time: *He pulled up alongside me at the traffic lights.* ◇ *A taxi pulled up outside.*
SYN **draw up**
✦ v + adv

,**pull sb 'up 1** (*BrE*) (**on/for sth**) (*informal*) to criticize or correct sb for sth they have done badly or wrong: *She pulled him up on his untidy handwriting.* ◇ *I was pulled up for not using the correct procedure.* **2** to make sb stop doing or saying sth very suddenly: *The shock of his words pulled me up short.* ◇ *The expansion of industry was pulled up sharply by an economic crisis.* SYN **draw sb up**
→ *see also* DRAW YOURSELF UP
✦ v + n/pron + adv ✦ v + adv + n

,**pull sth 'up 1** to move sth from a lower to a higher position: *She pulled her shorts up and put a T-shirt on.* **2** to remove sth from the ground with force: *Kids had pulled all the shrubs up.* **3** (**to sth**) to bring sth such as a chair closer to sb/sth: *Pull up a chair and sit down.* SYN **draw sth up**
✦ v + n/pron + adv ✦ v + adv + n

IDM **pull your 'socks up** (*BrE*) to try to develop a more serious, responsible attitude to your work; to improve your behaviour: *He'll have to pull his socks up if he wants to pass that exam.*

▸ **'pull-up** *n* an exercise in which you hold onto a high bar above your head and pull yourself up towards it: *She does 50 pull-ups and 100 sit-ups every morning.*

,**pull yourself 'up 1** to move your body into an upright position, especially by holding sth firmly and using force: *Julia pulled herself up from the sofa.* ◇ *I pulled myself up to my full height and glared angrily at Dan.* **2** to stop doing or saying sth very suddenly: *I started to ask about her family, but pulled myself up sharply when I saw she was getting upset.*
SYN **draw yourself up**
→ *see also* PULL SB UP
✦ v + pron + adv

IDM **pull yourself up by your** (**own**) '**bootstraps** (*informal*) to improve your situation yourself, without help from other people

pump /pʌmp/

,**pump sth 'in**; ,**pump sth 'into sth** to give large amounts of money or resources to sth: *Millions have been pumped into this industry.*
OBJ **money** SYN **inject sth** (**into sth**)
✦ v + n/pron + adv ✦ v + adv + n ✦ v + n/pron + prep

,**pump 'out**; ,**pump 'out of sth**; ,**pump sth 'out**; ,**pump sth 'out of sth 1** (of a liquid) to come out of somewhere or to be produced from somewhere with force and in large amounts: *Blood was pumping out of the wound.* ◇ *Cars are pumping out tons of pollutants every year.* **2** if music, sound, etc. **pumps out** or sb **pumps it out**, it is produced from somewhere very loudly and for a long time: *Heavy metal was pumping out of huge speakers.*
✦ v + adv ✦ v + adv + prep ✦ v + adv + n ✦ v + n/pron + adv ✦ v + n/pron + adv + prep

,**pump sth 'out**; ,**pump sth 'out of sth** to remove a gas, liquid, etc. from inside sth with a pump: *The fire brigade pumped out the basement.* ◇ *The fire brigade pumped the water out of the basement.*
✦ v + n/pron + adv ✦ v + adv + n ✦ v + n/pron + adv + prep

,**pump sb 'up**; ,**pump yourself 'up** (*informal, especially AmE*) to make sb feel more excited or determined about sth: *I was really pumped up for the race.*
NOTE **Pump sb up** is often used in the passive.
✦ v + adv + n ✦ v + n/pron + adv

,**pump sth 'up 1** to fill a tyre, etc. with air using a pump: *Pump your tyres up before you set off.* **2** (*informal, especially BrE*) to increase the amount, value or volume of sth: *They always pump their prices up before Christmas.*
✦ v + n/pron + adv ✦ v + adv + n

punch /pʌntʃ/

,punch 'in/'out; **,punch sb 'in/'out** (*AmE*) to record the time that you arrive at or leave work, by putting a card into a machine; to do this for sb else: *He punched in ten minutes late.* ◇ *I was in such a hurry to leave that I forgot to punch out.* ◇ *Would you punch me in? I'm going to be late.*
> **SYN** **clock in/on, clock sb in/on** (*BrE*), **clock off/out** (*BrE*)
> ◈ v + adv ◆ v + n/pron + adv

,punch sth 'in; **,punch sth 'into sth** to put information into a computer, etc. by pressing keys: *She punched in the security code and the door opened.*
> ◈ v + adv + n ◆ v + n/pron + adv ◆ v + n/pron + prep

,punch 'out; **,punch sb 'out** (*AmE*) = PUNCH IN/OUT, PUNCH SB IN/OUT

,punch sb 'out (*AmE, informal*) to hit sb repeatedly: *Touch my car and I'll punch you out.*
> **SYN** **beat sb up**
> → see also PUNCH IN/OUT, PUNCH SB IN/OUT
> ◈ v + n/pron + adv

,punch sth 'out 1 to press a combination of buttons or keys on a computer, telephone, etc: *He picked up the phone and punched out Donna's number.* **2** to hit sth very hard and make a hole in it or make sth fall out: *The burglar had punched out a pane of glass to open the window.*
> ◈ v + adv + n ◆ v + n/pron + adv

push /pʊʃ/

~ about	220	~ off
~ ahead/forward/on		~ on
~ around		~ on/onto
~ aside		~ out, out of
~ away		~ over
~ back		~ past
~ by/past		~ through
~ for		~ to
~ forward		~ towards
~ in		~ up

,push sb a'bout (*especially BrE*) = PUSH SB AROUND

,push a'head/'forward/'on (**with sth**) to continue with a plan in a determined way: *They pushed ahead with the modernization programme.*
> → see also PUSH ON
> ◈ v + adv

,push sb a'round (*also* ,push sb a'bout *especially BrE*) (*informal*) to order sb to do things in a threatening or unpleasant way: *Don't let him push you around.*
> ◈ v + n/pron + adv

,push sb/sth a'side 1 to move sb/sth to a position where they do not prevent you from going somewhere or doing sth: *He pushed her aside and went into the room.* ◇ *I pushed the curtain aside to*

get a better view. **2** to treat sb/sth as if they/it are not important; to avoid thinking about sb/sth: *When his sister brought home a school friend, he felt pushed aside and abandoned.* ◇ *Emma immediately pushed the unpleasant thought aside.*
> ◈ v + n/pron + adv ◆ v + adv + n

,push sb/sth a'way to remove sb/sth from in front of you with your hands or arms, to show that you do not want them/it: *He offered to help, but she pushed him away.* ◇ *She pushed her plate away. 'I'm not hungry.'* ◇ (*figurative*) *Had he lied to me? I pushed the thought away.*
> ◈ v + n/pron + adv ◆ v + adv + n

,push sb 'back 1 to use force to make sb move backwards, especially by using your hands or arms: *The police pushed the protesters back.* **2** if sb **pushes** soldiers, an army, etc. **back**, they force them to move away from a place: *Magnus's army was gradually pushed back into a defensive circle.*
> ◈ v + n/pron + adv ◆ v + adv + n

,push sth 'back 1 to make sth move backwards by using your hands, arms, legs, etc: *He pushed his chair back and stood up.* **2** to make the time or date of a meeting, etc. later than originally planned: *The release of their new album has been pushed back until early next year.*
> ◈ v + n/pron + adv ◆ v + adv + n

,push 'by/'past; **,push 'by/'past sb** to use force to go past other people, rudely making them move to one side: *She pushed by without saying a word.* ◇ *He followed me to the door and pushed past me into the house.*
> ◈ v + adv ◆ v + prep

'push for sth; **'push sb for sth** to keep asking for sth, or asking sb to do sth, because you think it is very important: *We are pushing hard for electoral reform.* ◇ *They're pushing me for a decision on the matter.*
> **SYN** **press for sth, press sb for sth**
> ◈ v + prep ◆ v + n/pron + prep

,push 'forward 1 to move forward through a group of people until you are near the front: *She pushed forward through the crowd.* **2** = PUSH AHEAD/FORWARD/ON **3** if soldiers, an army, etc. **push forward**, they move forward against the enemy, especially with some difficulty
> ◈ v + adv

,push sb/yourself 'forward to try to make sb notice sb/yourself, especially in order to obtain sth such as a job or a move to a more important job: *He's not the sort of person who pushes himself forward.*
> ◈ v + n/pron + adv

,push 'in (*BrE, informal*) to move in front of other people who are waiting in a line: *They thought I was trying to push in at the head of the queue.*
> **SYN** **cut in** (*AmE*)
> ◈ v + adv

,**push 'off 1** (*informal, especially BrE*) used to tell sb rudely to go away: *Push off and leave me in peace!* **2** to leave sb/a place, especially in order to go home: *It's time I pushed off and did some work.* **3** (**from sth**) to move away from the shore in a boat, or from the side of a swimming pool: *He pushed off from the bank and rowed downstream.*
◈ v + adv

,**push 'on 1** (**to…**) to continue travelling somewhere: *We decided to push on to Kobe.* **2** = PUSH AHEAD/FORWARD/ON
◈ v + adv

'**push sth on/onto sb** to try to make sb accept or buy sth they do not really want: *He keeps pushing his attentions on her.*
◈ v + n/pron + prep

,**push sb 'out**; ,**push sb 'out of sth** to make sb leave a place or an organization: *He refused to resign, so his colleagues pushed him out.* ◇ *Patients are being pushed out of hospital before they are really ready.*
◈ v + n/pron + adv ◆ v + adv + n ◆ v + n/pron + adv + prep

,**push sb/sth 'out** to make sb/sth less important than before; to replace sb/sth with sb/sth else: *My parents didn't want me to feel pushed out by my younger brother.* ◇ *'Harry Potter' is pushing out more traditional children's stories.*
◈ v + adv + n ◆ v + n/pron + adv

,**push sb/sth 'over** to make sb/sth fall to the ground; to make sth fall onto its side or turn over: *I was pushed over in the playground.*
◈ v + n/pron + adv ◆ v + adv + n
▶ '**pushover** n (*informal*) **1** a task that is easy to do; a contest that you win easily: *The game against Sheffield will be a pushover.* **2** a person who is easy to influence or persuade

,**push 'past**; ,**push 'past sb** = PUSH BY/PAST, PUSH BY/PAST SB

,**push 'through**; ,**push 'through sth** to use force to cross a barrier, especially one formed by a crowd of people: *He pushed his way through to the front of the crowd.*
◈ v + adv ◆ v + prep

,**push sth 'through**; ,**push sth 'through sth** to get a new law, plan or proposal officially accepted: *We're trying to push through the reforms as quickly as possible.* ◇ *The Prime Minister promised to push the bill through Parliament quickly.*
OBJ **bill, reforms, legislation**
◈ v + n/pron + adv ◆ v + adv + n ◆ v + n/pron + prep

,**push sth 'to** if you push a door or a window to, you close it or almost close it by moving it away from you: *I pushed the door to.*
OBJ only **door, window** SYN **shut sth**
OPP **pull sth to**
◈ v + n/pron + adv

,**push to'wards sth** to make progress towards achieving an aim: *We are pushing towards full monetary union in Europe.*
◈ v + prep

,**push sb to'wards sth**; ,**push sb to'wards doing sth** to make sb try to do or achieve sth: *The need for aid finally pushed them towards cooperation with the USA.*
◈ v + n/pron + prep

,**push sth 'up** to make sth rise or increase: *A shortage of land pushed property prices up.*
OBJ **prices, rates, costs**
◈ v + n/pron + adv ◆ v + adv + n

put /pʊt/ (putting, put, put)

	~ about		~ in for
	~ above	223	~ into
	~ across		~ off
221	~ aside	224	~ on
	~ at		~ onto
	~ away		~ out
	~ back	225	~ over
	~ before		~ over on
	~ behind		~ past
	~ by		~ through
	~ down	226	~ to
222	~ down as		~ together
	~ down for		~ towards
	~ down to		~ under
	~ forth		~ up
	~ forward	227	~ up to
	~ in		~ up with
	~ in/into		~ upon

,**put a'bout** (*technical*) if a ship puts about, it changes direction: *The ship put about and headed back to port.*
◈ v + adv

,**put sth a'bout** (*informal, especially BrE*) to spread information, stories etc. among a group of people: *Someone has been putting it about that you're leaving.* ◇ *This was an idea put about by the government.* ◇ *Rumours were put about that the shop was closing.*
OBJ **rumour, idea, it**
NOTE Put sth about is often used in the passive.
◈ v + n/pron + adv ◆ v + adv + n

'**put sb/sth above sb/sth** = PUT SB/STH BEFORE SB/STH

,**put sth a'cross** (*also* ,**put sth 'over**) (**to sb**) to communicate your ideas, feelings, etc. to sb clearly and successfully: *The campaign failed to put the message across.* ◇ *She's very good at putting across her ideas.*
OBJ **message, idea, point** SYN **get sth across**
◈ v + n/pron + adv ◆ v + adv + n
IDM **put one a'cross sb** (*informal*) to deceive or trick sb

,put yourself a'cross (*also* ,put yourself 'over) (to sb) (*BrE*) to make sb understand your ideas, your personality, etc: *She puts herself across well at interviews.*
◆ v + pron + adv

,put sth a'side 1 to place sth to one side: *She put the newspaper aside and stood up.* $\overline{\text{SYN}}$ **lay sth aside 2** to keep an item for a customer to collect later: *I asked them to put the dress aside for me.* **3** (*also* ,put sth 'by *especially BrE*, ,put sth a'way) to save some money to use later: *He had been putting some money aside every month.* OBJ **money 4** to decide to keep a period of time for a particular task or activity: *We need to put aside some time to deal with this.* OBJ **time 5** to ignore or forget sth: *Doctors have to put their personal feelings aside.* ◊ *They decided to put aside their differences.* $\overline{\text{SYN}}$ **set sth aside; disregard sth** (*more formal*)
◆ v + adv + n ◆ v + n/pron + adv

'put sth/sb at sth to calculate or estimate something to be a particular size, amount, etc: *I'd put his age at about sixty.* ◊ *I'd put him at about sixty.* ◊ *The cost of the project is put at two million pounds.*
OBJ **figure, cost**
◆ v + n/pron + prep + n

,put sb a'way (*informal*) **1** to send sb to prison, to a hospital for people who are mentally ill, etc: *He was put away for 15 years.* ◊ *If you're found guilty, they'll put you away for a long time.* NOTE **Put sb away** is often used in the passive in this meaning. **2** (*AmE, slang*) to kill sb: *He was ordered to put the hostage away.*
◆ v + n/pron + adv ◆ v + adv + n

,put sth a'way 1 to put sth in a box, drawer, etc. because you have finished using it: *He washed the dishes and put them away.* ◊ *I'm just going to put the car away* (= in the garage). ◊ *Kids — will you put away your toys now?* **2** = PUT STH ASIDE 3 *She's putting some money away for college.* ◊ *I'm putting something away for a rainy day* (= for difficult times). **3** (*informal*) to eat or drink large quantities of sth: *They put away five bottles of wine between them!* ◊ *I don't know how he manages to put it all away!* **4** (*AmE*) = PUT STH DOWN 4
◆ **1,2** v + n/pron + adv ◆ v + adv + n
   3 v + adv + n ◆ v + pron + adv ◆ v + n + adv (*less frequent*)

,put sth 'back 1 to return sth to its usual place; to return sth to the place it was before: *He uses my things and never puts them back.* ◊ *Put the book back on the shelf, will you?* ◊ *She carefully put the letters back where she'd found them.* $\overline{\text{SYN}}$ **replace sth** (*more formal*) **2** (to…) (*also* ,put sth 'back…) to move sth to a later time or date: *The meeting has been put back to next week.* ◊ *The game has been put back 24 hours.* $\overline{\text{SYN}}$ **postpone sth** (*more formal*) $\overline{\text{OPP}}$ **bring sth forward 3** to cause sth to be delayed: *The strike has put back*

our deliveries by over a month. $\overline{\text{SYN}}$ **set sth back 4** to move the hands of a clock back to give the correct earlier time, especially at the end of summer: *We forgot to put the clocks back last night.* OBJ **the clocks, your watch** $\overline{\text{OPP}}$ **put sth forward 5** (*informal*) to drink a large quantity of alcohol: *I had just put back my sixth beer of the evening.* $\overline{\text{SYN}}$ **knock sth back 6** (into sth) to give sth to or do sth for an organization, a society, etc. that has given you sth: *The school has been so good to me. I really want to put something back into it.* OBJ **something** $\overline{\text{SYN}}$ **give sth back 7** to spend more money on sth in order to make it better or more successful: *The government isn't putting enough money back into the economy.* OBJ **money**
◆ **1,2,4** v + n/pron + adv ◆ v + adv + n
   3,5 v + adv + n ◆ v + n/pron + adv
IDM **put the 'clock back** to return to a situation that existed in the past: *I wish I could put the clock back and give our marriage another chance.*

'put sb/sth before sb/sth (*also* 'put sb/sth above sb/sth) to give sb/sth more importance than sb/sth else: *He puts his children before anyone else.* ◊ *They have always put business before pleasure.* ◊ *Some young men put their own career above their partner's.*
◆ v + n/pron + prep

,put sth be'fore sb/sth to present sth to sb/sth: *She will be able to put her arguments before the committee.* ◊ *The new evidence was put before the court.*
OBJ **proposal, evidence, plan**
◆ v + n/pron + prep

,put sth be'hind you to try to forget about sth unpleasant that has happened and not allow it to affect your future: *She wanted to put the past behind her.*
OBJ **your/the past, your problems**
◆ v + n/pron + prep + pron

,put sth 'by (*especially BrE*) = PUT STH ASIDE 3 *He puts a few pounds by every week.* ◊ *She's got some money put by.*

put 'down (*especially BrE*) if an aeroplane or its pilot **puts down**, the plane comes down to the ground: *The plane put down at Manchester airport.* ◊ *He had to put down in a field.*
$\overline{\text{SYN}}$ **set down, set sth down; land, land sth**
◆ v + adv

,put sb 'down 1 (*also* ,put yourself 'down) to criticize sb and make them feel stupid, especially in front of other people; to say something that suggests that you have a low opinion of yourself: *She's always putting people down.* ◊ *Don't put yourself down!* $\overline{\text{SYN}}$ **do sb down, do yourself down** (*BrE, informal*) **2** (*BrE*) (of a bus, etc.) to allow sb to get off: *The bus stopped to put down some passengers.* ◊ *Ask the driver to put you down outside the City Hall.* OBJ **passengers**

SYN **set sb down** (*especially BrE*) **OPP** **pick sb up** **3** to put a baby to bed: *She's just put the baby down.* **OBJ** **baby**

✦ **1,3** v + n/pron + adv ♦ v + adv + n (*rare*)
  2 v + n/pron + adv ♦ v + adv + n

▶ **'put-down** n (*informal*) a remark or an action that is intended to make sb look stupid: *She produces some wonderful put-downs.*

,put yourself 'down 1 = PUT SB DOWN 1 **2** = PUT SB/STH DOWN, PUT YOURSELF DOWN

,put sb/sth 'down to place sb/sth that you are holding onto the floor or another surface: *She put her bag down by the door.* ◇ *Put me down!* ◇ (*figurative*) *It's a great book. I couldn't put it down!* (= stop reading it)
  OPP **pick sb/sth up**
  ✦ v + n/pron + adv ♦ v + adv + n

,put sb/sth 'down; ,put yourself 'down 1 (**for/as sth**) (**to do sth**) to add your name or someone else's to a list, etc. in order to arrange for you/them to do sth: *She put herself down for an aerobics class.* ◇ *I've put Jack's name down for the local school.* ◇ *We've been put down to go to a class at 4 p.m.* **2** (**as sth**) to write sth down; to make a note of sth: *I'll put the meeting down in my diary.* ◇ *He put himself down on the form as 'unfit'.* ◇ *I've put some ideas down on paper.* ◇ *Could you put down in writing what you feel?* ◇ *I've put you* (= your name) *down where it says 'next of kin'* (= on a form).
  ✦ v + n/pron + adv ♦ v + adv + n

,put sth 'down 1 to replace the receiver of a telephone and end your conversation: (*BrE*) *She put the phone down on me!* **OBJ** only **the phone, the receiver 2** to pay part of the cost of sth: *I've put down a deposit on our trip.* **OBJ** **deposit 3** to move sth from a higher to a lower position: *The sun's in my eyes — can I put the blind down?* ◇ *Put your feet down, please!* (= off the table/chair) ◇ *The rain stopped so she put her umbrella down.* **4** (*AmE* also **,put sth a'way**) to kill an animal because it is old or sick: *The horse was injured and had to be put down.* ◇ *We had to **have** our cat put down.* **NOTE** Put sth down is often used in the passive in this meaning. **5** to stop sth by force: *The revolt was swiftly put down.* **OBJ** **rebellion, uprising, revolt** **SYN** **suppress sth; crush sth 6** to spread sth on the floor or ground: *We decorated the room and put a new carpet down.* ◇ *I'm going to put some poison down for the rats.* **7** (in a game of cards) to play a card: *She put down the ace of spades.* ◇ *Each player puts down a card in turn.* **OBJ** **card, ace, etc. 8** to present sth formally for discussion by a parliament or a committee: *to put down a motion/an amendment* **SYN** **table sth** (*formal*)
  ✦ v + n/pron + adv ♦ v + adv + n

IDM **put your 'foot down 1** (*BrE*) to drive faster; to drive very fast **2** to be very firm in opposing sth: *You'll just have to put your foot down and say*

no. **put your 'head down** to go to sleep: *Why don't you put your head down for a while?*

,put sb 'down as sth to think that sb is a particular type of person, especially when you do not know them very well: *I put the boy down as a troublemaker as soon as I saw him.* ◇ *I would never have put you down as an athlete!*
  ✦ v + n/pron + adv + prep + n

,put sb 'down for sth to write down that sb is willing or wishes to buy sth, give an amount of money, etc: *Put me down for three tickets for the Saturday show.*
  ✦ v + n/pron + adv + prep

'put sth down to sth to consider that sth is caused by sth: *She tends to put everything down to fate.*
  SYN **attribute sth to sth** (*formal*), **chalk sth up to sth** (*informal*)
  ✦ v + n/pron + adv + prep

,put sth 'forth (*formal* or *literary*) **1** = PUT STH OUT 9 *The plant put forth new leaves.* **2** (*especially AmE*) = PUT STH FORWARD 3 **3** (*AmE*) to make a strong physical or mental effort to do sth: *He isn't putting forth the necessary effort.* **OBJ** **effort**
  ✦ v + adv + n ♦ v + n/pron + adv (*rare*)

,put sb/sth 'forward; ,put yourself 'forward (**for/as sth**) to suggest somebody or yourself as a candidate for a job, a position, etc: *Can I put your name forward for the job?* ◇ *Only one woman has put herself forward as a candidate.* ◇ *We would like to put you forward as head of department.* ◇ *My name was put forward for the scholarship by the principal.*
  OBJ **name**
  ✦ v + n/pron + adv ♦ v + adv + n

,put sth 'forward 1 to move sth to an earlier time or date: *We've put the meeting forward a couple of days.* **SYN** **bring sth forward 2** to move the hands of a clock forward to give the correct time, especially at the beginning of summer: *We forgot to put the clocks forward last night.* ◇ *France is an hour ahead, so you'll have to put your watch forward when you get there.* **OBJ** **the clocks, your watch** **OPP** **put sth back 3** (*also* **,put sth 'forth** *formal, especially AmE*) to suggest an idea or a plan so that it can be discussed: *She put forward several ideas for new projects.* ◇ *This theory was originally put forward by Darwin.* **OBJ** **argument, proposal, idea** **SYN** **bring sth forward**
  ✦ **1** v + n/pron + adv ♦ v + adv + n
  2 v + n/pron + adv ♦ v + adv + n (*rare*)
  3 v + adv + n ♦ v + n/pron + adv

,put 'in (**at …**), **,put 'into …** (*BrE*) (of a ship or its sailors) to stop in port for a short time: *The ship put in at Lisbon.* ◇ *The captain was instructed to put into Calais for repairs.*
  OPP **put out (to/from…)**
  ✦ v + adv ♦ v + prep

,put 'in; ,put 'in sth to interrupt another speaker in order to say sth: *'But what about us?' he put in quickly.* ◇ *Could I put in a word?*
SYN **interject sth** (*more formal*)
⬥ v + adv + speech ◆ v + adv + n ◆ v + n/pron + adv

,put sb 'in (*especially BrE*) to elect a political party as the government; to choose sb officially to do a particular job: *The voters put the Conservatives in with a large majority.*
⬥ v + n/pron + adv ◆ v + adv + n

,put sb 'in/'into sth 1 to make sb go to a particular institution, such as a school, hospital, etc: *He was put in prison for five years.* ◇ *An accident put him in hospital for three weeks.* ◇ *We had to put granny in/into a nursing home.* NOTE When this meaning of the phrasal verb is used with *hospital* and *prison*, in is usually rather than into. 2 to give sb a particular job to do: *We put her in/into sales and she did really well.*
⬥ v + n/pron + prep

IDM **put sb in the 'picture** (*informal*) to give sb the information they need in order to understand a situation: *You should put Mike in the picture as soon as possible.* **put sb in their 'place** to make sb feel stupid or embarrassed when they have shown too much confidence **put yourself in sb's shoes** to imagine that you are in another person's situation, especially when it is an unpleasant or difficult one: *Don't be angry with your brother. Try to put yourself in his shoes.*

,put sth 'in 1 to fit a piece of equipment, furniture, etc. into a particular place: *Steve put the shower in by himself.* ◇ *They had central heating put in when they moved into the flat.* SYN **install sth** (*more formal*) 2 to officially make a claim, a request, etc: *I've put in a request for some extra funding.* ◇ *They've put in an offer on the house* (= they've said they would pay a particular amount for it). OBJ **offer, claim** 3 to give sth, such as time or money, in order to help sb/sth: *We all put in five pounds for Lucy's present.* 4 to plant sth in the ground: *Have you put any bulbs in this autumn?* OBJ **bulbs, seeds**
⬥ v + n/pron + adv ◆ v + adv + n

IDM **put in an ap'pearance** to go somewhere for a short time: *I can't stay long at the party, but I'd better put in an appearance.*

,put sth 'in; ,put sth 'in/'into sth 1 to include sth in a story, a letter, etc: *He didn't put anything in his letter about coming to stay.* ◇ *When you write the report, make sure you put in the latest figures.* 2 to pay money into a bank account: *He put £500 into his account.* OBJ **money** SYN **pay sth in, pay sth into sth; deposit sth** 3 (*also put sth into doing sth*) to give a lot of time or effort to sth or to doing sth: *She's put a lot of effort into improving her French.* ◇ *Thank you for all the hard work you've put in.* OBJ **effort** 4 (*also put sth into doing sth*) to provide money for sth:

The school has put a lot of money into (*buying*) *new equipment.* OBJ **money, resources** SYN **invest sth**
⬥ v + n/pron + adv ◆ v + adv + n ◆ v + n/pron + prep
▶ '**input** *n* [C] [U] time, knowledge, ideas or work that you put into a project, etc. in order to make it succeed: *Nurses should have more input into the way patients are treated.* ◇ *Thank you for your input to the discussion.*
NOTE There is also a verb **input sth** meaning *to put information into a computer* and a related noun **input**.

,put 'in for sth (*especially BrE*) to apply formally for sth: *Are you going to put in for that job?* ◇ *She's going to put in for a transfer.*
OBJ **transfer, job**
⬥ v + adv + prep

,put sb/sth/yourself 'in for sth to enter sth/yourself for a competition: *She's put herself in for the 100 metres.* ◇ *You should put that photo in for the competition.*
⬥ v + n/pron + adv + prep

,put 'into... (*BrE*) = PUT IN (AT ...), PUT INTO...

,put sb 'into sth = PUT SB IN/INTO STH

,put sth 'into sth 1 to add a quality to sth: *Do you need to put some excitement into your life?* 2 = PUT STH IN, PUT STH IN/INTO STH
⬥ v + n/pron + prep

put sth into doing sth = PUT STH IN, PUT STH IN/INTO STH 3,4

,put 'off doing sth = PUT STH OFF 1

,put sb 'off 1 to cancel a meeting or sth you had arranged with sb: *He was supposed to come yesterday, but I put him off.* ◇ *Tell her you want to talk to her and don't be put off.* 2 (*BrE*) (of a vehicle, a driver, a ship, etc.) to stop in order to allow sb to get off: *I asked the bus driver to put me off near the town centre.*
⬥ v + n/pron + adv ◆ v + adv + n (*less frequent*)

,put sb 'off; ,put sb 'off sb/sth; ,put sb 'off doing sth to make sb stop liking sb/sth; to make sb lose interest in sb/sth: *His manner tends to put people off.* ◇ *Your story is putting me off my food!* ◇ *The accident put her off driving for life.* ◇ *The way he treated his wife really put me off him.* ◇ *Don't be put off by her appearance — she's really very sweet.*
⬥ v + n/pron + adv ◆ v + adv + n (*rare*) ◆ v + n/pron + prep
▶ '**off-putting** *adj* (*informal, especially BrE*) unpleasant; making sb dislike or not be interested in sth/sb: *The computer made a buzzing noise that she found off-putting.* ◇ *I find it very off-putting to have someone watching me all the time.* ◇ *His manner is very off-putting.*

,put sb 'off; ,put sb 'off sth to disturb sb who is trying to give all their attention to sth: *Don't put me off when I'm trying to concentrate.* ◇ *The sudden noise put her off her game.*

SYN **distract sb (from sth)**

◆ v + n/pron + adv ◆ v + adv + n (*rare*) ◆ v + n/pron + prep

,put sth 'off 1 (*also* ,put 'off doing sth) to change sth to a later date or time: *We'll have to put the meeting off until next week.* ◇ *He keeps putting off going to the dentist.* SYN **delay sth 2** (*especially BrE*) to switch sth off: *Could you put the lights off before you leave?* OBJ **lights, the television, etc.** SYN **switch sth off; turn sth off**

◆ v + n/pron + adv ◆ v + adv + n **1** also v + adv + -ing

,put sb 'on (*AmE, informal*) (*usually used in the progressive tenses*) to laugh at sb, especially by pretending that sth is true that is not: *I thought you were putting me on!*

SYN **have sb on** (*BrE*)

NOTE Put sb on is not used in the passive.

◆ v + n/pron + adv

▶ 'put-on *n* [C, usually sing.] (*AmE, informal*) an act of laughing at sb by telling them that sth is true that is not; a joke or trick: *Don't take it so seriously — it was just a put-on.*

→ *see also* PUT-ON at PUT STH ON

,put sb 'on; ,put sb 'on sth to give sb the telephone so that they can speak to the person calling: *She put Tim on the phone.* ◇ *Put Jane on for a minute, will you?*

◆ v + n/pron + adv ◆ v + n/pron + prep

,put sb 'on sth 1 to make sure that someone gets on a plane, train, etc: *We put Ruth on the bus to Carlisle.* **2** to make someone follow a particular diet, take a particular medicine, etc: *The doctor put him on antibiotics.* ◇ *Tim's been put on a low-fat diet.* **3** to decide that someone should do a particular job: *They're going to put someone else on that project.*

◆ v + n/pron + prep

,put sth 'on 1 to put an item of clothing, etc. on your body: *Aren't you going to put your coat on?* ◇ *Hang on, I need to put my glasses on.* ◇ *I can't find anything clean to put on!* ◇ *Have you put your seat belt on* (= in a car)? ◇ *Could you put his shoes on for him?* OBJ **coat, shoes, glasses, etc.** OPP **take sth off 2** to apply sth to your skin: *She's putting her make-up on.* ◇ *Make sure you put some sun cream on before you go out.* OBJ **lipstick, make-up, perfume** SYN **apply sth** OPP **take sth off 3** (*especially BrE*) to switch sth on: *Shall I put the light on — it seems very dark in here?* ◇ *Let's put the kettle on and have a cup of tea.* OBJ **the light, the heating, the radio, the kettle** SYN **switch sth on; turn sth on** OPP **put sth off; switch sth off; turn sth off 4** to begin to cook food: *I need to get home and put the dinner on.* SYN **get sth on 5** to make a tape, a CD, etc. begin to play: *Do you mind if I put some music on?* ◇ *She put on a Bob Marley CD.* OBJ **some music, CD, tape, video 6** to operate the brakes on a

vehicle (=a device for slowing or stopping the vehicle): *Don't forget to put the handbrake on.* ◇ *She put on the brakes suddenly.* OBJ **the brakes, the handbrake** SYN **apply sth** (*more formal*) **7** to grow heavier by the amount mentioned: *He's put on a lot of weight since I last saw him.* ◇ *I've put on two kilos in two weeks.* OBJ **weight** SYN **gain sth** (*more formal*) OPP **lose sth** NOTE Put sth on is not used in the passive in this meaning. **8** to provide sth specially: *They put on extra trains during the holiday period.* ◇ *A splendid lunch was put on for the visitors.* OBJ **bus, train** SYN **lay sth on** OPP **take sth off 9** to produce or present a play, an exhibition, etc: *The local drama group are putting on 'Macbeth'.* ◇ *The museum put on a special exhibition about dinosaurs.* OBJ **play, exhibition, show** SYN **stage sth** (*more formal*) OPP **take sth off 10** to pretend to have a particular feeling or quality: *He put on a hurt expression.* ◇ *Can you put on an American accent?* ◇ *She isn't really upset — she's just putting it on.* ◇ *He seemed furious, but I think it was all put on.* OBJ **accent, expression** SYN **assume sth** (*formal*)

◆ v + n/pron + adv ◆ v + adv + n

▶ 'put-on *n* [C, usually sing.] (*AmE, informal*) something that is done to trick or deceive people: *Kate's shabby appearance is just a put-on. Her parents are both lawyers.*

→ *see also* PUT-ON at PUT SB ON

,put sth 'on sth 1 to add an amount of money to the price or cost of sth: *The new tax put 20 pence on the price of a packet of cigarettes.* OPP **knock sth off sth 2** to bet money on sth: *I've put £10 on Sultan's Promise* (= the name of a horse) *in the next race.* OBJ **bet (on sth), money**

◆ v + n/pron + prep

,put sb 'onto sb/sth (*also* ,put sb 'on to sb/sth) **1** to tell sb about a person, an organization, etc. that could help them, or something that they might like or find useful: *Could you put me onto a good accountant?* **2** to connect sb by telephone to sb else: *Could you put me onto the manager, please?* **3** to inform the police, etc. about a crime or a criminal: *Do you know who put the police onto the hackers?*

◆ v + n/pron + prep ◆ v + n/pron + adv + prep

,put 'out 1 (to/from…) (*BrE*) (of a boat or a crew) to move out to sea from a harbour, port, etc: *The ship put out to sea by night.* ◇ *We put out from Liverpool.* OPP **put in (at …) 2** (*AmE, slang*) (of a woman) to agree to have sex with sb: *She won't put out on a first date.* NOTE Some people consider **put out** offensive in this meaning.

◆ v + adv

,put sb 'out 1 to make trouble, problems, extra work, etc. for sb: *I hope our arriving late didn't put you out at all.* **2** be ,put 'out to be upset or offended: *Jeff wasn't at all put out by what I said.* ◇ *I was a bit put out that I hadn't been invited*

3 (*informal*) to make sb go to sleep or become unconscious: *These pills should put him out for a few hours.* → *see also* PUT YOURSELF OUT

◆ v + n/pron + adv ◆ v + adv + n (*less frequent*)

‚put sth 'out 1 to make sth stop burning: *Fire-fighters soon put the fire out.* ◇ *He put his cigarette out with his foot.* OBJ **fire, cigarette, candle** SYN **extinguish sth** (*more formal*) **2** (*especially BrE*) to switch sth off: *Put the light out before you come to bed.* OBJ **the light** SYN **put sth off; switch sth off; turn sth off 3** to take sth out of your house and leave it, often for sb to collect: (*BrE*) *Remember to put the dustbins/rubbish out tonight.* ◇ (*AmE*) *Remember to put the gar-bage/trash out.* ◇ *She put the washing out to dry.* OPP **bring sth in 4** to place sth where it will be noticed and used: *Have you put out clean towels for the guests?* **5** to stretch part of your body away from yourself towards sb else: *He put his hand out to shake mine.* OBJ **hand, tongue 6** (*also* **‚put sth 'out of sth**) to make sth, especially part of your body, come out through a door or window to the outside: *She opened the window and put her head out.* ◇ *Sam put the cat out of the door roughly.* **7** (*BrE*) to broadcast sth; to publish or issue sth: *The programme will be put out on Channel Four.* ◇ *The CD was put out for the American market.* ◇ *The police put out an urgent appeal for witnesses.* OBJ **appeal, statement** SYN **broadcast sth 8** (*informal*) to produce sth: *The factory puts out 500 new cars a week.* ◇ *They put out a new software package last month.* SYN **produce sth 9** (*also* **‚put sth 'forth** *more formal*) (of a plant) to develop or produce new leaves, etc: *The roses are putting out new shoots already.* OBJ **flowers, shoots, leaves 10** to make a figure, a result, etc. wrong: *A price increase put our esti-mates out by a thousand pounds.* **11** (**to sb**) to give a job, a task, etc. to a worker who is not your employee or to another company so that the work will be done in another place: *A lot of edit-ing is put out to freelancers.* ◇ *The cleaning con-tract was put out to tender* (= companies were asked to make offers to supply these services). OBJ **work 12** (*informal*) to push a bone out of its normal position: *She fell off her horse and put her shoulder out.* ◇ *You're going to put your back out lifting those boxes.* OBJ **your back, shoulder** SYN **dislocate sth** (*formal*)

◆ v + n/pron + adv ◆ v + adv + n

▶ **'output** *n* [U] [sing.] **1** the amount of some-thing that a person, machine, company, etc. pro-duces: *The company aims to increase output in the coming year.* ◇ *His musical output has dimin-ished in recent years.* **2** (*computing*) the informa-tion produced by a computer: *data output* NOTE There is also a verb **output sth**, related to this meaning. **3** the power, energy, etc. produced by a piece of equipment: *an output of 100 watts*

‚put yourself 'out to make a special effort to do sth for sb: *Please don't put yourself out on our account.* ◇ *She really put herself out for the visitors.* → *see also* PUT SB OUT 1

◆ v + pron + adv

be ‚put 'out = PUT SB OUT 2

‚put yourself 'over (**to sb**) = PUT YOURSELF ACROSS (TO SB)

‚put sth 'over = PUT STH ACROSS

IDM **put one 'over on sb** (*spoken, informal*) **1** to persuade sb to accept sth that is not true; to deceive sb: *No one is going to put one over on him.* **2** to show that you are better, stronger, etc. than sb else by defeating them: *We'd love to put one over on the Welsh team.*

‚put sth 'past sb (**to do sth**) (*informal*) (*always used in negative sentences with wouldn't*) to be surprised that someone has done something wrong, illegal, etc: *I wouldn't put it past him to use force to get what he wants.* ◇ *'She won't tell the teacher, will she?' 'I wouldn't put it past her!'* ◇ *Personally I wouldn't put anything past him!* OBJ **only it, anything, that** NOTE **Put sth past sb** is not used in the passive.

◆ v + n/pron + prep

‚put sb/yourself 'through sth 1 to make sb/yourself experience sth unpleasant or diffi-cult: *He put his parents through hell.* ◇ *Why put yourself through it?* ◇ *She never forgot the ter-rible ordeal he had put her through.* **2** to pay for sb to attend a school, college, etc: *She worked part-time to put herself through university.*

◆ v + n/pron + prep

‚put sb/sth 'through (**to sb/to…**) to connect sb to sb else by telephone: *Could you put me through to the manager, please?* ◇ *The call was put through to the wrong extension.* ◇ *Hold the line, I'm put-ting you through.*

◆ v + n/pron + adv

‚put sb/sth 'through sth to test sb/sth to see what they are able to do: *We put the machines through a series of tests.* ◇ *The team are put through a fitness programme.*

◆ v + n/pron + prep

IDM **put sb/sth through their/its 'paces** to give someone or something tasks to perform in order to find out what they are able to do: *He put the car through its paces.* ◇ *She watched the team being put through their paces.*

‚put sth 'through; **‚put sth 'through sth** to complete a plan, programme, etc. successfully: *This was the last deal James put through.* ◇ *Has the legislation been put through parliament?*

◆ v + n/pron + adv ◆ v + adv + n ◆ v + n/pron + prep

‚put sth 'through sth to change sth by using a machine, a process, etc: *She put some oranges through the juicer.* ◇ *The fish is then put through the smoking process* (= to produce smoked fish).

◆ v + n/pron + prep

▶ 'throughput n [U] [C, usually sing.] (technical) the number of people that are dealt with, or the amount of work that is done, in a particular period: Hospitals have increased the throughput of patients.

'put sb to sth to make trouble, problems or extra work for sb: I hope we're not putting you to too much trouble.
◈ v + n/pron + prep + n

'put sth to sb 1 to suggest sth to sb for them to consider: Your proposal will be put to the board of directors. ◇ The question of strike action must be put to union members. ◇ When are you going to put the idea to your parents? ◇ I'll put it to you straight (= tell or ask you sth in an honest and direct way). OBJ proposal, idea, view 2 to ask sb a question: The audience were invited to put questions to the panel. OBJ question
◈ v + n/pron + prep

,put sth to'gether 1 to make or repair sth by fitting parts together: He took the clock apart and couldn't put it together again. ◇ Can you put a team together in time for the game on Saturday? SYN assemble sth (more formal) OPP take sth apart 2 to create sth: He's putting together a travel guide for the British Isles. ◇ The band are putting their first album together. 3 to combine things: What reaction will we get if we put these two chemicals together?
◈ 1,3 v + n/pron + adv ◆ v + adv + n (less frequent)
    2 v + adv + n ◆ v + n/pron + adv
IDM more, better, etc. than…put to'gether used when comparing sb/sth with a group of other people or things to mean 'combined' or 'in total': This painting is worth more than all the rest put together. put our/your/their 'heads together to discuss sth as a group in order to reach a plan of action, a solution to a problem, etc: We put our heads together and decided what had to be done.

'put sth towards sth to use or give an amount of money to pay part of the cost of sth: We will put the money towards a new computer. ◇ The city council will put £5 000 towards equipment for the nursery.
OBJ money
◈ v + n/pron + prep

,put sb 'under (informal, especially AmE) to make sb unconscious before a medical operation: I'm afraid we'll need to put you under for the operation.
◈ v + n/pron + adv

,put 'up [+ adv/prep] (old-fashioned, especially BrE) to stay somewhere for the night: We put up at a hotel.
◈ v + adv

,put 'up sth 1 to resist strongly or fight hard in a game, a contest, an argument, etc: The other team didn't put up much of a fight. ◇ She's not likely to put up much resistance to the idea. OBJ fight, resistance 2 to show a good level of skill in a game or a competition: The team put up a great performance (= played very well). OBJ performance, show 3 to suggest an idea for other people to discuss: to put up a proposal for a new book OBJ argument, proposal
◈ v + adv + n

,put sb 'up 1 to let sb stay at your home; to arrange for sb to stay somewhere: We can put you both up for the night. ◇ They put us up at a hotel in town. 2 (for sth) to present sb as a candidate in an election; to propose sb for an official position: We hope to put up more women candidates in the next election. ◇ We want to put you up for club secretary. OBJ candidates
◈ 1 v + n/pron + adv ◆ v + adv + n (less frequent)
    2 v + n/pron + adv ◆ v + adv + n

,put sth 'up 1 to raise sth from a lower to a higher position: Put your hand up if you want to ask a question. ◇ It started raining so I put my umbrella up. ◇ I've decided to put my hair up for the party. ◇ to put up a flag OBJ your hand, your hair 2 to fix or fasten sth in a place where it will be seen; to display sth: Several warning signs have been put up. ◇ The exam results haven't been put up on the noticeboard yet. ◇ Annie's put posters up all over her bedroom. ◇ The stores have put their Christmas decorations up already. OBJ sign, poster, curtains, notice OPP take sth down 3 to build sth; to put sth into an upright position: These apartment blocks were put up in the sixties. ◇ We had trouble putting the tent up in the dark. ◇ We need to put some shelves up for our books. OBJ tent, shelf, fence OPP take sth down; pull sth down 4 to increase the price or cost of sth: The theatre has put up ticket prices. ◇ The banks have put up their interest rates again. ◇ The landlord wants to put up the rent by £20 a month. OBJ prices SYN raise sth OPP bring sth down 5 (informal) to provide or lend money: James put up half the money for the car. ◇ A local businessman has put up the £500 000 needed to save the club. OBJ money 6 ,put sth 'up for sth to offer sth to sb else for them to buy, etc: The house has been put up for sale. ◇ Why did Jess put her baby up for adoption? OBJ house, baby, child
◈ 1,2,3,4 v + n/pron + adv ◆ v + adv + n
    5 v + adv + n ◆ v + pron + adv ◆ v + n + adv (less frequent)
    6 v + n/pron + adv ◆ v + adv + n (rare)
IDM put your 'feet up to sit down and relax: I can't wait to get home and put my feet up for a while. a ,put-up 'job (BrE, informal) a plan or an event that has been arranged secretly in order to trick or deceive sb: The kidnapping was a put-up job.

,put sb 'up to sth; **,put sb 'up to doing sth**
(*informal*) to encourage or persuade sb to do sth
wrong or foolish: *Some of the older boys must
have put him up to it.* ◇ *Her sister put her up to
climbing into the house through an open window.*
◆ v + n/pron + adv + prep

,put 'up with sb/sth to accept sb/sth that is
annoying, difficult or unpleasant, without complaining: *I don't know how your parents put up
with you!* ◇ *We put up with that car for years.* ◇ *I
don't see why I should put up with being spoken to
like that.* ◇ *I can put up with the rain — it's the
cold I don't like.* ◇ *She has a lot to put up with.*
SYN **tolerate sth** (*more formal*), **endure sth**
(*more formal*)
◆ v + adv + prep

'put upon sb (*BrE*) to use sb's kindness for your
own advantage by asking them to do things for
you that you should not expect them to do: *I felt
that my mother had been put upon.*
NOTE **Put upon sb** is often used in the passive.
◆ v + prep
▶ **'put-upon** *adj* badly treated by someone who
uses your kindness for their own advantage: *My
grandmother is the most put-upon member of the
family.*

putter /ˈpʌtə(r)/

,putter a'round; **,putter a'round sth** (*AmE*) =
POTTER ABOUT/AROUND, POTTER ABOUT/AROUND
STH

puzzle /ˈpʌzl/

,puzzle a'bout sth = PUZZLE OVER/ABOUT STH

,puzzle sth 'out to find the solution to a difficult
problem by thinking carefully about it: *She
couldn't puzzle out where her keys could have
gone.* ◇ *I spent hours trying to puzzle out an
explanation for his behaviour.* ◇ *I can't puzzle out
how the box opens.*
SYN **work sth out**
NOTE **Puzzle sth out** is often used with the question words *how, what, why,* etc. ◆ It cannot be
used in the passive.
◆ v + adv + n ◆ v + pron + adv ◆ v + n + adv (*less
frequent*)

'puzzle over/about sth to think hard about
something because you want to understand it:
Police are still puzzling over the incident. ◇ *She
puzzled over the postmark on the letter.*
◆ v + prep

Q q

quarrel /ˈkwɒrəl; *AmE* ˈkwɔːr-, ˈkwɑːr/ (**-ll-**, *AmE* **-l-**)

'quarrel with sth/sb (*especially BrE*) (*usually used in negative sentences*) to disagree with sth/sb: *Few would quarrel with the principle of free education for all.*
◈ v + prep

queue /kjuː/ (**queuing** *or* **queueing**)

,queue 'up (**for sth/to do sth**) (*BrE*) to wait or stand in a line with other people in order to get sth or do sth: *They spent four hours queueing up for tickets.* ◇ *We had to queue up to get our visas.*
NOTE Queue is often used with the same meaning: *We spent four hours queueing for tickets.*
→ *see also* LINE UP 1
◈ v + adv

be ,queuing 'up for sth; be ,queuing 'up to do sth if you say that people **are queuing up** for sth or to do sth, you mean that a lot of people are very eager to have sth or do sth: *Actors are queuing up to work with this company.*
◈ be + v + adv + prep ◆ be + v + adv + to inf

quiet (*AmE*) /ˈkwaɪət/

,quiet 'down; ,quiet sb 'down = QUIETEN DOWN, QUIETEN SB DOWN

quieten (*BrE*) /ˈkwaɪətn/ (*AmE* **quiet**)

,quieten 'down; ,quieten sb 'down to become, or to make sb, calmer, less noisy or less active: *We've been really busy at work during the summer but things should quieten down now.* ◇ *It took a long time for the baby to quieten down.* ◇ *Can you quieten the kids down?*
NOTE Quieten/quiet and **quieten/quiet sb** are also used with the same meaning, especially in more formal language: *The class quietened.*
◈ v + adv ◆ v + n/pron + adv ◆ v + adv + n (*less frequent*)

quit /kwɪt/ (**quitting, quit, quit,** *BrE also* **quitting, quitted, quitted**)

'quit on sb (*AmE, informal*) **1** to stop helping, working with or supporting sb when they need you most: *I can't believe he quit on the team after only two games!* ◇ *You can't quit on me now, we're almost there!* **2** if a machine, a vehicle, etc. **quits on** you, it stops working at a time when you really need it: *The air-conditioning quit on us in mid-July.*
◈ v + prep

Rr

rabbit /'ræbɪt/

,rabbit 'on (about sb/sth) (*BrE, informal, disapproving*) to talk about sth for a long time in a boring way: *What's he rabbiting on about?*
SYN go on (about sb/sth)
◆ v + adv

rack (*also* wrack *less frequent*) /ræk/

,rack 'up sth; ,rack it/them 'up (*informal, especially AmE*) to get or collect a large amount or quantity of sth, such as profits or losses in a business or points in a competition: *The company racked up $20 billion in sales.* ◇ *Bush has racked up victories in another five states.*
NOTE A noun must always follow up, but a pronoun comes between the verb and up.
◆ v + adv + n ◆ v + pron + adv (*less frequent*)

raffle /'ræfl/

,raffle sth 'off to offer sth as a prize in a raffle (= a way of making money when people buy tickets with a number on and some of the numbers are later chosen to win prizes): *The cake will be raffled off to raise money for the school.*
NOTE Raffle sth is used more frequently with this meaning.
◆ v + adv + n ◆ v + n/pron + adv

rail /reɪl/

'rail against/at sb/sth (*formal*) to protest about sb/sth in an angry or bitter way: *to rail against the government/authorities* ◇ *There's no point railing against the decision.*
◆ v + prep

rain /reɪn/

,rain 'down (on/upon sb/sth), ,rain sth 'down (on/upon sb/sth) to fall or to make sth fall on sb/sth in large quantities: *Huge boulders rained down on us.* ◇ *He rained blow after blow down on my skull.*
◆ v + adv ◆ v + n/pron + adv ◆ v + adv + n

be ,rained 'off (*BrE*) (*AmE* be ,rained 'out) (*informal*) if an event such as a sports game is rained off, it stops or it does not take place because of rain: *The game was rained off.* ◇ *It looks as if the concert is going to be rained off.*
◆ be + v + adv

rake /reɪk/

,rake sth 'in (*informal*) to earn large amounts of money without difficulty: *The company rakes in* about £190 million. ◇ *Since she moved to London she's been raking it in.*
◆ v + adv + n ◆ v + pron + adv ◆ v + n + adv (*less frequent*)

,rake 'over sth (*BrE, informal, disapproving*) to examine sth that happened in the past in great detail and keep talking about it, when it should be forgotten: *There's no point in raking over the events of the past.*
OBJ the past
◆ v + prep
IDM rake over old 'coals/'ashes to discuss sth that happened in the past in detail, when it should be forgotten rake sb over the 'coals (*AmE*) (*BrE* haul sb over the 'coals) to criticize sb severely because they have done sth wrong

,rake sth 'up 1 to talk about sth unpleasant that has happened in the past, which people would like to forget: *I didn't come here to rake up old arguments.* 2 to collect sth into a pile using a tool with a long handle and a row of metal points at the end (a rake): *I raked up all the leaves.*
◆ v + adv + n ◆ v + n/pron + adv

rally /'ræli/ (rallies, rallying, rallied, rallied)

,rally a'round/'round; ,rally a'round/'round sb if people rally around or rally around sb, they work together to help and support sb who is in a difficult or unpleasant situation: *When she was ill, the neighbours all rallied round to help her and bring her meals.* ◇ *His friends rallied around him as soon as they heard the news.*
◆ v + adv ◆ v + prep

ram /ræm/ (-mm-)

,ram 'into sb/sth; ,ram sth 'into sth to hit sth violently; to make sth hit sth violently: *He was going too fast and rammed into the car in front.* ◇ *The thieves rammed their truck into the jeweller's window.*
◆ v + prep ◆ v + n/pron + prep

ramble /'ræmbl/

,ramble 'on (about sb/sth) (*BrE*) to talk or write a lot about sb/sth in a confused and boring way: *What is she rambling on about?* ◇ *There's me rambling on, and you haven't told me your news yet.*
◆ v + adv

range /reɪndʒ/

be ,ranged a'gainst/'with sb/sth; ,range yourself a'gainst/'with sb/sth (*formal*) to join with other people to oppose sb/sth: *He felt as*

though the whole family was ranged against him.
◇ *She ranged herself more with her parents than with her brother.*
🔷 be + v + prep ♦ v + pron + prep

rap /ræp/ (**-pp-**)

‚rap sth 'out to say sth quickly and sharply: *The officer rapped out orders.*
[OBJ] **command, order** [SYN] **bark sth out**
🔷 v + adv + n ♦ v + pron + adv ♦ v + n + adv (*rare*) ♦ v + adv + speech

rat /ræt/ (**-tt-**)

'rat on sb (*informal*) to give information to people in authority, causing trouble for sb: *Say what you like about Ali but he has never ratted on his friends.*
🔷 v + prep

'rat on sth (*BrE, informal*) to fail to keep a promise you have made: *They accused the government of ratting on promises to the disabled.*
[OBJ] **promise, pledge**
🔷 v + prep

ratchet /'rætʃɪt/

‚ratchet sth 'up to make prices, etc. increase a little at a time: *The interest rates have been ratcheted up sharply.* ◇ *The hormone rushes around the brain, ratcheting the heart rate up from 60–80 to about a hundred.* ◇ (*figurative*) *The government have ratcheted up the pressure on the protest organizers.*
🔷 v + adv + n ♦ v + n/pron + adv

ration /'ræʃn/

‚ration sth 'out to divide sth that there is not very much of between a group of people in such a way that everyone gets a small share: *They rationed the water out among the survivors.*
[OBJ] **food, water**
🔷 v + n/pron + adv ♦ v + adv + n

rattle /'rætl/

‚rattle a'round; ‚rattle a'round sth (*informal*) to live, work, etc. somewhere that is much too big for your needs: *There are only two of us, rattling around in this massive office.* ◇ *They're rattling around that house now that the children have left.*
🔷 v + adv ♦ v + prep

‚rattle sth 'off to say or repeat sth from memory, quickly and without any effort: *She rattled off the names of the movies Hitchcock had directed.*
[SYN] **reel sth off**
🔷 v + adv + n ♦ v + pron + adv ♦ v + n + adv (*rare*)

‚rattle 'on (**about sth**) (*informal*) to talk quickly and for a long time about sth that is not important or interesting: *He rattled on about his job for*

over an hour.
[SYN] **waffle on** (**about sth**)
🔷 v + adv

‚rattle 'through sth (*BrE, informal*) to do something very quickly: *He rattled through his homework then went out.*
🔷 v + prep

reach /riːtʃ/

‚reach sth 'down (**for sb**) to get sth down from a high place: *Could you reach that vase down for me?* ◇ *She reached down a box from the top shelf.*
[NOTE] In informal spoken language **reach sb down sth** is also used: *Could you reach me down that vase?*
🔷 v + n/pron + adv ♦ v + adv + n

‚reach 'out; ‚reach sth 'out to stretch your arm or your hand in order to touch or get something: *He reached out to switch on the light.* ◇ ***I reached out a hand*** *to touch her face.* ◇ *The child reached out for her hand.*
🔷 v + adv ♦ v + adv + n ♦ v + pron + adv ♦ v + n + adv (*rare*)

‚reach 'out to sb to show sb that you are interested in them and/or want to help them; to try to get people's interest or attention: *The organization is trying to reach out to people of all ages and from all levels of society.* ◇ *The party has failed to reach out to young people.* ◇ *The makers of this movie have tried to reach out to an older audience.*
🔷 v + adv + prep
▶ **'outreach** *n* [U] the activity of an organization that provides a service or advice to people in the community, especially those who cannot or are unlikely to come to an office, a hospital, etc. for help: *a rural outreach programme* ◇ *outreach work*

read /riːd/ (**read, read** /red/)

‚read sth 'back to read a message, a letter etc. aloud in order to check that it is correct: *I got her to read the message back to me to make sure it was right.*
🔷 v + n/pron + adv ♦ v + adv + n

‚read sth 'into sth to think that something has a meaning or an importance that it probably does not have: *It's a mistake to read too much into the results of one opinion poll.* ◇ *You can read anything you want into horoscopes.* ◇ *Her voice was cold and I wasn't sure what to read into it.*
[OBJ] **too much, something, anything**
🔷 v + n/pron + prep

‚read sth 'off to look at the measurement shown on a machine or other measuring device: *The speed can be calculated or read off from the graph.* ◇ *I looked at the thermometer and read off the temperature.*
🔷 v + adv + n ♦ v + n/pron + adv

,**read** '**on** to continue reading: *The book was so exciting he read on until dawn.* ◇ *The idea is to make the reader want to read on.* ◇ *If you want to find out more, read on!*
◆ v + adv

,**read sth** '**out** (**to sb**) **1** to read sth aloud, especially to other people: *She read out the names of the winners.* ◇ *The teacher read my poem out to the class.* ◇ *There's a letter from Tom. Shall I read it out to you?* **2** (*especially AmE, computing*) to get back information that is stored on a computer; to produce a display of the information on a screen
◆ v + adv + n ◆ v + n/pron + adv ◆ v + adv + speech
▶ '**read-out** *n* (*computing*) a record or display of information on a computer screen: *The computer will work out the best route for you and give you a read-out on the screen.*

,**read sth** '**through** (*also* ,**read sth** '**over** *less frequent*) to read something from the beginning to the end, usually in order to find any mistakes: *I read through my translation, checking for mistakes.* ◇ *When she read her letter through the next day, she decided not to send it.* ◇ *When she'd finished, Emily read over what she'd written.*
◆ v + adv + n ◆ v + n/pron + adv

,**read** '**up on sb/sth**; ,**read sb/sth** '**up** (*also* ,**read** '**up about sb/sth** *less frequent*) to read a lot about a particular subject in order to learn about it: *Have you been reading up on the history of the island?* ◇ *I've been reading this place up in the library.*
◆ v + adv + prep ◆ v + adv + n ◆ v + n/pron + adv

rear /rɪə(r)/; *AmE* rɪr/

'**rear sb/sth on sth** to give a person or an animal a particular type of food, entertainment, etc. when they are young: *I was reared on jazz, but later discovered rock.*
NOTE Rear sb/sth on sth is usually used in the passive.
◆ v + n/pron + prep

,**rear** '**up 1** if a horse, etc. **rears up**, it stands on its back legs with its front legs in the air: *The horse reared up and she fell off.* **2** if a building, cliff, etc. **rears up**, it seems to lean over you in a threatening way: *The cliff reared up before them.*
NOTE Rear is also used with these meanings, especially meaning 1: *The horse reared and she fell off.*
◆ v + adv

reason /'riːzn/

,**reason sth** '**out** to think carefully about something in a logical way in order to understand it: *Let's try to reason out why he behaved as he did.* ◇ *Reason it out for yourself — why do you think she didn't say where she was going?*
SYN **figure sb/sth out**; **work sth out**
◆ v + n/pron + adv ◆ v + adv + n

'**reason with sb** to talk to sb in order to persuade them to be more sensible: *It's impossible to reason with her when she's in this mood.*
NOTE Reason with sb can be used in the passive: *He can't be reasoned with.*
◆ v + prep

rebound /rɪ'baʊnd/

re'**bound on sb** (*also* re'**bound upon sb** *more formal, less frequent*) if sth that you do, especially sth that is intended to be unpleasant for sb else, **rebounds on/upon** you, it has a bad or unpleasant effect for you instead: *His little trick seems to have rebounded on him.* ◇ *These measures could rebound on the poorest families* (= affect them instead of the people they were intended to affect).
◆ v + prep

reckon /'rekən/

'**reckon on sb/sth**; '**reckon on doing sth**; '**reckon on sb/sth doing sth** to rely on sb/sth or on sth happening; to expect sb to do sth or sth to happen: *We were reckoning on a profit of about half a million.* ◇ *You can reckon on my support.* ◇ *We hadn't reckoned on them arriving so early.* ◇ *You can't always reckon on having good weather in June.* ◇ *The company thought they would easily get permission to build a hotel, but they hadn't reckoned on the local people.*
SYN **count on sb/sth**, **count on doing sth**, **count on sb/sth doing sth**
◆ v + prep

,**reckon sth** '**up** (*especially BrE*) to add figures or numbers together: *That'll be £20.50, if I've reckoned it up correctly.*
SYN **add sth up**; **calculate sth** (*more formal*)
◆ v + n/pron + adv ◆ v + adv + n

'**reckon with sb/sth 1** (*usually used in negative sentences*) to consider sb/sth as a possible problem that you should be prepared for: *Unfortunately, we hadn't reckoned with Emily.* ◇ *We must reckon with the possibility of failure.* **2** to consider or deal with sb/sth as a serious opponent or problem: *He had to reckon with a great deal of opposition.* ◇ *The team are still **a force to be reckoned with*** (= they will be difficult to defeat).
NOTE In this meaning **reckon with sb/sth** can be used in the passive.
◆ v + prep

'**reckon without sb/sth** (*especially BrE*) to not consider sb/sth as a possible problem and therefore not be prepared for it: *We allowed an hour to get there, but we'd reckoned without the traffic* (= it took us much longer).
◆ v + prep

reconcile /ˈrekənsaɪl/

'reconcile sb/yourself to sth; 'reconcile sb/yourself to doing sth to make sb/your-self accept an unpleasant situation because there is nothing you can do to change it: *They were reconciled to the fact that he wouldn't be coming back.* ◊ *I've reconciled myself to having no money while I'm a student.*
◈ v + n/pron + prep

reduce /rɪˈdjuːs; *AmE* -ˈduːs/

re'duce sb/sth to sth to bring sb to a particular state, especially a worse one: *She was reduced to tears by their criticism.* ◊ *The building was reduced to a heap of rubble.* ◊ *Her questioning reduced him to a state of confusion.*
◈ v + n/pron + prep

re'duce sb to doing sth to make sb do something they do not approve of or are ashamed of because there is no other choice for them: *I was reduced to borrowing money from friends.*
NOTE Reduce sb to doing sth is nearly always used in the passive.
◈ v + n/pron + prep

re'duce sth to sth to change sth into a simpler or more general form: *His arguments can be reduced to four points.*
◈ v + n/pron + prep

reek /riːk/

'reek of sth (*disapproving*) **1** to smell very strongly of sth unpleasant: *His breath reeked of tobacco.* **2** if sth reeks of sth unpleasant or suspicious, it suggests very strongly that there is sth unpleasant or suspicious about it: *His statement reeks of hypocrisy.* ◊ *The whole place reeked of neglect.*
◈ v + prep

reel /riːl/

,reel sth 'in/'out to wind sth on/off a special round device (a reel), for example on a fishing rod: *He slowly reeled the fish in.* ◊ *The firefighters reeled out the hose.* ◊ *The line caught on something in the water as he reeled it in.*
◈ v + n/pron + adv ♦ v + adv + n

,reel sth 'off **1** to say a long list of things quickly and without having to think about it: *He reeled off the names of the people he'd invited.* **OBJ** list, names, figures **SYN** rattle sth off **2** (*informal, especially BrE*) (in a sports competition) to win a series of games or a number of points: *The Bulls reeled off nine consecutive points.* ◊ *Henman reeled off three straight games.* **OBJ** points, games **SYN** chalk up sth
◈ v + adv + n ♦ v + pron + adv ♦ v + n + adv (*less frequent*)

,reel sth 'out = REEL STH IN/OUT

refer /rɪˈfɜː(r)/ (-rr-)

re'fer to sb/sth **1** (as sth) to mention or talk about somebody or something: *She never referred to the incident again.* ◊ *Passengers are now referred to as 'customers'.* **2** to describe or be connected to sb/sth: *This paragraph refers to the events of last year.* ◊ *This phenomenon is referred to in detail in chapter nine.* ◊ *The term 'visually handicapped' refers to students who have serious difficulties in seeing.*
NOTE Refer to sb/sth can be used in the passive.
◈ v + prep

re'fer to sth to look at sth for information: *You don't need to refer to a dictionary for this exercise.* **OBJ** book, dictionary, manual, instructions **SYN** consult sth (*more formal*)
NOTE Refer to sth can be used in the passive: *It is important to provide a record that can be referred to.*
◈ v + prep

re'fer sb/sth to sb/sth to send sb/sth to a different place or person in order to get help, advice or a decision: *The case was referred to the Court of Appeal.* ◊ *My tutor referred me to a counsellor.* ◊ (*formal*) *I refer you to my letter of 2 June.*
◈ v + n/pron + prep

reflect /rɪˈflekt/

re'flect on sb/sth (*also* re'flect upon sb/sth *more formal*) to make sb have a particular opinion of sb/sth: *When the department performs badly, it reflects on me as manager* (= it makes people think I am a bad manager). ◊ *This incident reflects badly on everyone involved.* ◊ *When our students are successful it reflects well on the whole school.*
NOTE Reflect on sb/sth is often used with adverbs, especially *badly* or *well*.
◈ v + prep

IDM reflect great credit on sb/sth to show that sb/sth is very good or has done sth very well: *The fine condition of the cars reflects great credit on their owners.* ◊ *The young orchestra's performance reflected great credit on their training.*

regale /rɪˈɡeɪl/

re'gale sb with sth to entertain sb with stories, jokes, etc: *She was regaling us with tales of her youth.*
◈ v + n/pron + prep

rein /reɪn/

,rein 'in; ,rein sth 'in (*also* ,rein 'back, ,rein sth 'back *less frequent*) to pull on the reins of a horse (= the leather bands that go around its neck) to make it go more slowly or stop: *Felipe reined back and rode beside her.* ◊ *She reined in her horse and waited for John to catch up.*
◈ v + adv ♦ v + adv + n ♦ v + n/pron + adv

‚rein sb/sth 'in (*also* ‚rein sb/sth 'back *less frequent*) to control sb or sth more strictly: *We need to rein in public spending.* ◇ *The new President is faced with the task of reining in the military.* ◇ *He was unable to rein back his impatience.*
◈ v + adv + n ◆ v + pron + adv ◆ v + n + adv (*less frequent*)

relate /rɪˈleɪt/

rel'ate to sb/sth 1 to feel that you can understand a person, a situation, sth that sb does or feels, etc. and have sympathy with them/it: *She was unable to relate to her youngest child.* ◇ *I find him very difficult to relate to.* ◇ *I just couldn't relate to that movie at all.* ◇ *She could relate to his feelings of guilt about his children.* **2** to be connected to sb/sth; to refer to sb/sth: *All the documents relating to the matter were destroyed.* ◇ *The new law relates only to children born after 1996.*
◈ v + prep

relieve /rɪˈliːv/

re'lieve sb of sth 1 (*formal*) to carry out a difficult or unpleasant task for sb else, or instead of them: *Robots can relieve people of dull and repetitive work.* ◇ *Can I relieve you of some of your bags* (= carry them for you)? **2** (*formal*) to dismiss sb from a job or responsibility: *He was relieved of his post as manager.* NOTE In this meaning, **relieve sb of sth** is often used in the passive. **3** (*informal, ironic*) to rob sb of sth: *The thief relieved him of his wallet.*
◈ v + n/pron + prep

rely /rɪˈlaɪ/ (relies, relying, relied, relied)

re'ly on sb/sth (*also* re'ly upon sb/sth *more formal*) **1** (**for sth**) to need or be dependent on sb/sth: *She still has to rely on her parents for money.* ◇ *He hasn't got a car, and relies on public transport to get around.* ◇ *We relied on Anna to translate for us.* ◇ *Before they got a piped water supply, local people had to rely on getting their water from wells and tanks.* ⟨SYN⟩ **depend on/upon sb/sth** (**for sth**) **2** to trust or have confidence in sb/sth: *You can safely rely on her judgement.* ◇ *You can rely on Jon to turn up late!* (= he always does) ◇ *For the first time in years she had someone she could rely on.* ◇ *We relied on the advice of our solicitor.* ⟨SYN⟩ **count on/upon sb/sth**; **depend on/upon sb/sth** NOTE Rely **on/upon sb/sth** can be used in the passive in this meaning: *She cannot be relied on to tell the truth.*
◈ v + prep

remember /rɪˈmembə(r)/

re'member sb to sb (*BrE*) (*not used in the progressive tenses*) used to ask sb to give your greetings and good wishes to sb else: *Remember me to your mother.*
◈ v + n/pron + prep

remind /rɪˈmaɪnd/

re'mind sb of sb/sth (*not used in the progressive tenses*) if sb/sth **reminds you of** sb/sth, they make you think of sb/sth because they are similar: *The smell of bread baking reminds me of home.* ◇ *When Clare smiled, she reminded me of her mother.* ◇ *Watching his serious face, with its big round glasses, she was reminded of an owl.* NOTE **Remind sb of sb/sth** can be used in the passive: *Listening to her, he was reminded of Helen.*
◈ v + n/pron + prep

rent /rent/

‚rent sth 'out (**to sb**) to allow something that you own to be used by someone else in return for payment: *They rented the house out to students.* ◇ *Most of these houses are rented out.*
OBJ **room, house, etc.** ⟨SYN⟩ **hire sth out** (**to sb**); **let sth out** (**to sb**) (*BrE*) NOTE **Rent sth** can also be used with the same meaning: *You could rent a room to a student.*
◈ v + n/pron + adv ◆ v + adv + n

repair /rɪˈpeə(r); AmE -ˈper/

re'pair to... (*formal or humorous*) to go to a place: *After dinner, they repaired to the lounge for coffee.*
◈ v + prep

report /rɪˈpɔːt; AmE rɪˈpɔːrt/

re‚port 'back 1 (**to sb**) (**on sb/sth**) to give a spoken or written account of some information that you were asked to find out about: *I have to report back to the manager on our progress.* **2** (**to...**) to return to a place, especially in order to start work again: *When do you have to report back for duty?*
◈ v + adv

re‚port 'in (**to sb/sth**) to contact sb to let them know where you are or what you are doing: *The officer briefly reported in* (*to the police station*).

re'port to sb (*business*) (*not used in the progressive tenses*) if you **report to** sb in a company or an organization, they are responsible for your work and tell you what to do: *She reports directly to the chief executive.* ◇ *A new team will be put together for the project, reporting to Julia Healey.*
◈ v + prep

reside /rɪˈzaɪd/

re'side in sb/sth (*formal*) to be in sb/sth; to be caused by sth: *The attraction of the book resides in its illustrations.* ◇ *The interests of the child reside in getting the best possible education.*
◈ v + prep

re'side in/with sb/sth (*formal*) to be present in
  or belong to sb/sth: *Supreme authority resides*
  with the President. ◇ *Political power seems to res-*
  ide increasingly in the South of England.
  ✥ v + prep

resign /rɪ'zaɪn/

re'sign yourself to sth; re'sign yourself to
  doing sth to be ready to accept sth unpleasant
  because you cannot avoid it: *She resigned her-*
  self to her fate. ◇ *They resigned themselves to*
  being defeated. ◇ *I've resigned myself to staying*
  in again tonight.
  ✥ v + pron + prep

resolve /rɪ'zɒlv/; AmE rɪ'zɑːlv/

re'solve into sth; re'solve sth into sth to
  separate or to be separated into its parts: *The*
  design resolved into a number of different pat-
  terns. ◇ *a lawyer's ability to resolve facts into*
  their legal categories
  ✥ v + prep ✦ v + pron + prep

re'solve into sth; re'solve itself/them-
  selves into sth 1 if sth you see or hear at a distance **resolves into** sth or **resolves itself into**
  sth, you gradually see it or hear it clearly as a
  particular thing: *The grey shape resolved into a*
  group of walkers. ◇ *The white light resolved itself*
  into the headlights of a car. **2** to gradually
  become or be understood as sth: *The discussion*
  eventually resolved itself into two main issues. ◇
  The question resolves itself into whether individ-
  uals should be allowed to choose such a course of
  action.
  ✥ v + prep ✦ v + pron + prep

resort /rɪ'zɔːt/; AmE rɪ'zɔːrt/

re'sort to sth; re'sort to doing sth to make
  use of something, especially something bad or
  unpleasant, as a way of achieving sth, often
  because no other course of action is possible:
  They should be able to settle their differences with-
  out resorting to violence. ◇ *They resorted to brib-*
  ery to get what they wanted.
  OBJ violence, bribery
  NOTE Resort to sth/to doing sth can be used in
  the passive: *Various measures were resorted to.*
  ✥ v + prep

rest /rest/

'rest on sb/sth (*also* **'rest upon sb/sth** *more for-*
  mal) **1** to depend on sb/sth: *Britain's hopes of a*
  medal now rest on Henderson. **2** if your eyes **rest**
  on sb/sth, you look at them/it: *Her eyes rested on a*
  photograph on the desk. **SUBJ** eyes, gaze
  ✥ v + prep

'rest on sth (*also* **'rest upon sth** *more formal*) to
  be based on sth: *The whole case rests on one man's*
  evidence. ◇ *His argument seemed to rest on a false*
  assumption.
  ✥ v + prep

,rest 'up (*informal*) **1** (*old-fashioned, especially*
  BrE) to rest after an illness or injury: *He was*
  advised to rest up for a week after his fall. **NOTE**
  Rest is usually used with this meaning. **2** (*espe-*
  cially AmE) to rest in order to gain energy and
  strength, for example after an illness or before a
  sports competition: *You should rest up if you're*
  going to be fit for the game. ◇ *The climbers*
  decided to rest up for a couple of days before con-
  tinuing up to the summit. **NOTE** Rest can also be
  used with this meaning.
  ✥ v + adv

'rest with sb (to do sth) (*formal*) (*not used in the*
  progressive tenses) to be sb's responsibility: *The*
  decision rests entirely with you. ◇ *The responsi-*
  bility for bringing up children rests with the par-
  ents. ◇ *It rests with the bus company to prove*
  they were not responsible for the accident.
  SYN lie with sb (to do sth)
  ✥ v + prep

result /rɪ'zʌlt/

re'sult in sth to have a particular effect; to make
  sth happen: *The accident resulted in 67 deaths.* ◇
  The agreement will result in employers working
  more closely with students and teachers.
  OBJ death, increase, loss
  ✥ v + prep

retail /'riːteɪl/

'retail at/for sth (*business*) to be sold at a particular price: *The videos retail at £15 each.*
  ✥ v + prep

return /rɪ'tɜːn/; AmE rɪ'tɜːrn/

re'turn to sth 1 to go back to a previous state:
  Train services have returned to normal after the
  strike. **SYN** go back to sth **2** to start discussing
  a subject you were discussing earlier: *He returns*
  to this topic later in the report. **SYN** come back
  to sth
  ✥ v + prep

rev /rev/ (-vv-)

,rev 'up; ,rev sth 'up if the engine of a vehicle
  revs up, or sb **revs** it **up**, it runs quickly
  although the vehicle does not move: *The car*
  revved up and roared away.
  NOTE Rev and rev sth are also used with this
  meaning.
  ✥ v + adv ✦ v + n/pron + adv ✦ v + adv + n

,**rev 'up (for sth)**, ,**rev sb/sth 'up (for sth)** (*especially AmE*) to become, or to make sb/sth, more active or excited: *The team are revving up for next week's game.* ◇ *It's his job to rev up the audience before the show starts.*
◈ v + adv ◆ v + n/pron + adv ◆ v + adv + n

revel /'revl/ (**-ll-**, **-l-**)

'**revel in sth**; '**revel in doing sth** to enjoy a situation or an experience very much: *I think he's secretly revelling in all the attention.* ◇ *She seems to revel in annoying her parents.*
◈ v + prep

revert /rɪ'vɜːt; *AmE* rɪ'vɜːrt/

re'vert to sb (*law*) (of property and land) to return legally to the owner: *After his death the house reverted to its original owner.*
◈ v + prep

re'vert to sth; **re'vert to doing sth** (*formal*) **1** to go back to a previous condition or activity, especially a worse one: *When the pressure is on, players revert to bad habits.* ◇ *After a good year the team reverted to type in their last game* (= they played badly again). ◇ *After 80 years as a school, the building has reverted back to being a house again.* **2** to start talking or thinking again about a subject you were considering earlier: *To revert to your earlier question…*
◈ v + prep

revolve /rɪ'vɒlv; *AmE* rɪ'vɑːlv/

re'volve around sb/sth; **re'volve around doing sth** (*also* **revolve round sb/sth, revolve round doing sth** *especially BrE*) to have sb/sth as the main subject or interest: *His whole life revolved round cars.* ◇ *You think the whole world revolves around you.* ◇ *Much of a dolphin's life revolves around finding and eating food.*
◈ v + prep

re'volve around sth (*also* **re'volve round sth** *especially BrE*) to move around sth in a circle: *The earth revolves around the sun.*
◈ v + prep

rid /rɪd/ (**ridding, rid, rid**)

'**rid sb/sth/yourself of sb/sth** (*formal*) to remove sth/sb unpleasant from a person, a place or an organization: *The government pledged to rid the country of nuclear weapons.* ◇ *How could she rid herself of Charles?*
NOTE This phrasal verb is used mainly in written English.
◈ v + n/pron + prep

riddle /'rɪdl/

'**riddle sb/sth with sth** to fill sb/sth with bullets or with holes: *His body was riddled with bullets.* ◇ *wooden beams riddled with holes* ◇ *a bullet-riddled car*
NOTE **Riddle sb/sth with sth** is often used in the passive.
◈ v + n/pron + prep

be 'riddled with sth to be full of sth, especially sth unpleasant or bad: *The whole organization is riddled with corruption.*
◈ be + v + prep

ride /raɪd/ (**rode** /rəʊd; *AmE* roʊd/ **ridden** /'rɪdn/)

'**ride on sth** (*usually used in the progressive tenses*) to depend on sth: *My whole future is riding on this interview.* ◇ *There's a lot of money riding on this deal.* ◇ *She has a lot riding on this film after the failure of the last two.*
◈ v + prep

,**ride sth 'out** to manage to survive a difficult period or situation without suffering serious harm: *Do you think the president will be able to ride out this latest crisis?* ◇ *Of course your parents were angry, but you should have stayed to ride out the storm.*
OBJ **storm, recession**
◈ v + adv + n ◆ v + n/pron + adv

,**ride 'up** if an item of clothing **rides up**, it gradually moves upwards, out of position: *His waistcoat was riding up over his stomach.*
◈ v + adv

rifle /'raɪfl/

,**rifle 'through sth** to search quickly through sth such as drawers, cupboards or papers, in order to find or steal sth: *Sally rifled through her wardrobe looking for something to wear.* ◇ *The room looked as if a burglar had rifled through it* (= it was very untidy).
NOTE **Rifle through sth** can be used in the passive: *The drawers had been rifled through.*
◈ v + prep

rig /rɪg/ (**-gg-**)

'**rig sb/sth 'out (in/with sth)** (*old-fashioned, BrE*) to provide sb/sth with clothes or equipment: *They took the kids to a big store and rigged them out from top to bottom* (= bought them a set of new clothes, shoes, etc.). ◇ *The ship had been rigged out with state-of-the-art equipment.*
SYN **kit sb/sth out (in/with sth)** (*BrE*)
NOTE **Rig sb out** is often used in the passive.
◈ v + adv + n ◆ v + n/pron + adv

ˌrig sth ˈup 1 to fix a piece of equipment into place: *We've rigged up lights in the garden for the party.* ◊ *He was rigged up to a machine so that the nurses could check his heartbeat.* **2** to make or build sth quickly, using whatever materials are available: *He had rigged up a sort of tent, using his jacket and shirt.*
　◈ v + adv + n ◆ v + n/pron + adv

ring /rɪŋ/ (rang /ræŋ/ rung /rʌŋ/)

NOTE To **ring** is not used in American English to mean 'to telephone'. **To call** is the most common verb for this in American English. It is also used in British English, as well as **to phone**.

ˌring aˈround/ˈround; ˌring aˈround/ˈround sb/sth (*BrE*) to phone several people or places to find out information or discuss sth: *I've spent the morning ringing round travel agents to find a flight.*
　◈ v + adv ◆ v + prep

ˌring ˈback; ˌring sb ˈback (*BrE*) to telephone sb again or to telephone sb who telephoned you earlier: *I'll ring you back later with more details.* ◊ *Your mother called while you were out. She wants you to ring back.* ◊ *I've only got a few coins for this call* (= from a public telephone). *Can you ring me back?* ◊ *If he phones while I'm out, tell him to ring back later.*
　◈ v + adv ◆ v + n/pron + adv

ˌring ˈin (*BrE*) **1** to telephone the place where you work: *She felt so exhausted she rang in sick* (= to say she could not come to work). ◊ *The boss rings in several times a day, even when he's on holiday.* **2** to telephone a radio, television programme, etc: *Listeners were asked to ring in with their opinions.*
　◈ v + adv

ˌring ˈoff (*BrE*) to end a telephone conversation, and put the telephone down: *He rang off before I could explain.*
　SYN hang up
　◈ v + adv

ˌring ˈout to be heard loudly and clearly: *His clear voice rang out across the hall.* ◊ *Suddenly shots rang out nearby.*
　◈ v + adv

ˌring ˈround; ˌring ˈround sb/sth (*BrE*) = RING AROUND/ROUND, RING AROUND/ROUND SB/STH

ˌring ˈthrough (to sb/sth) (*BrE*) to make a telephone call to sb, especially within the same building: *Reception rang through to say my visitor had arrived.*
　◈ v + adv

ˌring ˈup; ˌring sb/sth ˈup (*BrE*) to telephone sb/sth: *He rang up to apologize.* ◊ *We must ring Jenny up tonight.* ◊ *Can you ring up the station to check the train times?* ◊ *My dad was once rung up by someone claiming to be John Lennon.*

NOTE **Ring** and **ring sb** are also frequently used with this meaning. **Ring up** and **ring sb up** are very common in spoken English.
　◈ v + adv ◆ v + n/pron + adv ◆ v + adv + n

ˌring sth ˈup to record the cost of goods being bought in a shop/store on a machine (a **cash register**); to make sales of the value mentioned: *She rang up the drinks on the till.* ◊ *The company rang up profits of $160 million last year.*
　◈ v + adv + n ◆ v + n/pron + adv

rinse /rɪns/

ˌrinse sth ˈout 1 to make sth clean by washing it in water: *Ruth finished her coffee and rinsed out her cup out under the tap.* ◊ *Rinse your mouth out to get rid of the taste.* **NOTE** **Rinse sth** is also used with the same meaning: *She quickly rinsed her cup and plate.* **2** (*also* **ˌrinse sth ˈout of sth**) to remove sth such as soap from sth else with water: *Leave the conditioner on your hair for three minutes and then rinse it out.*
　SYN wash sth out
　◈ v + n/pron + adv ◆ v + adv + n
　　2 also v + n/pron + adv + prep

rip /rɪp/ (-pp-)

ˈrip at sth to attack sth violently and tear it or cut it: *The bird ripped at its rival's throat.* ◊ *(figurative) The hurricane tore at their skin and ripped at their clothes.*
　◈ v + prep

ˌrip ˈinto sb/sth (with sth) (for sth/for doing sth) (*informal*) to criticize sb in an angry way for sth they have done or said: *He ripped into me for being late.*
　SYN lay into sb/sth (with sth) (for sth/for doing sth)
　NOTE **Rip into sb/sth** can be used in the passive
　◈ v + prep

ˌrip ˈinto/ˈthrough sb/sth to go very quickly or violently into or through sb/sth: *An explosion ripped through a four-storey apartment building.*
　◈ v + prep

ˌrip sb ˈoff (*informal*) to cheat sb, for example by charging them too much for sth, selling them sth of poor quality, etc: *The bank was accused of ripping off its customers.* ◊ *The tickets were very expensive, but the play was terrible. We felt we'd been ripped off.*
　NOTE **Rip sb off** is often used in the passive: *The law protects tenants from being ripped off by landlords.*
　◈ v + adv + n ◆ v + n/pron + adv
　▸ **ˈrip-off** *n* [usually sing.] (*informal*) a situation where you pay too much for sth; sth that is not worth what you pay for it: *They charged you £25 for a T-shirt? What a rip-off!* ◊ *The meal was a total rip-off.* ◊ *rip-off prices*

→ *see also* RIP-OFF at RIP SB/STH OFF; RIP-OFF at RIP STH OFF

,rip sb/sth 'off (*informal*) to copy sb/sth, by stealing ideas, designs, etc. especially in order to make money for yourself: *Another band has ripped off our song.* ◇ *She was accused of ripping off other people's ideas.*
  ✦ v + adv + n ◆ v + n/pron + adv
  ▶ 'rip-off (of sth) *n* (*informal*) a copy of sth, especially one that is not as good as the original: *He has a stall that sells designer rip-offs* (= clothes).
  → *see also* RIP-OFF at RIP SB OFF; RIP-OFF at RIP STH OFF

'rip sth 'off (*slang*) to steal sth: *Thieves broke in and ripped off five computers.*
  [SYN] nick sth (*BrE, slang*)
  ✦ v + n/pron + adv ◆ v + adv + n
  ▶ 'rip-off *n* (*informal*) an act of stealing sth: *It was a scandalous rip-off of public funds.*
  → *see also* RIP-OFF at RIP SB OFF; RIP-OFF at RIP SB/STH OFF

,rip sth 'off; ,rip sth 'off sb/sth to remove sth, especially clothing, very quickly by pulling sharply: *The fans were trying to rip his clothes off.* ◇ *She ripped the poster off the wall.*
  [SYN] tear sth off, tear sth off sb/sth
  ✦ v + n/pron + adv ◆ v + adv + n

,rip 'through sth = RIP INTO/THROUGH STH

,rip sth 'up 1 to tear sth to pieces: *I ripped the letter up without reading it.* 2 to pull sth quickly or violently from the floor or ground: *A gang of teenagers ripped up fences and plants.* ◇ *We've ripped up the old carpets and painted the walls.*
  [SYN] tear sth up
  ✦ v + n/pron + adv ◆ v + adv + n

rise /raɪz/ (rose /rəʊz/; AmE roʊz/risen /'rɪzn/)

,rise a'bove sth (*written*) 1 to not be affected or limited by problems, insults, etc.; to be able to deal with problems: *She was able to rise above her disability.* 2 to be too wise or good to do sth wrong or to think or behave in the way other people do: *He had an unusual ability to rise above the prejudices of his generation.* ◇ *There will always be gossip. You have to try and rise above it.* 3 to be better than other similar things: *Her articles never rise above the level of a gossip column.*
  ✦ v + prep

'rise to sth 1 to deal successfully with a situation or problem that you do not expect or do not usually have to face: *The job wasn't easy but Sam was ready to rise to the challenge.* ◇ *The play was a challenge for the actors but they rose to the occasion.* 2 to react when sb is deliberately trying to make you angry or get you interested in sth: *I refuse to rise to that sort of comment.* ◇ *I decided to flatter him and he rose to the bait* (= he reacted in the way that I wanted).
  ✦ v + prep

,rise 'up 1 (against sb/sth) (*formal*) to start to fight against or refuse to obey people in authority, for example a government or king: *The people rose up against the invaders.* [SYN] rebel (against sb/sth) 2 (*literary*) to appear as a tall shape above the surroundings: *A magnificent palace rose up before her.*
  ✦ v + adv
  ▶ 'uprising *n* a situation in which a group of people join together to fight against or to refuse to obey people in authority: *The uprising was ruthlessly suppressed.*

roll /rəʊl; AmE roʊl/

,roll a'round (*BrE also* ,roll 'round) (*informal*) 1 (*BrE also* ,roll a'bout) to be laughing so much that that you can hardly control yourself: *Her speech had everyone rolling around with laughter.* 2 (of a regular event) to arrive; to happen at the usual time: *We have to be ready when election time rolls around again.* [SYN] come round, come around
  ✦ v + adv

,roll sth 'back 1 to reduce the amount of influence, power or importance that sth has; to change sth so that it is the opposite of what it was: *They were determined to roll back union power.* 2 to reduce prices, wages, etc: *We must roll back inflation.* [OBJ] prices 3 to make sth go back or further away: *to roll back the frontiers of space/science* ◇ *The former international football player rolled back the years with a brilliant performance last night* (= he played as he did when he was younger). [OBJ] frontiers
  ✦ v + adv + n ◆ v + pron + adv ◆ v + n + adv (*rare*)
  ▶ 'rollback (of sth) *n* 1 (*especially AmE*) a reduction or decrease in sth: *a 2% rollback in taxes* 2 (*computing*) a return to the condition that existed before there was an error in a computer system

,roll sth 'down 1 to open out a piece of clothing, etc. that has been folded over and over: *She rolled down her sleeves.* [OBJ] sleeves 2 to lower sth; to open a window in a car, especially by turning a handle: *He rolled down the car window and waved to us.* [OBJ] car window
  [OPP] roll sth up
  ✦ v + adv + n ◆ v + n/pron + adv

,roll 'in (*informal*) 1 to arrive in great numbers or quantities: *Offers of help continue to roll in.* 2 to arrive somewhere, usually late and without being worried or sorry: *Rob finally rolled in at lunch time.*
  ✦ v + adv

,roll 'on 1 (of time) to pass steadily: *As the years rolled on the painful memories began to fade.* 2 to continue without changing very much: *For the next few weeks the debate rolled on.* 3 roll on... (*BrE, informal*) used to say that you wish sth would come soon: *Roll on summer!*
  ✦ v + adv

,**roll sb/sth 'out** (*informal, especially AmE*) to use sb/sth to help you achieve sth: *He rolled out all his old friends to help him win the election.* ◊ *The Moscow Circus rolled out dancing bears to announce its arrival in North America.*
◈ v + adv + n ♦ v + pron + adv ♦ v + n + adv

,**roll sth 'out 1** to make a substance such as pastry flat and thin by rolling sth over it: *Roll out the pastry with a clean rolling pin.* OBJ **pastry, dough 2** to unfold sth that is in a roll and put it flat on the ground: *I rolled out my sleeping bag and crawled in.* OPP **roll sth up 3** to officially make a new product available to the public: *The Air Force will roll out its new planes in November.* SYN **launch sth**
◈ v + adv + n ♦ v + n/pron + adv
IDM **roll out the red 'carpet (for sb)** to treat sb like a very important visitor
▸ **'roll-out** *n* an occasion when a company introduces a new product: *a roll-out ceremony*

,**roll 'over**; ,**roll sb/sth 'over 1** (of a person) to turn from lying on one side of your body to the other side; to move sb in this way: *She rolled over onto her back.* ◊ *I rolled the baby over and sat up.* **2** (of a vehicle, a boat, etc.) to turn onto its side or upside down; to move sth in this way: *The car rolled over into a ditch.*
SYN **turn over, turn sb/sth over**
◈ v + adv ♦ v + n/pron + adv

,**roll sth 'over 1** (*finance*) to allow money that sb owes to be paid at a later date: *The government agreed to roll over the debt.* OBJ **debt, loan 2** (*BrE*) to add the prize money in a competition in a particular week to the prize money the next week, if no one has won it: *This week's lottery jackpot will be rolled over until next week.*
◈ v + adv + n ♦ v + n/pron + adv
▸ **'rollover** *n* **1** [C] (*BrE*) a prize of money in a competition that is formed by adding the prize from one week when no one has won it to the prize for the next week: *This week there is a rollover of $14 million.* ◊ *a rollover jackpot/week* **2** [U] (*finance*) the act of allowing money that is owed to be paid at a later date

,**roll 'round** (*BrE*) = ROLL AROUND

,**roll 'up** (*informal*) to arrive: *He finally rolled up an hour late.* ◊ *Roll up! Roll up for the greatest show on earth!* (= used to invite people who are passing to come and form an audience)
◈ v + adv

,**roll sth 'up 1** to turn the end of a piece of clothing over and over to make it shorter: *He rolled up his sleeves and started washing the dishes.* OBJ **sleeves, trousers** OPP **roll sth down 2** to fold sth to make the shape of a tube or a ball: *She rolled up the sleeping bag.* OPP **roll sth out 3** to close the window in a car, especially by turning a

handle; to raise sth: *She rolled up the window and drove off.* OBJ **car window** OPP **roll sth down**
◈ v + adv + n ♦ v + n/pron + adv
▸ **'roll-up** *n* (*BrE, informal*) a cigarette that you make yourself by rolling tobacco in special paper: *Simon lit a roll-up.*

romp /rɒmp; *AmE* rɑːmp/

,**romp a'head/a'way** (*BrE*) to make progress, increase or win quickly and easily: *The home team romped away to win by 3 goals.*
NOTE This verb is mostly used in newspapers.
◈ v + adv

,**romp 'through sth** (*BrE, informal*) to do sth easily and quickly: *She romped through the exam questions.*
NOTE This verb is mostly used in newspapers.
◈ v + prep

root /ruːt/

,**root a'round**; ,**root a'round/'through sth** (*BrE also* ,**root a'bout**, ,**root a'bout sth**) **(for sth)** to move things around or turn them over to try to find sth: *He was rooting around in the drawer for his keys.* ◊ *Something or someone had been rooting through the piles of rubbish.*
◈ v + adv ♦ v + prep

'**root for sb/sth** (*informal*) (*usually used in the progressive tenses*) to support or encourage sb in a sports competition or when they are in a difficult situation: *Good luck — I'll be rooting for you!*
◈ v + prep

,**root sb/sth 'out 1** to find the person or thing that is causing a problem and remove or get rid of them: *The government has promised to root out police corruption.* ◊ *The trouble makers seem to have been rooted out.* OBJ **corruption 2** (*informal*) to find sb/sth when it is not easy or it takes a long time: *They eventually rooted out two witnesses.* ◊ *I've got some instructions for the camera somewhere — I'll see if I can root them out.* ◊ *I'll root out the photo for you.* SYN **dig sth out; hunt sth down/out**
◈ v + adv + n ♦ v + pron + adv ♦ v + n + adv (*less frequent*)

,**root 'through sth** = ROOT AROUND, ROOT AROUND/THROUGH STH

'**root sb to sth** if fear, shock, etc. **roots you to** a place, it makes you unable to move: *She stood rooted to the spot in horror.*
◈ v + n/pron + prep

,**root sth 'up** to dig or pull up a plant, tree, etc. with its roots: *Kids have been rooting up plants and carving their names on the trees.*
◈ v + adv + n ♦ v + n/pron + adv

rope /rəʊp; *AmE* roʊp/

,rope sb 'in; **,rope sb 'into sth;** **,rope sb 'into doing sth** (*informal*) to persuade sb to take part in an activity or to help you, even when they do not want to: *We'll rope Colin in to help us.* ◇ *I got roped into washing all the dirty dishes.*
NOTE This phrasal verb is often used in the passive.
✦ v + n/pron + adv ◆ v + adv + n ◆ v + n/pron + prep

,rope sth 'off to separate one area from another with ropes, in order to stop people from entering it: *The scene of the crime had been roped off.*
OBJ area
NOTE Rope sth off is often used in the passive.
✦ v + n/pron + adv ◆ v + adv + n

rot /rɒt; *AmE* rɑːt/ (**-tt-**)

,rot a'way to gradually decay: *The window frame had rotted away.*
✦ v + adv

rough /rʌf/

,rough sth 'out to draw or write the main parts of sth without including all the details: *She roughed out the design on the back of an envelope.* ◇ *I've roughed out a few ideas for the book.*
✦ v + adv + n ◆ v + pron + adv ◆ v + n + adv (*less frequent*)

,rough sb 'up (*informal*) to hurt sb by hitting or kicking them, especially in order to frighten or warn them: *They didn't want to kill him, just rough him up a little.* ◇ *Demonstrators claimed they had been roughed up by the police.*
✦ v + n/pron + adv ◆ v + adv + n

round /raʊnd/

,round sth 'down (to sth) = ROUND STH UP/DOWN (TO STH)

,round sth 'off 1 (*AmE also* **,round sth 'out**) (with sth) to end or complete sth in a satisfactory way: *We rounded off the meal with coffee.* ◇ *The team rounded off a successful season with another brilliant victory.* ◇ *The evening was rounded off with a disco.* **OBJ** the day, the evening **2** to give a smooth curved shape to the edge of sth: *I rounded off the corners with sandpaper.*
✦ v + adv + n ◆ v + n/pron + adv

'round on sb to suddenly speak angrily to sb and criticize or attack them: *He rounded on her angrily and told her to keep her mouth shut.*
✦ v + prep

,round sth 'out (*AmE*) = ROUND STH OFF 1

,round sb/sth 'up to bring together a number of people, animals or objects in one place: *to round up cattle/sheep* ◇ *The gang were rounded up and put in jail.* ◇ (*humorous*) *We've rounded up some good speakers for the conference.*
✦ v + adv + n ◆ v + n/pron + adv

▶ **'round-up** *n* [usually sing.] **1** a brief summary of the most important points of news or sport, for example on a television or radio news programme: *a news round-up* ◇ *a round-up of the day's events* **2** an act of bringing people or animals together in one place: *a round-up of wild ponies* ◇ *a round-up of suspects*

,round sth 'up/'down (to sth) to increase/ decrease a number to the next highest or lowest whole number: *He rounded the price down to $900.* ◇ *Totals should be rounded up to the nearest whole number.*
✦ v + n/pron + adv ◆ v + adv + n

rub /rʌb/ (**-bb-**)

,rub a'gainst sb/sth; **,rub 'up against sb/sth** if an animal **rubs** (**up**) **against** sb/sth, it moves backwards and forwards and presses itself against them/it: *The cat rubbed* (*up*) *against her legs.*
✦ v + prep ◆ v + adv + prep

,rub a'long (with sb/together) (*BrE, informal*) to live or work together with sb in a satisfactory way: *We rub along all right with the neighbours.*
SYN get on/along (with sb/together)
✦ v + adv

,rub sb/sth 'down; **,rub yourself 'down** to rub the skin of a person, an animal, etc. with sth such as a towel, to make it clean and dry: *She rubbed herself down with a towel.* ◇ *After exercise each horse must be rubbed down.*
✦ v + n/pron + adv ◆ v + adv + n
▶ **'rub-down** *n* [usually sing.] an act of rubbing sb/sth yourself with a towel, for example
→ *see also* RUB-DOWN at RUB STH DOWN

,rub sth 'down 1 (*especially BrE*) to make sth clean by wiping it with a cloth, etc: *Rub the walls down well before painting them.* **2** to make the surface of sth smooth by rubbing it with special paper, etc: *He rubbed the woodwork down with sandpaper.*
✦ v + n/pron + adv ◆ v + adv + n
▶ **'rub-down** *n* [usually sing.] (*especially BrE*) **1** an act of cleaning the surface of sth with a cloth, etc. **2** an act of rubbing the surface of sth to make it smooth
→ *see also* RUB-DOWN at RUB SB/STH DOWN, RUB YOURSELF DOWN

,rub sth 'in to say sth to sb which reminds them of sth that they feel embarrassed or guilty about and would like to forget: *I already know it was my fault — there's no need to rub it in.* ◇ *Was he trying to rub in the fact that he didn't like me?*
OBJ it
NOTE Rub sth in is not used in the passive.
✦ v + n/pron + adv ◆ v + adv + n
IDM **rub sb's 'nose in it** to remind sb of sth they feel embarrassed or guilty about and would like to forget

,**rub sth 'in**; ,**rub sth 'into sth** to spread a substance over a surface while pressing firmly with your fingers, a cloth, etc: *Rub the lotion into your skin with your fingers.* ◇ *Spray on the polish and rub it in well.*

OBJ **cream, lotion**

🌐 v + n/pron + adv ♦ v + adv + n ♦ v + n/pron + prep

,**rub 'off** (**on/onto sb**) if sth, such as a good quality that sb has, **rubs off** onto you, you gain some of that quality by spending time with the person: *Let's hope some of his good luck rubs off on me!* ◇ *None of her love for nature has rubbed off onto her children.*

🌐 v + adv

,**rub 'off**; ,**rub sth 'off**; ,**rub sth 'off sth** to be removed from sth by rubbing; to remove sth from sth by rubbing: *Somebody's used the wrong kind of pen on the whiteboard and it won't rub off.* ◇ *He quickly rubbed mud off his face.*

🌐 v + adv ♦ v + n/pron + adv ♦ v + adv + n ♦ v + n/pron + prep

,**rub sb 'out** (*AmE, slang*) to murder sb: *He was rubbed out before he could talk.*

SYN **bump sb off** (*informal*), **do away with sb** (*informal*), **murder sb**

NOTE **Rub sb out** is often used in the passive.

🌐 v + n/pron + adv ♦ v + adv + n

,**rub sth 'out** (*BrE*) to remove the marks made by a pen, pencil, piece of chalk, etc. from a piece of paper, a board, etc: *Draw the outline with a soft pencil, so that you can rub it out later.*

SYN **erase sth** (*more formal*)

🌐 v + n/pron + adv ♦ v + adv + n

,**rub 'up against sb/sth** = RUB AGAINST SB/STH, RUB UP AGAINST SB/STH

ruck /rʌk/

,**ruck 'up**; ,**ruck sth 'up** (*BrE*) to form untidy folds; to make sth do this: *Your blouse has rucked up at the back.* ◇ *Her skirt was rucked up.*

🌐 v + adv ♦ v + adv + n ♦ v + n/pron + adv

rule /ru:l/

,**rule sth 'in**; ,**rule sth 'into sth** (*formal*) if sb **rules sth in**, they decide that it is possible, or that it can or should happen: *He asked for all possible results to be ruled in to the discussions.*

OPP **rule sth out, rule sth out of sth**

🌐 v + n/pron + adv ♦ v + adv + n ♦ v + n/pron + prep

,**rule sb 'out** (**as sth**), ,**rule sb 'out of sth 1** if somebody **rules** somebody else **out**, they decide that it is not possible for them to have done sth or to do sth, or that they are not suitable for sth: *The police soon ruled out her husband as a suspect.* ◇ *The producer ruled out an older actress for the role.* ◇ *Ramsay has been ruled out as too old for the job.* **2** if something **rules sb out**, it makes it impossible for sb to have done sth or to do sth, or makes them unsuitable for sth: *Several people saw her at*

the restaurant at 9.00 p.m. so that seems to rule her out as the murderer. ◇ *Beckham has been ruled out of tonight's game with a knee injury.*

→ *see also* RULE YOURSELF, ITSELF, ETC. OUT, RULE YOURSELF, ITSELF, ETC. OUT OF STH

🌐 v + n/pron + adv ♦ v + adv + n ♦ v + n/pron + adv + prep

,**rule sth 'out** (**as sth**), ,**rule sth 'out of sth 1** if somebody **rules sth out**, they decide that it is not possible, or that it cannot or should not happen: *The police have ruled out suicide.* ◇ *I wouldn't rule anything out.* ◇ *Detectives have not ruled out the possibility that she was abducted.* ◇ *Manchester has been ruled out as the site for the next Olympics.* ◇ *Sabotage was ruled out of the investigation.* OPP **rule sth in, rule sth into sth 2** if something **rules sth out**, it makes it impossible for sth to happen, or makes sth unsuitable for a particular purpose: *The latest developments rule out the possibility of a lasting peace.* ◇ *The change in the weather ruled out any climbing the next day.* ◇ *The size of the house ruled it out as a family home* (= it was too small).

🌐 v + adv + n ♦ v + n/pron + adv ♦ v + n/pron + adv + prep

,**rule yourself, itself, etc. 'out**; ,**rule yourself, itself, etc. 'out of sth** to decide you do not want to or are not able to do sth; to decide that you are not suitable for sth: *Smith has not ruled himself out of Saturday's game.*

🌐 v + pron + adv ♦ v + pron + adv + prep

rumble /ˈrʌmbl/

,**rumble 'on** (*written, especially BrE*) if an argument, a dispute, etc. **rumbles on**, it continues slowly and steadily for much longer than it should: *The dispute rumbled on through the summer.* ◇ *The row has been rumbling on for two years.*

🌐 v + adv

run /rʌn/ (**running, ran** /ræn/**run**)

	~ about		~ in
241	~ across		~ into
	~ after	243	~ off
	~ along		~ off together
	~ around		~ off with
	~ around after		~ on
	~ around with		~ out
	~ at		~ out on
	~ away	244	~ over
	~ away from		~ past
	~ away with		~ round
	~ away/off		~ round after
	~ away/off together		~ through
	~ away/off with		~ to
242	~ by		~ up
	~ down		~ up against

,**run a'bout**; ,**run a'bout sth** (*BrE*) = RUN AROUND, RUN AROUND STH

▶ '**runabout** *n* (*informal*) **1** a small car, boat or aircraft, used mainly for short journeys **2** (*AmE*) a person who moves from place to place

,**run a'cross sb/sth** to meet sb or find sth by chance: *I ran across Mary in town yesterday.*
⟐SYN⟐ **come across sb/sth**
✦ v + prep

,**run 'after sb** (*informal*) to try to persuade sb to have a romantic or sexual relationship with you: *He's always running after younger women.*
✦ v + prep

,**run 'after sb/sth** to run to try to catch sb/sth; to chase sb/sth: *They ran after the thief but he got away.*
✦ v + prep

,**run a'long** (*old-fashioned, informal*) used to tell sb, especially a child, to go away and not disturb you: *Run along now, children, I'm busy.*
✦ v + adv

,**run a'round**; ,**run a'round sth** (*BrE also* ,**run a'bout/'round**, ,**run a'bout/'round sth**) **1** to run in different directions, especially in an excited way: *It's a lovely park to run around in.* ◇ *The children were running round the house with no clothes on.* ◇ *They stopped the car to let the dogs out to run about.* **2** to move very quickly from place to place, being very busy: *I ran around like a mad thing all day.* ◇ *He's been running about the place organizing the party.* ◇ *I've been running round everywhere looking for you!* ◇ *He's had the police **running around in circles** (= being very busy but not achieving anything).*
⟐SYN⟐ **rush around**, **rush around sth**; **tear around**, **tear around sth**
✦ v + adv ♦ v + prep

▶ '**runaround** *n* if you give sb the **run around**, you treat them badly by delaying them, giving them false information, not telling them the truth, etc: *You know where she is, don't you, but you're just **giving me the run around**.*

,**run a'round after sb** (*BrE also* ,**run 'round after sb**) to be very busy doing a lot of things for sb, when they should be able to do them for themselves: *His mother shouldn't have to run around after him.* ◇ *She spends all her time running round after the children.*
✦ v + adv + prep

,**run a'round with sb** (*disapproving*) to spend a lot of time with sb: *Their son is running around with a bad crowd.*
✦ v + adv + prep

'**run at sb** to run towards sb to attack them or as if you were going to attack them: *He ran at me with a knife.*
✦ v + prep

'**run at sth** (*often used in the progressive tenses*) to be at or near a particular level or rate: *Inflation is running at 26%.* ◇ *Interest rates were running at record levels.* ⟐SUBJ⟐ **inflation**, **unemployment**
✦ v + prep

,**run a'way 1** (**from sb/sth**) to move quickly away from sb/a place; to escape from sb/a place: *A man was seen running away from the shop.* ◇ *'Bye then,' she said, and ran away without looking back.* ◇ *His first instinct was to run away.* → *see also* RUN OFF 1 **2** (**from sth**) to leave the place where you are living or staying suddenly and secretly because you are unhappy: *She ran away from home on several occasions.* ◇ *He ran away and joined a circus.* → *see also* RUN OFF 2 **3** to leave a person or a place to try to avoid doing sth: *Don't run away — I want your advice.* **4** used to tell a child to go away and not disturb you: *Run away and play.*
✦ v + adv

▶ '**runaway** *adj* [only before noun] **1** (of a situation or an event) happening quickly and easily and not able to be controlled: *The movie has been a runaway success.* ◇ *The game was a runaway victory for Liverpool.* ◇ *runaway inflation* **2** (of an animal or a vehicle) moving, but no longer under the control of the rider or driver: *a runaway horse* **3** (of a person) having secretly left their home or the place where they are staying: *runaway children/ teenagers*

▶ '**runaway** *n* a person who has left their home or the place where they are staying suddenly and secretly because they are unhappy there: *a 16-year-old runaway*

,**run a'way/'off**; ,**run a'way/'off with sb**; ,**run a'way/'off together** to leave your home, husband, wife, etc. secretly with sb else in order to marry them or have a sexual relationship with them: *They ran away to Scotland.* ◇ *We think John and Susie have run off together.*
✦ v + adv ♦ v + adv + prep ♦ v + adv + adv

,**run a'way from sth** to try to avoid dealing with or thinking about sth because it is difficult or unpleasant: *He is running away from his responsibilities.* ◇ *You can't just run away from difficult situations — you must face up to them.*
⟐OBJ⟐ **responsibilities**
✦ v + adv + prep

,**run a'way with sb**; ,**run a'way together** = RUN AWAY/OFF, RUN AWAY/OFF WITH SB, RUN AWAY/OFF TOGETHER

,**run a'way with you** if a feeling, an emotion, etc. **runs away with you**, you are not able to control it: *Her imagination tends to run away with her.* ◇ *My tongue ran away with me and I said things I regretted.* ⟐SUBJ⟐ **imagination**, **tongue**
✦ v + adv + prep

,run a'way with sth 1 to win sth clearly or easily: *Their team are running away with the championship.* ◇ *She ran away with the show* (= she was easily the best performer). **2** (*especially AmE*) (*also* **,run 'off with sth**) to escape with sth that you have stolen or taken without asking: *The treasurer ran away with all the funds.* **3** (*informal*) to believe sth that is not true: *Don't run away with the idea that everything was perfect in our marriage.* OBJ **idea, impression**

◈ **1,2** v + adv + prep
　 3 v + adv + prep + noun

,run sth 'by/'past sb (*informal*) to show sb sth or tell them about an idea, a proposal, etc. in order to get their reaction to it: *I've got a few ideas I'd like to run by you.* ◇ *Run that past me again.*
◈ v + n/pron + prep

,run 'down; ,run sth 'down 1 to lose power or stop working; to make sth do this: *I think the batteries are running down.* ◇ *If you leave your headlights on, you'll run the battery down.* SUBJ **battery 2** to stop functioning gradually or become smaller in size or number; to make sth do this: *Oil supplies in the region will start to run down in the next decade.* ◇ *The company are running down their operations in the UK.*
◈ v + adv ◆ v + n/pron + adv ◆ v + adv + n
▶ **'rundown (in/of sth)** n [usually sing.] (*BrE*) **1** a reduction in the size, number, amount or importance of sth: *The public are complaining about the rundown of health services.* **2** a description or an explanation of sth, especially the main points: *a rundown of the history of each team*
→ *see also* RUNDOWN at RUN DOWN STH, RUN STH DOWN STH
▶ **,run-'down** adj **1** (of a building or an area) in poor condition; that has not been looked after: *a run-down area of East London* **2** (of a business, etc.) not as busy or as active as it used to be **3** [not before noun] (of a person) tired, weak and not in good health after having worked too hard, etc: *I'm feeling a bit run-down.*
→ *see also* RUNDOWN at RUN DOWN STH, RUN STH DOWN STH

,run 'down sth if a liquid **runs down** a surface, it flows downwards over it: *Tears were running down his cheeks.*
◈ v + prep

,run 'down sth; ,run sth 'down sth 1 to look quickly at a list; to quickly read and mention the items on it: *Her eyes ran down the figures on the page.* ◇ *She ran her eyes down the page.* **2** to pass, or to make sth pass, downwards over a surface: *She ran her finger down the page.*
▶ **'rundown (on/of sth)** n [usually sing.] an explanation or a description of sth: *I can give you a brief rundown on each of the job applicants.* ◇ *We would like a full rundown on the progress of*

the project so far.
→ *see also* RUNDOWN at RUN DOWN, RUN STH DOWN
◈ v + prep ◆ v + n/pron + prep

,run sb/sth 'down 1 (of a vehicle or its driver) to hit a person or an animal and knock them/it to the ground: *The cyclist was run down by a lorry.* ◇ *You nearly ran down that pedestrian.* SYN **knock sb down; knock sb over** NOTE In this meaning **run sb/sth down** is often used in the passive. It can also suggest that the driver of the vehicle intended to hit the person or animal: *The officer challenged the thief and tried to make the car stop, but the driver ran him down.* → *see also* RUN SB/STH OVER **2** to criticize sb/sth in an unkind way: *She's always running her husband down in front of their friends.* SYN **disparage sb/sth** (*formal*) NOTE In this meaning **run sb/sth down** is not used in the passive. → *see also* RUN YOURSELF DOWN **3** to find sb/sth after looking for a long time: *I finally ran the book down in the college library.* SYN **track sb/sth down; trace sb/sth** NOTE In this meaning **run sb/sth down** is not used in the passive.
◈ v + n/pron + adv ◆ v + adv + n

,run yourself 'down to criticize yourself, often unfairly: *You're always running yourself down!*
→ *see also* RUN SB/STH DOWN 2
◈ v + pron + adv

,run 'in; ,run 'into sth (*AmE, informal*) to visit sb for a short time in an informal way; to go somewhere quickly on your way to somewhere else: *I'll run in on my way home.* ◇ *Can you run into the dry-cleaner's on your way to work?*
◈ v + adv ◆ v + prep

,run sb 'in (*old-fashioned, informal*) to arrest sb and take them to a police station: *She was run in for shoplifting.*
◈ v + n/pron + adv ◆ v + adv + n (*rare*)
▶ **'run-in** n **1** (**with sb**) (*informal*) an argument or a quarrel: *I had a run-in with my mum this evening.* **2** (*also* **'run-up**) (**to sth**) (*BrE*) a period of preparation just before an event takes place: *the final run-in to the World Cup* **3** the action of approaching sth or the distance you cover: *the final run-in to the target*

,run sb 'in; ,run sb 'into sth/… to take sb by car to the centre of town, etc: *I need to go into town. Can you run me in?*
◈ v + n/pron + adv ◆ v + n/pron + prep

,run sth 'in (*BrE*) (in the past) to drive a vehicle slowly and carefully when it is new so that you do not damage the engine: *I'm not going on motorways until I've run the car in.*
◈ v + n/pron + adv ◆ v + adv + n

,run 'into sb to meet sb by chance: *Guess who I ran into today?* ◇ *You rarely run into people you know in London.*
SYN **bump into sb** (*informal*)
◈ v + prep

'run into sb/sth; **'run sth into sb/sth** to accidentally crash into sb/sth; to make a vehicle do this: *The car went out of control and ran into a tree.* ◇ *The lorry behind ran into the back of me* (= my car). ◇ *He ran his car into a tree.*
◉ v + prep ♦ v + n/pron + prep

'run into sth 1 to meet or enter an area of bad weather while travelling: *We ran into a patch of thick fog just outside the city.* OBJ **bad weather 2** to experience difficulties or problems: *We ran into problems right from the beginning of the project.* OBJ **trouble, difficulties, problems, opposition 3** to reach a particular level or amount: *The bill will run into hundreds of pounds.* **4** if things **run into** each other, or sth **runs into** sth else, they join so that they can only be separated with difficulty: *I tried to explain, but my words all ran into each other.*
◉ v + prep

'run sb 'into sth = RUN SB IN, RUN SB INTO STH

'run sth into sb/sth = RUN INTO SB/STH, RUN STH INTO SB/STH

'run 'off 1 to move quickly away from sb/a place; to escape from sb/a place: *The thief ran off down a side street.* ◇ *They ran off laughing.* → *see also* RUN AWAY 1 **2** to leave a place secretly: *She ran off in the middle of the night.* → *see also* RUN AWAY 2
→ *see also* RUN AWAY/OFF, RUN AWAY/OFF WITH SB, RUN AWAY/OFF TOGETHER
◉ v + adv

'run 'off; **'run 'off sth** if a road, path, etc. **runs off** or **runs off** a place, it leads away from it: *Can you see that road running off to the right?* ◇ *Several doors ran off the corridor.*
◉ v + adv ♦ v + prep

'run 'off; **'run 'off with sb**; **'run 'off together** = RUN AWAY/OFF, RUN AWAY/OFF WITH SB, RUN AWAY/OFF TOGETHER

'run 'off sb/sth to drain or flow from sb/sth: *Water runs off the fields into the valley.* ◇ *Sweat was running off her.*
SUBJ **water, sweat**
◉ v + prep
▶ **'run-off** *n* [C] (*technical*) rain, water or other liquid that runs off land and into rivers, etc.

'run 'off sth; **'run sth 'off sth** (of a machine, etc.) to use a particular type of power in order to operate a machine: *The outboard motor runs off an ordinary car battery.*
→ *see also* RUN ON STH, RUN STH ON STH
◉ v + prep ♦ v + n/pron + prep

'run sth 'off 1 to produce copies of a piece of writing, etc. on a machine: *They ran off hundreds of copies of the leaflet.* ◇ *Can you run these letters off for me?* NOTE In informal spoken language **run sb off sth** and **run sb sth off** are also used: *I'll just run you off a copy.* ◇ *I'll run you a copy off now.* **2** to produce sth that is usually difficult to write, such as a poem, speech, etc. quickly and easily: *She ran off a fantastic speech in no time at all.*
◉ v + adv + n ♦ v + n/pron + adv

'run 'off with sb; **'run 'off together** = RUN AWAY/OFF WITH SB, RUN AWAY/OFF TOGETHER

'run 'off with sth = RUN AWAY WITH STH 2

'run 'on 1 to continue to run in the same direction: *I'll stop here, you run on ahead.* **2** to continue longer than is necessary or expected: *I don't want the meeting to run on.* **3 (about sth)** (*especially AmE*) to continue talking for a long time about unimportant things: *She does tend to run on!* ◇ *She ran on with great enthusiasm about her latest project.* **4 [+ adv/prep]** (of a road or a track) to continue in the same direction: *The road runs on into the desert.* **5** (of a line of text) to continue into the next line: *This line runs on into the next verse of the poem.*
SYN **go on**
◉ v + adv

'run on sth if your thoughts etc. **run on** a particular subject, you think or talk about it a lot: *Her thoughts kept running on their last meeting.*
◉ v + prep

'run on sth; **'run sth on sth** to use a particular type of power or fuel to make a machine or a vehicle work: *You can run the car on any type of unleaded petrol.*
→ *see also* RUN OFF STH, RUN STH OFF STH
◉ v + prep ♦ v + n/pron + prep

'run 'out 1 if a supply of sth **runs out**, it is finished or used up: *I'm going to keep travelling until my money runs out.* ◇ *We have to eat quickly as time is running out.* ◇ *One day his luck will run out.* ◇ *My patience with her suddenly ran out.* SUBJ **money, petrol, time, luck, patience 2** (*also* **'run 'out of sth**) if a person or a machine **runs out** of a supply of sth, they finish it or use it all up: *We're running out of money.* ◇ *Could you get some more milk? We've run out.* ◇ *I've run out of patience with her.* ◇ *You've run out of space on the disk.* ◇ *The band seems to have run out of ideas.* OBJ **money, ideas, petrol, patience, time 3** if a contract or other legal document **runs out**, it is no longer valid: *His contract with the club runs out at the end of the season.* SYN **expire** (*more formal*)
◉ v + adv **2** also v + adv + prep
IDM **'run out of 'steam** (*informal*) to have less energy and enthusiasm and stop doing sth or do it less well: *I ran out of steam halfway up the hill.* ◇ *The campaign seems to have run out of steam.*

'run sb 'out; **'run sb 'out of sth/**… (*especially AmE*) to force sb to leave a place: *He vowed to run them out of town.*
◉ v + n/pron + adv ♦ v + n/pron + adv + prep

run sb 'out; **run yourself 'out** (in cricket, etc.) to make a player end their turn at hitting the ball by throwing the ball so that it hits the set of upright sticks, (the **wicket**), while they are still running: *He was run out for 73.*
NOTE Run sb out is often used in the passive.
✪ v + n/pron + adv ♦ v + adv + n

run 'out on sb to leave sb that you live or work with, especially when they need your help: *She ran out on him as soon as things got difficult.*
✪ v + adv + prep

run 'over 1 if a container or the liquid in it **runs over**, the liquid flows out of it over the edge: *Don't let the bath run over!* ◇ *The tea ran over into the saucer.* ⟨SYN⟩ **overflow 2** to continue longer than expected or planned: *We've already run over so let's try to end the meeting soon.*
✪ v + adv

run 'over sb/sth; **run sth 'over sb/sth** to move over a surface; to make sth do this: *I let the cold water run over me.* ◇ *She ran her eye over the figures on the page.*
✪ v + prep

run 'over sth to read through or think about sth quickly; to practise sth: *Let's run over the plans again.* ◇ *I ran over the possibilities in my mind.*
⟨SYN⟩ **go over sth**
✪ v + prep

run sb/sth 'over (of a vehicle or its driver) to knock a person or an animal down and often pass over their body or part of it: *Two children were run over by a truck and killed.* ◇ *I ran over a cat last night.* ◇ *You nearly ran me over!*
⟨SYN⟩ **knock sb over**
→ *see also* RUN SB/STH DOWN 1
✪ v + n/pron + adv ♦ v + adv + n

run sth 'past sb (*informal*) = RUN STH BY/PAST SB

run 'round; **run 'round sth** (*BrE*) = RUN AROUND, RUN AROUND STH

run 'round after sb (*BrE*) = RUN AROUND AFTER SB

run 'through sb/sth if a feeling **runs through** sb/sth, it passes quickly through them/it: *A thrill of excitement ran through her.* ◇ *She felt a tremor run through his body.* ◇ *An angry murmur ran through the crowd.*
SUBJ tremor, shiver, shudder, fear, relief
✪ v + prep

run 'through sth 1 to be present in every part of sth: *There is a common theme running through all of her novels.* ◇ *The English title picks up a thread running through the film.* **2** to discuss, examine or read sth quickly: *He ran through his check list one more time.* ◇ *Can you run through some of these figures with me?* ◇ *She mentally ran through the list of who to invite.* ◇ *Let's run through what I'm meant to do again.* ⟨SYN⟩ **go through sth 3** to perform, act or practise sth:

Could we run through Act 3 again, please? ⟨SYN⟩ **go through sth 4** (*informal*) to use up or spend money carelessly: *She ran through a lot of money in her first year at college.* ⟨SYN⟩ **go through sth**
NOTE Run through sth can be used in the passive in meanings 2, 3 and 4: *That scene's been run through plenty of times.*
✪ v + prep
▶ **'run-through** *n* a practice for an event or a performance: *We're having the main technical run-through of the play tonight.*

run to sb to go to sb for help, advice, protection, etc: *If you get hurt, don't come running to me.*
✪ v + prep

run to sth 1 to reach the amount, or size mentioned, especially a large one: *The total cost runs to hundreds of pounds.* ◇ *The report already runs to 800 pages.* **2** (*BrE*) (*often used in negative sentences and with can*) if a person or their money can **run to** sth, they have enough money to pay for it: *We couldn't quite run to private education for the children.* **3** if your taste or your mind, etc. **runs to** sth, you enjoy it or can do it: *His taste in music runs to pop and jazz, but that's about it.*
✪ **1** v + prep + n
2,3 v + prep

run 'up 1 to move quickly towards sb/sth: *She ran up to me, smiling.* **2** (in cricket and other sports) to run in order to gain speed before you throw a ball, jump a long distance, etc: *Gough is now running up to bowl.*
✪ v + adv
▶ **'run-up** *n* (*BrE*) **1** (*sport*) the act of running or the distance you run in order to gain speed before you throw a ball, jump a long distance, etc: *She took a run-up and kicked the ball.* **2** (*also* **'run-in** *less frequent*) (to sth) the period of preparation before an important event: *She's been training hard in the run-up to the big competition.* ◇ *the run-up to the election*

run sth 'up 1 to allow a bill, debt, etc. to reach a large total: *I ran up a few debts while I was abroad.* ◇ *He's run up a huge bill on his credit card.* **OBJ** bill, debts, overdraft **2** (for sb) to make sth very quickly, especially an item of clothing: *I'll run up some new dresses for the girls.* **NOTE** In informal spoken language run sb up and, less often, run sb sth up can also be used: *Could you run me up some curtains/run me some curtains up?* **3** to raise sth, especially a flag: *They ran up a white flag and surrendered.* **OBJ** flag **4** to achieve sth: *The team have run up their best victory yet.* **OBJ** victory, results
✪ v + adv + n ♦ v + pron + adv ♦ v + n + adv (*less frequent*)

run 'up against sb/sth to experience a difficulty or a problem: *The project keeps running up against the problem of lack of funds.* ◇ *In this* *round, he will run up against the previous year's champion.*

OBJ **problems** SYN **come up against sb/sth**
◈ v + adv + prep

rush /rʌʃ/

,**rush a'round**; ,**rush a'round sth** (*BrE also* ,**rush a'bout/'round**, ,**rush a'bout/'round sth**) to move very quickly from place to place, being very busy: *I've been rushing around all day.* ◇ *He rushed about the room tidying.*
SYN **run around, run around sth; tear around, tear around sth**
◈ v + adv

,**rush 'in** to do or decide sth very quickly, often without thinking about it for long enough: *He's very wary of rushing in and making changes.*
◈ v + adv ♦ v + prep

IDM **fools rush in (where angels fear to tread)** used to say that people with little experience will try to do the difficult or dangerous things that people with more experience would not do

,**rush 'into sth**; ,**rush 'into doing sth**; ,**rush sb 'into doing sth** to do or decide sth quickly without thinking about it carefully; to make sb do this: *Don't go rushing into anything.* ◇ *You shouldn't rush into getting married.* ◇ *She won't*

be rushed into a decision. ◇ *Don't let anyone rush you into accepting the job.*
◈ v + prep ♦ v + n/pron + prep

,**rush 'off** to leave quickly: *Don't rush off, I haven't finished.*
◈ v + adv

,**rush sth 'out** to produce sth very quickly: *They rushed out the posters in time for the festival.* ◇ *The book was rushed out by the publishers.*
◈ v + adv + n ♦ v + n/pron + adv

,**rush 'round**; ,**rush 'round sth** (*BrE*) = RUSH AROUND, RUSH AROUND STH

,**rush sth 'through**; ,**rush sth 'through sth** to make sth become official policy, etc. much quicker than normal: *The legislation has been rushed through.* ◇ *They rushed the bill through Parliament.*
OBJ **bill, legislation**
◈ v + n/pron + adv ♦ v + adv + n (*rare*) ♦ v + n/pron + prep

rustle /'rʌsl/

,**rustle sb/sth 'up** (*informal*) to prepare or provide sth for sb very quickly without planning; to find sb very quickly: *I'll rustle up some lunch for you.* ◇ *I rustled up a few helpers to hand out leaflets.*
◈ v + adv + n ♦ v + n/pron + adv

S s

sack /sæk/

,sack 'out (*AmE, informal*) to lie down to rest or relax: *We sacked out on the couch and watched a video.*
⊕ v + adv

saddle /'sædl/

,saddle 'up; **,saddle sth 'up** to prepare to ride a horse by placing a leather seat (**a saddle**) on it: *Have you saddled up the horses yet?* ◇ *Saddle up, we're leaving right away.*
[OBJ] **horse**
⊕ v + adv ♦ v + adv + n ♦ v + n/pron + adv

'saddle sb/yourself with sb/sth; **'saddle sb/yourself with doing sth** to give sb/yourself a difficult or unpleasant task or responsibility to deal with: *I've been saddled with my brother's kids for the weekend* (= I have to take care of them). ◇ *He had saddled himself with huge debts.* ◇ *I've been saddled with organizing the conference.*
[SYN] **land sb/yourself with sb/sth, land sb/yourself with doing sth**
[NOTE] **Saddle sb with sb/sth** is often used in the passive.
⊕ v + n/pron + prep

safeguard /'seɪfɡɑːd; AmE -ɡɑːrd/

,safeguard a'gainst sth; **,safeguard sb/sth/yourself a'gainst sth** (*formal*) to prevent sth bad from happening to sth; to keep sth safe from harm or damage: *Safeguard against theft by installing a burglar alarm.* ◇ *The leaflet shows you how to safeguard your home against electrical dangers and accidents.*
⊕ v + prep ♦ v + n/pron + prep

sail /seɪl/

,sail 'through; **,sail 'through sth** to succeed in an examination, a test, etc. very easily: *She sailed through her final exams.*
[OBJ] **exam**
⊕ v + adv ♦ v + prep

sally /'sæli/ (**sallies, sallying, sallied, sallied**)

,sally 'forth (*also* **,sally 'out** *less frequent*) (*old-fashioned or literary*) to leave a place in a determined or enthusiastic way: *After lunch she sallied forth for a short walk.*
⊕ v + adv

salt /sɔːlt, BrE also sɒlt/

,salt sth a'way to save money, etc. for the future, often secretly or dishonestly: *He claimed she had salted money away in Brazil.* ◇ *$10 billion had been salted away in banks.*
[OBJ] **money**
⊕ v + n/pron + adv ♦ v + adv + n

sand /sænd/

,sand sth 'down to make sth smooth by rubbing it with strong, rough paper: *Sand the doors down before you paint them.*
[NOTE] **Sand sth** can be used with the same meaning: *Sand the doors before you paint them.*
⊕ v + n/pron + adv ♦ v + adv + n

sandwich /'sænwɪtʃ, -wɪdʒ/

'sandwich sb/sth between sb/sth to fit sth/sb into a very small space between two other things or people: *I was sandwiched between two large men on the back seat.* ◇ *The shop is sandwiched between a bank and a café.*
[NOTE] **Sandwich sb/sth between sb/sth** is nearly always used in the passive.
⊕ v + n/pron + prep

,sandwich A and B to'gether (**with sth**) to put sth between two things to join them: *Sandwich the cakes together with cream.*
⊕ v + n/pron + adv ♦ v + adv + n

save /seɪv/

'save on sth; **'save sth on sth** to use less of sth or not more than necessary: *He saved on electricity by using candles.* ◇ *Get your tickets early and save $5 on the cost of an adult ticket.*
⊕ v + prep ♦ v + n/pron + prep

,save 'up; **,save sth 'up** (**for sth**) to keep your money instead of spending it, especially because you want to buy a particular thing: *She's saving up for a new computer.* ◇ *I saved up all my wages to buy my parents a present.*
[NOTE] **Save** and **save sth** are used more frequently with this meaning, especially in more formal English.
⊕ v + adv ♦ v + adv + n ♦ v + n/pron + adv

,save sth 'up to keep sth to use or enjoy in the future: *I save up the week's newspapers to read at weekends.*
[NOTE] **Save sth** is used more frequently with this meaning, especially in more formal English.
⊕ v + adv + n ♦ v + n/pron + adv

saw /sɔː/ (**sawed, sawn** /sɔːn/, *AmE also* **sawed, sawed**)

,saw sth '**down** to cut sth down and bring it to the ground, using a tool with a long blade and sharp points along the edge (a **saw**): *We had to saw down two trees.*
[OBJ] **tree**
◈ v + adv + n ◆ v + n/pron + adv

,saw sth '**off**; ,saw sth '**off** sth to remove sth from sth by cutting it with a tool with a long blade and sharp points along the edge, (a **saw**): *I sawed the lower branches off the apple tree.*
[OBJ] **branch**
◈ v + n/pron + adv ◆ v + adv + n ◆ v + n/pron + prep
▸ '**sawn-off** (*BrE*) (*AmE* '**sawed-off**) [only before noun] (of a gun) having had the long tube through which the bullets are fired, (the **barrel**), cut short: *a sawn-off shotgun*

,saw sth '**up** (into) to cut sth into pieces using a tool with a long blade and sharp points along one edge (a **saw**): *All the trees were sawn up into logs.*
◈ v + adv + n ◆ v + n/pron + adv

scale /skeɪl/

,scale sth '**down** (*AmE also* ,scale sth '**back**) to reduce sth in size or importance: *The company has scaled down its training programmes this year.* ◇ *Police are scaling down the search for the attacker.* ◇ *Jonnie's tools were a scaled-down version of his father's.*
[OBJ] **programme, project** [OPP] **scale sth up** (*less frequent*)
◈ v + adv + n ◆ v + n/pron + adv

,scale sth '**up** to increase the size or importance of sth: *We're deciding how to scale up our operation.*
[OPP] **scale sth down**
◈ v + adv + n ◆ v + n/pron + adv

scare /skeə(r); *AmE* sker/

,scare sb/sth a'**way**/'**off** to make sb/sth leave or stay away by frightening them: *She used a whistle to scare away her attacker.* ◇ *The noise scared the birds off.*
[SYN] **frighten sb/sth away/off** (*especially BrE*)
◈ v + adv + n ◆ v + n/pron + adv

,scare sb **into** sth; ,scare sb '**into doing sth** to make sb do sth by frightening them: *He was scared into signing a confession.* ◇ *Her threats finally scared him into action.*
◈ v + n/pron + prep

,scare sb '**off** to accidentally make sb afraid of or nervous about sth they were planning to do: *Many investors were scared off by the rumours.* ◇ *Don't act too interested or you'll scare him off* (= a boyfriend).
[SYN] **frighten sb off** (*especially BrE*)
◈ v + n/pron + adv ◆ v + adv + n

,scare sb/sth '**off** = SCARE SB/STH AWAY/OFF

,scare '**up** sth; ,scare it, him, etc. '**up** (*AmE, informal*) to find sb/sth or to make sth by using whatever is available: *I'll see if I can scare up enough chairs for us all.* ◇ *I'll try to scare up some friends to come and help us.*
[NOTE] A noun must always follow **up**, but a pronoun comes between the verb and **up**.
◈ v + adv + n ◆ v + pron + adv (*less frequent*)

scoop /skuːp/

,scoop sth '**out 1** (*also* ,scoop sth '**out of** sth) to remove sth from the inside of sth else using a curved tool, such as a spoon, or your hand: *Scoop all the seeds out of the fruit.* [OBJ] **seeds, flesh 2** to make sth hollow by removing the inside with a curved tool such as a spoon: *First scoop out the melon using a spoon.* [SYN] **hollow sth out**
◈ **1** v + n/pron + adv ◆ v + adv + n ◆ v + n/pron + adv + prep
2 v + adv + n ◆ v + n/pron + adv

,scoop sb/sth '**up** to move or lift sb/sth using a quick continuous movement: *I scooped up a handful of sweets.* ◇ *She scooped the baby up into her arms.*
◈ v + adv + n ◆ v + n/pron + adv

,scoop '**up** to win or get sth easily, especially a large sum of money or a prize: *The Democrat party scooped up four fifths of the seats.*
[OBJ] **seats, prizes**
[NOTE] Scoop sth can also be used with the same meaning: *The movie scooped nine Oscars.*
◈ v + adv + n ◆ v + n/pron + adv

scoot /skuːt/

,scoot '**over** (*AmE, informal*) to move along on a seat to make room for another person: *Scoot over and make room for your sister.* ◇ (*figurative*) *Scoot over, men! Women golfers are on the increase.*
[SYN] **move over**
◈ v + adv

scope /skəʊp; *AmE* skoʊp/

,scope sb/sth '**out** (*AmE, informal*) to look for sb/sth interesting or attractive; to search out sb/sth: *We scoped out a place to spend the weekend.*
◈ v + adv + n ◆ v + n/pron + adv

score /skɔː(r)/

'score off sb (*especially BrE*) to show that you are better than sb, especially by making clever remarks, for example in an argument: *He's always trying to score off his colleagues.*
◈ v + prep

,score sth '**out**/'**through** (*BrE*) to draw a line or lines through sth in a text to show that you do not

want it: *The last paragraph had been scored out.*
◇ *He neatly scored through the word 'impossible'.*
$\overline{\text{SYN}}$ **cross sth out/through; delete sth**
⊕ v + adv + n ◆ v + n + adv (*rare*)

scout /skaʊt/

,scout a'round; ,scout a'round sth (*BrE also*
,scout 'round, ,scout 'round sth) (for sb/sth) to
search an area or different places to try to find
sb/sth: *I'll go and scout around for some water.*
⊕ v + adv ◆ v + prep

,scout sth 'out to find out what sth is like or
where sth is, by searching: *A team travelled to
Moscow to scout out possible places for a meeting.*
◇ *The company is scouting out business opportunities in Vietnam.*
⊕ v + adv + n ◆ v + n/pron + adv

scrabble /'skræbl/

,scrabble a'round (*BrE also* ,scrabble a'bout,
,scrabble 'round) (for sth) to use your fingers to
search for sth quickly or with difficulty: *She
scrabbled around in her bag for her glasses.*
⊕ v + adv

,scrabble at sth to scratch at sth with small,
hurried movements: *She was scrabbling at the
earth with her fingers.*
⊕ v + prep

scrape /skreɪp/

,scrape 'by (on sth) to manage to live on the
money you have, although you do not have much:
I can just scrape by on what my parents give me.
⊕ v + adv

,scrape 'in; ,scrape 'into sth (*BrE*) to manage
to get a job, a position, a place at college, etc., but
with difficulty: *I just managed to scrape into university.* ◇ *He scraped in with 180 votes.* ◇ *Our team
just scraped into the semi-finals.*
⊕ v + adv ◆ v + prep

,scrape sth 'off; ,scrape sth 'off sth to
remove sth from a surface by moving sth sharp
and hard like a knife across it: *He spent all day
scraping paint off the walls.*
⊕ v + n/pron + adv ◆ v + adv + n ◆ v + n/pron + prep

,scrape sth 'out 1 (*also* ,scrape sth 'out of sth)
to remove sth from the inside of sth else using
sth sharp and hard like a knife: *I scraped all the
seeds out of the melon.* ◇ *He scraped out the bowl*
(= removed everything from it) *with a teaspoon.* **2**
(*AmE*) to just manage to make enough money to
live: *He scraped out a living by drawing car-
toons for local newspapers.* $\overline{\text{OBJ}}$ **living, existence**
⊕ v + adv + n ◆ v + n/pron + adv
    1 also v + n/pron + adv + prep

,scrape 'through; ,scrape 'through sth to
succeed with difficulty in doing sth, especially in
passing an exam: *I might scrape through* (*the
exam*) *if I'm lucky.* ◇ *She just scraped through
law school.*
$\overline{\text{OBJ}}$ **exam**
⊕ v + adv ◆ v + prep

,scrape sth to'gether (*also* ,scrape sth 'up *less
frequent*) to obtain or collect sth such as an
amount of money with difficulty: *They managed
to scrape together $1 200 and printed 3 000 copies of
the comic.* ◇ *We **scraped up enough money** to
buy a small car.*
⊕ v + adv + n ◆ v + n/pron + adv

scratch /skrætʃ/

,scratch a'round (*BrE also* ,scratch a'bout) (for
sth) to search for sth in a way that is not very
organized, by looking at different things, looking on the ground, etc: *He was scratching around
on the ground for clues.*
⊕ v + adv

,scratch sth 'off; ,scratch sth 'off sth to
remove sth from a surface by rubbing with your
nails, etc: *She scratched the paint off to see what
was underneath.*
⊕ v + n/pron + adv ◆ v + adv + n ◆ v + n/pron + prep

,scratch sth 'out to remove a word, especially a
name, from sth written, usually by putting a line
through it: *Their names had been scratched out.*
⊕ v + n/pron + adv ◆ v + adv + n

scream /skri:m/

,scream 'out (for sth) to be very obvious or
noticeable; to demand attention: *The mistakes
just scream out at you.* ◇ *The cake was screaming
out to be eaten.*
⊕ v + adv

screen /skri:n/

,screen sth 'off to separate or hide an area of a
room etc. from another area by putting a tal
piece of furniture or equipment in front of it o
around it: *Part of the room had been screened of
with a curtain.*
$\overline{\text{NOTE}}$ **Screen sth off** is often used in the passive.
⊕ v + adv + n ◆ v + n/pron + adv

,screen sb/sth 'out to decide not to includ
sb/sth, or not to allow sb to join an organizatio
enter a country, etc. because you think they ma
not be suitable or may cause trouble: *Unsuitabl
candidates were screened out.* ◇ *His job is t
screen out inquiries unlikely to result in a sale.*
*Insurance companies often screen out people wh
are high risk.*
⊕ v + adv + n ◆ v + n + adv (*less frequent*) ◆
    v + pron + adv

,screen sth 'out to prevent sth harmful from entering or going through sth: *It is essential to screen out ultraviolet rays.* ◊ *A window blind will screen out too much light.*
◈ v + adv + n ◆ v + n + adv (*less frequent*) ◆ v + pron + adv

screw /skruː/

,screw a'round (△, *slang*) **1** to have sex with a lot of different people NOTE A more polite, informal way to say this is **sleep around**. **2** (*AmE*) to waste time doing silly or useless activities: *Stop screwing around and do some work!* NOTE A more polite, informal way to say this is **mess around**, or, in British English, **mess about**.
◈ v + adv

,screw sb a'round (*BrE*, △, *slang*) to treat sb in a way that is deliberately not helpful to them or wastes their time: *Stop screwing me around and tell me the truth!* NOTE A more polite, informal way of saying this is **mess sb about/around** (*BrE*).
◈ v + n/pron + adv

,screw sth 'down to attach sth firmly to sth else using screws: *Screw the lid of the box down securely.*
◈ v + n/pron + adv ◆ v + adv + n

,screw sth 'on; **,screw sth 'onto sth** to fasten the top on a container by twisting it around: *Is the top screwed on tightly?*
OBJ lid, top
◈ v + n/pron + adv ◆ v + adv + n ◆ v + n/pron + prep
IDM **have your head screwed on (right/the right way)** (*informal*) to be a sensible person

,screw sb 'out of sth (*slang*) to cheat sb and prevent them from having sth that they should have: *She tried to screw him out of his winnings.* NOTE A more polite way to say this is **cheat sb out of sth**.
◈ v + n/pron + adv + prep

,screw sth 'out of sb (*slang*) to force sb to give you sth; to get sth from sb with great difficulty: *They screwed the money out of her by threatening to hit her.*
◈ v + n/pron + adv + prep

screw sb 'over (*AmE*, △, *slang*) to trick sb in order to obtain sth valuable from them; to treat sb badly, especially by deceiving them: *He screwed her over and took all her money.*
◈ v + n/pron + adv ◆ v + adv + n

screw 'up; **,screw sth 'up** (*slang, especially AmE*) to do sth badly or spoil sth: *I was trying to be helpful, but I screwed up again.* ◊ *She screwed up all the arrangements.*
SYN **mess up, mess sth up**
◈ v + adv ◆ v + adv + n ◆ v + n/pron + adv
▶ **'screw-up** n (*slang, especially AmE*) a situation that has been dealt with very badly; a bad mistake: *There was a screw-up over the bookings.*

,screw sb 'up (*slang*) to make sb so upset or confused that they are unable to deal with problems in life: *Her parents have really screwed her up.*
SYN **mess sb up**
◈ v + n/pron + adv ◆ v + adv + n
▶ **,screwed-'up** adj (*informal*) upset and anxious, especially because of sth bad that has happened to you in the past: *a screwed-up kid*
→ see also SCREWED-UP at SCREW STH UP

,screw sth 'up 1 (*BrE*) to squeeze sth into a tight ball: *She screwed up the note and threw it away.*
OBJ **paper, letter** SYN **scrunch sth up 2** if you **screw up** your eyes or your face, you tighten the muscles because you are in pain, the light is too bright, etc: *He screwed up his face in disgust.* OBJ **face, eyes**
◈ v + adv + n ◆ v + n/pron + adv
IDM **screw up your 'courage** (*especially BrE*) to force yourself to be brave enough to do sth: *I finally screwed up my courage and went to the dentist.*
▶ **,screwed-'up** adj (*BrE*) squeezed and twisted into a ball: *a screwed-up sheet of paper*
→ see also SCREWED-UP at SCREW SB UP

scribble /'skrɪbl/

,scribble sth 'down to write sth quickly and carelessly: *She scribbled down the directions on her pad.*
◈ v + adv + n ◆ v + n/pron + adv

scroll /skrəʊl; AmE skroʊl/

,scroll 'down/'up (*computing*) to move down/up or backwards/forwards in the text on a computer screen so that you can read different parts of it: *She scrolled down to the end of the document.*
◈ v + adv

scrounge /skraʊndʒ/

,scrounge a'round (for sth) (*AmE, informal*) to search around in different places for sth, especially if it is difficult to find or there is not much available: *He scrounged around in his desk drawer for a paper clip.*
◈ v + adv

scrub /skrʌb/ (-bb-)

scrub 'in (*AmE*) = SCRUB UP

,scrub sth 'off; **,scrub sth 'off sth** to remove sth from the surface of sth by rubbing it hard with a brush, etc: *Scrub all that mud off the walls.*
◈ v + n/pron + adv ◆ v + adv + n ◆ v + n/pron + prep

,scrub sth 'out to clean the inside of sth by rubbing it hard with a brush and usually with soap and water: *He scrubbed out the pans and left them to drain.* ◊ *The cupboards are scrubbed out every week.*
◈ v + adv + n ◆ v + n/pron + adv

,scrub 'up (*especially BrE*) (*AmE usually* **,scrub 'in**) (of a doctor, nurse, etc.) to wash your hands and arms very thoroughly before performing a medical operation: *The surgeon scrubbed up and put on his gloves.* ◇ *He asked to scrub in for surgery.*
◈ v + adv
IDM **scrub 'up well** if sb/sth **scrubs up well**, they look very attractive when they are clean and tidy

scrunch /skrʌntʃ/

,scrunch sth 'up (*informal*) **1** to squeeze sth into a small round shape in your hands: *He scrunched up the piece of paper and threw it at me.* **OBJ paper, letter 2** to twist your face or part of it into a different shape: *He scrunched up his face, trying to concentrate.* **OBJ face, eyes**
◈ v + adv + n ◆ v + n/pron + adv

seal /siːl/

,seal sth 'in to keep sth inside a container so that none of it can escape: *The foil packet seals in the flavour.*
◈ v + adv + n ◆ v + n/pron + adv

,seal sth 'off if the police, the army, etc. **seal** a place or an area **off**, they put barriers there to prevent anyone from entering it: *The police have sealed off the town centre.* ◇ *Seal off all the exits!* **OBJ area, road, building**
◈ v + adv + n ◆ v + n + adv (*less frequent*) ◆ v + pron + adv

,seal sth 'up 1 to close an envelope, etc. by sticking the edges of the opening together: *He sealed up the envelope and wrote the address on it.* **2** to close sth completely so that nothing can get in or out: *I sealed up the windows to keep out the fumes.* **NOTE** Seal sth is used more frequently with these meanings.
◈ v + adv + n ◆ v + n/pron + adv

search /sɜːtʃ; AmE sɜːrtʃ/

,search sb/sth 'out to look for sb/sth until you find them: *He's searching out some old pictures to show us.* ◇ *She wanted to search out her real parents.* ◇ *John searched me out and gave me a note.* **SYN seek sb/sth out**
◈ v + adv + n ◆ v + n + adv (*less frequent*) ◆ v + pron + adv

see /siː/ (saw /sɔː/ seen /siːn/)

,see a'bout sth; ,see a'bout doing sth to deal with sth; to make arrangements for sth to be done: *I'll go and see about lunch.* ◇ *I must see about getting someone to help you with the kids.*
◈ v + prep

,see sb 'in; ,see sb 'into sth to go with sb into a room, building, etc. to make sure that they get there safely: *After seeing her in (= into her home), he rode off without a word.*

NOTE See sb out, see sb out of sth are used much more often than these verbs.
→ *see also* SEE SB/OUT, SEE SB/YOURSELF OUT OF STH
◈ v + n/pron + adv ◆ v + n/pron + prep

,see sth 'in if you **see in** an occasion such as New Year, you are there when it happens: *They saw in the New Year with friends.* ◇ *He lived long enough to see in the new millennium.* **OBJ New Year**
◈ v + adv + n ◆ v + n/pron + adv

,see sth in sb/sth to believe that sb/sth has a particular quality or characteristic, especially a good one: *I don't know what she sees in him* (= I can't understand why she likes him or finds him attractive). ◇ *He sees good in everyone.* ◇ *I can see value in each argument.*
◈ v + n/pron + prep

,see sb/sth 'off 1 to go to a station, an airport, etc. to say goodbye to sb who is going on a journey: *We all went to the airport to see her off.* **2** (*BrE*) to force sb to leave a place, for example by chasing them: *The dogs soon saw off the burglars.* **3** to defeat sb: *She saw off her opponent and now goes into the final.*
◈ v + n/pron + adv ◆ v + adv + n

,see sth 'off (*BrE*) to be strong enough to resist sth: *The company saw off the threat of a takeover.*
◈ v + adv + n ◆ v + n/pron + adv

,see sb/yourself 'out; ,see sb/yourself 'out of sth to go with sb out of a building, etc. to make sure that they find the way: *Jay saw the last guests out and locked the door.* ◇ *Don't get up. I'll see myself out.* → *see also* SEE SB IN, SEE SB INTO STH
◈ v + n/pron + adv ◆ v + adv + n ◆ v + n/pron + adv + prep

,see sth 'out (*not used in the progressive tenses*) **1** to stay in the same place, do the same things, or survive, until the end of sth: *She promised to see out the rest of her contract.* **2** to last until the end of sth: *We have enough fuel to see the winter out.* **NOTE** See sth out is not used in the passive.
◈ v + adv + n ◆ v + n/pron + adv

,see 'over/'round sth (*BrE*) to visit and look at a place carefully: *We'd like to see over the flat again before we rent it.* **SYN look over sth; look around sth**
◈ v + prep

,see 'through sb/sth (*not used in the progressive tenses*) to realize the truth about sb/sth so that you are not deceived: *We saw through him straight away.* ◇ *I can see through your little game* (= trick).
◈ v + prep

,see sb 'through; ,see sb 'through sth to give sb support to enable them to survive a difficult experience or a particular period of time: *His courage and good humour saw him through*

◇ *She saw him through the months after his accident.* ◇ *I only have $20 to see me through the week.*
✦ v + n/pron + adv ◆ v + n/pron + prep

,see sth 'through (*not usually used in the progressive tenses*) to not give up a task, project, etc. until it is completed: *She's determined to see the job through.*
[OBJ] **project, job**
✦ v + n/pron + adv

'see to sb/sth to deal with sb/sth that needs attention: *I'll see to the kids.* ◇ *Lin was great and saw to everything.* ◇ *Don't worry, I'll see to it!*
[SYN] **attend to sb/sth** (*formal*)
[NOTE] See to sth can be used in the passive: *We must get that door seen to.*
✦ v + prep

'see to it that... to make sure that sth happens: *Can you see to it that everyone knows the date of the meeting?*
✦ v + prep

seek /siːk/ (**sought, sought** /sɔːt/)

,seek sb/sth 'out to look for and find sb/sth, especially when this means using a lot of effort: *He sought her out to ask her advice.* ◇ *She's always seeking out new business opportunities.*
[OBJ] **opportunities, information**
[SYN] **track sb/sth down** (*less formal*)
✦ v + adv + n ◆ v + n/pron + adv

seep /siːp/

,seep a'way to flow away slowly and in small quantities: *Water had been slowly seeping away from the pond.* ◇ (*figurative*) *My anger began to seep away.*
✦ v + adv

segue /'segweɪ/

,segue 'into sth to move smoothly from one song, subject, place, etc. to another: *a spiritual that segued into a singalong chorus* ◇ *He then segued into a discussion of children's rights.*
✦ v + prep

seize /siːz/

'seize on sth (*also* 'seize upon sth *more formal*) to suddenly show a lot of interest in sth, especially because you can use it to your advantage: *The scandal was immediately seized upon by the press.* ◇ *Peter seized eagerly on all opportunities for conversation.*
[SYN] **pounce on sth**
[NOTE] Seize on/upon sth can be used in the passive.
✦ v + prep

,seize 'up 1 if a machine or a part of a machine seizes up, it stops moving or working correctly: *The engine seized up after only three weeks.* ◇

(*figurative*) *The whole city seized up* (= no traffic, etc. was able to move) *during the blizzard.* 2 if a part of your body seizes up, it becomes stiff and you are unable to move it easily: *My legs were beginning to seize up and I needed a rest.*
✦ v + adv

sell /sel/ (**sold, sold** /səʊld; *AmE* soʊld/)

,sell sth 'off 1 to sell all or part of an industry, a company or a piece of land: *Unwanted land next to the farm was sold off.* ◇ *The government decided to sell off state companies.* [OBJ] **assets, land, business, company** 2 to sell things cheaply because you no longer want them or because you need the money: *The store is selling off the old stock.* ◇ *The family silver was sold off to pay the debts.*
✦ v + adv + n ◆ v + n/pron + adv
▸ 'sell-off *n* (*BrE*) 1 the sale by the government of an industry or a service to individual people or private companies: *the proposed sell-off of the rail company* ◇ *sell-off plans* 2 (*AmE, business*) the sale of a large number of shares in a company, after which their value usually falls

,sell sth 'on (to sb) to sell sth to sb else that you have bought not long before, usually in order to make a profit: *She managed the business for a year and then sold it on.*
✦ v + n/pron + adv ◆ v + adv + n

be 'sold on sth (*informal*) to be convinced that sth is very good: *I could see she was sold on the idea.* ◇ *I'm not really sold on American music.*
[OBJ] **idea**
✦ be + v + prep

,sell 'out; be ,sold 'out 1 if tickets for a concert, a game, etc. sell out or are sold out, they are all sold and there are none left: *The tickets for the game will sell out quickly.* ◇ *Tonight's performance is completely sold out.* ◇ *The first 5 000 copies of the book have sold out.* 2 (*also* ,sell 'out of sth, be ,sold 'out of sth) if sb sells out of sth or is sold out of sth, they have sold all of it and have nothing left: *I'm sorry, we've sold out of milk.* ◇ *We are already sold out for tonight's concert.*
✦ v + adv ◆ be + v + adv
2 *also* v + adv + prep ◆ be + v + adv + prep
▸ 'sell-out *n* [usually sing.] a play, concert, etc. for which all the tickets have been sold: *The gig is a sell-out.* ◇ *a sell-out tour/crowd*
→ *see also* SELL-OUT at SELL OUT (TO SB/STH)

,sell 'out (to sb/sth) (*disapproving*) 1 to ignore or change your principles or beliefs, especially to gain an advantage for yourself: *The rest of the gang accused him of selling out to the law.* ◇ *a talented British movie director who's sold out to Hollywood* 2 to sell your business or a part of your business: *The company sold out to its rival.*
✦ v + adv

▸ **'sell-out** *n* [usually sing.] a situation in which sb betrays sb who trusted them, by not doing sth that they promised to do, or by doing sth that they promised not to do: *a dreadful sell-out of their cause* ◇ *The deal was seen as a union sell-out to management.*
→ *see also* SELL-OUT at SELL OUT, BE SOLD OUT

,sell sb/sth 'out (to sb/sth) to betray sb: *They discovered who had sold them out to the enemy.*
   ⊕ v + n/pron + adv ◆ v + adv + n

,sell 'out of sth; be ,sold 'out of sth = SELL OUT; BE SOLD OUT 2

,sell 'up; ,sell sth 'up to sell your home, possessions, business, etc., usually because you need the money, are moving to another place or stopping work: *They sold up and moved to France.* ◇ *We decided to sell up everything and buy a farm.*
   ⊕ v + adv ◆ v + adv + n ◆ v + pron + adv

send /send/ (**sent, sent** /sent/)

,send sb/sth a'head to arrange for sb/sth to go or be taken to the place you are going to, before you arrive there: *The rest of the equipment was sent ahead by air.*
   ⊕ v + n/pron + adv

,send a'way (for sth) = SEND OFF (FOR STH)

,send sb a'way 1 to tell sb to leave: *The reporters were sent away empty-handed* (= without any news). **2 (to…)** to arrange for sb to go somewhere away from home: *He was sent away to boarding school at the age of 7.*
   ⊕ v + n/pron + adv ◆ v + adv + n (*less frequent*)

,send sb/sth 'back (to sb/sth) to return sb/sth to where they/it came from: *The refugees were sent back to their own country.* ◇ *You can send the goods back if you're not satisfied.*
   ⟨SYN⟩ **return sb/sth (to sb/sth)** (*more formal*)
   ⊕ v + n/pron + adv ◆ v + adv + n

,send sb 'down (*BrE*) **1** (*informal*) to send sb to prison: *He was sent down for ten years.* ⟨SYN⟩ **put sb away 2** (*old-fashioned*) to make a student leave a university, especially Oxford or Cambridge, because of bad behaviour: *She was sent down from Oxford.* ⟨SYN⟩ **expel sb**
   ⟨NOTE⟩ Send sb down is often used in the passive.
   ⊕ v + n/pron + adv ◆ v + adv + n

'send for sb to send a message to sb to ask them to come and see you, especially in order to help you: *Send for a doctor.*
   ⟨OBJ⟩ **doctor, police** ⟨SYN⟩ **call sb in**
   ⟨NOTE⟩ Send for sb can be used in the passive: *Has the doctor been sent for?*
   ⊕ v + prep

'send for sth to ask sb to bring or deliver sth to you: *Send for an ambulance.* ◇ *Have you sent for a catalogue* (= by post/mail)*?*
   ⟨NOTE⟩ Send for sth can be used in the passive: *More equipment has been sent for.*
   ⊕ v + prep

,send sb 'in 1 to order sb to go to a place to deal with a difficult situation: *Troops were sent in to restore order.* ⟨OBJ⟩ **troops, police, army 2** to tell sb to go into a room, where sb else is waiting to see them: *Send the next candidate in, please.*
   ⊕ v + n/pron + adv ◆ v + adv + n

,send sth 'in to send sth by post/mail to a place where it will be dealt with: *500 schools sent in entries for the competition.* ◇ *Viewers are invited to send in their suggestions for the programme.*
   ⊕ v + n/pron + adv ◆ v + adv + n

,send 'off (*also* ,**send a'way** *especially AmE*) (**for sth**) to write to sb and ask them to send you sth by post/mail: *If you save enough packets, you can send off and get a free toy.* ◇ *You can send off for a free booklet.*
   ⟨SYN⟩ **write away/off (to sb) (for sth)**
   ⊕ v + adv

,send sb 'off 1 (for sth) (*BrE*) (in a sports game) to make sb leave the field because they have broken the rules of the game: *He was sent off for a foul.* ◇ *Three players got sent off in the first half.* ⟨OBJ⟩ **player** ⟨NOTE⟩ In this meaning **send sb off** is often used in the passive. **2 (to …)** to ask or tell sb to go somewhere: *The bank sent him off for four months study at Harvard.* ◇ *I always send the kids off to school looking clean and tidy.* ◇ *The men were sent off to find water.*
   ⊕ **1** v + n/pron + adv ◆ v + adv + n
     2 v + n/pron + adv

▸ **,sending-'off** *n* (*BrE*) (in a sports game) a situation when a player is told to leave the field because they have broken the rules: *It's his third sending-off this year.* ◇ *The match saw three penalties and two sendings-off.*

▸ **'send-off** *n* (*informal*) an occasion when people come together to say goodbye to sb who is leaving: *She was given a good send-off by all her colleagues.*

,send sth 'off (to sb) to send sth by post/mail: *Have you sent that letter off yet?*
   ⟨OBJ⟩ **letter, parcel** ⟨SYN⟩ **mail sth off (to sb)** (*AmE*), **post sth off (to sb)** (*BrE*)
   ⊕ v + n/pron + adv ◆ v + adv + n

,send sth 'on 1 (to…) to send a letter, etc. that has arrived at sb's old address to their new one: *I've asked a neighbour to send on any important letters.* ⟨OBJ⟩ **letter** ⟨SYN⟩ **forward sth (to sb/sth)** (*more formal*) **2 (to sb/sth)** to send sth you have received to sb else for them to see or deal with: *I'll send the photos on to you.* **3** to send sth to a place so that it arrives before you get there: *We sent our furniture on by ship.* ◇ *We've arranged for your belongings to be sent on.*
   ⊕ v + n/pron + adv ◆ v + adv + n

,send sb 'out to send sb somewhere for a particular purpose: *I'll ask them to send someone out straightaway to fix the car.* ◇ *If I'm not back by midnight, send out a search party!*
   ⊕ v + n/pron + adv ◆ v + adv + n

,send sth 'out 1 to send sth to a lot of different people or places: *I sent out fifty invitations.* ◇ *Have we sent letters out to all the applicants?* OBJ **letter, information** SYN **mail sth out 2** to produce sth, such as light, a signal, sound, etc: *a fire sending out waves of warmth* ◇ *His brain was sending out warning signals telling him to be careful.* OBJ **signal** SYN **emit sth** (*more formal*)
◈ v + n/pron + adv ◆ v + adv + n

,send 'out for sth to ask a restaurant or shop/store to deliver food to you at home or at work: *We could send out for a takeaway.*
◈ v + adv + prep

,send sb/sth 'up (*BrE, informal*) to make people laugh, especially by copying them/it in an amusing way: *a TV programme that sends up politicians* ◇ *Everyone was sending her up.* ◇ *The teacher heard me sending up her accent.*
◈ v + adv + n ◆ v + pron + adv ◆ v + n + adv (*rare*)
▸ **'send-up** n (*BrE, informal*) an act of making sb/sth look silly by copying them in an amusing way: *The movie is a hilarious send-up of the Hollywood western.*

separate /'sepəreɪt/

,separate sth 'off (**from sth**) to remove sth from a larger thing or group; to keep sth apart: *The property agency has been separated off from the main business.*
◈ v + adv + n ◆ v + pron + adv ◆ v + n + adv (*rare*)

,separate 'out; ,separate sb/sth 'out (**from sth**) to divide into different parts; to divide sb/sth into different parts or groups: *The mixture separates out into layers.* ◇ *Plastics must be separated out into different types for recycling.* ◇ *We need to separate out fact from speculation.* ◇ *The process separates out the different gases.*
NOTE **Separate** and **separate sb/sth** can also be used with this meaning.
◈ v + adv + n ◆ v + pron + adv ◆ v + n + adv (*rare*)

serve /sɜːv; AmE sɜːrv/

'serve as/for sth to be used instead of sth else when there is nothing better available: *An old box served as a table.* ◇ *Small temporary buildings had to serve for offices.*
SYN **act as sth**
◈ v + prep

'serve sth on sb (*also* **'serve sth upon sb** *more formal*) **'serve sb with sth** (*law*) to give or send sb an official document, especially one that orders them to appear in a court of law: *The police have served a summons on Mr Jackson.* ◇ *The police have served him with a summons.*
OBJ **summons, notice, writ**
◈ v + n/pron + prep

,serve sth 'out 1 to continue doing sth until the end of a fixed period of time: *She served out the rest of her sentence in an open prison.* OBJ **notice,**

sentence, term NOTE In this meaning **serve sth out** cannot be used in the passive. **2** (*especially BrE*) = SERVE STH UP
◈ v + adv + n ◆ v + pron + adv ◆ v + n + adv (*rare*)

,serve sth 'up 1 (*also* **,serve sth 'out** *especially BrE*) to put food onto plates and give it to people: *He served up a delicious meal.* SYN **dish sth out**; **dish up, dish sth up 2** (*disapproving*) to give or offer sth: *All the TV channels served up the usual old movies during the holidays.*
◈ v + n/pron + adv ◆ v + adv + n

,serve sth u'pon sb = SERVE STH ON SB, SERVE SB WITH STH

'serve sb with sth = SERVE STH ON SB, SERVE SB WITH STH

set /set/ (setting, set, set)

~ about		~ in/into
~ against	255	~ off
254 ~ ahead		~ off against
~ apart		~ on
~ aside		~ out
~ back		~ to
~ down		~ up
~ forth	256	~ up as
~ in		~ upon

'set about sb (**with sth**) (*BrE, old-fashioned*) to attack sb: *He set about me with a stick.*
◈ v + prep

'set about sth; 'set about doing sth 1 to begin a task or an activity, especially with energy or enthusiasm: *We set about the task of cleaning the apartment.* **2** to approach a problem or task in a particular way: *You've set about this problem the wrong way.* ◇ *How should I set about finding a job?* SYN **go about sth, go about doing sth**
◈ v + prep

'set sb a'gainst sb to make sb oppose a friend, relative, etc: *The civil war set brother against brother.*
◈ v + n/pron + prep

,set sth a'gainst sth 1 to consider sth by comparing good points with bad ones: *Set against the benefits of the new technology is the possibility that jobs will be lost.* SYN **balance A against B 2** (*also* **'set sth 'off against sth**) (*finance*) to record sth as a business cost as a way of reducing the amount of tax you must pay: *The cost of looking for oil can be set against tax as business expenditure.* **3 be set against sth** if sth is **set against** sth else, it is placed near it or next to it so that the difference between the two is very noticeable: *views of rocky islands set against fiery sunsets* ◇ *Set against her white dress, her hair seemed even darker.* **4 be set against sth** if a story, a film/movie, etc. is **set against** a particular time, event or place, the action happens at that time or place: *It is a love story set against a backdrop of rural Irish life.*

NOTE In meanings 3 and 4 **set sth against sth** is only used in the passive.

◆ **1,2** v + n/pron + prep
   3,4 be + v + prep

,set sth a'head (*AmE*) to change a clock or watch to show the correct later time: *Don't forget to set your clocks ahead tonight* (= because the time has officially changed).

OBJ clock, watch **SYN** **put sth forward** (*BrE*)
OPP **set sth back** (*AmE*), **put sth back** (*BrE*)
◆ v + n/pron + adv

,set sb/sth a'part (from sb/sth) to make sb/sth different from or better than others: *His confidence sets him apart from his classmates.* ◇ *It's the service at the restaurant that sets it apart.*
◆ v + n/pron + adv ◆ v + adv + n (*less frequent*)

,set sth a'part (*BrE*) (*also* ,set sth a'side *AmE*, *BrE*) to keep sth such as money or time for a special use or purpose: *A room was set apart for quiet reading.*
◆ v + adv + n ◆ v + pron + adv ◆ v + n + adv (*less frequent*)

,set sth a'side 1 to place sth to one side: *I set her letter aside, meaning to read it later.* **SYN** **put sth aside 2** to save or keep sth for a particular purpose: *She sets aside £50 every month for her daughter's college fees.* ◇ *We need to set aside some time to deal with this.* **OBJ** money, time **SYN** **put sth aside 3** to ignore sth such as your feelings or opinions, because other things are important: *We decided to set our differences aside.* ◇ *Let's set aside my personal feelings for now.* **SYN** **put sth aside 4** = SET STH APART *Restaurants must set aside an area for non-smokers.* **OBJ** area, room **SYN** **put sth aside 5** (*law*) to reject a previous decision made by a court of law: *The verdict was set aside by the Appeal Court.* **OBJ** decision, conviction **SYN** **overturn sth** (*more formal*)
◆ v + adv + n ◆ v + n/pron + adv
▸ **'set-aside** n [U] a system in which the government pays farmers not to use some of their land for growing crops; the land that the farmers are paid not to use: *750 acres of set-aside*

,set sb 'back sth (*informal*) to cost sb a large amount of money: *That new car must have set her back a bit.* ◇ *This watch set me back £200.*
SYN **knock sb back sth** (*BrE, informal*)
NOTE Set sb back sth cannot be used in the passive.
◆ v + n/pron + adv + n

,set sb/sth 'back to delay the progress of sb/sth: *The rain set the building programme back by several weeks.* ◇ *He was starting to play very well, but his injury has really set him back.*
◆ v + n/pron + adv ◆ v + adv + n

▸ **'setback** n a problem or difficulty that delays the progress of sb/sth: *Parry's broken ankle was a major setback for the team.*

,set sth 'back (*AmE*) to change a clock or watch to show the correct earlier time: *I forgot to set my watch back last night* (= when the time officially changed).

OBJ clock, watch **SYN** **put sth back** (*BrE*)
OPP **put sth forward** (*BrE*), **set sth ahead** (*AmE*)
◆ v + n/pron + adv

be ,set 'back (from sth) if a building is **set back**, it is a long way from sth, especially a road: *Their house is the only one that's set back (from the road).*
◆ be + v + adv

,set 'down; **,set sth 'down** (of a plane, a pilot, passengers, etc.) to land: *We set down on the beach.* ◇ *The pilot tried to set the plane down in a field.*
SYN **put down** (*especially BrE*), **land**, **land sth**
◆ v + adv ◆ v + n/pron + adv ◆ v + adv + n

,set sb 'down (*BrE*) (of a vehicle or its driver) to stop and allow sb to get off/out: *The taxi set me down at the end of the road.*
SYN **drop sb/sth off** **OPP** **pick sb up**
◆ v + n/pron + adv ◆ v + adv + n

,set sth 'down 1 (on sth) (*literary*) to place an object down on a surface: *He set his glass down before he spoke.* ◇ *She made space so that I could set the tray down on the table.* **SYN** **put sth down 2** to write sth down on paper in order to record it: *I wanted to set my thoughts down on paper.* ◇ *It's a good idea to set down your complaint in writing.* **SYN** **put sth down 3** to give sth as a rule, etc: *to set down guidelines/rules* ◇ *qualifying standards set down by the Athletics Association*
◆ **1,2** v + n/pron + adv ◆ v + adv + n
   3 v + adv + n ◆ v + pron + adv ◆ v + n + adv (*rare*)

,set 'forth (*literary*) to start a journey: *They set forth for Crete.*
SYN **set out** (*less formal*)
◆ v + adv

,set 'forth sth; **,set it/them 'forth** (*formal*) to state sth clearly; to make sth known: *The President set forth his views in a long television broadcast.*
NOTE This phrasal verb can be used in the passive: *Her beliefs have been clearly set forth.* ◆ A noun must always follow **forth**, but a pronoun comes between the verb and **forth**.
◆ v + adv + n ◆ v + pron + adv

,set 'in if bad weather, an unpleasant feeling, an illness, etc. **sets in**, it begins and seems likely to continue: *I need to mend the roof before winter sets in.* ◇ *Panic set in when she realized how much work there was to do.* ◇ *He eventually agreed to stay in bed, but it was too late — pneumonia had set in.* **SUBJ** panic, winter
◆ v + adv

IDM **the 'rot set in** used to describe the fact that a situation has become very bad and will continue like that: *She had problems at her first school, but when she changed schools the rot really set in.*

,set sth 'in/into sth to fix sth in a space so that it does not stick out beyond the surface: *A small safe had been set into the wall.*

NOTE Set sth **in/into sth** is usually used in the passive. ♦ The verb **inset sth** has a similar meaning.

♦ v + n/pron + prep

▶ **'inset** *n* **1** a small picture, map, etc. inside a larger one: *Brad Pitt at the premiere, and his wife (inset)* (= about a photograph in a newspaper) **2** a piece of material, a small stone, etc. that is added on to sth else or put inside sth else: *a silver brooch with ruby insets*

,set 'off to begin a journey: *I set off for work at seven.* ◇ *Check your oil before setting off on a long journey.* ◇ *When are you planning to set off?*

♦ v + adv

,set sb 'off; ,set sb 'off doing sth (*informal, especially BrE*) to make sb start doing sth such as laughing, crying or talking: *Those photos always set her off (crying).* ◇ *Just seeing him laughing sets me off!* (= makes me start laughing)

SYN **start sb off, start sb off doing sth**

♦ v + n/pron + adv

,set sth 'off 1 to make a bomb, etc. explode: *to set off fireworks* ◇ *They set the bomb off as soon as they were a safe distance away.* **OBJ** **bomb, firework 2** to make an alarm (= a loud warning noise or signal) start: *The burglars set the alarm off.* ◇ *If you burn the toast you'll set the smoke alarm off.* **OBJ** **alarm 3** to start a process or series of events: *The news set off a wave of panic on world markets.* ◇ *The girl's death set off a terrible chain of events* → *see also* SET STH UP 4 **4** to make sth appear more attractive by being placed near it: *That scarf sets off the blue of her eyes.*

♦ **1,2** v + n/pron + adv ♦ v + adv + n
3,4 v + n/pron + adv ♦ v + n/pron + adv

,set sth 'off against sth= SET STH AGAINST STH 2
NOTE The verb **offset sth (against sth)** has a similar meaning: *There are certain expenses that you can offset against tax.*

'set on/upon sb (*formal*) to attack sb: *I was set upon by a gang of youths.*

NOTE Set **on/upon sb** is often used in the passive.

♦ v + prep

'set sb/sth on sb to make a person or an animal attack sb: *The farmer threatened to set his dogs on us if we didn't leave at once.*

♦ v + n/pron + prep

,set 'out 1 to leave a place and begin a journey, especially a long journey: *They set out on the last stage of their journey.* ◇ *We set out at dawn.* **2** **,set 'out to do sth** to begin to do sth with a particular

aim or purpose: *She set out to break the world record.* ◇ *They succeeded in what they had set out to do.*

♦ v + adv **2** also v + adv + to inf

▶ **'outset** *n* the beginning of sth: *We knew the danger at/from the outset.*

,set sth 'out 1 to arrange or display sth: *She began setting out plates and glasses.* ◇ *Set out your answers neatly.* **2** to present ideas, facts, etc. in a clear, organized way, in speech or writing: *This document sets out our objections to the proposal.* **OBJ** **terms, reasons, policies, conditions**

♦ **1** v + adv + n ♦ v + n/pron + adv
2 v + adv + n ♦ v + pron + adv ♦ v + n + adv (*rare*)

,set 'to (*old-fashioned, formal, especially BrE*) **1** to begin doing sth in a busy or determined way: *She set to with a scrubbing brush* (= she started cleaning). **2** to begin fighting: *They took off their jackets and set to.*

♦ v + adv

▶ **,set-'to** *n* [sing.] (*informal, especially BrE*) a fight or an argument: *He had a set-to with one of his workmates.*

,set 'up; ,set sth 'up to make a machine, some equipment, etc. ready to use: *He helped me to carry my equipment in and set up.* ◇ *It took hours to set up all the equipment.*

♦ v + adv ♦ v + adv + n ♦ v + n/pron + adv

,set 'up; ,set yourself 'up to start running your own business: *He left the firm and set up in business on his own.* ◇ *She set herself up as a hairdresser.*

♦ v + adv ♦ v + pron + adv

,set sb 'up 1 to provide sb with the money they need, for example to start a business, buy a home, etc: *A bank loan helped to set her up in business.* ◇ *He set his daughter up in her own apartment.* ◇ *If you win tonight's fight, you'll **be set up for life*** (= have all the money you will ever need). **2** (*informal*) to trick sb, especially by making them appear to be guilty of sth that they have not done: *He claimed he had been set up by the police.* **3** (*informal*) to make sb feel healthier, stronger, more active, etc: *A good breakfast will set you up for the day.* **4** (**with sb**) (*informal*) to arrange for sb to meet sb so that they can have a romantic or sexual relationship: *He set me up with his sister.*

♦ v + n/pron + adv ♦ v + adv + n ♦ v + n + adv (*less frequent*)

▶ **'set-up** *n* [usually sing.] (*informal*) **1** a situation in which sb tricks you or makes it seem as if you are guilty of sth that you have not done: *I didn't do it, this is a set-up!* **2** a situation when sb arranges for you to meet sb in order to begin a romantic or sexual relationship: *a set-up date*
→ *see also* SET-UP at SET STH UP

,set sth 'up 1 to create sth or start a business, an organization, etc: *She gave a talk on setting up a business.* ◇ *A committee was set up to investigate* *the problem.* ◇ *young people* setting up home *for the first time* OBJ **business, committee, system, company 2** to build sth or put sth somewhere: *The police set up roadblocks on all main roads.* **3** to organize or arrange sth; to make the arrangements for sth to happen: *to set up a meeting* ◇ *We'll set up the transport arrangements.* OBJ **meeting 4** to start a process or a series of events: *The crisis set up a chain reaction in other European markets.* OBJ **chain reaction, chain of events** → *see also* SET STH OFF 3

◆ v + adv + n ♦ v + n/pron + adv

▸ **'set-up** *n* [usually sing.] (*informal*) the way sth is organized or arranged; a system: *I've only been here a week so I don't really know the set-up.*
→ *see also* SET-UP *at* SET SB UP

,**set yourself 'up** = SET UP, SET YOURSELF UP

,**set yourself 'up as sth** to claim to be very important, know a lot about sth, etc: *He set himself up as an authority on modern art.*

◆ v + pron + adv + prep

'**set upon sb** (*formal*) = SET ON/UPON SB

settle /'setl/

,**settle 'down 1** (*also* ,settle yourself 'down) to get yourself into a comfortable position when you are sitting or lying: *She settled down in an armchair to read.* ◇ *Tom settled himself down at the table.* **2** to start to have a calmer or quieter way of life, without many changes, especially living in one place: *He got married and settled down.* **3** to become relaxed and confident in a new situation; to get used to a new way of life, job, etc: *She's settling down well at her new school.* ◇ *He just couldn't settle down in the city.* **4** to become calmer and less active: *I've been really busy at work, but things should settle down again soon.* ◇ *Their speed settled down to a steady fifty miles an hour.*

◆ v + adv **1** also v + pron + adv

,**settle 'down**; ,settle sb 'down to become or to make sb become calmer, less excited, etc: *The children finally settled down and started work.* ◇ *The teacher had trouble settling the class down.*

◆ v + n/pron + adv

,**settle yourself 'down** = SETTLE DOWN

,**settle 'down to sth** (*also* 'settle to sth *BrE*) to begin to think about sth or give your attention to doing sth: *They had just settled down to dinner when the phone rang.* ◇ *I'm so worried that I can't settle to anything.*

◆ v + adv + prep ♦ v + prep

'**settle for sth**; 'settle for doing sth to accept sth that is not quite what you wanted but is the best that you can get: *Both teams were happy to settle for a draw.* ◇ *He'd hoped to get £8 000 for the car but had to settle for a lot less.* ◇ *I refuse to settle for (being) second best!*

OBJ **less**

◆ v + prep

,**settle 'in**; ,settle 'into sth to become used to something new, such as a new home, school or job: *She soon settled in at school.* ◇ *It took her a while to settle into her new job.*

OBJ **routine, school, job**

◆ v + adv ♦ v + prep

'**settle on sth** (*also* 'settle upon sth *more formal*) to choose sth; to make a decision about sth: *We couldn't decide where to go but we eventually settled on Italy.*

SYN **decide on/upon sth**

NOTE Settle on/upon sth can be used in the passive: *A date was finally settled on.*

◆ v + prep

'**settle sth on/upon sb** (*formal, law*) to arrange to give property or money to sb, for example after your death: *He settled his entire estate on his son.*

OBJ **money, estate**

◆ v + n/pron + prep

'**settle to sth** (*BrE*) = SETTLE DOWN TO STH

,**settle 'up** (with sb) to pay sb the money you owe them: *We need to settle up with them for the hire of the room.* ◇ *I'll pay now — we can settle up later.*

◆ v + adv

'**settle upon sth** = SETTLE ON STH

'**settle sth upon sb** = SETTLE STH ON/UPON SB

sew /səʊ; *AmE* soʊ/ (sewed, sewn /səʊn; *AmE* soʊn/ *or* sewed)

,**sew sth 'up 1** to join or mend sth using a needle and thread: *Sew up the tear before it gets any worse.* ◇ *They cleaned the wound and sewed it up.* OBJ **seam, tear, wound 2** (*informal*) to arrange sth in a satisfactory way; to bring sth to a favourable conclusion: *They'd sewn the deal up by midday.* OBJ **deal 3** (*informal*) to have control of sth; to be likely to win sth: *Her company have got the market sewn up.* ◇ *By half time they had the game sewn up.* OBJ **market, game, election**

NOTE In meanings 2 and 3 sew sth up is often used in the passive and in the phrase have (got) sth sewn up.

◆ v + adv + n ♦ v + n/pron + adv

shack /ʃæk/

,**shack 'up with sb**; be ,shacked 'up with sb (*also* ,shack 'up together) (*slang, disapproving*) to live with sb you are having a sexual relationship with but are not married to: *He's shacked up with some girl he met in Berlin.*

◆ v + adv + prep ♦ be + v + adv + prep ♦ v + adv + adv

shade /ʃeɪd/

,**shade sth 'in** to make part of a picture darker, either with colours or using black: *He shaded in part of the graph.*

◆ v + adv + n ♦ v + n/pron + adv

,**shade** '**into sth** to gradually change into sth else so that you cannot tell where one thing ends and the other begins: *The blue gradually shades into purple.* ◇ *Sometimes nervousness can shade into fear.*

◈ v + prep

shake /ʃeɪk/ (**shook** /ʃʊk/**shaken** /ˈʃeɪkən/)

,**shake** '**down** (*informal*) to become comfortable and confident in a new situation: *Once the team shakes down, results should improve.*

◈ v + adv

▶ '**shakedown** *n* (*AmE, informal*) the test of a vehicle or an aircraft before it is generally used, to see if there are any problems and to make the crew familiar with it: *a shakedown flight*

→ *see also* SHAKEDOWN at SHAKE SB DOWN; SHAKEDOWN at SHAKE SB/STH DOWN

,**shake sb** '**down** (*AmE, slang*) to threaten sb in order to get money from them: *They've found the guy who shook George down.* ◇ *police who shake down motorists for bribes*

◈ v + n/pron + adv ◆ v + adv + n

▶ '**shakedown** *n* (*AmE, slang*) an act of trying to get money from sb with violence or threats: *He was stabbed during a shakedown.*

→ *see also* SHAKEDOWN at SHAKE DOWN; SHAKE-DOWN at SHAKE SB/STH DOWN

,**shake sb/sth** '**down** (*AmE, informal*) to search a person or place in a very thorough way: *Police shook down the club, looking for drugs.*

◈ v + adv + n ◆ v + n/pron + adv

▶ '**shakedown** *n* (*AmE, informal*) a thorough search of sb/sth: *a police shakedown of the area*

→ *see also* SHAKEDOWN at SHAKE DOWN; SHAKE-DOWN at SHAKE SB DOWN

,**shake sb** '**off 1** to escape from sb; to get rid of sb who is following you: *He twisted and turned in a desperate attempt to shake off his pursuer.* ◇ *I think we've shaken them off.* **2** to escape from sb who is holding you and will not let go: *She clung to him, but he shook her off.*

◈ v + adv + n ◆ v + n/pron + adv

,**shake sth** '**off** to get rid of sth, such as an illness, that is causing you problems: *I can't shake off this cold.* ◇ *She struggled to shake off her image as a beauty with no brains.*

OBJ (a) **cold**

◈ v + adv + n ◆ v + n/pron + adv

'**shake on sth** to shake hands with sb in order to show that you agree to sth: *Let's shake on it.*

OBJ **deal**, **agreement**, **it**

◈ v + prep

,**shake sth** '**out 1** to open or spread sth by shaking it: *He shook the blanket out and spread it on the grass.* **2** to open sth by shaking it in order to get rid of bits of dirt, dust, etc: *She went outside to shake out the tablecloth.*

→ *see also* SHAKE-OUT at SHAKE STH UP

◈ v + n/pron + adv ◆ v + adv + n

,**shake sb** '**up 1** to shock or upset sb: *She has been badly shaken up by the experience.* NOTE Shake sb up is often used in the passive in this meaning.
◆ **Shake sb** is also used frequently with this meaning: *She was badly shaken by the experience.* **2** to surprise sb in order to make them think or behave in a different way, become more active, etc: *He was asked to shake the staff up a bit.* ◇ *Shaken up by the early goal against them, the team began to fight back.*

◈ v + n/pron + adv ◆ v + adv + n

,**shake sth** '**up** to make important changes in an organization, a profession, etc. in order to make it more efficient: *The company needs shaking up.*

◈ v + n/pron + adv ◆ v + adv + n

▶ '**shake-up** (*also* '**shake-out**) *n* a major change to a company or an organization in order to improve it: *The police force is facing the biggest shake-up in its history.*

shame /ʃeɪm/

'**shame sb into sth**; '**shame sb into doing sth** to persuade sb to do sth by making them feel ashamed not to do it: *They shamed him into apologizing.*

◈ v + n/pron + prep

shape /ʃeɪp/

,**shape** '**up** (*informal*) **1** [+ adv/prep] to develop in a particular way, often in the way that you had hoped for: *Our plans are shaping up nicely.* ◇ *How's the new team shaping up?* **2** to improve your work or your behaviour: *If you don't shape up, you'll lose your job.* **3** (*especially BrE*) to become slim and physically fit: *It's time to slim down and shape up for the summer.*

◈ v + adv

IDM **shape up or ship** '**out** (*AmE, informal*) used to tell sb that if they do not improve their work or their behaviour they will have to leave their job, etc.

share /ʃeə(r); AmE ʃer/

,**share sth** '**out** (**among/between sb**) to divide something such as money, food or work and give an amount to each person: *The work was shared out equally.* ◇ *How can we share out the pizza between the five of us?*

◈ v + adv + n ◆ v + n/pron + adv

sharpen /ˈʃɑːpən; AmE ˈʃɑːrpən/

,**sharpen** '**up**; ,**sharpen sb/sth** '**up** to become, or to make sb/sth, better, more skilful, more effective, etc. than before: *She needs to sharpen up before next month's competition.* ◇ *This exercise will help students sharpen up their reading skills.* ◇ *Discipline has sharpened them up.*

◈ v + adv ◆ v + adv + n ◆ v + n/pron + adv

shave /ʃeɪv/

,shave sth 'off to remove hair from your face, head, etc: *Dad's shaved his beard off.* ◇ *She shocked everyone by shaving all her hair off.*
[OBJ] **beard, moustache, hair**
✦ v + n/pron + adv ♦ v + adv + n

,shave sth 'off; ,shave sth 'off sth 1 to cut very thin pieces from the surface of a piece of wood, etc: *I had to shave a bit off the door to make it shut.* ◇ *Use a sharp knife to shave off thin rolls of chocolate.* **2** to make something smaller or lower by a very small amount: *We managed to shave 5% off the cost.* ◇ *He shaved half a second off the world record.*
✦ v + n/pron + adv ♦ v + adv + n ♦ v + n/pron + prep

shear /ʃɪə(r); AmE ʃɪr/ (sheared, shorn /ʃɔːn; AmE ʃɔːrn/ or sheared)

be 'shorn of sth (*literary*) to have sth important taken away from you: *a political party shorn of power*
✦ be + v + prep

,shear 'off; ,shear sth 'off (*technical*) (especially of sth metal) to break under pressure; to cut through sth and make it break: *The bolts holding the wheel in place sheared off.*
✦ v + adv ♦ v + n/pron + adv ♦ v + n + adv

sheer /ʃɪə(r); AmE ʃɪr/

,sheer a'way/'off to suddenly move away in a different direction, especially to avoid hitting sth: *The car sheered wildly away, just missing the truck.* ◇ *Her mind sheered away from images she did not wish to dwell on.*
[SYN] **veer off, veer away (from sth)**
✦ v + adv

shell /ʃel/

,shell 'out (for sth), ,shell sth 'out (for sth) (*informal*) to pay for sth, especially when it is a lot of money or you do not really want to: *I'm not shelling out for another computer.* ◇ *I had to shell out $500 for the air fare.*
[SYN] **fork out (for sth), fork sth out (for sth)**
✦ v + adv ♦ v + adv + n ♦ v + pron + adv ♦ v + n + adv
(*less frequent*)

shin (BrE) /ʃɪn/ (-nn-) (AmE shinny)

,shin 'down/'up; ,shin 'down/'up sth (*BrE*) (*informal*) to climb down or up sth, using your hands and legs to hold it tightly: *He shinned down the drainpipe.* ◇ *You might be able to see if you shin up that tree.*
[OBJ] **drainpipe, rope**
✦ v + adv ♦ v + prep

shine /ʃaɪn/ (shone, shone /ʃɒn; AmE ʃoʊn/)

,shine 'out 1 to shine brightly: *A light shone out across the field.* **2** if a person or a thing **shines out**, you notice them because they are very much better than the others: *She seemed to shine out from the rest.*
✦ v + adv

,shine 'through; ,shine 'through sth to be seen clearly and easily: *In the last game her talent really shone through.* ◇ *His love of life shines through the pages of his book.*
✦ v + adv ♦ v + prep

shinny (AmE) /'ʃɪni/ (shinnies, shinnying, shinnied, shinnied)

,shinny 'down/'up; ,shinny 'down/'up sth (*AmE*) = SHIN DOWN/UP, SHIN DOWN/UP STH *Burglars broke into the art gallery through the roof, shinnied down the rope and stole five valuable paintings.*

ship /ʃɪp/ (-pp-)

,ship sb 'off (to…) (*informal*) to send sb away somewhere, especially when they do not want to go: *They shipped the children off to summer camp.*
[NOTE] **Ship sb off** is often used in the passive: *I was shipped off to Canada.*
✦ v + n/pron + adv ♦ v + adv + n

,ship sb/sth 'off (to…) to send goods or people somewhere by ship: *They shipped all their possessions off to Australia.*
[NOTE] **Ship sb/sth off** is often used in the passive: *The goods were shipped off last week.*
✦ v + n/pron + adv ♦ v + adv + n

,ship sb/sth 'out (to…) to send goods or people somewhere, especially by ship: *They shipped the sculpture out to the States.*
[NOTE] **Ship sb/sth out** is often used in the passive: *Fresh supplies were shipped out.*
✦ v + n/pron + adv ♦ v + adv + n

[IDM] **shape up or ship 'out** (*AmE, informal*) used to tell sb that if they do not improve their work or their behaviour they will have to leave their job, etc.

shoot /ʃuːt/ (shot, shot /ʃɒt; AmE ʃɑːt/)

,shoot sb/sth 'down 1 to shoot at sb/sth and make them/it fall to the ground: *They were shot down in cold blood.* ◇ *They shot down a civilian aircraft by mistake.* **2** (*informal*) to strongly criticize sb or their ideas, etc: *When I made a suggestion they shot me down in flames.* ◇ *My ideas were shot down one by one.*
✦ v + adv + n ♦ v + n/pron + adv

'shoot for sth (*AmE, informal*) (*usually used in the progressive tenses*) to try to get or achieve sth difficult: *They're shooting for another victory this season.*
◆ v + prep

,shoot 'off (*informal*) to leave somewhere very quickly: *She had to shoot off to meet someone.* ◊ *I'm sorry, I've got to shoot off.*
◆ v + adv

,shoot sth 'off to remove sth by shooting: *They shot the lock off.*
◆ v + n/pron + adv ◆ v + adv + n

,shoot 'through (*informal, especially AustralE*) to leave, especially in order to avoid sb/sth: *I was only five when my Dad shot through.*
◆ v + adv

,shoot 'up 1 (to sth) to rise or increase very quickly: *The inflation rate has shot up to 20%.* **2** to grow taller in a short time: *She's shot up in the last few months.*
◆ v + adv

,shoot 'up; **,shoot 'up sth** (*slang*) to inject an illegal drug
OBJ **heroin, drugs**
◆ v + adv ◆ v + adv + n

,shoot sb/sth 'up to injure sb or damage sth severely by shooting: *An armed gang shot up the nightclub.*
OBJ **house, bar, club**
◆ v + adv + n ◆ v + n/pron + adv

shop /ʃɒp; *AmE* ʃɑːp/ (**-pp-**)

,shop a'round (for sth), **,shop a'round sth** (for sth) to look at different shops/stores to compare the prices of goods or services so that you can buy the ones that are the best value: *If you're buying a new hi-fi, shop around for the best price.* ◊ *It's worth shopping around the travel agents to find the best deal.* ◊ *When you open a bank account, it's a good idea to shop around first.*
◆ v + adv ◆ v + prep

shore /ʃɔː(r)/

,shore sth 'up 1 to support part of a building or other large structure by placing large pieces of wood or metal against or under it so that it does not fall down: *Engineers shored up the tunnel with wooden beams.* ◊ *The building was shored up to make it safe.* **2** to strengthen or support sth that is weak or failing: *to shore up the economy/dollar/pound*
◆ v + adv + n ◆ v + pron + adv ◆ v + n + adv (*less frequent*)

shout /ʃaʊt/

,shout sb 'down to shout to prevent sb who is speaking from being heard, because you do not like them, or you disagree with what they are

saying: *I tried to explain but they just shouted me down.* ◊ *The speaker was shouted down by angry protesters.*
◆ v + n/pron + adv ◆ v + adv + n

,shout 'out (to sb), **,shout sth 'out** (to sb) to suddenly say sth in a loud voice: *I shouted out to them but they didn't hear me.* ◊ *She shouted out a warning.* ◊ *He shouted out, 'Over here!'*
SYN **call out** (to sb), **call sth out** (to sb)
◆ v + adv ◆ v + adv + n ◆ v + n/pron + adv ◆ v + adv + speech

shove /ʃʌv/

,shove 'off (*BrE, spoken*) used to tell sb rather rudely to go away: *Just shove off and leave me alone!*
SYN **push off**
◆ v + adv

,shove 'up (*BrE, spoken*) used to ask sb to move to make a space for sb else to sit down: *We can get one more in if you shove up.* ◊ *Shove up a bit!*
SYN **budge up** (*BrE*), **move up**
◆ v + adv

show /ʃəʊ; *AmE* ʃoʊ/ (**showed, shown** /ʃəʊn; *AmE* ʃoʊn/ or, rarely, **showed**)

,show sb a'round; **,show sb a'round sth** (*BrE also* **,show sb 'round**, **,show sb 'round sth**) to go with sb when they visit a place for the first time, showing them what is interesting: *There are guides in the palace who will show visitors around.* ◊ *I'll arrange for someone to show you around the school.*
SYN **take sb around, take sb around sth**
→ *see also* SHOW SB OVER STH
◆ v + n/pron + adv ◆ v + n/pron + prep

,show sb 'in; **,show sb 'into sth** to lead a visitor to a place where they can wait, or to the room where sb is waiting to see them: *Sarah showed the visitors in.* ◊ *I was shown into a waiting room.*
OPP **show sb out, show sb out of sth**
◆ v + n/pron + adv ◆ v + adv + n ◆ v + n/pron + prep

,show 'off (*informal, disapproving*) to try to impress other people with your abilities, wealth, intelligence, etc: *Stop showing off!* ◊ *Bonnie was showing off to her friends, doing handstands on the grass.*
◆ v + adv
▶ **'show-off** *n* (*informal, disapproving*) a person who likes to impress other people with their abilities, wealth, etc: *You're such a show-off!*

,show sb/sth 'off (to sb) **1** to try to make people pay attention to sb/sth because you are proud of them/it: *He was showing his CD collection off to his friends.* ◊ *She brought her new boyfriend along to show him off.* **2** to make sb/sth look attractive or seem interesting or exciting by

showing their best features: *The black sweater showed off her figure to full advantage.* ◇ *The music shows the band off in their best light.*
✦ v + n/pron + adv ◆ v + adv + n

,show sb 'out; **,show sb 'out of sth** to lead a visitor to the door out of a room, a building, etc: *I'll show you out.*
》OPP《 **show sb in, show sb into sth**
✦ v + n/pron + adv ◆ v + adv + n ◆ v + n/pron + prep

,show sb 'over sth (*BrE*) to take sb around a place they are visiting and show them what is interesting: *They showed me over the house.*
→ *see also* SHOW SB AROUND, SHOW SB AROUND STH
✦ v + n/pron + prep

,show sb 'round; **,show sb 'round sth** (*BrE*)
= SHOW SB AROUND, SHOW SB AROUND STH

,show 'through; **,show 'through sth** to be visible through something or behind sth: *This paper is so thin the ink shows through.* ◇ *His skull showed through his thin hair.* ◇ *When he spoke, his bitterness showed through.*
✦ v + adv ◆ v + prep

,show 'up (*informal*) to arrive or appear at the place you have arranged: *She finally showed up at lunchtime.* ◇ *I arranged to meet him but he didn't show up.*
》SYN《 **turn up**
✦ v + adv

,show 'up; **,show sth 'up** to become or to make sth easy to see: *His striped tie showed up well against his dark red shirt.* ◇ *Something odd has shown up on the X-ray.* ◇ *Her lack of experience was shown up by the test.*
✦ v + adv ◆ v + adv + n ◆ v + n/pron + adv

,show sb 'up (*informal*) to make sb else feel embarrassed by behaving badly or by doing sth better than them: *He said I'd shown him up in front of his friends.* ◇ *You really showed me up by snoring during the concert!* ◇ *Don't worry about being shown up by the kids — they've always used computers.*
✦ v + n/pron + adv ◆ v + adv + n

,show sb/sth 'up as/for sth to show what sb/sth is really like, when this is worse than people thought: *The book shows her up for what she really is: a fraud.* ◇ *We were shown up as the second-rate team that we were.*
✦ v + n/pron + adv + prep

shower /'ʃaʊə(r)/

,shower 'down; **,shower 'down on sb/sth**; **'shower on sb/sth**; **,shower sth 'down on sb/sth**; **'shower sth on sb/sth** to fall onto sb/sth, especially in a lot of small pieces: *Volcanic ash showered down on the town after the eruption.* ◇ *The bottle broke and showered glass fragments on us.*
✦ v + adv ◆ v + adv + prep ◆ v + prep ◆ v + n/pron + adv + prep ◆ v + n/pron + prep

'shower sb with sth to drop a lot of small things onto sb: *The bride and groom were showered with rice as they left the church.* ◇ *The roof collapsed, showering us with dust and debris.* ◇ (*figurative*) *He showered her with gifts.*
✦ v + n/pron + prep

shrink /ʃrɪŋk/ (shrank /ʃræŋk/shrunk /ʃrʌŋk/ or shrunk, shrunk)

,shrink a'way/'back (from sb/sth) to move backwards or away from sb/sth, especially because you are frightened or disgusted: *She shrank away from him in horror.*
✦ v + adv

'shrink from sth; **'shrink from doing sth** (*often used in negative sentences*) to be unwilling to do or to accept sth that you find frightening, unpleasant or immoral: *She recognized her responsibility and did not shrink from it.* ◇ *He shrank from confronting his son face to face.* ◇ *She never shrank from difficult tasks.*
OBJ **task, duty** 》SYN《 **back away from sth**
NOTE **Shrink from sth/from doing sth** are usually used in written English.
✦ v + prep

shrivel /'ʃrɪvl/ (-ll-, *AmE* -l-)

,shrivel 'up to become dry and wrinkled (= having many small lines or folds) because of heat, lack of water, etc: *The apples left on the tree had shrivelled up.*
NOTE **Shrivel** is used with a similar meaning.
✦ v + adv
▶ **,shrivelled 'up** *adj* dry and wrinkled (= with many small lines or folds): *shrivelled-up apples*

shroud /ʃraʊd/

be 'shrouded in sth 1 to be covered or hidden by sth: *The city was shrouded in mist.* ◇ *furniture shrouded in dust sheets* **2** if information, etc. is shrouded in mystery, it is hidden or kept secret: *His family background is shrouded in mystery.* ◇ *Their work is shrouded in secrecy.*
✦ be + v + prep

shrug /ʃrʌg/ (-gg-)

,shrug sth 'off 1 (*also* **,shrug sth a'way** *less frequent*) to push sth back or away with your shoulders: *She shrugged off her jacket.* ◇ *She put her hand on his shoulder but he shrugged it away.* OBJ **jacket, hand 2** (*also* **,shrug sth a'side** *less frequent*) to treat sth as if it is not important: *He shrugged off all the objections I raised.* ◇ *Barnes is trying to shrug off an ankle injury.* OBJ **injury, criticism**
✦ v + adv + n ◆ v + n/pron + adv

shut /ʃʌt/ (shutting, shut, shut)

,shut sb/sth a'way to put sb/sth in a place where other people cannot see or find them/it: *He shut the files away in the safe.* ◊ *prisoners shut away in jail for a long time*
〔SYN〕 **lock sb up/away; lock sth up/away**
⊕ v + n/pron + adv ◆ v + adv + n

,shut yourself a'way (from sb/sth) to stay in your room or go somewhere where you will be completely alone: *He shut himself away in his study to finish the book.* ◊ *You can't just shut yourself away from the world.*
〔SYN〕 **lock yourself away**
⊕ v + pron + adv

,shut 'down; ,shut sth 'down 1 to stop opening for business; to stop sth from opening: *The mine shut down last month.* ◊ *The club was shut down by the police.* 〔SYN〕 **close down, close sth down 2** if a machine **shuts down**, or sb **shuts it down**, it stops working: *The machine shuts down if there's an overload.* ◊ *The computer system will be shut down over the weekend.*
⊕ v + adv ◆ v + adv + n ◆ v + n/pron + adv
▶ **'shutdown** *n* **1** the act of closing a factory or business, either temporarily or permanently: *The shutdown has put hundreds out of work.* **2** the act of stopping a large machine from working, either temporarily or permanently: *There was a fault in the nuclear reactor's emergency shutdown procedures.*

,shut sb/sth 'in; ,shut sb/sth 'in sth; ,shut yourself 'in; ,shut yourself 'in sth to put sb/sth in a room, a vehicle, etc. and keep them there; to go into a room, a building, a vehicle, etc. and stay there: *They shut the animals in at night.* ◊ *Liz rushed out of the kitchen and shut herself in her room.*
⊕ v + n/pron + adv ◆ v + adv + n ◆ v + n/pron + prep
▶ **'shut-in** *n* (*AmE, old-fashioned*) a person who cannot leave their home because they are ill/sick or cannot move easily

'shut sth in sth to trap or injure sth by closing sth tightly around it: *I shut my finger in the car door.*
〔OBJ〕 **finger**
⊕ v + n/pron + prep

,shut 'off; ,shut sth 'off 1 if a machine **shuts off**, or sb **shuts it off**, it stops working: *The central heating shuts off automatically at 9.30.* ◊ *I stopped the car and shut off the engine.* 〔SYN〕 **switch off, switch sth off; turn off, turn sth off** 〔OPP〕 **switch on, switch sth on; turn on, turn sth on 2** if a supply of gas, water, electricity, etc. **shuts off** or sb/sth **shuts it off**, it stops flowing: *The water shuts off automatically when the tank is full.* ◊ *A valve shuts off the gas when the lid is closed.*
⊕ v + adv ◆ v + n/pron + adv ◆ v + adv + n

▶ **'shut-off** *n* **1** a device that stops sth working or stops power, water, gas, etc. from flowing: *a shut-off valve* **2** a period when power, water, gas, etc. is prevented from flowing: *a shut-off of the water supply*

,shut sb/sth 'off (from sth) to keep sb/sth separate from other people or things: *A range of mountains shuts Bosnia off from the Adriatic.* ◊ *The kitchen area could be shut off from the rest of the room.*
⊕ v + n/pron + adv ◆ v + adv + n

,shut yourself 'off (from sb/sth) to deliberately separate yourself physically or socially from other people: *After her son died, she just wanted to shut herself off from the world.*
〔SYN〕 **cut yourself off (from sb/sth)**
⊕ v + pron + adv

,shut sb 'out 1 (*also* **,shut sb 'out of sth**) to refuse to allow a person to share your thoughts, feelings or activities: *Don't shut me out* (= Tell me about your problems) — *I want to help you.* ◊ *I was shut out of the decision-making process.* ◊ *When he saw her with the baby he felt shut out.*
〔SYN〕 **exclude sb** (*more formal*) **2** (*AmE, informal*) to stop an opponent from scoring in a game or contest: *They shut out the Mets in their last game.*
⊕ v + n/pron + adv ◆ v + adv + n
1 also v + n/pron + adv + prep
▶ **'shut-out** *n* (*AmE, informal*) a game in which one team does not score

,shut sb/sth 'out; ,shut sb/sth 'out of sth to stop sb/sth from entering a place: *He closed the door firmly, shutting us out of the room.* ◊ *I drew the curtains to shut out the light.*
〔OBJ〕 **light, noise**
⊕ v + adv + n ◆ v + n/pron + adv ◆ v + n/pron + adv + prep

,shut sth 'out; ,shut sth 'out of sth to stop yourself from having particular feelings or from thinking about particular things: *She tried to shut out all the painful memories.*
〔OBJ〕 **pain, memories** 〔SYN〕 **block sth out, block sth out of sth**
⊕ v + adv + n ◆ v + n/pron + adv ◆ v + n/pron + adv + prep

,shut yourself 'out; ,shut yourself 'out of sth to be unable to enter your home because you have closed the door and left your keys inside: *I've shut myself out of the house again!*
〔SYN〕 **lock yourself out, lock yourself out of sth**
⊕ v + pron + adv ◆ v + pron + adv + prep

,shut 'up (*spoken, informal*) used to tell sb rudely to stop talking or making a noise: *Shut up and go away!* ◊ *If you'd shut up, I could hear what she's saying.*
〔SYN〕 **belt up** (*BrE*)
⊕ v + adv

,**shut sb 'up** (*informal*) to make sb stop talking or making a noise: *I couldn't shut the kids up!*
  ◆ v + n/pron + adv

,**shut sb/sth 'up** (**in sth**), ,**shut yourself 'up** (**in sth**) to keep sb/sth in a place and prevent them from going anywhere; to stay in a room and not go out: *He had been shut up in a cell for ten years.* ◇ *Shut the dog up in the shed.* ◇ *My father used to shut himself up with his books for days.*
  ◆ v + n/pron + adv ◆ v + adv + n

,**shut sth 'up** (*especially BrE*) to close a room, house, etc. and not use it for a period of time: *We shut the summer house up for another year.*
  ⟨SYN⟩ **close sth up**
  ◆ v + n/pron + adv ◆ v + adv + n
  ⟨IDM⟩ **shut up 'shop** (*BrE, informal*) to close a business permanently; to stop working for the day: *It's time to shut up shop and go home.*

shy /ʃaɪ/ (**shies, shying, shied, shied** /ʃaɪd/)

,**shy a'way** (**from sth/from doing sth**) to avoid doing sth because you are nervous or frightened: *She shies away from close friendships.* ◇ *Don't shy away from saying what you think.*
  ◆ v + adv

sic (*also* **sick**) /sɪk/ (**-cc-**)

'**sic sth on sb** (*AmE, informal*) to tell a dog to attack sb: *Back off or I'll sic the dog on you.*
  ⟨OBJ⟩ **dog** ⟨SYN⟩ **set sth on sb** (*BrE*)
  ◆ v + n/pron + prep

sick /sɪk/

,**sick sth 'up** (*BrE, informal*) to bring food up from the stomach: *The baby sicked up her milk.*
  ⟨SYN⟩ **throw sth up; vomit sth** (*more formal*)
  ◆ v + adv + n ◆ v + n/pron + adv

'**sick sth on sb** (*AmE, informal*) = SIC STH ON SB

sicken /'sɪkən/

'**sicken for sth** (*BrE*) (*usually used in the progressive tenses*) to show signs that you may be becoming ill/sick: *I feel as if I'm sickening for something.* ◇ *You look as if you're sickening for flu.*
  ⟨SYN⟩ **go down with sth; get sth**
  ◆ v + prep

side /saɪd/

'**side with sb** (**against sb**) to support sb in an argument, a dispute, etc: *The children always sided with their mother* (*against their father*).
  ◆ v + prep

sidle /'saɪdl/

,**sidle 'over/'up** (**to sb**) to approach sb in a shy, uncertain or secret way: *She sidled up to him and whispered in his ear.*
  ◆ v + adv

sift /sɪft/

'**sift sth from sth**; ,**sift sth 'out from sth** to separate sth, usually sth you want, from a group of things: *to sift (out) the good from the bad*
  ◆ v + n/pron + prep ◆ v + adv + n + prep ◆ v + n/pron + adv + prep

,**sift sth 'out** to separate sth, usually sth you do not want, from a group of things: *We need to sift out unsuitable applications.* ◇ *He helped me sift out the bad songs I'd written.*
  ◆ v + adv + n ◆ v + n/pron + adv

,**sift 'through sth** (**for sth**) to carefully examine a large amount of sth in order to find sth important or decide what is useful and what is not: *I sifted through his papers for clues.* ◇ *The judges sifted through 8 000 entries and finally picked the winner.*
  ⟨NOTE⟩ **Sift through sth** can be used in the passive: *This pile of reports needs to be sifted through by the end of this week.*
  ◆ v + prep

sign /saɪn/

,**sign sth a'way** to give up your rights, property, etc. by signing a document: *The artist lost millions by signing away his rights to the cartoon character he created.*
  ⟨OBJ⟩ **rights**
  ◆ v + adv + n ◆ v + n/pron + adv

'**sign for sth 1** to sign a form, etc. as proof that you have received sth: *The postman asked me to sign for the packet.* ⟨NOTE⟩ **Sign for sth** can be used in the passive in this meaning: *This letter hasn't been signed for.* **2** if a football player **signs for** a club, he formally agrees to play for that team: *When did Cantona sign for United?*
  ◆ v + prep

,**sign 'in**; ,**sign sb 'in** to write your name or the name of a guest when you arrive at an office, a club, etc: *All visitors must sign in on arrival.* ◇ *You have to be signed in by a member.*
  ⟨OPP⟩ **sign out, sign sb out**
  ◆ v + adv ◆ v + n/pron + adv ◆ v + adv + n

,**sign 'off 1** (*BrE*) to end a letter, a postcard, etc: *I'll sign off now and post this.* **2** to end a broadcast by saying goodbye or playing a piece of music: *I'll sign off with a reminder to tune in again tomorrow.*
  ◆ v + adv

,**sign sb 'off** (*BrE*) to say officially that sb is too ill/sick to work for a particular period: *The doctor signed him off for a week.* ⟨SUBJ⟩ **doctor**
  ◆ v + n/pron + adv ◆ v + adv + n

,**sign sth 'off** (*BrE*) to give your formal approval to sth, by signing your name: *She signed off all the invoices.*
  ◆ v + adv + n ◆ v + n/pron + adv

,sign 'off on sth (*AmE, informal*) to express
your approval of sth formally and definitely: *The
President hasn't yet signed off on this report.*
◆ v + adv + prep

,sign 'on 1 (*BrE, informal*) to sign a form stating
that you are unemployed so that you can receive
payment from the government: *He had to sign on
when the factory closed.* 2 (*old-fashioned, AmE*) to
announce the start of broadcasting for the day:
This is Jack Grainger signing on.
◆ v + adv

,sign 'on; ,sign sb 'on = SIGN UP, SIGN SB UP *Eric
has been signed on for the team as goalkeeper.* ◇
Shall I sign you on for the painting class? ◇ *I tried
to sign on as a medical assistant.*
◆ v + adv ◆ v + n/pron + adv

,sign 'out; ,sign sb 'out to write your name or the
name of a guest when you leave an office, a club,
etc: *Don't forget to sign out when you go.* ◇ *You must
sign your guests out when they leave the club.*
[OPP] **sign in, sign sb in**
◆ v + adv ◆ v + n/pron + adv

,sign sth 'out to sign a document to say officially
that sth can be removed from a place or that you
have taken it: *There is no record of the file being
signed out again.*
◆ v + n/pron + adv ◆ v + adv + n

,sign sth 'over (to sb) to give your rights or property to sb else by signing a document: *He signed
the house over to his daughter.*
◆ v + n/pron + adv ◆ v + adv + n

,sign 'up; ,sign sb 'up (*also* ,sign 'on, ,sign sb
'on *less frequent*) 1 (with/for sb) to sign a document saying that you agree to work for sb, play
for their team, etc.; to persuade sb to do this:
She's signed up with an employment agency. ◇
We've signed up three new players. ◇ *Who has
been signed up to star in the new movie?* 2 (for sth)
to arrange to do a course of study by adding your
name or sb else's name to the list of people doing
it: *I've signed up for a pottery course.* ◇ *Shall I
sign you up for the workshop too?* 3 to agree to
become a member of the armed forces; to persuade sb to do this: *He tried to sign up when he
was only fifteen.*
◆ v + adv ◆ v + adv + n ◆ v + n/pron + adv

silt /sɪlt/

,silt 'up; ,silt sth 'up to become blocked with
sand, mud, etc. that has been brought by flowing
water; to block sth in this way: *The old harbour
has silted up.* ◇ *Mud is silting up the stream.*
◆ v + adv ◆ v + adv + n ◆ v + n/pron + adv

simmer /'sɪmə(r)/

,simmer 'down (*informal*) to become calm after
a period of anger, excitement, violence, etc: *Just
simmer down and we'll discuss this calmly.*
[SYN] **cool down, calm down**
◆ v + adv

sing /sɪŋ/ (sang /sæŋ/, sung /sʌŋ/)

,sing a'long (with sb/sth), ,sing a'long (to sth)
to sing together with sb who is already singing
or while a record, radio, or musical instrument
is playing: *He sang along with the CD.* ◇ *We sang
along to all the songs.*
◆ v + adv
▶ 'singalong *n* an informal occasion at which
people sing songs together: *We had a great singalong in the pub last night.*

,sing 'out; ,sing sth 'out to sing or say sth
clearly and loudly: *Sing out so that everyone can
hear.* ◇ *If you need anything, just sing out.*
◆ v + adv ◆ v + adv + speech ◆ v + adv + n ◆
v + n/pron + adv

,sing 'up (*BrE*) to sing more loudly: *Sing up, I
can't hear you.*
◆ v + adv

single /'sɪŋgl/

,single sb/sth 'out (for sth/as sb/sth) to choose
sb/sth from among a group for special comment
or treatment: *They singled her out for particular
praise.* ◇ *He was singled out as the best student.*
[NOTE] **Single sb/sth out** is often used in the passive: *Why had Aidan been singled out for special
treatment?*
◆ v + adv + n ◆ v + n/pron + adv

sink /sɪŋk/ (sank /sæŋk/ sunk /sʌŋk/) or (*less
frequent* sunk, sunk)

,sink 'back (into sth) to move or fall backwards,
or lie down, especially when you are feeling
tired: *She sank back into her chair.* ◇ *He sank
back against the pillows, exhausted.*
◆ v + adv

,sink 'in; ,sink 'into sth 1 (of liquids) to go down
into another substance: *Apply the moisturiser
and let it sink in.* ◇ *The rain sank into the dry
ground.* [SYN] **be absorbed** (into sth) 2 (of
words, etc.) to be fully understood or realized:
It took a while for the news to sink in. ◇ *He paused
to let his words sink into her brain.* [SUBJ] **words,
news, meaning**
◆ v + adv

[IDM] **be 'sunk in sth** to be in a state of unhappi-
ness or deep thought: *She just sat there, sunk in
thought.*

'sink into sth to go gradually into a less active,
happy or pleasant state: *She sank into a deep
sleep.* ◇ *He sank deeper into depression.*
[OBJ] **depression** [SYN] **descend into sth** (*more
formal*)
◆ v + prep

,sink 'into sth; ,sink sth 'into sth to go deep
into sth solid; to make sth sharp do this: *Sharp
teeth sank into his arm.* ◇ *The dog sank its teeth
into my leg.*
◆ v + prep ◆ v + n/pron + prep

,sink sth 'into sth to spend a lot of money on a business or an activity, for example in order to make money from it in the future: *We sank all our savings into the new company.*
[OBJ] **a fortune** [SYN] **plough sth into sth**
◆ v + n/pron + prep

sip /sɪp/ (-pp-)

'sip at sth to drink sth slowly, taking a very small amount each time: *She sipped at her coffee.*
[OBJ] **drink**
◆ v + prep

siphon (*also* syphon) /'saɪfn/

,siphon sth 'off (from sth) (*informal*) to move money or resources from one place to another, usually illegally: *She siphoned off profits into her own bank account.*
[OBJ] **money, funds** [SYN] **divert sth** (*more formal*)
◆ v + adv + n ◆ v + n/pron + adv

sit /sɪt/ (sitting, sat, sat /sæt/)

,sit a'round; ,sit a'round sth (*BrE also* ,sit a'bout/'round, ,sit a'bout/'round sth) to spend time sitting down doing very little: *I'm far too busy to sit around here all day.* ◇ *We sat about talking for most of the morning.* ◇ *All we could do was sit around and wait.* ◇ *They were sitting around the house chatting.*
◆ v + adv ◆ v + prep

,sit 'back 1 to sit or lean comfortably in a chair: *He sat back in his chair and closed his eyes.* **2** (**and do sth**) to relax, especially by not getting too involved in or anxious about sth: *Now all the work's done we can **sit back and** enjoy things!* ◇ *Are you going to sit back and let me do everything?*
◆ v + adv

,sit 'by to do nothing to stop sth bad or unpleasant happening: *I'm not going to sit by and let an innocent man go to jail.*
[SYN] **stand by**
◆ v + adv

,sit 'down 1 to lower your body until you are sitting on a chair, etc: *Please sit down!* ◇ *We sat down on the sofa.* ◇ *When everyone was sitting down, he began.* → *see also* SIT YOURSELF DOWN **2** (**and do sth**) to give time and attention to sth in order to try to solve a problem or achieve sth: *We've never actually **sat down and** talked the problem through.*
◆ v + adv
▶ **'sit-down** *n* **1** [C] a strike, demonstration, protest, etc. involving people sitting down and refusing to leave a place: *to stage a sit-down* ◇ *a sit-down protest* **2** [sing.] (*BrE, informal*) a short rest while sitting: *I need a sit-down.*

,sit 'sb down to help or persuade sb to sit down either for a rest or to discuss sth: *She sat him down in front of the fire.* ◇ *We need to sit him down and explain the situation.*
[NOTE] Sit sb down is not used in the passive.
◆ v + n/pron + adv

,sit yourself 'down (*informal*) to lower your body until you are sitting on a chair, etc: *Come in and sit yourself down.*
→ *see also* SIT DOWN 1
◆ v + pron + adv

'sit for sb/sth to be a model for an artist or a photographer: *She sat for some of the most famous artists of her day.*
◆ v + prep

,sit 'in (on sth) to attend a meeting, a class, etc. to watch it, not to take part: *I was allowed to sit in on the meeting.* ◇ *I sat in on some English classes.*
◆ v + adv
▶ **'sit-in** *n* a form of protest in which people refuse to leave a factory, a building, etc: *Workers decided to stage a sit-in.*

,sit 'in for sb to do sb's job or perform sb's duties while they are away: *The chief reporter often sat in for George as editor.*
[SYN] **stand in for sb**
◆ v + adv + prep

'sit on sth 1 to be a member of a group of people such as a committee: *How many people sit on the committee?* ◇ *My mother sat on the jury during a famous murder trial.* [OBJ] **committee, council 2** (*informal*) to do nothing about a letter, report, etc. that sb has sent you: *They've been sitting on my application for a month now.*
◆ v + prep
[IDM] **sit on the 'fence** to avoid becoming involved in deciding or influencing something: *You can't go on sitting on the fence trying not to upset anybody.* (**be**) **sitting on a 'fortune/'gold mine** (*informal*) to own sth very valuable, often when you do not realize it: *His paintings are in great demand. If you have one, you could be sitting on a gold mine.*

,sit 'out to sit outside somewhere rather than inside: *It's too cold now to sit out.* ◇ *Let's sit out on the balcony.*
◆ v + adv

,sit sth 'out 1 to not take part in a dance, game or other activity: *I think I'm going to sit this one out.* [OBJ] **dance 2** to stay in a place and wait for sth unpleasant or boring to finish: *to sit out a recession/slump/war* ◇ *We'll just have to sit it out here until things improve.*
[NOTE] Sit sth out is not used in the passive.
◆ v + adv + n ◆ v + pron + adv ◆ v + n + adv (*rare*)

'sit over sth to have a meal or a drink in a slow relaxed way: *We sat over breakfast and planned the day ahead.*
[OBJ] **breakfast, dinner, etc.**
◆ v + prep

,sit 'round; ,sit 'round sth (*BrE*) = SIT AROUND,
SIT AROUND STH

'sit **through** sth to stay until the end of a performance, speech, meeting, etc. that you think is
boring or too long: *We had to sit through a whole
dinner without a cigarette.* ◊ *I can't sit through
four hours of Shakespeare!*
  ✚ v + prep

,sit 'up **1** to be or to move yourself into a sitting
position, for example, from lying down: *He sat
up, turned the light on, and looked at his watch.* ◊
Do you feel well enough to sit up yet? **2** to not go to
bed until later than usual: *We sat up late watching a movie.* SYN **stay up 3 (and do sth)** to suddenly give your attention to sth: *We need an
advert that will make people **sit up and take
notice**.* ◊ *This will make them sit up and listen.*
  ✚ v + adv
  ▶ '**sit-up** *n* an exercise in which you move from
  lying down to a sitting position: *I do about sixty
  sit-ups a day.*

,sit sb 'up to move sb from lying to a sitting position: *She sat the baby up in the pram.*
  ✚ v + n/pron + adv

size /saɪz/

,size sb/sth 'up (*informal*) to form a judgement
or an opinion of sb/sth: *The two opponents were
sizing each other up.* ◊ *I sized up the situation
very quickly.*
  OBJ **situation** SYN **sum sb/sth up (as sb/sth)**
  ✚ v + n/pron + adv ♦ v + adv + n

skate /skeɪt/

,skate 'over/a'round sth (*BrE also* ,skate
'round sth) to talk about sth difficult or embarrassing quickly, without giving attention to
details: *She skated over the next part of her story.*
  ✚ v + prep

sketch /sketʃ/

,sketch sth 'in **1** to give more information or
details about sth: *He sketched in the background
to the case.* ◊ *I'll sketch in the details later for you.*
◊ *You need to sketch in his character a little more.*
  OBJ **background, history 2** to add sth to a drawing quickly or roughly: *She sketched in a few
  more trees.* ◊ *I sketched in the outline of the house.*
  ✚ v + adv + n ♦ v + n/pron + adv

,sketch sth 'out **1** to draw all the main features
of sth without showing exact details: *He sketched
out some preliminary designs.* **2** to give a brief
general description of a plan or an idea: *She
sketched out the plots of her novels in an exercise
book.* SYN **outline sth** (*more formal*)
  ✚ v + adv + n ♦ v + n/pron + adv

skim /skɪm/ (**-mm-**)

,skim sth 'off **1** to remove a substance such as fat
from the surface of a liquid: *Skim off the fat and
reheat the stew.* **2** to take the best part of sth for
yourself, often in an unfair or dishonest way:
*She's been skimming off a percentage of the
profits for years.*
  ✚ v + adv + n ♦ v + n/pron + adv

,skim 'through sth to read sth very quickly in
order to get a general impression or to find a particular point: *I only had time to skim through the
report.* ◊ *He skimmed through the article trying
to find his name.*
  OBJ **book, letter**
  ✚ v + prep

skimp /skɪmp/

'skimp **on** sth to spend less money or time on sth
than is normal or necessary: *Older people
shouldn't skimp on food or heating.*
  SYN **hold back on sth**
  ✚ v + prep

skip /skɪp/ (**-pp-**)

,skip 'off (*BrE*) (*also* ,skip 'out *AmE, BrE*) (*informal*) to leave a place secretly or suddenly, especially for a dishonest reason, for example to
avoid paying for sth: *They skipped off without
paying.*
  ✚ v + adv

,skip 'out on sb/sth (*AmE, informal*) to leave sb,
especially when they need you, or when you have
a responsibility towards them; to try to avoid a
difficult situation by leaving a place: *He just
skipped out on his wife leaving her with four kids
to take care of.* ◊ *He was found 12 years after he
skipped out on drugs charges.*
  SYN **run out on sb** (*especially BrE*)
  ✚ v + adv + prep

skirt /skɜːt; *AmE* skɜːrt/

,skirt a'round sth (*BrE also* ,skirt 'round sth) **1**
to be or move around the edge: *We skirted around
the pond and crossed the bridge.* **2** to avoid discussing or dealing with a difficult or embarrassing subject: *She tactfully skirted around the
subject of money.* OBJ **subject, question** NOTE
Skirt **around/round** sth can be used in the passive in this meaning: *The issue was skirted
around for years.*
  NOTE Skirt **sth** is also used with both these
  meanings: *the road that skirted the lake* ◊ *to skirt
  laws/duties.*
  ✚ v + prep

skive /skaɪv/

,**skive 'off**; ,**skive 'off sth** (*BrE, informal*) to avoid work or school by staying away or leaving early: *I can skive off for a few hours.* ◇ *I decided to skive off school and tell my mum I had a bad headache.*
> **OBJ** **school, work** **SYN** **bunk off, bunk off sth** (*BrE*)
> **NOTE** Skive can also be used, but not *skive sth*: *Where's Tom? I expect he's skiving again!*
> ✦ v + adv ◆ v + prep

slack /slæk/

,**slack 'off** to do sth more slowly or work less hard than before: *We can't slack off until everything is finished.*
> **SYN** **ease off**
> ✦ v + adv

slacken /'slækən/

,**slacken 'off** to become less busy or active: *We've been really busy, but things are starting to slacken off now.*
> ✦ v + adv

slag /slæg/ (-gg-)

,**slag sb/sth 'off** (*BrE, slang*) to criticize sb/sth in a cruel, unkind way: *He's always slagging his brother off.*
> **SYN** **run sb/sth down** (*BrE*), **cut sb/sth down** (*AmE, more formal*)
> ✦ v + n/pron + adv ◆ v + adv + n

slam /slæm/ (-mm-)

,**slam a'gainst sb/sth**; ,**slam sb/sth a'gainst sb/sth** = SLAM INTO/AGAINST SB/STH, SLAM SB/STH INTO/AGAINST SB/STH

,**slam sth 'down** (**on/onto sth**) to put sth down with a lot of force, especially when you are angry: *She slammed the book down on the table.* ◇ *I slammed down the phone* (= put the receiver down and ended the phone conversation) *in a rage.*
> **OBJ** **phone, receiver**
> ✦ v + n/pron + adv ◆ v + adv + n

,**slam 'into/a'gainst sb/sth**; ,**slam sb/sth 'into/a'gainst sb/sth** to crash, or to make sth crash, into sth with a lot of force: *The jeep slammed into the wall.* ◇ *In the crash she was slammed against the back of the seat.*
> ✦ v + prep ◆ v + n/pron + prep

,**slam sth 'on** if you **slam on** the brakes of a vehicle, you press your foot very hard on the brake and make the vehicle stop very quickly: *A child suddenly ran out into the road and I had to slam on the brakes.*
> **OBJ** only **brakes** **SYN** **jam sth on**
> ✦ v + adv + n ◆ v + n/pron + adv

slap /slæp/ (-pp-)

,**slap sb a'bout/a'round** (*informal, especially BrE*) to hit sb regularly or often, used especially of a man hitting a woman: *He used to come back drunk and slap his wife around.*
> **SYN** **knock sb around**
> ✦ v + n/pron + adv

,**slap sb 'down** (*informal*) to criticize sb or their ideas or suggestions in an unfair way, often in public: *He tried to object, but was immediately slapped down.* ◇ *If you ask a question, she just slaps you down.*
> **SYN** **cut sb down** (*AmE*)
> ✦ v + n/pron + adv ◆ v + adv + n

,**slap sth 'down** (**on/onto sth**) to put sth onto a surface in a quick and often noisy way, especially because you are angry: *He slapped down a copy of the book on the table.*
> ✦ v + n/pron + adv ◆ v + adv + n

,**slap sth 'on**; ,**slap sth on sb/sth** (*informal*) to announce suddenly that sb must have a punishment, obey a new rule etc., often when this is unfair: *Judges have been slapping on longer prison sentences.* ◇ *The government slapped a new tax on high earners.*
> ✦ v + n/pron + prep

,**slap sth 'on**; ,**slap sth 'on/'onto sth** (*informal*) to spread a substance on a surface quickly and carelessly: *I'd better slap some make-up on before I go out.*
> **OBJ** **paint, make-up**
> ✦ v + n/pron + adv ◆ v + adv + n ◆ v + n/pron + prep

,**slap sth on sth** (*informal*) to increase the price of sth suddenly: *They've slapped 50p on the price of cigarettes.*
> ✦ v + n/pron + prep

,**slap sth 'onto sth** = SLAP STH ON, SLAP STH ON/ONTO STH

slash /slæʃ/

'**slash at sb/sth** (**with sth**) to attack sb violently with a knife, etc. and try to cut them/it: *He slashed at his opponent's face with a knife.*
> ✦ v + prep

slave /sleɪv/

,**slave a'way** (**at sth**) (*usually used in the progressive tenses*) used to emphasize how hard you are working, especially when you think people do not recognize this or feel grateful: *I've been slaving away all day trying to get this work finished.*
> ✦ v + adv

sleep /sliːp/ (**slept, slept** /slept/)

,**sleep a'round** (*informal, disapproving*) to have sex with many different partners
> ✦ v + adv

,sleep 'in to remain in bed longer than usual in the morning: *She usually sleeps in on Sundays.*
SYN **lie in** (*BrE, informal*)
NOTE Compare **oversleep**, which means to sleep longer than you intended.
◆ v + adv

,sleep sth 'off to get better after sth, especially drinking too much alcohol, by sleeping: *He's still sleeping off yesterday's hangover.* ◇ *Go home and sleep it off.*
◆ v + adv + n ◆ v + n/pron + adv

'sleep on sth to delay making a decision about sth until the next day so that you can think about it: *Sleep on it and let me know tomorrow.*
◆ v + prep

,sleep 'out to sleep outdoors: *We slept out most nights when we were in Greece.*
◆ v + adv

,sleep 'over to stay the night at sb else's home: *The kids are sleeping over with friends.* ◇ *It's very late now — why don't you sleep over?*
NOTE Compare **oversleep**, which means to sleep longer than you intended.
◆ v + adv

▶ **'sleepover** *n* a party for children or young people when a group of them spend the night at one house

,sleep 'through sth to not be woken up by sth such as a loud noise or a lot of activity: *She slept right through the thunderstorm.* ◇ *I'm afraid I slept through the alarm.* ◇ *Did he sleep through the whole incident?*
◆ v + prep

'sleep together; **'sleep with sb** (*informal*) to have sex with sb, especially sb you are not married to: *They have been sleeping together for months now.*
◆ v + adv ◆ v + prep

slice /slaɪs/

,slice sth 'off; **,slice sth 'off sth 1** to remove a thin piece of sth from sth larger by cutting: *The top of his finger was sliced off in an accident.* ◇ *She sliced a piece of meat off the joint.* **2** to reduce sth by a particular amount: *He sliced two seconds off the world record.*
◆ v + adv + n ◆ v + n/pron + adv ◆ v + n/pron + prep

,slice 'through sth (*especially BrE*) to pass through sth very easily: *The axe sliced through the wood like butter.* ◇ (*figurative*) *He sliced through all my objections.*
◆ v + prep

,slice sth 'up to cut sth into flat thin pieces: *Would you slice the cucumber up?*
◆ v + n/pron + adv ◆ v + adv + n

slick /slɪk/

,slick sth 'back/'down if you **slick** your hair **back/down** you make it lie flat by putting oil, water, etc. on it: *His hair was slicked back.* ◇ *He still slicks down his hair with oil.*
OBJ hair
NOTE **Slick sth down** is often used in the passive.
◆ v + n/pron + adv ◆ v + adv + n

slim /slɪm/ (**-mm-**)

,slim 'down to become thinner, for example as a result of eating less: *She slimmed down to 60 kilos before her wedding.*
SYN **trim down**
◆ v + adv

,slim 'down; **,slim sth 'down** to make sth, such as an organization or a company, smaller by employing fewer people, reducing the amount of work done, etc: *The coal industry has had to slim down.* ◇ *The firm had to slim down its workforce.* ◇ *a slimmed down curriculum*
SYN **trim down, trim sth down**
◆ v + adv ◆ v + adv + n ◆ v + n/pron + adv

slip /slɪp/ (**-pp-**)

,slip a'way 1 (*also* **,slip 'off**) to leave quietly without attracting attention: *I slipped away to my room to write some letters.* ◇ *He managed to slip off alone for an hour.* **2** (*also* **,slip 'by**) if a period of time **slips away**, it passes more quickly than you realize: *She could see her childhood slipping away.* ◇ *The afternoon slipped away.* **3** (**from sb**) to disappear; to die or to stop existing: *He slipped away* (= died) *peacefully during the night.* ◇ *I felt the game was slipping away from me* (= I was losing).
◆ v + adv

,slip 'by 1 = SLIP AWAY 2 *Time just seemed to slip by.* **2** if an opportunity, etc. **slips by**, it passes and you do not use it: *I try never to let a chance to travel slip by.*
◆ v + adv

,slip sth 'in; **,slip sth 'into sth** to add sth to a speech, conversation or written text quickly or secretly: *He usually slips a couple of jokes into his lectures.* ◇ *She slipped in a few comments about her boyfriend.*
◆ v + adv + n ◆ v + n/pron + adv ◆ v + n/pron + prep

,slip 'into sth 1 to put clothes on quickly and easily: *I'll just slip into something more comfortable.*
OBJ dress, shoes, etc. **OPP** slip out of sth → *see also* SLIP STH OFF; SLIP STH ON **2** to pass into a particular state or situation, especially a difficult or unpleasant one: *The patient slipped into a coma.* ◇ *The economy has slipped into recession.*
OBJ coma, sleep, recession, debt
◆ v + prep

,slip 'off = SLIP AWAY 1

‚slip sth 'off to take clothes or shoes off quickly and easily: *She slipped her shoes off by the door.* ◇ *Slip off your coat and I'll make some tea.*
> OBJ **coat, shoes, etc.** OPP **slip sth on**
→ *see also* SLIP INTO STH; SLIP OUT OF STH
⊕ v + n/pron + adv ◆ v + adv + n

‚slip sth 'on to put clothes or shoes on quickly and easily: *Hold on, I'll just slip my coat on, then I'll be ready.*
> OBJ **shoes, jacket, etc.** OPP **slip sth off**
→ *see also* SLIP INTO STH; SLIP OUT OF STH
⊕ v + n/pron + adv ◆ v + adv + n
▶ **'slip-on** n [usually pl.] a shoe that you can put on and take off quickly and easily without having to tie or fasten anything: *a pair of cheap slip-ons* ◇ *slip-on shoes*

‚slip 'out (*informal*) if sth **slips out**, you say it when you do not intend to: *I didn't mean to tell him — it just slipped out.*
⊕ v + adv

‚slip 'out of sth to take off clothes quickly and easily: *She slipped out of her clothes and got into the shower.*
> OBJ **clothes, dress, etc.** OPP **slip into sth**
→ *see also* SLIP STH OFF; SLIP STH ON
⊕ v + prep ◆ v + adv + prep

‚slip 'over to slide a short distance and fall: *He slipped over on the ice and broke his leg.*
⊕ v + adv

‚slip 'through; **‚slip 'through sth** if sth or sb **slips through** or **slips through** a system, etc., a person or a system fails to find and deal with it/them: *Mistakes occasionally slip through.* ◇ *Somehow he slipped through the company's screening process.*
⊕ v + adv ◆ v + prep
> IDM **(let sth) slip through your 'fingers** if sb/sth **slips through your fingers**, you fail to keep or use it/them: *The thief had slipped through their fingers yet again.* ◇ *You've wasted your time at college and let your chances slip through your fingers.* **slip through the 'net** when sb/sth slips through the net, an organization or a system fails to find them and deal with them: *We tried to contact all the former students, but some slipped through the net.*

‚slip 'up (over sth) (*informal*) to make a careless mistake: *I slipped up over the date of the meeting.* ◇ *He slipped up in his calculations.* ◇ *We slipped up there, didn't we?*
⊕ v + adv
▶ **'slip-up** n (*informal*) a careless mistake: *One small slip-up could cost us the election.*

slob /slɒb; *AmE* slɑːb/ (**-bb-**)

‚slob a'round/'out; **‚slob a'round sth** (*BrE, slang*) to spend time being lazy and doing nothing: *We just slobbed out in front of the telly last night.* ◇ *Are you going to slob around in your* pyjamas all morning? ◇ *I decided to slob around the campsite instead of going swimming.*
⊕ v + adv ◆ v + prep

slog /slɒg; *AmE* slɑːg/ (**-gg-**)

‚slog a'way (at sth) (*informal*) to work hard and steadily at sth, especially a boring or difficult task, for a long time: *He slogged away at that report for weeks.*
⊕ v + adv

‚slog it 'out (*BrE, informal*) = SLUG IT OUT

‚slog 'through sth (*informal*) to work hard and steadily at sth, especially a boring or difficult task, for a long time: *I seem to have been slogging through this book for weeks.*
⊕ v + prep

slop /slɒp; *AmE* slɑːp/ (**-pp-**)

‚slop a'bout/a'round 1 (in sth) (of a liquid) to move around in a container, often so that some liquid comes over the edge: *Water was slopping about in the bottom of the boat.* SYN **slosh around/about 2 (in sth)** to move around in water, mud, etc: *She slopped around in the cooling water.* SYN **slosh around/about 3** (*BrE, informal, disapproving*) to spend time relaxing or being lazy: *She used to slop around all day in old jeans and sweatshirts.* SYN **slouch about/around** (*BrE*), **hang around**
⊕ v + adv

‚slop 'out (*BrE*) when prisoners **slop out**, they empty the containers that they use as toilets
⊕ v + adv

‚slop 'over; **‚slop 'over sth** (of a liquid) to move around in a container so much that some liquid comes out over the edge: *Some tea had slopped over into the saucer.* ◇ *Water slopped over the edge of the bath.*
⊕ v + adv ◆ v + prep

slope /sləʊp; *AmE* sloʊp/

‚slope 'off (*BrE, informal*) to go away, especially without being noticed, in order to avoid doing work, talking to sb, etc: *He always slopes off if there's any work to be done.* ◇ *Where are you trying to slope off to?*
⊕ v + adv

slosh /slɒʃ; *AmE* slɑːʃ/

‚slosh a'round (*also* **‚slosh a'bout** *especially BrE*) **(in sth)** (*informal*) **1** (of a liquid) to move around noisily in a container: *The water was sloshing about in the bucket.* SYN **slop about/around 2** to move around noisily in sth liquid: *The children were sloshing around in the puddles.* SYN **slop about/around 3** (*BrE*)

(especially of money) to be present in large quantities: *There seems to be lots of money sloshing around in professional tennis.*
⊕ v + adv

slot /slɒt; *AmE* slɑːt/ (**-tt-**)

,slot 'in; ,slot 'into sth if sth **slots in** or **slots into sth**, it fits easily and exactly into a space, especially the space made or designed for it: *This bit slots in neatly just here.* ◇ *This piece is meant to slot into this groove.* ◇ *(figurative) I didn't understand everything at the time, but later it all slotted into place.*
→ *see also* SLOT STH IN, SLOT STH INTO STH
⊕ v + adv ◆ v + prep

,slot sb/sth 'in to manage to find a time to see sb or to do sth: *I can slot you in tomorrow at four.*
⟨SYN⟩ **fit sb/sth in**
⊕ v + n/pron + adv ◆ v + adv + n

,slot sth 'in; ,slot sth 'into sth to put something into a space that is available or designed for it: *He slotted a coin into the machine.* ◇ *(figurative) The final pieces of the puzzle had been slotted into place and I understand what was happening.*
→ *see also* SLOT IN, SLOT INTO STH
⊕ v + n/pron + adv ◆ v + adv + n ◆ v + n/pron + prep

,slot to'gether; ,slot A and B to'gether if two things **slot together**, or sb **slots them together**, they fit together easily and exactly: *The base comes in two sections that simply slot together.* ◇ *The parts are pre-cut, ready to be slotted together.*
⊕ v + adv ◆ v + n/pron + adv ◆ v + adv + n

slouch /slaʊtʃ/

,slouch a'bout/a'round; ,slouch a'bout/ a'round sth (*BrE, disapproving*) to spend time relaxing or being lazy: *He slouches around all day reading comics.* ◇ *She wasted the day slouching about the house.*
⟨SYN⟩ **slop about/around** (*BrE*), **hang around**
⊕ v + adv ◆ v + prep

slough /slʌf/

,slough sth 'off 1 to remove or get rid of a layer of dead skin, etc: *Slough off dry skin once a week.* ⟨SYN⟩ **shed sth 2** (*formal*) to get rid of sth that you no longer want: *He was not able to slough off the memories of the past.* ◇ *Responsibilities are not sloughed off so easily.*
⊕ v + adv + n ◆ v + pron + adv ◆ v + n + adv (*rare*)

slow /sləʊ; *AmE* sloʊ/

,slow 'down; ,slow sb/sth 'down (*also* ,slow 'up, ,slow sb/sth 'up *less frequent*) 1 to go, or to make sb/sth go, at a slower speed: *Slow down, I can't keep up with you.* ◇ *The bus slowed up as it*

approached the junction. ◇ *The heat slowed us down.* ◇ *The roadworks are slowing the traffic up in the mornings.* 2 to be less active or develop more slowly; to make sb/sth do this: *He looks ill, he should slow down.* ◇ *The economy has slowed down.* ◇ *They claim they can slow up the ageing process.*
⊕ v + adv ◆ v + n/pron + adv ◆ v + adv + n
▶ 'slowdown *n* 1 a decrease in the rate of activity or production: *a slowdown in the economy* 2 (*AmE*) a protest that workers make by doing their work more slowly than usual: *The union threatened a slowdown if their demands were not met.*

slug /slʌg/ (**-gg-**)

,slug it 'out (*BrE also* ,slog it 'out) (*informal*) to fight; to compete until sb has won: *The two companies slugged it out for their share of the market.* ◇ *The Democrats and the Republicans will be slugging it out in November.*
⊕ v + it + adv

sluice /sluːs/

,sluice sth 'down/'out (*especially BrE*) to wash or clean the surface of sth with large amounts of water: *They sluice the streets down every morning.* ◇ *An attendant was sluicing out the changing rooms.*
⊕ v + adv + n ◆ v + n/pron + adv

smack /smæk/

'smack of sth to seem to contain an unpleasant attitude or quality: *His comments smack of racism.*
⊕ v + prep

smarten /'smɑːtn; *AmE* 'smɑːrtn/

,smarten 'up 1 (*also* ,smarten yourself 'up) to make yourself neater, tidier, or more attractive: *You need to smarten (yourself) up before you go out.* ⟨SYN⟩ **spruce yourself up 2** (*especially AmE*) to become more clever and aware of things: *You'll have to smarten up if you want to pass those exams.*
⊕ v + adv 1 also v + pron + adv

'smarten sb/sth 'up (*especially BrE*) to make a person or a place neater, tidier or more attractive: *The hotel has been smartened up by the new owners.* ◇ *She did her best to smarten her husband up.*
⟨SYN⟩ **spruce sb/sth up**
⊕ v + adv + n ◆ v + n/pron + adv

smash /smæʃ/

,smash sth 'down to make sth fall by hitting it very hard and breaking it: *The police decided to smash the door down.*
⟨OBJ⟩ **door**
⊕ v + n/pron + adv ◆ v + adv + n

,**smash sth 'in** to make a hole in sth or destroy it by hitting it very hard: *The doll's face had been smashed in.* ◇ (*informal*) *He threatened to smash my head in* (= hit my head very hard).
[OBJ] **door, face, head** [SYN] **bash sth in** (*informal, especially BrE*)
◈ v + n/pron + adv ♦ v + adv + n

,**smash sth 'up** to damage or destroy sth by hitting it very hard: *A bunch of thugs broke in and smashed the place up.* ◇ *He smashed his car up last week* (= he had a crash).
[OBJ] **car, things, place**
◈ v + n/pron + adv ♦ v + adv + n

smell /smel/ (**smelled, smelled**, *BrE also* **smelt, smelt** /smelt/)

'**smell of sth** to have the smell of sth: *The baby smelled of soap and milk.* ◇ *Can you put your cigarette out? I don't want my room smelling of smoke.*
◈ v + prep
[IDM] **come up/out of sth smelling of 'roses** (*informal*) to still have a good reputation, even though you have been involved in sth that might have given people a bad opinion of you

,**smell sb/sth 'out 1** to be aware of fear, danger, trouble, etc. in a situation: *He could smell out weakness in others.* **2** (of dogs) to detect sb/sth, by smelling: *The dogs are trained to smell out drugs.*
[SYN] **sniff sb/sth out**
◈ v + adv + n ♦ v + n/pron + adv

,**smell sth 'out** (*BrE*) (*AmE* **smell sth 'up**) to fill a place with an unpleasant smell: *That fish smelt the whole house out.*
[SYN] **stink sth out** (*BrE*), **stink sth up** (*AmE*)
◈ v + n/pron + adv ♦ v + adv + n

smile /smaɪl/

'**smile on/upon sb/sth** (*formal* or *literary*) if fortune, fate, etc. **smiles on** you, you are very lucky and successful: *Fortune smiled on us that night and the plane landed safely.*
→ *see also* FROWN ON SB/STH
◈ v + prep

smoke /sməʊk/; *AmE* smoʊk/

,**smoke sb/sth 'out 1** to make sb/sth come out of a place by filling it with smoke: *The fire is used to smoke the bees out.* **2** to find sb/sth that is causing a problem; to make sth that is secret publicly known: *The police are determined to smoke out the leaders of the gang.*
◈ v + adv + n ♦ v + n/pron + adv

smooth /smuːð/

,**smooth sth a'way/'out** to reduce or remove problems and difficulties: *The group was set up to smooth away local difficulties.* ◇ *His anxieties were quickly smoothed away.*
◈ v + adv + n ♦ v + n/pron + adv

,**smooth sth 'down** to make your hair or your clothes smooth and flat with your hands: *He smoothed down his hair.*
[OBJ] **hair, skirt**
◈ v + adv + n ♦ v + n/pron + adv

,**smooth sth 'out 1** to make sth such as a piece of paper or cloth smooth and flat with your hands: *She tried to smooth out the crumpled letter.* [OBJ] **wrinkles, paper 2** = SMOOTH STH AWAY/OUT *We are here to smooth out any practical problems for you.* [OBJ] **differences, problems**
◈ v + adv + n ♦ v + n/pron + adv

,**smooth sth 'over** to make a problem or difficulty seem less serious or easier to deal with, especially by talking to the people involved: *She tried to calm her parents down and smooth things over.* ◇ *The leaders managed to smooth over their differences.*
[OBJ] **differences, things**
◈ v + adv + n ♦ v + n/pron + adv

snack /snæk/

'**snack on sth** to eat small amounts of food between or instead of meals: *It's healthier to snack on fruit rather than chocolate.*
◈ v + prep

snap /snæp/ (**-pp-**)

,**snap 'back** (**into sth**) (*AmE*) (*informal*) = BOUNCE BACK (FROM STH) *After the initial shock, he soon snapped back.* ◇ *She snapped back into her daily routine soon after the operation.*
[SYN] **recover (from sth)**
◈ v + adv

,**snap sth 'out** to say sth in a sharp or unpleasant way: *The sergeant snapped out an order.*
[NOTE] **Snap sth** can be used with this meaning: *She snapped instructions to the team.*
◈ v + adv + n ♦ v + pron + adv ♦ v + n + adv (*less frequent*) ♦ v + adv + speech

,**snap 'out of sth**; ,**snap sb 'out of sth** (*informal*) to make yourself, or help sb else, stop feeling upset, in a bad mood, etc.; to wake up from a day dream: *Come on, Joe. Snap out of it.* ◇ *She was snapped out of her reverie by the sound of the door opening.*
◈ v + adv + prep ♦ v + n/pron + adv + prep

,**snap 'to it** (*informal*) used to tell sb to start working harder or more quickly: *This place has to be clean by this evening so snap to it!*
◈ v + prep + it

,**snap sb/sth 'up** to buy or seize sth quickly and eagerly: *Fans quickly snapped up the tickets.* ◇ (*figurative*) *He was snapped up by United.*
◈ v + adv + n ♦ v + n/pron + adv

snarl /snɑːl; *AmE* snɑːrl/

,snarl 'up; ,snarl sth 'up if sth **snarls up**, or sth **snarls it up**, it becomes so confused, twisted, etc. that no part of it can move: *The dog's lead got snarled up in a bush.* ◇ *The traffic snarls up at that junction every evening.* ◇ *The accident snarled up the traffic for the whole day.*
NOTE **Snarl sth up** is often used in the passive with *get*: *The city centre gets snarled up with tourists in the summer.*
◈ v + adv ◆ v + adv + n ◆ v + n/pron + adv
▶ **'snarl-up** *n* (*BrE*, *informal*) a situation in which traffic is unable to move

snatch /snætʃ/

'snatch at sth **1** to try to take hold of sth: *She snatched at the letter in his hand.* **2** (*BrE*) to take an opportunity to do sth eagerly and quickly: *They snatched at the chance to be happy.*
◈ v + prep

sneak /sniːk/

NOTE The usual past form is **sneaked**, but **snuck** is now very common in informal speech in American English and some people use it in British English too. However, many people consider it incorrect and it should not be used in formal writing.

,sneak 'up (on sb) to approach sb very quietly, so that they do not see or hear you until you reach them: *He loves sneaking up on me to scare me.* ◇ *She snuck up behind them and suddenly shouted.*
◈ v + adv

sniff /snɪf/

,sniff a'round; ,sniff a'round sth/sb (*BrE* *also* ,sniff 'round, ,sniff 'round sth/sb) (*informal*) to go somewhere to try to find secret information about sth/sb or to look for a particular person or thing: *Representatives from the studio were sniffing around for new talent.* ◇ *It won't be long before the press come sniffing around the club.*
◈ v + adv ◆ v + prep

'sniff at sth (*informal*) to show a lack of interest in or respect for sth: *At first he sniffed at her foreign ways.*
◈ v + prep
IDM not to be 'sniffed at (*informal*) good enough to be accepted or considered seriously: *Her achievement is not to be sniffed at.*

,sniff sb/sth 'out **1** (especially of dogs) to find sb/sth by smelling: *These dogs can sniff out explosives.* **SYN** smell sb/sth out **2** (*informal*) to find information about sb/sth: *journalists trained to sniff out a sensation or a scandal* ◇ *They're quick to sniff out a deception.* **SYN** nose sth out
◈ v + adv + n ◆ v + n/pron + adv

,sniff 'round; ,sniff 'round sth (*BrE*) = SNIFF AROUND, SNIFF AROUND STH/SB

snow /snəʊ; *AmE* snoʊ/

be/get ,snowed 'in/'up to be unable to go anywhere or leave a place because of heavy snow: *We got snowed in for three days.*
◈ be/get + v + adv

be/get ,snowed 'under (with sth) to have so much work that you have problems dealing with it: *We're snowed under with work at the moment.*
◈ be/get + v + adv

be/get ,snowed 'up (*BrE*) **1** = BE/GET SNOWED IN/UP **2** (of a road, etc.) to be/become blocked with snow: *The driveway was still snowed up.*
◈ be/get + v + adv

snuff /snʌf/

,snuff sb 'out (*especially AmE*) to kill sb: *He was snuffed out by the Mafia.*
◈ v + n/pron + adv ◆ v + adv + n

,snuff sth 'out **1** to stop a flame from burning: *She snuffed out the candles.* **OBJ** candle, flame **NOTE** **Snuff sth** can also be used with this meaning. **2** (*written*) to suddenly end or destroy sth: *A moment of mindless violence snuffed out his life.* ◇ *The revolution was quickly snuffed out.* **OBJ** life, hope
◈ v + adv + n ◆ v + pron + adv ◆ v + n + adv (*less frequent*)

snuggle /'snʌgl/

,snuggle 'down to make yourself warm and comfortable in your bed: *He snuggled down and went to sleep.*
◈ v + adv

,snuggle 'up (to/against sb/sth), ,snuggle 'up (in sth) to get into a warm and comfortable position close to sb/sth or in sth: *She snuggled up to him on the sofa.* ◇ *I'd love to snuggle up in bed right now!*
SYN cuddle up (to/against sb)
◈ v + adv

soak /səʊk; *AmE* soʊk/

,soak 'in; ,soak 'into sth (of a liquid) to pass into sth: *Apply the oil to the wood and leave it to soak in.* ◇ *The wine had soaked into the carpet.*
◈ v + adv ◆ v + prep

,soak 'through; ,soak 'through sth (of a liquid) to pass into or through sth: *Blood had soaked through the bandage.*
◈ v + adv ◆ v + prep

,soak sth 'up **1** to take in or absorb sth, especially a liquid: *Use a paper towel to soak up the excess oil.* ◇ (*figurative*) *The farmers soak up* (= use up) *£1 billion of government aid a year.* **OBJ** water, debts **2** to absorb sth into your senses, your body or your mind: *We walked around the town, soaking up the atmosphere.* OBJ **the sun, the atmosphere**

SYN **absorb sth** (*more formal*)

✦ v + adv + n ◆ v + n/pron + adv (*less frequent*)

sober /'səʊbə(r); AmE 'soʊ-/

,sober 'up; ,sober sb 'up to become, or to make sb, no longer drunk: *I decided to walk home to sober up.* ◇ *I need a black coffee to sober me up.* ◇ (*figurative, especially BrE*) *We all laughed at what Liam said, but soon sobered up* (= became serious) *when we saw his wife's expression.*

✦ v + adv ◆ v + n/pron + adv ◆ v + adv + n

sock /sɒk; AmE saːk/

,sock sth a'way (*AmE, informal*) to save money by putting it in a bank or by buying shares in a company, etc: *She already has $500 socked away for college.* ◇ *He socks away half his salary every month for the house.*

OBJ **money**

✦ v + adv + n ◆ v + n/pron + adv

'sock it to sb (*informal or humorous*) used to encourage sb to do or say sth that will have a strong effect, for example before an interview, a sports game, etc: *You'll be fine. Just get in there and sock it to them.*

NOTE **Sock it to sb** is not used in the passive.

✦ v + it + prep

sod /sɒd; AmE saːd/ (-dd-)

,sod 'off (*BrE*, △, *slang*) used to tell sb to go away: *Just sod off and leave me in peace!*

✦ v + adv

soften /'sɒfn; AmE 'sɔːfn/

,soften sb 'up (*informal*) to try to make sb more willing to do sth for you by being very nice to them first: *I know you, you're just trying to soften me up!* ◇ *They softened the voters up with promises they had no intention of keeping.*

SYN **butter sb up**

✦ v + adv + n ◆ v + n/pron + adv

,soften sb/sth 'up to make an enemy weaker and easier to attack: *It'll take more than a few bruises to soften him up.* ◇ *The artillery was used to soften up the advancing enemy.*

✦ v + n/pron + adv ◆ v + adv + n

soldier /'səʊldʒə(r); AmE 'soʊl-/

,soldier 'on (with sth) to continue with sth you are doing although it is difficult or unpleasant: *She soldiered on with the course in spite of her personal problems.* ◇ *I'm having to soldier on alone since Bill left.*

✦ v + adv

sort /sɔːt; AmE sɔːrt/

,sort sb 'out (*informal, especially BrE*) to deal with sb who has been causing trouble: *They sent the lads round to sort him out.*

SYN **deal with sb**

✦ v + n/pron + adv ◆ v + adv + n

,sort sb/yourself 'out (*BrE, informal*) **1** to find a solution to sb's/your own problems, etc: *It took her months to sort herself out after the divorce.* ◇ *He was so upset it took us an hour to calm him down and sort him out.* SYN **straighten sb/yourself out 2** to organize sb or yourself: *You load the car and I'll sort the kids out.* ◇ *She's in her room sorting herself out for the trip* (= packing clothes, etc.).

✦ v + n/pron + adv

,sort sb 'out with sth (*informal, especially BrE*) to provide sb with something they need: *I'm sure we can sort you out with some dry clothes.*

✦ v + n/pron + adv + prep

,sort sth 'out **1** to put sth in order; to tidy and organize sth: *I spent the afternoon sorting out my study.* OBJ **room, stuff 2** (*especially BrE*) to organize or arrange sth: *First you have to sort out a work permit.* **3** (*especially BrE*) to decide on sth: *I need to sort out what clothes to take with me on the trip.* OBJ **details, priorities** NOTE In this meaning **sort sth out** is usually used with question words such as *what, where,* etc. **4** to solve a problem: *We've sorted the problem out.* OBJ **problem, mess 5** (from sth) to separate sth from a larger group: *Sort out the ripe pears from the rest.* ◇ *She sorted out the clothes that she didn't wear any more.*

✦ v + n/pron + adv ◆ v + adv + n

▶ 'sort-out n (*BrE, informal*) an act of arranging or organizing things in a neat and tidy way and getting rid of things you don't want

,sort itself 'out (*especially BrE*) if a problem sorts itself out, it stops being a problem without anyone having to do anything: *He woke up feeling ill, but thought the problem would soon sort itself out.*

SYN **work itself out**

✦ v + pron + adv

,sort 'through sth to look through a number of things either in order to find a particular thing or to put them in groups: *She sorted through her wardrobe for something to wear.* ◇ *They sorted through thousands of old photos.*

✦ v + prep

sound /saʊnd/

,sound 'off (about sth) (*informal, disapproving*) to express your opinions loudly or in an aggressive way: *He should check his facts before sounding off like that.*

✦ v + adv

,**sound sb/sth 'out** (**about/on** sth) to try to discover sb's views, opinions, etc. on sth, especially in an indirect way: *I want to sound him out about a possible job.* ◇ *We should sound out opinions on these changes.*
◆ v + adv + n ◆ v + pron + adv ◆ v + n + adv (*less frequent*)

soup /suːp/

,**soup sth 'up** (*informal*) if you **soup up** a car, a computer, etc., you make changes to it so that it is more powerful or exciting: *He makes a living buying old cars and souping them up.*
◆ v + adv + n ◆ v + pron + adv ◆ v + n + adv (*less frequent*)

▶ '**souped-up** *adj* [only before noun] (*informal*) a **souped-up** car, computer, etc. has been changed to make it more powerful or exciting: *a souped-up Mini*

space /speɪs/

,**space 'out**; ,**space sb 'out** (*slang, especially AmE*) to be confused, unable to think clearly, or not aware of what is happening around you, for example as a result of taking drugs; to put sb in a state like this: *I was supposed to meet her for lunch but I spaced out and forgot.* ◇ *The drugs I was taking for my illness spaced me out so I couldn't think clearly.*
◆ v + adv ◆ v + n/pron + adv

▶ ,**spaced 'out** *adj* (*slang*) confused, unable to think clearly and not completely conscious of what is happening around you, for example because of taking drugs: *He sat in the corner looking completely spaced out.*

,**space sth 'out** to arrange things with a regular distance or time between them, especially a fairly large amount: *Try spacing the words out more on the page.* ◇ *Should I space out the baby's feeds over 24 hours?*
◆ v + n/pron + adv ◆ v + adv + n

spark /spɑːk; AmE spɑːrk/

,**spark sth 'off** (*informal*) to cause something to suddenly happen or develop: *The incident sparked off riots across the country.* ◇ *His resignation sparked off a political crisis.*
OBJ riots, debate, incident, protest, crisis
NOTE Spark sth is also used with this meaning: *The TV programme sparked a storm of protest.*
◆ v + adv + n ◆ v + pron + adv ◆ v + n + adv (*less frequent*)

,**spark 'up** if a fire **sparks up**, it starts to burn brightly again after a period when it was almost out: *The fire is still smoking and could spark up at any moment.* ◇ (*figurative*) *They sparked up* (= became more lively and interested) *when they heard the music.*
◆ v + adv

,**spark sth 'up** (*informal*) **1** if you **spark up** a conversation, a debate, a friendship, etc., you start one, often suddenly: *I sat down beside Helen and tried to spark up a conversation with her.* **2** to add interest or excitement to sth: *Spark up pasta dishes with fresh herbs.* ◇ *Send a card and spark up someone's day.* **SYN** **spice sth up 3** spark up **sth**, **spark it/them up** to light a fire, etc: (*slang*) *Time to spark up a cigarette.* ◇ (*figurative*) *There is nothing in the book to spark up the reader's interest.* **NOTE** A noun must come after **up**, but a pronoun comes between the verb and **up**.
◆ v + adv + n ◆ v + pron + adv ◆ v + n + adv (*rare*)

speak /spiːk/ (*past* **spoke** /spəʊk; AmE spoʊk/**spoken** /'spəʊkən; AmE 'spoʊ-/)

'**speak for sb 1** to state the wishes or views of sb; to act as a representative for sb: *I can't speak for the others, but I'd love to come.* ◇ *She speaks for a whole generation of disillusioned youngsters.* **SYN** **answer for sb 2** to give evidence to support sb in a court of law: *Many people spoke for her at the trial.*
◆ v + prep

IDM **speak for it'self/them'selves** if something **speaks for itself** it is so clear and easy to understand that it does not need to be explained: *The facts speak for themselves.*

,**speak for your'self** to express your own opinion, although you know that others might not agree with you: *Speaking for myself, I'd prefer to go by train.* ◇ *He speaks for himself when he says we need a smoking area.*
◆ v + prep

IDM **speak for my'self/her'self/him'self/them-'selves** to express your opinion yourself, rather than sb else doing it for you: *I can speak for myself, thank you!* **speak for your'self** (*spoken, informal*) used to tell sb that sth they have said is not true of you: *'We're all tired.' 'Speak for yourself — I'm fine!'*

be 'spoken for 1 to be married or to have a partner already: *You can forget about him, he's spoken for!* **2** to be set aside for a particular purpose: *Half the money is already spoken for.*
◆ be + v + adv

'**speak of sth** (*formal* or *literary*) to be evidence of sth; to suggest sth: *The pictures and ornaments in the room spoke of dreams of faraway places.*
◆ v + prep

,**speak 'out** (**against/in favour of/on** sth) to say what you think clearly and publicly, often criticizing or opposing sb/sth, in a way that needs courage: *People are no longer afraid to speak out.* ◇ *She spoke out against the regime.*
◆ v + adv

▶ **out'spoken** *adj* saying openly exactly what you think, even if you know other people will disagree or be offended: *Her outspoken views often get her into trouble.*

,**speak 'up 1** used to ask sb to speak louder: *Please speak up — we can't hear you at the back.* **2** **(for sb/sth/yourself)** to say what you think clearly and freely, especially to support or defend sb/sth: *Several players spoke up for their manager.* ◇ *She's learned to speak up for herself.* ◇ *It's time to speak up about what is happening in our schools* (= to say we do not like it).
⊕ v + adv

speed /spiːd/ **(speeded, speeded,** or **sped, sped)**

,**speed a'way/'off** to leave very quickly, usually in a vehicle of some kind: *The car sped away from the house.* ◇ *She sped off on her bike to get help.*
NOTE Sped is usually used as the past tense and past participle of this verb.
⊕ v + adv

,**speed 'up**; ,**speed sth 'up** to start to move or happen faster; to make sth do this: *The train started to speed up.* ◇ *Parking restrictions were introduced to try to speed up the traffic.* ◇ *They worked slowly at first, speeding up as they got used to it.* ◇ *The new tool bar on the screen definitely **speeds things up**.*
NOTE Speeded is used as the past tense and past participle of this verb.
⊕ v + adv ◆ v + adv + n ◆ v + n/pron + adv

spell /spel/ **(spelt, spelt** /spelt/ or **spelled, spelled)**

,**spell sth 'out 1** to make sth clear and easy to understand; to explain sth in detail: *His reasons for leaving are spelt out in detail in his letter.* ◇ *Surely I don't have to spell it out?* (= it should be obvious) **2** to say or write the letters of a word in the correct order: *Could you spell that word out for me again?* **NOTE** Spell sth is usually used with this meaning.
⊕ **1** v + adv + n ◆ v + pron + adv ◆ v + n + adv (*less frequent*)
2 v + adv + n ◆ v + n/pron + adv ◆ v + adv + speech

spew /spjuː/

,**spew 'out**; ,**spew sth 'out** to flow out quickly in large amounts; to make sth do this: *lava spewing out from a volcano* ◇ *fumes spewed out by cars and trucks*
NOTE Spew and spew sth are also used with this meaning: *a volcano spewing clouds of ash*
⊕ v + adv ◆ v + adv + n ◆ v + n/pron + adv

,**spew 'up**; ,**spew sth 'up** (*BrE, slang*) to bring food from the stomach back out through the mouth: *He spewed up all over my jacket.*
SYN throw up, throw sth up; vomit, vomit sth (*more formal*)
⊕ v + adv ◆ v + n/pron + adv ◆ v + adv + n

spice /spaɪs/

,**spice sth 'up** to add spice to food in order to give it more flavour and make it more interesting: *Casseroles can be spiced up with a dash of tabasco sauce.* ◇ (*figurative*) *He exaggerated the details to spice up the story.*
SYN jazz sth up (*informal*), liven sth up
⊕ v + adv + n ◆ v + n/pron + adv

spiff /spɪf/

,**spiff sb/sth 'up**; ,**spiff yourself 'up** (*AmE, informal*) to make sb/sth/yourself look more attractive: *We went home to **get spiffed up** for the party.* ◇ *Here are some easy ways to spiff up spreadsheets.*
⊕ v + adv + n ◆ v + n/pron + adv ◆ v + n + adv (*less frequent*)

spill /spɪl/ **(spilled, spilled,** *BrE also* **spilt, spilt** /spɪlt/)

,**spill 'out**; ,**spill 'out of sth 1** to accidentally flow out of a container: *The contents of her bag spilled out everywhere.* ◇ *Water had spilled out onto the floor.* **2** to come out in large numbers or amounts: *The theatre crowds spilled out onto the pavement.* ◇ *The children spilled out into the yard.* **SYN** pour out, pour out of sth
⊕ v + adv

,**spill 'out**; ,**spill sth 'out** to tell sb a secret, your fears, worries, etc. in a hurried and unplanned way: *When she started to speak, the words just came spilling out.* ◇ *She spilled out her troubles to her parents.*
⊕ v + adv ◆ v + adv + n ◆ v + n/pron + adv

,**spill 'over (into/to sth)** to start in one situation or area and then have an effect on another situation or in another area: *Unrest has spilt over into areas outside the city.* ◇ *Anger spilled over into violence at yesterday's demonstration.* ◇ *Her excitement spilled over to the rest of the group.*
⊕ v + adv

▶ **'overspill** *n* [U] [sing.] (*BrE*) people who move from a town or city because it is too crowded and go and live somewhere else: *These towns were built to house overspill populations from the big cities.*

▶ **'spillover** [C] [U] **1** something that is too large or too much for the place where it starts and spreads to other places: *a spillover of riots* ◇ *a spillover room for guests and friends* (= a room where extra guests and friends can go) **2** the results and effects of sth that have spread to other situations or areas: *Other resorts could benefit from the spillover (of tourists).* ◇ *spillover effects/benefits*

,spill 'over; **,spill 'over sth** to flow over the edge of a container that is too full: *The water spilled over the rim of the glass.* ◇ *Her tears suddenly spilled over* (= she started to cry). ◇ *The goods were spilling over from the shops onto the pavements.* ◇ *(figurative) His emotions suddenly spilled over.*
◈ v + adv ♦ v + prep

spin /spɪn/ (**spinning, spun, spun** /spʌn/)

,spin a'round; **,spin sb/sth a'round** (*BrE also* **,spin 'round**, **,spin sb/sth 'round**) **1** to turn very quickly to face in the opposite direction; to turn sb/sth in this way: *She jumped when she heard her name and spun around to see the speaker.* ◇ *He spun her round to face him.* **2** to turn round and round quickly; to make sth do this: *The propeller started to spin around.* ◇ *The room seemed to be spinning round.* ◇ *to spin a ball/coin*
◈ v + adv ♦ v + n/pron + adv

,spin 'off (**from sth**), **,spin sth 'off** (**from sth**) (*especially BrE, business*) to produce a new product, material, service, etc. that is connected with sth successful that already exists; to be produced in this way: *Calendars and diaries spinning off from familiar books and TV shows are always popular.* ◇ *'A Different World' was spun off from 'The Cosby Show'.* ◇ *Their research has spun off many useful applications.*
◈ v + adv ♦ v + adv + n ♦ v + pron + adv ♦ v + n + adv (*rare*)
▶ **'spin-off** *n* **1** an unexpected but useful result of an activity that is designed to produce sth else: *commercial spin-offs from medical research* ◇ *spin-off effects* **2** a product or a book, film/movie, etc. that is based on a very successful book, film/movie or television series: *'The Cosby Show' and its spin-off 'A Different World'* ◇ *a spin-off movie*

,spin sth 'off (*especially AmE, business*) to separate part of a company or an organization from the main part in order to form a new one: *The fast food chain could be spun off as a separate company.*
◈ v + adv + n ♦ v + pron + adv ♦ v + n + adv (*rare*)

,spin sth 'out to make sth last as long as possible: *I managed to spin my talk out to an hour.* ◇ *She had to spin out her money until pay day.*
◈ v + adv + n ♦ v + n/pron + adv

,spin 'round; **,spin sb/sth 'round** (*BrE*) = SPIN AROUND, SPIN SB/STH AROUND

spirit /'spɪrɪt/

,spirit sb/sth a'way/'off (**to sth**) to remove sb/sth quickly, secretly or as if by magic: *He was spirited away by his friends before the police arrived.* ◇ *An enormous amount of money had been spirited away in only two months.*
◈ v + n/pron + adv ♦ v + adv + n

spit /spɪt/ (**spitting, spat, spat** /spæt/ *or* **spitting, spit, spit,** *especially AmE*)

,spit it 'out (*spoken*) used to tell sb to reveal a piece of information or to say sth when they are feeling nervous or unwilling to speak: *Come on, spit it out! Who did it?*
◈ v + it + adv

,spit sth 'out 1 to force sth out of your mouth: *It tasted so horrible he had to spit it out.* **2** to say sth very angrily: *'Men!' She spat the word out.* OBJ **word**
◈ v + n/pron + adv ♦ v + adv + n
2 *also* v + adv + speech

,spit 'up; **,spit sth 'up** (*AmE*) if a baby **spits up** or **spits sth up**, it brings milk back from its stomach out through its mouth: *Put this cloth on your shoulder in case she spits up.* ◇ *Lots of babies spit up a bit of milk after feeding.*
◈ v + adv ♦ v + n/pron + adv ♦ v + adv + n
⊃SYN **vomit, vomit sth; be sick** (*BrE*)
▶ **'spit-up** *n* [U] the milk that a baby brings back out of its mouth

splash /splæʃ/

,splash a'bout (*BrE*) = SPLASH AROUND

,splash sth a'bout/a'round (*informal, especially BrE*) to spend money freely or carelessly: *He splashes his wages about just to impress her.*
◈ v + n/pron + adv ♦ v + adv + n

,splash sth a'cross/o'ver sth to publish a photograph, a news story, etc. in a place where a lot of people will see it, especially in a newspaper: *The next day her name was splashed across all the front pages.* ◇ *I don't want my private life splashed all over the tabloids.*
NOTE **Splash sth across/over sb** is often used in the passive.
◈ v + n/pron + prep

,splash a'round (*BrE also* **,splash a'bout**) (**in sth**) to move about in water making it fly everywhere: *The children splashed about in the river all afternoon.*
◈ v + adv

,splash sth a'round = SPLASH STH ABOUT/AROUND

,splash 'down when a spacecraft **splashes down**, it returns to earth and lands in the sea/ocean: *The capsule splashed down in the Pacific.*
◈ v + adv

▶ **'splashdown** n [C] [U] the return of a spacecraft to earth when it lands in the sea/ocean: *Splashdown is expected 300 kilometres west of Valparaíso.*

,**splash 'out (on sth)**, ,**splash sth 'out (on/for sth)** *(informal)* to spend a lot of money on sth: *She splashed out on a new pair of shoes.* ◇ *Why don't we splash out and go out for a meal?* ◇ *The band splashed out thousands of pounds on new equipment.* ◇ *Don't splash it all out at once!*
➔ v + adv ◆ v + adv + n ◆ v + pron + adv ◆ v + n + adv *(rare)*

,**splash sth 'over sth** = SPLASH STH ACROSS/ OVER STH

split /splɪt/ (splitting, split, split)

,**split a'way/'off (from sth)**, ,**split sth a'way/'off (from sth)** to separate from, or be separated from, a large object or a group: *The branch had split away from the main trunk.* ◇ *The wind split the door away from its frame.* ◇ *Some of the members split away to form a new party.* ◇ *Should the ownership of the rail track be split off from the running of the train services?*
➔ v + adv ◆ v + adv + n ◆ v + n/pron + adv

'split on sb (to sb) *(BrE, informal)* to tell sb in authority about sth bad or wrong that sb has done: *Promise you won't split on me.*
⟩SYN⟨ tell on sb
➔ v + prep

,**split 'up (with/from sb)**, ,**split sb 'up** *(informal)* to end a relationship or a marriage; to make two people stop having a relationship with each other: *He told me he had split up with his girlfriend.* ◇ *The band split up at the height of their fame.* ◇ *My friend is doing her best to split Maria and me up.*
⟩SYN⟨ break up (with sb), break sb up
➔ v + adv ◆ v + n/pron + adv ◆ v + adv + n

,**split 'up (into sth)**, ,**split sb/sth 'up (into sth)** if a group of people or a family **splits up**, or sb **splits it up**, the members separate and do not stay together: *We split up into groups to discuss the question.* ◇ *The class was split up into groups.* ◇ *We got split up in the crowd.*
⟩SYN⟨ break up, break sb/sth up
➔ v + adv ◆ v + n/pron + adv ◆ v + adv + n

,**split sth 'up (into sth)** to divide sth into smaller parts: *The day was split up into 6 one-hour classes.* ◇ *We split the profits up between us.*
➔ v + n/pron + adv ◆ v + adv + n

spoil /spɔɪl/ (spoiled, spoiled /spɔɪld/, *BrE* also spoilt, spoilt /spɔɪlt/)

'spoil for sth *(informal)* *(only used in the progressive tenses)* to be very eager to fight sb: *He was spoiling for a fight.*
OBJ a fight
➔ v + prep

sponge /spʌndʒ/

,**sponge sb/sth 'down** to wash sb/sth with a wet cloth or a soft material: *I sponged the coat down to remove the mud.* ◇ *She tried sponging the baby down to lower his temperature.*
➔ v + n/pron + adv ◆ v + adv + n

'sponge off sb *(also* **'sponge on sb** *less frequent)* *(informal, disapproving)* to get money, food, etc. from other people, without doing anything for them or offering to pay: *He's constantly sponging off his friends.*
➔ v + prep

,**sponge sth 'off**; ,**sponge sth 'off sth** *(especially BrE)* to remove a mark, some dirt, etc. with a wet cloth or a piece of a soft material: *It was impossible to sponge the mark off.* ◇ *I couldn't sponge the stain off my dress.*
➔ v + n/pron + adv ◆ v + adv + n ◆ v + n/pron + prep

'sponge on sb = SPONGE OFF SB

spout /spaʊt/

,**spout 'off/'on (about sth)** *(informal, disapproving)* to talk about sth in a boring or annoying way: *He's always spouting off about the behaviour of young people today.* ◇ *What are you spouting on about now?*
➔ v + adv

sprawl /sprɔːl/

,**sprawl 'out** to sit or lie down with your arms and legs spread out in a relaxed or awkward way: *He came home and just sprawled out on the sofa.*
NOTE Sprawl is used more frequently with the same meaning: *Tom sprawled in the armchair.*
➔ v + adv

spread /spred/ (spread, spread)

,**spread 'out 1** to gradually cover a wider area: *The city has spread out into what used to be countryside.* ◇ *The ripples spread out across the water.* ◇ *(figurative) A bright future spread out before him.* **NOTE Spread** is also frequently used with this meaning: *The fields spread for miles along the river.* **2** *(also* ,**spread yourselves 'out)** to move away from others in a group so as to cover a wider area: *The search party spread out over the moor.* ◇ *Don't all sit together. Spread yourselves out.* **NOTE** When this phrasal verb is used with a reflexive pronoun, the pronoun is always plural: *ourselves, yourselves* or *themselves.* **3** *(also* ,**spread yourself 'out)** to stretch your body or arrange your things over a large area: *There's more room to spread out in business class.* ◇ *Do you have to spread yourself out all over the sofa?*
➔ **1** v + adv
    2,3 also v + pron + adv

,spread 'out; be ,spread 'out to cover a wide area: *The valley spread out beneath us.* ◊ *We looked down at the city spread out below us.*
NOTE This verb is often used in descriptions of cities, views, etc. ♦ **Spread** and **be spread** are also frequently used with this meaning: *The valley lay spread before us.*
🔄 v + adv ♦ be + v + adv

,spread sth 'out 1 to arrange a group of objects on a surface so that you can see them all clearly: *Spread out all the pieces before you begin the jigsaw.* ◊ *All the brochures were spread out on the floor.* **2** to unfold sth and put it down on a flat surface: *They spread the blanket out on the grass.* ◊ *The map had been spread out on the table.* **OBJ** **map, newspaper, blanket 3** to stretch your fingers, arms, etc. so that they are apart: *The boy spread out his arms, pretending to be an aeroplane.* **OBJ** **arms, hands** **NOTE** **Spread sth** is also frequently used with this meaning. **4 (over sth)** to separate sth into parts and arrange them over a period of time or divide them between different people: *The cost can be spread out over two years.* ◊ *I'll try to spread out the work evenly.* **OBJ** **cost, work** **SYN** **divide sth** (*more formal*)
NOTE **Spread sth (over sth)** is also frequently used with this meaning: *Payments can be spread (over five years).*
🔄 v + n/pron + adv ♦ v + adv + n

,spread yourself 'out = SPREAD OUT 3
,spread yourselves 'out = SPREAD OUT 2

spring /sprɪŋ/ (**sprang** /spræŋ/**sprung** /sprʌŋ/, *AmE also* **sprung, sprung**)

'spring for sth (*AmE, slang*) to pay for sth for other people: *I'll spring for lunch.*
🔄 v + prep

'spring from sth 1 (*written*) to be caused by sth; to start from sth: *The idea for the novel sprang from a trip to India.* ◊ *Aggression often springs from fear.* **2** (*informal*) (*usually used in questions*) to appear suddenly or unexpectedly from somewhere: *Where on earth did you spring from?*
🔄 v + prep

'spring sth on sb to suddenly do, say or suggest sth that people do not expect: *I hate to spring this on you at such short notice.* ◊ *They were planning to spring a surprise on us.* ◊ *I didn't know a thing about Rob's new job until he sprang it on me this morning.*
🔄 v + n/pron + prep

,spring 'up to appear, develop, grow, etc. quickly or suddenly: *Weeds were springing up everywhere.* ◊ *Several new cafés sprang up in the area.* ◊ *A cool breeze had sprung up.* ◊ *New industries were springing up all over the country.*
🔄 v + adv

spruce /spruːs/

,spruce sb/sth 'up; ,spruce yourself 'up to make sb/sth/yourself tidy and clean: *We spruced up the room with a coat of paint.* ◊ *He spruced himself up for the interview.*
SYN **smarten up, smarten yourself up; smarten sb/sth up**
🔄 v + adv + n ♦ v + pron + adv ♦ v + n + adv (*less frequent*)

spur /spɜː(r)/ (**-rr-**)

,spur sb 'on (to sth/to do sth) to encourage sb to act in a particular way, especially to work harder or to try to achieve sth: *Her difficult childhood spurred her on to succeed.* ◊ *His parents' encouragement spurred him on to greater efforts.* ◊ *Spurred on by this victory, we went on to win the championship.* ◊ *Their shouts of encouragement spurred us on.*
SYN **encourage sb**
NOTE **Spur sb on** is often used in the passive: *He was spurred on by new hope.* ♦ **Spur sb** followed by an infinitive or a phrase beginning with a preposition is also used with this meaning: *His criticism spurred me to try harder.*
🔄 v + n/pron + adv ♦ v + adv + n

spurt /spɜːt; *AmE* spɜːrt/

,spurt 'out; ,spurt 'out of sth; ,spurt sth 'out; ,spurt sth 'out of sth to come out of sth in a sudden or fast stream; to pour out a sudden fast stream of liquid or flames: *Water spurted out of the hole.* ◊ *The volcano was spurting out rivers of molten lava.*
🔄 v + adv ♦ v + adv + prep ♦ v + adv + n ♦ v + n/pron + adv ♦ v + n/pron + adv + prep

spy /spaɪ/ (**spies, spying, spied, spied**)

'spy on sb/sth (*also* **'spy upon sb/sth** *more formal*) to watch sb/sth secretly: *He hired a detective to spy on his wife.*
NOTE **Spy on sb/sth** can be used in the passive: *He knew he was being spied on.*
🔄 v + prep

,spy sth 'out (*BrE*) to go somewhere secretly to try to find out information: *I arrived early to spy out the land* (= collect information before deciding what do do). ◊ *He studied the map and spied out the quickest route.*
🔄 v + adv + n ♦ v + pron + adv ♦ v + n + adv (*rare*)

square /skweə(r); *AmE* skwer/

,square sth a'way (*AmE*) to finish dealing with sth; to put sth in order: *We need to get everything squared away before you leave.*
NOTE **Square sth away** is often used in the passive.
🔄 v + n/pron + adv ♦ v + adv + n

,square 'off (against sb) (AmE) to fight or to prepare to fight sb: *The two candidates will square off in a TV debate tomorrow.* ◇ *Protesting students squared off against police.*
◆ v + adv

,square 'up 1 (to sb) (BrE) to stand facing sb as if you are prepared to fight or argue with them: *Kath put her hands on her hips and squared up to him.* 2 (to sb/sth) to face a difficult situation and deal with it in a determined way: *He must square up to the reality of being out of work.* ⟨SYN⟩ **face up to sth 3** (with sb) to pay sb the money you owe them: *Can I leave you to square up with the waiter?* ⟨SYN⟩ **settle up** (with sb)
◆ v + adv

'square with sth; 'square sth with sth to agree with another fact, idea or situation; to make two facts, ideas or situations agree with each other: *This doesn't square with what you told us earlier.* ◇ *How do you square your profession with your religious beliefs?* ◇ *We must remember that the interests of the farmers need to be squared with those of consumers.*
◆ v + prep ◆ v + n/pron + prep

'square sth with sb to get sb's approval before you do sth: *You'd better square it with the boss if you want to leave early.*
◆ v + n/pron + prep

squash /skwɒʃ; AmE skwɑːʃ, skwɔːʃ/

,squash 'in; ,squash 'into sth = SQUEEZE IN, SQUEEZE INTO STH *Can I squash in?* ◇ *We all squashed into the back of the van.*

,squash sb/sth 'in; ,squash sb/sth 'into sth = SQUEEZE SB/STH IN, SQUEEZE SB/STH INTO STH *We can squash you in.*

,squash sb/sth to'gether to press people or things tightly together in a small space: *people living squashed together in terrible conditions* **NOTE** Squash sb/sth together is usually used in the passive.
◆ v + n/pron + adv ◆ v + adv + n (rare)

,squash 'up (against sb/sth), ,squash sb/sth 'up (against sb/sth) (BrE) = SQUEEZE UP, SQUEEZE SB/STH UP *If we squash up there'll be room for one more.* ◇ *I was squashed up against Jo in the back of the van.*

squeak /skwiːk/

,squeak 'by (AmE, informal) to achieve a successful result with great difficulty: *We just squeaked by in the semi-final.*
◆ v + adv

,squeak 'through; ,squeak 'through sth (informal) to manage to achieve sth or get a successful result with great difficulty: *Andrew squeaked through the qualifying rounds of the championship.*
◆ v + adv ◆ v + prep

squeeze /skwiːz/

,squeeze 'in; ,squeeze 'into sth (also ,squash 'in, ,squash 'into sth) to just manage to fit into a small space: *The bus was so full not one more passenger could have squeezed in.*
◆ v + adv ◆ v + prep

,squeeze sb/sth 'in; ,squeeze sb/sth 'into sth 1 (also ,squash sb/sth 'in, ,squash sb/sth 'into sth) to just manage to put sb/sth into a small space: *Can you squeeze anything else into that case?* 2 to just manage to fit sb/sth into a short period of time: *The doctor can squeeze you in on Tuesday morning.* ◇ *All my classes are squeezed into four days a week.*
◆ v + n/pron + adv ◆ v + adv + n ◆ v + n/pron + prep

,squeeze sb/sth 'out; ,squeeze sb/sth 'out of sth to prevent sb/sth from doing sth or from doing business: *Small firms are being squeezed out by larger companies.* ◇ *One candidate has already been squeezed out of the leadership race.* ⟨SYN⟩ **crowd sb/sth out, crowd sb/sth out of sth; exclude sb/sth (from sth)**
◆ v + n/pron + adv ◆ v + adv + n ◆ v + n/pron + adv + prep

,squeeze sth 'out 1 (also ,squeeze sth 'out of sth) to remove liquid from sth by pressing it hard: *She squeezed the cloth out.* ◇ *You'll need to squeeze the juice out of four oranges.* 2 (also ,squeeze sth 'out of sb/sth) to get sth such as information or money from sb by putting pressure on them, threatening them, etc: *The government will always try to squeeze more money out of the taxpayer.* ◇ *The police squeezed the truth out of him.* ◇ *They finally squeezed some concessions out of the employers.*
◆ v + n/pron + adv ◆ v + adv + n ◆ v + n/pron + adv + prep

,squeeze 'up (against sth), ,squeeze sb/sth 'up (against sth) (also ,squash 'up, ,squash sb/sth 'up) to move closer towards sb so that you are pressed tightly together: *There'll be enough room if we all squeeze up a bit.* ◇ *I'll walk — it's better than being squeezed up in the back of the car.*
◆ v + adv ◆ v + n/pron + adv ◆ v + adv + n

squirrel /'skwɪrəl; AmE 'skwɜːrəl/ (-ll-, AmE -l-)

,squirrel sth a'way to put sth, especially money, in a safe place so that you can use it later: *She had money squirrelled away in various bank accounts.*
◆ v + n/pron + adv ◆ v + adv + n

stack /stæk/

,stack 'up 1 to increase gradually until there is a large pile, a long line, etc: *Over the months he just let the paperwork stack up.* ◇ *The traffic quickly stacked up behind the bus.* ⟨SYN⟩ **pile up 2** (**against** sb/sth) (*informal*) to compare with sb/sth: *How does this washing powder stack up against your usual brand?* ◊ *Let's try him in the team and see how he stacks up.* SYN **compare** (**with sb/sth**)

◆ v + adv

,**stack 'up**; ,**stack sth 'up** if planes **stack up** or are **stacked up** over an airport, there are a lot of them flying around waiting to land: *Planes stacked up at Heathrow after an accident on the runway.*

NOTE **Stack** and **stack sth** are sometimes used with this meaning: *a queue of planes stacked in the air over the closed airport*

◆ v + adv ◆ v + adv + n ◆ v + n/pron + adv

,**stack sth 'up 1** to arrange things in a tall pile: *He stacked up the dishes on the draining board.* SYN **pile sth up** NOTE **Stack sth** is often used with this meaning. **2** (*AmE, informal*) to gradually get more of sth: *She's stacking up the college credits with all of her night classes.*

◆ v + n/pron + adv ◆ v + adv + n

stake /steɪk/

'**stake sth on sth**; '**stake sth on doing sth** to risk money or sth very important on the result of sth or on sth happening: *He staked twenty pounds on the favourite* (= in horse racing, for example). ◊ *Several journalists staked their reputation on Bush winning the election.* ◊ *He'll never let you down—I'd stake my life on it.*

◆ v + n/pron + prep

stake sth 'out 1 to mark the position and the limits of a piece of land or an area to show that you own it: *The male stakes out his territory and defends it from other birds.* **2** to state your position or opinion on sth clearly: *The President staked out his position on the issue.* **3** if police **stake out** a building, they watch it secretly and continuously because they think sth illegal is happening there: *Armed police have been staking out the house for two weeks.* ◊ *The cops had the building staked out.*

◆ v + adv + n ◆ v + pron + adv ◆ v + n + adv (*rare*)

▶ '**stake-out** *n* a situation when police watch a building continuously and secretly because they think sth illegal is happening there: *The stake-out at the house produced nothing.*

stamp /stæmp/

stamp on sth 1 to bring your foot down on sth with force: *The child stamped on the spider.* ◊ *She stamped on his foot as hard as she could.* ◊ *The victim had been kicked and stamped on.* ◊ *A child ran out into the road and I had to stamp on the brakes.* **2** (*especially BrE*) to control sth or stop sth from happening by force: *This kind of disobedience must be stamped on at once.*

NOTE **Stamp on sb/sth** can be used in the passive.

◆ v + prep

'**stamp sth on sth** to make sth have an important effect or influence on sth: *She stamped her own interpretation on the role.* ◊ *The new director has worked hard to stamp his authority on the board.* ◊ *The date is forever stamped on her memory.*

OBJ **your authority, your mark**

◆ v + n/pron + prep

,**stamp sth 'out 1** to destroy or get rid of sth bad or unpleasant by force or with a lot of effort: *They aim to stamp out drug dealing in schools.* ◊ *The party chairman is determined to stamp out corruption.* OBJ **a problem, drug abuse** SYN **eradicate sth** (*more formal*) **2** to put out a fire by pressing down on it hard with your foot: *He stamped out the flames before they spread any further.*

◆ **1** v + n/pron + adv ◆ v + adv + n
   2 v + adv + n ◆ v + pron + adv ◆ v + n + adv (*rare*)

stand /stænd/ (**stood, stood** /stʊd/)

~ about		~ in
~ around		~ out
~ aside		~ over
~ back		~ round
280	~ between	~ up
~ by	281	~ up for
~ down		~ up to
~ for		

,**stand a'round**; ,**stand a'round sb/sth** (*also* (*BrE also*, ,**stand a'bout/'round**, ,**stand 'round sb/sth** *BrE*) to stand in a place doing nothing, either waiting for sb/sth or with no particular purpose: *Don't just stand around watching me, give me a hand.* ◊ *There were a few people standing around the square.* ◊ *A group of people stood around watching.* ◊ *Young men stood about in groups, chatting.*

◆ v + adv ◆ v + prep

,**stand a'side 1** to move to one side to let sb/sth pass: *Stand aside please and let her through.* **2** to take no part in events; to do nothing: *I can't stand aside and let you waste an opportunity like that.* **3** to stop doing a job so that sb else can do it: *It's time he stood aside and let somebody younger take his place.*

◆ v + adv

,**stand 'back** (**from sth**) **1** to move a short distance away from sb/sth: *Stand well back from the flames.* **2** to be situated at a distance from sth: *The house stands back from the road.* **3** to think about a situation as if you are not involved in it: *She found it hard to stand back from the situation.* ◊ *This is an opportunity to stand back and think about what you have achieved.* SYN **step back** (**from sth**)

◆ v + adv

,**stand be'tween A and B** to prevent sb from doing or having sth, or being in a particular situation: *Only three people stood between him and the crown* (= becoming king). ◇ *Your lack of confidence is all that stands between you and a much better job.*

◈ v + prep

,**stand 'by 1** to be present when sth bad or unpleasant is happening, but not become involved: *I can't stand idly by and let him take the blame for what happened.* ◇ *I can't stand by and see you ruin your life.* **2 (for sth)** to be ready to take appropriate action: *The pilot was instructed to stand by for take-off.* ◇ *Fire crews are standing by in case of an explosion.*

◈ v + adv

▸ '**bystander** *n* a person who is present but is not involved in sth: *Two innocent bystanders were hit by stray bullets.*

▸ '**standby** *n* **1** [C] a person or a thing that can be used if sb/sth else is not available: *Keep some candles as a standby in case the power fails.* ◇ *Mia made a delicious meal from standbys in the store cupboard.* **2** [U] a state of being ready to act if necessary: *All local hospitals have been put on standby.*

▸ '**standby** *adj* [only before noun] **1** that can be used if other things are not available: *standby supplies* ◇ *Two divers work together while a standby diver remains on the surface.* **2** a **standby** ticket for a flight, a theatre, etc. is one that cannot be bought in advance and is only available a very short time before the plane leaves or the performance starts: *standby passengers* ◇ *to fly standby* (= with a standby ticket)

,**stand 'by sb** to support or help sb in a difficult situation: *I'll stand by you whatever happens.*

〉SYN〈 **stick by sb** (*informal*)

◈ v + prep

'**stand by sth** to continue to believe sth you said earlier even though the situation may now be different: *I'll stand by what I said earlier.* ◇ *He appealed against his suspension, but the committee stood by their decision.*

◈ v + prep

,**stand 'down 1 (as/from sth)** to leave a job or position; to stop taking part in a race or a competition, etc: *She stood down after only three months as chairman.* ◇ *He stood down from the committee for personal reasons.* 〉SYN〈 **step down (as/from sth) 2** (in a court of law) to leave the place where you stand to give evidence: *The witness was allowed to stand down.*

◈ v + adv

'**stand for sth 1** (*not used in the progressive tenses*) to be an abbreviation of sth: *What does DVD stand for?* **2** to support sth; to be in favour of sth: *Our party stands for racial harmony.* ◇ *I hated him and all he stood for.* **3** (*used in negative*

sentences and questions) to allow sth to happen or sb to do sth: *I won't stand for this behaviour.* 〉SYN〈 **put up with sth; tolerate sth** (*more formal*)

◈ v + prep

,**stand 'in (for sb)** to take sb's place: *We'll need someone to stand in for you while you're away.* 〉SYN〈 **deputize (for sb)** (*formal*)

◈ v + adv

▸ '**stand-in** *n* **1** a person who does sb's job for a short time while they are away or not available: *Tom acted as my stand-in while I was abroad.* ◇ *a stand-in captain/goalkeeper* (= for example, in a football game) **2** a person who replaces an actor in some scenes in a film/movie, especially dangerous ones: *rehearsing with stand-ins*

,**stand 'out 1 (against/from sth)** to be clearly visible: *His yellow jacket stood out clearly against the grey hillside.* ◇ *The church tower stands out against the sky.* ◇ *A small figure in red stood out from the rest of the group.* 〉SYN〈 **stick out 2 (as/from sb/sth)** to be much better or more important than other people or things: *This building stands out from the rest because of its superior design.* ◇ *She's the sort of person who always stands out in a crowd.* **3 (against/fo sb/sth)** to oppose or refuse to accept sth that you believe is wrong: *Parents often stand out against troublesome behaviour for some time, then give in.* 〉SYN〈 **stick out for sth; hold out against for sth**

◈ v + adv

IDM **stand out like a sore thumb** to be very noticeable in an unpleasant way: *Dressed lik that, you'll stand out like a sore thumb.*

▸ **out'standing** *adj* **1** excellent: *an outstandin young actress* **2** [usually before noun] very obv ous or important: *Lake Baykal is one of earth outstanding features.* **3** (of payment, work, prob lems, etc.) not yet paid, done, solved, etc: *to repa outstanding debts* ◇ *I don't have any urgent wor outstanding.*

▸ **out'standingly** *adv* **1** used to emphasize th good quality of sth: *outstandingly beautiful/su cessful* **2** extremely well: *Owen has played ou standingly this season.*

,**stand 'over sb** to remain close to sb and watc them, usually to make sure that they behave do sth correctly: *She won't do her homewor unless I stand over her.* ◇ *I can't concentrate wi you standing over me.*

◈ v + prep

,**stand 'round; ,stand 'round sb/sth** (*BrE*) STAND AROUND, STAND AROUND SB/STH

,**stand 'up 1** to rise to your feet from a sitting lying position; to be on your feet: *Darcy stood when Emma came into the room.* ◇ *There was s ence when the President stood up to speak.* **Stand up straight** instead of slouching. ◇ *Hors can sleep standing up.* **2 (to sth)** to remain true correct even when tested, examined closely, e

Your theory doesn't stand up to close examination. ◇ *His story won't stand up under cross-examination.* ⟨SYN⟩ **hold up 3 (to sth)** to be strong enough not to be harmed by sth: *The children stood up well under questioning from the police.* ◇ *The players are standing up to the tour well.*

◈ v + adv

▸ **'stand-up** *adj* [only before noun] **1** a **stand-up** comedian (= an entertainer who makes people laugh by telling jokes) is sb who stands in front of an audience and tells jokes or funny stories: *stand-up comedy* ◇ *a stand-up act* **2** (*especially BrE*) a **stand-up** argument, fight, etc. is one in which people shout loudly at each other or are violent towards each other: *He had a stand-up row with the team captain.*

stand sb 'up (*informal*) to deliberately fail to meet sb you have arranged to meet, especially sb you are having a romantic relationship with: *We agreed to meet at the cinema but she stood me up.* ◇ *I've been stood up!*

◈ v + n/pron + adv ◆ v + adv + n (*less frequent*)

stand 'up for sb/sth/yourself to support or defend sb/sth/yourself, especially when sb is criticizing them/it/you: *She's always stood up for her friends.* ◇ *You should stand up for what you believe in.* ◇ *He's always telling her what to do. It's time she stood up for herself!* ◇ *James doesn't need you to stand up for him.*

⟨OBJ⟩ **your rights, your interests**
◈ v + adv + prep

stand 'up to sb/sth to resist sb/sth; to defend your position against a more powerful person or organization that is treating you badly or unfairly: *If you don't stand up to him he'll treat you like dirt.* ◇ *It was difficult for Paul to stand up to his father's rage.*

◈ v + adv + prep

stand 'up to sth (of a product, material, etc.) to be able to stay in good condition even though it is treated roughly: *Will your china and glass stand up to family wear and tear?*

⟨SYN⟩ **withstand sth** (*formal*)
◈ v + adv + prep

stare /steə(r); *AmE* ster/

stare sb 'out (*BrE*) (*also* **stare sb 'down** *AmE, BrE*) to look sb directly in the eyes for a long time until they feel forced to lower their eyes or look away: *He was looking at her intently but she stared him out.* ◇ (*figurative*) *The two nations are trying to stare each other down.*

◈ v + n/pron + adv ◆ v + adv + n (*less frequent*)

start /stɑːt; *AmE* stɑːrt/

start 'back to begin to return somewhere: *It's time we started back.*

◈ v + adv

'start for … to leave one place to go to another: *We started for home.*

⟨SYN⟩ **head for** …
◈ v + prep

start 'in (on sth) (*informal, especially AmE*) to begin to do sth: *Let's start in now and get the job done quickly.* ◇ *It's time you started in on your homework.*

◈ v + adv

start 'in on sb/sth (*especially AmE*) **1** = START ON SB/STH **2** = START ON AT SB

start 'off 1 (*also* **start 'off doing sth, start sth 'off**) [+ adv/prep/adj] to begin happening in a particular way; to begin doing sth in a particular way: *The game started off well, but gradually got worse.* ◇ *We started off with some gentle exercises.* ◇ *She started off by welcoming everyone.* ◇ *He started off as a plumber.* ◇ *I started off working quite hard, but it didn't last.* ◇ *The discussion started off calmly enough.* ◇ *The leaves start off green but turn red later.* ◇ *We always started off the lessons with a quiz.* ◇ *The teacher started things off by asking us what we had done at the weekend.* ⟨NOTE⟩ In this meaning, **start off** and **start off sth** are always followed by an adverb, an adjective, a phrase beginning with a preposition, or the *-ing* form of a verb. **2** [+adv/prep] to begin to move or travel: *The bus started off with a jolt.* ◇ *We started off for home.*

◈ **1** v + adv ◆ v + adv + -ing ◆ v + adv + n ◆
v + pron + adv ◆ v + n + adv (*rare*)
2 v + adv

start sb 'off 1 (on sth) (*also* **start sb 'off doing sth**) to help sb begin an activity, an exercise, a job, etc: *I'll start you off on the first exercise.* ◇ *His father started him off farming.* **2** (*also* **start sb 'off doing sth**) to make sb react in a particular way or begin doing sth: *Just mentioning 'The Simpsons' started her off again* (= made her start laughing). ◇ *Don't shout — you'll start the baby off* (*crying*) *again.* ⟨SYN⟩ **set sb off, set sb off doing sth**

⟨NOTE⟩ **Start sb off** cannot be used in the passive in this meaning.
◈ v + n/pron + adv

start sth 'off
→ *see also* START OFF 1

'start on sb/sth (*also* **start 'in on sb/sth** *especially AmE*) (*informal*) to attack sb physically or with words: *He hit me first and then he started* (*in*) *on my friend.* ◇ *Don't start on me, I'm tired.* ◇ *My mum started on me about doing my homework as soon as I got home.*

◈ v + prep ◆ v + adv + prep

'start on sth to begin to deal with sth; to begin to do sth: *When she'd finished cleaning the kitchen, she started on the bathroom.*

⟨NOTE⟩ **Start sth** has a similar meaning.
◈ v + prep

,start 'on at sb (*BrE*) (*also* ,start 'on about sth, ,start 'in on sb/sth *AmE, BrE*) (*informal*) to begin to criticize sb/sth or complain to sb about sth: *He started on at me again about my hair.* ◇ *Don't start on about that dog barking.*
◈ v + adv + prep

,start 'out 1 to begin a journey: *Check the engine before you start out.* ◇ *What time did they start out?* ⟩SYN⟨ set off 2 (as sth) to begin in a particular way, especially in business or work: *We started out originally as a taxi firm.* ◇ *When the band started out, they had hardly any equipment.* ◇ *Did you know the tower started out leaning the other way?* 3 (*also* ,start 'out to do sth, ,start 'out doing sth) to have a particular idea or intention when you begin to do sth: *I had no idea what I was going to write about when I started out.* ◇ *She had started out to write a short story but it ended up as a novel.* ◇ *He started out with no political opinions, but soon got involved in student politics.* ◇ *She'd started out meaning to apologize but couldn't.* ⟩SYN⟨ set out to do sth
◈ v + adv 3 also v + adv + to inf ◆ v + adv + -ing

,start 'over; ,start sth 'over (*especially AmE*) to begin doing sth again, especially because you were not successful the first time: *I messed up and had to start over.* ◇ *She spelled my name wrong and had to start over.* ◇ *His wife has walked out on him and he must start life over.*
◈ v + adv ◆ v + n/pron + adv

,start 'up to begin happening: *After a moment's silence, the music started up again.*
◈ v + adv

,start 'up; ,start sth 'up 1 to start operating; to make sth start operating: *The engine started up with a roar.* ◇ *It took me a while to start up the generator.* ◇ *I heard the car starting up.* 2 (in sth) to start operating or trading; to establish a business: *When I started up in business, I needed a lot of help.* ◇ *There are a lot of small businesses starting up in the area.* ◇ *My father helped me start up my own company.* ⟨OBJ⟩ business, company
◈ v + adv ◆ v + adv + n ◆ v + n/pron + adv
▶ 'start-up *adj* connected with beginning a new business: *the new company's start-up costs*
▶ 'start-up *n* a company that is just beginning to operate, especially an Internet company: *This is just one of the problems facing start-ups in this highly competitive area.*

starve /stɑːv; *AmE* stɑːrv/

'starve for sth; 'starve sb/sth for sth (*AmE*) to feel you do not have something that you really need; to prevent sb/sth from having sth necessary or very important: *Sam was starving for a kind word from Clare.* ◇ *The children were starved for affection.*

⟨NOTE⟩ Starve for sth is usually used in the progressive tenses. ◆ Starve sb/sth for sth is usually used in the passive.
→ *see also* STARVE SB/STH OF STH
◈ v + prep ◆ v + n/pron + prep

'starve sb into sth; 'starve sb into doing sth to force sb to do sth or accept sth by preventing them from getting food or money: *The aim was to starve the enemy into submission.*
◈ v + n/pron + prep

'starve sb/sth of sth to prevent sb/sth from having sth that they want or need: *The project is being starved of funds.* ◇ *The baby had been starved of oxygen at birth.* ◇ *Teachers described the students as starved of attention and affection.* ⟩SYN⟨ deprive sb/sth/yourself of sth
⟨NOTE⟩ Starve sb/sth of sth is usually used in the passive.
→ *see also* STARVE FOR STH, STARVE SB/STH FOR STH
◈ v + n/pron + prep

,starve sb 'out to force sb to leave a place by not allowing them to get food: *It took a month to starve them out.* ◇ *A few rebels remain in the area. The rest have been starved out.*
◈ v + n/pron + adv ◆ v + adv + n

stash /stæʃ/

,stash sth a'way (*informal*) to store sth in a secret or safe place: *She has a fortune stashed away in various bank accounts.*
⟩SYN⟨ hide sth away
◈ v + n/pron + adv ◆ v + adv + n

stave /steɪv/

,stave sth 'in to break sth by hitting it with force and making part of it fall inwards: *The side of the boat was staved in when it hit the rocks.*
◈ v + n/pron + adv ◆ v + adv + n

,stave sth 'off to prevent sth unpleasant from happening for a period of time; to delay sth unpleasant: *to stave off hunger/illness* ◇ *desperate attempts to stave off civil war* ◇ *I staved off jet lag with a bath and an early night.*
⟩SYN⟨ avert sth
◈ v + adv + n ◆ v + pron + adv ◆ v + n + adv (*rare*)

stay /steɪ/

	~ ahead	~ off
283	~ around	~ on
	~ away	~ out
	~ back	~ out of
	~ behind	~ over
	~ down	~ up
	~ in	~ with

,stay a'head; ,stay a'head of sb/sth to succeed in remaining further forward in space, time, development, success, etc: *We need to ke* an eye on our competitors if we want to stay ahead. ◇ He stayed ahead of me throughout the race. ◇ More investment is needed if we are to **stay ahead of the game** (= be more successful than our competitors).

[OBJ] competitors
[SYN] **keep ahead**, **keep ahead of sb/sth**
✦ v + adv ✦ v + adv + prep

,**stay a'round** to not leave somewhere: I'll stay around in case you need me. ◇ I don't know if he'll be angry with us or not, but I'm not staying around to find out!
✦ v + adv

,**stay a'way** (**from sb/sth**) to not go near sb/sth dangerous or unpleasant; to have nothing to do with sb/sth: Stay away from the edge! ◇ He advised us to stay away from drugs. ◇ The police have asked the public to stay away.
[SYN] **keep away** (**from sb/sth**)
✦ v + adv

,**stay 'back** to remain in a place and not move forward: The police shouted to the crowd to stay back.
[SYN] **keep back** (**from sb/sth**)
✦ v + adv

,**stay be'hind** (**after sth**) to remain in a place at the end of an event after other people have left: I had to stay behind after class. ◇ She stayed behind after the meeting for a chat.
✦ v + adv

,**stay 'down 1** to remain in a low position: The blind won't stay down. ◇ Get down and stay down or he'll see you! [SYN] **keep down 2** (of food) to remain in the stomach: Nothing she ate would stay down.
✦ v + adv

,**stay 'in 1** to remain in a position inside sth: This nail won't stay in. **2** to remain at home or inside a building: I was ill and had to stay in all week. ◇ Let's stay in this evening.
✦ v + adv

,**stay 'off** to keep away; to not return: If the rain stays off, we'll get out for a walk. ◇ She's always dieting, but she can never get the weight to stay off.
✦ v + adv

,**stay 'off**; ,**stay 'off sth** (BrE) to not go to work, school, etc., especially because you are ill/sick: He injured his back and stayed off for a week. ◇ Can I stay off school today?
[OBJ] **work**, **school**
✦ v + adv ✦ v + prep

,**stay 'off sth** to stop yourself from eating or drinking sth, especially sth that could be harmful: The doctor told him to stay off alcohol.
[SYN] **keep off sth**
✦ v + prep

,**stay 'on 1** to remain in position on top of sth: The lid won't stay on. **2** to not leave a job, school, place, etc. when you are expected to, or when other

people do: We hope he will stay on as manager at the end of his contract. ◇ We couldn't persuade Jane to stay on at school for an extra year. **3** to continue operating: The light stays on until dawn.
✦ v + adv

,**stay 'out 1** to remain out of the house or outdoors, especially at night: Sam was allowed to stay out until 11.30 on a Saturday. ◇ I don't like you staying out so late. Try to come home earlier next time. **2** to remain on strike: The miners stayed out for fifteen months.
✦ v + adv

,**stay 'out**; ,**stay 'out of sth** to remain outside a place: Stay out, the floor's wet. ◇ Stay out of the kitchen, I'm busy.
✦ v + adv ✦ v + adv + prep

,**stay 'out of sth 1** to not become involved in sth that does not concern you: I try to stay out of their little quarrels. ◇ Stay out of this, it's none of your business. **2** to avoid sth: Try to stay out of trouble!
[SYN] **keep out of sth**, **keep sb out of sth**
✦ v + adv + prep

,**stay 'over** to sleep at sb's house for a night: It got late, so we stayed over. ◇ Can I stay over at Gareth's (house) tonight?
[SYN] **sleep over**
✦ v + adv

,**stay 'up 1** if something **stays up**, it remains in an upright or higher position where it has been put, built, etc: These trousers won't stay up without a belt. ◇ I'm not very good at putting up shelves — I'm amazed they've stayed up! **2** to not go to bed: Don't **stay up** too **late**. ◇ We let him stay up to watch the movie.
✦ v + adv

'**stay with sth/sb** (informal) to continue to do sth, especially when it is difficult or you do not really want to; to wait until sb has finished sth: Several students said they weren't enjoying the course, but they stayed with it. ◇ Stay with me, I've nearly finished this list.
[SYN] **stick with sth**
✦ v + prep

steal /stiːl/ (**stole** /stəʊl/; AmE stoʊl/**stolen** /'stəʊlən/; AmE 'stoʊ-/)

,**steal a'way** to go away from a place quietly and secretly: He stole away under cover of darkness.
✦ v + adv

,**steal 'over sb** (formal) if a feeling **steals over** you, you gradually feel it: A chill stole over her body. ◇ Exhaustion stole over me as I sat there.
✦ v + prep

,**steal 'up** (**on sb**) to approach sb silently so that they do not see or hear you coming: She stole up on him in the dark.
✦ v + adv

steam /sti:m/

,steam sth 'off; ,steam sth 'off sth to remove a piece of paper from another piece using steam to soften the glue that is holding them together: *He steamed the stamp off the envelope.*
⬦ v + n/pron + adv ◆ v + adv + n ◆ v + n/pron + prep

,steam 'up; ,steam sth 'up to become, or to make sth become, covered with steam: *The windows had steamed up.* ◇ *The warmth in the room steamed all the windows up.*
》SYN《 **fog up; mist up, mist sth up**
⬦ v + adv ◆ v + n/pron + adv ◆ v + adv + n

▣ **be/get (all) steamed 'up (about/over sth)** (*BrE, informal*) to be/become very angry or excited about sth: *I realized I had got all steamed up over nothing.*

steep /sti:p/

'steep sth in sth to put food in a liquid and leave it for some time so that it becomes soft and flavoured by the liquid: *Raspberries are delicious steeped in brandy.*
⬦ v + n/pron + prep

'steep yourself in sth; be 'steeped in sth (*formal*) to spend a lot of time doing sth or thinking about sth and learn a lot about it: *teenagers steeping themselves in pop culture* ◇ *He was steeped in the family business from an early age.*
▣ **NOTE** This phrasal verb is mainly used in written English.
⬦ v + pron + prep ◆ be + v + prep

be 'steeped in sth (*written*) to have a lot of a particular quality: *a city steeped in history and tradition*
▣ **OBJ** history, tradition
⬦ be + v + prep

steer /stɪə(r); AmE stɪr/

,steer a'way from sth to avoid discussing sth or becoming involved with sb/sth, because it may cause problems: *I tried to steer away from the subject of divorce.* ◇ *Jane tends to steer away from sugary foods.*
⬦ v + adv + prep

stem /stem/ (-mm-)

'stem from sth (*not used in the progressive tenses*) to be caused by sth; to be the result of sth: *Many of her problems stem from the fact that her parents are famous.* ◇ *Their opposition stems from fear and ignorance.*
▣ **SUBJ** problem, difficulty ▣ **OBJ** the fact that...
⬦ v + prep

step /step/ (-pp-)

,step a'side/'down (as/from sth) to leave an important job or position in order to let sb else take your place: *After 10 years as party leader, it's*

time for him to step aside. ◇ *He decided to step aside as company director to make way for his son.* ◇ *I intended to step down as Chairman.* ◇ *She's stepping down from her post next year.*
⬦ v + adv

,step 'back 1 (from sth) to try to think calmly about a situation in which you have been closely involved, as if you are not involved in it: *You should try to step back from the problem and look for a new way to deal with it.* 》SYN《 **stand back (from sth) 2** to feel as if you have moved backwards to an earlier period of history: *When you enter the cathedral you step back in time to the 15th Century.*
⬦ v + adv

,step 'down (as/from sth) = STEP ASIDE/DOWN
》SYN《 **stand down (as/from sth)**

,step 'forward to offer to help sb, give information, money, etc: *A soft drinks company has stepped forward to sponsor the team.*
⬦ v + adv

,step 'in to help in an argument or a difficult situation: *When my mum was ill, my aunt stepped in to help.* ◇ *The Youth Club was going to close, but a local bank stepped in with a generous donation.*
⬦ v + adv

'step on it (*spoken, informal*) used especially to tell sb to drive faster: *Step on it! We're late already!* ◇ *We'll have to really step on it to be there by noon.* ◇ (*figurative*) *Step on it! I need those figures by lunchtime.*
⬦ v + prep + it

,step 'out (*especially AmE*) to leave a place for a short period: *He's just stepped out for ten minutes.*
⬦ v + adv

,step 'up (to sb/sth) to come forward: *He stepped up to receive his award.* ◇ *The runners stepped up to the line.*
⬦ v + adv

,step sth 'up to increase the rate, level, amount, etc. of sth: *Security has been stepped up at the airport since the bomb scare.* ◇ *Police have stepped up their search for the missing schoolgirl.*
▣ **OBJ** campaign, pressure, security, production, efforts
⬦ v + adv + n ◆ v + n/pron + adv

stick /stɪk/ (stuck, stuck /stʌk/)

285	~ around		~ out, out of
	~ at		~ out for
	~ back	286	~ through
	~ by		~ to
	~ down		~ together
	~ in		~ up
	~ in/into		~ up for
	~ on		~ with
	~ on, onto		

▣ **NOTE** **Stick** is often used as an informal way of saying **put**.

,stick a'round (*informal*) to stay in or near a place, waiting for sth to happen, sb to arrive, etc: *Stick around, we need all the help we can get.* ◇ *I'll stick around here in case Maya arrives.*
◆ v + adv

'stick at sth to work continuously at sth in a determined way: *If we stick at it, we should finish the job today.* ◇ *She never sticks at anything for very long.*
⟨SYN⟩ keep at sth; persevere with sth (*more formal*)
◆ v + prep

,stick sth 'back (*informal*) to return sth to its usual place; to return sth to the place it was before: *Stick the cake back in the oven for ten minutes.* ◇ *When you've finished with the dictionary, just stick it back on the shelf.*
⟨SYN⟩ put sth back
◆ v + n/pron + adv

'stick by sb (*informal*) to be loyal to sb and continue to support them in difficult times: *She stuck by him through thick and thin.*
⟨SYN⟩ stand by sb
◆ v + prep

'stick by sth to do what you said, planned or promised you would do, even though the situation might have changed: *In spite of what's happened, we must stick by our decision.* ◇ *The developer wants to stick by his original plan.*
⟨SYN⟩ stand by sth
◆ v + prep

'stick sth 'down 1 to fix a piece of paper, etc. to sth else using glue: *I can't stick the corners of this wallpaper down.* ◇ *The envelope hadn't been stuck down properly.* 2 (*informal*) to place sth that you are holding onto the floor or another surface: *Stick your coat on the chair and come and sit down here.* ⟨SYN⟩ put sth down 3 (in/on sth) (*informal*) to write or note sth down quickly: *Stick it all down on paper before you forget.* ⟨SYN⟩ put sth down; jot sth down; note sth down
◆ v + n/pron + adv ◆ v + adv + n

'stick in sth 1 if something sharp sticks in sth, it goes into sth, making a small hole, and stays there: *The arrow whizzed past and stuck in the tree.* ◇ *These poles stick in the ground easily.* ◇ *Something was sticking in my back.* 2 if something sticks in a place, it stays there and does not move: *A crumb stuck in my throat.* ◇ *I've got my finger stuck in the bottle.* ◇ (*figurative*) *The words stuck in my throat* (= I couldn't say them). ◇ (*figurative*) *Her words stuck in my mind/memory.*
◆ v + prep

,stick sth 'in/'into sth; ,stick sth 'in 1 (*informal*) to put sth into sth: *I stuck the letter in my pocket to read later.* ◇ *He saw the hole and stuck his finger in.* ◇ *I stuck my feet into my slippers.* ◇ *Timmy stuck his thumb in his mouth.* ⟨SYN⟩ put sth in, put sth in/into sth 2 to put sth sharp into

sth, making a small hole: *Ouch! I've stuck the needle in my finger!* ⟨OBJ⟩ knife, needle 3 (*informal*) to include sth in a story, a letter, etc: *Should I stick this paragraph in or leave it out?* ◇ *I'll stick in something about football to make the article more interesting.* ⟨SYN⟩ put sth in, put sth in/into sth 4 to attach sth firmly to sth, using tape or glue: *I'm going to stick the new photos in my album.*
◆ v + n/pron + adv ◆ v + adv + n ◆ v + n/pron + prep

⟨IDM⟩ stick/poke your 'oar/'nose into sth (*informal*) to try to become involved in sth that does not concern you

,get stuck 'in; ,get stuck 'into sth (*BrE*, *informal*) to start doing sth in an enthusiastic way; to become very interested and involved in sth: *You must be hungry. Get stuck in!* (= start eating) ◇ *I was too tired to get really stuck into the debate.*
◆ get + v + adv ◆ get + v + prep

,stick sth 'on (*informal*) 1 to switch on a piece of electrical equipment: *I'll stick the kettle on for a cup of tea.* 2 to put on clothes: *I'll just stick a jacket on, and I'm ready.* 3 to begin to cook food: *I'll stick the potatoes on and then I'll make us a coffee.* 4 to make a tape, a CD, etc. begin to play: *Stick on some music, if you like.*
⟨SYN⟩ put sth on
◆ v + n/pron + adv ◆ v + adv + n

,stick sth 'on; ,stick sth 'on/'onto sth to attach sth firmly to a surface, using glue, tape, etc: *I stuck the label on with adhesive tape.* ◇ *He sealed the envelope, and stuck a stamp on it.*
◆ v + n/pron + adv ◆ v + adv + n ◆ v + n/pron + prep
▶ 'stick-on adj [only before noun] a stick-on object has glue on one side so that it can be attached to sth: *stick-on badges/labels*

,stick sth 'on sth (*informal*) 1 to put sth somewhere in a casual way: *Stick your report on my desk when you've finished it.* 2 to add an amount of money to the price or cost of sth: *They can't just stick an extra 20p on the price of cigarettes!*
⟨SYN⟩ put sth on sth
◆ v + n/pron + prep

,stick 'out to be very noticeable or easy to see: *They wrote the notice in red so that it would stick out.* ◇ (*figurative*) *One of the boys in the class sticks out in my mind.*
⟨SYN⟩ stand out (*more formal*)
◆ v + adv

⟨IDM⟩ stick out a 'mile to be very noticeable or easy to see: *Dressed like that, you stick out a mile.* ◇ *It stuck out a mile that she was lying.* stick out like a sore 'thumb to be very different from others, especially in an unpleasant way: *The red house stuck out like a sore thumb among the old stone cottages.*

,stick 'out; ,stick 'out of sth to be further out than sth else; to be partly outside sth such as a container: *His ears stick out.* ◇ *There was a newspaper sticking out of her coat pocket.*
◆ v + adv ◆ v + adv + prep

,**stick sth 'out**; ,**stick sth 'out of sth** to make sth, especially part of your body, come through a hole: *If you want to turn right, stick out your hand.* ◇ *I stuck my head out of the window to see what was happening.*

[OBJ] **head, tongue** [SYN] **poke sth out, poke sth out of sth**

◆ v + adv + n ◆ v + n/pron + adv ◆ v + n/pron + adv + prep

[IDM] **stick your 'neck out** (*informal*) to do or say sth when there is a risk you may be wrong: *I'm going to stick my neck out and say that we'll have a dry summer.*

,**stick it/sth 'out** to continue doing sth difficult or boring until it is finished: *I don't like being on my own, but I'll stick it out until my parents come back.* ◇ *I'm amazed that she's stuck the course out.*

◆ v + n/pron + adv

,**stick 'out for sth** (*BrE, informal*) to refuse to give up until you get what you want: *They're sticking out for a higher pay rise.*

[SYN] **hold out for sth**

◆ v + adv + prep

,**stick 'through**; ,**stick 'through sth** if sth **sticks through** or **sticks through sth**, it goes from one side of sth to the other and it is partly outside: *His head was sticking through the railings.*

◆ v + adv ◆ v + adv + prep

'**stick to sth 1** to continue doing sth even if it is difficult or you have problems: *He found it difficult to stick to a diet.* → *see also* STICK WITH STH 1; STAY WITH STH **2** to continue doing or using sth and not want to change it: *I'm sticking to my previous statement.* ◇ *That's her story and she's sticking to it.* → *see also* STICK WITH STH 2 **3** to keep inside the limits of a particular subject, etc: *I'm not interested in your opinions — just stick to the facts.*

◆ v + prep

[IDM] **stick to your 'guns** to refuse to change your mind about sth even when other people are trying to persuade you that you are wrong

,**stick to'gether** (*informal*) **1** to remain friendly and loyal to one another; to support each other: *The family should stick together at a time like this.* ◇ *The children from the village tended to stick together.* **2** (*informal*) to stay physically close to each other: *Let's all stick together until we find the way out.* → *see also* STICK WITH SB 1

◆ v + adv

,**stick sth to'gether** to attach things or parts of things to each other: *Cut out the shapes and stick them together to make a bird.*

◆ v + n/pron + adv ◆ v + adv + n

,**stick 'up** to point upwards; to be upright: *The branch was sticking up out of the water.* ◇ *Is my hair sticking up?*

◆ v + adv

,**stick sb/sth 'up** (*AmE, informal*) = HOLD SB/STH UP *He stuck up a liquor store in Oregon.*

▶ '**stick-up** *n* (*AmE, informal*) an act of robbing sb/sth using a gun: *This is a stick-up, nobody move!*

,**stick sth 'up** to attach sth to a wall, a noticeboard, a window, etc. so that people can see it: *They had stuck up posters everywhere advertising the show.* ◇ *If you want to sell your bike, just stick a notice up in the shop window.*

[SYN] **put sth up**

◆ v + adv + n ◆ v + n/pron + adv

,**stick sth 'up**; ,**stick sth 'up sth** (*informal*) to place sth in a high position; to move sth upwards, especially inside sth: *Stick your hand up if you know the answer.* ◇ *Jeff stuck his hand up the pipe to see what was blocking it.*

[OBJ] **hand, finger** [SYN] **put sth up**

◆ v + n/pron + adv ◆ v + n/pron + adv + n

,**stick 'up for sb/yourself/sth** (*informal*) to support or defend sb, yourself or sth, when they are being criticized: *She always sticks up for her little sister.* ◇ *You must stick up for what you believe in.* ◇ *Don't be so weak — you should stick up for yourself.*

◆ v + adv + prep

'**stick with sb 1** (*informal*) to stay physically close to sb: *Stick with me until we get out of the forest.* → *see also* STICK TOGETHER **2** (*informal*) to remain in sb's memory: *His words will stick with me for ever.*

◆ v + prep

'**stick with sth** (*informal*) **1** to continue to do sth in spite of difficulties: *If we stick with it we should finish by Friday.* ◇ *I stuck with the job for as long as I could, although I didn't enjoy it.* **2** to continue doing or using sth and not want to change it: *I've decided to stick with my usual method.* → *see also* STICK TO STH 2

◆ v + prep

be/get 'stuck with sb/sth (*informal*) to be forced to do sth, take care of sb/sth, etc. that you do not want to: *How did I get stuck with all the cleaning?* ◇ *If we're stuck with each other for the next two weeks, we might as well be polite.* ◇ *I got stuck with defending my brother's wild behaviour* (= but I really thought he was wrong).

◆ be/get + v + prep

sting /stɪŋ/ (**stung, stung** /stʌŋ/)

'**sting sb for sth** (*informal*) **1** to trick or cheat sb into paying more money than they should or than they expected to: *Motorists are being stung for another £25 road tax.* **2** (*BrE*) to borrow money from sb, especially when they are unwilling to give it to you: *Can I sting you for a fiver* (= five pounds)?

◆ v + n/pron + prep

stink /stɪŋk/ (**stank** /stæŋk/**stunk** /stʌŋk/ or **stunk**, **stunk**)

,stink sth 'out (*BrE*) (*AmE* **,stink sth 'up**) (*informal*) to fill a room, a building, etc. with a very unpleasant smell: *He stank the whole place out with his cigarettes.*

‖OBJ‖ **the place** ‖SYN‖ **smell sth out** (*BrE*), **smell sth up** (*AmE*)

⊕ v + n/pron + adv ◆ v + adv + n

stir /stɜ:(r)/ (**-rr-**)

,stir sth 'in; **,stir sth 'into sth** to mix one substance into another by moving a spoon or sth similar in circles: *Stir in the cream.* ◇ *Stir the pasta into the sauce.*

‖SYN‖ **mix sth in** (**with sth**), **mix sth into sth**

⊕ v + adv + n ◆ v + n/pron + adv ◆ v + n/pron + prep

,stir sb 'up to encourage sb to do sth; to make sb feel they must do sth: *He was accused of stirring up the slaves against their masters.*

⊕ v + adv + n ◆ v + n/pron + adv

,stir sb/sth 'up 1 to cause trouble, especially by making people feel strong emotions: *I don't want to stir up any more trouble.* ◇ *The government has been accused of stirring up racial hatred.* ‖OBJ‖ **hatred, trouble, things, controversy** ‖SYN‖ **rouse sb/sth 2** to make sb have a particular feeling or attitude: *Her story stirred up a lot of old memories for me.* ◇ *I can't seem to stir up any interest in the campaign.* ‖OBJ‖ **memories, interest, emotions 3** to make sth such as sand or dust move around in water or air: *The helicopter stirred up a cloud of dust.* ‖OBJ‖ **dust**

⊕ v + adv + n ◆ v + n/pron + adv

‖IDM‖ **stir up a 'hornet's nest** to cause a difficult situation in which a lot of people get very angry: *His criticisms of the president stirred up a hornet's nest.*

stitch /stɪtʃ/

,stitch sb 'up (*BrE*, *informal*) to make sb appear to be guilty of sth they have not done, for example by giving false information; to cheat sb: *I didn't do it! I've been stitched up!*

‖SYN‖ **frame sb**

⊕ v + n/pron + adv ◆ v + adv + n

,stitch sth 'up 1 to join things together using a needle and thread: *This wound has to be stitched up urgently.* ‖OBJ‖ **wound 2** (*BrE*, *informal*) to arrange sth; to complete a business deal: *He has managed to stitch up major deals all over the world.* ◇ *The company has the US market stitched up.* ‖OBJ‖ **deal**

‖SYN‖ **sew sth up**

⊕ v + adv + n ◆ v + n/pron + adv

stock /stɒk; *AmE* stɑ:k/

,stock 'up (**on/with sth**) to buy or get a lot of sth so that you can use it later: *The shops are very busy with people stocking up for the holidays.* ◇ *I need to stock up on food before all the family arrive.*

⊕ v + adv

,stock sth 'up (**on/with sth**) to fill sth with goods, food, etc: *Mum stocked up the freezer for us before she went to the conference.*

⊕ v + adv + n ◆ v + n/pron + adv

stoke /stəʊk; *AmE* stoʊk/

,stoke 'up (**on/with sth**) (*informal*) to eat a lot of sth so that you will not feel hungry later: *We'd better stoke up now — we've got a long journey in front of us.*

⊕ v + adv

,stoke sth 'up 1 to keep a fire, etc. burning by adding more fuel: *He stoked up the fire before going to bed.* ‖OBJ‖ **fire 2** to make people feel sth more strongly: *He continued to stoke up hatred in his speeches.*

‖NOTE‖ **Stoke sth** can also be used with the same meanings.

⊕ v + adv + n ◆ v + n/pron + adv

stoop /stu:p/

'stoop to sth; **'stoop to doing sth** to do sth bad or unpleasant in order to gain an advantage for yourself: *I can't believe he would stoop to blackmail.* ◇ *He's the kind of person who would stoop to making personal attacks on a rival.*

‖SYN‖ **descend to sth** (*more formal*)

⊕ v + prep

stop /stɒp; *AmE* stɑ:p/ (**-pp-**)

,stop a'round; **,stop a'round sth** (*AmE*) to make a short visit to sb, usually at their home: *I'll stop around this evening when I finish work.* ◇ *Let's stop around the Smiths' house for a quick drink.*

‖SYN‖ **drop round**; **pop over/round** (*both BrE*)

⊕ v + adv ◆ v + prep

,stop a'way to deliberately decide not to go somewhere: *Many of the people invited to the dinner had stopped away in protest.*

‖SYN‖ **stay away**

‖NOTE‖ **Stay away** is used much more frequently than **stop away**.

⊕ v + adv

,stop 'back (*AmE*) to return to somewhere that you have visited earlier: *I'll stop back on my way home.*

⊕ v + adv

,stop be'hind (**after sth**) (*informal*) to remain somewhere at the end of an event after other

people have left: *She stopped behind after the meeting to talk to him.*
⟨SYN⟩ **stay behind (after sth)**
NOTE **Stay behind** is used more frequently than **stop behind**.
◈ v + adv

,stop 'by; ,stop 'by sth to make a short visit to sb/somewhere, especially when you are on the way to somewhere else: *Stop by for a chat on your way home.* ◇ *Could you stop by the store for some milk?*
⟨SYN⟩ **come by, come by sth; drop by**
◈ v + adv ♦ v + prep

,stop 'in (*BrE, informal*) to stay at home rather than go out: *We've decided to stop in tonight because it's raining.*
⟨SYN⟩ **stay in**
NOTE **Stay in** is used much more frequently than **stop in**.
◈ v + adv

,stop 'off (at/in…) to stop somewhere for a short time when you are on the way to somewhere else: *We stopped off for lunch just north of Paris.* ◇ *I stopped off at the supermarket on the way home.*
◈ v + adv
▶ **'stop-off** n **1** a short stay somewhere during a trip: *a stop-off in Sydney* **2** a place where you stop for a short time during a trip

,stop 'on [+ adv/prep] (*BrE, informal*) to stay somewhere longer than you planned or after other people have left: *I'll be late home tonight — the boss wants me to stop on an hour after work and help tidy up after the meeting.*
⟨SYN⟩ **stay on**
NOTE **Stay on** is used more frequently than **stop on**.
◈ v + adv

,stop 'out (*BrE, informal*) to stay out late at night or all night instead of going home: *He often stops out till three in the morning.*
⟨SYN⟩ **stay out**
NOTE **Stay out** is used much more frequently than **stop out**.
◈ v + adv

,stop 'over (in/at …) to stop somewhere for a short time when you are on a long journey, especially a journey by plane: *I stopped over in Mérida on the way to Havana.*
◈ v + adv
▶ **'stopover** n **1** a short stay somewhere during a long journey: *We had a three-day stopover in Hawaii.* **2** a place where you stay for a short time during a long journey

,stop 'up (*BrE, informal*) to not go to bed until later than usual: *She stopped up to see the football match.*
⟨SYN⟩ **stay up**

NOTE **Stay up** is used much more frequently than **stop up**.
◈ v + adv

,stop sth 'up to cover or fill a hole, a crack, etc. so that nothing can get through: *I stopped up all the holes to keep out the draught.*
⟨SYN⟩ **block sth up**
◈ v + adv + n ♦ v + n/pron + adv

store /stɔː(r)/

,store sth a'way to put sth in a safe place and keep it there so that you can use it later: *We stored away the baby clothes until we had another child.* ◇ *It's amazing how much knowledge he's got stored away in his memory.* ◇ *I stored away the information for future use.*
◈ v + adv + n ♦ v + n/pron + adv

,store 'up sth; ,store it 'up to not express strong feelings or deal with problems when you have them, often making trouble for yourself in future: *Smokers may be storing up health problems for their unborn children.* ◇ *Children who store up their bad feelings often develop headaches or stomach pains.*
OBJ **problems, trouble**
NOTE A noun must always follow **up**, but a pronoun comes between the verb and **up**.
◈ v + adv + n ♦ v + pron + adv

,store sth 'up 1 to keep sth so that it can be used later: *animals storing up food for the winter* ◇ *The batteries store up enough energy for a week.*
NOTE **Store sth** is also used with this meaning. **2** to keep information or facts in your memory to use later: *He stored up all the amusing and interesting things that happened during the day to tell his family in the evening.*
◈ v + adv + n ♦ v + n/pron + adv

storm /stɔːm; AmE stɔːrm/

,storm 'off to leave a place or a person suddenly because you are very angry: *We had a big argument and he stormed off.*
◈ v + adv

stow /stəʊ; AmE stoʊ/

,stow a'way (on sth) to hide on a vehicle, especially a ship or a plane, in order to travel without paying or without being seen: *He stowed away on a ship bound for Vigo.*
◈ v + adv
▶ **'stowaway** n a person who hides on a ship or a plane in order to travel without paying or without being seen

,stow sth a'way to put sth in a place where it will be safe or will not be found: *He stowed his passport away safely in a drawer.*
◈ v + n/pron + adv ♦ v + adv + n

straighten /'streɪtn/

,straighten 'out; ,straighten sth 'out to become or to make sth straight: *After the bridge, the road straightens out.* ◇ *attempts to straighten out the river*
◆ v + adv ◆ v + adv + n ◆ v + n/pron + adv

,straighten sb 'out; ,straighten yourself 'out to help sb deal with problems or understand a difficult situation which may be making them behave badly; to help yourself in this way: *A few sessions talking to a counsellor should straighten him out.*
⟨SYN⟩ **sort sb/yourself out**
◆ v + n/pron + adv ◆ v + adv + n

,straighten sth 'out to deal with problems or a difficult situation; to organize things that are confused: *I was left to straighten out the mess.* ◇ *He's trying to straighten out his finances.*
⟨SYN⟩ **sort sth out**
◆ v + adv + n ◆ v + n/pron + adv

,straighten 'up to stand up straight from a bent position: *She slowly straightened up and rubbed her back.*
◆ v + adv

,straighten sth 'up to make a room, etc. neat and tidy: *We'd better straighten up the house before they get back.*
⟨SYN⟩ **tidy sth up**
◆ v + adv + n ◆ v + n/pron + adv

strain /streɪn/

'strain at sth to pull very hard on sth: *The dog was straining at its lead.*
◆ v + prep
⟨IDM⟩ **strain at the 'leash** (*informal*) to want to do sth very much, especially when sb/sth is trying to stop you: *He's straining at the leash to get on with his research.*

,strain sth 'off to separate a liquid from sth solid by pouring it through sth that has very small holes in it: *Strain off any excess liquid.*
◆ v + adv + n ◆ v + n/pron + adv

strap /stræp/ (-pp-)

,strap sb 'in; ,strap yourself 'in; ,strap sb/yourself 'into sth to fasten sb/yourself in a seat, etc. using straps: *All passengers in the plane must be securely strapped in.* ◇ *Make sure you strap the baby firmly into the high chair.* ◇ *Have you strapped yourselves in?*
◆ v + n/pron + adv ◆ v + n/pron + prep

,strap sth 'on; ,strap sth 'onto sth to attach sth to sth else with straps: *He strapped on his helmet and rode away.* ◇ *She strapped the suitcases onto the roof of the car.*
◆ v + adv + n ◆ v + n/pron + prep

,strap sth 'up to tie strips of cloth (a **bandage**) around sth, especially an injured part of the body, to support it or prevent it from moving: *Your wrist needs to be strapped up.*
◆ v + n/pron + adv ◆ v + adv + n

stress /stres/

,stress sb 'out (*informal*) to make sb very anxious and tired so that they are unable to relax: *My job really stresses me out.* ◇ *My Dad stressed me out by criticizing me all the time.*
◆ v + n/pron + adv
▶ **,stressed 'out** *adj* too anxious and tired to be able to relax: *When I'm stressed out, I try to go for a long walk.* ◇ *stressed-out executives*

stretch /stretʃ/

,stretch a'way/'out [+ adv/prep] to spread over a large area of land, especially away from where you are: *The mountains stretched away into the distance.* ◇ *Banana plantations stretched away as far as the eye could see.*
⟨SYN⟩ **extend**
◆ v + adv

,stretch 'out; ,stretch yourself 'out to lie down, with your arms or legs out straight, especially in order to relax or sleep: *He stretched out on the floor and fell asleep.*
◆ v + adv ◆ v + pron + adv

,stretch sth 'out 1 to put your arm or leg out straight, especially in order to reach sth: *She stretched out a hand to touch his face.* ◇ *He leant back and stretched his legs out in front of him.* ⟨OBJ⟩ **arm, hand, leg 2** to make sth last as long as possible by not using very much at a time: *It's hard to stretch my money out to the end of the month.* ⟨SYN⟩ **spin sth out**
◆ v + n/pron + adv ◆ v + adv + n

strew /struː/ (strewed, strewed or strewn /struːn/)

be 'strewn with sth to be covered with a lot of things: *The floor was strewn with clothes.* ◇ (*figurative*) *The way ahead is strewn with difficulties.*
◆ be + v + prep

strike /straɪk/ (struck, struck /strʌk/, *AmE* also struck, stricken /'strɪkən/)

'strike at sb/sth 1 to try to hit sb/sth, especially with a weapon: *She screamed and struck at the wolf with a stick.* **2** to cause damage or have a serious effect on sb/sth: *The proposals strike at the roots of community life.* ◇ *This legislation strikes at the most vulnerable people in society.*
◆ v + prep

,**strike 'back** (at/against sb/sth) to criticize or attack sb who has criticized or attacked you: *Sarah used the article to strike back at her critics.* ⟩SYN⟨ **hit back (at sb/sth)**
◆ v + adv

,**strike sb 'down** (*formal*) **1** if a disease **strikes sb down**, it kills them or makes them seriously ill: *She was struck down by polio at the age of four.* ◇ *I was struck down by flu and had to cancel the trip.* **2** to hit sb very hard so that they fall to the ground; to kill sb: *Fights broke out near the shop and one girl was struck down by a handbag.* ◇ *the spot where Kennedy was struck down* NOTE **Strike sb down** is often used in the passive.
◆ v + n/pron + adv ♦ v + adv + n

,**strike sth 'down** (*especially AmE*) to reject sth; to make sth no longer valid: *Only the Supreme Court has the power to strike down this legislation.* ◇ *Parents tried to have the dance ban struck down.*
◆ v + adv + n ♦ v + n/pron + adv

,**strike 'off** = STRIKE OUT 3

,**strike sb/sth 'off**; ,**strike sb/sth 'off sth** (*BrE*) to remove sb's name from the list of members of a profession so that they can no longer work in that profession: *She was struck off for professional misconduct.* ◇ *These doctors should be struck off the medical register.* ◇ *I'm going to strike Ashok off my guest list for the party.*
◆ v + n/pron + adv ♦ v + adv + n ♦ v + n/pron + prep

,**strike sth 'off** (*formal*) to remove sth with a sharp blow; to cut sth off: *They struck off his head with a sword.* ⟩SYN⟨ **chop sth off** (*less formal*)
◆ v + adv + n ♦ v + n/pron + adv

,**strike 'out 1** (at sb/sth) to aim a violent blow at sb: *He struck out at me with his fist.* ⟩SYN⟨ **hit out (at sb/sth) 2** to start being independent and do sth new: *Sanjay left the firm and struck out on his own.* **3** (*also* ,**strike 'off** *less frequent*) [+ adv/prep] to start to go somewhere in a determined way: *He struck out across the fields towards the farmhouse.* **4** (with sb) (*AmE, informal*) to fail; to be unsuccessful: *I tried to get a job but struck out completely.* ◇ *He must have struck out with her because he came home early.* **5** (at sb/sth) to criticize sb/sth, especially publicly: *striking out at your critics* ⟩SYN⟨ **hit out (at sb/sth)**
◆ v + adv

,**strike 'out**; ,**strike sb 'out** (*AmE*) (in baseball) to fail to hit the ball successfully three times and so finish your turn; to make sb do this: *He struck out in the third inning.* ◇ *The pitcher struck out three batters.*
◆ v + adv ♦ v + adv + n ♦ v + n/pron + adv

,**strike sth 'out/'through** (*especially BrE*) to remove sth from a text or a list by drawing a line through it: *I struck out some words to make the*

telegram shorter. ◇ *He insisted that I strike out all references to his family.*
⟩SYN⟨ **cross sth out/through**
◆ v + adv + n ♦ v + n/pron + adv

,**strike 'up** (with sth), ,**strike 'up sth** if a band or an orchestra **strike up**, they begin to play: *Everyone was waiting for the band to strike up.* ◇ *The orchestra struck up a lively tune.*
OBJ **tune**
◆ v + adv ♦ v + adv + n

,**strike 'up sth** (with sb) to begin a friendship, a relationship, a conversation, etc. with sb: *My mother will strike up a conversation with anyone she meets.* ◇ *Children of the same age don't always strike up friendships (with each other).*
OBJ **conversation, friendship, relationship**
◆ v + adv + n

string /strɪŋ/ (strung, strung /strʌŋ/)

,**string a'long** (with sb) (*informal*) to go somewhere or do sth with sb else, especially because you have nothing else to do: *I'm free this morning. Can I string along with you when you go to the shops?*
⟩SYN⟨ **tag along (behind/with sb)**
◆ v + adv

,**string sb a'long** (*informal*) to allow sb to believe sth that is not true for a long period of time, especially when you encourage them to have false hopes: *They never really intended to give her a job. They were just stringing her along.* ◇ *He strung her along for years and then married somebody else.*
◆ v + n/pron + adv

,**string 'out** (across/along sth) to spread out in a line: *As we climbed, we tended to string out, with the fittest people taking the lead.*
◆ v + adv

,**string sth 'out** to make sth last longer than expected or necessary: *I didn't want to string out the argument.*
◆ v + adv + n ♦ v + n/pron + adv

,**string sth to'gether 1** to combine words, phrases, sentences, etc. to form sth that has some meaning: *I can barely string together two words of German.* ◇ *The report should be written by somebody who can string two sentences together.*
OBJ **words, a sentence 2** to join a series of things together: *pearls strung together on a necklace* ◇ *The student of kung fu learns various movements that are then strung together.*
◆ v + n/pron + adv ♦ v + adv + n

,**string sb 'up** (*informal*) to kill sb by hanging them, especially illegally: *They'll string him up if they catch him.*
◆ v + n/pron + adv ♦ v + adv + n

,**string sth 'up** to hang or tie sth in place: *She strung up a banner saying 'Happy 40th Birthday'.*
◆ v + n/pron + adv ♦ v + adv + n

strip /strɪp/ (-pp-)

,**strip sth a'way 1** (from sth) to completely remove a layer of sth that is covering sth else: *Strip away the paint to reveal the wood underneath.* ◊ *The bark has been stripped away from the tree.* **2** to remove anything that is not true and necessary to reveal what sb/sth is really like: *When you strip away the jargon, he really has nothing sensible to say.* ◊ *The programme stripped away the mystery surrounding the royal family.* **3** to remove or get rid of sth that has existed for a long time: *Our basic rights are being stripped away by these laws.*
  ✪ v + adv + n ◆ v + n/pron + adv

,**strip sth 'down** to separate a machine or an engine into parts, especially in order to clean or repair it: *We had to strip down the engine and replace the worn parts.* ◊ *The car was stripped down and sold for parts.*
  ⟨SYN⟩ **dismantle sth** (*more formal*)
  ✪ v + adv + n ◆ v + n/pron + adv

,**strip 'down to sth** to take off your clothes until you are only wearing the items mentioned: *I stripped down to my underwear for the massage.*
  ✪ v + adv + prep + noun

,**strip sth 'from sth** = STRIP STH OFF, STRIP STH OFF/FROM STH

'**strip sb/sth of sth** to take away a right, a privilege, property, etc. that sb has, as a punishment: *He was stripped of his title for refusing to fight in Britain* (= for example, in boxing). ◊ *They stripped me of my citizenship and deported me.*
  ⟨SYN⟩ **divest sb/sth of sth** (*formal*)
  NOTE Strip sb of sth is often used in the passive.
  ✪ v + n/pron + prep

,**strip 'off**; ,**strip sth 'off** (*BrE, informal*) if you **strip off**, or **strip sth off**, you take off all or nearly all your clothes: *She stripped off and dived into the water.* ◊ *Strip off your wet clothes and put on these dry ones.*
  ✪ v + adv ◆ v + adv + n ◆ v + n/pron + adv

,**strip sth 'off**; ,**strip sth 'off/'from sth** to remove a layer of sth: *It was hard work stripping the old wallpaper off.* ◊ *All the leaves had been stripped off the branches.*
  ✪ v + n/pron + adv ◆ v + adv + n ◆ v + n/pron + prep

,**strip sth 'out** to completely remove things you do not want; to remove everything from a place and leave it empty: *They had stripped out all the original features of the house.*
  ✪ v + adv + n ◆ v + n/pron + adv

struggle /'strʌgl/

,**struggle a'long/'on** to manage to continue in spite of great difficulties: *The country's economy is still struggling along.* ◊ *The government struggled on with a tiny majority.*
  ✪ v + adv

stub /stʌb/ (-bb-)

,**stub sth 'out** to stop a cigarette, etc. burning: *He stubbed the cigarette out with his foot.*
  ⟨OBJ⟩ **cigarette, cigar** ⟨SYN⟩ **grind sth out; put sth out; extinguish sth** (*more formal*)
  ✪ v + n/pron + adv ◆ v + adv + n

stuff /stʌf/

,**stuff 'up**; ,**stuff sth 'up** (*BrE, slang*) to do sth very badly; to fail at sth: *I'm afraid I stuffed up again.* ◊ *I'm not having them stuff up my plans.*
  ⟨SYN⟩ **mess up, mess sth up**
  ✪ v + adv ◆ v + adv + n ◆ v + n/pron + adv

stumble /'stʌmbl/

,**stumble a'cross/'on/u'pon sb/sth** to find sb/sth unexpectedly or by chance: *We stumbled on the solution by accident.* ◊ *I stumbled across an old school friend today.*
  ✪ v + prep

'**stumble into sth** to become involved in sth by chance: *She stumbled into engineering because of her love of maths.*
  ✪ v + prep

stump /stʌmp/

,**stump 'up** (for sth), ,**stump 'up sth** (for sth) (*BrE, informal*) to pay the amount of money for sth that sb asks, often when you do not want to: *He had no money so I had to stump up for his ticket.* ◊ *We had to stump up an extra five hundred pounds for insurance.*
  ⟨OBJ⟩ **the cash** ⟨SYN⟩ **cough up, cough sth up**
  ✪ v + adv ◆ v + adv + n

subject /'sʌbdʒekt/

sub'ject sb/sth/yourself to sth (*formal*) to make sb/sth/yourself experience, suffer or be affected by sth, usually sth unpleasant: *to subject sth to scrutiny/analysis* ◊ *All our products are subjected to thorough tests.* ◊ *to be subjected to criticism/harassment/abuse/torture* ◊ *Why did I subject myself to another evening of arguments?* ◊ *The city was subjected to repeated bombings.*
  NOTE Subject sb/sth/yourself to sth is often used in the passive. ◆ It is mainly used in written English.
  ✪ v + n/pron + prep

subscribe /səb'skraɪb/

sub'scribe to sth (*formal*) to agree with an opinion, a theory, etc: *It's not an opinion I tend to subscribe to.* ◊ *The company subscribe to the view that if you can encourage children to use your products, they will continue to use them when they are adults.*
  ⟨OBJ⟩ **view, theory, opinion**

NOTE Subscribe to sth can be used in the passive: *It is not a theory that is commonly subscribed to.*

◈ v + prep

substitute /'sʌbstɪtjuːt; *AmE* -tuːt/

'**substitute for sb/sth** to take the place of sb/sth else: *Can you substitute for me at the meeting?* ◊ *Nothing can substitute for the advice your doctor is able to give you.*

◈ v + prep

succeed /sək'siːd/

suc'ceed in doing sth to achieve sth that you have been trying to do or get; to have the result or effect that was intended: *He succeeded in getting top marks in chemistry.* ◊ *The Labour Party succeeded in capturing the female vote* (= they persuaded women to vote for them). ◊ *(ironic) I tried to mend my watch, but only succeeded in breaking it* (= that was not what I intended).

◈ v + prep

suck /sʌk/

,**suck sb 'in**; ,**suck sb 'into sth** to gradually involve sb in an activity, a situation, etc., especially one that they do not at first want to be involved in: *There is a danger we could be sucked into a war.* ◊ *Don't let yourself get sucked in.* ◊ *In his youth he had been sucked into a hippy cult.*
NOTE Suck sb in/suck sb into sth is nearly always used in the passive.

◈ v + n/pron + adv ◆ v + adv + n ◆ v + n/pron + prep

,**suck 'up to sb** (*informal, disapproving*) to try to please sb by helping them, saying nice things to them, etc. in order to gain an advantage for yourself: *He's always sucking up to the teacher.* ◊ *We don't suck up to anyone!*

◈ v + adv + prep

sucker /'sʌkə(r)/

,**sucker sb 'into sth**; ,**sucker sb 'into doing sth** (*AmE, informal*) to persuade sb to do sth they do not really want to do, especially by using their lack of knowledge or experience: *He got suckered into the scheme.* ◊ *I was suckered into helping.*
NOTE This phrasal verb is usually used in the passive.

◈ v + n/pron + prep

sue /suː/ *BrE also* sjuː/

'**sue for sth** (*formal*) to formally ask for sth, especially in a court of law: *to sue for divorce* ◊ *The rebels were forced to sue for peace.*
OBJ divorce, peace

◈ v + prep

suit /suːt *BrE also* sjuːt/

'**suit sth to sb/sth** to make sth appropriate for sb/sth: *He can suit his conversation to whoever he's with.*

◈ v + n/pron + prep

sum /sʌm/ (-mm-)

,**sum 'up**; ,**sum sth 'up 1** to give the main points of sth in a few words: *Before we conclude the meeting, let me sum up.* ◊ **To sum up**, *there are three main ways of tackling the problem...* ◊ *In her conclusion, she summed up what had been agreed.*
SYN summarize, summarize sth (*more formal*) **2** (of a judge) to give the main points of the evidence or arguments in a legal case, near the end of the trial: *When he summed up, the judge reminded the jury of the seriousness of the case.*

◈ v + adv ◆ v + adv + n ◆ v + pron + adv ◆ v + n + adv (*less frequent*)

▶ ,**summing-'up** *n* **1** a speech made by the judge to the jury near the end of the trial, giving the main points of the evidence and the arguments in the case: *The judge will begin her summing-up on Monday.* **2** an occasion when sb states the main points of an argument, etc: *There was a final summing-up by each of the speakers.* ◊ *The speakers gave brief summings-up of their talks.*

,**sum sb/sth 'up 1** to describe or show the most typical characteristics of sb/sth, especially in a few words: *His speech summed up the mood of the whole country.* ◊ *Totally lazy — that just about sums him up.* **2** (as sb/sth) to decide or express what you think about sb/sth: *The two of them stood there, summing each other up.* ◊ *He had already summed her up as someone who hated to admit defeat.* ◊ *I summed up the situation immediately* (= realized what was happening and what needed to be done). **SYN** size sb/sth up

◈ v + adv + n ◆ v + pron + adv ◆ v + n + adv (*less frequent*)

summon /'sʌmən/

,**summon sth 'up 1** to manage to produce a particular feeling in yourself, although this is difficult: *She eventually summoned up the courage to knock at the door.* ◊ *He managed to summon up a smile.* ◊ *I can't summon up much enthusiasm for grammar!* ◊ *I don't think I can summon up the energy to go for a run.* **OBJ** courage, smile, energy, strength **SYN** muster sth up **NOTE** In this meaning **summon sth up** is not used in the passive. ◆ **Summon sth** is sometimes used with this meaning. **2** to make an idea, a feeling, a memory, etc. come into your mind: *It's a smell that summons up memories of my childhood.* **OBJ** memories, vision, image **SYN** evoke sth (*more formal*)

◈ v + adv + n ◆ v + pron + adv ◆ v + n + adv (*rare*)

surge /sɜːdʒ; *AmE* sɜːrdʒ/

,surge 'through sb if a feeling **surges through**
you, you suddenly feel it very strongly: *A thrill of*
excitement surged through Isobel. SUBJ **relief,**
excitement, anger
→ *see also* SURGE UP
◈ v + prep

,surge 'up (*literary*) if an emotion **surges up** in
you, you suddenly feel it very strongly: *Panic*
surged up inside her.
NOTE **Surge up** is usually used with another
adverb or a phrase beginning with a preposition.
→ *see also* SURGE THROUGH SB
◈ v + adv

▶ **'upsurge** (**in/of sth**) *n* [*usually* sing.] a sudden
great increase in sth: *There has been a recent*
upsurge of violence in the area. ◇ *an upsurge of*
interest in science and technology

surrender /səˈrendə(r)/

sur'render to sb/sth; sur'render yourself
to sb/sth (*formal*) to stop trying to resist a feeling, a particular person, etc. and let them control
what you do: *He surrendered to his natural*
instinct to run away. ◇ *She surrendered to Leo's*
charm. ◇ *He surrendered himself to sleep.*
◈ v + prep ◆ v + pron + prep

suss /sʌs/

,suss sb/sth 'out (*BrE, informal*) to find out
what sb/sth is really like; to understand the
important things about sb/sth: *My classmates*
were sussing me out, seeing how tough I was. ◇
We'll need to suss out our opponents before the
game. ◇ *I've got him sussed out now.* ◇ *Jen had*
sussed out right away that there was something
strange going on. ◇ *Simon always did what his*
family wanted. I soon sussed that out.
NOTE **Suss sb/sth** can be used with a similar
meaning: *I've got him sussed.*
◈ v + n/pron + adv ◆ v + adv + n

swallow /ˈswɒləʊ; *AmE* ˈswɑːloʊ/

,swallow sb/sth 'up to completely cover sb/sth
or absorb them/it, so that they can no longer be
seen or do not exist separately: *He watched them*
walk away until the darkness swallowed them up.
◇ *She was so embarrassed she wished that the*
ground would open and swallow her up. ◇ *The*
countryside is rapidly being swallowed up by
building developments. ◇ *Many small businesses*
have been swallowed up by larger companies.
NOTE **Swallow sb/sth** is sometimes used with
this meaning: *She wished that the ground would*
open up and swallow her.
◈ v + n/pron + adv ◆ v + adv + n

,swallow sth 'up to use sth such as money or
resources completely: *Practising the piano swal-*
lows up all her free time. ◇ *Pay rises were quickly*
swallowed up by price increases. ◇ *Nuclear*
weapons swallowed up a third of the country's
defence spending. ◇ *The extra money was swal-*
lowed up by debts.
OBJ **time, money** SYN **use sth up**
NOTE **Swallow sth up** is often used in the
passive.
◈ v + adv + n ◆ v + pron + adv ◆ v + n + adv (*rare*)

swan /swɒn; *AmE* swɑːn/ (**-nn-**)

,swan   a'bout/a'round; ,swan   a'bout/
a'round sth (*BrE, informal, disapproving*) to
move around or go from one place to another
enjoying yourself, but with no real purpose: *Stop*
swanning about pretending to be clever. ◇ *She's*
swanning around Europe for the summer.
◈ v + adv ◆ v + prep

,swan 'off (**to…**) (*BrE, informal, disapproving*) to
go off to enjoy yourself with no real purpose:
He's always swanning off to Spain on holiday!
◈ v + adv

swap (*also* **swop**) /swɒp; *AmE* swɑːp/ (**-pp-**)

,swap a'round/'over/'round (*informal, espe-*
cially BrE) if two people **swap around/over/**
round, they move to where the other person was
before or start doing each other's jobs: *I'll drive*
there and you can read the map. We'll swap over
on the way back.
SYN **change over/round** (*BrE*)
◈ v + adv

,swap sb/sth a'round/'over/'round (*informal,*
especially BrE) to replace sb/sth with sb/sth else:
At half-time the manager swapped some of the
players around.
SYN **change sb/sth round/around**
◈ v + n/pron + adv ◆ v + adv + n (*rare*)

,swap 'over (**to sth**), **,swap sb/sth 'over** (**to sth**)
to change from one situation, position, etc. to
another; to make sb do this: *We swapped over*
from an electric cooker to a gas cooker. ◇ *Have you*
been swapped over to the new computer system
yet?
SYN **switch over, switch sth over, switch sb**
over
◈ v + adv ◆ v + n/pron + adv ◆ v + adv + n (*less*
frequent)

swarm /swɔːm; *AmE* swɔːrm/

'swarm with sb/sth (*usually used in the progres-*
sive tenses) if a place is **swarming with** sb/sth, it
is very full of people or things moving around:
The museum was swarming with tourists. ◇ *The*
room was hot and swarming with flies.
◈ v + prep

swear /sweə(r); *AmE* swer/ (**swore**
/swɔː(r)/**sworn** /swɔːn; *AmE* swɔːrn/)

'swear by sb (*not used in the progressive tenses*)
to name sb in order to show that you are making
a serious promise: *I swear by Almighty God that I
will tell the truth* (= for example, said in a British
court of law).
◆ v + prep

'swear by sth/sb (*not used in the progressive
tenses*) to believe strongly that sth/sb is very useful and helpful: *My brother swears by lemon and
honey drinks as a cold remedy.* ◇ *Why don't you go
and see Dr. Nash? My mother swears by him.*
◆ v + prep

,swear sb 'in; **,swear sb 'into sth** to introduce
sb publicly to a new position, responsibility, etc.
by getting them to promise that they will do the
job correctly, be loyal to the organization, their
country, etc: *He was sworn in as President in
January.* ◇ *The new President was hurriedly
sworn into office.*
NOTE Swear sb in and swear sb into sth are
often used in the passive.
◆ v + adv + n ◆ v + n/pron + adv ◆ v + n/pron + prep
▶ **,swearing-'in** *n* [U] [sing.] the act of getting sb
to promise publicly to do their job correctly, be
loyal to their organization or country, etc. before
they begin a new job or responsibility: *The
swearing-in of the new president will take place
tomorrow.* ◇ *a swearing-in ceremony*

,swear 'off sth (*informal, especially AmE*) to
make a serious promise that you will give sth up,
especially sth that is bad or harmful: *He's intending to swear off alcohol.* ◇ *Ever since her boyfriend left she has sworn off men.*
◆ v + prep

'swear to sth (*informal*) to say that sth is definitely true: *I think I've met him somewhere before,
but I **couldn't swear to it*** (= I'm not completely
certain).
◆ v + prep

'swear sb to sth to make sb promise sth, especially that they will not tell other people sth: *The
actors know how the series will end but they are
sworn to secrecy.* ◇ *Jeff told me about his promotion and swore me to silence.*
◆ v + n/pron + prep

sweat /swet/

,sweat sth 'off to lose weight by doing a lot of
hard exercise to make yourself hot and produce
sweat: *I sweated off the extra weight by playing
squash every day.*
◆ v + adv + n ◆ v + pron + adv ◆ v + n + adv (*rare*)

,sweat sth 'out 1 to get rid of a cold, fever, etc. by
staying warm so that you produce sweat: *Whenever I get a bad fever I go to bed and sweat it out.*

OBJ cold, fever **2** **,sweat it 'out** to wait for sth
that you feel nervous or anxious about to happen
or to end: *They made us sweat it out for two hours
until the result was announced.*
NOTE Sweat sth out is not used in the passive.
◆ v + pron + adv ◆ v + n + adv ◆ v + adv + n (*less
frequent*)

'sweat over sth (*informal*) to work very hard on
sth; to spend a lot of time doing sth or worrying
about sth: *I've been sweating over my letter of resignation for several days.*
◆ v + prep

sweep /swiːp/ (**swept, swept** /swept/)

,sweep sb a'long/a'way to make sb feel very
enthusiastic about sth or involved in sth; to
affect sb so much they forget everything else:
Ana was swept along by her father's enthusiasm.
SYN carry sb along; be/get carried away
NOTE Sweep sb along/away is usually used in
the passive.
◆ v + n/pron + adv

,sweep sb a'side to defeat sb easily: *United
swept Liverpool aside with ease.*
◆ v + n/pron + adv ◆ v + adv + n

,sweep sth a'side to ignore sth; to treat sth as
though it is not important: *All their objections
were swept aside.* ◇ *She sweeps aside every suggestion I make.*
OBJ objections, protests, restrictions, opposition, criticism
NOTE Sweep sth aside is often used in the
passive.
◆ v + n/pron + adv ◆ v + adv + n

,sweep sb a'way = SWEEP SB ALONG/AWAY

,sweep sth a'way to destroy or get rid of sth
completely: *The President's speech swept away
all our doubts.* ◇ *Poverty will be swept away!* ◇
*The old way of life has been swept away by the
electronic revolution.*
◆ v + adv + n ◆ v + n/pron + adv

,sweep sth 'back/'up if you **sweep** your hair
back or **up**, you brush or push it away from your
face: *She swept her hair back from her face with
both hands.* ◇ *Long hair can be swept up on top of
your head.*
OBJ hair
◆ v + n/pron + adv ◆ v + adv + n

,sweep sth 'off; **,sweep sth 'off sth** to remove
sth from somewhere, especially by brushing
with your hands, a brush, etc: *He swept the
crumbs off the table.* ◇ (*figurative*) *The wind
swept her hat off.*
◆ v + n/pron + adv ◆ v + adv + n ◆ v + n/pron + prep
IDM **sweep sb off their 'feet** to make sb fall suddenly and deeply in love with you: *Maria was
swept off her feet by Mark's charm.*

,sweep sth 'out to clean a room, a cupboard, etc. with a large brush with a long handle (a **broom**): *Brad was busy sweeping out the yard.*
◆ v + adv + n ♦ v + n/pron + adv

,sweep sb 'up 1 to lift sb with a sudden smooth movement: *He ran forward and swept her up in his arms.* **2** to make sb become very involved in sth so that they are unable to think clearly: *The whole country was swept up in the excitement.* ⟩SYN⟩ **be/get caught up (in sth)** NOTE Sweep sb up is often used in the passive in this meaning.
◆ v + n/pron + adv ♦ v + adv + n (*rare*)

,sweep 'up; ,sweep sth 'up to remove dust, dirt, etc. from a floor with a brush: *We had to sweep up before we left.* ◇ *We'd better sweep up all the bits of broken glass quickly.*
◆ v + adv ♦ v + adv + n ♦ v + n/pron + adv

,sweep sth 'up = SWEEP STH BACK/UP

sweeten /'swiːtn/

,sweeten sb 'up (*informal*) to try to persuade sb to help you, agree to sth, etc. by giving them gifts, being very nice to them, etc: *If you sweeten him up he'll do the work for you.* ◇ *They sweeten up customers with special offers.*
◆ v + n/pron + adv ♦ v + adv + n

swell /swel/ (swelled /sweld/swollen /'swəʊlən; AmE 'swoʊ-/ or swelled, swelled)

,swell 'up if part of the body **swells up**, it becomes much larger and rounder than usual as a result of illness, injury, etc: *My foot swelled up to twice its normal size.* ◇ (*figurative*) *A feeling of admiration swelled up in her.*
◆ v + adv

swill /swɪl/

,swill sth 'down (*informal*) to drink a large amount of sth quickly: *He just swilled down his beer and walked out.*
◆ v + adv + n ♦ v + n/pron + adv

swing /swɪŋ/ (swung, swung /swʌŋ/)

,swing a'round; ,swing sb/sth a'round (*BrE also* ,**swing 'round, ,swing sb/sth 'round**) **1** to turn around fast to face the other way; to make sb/sth do this: *Luke suddenly swung round and glared at me.* ◇ *I swung the car round and drove back down the road.* **2** to change from one idea, opinion, etc. to another, especially the opposite one: *The Labour Party has now swung round to supporting Europe.* ◇ *You should be able to swing people round to your point of view.*
◆ v + adv ♦ v + n/pron + adv

'swing at sb; 'swing sth at sb to try to hit sb: *She swung at me with the iron bar.*
◆ v + prep ♦ v + n/pron + prep

,swing 'by; ,swing 'by sth (*AmE, informal*) to visit a person or place for a short time, especially when you are going somewhere else: *She swung by* (= came here) *on her way home.* ◇ *Let's swing by Dave's house after the movie.*
⟩SYN⟩ **drop by**
◆ v + adv ♦ v + prep

,swing 'round; ,swing sb/sth 'round (*BrE*) = SWING AROUND, SWING SB/STH AROUND

switch /swɪtʃ/

,switch 'off (*informal*) to stop giving your attention to sb or sth: *I just switch off when Jo starts talking.* ◇ *Do you find it hard to switch off* (= stop thinking about work) *when you get home?*
⟩SYN⟩ **turn off**
◆ v + adv

,switch 'off; ,switch sth 'off; ,switch itself 'off to stop an electrical device, a machine or an engine working by pressing a switch, a button, etc: *The heating switches off at 10.00 p.m.* ◇ *Shall I switch the lights off?* ◇ *The electricity has been switched off.* ◇ (*figurative*) *Her smile switched off suddenly when she saw him come in.*
⟩SYN⟩ **turn off, turn itself off, turn sth off**
⟩OPP⟩ **switch on, switch sth on, switch itself on**
◆ v + adv ♦ v + n/pron + adv ♦ v + adv + n

,switch 'on; ,switch sth 'on; ,switch itself 'on to start an electrical device, a machine or an engine by pressing a switch, a button, etc: *She walked in and switched on the light.* ◇ *The machine switches* (*itself*) *on automatically.* ◇ *How do you switch this thing on?* ◇ (*figurative*) *He can switch on the charm whenever he likes.*
⟩SYN⟩ **turn on, turn itself on; turn sth on**
⟩OPP⟩ **switch off, switch sth off, switch itself off**
◆ v + adv

,switch 'over (to sth), ,switch sth 'over (to sth) 1 (*BrE*) to change from one television station to another: *I switched over to watch the news.* ⟩SYN⟩ **change over (to sth); turn over (to sth), turn sth over (to sth) 2** (*also* ,**switch sb 'over**) to change from one position, situation, job, etc. to another: *We've finally switched over to a computerized system.* ◇ *The country gradually switched over from imperial to metric.* ◇ *35 000 customers have been switched over to the new system.* ⟩SYN⟩ **change over (from sth) (to sth)**
◆ v + adv ♦ v + n/pron + adv ♦ v + adv + n

swivel /'swɪvl/ (-ll-, AmE -l-)

,swivel a'round; ,swivel sb/sth a'round (*also* ,**swivel 'round, ,swivel sb/sth 'round** *especially BrE*) **1** to turn or move your body, eyes or head around quickly to face another direction: *He swivelled around to look at her.* **2** to turn or make sth turn around a fixed central point: *She swivelled the chair around to face them.*
◆ v + adv ♦ v + n/pron + adv

swop /swɒp; *AmE* swɑːp/ (**-pp-**)

,**swop a'round**/'**over**/'**round** = SWAP AROUND/
OVER/ROUND

,**swop sb/sth a'round**/'**over**/'**round** = SWAP
SB/STH AROUND/OVER/ROUND

swot /swɒt; *AmE* swɑːt/

,**swot 'up (on sth)** (*BrE, informal*) to study a subject very hard, especially when you are preparing for an exam: *I have to swot up on phrasal
verbs for a test tomorrow.* ◇ *It's time to start swot-
ting up for the exam.*
　▶SYN **brush sth up, brush up on sth** (*especially
BrE*), **mug up (on sth), mug sth up** (*BrE*),
review sth (*especially AmE*), **revise sth** (*BrE*)

syphon /'saɪfn/

,**syphon sth 'off** = SIPHON STH OFF

Tt

tack /tæk/

,tack sth 'on; ,tack sth 'on to sth (*informal*)
to add sth as an extra item, especially in a careless way: *The last paragraph seems to have been
tacked on at the last minute.* ◇ *An extra day has
been tacked onto the New Year holiday.* ◇ *a porch
tacked on to the front of the house*

⟨SYN⟩ **add sth on, add sth on to sth**

NOTE **Tack sth on** and **tack sth on to sth** are
often used in the passive.

→ *see also* TAG STH ON, TAG STH ON TO STH

◈ v + n/pron + adv ♦ v + adv + n ♦
v + n/pron + adv + prep

tag /tæg/ (-gg-)

,tag a'long (behind/with sb) (*informal*) to go
somewhere with sb, especially when you have
not been invited: *The children tagged along
behind their mother.* ◇ *Can I tag along (with you)
when you go to the shops?*

⟨SYN⟩ **string along (with sb)**

→ *see also* TAG ON, TAG ON TO SB

◈ v + adv

,tag 'on; ,tag 'on to sb/sth (*especially BrE*) to
follow sb closely and go somewhere with them,
although you have not been invited: *Kate's friend
tagged on and spoiled the day.* ◇ *We tagged on to
the end of the procession.*

→ *see also* TAG ALONG (BEHIND/WITH SB)

◈ v + adv ♦ v + adv + prep

,tag sth 'on; ,tag sth 'on to sth (*informal*) to
add sth as an extra item to the end of sth, especially in a careless way: *An apology was tagged
on to the end of the letter.* ◇ *Online security is
being built in to the system, not tagged on.*

⟨SYN⟩ **add sth on, add sth on to sth**

NOTE **Tag sth on** and **tag sth on to sth** are often
used in the passive.

→ *see also* TACK STH ON, TACK STH ON TO STH

◈ v + n/pron + adv ♦ v + adv + n ♦
v + n/pron + adv + prep

tail /teɪl/

,tail a'way = TAIL OFF

,tail 'back (*BrE*) if traffic **tails back**, it forms a
long line that moves very slowly or does not
move at all: *After the accident, traffic tailed back
eight miles.*

◈ v + adv

▶ **'tailback** *n* (*BrE*) a long line of traffic that
moves very slowly or does not move at all: *The
crash caused a six-mile tailback.*

,tail 'off (*also* **,tail a'way** *less frequent*) to become
smaller, fewer, weaker, etc: *Sales tailed off in the
autumn/fall.* ◇ *The number of tourists starts to
tail off in September.* ◇ *Her voice tailed away.* ◇
'Did you want to see…' she tailed off.

◈ v + adv

tailor /'teɪlə(r)/

'tailor sth to/for sb/sth to make or adapt sth for
a particular purpose, a particular person, etc:
*Special programmes of study are tailored to the
needs of specific students.*

◈ v + n/pron + prep

take /teɪk/ (took /tʊk/ taken /'teɪkən/)

	~ aback	301	~ on
	~ after		~ out
	~ against	302	~ out of
	~ along		~ out on
298	~ apart		~ over
	~ around		~ round
	~ aside		~ through
	~ away		~ to
	~ away from	303	~ up
	~ back		~ up on
299	~ down		~ up with
	~ in		~ upon
300	~ into		~ with
	~ off		

,take sb a'back to shock or surprise sb: *I was
taken aback by his rudeness.*

NOTE **Take sb aback** is usually used in the
passive.

◈ v + n/pron + adv

,take 'after sb 1 (*not used in the progressive
tenses*) to look like or behave like an older member of your family: *I'm told I take after my grandmother.* ◇ *Your daughter doesn't take after you at
all.* ◇ *He's always been shy — he takes after his
father.* **2** (*old-fashioned, AmE*) to begin to follow
sb quickly in order to catch them: *A man rushed
out of the bank and two men took after him.* ◇ *She
ran out into the night and he took after her.*

◈ v + prep

,take a'gainst sb/sth (*old-fashioned, BrE*) to
begin to dislike sb/sth: *Why have you suddenly
taken against Laura?*

⟨OPP⟩ **take to sb/sth**

◈ v + prep

,take sb/sth a'long (to sth) to take sb or sth with
you when you go somewhere: *Tom took his sister
along to the party.* ◇ *When you travel with young
children, take along some favourite toys or a book.*

◈ v + n/pron + adv ♦ v + adv + n

,take sb/sth a'part (*informal*) **1** (in sport) to defeat sb easily: *He took the American apart in the third set* (= in a game of tennis). ◊ *We took the other team apart.* ◊ *Touch her again and I'll take you apart!* **2** to attack or criticize sb/sth severely: *Her second novel was taken apart by the critics.*
◈ v + n/pron + adv ◆ v + adv + n (*less frequent*)

,take sth a'part to separate a machine, a piece of equipment, etc. into its parts: *She took the clock apart and couldn't put it back together.* ◊ *You can take the mixer apart to clean it.* ◊ *The police took the room apart* (= examined everything very carefully), *looking for evidence.*
⟨SYN⟩ **dismantle sth** (*more formal*)
⟨OPP⟩ **put sth together**
◈ v + n/pron + adv ◆ v + adv + n (*less frequent*)

,take sb a'round; **,take sb a'round sth** (*BrE also* **,take sb 'round**, **,take sb 'round sth**) to visit a place with sb; to show sb the interesting or important parts of a place: *If you'd like to see the town, I could take you around.* ◊ *We got a guide to take us round the temples.*
⟨SYN⟩ **show sb around**, **show sb around sth**; **take sb over sth**
◈ v + n/pron + adv ◆ v + n/pron + prep

,take sb/sth a'round (*especially AmE*) = TAKE SB/STH ROUND

,take sb a'side to separate sb from the rest of a group in order to talk to them privately: *She took me aside and explained the situation.*
◈ v + n/pron + adv

,take sb a'way (from sb/sth) 1 to remove sb from somewhere; to lead or move sb to another place: *The injured were taken away by ambulance.* ◊ *I can take you away from all this* (= all this trouble). **2** to remove sb, especially a child, from sb's care: *The children were taken away from them and put into a children's home.* ◊ *My father took me away from school and taught me himself.* **3** to take sb with you on a trip or holiday/vacation: *He takes the whole family away for two weeks in the summer.* **4** to make it necessary for sb to leave a place, especially temporarily: *Sam's work takes him away from his family for months at a time.*
◈ v + n/pron + adv ◆ v + adv + n (*less frequent*)

,take sth a'way 1 to remove sth and place it somewhere else: *They had to take the computer away to fix it.* ◊ *You can take the book away with you.* **2** (*from sb/sth*) to remove something from a person, a place or an organization so that they no longer have it: *These books must not be taken away from the library.* ◊ *They can't take our rights away from us.* **3** to make a feeling, pain, etc. disappear: *These tablets should help take the pain away.* ◊ *That was disgusting! I need a drink of water to take the taste away.* ⟨OBJ⟩ **pain**, **taste**, **appetite 4** (*from sth*) (*mathematics*) to take one number from another: *If you take four away from ten, that leaves six.* ◊ *Ten take away four*

leaves six (10 – 4=6). **5** (*BrE*) (*AmE* **,take sth 'out**) (*usually used in the infinitive with 'to'*) to buy a cooked dish at a restaurant and carry it away to eat at home, in the street, etc: *A cheeseburger and a coffee to take away, please.* ◊ *Is that to eat here or take away?* **6** (*from sth*) to form an opinion or impression of sb/sth that is still there when you go away: *We didn't take away a very favourable impression of the hotel.* ◊ *What do we want students to take away* (= to learn) *from this course?*
◈ v + n/pron + adv ◆ v + adv + n

IDM **take sb's 'breath away** to surprise or please somebody very much: *The first sight of the waterfall takes your breath away.*

▶ **'takeaway** (*BrE*) *n* **1** a restaurant that cooks and sells food that you eat somewhere else: *a Chinese/Indian takeaway* ◊ *a takeaway restaurant* **2** (*AmE* **'takeout**, **'carry-out**) a meal that you buy from this type of restaurant: *We could get a takeaway tonight.* ◊ *a takeaway pizza*

,take a'way from sth to make the effect or value of sth seem less: *I don't wish to take away from his achievements, but he couldn't have done it without our help.*
⟨SYN⟩ **detract from sth** (*more formal*)
◈ v + adv + prep

,take sb a'way from sth to take sb's attention away from what they are trying to do: *These minor problems are taking us away from the real issue.*
⟨SYN⟩ **distract sb** (*from sth*)
◈ v + n/pron + adv + prep

,take sb 'back 1 (*to sth*) to go with someone to the place where they were or to your/their home: *Can you take me back to the hotel?* ◊ *I'll take the kids back now — they're getting tired.* **2** to allow sb such as your husband, wife or partner to come home after they have left because of a problem; to allow sb to return to their job: *I agreed to take her back if she promised to be faithful in future.* ◊ *An employer cannot be forced to take you back.*
⟨SYN⟩ **have sb back 3** (*to sth*) to make sb's thoughts return to a past time: *The smell of the sea took me back to my childhood.* ◊ *That song takes me back a bit!* ⟨SYN⟩ **carry sb back** (*to sth*)
◈ v + n/pron + adv

,take sth 'back 1 (*to sb/sth*) if you **take sth back** to a shop/store, or a shop/store **takes sth back**, you return sth that you have bought because it is the wrong size or does not work, for example: *The sweater had a hole in it so I took it back.* ⟨SYN⟩ **return sth** (*more formal*) **2** to return sth you have borrowed, hired, etc: *I forgot to take my books back to the library.* ◊ *It's your turn to take the videos back.* ⟨SYN⟩ **return sth** (*more formal*) **NOTE** In informal spoken language **take sb back sth**, or, less often, **take sb sth back** can also be used: *I took him back his CD.* ◊ *I took him his CD back.* **3** to take something you have bought, etc. home with you after you have been

away: *We spent a lot of the holiday looking for presents to take back for the kids.* NOTE In informal spoken language **take sb back sth** is also used: *We took the kids back some presents.* **4** to receive or take sth that you own from sb who has borrowed it: *When I'd read the letter he took it back and put it in his pocket.* ◇ *No attempt was ever made to take back the land* (= to take control of it again). **5** to admit that sth you said was wrong or that you should not have said it: *I take back what I said about you being lazy.* SYN **retract sth**; **withdraw sth** (*both more formal*)
🔷 v + n/pron + adv ◆ v + adv + n **5** v + adv + n ◆ v + pron + adv ◆ v + n + adv (*less frequent*)

take sb/sth 'down; take sb/sth 'down sth
to go with sb/sth to a lower level, to a more southern part of a country, etc., or to a different part of a building, town, country, etc: *The nurse will take you down in the lift.* ◇ *The injured climbers were taken down the mountain on a sledge.* ◇ *You promised to take me down to London next time you went!* ◇ *Tony's just taking the car down to the garage — he'll be back soon.*
OPP **take sb/sth up, take sb/sth up sth**
🔷 v + n/pron + adv ◆ v + adv + n (*less frequent*) ◆ v + n/pron + prep

take sth 'down 1 to remove sth from a high level: *She took a book down from the top shelf.* **2** to remove sth that is hanging on a rail, etc: *Will you help me take the curtains down?* OBJ **curtains, pictures** OPP **put sth up 3** to remove a structure by separating it into pieces: *They were taking their tent down as we left.* OBJ **a tent, scaffolding** OPP **put sth up 4** to pull down a piece of clothing worn below the waist, without actually removing it: *She took her trousers down to show the doctor her leg wound.* OBJ **trousers, pants 5** to write sth down: *She took down my name, address and phone number.* OBJ **details, (telephone) number** SYN **note sth down**
🔷 v + n/pron + adv ◆ v + adv + n

take sb 'in 1 to allow sb to stay in your home: *She takes in paying guests.* ◇ *When my parents died, my uncle took me in and brought me up.* OBJ **guests, lodgers 2** if the police **take sb in**, they take them to a police station to question them about a crime: *Two young men have been taken in for questioning.* **3** (of an organization, an institution, etc.) to accept sb as a member, a student, a patient, etc: *The college took in more students than ever before last year.* **4** to make sb believe sth that is not true: *How could I have been taken in by his charm?* ◇ *She took me in completely with her story.* SYN **deceive sb** (*more formal*) NOTE In this meaning **take sb in** is usually used in the passive.
🔷 v + n/pron + adv ◆ v + adv + n
▶ **'intake** n **1** [C] [U] the number of people who join a college or other organization at a particular time: *a new intake of students* **2** (*AmE*) a first

test, meeting, etc. that you have when you go to a hospital or have an interview for a job or school, etc. → *see also* INTAKE at TAKE STH IN, TAKE STH INTO STH

take sb/sth 'in (to sth), take sb/sth 'into sth
to go with sb or to take sth into a building or another place: *I'm going into town, so I'll take you in if you like.* ◇ *I took Jack into the kitchen for a quiet chat.* ◇ *I'll take you in to meet the manager now.* ◇ *If you take your camera in (to the shop), they'll have a look at it for you.* ◇ *My dad has been taken into hospital.*
NOTE In informal spoken language **take sth in (for sb)** can also be used in the patterns **take sb in sth** and, less often, **take sb/sth in**: *I took him in a cup of tea.* ◇ *I took him a cup of tea in.*
→ *see also* TAKE STH IN, TAKE STH INTO STH
🔷 v + n/pron + adv ◆ v + adv + n ◆ v + n/pron + prep

take sth 'in 1 to notice sth with your eyes: *He took in every detail of her appearance.* ◇ *She started to relax and take in her surroundings.* **2** to understand or absorb sth that you hear or read; to accept sth as true: *I read the whole page without taking anything in.* ◇ *He just couldn't take in what had happened.* **3** to include or cover sth: *The trip takes in six European capitals.* ◇ *The study takes in women from 15 different countries.* NOTE In this meaning **take sth in** is not used in the passive. **4** (*informal*) to go to see or visit sth such as a film/movie, especially when you are in a place for a different reason: *She always tries to take in a show when she's in New York.* OBJ **a show, the sights** NOTE In this meaning **take sth in** is not used in the passive. **5** to make a piece of clothing narrower or tighter: *This dress needs to be taken in at the waist.* OBJ **a dress, a skirt, etc.** OPP **let sth out 6** if a boat **takes in** water, water comes in to it, usually through the bottom or sides OBJ only **water 7** (*old-fashioned*) to do particular kinds of work for other people in your home, in order to earn money: *My grandmother used to take in washing.* OBJ **washing, ironing, sewing 8** (*AmE*) to receive or earn an amount of money: *How much did the show take in?*
🔷 v + adv + n ◆ v + pron + adv ◆ v + n + adv (*less frequent*)

take sth 'in; take sth 'into sth to absorb sth into the body by breathing or swallowing it: *Fish take in oxygen through their gills.* ◇ *She took in deep breaths of sea air.* ◇ *When we breathe we take oxygen into the body.*
🔷 v + adv + n ◆ v + n/pron + adv ◆ v + n/pron + prep
▶ **'intake** n **1** [U] [C] the amount of food, drink, etc. that you take into your body: *a high intake of vitamin C* ◇ *to reduce your calorie intake* **2** [C, usually sing.] an act of taking sth in, especially a breath: *a sharp intake of breath*
→ *see also* INTAKE at TAKE SB IN

,**take sb 'into sth** to accept sb into an institution, an organization, etc: *They had to take the children into care* (= to be looked after by the local authority). ◊ *Five men were taken into custody* (= to prison). ◊ *They took him into the firm as a partner last year.*
NOTE Take **sb into sth** is often used in the passive.
✦ v + n/pron + prep

,**take sb/sth 'into sth** to bring sb/sth into a particular situation, activity, period of time, etc: *Improved graphics took computer games into a new era.* ◊ *Owen's goal took England into the lead* (= they were winning). ◊ *the government that took Britain into Europe*
✦ v + n/pron + prep

,**take 'off 1** (of an aircraft, etc.) to leave the ground and begin to fly: *The flight was due to take off from Heathrow at 13.15.* ◊ *(figurative) The high jumper took off at a bad angle.* $\overline{OPP}$ **land 2** (*informal*) if an idea, a product, etc. **takes off**, it suddenly becomes successful or popular: *The new dictionary has really taken off.* ◊ *Her career is just starting to take off.* ◊ *Sales of mobile phones have really taken off in the last few years.*
✦ v + adv
▸ **'take-off** *n* [U] [C] **1** the moment when an aircraft, etc. leaves the ground: *The plane is ready for take-off.* ◊ *take-off point/speed/run* ◊ *(figurative) The economy is poised for take-off.* **2** the moment when your feet leave the ground when you jump
→ *see also* TAKE-OFF at TAKE SB OFF

,**take 'off**; ,**take yourself 'off** to leave somewhere suddenly or in a hurry: *Whenever things get tough, she takes off.* ◊ *He stayed for a year, then took off for a job in New York.* ◊ *I'm going to take myself off to bed.*
✦ v + adv ✦ v + pron + adv

,**take sb 'off** (*especially BrE*) **1** to copy sb in an annoying way: *She was taking off the woman next door.* **2** (in sports, entertainment, etc.) to remove a player from the field, an actor from the stage, etc. and not allow them to continue playing, or acting: *Their best striker was taken off after 30 minutes.*
✦ **1** v + adv + n ✦ v + pron + adv ✦ v + n + adv
2 v + n/pron + adv ✦ v + adv + n (*less frequent*)
▸ **'take-off** *n* an act of copying sb in an amusing way
→ *see also* TAKE-OFF at TAKE OFF

,**take sb 'off**; ,**take sb 'off sth** to rescue sb from a ship, a mountain, etc: *The injured men were taken off the boat by helicopter.*
NOTE This phrasal verb is often used in the passive.
✦ v + n/pron + adv ✦ v + adv + n (*less frequent*) ✦ v + n/pron + prep

'**take sb/sth 'off** (**to sth**) to make sb go with you to another place; to take sth to another place: *They took him off to the police station.* ◊ *She collected our passports and took them off somewhere.*
✦ v + n/pron + adv ✦ v + adv + n (*rare*)

,**take sb 'off sth 1** to stop sb from continuing a particular medicine, treatment, etc: *His doctor took him off tranquillizers.* $\overline{OPP}$ **put sb on sth 2** to remove sb from a job, position, etc. and not allow them to continue: *One of the lawyers has been taken off the case.*
✦ v + n/pron + prep

,**take sth 'off 1** to remove an item of clothing from your/sb's body: *She took her coat off and hung it up.* ◊ *It's the custom to take off your shoes when you go into the house.* ◊ *Can you take off Tommy's jacket for me?* **OBJ** **clothes**, **shoes**, **coat**, **jacket, etc.** $\overline{OPP}$ **put sth on 2** to remove a bus, train, etc. from service; to stop a television or radio programme, performances of a show, etc: *The 17.13 bus to Bristol will be taken off next month.* ◊ *The play was taken off after a week.* $\overline{OPP}$ **put sth on 3** to cut off hair or a part of the body: *The hairdresser asked me how much she should take off.* ◊ *His leg had to be taken off above the knee.*
✦ v + n/pron + adv ✦ v + adv + n
IDM **I take my 'hat off to sb** (*informal, especially BrE*) used to say that you admire sb very much for sth they have done

,**take sth 'off**; ,**take sth 'off sth 1** to remove sth from somewhere: *Sam took off the lid and looked inside.* ◊ *Sam took the lid off the box and looked inside.* ◊ *Can you take your feet off the sofa?* ◊ *I've got an assistant now, which will take the pressure off a bit.* ◊ *Always take your make-up off before you go to bed.* **SYN** **remove sth** (*more formal*) $\overline{OPP}$ **put sth on 2** to remove an amount of money, a number of marks or points, etc. from sth in order to reduce the total: *Can you take any money off this shirt* (= sell it at a cheaper price)? ◊ *Marks will be taken off for bad spelling.* **3** to have a period of time as a break from work or school: *I'm going to take next week off.* ◊ *She took a day off work.* **4** to remove a name, an item, etc. from a list: *The soup has been taken off* (*the menu*). ◊ *I took my name off the list.*
✦ v + n/pron + adv ✦ v + adv + n ✦ v + n/pron + prep
IDM **take your 'eyes off sb/sth** to stop looking at sb/sth: *He couldn't take his eyes off the cake.* ◊ *I only took my eyes off her for a second and she disappeared.* **take your 'mind off sb/sth** to make you stop thinking about sb or about sth unpleasant: *We thought going out for the evening might take her mind off things.*

,**take sth 'off sb** (*informal, especially BrE*) to use force or your authority to get sth from sb: *Another child took his teddy off him.* ◇ *The teacher took the cigarettes off me.*
⊕ v + n/pron + prep
IDM **take 'years off sb** to make sb feel or look younger than they are: (*informal*) *That hairstyle takes ten years off you!*

,**take 'off sth** (*informal*) to make sth shorter by the amount mentioned: *Smoking takes six years off the average life.*
⊕ v + n/pron + prep

,**take yourself 'off** = TAKE OFF, TAKE YOURSELF OFF

,**take 'on sth** to begin to have a particular quality, appearance, etc: *Lisa's voice took on a more serious tone.* ◇ *His words suddenly took on a different meaning.* ◇ *The car suddenly seemed to take on a life of its own* (= move by itself without anyone controlling it).
OBJ **meaning, shape, expression, appearance** ‹SYN› **assume sth** (*more formal*)
⊕ v + adv + n

,**take sb 'on 1** to employ sb: *She was taken on as a graduate trainee.* ◇ *They take on extra staff for the summer.* ‹SYN› **employ sb 2** to accept sb as a patient, a customer, etc: *The practice* (= group of doctors or dentists) *has stopped taking on new patients.* **OBJ** **patients, clients 3** to play against sb in a game or contest; to fight against sb: *She took her father on at chess and beat him.* ◇ *The rebels took on the entire Roman army.*
⊕ v + n/pron + adv ◆ v + adv + n

,**take sb/sth 'on** (of a bus, plane, ship, etc.) to allow sb/sth to enter or come on board: *The bus stopped to take on more passengers.* ◇ *The plane was taking on fuel from a tanker.*
⊕ v + adv + n ◆ v + n/pron + adv

,**take sth 'on** to decide to do sth; to agree to be responsible for sth: *She took on more responsibilities when she was promoted.* ◇ *If we're short of money, I'll just have to take on extra work.*
OBJ **responsibility, job, task, work**
⊕ v + adv + n ◆ v + n/pron + adv

'**take sth on/upon yourself** to decide to do sth without asking permission or talking to anyone else: *She took the responsibility for what had happened upon herself.* ◇ *Reg took it upon himself to tell the newspapers the truth.*
⊕ v + n/pron + prep + pron

,**take sb 'out** (**for/to sth**) to invite sb to go with you to the theatre, a restaurant, etc: *He took Susie out for a meal.*
⊕ v + n/pron + adv

take sb 'out; ,take sb 'out of sth to remove sb from a place; to take sb outside a building: *The prisoners were taken out and shot.*
⊕ v + n/pron + adv ◆ v + n/pron + adv + prep

,**take sb/sth 'out** (*informal*) to kill sb or destroy sth; to injure or damage sb/sth so that they cannot work or be used: *Enemy missiles took out two of our planes.* ◇ *Police think he was taken out by a rival gang.*
⊕ v + adv + n ◆ v + n/pron + adv

,**take sth 'out 1** to remove a part of the body from inside sb: *She had to have her appendix taken out.* ◇ *I'm afraid we'll have to take the tooth out.* **OBJ** **your/sb's tonsils, your/sb's teeth, your/sb's appendix** ‹SYN› **remove sth** (*more formal*) **2** to obtain an official document or a service: *She took out a loan to buy a new car.* ◇ *Did you remember to take out travel insurance?* **OBJ** **insurance, loan, mortgage 3** (**against sb**) to start a legal process against sb by means of an official document: *They took out an injunction against the newspaper.* **OBJ** **summons, injunction 4** (**for sth**) to leave your house with sth in order to do a particular activity: *Shall we take the car out for a drive this afternoon?* **5** (*AmE*) = TAKE STH AWAY 5
⊕ v + adv + n ◆ v + n/pron + adv

,**take sth 'out; ,take sth 'out of sth 1** to remove sth from somewhere: *Jack felt in his pocket and took out his keys.* ◇ *How many books did you take out of* (= borrow from) *the library?* ◇ *You're not allowed to take so much money out of the country.* ◇ *He took out his wallet and pulled out a £50 note.* **2** to carry sth with you outside: *I'll take the cases out to the car.* **3** to remove money from your bank account: *I took some more money out* (*of my account*) *yesterday.* **OBJ** **money** ‹SYN› **draw sth out, draw sth out of sth; withdraw sth** (**from sth**) (*more formal*) **4** to remove an amount of money from a larger amount to pay for sth: *£20 will be taken out of your wages to pay for the damage.* ◇ *Contributions to your pension will be taken out of your salary.* **5** to stop your career, studies, etc. for a period of time in order to do sth else: *She took a year out of college to work abroad.* ◇ *He took a year out between school and college.* ◇ *We need to take time out to think things through.* **OBJ** **a year, time** **NOTE** Take sth out is not used in the passive in this meaning. **6** to make sth disappear from somewhere: *Soaking should help to take the stain out.* **OBJ** **stain**
⊕ v + adv + n ◆ v + n/pron + adv ◆ v + n/pron + adv + prep
5 v + n + adv ◆ v + n + adv + prep ◆ v + adv + n (*rare*)

IDM **take a leaf out of sb's 'book** to follow sb's example: *I'm going to take a leaf out of your book and get to work early.* **take sth out of sb's 'hands** to remove sth from sb's control and deal with it yourself: *The decision has been taken out of my hands.* **take the 'mickey out of sb/sth** (*also* **take the 'piss out of sb** △, *slang*) both (*BrE, informal*) to make sb look or feel silly by copying sth that they do, or making them believe sth that is not true: *They used to take the mickey out of Ade because of the way he spoke.*

▸ **'takeout** (*AmE*) = TAKEAWAY at TAKE STH AWAY

'take it/sth 'out of sb to make sb feel very tired: *That flu really took it out of me.* ◊ *Looking after three young children really takes a lot out of you.*
OBJ **a lot, so much** SYN **wear sb out**
✦ v + it + adv + prep ◆ v + pron + adv + prep

,**take sb 'out of themselves** (*especially BrE*) to make sb forget their worries, thoughts, concerns, etc: *Seeing his old friends again took him out of himself.*
✦ v + n/pron + adv + prep

,**take sth 'out on sb/sth** to behave in an unpleasant way towards sb/sth because you feel angry, disappointed, etc: *When he's had a bad day, he always takes it out on me.* ◊ *You shouldn't take your frustrations out on the kids.*
✦ v + it + adv + prep ◆ v + n/pron + adv + prep

,**take 'over 1** (from sth) (as sth) to become more important than sth else and replace it: *Computers are rapidly taking over from books as children's learning resources.* ◊ *Glasgow took over from Lisbon as cultural capital of Europe.* **2** to become stronger, more powerful or more noticeable: *It's hard not to let negative feelings take over.* ◊ *When she saw the accident, her training as a doctor immediately took over.*
✦ v + adv

,**take 'over**; ,**take sth 'over 1** (from sb) (as sth) to take responsibility for sth after sb else has finished; to do sth instead of sb else: *Who's going to take over from Bill as manager when he retires?* ◊ *If you're tired of driving, I'll take over for a while.* ◊ *I'll take over the driving if you want.* **2** to gain control of a political party, a country, etc: *Things will change when the Socialist Party takes over.* ◊ *In the film, aliens take over the world.*
✦ v + adv ◆ v + adv + n ◆ v + pron + adv
1 also v + n + adv (*rare*)

,**take sb 'over sth 1** to go with sb around a building and show them what is interesting or important: *A guide took us over the house.* SYN **take sb around/round sth 2** to look at or discuss sth with sb and explain important points: *Would you mind taking us over the procedure again?* → *see also* TAKE SB THROUGH STH
✦ v + n/pron + prep

,**take sb/sth 'over 1** to affect sb so strongly that they are unable to think of anything else or do anything else: *His ambition had taken him over.* ◊ *My job is starting to take over my life.* **2** [+ adv/prep] to take sb/sth from one place to another: *I took Mia over to Cambridge to meet my parents.*
✦ **1** v + n/pron + adv ◆ v + adv + n
  2 v + n/pron + adv

'take sth 'over 1 to gain control of a business, a company, etc. by buying it or by buying the most of its shares: *The company was taken over last September.* ◊ *They have already taken over several smaller airlines.* OBJ **company** SYN **buy sth out 2** if you **take over** a place, you fill it or use the whole of it so that other people cannot use it: *We're taking over the whole hotel for the conference.* **3** to start living in a place or using it: *The flat was a mess when we took it over.* ◊ *This building used to be a school until the hotel took it over.*
✦ v + adv + n ◆ v + n/pron + adv

▸ **'takeover** *n* [C] [U] **1** an act of gaining control of a company by buying most of its shares: *The company have abandoned their takeover bid.* **2** an act of gaining control of a country, region or city, especially by force: *a military takeover*

,**take sb 'round**; ,**take sb 'round sth** (*BrE*) = TAKE SB AROUND, TAKE SB AROUND STH

,**take sb/sth 'round** (*BrE*) (*also* ,**take sb/sth a'round** *AmE, BrE*) to take sb/sth with you to another place, sb else's home, etc: *I'm taking the photos straight round to Phil's to show him.* ◊ *Joe took us round to see his mother.*
✦ v + n/pron + adv ◆ v + adv + n

,**take sb/sth 'through**; ,**take sb/sth 'through sth** to lead or carry a person or a thing through one place to another: *Let's take our tea through to the lounge.* ◊ *The journey takes you through some beautiful scenery.* ◊ (*figurative*) *We have plenty of work to take us through to the end of the year.*
✦ v + n/pron + adv ◆ v + n/pron + prep

'take sth 'through sth to discuss sth with sb or explain it to them so that they know what to do: *Your solicitor will take you through the contract.* ◊ *The director took us through the play scene by scene.*
→ *see also* TAKE SB OVER STH 2
✦ v + n/pron + prep

'take to sb/sth to start liking sb/sth: *I didn't take to Elena's husband at all.* ◊ *He hasn't taken to his new school.*
OPP **take against sb/sth**
✦ v + prep
IDM **not take 'kindly to sb/sth** to not like sb/sth: *I don't take kindly to being told how to run my life.*

'take to sth to go away to a particular place, especially to escape from sth difficult or dangerous: *She felt so ill that she took to her bed.* ◊ *The rebels took to the hills.* ◊ *Thousands of people took to the streets* (= went out into the streets) *in protest.*
✦ v + prep
IDM **take to your 'heels** to start running: *They took to their heels and fled.*

'take to sth 1 (*also* **'take to doing sth**) to begin to do sth, especially as a habit: *For some reason he took to walking the New York streets at night.* ◊

She gave up painting and took to sculpture. **2** to develop an ability for sth: *He took to tennis as if he'd been playing all his life.* ◇ *Jay took to teaching like a duck to water* (= very naturally).
◈ v + prep

'take sth to sth (*informal*) to use a tool or piece of equipment in order to do sth, especially sth violent: *He took a hammer to the radio* (= he destroyed it).
◈ v + n/pron + prep

take 'up to continue with sth, especially after sb/sth else has finished: *The band's new album takes up where the last one left off.*
◈ v + adv

take sb/sth 'up; **take sb/sth 'up sth** to go with sb or take sth to a higher place or to another part of a building, country, etc: *Someone will take you up to your room.* ◇ *Why don't we take our picnic up the hill?* ◇ *She took a hot drink up to bed with her.*
〉OPP〈 **take sb/sth down**, **take sb/sth down sth** **NOTE** In informal spoken language **take sb up sth** and, less often, **take sb sth up** are also used: *He took her up a cup of tea.* ◇ *He took her a cup of tea up.*
◈ v + n/pron + adv ◆ v + adv + n (*less frequent*) ◆ v + n/pron + prep

take sth 'up 1 to remove sth that is fixed on a floor or on the ground: *They took the road up to repair the water pipes.* **OBJ** **road, pavement, carpet, floorboards** 〉SYN〈 **pull sth up 2** to fill a particular amount of space or time: *This table takes up too much room.* ◇ *Virtually all the memory is taken up with this one program.* ◇ *I mustn't take up any more of your time.* ◇ *Her whole day was taken up with making phone calls.* **OBJ** **room, space, time** 〉SYN〈 **occupy sth 3** to start to do a new activity, especially for pleasure: *She took up yoga a few years ago.* ◇ *I've decided to take up Japanese.* ◇ *Alex only took up the piano when he was 14.* **4** to start or begin sth, especially a job: *She took up a post at Kyoto University.* **OBJ** **post 5** to make an item of clothing, a curtain, etc. shorter: *This skirt will need taking up.* 〉OPP〈 **let sth down 6** to absorb sth such as a liquid, a gas, etc: *Plants take up carbon dioxide from the atmosphere.* 〉SYN〈 **absorb sth 7** to continue sth after sb else has stopped; to continue to discuss sth that was mentioned earlier: *I'd like to take up the point you raised earlier.* ◇ *Paula took up the story.* **OBJ** **story** 〉SYN〈 **pick sth up 8** to accept a suggestion, a policy, an invitation, etc: *The union have taken up her case.* ◇ *The idea was never taken up.* ◇ *I'd like to take up their invitation to visit them in Rio.* **OBJ** **case, idea, challenge, offer 9** to join in saying or singing sth: *The cry was taken up by the rest of the crowd.* **OBJ** **the cry, the refrain 10** to move into a particular position: *We took up our positions by the door.* ◇ (*formal*) *She has **taken up residence** (= begun to live) in London.* **OBJ** **position 11** (*old-fashioned*, *formal*) to take sth in

your hand: *She took up a book and began to read.*
〉SYN〈 **pick sth up**
◈ v + adv + n ◆ v + n/pron + adv (*less frequent*)**1**
v + n + adv ◆ v + adv + n ◆ v + pron + adv

▶ **'uptake** *n* [U] [sing.] **1** the process by which sth is taken into a body or system; the rate at which this happens: *The experiment measured the uptake of oxygen by the muscles.* **2** an act of making or starting sth; the number of people who do this: *There has been an increase in the uptake of these courses.*

take sb 'up on sth (*informal*) **1** to question sb or argue with sb about sth because you do not agree: *I thought he was wrong but I didn't take him up on it.* ◇ *I'd like to take you up on what you said about unemployment.* 〉SYN〈 **pick sb up on sth 2** to accept an offer, an invitation that sb has made: *I think I'll take you up on your offer to help.* ◇ *'You can borrow the car if you like.' 'I might take you up on that.'*
◈ v + n/pron + adv + prep

take 'up with sb (*informal*) to become friendly with sb; to start a relationship with sb, especially sb who might have a bad influence on you: *I heard Tom has taken up with a supermodel!* ◇ *She's taken up with a bunch of losers* (= people who will never be successful).
◈ v + adv + prep

take sth 'up with sb to speak or write to sb about sth they may be able to help you with: *You'll have to take your complaint up with the manager.*
◈ v + n/pron + adv + prep

be ,taken 'up with sb/sth; **be ,taken 'up with doing sth** to be very busy with sb or with doing sth: *She is very taken up with the children.* ◇ *I've been completely taken up with preparing for exams.*
◈ be + v + adv + prep

take sth u'pon yourself = TAKE STH ON/UPON YOURSELF

be 'taken with sb/sth to find sb/sth attractive or interesting: *We were all very taken with Zoe.*
◈ be + v + prep

talk /tɔːk/

	~ around		~ out of
304	~ at		~ over
	~ away		~ round
	~ back		~ through
	~ down	305	~ to
	~ down to		~ up
	~ into		~ with
	~ out		

talk a'round sth (*BrE also* **,talk 'round sth**) to talk in a general way about a subject or a problem without discussing the difficult or important parts of it: *We talked around the subject for some time before coming to the real issue.*
OBJ **subject**
◈ v + prep

'talk at sb to speak to sb without listening to what they say in reply: *My father always listened to our point of view — he never just talked at us.* NOTE Talk at sb can be used in the passive: *I was being talked at rather than talked to.*
◈ v + prep

talk a'way (to sb) to talk without stopping for a period of time: *They were soon talking away to each other as if they'd known each other for years.* ◊ *Marie was talking away nineteen to the dozen* (= talking a lot without stopping).
◈ v + adv

talk 'back (to sb) to reply rudely to sb in authority: *She was sent out for talking back to the teacher.*
SYN answer back, answer sb back (*especially BrE*)
◈ v + adv

▶ **'back talk** *n* [U] (*AmE, informal*) a rude reply or comment: *I said no, and don't give me any more back talk.*

talk sb 'down 1 to talk to sb who is threatening to kill themselves and persuade them not to jump from a tall building, a bridge, etc: *The police were trying to talk down a youth threatening to jump from the roof of the car park.* **2** to prevent sb from speaking by talking loudly or without stopping: *I tried to argue but they talked me down.*
◈ v + n/pron + adv ◆ v + adv + n

talk sb/sth 'down 1 to help a pilot bring a plane to the ground by giving detailed instructions from the ground: *The pilots were talked down through the fog by the Ground Controllers.* ◊ *to talk a plane down* **2** to persuade sb to lower their prices: *He's asked for $1 000. Can we talk him down any further?* **3** to talk about sth in a way that makes it seem less important or successful than it really is: *The opposition was attacked for talking the country down.* ◊ *He tends to talk his achievements down.*
OPP talk sb/sth up
◈ v + n/pron + adv ◆ v + adv + n

talk 'down to sb to speak to sb as if they are younger or less intelligent than you or than they really are: *He makes the mistake of talking down to his students.*
SYN patronize sb
NOTE Talk down to sb can be used in the passive: *I hate being talked down to.*
◈ v + adv + prep

talk sb/yourself 'into/'out of sth; talk sb/yourself 'into/'out of doing sth to persuade sb/yourself to do/not to do sth: *Why did you let James talk you into this crazy scheme?* ◊ *I*

talked myself into believing I was happy. ◊ *I'm leaving now and don't try to talk me out of it.*
◈ v + n/pron + prep ◆ v + n/pron + adv + prep

IDM **talk your way out of sth/of doing sth** to make excuses and give reasons for not doing sth; to manage to get yourself out of a difficult situation: *I managed to talk my way out of having to give a speech.* ◊ *His wife's found out about everything! I'd like to see him talk his way out of this one!*

talk sth 'out to discuss sth thoroughly until you find a solution, an agreement, etc. or make a decision: *to talk out your thoughts/feelings/problems with sb* ◊ *It might help to talk things out.*
OBJ things, problem
◈ v + n/pron + adv ◆ v + adv + n

talk yourself 'out to talk until you have nothing left to say: *They spent all the evening discussing the problem until they talked themselves out.*
◈ v + pron + adv

talk sb/yourself 'out of sth; talk sb/yourself 'out of doing sth = TALK SB/YOURSELF INTO/OUT OF STH, TALK SB/YOURSELF INTO/OUT OF DOING STH

talk sth 'over (with sb) to discuss sth thoroughly with sb in order to find a solution, make a decision, etc: *I need to talk it over with my parents.* ◊ *You'll find it helpful to talk things over with a friend.* ◊ *You and Len both need to talk over what happened.*
OBJ things, feelings, problems
◈ v + n/pron + adv ◆ v + adv + n

talk 'round sth (*BrE*) = TALK AROUND STH

talk sb 'round (to sth) (*BrE*) to persuade sb to accept sth or to agree to sth: *My parents didn't want me to go to study in Britain, but I managed to talk them round (to the idea).*
◈ v + n/pron + adv

talk sb 'through sth to explain sth to sb in detail so that they understand it: *The technical support staff will talk you through any difficulties you have with the software.* ◊ *I can talk you through the application form.*
SYN walk sb through sth (*AmE*)
◈ v + n/pron + prep

talk sth 'through to discuss sth thoroughly so that you can understand it, come to an agreement, or make a decision about it: *Throughout their marriage they have always talked things through.* ◊ *It's helpful to talk the problem through with a counsellor.* ◊ *We talked through what had happened.*
OBJ things, problems
◈ v + n/pron + adv ◆ v + adv + n

'**talk to sb 1** (*also* '**talk with sb** *especially AmE*) to have a conversation with sb **2** to speak to sb seriously, especially about sth wrong that they have done, or sth that they have not done: *I'd like to talk to you in my office now.*

◆ v + prep

▶ '**talking-to** *n* [sing.] (*informal*) a serious talk with sb who has done sth wrong: *to give sb a good talking-to*

,**talk sb/sth 'up** to praise sb/sth in order to make other people interested in them/it; to describe sb/sth in a way that makes them sound better or more successful than they really are: *They talked up the tourist attractions to encourage more visitors.* ◇ *He was being talked up as a future presidential candidate.* ◇ *It's too early to tell if the new President will talk the dollar up or down.*

⟩OPP⟨ **talk sb/sth down**

◆ v + n/pron + adv ◆ v + adv + n

'**talk with sb** (*especially AmE*) = TALK TO SB 1

tamper /'tæmpə(r)/

'**tamper with sth** to do something to sth to change it without permission: *Two policemen were accused of tampering with the evidence.*

OBJ **evidence, controls, brakes** SYN **interfere with sth**

NOTE **Tamper with sth** can be used in the passive: *The lock has been tampered with.*

◆ v + prep

tangle /'tæŋgl/

,**tangle sth 'up; be/get ,tangled 'up** (**in/with sth**) to twist sth into an untidy mass; to become twisted in this way: *My long skirt got tangled up in the wheel of my bike.* ◇ (*figurative*) *Kurt didn't want to get tangled up with a girl while he was trying to study.*

NOTE **Tangle sth up** is usually used in the passive.

◆ v + n/pron + adv ◆ v + adv + n ◆ be/get + v + adv

'**tangle with sb** (*informal*) to become involved in an argument or a fight with sb: *You've chosen the wrong man to tangle with.*

◆ v + prep

tank /tæŋk/

,**tank 'up**; ,**tank sth 'up** (*AmE, informal*) to fill a vehicle with fuel: *We'd better tank up before we get on the thruway.*

◆ v + adv ◆ v + n/pron + adv ◆ v + adv + n

,**tank 'up** (**on sth**) (*slang*) to drink a lot of alcohol: *The lads had spent all evening tanking up on scotch.*

◆ v + adv

▶ ,**tanked 'up** *adj* very drunk: *She got totally tanked up and couldn't drive home.*

tap /tæp/ (**-pp-**)

'**tap sb for sth 1** (*BrE, informal*) to persuade sb to give you sth, especially money: *Can't you tap your father for a loan?* ◇ *to tap sb for information* **2** (*AmE, informal*) to choose sb for a particular role or job: *A British actress has been tapped for a part in the movie.* NOTE **Tap sb for sth** is usually used in the passive in this meaning.

◆ v + n/pron + prep

,**tap sth 'in/'out** to put information, numbers, letters, etc. into a machine by pressing buttons: *Tap in your password.* ◇ *I picked up the phone and tapped out Joe's number.*

= TAP STH OUT

◆ v + adv + n ◆ v + n/pron + adv

,**tap 'into sth 1** to use a computer to obtain information from another computer: *He had managed to tap into the company's database.* **2** to use sth from a supply of energy, knowledge, etc. for your own advantage: *Schools should tap into the knowledge and experience of people in the local community.* ◇ *His talk about bullying tapped into parents' anxieties.*

◆ v + prep

,**tap sth 'out 1** to hit a surface lightly, making a rhythm: *He tapped out the rhythm with his foot.* **2** = TAP STH IN/OUT

◆ v + n/pron + adv ◆ v + adv + n

tape /teɪp/

,**tape sth 'up 1** to fasten tape around sth firmly: *Put it in a box and tape it up securely.* **2** (*AmE*) to tie a long strip of fabric (a **bandage**) firmly around an injury or a wound: *That's a nasty cut — come on, we'll get it all taped up.*

NOTE **Tape sth** can also be used: *Put it in a box and tape it securely.*

◆ v + n/pron + adv ◆ v + adv + n

taper /'teɪpə(r)/

,**taper 'off** to gradually become smaller in size, volume, amount, etc: *Our profits have begun to taper off.*

◆ v + adv

tart /tɑːt; *AmE* tɑːrt/

,**tart sth 'up** (*BrE, informal*) to decorate or improve the appearance of sth, often in a way that other people do not think is attractive: *They've tarted up the restaurant but the food hasn't improved.*

◆ v + adv + n ◆ v + n/pron + adv

,**tart yourself 'up** (*BrE, informal, disapproving*) (especially of a woman) to try and make yourself more attractive by putting on special clothes and jewellery, and putting substances on your face (make-up): *She spends ages tarting herself up for a night out.*

⟩SYN⟨ **doll yourself up (in sth)**

◈ v + pron + adv

task /tɑːsk; *AmE* tæsk/

'**task sb with sth** to give sb a task to do: *forces tasked with keeping the peace*

NOTE **Task sb with sth** is usually used in the passive. ♦ You can also use the pattern **task sb to do sth**: *soldiers tasked to provide medical support*

◈ v + n/pron + prep

tax /tæks/

'**tax sb with sth** (*formal*) to accuse sb of doing sth wrong: *Critics taxed the government with not acting quickly enough.*

◈ v + n/pron + prep

team /tiːm/

,**team 'up** (**with sb**) to work together with another person or group in order to do sth: *The two companies have teamed up to produce new software.* ◊ *We've teamed up with XL Records to give away 25 pairs of tickets for the live concert.* ◊ *How did the two of you come to team up?*

◈ v + adv

tear /teə(r); *AmE* ter/ (**tore** /tɔː(r)/ **torn** /tɔːn; *AmE* tɔːrn/)

,**tear a'bout**; ,**tear a'bout sth** (*BrE*) = TEAR AROUND, TEAR AROUND STH

,**tear sb/yourself a'part** to make sb/yourself suffer very much or feel very unhappy: *Being separated from the children was tearing her apart.* ◊ *Don't tear yourself apart thinking about the past.*

◈ v + n/pron + adv

,**tear sb/sth a'part 1** (*also* ,**tear itself, themselves, etc. a'part**) to separate people in a family, an organization, a country, etc. and make them argue with or fight against each other: *The civil war is tearing the country apart.* ◊ *The family was torn apart by conflicting loyalties.* ◊ *The region was tearing itself apart.* ◊ *Jealousy tore them apart.* **2** to destroy or defeat sb/sth; to criticize sb/sth severely: *We tore the other team apart in the second half.* ◊ *You can't write that — you'll be torn apart.*

◈ v + n/pron + adv ♦ v + adv + n

,**tear sth a'part 1** to destroy sth by pulling it violently so that it breaks into pieces: *The dogs tore the fox apart.* OBJ **prey** ⟩SYN⟨ **rip sth apart 2** to destroy a building, etc: *Hundreds of homes were torn apart by the hurricane.* ◊ *The police tore the room apart looking for drugs.*

◈ v + n/pron + adv ♦ v + adv + n (*rare*)

,**tear itself, themselves, etc. a'part** = TEAR SB/STH APART 1

,**tear a'round**; ,**tear a'round sth** (*BrE also* ,**tear a'bout/'round**, ,**tear a'bout/'round sth**) to move very quickly from place to place, being very busy: *The children were tearing around shouting.* ◊ *No wonder you're tired, tearing about like that all the time.*

⟩SYN⟨ **run around, run around sth; rush around, rush around sth**

◈ v + adv ♦ v + prep

'**tear at sth** (**with sth**) to attack sth violently, especially by pulling pieces off it: *The brambles tore at her legs.* ◊ *He tore at the meat with his bare hands.*

◈ v + prep

,**tear sb/yourself/sth a'way** (**from sb/sth**) to make sb/yourself stop doing sth they/you enjoy in order to do sth else: *I can't tear myself away from this book.* ◊ *Come and visit us, if you can tear Bill away from his computer!* ◊ *He couldn't tear his eyes away from* (= stop looking at) *Mina.*

⟩SYN⟨ **drag sb/sth/yourself away (from sb/sth)**

◈ v + n/pron + adv

▶ '**tearaway** *n* (*informal*) a young person who behaves in a wild way or who is not responsible or reliable: *Her son's a bit of a tearaway.* ◊ *The 11-year-old tearaway had burgled several houses.*

,**tear sth a'way** to pull sth violently from the thing it is attached to: *The floods had torn away the base of the bridge.*

◈ v + n/pron + adv ♦ v + adv + n

be '**torn between A and B** to have to make a very difficult choice between two things, people, etc: *I was torn between my parents and my friend.* ◊ *Jenni was torn between staying at school or going to music college.*

◈ be + v + prep

,**tear sth 'down** to pull or knock down a building, a wall, etc: *They're tearing down some old houses to build a new office block.*

OBJ **building, house, trees** ⟩SYN⟨ **pull sth down; demolish sth** (*more formal*)

◈ v + adv + n ♦ v + n/pron + adv

,**tear 'into sb/sth** to attack sb/sth physically or with words: *He tore into Jed with his fists.* ◊ *She tore into the students if they were late.* ◊ (*figurative*) *They tore into their food* (= started eating) *as if they were starving.*

◈ v + prep

,**tear sth 'off**; ,**tear sth 'off sb/sth** to remove sth quickly by pulling violently: *Alice tore off her ring and threw it on the ground.* ◊ *The door was nearly torn off its hinges.* ◊ *If you need a piece of paper I'll tear some off my pad.*

◈ v + n/pron + adv ♦ v + adv + n ♦ v + n/pron + prep

IDM **tear sb 'off a strip; tear a 'strip off sb** (*BrE*, *informal*) to speak angrily to sb you think has done sth wrong: *The boss tore him off a strip.*

,**tear sth 'out; ,tear sth 'out of sth** to separate sth from sth it is attached to, especially with your hands: *Several pages had been torn out of the book.*
✦ v + n/pron + adv ◆ v + adv + n ◆ v + n/pron + adv + prep

IDM **tear your 'hair out** (*informal*) to show that you are very angry or very worried about sth: *I was tearing my hair out trying to work out what to do.*

,**tear 'round; ,tear 'round sth** (*BrE*) = TEAR AROUND, TEAR AROUND STH

,**tear sth 'up 1** to destroy a piece of paper, a letter, etc. by pulling it into pieces: *She tore up all the letters he had sent her.* ◊ (*figurative*) *The union accused the management of tearing up* (= ignoring) *the agreement.* **OBJ** **letter**, **agreement**, **treaty** **SYN** **rip sth up 2** to destroy or damage sth, especially by removing it violently from the ground: *Trees and bushes were torn up by the storm.* **OBJ** **trees** **SYN** **pull sth up; rip sth up**
✦ v + n/pron + adv ◆ v + adv + n

tease /tiːz/

,**tease sth 'out; ,tease sth 'out of sth 1** to try to find some information or the meaning of sth when this is hidden or not clear: *teasing out meanings from texts* ◊ *to tease information/the truth out of somebody* **OBJ** **information**, **answers**, **truth 2** to remove sth such as knots from hair, wool, etc. by gently pulling or brushing it: *Lisa dried her hair carefully, teasing it out between her fingers.* **3** to separate sth carefully from sth else: *birds teasing out ripe seeds (from plants)* ◊ *He took a screwdriver and teased out the remaining screws.*
✦ v + n/pron + adv ◆ v + adv + n ◆ v + n/pron + adv + prep

tee /tiː/ (**teed, teed**)

,**tee 'off** to start a game of golf by hitting the ball for the first time: *The players eventually teed off two hours late.*
✦ v + adv

,**tee sb 'off** (*AmE*, *informal*) to make sb angry or annoyed
NOTE This phrasal verb is usually used as an adjective **teed off**.
✦ v + n/pron + adv ◆ v + adv + n
▶ ,**teed 'off** *adj* (*AmE*, *informal*) annoyed or angry: *Her friend was teed off about what she said.*

,**tee 'up; ,tee sth 'up** to prepare to hit a golf ball by placing it on a small piece of plastic or wood stuck in the ground (a **tee**): *The crowd fell silent as he teed up.*
✦ v + adv ◆ v + n/pron + adv

teem /tiːm/

,**teem 'down** to rain hard: *It was absolutely teeming down.*
SUBJ only **the rain, it** **SYN** **pour down**
NOTE You can also say: *It was teeming with rain.*
✦ v + adv

'**teem with sb/sth** (*usually approving*) (*usually used in the progressive tenses*) to have large numbers of people or things moving around: *cities teeming with life/people* ◊ *The lake was teeming with fish.*
✦ v + prep

tell /tel/ (**told, told** /təʊld; *AmE* toʊld/)

,**tell a'gainst sb** (*formal, especially BrE*) to be a serious disadvantage to sb: *Her lack of experience told against her.*
SYN **count against sb** (*less formal*)
✦ v + prep

,**tell sb/sth a'part** to be able to distinguish sb/sth from other similar people or things: *I can never tell the twins apart.*
✦ v + n/pron + adv

'**tell sb/sth from sb/sth** to distinguish sb/sth from another person or thing: *It needs skill to tell a real diamond from a fake.* ◊ *Can you tell Tom from his twin brother?*
NOTE Tell sb/sth from sb/sth is not used in the passive.
✦ v + n/pron + prep

'**tell of sth** (*formal* or *literary*) to make sth known; to give an account of sth: *The report told of a series of design errors.* ◊ *The story tells of the love between a prince and a young girl.*
✦ v + prep

,**tell sb 'off** (**for sth/for doing sth**) (*informal*) to speak angrily to sb, especially a child, because they have done sth wrong: *I told the boys off for making so much noise.* ◊ *You'll get told off if you're caught doing that.*
SYN **tick sb off; reprimand sb; scold sb** (*both formal*)
✦ v + n/pron + adv ◆ v + adv + n (*less frequent*)
▶ ,**telling-'off** (**for sth/for doing sth**) *n* [C, usually sing.] (*informal, especially BrE*) an act of speaking angrily to sb, especially a child, because they have done sth wrong: *You've already had one telling-off today!* ◊ *How many tellings-off have you had this week?*

'**tell on sb 1** (*informal*) (*used mainly by children*) to tell a teacher or sb in authority that sb has done sth wrong: *Don't tell on me, will you?* **2** (*formal*) to have a bad effect on sb/sth: *The long wait was telling on his nerves.*
✦ v + prep

tend /tend/

'tend to sb/sth to care for sb/sth, especially when there is a problem: *I'll look after the child — you tend to the mother.* ◇ *The injured were already being tended to.*
〉SYN〈 **attend to sb/sth; see to sb/sth**
〉NOTE〈 Tend to sb/sth can be used in the passive ◆ **Tend sb/sth** can also be used: *farmers tending their cattle*
✦ v + prep

'tend towards sth; 'tend towards doing sth (*less frequent*) to take a particular direction or have a particular opinion; to have a lot of a particular quality: *We're tending towards the view that all students should study English.* ◇ *His views tend towards the extreme.*
〉SYN〈 **incline to/towards sth**
✦ v + prep

tense /tens/

,tense 'up; ,tense sth 'up if you **tense up** or **tense sth up**, you make your muscles stiff and tight because you are not relaxed: *If you feel that you're tensing up, take a few moments to relax.* ◇ *Tense up your arm and leg muscles and then let them go.*
〉NOTE〈 Tense and tense sth are used with the same meaning.
✦ v + adv ◆ v + adv + n ◆ v + pron + adv ◆ v + n + adv

test /test/

'test for sth; 'test sb/sth for sth to examine sb/sth to see if a particular substance, etc. is present: *They are testing for oil in the area.* ◇ *She was tested for hepatitis.* ◇ *The software has been tested for viruses.*
✦ v + prep ◆ v + n/pron + prep

,test sb 'out to try to find out what qualities sb has, how they will react in a particular situation, etc: *My new boss gave me the most difficult clients to deal with. I felt he was really testing me out to see if I would cope.*
✦ v + n/pron + adv ◆ v + adv + n (*less frequent*)

,test sth 'out (on sb/sth) to try an idea, a machine, a product, etc. to see if it works well or if people like it: *Let me test this idea out on you.* ◇ *When you buy a bed, test it out in the shop.*
〉OBJ〈 **idea, theory, equipment** 〉SYN〈 **try sb/sth out (on sb/sth)**
〉NOTE〈 Test sth can also be used with the same meaning.
✦ v + n/pron + adv ◆ v + adv + n

testify /'testɪfaɪ/ (testifies, testifying, testi-fied, testified)

'testify to sth to show or be evidence that sth is true: *Vijay's school reports testified to his ability.*
✦ v + prep

thaw /θɔː/

,thaw 'out if ice or snow **thaws out**, it becomes water again: *Britain is thawing out after the big freeze* (= there has been a lot of snow and ice).
✦ v + adv

,thaw 'out; ,thaw sth 'out 1 to become, or to let frozen food become, soft and ready to cook: *He took the meat out of the freezer and left it to thaw out.* ◇ *to thaw out meat/fish* 〉SYN〈 **defrost, defrost sth 2** (*informal*) to become, or to let sth become, warmer after being very cold: *Come in and thaw out by the fire!* ◇ *My feet are frozen! I need to thaw them out.* ◇ (*figurative*) *She was very shy at first, but she soon thawed out.*
〉NOTE〈 Thaw and thaw sth can also be used with these meanings.
✦ v + adv ◆ v + n/pron + adv ◆ v + adv + n

thin /θɪn/ (-nn-)

,thin sth 'down (with sth) to make a liquid less thick or strong, for example by adding water to it: *The paint needs to be thinned down with water before you use it.*
〉NOTE〈 Thin sth is used more frequently.
✦ v + adv + n ◆ v + n/pron + adv

,thin 'out to become fewer in number, or less thick: *The crowd had thinned out and only a few people were left.* ◇ *Once they were clear of the city, the traffic started to thin out.* ◇ *The trees began to thin out as we climbed higher.*
〉SUBJ〈 **crowd, trees, traffic**
✦ v + adv

,thin sth 'out to reduce the number of sth so that there is more space between them: *Thin out the seedlings to about 10 cm apart.*
〉OBJ〈 **plants**
✦ v + adv + n ◆ v + n/pron + adv

think /θɪŋk/ (thought, thought /θɔːt/)

'think about sb/sth 1 to have ideas or images in your mind; to remember sb/sth: *I can't stop thinking about her.* ◇ *All he ever thinks about is money.* ◇ *It doesn't bear thinking about.* ◇ *When I was alone, I just sat and thought about things.* **2** (*also* **'think of sb/sth**) to consider sb/sth: *It's time you stopped being so selfish and started thinking about other people!* 〉SYN〈 **take sb/sth into account**
✦ v + prep
〉IDM〈 **if/when you 'think about it** used to draw attention to a fact that is not obvious or has not been mentioned before: *It must have been terrible when you think about it.*

'think about sth; 'think about doing sth to use your mind to consider sth, such as your future plans, to try to solve problems, etc: *I'll think about it and let you know tomorrow.* ◇ *She's thinking about changing her job.* ◇ *Have you* *thought about what you'll do if you don't get a place at college?* ◇ *'What did I do wrong?' 'Just think about it!'*

◉ v + prep

IDM **think 'twice about sth/about doing sth** to think carefully before you decide to do sth: *I'd think twice about calling him if I were you.*

,**think a'head** (**to sth**) to think carefully about what might happen in the future; to plan for the future: *Even when their children are very young, parents are thinking ahead to exams and jobs.* ◇ *Pilots are trained to think ahead.*

◉ v + adv

,**think 'back** (**to sth**) to remember or think about sth that happened in the past: *She thought back to the day they first met.* ◇ *Thinking back, I'm sure I noticed there was something strange.*

◉ v + adv

,**think for your'self** to make your own decisions, form your own opinions, etc. without depending on other people: *You need to learn to think for yourself.* ◇ *Our parents always encouraged us to think for ourselves.*

◉ v + prep + pron

'**think of sb/sth 1** to have an image or idea of a particular person or thing in your mind: *When I said that, I wasn't thinking of anyone in particular.* ◇ *He thought of how happy his parents would be to see him.* **2** = THINK ABOUT SB/STH 2 *Just think of the consequences if you give up your job.* **3** to create an idea in your imagination: *Who first thought of the idea?* ◇ *Can you think of anyone who could help?* ◇ *Hasn't this idea ever been thought of before?* **4** (*used especially with* **can**) to remember sb/sth: *I can't think of his name at the moment.* ◇ *I was just thinking of the wonderful trip we had.* **5** (**as sb/sth**) to consider sb/sth from a particular point of view: *I still think of Oxford as my home.* ◇ *Franco thought of his landlady as his 'English mother'.* ◇ *I don't really think of myself as a businesswoman.* ◇ *Jenni hates being thought of as a little girl.*
NOTE Think of sb/sth can be used in the passive, especially in meanings 3 and 5

◉ v + prep

IDM **come to 'think of it** used when you suddenly remember sth or realize that it might be important: *Come to think of it, he did mention seeing you yesterday.* **not think much of sb/sth** to not have a very high opinion of sb/sth: *I didn't think much of her new boyfriend.* **think 'better of it/of doing sth** to decide not to do sth you had planned to do after you have thought about it: *I was about to tell him the truth, but I thought better of it.* **think the 'world of sb** to have a very high opinion of sb; to love sb very much: *He thinks the world of his daughter.*

◀**think of doing sth 1** to consider that you might do sth: *They're thinking of moving to America.* ◇ *I did think of resigning, but I decided against it.*

〉SYN〈 **contemplate** sth (*more formal*) **2** to imagine an actual or a possible situation: *I'd never have thought of doing that!* ◇ *I couldn't think of letting you take the blame* (= I wouldn't allow you to do this). **NOTE** In this meaning **think of doing sth** is often used in negative sentences.

IDM **think 'nothing of doing sth** to consider that doing sth is normal and not very difficult: *She thinks nothing of walking all the way home in the rain.*

,**think sth 'out** to consider all the details of sth carefully, especially in order to find an answer or a solution to a problem: *She needed to be alone to think things out.* ◇ *I thought out what I was going to say before I phoned.* ◇ *a well-thought-out training programme*

◉ v + n/pron + adv ◆ v + adv + n

,**think sth 'over** to consider sth carefully especially before making a decision: *Please think over what I've said.* ◇ *I'd like more time to think things over.*

〉SYN〈 **mull sth over**

◉ v + adv + n ◆ v + n/pron + adv

,**think sth 'through** to consider a problem fully: *Careers advisers can help you think through your choices.* ◇ *Take my advice and think things through before you do anything.*

◉ v + adv + n ◆ v + n/pron + adv

,**think sth 'up** (*informal*) to create an idea, a plan, a story, etc. in your mind: *We need to think up a new name for the group.* ◇ *Can't you think up a better excuse than that?*

〉SYN〈 **devise sth** (*more formal*), **invent sth** (*more formal*)

◉ v + adv + n ◆ v + pron + adv ◆ v + n + adv (*rare*)

thirst /θɜːst; *AmE* θɜːrst/

'**thirst for sth** (*literary*) to be eager for sth; to want sth very much: *Our opponents were thirsting for revenge.*

◉ v + prep

thrash /θræʃ/

,**thrash a'round** (*also* ,**thrash a'bout** *especially BrE*) to move about in a violent, uncontrolled way: *He thrashed around in the water, gasping for breath.*

◉ v + adv

,**thrash sth 'out** to discuss sth thoroughly and in an open and honest way to try to find a solution: *He called a meeting to thrash out the problem.* ◇ *Eventually they thrashed out an agreement.*

OBJ **problem, details, agreement, deal** 〉SYN〈 **hash sth out** (*AmE, informal*)

◉ v + adv + n ◆ v + pron + adv ◆ v + n + adv (*less frequent*)

thrill /θrɪl/

'thrill to sth (*formal*) to feel very excited at sth: *Audiences thrilled to his performance in Macbeth.*
◆ v + prep

thrive /θraɪv/ (**thrived, thrived**, *AmE also* **throve** /θrəʊv/; *AmE* θroʊv/ **thriven** /'θrɪvn/)

'thrive on sth to enjoy or be successful in a situation or condition that other people would not like: *He thrives on hard work.* ◇ *Sue and Jack seem to thrive on arguments.*
◆ v + prep

throttle /'θrɒtl; *AmE* 'θrɑːtl/

,throttle 'back (*also* **,throttle 'down** *less frequent*) to control the supply of fuel or power to an engine in order to reduce the speed of a vehicle: *The pilot got very low before he throttled back.*
◆ v + adv

,throttle 'up (*rare*) to control the supply of fuel or power to an engine in order to increase the speed of a vehicle
◆ v + adv

throw /θrəʊ; *AmE* θroʊ/ (**threw** /θruː/, **thrown** /θrəʊn; *AmE* θroʊn/)

	~ about	312	~ into
	~ around		~ off
	~ aside	313	~ on
	~ at		~ onto
311	~ away		~ out, out of
	~ back		~ over
	~ back at	314	~ round
	~ back on		~ together
	~ down		~ up
	~ in		~ upon

,throw sb/yourself a'bout; **,throw sb/yourself a'bout sth** (*especially BrE*) = THROW SB/YOURSELF AROUND, THROW SB/YOURSELF AROUND STH

,throw sth a'bout (*especially BrE*) = THROW STH AROUND

,throw sth a'bout; **,throw sth a'bout sth** (*especially BrE*) = THROW STH AROUND, THROW STH AROUND STH

,throw sth a'bout sb/sth (*BrE*) = THROW STH AROUND SB/STH

,throw sb/yourself a'round; **,throw sb/yourself a'round sth** (*BrE also* **,throw sb/yourself a'bout**, **,throw sb/yourself a'bout sth** *especially BrE*) to make sb/yourself move about suddenly and violently, often causing injury: *The passengers were thrown around in the crash.* ◇ *The child was screaming and throwing himself around.* ◇ *The band threw themselves around the stage like madmen.*
◆ v + n/pron + adv ◆ v + n/pron + prep

,throw sth a'round (*BrE also* **,throw sth a'bout**)
1 to say sth, discuss sth, etc. in a general way: *You can't just throw accusations around like that!* ◇ *Let's have an initial meeting to throw some ideas about.* [OBJ] **accusations, ideas** [SYN] **toss sth around 2** to spend time throwing sth such as a ball from one person to another, in a not very serious way: *They were in the yard throwing a ball around.* [OBJ] **ball 3** to move part of your body around violently: *She was speaking excitedly, throwing her arms around.* [OBJ] **arms, head**
◆ v + n/pron + adv

[IDM] **throw your 'money around** to spend a lot of money in a very careless way, often in order to impress people: *John hates people being well off and throwing their money about.* **throw your 'weight around** (*informal*) to use your authority too aggressively to achieve what you want: *She enjoys throwing her weight about and making people do what she wants.*

,throw sth a'round; **,throw sth a'round sth** (*also* **,throw sth a'bout/'round**, **,throw sth a'bout/'round sth** *especially BrE*) to send sth from your hand in different directions, often because you are angry: *How do you stop babies throwing their food around?* ◇ *Jeff got so angry that he started throwing furniture about.* ◇ *People were throwing glasses round the room.*
◆ v + n/pron + adv ◆ v + n/pron + prep

,throw sth a'round sb/sth (*BrE also* **,throw sth a'bout/'round sb/sth**) **1** if you **throw** your arms **around** sb, you hold them tightly to show that you love them or wish to thank them for sth: *Diana rushed up to her father, threw her arms around him/his neck and kissed him.* **2** to put sth quickly around sb/sth: *We threw blankets around ourselves to keep warm.* ◇ *a silk scarf thrown casually around the shoulders* **3** to put a barrier around a place so that people cannot enter or leave: *A security cordon had been thrown around the area.*
◆ v + n/pron + prep

,throw sth a'side 1 to put sth quickly to one side, often because you are angry or in a hurry: *She read the letter and immediately threw it aside.* [SYN] **cast sth aside** (*formal*), **toss sth aside** (*formal*) **2** to reject sth such as an attitude, an idea, a way of life, etc: *All loyalties were thrown aside once the competition started.* ◇ *to throw aside sentimentality/nervousness* ◇ *to throw aside a system* [SYN] **cast sth aside** (*formal*)
◆ v + n/pron + adv ◆ v + adv + n

'throw sth at sb 1 to direct sth such as a remark, a question, etc. at sb, often in an aggressive way: *She threw a look of contempt at me.* ◇ *to throw insults/accusations at somebody* ◇ *He has an answer for any question you can throw at him.* [OBJ] **question, look, accusation** [NOTE] You can also say: *She threw me a look of contempt.* **2** to do sth or give sb sth that tests their abilities and skills: *You never know what life's going to throw at you.* ◇ *We can cope with anything our opponents throw at us.* OBJ **everything, anything, whatever**

⟐ v + n/pron + prep

'throw sth at sb/sth to throw an object in the direction of sb/sth, trying to make it hit them: *He threw stones at the window to try to catch their attention.*

⟐ v + n/pron + prep

IDM **throw the 'book at sb** (*informal*) to punish sb who has committed an offence very severely **throw 'money at sth** (*disapproving*) to try to solve a difficult situation or problem by spending lots of money on it rather than considering other ways of dealing with it: *You can't solve the problem by throwing money at it.*

'throw yourself at sb (*informal, disapproving*) (usually of a woman) to be too eager to try to attract sb, because you want to have a romantic relationship with them: *He was flattered that such an attractive woman as Nell was throwing herself at him.*

SYN **fling yourself at sb**

⟐ v + pron + prep

'throw yourself at sb/sth to rush or jump violently towards or onto sb/sth: *The dogs threw themselves at the gate.*

⟐ v + pron + prep

'throw sth a'way 1 (*also* **throw sth 'out**) to get rid of sth that has no use or that you no longer need: *She never throws anything away.* ◇ *The average household throws away 3 kilos of waste every week.* SYN **discard sth** (*more formal*) **2** to fail to make good use of sth; to waste sth: *She's throwing away a great opportunity.* ◇ *The team threw away a 2-0 lead* (= they were winning, but then lost the game). OBJ **chance, lead, money, opportunity**

⟐ v + n/pron + adv ◆ v + adv + n

▶ **'throwaway** *adj* [only before noun] **1** a **throwaway** product is intended to be used only once, or for a short time and then to be got rid of: *a throwaway lighter/razor* ◇ *our throwaway culture/society* (= we expect to use things once and then throw them away) **2** a **throwaway** remark, line or comment is sth you say casually, without careful thought, often in order to be funny: *Some people overreacted to what was only a throwaway remark.*

throw yourself a'way (on sb) to have a relationship with sb, or work for sb, who is not good enough for you or does not deserve you: *Don't throw yourself away on somebody like him.*

⟐ v + pron + adv

throw sth 'back 1 to return sth with a sharp movement of your arm or wrist: *Can you throw the ball back to me?* **2** to put sth quickly and care-

lessly in the place where it was before: *Just throw those papers back in the drawer when you've finished with them.* **3** if you **throw back** your head or your shoulders, you move them backwards suddenly: *She threw back her head and laughed.* OBJ **head, shoulders 4** to pull or fold back a covering, especially on a bed: *He threw back the bedclothes and jumped out of bed.* OBJ **covers, bedclothes**

⟐ v + n/pron + adv ◆ v + adv + n

▶ **'throwback (to sth)** *n* [C, usually sing.] sb/sth that is very similar to sb/sth that existed a long time ago: *This music is a real throwback to the seventies.*

,throw sth 'back at sb 1 to remind sb of sth they have said or done in the past, especially to upset or annoy them: *His unwise remark was frequently thrown back at him by his colleagues.* OBJ **words, remark 2** to reply angrily to sb: '*It was your fault!' he threw back at her.*

⟐ **1** v + n/pron + adv + prep
   2 v + speech + adv + prep

be ,thrown 'back on sth to be forced to rely on sth which you have not needed for a while because nothing else is available: *The television broke down so we were thrown back on our own resources* (= we had to entertain ourselves).

⟐ be + v + adv + prep

,throw sb/sth 'down; ,throw sb/sth 'down sth to send sb/sth from your hand suddenly and violently downwards: *Ellie threw the book down on the table.* ◇ *Jed threw her down on the sofa.* ◇ *Throw the rest of the medicine down the sink.* ◇ *Her husband threw her down the stairs.*

⟐ v + n/pron + adv ◆ v + adv + n ◆ v + n/pron + prep

,throw sth 'down 1 to drop or put your weapons down to show that you do not wish to fight any longer: *The rebels have thrown down their arms.* OBJ **weapons, arms 2** to eat or swallow food or drink very quickly: *He threw his dinner down in two minutes and raced out of the house.* **3** to suggest that sb should do sth you think they will not be willing or able to do: *She threw down a direct challenge for him to tell them the truth.* OBJ **only challenge**

⟐ **1,2** v + adv + n ◆ v + pron + adv ◆ v + n + adv (*rare*)
   3 v + adv + n ◆ v + n + adv (*rare*)

IDM **throw down the 'gauntlet** to invite sb to fight or compete with you

,throw yourself 'down to move suddenly and violently so that you fall down to the ground: *She threw herself down on the grass.*

→ *see also* THROW SB/STH DOWN

⟐ v + pron + adv

,throw sb 'in/into sth (*usually used in the passive*) to force or order sb to enter a prison and stay there: *I'll have you thrown in jail for that!* ◇ *He was thrown into a police cell overnight.*

⟐ v + n/pron + prep

,**throw sb/sth/yourself 'in**; ,**throw sb/sth/ yourself 'in**/**'into sth** to push or move sb/sth/ yourself roughly or violently into sth, such as water or a building: *Sam opened the door of the shed and threw his bike in.* ◇ *Did Eva throw herself in the river or was she pushed?*

✦ v + n/pron + adv ◆ v + adv + n (*less frequent*) ◆ v + n/pron + prep

IDM **throw sb in at the 'deep end** (*informal*) (*usually used in the passive*) to introduce sb to the most difficult part of an activity or job, especially an activity they have not been prepared for

▶ '**throw-in** *n* (in football and rugby) the act of throwing the ball back onto the playing field after it has gone outside the area

,**throw sth 'in 1** to include sth with what you are selling or offering, without increasing the price: *The job pays £25 000, with a company car thrown in.* **2** to add a remark, comment, etc. casually or unexpectedly: *Jack threw in the odd encouraging comment.* ◇ *'I wouldn't mind coming,' she threw in casually.*

✦ v + adv + n ◆ v + n/pron + adv

2 also v + adv + speech

IDM **throw in your 'lot with sb/sth** (*informal*) to decide to join sb/sth and share all their successes and problems **throw in the 'towel; throw in your 'hand** (*informal*) to admit that you are defeated and stop trying to do sth: *Decorating my apartment isn't easy, but I'm not ready to throw in the towel yet.*

'**throw sb into sth** = THROW SB IN/INTO STH

,**throw sb/sth 'into sth** to put sb/sth suddenly in a particular state, especially a bad one: *His announcement threw everyone into confusion.* ◇ *Her arrival threw him into a panic.* ◇ *Traffic was thrown into chaos by the accident.*

✦ v + n/pron + prep

IDM **throw sth into 'doubt/'question** to make people wonder whether sth is true, correct, appropriate, etc. or whether it will be able to continue: *The future of the company has been thrown into question by recent events.* **throw sth into (sharp) relief 1** to make an object more noticeable than others around it: *The sunlight threw the objects in the room into sharp relief.* **2** to make a particular situation, problem, etc. more noticeable than before: *Their differences have been thrown into sharp relief by the present crisis.*

,**throw sb/sth/yourself 'into sth** = THROW SB/ STH/YOURSELF IN, THROW SB/STH/YOURSELF IN/ INTO STH

,**throw sth 'into sth 1** to use a lot of energy or resources to try to make sth successful: *He's thrown all his energy into this project.* **2** = THROW SB/STH/YOURSELF IN, THROW SB/STH/YOURSELF IN/INTO STH

✦ v + n/pron + prep

,**throw yourself 'into sth 1** (*also* ,**throw yourself 'into doing sth**) to begin to do sth with energy and often enthusiasm: *Laura threw herself into her work to try and forget him.* ◇ *He threw himself into writing his report.* **SYN** **fling yourself into sth 2** = THROW SB/STH/YOURSELF IN, THROW SB/STH/YOURSELF IN/INTO STH

✦ v + pron + prep

,**throw sb 'off**; ,**throw sb 'off sth** to order sb to leave a place: *Farmers are being thrown off their land.* ◇ *If he finds you on his property, he'll throw you off.*

✦ v + n/pron + adv ◆ v + adv + n (*less frequent*) ◆ v + n/pron + prep

,**throw sb/sth 'off**; ,**throw sb/sth 'off sth 1** to get rid of sb/sth that is making you suffer, annoying you, following you, etc.; to free yourself from sb/sth: *to throw off repression/domination* ◇ *to throw off anger/family worries/troublesome thoughts* ◇ *They waded through a stream to throw the dogs off* (= so that they could not follow them). ◇ *I tried every way I could think of to throw him off.* ◇ *She wants to throw off her old image and start again.* ◇ *I can't seem to throw off this cold.* **2** to disturb sb/sth who is trying to do sth, making them fail or not behave as usual: *The director came in while I was speaking and that threw me off a bit.* **SYN** **put sb off, put sb off sth**

✦ v + n/pron + adv ◆ v + adv + n ◆ v + n/pron + prep

IDM **throw sb off 'balance 1** to make sb unsteady and likely to fall: *I was thrown off balance by the sudden gust of wind.* **2** to make sb surprised and no longer calm: *The senator was thrown off balance by the unexpected question.* **throw sb off 'course 1** if sb/sth is **thrown off course**, they are forced away from the direction they should be travelling in: *The plane was thrown off course in dense fog.* **2** to force sb to change the direction in which their ideas or actions are moving: *The government was thrown off course by labour and economic problems.* **throw sb off the 'scent** to deceive sb to stop sb finding you or discovering a secret: *She changed taxis to throw her pursuers off the scent.* ◇ *Lisa told her parents she was going to a friend's house to throw them off the scent* (= she was really going somewhere else).

,**throw sth 'off** to remove your clothes or sth covering your body quickly and carelessly: *She threw off her clothes and leapt into the river.* **SYN** **fling sth off** **OPP** **throw sth on**

✦ v + adv + n ◆ v + n/pron + adv

,**throw sb/sth/yourself 'off**; ,**throw sb/sth/ yourself 'off sth** to send or push sb/sth violently from a high place; to jump from a high place: *Ed was threatening to throw himself off the roof.* ◇ *The sledge hit a bump and threw me off.*

✦ v + n/pron + adv ◆ v + n/pron + prep

,**throw sth 'on** to put on a piece of clothing quickly and carelessly: *He threw on his clothes and ran downstairs.* ◇ *I'll just throw a coat on and then I'll be ready.*
⟨SYN⟩ fling sth on ⟨OPP⟩ throw sth off
◈ v + adv + n ♦ v + n/pron + adv

,**throw sb/sth 'on**; ,**throw sb/sth 'on/'onto sth**; ,**throw yourself 'on/'onto sth** to send or push sb/sth violently onto sth: *Jamie angrily threw the book onto the table.* ◇ *The fire wasn't burning well, so we threw on more wood.*
◈ v + adv + n ♦ v + n/pron + adv ♦ v + n/pron + prep

'**throw sth on sb/sth** (*also* ,**throw sth u'pon sb/sth** *more formal*) **1** if sb/sth **throws** doubt or suspicion **on** sb/sth, people start to wonder if sth is true, is what it seems to be, will continue, etc: *New evidence threw doubt on Tom's innocence.* ◇ *This controversy throws doubt on her political future.* ◇ *The murder was carefully planned to throw suspicion on the woman's husband* (= to make him appear guilty). ◇ *They tried to throw suspicion on us.* **OBJ** **doubt, suspicion 2** (*formal*) to cover sb/sth in light or shadows: *The lamp threw strange shadows on his face.* **OBJ** **light, shadows**
◈ v + n + prep
IDM **throw 'light on sth** to make a problem, etc. easier to understand: *I thought you might be able to throw some light on the matter.* ◇ *Recent research has thrown new light on the cause of the disease.*

throw yourself on sb/sth (*also* '**throw yourself onto sb/sth** *less frequent*) to run towards sb/sth and fall onto them: *She threw herself on him and burst into tears.*
→ *see also* THROW SB/STH ON, THROW SB/STH ON/ONTO STH, THROW YOURSELF ON/ONTO STH
◈ v + pron + prep
IDM **throw yourself on sb's 'mercy** (*formal*) to put yourself in a position where you must rely on sb to be kind to you and not harm or punish you: *He threw himself on the mercy of his captors.*

throw sb/sth/yourself 'onto sth = THROW SB/STH ON, THROW SB/STH ON/ONTO STH, THROW YOURSELF ON/ONTO STH

throw sb 'out; ,**throw sb 'out of sth** to force sb to leave a place, their home, a job, etc: *Tim's parents threw him out when he was 18.* ◇ *When the mine closed down, 50 people were thrown out of their jobs.* ◇ *When she failed her exams, she was thrown out of college.* ◇ *Many families have been thrown out into the street* (= made to leave their homes).
⟨SYN⟩ boot sb out, boot sb out of sth; kick sb out, kick sb out of sth (*both informal*)
NOTE **Throw sb out** is often used in the passive.
◈ v + n/pron + adv ♦ v + adv + n ♦ v + n/pron + adv + prep

,**throw sb/sth 'out** to confuse sb/sth; to make sb make a mistake; to make sth wrong: *One of the figures was wrong and it threw me out completely.* ◇ *Some unexpected costs threw our calculations out by £4 000.*
OBJ **calculations**
◈ v + n/pron + adv ♦ v + adv + n

,**throw sth 'out 1** = THROW STH AWAY 1 *It's time we threw that old chair out.* **2** to reject sth such as a proposal, an idea, etc: *The committee have thrown out the proposal for a new supermarket.* ◇ *The case was thrown out of court* (= in a court of law). **OBJ** **bill, case, proposals** **NOTE** **Throw sth out** is often used in the passive in this meaning. **3** to mention sth, usually in a casual way, for people to think about: *She threw out a few ideas for us to consider.* ◇ *We are throwing out a challenge to residents to help clean up our neighbourhood.* **OBJ** **idea, challenge 4** to produce sth such as heat, light, smoke, etc: *The fire throws out a lot of heat.* ◇ *The lamp threw out just enough light to read by.* **OBJ** **heat, light** **⟨SYN⟩ emit sth 5** to move a hand or arm suddenly away from your body: *She threw her arm out to protect herself as she fell.* **OBJ** **hand, arm**
◈ v + adv + n ♦ v + n/pron + adv
IDM **throw the baby out with the 'bathwater** (*informal*) to lose sth that you want at the same time as you are trying to get rid of sth that you do not want

,**throw sb/sth 'out**; ,**throw yourself 'out**; ,**throw sb/sth 'out of sth**; ,**throw yourself 'out of sth** to push or send sb/sth/yourself forward and out of a place: *Frank quickly opened the window and threw his cigarette out.* ◇ *He threw himself out of the window and was killed.*
◈ v + n/pron + adv ♦ v + adv + n ♦ v + n/pron + adv + prep

,**throw sb 'over** (*old-fashioned*) to end a relationship with sb: *His girlfriend threw him over for somebody else.*
⟨SYN⟩ chuck sb (*BrE, slang*)**, dump sb** (*informal*)
◈ v + n/pron + adv ♦ v + adv + n

,**throw sb/sth 'over**; ,**throw yourself 'over**; ,**throw sb/sth/yourself 'over sth** to move or push sb/sth so that they move over the top of sth and land on the other side of it; to move yourself violently in this way: *Throw a rope over and I'll catch it on the other side.* ◇ *I threw myself over the wall to escape from the dog.* ◇ *Jay took off his coat and threw it over a chair* (= so it rested on the back of a chair).
◈ v + n/pron + adv ♦ v + adv + n (*less frequent*) ♦ v + n/pron + prep
IDM **throw sth over your 'shoulder** if you **throw** a remark, a comment, or a look **over your shoulder**, you turn your head to say sth to sb or to look at sb: *'And don't bother phoning me!' she threw over her shoulder as she left.*

,**throw sth 'over (to sb)** (*informal*) to pass sth to sb in a casual way: *He threw the paper over to me.* ◇ *Will you throw over those keys?*
NOTE You can also use **throw sb over sth** and **throw sb sth over**: *Will you throw me over the paper?* ◇ *Will you throw me the paper over?*
⬧ v + n/pron + adv ◆ v + adv + n

,**throw sth 'over sb/sth** to quickly place sth so that it covers sb/sth: *I threw a blanket over the baby to keep him warm.* ◇ *He threw a coat over his pyjamas and ran out into the street.*
⬧ v + n/pron + prep

,**throw sth 'round**; ,**throw sth 'round sth** = THROW STH AROUND, THROW STH AROUND STH

,**throw sth 'round sb/sth** (*especially BrE*) = THROW STH AROUND SB/STH 1 *We threw blankets round ourselves to keep warm.* ◇ *She threw her arms round me/my neck.*

,**throw sth 'round sth** (*BrE*)
→ *see also* THROW STH AROUND, THROW STH AROUND STH

,**throw sb to'gether** to bring people into contact with each other, often casually: *Fate had thrown them together.*
NOTE **Throw sb together** is often used in the passive: *We were strangers, thrown together by circumstance.*
⬧ v + n/pron + adv ◆ v + adv + n

,**throw sth to'gether** to make or produce sth roughly or quickly, often with things that you can find easily: *I'll just throw together a quick supper.* ◇ *Can you throw a report together by tomorrow morning?*
⬧ v + adv + n ◆ v + n/pron + adv

,**throw 'up** (*also* ,**throw sth 'up** *less frequent*) (*informal*) to bring food you have eaten back out of your mouth: *The smell made me want to throw up.* ◇ *He ate the meal and immediately threw it all up.*
SYN **bring sth up; vomit, vomit sth**
⬧ v + adv ◆ v + adv + n ◆ v + n/pron + adv

,**throw sb/sth 'up** to lift sb/sth and make them move upwards into the air by moving your hand quickly: *The baby loved being thrown up into the air.* ◇
⬧ v + n/pron + adv

,**throw sth 'up 1** to produce sth; to show or make people notice sth: *Her research has thrown up some interesting facts.* ◇ *The competition threw up some promising players.* **OBJ** **problems, ques-tions, ideas, facts 2** (*BrE, informal*) to leave your job suddenly and often unexpectedly: *He threw up a highly paid job to travel round the world.* **OBJ** **job** **SYN** **chuck sth in/up** (*BrE, infor-mal*), **give sth up** (*informal*) **3** to build sth sud-denly or quickly, and often carelessly: *These buildings were thrown up hurriedly after the war.* **OBJ** **buildings 4** if you **throw up** your arms or hands, you raise them quickly in the air: *He threw up his hands to protect his face as he fell.* ◇

She threw her arms up in horror. **OBJ** **hand, arm 5** to make sth such as dust or water rise up into the air: *The wheels threw up a shower of mud and water.* **OBJ** **dust, mud**
⬧ v + adv + n ◆ v + n/pron + adv

,**throw sth u'pon sb/sth** = THROW STH ON SB/STH

thrust /θrʌst/ (**thrust**, **thrust**)

,**thrust sth a'side** to refuse to listen to sb's com-plaints, comments, etc: *All our objections were thrust aside.*
⬧ v + n/pron + adv ◆ v + adv + n

'**thrust sb/sth on sb** (*also* '**thrust sb/sth upon sb** *more formal*) to force sb to accept sb/sth or do sth that they do not want to: *Responsibility for the family was thrust upon him at an early age.* ◇ *She was annoyed at having three extra guests sud-denly thrust upon her.*
OBJ **role, responsibility, change**
NOTE **Thrust sb/sth on/upon sb** is often used in the passive.
⬧ v + n/pron + prep

thumb /θʌm/

,**thumb 'through sth** to turn the pages of a book, a magazine, etc. looking at them quickly: *She thumbed through her diary.*
OBJ **book, pages** **SYN** **flick through sth**
⬧ v + prep

tick /tɪk/

,**tick a'way**; ,**tick sth a'way** if a clock ticks away or ticks the minutes or seconds away, it makes continuous short light regular sounds to mark time passing: *The clock ticked away in the silence.* ◇ *We waited as the clock ticked away the last few seconds of the old millennium.*
⬧ v + adv ◆ v + adv + n ◆ v + n/pron + adv

,**tick a'way/'by/'past** (of time) to pass, espe-cially when you feel it is passing too quickly or too slowly: *The seconds ticked by as I tried to think of something to say.* ◇ *Two long minutes ticked past.* **SUBJ** **minutes, seconds, time**
⬧ v + adv

,**tick sb 'off 1** (**for sth/for doing sth**) (*BrE, infor-mal*) to speak angrily to sb, especially a child because they have done sth wrong: *I was ticked off for forgetting my books.* **SYN** **tell sb off, scold sb** (*more formal*) **2** (*informal, especially AmE*) to annoy sb: *This type of thing really ticks me off.* **SYN** **hack sb off** (*BrE*)
⬧ v + n/pron + adv ◆ v + adv + n
▸ ,**ticked 'off** *adj* (*informal, especially AmE*) annoyed: *I was really ticked off about it.*
▸ ,**ticking 'off** (**for sth/for doing sth**) *n* [sing.] (*old-fashioned, BrE, informal*) the act of speaking somebody angrily because they have done sth wrong: *He gave me a ticking off for being late for class.*

,**tick sb/sth 'off** (*BrE*) (*AmE* ,**check sb/sth 'off**)
to put a mark next to sth on a list to show that it
has been dealt with: *Al ticked off the names of the
people who had replied.* ◇ *Everything on the list
had been ticked off.* ◇ *She ticked the points off on
her fingers.*
OBJ **points, items**
◈ v + adv + n ♦ v + n/pron + adv

,**tick 'over** (*especially BrE*) (*usually used in the
progressive tenses*) **1** if an engine is **ticking over**
it is running slowly but the vehicle is not moving: *Don't leave the engine ticking over while you
are in the shop.* ◇ (*figurative*) *Learning Japanese
keeps my brain ticking over!* SUBJ **engine** SYN
idle 2 to continue slowly without producing or
achieving much: *Try and keep things ticking over
while I'm away.* SUBJ **things**
◈ v + adv

,**tick 'past** = TICK AWAY/BY/PAST

tide /taɪd/

,**tide sb 'over**; ,**tide sb 'over sth** to help sb
through a difficult period by providing what
they need: *We've got enough money to tide us over
until next month.* ◇ *Our savings should tide us
over the next couple of months.* SUBJ **money, loan**
NOTE **Tide sb over** is usually used in the infinitive form. It cannot be used in the passive.
◈ v + n/pron + adv ♦ v + n/pron + prep

tidy /'taɪdi/ (**tidies, tidying, tidied, tidied**)

,**tidy sth a'way** (*BrE*) to put things in a particular place where they cannot be seen so that a
room, etc. appears tidy: *Harry was busy tidying
away his papers in the office.*
SYN **clear away, clear sth away**
◈ v + adv + n ♦ v + n/pron + adv

,**tidy sth 'out** (*BrE*) to make a room, a cupboard,
etc. tidy by removing things you do not want and
arranging the rest neatly: *It's time to tidy out the
kitchen cupboards.*
OBJ **cupboard, drawer, room** SYN **clear sth
out**
◈ v + adv + n ♦ v + n/pron + adv

,**tidy 'up**; ,**tidy sth 'up** (*especially BrE*) to make a
room, a group of things, etc. tidy by arranging
things neatly in the correct places: *Don't forget to
tidy up when you've finished.* ◇ *The whole place
needs tidying up.* ◇ *I've just got a bit of tidying up
to do.* ◇ *I'd better tidy my desk up.*
SYN **clear up, clear sth up**
◈ v + adv ♦ v + n/pron + adv ♦ v + adv + n

,**tidy sb 'up**; ,**tidy yourself 'up** (*especially BrE*)
to make sb/yourself look cleaner and smarter:
*How about tidying yourself up a bit before we go
out?*
◈ v + n/pron + adv ♦ v + adv + n

,**tidy sth 'up** (*BrE*) **1** to finish sth such as a piece
of written work by dealing with the last details
well or correctly: *My lecture still needs tidying up.*
OBJ **room, mess, house** SYN **clear sth up 2** to
make sure that things are dealt with correctly:
*He had to go to Boston to tidy up his brother's
affairs* (= after his brother had died).
◈ v + n/pron + adv ♦ v + adv + n

tie /taɪ/ (**ties, tying, tied, tied**)

,**tie sb 'down 1** (*also* ,**tie yourself 'down**) (**to
sth/to doing sth**) to restrict sb's activities or freedom, for example by making them accept particular conditions or by keeping them busy: *We
managed to tie him down to a date for the meeting.*
◇ *She didn't want to be tied down by a full-time
job.* ◇ *I don't want to be tied down to coming back
at a particular time.* ◇ *Do you really want to tie
yourself down at 18 with a husband, a home and a
baby?* **2** to do sth so that an enemy force is kept
busy and has to stay in a particular area:
*Guerrilla activity kept the army tied down in the
mountains.* OBJ **troops, police**
◈ **1** v + n/pron + adv
   2 v + n/pron + adv ♦ v + n/pron + adv

,**tie 'in** (**with sth**) to fit or be in agreement with sth:
*This new evidence ties in with the witness's state-
ment.* ◇ *That doesn't tie in with what you said
yesterday.*
◈ v + adv

,**tie 'in** (**with sth**), ,**tie sth 'in** (**with sth**) to link sth
or be linked to sth; to happen or to arrange for sth
to happen at the same time as sth else: *The book
was intended to tie in with the TV series.* ◇ *Jack
couldn't be tied in with the murder.* ◇ *The release
of their new album will be tied in with the tour.*
◈ v + adv ♦ v + n/pron + adv ♦ v + adv + n
   ▶ '**tie-in** n **1** (*BrE*) a product such as a book or a
   toy that is sold in close connection with a
   film/movie, television programme, etc: *televi-
   sion/film tie-ins* ◇ *tie-in books/toys/sales* **2** (*especially AmE*) a link or a relationship with sth: *a
   tie-in to the main subject*

,**tie sth 'off** to put a knot in the end of sth; to close
sth with string, thread, etc: *to tie off a rope/an
artery*
◈ v + adv + n ♦ v + n/pron + adv

,**tie 'up**; ,**tie sth 'up 1** to attach a boat to a fixed
point with a rope: *The barge tied up at the quay.* ◇
Ben tied the boat up and jumped ashore. **2** to close
or fasten sth with a knot; to be closed or fastened
in this way: *I'm so fat my bathrobe won't tie up!* ◇
to tie up a garbage bag
◈ v + adv ♦ v + n/pron + adv ♦ v + adv + n

,**tie sb 'up 1** to tie sb's arms and legs tightly so
that they cannot move or escape: *The gang tied
up the security guard and put a gag in his mouth.*
2 to keep sb so busy that they have no time for
other things: *I'm tied up in a meeting until three.*

tie up

off**316**

◇ *Sorry I'm late — I was tied up at the office.* NOTE
Tie sb up is usually used in the passive in this
meaning.
✦ v + n/pron + adv ◆ v + adv + n

,**tie sth 'up 1** to make sth secure by putting
string, rope, etc. around it, or attaching it to sth
else: *He tied the parcel up with a ribbon.* ◇ *He tied
the dog up outside.* **2 (with sth)** to connect or link
sth to sth else: *Her behaviour is tied up with her
feelings of guilt.* ◇ *Do you think these two incidents are tied up?* NOTE **Tie sth up** is usually used
in the passive in this meaning. **3 (in sth)** to invest
money so that it is not easily available for use:
Most of our capital is tied up in property. OBJ
money, capital, resources, assets SYN **lock
sth up** NOTE **Tie sth up** is often used in the passive in this meaning. **4** to deal with all the
remaining details of sth: *to tie up a deal* ◇ *We're
hoping to **tie up all the loose ends** as quickly as
possible.* OBJ **deal, loose ends 5** to bring sth to a
stop; to prevent sb from doing sth or using sth:
The strike tied up production for a week. ◇
*Haven't you finished yet? You've been tying up the
phone for hours!*
✦ v + n/pron + adv ◆ v + adv + n

▸ '**tie-up** *n* **1 (with sb/sth)** *(BrE)* an agreement
between two companies to join together: *They're
negotiating a tie-up with Ford.* **2 (between A and
B)** *(BrE)* a connection between two or more
things: *a tie-up between politics and economics* **3**
(especially AmE) a situation in which sth, especially traffic, stops moving: *A tie-up on the highway caused major delays.*

tighten /'taɪtn/

,**tighten 'up; ,tighten sth 'up 1** to become or
to make sth tight or tighter: *His face muscles
tightened up in anger.* ◇ *to tighten up a screw/
wheel/muscle* NOTE **Tighten** and **tighten sth** can
also be used with this meaning **2** to become more
careful or strict about sth; to make sth more
strict: *Laws on gambling have tightened up
recently.* ◇ *The police are **tightening up on**
drink–driving.* ◇ *to tighten up laws/rules/legisla-
tion/security*
✦ v + adv ◆ v + adv + n ◆ v + pron + adv ◆ v + n + adv
(less frequent)

tinker /'tɪŋkə(r)/

,**tinker a'round** *(also ,tinker a'bout especially
BrE)* **(with sth)** to make small changes to sth in
order to repair or improve it, especially in a way
that may not be helpful: *He's outside tinkering
around with his bike.* ◇ *They haven't made any
real changes to the system — they've just been tinkering around a bit.*
✦ v + adv

tip /tɪp/ (-pp-)

,**tip sb 'off (about sth)** *(informal)* to give sb a
warning about sth which will affect them and
which they should know about, especially sth
illegal: *The police were tipped off about the bank
robbery.*
OBJ **police**
✦ v + adv + n ◆ v + pron + adv ◆ v + n + adv *(less
frequent)*

▸ '**tip-off** *n* *(informal)* a piece of useful or secret
information that sb gives, for example to the
police, to warn them about an illegal or unexpected activity: *The police received an anonym-
ous tip-off about the attack.*

,**tip 'over; ,tip sth 'over** to become unstable and
fall over; to make sth do this: *The bottle tipped
over and all the water spilled out.* ◇ *Watch you
don't tip the jug over.*
SYN **overturn, overturn sth** *(more formal)*
✦ v + adv ◆ v + n/pron + adv ◆ v + adv + n

,**tip 'up; ,tip sth 'up** to become unsteady and fall
forwards, backwards or sideways; to make sth do
this: *One after another the canoes tipped up.* ◇
*The pile of books on the end of the table nearly
tipped it up.*
✦ v + adv ◆ v + n/pron + adv ◆ v + adv + n

,**tip sth 'up** to change the angle of sth so that it
leans to one side: *She tipped her glass up and
drained it.* ◇ *He tipped his face up towards the
light.*
✦ v + n/pron + adv ◆ v + adv + n

tire /'taɪə(r)/

'**tire of sb/sth; 'tire of doing sth** to become
bored with sb/sth or begin to enjoy them/it less:
They soon tired of the beach and went for a walk.
✦ v + prep

IDM **never tire of doing sth** to do sth a lot, especially in a way that annoys people: *Jack travelled
all over the world when he was a student, as he
never tires of telling us.*

,**tire sb 'out; ,tire yourself 'out** to make
sb/yourself feel very tired: *I took the children to
the beach to tire them out.* ◇ *Try not to tire yourself out too soon in the race.*
SYN **wear sb/yourself out** *(with sth)*
✦ v + n/pron + adv ◆ v + adv + n *(less frequent)*

▸ ,**tired 'out** *adj* very tired: *We finally reached
home tired out.*

toddle /'tɒdl; AmE 'tɑːdl/

,**toddle 'off** *(BrE, informal, humorous)* to leave; to
depart: *It's late — it's time you toddled off to bed.*
✦ v + adv

tog /tɒg; *AmE* tɑːg, tɔːg/ (**-gg-**)

be/get ˌtogged 'out/'up (**in sth**) (*BrE, informal*) to be wearing clothes for a particular activity or occasion: *He got togged up in a suit and tie for the interview.* ◇ *We were all togged out in our best clothes.*
⊕ be/get + v + adv

toil /tɔɪl/

ˌtoil a'way (**at sth**) to work extremely hard at sth difficult or boring: *He toiled away at his homework all the evening.*
⊕ v + adv

tone /təʊn; *AmE* toʊn/

ˌtone sth 'down 1 to make sth such as a speech, an opinion, etc. less offensive, critical or harsh than it was originally: *He had to tone down his article before it was published.* **2** to make sth, especially your clothes, less bright, colourful and noticeable: *She toned down her style of dress when she started her new job.* **3** to make a colour less bright: *We toned down the yellow paint with a little white.* ◇ *Petra used powder to tone down her rosy cheeks.*
⊕ v + adv + n ◆ v + pron + adv ◆ v + n + adv (*less frequent*)

ˌtone 'in (**with sth**) (*BrE*) to match or fit with the colour or style of sth else: *The cushions tone in well with the carpet.* ◇ *The new bridge doesn't tone in with the buildings around it.*
⊕ v + adv

ˌtone 'up; **ˌtone sth 'up** to make your muscles or a part of your body firmer, stronger, and healthier: *It's time I toned up and slimmed down.* ◇ *This exercise will tone up your stomach muscles.*
[OBJ] **body, muscles**
⊕ v + adv ◆ v + adv + n ◆ v + pron + adv ◆ v + n + adv (*less frequent*)

tool /tuːl/

ˌtool 'up; **ˌtool sth 'up** (**for sth/to do sth**) (*BrE, technical*) to get or provide sb/sth with the equipment, machines, etc. necessary to do or produce sth: *It took several months to tool up to produce the new model.* ◇ *A new plant in Scotland is being tooled up to produce these screws.*
⊕ v + adv ◆ v + adv + n ◆ v + pron + adv ◆ v + n + adv (*rare*)

▶ **ˌtooled 'up** *adj* (*slang*) **1** having the equipment necessary for a particular job **2** (*BrE*) carrying a gun

top /tɒp; *AmE* tɑːp/ (**-pp-**)

ˌtop sth 'off (**with sth**) to complete sth in a successful or pleasant way, especially by adding one final thing: *Jane was wearing a very colourful outfit, topped off with a dramatic hat.*
[NOTE] **Top sth off** is often used in the passive.
⊕ v + n/pron + adv ◆ v + adv + n

ˌtop 'out (**at sth**) to stop increasing after reaching a high level: *Your annual salary will top out at seventy thousand dollars.*
⊕ v + adv

ˌtop sb 'up (*BrE*) to fill sb's glass or cup by adding some more liquid: *Can I top you up?*
⊕ v + n/pron + adv ◆ v + adv + n

▶ **'top-up** *n* (*BrE*) an amount of liquid that you add to some already in a glass, cup or other container: *Can I give you a top-up?*
→ *see also* TOP-UP at TOP STH UP

ˌtop sth 'up (*especially BrE*) **1** (**with sth**) to add some more liquid to some already in a glass, cup or other container in order to fill it: *Can I top your glass up?* ◇ *We should top the car up with oil before we set off.* [OBJ] **glass, cup 2** to increase the amount of sth, especially money, to the level you want or need: *She relies on tips to top up her wages.* [OBJ] **income, pension**
⊕ v + adv + n ◆ v + n/pron + adv

▶ **'top-up** *n* (*BrE*) a sum of money that is added to what you already have in order to increase it to the amount that you need: *a salary top-up* ◇ *a top-up loan* ◇ *top-up fees* (= extra money that university students must pay, in addition to the money that they already pay, in order to provide the university with the money it needs)
→ *see also* TOP-UP at TOP SB UP

▶ **'top-up card** *n* a card that you buy for a mobile phone that enables you to make calls to the value of the card

topple /'tɒpl; *AmE* 'tɑːpl/

ˌtopple 'over to become unsteady and fall over: *The vase wobbled and then toppled over.*
⊕ v + adv

toss /tɒs; *AmE* tɔːs/

ˌtoss sth a'round (*also* **ˌtoss sth a'bout** *especially BrE*) to discuss ideas in a casual or general way: *We sat and tossed around a few suggestions.* ◇ *This is a problem that has been tossed around for more than a century.*
[SYN] **throw sth around**
⊕ v + n/pron + adv ◆ v + adv + n

ˌtoss sth a'side 1 to put sth quickly to one side because you are angry or in a hurry: *He tossed aside the newspaper angrily and stood up.* ◇ (*figurative*) *When he's bored with people he just tosses them aside.* [SYN] **cast sth aside** (*formal*), **throw sth aside 2** to reject sth such as an attitude, an idea, a way of life, etc: *The idea of buying a new car was quickly tossed aside.* [SYN] **cast sth aside** (*formal*), **throw sth aside**
⊕ v + n/pron + adv ◆ v + adv + n

ˌtoss sth a'way to throw sth away carelessly: *She finished her drink and tossed the can away.* ◇ (*figurative*) *He's tossed away so many opportunities.*
⊕ v + adv + n ◆ v + n/pron + adv

ˌtoss sth 'back 1 (*also* ˌtoss sth 'down *less frequent*) to drink sth very quickly, especially alcohol: *She tossed back glass after glass of champagne.* ◇ *He tossed back the rest of his drink and walked out.* ⟨OBJ⟩ **drink, whisky, wine, etc. 2** to move sth, especially your head, quickly backwards, especially when you are angry or impatient: *Sam tossed back his head in defiance.* ◇ *She tossed back her hair and smiled.* ⟨OBJ⟩ **hair, head**
◆ v + adv + n ◆ v + n/pron + adv

'toss for sth; 'toss sb for sth (*especially BrE*) (*BrE also* ˌtoss 'up (for sth)) (*AmE also* 'flip for sth, 'flip sb for sth) to make a decision about sth by spinning a coin in the air and seeing which side is on top when it lands: *We can't both go, so why don't we toss for it?* ◇ *There's only one ticket left — I'll toss you for it.*
→ *see also* FLIP FOR STH
◆ v + prep ◆ v + n/pron + prep

ˌtoss 'off; ˌtoss sb 'off; ˌtoss yourself 'off (*BrE*, △, *slang*) to give yourself sexual pleasure by rubbing your sex organs; to give sb else sexual pleasure in this way
◆ v + adv ◆ v + n/pron + adv ◆ v + adv + n

ˌtoss sth 'off (*especially BrE*) to do sth quickly, easily and often with little care or effort: *He tossed this novel off in two months.*
◆ v + n/pron + adv ◆ v + adv + n

ˌtoss 'up (for sth) (*BrE*) = TOSS FOR STH, TOSS SB FOR STH *They tossed up for the best seat.*
◆ v + adv
▶ 'toss-up *n* [sing.] (*informal*) a situation where it is difficult to decide between two things, or where there are two possible results: *It was a toss-up between spending the night in the van and walking ten miles for help.*

tot /tɒt; *AmE* tɑːt/ (**-tt-**)

ˌtot sth 'up (*informal, especially BrE*) to add together several numbers or amounts in order to get a total: *Can you tot up how much I owe you?*
⟨OBJ⟩ **figures, the number of sth** ⟨SYN⟩ **add sth up**
◆ v + adv + n ◆ v + pron + adv ◆ v + n + adv (*less frequent*)

total /'təʊtl; *AmE* 'toʊtl/ (**-ll-**, *AmE also* **-l-**)

ˌtotal 'up (to sth) to reach a particular total: *The costs total up to over a million.*
◆ v + adv

ˌtotal sth 'up to add amounts together to get a total: *Let's total up what we've spent.*
◆ v + adv + n ◆ v + n/pron + adv

touch /tʌtʃ/

ˌtouch 'down 1 (of a plane, a spacecraft, etc.) to land: *The plane touched down safely at Kennedy Airport at about midday.* ◇ (*figurative*) *A tornado touched down in Colorado, injuring five people.*

⟨SUBJ⟩ **plane, aircraft, helicopter** ⟨SYN⟩ **land** ⟨OPP⟩ **take off 2** (in rugby) to score points (a **try**) by putting the ball on the ground behind the other team's goal line: *Williams touched down in the first few minutes of the game.*
◆ v + adv
▶ 'touchdown *n* **1** the moment when a plane or a spacecraft touches down **2** (in rugby) an act of scoring points by putting the ball down on the area of ground behind the other team's goal line **3** (in American football) an act of scoring points by crossing the other team's goal line while carrying the ball, or receiving the ball when you are over the other team's goal line

ˌtouch sb for sth (*BrE, informal*) to persuade sb to give or lend you money: *He tried to touch me for twenty pounds.*
◆ v + n/pron + prep

ˌtouch sth 'off to make sth begin, especially an explosion or a violent or difficult situation: *The explosion was touched off by a single spark.* ◇ *His arrest touched off a riot.*
◆ v + adv + n ◆ v + pron + adv ◆ v + n + adv (*rare*)

'touch on/upon sth to mention or deal briefly with a topic, a problem, etc: *He touched on the need for increased funding.* ◇ *Some of these issues were touched on in Chapter 7.*
⟨OBJ⟩ **subject, point, issue**
⟨NOTE⟩ Touch **on/upon** sth can be used in the passive.
◆ v + prep

ˌtouch sb 'up (*BrE, informal*) to touch sb in an unpleasant sexual way
◆ v + adv + n ◆ v + n/pron + adv

ˌtouch sth 'up to improve sth by making small changes or additions: *He had to touch up the paintwork to cover the scratches.* ◇ *The photo had been touched up.*
◆ v + adv + n ◆ v + pron + adv ◆ v + n + adv (*less frequent*)

'touch upon sth = TOUCH ON/UPON STH

tough /tʌf/

ˌtough sth 'out to stay firm and determined in a difficult situation: *He decided not to resign, but to stay and tough it out.*
◆ v + n + adv ◆ v + pron + adv ◆ v + adv + n (*less frequent*)

toughen /'tʌfn/

ˌtoughen 'up; ˌtoughen sb 'up to become stronger and better able to deal with difficult situations; to make sb stronger in this way: *He had toughened up during military service.* ◇ *His parents sent him away to boarding school to toughen him up.*
◆ v + adv ◆ v + n/pron + adv ◆ v + adv + n

,toughen sth 'up to make sth such as a law or a rule more strict: *The legislation on this trade needs to be toughened up.*
🔷 v + adv + n ◆ v + n/pron + adv

tout /taʊt/

,tout sth a'round; **,tout sth a'round sth** (*BrE also* **,tout sth 'round**, **,tout sth 'round sth**) to take sth to many different places or companies in the hope of selling it: *He's been touting his novel around publishers for years.*
🔷 v + n/pron + adv ◆ v + adv + n ◆ v + n/pron + prep

'tout for sth (*especially BrE*) to try to get business, work, etc. by asking people directly: *cab drivers touting for business at the airport*
[OBJ] **business, trade, custom**
🔷 v + prep

tow /təʊ; *AmE* toʊ/

,tow sth a'way (from sth) to remove sth, especially a vehicle, from a place, by pulling it behind another one: *They'll tow your car away if you park it here.*
🔷 v + n/pron + adv ◆ v + adv + n

tower /'taʊə(r)/

,tower a'bove/'over sb/sth 1 to be much higher or taller than other things or people that are near: *The new offices tower above the rest of the town.* ◇ *Amy towers over her mother.* **2** to be much better, more famous, etc. than other people or things: *He towers above all other poets of his generation.*
🔷 v + prep

toy /tɔɪ/

'toy with sth 1 to consider sth but not very seriously or for very long: *He had toyed with the idea of living in Germany.* [OBJ] **the idea of 2** to play with sth; to move sth around carelessly without really thinking about it: *Stop toying with your food!* ◇ (*figurative*) *He accused the young man of toying with his daughter's affections.*
[SYN] **dally with sth/sb**
[NOTE] **Toy with sth** can be used in the passive: *The possibility had been toyed with but rejected.*
🔷 v + prep

trace /treɪs/

,trace sth 'back (to sth) to find the origin or cause of sth by following clues or evidence backwards from the present time: *Many different childhood illnesses can be traced back to certain foods.* ◇ *Boston has a large population that traces its roots back to Ireland.* ◇ *She can trace her family back as far as the 13th century.*
[OBJ] **roots, origins, history**
🔷 v + n/pron + adv ◆ v + adv + n

,trace sth 'out to draw a shape or a mark clearly: *I traced out our route on the map.* ◇ (*figurative*) *She traced out how working patterns had changed in the last 50 years.*
🔷 v + n/pron + adv ◆ v + adv + n

track /træk/

,track sb/sth 'down (to sth) to find sb/sth after a long and difficult search: *We finally tracked Sam down to his parents' house.* ◇ *It has taken ten years to track down the wreckage of the plane.*
🔷 v + n/pron + adv ◆ v + adv + n

trade /treɪd/

,trade 'down (to sth) **1** to spend less money on things than you used to: *People are trading down and buying cheaper food.* **2** to sell sth large or expensive and buy sth smaller or less expensive: *They traded down to a house with fewer bedrooms.* [OPP] **trade up** (to sth)
🔷 v + adv

,trade sth 'in (for sth) to give sth that you have used to sb you are buying sth new from as part of your payment: *He traded his motorbike in for a new van.*
🔷 v + n/pron + adv ◆ v + adv + n
▶ **'trade-in** *n* a method of buying something by giving a used item as part of the payment for a new one; the used item that you give: *the trade-in value of a car* ◇ *Do you have a trade-in?*

,trade sth 'off (against sth) to balance two things or situations that are opposed to each other: *The government were attempting to trade off inflation against unemployment.* ◇ *They were willing to trade off information to keep the hostages alive* (= to give information in exchange for their lives).
🔷 v + adv + n ◆ v + pron + adv ◆ v + n + adv (*less frequent*)
▶ **'trade-off** (between sth and sth) *n* the act of balancing two things that you need or want but which are opposed to each other: *a trade-off between inflation and unemployment* ◇ *There is a trade-off between the benefits of the drug and the risk of side effects.*

'trade on sth (*also* **'trade upon sth** *more formal, less frequent*) (*disapproving*) to unfairly make use of sth for your own advantage: *He traded on his father's name to get himself a job.*
[SYN] **exploit sth**
🔷 v + prep

,trade 'up (to sth) to sell sth small or not expensive in order to buy sth larger or more expensive: *He traded up to a larger car.*
[OPP] **trade down** (to sth)
🔷 v + adv

'trade upon sth = TRADE ON STH

traffic /ˈtræfɪk/ (-ck-)

ˈtraffic in sth to buy and sell sth, especially drugs or weapons, illegally: *He was accused of trafficking in stolen works of art.*
OBJ drugs, weapons
◆ v + prep

trail /treɪl/

ˌtrail aˈway/ˈoff if sb's speech **trails away/off**, it gradually becomes quieter and then stops: *Mark's voice trailed away to a whisper.* ◇ *'I only hope…' She trailed off.*
SUBJ voice
◆ v + adv

train /treɪn/

ˈtrain sth on/upon sb/sth (*formal*) to point sth such as a gun, a camera, a light, etc. at sb/sth: *The police marksmen trained their weapons on the building.* ◇ *She trained the camera on the bride and groom.* ◇ *He kept his eyes trained on the road ahead.*
OBJ gun, camera, eyes
NOTE This phrasal verb is used mainly in written English.
◆ v + n/pron + prep

ˌtrain sb ˈup to make sb ready to do a job or an activity by teaching them the skills they need: *We need to train up extra staff for the Christmas period.*
◆ v + adv + n ♦ v + n/pron + adv

traipse /treɪps/

ˌtraipse aˈround; ˌtraipse aˈround sth (*BrE also* ˌtraipse ˈround, ˌtraipse ˈround sth) (*informal*) to walk from place to place slowly because you are tired and unwilling: *I've been traipsing around all day with Jenny trying to buy a coat for her.* ◇ *We spent the afternoon traipsing around the town.*
◆ v + adv ♦ v + prep

trample /ˈtræmpl/

ˈtrample on/over sb/sth to ignore sb's feelings or rights and treat them as if they are not important: *The government is trampling on the views of ordinary people.* ◇ *Don't let Jack trample all over you!*
◆ v + prep

treat /triːt/

ˈtreat sb to sth to entertain sb with sth special: *Visitors will be treated to a spectacular show.* ◇ (*ironic*) *We were treated to (= we had to suffer) a two-hour lecture.*
NOTE Treat sb to sth is often used in the passive.
◆ v + n/pron + prep

trick /trɪk/

ˌtrick sb ˈinto sth; ˌtrick sb ˈinto doing sth to manage to get sb to do sth by deceiving them or not telling them the truth: *She felt she'd been tricked into marriage.* ◇ *He tricked me into lending him £100.*
NOTE Trick sb into sth/into doing sth is often used in the passive.
◆ v + n/pron + prep

ˌtrick sb ˈout of sth to take sth away from sb by deceiving them: *An 80-year old woman was tricked out of her life savings.*
◆ v + n/pron + adv + prep

trickle /ˈtrɪkl/

ˌtrickle ˈdown (especially of money) to spread from rich to poor people through the economic system of a country: *If the wealthy pay less tax, the benefits should trickle down to people on lower incomes.*
◆ v + adv
▶ **ˈtrickle down** *n* [U] the theory that if the richest people in society become richer this will have a good effect on poorer people as well, for example by creating more jobs

trifle /ˈtraɪfl/

ˈtrifle with sb/sth (*used especially in negative sentences*) to treat sb/sth without respect as if they are not very important: *He is not a man to be trifled with.* ◇ *He was a man who trifled with women's affections.*
◆ v + prep

trim /trɪm/ (-mm-)

ˌtrim sth aˈway/ˈoff to cut off a small part of sth because it is not needed: *My hair is too long now. Can you trim off about two centimetres?*
◆ v + adv + n ♦ v + n/pron + adv

ˌtrim ˈdown; ˌtrim sth ˈdown to become, or to make sth, smaller in size: *He's trimmed down from 90 kilos to 70.* ◇ *The movie was trimmed down to 2½ hours.*
SYN slim down; slim down, slim sth down
◆ v + adv ♦ v + adv + n ♦ v + n/pron + adv

trip /trɪp/ (-pp-)

ˌtrip ˈover; ˌtrip ˈover sb/sth to fall or almost fall because you have accidentally hit your foot against sth while you are walking or running: *I tripped over the rug and fell heavily.* ◇ *He kept tripping over.* ◇ (*figurative*) *He tripped over his words in his excitement.*
◆ v + adv ♦ v + prep

ˌtrip ˈup; ˌtrip sb ˈup 1 (*especially BrE*) to fall or almost fall because you have accidentally hit your foot against sth while walking or running; to make sb fall or almost fall by catching their

foot while they are walking or running: *I tripped up as I ran across the room.* ◇ *She tripped him up with her stick.* **2** to make a mistake; to deliberately make sb do this: *I knew I had to think carefully in the interview or I might trip up.* ◇ *She was trying to trip me up with her questions.*
◈ v + adv ♦ v + n/pron + adv ♦ v + adv + n

trot /trɒt; *AmE* trɑːt/ (-tt-)

,trot 'off to go somewhere, walking quite quickly: *She trotted off to school happily with her new lunch box.*
◈ v + adv

,trot sth 'out (*informal, disapproving*) to say or repeat sth such as an excuse, an explanation, etc. without thinking about it or being sincere about it: *The airline trotted out the same old excuses to explain the delays.* ◇ *He's just trotting out the party line again* (= in politics).
◈ v + adv + n ♦ v + pron + adv (*less frequent*)

trump /trʌmp/

,trump sth 'up to make up a false story about sb/sth, especially accusing them of doing sth wrong: *Several of his colleagues trumped up a complaint to get him removed from the job.* ◇ *She was arrested on trumped-up charges.*
[OBJ] **charge(s)**
◈ v + adv + n ♦ v + pron + adv ♦ v + n + adv (*rare*)

trundle /'trʌndl/

,trundle sth 'out (*disapproving, especially BrE*) to mention sb/sth or do sth that you have often mentioned or done before: *The government trundled out the same old clichés to justify their actions.*
◈ v + adv + n ♦ v + n/pron + adv

truss /trʌs/

,truss sb/sth 'up (*old-fashioned*) to tie a person or an animal up very tightly so that they cannot move or escape: *The victims had been trussed up with rope and beaten.*
[NOTE] **Truss sb/sth up** is often used in the passive.
◈ v + n/pron + adv ♦ v + adv + n

trust /trʌst/

'trust in sb/sth (*formal*) to have confidence in sb/sth; to rely on sb completely: *I was scared before the operation, but I trusted in the skill of the doctors and nurses.* ◇ *He urged them to trust in God.*
[OBJ] **God**
◈ v + prep

'trust to sb/sth to leave the result or progress of events to be decided by luck, chance, etc., because there is nothing or no one else to help

you: *I stumbled along in the dark, trusting to luck to find the right door.*
[OBJ] **luck**
◈ v + prep

'trust sb with sb/sth to give sb/sth to a person to take care of because you believe they will be careful with them/it: *Would you trust her with the children?* ◇ *I'd trust him with my life.*
◈ v + n/pron + prep

try /traɪ/ (**tries, trying, tried, tried**)

,try 'back; ,try sb 'back (*AmE*) to telephone sb again when you have already telephoned them but have not managed to speak to them: *Can you try back later?* ◇ *She's not there. I'll have to try her back after lunch.*
[SYN] **phone back, phone sb back** (*especially BrE*), **call back, call sb back**
◈ v + adv ♦ v + n/pron + adv ♦ v + adv + n

'try for sth (*especially BrE*) to make an attempt to get or win sth: *Are you going to try for that job?* ◇ *They've been trying for a baby for several years now* (= the woman has been trying to become pregnant).
[OBJ] **a baby**
◈ v + prep

,try it 'on (with sb) (*informal, disapproving, especially BrE*) to behave badly towards sb or try to get sth from them just to see what you can do before they become angry or stop you: *The kids sometimes try it on with a new babysitter.*
◈ v + it + adv
▶ 'try-on *n* (*BrE*) an act of trying to behave badly and hoping that no one will stop you

,try sth 'on to put on a piece of clothing to see if it fits and how it looks: *Can I try on the blue one?* ◇ *If you like it, why don't you try it on?*
◈ v + adv + n ♦ v + n/pron + adv

,try 'out (for sth) (*especially AmE*) to compete for a place in a sports team, a part in a play, etc: *He tried out for the school band.* ◇ *It's a pretty good team. I think I'll try out.*
◈ v + adv
▶ 'try-out *n* (*AmE*) a test, etc. to choose players for a team, actors for a play, etc: *The team is holding try-outs this Thursday.* ◇ *Did you have a try-out for the school play?*
→ *see also* TRY-OUT at TRY SB/STH OUT (ON SB)

,try sb/sth 'out (on sb) to test sb/sth to see how good and useful they are or how suitable for a particular task or purpose before you decide to use them/it: *We've been trying out some new musicians for our band.* ◇ *He couldn't wait to try out his new invention.* ◇ *I've got an idea I'd like to try out on you.* ◇ *The drug has not been tried out on humans yet.*
[SYN] **test sth out (on sb/sth)**
◈ v + n/pron + adv ♦ v + adv + n

► **'try-out** *n* an act of testing how good or suitable sb/sth is before you decide to use them/it: *The play had an out-of-town try-out in Oxford.*
→ *see also* TRY-OUT *at* TRY OUT (FOR STH)

tuck /tʌk/

,**tuck sth a'way 1 be ,tucked a'way** to be in a quiet or hidden place where not many people go: *The house is tucked away right at the end of a rough track.* ⟨SYN⟩ **hide sth away** NOTE Be **tucked away** is usually followed by a phrase with a preposition: *The café was tucked away in the basement.* **2 (in sth)** to put sth in a safe place, especially sth valuable: *She tucked the photos away in her wallet.* ◇ *We've got some money tucked away for emergencies.* ⟨SYN⟩ **stash sth away 3** (*BrE, informal*) to eat a lot of food: *He can certainly tuck it away!* ⟨SYN⟩ **put sth away**
◈ **1** be + v + adv
2,3 v + n/pron + adv ♦ v + adv + n

,**tuck 'in; ,tuck 'into sth** (*informal, especially BrE*) to eat food, especially quickly or with enthusiasm: *We tucked in hungrily.* ◇ *He was tucking into a huge plateful of pasta.* ◇ *Tuck in, everybody!*
⟨SYN⟩ **dig in; dig into sth**
◈ v + adv ♦ v + prep

,**tuck sb 'in/up** to cover sb, especially a child, comfortably in bed by pulling the covers around them: *Will you come and tuck me in, Mummy?* ◇ *The children were all tucked up in bed by 8 p.m.*
◈ v + n/pron + adv ♦ v + adv + n

,**tuck sth 'in; ,tuck sth 'into sth 1** to push or fold the loose end of a piece of clothing, a sheet, rope, hair, etc., in sth, to make it tidy or hold it in position: *Tom, tuck your shirt in!* ◇ *Why don't you tuck your trousers into your socks?* ◇ *Tuck the flap of the envelope in.* OBJ **shirt 2** to pull a part of your body inwards, especially by making your muscles tight: *Stand up straight and tuck your bottoms in!* ◇ *Keep your chin tucked in.*
◈ v + n/pron + adv ♦ v + adv + n ♦ v + n/pron + prep

,**tuck sb 'up** = TUCK SB IN/UP

,**tuck sth 'up** to move or put sth in a small space, especially to hide it or keep it safe or comfortable: *She kicked off her shoes and tucked her feet up under her.* OBJ **legs, feet** NOTE **Tuck sth up** is often used in the passive: *She sat with her legs tucked up under her.*
◈ v + n/pron + adv ♦ v + adv + n

tug /tʌg/ (-gg-)

'**tug at sth** to give sth a quick, strong pull: *Daniel tugged at my sleeve.*
OBJ **sb's arm, sb's hair, sb's sleeve** ⟨SYN⟩ **pull at sth**
◈ v + prep

tumble /'tʌmbl/

,**tumble 'down** to fall suddenly to the ground in a dramatic way: *One push and the wall came tumbling down.* ◇ *Her long dark hair tumbled down around her face.* ◇ (*figurative*) *She felt herself tumbling down into the hole.*
◈ v + adv
► '**tumbledown** *adj* [usually before noun] a **tumbledown** building is old and in a very bad condition, with parts falling down: *He lived in a small, tumbledown hut.*

,**tumble 'over** to fall to the ground: *She knocked the statue and it tumbled over.*
◈ v + adv

'**tumble to sb/sth** (*BrE, informal*) to suddenly realize, understand, or become aware of what sb/sth is really like: *I've tumbled to Isabel now.* ◇ *I've tumbled to what he is trying to do.*
◈ v + prep

tune /tjuːn; AmE tuːn/

,**tune 'in (to sth), ,tune 'into sth 1** to turn on the radio or television in order to listen or watch a particular programme or channel: *We tuned in to watch the football.* ◇ *Tune into* (= watch) *next week's exciting episode!* **2** to be aware of or understand other people's thoughts, feelings or needs: *You must tune into the needs of the people you love.*
◈ v + adv ♦ v + prep

,**tune sth 'in 1** to adjust the controls on a radio or television so that you can hear or see a particular programme or channel clearly: *The radio isn't properly tuned in.* ◇ *I keep the radio tuned in to the BBC World Service.* **2** (*AmE*) to turn on the radio or television in order to listen to or watch a particular programme: *Tune in our TV special tonight at nine.*
◈ v + adv + n ♦ v + n/pron + adv

be ,tuned 'in (to sth); be ,tuned 'into sth to be aware of or understand sth, especially other people's feelings: *Parents should be tuned in to the needs of their child.* ◇ *I'm tuned in to what I have to do.*
◈ be + v + adv ♦ be + v + adv + prep

,**tune 'out; ,tune sb/sth 'out** (*informal, especially AmE*) to stop listening to sb/sth; to ignore sb/sth: *When Lee started talking about her job, Tim just tuned out.*
◈ v + adv ♦ v + n/pron + adv ♦ v + adv + n

'**tune sth to sth** to adjust the controls of a radio or television so that you can listen to or watch a particular programme: *All the TVs in the store were tuned to the same channel.*
◈ v + n/pron + prep

,tune 'up when an orchestra **tunes up**, the players adjust the instruments so that they can play together: *We could hear the orchestra tuning up.* ◇ *The quartet tuned up and began to play.*
◈ v + adv

turf /tɜːf; *AmE* tɜːrf/

,turf sb/sth 'out; **,turf sb/sth 'out of sth** (*also* **,turf sb 'off, ,turf sb 'off sth**) (*BrE, informal*) to force sb/sth to leave a particular place or an organization: *We need to turf the Democratic party out.* ◇ *Several families have been turfed out of their homes.* ◇ *The boys should have been turfed off the bus.*
SYN kick sb out, kick sb out of sth; throw sb/sth out, throw sb/sth out of sth
◈ v + n/pron + adv ◆ v + adv + n (*less frequent*) ◆ v + n/pron + adv + prep ◆ v + n/pron + prep

,turf sth 'out (*BrE, informal*) to get rid of sth you do not want: *The shop is full of beautiful clothes that people have turfed out.*
◈ v + adv + n ◆ v + n/pron + adv

turn /tɜːn; *AmE* tɜːrn/

	~ about	325	~ off
	~ against		~ on
	~ around		~ on to
	~ aside		~ out, out of
324	~ away	326	~ over
	~ away from	327	~ over to
	~ back		~ round
	~ down		~ to
	~ in		~ up
	~ in on		~ upon
	~ inside out		~ upside down
	~ into		

,turn a'bout (*especially BrE*) to turn around quickly so as to face in the opposite direction: *She turned about and went into the kitchen.*
→ *see also* TURN AROUND, TURN SB/STH AROUND; TURN AROUND, TURN STH AROUND
◈ v + adv
▶ **a,bout-'turn** *n* (*BrE*) **1** an act of turning around quickly so as to face in the opposite direction: *He did a rapid about-turn when he saw me and went back inside.* **2** a complete change of opinion, plan or behaviour: *Hours later the management did an about-turn and agreed to our demands.* ◇ *a dramatic about-turn in government policy*
▶ **'turnabout** *n* [sing.] **1** an act of turning around quickly so as to face in the opposite direction **2** a sudden and complete change in attitude or opinion

,turn a'gainst sb/sth; **,turn sb a'gainst sb/sth** to stop, or to make sb stop, being friendly towards sb; to stop, or to make sb stop, supporting sb/sth: *Her old friends were turning against her.* ◇ *He's trying to turn his family*

against me. ◇ *What has made them turn against the government?*
◈ v + prep ◆ v + n/pron + prep

turn a'round (*BrE also* **,turn 'round**) if sb **turns around** and does sth, they do sth unexpectedly and often unfairly: *What will we do if he turns around and says it was all our fault?*
◈ v + adv

,turn a'round; **,turn sb/sth a'round** (*BrE also* **,turn 'round, ,turn sb/sth 'round**) to move your head and shoulders or your whole body so that you face in the opposite direction; to make sb/sth change position in this way: *She turned around to stare at the man behind her.* ◇ *He walked away without turning round.* ◇ *I turned the bottle round to look at the label.* ◇ *The nurse turned him around to face the window.*
→ *see also* TURN ABOUT
◈ v + adv ◆ v + n/pron + adv ◆ v + adv + n (*less frequent*)
▶ **'turnaround** (*BrE also* **'turnround**) *n* [usually sing.] **1** the amount of time it takes to unload a plane or ship at the end of a journey and load it ready for the next one **2** the amount of time that it takes to do a piece of work that you have been given and return it **3** a complete change in sb's opinion, plans, behaviour, etc.
→ *see also* TURNAROUND at TURN AROUND, TURN STH AROUND

,turn a'round; **,turn sth a'round** (*BrE also* **,turn 'round, ,turn sth 'round**) if a business or an economy **turns around**, or sb **turns it around**, it becomes successful after it has been unsuccessful for a time: *The economy is slowly turning around.* ◇ *His job is to try to turn the company around.*
◈ v + n/pron + adv ◆ v + adv + n
▶ **'turnaround** (*BrE also* **'turnround**) *n* [C, usually sing.] a sudden improvement in a business, an economy, etc: *The predicted economic turnaround failed to happen.*
→ *see also* TURNAROUND at TURN AROUND, TURN SB/STH AROUND

,turn sth a'round (*BrE also* **,turn sth 'round**) to deliberately understand sth that sb says in the wrong way, especially for your own advantage: *You turn everything I say around to make me look stupid.*
◈ v + n/pron + adv ◆ v + adv + n

,turn a'side to change direction and go to one side, especially in order to avoid sb/sth: *He turned aside in embarrassment.*
◈ v + adv

,turn sb/sth a'side to make sb/sth move to one side, especially in order to avoid sth difficult or dangerous: *As he bent to kiss her, she turned her head aside.* ◇ (*figurative*) *He cleverly turned all her questions aside* (= he did not answer them).
◈ v + n/pron + adv ◆ v + adv + n (*less frequent*)

,turn a'way; ,turn sth a'way (from sb/sth) to
move or to move your head to face in a different
direction, often to avoid sth difficult or dangerous: *Will turned quickly away and walked out of
the door.* ◇ *He turned away from her with a sigh.* ◇
*Tina turned her head away and looked out of the
window.*
  ◈ v + adv ◆ v + n/pron + adv ◆ v + adv + n

,turn sb a'way 1 (from sth) to refuse to allow sb
to enter a place: *We had to turn hundreds of fans
away from the game* (= because the place was
full). 2 to refuse to help sb: *They had nowhere to
stay so I couldn't just turn them away.*
  ◈ v + n/pron + adv ◆ v + adv + n

,turn a'way from sth; ,turn sb a'way from
sth to stop, or to make sb stop, supporting sb/sth
or being interested in sth: *Younger voters are
turning away from the party.* ◇ *The recent scandals have turned many people away from politics.*
  ◈ v + adv + prep ◆ v + n/pron + adv + prep

,turn 'back; ,turn sb/sth 'back to return in the
direction that you have come from; to make
sb/sth do this: *The weather got so bad that we
turned back.* ◇ *We were turned back at the border.*
◇ (*figurative*) **There'll be no turning back** (=
you can't change your mind) *once you sign the
agreement.*
  ◈ v + adv ◆ v + n/pron + adv ◆ v + adv + n
  IDM **turn the 'clock back** to return to a situation
that existed in the past; to return to old-
fashioned methods or ideas: *This new law is an
attempt to turn the clock back.*

,turn sth 'back to fold sth back on itself: *She
straightened the bedclothes and turned back the
top sheet.*
  ◈ v + n/pron + adv ◆ v + adv + n

,turn 'down (*rare*) if your mouth **turns down**, it
forms a line with the ends curved downwards,
because you are sad or annoyed: *'Don't be cross
with me,' she said, her mouth turning down at the
corners.*
  OPP **turn up**
  ◈ v + adv

,turn sb/sth 'down to reject or refuse sb/sth:
Why did Clare turn down your invitation? ◇ *He
asked her to marry him, but she turned him down.*
◇ *They turned down my offer of help.* ◇ *She
turned the job down because it paid too little.* ◇
My book was turned down by eight publishers.
  OBJ **offer, application, invitation, request, job,
proposal** **SYN** **reject sb/sth**
  ◈ v + adv + n ◆ v + n/pron + adv

,turn sth 'down 1 to adjust the controls on a
piece of equipment in order to reduce the
amount of heat, noise, light, etc. produced: *Turn
that radio down, I can't sleep.* ◇ *It's warmer
today. I'll turn down the heating.* ◇ *She turned the
lights down low.* **OBJ** **volume, heating, sound,
television** **OPP** **turn sth up** 2 to fold sth so that

one part is covering another: *The corner of the
page had been turned down.* ◇ *He turned down
the blankets and the children climbed into bed.*
  ▶ **'downturn** *n* [C, usually sing.] a fall in economic activity or profits: *a downturn in sales*

,turn 'in (*old-fashioned, informal*) to go to bed: *It's
time for me to turn in.*
  SYN **retire** (*formal*)
  ◈ v + adv

,turn 'in sth to achieve a good result, performance, profit, etc: *The champion turned in a brilliant performance.* ◇ *The company turned in
nearly $150 000 last month.*
  OBJ **performance, profit**
  ◈ v + adv + n

,turn sb 'in; ,turn sth 'in to fold sth so that it
bends or faces inwards; to be folded in this way:
Her feet turn in as she walks.
  ◈ v + adv ◆ v + n/pron + adv ◆ v + adv + n

,turn sb 'in (to sb), ,turn yourself 'in (to sb)
(*informal*) to give sb or yourself to sb in authority because they/you have done sth wrong: *He
turned his own brother in to the police.* ◇ *Things
will be better for you if you turn yourself in.*
  ◈ v + n/pron + adv ◆ v + adv + n

,turn sth 'in 1 to give back sth that you no longer
need or should have: *Turn in your pass before you
leave.* 2 (*especially AmE*) to give sth such as a
piece of written work to the person who asked
you to do it: *Have you turned in your assignment
yet?* **SYN** **hand sth in (to sb)** 3 to give sth to the
police or sb in authority: *Only a few guns have
been turned in so far.* **SYN** **hand sth in (to sb)**;
give sth in
  ◈ v + adv + n ◆ v + n/pron + adv

,turn 'in on yourself to become very concerned
with your own problems and stop communicating with others: *He completely turned in on himself after his wife left him.*
  ◈ v + adv + prep

,turn inside 'out; ,turn sth inside 'out to
make the inside of sth face outwards: *It was so
windy my umbrella turned inside out.* ◇ *She
pulled off her jumper, turning the sleeves inside
out.*
  ◈ v + adv + adv ◆ v + n/pron + adv + adv

,turn sb/sth inside 'out to make great changes
in sb's life: *The shock turned her world inside out.*
  ◈ v + n/pron + adv + adv
  SYN **turn sb/sth upside down**

,turn 'into sth; ,turn sb/sth 'into sth to
change, or to make sth change, into sth different:
*We need to stop this problem from turning into a
crisis.* ◇ *The house had been turned into three
apartments.* ◇ *As the fruit ripens, the starch turns
into sugar.* ◇ *The director turned her into a star!*
  SYN **change into sth, change sb/sth into sth**
  ◈ v + prep ◆ v + n/pron + prep

,**turn 'off** (*informal*) to stop listening to or thinking about sb/sth: *I couldn't understand the lecture so I just turned off.*
> [SYN] **switch off**
> ⊕ v + adv

,**turn 'off**; ,**turn 'off sth** to leave one road in order to travel on another: *She turned off onto a side street.* ◇ *The car turned off the main road.*
> ⊕ v + adv ♦ v + prep
> ▶ '**turn-off** *n* a place where one road leads off a larger or more important road: *the turn-off for the airport*
> → *see also* TURN-OFF *at* TURN SB OFF, TURN SB OFF SB/STH

,**turn 'off**; ,**turn itself 'off** if a machine or a piece of equipment **turns off**, or **turns itself off**, it stops operating: *The heating turns off automatically at 9.30.* ◇ *The computer will turn itself off if you leave it.*
> [SYN] **switch off, switch itself off**
> [OPP] **turn on, turn itself on**
> ⊕ v + adv ♦ v + pron + adv

,**turn sb 'off**; ,**turn sb 'off sb/sth 1** (*informal*) to make sb lose interest or become bored: *People had been turned off by both candidates in the election.* ◇ *His political views turned her off him.* **2** (*informal*) to stop sb feeling attracted to sb/sth; to make sb feel disgusted: *If I tell her I'm only 17 it might turn her off.* ◇ *The sight of all that raw meat turned me off.* ◇ *The smell turned me off my food.*
> [OPP] **turn sb on; turn sb on to sb/sth**
> ⊕ v + n/pron + adv ♦ v + adv + n ♦ v + n/pron + prep
> ▶ '**turn-off** *n* [C, usually sing.] (*informal*) something or somebody that people do not find interesting or attractive: *Unlike many other women she found his beard a real turn-off.*
> → *see also* TURN-OFF *at* TURN OFF, TURN OFF STH

,**turn sth 'off** to stop the flow of electricity, gas, water, etc. by moving a switch or a button: *to turn the radio/television off* ◇ *I forgot to turn the tap off.* ◇ *Turn all the lights off when you leave.* ◇ *You'll need to turn off the water to mend the pipe.*
> [OBJ] **light, television, tap, water, gas, etc.**
> [SYN] **switch sth off** [OPP] **turn sth on**
> → *see also* TURN STH OUT
> ⊕ v + n/pron + adv ♦ v + adv + n

'**turn on sb** to attack sb suddenly and unexpectedly: *The dog turned on him and bit his finger.* ◇ *She suddenly turned on me and started shouting.*
> ⊕ v + prep

'**turn on sth** (*also* '**turn upon sth** *more formal*) **1** (*BrE*) to depend on sth in order to have a successful outcome: *Her future career turns on this interview.* ◇ *The case turns on whether the police can prove that the driver knew he had hit something.* ◇ *Much turns on the outcome of the peace talks.*
> [SYN] **hinge on sth 2** if a conversation, an argu-

ment, etc. **turns on** sth, it has that as its main subject: *Their talk turned on the likelihood of his return* (= if he was likely to return or not).
> ⊕ v + prep

,**turn 'on**; ,**turn itself 'on** if a machine or a piece of equipment **turns on**, or **turns itself on**, it starts operating: *I've set the oven to turn on at 5 p.m.* ◇ *I don't know why the radio suddenly turned itself on.*
> [SYN] **switch on, switch itself on**
> [OPP] **turn off, turn itself off**
> ⊕ v + adv ♦ v + pron + adv

,**turn sb 'on** (*informal*) **1** to make sb enthusiastic about sth: *What really turns him on is motorbikes.* ◇ *If live theatre turns you on, there is plenty to choose from.* **2** to make sb feel sexually excited: *That's not the kind of thing that turns me on.* ◇ *She says she gets turned on by men in uniform!*
> [OPP] **turn sb off**
> ⊕ v + n/pron + adv ♦ v + adv + n
> ▶ '**turn-on** *n* [C, usually sing.] (*informal*) a person, a thing, a situation, etc. that sb finds sexually exciting: *Being the centre of attention for four or five guys was a real turn-on.*

,**turn sth 'on** to start the flow of electricity, gas, water, etc. by moving a switch or a button: *Did you turn the central heating on?* ◇ *Turn the tap on slowly.* ◇ *I checked the fuses and turned the electricity back on.* ◇ *I didn't know you were in the room until I turned the light on.* ◇ *Leo turns the television on as soon as he comes home from school.*
> [OBJ] **light, tap, television, water, gas, etc.**
> [SYN] **switch sth on** [OPP] **turn sth off**
> ⊕ v + n/pron + adv ♦ v + adv + n
> [IDM] **turn on the 'charm** to be very pleasant and polite to sb in order to gain sth for yourself: *She's good at turning on the charm to get what she wants.*

'**turn sth on sb/sth** (*also* '**turn sth upon sb/sth** *more formal*) to point sth such as gun, a camera, a light, etc. at sb/sth: *Officers turned hoses on the demonstrators.*
> [SYN] **train sth on sb/sth**
> ⊕ v + n/pron + prep

,**turn sb 'on to sb/sth** (*informal*) to make sb interested in sb/sth or use sth for the first time: *What was it that first turned you on to jazz?*
> [OPP] **turn sb off sb/sth**
> ⊕ v + n/pron + adv + prep

,**turn 'out 1** to be present at an event; to attend sth or to go somewhere: *The whole village turned out to welcome us.* ◇ *Only half the team turned out for the practice.* ◇ *I'm not going to turn out to meet you in this weather.* **2** (*used with an adverb, an adjective or in questions with how*) to take place or happen in the way mentioned; to develop or end in a particular way: *The article she wrote had turned out well.* ◇ *The day turned out fine again.* ◇ *You never know how things will turn out.* ◇ *I* *couldn't have gone anyway, as it turned out.* ◇ *The children have turned out well in spite of their upbringing.* **3** to be discovered to be; to prove to be: *It turned out that she was a friend of my sister.* ◇ *My decision turned out to have been a mistake.* ◇ *Ruth's illness turned out not to be serious after all.*

✥ v + adv

▸ **'turnout** *n* [C, usually sing.] [U] **1** the number of people who come to take part in or watch an activity: *There was a good turnout for the concert.* **2** the number of people who vote in a particular election: *a high/low/poor turnout*

,turn 'out; ,turn sth 'out to point, or to make sth point, outwards: *His feet turn out as he walks.* ◇ *She turns her toes out when she walks.*

✥ v + adv ◆ v + n/pron + adv ◆ v + adv + n

,turn sb 'out (from sth), ,turn sb 'out of sth to force sb to leave or go out of a place: *The landlord turned them out of their house just before the New Year.* ◇ *You can't turn us out in this storm!*

SYN **chuck sb out, chuck sb out of sth; kick sb out, kick sb out of sth; turf sb out, turf sb out of sth** (*BrE, informal*)

✥ v + n/pron + adv ◆ v + n/pron + adv + prep

,turn sth/sb 'out to produce sth/sb: *The factory turns out 900 cars a week.* ◇ *This school has turned out several well-known engineers.*

✥ v + adv + n ◆ v + n/pron + adv (*less frequent*)

,turn sth 'out **1** to switch off sth such as a light or a source of heat: *Remember to turn out the lights.* OBJ only **light, gas** SYN **switch sth off** OPP **turn sth on →** *see also* TURN STH OFF **2** (*BrE*) to clean a room, a cupboard, etc. thoroughly by removing the contents and organizing them again: *She turned the kitchen cupboards out at the beginning of the year.* ◇ *I'm going to turn out my bedroom during the holidays.* SYN **clear sth out 3** to remove the contents of sth; to empty sth completely: *I turned out all the drawers looking for my keys.* ◇ *Turn out your pockets.* ◇ *She turned the rice out of the packet into a bowl.* SYN **empty sth**

✥ v + adv + n ◆ v + n/pron + adv

be ,turned 'out [+ adv/prep] to dress sb/yourself with special care or effort: *The children were always beautifully turned out.* ◇ *She was fashionably turned out in cream trousers and a red sweater.*

NOTE This phrasal verb is always used in the passive.

✥ be + v + adv

,turn 'over; ,turn sb/sth 'over to change your position, or the position of sb/sth, so that the other side is facing outwards or upwards: *He turned over onto his back.* ◇ *The van skidded and turned over.* ◇ *Jack was driving too fast and turned the car over on the bend.* ◇ *The nurse*

turned Adam over onto his back. ◇ *Turn the pancake over when one side is cooked.* ◇ (*figurative*) *The smell made my stomach turn over.*

✥ v + adv ◆ v + n/pron + adv ◆ v + adv + n (*less frequent*)

▸ **'turnover** *n* a small piece of pastry filled with fruit or jam, folded over and baked

→ *see also* TURNOVER at TURN OVER, TURN STH OVER; TURNOVER at TURN STH OVER

,turn 'over; ,turn sth 'over **1** (of an engine) to run steadily at a low speed; to start: *I turned the key and the engine turned over quietly.* ◇ *The engine was turning over too fast.* SYN **tick over 2** (to sth) (*BrE*) to change to a different channel when watching television: *Can I turn over to Channel Four?* ◇ *This is boring. Let's turn it over.* SYN **change over** (to sth); **switch over** (to sth); **switch sth over** (to sth) **3** to move a page or a piece of paper so that you can see the other side: *Turn over (the page) for more details.* NOTE **Turn** or **turn sth** is used more frequently in this meaning: *I turned the page quickly.* ◇ *Turn to page 23.* **4** to sell goods and replace them; to be sold and replaced: *Large supermarkets turn over their stock very rapidly.* ◇ *This brand turns over twice as fast as the others.*

✥ v + adv ◆ v + n/pron + adv ◆ v + adv + n

IDM **turn over a new 'leaf** to change your way of life to become a better, more responsible person

▸ **'turnover** *n* [sing.] **1** the rate at which employees leave a company and are replaced by others: *a high turnover of staff* **2** the rate at which goods are sold in a shop/store and are replaced by others: *a fast turnover of stock*

→ *see also* TURNOVER at TURN OVER, TURN STH/SB OVER; TURNOVER at TURN STH OVER

,turn sb/sth 'over (to sb/sth) to deliver sb/sth to the control and care of sb in authority, especially the police: *He was turned over to the Belgian police at the border.*

✥ v + n/pron + adv ◆ v + adv + n

,turn sth 'over **1** (to sb) to give the responsibility for sth important to sb else: *He had to turn over some of his duties to his assistant.* ◇ *She's planning to turn the business over to her daughter.* SYN **hand sth over to sb, hand sth over to sb 2** if a business **turns over** a particular amount of money, it deals with that amount in a particular period of time: *The company turned over a million pounds in its first year.* **3** to think about sth carefully: *Diana turned over what James had said in her mind.* ◇ *He lay in the dark, turning over the day's extraordinary events.* SYN **chew sth over; mull sth over 4** (*BrE, slang*) to enter a place illegally and steal valuable things from it: *The burglars had turned the house over.* NOTE **Turn sth over** is often used in the passive in this meaning. **5** (*BrE*) to search a place very thoroughly, making it very untidy: *His room had been turned over by the police.* NOTE **Turn sth over** is often used in the passive in this meaning.

⊕ **1,3,4,5** v + adv + n ◆ v + n/pron + adv
    2 v + adv + n ◆ v + pron + adv

▶ **'turnover** *n* [C, usually sing.] [U] the total amount of goods and services sold by a company during a particular period of time: *an annual turnover of twenty million*

→ *see also* TURNOVER at TURN OVER, TURN SB/STH OVER; TURNOVER at TURN OVER, TURN STH OVER

,**turn 'over to sth**; ,**turn sth 'over to sth** if an area, a factory, etc. **turns over** or sb **turns it over** to sth, it starts to be used for sth different: *The whole area has turned over to rice production.* ◇ *The factory was turned over to the production of aircraft parts.*

⊕ v + adv + prep ◆ v + n/pron + adv + prep

,**turn 'round** (*BrE*) = TURN AROUND

,**turn 'round**; ,**turn sb/sth 'round** (*BrE*) = TURN AROUND, TURN SB/STH AROUND

,**turn 'round**; ,**turn sth 'round** (*BrE*) = TURN AROUND, TURN STH AROUND

,**turn sth 'round** (*BrE*) = TURN STH AROUND

'**turn to sb 1** to move your head or body so as to face sb: *He turned to me and smiled.* **2 (for sth)** to approach sb for help, sympathy or advice: *Sue turns to her friends for support rather than her family.* ◇ *You're the only person I can turn to for advice.* ◇ *She has nobody she can turn to.*

⊕ v + prep

'**turn to sth** to start to become involved in sth or start to do sth, especially sth illegal or harmful, often because you are in a difficult situation: *He was forced to turn to crime to pay off his debts.* ◇ *People often cope with stress by turning to food for comfort.*

⊕ v + prep

'**turn to sth**; '**turn sth to sth** to turn your attention, your thoughts, etc. to a new subject: *Our conversation soon turned to the kind of music that we liked.* ◇ *Let's turn our attention to next week's conference.*

OBJ **attention**

⊕ v + prep ◆ v + n/pron + prep

,**turn 'up 1** (of a person) to arrive: *He finally turned up at three o'clock.* ◇ *The taxi didn't turn up so we walked.* SYN **show up** (*informal*) **2** to be found, especially by chance, after being lost: *The missing letter turned up in the waste basket.* **3** (of an opportunity) to happen, especially unexpectedly: *I haven't got a job at the moment, but I'm sure that something will turn up.* ◇ *References to Irina turn up in many of his poems.*

⊕ v + adv

IDM **turn up/come up 'trumps** to do more than people expect and so make a situation very suc-

cessful: *The team's new player turned up trumps and scored three goals.* ◇ *That was a wonderful meal! You've turned up trumps again.*

▶ '**turn-up** *n* [sing.] (*BrE, informal, humorous*) something surprising or unexpected that happens: *Nick's handed his work in on time? That's a turn-up for the books!*

→ *see also* TURN-UP at TURN STH UP

▶ '**upturn** *n* an improvement or an increase in sth: *an upturn in the economy*

,**turn 'up**; ,**turn sth 'up** to point, or to make sth point, upwards: *Her nose turns up at the end.* ◇ *She turned her face up towards him.*

OPP **turn down**; **turn sth down**

⊕ v + adv ◆ v + n/pron + adv ◆ v + adv + n

▶ '**turned-up** *adj* [only before noun] pointing upwards: *a turned-up nose*

▶ '**upturned** *adj* [only before noun] pointing or facing upwards: *an upturned nose* ◇ *upturned faces*

→ *see also* UPTURNED at TURN STH UPSIDE DOWN

,**turn sth 'up 1** to adjust the controls of a piece of electrical equipment in order to increase the heat, noise, etc: *Turn the TV up, I can't hear what she's saying.* ◇ *Let's turn the heating up, I'm freezing.* ◇ *The music was turned up loud.* OBJ **heating**, **music**, **radio/television** OPP **turn sth down 2** to make a piece of clothing, or part of a piece of clothing, shorter by folding it back and sewing it: *The sleeves were too long and had to be turned up.* ◇ *Will you turn the hem up for me?* OBJ **hem** OPP **let sth down 3** to discover sth, such as information or sth hidden: *Their enquiries turned up a number of interesting facts.* ◇ *Our efforts to trace him turned up nothing.*

⊕ **1,2** v + n/pron + adv ◆ v + adv + n
    3 v + adv + n ◆ v + n/pron + adv

▶ '**turn-up** *n* (*BrE*) the bottom of the leg of a pair of trousers/pants that has been folded over on the outside: *Turn-ups seem to be coming back into fashion.*

→ *see also* TURN-UP at TURN UP

'**turn upon sth** (*formal*) = TURN ON STH

'**turn sth upon sb/sth** = TURN STH ON SB/STH

,**turn upside 'down**; ,**turn sth upside 'down** to move sth so that the bottom is facing upwards: *The car hit a wall, turned upside down, and ended up in a field.* ◇ *I turned the box upside down and everything fell out.*

⊕ v + adv + adv ◆ v + n/pron + adv + adv

,**turn sth upside 'down 1** to make a place very untidy while you are searching for sth: *The burglars turned the flat upside down.* **2** to make large changes and confusion in sb's life: *The divorce turned his whole world upside down.*

SYN **turn sb/sth inside out**

⊕ v + n/pron + adv + adv

▶ **'upturned** *adj* [only before noun] turned upside down: *upturned chairs* ◇ *We sat on an upturned box.*

→ *see also* UPTURNED at TURN UP, TURN STH UP

twist /twɪst/

,twist sth 'off; **,twist sth 'off sth** to remove sth or break sth off by turning and pulling it with your hand: *He twisted off the lid and looked inside.* ◇ *She twisted the cap off the bottle and took a mouthful of water.*

✦ v + n/pron + adv ◆ v + adv + n ◆ v + n/pron + prep

type /taɪp/

,type sth 'in; **,type sth 'into sth** to put data into a document using a computer or a type-writer: *Type in the file name then press return.* ◇ *Type the relevant details into the boxes provided.*

〉SYN〈 **key sth in, key sth into sth**

✦ v + adv + n ◆ v + n/pron + adv ◆ v + n/pron + prep

,type sth 'out/'up to produce a copy of sth on a computer (or **word processor**) or a typewriter: *I'm typing up the report this morning.* ◇ *It took me ages to type my notes out.*

✦ v + adv + n ◆ v + n/pron + adv

Uu

urge /ɜːdʒ; *AmE* ɜːrdʒ/

ˌurge sb/sth 'on (to sth/to do sth) to encourage
sb; to support sb so that they can do sth better:
The supporters were urging the team on. ◇ *Urged
on by the Prime Minister the police tried to end the
strike.* ◇ *The driver urged the horses on.*
 > **SYN** **encourage sb/sth**
 ◈ v + n/pron + adv ◆ v + adv + n

use /juːz/ (**used, used** /juːzd/)

ˌuse sth 'up to use all of sth until no more is left:
I've used up all the milk. ◇ *These eggs need to be
used up quickly.* ◇ *This program will use up a lot
of memory on the hard disk.* `
 ◈ v + n/pron + adv ◆ v + adv + n

usher /ˈʌʃə(r)/

ˌusher sth 'in (*formal*) to mark or be the start of
sth new: *The elections ushered in a new period of
change in the country.* ◇ *Firework displays
ushered in the New Year.*
 > **OBJ** **period, era** **SYN** **herald sth** (*formal*)
 ◈ v + adv + n ◆ v + pron + adv

Vv

veer /vɪə(r); *AmE* vɪr/

veer 'off; **veer 'off sth** (*also* **veer a'way (from sth)**) **1** to suddenly change direction: *The car suddenly veered off to the left.* ◇ *The truck veered off the road and crashed into a tree.* ◇ *The plane was going straight towards the mountain, but veered away at the last minute.* **2** (of a conversation or a way of behaving or thinking) to change in the way it develops: *The conversation veered off into more personal matters.* ◇ *Throughout his career, he's veered away from jazz into other areas.*
◈ v + adv ◆ v + prep

veg /vedʒ/ (**vegges, vegging, vegged, vegged**)
NOTE Although these forms are spelt with *-gg-*, they are all pronounced /vedʒ-/.

veg 'out (*spoken, informal*) to relax and do very little: *All she does is veg out in front of the telly.*
SYN **laze about/around; lounge about/around**
◈ v + adv

venture /'ventʃə(r)/

venture into/on sth (*also* **venture upon sth** *more formal*) to dare to do sth that could be dangerous or involve risk: *As soon as he arrived in the country, he ventured on a trip up the Amazon.* ◇ *This is the first time the company has ventured into movie production.*
◈ v + prep

verge /vɜːdʒ; *AmE* vɜːrdʒ/

verge on sth (*also* **verge upon sth** *more formal*) to be very close or similar to an extreme state or condition: *I was treated with suspicion that verged on hostility.* ◇ *Her hair was dark brown, verging on black.*
SYN **border on sth**
◈ v + prep

vest /vest/

vest sth in sb/sth; **vest sb with sth** (*formal*) **1** to officially or legally give sb the power or authority to do sth: *It is unwise to vest absolute power in a single institution.* ◇ *The court is vested with certain rights.* **2** to make sb the legal owner of land or property NOTE **Vest sth in sb/sth** and **vest sb with sth** are often used in the passive.
◈ v + n/pron + prep

vie /vaɪ/ (**vies, vying** /'vaɪɪŋ/ **vied, vied**)

vie with sb/sth (for sth/to do sth), **vie for sth** (*formal*) (*often used in the progressive tenses*) to compete strongly with sb/sth: *There'll be a lot of people vying for those posts.* ◇ *The children were vying for the teacher's attention.* ◇ *The boys were vying with each other to impress her.* ◇ *There were several restaurants vying with each other for customers.*
SYN **compete (with sb/sth) (for sth)**
NOTE You can also use **vie to do sth**: *The boys were vying to impress her.*
◈ v + prep

visit /'vɪzɪt/

visit with sb (*AmE, informal*) to spend time with sb talking in an informal and casual way: *I visited with my neighbour while the kids were playing.*
◈ v + prep

be 'visited on sb/sth (*also* **be 'visited upon sb/sth**) (*old-fashioned, formal*) to be punished with sth: *He listed the horrors visited upon the region during the conflict.* ◇ *Each new indignity visited on her was worse than the previous one.*
◈ be + v + prep

vote /vəʊt; *AmE* voʊt/

vote sb/sth 'down to reject or defeat a candidate or a proposal by voting: *The Senate has voted down efforts to raise taxes.* ◇ *If Mr Smith demands too much, the unions will vote him down.*
◈ v + n/pron + adv ◆ v + adv + n

vote sb 'in; **vote sb 'into/'onto sth** to choose sb for a particular position by voting: *I was voted in as treasurer.* ◇ *When was this government voted into office?* ◇ *Who voted her onto the Board of Governors?*
SYN **elect sb (to sth)** (*more formal*)
NOTE **Vote sb in** and **vote sb into/onto sth** are often used in the passive.
◈ v + adv + n ◆ v + pron + adv ◆ v + n + adv (*rare*) ◆ v + n/pron + prep

vote sb 'off sth = VOTE SB OUT, VOTE SB OUT OF/OFF STH

vote on sth to make a decision about sth by voting: *The committee is voting on the proposal tonight.* ◇ *Workers have begun voting on whether to hold a series of one-day strikes.*
OBJ **proposal, resolution, issue**
NOTE **Vote on sth** can be used in the passive: *The proposal was voted on and agreed.*
◈ v + prep

vote sb 'onto sth = VOTE SB IN, VOTE SB INTO/ONTO STH

vote sb 'out; **vote sb 'out of/'off sth** to decide as a group to remove sb from a particular position by voting: *The government may be voted*

out of office at the next election. ◇ What will he do
if he gets voted out? ◇ Parsons was voted off the
Board.

OBJ **government**, **party**

NOTE **Vote sb out** and **vote sb out of/off sth** are
often used in the passive.

◈ v + n/pron + adv ◆ v + adv + n ◆
     v + n/pron + adv + prep ◆ v + n/pron + prep

‚vote sth 'through to approve sth or bring a proposal, etc. into force by voting for it: Congress
voted the bill through without a debate.

OBJ **bill**, **proposal**

NOTE **Vote sth through** is often used in the
passive.

◈ v + n/pron + adv ◆ v + adv + n

vouch /vaʊtʃ/

'vouch for sb/sth 1 to say that you know sb, that
you believe they have a good character and that
you are prepared to be responsible for their
actions: They asked whether I was prepared to
vouch for him. ◇ You should give the names of
two people who can vouch for your honesty and
reliability. ◇ I can vouch for the fact that he is a
good worker. SYN **answer for sth 2** to say that
you know sth is true because you have seen it
yourself: I was in bed with flu. My wife can vouch
for that/me. ◇ I can't vouch for this hotel (= I have
no personal experience of it) but it looked wonderful from the brochure.

NOTE **Vouch for sb/sth** can be used in the
passive: I had to be vouched for by a responsible
person.

◈ v + prep

Ww

wade /weɪd/

,wade 'in; ,wade 'into sth (*informal*) to get involved in a discussion, an argument, a difficult situation, etc. in a forceful and not very sensitive way: *She waded in with an attack on company policy.* ◇ *The Senator waded into a new argument over defence spending.*
◈ v + adv ◆ v + prep

,wade 'into sb (*informal*) to attack sb physically or with words: *Marty was terrific — he just waded into the skinheads without a thought.* ◇ *She waded straight into her critics with her opening remarks.*
⟩SYN⟨ **launch into sb; attack sb** (*more formal*)
◈ v + prep

,wade 'through sth to spend a lot of time and effort reading sth or dealing with sth: *I had to wade through pages and pages of statistics.*
[OBJ] **pages** ⟩SYN⟨ **plough through sth**
◈ v + prep

waffle /'wɒfl; AmE 'wɑːfl/

,waffle 'on (about sth) (*informal, especially BrE*) to talk or write a lot about sth without giving any useful information: *He waffled on for ages about his garden.*
⟩SYN⟨ **go on (about sth); rattle on (about sth)**
◈ v + adv

wait /weɪt/

,wait a'round (*BrE also* ,wait a'bout) **(for sb/sth)** to stay in a place without doing anything, waiting for sth to happen or for sb to arrive: *I wouldn't bother waiting around for him.* ◇ *She didn't wait about to hear his reply.*
⟩SYN⟨ **hang around**
◈ v + adv

,wait be'hind (*especially BrE*) to stay after other people have gone, especially in order to speak to sb privately: *He asked her to wait behind after the meeting.*
◈ v + adv

,wait 'in (for sb/sth) (*BrE*) to stay at home because you are expecting sb to arrive or telephone: *I've got to wait in for the TV repair man.* ◇ *She waited in all day in case he called.*
◈ v + adv

'wait on sb 1 (*also* 'wait on sth *especially AmE*) to bring food and drink to people at a table, usually in a restaurant: *My daughter will wait on us this evening!* ◇ *When I started, I didn't know anything about waiting on tables.* ◇ *We were waited on by a very polite young man.* **2** (*also* 'wait upon sb *more formal*) to bring sb everything they want or need: *She spoiled the children, always waiting*

on them hand and foot (= doing everything for them, like a servant). **3** (*AmE*) to serve customers in a shop/store: *Is anybody waiting on you?* ◇ *There is no one in the furniture department to wait on me.*
◈ v + prep

'wait on sb/sth (*informal, especially AmE*) to wait until sb arrives or until sth is available: *Judd was late and she was sick of waiting on him.* ◇ *I'm still waiting on the result of the blood test.* ◇ *She was waiting on my decision.*
[NOTE] In British English, **wait (for sb/sth)** is usually used.
◈ v + prep

'wait on sth (*especially AmE*) = WAIT ON SB 1

,wait sth 'out to stay in a place until sth difficult or unpleasant has passed or finished: *We sheltered in a doorway to wait out the storm.* ◇ *It was difficult to wait out the hours until I could phone her to hear the news.* ◇ *Their strategy has been to wait the recession out.*
◈ v + adv + n ◆ v + n/pron + adv

,wait 'up 1 (for sb) to not go to bed until sb comes home or arrives: *Don't wait up (for me), I may be late.* ⟩SYN⟨ **stay up 2** (*informal, especially AmE*) used to tell sb to stop so that you can reach them and talk to them or go with them: *Wait up! I'll be right there.* ◇ *Hey guys, wait up.* ⟩SYN⟨ **hang on**
◈ v + adv

'wait upon sb = WAIT ON SB 2

wake /weɪk/ (woke /wəʊk/ woken /'wəʊkən/ or waked, waked)

,wake 'up; ,wake sb 'up; ,wake yourself 'up 1 to stop sleeping; to make sb stop sleeping: *How many times does the baby wake up in the night?* ◇ *I usually wake up early in the summer.* ◇ *You look as if you've only just woken up!* ◇ *Can you wake me up at 8?* ◇ *He was woken up by the sound of breaking glass.* [NOTE] **Wake** and **wake sb** can also be used with this meaning, but usually only in more formal language. **Wake up** and **wake sb/yourself up** are much more common than *awake/awake sb, awaken/awaken sb* and *waken/waken sb*, which are formal and usually only used in writing. **2** to become, or to make sb, more lively and interested: *You need to wake up and start paying attention.* ◇ *Wake up! I don't want to have to repeat all this.* ◇ *The class needs waking up.*
◈ v + adv ◆ v + n/pron + adv ◆ v + adv + n

▶ **'wake-up** adj [only before noun] that is intended to wake you up: *What time would you like your wake-up call* (= for example, in a hotel)?

,wake 'up to sth to become aware of sth; to realize sth: *People are finally waking up to the fact*

that the natural world must be conserved. ◇ *The hospitals have woken up to the value of experienced nurses.* ◇ *He hasn't yet woken up to the seriousness of the situation.*
◈ v + adv + prep

walk /wɔːk/

,walk a'way (from sb/sth) 1 to leave a difficult or unpleasant situation in order to avoid it, instead of staying to deal with it: *to walk away from a situation/deal* ◇ *You can't just walk away from the problem.* ◇ *He just walked away from everything — his job, his home and his family.* **2** if you **walk away** from an accident, etc. you are not seriously injured: *Both drivers walked away with minor cuts and bruises.* ◇ *He walked away unhurt.* NOTE Walk away is usually used with an adjective or a phrase beginning with a preposition in this meaning.
◈ v + adv

,walk a'way/'off with sth 1 to win sth very easily: *The team walked away with the championship.* **2** to steal sth; to take sth without the owner's permission: *The thief walked away with jewellery worth £24 000.*
◈ v + adv + prep

,walk 'in on sb/sth to go into a room and see what sb is doing when they did not expect you and did not want anyone to see them: *Sorry, I didn't mean to walk in on you.* ◇ *I'd obviously walked in on a very serious conversation.*
◈ v + adv + prep

,walk 'into sb/sth to crash into sb/sth while you are walking: *Look where you're going! You walked straight into me.* ◇ *He keeps bumping into things and walking into walls.*
◈ v + prep

,walk 'into sth (*informal*) **1** to become caught in sth that you are not expecting, especially because you are not careful: *He realized he'd walked into a trap.* **2** to succeed in getting a job without having to make an effort: *She walked straight into a job in publishing.*
◈ v + prep

,walk 'off; ,walk 'off sth to leave a place or a person suddenly because you are angry or upset: *She turned and walked off without a word.* ◇ *The rest of the team walked off the field in protest.*
◈ v + adv ◆ v + prep

,walk sth 'off to go for a walk in order to get rid of the feeling that you have eaten too much or an emotion such as anger: *I need to walk off that lunch.* ◇ *It'll do her good to walk some of her temper off.*
NOTE Walk sth off is not used in the passive.
◈ v + adv + n ◆ v + n/pron + adv

,walk 'off with sth (*informal*) **1** = WALK AWAY/OFF WITH STH 1 *They've walked off with most of the film awards.* **2** (*humorous*) = WALK AWAY/OFF

WITH STH **2** *Who's walked off with my pen?* ◇ *That dog's just walked off with our ball!*

,walk 'out 1 (*also* ,walk 'out of sth) to leave a meeting, a performance, etc. suddenly before the end, because you do not like it or are angry: *Several students walked out of the debate before the vote.* ◇ *Some of the audience walked out in disgust.* **2** (of workers) to stop working and go on strike: *The cameramen have walked out over working conditions.* **3** (on sb/sth) (*informal*) to leave sb you have a close relationship with and a responsibility for: *He walked out on his wife/marriage after 35 years.*
◈ v + adv **1** also v + adv + prep
▶ 'walkout *n* **1** a sudden strike by workers: *The staff staged a one-day walkout.* **2** a protest in which you leave a meeting, a performance, etc. to show your anger or disapproval

,walk 'over sb (*informal*) **1** to treat sb badly and not consider their wishes or feelings: *We're not prepared to let the management walk all over us.* **2** to defeat sb easily in a competition: *They'll walk all over you on Saturday.*
NOTE Walk over sb can be used in the passive: *Don't let yourselves be walked over.*
◈ v + prep
▶ 'walkover *n* (*informal*) an easy victory in a game or competition; a situation in which you are considered to have won a game although you did not in fact play: *The race was no walkover* (= it was not easy to win). ◇ *The other team didn't turn up so we had a walkover into the final.*

,walk 'through sth (*especially AmE*) **1** to practise or perform a play in a simple way, just using basic moves and positions **2** to practise a television programme without the cameras
◈ v + prep
▶ 'walk-through *n* [usually sing.] **1** a practice of a play without costumes or the objects you need, to practise basic moves and positions **2** a practice of a television programme without the cameras

,walk sb 'through sth (*AmE*) to show or tell sb how to do sth by carefully explaining or showing each part separately: *She walked me through the complicated document.* ◇ *He'll walk you through the procedure.*
SYN talk sb through sth
◈ v + n/pron + prep

,walk 'up (to sb/sth) to approach sb/sth in a confident way: *She walked straight up to the desk and asked to see the manager.*
◈ v + adv

wall /wɔːl/

,wall sth 'in to put a wall or a barrier around sth: *Apartment blocks walled in the playground completely.*
◈ v + adv + n ◆ v + n/pron + adv

,**wall sth 'off** to build a wall or a barrier around an area to separate it from another area: *Part of the yard had been walled off.*
NOTE **Wall sth off** is often used in the passive.
⬥ v + adv + n ♦ v + n/pron + adv

,**wall sb 'up** to keep sb as a prisoner in a place surrounded by walls: *a story of a woman who was walled up in a small room and left to die*
NOTE **Wall sb up** is often used in the passive.
⬥ v + adv + n ♦ v + n/pron + adv

,**wall sth 'up** to block a space with bricks or a wall so that it can no longer be used: *The entrance had been walled up in the 17th century.*
NOTE **Wall sth up** is often used in the passive.
⬥ v + adv + n ♦ v + n/pron + adv

wallow /'wɒləʊ; *AmE* 'wɑːloʊ/

'**wallow in sth** (*often disapproving*) to enjoy sth that gives you pleasure, especially when it is sth unpleasant and you do it in a way that makes other people think you enjoy being unhappy or want sympathy from them: *Stop wallowing in self-pity.* ◇ *She wallows in nostalgia for the past.*
OBJ **self-pity, nostalgia**
⬥ v + prep

waltz /wɔːls; *AmE* wɔːlts/

,**waltz 'off** (**with sth**) (*informal*) to leave a person or place in an annoying way, often taking sth without the owner's permission: *The tenants waltzed off with half our possessions.* ◇ *He just waltzed off and left me!*
SYN **walk away/off (with sth)**
⬥ v + adv

wander /'wɒndə(r); *AmE* 'wɑːn-/

,**wander 'off/a'way**; ,**wander 'from/'off sth** to leave the place where you ought to be, or the person or group of people you are with, without thinking about it: *Don't wander off and get lost.* ◇ *The child had wandered away from her mother.* ◇ *We had wandered off the path.*
⬥ v + adv ♦ v + prep

want /wɒnt; *AmE* wɑːnt, wɔːnt/

'**want for sth** (*formal*) (*usually used with a negative word*) to suffer because you do not have sth: *I work hard so that my children want for nothing.*
OBJ **little, nothing**
⬥ v + prep

,**want 'in** (**on sth**) **1** (*also* ,**want 'into sth**) (*informal, especially AmE*) to want to be involved in sth, especially a business deal: *Do you want in* (*on this project*)? ◇ *Does Jack want into the club?* **2** (*informal, especially AmE*) to want to come inside a place: *The cat wants in. Can you open the door?*
OPP **want out, want out of sth**
⬥ v + adv **1** also v + prep

,**want 'out**; ,**want 'out of sth 1** (*informal*) to no longer want to be involved in sth, especially a business deal: *I want out before we get into difficulties.* ◇ *I want out of this mess.* **OPP** **want in** (**on sth**), **want into sth 2** (*informal, especially AmE*) to want to go out of a place: *I want out of here.* **OPP** **want in**
⬥ v + adv ♦ v + adv + prep

ward /wɔːd; *AmE* wɔːrd/

,**ward sb/sth 'off** to prevent sb/sth dangerous or unpleasant from affecting or harming you: *She put up a hand to ward off the blows.* ◇ *I'm taking vitamin C to ward off a cold.* ◇ *He keeps dogs to ward off unwanted visitors.*
OBJ **evil, blows, criticism, danger**
⬥ v + adv + n ♦ v + n/pron + adv

warm /wɔːm; *AmE* wɔːrm/

'**warm to sb** to start to like a person: *I warmed to the teacher immediately.*
⬥ v + prep

'**warm to sth** to become more interested in or enthusiastic about sth: *The speaker was warming to his theme now.*
OBJ **theme, task, idea**
⬥ v + prep

,**warm 'up 1** (of the weather, the earth, etc.) to become warmer: *Research shows that the sea is warming up.* ◇ *When spring comes the earth begins to warm up.* **2** to do gentle exercise or practice to prepare for an athletic activity or a performance: *I'm always careful to warm up before I go jogging.* ◇ *Peter was warming up with a few scales.* **SYN** **limber up (for sth) 3** (of a machine, an engine, etc.) to run for a short time in order to reach the temperature at which it will operate well: *This computer takes a long time to warm up.*
⬥ v + adv

▶ '**warm-up** *n* [usually sing.] a series of gentle exercises or a short practice to prepare for an athletic activity or a performance: *What do you do as a warm-up?* ◇ *warm-up exercises*

,**warm 'up**; ,**warm sb/sth 'up 1** to become, or to make sb or a part of sb's body, feel warmer: *Come and warm up by the fire.* ◇ *They stamped their feet to warm them up.* **2** to become, or to make sb/sth, more lively or enthusiastic: *By midnight the party was only just warming up.* ◇ *His role is to warm up the audience before the main event.*
⬥ v + adv ♦ v + n/pron + adv ♦ v + adv + n

,**warm sth 'up 1** to make sth become warmer: *The fire had begun to warm the room up.* **2** to heat cooked food again before you eat it: *The soup just needs warming up.*
SYN **heat sth up**
⬥ v + n/pron + adv ♦ v + adv + n

warn /wɔːn; *AmE* wɔːrn/

,**warn sb/sth a'way** to tell a person, a ship, an aircraft, etc. not to come near a place because it is dangerous: *The male birds sing to warn other males away.* ◇ *An electric fence warned away anyone who came too close.*
◈ v + n/pron + adv ◆ v + adv + n

,**warn sb 'off**; ,**warn sb 'off sb/sth**; ,**warn sb 'off doing sth 1** to tell sb to leave or not to come near a place, often in a threatening way: *The farmer warned us off his land when we tried to camp there.* **2** to advise sb not to do sth or to stop doing sth: *He was warned off smoking after his first heart attack.* ◇ *She warned him off a career in acting.* ◇ *We were warned off renting the apartment.*
◈ v + n/pron + adv ◆ v + n/pron + prep

wash /wɒʃ; *AmE* wɑːʃ, wɔːʃ/

,**wash sb/sth a'way** if water, a wave, etc. **washes sb/sth away**, it removes or carries them/it away to another place: *A freak wave washed the two children away.* ◇ *The bridge was washed away by the floods.*
◈ v + n/pron + adv ◆ v + adv + n

,**wash sth a'way** to use water to remove a mark, dirt, etc. from sth: *She tried to wash away some of the dirt and blood from the boy's face.* ◇ *(figurative) A hot bath soon washed my tiredness away.*
◈ v + adv + n ◆ v + n/pron + adv

,**wash sth 'down 1** (**with sth**) to clean sth by using a large quantity of water: *I washed the car down with a hose.* **2** (**with sth**) to drink sth after, or at the same time as, eating food: *We washed our lunch down with iced tea.* ◇ *He had a huge plate of pasta washed down with several bottles of beer.* **3** (of a river, a flood, etc.) to carry sth downwards away from its original position: *Tons of earth had been washed down by the storm.*
◈ v + n/pron + adv ◆ v + adv + n

,**wash 'off**; ,**wash sth 'off**; ,**wash sth 'off sth** to be removed from the surface of sth or from a fabric by washing; to remove sth in this way: *However hard you rub, an ink stain won't wash off.* ◇ *Wash off the dirt with soap and water.* ◇ *Wash the mud off your boots before you go in.*
◈ v + adv ◆ v + n/pron + adv ◆ v + adv + n ◆ v + n/pron + prep

,**wash 'out**; ,**wash sth 'out**; ,**wash sth 'out of sth** to be removed from a fabric, hair, etc. by washing; to remove sth in this way: *The hair colour isn't permanent. It will wash out in a few weeks.* ◇ *Take care to wash all the shampoo out of your hair.*
◈ v + adv ◆ v + n/pron + adv ◆ v + adv + n ◆ v + n/pron + prep
▶ ,**washed 'out** *adj* (of fabric, clothes or colours) no longer brightly coloured, often as a result of

frequent washing: *Washed-out jeans were very fashionable at that time.*
→ see also WASHED OUT at WASH SB OUT; WASHED OUT at WASH STH OUT

,**wash sb 'out** to make sb very tired: *That long walk has washed me out.*
◈ v + n/pron + adv ◆ v + adv + n
▶ ,**washed 'out** *adj* (of a person) tired and pale: *You look washed out — go and rest.*
→ see also WASHED OUT at WASH OUT, WASH STH OUT, WASH STH OUT OF STH; WASHED OUT at WASH STH OUT

,**wash sb/sth 'out** (**to ...**), ,**wash sb/sth 'out of sth** (of water, a wave, etc.) to carry sb/sth away from their/its original position: *If you'd fallen in you would have been washed out to sea.*
◈ v + n/pron + adv ◆ v + n/pron + adv + prep

,**wash sth 'out 1** (**with sth**) to wash the inside of a container in order to remove dirt, etc: *He carefully washed the bottles out with disinfectant.* **2** if rain **washes out** a sports game, an event, etc. it makes it end early or prevents it from starting: *The game was washed out.* **3** (*AmE, formal*) to end sth: *Baltimore washed out the Indians' six-game win streak with an 8-3 win.*
◈ **1,3** v + n/pron + adv ◆ v + adv + n
     2 v + adv + n ◆ v + n/pron + adv
▶ ,**washed 'out** *adj* [only before noun] flooded; damaged by floods: *Washed-out towns are appealing for help.*
→ see also WASHED OUT at WASH SB OUT; WASHED OUT at WASH OUT, WASH STH OUT, WASH STH OUT OF STH
▶ '**washout** *n* (*informal*) **1** an event that stops early or does not happen, because of rain: *The game was a washout.* **2** an event that is a complete failure: *The party was a total washout.*

,**wash 'over sb 1** (*also* ,**wash 'through sb**) to suddenly affect sb very strongly: *A wave of guilt washed over her.* **2** (*informal*) to happen all around sb without affecting them: *All their criticism seems to wash over him.*
◈ v + prep

,**wash 'up** (*AmE*) to wash your hands and face: *I went to the men's room to wash up.*
◈ v + adv

,**wash 'up**; ,**wash sth 'up 1** (*BrE*) to wash dirty plates, glasses, etc. after a meal: *It's your turn to wash up.* ◇ *Don't forget to wash up the glasses as well.* **2** to be carried along in the water and then left on land; to carry sth along and leave it in this way: *A number of dead dolphins have washed up on the shore.* ◇ *His body was washed up on the beach two days later.*
◈ v + adv ◆ v + n/pron + adv ◆ v + adv + n
▶ ,**washed 'up** *adj* (*informal, especially AmE*) to be no longer successful and unlikely to succeed again in the future: *a washed-up cabaret singer*
▶ ,**washing-'up** *n* [U] (*BrE*) **1** the act of washing dirty dishes, glasses, etc. after a meal: *Don't*

forget to do the washing-up before you go out. ◇
washing-up liquid **2** the dirty dishes, glasses, etc.
that have to be washed after a meal: *a sink full of
washing-up*

waste /weɪst/

,waste a'way (of a person, part of the body, etc.)
to grow thin or weak in an unhealthy way: *He
was clearly wasting away.* ◇ *The muscles in her
arm had wasted away.*
◈ v + adv

watch /wɒtʃ; *AmE* wɑːtʃ, wɔːtʃ/

'watch for sb/sth 1 to look and wait for sth to
happen or for sb to come: *My parents were watching for me coming off the plane.* ◇ *Watch for the
sign.* **2** = WATCH OUT FOR SB/STH 1 *There are several points to watch for.*
◈ v + prep

,watch 'out (*spoken*) used to warn sb about sth
dangerous: *Watch out, there's a car coming!* ◇
He'll get in a terrible mess if he doesn't watch out.
SYN **look out**
◈ v + adv

,watch 'out for sb/sth 1 (*also* **'watch for
sb/sth**) to be quick to notice or be aware of
sb/sth, especially sb/sth that might cause you
trouble: *The staff were asked to watch out for
forged banknotes.* ◇ *Watch out for their striker; he
could cause us all sorts of problems.* **2** to be ready
to see sb/sth new or interesting: *Watch out for a
new feature in next month's magazine.*
SYN **look out for sb/sth**
◈ v + adv + prep ◆ v + prep

,watch 'over sb/sth (*formal*) **1** to take care of
sb/sth, by being near them; to protect or guard
sb/sth: *The child needed to be watched over 24
hours a day.* ◇ *He believed his mother was still
watching over him, even though she had died
when he was very young.* **SYN** **protect sb/sth**
(*more formal*) **2** to watch sb/sth carefully to make
sure that everything is done or happens correctly: *There is a committee to watch over each
different area of government policy.* **SYN** **super-
vise sb/sth** (*more formal*)
NOTE Watch over sb/sth can be used in the passive: *I don't like being watched over like a child.*
◈ v + prep

water /'wɔːtə(r); *AmE also* 'wɑːt-/

,water sth 'down 1 to make a liquid weaker by
adding water: *The beer had been watered down.*
OBJ **beer** **SYN** **dilute sth** (*more formal*) **2** to
change sth such as a speech, a piece of writing,
etc. to make it less strong and less likely to offend
people: *The criticisms had been watered down to
avoid giving offence.* **OBJ** **proposal** **SYN** **dilute
sth** (*more formal*)

NOTE Water sth down is often used in the
passive.
◈ v + adv + n ◆ v + pron + adv ◆ v + n + adv (*rare*)
▶ **watered 'down** *adj* **1** made weaker because
water has been added: *watered-down beer* **2**
made less strong or critical in order not to offend
people: *watered-down language* ◇ *It's a watered-
down version of the original proposal.*

wave /weɪv/

,wave sth a'round (*BrE also* **,wave sth a'bout**) if
you **wave** your arms, hands, etc. **around** in the
air, you move them violently about, often in
order to attract attention: *She ran out into the
yard, waving her arms about.* ◇ *Stop waving that
knife around!*
◈ v + n/pron + adv

,wave sth a'side/a'way to not accept sth
because you think it is not important or necessary: *Their protests were waved aside.* ◇ *He
waved away my question without trying to
answer it.*
OBJ **objection, protest** **SYN** **brush sth aside**;
dismiss sth (*more formal*)
◈ v + n/pron + adv ◆ v + adv + n

,wave sb/sth 'down to signal to sb/sth to stop, by
waving your hand: *We waited while Richard
waved down a taxi.* ◇ *The police had set up a
roadblock and waved several drivers down.*
OBJ **driver, taxi, vehicle** **SYN** **flag sb/sth down**
◈ v + n/pron + adv ◆ v + adv + n

,wave sb 'off to wave goodbye to sb as they leave:
*I waved the children off to school and went back
inside.*
◈ v + n/pron + adv ◆ v + adv + n

,wave sb/sth 'on to signal to sb/sth to go forwards, by waving your hand or arm: *The police
waved the traffic on.* ◇ *We stopped, but the cab
driver waved us on.*
◈ v + n/pron + adv ◆ v + adv + n

,wave sb/sth 'through; **,wave sb/sth
'through sth** to signal to sb to continue forwards through a gate or a barrier, by waving
your hand or arm: *The soldier gave us back our
passports and waved us through.*
◈ v + n/pron + adv ◆ v + adv + n ◆ v + n/pron + prep

wean /wiːn/

be 'weaned on sth to have learned about or
experienced sth from an early age: *I was weaned
on a regular diet of Hollywood fantasy.*
◈ be + v + prep

'wean sb/yourself off/from sth to make
sb/yourself gradually stop doing sth or using sth
that is bad or harmful: *The hospital managed to
wean her off the drug.* ◇ *The patch enables
smokers to wean themselves off cigarettes very*

gradually. ◇ *It can be extremely difficult to wean children off junk food.*
◆ v + n/pron + prep

wear /weə(r); *AmE* wer/ (*past* **wore** /wɔː(r)/**worn** /wɔːn; *AmE* wɔːrn/)

,wear a'way (*written*) if time **wears away**, it passes very slowly: *The afternoon was wearing away.*
⟨SYN⟩ **pass by**
◆ v + adv

,wear a'way; **,wear sth a'way** to become, or to make sth become thinner, smoother, etc. by continually using or rubbing it: *The picture on the coin had worn away.* ◇ *The steps had been worn away by the feet of thousands of visitors.*
◆ v + adv ♦ v + adv + n ♦ v + pron + adv ♦
v + n + adv (*rare*)

,wear a'way at sb/sth to slowly and gradually make sth thinner or smoother: *a drop of water wearing away at a stone* ◇ (*figurative*) *Stress can wear away at your ability to think straight.*
⟨OBJ⟩ **stone** ⟨SYN⟩ **erode sth** (*more formal*)
◆ v + adv + prep

,wear 'down; **,wear sth 'down** to become or to make sth become, gradually smaller, thinner, etc. by continuously using or rubbing it: *The tyres had worn right down.* ◇ *The path has been worn down in places to bare rock.*
◆ v + adv ♦ v + adv + n ♦ v + n/pron + adv

,wear sb/sth 'down to make sb/sth weaker or less determined, especially by continuously attacking or putting pressure on them/it over a period of time: *Constantly being criticized was wearing her down.* ◇ *to wear down sb's patience/resistance*
⟨SYN⟩ **grind sb down**
◆ v + adv + n ♦ v + pron + adv ♦ v + n + adv (*rare*)

,wear sth 'in (*BrE*) to wear boots or shoes for a short period of time until they become comfortable: *These boots were so comfortable they didn't need to be worn in at all.*
⟨OBJ⟩ **boots, shoes** ⟨SYN⟩ **break sth in**
◆ v + n/pron + adv ♦ v + adv + n

,wear 'off if a feeling or an effect **wears off**, it gradually disappears: *The effects of the medicine slowly wore off.* ◇ *Children love new toys, but the novelty soon wears off.*
◆ v + adv

,wear 'on (*written*) when time **wears on**, it passes in a way that seems slow: *As the evening wore on, she became more and more nervous.*
◆ v + adv

,wear 'out; **,wear sth 'out** to become, or to make sth become, thin or no longer able to be used, usually because it has been used too much: *Our*

carpets always seem to wear out quickly. ◇ *I wore out two pairs of boots on the walking trip.* ◇ (*figurative*) *Her patience finally wore out.*
◆ v + adv ♦ v + adv + n ♦ v + n/pron + adv
▶ **,worn 'out** *adj* badly damaged and no longer useful because it has been used a lot: *worn-out clothes/equipment*
→ *see also* WORN OUT *at* WEAR SB/YOURSELF OUT (WITH STH)

,wear sb/yourself 'out (with sth) to make sb/yourself extremely tired: *It's no good wearing yourself out by working so late.* ◇ *The kids have worn me out today.*
⟨SYN⟩ **tire sb out**; **exhaust sb** (*more formal*)
◆ v + n/pron + adv
▶ **,worn 'out** *adj* [not usually before noun] extremely tired: *I went to bed feeling worn out after the busy week.* ◇ *You look worn out!* ◇ *He died a worn-out man overcome by the injustices of life.*
→ *see also* WORN OUT *at* WEAR OUT, WEAR STH OUT

weary /'wɪəri; *AmE* 'wɪri/ (**wearies, weary- ing, wearied, wearied**)

'weary of sb/sth; **'weary of doing sth** (*literary*) to lose your interest in or enthusiasm for sb/sth: *As the day went on, we wearied of the long journey.*
⟨SYN⟩ **tire of sb/sth**, **tire of doing sth** (*less formal*)
◆ v + prep

weasel /'wiːzl/ (**-ll-**, *AmE* **-l-**)

,weasel 'out; **,weasel 'out of sth** (*informal, disapproving, especially AmE*) to avoid keeping a promise, doing your duty, etc: *What I did was wrong and I should be punished. I'm not going to try and weasel out.* ◇ *He's trying to figure out a way to weasel out of the deal.*
◆ v + adv ♦ v + adv + prep

weed /wiːd/

,weed sb/sth 'out to remove or get rid of sb/sth that you do not want from a group of people or things: *a plan intended to weed out poor teachers* ◇ *Weak or sick animals were weeded out.*
◆ v + adv + n ♦ v + n/pron + adv

weigh /weɪ/

,weigh a'gainst sb/sth (*formal*) to make sb less likely to achieve sth or to be successful: *The fact that he's had five jobs in two years will weigh against his application.*
⟨SYN⟩ **count against sb**
◆ v + prep

,**weigh sth a'gainst sth** to consider the importance or the advantages of sth compared to sth else: *Potential benefits need to be weighed against the obvious risks.*

▷SYN◁ **set sth against sth**

◈ v + n/pron + prep

,**weigh sb 'down** (**with sth**) to make sb feel anxious or depressed: *The responsibilities of the job are weighing her down.* ◇ *He was weighed down with grief.*

NOTE **Weigh sb down** is often used in the passive.

◈ v + adv + n ◆ v + pron + adv ◆ v + n + adv (*rare*)

,**weigh sb/sth 'down** (**with sth**) to put a heavy weight on sb/sth so that it is difficult for them to move easily: *We were weighed down with bags of shopping.* ◇ *The snow was weighing down the branches of the fir trees.*

▷SYN◁ **burden sb** (**with sth**)

NOTE **Weigh sb down** is often used in the passive.

◈ v + adv + n ◆ v + pron + adv ◆ v + n + adv (*rare*)

,**weigh 'in 1** (**at sth**) to have your weight measured, especially before a race, a competition, etc: *Both boxers weighed in at several pounds below their limit.* ◇ *Baby Sam weighed in at 4 kilos.* **2** (**with sth**) (*informal*) to join in a discussion, an argument, etc. by saying sth important or doing sth to help: *We all weighed in with helpful suggestions.*

◈ **1** v + adv

   2 v + adv ◆ v + adv + speech

▶ ,**weigh-in** *n* the occasion when the weight of a sports person such as a boxer is measured just before a fight, a race, etc: *The champion arrived five minutes late for the weigh-in*

'**weigh on sb/sth** (*also* '**weigh upon sb/sth** *more formal*) to make sb feel worried or depressed; to be a difficult duty or task for sb/sth: *The responsibilities are clearly **weighing heavily on his shoulders**.* ◇ *The debt burden weighs heavily on the government.*

▷SYN◁ **burden sb/sth**

◈ v + prep

,**weigh sth 'out** to measure a quantity of sth by weight: *Weigh out all the ingredients before you start making the cake.*

◈ v + adv + n ◆ v + pron + adv ◆ v + n + adv (*rare*)

,**weigh sb 'up** to form an opinion of sb by watching them or talking to them: *She stared at him, weighing him up.* ◇ *The two women weighed each other up for a few moments.* ◇ *He's certainly got Jeff weighed up.*

◈ v + adv + n ◆ v + pron + adv ◆ v + n + adv (*rare*)

,**weigh sth 'up** (**against sth**) to think carefully about a situation before you decide what to do: *I weighed up the pros and cons* (= the advantages and disadvantages) *of giving up my job.* ◇ *We have to weigh up whether we can afford a trip to*

Italy this year. ◇ *It's important to weigh up all possible courses of action.*

◈ v + adv + n ◆ v + pron + adv ◆ v + n + adv (*rare*)

'**weigh upon sb/sth** = WEIGH ON SB/STH

weight /weɪt/

,**weight sth 'down** (**with sth**) to add a weight to sth so that it feels very heavy, bends down, sinks, etc: *The canvas sheet was weighted down to stop it blowing away.* ◇ *My pockets were weighted down with lots of small coins.*

NOTE **Weight sth down** is often used in the passive.

◈ v + adv + n ◆ v + pron + adv ◆ v + n + adv (*rare*)

welch /weltʃ, welʃ/

'**welch on sb/sth** = WELSH ON SB/STH

weld /weld/

,**weld sb/sth 'into sth**; ,**weld sb/sth to'gether** to unite sb/sth into an effective whole: *The manager has welded the players into a strong team.* ◇ *The crisis helped to weld the community together.*

◈ v + n/pron + prep ◆ v + n/pron + adv

well /wel/

,**well 'up 1** if a liquid **wells up**, it rises to the surface and starts to flow: *Tears welled up in his eyes.* ◇ *Spots of blood began to well up on her skin.* **2** (**in/inside sb**) if an emotion **wells up**, you start to feel it very strongly: *She felt anger welling up inside her.*

◈ v + adv

welsh /welʃ/ (*also* welch)

'**welsh on sb/sth** (*informal, disapproving*) to not do sth that you have promised to do, for example to not pay money that you owe a person: *'I'm not in the habit of welshing on deals,' said Don.*

◈ v + prep

whale /weɪl/

'**whale into/on sb** (*AmE, informal*) to attack sb by hitting them again and again with great force: *Jo really whaled on Steve and was surprised he was still standing afterwards.* ◇ *I was so angry, I simply whaled into him.* ◇ (*figurative*) *She whaled into me for being late again.*

◈ v + prep

wheel /wiːl/

,**wheel a'round**; ,**wheel sb/sth a'round** (*BrE also* ,**wheel 'round**, ,**wheel sb/sth 'round**) (*literary*) to turn around very quickly to face the opposite direction; to make sb/sth do this: *I* *wheeled around to scream at Miles.* ◇ *He wheeled his horse around and started for home.*

[SYN] **spin around, spin sb/sth around**

◈ v + adv ♦ v + n/pron + adv

,**wheel sb/sth 'out** (*BrE, informal*) to produce sb/sth and use them to help you do sth, even though they have often been used before: *He wheels out the same old arguments every time he makes a speech.* ◇ *The company wheeled out some big guns* (= very important people) *to launch the new car.*

◈ v + n/pron + adv ♦ v + adv + n

while /waɪl/

,**while sth a'way** if you **while away** a period of time, you spend it in a pleasant, lazy way: *There were plenty of cafés in which to while away a pleasant evening.* ◇ *We whiled away the time at the airport reading magazines.*

◈ v + adv + n ♦ v + pron + adv ♦ v + n + adv (*rare*)

whip /wɪp/ (-pp-)

,**whip sth 'out**; ,**whip sth 'out of sth** to take sth out quickly and suddenly: *He whipped out his camera and started taking photos.*

◈ v + n/pron + adv ♦ v + adv + n ♦ v + n/pron + adv + prep

,**whip 'through sth** (*informal*) to do sth very quickly: *She whipped through the routine paperwork.*

◈ v + prep

,**whip sb/sth 'up** to deliberately make sb feel strong emotions or get excited about or interested in sth: *The studio audience was whipped up into a frenzy.* ◇ *They're trying to whip up support for their candidate.*

[OBJ] **crowd, support, resistance** [SYN] **stir sb/sth up; rouse sb/sth** (*more formal*)

◈ v + n/pron + adv ♦ v + adv + n

,**whip sth 'up 1** to prepare a meal or some food very quickly: *I can easily whip up an omelette.*

[SYN] **put sth together; throw sth together** (*informal*) **2** if the wind **whips up** dust, waves, etc. it makes it/them rise quickly: *The wind whipped up the sand in gusts.* [SUBJ] **wind**

◈ v + adv + n ♦ v + pron + adv ♦ v + n + adv (*less frequent*)

whisk /wɪsk/

,**whisk sb/sth a'way/'off** to remove sb/sth from a place very quickly: *The president was whisked away by his bodyguards.* ◇ *The food was whisked away before we had finished.*

◈ v + n/pron + adv ♦ v + adv + n

whittle /'wɪtl/

,**whittle sth a'way** to gradually reduce the size, importance or value of sth: *Inflation has been*

whittling away their savings. ◇ *Our lead* (= in a sports competition, for example) *was being gradually whittled away.*

◈ v + adv + n ♦ v + n/pron + adv

,**whittle sth 'down** to reduce the size or number of sth/sb gradually: *The government's majority has been whittled down to eight.*

[SYN] **reduce sb/sth**

◈ v + adv + n ♦ v + n/pron + adv

whizz (*especially BrE*) (*AmE usually* **whiz**) /wɪz/

,**whizz 'through sth** to do, read sth, etc. very quickly: *She whizzed through the work and was finished before lunch.*

◈ v + prep

whoop /wuːp; *AmE* wʊp/

,**whoop it 'up** (*informal*) **1** to enjoy yourself in a noisy and excited way: *I've been working hard while you've been whooping it up in Berlin.* **2** (*AmE*) to try to make people excited or enthusiastic about sb/sth

[SYN] **live it up**

[NOTE] **Whoop it up** cannot be used in the passive.

◈ v + it + adv

wig /wɪg/

,**wig 'out**; ,**wig sb 'out** (*AmE, slang*) to become, or to make sb, very excited or very anxious about sth; to go, or to make sb, crazy, often as a result of the effect of drugs

◈ v + adv ♦ v + n/pron + adv

wimp /wɪmp/

,**wimp 'out** (**on sb/sth**) (*informal, disapproving*) to decide not to do sth you had intended to do because you are too frightened: *Did you wimp out on any of the tests?* ◇ *Dave wimped out and refused to dive off the top board.*

[SYN] **bottle out, bottle out of sth, bottle out of doing sth; chicken out, chicken out of sth, chicken out of doing sth**

◈ v + adv

win /wɪn/ (**winning, won, won** /wʌn/)

,**win sb/sth 'back** to get again by your own efforts sb/sth that you had before: *I'm hoping to win back my place in the team soon.* ◇ *Jack had tried everything to win Martha back.* ◇ *You do have a chance to win your money back.*

◈ v + n/pron + adv ♦ v + adv + n

,**win 'out** (**over sb/sth**) (*informal*) if sth **wins out**, it is stronger or more successful than other things: *It is not clear if the archaeologists will win out over the builders and save the temple.*

[SYN] **prevail** (*more formal*)

◈ v + adv

,**win sb 'over** (*BrE also* ,**win sb 'round**) (**to sth**) to gain sb's support or approval, especially by persuading them that you are right: *My dad's against the idea, but I'm sure I can win him over.* ◇ *Jenny's parents were soon won over by Anthony's easy charm.*

SYN **bring sb round/around** (**to sth**)

✪ v + n/pron + adv ◆ v + adv + n

,**win 'through** to finally succeed after trying very hard: *We are faced with a lot of problems but we'll win through in the end.* ◇ *United won through to the final in an exciting game.*

✪ v + adv

wind /waɪnd/ (**wound, wound** /waʊnd/)

,**wind 'down 1** to relax, after a period of stress or excitement: *It takes a while for me to wind down after work.* SYN **unwind 2** if a machine **winds down**, it goes slowly and then stops: *The old clock had wound right down.* **3** if a business **winds down**, it gradually reduces the amount of work it does until it closes completely: *Next week the mill winds down for a summer break.*

✪ v + adv

,**wind sth 'down 1** to bring a business or an activity gradually to an end over a period of time: *The government is winding down its nuclear programme.* OBJ **business, programme** SYN **reduce sth** OPP **expand sth 2** to make the window of car open and go downwards by moving a handle, pushing a button, etc: *She wound down the driver's window and called to him.* OBJ **car window** SYN **open sth** OPP **wind sth up**

✪ v + n/pron + adv ◆ v + adv + n

,**wind 'up**; ,**wind 'up doing sth** (*informal*) to find yourself after a long time in a particular place or situation: *I always said she would wind up in jail.* ◇ *Bill wound up marrying the girl next door!* ◇ *If he isn't more careful, he'll wind up dead.*

SYN **end up, end up doing sth; finish up, finish up doing sth**

NOTE In this meaning, **wind up** is nearly always used with either an adjective, a phrase beginning with a preposition, or *doing sth*.

✪ v + adv

,**wind 'up**; ,**wind sth 'up 1** to bring sth such as a speech, a meeting or a discussion to an end: *Before I wind up, I'd like to make one final point.* ◇ *If we all agree, let's wind up the discussion.* **2** to make sth mechanical work by turning a handle several times: *Does this clock have a battery or does it wind up?* ◇ *This is a great little toy. You just wind it up and off it goes!*

✪ v + adv ◆ v + adv + n ◆ v + n/pron + adv

▶ '**wind-up** *adj* [only before noun] a **wind-up** mechanism is one that you operate by turning a handle several times: *a wind-up clock/toy*

,**wind sb 'up** (*BrE, informal*) **1** to deliberately make sb very angry or annoyed: *Are you deliberately winding me up?* ◇ *Ignore them. They're just trying to wind you up.* SYN **annoy sb** (*more formal*) **2** to tell sb sth that is not true in order to make a joke: *Come off it, you're winding me up!* SYN **tease sb**

✪ v + n/pron + adv ◆ v + adv + n

▶ '**wind-up** *n* (*BrE, informal*) sth that sb says or does in order to annoy sb or to make a joke: *It sounded so crazy I thought it was a wind-up.*

,**wind sth 'up 1** to close a business, a company, etc: *The company was wound up last year.* OBJ **business, company 2** to close a car window, making it move upwards, by turning a handle, pressing a button, etc: *I wound up the window and locked the door.* OBJ **car window** OPP **wind sth down**

✪ v + adv + n ◆ v + n/pron + adv

▶ ,**winding-'up** *n* the act of officially closing a business, a company, etc: *a voluntary winding-up of the company* ◇ *a winding-up order/petition*

wink /wɪŋk/

'**wink at sth** to pretend that you have not noticed sth, especially sth bad or illegal: *The authorities have chosen to wink at the illegal trade.*

✪ v + prep

winkle /'wɪŋkl/

,**winkle sb/sth 'out**; ,**winkle sb/sth 'out of sth** (*BrE*) to get sb/sth out of somewhere slowly and with difficulty: *The bird uses its sharp beak to winkle insects out of tree trunks.* ◇ *The terrorists have been winkled out of their hiding place.* ◇ *Leila had been working in the library all the week, so we sent Tim to winkle her out.*

✪ v + n/pron + adv ◆ v + adv + n ◆
v + n/pron + adv + prep

,**winkle sth 'out**; ,**winkle sth 'out of sb** (*BrE*) to get sth such as information, money, etc. from sb with difficulty: *She's very good at winkling out secrets.* ◇ *He wouldn't tell you? Don't worry, I'll winkle it out of him.*

✪ v + n/pron + adv ◆ v + adv + n ◆
v + n/pron + adv + prep

wipe /waɪp/

,**wipe sth a'way** to remove sth, such as dirt or tears, with a cloth or your hand: *Wipe away mud splashes with a wet cloth.* ◇ *He wiped away a tear.* OBJ **tear**

✪ v + adv + n ◆ v + n/pron + adv

,**wipe sth 'down** to clean a surface with a cloth: *I'll just wipe the table down before you put your books there.*

✪ v + n/pron + adv ◆ v + adv + n

,wipe sth 'off; **,wipe sth 'off sth 1** to remove
sth from a surface with a cloth: *Wipe off any surplus glue with a rag before it dries.* ◇ *Tom had
carefully wiped his fingerprints off the glass.* **2** to
remove sth that has been recorded on a tape or a
video tape: *He wiped the conversation off the tape.*
3 to reduce the value of sth, especially shares:
*Over £5 billion was wiped off share values world-
wide today.*
◈ v + n/pron + adv ♦ v + adv + n ♦ v + n/pron + prep

,wipe 'out (on sth) (*informal, especially AmE,
sport*) to fall or crash in a sport, especially to fall
from a board (a **surfboard**) when you are riding
the waves: *I caught a huge wave but then wiped
out on the next.*
◈ v + adv
▶ **'wipe-out** *n* (*informal, especially AmE, sport*) a
fall or a crash, especially a fall from a board (a
surfboard) when you are riding on waves: *I had
so many bad wipe-outs while I was learning to
surf.*

,wipe sb 'out 1 (*informal*) to defeat sb easily in a
sports competition: *The Welsh side was wiped out
24-3.* **2** (*informal, especially AmE*) to make sb
very tired: *All that travelling wiped her out.* **3**
(*slang*) to murder sb
◈ v + n/pron + adv ♦ v + adv + n
▶ **,wiped 'out** *adj* [not before noun] (*informal*)
very tired

,wipe sb/sth 'out to kill large numbers of people
or animals: *The whole village was wiped out by
the flood.* ◇ *Pollution has wiped out half the species of fish in the river.*
NOTE Wipe sb/sth out is often used in the
passive.
◈ v + adv + n ♦ v + n/pron + adv

,wipe sth 'out 1 to destroy sth completely: *The
disease has been virtually wiped out.* ◇ *The government is trying to wipe out drug trafficking.* **OBJ**
memory 2 to remove information from a computer, writing from a board, etc: *The virus could
wipe out your hard disk.* ◇ (*figurative*) *I'll never
be able to wipe out the memory of that day.* **OBJ**
disease 3 to remove or deal with a debt completely: *He secured a loan to wipe out the club's
debts.* ◇ *Their lead was wiped out* (= destroyed)
by four goals in ten minutes. ◇ *This year's losses
have wiped out last year's profits.* **OBJ** profits,
debts
◈ v + adv + n ♦ v + n/pron + adv

,wipe 'up; **,wipe sth 'up** (*BrE, informal*) to dry
dishes with a cloth: *You wash and I'll wipe up.*
SYN dry up, dry sth up; dry, dry sth
◈ v + adv ♦ v + n/pron + adv ♦ v + adv + n

,wipe sth 'up to clean a substance, especially a
liquid, from a surface with a cloth: *Keep a cloth
handy to wipe up any mess.*
◈ v + adv + n ♦ v + n/pron + adv

wire /'waɪə(r)/

,wire sb/sth 'up (to sth) to connect sb/sth to a
piece of electrical equipment by using electrical
wires: *You will be wired up to a machine which
will record your heartbeat.* ◇ *The police suggested
I should be wired up* (= to record the conversation) *before I met the dealer.* ◇ *The band's instruments were all wired up for sound.* ◇ *The
microphone hadn't been wired up properly.*
NOTE Wire sb/sth up is often used in the passive.
◈ v + adv + n ♦ v + n/pron + adv

wise /waɪz/

,wise 'up (to sth) (*informal, especially AmE*) to
understand sth better; to become aware of the
unpleasant truth about a situation: *Employees
should wise up about how the industry works.* ◇
*You need to wise up to the fact that he's never com-
ing back.* ◇ *Wise up! Try and see her for what she
really is.* ◇ *You need to wise up to how serious this
situation is.*
◈ v + adv

wish /wɪʃ/

,wish sb/sth a'way to try to get rid of sth by
wishing it did not exist; to wish that sb was somewhere else: *These complications can't just be
wished away, you know.* ◇ *Don't wish your life
away* (= said to sb who spends a lot of time looking forward to sth that is going to happen in the
future).
◈ v + n/pron + adv ♦ v + adv + n

'wish sb/sth on sb (*also* **'wish sb/sth upon sb**
more formal) (*used in negative sentences, especially with* ***wouldn't***) to hope very much that sth
unpleasant will happen to sb or that they will
have to deal with sb unpleasant: *I wouldn't wish
this pain on my worst enemy.* ◇ *I wouldn't wish
my daughter on anyone at the moment — she's
very difficult!*
◈ v + n/pron + prep

wither /'wɪðə(r)/

,wither a'way to become less or weaker, especially before disappearing completely: *All our
hopes just withered away.* ◇ *They predicted that
the bad schools would wither away.*
◈ v + adv

wolf /wʊlf/

,wolf sth 'down (*informal*) to eat sth very
quickly, especially in large quantities: *He wolfed
down his breakfast and rushed out of the house.*
SYN gobble sth down/up
NOTE Wolf sth is also sometimes used with this
meaning: *wolfing tea and cakes*
◈ v + adv + n ♦ v + n/pron + adv

wonder /ˈwʌndə(r)/

'wonder at sth to be very surprised by sth: *He wondered at her beauty.* ◇ *She wondered at her own stupidity.* ◇ ***It's hardly to be wondered at** that he behaves as he does, considering his family background.*
SYN marvel at sth
NOTE Wonder at sth can be used in the passive.
◈ v + prep

work /wɜːk; *AmE* wɜːrk/

~ against	~ out
~ around	343 ~ over
~ around to	~ round
~ at	~ round to
~ away	~ through
~ in	~ to
~ into	~ towards
~ off	~ up
~ on	344 ~ up to

work a'gainst sb/sth if sth **works against** sb/sth, it has the effect of making it harder for sb to do or achieve sth: *The engineering career structure works against women.* ◇ *The government's new policy has worked against the interests of small farmers.*
◈ v + prep

work a'round sth (*BrE also* **work 'round sth**) to find a way of doing what you want to in spite of situations, rules, etc. that could prevent you doing it: *If we can't get rid of the problem, we'll just have to work round it.* ◇ *He urged the two sides to work around their disputes and reach an agreement.* ◇ *My uncle couldn't read, but he'd found ways to work around it because he was too embarrassed to tell anyone.*
◈ v + prep

work a'round to sth (*BrE also* **work 'round to sth**) to gradually turn a conversation towards a particular topic: *I wondered when he would work around to the subject of money.*
◈ v + adv + prep

'work at sth; **'work at doing sth** to make great efforts to achieve sth or do sth well: *She worked hard at her French and passed the exam.* ◇ *You've got to work at losing weight.* ◇ *You've got to work at it.*
NOTE Work at sth/at doing sth can be used in the passive: *Marriage has to be worked at.*
◈ v + prep

work a'way (at sth) (*often used in the progressive tenses*) to continue to work hard for a period of time: *I've been working away in the gym, trying to get fit.* ◇ *Ruth spends hours in the library, working away at Japanese.*
◈ v + adv

work sth 'in; **work sth 'into sth 1** to add one substance to another and mix them together: *Work the butter in with your fingers.* ◇ *Use plenty of polish and work it well into the wood.* **2** to try to include sth in a piece of writing, a speech, etc: *Try and work in something about your own experience.* ◇ *He usually manages to work something topical into his act.*
◈ **1** v + n/pron + adv ♦ v + adv + n ♦ v + n/pron + prep **2** v + adv + n ♦ v + n/pron + adv ♦ v + n/pron + prep

work yourself 'into sth to become very angry, excited, etc: *She's working herself into a state about the exams.* ◇ *He was working himself into a rage.*
→ *see also* WORK SB UP, WORK YOURSELF UP
◈ v + pron + prep

'work off sth (of a machine, a piece of electrical equipment, etc.) to use a supply of power or another machine in order to operate: *The lighter works off the car battery.*
◈ v + prep

'work sth 'off 1 to get rid of sth by physical effort: *He went for a run to work off some calories* (= the food that he had eaten). ◇ *By the time she had finished cleaning, she had worked off her anger.* **2** to earn money in order to pay off a debt; to work for the person you owe money to: *They worked off their huge bank loan over five years.* **3** if you **work off** a punishment, etc., you do what you have been told to do because you have done sth wrong or committed a crime: *Grima has started to work off his eight-match suspension.*
◈ v + adv + n ♦ v + n/pron + adv

'work on sb to try to persuade sb to agree to sth or to do sth: *My father hasn't said he will lend me the car yet, but I'm working on him.*
◈ v + prep

'work on sth 1 to be busy with a particular activity, project, piece of research, etc: *What are you working on at the moment?* ◇ *The committee worked on ways to raise money for the project.* ◇ *Tara is currently working on a solo album.* **2** to practise or work hard in order to improve sth: *Your designs are great, but you need to work on them a bit more.* ◇ *You need to work on your technique* (= for example, in a sport). ◇ *Jack's been working on building up his confidence.* ◇ *'Have you sorted things out with your parents yet?' 'No, but I'm working on it* (= I'm trying hard to do this).' **3** to consider that sth is true when you are saying or doing sth, planning sth, etc: *We are **working on the assumption** that everyone invited will come.* ◇ *The police are working on the theory that she was attacked by somebody she knew.*
◈ v + prep

'work 'out 1 to happen or develop in a particular way, especially a successful way: *I'm glad my plan worked out* (= was successful). ◇ *Their marriage didn't work out* (= was not successful). ◇ *It is all working out very well.* ◇ *Don't worry now,*

everything will work out all right in the end. **2 (at sth)** if sth **works out** at sth, you calculate that it will be a particular amount: *The rent works out at £50 a week each.* ◊ *It'll* **work out cheaper** *to go by bus.* NOTE **Work out** is often used with *cheaper, more expensive,* etc. in this meaning **3** to train the body by physical exercise: *I try and work out two or three times a week.* **4** if a sum, a mathematical problem, etc. **works out,** it gives a result: *The equation won't work out if* x *is negative.*
◈ v + adv
▶ **'workout** *n* a period of physical exercise: *I did a two-hour workout in the gym.*

,**work sb 'out** (*especially BrE*) to understand sb's character: *I've never been able to work my mother out.*
SYN **figure sb out**
NOTE **Work sb out** cannot be used in the passive.
◈ v + n/pron + adv ◆ v + adv + n (*rare*)

,**work sth 'out 1** to calculate sth: *You'll have to work out the costs involved.* ◊ *Can you work out the answer to number 2?* ◊ *I worked out that we owe him £30.* ◊ *Let me pay for now and we'll work it out later.* OBJ **cost, answer** SYN **figure sth out 2** to find the answer to a question or sth that is difficult to understand or explain: *I couldn't* **work out how** *Jack had got there so quickly.* ◊ *We worked out that we were second cousins.* ◊ *Can you work out what's going on?* ◊ *The game was fairly simple once we'd worked out the rules.* SYN **figure sth out** NOTE **Work sth out** is often used with *how, where, why,* etc. in this meaning. **3** to plan sth; to think of sth: *I've worked out a better way of doing it.* ◊ *The details still have to be worked out.* OBJ **details, plan, way 4** to organize sth or deal with problems in a satisfactory way: *Ed and Jane seem to have* **worked things out** *between them.* SYN **sort sth out 5** to continue to work at your job until the end of the period of time mentioned: *They didn't make me work out my notice* (= the period of time that is officially fixed before you can leave your job). ◊ *He didn't want to work out the rest of his years in an office.* **6** to remove all the coal or metal from a mine: *Most of the mines had been worked out.* SYN **exhaust sth** NOTE **Work sth out** is often used in the passive in this meaning.
◈ v + n/pron + adv ◆ v + adv + n

,**work itself 'out** if a problem **works itself out,** it gradually stops being a problem without anyone having to do anything: *Did you think everything would just work itself out?*
SYN **sort itself out**
◈ v + pron + adv

,**work sb 'over** to attack sb physically and injure them, either as a punishment or to get information from them: *They sent the boys round to work him over.*
◈ v + n/pron + adv ◆ v + adv + n

,**work 'round sth** (*BrE*) = WORK AROUND STH

,**work 'round to sth** (*BrE*) = WORK AROUND TO STH

,**work 'through** to work without stopping for a particular period of time: *At harvest time we work through until it gets dark.*
◈ v + adv

,**work 'through;** ,**work 'through sth 1** to start to have an effect somewhere: *These pressures have worked through to the staff.* ◊ *The full effects of the change will take time to work through the system.* **2** to move or pass through sth gradually until you reach a particular point: *I started at page one and slowly* **worked my way through** *to the end.* ◊ *You shouldn't try to work through the course too fast.* ◊ *Allow time for the drug to work through your body.*
◈ v + adv ◆ v + prep

,**work 'through sth 1** to experience a problem, a difficult situation, etc., and deal with it until you eventually find a solution: *to work through grief/emotions* ◊ *Counselling is helping him work through this trauma.* ◊ *The situation was difficult for the family, but they were able to work through it and come out the other side.* **2** (*also* **work sth 'through** *less frequent*) to think or talk about sth carefully until you can find a solution: *If you are having problems in your relationship, take time to work through it with your partner.* ◊ *Work the problem through together.*
◈ **1** v + prep
2 v + prep ◆ v + n/pron + adv (*less frequent*)

'**work to sth** to follow a plan, etc: *We're working to a very tight schedule.* ◊ *They have to work to a budget.*
◈ v + prep

,**work to'wards sth** (*also* ,**work to'ward sth** *especially AmE*) to try to reach or achieve a goal: *She's working towards her PhD.* ◊ *The two groups are working towards the same end.* ◊ *Jo's working towards obtaining a Master's degree.*
◈ v + prep

,**work sb 'up;** ,**work yourself 'up (into sth)** to gradually make sb/yourself become very upset, angry or excited about sth: *She had worked herself up into a rage.* ◊ *He worked the crowd up into a frenzy.* ◊ *You've worked yourself up into a state again. Try and relax.*
◈ v + n/pron + adv ◆ v + adv + n
▶ ,**worked 'up (about sth)** *adj* [not before noun] (*informal*) very excited, upset or angry about sth: *What was Ben so worked up about?* ◊ *I can't get at all worked up about cars* (= I am not interested in or excited by cars). ◊ *She gets terribly* **worked up** (= nervous) *about exams.*

,**work sth 'up 1** to gradually develop or increase sth until you have enough: *We jogged up the hill to work up an appetite.* ◊ *I can't work up much enthusiasm for this subject.* ◊ *She soon worked up a sweat.* **2** (**into sth**) to spend time and effort on a piece of work in order to improve or complete it: *The idea needs a lot of working up.* ◊ *You could work up this idea into a story.* ◊ *Some of the sketches were worked up into paintings.*
◆ v + adv + n ♦ v + n/pron + adv

,**work 'up to sth 1** to gradually prepare for and move towards sth that is more exciting or extreme: *He started slowly and worked up to running ten miles a day.* ◊ *The tension works up to a climax towards the end of the film.* **2** to prepare yourself to do sth difficult or unpleasant: *I haven't told him yet but I'm working up to it.* ⟨SYN⟩ **build up** (**to sth**)
◆ v + adv + prep

worm /wɜːm; *AmE* wɜːrm/

,**worm your way/yourself 'into sth** (*informal, disapproving*) to gradually make sb like or trust you, especially in order to gain an advantage for yourself: *Somehow he managed to worm his way into her confidence.*
⟨OBJ⟩ **confidence, affections, heart**
◆ v + n/pron + prep

,**worm sth 'out of sb** (*informal*) to manage to obtain information from sb, often by asking them questions in a clever way for a long period of time: *It took me days to worm the truth out of my daughter.*
◆ v + n/pron + adv + prep

worry /'wʌri; *AmE* 'wɜːri/ (**worries, worrying, worried, worried**)

'**worry at sth** (*often used in the progressive tenses*) **1** if an animal such as a dog **worries at sth,** it holds it in its teeth and shakes it about: *a dog worrying at a bone* ◊ (*figurative*) *She worried at the knot in the string* (= with her fingers). **2** to think or talk about a problem and try to find a solution: *He lay awake all night, worrying at the problem.*
◆ v + prep

wrap /ræp/ (**-pp-**)

,**wrap sth a'round sb/sth** (*BrE also* ,**wrap sth 'round sb/sth**) to put sth firmly around sth/sb: *He wrapped his arms tightly around my waist.* ◊ *A long scarf was wrapped round her neck.*
◆ v + n/pron + prep

,**wrap 'up**; ,**wrap it 'up** (*slang*) used to tell sb rudely to stop talking and be quiet: *Oh wrap up and let somebody else say something!*
◆ v + adv ♦ v + it + adv

,**wrap 'up** (**in sth**), ,**wrap sb 'up** (**in sth**), ,**wrap yourself 'up** (**in sth**) to put warm clothes, etc. on yourself/sb: *Wrap up warm — it's really cold outside.* ◊ *I wrapped the twins up before letting them go out.* ◊ *We were all well wrapped up against the weather.* ◊ *I wrapped myself up against the cold.*
⟨SYN⟩ **bundle up, bundle sb up** (**in sth**)
◆ v + adv ♦ v + n/pron + adv ♦ v + adv + n

,**wrap sth 'up 1** (**in sth**) to cover sth in a layer of paper or other material, either to protect it or because you are giving it to sb as a present: *I wrapped the vase up in tissue paper.* ◊ *It took all the evening to wrap up the kids' Christmas presents.* ◊ (*figurative*) *There's a simple explanation wrapped up in all those long words.* ⟨SYN⟩ **do sth up** (**in sth**) ⟨NOTE⟩ **Wrap sth** is often used with this meaning. **2** to complete sth in a satisfactory way: *The discussions should be wrapped up by Friday.* ◊ *Well, I think that just about wraps it up for today.*
◆ v + n/pron + adv ♦ v + adv + n
▸ '**wrap-up** n (*especially AmE*) **1** a short summary of what has gone before, especially at the end of a news broadcast: *And to close, here is a wrap-up of today's developments.* **2** the final actions that complete sth: *the wrap-up of the campaign*

be ,wrapped 'up in sb/sth to be so involved in a person or an activity that you do not notice other people or what is happening around you: *He was so wrapped up in his book that he didn't notice me leaving.* ◊ *Julia is completely wrapped up in her children.*
◆ be + v + adv + prep

wrench /rentʃ/

,**wrench sth 'off**; ,**wrench sth 'off sth** to remove sth from sth by force with a strong twisting movement: *The tug of the rope nearly wrenched my arm off.* ◊ *He wrenched the picture off the wall and threw it to the ground.*
◆ v + n/pron + adv ♦ v + adv + n ♦ v + n/pron + prep

wrest /rest/

'**wrest sth from sb/sth** (*formal*) **1** to take sth such as power or control from sb/sth with great effort: *The rebels tried to wrest control of the town from government forces.* **2** to take sth from sb that they do not want to give, suddenly or violently: *The officer managed to wrest the gun from his grasp.*
◆ v + n/pron + prep

wrestle /'resl/

'**wrestle with sth** to struggle to deal with sth difficult: *Farmers are wrestling with the problem of the wet weather.* ◊ *He spent several more weeks* *wrestling with his conscience and then finally decided to resign.* ◇ *He wrestled with the reins as the horse galloped towards the cliff edge.*

SYN **grapple with sth**

✦ v + adv + prep

wriggle /ˈrɪɡl/

,wriggle 'out of sth; ,wriggle 'out of doing sth *(informal)* to avoid doing sth unpleasant or sth that you do not want to do by making clever excuses: *to wriggle out of your responsibilities* ◇ *I've got an appointment I can't wriggle out of.* ◇ *Don't let Tom wriggle out of helping you.*

✦ v + adv + prep

wring /rɪŋ/ (wrung, wrung /rʌŋ/)

'wring sth from sb = WRING STH OUT OF/FROM SB

,wring sth 'out to remove water or other liquid from a cloth, etc. by twisting it tightly and squeezing it: *Rinse the cloth and wring it out well.* ◇ *My clothes got so wet I could wring the water out!*

✦ v + n/pron + adv ◆ v + adv + n

'wring sth out of/from sb to obtain sth from sb with difficulty, especially by putting pressure on them: *She eventually wrung an apology out of him.* ◇ *A few concessions were wrung from the government.*

✦ v + n/pron + prep

write /raɪt/ (wrote /rəʊt/ written /ˈrɪtn/)

,write a'way (to sb) (for sth) = WRITE OFF/AWAY *I wrote away to the company for a free sample.*

,write 'back (to sb) to write in reply to sb's letter: *I wrote and apologized, but he never wrote back.* ◇ *The school wrote back to me saying that all the courses were full.*

✦ v + adv

,write sth 'down (in/on sth) **1** to write sth on paper so that you do not forget it: *I wrote her address down in my notebook.* ◇ *There is a handout so you needn't write all this down.* SYN **take sth down 2** *(business)* to reduce the value of what a company owns when stating it in the company's accounts: *All stock over six months old was written down to 50%.*

✦ v + n/pron + adv ◆ v + adv + n

▶ 'write-down *n (business)* a reduction in the value of what a company owns, etc.

,write 'in (to sb/sth) to write a letter to an organization to state an opinion or to ask a question: *Write in to the programme and tell us your own opinion on this.* ◇ *500 viewers wrote in to complain about the advertisement.*

✦ v + adv

write sb/sth 'in *(AmE)* to add an extra name to a list of candidates in an election so that you can vote for them: *She wrote Carrasco in on the ballot*

paper. ◇ *Workers were handing out sample ballots with their candidate's name written in.*

✦ v + n/pron + adv ◆ v + adv + n

▶ 'write-in adj *(AmE)* a vote for sb who is not an official candidate in an election, in which you write their name on your voting paper: *He qualified as a write-in in 15 states.* ◇ *a write-in candidate/vote*

,write sb/sth 'in; ,write sb/sth 'into sth to add a character or a scene to a play, a film/movie, a regular series, etc: *Why did you write the plane crash in?* ◇ *It was the first time a disabled child had been written into a TV soap.* ◇ *He wrote himself into the history books by becoming the first player to win the championship five times.*

OPP **write sb/sth out, write sb/sth out of sth**

✦ v + n/pron + adv ◆ v + adv + n ◆ v + n/pron + prep

,write sth 'in; ,write sth 'into sth to include sth such as a special rule or a condition in a document, a contract, an agreement, etc: *A yearly visit to both families was written into their marriage contract.*

✦ v + n/pron + adv ◆ v + adv + n ◆ v + n/pron + prep

,write 'off/a'way (to sb) (for sth) to write to an organization or a company, asking them to send you sth: *She wrote off to an agency for advice.*

SYN **send off (for sth), send away (for sth)**

✦ v + adv

,write sb/sth 'off (as sth) to consider that sb/sth is a failure or not important: *Don't write John off too soon — he may surprise you!* ◇ *I wrote off my symptoms as tiredness.*

✦ v + n/pron + adv ◆ v + adv + n

▶ 'write-off *n* [sing.] *(informal)* a failure; a time when you do not achieve anything: *Today has been a write-off as far as work is concerned.*

→ *see also* WRITE-OFF at WRITE STH OFF

,write sth 'off **1** *(business)* to cancel a debt; to recognize that sth is a failure, has no value, etc: *All outstanding Third World debts should now be written off.* **2** *(BrE)* to damage a vehicle so badly that it is not worth spending money to repair it: *That's the third car he's written off this year.*

✦ v + n/pron + adv ◆ v + adv + n

▶ 'write-off *n* **1** *(business)* an act of cancelling a debt and accepting that it will never be paid: *a £4.9 billion debt write-off* **2** *(BrE, informal)* a vehicle that is so badly damaged that it is not considered worth repairing: *They escaped with minor injuries but the van was a write-off.*

→ *see also* WRITE-OFF at WRITE SB/STH OFF (AS STH)

,write sb/sth 'out; ,write sb/sth 'out of sth to remove a character, a scene, etc. from a play, a film/movie, a regular series, etc: *He got bored and asked to be written out of the series.* ◇ *The censor demanded that the scene be written out.*

OPP **write sb/sth in, write sb/sth into sth**

✦ v + n/pron + adv ◆ v + adv + n ◆
v + n/pron + adv + prep

,**write sth 'out** to write sth on paper clearly, including all the details: *Use symbols and abbreviations instead of writing things out in full.* ◊ *I wrote out the poem in my best handwriting.* ◊ *I watched him write out a cheque for five thousand pounds for her.*

NOTE In informal spoken language **write sb out sth** is also used: *He wrote her out a cheque.*

◈ v + adv + n ♦ v + n/pron + adv

,**write sb 'up** (*AmE*) to report sb in writing because they have done sth illegal: *He wrote me up for illegal parking.*

◈ v + n/pron + adv ♦ v + adv + n

,**write sth 'up 1** to write sth in a complete and final form, especially from notes that you have made: *She writes her lecture notes up every night before going out.* **OBJ** **notes**, **research**, **experiment 2** to write a review of a play, a concert, a book, etc. for a newspaper or magazine: *She wrote the movie up in glowing terms.*

◈ v + n/pron + adv ♦ v + adv + n

▶ '**write-up** *n* a review of a concert, a play, a book, etc. in a newspaper or magazine: *The concert got a good write-up in all the papers.*

Yy

yank /jæŋk/

'yank at sth to pull at sth hard and quickly:
Someone yanked at my hair.
◆ v + prep

,yank sth 'off; ,yank sth 'off sth to remove sth
by pulling it quickly and hard: *He yanked off his
shoes. ◇ She yanked the lid off the tin.*
◆ v + adv + n ◆ v + n/pron + adv ◆ v + n/pron + prep

,yank sb/sth 'out; ,yank sb/sth 'out of sth
(*informal*) to remove sb/sth from somewhere by
pulling hard and quickly: *He was yanked out of
the house and bundled into a car.*
◆ v + n/pron + adv ◆ v + n/pron + adv + prep

yearn /jɜːn; AmE jɜːrn/

'yearn for sb/sth (*literary*) to want sb/sth very
much, especially when this is difficult to get:
Mira yearned for a child.
⟨SYN⟩ **long for sb/sth**
◆ v + prep

yell /jel/

,yell 'out; ,yell sth 'out to suddenly shout sth in
a loud voice: *She was yelling out in terror. ◇ He
yelled out the names of the winners.*
◆ v + adv ◆ v + adv + n ◆ v + n/pron + adv ◆
v + adv + speech

yield /jiːld/

'yield to sth (*formal*) to be replaced by sth:
*Barges yielded to road vehicles for transporting
goods.*
◆ v + prep

'yield sth 'up (*formal*) **1** to allow sb else to take
sth that you own and feel is very important for
you: *He swore he would never yield up the castle to
the English.* **2** to reveal sth that has been hidden:
*A thorough search of the site yielded up only a few
ancient coins.*
◆ v + adv + n ◆ v + n/pron + adv

Zz

zero /'zɪərəʊ; AmE 'zɪroʊ, 'ziː-/ (**zeroes, zero-**
ing, zeroed, zeroed)

,zero 'in on sb/sth 1 to aim weapons at sb/sth:
They zeroed in on the target. ◇ (*figurative*) *Clare*
zeroed in on Craig (= went to talk to him) *as soon*
as he entered the room. **2** to fix all your attention
on sb/sth: *Wasting no time she zeroed in on the*
main topic.
◆ v + adv + prep

zip /zɪp/ (-pp-)

,zip 'through sth to do, read, etc. sth very
quickly: *Could you zip through my report and*
check it's OK?
◆ v + prep

,zip 'up; **,zip sb/sth 'up** to be fastened with a
zip/zipper (= a device consisting of two rows of
metal or plastic teeth that you can pull together
or pull apart); to fasten sth with a zip/zipper: *The*
skirt zips up at the side. ◇ *Will you zip me up* (=
my dress), *please?* ◇ *I can't zip my jacket up!*
◆ v + adv ◆ v + n/pron + adv ◆ v + adv + n
▶ **'zip-up** *adj* [only before noun] fastened with a
zip/zipper: *a zip-up jacket*

zone /zəʊn; AmE zoʊn/

,zone sth 'off (**for sth**) to keep an area of land to
be used for a particular purpose: *The city centre*
has been zoned off for pedestrians.
◆ v + adv + n ◆ v + n/pron + adv

,zone 'out (*AmE, slang*) to stop thinking or
noticing what is going on around you: *Relax your*
muscles, take a deep breath, and zone out for a
while.
〉SYN **space out, space sb out** (*slang*)
◆ v + adv
▶ **'zone-out** *n* a time when you stop thinking or
noticing what is going on around you
▶ **,zoned 'out** *adj* (*AmE, informal*) unable to
think or to notice what is going on around you
because of the effects of drugs or alcohol

zonk /zɒŋk/

,zonk 'out; **,zonk sb 'out** (*slang, especially*
AmE) to fall asleep, become unconscious or
unable to think, either because you are very
tired or because of the effects of drugs or
alcohol; to make sb do this: *He zonked out after*
the big exam. ◇ *I usually zonk out about 11 p.m.*
◆ v + adv ◆ v + n/pron + adv
▶ **,zonked 'out** *adj* (*slang, especially AmE*) sleeping, unconscious, or unable to think, especially
from the effects of drugs or alcohol: *I feel totally*
zonked out after the day's work.

zoom /zuːm/

,zoom 'in/'out (**on sb/sth**) if a camera **zooms**
in/out, it shows the object that is being photo-
graphed from closer/further away, by using a
special lens (a **zoom lens**): *The camera zoomed in*
on her beautiful eyes.
◆ v + adv

,zoom 'off (*informal*) to hurry away: *He jumped*
into his car and zoomed off.
◆ v + adv

GUIDE to the PARTICLES

Introduction

This Guide deals with the main categories of meaning of the particles that occur most frequently in the verbs in this dictionary. Knowing something about the different meanings of particles can help you learn and understand how phrasal verbs or combinations of verbs and particles are formed and help you understand new ones when you meet them.

When you look at verbs used with a particular particle, you can see that one particle can have several different meanings. The most obvious starting point is the basic or literal meaning of the particle since it often combines with verbs to produce a meaning that you can easily recognize. For example, the basic meaning of the particle **down** involves movement from a higher position to a lower position. It can be used in combination with a verb as a preposition: '*He **climbed down** the mountain.*', or as an adverb: '*What are you doing up there? **Come down** at once!*' '**Put** the book **down** there.*' This meaning of **down** can help you to understand its more figurative use in other verbs. For example, **down** can be used to express the related ideas of making something lower, or reducing something, (for example *Turn down that radio*), keeping something low (*to **keep down** the rate of inflation*), or removing somebody or something from a powerful position (for example, *to **bring down** the government.*)

What this also shows is that there is a system to the way phrasal verbs are formed. In other words, the combination of particles and verbs is to a large extent systematic and not totally random. It also explains how new phrasal verbs come to be created and can be easily understood by everybody. For example, the phrasal verb *to rule something in*, meaning to include something, is a relatively new expression which you might hear. It was created in contrast to the phrasal verb *to rule something out*, meaning to exclude something. Both these phrasal verbs are related to the meaning of their particles, **out** suggesting excluding and **in** suggesting including. (You can find more about new verbs on page S20 − 21.)

As this last example shows, particles which have opposite meanings, such as **up** and **down** , **in** and **out** , **on** and **off** , can form phrasal verbs which have opposite meanings as well. For example, the opposite of *to turn on* is *to turn off*. However, there are exceptions. The opposite of *to put on your clothes* is *to take off your clothes*. The particles **on** and **off** are opposite in meaning, but combine with different verbs to produce phrasal verbs with opposite meanings.

The meanings of particles that you will find in this Guide are only the main meanings, usually figurative, that occur in groups of verbs. After the explanation of the meaning, some verbs belonging to the group are given, first the ones that appear in the examples, and then a few other important verbs, arranged in alphabetical order. The examples that have been chosen to illustrate each meaning show you the most frequent contexts. You will find that sometimes one phrasal verb appears in more than one category, for example, *build up* in 'Increasing' and 'Creating and constructing', reflecting two different senses of the verb. For more information on how each verb in the lists is used, you should look the verb up in the dictionary.

ABOUT

About is used in approximately 120 verbs (2%) in this dictionary, as an adverb and a preposition. It is often used to show the connection between the verb and its object, for example *talk about something, worry about something*. In some of the verbs, the particles **around** and, especially in British English, **round** can be used instead of **about** without changing the meaning. The most common categories of meaning are:

Moving in different directions

About can be used to indicate that you are moving here and there or making rough or violent movements. The verb shows what kind of movement it is. Example verbs are:

run about   **crash about**   **throw about**

1 The kids love *running about* in the park.
2 I can hear someone *crashing about* upstairs.
3 She got very angry and started *throwing* things *about* the room.

Around and **round** can usually be used with the same meaning. You can also add **about** to a variety of other verbs to make a similar meaning: for example, *jump about, scatter about*.

Doing nothing

About is used with many verbs that suggest you are spending your time in a lazy way. Other verbs refer to a silly way of behaving.

hang about   **wander about**   **mess about**

1 Groups of youths were *hanging about* the shopping centre with nothing to do.

2 We spent the afternoon *wandering about* the town and looking in shop windows.
3 Stop *messing about* and start doing your homework.

Around and **round** can usually be used with the same meaning. You can also add **about** to a variety of other verbs to make a similar meaning: for example, *faff about, muck about, potter about*.

Making something happen

About is used with some verbs to indicate something happening or somebody making something happen. Example verbs are:

come about   **bring about**   **set about**
go about   **see about**

1 More and more people are deciding to retire early. How has this *come about*?
2 What do you think has *brought about* this change in public opinion?
3 In the afternoon he *set about* cleaning the kitchen.

Surrounding and enclosing

About can be used with some verbs to give the idea of something going around something and surrounding or enclosing it.

throw about   **gather about**

1 She *threw* her arms *about* me and hugged me tightly.
2 He *gathered about* him a group of people with the same political views.

Around and **round** are more common with this meaning.

AROUND

Around is used in approximately 280 verbs (5%) in this dictionary, as an adverb and a preposition. Its basic meaning is of movement in a circle or curve to face in the opposite direction or to arrive at the other side of something, for example, *spin around, turn around, go around*. **Round** is often used instead of **around**, especially in British English. **About** is also sometimes used. In verb plus particle combinations, the most common categories of meaning are:

Moving in different directions

Around is used with some verbs to indicate movement in different directions or to

many different places. Example verbs are:

run around   **dance around**   **shop around**

1 The playground was full of children *running around* and shouting.
2 She was so happy when she got her results that she started *dancing around* the room.
3 You have to *shop around* if you want to find the best products at the lowest prices.

Round and **about** can be used in these verbs except *shop around*. **Around** can be used with many other verbs with a similar meaning: *blunder around, bustle around, rush around, crash around*, etc.

Doing nothing

Around can be used in verbs that suggest that you are spending your time in a lazy way. Other verbs refer to a silly way of behaving. Example verbs are:

hang around   fool around   mess around

1 They spend their time *hanging around* the streets.
2 You can't take her seriously because she is always *fooling around*.
3 Stop *messing around* and find something useful to do.

About can also be used with these verbs.

Surrounding and enclosing

Around can be used with some verbs to suggest surrounding someone or something.

crowd around   throw around   cluster around

1 People *crowded around* the entrance waiting for her to come out.
2 She rushed up to him and *threw* her arms *around* his neck.

Round can also be used with these verbs.

Being centred on something

Around is used as a preposition with some verbs to suggest the idea of something having a particular idea, object, etc. as its centre or focus. Example verbs are:

centre around   revolve around pivot around

1 Her whole life is *centred around* her research.
2 Their social life *revolves around* going to parties.

Avoiding

Around with verbs can be used to indicate that you are avoiding something.

skirt around   get around   skate around work around

1 He *skirted around* the issues without discussing any of them in depth.
2 We'll have to find a way of *getting around* the problem.

AT

At is a preposition used in 87 verbs (1½%) in this dictionary. It is a common word in English and is often used to show where something or somebody is in space or time. It has two main meanings in verb and particle combinations:

Aiming and directing

At is used with many verbs to give the idea of aiming or directing something at someone or something. Example verbs are:

laugh at   look at   stare at   talk at aim at   nag at   wonder at

1 I felt everybody was *laughing at* me so I left the room.
2 When I entered the room she was *looking at* the painting.
3 She *stared at* me in amazement when I

told her the news.
4 He *talked at* us rather than involve us in what he was saying.

Attacking, striking and holding

At can be used with verbs to give the idea of trying to attack, hit or hold someone or something. Example verbs are:

strike at   fly at   grab at   get at

1 He *struck at* me several times with a knife but missed.
2 She lost her temper and *flew at* them, punching and kicking.
3 She *grabbed at* my coat and pulled me back from the edge of the cliff.
4 My parents are always *getting at* me (= criticizing me) for not finishing my college course.

AWAY

Away is used in 210 verbs (3%) in this dictionary, as an adverb. The basic meaning of **away** indicates movement to a different place and it can be used with most verbs of

movement, for example, *go away, run away, hurry away, drive away*. **Off** can be used instead of **away** with a similar meaning. **Away** often combines with another particle, particularly **from**, for example *run away from*, *walk away from*, *do away with*. The most common uses of the particle with verbs are as follows:

Avoiding and not doing something

Away is used with some verbs to show that somebody is avoiding a person, a place or a situation or is stopping being involved in something. Example verbs are:

keep away   **look away**   **back away**
walk away from   **shrink away**   **stay away**

1 *Keep away* from the edge of the cliff - you might fall.
2 I looked at her but she *looked away*.
3 He moved towards her and she *backed away* in alarm.
4 You can't just *walk away from* every difficult situation.

Separating

Away is used with some verbs giving the meaning of becoming separated from something or from a group of people or of making this happen.

come away   **break away**   **call away**
peel away   **sheer away**   **strip away**

1 The handle of the bag *came away* in my hand.
2 They *broke away* from the rest of the group and started to explore the area on their own.
3 The doctor was *called away* from the meeting to attend to a patient.

Removing

Away is used with some verbs to give the idea of removing something from a particular place because you no longer want or need it, or of destroying something.

throw away   **frighten away**   **do away with**
blast away   **drive away**   **give away**

1 This is all rubbish. Please *throw* it *away*.
2 He is so rude and aggressive that he *frightens* customers *away*.

3 We need to *do away with* old and outdated laws.

Disappearing

Away is used with some verbs to give the idea of something disappearing gradually.

die away   **fade away**   **waste away**
wear away   **pass away**   **pine away**

1 The shouts and cheers gradually *died away* as the President stood up to speak.
2 The excitement of the day began to *fade away* as night fell.
3 The animal was *wasting away* through illness and lack of food.
4 The rock had been *worn away* by the action of the sea.
5 She *passed away* (= died) peacefully in her sleep.

Storing and hiding

Away can be used with some verbs to convey the idea of putting something in a place either to keep it safe or to stop people finding it. Example verbs are:

put away   **file away**   **tidy away**
hide away   **clear away**   **lock away**

1 *Put away* your books – you won't need them for the rest of the lesson.
2 All the records relating to the case have been *filed away*.
3 Can you *tidy away* everything on the floor.
4 The letter was *hidden away* where no one would find it.

Working hard or continuously

Away can be used to indicate that you are doing something, especially working hard or doing something difficult or boring, for a long period of time. Example verbs are:

slog away   **work away**   **slave away**
bang away   **beaver away**   **plod away**

1 I've been *slogging away* at this for days and I still haven't finished.
2 He spent hours *working away* at the problem.
3 She has been *slaving away* at the report all day.

BACK

Back is an adverb and is used in 175 verbs (3%) in this dictionary. The basic meaning of this particle is returning to the place where you were before or to an earlier time. Many verbs of movement use **back** with this meaning, for example *walk back*, *drive back*.

The other most common uses are:

Returning something

Back can be used to convey the idea of giving or taking something back to the place it came from. It can also mean reacting or replying to someone in a similar way to the way they have acted or spoken.

take back   give back   write back
call/ring back   fight back

1 I *took* the clock *back* to the shop because it broke after a few days.
2 Have you *given back* all the money you borrowed from him?
3 You must *write back* and thank her for her letter.

Moving backwards; being behind or at a distance

Back can be used with verbs to give the idea of moving away from the front or edge of something or of being at a distance from something. Example verbs are:

fall back   stand back   keep back
pull back   push back

1 The British runner tried to catch up, but *fell back* and finished fifth.
2 Please *stand back* and let the people get off the train.
3 *Keep back*! The bomb may explode at any moment.

Not making progress

Back in some combinations suggests being kept or held in a position without making any progress. Example verbs are:

hold back   set back   keep back

1 I feel I'm being *held back* in class. I want to move faster.
2 The fire at the office *set* the project *back* several months.

Repeating

Back can be used in verbs that express the idea of doing something again.

play back   go back over
read back   call/phone back

1 Can you *play back* the recording once more? I missed part of it.
2 I think we need to *go back over* it so that all the details are clear in our minds.
3 Can you *read* that *back* to me? I want to be sure that you wrote it down correctly.

Regaining

Back in combinations can be used with the idea of getting again something that was lost or of recovering from something.

win back   get back   bounce back   claw back
ease back   grow back   snap back

1 We were very lucky. We *won back* all the money we had lost.
2 I don't think I will ever *get back* all those books I lent him.
3 She's feeling a bit down at the moment, but she'll soon *bounce back*.

Being under control

Back in combinations often means reducing something or keeping something such as an emotion under control. Example verbs are:

cut back on   force back   choke back
bite back   hold back

1 You need to *cut back on* the number of cigarettes you smoke.
2 He tried to *force back* the urge to punch him on the nose.
3 She *choked back* the tears as she told us what had happened.

Looking at the past

Back can be used to talk about the past.

date back   go back   take back
look back   think back

1 This castle *dates back* to the 12th century.
2 John and I are great friends. We *go back* a long way.
3 This music *takes* me *back* to the years I lived in Paris.

DOWN

Down is used in about 310 verbs (7%) in this dictionary, mainly as an adverb. It often has meanings that are the opposite of **up**. The literal meaning is movement in a downwards direction, moving from a higher to a lower position, for example, *climb down, bend down, fall down*. Many combinations of a verb and **down** refer to somebody putting something on a surface, for example, *bang down, lay down*. It is also used to express figurative ideas related to downward movement, such as decreasing, being reduced or failing. As an adverb it combines with some prepositions to make three-word verbs such as *get down to*, *look down on*, *come down with*. The most common uses of **down** are:

Falling and destroying

This use of the particle is most closely connected to the literal meaning of **down**, and suggests something or somebody falling to the ground and being destroyed or suffering damage. Examples of verbs are:

pull down	burn down	tear down
knock down	run down	beat down

1 The builders were in the process of *pulling down* a wall.
2 The whole forest was *burnt down*.
3 The protesters *tore down* the barriers.
4 He was *knocked down/run down* by a car.

Reducing

Down is used in many verbs that express the idea of something decreasing in amount, strength, speed, cost, importance, etc., or of somebody making something do this. Examples of verbs are:

turn down	bring down	calm down come down
play down	cut down	die down narrow down
put down	run down	slow down wear down

1 Can you *turn* the music *down*, please? It's deafening.
2 We have to *bring down* our costs in order to remain competitive.
3 Please *calm down* – there's no need to get so excited about it.
4 Fortunately his temperature is starting to *come down*.
5 The government are trying to *play down* the importance of the meeting.

Suppressing

Down can be used with verbs to express the idea of keeping somebody or something under control or ending something, often using authority or force. Examples of verbs are:

keep down	clamp down	come down on
break down	crack down	pin down

1 The government is trying to *keep down* wage demands.
2 The police are going to *clamp down on* motorists who break the speed limit.

3 The teacher said he would *come down* hard *on* anyone he caught cheating.

Defeating

Down can be used to express the idea of defeating someone or something or being defeated in an argument, a competition, etc.

bring down	put down	vote down
back down	shout down	stare down

1 The aim of the rebels is to *bring down* the government.
2 The rebellion was quickly *put down* by troops loyal to the president.
3 Her proposal for stricter safety measures was *voted down*.
4 The government *backed down* over the idea of increasing taxes.

Failing

Down can be used to express the idea of something stopping, failing or not working properly. Examples of verbs are:

break down	close down	turn down
let down	wind down	

1 The car *broke down* on the way to the coast.
2 The company was making huge losses and in the end was forced to *close down*.
3 She applied for the job but was *turned down*.
4 My PC has never *let* me *down*.

Fixing

Down can be used with the idea of fixing something firmly to something else. Example verbs are:

tie down	nail down	strap down
batten down	screw down	stick down

1 Make sure you *tie* everything *down* so that the wind doesn't blow it away.
2 This floorboard needs *nailing down* before it causes an accident.
3 Everything on the boat was *strapped down* so it wouldn't be lost in a storm.

Recording in writing

Down is used with verbs meaning writing or copying to give the idea of recording something in writing. Examples of verbs are:

write down	get down	note down
jot down	copy down	put down
set down		

1 Could you *write* it *down* for me, please?
2 He was speaking too fast for me to *get* it *down* on paper.

3 I'll *note/jot down* the things we have to do before Sunday.

Eating

Down is used with some verbs to describe ways of eating or drinking. Example verbs are:

gulp down   gobble down   bolt down

FOR

For is a preposition, used in about 115 verbs (2%) in this dictionary. It is one of the most common words in English. It often combines with verbs to link the verb and its object, for example, ask for something, *pay for* something. It has two common meanings when used with verbs:

Aims and purposes

For can be used to refer to the aim or purpose of an action or to where you are going. Example verbs are:

**apply for   press for   live for
make for   head for**

1 I've *applied for* more than twenty jobs in the past month.
2 We're *pressing for* a change in the way animals are transported to markets.
3 I *live for* my children. They are the most

IN

In is used in about 380 verbs (6½%) in this dictionary, as an adverb and a preposition. The basic meaning is (being) contained inside something or somewhere, or movement from outside to inside. It is often the opposite of **out**. The preposition **into** can also be used with verbs of movement (*Please come in. She came into the room in a hurry.*) The most common uses are:

Entering

In is used with many verbs with the literal meaning of entering somewhere, for example, go in, come in, walk in, invite in. (**Into** has similar uses).

**break in   get in   let in   ask in
breeze in   drop in   squeeze in**

1 Thieves *broke in* and stole all the paintings.
2 I'll never understand how they *got in*

**keep down   stay down   wash down
wolf down**

1 She was in such a hurry she had to *gulp down* her coffee.
2 'This is delicious,' he said as he *gobbled down* another piece of cake.

important thing in my life.
4 We're *making for* Edinburgh and hope to be there by tonight.

States and actions in relation to other people

For can be used with some verbs to show how you feel about somebody or something, or to show how you are dealing with a person or a situation. Example verbs are:

**feel for   fall for   fear for
root for   care for   stand up for**

1 I really *feel for* her. She has lost all her family in the past year.
2 I *fell for* her the moment I saw her and two years later we were married.
3 When we heard the sound of gunfire we all *feared for* our lives.
4 Good luck, we'll be *rooting for* you.

without anyone noticing.
3 That'll be Stuart at the door. Can you *let him in*?

Arriving

In can be used in verb plus particle combinations that refer to a person, a vehicle, etc. arriving at a particular place.

**clock in   check in   pull in
draw in   flood in**

1 What time do you have to *clock in* in the morning?
2 Our flight is delayed so there is no hurry to *check in*.
3 We arrived at the station just as the train *pulled in*.

Absorbing

In can be used with certain verbs to give

the idea of absorbing something.

take in   **sink in**   **drink in**
breathe in   **soak in**

1 We had to try and *take in* a lot of information in a very short period of time.
2 It was only after a few minutes that the awful truth started to *sink in*.
3 For the first few minutes I *drank in* the atmosphere of the place.

Including

In can be used with some verbs that give the idea of adding or mixing something in something else, or of including something with something else. Example verbs are:

stir in   **throw in**   **take in**
blend in   **fold in**

1 *Stir in* the ingredients gradually until all of them have been used.
2 If you buy the car I'll *throw in* the radio for free.
3 While we're in London we could *take in* a visit to the theatre or the opera.

Putting inside or between

In can be used with some verbs, giving the idea of one thing being put into or going into another. Example verbs are:

plug in   **put in**   **key in**   **lay in**
pump in   **punch in**   **type in**

1 First you have to *plug* it *in* and then you switch it on.
2 I'd like to *put* some money *in* my bank account.
3 I need someone to *key in* all this information on my computer.

Beginning; introducing something new

In can be used in verbs that give the idea of something starting or of somebody introducing something new.

set in   **bring in**   **phase in**
creep in   **usher in**

1 The cold weather has started to *set in*.
2 The government wants to *bring in* stricter laws to protect the environment.
3 The new production scheme will be *phased in* gradually.

Collecting

In can be used in combinations that refer to collecting things. Example verbs are:

gather in   **get in**   **pull in**
fetch in   **pack in**

1 They *gathered in* the grapes ready for making wine.
2 It's starting to rain. I'd better *get* the washing *in*.
3 The band have been *pulling in* the crowds wherever they perform.

Filling and completing

In is used in some combinations that refer to filling a drawing, a shape, a hole etc. with something and completing it. Other similar verbs refer to writing something somewhere.

colour in   **fill in**   **pencil in**
block in   **ink in**   **shade in**

1 Listen, children. When you have finished your drawing you can *colour* it *in*.
2 I'd like you to *fill in* this form
3 I'll *pencil in* next Wednesday for a meeting.

Taking part

In is used with many verbs to suggest the idea of joining an activity and being involved in something. Sometimes the involvement of the person is not welcome.

join in   **go in for**   **call in**
meddle in   **interfere in**   **jump in**
pitch in   **want in**

1 Why don't you *join in* and have some fun? Everybody's dancing.
2 She decided to *go in for* the competition because she had a good chance of winning.
3 The police were *called in* to investigate the robbery.
4 I don't like you *meddling in* my affairs.

Interrupting

In can be used with verbs to express the idea of someone interrupting a conversation or a meeting when the interruption is not wanted or welcome.

cut in   **barge in**   **break in**

1 She *cut in* while I was talking in order to make her own suggestions.
2 We were talking quietly in the kitchen when he *barged in* and said he wanted a drink.
3 'I'm sorry, but I simply can't agree with that,' he *broke in*.

Limiting

In can be used in combinations that refer to somebody being prevented from leaving a place. Example verbs are:

snow in   block in   lock in
box in   fence in   hem in

1 No planes are flying out today. We are completely *snowed in*.
2 Look at that! Someone has parked their car so close to mine and *blocked* me *in*.
3 Some prisoners are *locked in* for twenty three hours a day.

Staying inside

In can be used in combinations that mean remaining inside or at home instead of going out somewhere. The particle **out** can be used with the same verbs with the opposite meaning. **In** is also used with verbs meaning that you remain in bed later than you usually do. Example verbs are:

stay in   eat in   sleep in   lie in   stop in

1 We decided to *stay in* and watch a film on television.
2 Why don't we *eat in* tonight instead of going out for a meal?
3 I was so tired I *slept in* until 11.

Damaging, destroying, falling

In is used in combinations that mean damaging or destroying things, especially by making them fall inwards. Other verbs refer to things falling inwards.

smash in   kick in   cave in

1 The car door was completely *smashed in*.
2 The police *kicked in* the door and entered the apartment.
3 The whole building is going to *cave in* at any moment.

Stopping doing something

In is used in combination with some verbs that mean stopping trying to resist something or giving up something such as your job. Example verbs are:

give in   throw in   cave in   jack in

1 We will never *give in* to threats of violence.
2 I sometimes feel like *throwing* it all *in* and looking for a job abroad.

INTO

Into is a preposition and it is used in 260 verbs (4%) in this dictionary. The literal meaning of **into** is movement from the outside of something to the inside, so it is used with many verbs that give the idea of of entering something, for example, *He walked into the room*. It is often used in the same verbs and with the same meanings as the adverb **in**, for example, *burst in* (on sb), *burst into* (a place). The particle can also be used in verbs that express metaphorical meanings, for example, changing or being transformed. The most common uses are:

Entering

Into is used in many combinations meaning to enter somewhere. Example verbs are:

break into   get into   check into
crowd into   invite into

1 Burglars *broke into* my house last night and stole all my video equipment.
2 He *got into* the car and drove off.
3 We *checked into* the hotel.
4 Everybody *crowded into* the room to listen to the Minister speak.
5 She *invited* us *into* her room.

Out of is often used with similar verbs as an opposite, for example *get out of*, *check out of*.

Putting in, going in

Into is used in many combinations referring to putting or going in or inside something.

plug into   tuck into   pay into
bore into   dip into

1 You can *plug* the TV *into* the socket in the wall.
2 She never wears her blouse *tucked into* her skirt.
3 I need to *pay* some money *into* my bank account.

Combining

Into is used in combinations that mean mixing one substance into another so that they become one. Example verbs are:

blend into   shade into   mix into
fade into   fold into

1 *Blend* the cream *into* the sauce.
2 The scarlet of the bird's wings *shades into* pink at the tips.

Transforming and changing

Into can be used to describe things that change or are transformed. Example verbs are:

turn into   grow into   make into   change into

1 The discussion soon *turned into* an argument about politics.
2 She *grew into* a very loving person.

Persuading and forcing

Into is used with some verbs to convey the idea of persuading or making someone do something that they do not really want to do. The verb describes the way you try to persuade somebody. Example verbs are:

talk into   press into   frighten into
force into   shame into   starve into

1 She *talked* me *into* going on holiday with her.
2 I was *pressed into* giving a speech at her farewell dinner.
3 He was *frightened into* confessing the crime.

Out of is often used with these verbs with the opposite meaning: *talk somebody out of something*.

Hitting and meeting

Into can be used with verbs that describe objects hitting one another, and to describe people meeting by accident.

crash into   run into   bump into

1 The car left the road and *crashed into* a tree.
2 I *ran into* Steve (= met him by chance) the other day. He hasn't changed at all.

Investigating

Into can be used with some verbs that give the idea of investigating something in detail in order to discover the truth.

go into   look into   delve into   dig into

1 The third chapter of the book *goes into* the subject in great detail.
2 The police are *looking into* the matter.

Starting

Many combinations with **into** suggest starting doing something, often suddenly.

burst into   plunge into   rush into   get into

1 She *burst into* tears.
2 The aircraft *burst into* flames.
3 The country was *plunged into* recession.

OF

Of is a preposition. It occurs in 55 verbs (almost 1%) in this dictionary. When it is used in verb plus particle combinations it shows the relationship between the verb and somebody or something that is involved in the action. The different kinds of relationship are shown below:

Communicating and interpreting

Of with some verbs shows that a particular piece of information or knowledge is being communicated to or interpreted by somebody. Example verbs are:

hear of   know of   make of
remind of   speak of

1 I'm sorry, I've never *heard of* him.
2 I *know of* the place but I've never been there.
3 What do you *make of* her most recent paintings?

Characteristics and qualities

Of can be used with verbs to show the characteristics or qualities of someone or something, or what something contains.

smell of   remind of   make of   consist of

1 This soap *smells of* spring flowers.
2 The piece of music *reminds* me *of* holidays in Greece.
3 It's *made of* cheese and potatoes.

Removing, lacking

Of can be used with some verbs to indicate something is being removed from someone or something or that they do not have something. Example verbs are:

rob of   starve of   deprive of
dispose of   strip of

1 They *robbed* me *of* everything I was carrying with me.
2 She was *starved of* affection during her childhood.

OFF

Off is used in about 520 verbs (8½%) in this dictionary, as an adverb and a preposition. It has a wide variety of meanings. It is often used with verbs of movement to indicate movement away from a place, for example, *run off, dash off, hurry off, march off*, where the verb shows how somebody departs. **Off** can sometimes be replaced by **away** in this meaning. The most common uses are:

Departing
The particle **off** can be used to give the idea of somebody starting a journey or leaving a place or of making somebody or something do this. Example verbs are:

set off   take off   see off   make off
clear off   blast off   head off   start off

1 We *set off* at four in the morning to climb the mountain.
2 What times does the plane *take off*?
3 He came to *see* us *off* at the airport.
4 The robbers *made off* in a blue car.

Starting
Off in combinations can also suggest that something is beginning. Example verbs are:

start off   spark off   kick off
lead off   touch off

1 The day *started off* well, but gradually got worse.
2 Small things can sometimes *spark off* a row between people.

Ending; not happening
Some verbs can be used with **off** to give the idea of something ending or being cancelled. Example verbs are:

break off   ring off   put off   call off
cut off   log off   switch off

1 The unions have decided to *break off* their negotiations with management.
2 I'm afraid he *rang off* before I had a chance to ask him what his name was.
3 We've *put off* the meeting till the end of next week.

Finishing completely
Off can be used with some verbs to emphasize that something is completely finished. Often these are verbs that can also be used on their own with a similar, but weaker, meaning. Example verbs are:

finish off   pay off   sell off   go off
polish off   round off   work off

1 I'd like to *finish off* what I'm doing before I go home.
2 Our aim is to *pay off* all our debts by the end of the year.
3 They decided to *sell off* their entire stock and invest in a new range of products.
4 The demonstration *went off* quietly without any serious incidents.

Becoming less
Off can be used with some verbs to express the idea of something gradually decreasing in strength or effect. Example verbs are:

wear off   level off   cool off   fall off
die off   ease off   tail off

1 The pain started to return when the effect of the drugs began to *wear off*.
2 The rate of inflation was rising dramatically but now it has started to *level off*.
3 We need time to *cool off* (= become less hot) and have a shower before lunch.

Rejecting or dismissing
Off is used with some verbs to suggest the idea of rejecting, dismissing or trying to ignore somebody or something. Example verbs are:

write off   lay off   shrug off
laugh off   brush off   shake off

1 I know he hasn't been playing very well recently, but we can't *write* him *off*.
2 The company has had to *lay off* several hundred workers.
3 It's only a cold. I'll soon *shrug* it *off*.
4 She tried to *laugh off* the whole matter, but I knew that it worried her terribly.

Resisting
Some verbs using the particle **off** indicate that you are trying to stop something happening or trying to protect somebody or yourself from something harmful or unpleasant. Example verbs are:

fight off   hold off   ward off   beat off
fend off   keep off   stave off   warn off

1 I am doing everything I can to *fight off* another attack of flu.
2 We can't *hold off* the enemy much longer.
3 He put up his hand to *ward off* the blows.

Removing

Off is used with some verbs to give the idea of removing something from somewhere, for example by cutting or chopping. Some combinations of verbs have the idea of removing someone from your responsibility.

cut off	cross off	take off
palm off on	bump off	rub off

1 I had to *cut* a bit *off* the top of the photo.
2 I think we can *cross* them *off* our list. I'm sure they won't come to the party.
3 *Take off* those dirty boots before you come into the house.
4 Don't *palm* your visitors *off on* me – you should entertain them yourself.

Dividing and separating

In these combinations **off** indicates that one area is divided or separated from another, for example with a barrier, to stop somebody or something going into it.

block off	fence off	seal off
curtain off	divide off	shut off

1 The police *blocked* the road *off* to prevent anyone from entering the city.
2 The field was *fenced off* to stop animals eating the crops.
3 The area has been *sealed off* to stop the spread of contamination.

Being absent from work or school

Off can be used with some verbs to talk about not going to work or school or leaving early. Example verbs are:

take off   skive off   slip off   bunk off

1 She *took* three weeks *off* (work) to be with her sick mother.
2 As a teenager he was always *skiving off* school.

Drawing attention

Off occurs in combination with some verbs that indicate that someone is drawing attention to themselves or their opinions in some way. Other combinations describe how something draws attention to something else

or makes it easy to see. Example verbs are:

show off   set off   sound off   mouth off

1 Ignore him. He's just *showing off* in front of the girls.
2 I think the white background is ideal for *setting off* the rich colours of the painting.

Using

Off can be used with some verbs to talk about things that are used, such as money, food, etc. Example verbs are:

live off   feed off   run off   work off

1 Although he's nearly thirty he still *lives off* his parents.
2 The birds *feed off* the meat that has been left behind by the lions.
3 You can *run* the CD player *off* a battery.

On can also be used with these verbs with a similar meaning.

Exploding

This group of verbs is used for things such as weapons, that explode or are fired.

set off   blast off   go off   let off   fire off

1 The bomb was *set off* by someone using a remote control device.
2 The rocket *blasted off* towards space.
3 The gun *went off* before he was ready.

Cheating

Off is used with some verbs to indicate that something is done dishonestly or with the intention of cheating someone.

rip off   fob off   palm off   pass off as

1 We were *ripped off* by the taxi driver. He charged more than double the normal price.
2 When I said I wanted to buy a good watch he tried to *fob* me *off* with a cheap plastic thing.

ON

On is used in 380 verbs (about 6%) in this dictionary, as an adverb and a preposition. Its basic meaning describes the position of one

thing above or on top of another or resting on something. For example: He put the lid on the pot. He put the lid on. It is also used in combination with verbs of movement, where the preposition **onto** is also sometimes used, for example *get on the bus*, *get onto the bus*. With some of these verbs it is the opposite of off, for example *get on the bus*, *get off the bus*. The most common uses of the particle **on** are as follows:

Continuing

The particle **on** can be used with many verbs to show that something continues and does not stop. For example, if someone decides to continue driving instead of stopping, we can say the person *drove on*. It can also mean that you stop for a short time and then continue: *We spent a few days in Seattle and then flew on to L.A.* It can also be used in this way to express the idea of continuing to do something difficult or unpleasant, for example *fight on*, *struggle on*, *battle on*, *soldier on*. In other cases it suggests that something is continuing for too long, for example *drag on*, *drone on*, *ramble on*. Other commonly used verbs are:

keep on	stay on	go on
carry on	hurry on	move on

1 Many people tried to interrupt him but he *kept on* talking.
2 We liked the town so much we decided to *stay on* another month.
3 He paused, then *went on* as if nothing had happened.

Developing and changing

On can be used with some verbs to talk about the way things are progressing or changing. Example verbs are:

get on	come on	move on

1 She is *getting on* very well at school.
2 How is your new novel *coming on*?
3 Technology has *moved on* and made the world a different place.

Encouraging

On in combination with some verbs gives the idea of supporting somebody or encouraging someone to do something. Example verbs are

urge on	come on	egg on	spur on

1 The team captain *urged* them *on* to produce their best performance.
2 *Come on*! I know you can do it if you try!
3 They *egged* him *on*, telling him to steal the apples.

Starting

On can be used in verbs that talk about starting an activity or making a machine begin to work. Example verbs are:

bring on	sign on	turn on
switch on	put on	

1 The dust in the air *brought on* an attack of coughing and sneezing.
2 He had to *sign on* at the unemployment office.
3 She *turned on* the radio.
4 He *put on* the kettle to make a cup of tea.

Off is often used with the some of these verbs with the opposite meaning. For example: *She turned on the radio. She turned off the radio.*

Holding and connecting

On can be used in combinations to express the idea of holding something tightly. Other verbs describe how things are connected or attached to each other. Example verbs are:

hang on	hold on	strap on	latch on
cling on	fasten on	screw on	stick on

1 *Hang on* to this rope and don't let go.
2 Can you *hold on* (= said on the phone) while I find the information you need?
3 The luggage was *strapped on* to the car roof.
4 People are *latching on* to the idea very quickly.

Dressing

On can be used with different verbs to talk about ways of getting dressed.

put on	try on	pull on	slip on

1 I *put on* my best clothes for the interview.
2 I *tried on* several jackets before choosing one.

Having an effect on someone or something

On is often used as a preposition with verbs to talk about what somebody does to a person or a thing, or the effect that somebody or something has. Example verbs are:

dote on	impress on	dawn on	cheat on
descend on	elaborate on	spy on	work on

1 He absolutely *dotes on* her and gives her gifts all the time.
2 I want to *impress on* you the importance of these new safety rules.
3 It suddenly *dawned on* me why she was so angry.

Upon can also be used with many of these verbs, but it is more formal: *The importance of education was impressed upon me from an early age*.

Attacking

Some verbs with on indicate that someone is being attacked, either physically or with words. Example verbs are:

turn on   pick on   round on   jump on
set on   start on

1 She suddenly *turned on* me and criticized everything I had done.
2 Why does my boss keep *picking on* me?
3 He *rounded on* me for not supporting him at the meeting.

Thinking and commenting

On is used with some verbs of thinking or deciding to show what you are thinking or talking about. Example verbs are:

reflect on   decide on   touch on   sleep on

1 I've *reflected on* what happened and I've decided to forgive you.
2 We have to *decide on* several things at today's meeting.

3 I'll *sleep on* it and let you know my decision by the end of the week.

Finding

On is used with some verbs that mean finding something or someone suddenly or unexpectedly. Examples of verbs are:

hit on   stumble on   chance on

1 We *hit on* a good idea for making some money.
2 I *stumbled on* the information while I was looking for something else.
3 Jill *chanced on* an old school friend at the party.

Depending

On is often used with verbs to indicate that one thing is affected by or decided by something else. **On** can also indicate the person or thing that you trust or feel sure about. Example verbs are:

depend on   rely on   count on   hinge on

1 The success of the trip will *depend on* whether it rains or not.
2 You can *depend on* James to deal with the situation.
3 Our work *relies on* voluntary donations.

OUT

Out is used in 815 verbs (14%) in this dictionary, as an adverb. The basic meaning is of movement from inside to outside, so it combines with many verbs of movement, for example, *storm out, rush out, go out*. Many verbs that combine with **out** also combine with the adverb plus preposition **out of**, for example, *storm out, storm out of the room*; *Don't leave me out*; *He was left out of the team*. **Out** and **in** can sometimes be used with the same verbs to express opposite meanings, for example, *go out, go in*. The most common uses of this particle are:

Leaving

Out can be used in verbs that mean starting a journey or going away from a person or a place. Example verbs are:

set out   pop out   check out   start out

1 We *set out* in the early morning to climb the mountain.
2 I'm just going to *pop out* for a few minutes to get some milk.
3 We have to *check out* of the hotel by midday.

Searching, observing, solving

Out in some combinations gives the idea of searching for something such as a piece of information, the answer to a difficult problem, etc. and then finding it.

find out   dig out   make out
turn out   hunt out   sort out
spy out   try out   work out

1 Can you *find out* how many people in the company are aged over forty?
2 I'll try and *dig out* some old college photos for you.
3 I can't *make out* the handwriting. What is this word here?
4 Let's wait and see how things *turn out*.

Disappearing; using completely

Out can be used in phrasal verbs to suggest that something is gradually disappearing or has been used completely so that there is none left. Example verbs are:

die out   run out   go out   phase out

1 The change in weather conditions is

causing many species to *die out*.
2 I think we've *run out* of petrol.

Stopping an activity

Out is used in some verbs that describe an activity being stopped, often by using force or authority. Some verbs describe people or places being completely destroyed. Other verbs refer to a fire, etc. going out or being put out. Example verbs are:

stamp out   cut out   wipe out   burn out
beat out   blow out   drown out

1 The rebellion was quickly *stamped out*.
2 I should really try to *cut out* chocolate (= stop eating it)!
3 The town was almost completely *wiped out* by the earthquake.
4 The fire had *burnt out* before the fire engines arrived.

Stopping being involved

Out can be used in combinations that show that you are no longer involved in something or no longer want to be involved. Example verbs are:

fall out   pull out   bottle out   chicken out
drop out   opt out   sell out

1 Mike and Janet have *fallen out* and are not talking to one another.
2 The company has decided to *pull out* of the project.

Producing

Out can be used with verbs to talk about things being produced, especially when they are produced quickly and in large quantities. Example verbs are:

turn out   churn out   spill out   pour out

1 The factory *turns out* 200 washing machines a day.
2 This magazine *churns out* the same stories every week of the year.
3 All her worries came *spilling out*.

Being outside

Out can be used in combinations that express the idea of somebody going out of a place, such as their home, or doing something outside. Example verbs are:

get out   camp out   eat out
stay out   go out   lock out

1 The prisoners *got out* through a hole in the fence.

2 We *camped out* in a field in the pouring rain.
3 We like to *eat out* at least once a month
4 They *stayed out* all night and only returned in the early morning.

Appearing

Out can be used with some verbs that give the idea of something or somebody appearing, sometimes suddenly, or of something being brought out of a place where it was hidden. Example verbs are:

leap out   turn out   take out
break out   come out

1 My name *leapt out* at me from the page.
2 Two thousand people *turned out* to watch the parade.
3 He *took out* a gun and pointed it at me.

Speaking or shouting loudly

Out can be used with some verbs that suggest that somebody is speaking loudly or angrily, perhaps to call for help or shout a warning. Example verbs are:

bark out   call out   scream out
shout out   snap out   yell out

1 She was *barking out* orders at the children.
2 Everyone was *calling out* for help
3 People were *screaming out* to the driver to tell him to stop.

Sharing

Out can be used to convey the idea of something being distributed to or shared among people. Example verbs are:

hand out   give out   share out
dish out   dole out   serve out

1 They were *handing out* free samples of cheese in the supermarket today.
2 We need to *give out* more information to our clients.
3 We *shared out* the prize money amongst the three of us.

Finishing

Out can be used to convey the idea of something being completely finished or done. Example verbs are:

hear out dry out talk out tire out wear out

1 Don't interrupt - *hear* me *out*.
2 If the soil in the garden *dries out*, this particular plant will not survive.
3 It might help to *talk* things *out*.

Out is often added to other verbs or past participles to create new verbs that mean you have completely finished doing something and can do no more. For example: *I'm all partied out* (= I have been to so many parties that I can't go to any more).

Removing

Out is used with some verbs that mean removing something or somebody from somewhere, or removing yourself from somewhere. The verb tells you how this is done. Example verbs are:

take out	knock out	pull out	bomb out
push out	rinse out	throw out	wash out

1 I'd like to *take out* three thousand pounds from my account.
2 She was *knocked out* of the competition in the first round.
3 The army has decided to *pull out*.

Excluding

Out can be used in combinations that express the idea that someone or something is not included in an activity, a list, etc. Example verbs are:

leave out	cross out	rule out
filter out	keep out	weed out

1 We must be sure not to *leave* anyone *out* when we invite people to the party.
2 *Cross out* the wrong answers.
3 The government has *ruled out* the possibility of giving any financial aid.

Supporting

Out is used with verbs that suggest helping or supporting somebody, especially with money or encouragement.

help out	bear out	bring out
draw out	reach out to	

1 I wonder if you could *help* me *out*. I've got a problem.
2 David will *bear* me *out* and confirm that everything I have said is true.

Choosing

Out can be used to convey the idea of something being chosen from among many others. Example verbs are:

pick out	single out	pull out
mark out	separate out	sort out

1 She was *picked out* as the person most likely to succeed in the company.

2 Some of the animals were *singled out* for special medical treatment.
3 Can you *sort out* all the books you don't want any more?

Lasting

Out can be used to convey the idea of resisting some kind of pressure or enduring a difficult situation. Example verbs are:

hold out	stick out	last out	ride out

1 The unions are *holding out* for a better pay deal.
2 I don't like the job but I'll *stick* it *out* until the end of the year.
3 They say they can't *last out* much longer. They need help now.

Attacking; reacting violently

Out can be used in verbs that show that someone is attacking somebody or reacting violently to something. Examples verbs are:

lash out	strike out	fight out
hit out	kick out	shoot out

1 The lion *lashed out* if any of the other lions came near him.
2 As soon as the fight started, he *lashed out* at everyone standing near him.
3 When the man said something rude, I *struck out* at him.

Recording and putting down on paper

Out can be used with verbs connected with writing or drawing to give the idea of something being recorded or written down on paper.

copy out	sketch out	map out	write out

1 Could you *copy* this *out* for me so it is easy to read?
2 I'll *sketch out* a few ideas for you on paper.
3 They have *mapped out* the area where they will be digging.

Increasing

Out is used with some verbs that show that something or somebody is increasing in size, shape, extent, etc.

broaden out	fill out	flesh out
open out	spread out	

1 The river *broadens out* just outside the town.
2 Hasn't the baby *filled out* now (= become fatter)?
3 These points were *fleshed out* in the later part of the speech.

OVER

Over is used in approximately 200 verbs (about 3%) in this dictionary as an adverb and a preposition. The basic meaning of the particle indicates movement from one side of something to the other, especially over the top of something, for example: *climb over a wall*, *fly over a city*, *cross over a road*. It can also indicate a position above something: *bend over* something, *lean over* someone. The most common uses are:

Having a higher position

Over can be used to suggest that someone or something is taller or in a higher position than somebody or something else. It can also refer to somebody in a position of greater authority or responsibility.

tower over   **stand over**   **rule over**
preside over   **watch over**

1 My son is only 15 but he *towers over* his father already.
2 I don't want my boss *standing over* me and watching everything I do.
3 She has *ruled over* the country for twenty years.

Covering

Over can be used in combination with verbs to show that something is completely covered with something such as ice or clouds. It is also used in a more figurative way to suggest that a difficulty or the truth is being hidden. Example verbs are:

freeze over   **cloud over**   **gloss over**
paint over   **paper over**

1 Last winter the lake was completely *frozen over*.
2 What a pity! It's starting to *cloud over*.
3 He avoided answering difficult questions by *glossing over* the problem.

Moving to the side

A few verbs use **over** to indicate movement to the side of something. Example verbs are:

pull over   **move over**

1 The driver *pulled over* to the side of the road to take a short break.
2 Can you *move over*? I haven't got enough space.

Visiting

Over with some verbs suggests going from your house to somebody else's for a visit.

ask over   **drop over**   **come over**
invite over   **pop over**

1 The neighbours have *asked* us *over* for tea.
2 Why don't you *drop over* this evening?

Considering, thinking about or examining

Over can be used with verbs that mean thinking about something carefully before you make a decision, or inspecting something to see if it is correct.

think over   **talk over**   **check over**
go over   **look over**

1 I'd like some time to *think over* your offer before making a decision.
2 Let's *talk* it *over* and see if we can come to some kind of agreement.
3 Can you *check* this *over* for me to see if there are any mistakes?

Remaining

Over can be used to convey the idea of something remaining in the same place or being kept to use at a later date.

stay over   **hold over**   **be left over**   **sleep over**

1 She decided to *stay over* with her parents for a couple of days.
2 I think we should *hold* that agenda item *over* until the next meeting.

Changing position

Over can be used in combination with verbs suggesting the idea of two people or things changing places, jobs etc., or of a person changing their opinion or ideas.

take over   **swap over**   **win over**
change over   **hand over**   **swap over**

1 She is *taking over* the management of the company from next spring.
2 I'll drive the first part of the journey, then we'll *swap over*.
3 I think I've managed to *win* her *over* to our side of the argument.

Falling

Over can be used with verbs to express the idea of something falling to the ground, usually from an upright position. The verb shows what the movement is.

fall over	knock over	trip over
keel over	kick over	run over

1 I *fell over* and hurt my knee.
2 She *knocked over* the vase as she entered the room.
3 I *tripped over* someone's bag and fell.

Finishing and recovering

Over can be used in combinations that mean that something is temporary and will soon end. Example verbs are:

blow over	get over	get over with

1 It wasn't a serious argument. I'm sure it will *blow over* and soon be forgotten.
2 She's upset now, but she'll soon *get over* it.

Communicating a message or an impression

Over can be used to convey the idea of giving somebody a message or a particular impression. Example verbs are:

put over	get over	come over

1 She is very good at *putting over* her ideas to an audience.
2 I think we succeeded in *getting over* the idea that the situation is serious.
3 He *came over* as rather arrogant in the interview.

Across can be used instead of **over** with these verbs with a very similar meaning.

Overflowing

Over can be used in combinations that mean that something such as a liquid flows over the edge of a container. These verbs can also have a figurative meaning referring to very strong feelings. Example verbs are:

boil over	spill over	brim over	bubble over

1 Please watch this saucepan of milk so that it doesn't *boil over*.
2 The enormous crowd *spilled over* into the neighbouring streets.
3 Her heart was *brimming over* with happiness.

ROUND

Round is used in approximately 150 verbs (2½ %) in the dictionary, as an adverb and a preposition. The basic meaning is of movement in a circle or curve in order to face in the opposite direction or to arrive at the other side of something. It can sometimes be replaced by **about** and **around** with very little change of meaning. The most common categories of use are:

Moving

Round is used with some verbs to indicate movement in different directions.

move round	run round	hand round
phone/call round		

1 At the first class we were told to *move round* the room and talk to different people.
2 It was a cold day so the kids *ran round* in the playground to keep warm.

Lack of activity and purpose

Round can be used to suggest lack of activity or specific purpose. Example verbs are:

stand round	hang round	sit round

1 We all *stood round*, waiting for

something to happen.
2 He *hangs round* bars and talks to anyone who will listen to him.

Surrounding and enclosing

Round can be used to indicate that something is surrounded by something.

wrap round	throw round	go round
gather round		

1 *Wrap* this scarf *round* your neck - it's cold outside.
2 He *threw* his arms *round* me.
3 The belt won't *go round* my waist now!

Being centred on something

Round can be used with a few verbs to indicate how something or somebody has a particular person or thing as the focus of their attention. Example verbs are:

revolve round	centre round

1 My whole life seems to *revolve round* cooking, cleaning and shopping.
2 Our holiday *centred round* sitting by the pool, swimming and sunbathing.

Turning

Round is sometimes used in combinations with the idea of something turning in circles or turning to face the other way. Example verbs are:

spin round   swing round   wheel round

1 The car *span round* several times and then hit a tree.
2 She *swung round* with the hammer in her hand and almost hit me.

Avoiding

Round can be used with verbs to express the idea that you are avoiding something.

talk round   skate round

1 We *talked round* the subject but we never really discussed it in any real detail.
2 Politicians tend to *skate round* most issues without answering any questions directly.

Persuading

Round can be used with verbs to express the idea of persuading someone to change their minds about something. The verb shows how you do this. Example verbs are:

talk round get round come round win round

1 I managed to *talk* them *round* and they finally signed the contract.
2 At first her parents refused to let her go on holiday alone, but she finally *got round* them.

Visiting informally

Round is used with some verbs to indicate going to a particular place to visit a person briefly on an informal basis.

**call round   drop round   pop round
come round**

1 *Call round* any time. We're always happy to see you.
2 I'll *drop round* later and give you that book I mentioned.

Sharing or distributing

Round in combinations can give the idea of sharing or distributing something between people. Example verbs are:

hand round   pass round   go round

1 Could you help to *hand round* the sandwiches?
2 *Pass* the photos *round* so that everyone can see them.
3 I don't think there is enough cake to go *round*.

Recovering

Round can be used with the idea of someone becoming conscious again, for example after an operation or after fainting. Other verbs mean recovering from an illness. Example verbs are:

come round   bring round   pull round

1 She started to *come round* three hours after the operation.
2 They tried to *bring* him *round* but he remained unconscious.
3 Don't worry about him. He'll soon *pull round* and be back to normal.

THROUGH

Through is used in 150 verbs (2½%) in the dictionary, as an adverb and a preposition. The basic meaning refers to passing from one side of something solid to the other side, for example, to *go through* a hole in a wall or to *see through* a window. It can be used with this meaning with many other verbs such as *to slice through*, *to cut through*, and *to break through something*. The most common categories are:

Doing something thoroughly and completely

Through can be used with verbs to give the idea of going from the beginning to the end of something and finishing it. The verb tells you what the activity is and how someone is doing it. It is often used to suggest doing something in a logical and thorough way and completing it. Example verbs are:

**look through   rush through   sit through
talk through   think through   read through**

1 Can you *look through* this letter for me and tell me if it's alright?
2 Don't *rush through* your homework – take your time.
3 We had to *sit through* a very boring talk that lasted almost two hours.
4 If the two of you have a problem then I suggest you sit down together and *talk* it *through*.

Surviving, achieving

Through can be used in combinations to express the idea of surviving a bad situation or getting past something difficult such as a test or a barrier. Example verbs are:

live through	come through	get through
sail through	pull through	see through

1 My grandmother *lived through* the horrors of two world wars.
2 She *came through* the operation and made a rapid recovery.
3 You won't *get through* the exam if you don't study hard.
4 You won't have any difficulties with the driving test. You'll *sail through*.

Communicating

Through can be used in combinatons that express the idea of communicating with somebody, for example by telephone. It can also be used to talk about attempts to make someone understand a message or an idea.

put through	get through	fax through

1 Hello, operator? Can you *put* me *through* to extension 437 please?
2 He won't listen to me. I can't *get through* to him how serious the problem is.

Seeing clearly

Through can be used with a few verbs to suggest that you can see or understand something or somebody very clearly.

see through	shine through	come through

1 He was able to fool everybody else, but I *saw through* him immediately.
2 Her qualities *shine through* in everything she does.

 TO

To is used in about 170 verbs (nearly 3%) in this dictionary, mainly as a preposition, although there are a few verbs where it is an adverb (*pull the door to, come to/round*.) With verbs of movement, it expresses the idea of direction, for example, *I walked to the office; It fell to the ground*. It generally shows the relationship between the verb and the person or thing that is affected by it, for example, *She is devoted to her children; We fixed a rope to the boat*. In the verbs in this dictionary, the most frequent groups are:

Directing or aiming

To used with verbs shows the direction that somebody or something is going or what is being aimed at. Example verbs are:

gravitate to	devote to	gear to
pander to	point to	

1 Many young people are *gravitating to* the cities in search of work.
2 She *devoted* herself *to* her career.

3 The course is *geared to* the needs of the students.

Showing relationships

To is used with verbs to indicate the relationship between people or things. The verb itself shows the nature of the action, feeling, etc, and **to** shows who or what is involved or affected. Example verbs are:

belong to	cling to	warm to
resort to	look up to	stick to
defer to	endear to	face up to
fall to	surrender to	stoop to

1 Who does this book *belong to*?
2 They *clung to* each other for comfort.
3 I *warmed to* Chris immediately.
4 You shouldn't need to *resort to* violence to achieve your aims.
5 Jack's always *looked up to* his older brothers.
6 I'm *sticking to* what I said before.

UP

The particle **up** is the most common particle in phrasal verbs. It is used in about 15% of verbs in this dictionary, mostly as an adverb. The literal meaning of **up** is movement upwards, from a lower to a higher position, so it occurs with many verbs describing movement, such as *climb up, jump up, look up*, and *sit up*. It is also used with verbs of lifting to express the idea of raising something to a higher level, for example *pick up*, *lift up*, *snatch up*. You will also find it used to express the related ideas of increase and improvement. As an adverb, it frequently combines with a preposition to form three-word verbs, for example, *come up against*, *keep up with*. The most common and important meanings are:

Increasing

Up is often used to give the idea of something increasing in volume, speed, price, strength, and reputation. Examples of such verbs are:

go up	speed up	turn up	grow up
build up	speak up	play up	flare up
hurry up	push up	step up	talk up

1 Petrol is *going up* next week.
2 The train started to *speed up* after it left the station.
3 It's freezing in here. Can you *turn up* the heat?
4 People say that children *grow up* very quickly nowadays.
5 You need to *build up* your strength before you go back to work.
6 I'm sorry, I can't hear you. Can you *speak up* a bit?
7 The government wants to *play up* the importance of the meeting.

The opposite of the particle **up** is **down**, so these particles can be used in verbs that have opposite meanings. For example, the opposite of *turn up* the heating is *turn down* the heating.

Improving

Up can be used to express the idea of things improving, such as the economy, your health or your knowledge. Example verbs are:

look up	brush up	clear up
smarten up	cheer up	brighten up
dress up	jazz up	pick up

1 The year started badly but I think things are starting to *look up*.
2 I'd like to *brush up* my knowledge of Italian.
3 The weather looks as if it's starting to *clear up*.
4 Well, I think you could *smarten up* your appearance.
5 They tried to *cheer* me *up* by telling me funny stories.

Note that *dress down* is now used as an

opposite for *dress up*, and means *to wear more casual clothes*.

Supporting

Up can be used to give the idea of providing support. Example verbs are:

back up	shore up	speak up for
stand up for	bolster up	stick up for

1 Will you *back* me *up* if I tell them what really happened?
2 The bank took action to *shore up* the value of sterling.
3 Nobody *spoke up for* him when he was falsely accused of stealing the money.
4 It's time for us to *stand up for* what we believe in.

Preparing

Up is used with a group of verbs to give the idea of preparing for doing something.

draw up	set up	warm up	butter up
fix up	limber up	soften up	tune up

1 She's busy *drawing up* a plan of how the whole scheme will work.
2 We are *setting up* a research project to investigate the effects of radiation on plant life.
3 He tried to *warm up* the audience by telling them a few jokes at the start of his talk.
4 We'd better *butter* him *up* before we ask him to give us so much money.

Creating and constructing

Up is also used to suggest creating, producing, inventing or constructing something, either physically or in your mind. Example verbs are:

make up	dream up	build up
come up with	conjure up	put up
rise up	think up	

1 My grandmother was fantastic at *making up* stories for us.
2 I would like to know who *dreamed up* this whole idea. It's complete madness.
3 She *built* the business *up* from nothing.
4 She has *come up with* a fantastic idea for solving the problem we're having with recruiting people.

Completing and finishing

With some verbs that can be used on their own, **up** adds the idea of completing something. For example, in the sentence *I ate fish for dinner*, *ate* means *took food*. If you tell somebody to *Eat up*, you want them to finish eating quickly. It is also used in this way in verbs like *tidy up*, *dry up* and *clear up*. Other examples of verbs are:

| end up | use up | wind up | dry up |
| dummy up | follow up | sum up | wake up |

1 Although he wanted to work in advertising, he *ended up* working in a bank.
2 We will have *used up* all our coal reserves by the end of the year.
3 Could I ask you to *wind up* the meeting?

Damaging and destroying
Up can be used to express the idea of something being damaged or spoilt in some way or not working well. Example verbs are:

| tear up | blow up | mess up | beat up |
| play up | slip up | smash up | |

1 After looking at the letter for a few moments, she *tore it up* and threw it in the bin.
2 Explosive experts *blew up* the building as part of a new building programme.
3 What a stupid mistake! Now you've really *messed* things *up*.

Stopping, delaying and disrupting
Up can be used to give the idea of something stopping, being delayed or prevented from operating normally. Example verbs are:

break up give up pull up hold up slow up

1 The police *broke up* the demonstration.
2 I've decided to *give up* smoking.
3 A car *pulled up* in front of the bank.
4 I'm sorry we're late. We were *held up* in traffic on the motorway.

Note that *slow up* and *slow down* have the same meaning: *to become slower*.

Things happening
Up can be used to convey the idea of something happening or of something/somebody appearing, sometimes unexpectedly. Example verbs are:

turn up come up bring up crop up pop up

1 To everybody's amazement she *turned up* at the party and behaved as if nothing had happened.
3 Can you come to the office as soon as possible? Something serious has *come up*.
4 I'd like to *bring up* the question of installing air conditioning in the new offices.

Approaching and getting closer for comfort
Up can be used to give the idea of something or somebody approaching or getting closer to somebody/something, sometimes in a rather secretive way. It can also be used to give the idea of getting closer to somebody or something for warmth and comfort. Example verbs are:

| creep up | loom up | snuggle up | curl up |
| nuzzle up | sneak up | steal up | |

1 The two children *crept up* close to the edge of the garden.
2 The exams are *looming up*.
3 It's lovely to *snuggle up* by the fire and listen to the rain outside.

Dividing and separating
Up can be used to give the idea of something being divided in some way, for example by being cut or chopped into small pieces. When it is used in connection with a group of people or a couple, it has the idea of separation. Example verbs are:

| slice up | divide up | split up | break up |
| cut up | chop up | | |

1 First you need to *slice up* the tomatoes and add them to the mixture.
2 We've decided to *divide up* the money equally.
3 Pam and Paul have *split up* after twenty years of marriage.

Gathering and collecting
Up can be used with the idea of collecting things or people together. Example verbs are:

| match up | stock up | team up | join up |
| meet up | pair up | pile up | save up |

1 The task is to *match up* all the cards in front of you.
2 We had better *stock up* on sugar as there is going to be a shortage.
3 I think it's best if we *team up* with people from other departments.

Fastening
Up can be used to talk about fastening things like clothes or objects. It can be used with the name of an object or a material to show how something is fastened, or with the name of a container to show where things are placed. Related to this is the idea of restricting the movement of somebody/

something. Example verbs are:

do up	zip up	parcel up	tie up
bag up	bandage up	brick up	chain up
lace up	lock up		

1 Remember to *do up* all the buttons on your coat.

WITH

With is a preposition and is used in about 125 verbs (2%) in the dictionary, sometimes combining with an adverb to form a three-word verb, such as *fall in with, fit in with*. It is generally used to describe the connections and relationships between people, things, facts or situations. The most common uses are:

Relationships between people

With is used with verbs that describe relationships between people. These often involve difficulties or the ending of a relationship. Example verbs are:

mess with	reason with	finish with
argue with	associate with	level with
trifle with	vie with	

1 I wouldn't *mess with* him. He has a terrible temper and can get violent.
2 I've tried *reasoning with* her, but she won't change her mind.
3 Maria is going to *finish with* Pierre. Their relationship just isn't working.

Relationships between things

Verbs plus **with** often show connections between things, such as comparing, including, involving or separating. Example verbs are:

| go with | crawl with | do away with |
| riddle with | square with | |

1 I wouldn't wear that tie. It doesn't *go with* the shirt.
2 The town is *crawling with* tourists at the

2 You'd better *zip up* your bag so no one steals anything from it.
3 I'm going to *parcel up* the gifts to send your cousins.
4 The security guard was *tied up* in a corner of the room.

moment.
3 He thinks it's time we *did away with* the monarchy.

Relationshps between people and things

With can be used to convey the idea of somebody taking action and getting involved in something, sometimes when they should not. Example verbs are:

deal with	wrestle with	juggle with
meddle with	catch up with	land with
lumber with	tamper with	

1 I'm very busy at the moment, so I'll *deal with* that later.
2 It's a problem I've been *wrestling with* for months.
3 In my job I have to *juggle with* several different things at the same time.
4 Please don't *meddle with* things you don't understand.

Giving support

With is used with verbs that express the idea of agreeing with a person or an idea or providing support. Example verbs are:

| agree with | side with | bear with | hold with |

1 I *agree with* everything you've said.
2 She always *sides with* her sister in any family arguments.
3 She's under a lot of strain at the moment - just *bear with* her.

S5 Phrasal Verb or Single Word?

For me, the highlight of the whole holiday was the trip to the temple. We *set off* at nine in the morning and were soon *going up* some hair-raisingly steep roads. We *got to* the temple about half ten. We had to wear long-sleeved tops and long trousers or they wouldn't have *let* us *in*. Of course, we had to *take* our shoes *off* before we *went in* the temple, too. A local guide *showed* us *round*, which was good, because lots of questions *came up* about how we were supposed to behave, and about the history of the place. The temple itself was absolutely breathtaking, but that wasn't the best thing because we *came back* through what they call the 'Lost Valley'. Lunch was *laid on* for the people who'd *asked for* it, but we'd taken a packed lunch with us and we agreed that it was the most spectacular picnic spot we'd ever seen!

S6–7 Are You a Natural Born Student?

Study quiz score

1 A–0, B–2, C–0	4 A–2, B–1, C–0	7 A–2, B–2, C–1	10 A–2,B–1,C–0
2 A–1, B–0, C–2	5 A–0, B–1, C–2	8 A–2, B–0, C–2	11 A–0,B–2,C–2
3 A–1, B–1, C–2	6 A–1, B–2, C–2	9 A–2, B–1, C–0	12 A–0,B–2,C–2

1 (a) did teachers always *pick on* you and *tell* you *off* for no reason?;
   (b) did kids who *messed around* in class annoy you?; (c) did you ever get *kept back* for extra study?

2 (a) *get on* with it straight away and finish it early?; (b) *put off* starting it until the last possible moment? (c) do some work on it immediately then *put* it *aside* for a while?

3 (a) *jot down* some notes then write it and *hand* it *in*?; (b) do it in rough first, and then *write* it *out* neatly or *type* it *up*?; (c) *plan* it *out* carefully then write and edit it?

4 (a) work steadily and *sail through* your exams?; (b) *scrape through* your exams despite *beavering away* all year?; (c) just do enough to *get by*?

5 (a) *rattle through* it and *hand* it *in* early?; (b) *go over* each question carefully before *moving on* to the next one?; (c) answer all the questions then *check through* your answers?

6 (a) as soon as you *come across* a word you don't know?; (b) only to *look up* a word whose meaning you can't guess?; (c) only after you've *read through* the article once without a dictionary?

7 (a) *sign up* for evening classes?; (b) *throw away* your books and find someone to talk with in English? (c) *swot up* on vocabulary every night?

8 (a) did you study while you were sick in order not to *fall behind*?; (b) were you just happy to have *got out of* lessons?; (c) did you borrow a friend's notes and *write* them *up*?

9 (a) do it as well as you could?; (b) *scribble* it *down* as quickly as possible; (c) *talk* a friend *into* letting you copy theirs at the last minute?

10 (a) *plan out* a revision timetable in plenty of time?; (b) *read up* the subject the night before each exam?; (c) just take it easy and hope easy questions *came/would come up*?

11 (a) *switch over* to something more interesting?; (b) *shout out* an answer quickly, even if you're not sure?; (c) get annoyed if the answer doesn't *come to* you quickly?

12 (a) *chill out* and gaze out of the window?; (b) buy a paper and *catch up on* the news?; (c) *settle down* with a good book?

S8–9 Sport

Football, and tonight's match in the European Cup ended in controversy after Italy *came back* from 2–0 down to beat Spain. At 2–2, the Italian goalkeeper Alberti appeared to *bring down* Rojas, the Spanish centre forward. As the Spanish players *appealed for* a penalty, the Italians *played on* and *broke away* to score. The Spanish captain Martín was then *sent off* for arguing with the referee. Italy *ended up* fortunate winners, but their goalkeeper Pollo *picked up* a hand injury and has been *ruled out* of the next two games.

The Tokyo marathon has been won by Takeshi Saito of Japan. *Urged on* by the home crowd, Saito *forged ahead* after just 5 kilometres and built up a 2-minute lead. The chasing runners did not *give up*, and gradually reduced the lead. The hot weather and the fast pace caused several leading athletes to *drop out*. Saito's recent training in the Sahara desert *paid off* as he *held off* the strong challenge of the Kenyan Daniel Nyanga, who *caught up* with 5 kilometres to go, then *fell back* in the final kilometre.

Tennis, and the unseeded Sofia Adamou of Greece has beaten Russia's Irena Markova in three sets to *go through* to the final of the French Open. Adamou said afterwards, "I've never *come up against* such a tough opponent. Before I came here I thought I'd get *knocked out* in the first round, but now I've got a chance of winning." Adamou, who only *took up* the sport four years ago, will *pick up* a cheque for $100,000. The loser will have to *settle for* just $50,000 !

Extract 1

1 c 2 d 3 a 4 i 5 e 6 h 7 f 8 b 9 g

Extracts 2 and 3

1 b 2 d 3 k 4 a 5 h 6 l 7 n 8 g 9 c 10 j
11 f 12 e 13 i 14 m

S10 Computers

Down

1 click on
2 pull-down
3 switch on
4 printout
6 shut down
7 scan in
9 back up
10 boot up
11 log in

Across

5 add-ons
8 hack into
12 go down
13 scroll down
14 type in
15 pop-up

S11 Environmental Problems

The Greenhouse effect

1 Carbon dioxide and other greenhouse gases are *given off* when fossil fuels are burned.
2 Greenhouse gases *soak up* heat that should escape into space.
3 Temperatures on earth *go up*.

Algae

1 Nitrates from fertilizers *soak through* the soil and end up in rivers and lakes.
2 Algae *feeds on* the nitrates and multiplies uncontrollably.
3 The algae *uses up* the oxygen in the water, and fish die.

Deforestation

1 Too many trees are burnt or *cut down*.
2 Some areas *turn into* desert.
3 Some species of animals and plants lose their habitat and *die out*.
4 Less carbon dioxide is *soaked up* by trees, which adds to global warming.

S12 Phrasal Verbs in Newspapers

1 d 2 k 3 a,g 4 e 5 c 6 j 7 l 8 f 9 h 10 i

S13 Business

1888 catches *on*, take *on*; 1902 teams *up*, set *up*, sell *off*; 1906 turning *out*;
1945 takes *over*; 1954 comes *up with*; 1963 take *off*, bringing *in*; 1969 buys
out; 1974 walk *out*, sparking *off*; 1987 swallowed *up*, turned *around*; 1992
worn *away*, falling *off*, mount *up*, go *under*, bailed *out*; 1999 takes *over*, caught
out, shoots *up*, wind *up*; 2000 laid *off*, closes *down*

S14–15 Informal

Using this dictionary

Formal	Informal	Neutral
provide for sth attend to sb/sth	boot sb out barge into sb tune out	turn up throw sth aside put sb down

Practice

The 11 phrasal verbs are:

swot up
mess up
beaver away
veg out
breeze through (sth)
jabber away

jack sth in
swan around
muck around
look sb up
catch up with sb

Matching Exercise:

a beaver away
b swot up
c swan around
d jabber away
e look sb up
f catch up

g jack sth in
h breeze through (sth)
i veg out
j mess up
k muck around

Sentences:

a OK, I'll level with you.
b at the last moment he chickened out.
c We're going to check out the new bar
d I'll be able to rustle something up.
e we whipped through the last three chapters.

f – they really freak me out.
g it took him ages to catch on.
h she just clammed up.

S16–17 Using Phrasal Verbs in Writing

Exercise 1

1 refers to	4 drawn up	7 sets out	10 accounts for
2 reported back	5 gone through	8 consists of	11 deals with
3 summed up	6 puts forward	9 enlarges upon	

Exercise 2: Sample Report

This report refers to the Intermediate English Course, which I attended last summer. Firstly, I will deal with the positive aspects of the course. The lessons were very enjoyable and the teachers were very helpful. I especially liked the opportunity to meet other students and speak to them in English.

However, I would also like to point out that there were some problems. The cafeteria was expensive and the meals consisted of only one course. Our opportunities for self-study were limited resulting from the fact that there were not enough books in the library. In addition, the trips and visits were not very interesting and I have enlarged upon this problem in a report I have submitted to the Social Secretary.

For next year, I suggest that a list of events is given to students to go through and perhaps they should be given the chance to put forward their own ideas. The college should also draw up a plan of action for improving the cafeteria and library.

To sum up, it was a positive experience but a few changes would make it even better.

Exercise 3

1 b   2 c   3 a   4 a   5 b   6 c   7 c   8 a

S18–19 Using Phrasal Verbs in the Passive

Exercise 1

1 No	5 Yes
2 Yes	6 No
3 Yes	
4 No	

Exercise 2

Separable	Inseparable
turn off	look for
turn down	

Exercise 3

Separable phrasal verbs can generally be used in the passive, whereas inseparable phrasal verbs cannot.

Exercise 4

1 She's been charged with shoplifting.
2 If you carry on like this you'll be kicked out of college.
3 The building was burnt down in the riots.
4 No one knows where Jerry is. He hasn't been heard of since the summer.
5 The twins look so alike that they are often mixed up.
6 £10 for this? You've been ripped off!

S20–21 New Phrasal Verbs

Task A
free up, hype up, tense up, test out, drown out

Task B
Suggested answers
a sports car – flashes past/by
a butterfly – flutters by/past/around
a boy with his leg in plaster – hobbles by/past/along
a bee – buzzes past/by/around
a train – steams past/by/along
tourists visiting a palace – wander around/past
a small child in a park – runs around
a group of boys going to school – muck around
a teacher going home at the end of a long day – hurries along/past

S22–25 The Most Common Phrasal Verbs

Up
i 1 b, 2 c, 3 d, 4 a
ii 1 c, 2 a, 3 d, 4 b

Down
i 1 breaks 2 lets 3 turn
ii 1 sit 2 keep 3 put 4 bend 5 lie

On
1 c, 2 d, 3 b, 4 a

Off
1 b, 2 c, 3 d, 4 a

In
1 come in 2 check in 3 let sb in 4 breaks in

Out
1 fall 2 getting 3 broken 4 came

Verbs with an adverb and a preposition
1 hang on to   4 put up with
2 looking forward to 5 get on with
3 run out of

Further practice: class activities

1 Work with a partner. See who can be first to remember all the verbs in each particle group. Remember to use example sentences.

2 In groups, make up an oral story using the verbs in two or three of the participle groups. One person starts the story with a sentence using one of the phrasal verbs and the next person has to continue the story using a different phrasal verb. Your sentences must show that you understand the meaning of the verb. For homework write the story down correctly.

3 In pairs learn one group of verbs, then teach them, together with their context, to another pair in your class. Then test your classmates by asking them to give you correct sentences using the verbs you have taught them.

Meaning Groups

Daily Routine

a come from	c had .... on	e get off	g catch up	i get back	k phone up
b got up	d set off	f met up	h got to	j look after	

Business

c, h, b, d, f, e, a, g

Opposites

1 c, 2 e, 3 d, 4 b, 5 f, 6 a

Further practice: class activity

Work with a partner. One of you starts a sentence with one of the verbs in the opposites group and the other must complete the sentence using a verb which is opposite in meaning.

Multi-Meaning Verbs

1 catch up   3 takes off   5 pick her up, pick it up   7 meet up
2 fall out   4 give up   6 come out

S26 Test Yourself

1 b, 2 c, 3 b, 4 c, 5 c, 6 c, 7 b, 8 a, 9 b

Which meaning?

i   increasing or improving: grow up, bring up, cheer up, hurry up
     completing or finishing: add up, hang up, give up, wake up, shut up
ii   failing: let down, turn down, break down
     movement: sit down, lie down, put down, keep down, bend down

Pronunciation

Phonetic symbols

Consonants

p	pen	/pen/
b	bad	/bæd/
t	tea	/tiː/
d	did	/dɪd/
k	cat	/kæt/
g	get	/get/
tʃ	chain	/tʃeɪn/
dʒ	jam	/dʒæm/
f	fall	/fɔːl/
v	van	/væn/
θ	thin	/θɪn/
ð	this	/ðɪs/

Vowels and diphthongs

iː	see	/siː/	ɜː	fur	/fɜː(r)/
i	happy	/ˈhæpi/	ə	about	/əˈbaʊt/
ɪ	sit	/sɪt/	eɪ	say	/seɪ/
e	ten	/ten/	əʊ	go	/gəʊ/ (BrE)
æ	cat	/kæt/	oʊ	go	/goʊ/ (AmE)
ɑː	father	/ˈfɑːðə(r)/	aɪ	my	/maɪ/
ɒ	got	/gɒt/	ɔɪ	boy	/bɔɪ/
ɔː	saw	/sɔː/	aʊ	now	/naʊ/
ʊ	put	/pʊt/	ɪə	near	/nɪə(r)/
u	actual	/ˈæktʃuəl/	eə	hair	/heə(r)/
uː	too	/tuː/	ʊə	pure	/pjʊə(r)/
ʌ	cup	/kʌp/			

The symbol /(r)/ indicates that British pronunciation will have /r/ only if a vowel sound follows directly at the beginning of the next word, as in **pore over**; otherwise /r/ is omitted. For Amercian English, all the /r/ sounds should be pronounced.

Stress in phrasal verbs

In speech it is important to use the correct stress patterns for phrasal verbs. To help with this, verbs are shown in this dictionary with stresses marked using the symbols /'/ (= a main stress) and /ˌ/ (= a weaker secondary stress).

There are two patterns of stress in phrasal verbs. One type has a single stress, and it is always on the first word of the verb. Examples are 'come to sth, 'go for sb, 'look at sth. The other type has two stresses; the first word is marked with a secondary stress, and a main stress is put on the second word. Examples are ˌget 'up, ˌput sth 'off, ˌgo 'off sth/sb. Remember that **sth, sb** are not really parts of the verb; they just show where other words may be fitted in. So in ˌput sth 'off, the second word of the verb is **off**.

One-stress verbs

One-stress verbs keep the single main stress on the first word in all situations. No stress is put on the second word of the verb (or on any other words which the verb may contain). Often the second word of these verbs is a word such as **for** or **at** which has both strong and weak forms. Generally the weak form of the word should be used, but if that word happens to come at the end of a phrase, the strong form must be used, even though the word remains unstressed. For example: *The washing machine is broken. I'll have to get it 'looked at.* 'Look at is a one-stress verb so the main stress is on **looked** and there is no stress on **at**. But because **at** is at the end of a phrase it is pronounced in its strong form with vowel /æ/ and not /ə/.